Poland

Krzysztof Dydyński

D1044476

LONELY PLANET PUBLICATIONS
Melbourne • Oakland • London • Paris

POLAND

BALTIC SEA

SŁOWIŃSKI NATIONAL PARK
Possibly the finest and
most unusual bit of
Polish Baltic coast

Łeba • Puck • *Zatok*
Ustka • Wejherowo • *Gdańs*
Łebork • **GDYNIA**
• **SOPOT**
Darłowo • Sławno • **SŁUPSK** Kartuzy • **GDAŃSK**
KOŁOBRZEG • **KOSZALIN** Bytów • Kościerzyna Tczew
Zatoka Białogard Miastko • Starogard Malbo
Pomorska • Gryfice • Chojnice Gdanski • Kwidz
Świnoujście • Szczecinek Tuchola Świecie Grudzią
Zalew Goleniów Połczyn Zdrój Złotów Chełmno
Szczeciński Złocieniec Czaplinek • **BYDGOSZCZ** • **TORUŃ**
• **SZCZECIN** • Stargard Szczecin Wałcz • **PIŁA** **TORUŃ**
• Choszczno Chodzież

TORUŃ
A gothic city with mighty
churches, this was
Copernicus' birthplace

Myślibórz Strzelce Kraj Żnin • Inowrocław
• **GORZÓW WLKP.** Wronki • Strzelno
Kostrzyn Skwierzyna Szamotuły Oborniki Gniezno
BERLIN Śwebodzin **POZNAŃ** Września • **KONIN** • Koło
Środa
Śrem Jarocin Turek

WROCŁAW
A large cultured city with
a marvellous old market
square and other attractions

GERMANY Gubin • **ZIELONA GÓRA** **LESZNO** • Gostyń • **KALISZ**
COTTBUS Lubsko Nowa Sól Krotoszyn
Żary Zagań Głogów Rawicz Ostrów Wlkp. **SIERAD**
Lubin
Trzebnica Wieluń
Zgorzelec Bolesławiec Brzeg Dln Oleśnica Kępno
DRESDEN Lubań **LEGNICA** Namysłów Kluczbork
Jawor Strzegom **WROCŁAW**
Bogatynia **JELENIA GÓRA** Świdnica Oława • **OPOLE** Lublin
WAŁBRZYCH Brzeg Strzelce Opo
Dzierżoniów Strzelin
Ząbkowice Śl **GLIWICE**
Nysa Kędzierzyn
Kłodzko Paczków Prudnik Ryb
HRADEC Głuchołazy Racibórz
KRÁLOVÉ Głubczyce Jastrzę

AUSCHWITZ
The largest Nazi concentration
camp and possibly Poland's
most moving sight

PRAGUE **OSTRAVA** Cieszyn

OLOMOUC

KRAKÓW
Poland's most important
historic city, this was the
royal capital for over 500 years

CZECH REPUBLIC

ELEVATION

	1500 m
	1200 m
	900 m
	600 m
	300 m
	150 m
	0

0   30   60km
0   15   30mi

POLAND

GDAŃSK
A rich old Hanseatic
city with much charm
and character

MALBORK
The largest and arguably
the best castle in Poland

THE GREAT MASURIAN LAKES
A beautiful world of lakes
and forests and a favourite
haunt of sailors and kayakers

BIAŁOWIEŻA NATIONAL PARK
Europe's largest original lowland
forest with much of its primeval
plant and animal life

WARSZAWA
A fast, bustling, cosmopolitan
melting pot of old and new

TATRA MOUNTAINS
An amazing alpine range
with much to delight
hikers and nature lovers

RUSSIA
(KALININGRAD REGION)

LITHUANIA   To Vilnius
(Wilno)

BELARUS   To Minsk

UKRAINE   To Łuck

SLOVAKIA

KALININGRAD
(KRÓLEWIEC)
Braniewo
Zalew Wiślany
Bartoszyce
ELBLĄG
Lidzbark Warm
Kętrzyn
Giżycko
Olecko
SUWAŁKI
Mrągowo
Ełk
Augustów
GRODNO
Lida
Ostróda
OLSZTYN
J. Śniardwy
Grajewo
Iława
Szczytno
Nidzica
Łomża
Brodnica
Mława
OSTROŁĘKA
Zambrów
Łapy
BIAŁYSTOK
lub-Dobrzyń
Sierpc
CIECHANÓW
Narew
Ostrów Maz
Hajnówka
Bielsk Podl
Białowieża
VŁOCŁAWEK
Płońsk
Nasielsk
Wyszków
Sokołów Podl
Bug
PŁOCK
Nowy Dwór Maz
Wyszogród
Gostynin
WARSZAWA
(WARSAW)
BRIEST
(BRZEŚĆ)
Kutno
Sochaczew
Pruszków
Otwock
Mińsk Maz
SIEDLCE
Biała Podlaska
Łowicz
Żyrardów
Góra Kalwaria
Łuków
Międzyrzec Podl
Zgierz
SKIERNIEWICE
Grójec
ŁÓDŹ
Pabianice
Włodawa
urska Wola
Tomaszów Maz
Dęblin
RADOM
Puławy
PIOTRKÓW
TRYB
Opoczno
LUBLIN
Bełchatów
Skarżysko Kam
Starachowice
CHEŁM
Radomsko
Ostrowiec Św
Kraśnik
Krasnystaw
obuck
KIELCE
ZAMOŚĆ
Hrubieszów
CZĘSTOCHOWA
Sandomierz
Stalowa Wola
Jędrzejów
Tarnobrzeg
Biłgoraj
Tomaszów Lub
Zawiercie
Mielec
San
TOM
KATOWICE
Olkusz
Dębica
horzów
Chrzanów
Jarosław
Pszczyna
Oświęcim
KRAKÓW
Bochnia
TARNÓW
RZESZÓW
PRZEMYŚL
BIELSKO-BIAŁA
Myślenice
Jasło
KROSNO
Żywiec
NOWY SĄCZ
Gorlice
Sanok
Nowy Targ
Krynica
Zakopane
Rysy
(2499m)
Vistula

Poland
4th edition – May 2002
First published – February 1993

Published by
Lonely Planet Publications Pty Ltd ABN 36 005 607 983
90 Maribyrnong St, Footscray, Victoria 3011, Australia

Lonely Planet offices
Australia Locked Bag 1, Footscray, Victoria 3011
USA 150 Linden St, Oakland, CA 94607
UK 10a Spring Place, London NW5 3BH
France 1 rue du Dahomey, 75011 Paris

Photographs
Many of the images in this guide are available for licensing from
Lonely Planet Images.
w www.lonelyplanetimages.com

Front cover photograph
The spires of the modern Orthodox Church at Hajnówka,Podlasie,
Poland (Krzysztof Dydyński)

ISBN 1 74059 082 1

text & maps © Lonely Planet Publications Pty Ltd 2002
photos © photographers as indicated 2002

Printed by The Bookmaker International Ltd
Printed in China

Contents – Text

4 Contents – Text

LANGUAGE   549

GLOSSARY   554

THANKS   556

INDEX   570

MAP LEGEND   back page

METRIC CONVERSION   inside back cover

Contents – Maps

6 Contents – Maps

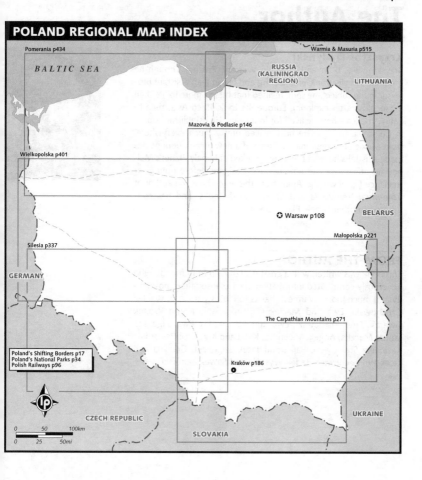

POLAND REGIONAL MAP INDEX

Pomerania p434

Warmia & Masuria p515

BALTIC SEA

RUSSIA
(KALININGRAD
REGION)

LITHUANIA

Mazovia & Podlasie p146

Wielkopolska p401

✪ Warsaw p108

BELARUS

Małopolska p221

Silesia p337

GERMANY

The Carpathian Mountains p271

Poland's Shifting Borders p17
Poland's National Parks p34
Polish Railways p96

Kraków p186

0   50   100km
0   25   50mi

CZECH REPUBLIC

UKRAINE

SLOVAKIA

The Author

Krzysztof Dydyński

Krzysztof was born and raised in Warsaw, Poland. Though he graduated in electronic engineering and became an assistant professor in the subject, he soon realised that there's more to life than microchips. After exploring Europe, he took off to Asia, then to Latin America where he lived for four years. He established a base in Colombia from where he travelled pretty much everywhere, from Mexico to Argentina. In search of a new incarnation, he has made Australia his next home and worked at Lonely Planet's Melbourne office as a cartographer and designer before opting for freelance travel writing. Apart from this guide he is the author of *Colombia*, *Venezuela* and *Kraków* guidebooks, and has contributed to other Lonely Planet books.

FROM THE AUTHOR

This book was written with a great deal of help from friends, who generously contributed information, advice, inspiration, hospitality and much more. Warmest thanks to Piotr Chamerski, Waldek Czechowski, Ewa and Maciek Gajewski, Aniuta and Wojtek Gwarek, Jarek Kisielewski, Ewa Kudokas, Ela Lis, Ewa, Jaga and Janusz Mączka, Angela Melendro, Kasia and Krzysztof Pasternak, Kazimierz Stagrowski, Bajka and Jacek Szelegejd, Grażyna and Jacek Wojciechowicz, Tadek Wysocki and Šawek Zagórski.

This Book

FROM THE PUBLISHER

The 4th edition of Poland was produced in Lonely Planet's Melbourne office. Editing was coordinated by Kalya Ryan and cartography and design by Celia Wood. Craig MacKenzie and Nina Rousseau assisted with editing and proofing. Huw Fowles, Jacqui Saunders and Mark Griffiths assisted with mapping. General credits go to Liz Filleul, Rachel Imeson, Chris Wyness and Mark Germanchis.

Thanks also to LPI for the images, Quentin Frayne for the language section, Wendy Wright (design) and Simon Bracken (artwork) for the front cover and Kate Nolan (KN), Tamsin Wilson (TW) and Martin Harris (MH) for the illustrations.

THANKS

Many thanks to the travellers who used the last edition and wrote to us with helpful hints, advice and interesting anecdotes. Your names appear in the back of this book.

Foreword

ABOUT LONELY PLANET GUIDEBOOKS

The story begins with a classic travel adventure: Tony and Maureen Wheeler's 1972 journey across Europe and Asia to Australia. There was no useful information about the overland trail then, so Tony and Maureen published the first Lonely Planet guidebook to meet a growing need.

From a kitchen table, Lonely Planet has grown to become the largest independent travel publisher in the world, with offices in Melbourne (Australia), Oakland (USA), London (UK) and Paris (France).

Today Lonely Planet guidebooks cover the globe. There is an ever-growing list of books and information in a variety of media. Some things haven't changed. The main aim is still to make it possible for adventurous travellers to get out there – to explore and better understand the world.

At Lonely Planet we believe travellers can make a positive contribution to the countries they visit – if they respect their host communities and spend their money wisely. Since 1986 a percentage of the income from each book has been donated to aid projects and human rights campaigns, and, more recently, to wildlife conservation.

Although inclusion in a guidebook usually implies a recommendation we cannot list every good place. Exclusion does not necessarily imply criticism. In fact there are a number of reasons why we might exclude a place – sometimes it is simply inappropriate to encourage an influx of travellers.

UPDATES & READER FEEDBACK

Things change – prices go up, schedules change, good places go bad and bad places go bankrupt. Nothing stays the same. So, if you find things better or worse, recently opened or long-since closed, please tell us and help make the next edition even more accurate and useful.

Lonely Planet thoroughly updates each guidebook as often as possible – usually every two years, although for some destinations the gap can be longer. Between editions, up-to-date information is available in our free, quarterly *Planet Talk* newsletter and monthly email bulletin *Comet*. The *Upgrades* section of our website (**w** www.lonelyplanet.com) is also regularly updated by Lonely Planet authors, and the site's *Scoop* section covers news and current affairs relevant to travellers. Lastly, the *Thorn Tree* bulletin board and *Postcards* section carry unverified, but fascinating, reports from travellers.

Tell us about it! We genuinely value your feedback. A well-travelled team at Lonely Planet reads and acknowledges every email and letter we receive and ensures that every morsel of information finds its way to the relevant authors, editors and cartographers.

Everyone who writes to us will find their name listed in the next edition of the appropriate guidebook, and will receive the latest issue of *Comet* or *Planet Talk*. The very best contributions will be rewarded with a free guidebook.

We may edit, reproduce and incorporate your comments in Lonely Planet products such as guidebooks, websites and digital products, so let us know if you don't want your comments reproduced or your name acknowledged.

How to contact Lonely Planet:
Online: **e** talk2us@lonelyplanet.com.au, **w** www.lonelyplanet.com
Australia: Locked Bag 1, Footscray, Victoria 3011
UK: 10a Spring Place, London NW5 3BH
USA: 150 Linden St, Oakland, CA 94607

Introduction

Poland is 1000 years old and many of its towns and cities date back to its early days. They shelter a rich architectural and artistic heritage that has survived all the battles fought on Polish soil over the centuries. A huge amount of damage was done during WWII, but the energy and resources that have gone into the rebuilding are astonishing – the old quarters of Warsaw and Gdańsk are miracles of loving reconstruction. Few cities were lucky enough to have survived the war without damage, and one of these was the illustrious old royal capital of Kraków – a place not to be missed. Other great historic cities include Toruń, Wrocław and Poznań.

Poland also has a lot to offer outside its cities. The southern border follows mountain ranges, where walkers can marvel at spectacular landscapes and scenery. The northern part of the country is skirted by the 500km Baltic coast, with an almost uninterrupted ribbon of white sandy beaches. For those who prefer fresh water, northeastern Poland offers gently rolling woodland with thousands of lakes, a paradise for yachting and canoeing. There's also an abundance of good, flat cycling country.

For centuries a bridge between East and West, set in the heart of Europe, Poland is still a largely unexplored country that retains much of its traditional way of life. You'll still see horse-drawn ploughs in remote areas, and carts laden with vegetables clogging up tiny back roads on their way to markets. There are villages which look as though the 20th century got lost somewhere down the road. The locals fill their rustic wooden churches to overflowing, and every small country road is dotted with wayside chapels and shrines, usually with fresh flowers. Here is a Poland to be savoured.

Poland has been one of the most cosmopolitan countries in Europe, thanks in part to its constantly shifting borders. It has incorporated Lithuanians, Ukrainians, Belarusians and Germans, and was a refuge for persecuted minorities – the Jews in particular – from all over the continent. The ethnic

POLAND

homogeneity you see today is quite recent – only 50 years old – and is set against the cultural complexity of Poland's past which has left behind a fascinating architectural mosaic, including Teutonic castles, Italian Renaissance palaces, French baroque country mansions and Eastern Orthodox churches crowned with onion domes.

While some parts of Europe have torn themselves apart for ethnic, religious or nationalistic reasons, Poland has a unity few other nations in the region can match. Bound together by Catholicism, language, nationality and shared experience, the country has swiftly got on after the collapse of communism, building a better home for its people – an opportunity for Westerners to see history in the making.

A reflective land of Chopin and Copernicus, Poland remains reasonably cheap and safe, with hospitable people who welcome visitors. Over the past decade, Poland has hugely improved its tourist infrastructure and developed into a modern, vibrant and progressive state, yet at the same time it maintains its traditional culture relatively unchanged. It's a fascinating destination and now is a great time to go.

Facts about Poland

HISTORY

Poland has not perished yet
As long as we (Poles) still live.
That which foreign force has seized
We at swordpoint shall retrieve.

The first lines of the Polish national anthem reflect the proud and irrepressible nature of the nation. One of the most patriotic and rebellious of peoples, Poles have had innumerable occasions to defend their freedom and sovereignty throughout more than 1000 turbulent years of history.

Nearly all the historical wrongs and atrocities the world could inflict have been experienced by the Poles. Geographically squeezed between two aggressive powers, Germany and Russia, Poland was repeatedly invaded and fought upon. Its boundaries have shifted east and west as its power waxed and waned, from being the largest country in Europe in the 17th century, to being completely wiped off the map from the end of the 18th century until after WWI. The nation re-emerged at this point, only to be devastated just two decades later in WWII, losing six million people.

Poland changed the course of history in 1989 by becoming the first Eastern European state to break free of communism, proving the truth of Stalin's 1944 comment that fitting communism onto Poland was like putting a saddle on a cow. Since then, the economic, social and psychological changes have been tremendous.

Origins

Some time in the Neolithic period (4000 to 2000 BC), permanent agricultural settlements began to appear in what is now Poland, and trading routes started to crisscross the thick forests which covered the area. In the last millennium BC and the early centuries AD, such diverse groups as Celts, Scythians, Balts, Goths, Huns and numerous Germanic tribes invaded, crossed and occasionally settled in the region. It's almost certain that the Slavs, the ethnic group to which the Poles belong, were among them, though some scholars believe it wasn't until the 6th or 7th century AD that the Slavs arrived from the south-east.

Diverse Slavonic tribes eventually settled various regions between the Baltic Sea and the ridge of the Carpathian Mountains. Toward the 10th century, one of these groups, the Polanie (literally, the people of the fields or open country dwellers), who had settled on the banks of the Warta River near present-day Poznań, attained dominance over the region.

Their tribal chief, the legendary Piast, managed to unite the scattered groups of the surrounding areas into a single political unit, and gave it the name Polska, or Poland, after the tribe's name. The region was later to become known as Wielkopolska or Great Poland and its first recorded ruler, Duke Mieszko I, was converted to Christianity in 966. This date is recognised as the formal birth of the Polish state.

The Piast Dynasty (966–1370)

Sandwiched between two expansive powers, Germany (the Holy Roman Empire in those days) and Russia (then comprising a myriad principalities dominated by Kyivan Rus), Poland was engaged in numerous armed conflicts with one or the other, or with both at the same time.

The first important break with the East came in 988, when Vladimir the Great of Kyiv accepted the Byzantine version of Christianity, thereby linking his principality to the Eastern Orthodox Church. The religious divergence between the Orthodox Russians and the Roman Catholic Poles subsequently fuelled cultural and political rivalry, which often led to armed struggle.

Duke Mieszko I was a talented leader. He managed to conquer the entire coastal region of Pomorze (Pomerania) and soon thereafter extended his sovereignty to include Śląsk (Silesia) to the south and Małopolska (Little

Poland) to the south-east. By the time of his death in 992, the Polish state was established within boundaries similar to those of Poland today, stretching over about 250,000 sq km. The first capital and archbishopric were established in Gniezno. By that time, towns such as Gdańsk, Szczecin, Poznań, Wrocław and Kraków already existed.

The son of Mieszko I, Bolesław Chrobry (Boleslaus the Brave, 992–1025), further enlarged and strengthened the empire. Shortly before his death in 1025 he was crowned the first Polish king by papal bull.

Wars continued unabated; the Germans were repeatedly invading the north, and expanded over the coastal regions. Due to these pressures, the administrative centre of the country was moved from Great Poland to the less vulnerable Little Poland. By the middle of the 11th century, Kraków was established as the royal seat.

Bolesław Krzywousty (Boleslaus the Wry-Mouthed, 1102–38) reconquered Pomerania and temporarily reinforced internal unity, but then, hoping to establish an ideal formula for succession, he divided the kingdom among his sons. This proved to be a disaster: Poland's short-lived unity was lost, and the rivalries and struggles between independent principalities left them all weak and vulnerable to foreign invaders. Enemies were quick to take advantage of the internal chaos.

When pagan Prussians from the region that is now the north-eastern tip of Poland attacked the province of Mazovia in 1226, Duke Konrad of Mazovia called for help from the Teutonic Knights, a Germanic military and religious order which had made its historical mark during the Crusades. Once the knights had subjugated the pagan tribes, they set up a state on the conquered territories that they ruled from their castle at Malbork. The knights soon became a major European military power, and after capturing all of northern Poland they controlled most of the Baltic coast, including the port of Gdańsk.

Things were not going much better in southern Poland. In their great 13th-century invasion, the Mongols (or Tatars, as they are commonly referred to in Poland) conquered Kyiv and most of the Russian principalities, then pushed farther west into Poland. They had devastated much of Little Poland and Silesia by 1241–42, and launched yet another destructive raid in 1259.

Not until 1320 was the Polish crown restored and the state reunified. Under the rule of Kazimierz III Wielki (Casimir III the Great, 1333–70), Poland gradually became a mighty, prosperous state. Kazimierz regained suzerainty over Mazovia, then captured vast areas of Ruthenia (today's Ukraine) and Podolia, thus greatly expanding his monarchy towards the south-east.

Kazimierz Wielki was also an enlightened and energetic ruler on the domestic front. Promoting and instituting reforms, he laid down solid legal, economic, commercial and educational foundations. Over 70 new towns were founded, existing towns expanded rapidly and the royal capital of Kraków flourished. In 1364, one of Europe's first universities was established at Kraków. An extensive network of castles and fortifications was constructed to improve the nation's defences. There is a saying that Kazimierz Wielki 'found Poland built of wood and left it built of masonry'.

The Jagiellonian Dynasty (1382–1572)

Kazimierz Wielki died in 1370 leaving no heir, and the Polish crown passed to his nephew, Louis I of Hungary. On his death in 1382, the Polish succession passed to his 10-year-old daughter Jadwiga, whereas the Hungarians chose her older sister Maria as their queen. The Polish aristocracy, which already enjoyed significant political clout, decided on a dynastic alliance with Lithuania, a vast and still pagan country. Grand Duke Jagiełło of Lithuania married the young Crown Princess Jadwiga, accepted the Catholic faith and assumed the name of Władysław II Jagiełło (1386–1434). This political marriage increased Poland's territory fivefold overnight and formed the Polish-Lithuanian alliance, which would continue through the next four centuries.

Under Jagiełło, Polish territory continued to expand. The king led a series of successful

Kazimierz III Wielki, one of Poland's most
enlightened and energetic leaders

wars, and at the Battle of Grunwald in 1410
the Polish-Lithuanian army defeated the Teutonic Knights, marking the beginning of the
order's decline. In the Thirteen Years' War of
1454–66, the Teutonic Order was eventually
disbanded and Poland recovered eastern
Pomerania, part of Prussia and the port of
Gdańsk, regaining access to the Baltic Sea.
For 30 years, the Polish empire extended
from the Baltic Sea to the Black Sea and was
the largest European state.

It was not to last, however. Another period of invasions began in 1475. This time
the main instigators were the Ottomans, the
Tatars of Crimea and the tsars of Moscow.
Independently or together, they repeatedly
invaded and raided the eastern and southern
Polish territories and on one occasion managed to penetrate as far as Kraków.

Despite the wars, the Polish kingdom's
power was firmly established. In addition to
prospering economically, the country advanced both culturally and spiritually. The
early 16th century brought the Renaissance
to Poland. The incumbent king, Zygmunt I

Stary (Sigismund I the Old, 1506–48), was
a great promoter of the arts. The Latin language was gradually supplanted by Polish
and a national literature was born. Printing
presses came into use and books began to
appear. Architecture blossomed and many
buildings of the period survive to this day.
In 1543, Nicolaus Copernicus (Mikołaj
Kopernik) published his work *On the Revolutions of the Celestial Spheres*, which altered the course of astronomy by proposing
that the earth moves around the sun.

The next and last king of the Jagiellonian
Dynasty, Zygmunt II August (Sigismund II
Augustus, 1548–72), continued his father's
patronage of arts and culture. Thanks to
their inspiring and protective policies, the
arts and sciences flourished and the two
reigns came to be referred to as Poland's
golden age.

The bulk of Poland's population at that
time was made up of Poles and Lithuanians,
but included significant minorities of Germans, Ruthenians (Ukrainians), Tatars, Armenians and Livonians (Latvians). Jews
constituted an important and steadily growing part of the community, and by the end of
the 16th century Poland had a larger Jewish
population than the rest of Europe combined.

Religious freedom was constitutionally
established by the *Sejm* (or Diet – the Polish parliament) in 1573 and the equality of
creeds officially guaranteed. Such diverse
faiths as Roman Catholicism, Eastern Orthodoxy, Protestantism, Judaism and Islam
were able to coexist relatively peacefully.

On the political front, Poland evolved during the 16th century into a parliamentary
monarchy with most of the privileges going
to the *szlachta* (gentry or the feudal nobility),
who comprised roughly 10% of the population. In contrast, the status of the peasants declined, and they gradually found themselves
falling into a state of virtual slavery.

The Royal Republic (1573–1795)

During the reign of Zygmunt August, the
threat of Russian expansionism increased.
Hoping to strengthen the monarchy, the
Sejm convened in Lublin in 1569 and unified Poland and Lithuania into a single

state. It also made Warsaw the seat of the Sejm's future debates. Since there was no heir apparent to the throne, it also established a system of royal succession based on direct voting in popular elections by the nobility, who would all come to Warsaw with their servants, horses, tents etc to vote. In the absence of a serious Polish contender, a foreign candidate would be considered.

The experiment proved disastrous. For each royal election, foreign powers promoted their candidates by bargaining and bribing voters. During the period of the Royal Republic, Poland was ruled by 11 kings, only four of whom were native Poles.

The first elected king, Henri de Valois, retreated to France after only a year on the Polish throne. His successor, Stefan Batory (Stephen Bathory, 1576–86), prince of Transylvania, was fortunately a much wiser choice. Batory, together with his gifted commander and chancellor Jan Zamoyski, conducted a series of successful battles against Tsar Ivan the Terrible.

After Batory's premature death, the crown was offered to the Swede Zygmunt III Waza (Sigismund III Vasa, 1587–1632), the first of three kings of Poland of the Vasa dynasty. Five years later Zygmunt also inherited the Swedish throne. As ruler of both countries, he tried to establish a Polish-Swedish alliance. This drew strong opposition in Sweden on the basis of religious differences, and the king, a devout Catholic, was dethroned by the predominantly Protestant (Lutheran) Swedes. The subsequent Swedish-Polish war caused Poland to lose part of Livonia (today Latvia and southern Estonia).

Meanwhile, on the eastern front, Polish troops were fighting the Russian army, eventually capturing vast new frontier provinces and giving Poland its greatest ever territorial extent. In effect, Zygmunt Waza ruled over an area of roughly one million sq km, or more than three times the size of present-day Poland. However, he probably better remembered for moving the Polish capital from Kraków to Warsaw between 1596 and 1609.

Economically, Poland was still a wealthy power serving as the granary of Europe, but the beginning of the 17th century was the turning point. From then on, the Royal Republic gradually declined in almost every way. The main source of further misfortune lay not in foreign aggression but in domestic policies that undermined the country from within. Ironically, it was all done in the name of the freedom, liberty and equality of which the Poles have always been so proud.

The economic and political power of the szlachta grew dangerously throughout the 17th century. The nobility not only divided most of the country into huge estates, which they distributed among themselves, but also usurped political privileges that significantly reduced governmental authority. The most ill-fated move was the introduction of the *liberum veto*: assuming the equality of each voter, no bill introduced to the Sejm could be adopted without a unanimous vote. In other words, each member of the Sejm had a veto over every bill. The height of this utopian concept was the rule that a single veto was sufficient to dissolve the Sejm at any time and to subject all law passed during the previous session to a re-vote during the following convention. This version of democracy (or anarchy, if you prefer) effectively paralysed the Sejm.

The liberum veto was first used in 1652, and later on, particularly in the 18th century, it was applied recklessly. During the 30-year rule of the next-to-last Polish king, August III Wettin, the Sejm only once succeeded in passing any legislation at all. To make things worse, some frustrated nobles judged the Sejm worthless and resorted to their own brand of justice, the armed rebellion.

Meanwhile, foreign invaders were systematically carving up the land. Jan II Kazimierz Waza (John II Casimir Vasa, 1648–68), the last of the Vasa dynasty on the Polish throne, was unable to resist the aggressors – Russians, Tatars, Ukrainians, Cossacks, Ottomans and Swedes – who were moving in on all fronts. The Swedish invasion of 1655–60, known as the Deluge, was particularly disastrous. During the rule of Kazimierz Waza, the country lost over a quarter of its national territory, cities were burned and plundered, the countryside was

POLAND'S SHIFTING BORDERS

1000

1370

1650

1750

1900

1930

 Present Polish Boundary

 Historical Polish Territory

devastated and the economy destroyed. Of the population of 10 million, four million people succumbed to war, famine and bubonic plague.

The last bright moment in the long decline of the Royal Republic was the reign of Jan III Sobieski (1674–96), a brilliant commander who led several victorious battles against the Ottomans. The most famous of these was the Battle of Vienna in 1683, in which he defeated the Turks and forced their retreat from Europe. Ironically, the victory only strengthened Austria, a country which would later take its turn at invading Poland.

The 18th century saw the agony of the Polish state. By then, Russia had evolved into a mighty, expansive empire which systematically strengthened its grip over Poland. This was somewhat facilitated by the corrupt Polish nobility which, given the disastrous state of affairs at home, was increasingly seeking benefits and favours abroad, principally in Russia. A significant nail in the coffin of Polish independence was the infamous Silent Sejm of 1717, in which Peter the Great succeeded in imposing a protectorate over Poland, effectively allowing Russia to intervene in Poland's internal matters. Although the last Polish king, Stanisław August Poniatowski (1764–95), was a patron of literature and the arts, he was essentially a puppet of the Russian regime. It was only during his reign that the Poles became aware of the severity of their country's situation, with direct intervention in Poland's affairs from Catherine the Great, Empress of Russia.

The Partitions

When anti-Russian rebellion broke out in Poland, Russia entered into treaties with Prussia and Austria, and the three countries agreed to annex three substantial chunks of Poland, amounting to roughly 30% of Polish territory. The Sejm was forced to ratify the partition in 1773.

The First Partition had the effect of a cold shower and led to immediate reforms in the administrative, military and educational spheres. The economy began to recover, and there were new developments in industry. In 1791, a new, fully liberal constitution was passed. It was known as the Constitution of the 3rd of May, and it was the world's second written delineation of government responsibility (the first was that of the USA). It abolished the old machinery of government, including the liberum veto.

Catherine the Great could tolerate no more of this dangerous democracy. Russian troops were sent into Poland, and crushed fierce resistance. The reforms were abolished by force. The Second Partition came in 1793, with Russia and Prussia strengthening their grip by grabbing over half the remaining Polish territory.

In response, patriotic forces under the leadership of Tadeusz Kościuszko, a hero of the American War of Independence, launched an armed rebellion in 1794. The campaign soon gained popular support and the rebels won some early victories, but the Russian troops, stronger and better armed, finally defeated the Polish forces.

This time the three occupying powers decided to eradicate the troublesome nation altogether, and in the Third Partition, effected in 1795, they divided the rest of Poland's territory among themselves. Poland disappeared from the map for the next 123 years.

Under the Partitions (1795–1914)

Despite the partitions, Poland continued to exist as a spiritual and cultural community, and a number of secret nationalist societies were soon created. Since revolutionary France was seen as their major ally in the struggle, some leaders fled to Paris and established their headquarters there.

When Napoleon attacked Prussia in 1806, a Polish popular insurrection broke out in his support as he advanced on Moscow. In 1807, Napoleon created the Duchy of Warsaw, a sovereign Polish state that consisted of former Polish territories, which had been annexed by Prussia. However, when Napoleon lost his war with Russia in 1812, Poland was again partitioned.

In 1815, the Congress of Vienna established the Congress Kingdom of Poland, a

Tadeusz Kościuszko – Polish-American Hero of Independence

Born in 1746 to a family of Polish nobility in Poland's far eastern province (now part of Belarus), Kościuszko completed military school in Warsaw and went to Paris to continue his military studies. On returning to Poland he fell in love with the daughter of a general, but was unable to win his permission for the marriage and, following an unsuccessful attempt to elope with her, he was forced to flee the country. He went to France then, in 1776, to America, where he joined the local forces fighting for independence from Britain.

During the following five years, he was involved in most major engagements of the American independence campaign, including the Battle of Saratoga, the Battle of Ninety-Six and the blockade of Charleston. In recognition for his contribution, he was granted US citizenship and made a brigadier general in the US Army. Yet, in 1784 he decided to go back to Poland, which was experiencing difficult political times.

His homecoming was disappointing, and it wasn't until 1789 that he was offered a major military position. Meanwhile, he lived a humble life in the countryside.

Following the invasion of Poland by the Russian army in 1792 Kościuszko was able to prove his military prowess once again. The Russian attack was launched by the Empress Catherine the Great to break the local reforms introduced in the aftermath of the fully liberal constitution of 1791. Russian aggression was met with strong resistance by the Poles, culminating in the Battle of Dubienka (1792). Kościuszko played a large part in the Polish victory. By this time his fame was reaching international proportions, so much so that the new French government gave him honorary French citizenship. King Stanisław August Poniatowski raised him to the rank of general.

In March 1794, Kościuszko solemnly swore the oath of national uprising against the occupants at Kraków's main square. A few months later he commanded the famous Battle of Racławice, in which legions of Polish peasants, equipped with just scythes, were victorious over the well-armed Russian troops.

In order to attract more peasant volunteers to form further military squads, Kościuszko issued a manifesto suspending serfdom, but this was met with resistance by the aristocracy, and proved to be a turning point in the campaign's fortunes. Kościuszko was forced to retreat to Warsaw where he led a heroic two-month defence of the city against the massive attacks of the combined Prussian-Russian armies. Despite the best efforts of the Polish forces the city was captured. Kościuszko tried to continue fighting in Wielkopolska, but was wounded and taken prisoner by the Russians at Maciejowice. Without its leader, the insurrection was soon over and it was just a matter of months before the three occupying powers divided the remaining chunk of Poland among themselves.

Jailed in St Petersburg, Kościuszko was freed in 1796 soon after the death of the Empress Catherine the Great. He went to the USA, where he became a close friend of Thomas Jefferson, but returned to France in 1798, hoping to gain Napoleon's aid in Poland's independence cause. Napoleon didn't want to commit himself, however.

Disillusioned and embittered, Kościuszko retired from public life, retreating to a country estate in France, then in Switzerland, where he died in 1817. A year later, his remains were brought to Kraków and buried among the Polish kings in the crypt of the Wawel Cathedral.

supposedly autonomous Polish state which nevertheless had the Russian tsar as its king. From its inception, its liberal constitution was violated by Tsar Alexander and his successors.

In response to continuing Russian oppression, several armed uprisings broke out.

The most significant were the November Insurrection of 1830 and the January Insurrection of 1863, both of which were crushed by the Russians and followed by harsh repression, executions and deportations to Siberia.

As it became increasingly clear that armed protest was not going to succeed, the Polish patriots reconsidered their strategy and advocated 'organic work', a pacifist endeavour to recover the economy, education and culture from the Russians. This change was reflected in the arts and literature, which moved from the visionary political poetry of the Romantics to the more realistic prose of the Positivists.

In the 1870s Russia dramatically stepped up its efforts to eradicate Polish culture, suppressing the Polish language in education, administration and commerce, and replacing it with Russian. Soon after, Prussia imitated the Russian system and introduced Germanisation. Only in the Austrian sector (Galicia) were the Poles given any degree of autonomy.

Towards the end of the 19th century, steady economic growth was evident. Political activity was revived and the first political parties were established in the 1890s. On the other hand, this was also a time of mass emigration. Due to the poverty of the rural areas, mainly in Galicia, peasants had no choice but to seek a better life abroad. By the outbreak of WWI about four million out of a total Polish population of 20 to 25 million had emigrated, primarily to the USA.

WWI (1914–18)

WWI broke out in August 1914. On one side were the Central Powers, Austria and Germany (including Prussia); on the other, Russia and its Western allies. With Poland's three occupying powers at war, most of the fighting was staged on the territories inhabited by the Poles, resulting in staggering losses of life and livelihood. Since no formal Polish state existed, there was no Polish army to fight for the national cause. Even worse, some two million Poles were conscripted into the Russian, German or Austrian armies, depending on whose territory they lived in, and were obliged to fight one another.

Paradoxically, the war eventually brought about Polish independence. It came as a result of a combination of external circumstances and the participation of the Poles. After the October Revolution in 1917, Russia plunged into civil war and no longer had the power to oversee Polish affairs. The final

collapse of the Austrian Empire in October 1918 and the withdrawal of the German army from Warsaw in November brought the opportune moment. Marshal Józef Piłsudski took command of Warsaw on 11 November 1918, declared Polish sovereignty, and usurped power as the head of state. This date is recognised as the day of the founding of the Second Republic, so named to create a symbolic bridge between itself and the Royal Republic that existed before the partitions.

Between the Wars (1918–39)

Poland began its new incarnation in a desperate position. After the war, the country and its economy were in ruins. It's estimated that over one million Poles lost their lives in WWI. All state institutions – including the army, which hadn't existed for over a century – had to be built up from scratch. Even the borders, which had been obliterated in the partitions, had to be redefined, and they weren't made official until 1923.

The Treaty of Versailles in 1919 awarded Poland the western part of Prussia, thereby providing access to the Baltic Sea. The city of Gdańsk, however, was omitted and became the Free City of Danzig. The rest of Poland's western border was drawn up in a series of plebiscites which resulted in Poland acquiring some significant industrial regions of Upper Silesia.

The eastern boundaries were established when Polish forces led by Piłsudski defeated the Red Army during the Polish-Soviet war (1919–20). The victory brought Poland vast areas of what are now western Ukraine and Belarus.

When Poland's territorial struggle was over, the Second Republic covered nearly 400,000 sq km and was populated by 26 million people. One-third of the population was of non-Polish ethnic background, mainly Jews, Ukrainians, Belarusians and Germans.

Piłsudski retired from political life in 1922, giving way to a series of unstable parliamentary governments. For the next four years, frequently changing coalition cabinets struggled to overcome enormous economic and social problems.

Quite unexpectedly, Piłsudski seized power in a military coup in May 1926, and then held on until his death in 1935. Parliament was gradually phased out. Despite the dictatorial regime, political repression had little effect on ordinary people. The economic situation was relatively stable, and cultural and intellectual life prospered.

On the international front, Poland's situation in the 1930s was unenviable. In an

Marshal Józef Piłsudski – Father of the Second Republic

Marshal Józef Piłsudski is widely admired in Poland, for various reasons. It was he who realised the long-awaited dream of a sovereign Poland after WWI, thus becoming the father of national independence. He was also the last great independent Polish leader, who commanded respect and contrasted sharply with the subsequent communist puppets, and was the last of Poland's rulers to defeat the Russians in battle.

Piłsudski was born in 1867 in the Vilnius region, then part of Poland under Russian occupation. As a teenager, he entered the underground anti-tsarist circles in Vilnius, but was arrested in 1887 and sent to a prison in Siberia for five years. Once freed, he returned to Poland and joined the newly founded Polish Socialist Party (PPS) in Warsaw. He was again arrested in 1900 and sent to a jail in St Petersburg, but escaped the following year and took refuge in Kraków (then under the less oppressive Austrian occupation), which became the base for his anti-tsarist activities until WWI.

In 1908 the PPS, then under the leadership of Piłsudski, formed paramilitary squads, which in time developed into the Polish Legions, the military force of the still formally nonexistent Poland. During WWI, the legions fought under Piłsudski for the nation's independence. The opportune moment came in November 1918, after Germany's capitulation. Marshal Piłsudski came to Warsaw, took power on 11 November and proclaimed Poland a sovereign state.

In 1919 Piłsudski launched a massive offensive towards the east, capturing vast territories that had been Polish before the 18th-century partitions. However, the Soviet counter-offensive pushed westward, and by mid-1920 the Red Army approached Warsaw. In the battle for the city in August 1920 (known as the Miracle on the Vistula), the Polish Army under Piłsudski outmanoeuvred and defeated the Soviets. It may well be that this victory saved the weakened Western Europe, or at least Germany, from the Bolshevik conquest.

After independent Poland was safely back on the map and a modern democratic constitution was adopted in 1921, Piłsudski stepped down. However, disillusioned with the economic recession and governmental crisis, he reappeared on the political scene in May 1926. In a classic coup d'etat, he marched on Warsaw at the head of the army. The three-day street fighting that broke out resulted in 400 dead and over 1000 wounded. After the government resigned, the National Assembly elected Piłsudski as president. However, he refused to take the post, opting instead for the office of Defence Minister, which he maintained until his death. There are no doubts, though, that it was Piłsudski who ran the country from behind the scenes for a decade, until he died of cancer in 1935.

Despite his obvious faults and dictatorial governing style, Piłsudski was buried in the crypt of Kraków's Wawel Cathedral among Polish kings, which in itself reflects the degree of national respect and admiration held for him. He continues to be widely admired today.

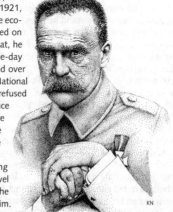

attempt to regulate relations with its two inexorably hostile neighbours, Poland signed nonaggression pacts with both the Soviet Union and Germany. Nevertheless, it soon became clear that the pacts didn't offer any real guarantee of safety.

On 23 August 1939, a pact of nonaggression between Germany and the Soviet Union was signed in Moscow by their foreign ministers, Ribbentrop and Molotov. This pact contained a secret protocol defining the prospective partition of Eastern Europe between the two great powers. Stalin and Hitler planned to carve up the Polish state between themselves.

WWII (1939–45)

WWII began at dawn on 1 September 1939 with a massive German invasion of Poland. Fighting began in Gdańsk (at that time the Free City of Danzig) when German forces encountered a stubborn handful of Polish resisters at Westerplatte. The battle lasted a week. Simultaneously, another German line stormed Warsaw, which finally surrendered on 28 September. Despite valiant resistance there was simply no hope of withstanding the numerically overwhelming and well-armed German forces; the last resistance groups were quelled by early October. Hitler intended to create a Polish puppet state on the newly acquired territory, but since no collaborators could be found, western Poland was directly annexed to Germany while the central regions became the so-called General Government, ruled by the Nazi governor from Kraków.

Winston Churchill observed: 'Poland was the only country which never collaborated with the Nazis in any form and no Polish units fought alongside the German army'.

On 17 September eastern Poland was invaded by the Soviet Union, and by November had been swallowed up. Thus within two months Poland was yet again partitioned. Mass arrests, exile and executions followed in both invaded parts. It's estimated that between one and two million Poles were sent by the Soviets to Siberia, the Soviet Arctic and Kazakhstan in 1939–40. Many of them never returned. One of the most tragic events of that

period was the massacre at Katyń and two other sites, where the Soviets shot and killed nearly 22,000 Polish prisoners, including many intellectuals and senior army officers.

Soon after the outbreak of the war, a Polish government-in-exile was formed in France under General Władysław Sikorski. It was shifted to London in June 1940. In July 1943 Sikorski died in an aircraft crash at Gibraltar, and Stanisław Mikołajczyk succeeded him as prime minister.

The course of the war changed dramatically when Hitler unexpectedly attacked the Soviet Union on 22 June 1941. The Germans pushed the Soviets out of eastern Poland and extended their power deep into Russia. For over three years, the whole of Poland lay under Nazi occupation. Hitler's policy was to eradicate the Polish nation and Germanise the territory. The Polish education system was dismantled, apart from primary schools. Hundreds of thousands of Poles were deported en masse to forced-labour camps in Germany, while others, primarily the intelligentsia, were executed in an attempt to exterminate spiritual and intellectual leadership. Jews were to be eliminated completely. They were at first segregated and confined in ghettos until a more efficient method was applied – the death camps.

The death camps were probably the most horrifying and inhumane chapter of WWII. They were initially established in 1940, and by the following year there was already a large network, with the largest at Oświęcim (Auschwitz). They proved *very* efficient and some five million people were put to death in the gas chambers. Almost the whole of Poland's Jewish population (three million) and roughly one million Poles died in the camps. There was desperate resistance from within the ghettos; the biggest single act of defiance came with the tragic Warsaw Ghetto Uprising that broke out in April 1943.

The Polish national resistance was organised in the cities, and formed and operated the Polish educational, communications and judicial systems. Armed squads were created in 1940 within Poland by the government-in-exile, and later became the Armia Krajowa (AK) or Home Army.

Massacre at Katyń

In April 1943, German troops fighting Soviets on the eastern front came across extensive mass graves at Katyń, near Smolensk, in present-day Belarus. Introductory exhumation revealed the remains of several thousand Polish soldiers and civilians shot dead, execution-style. The news immediately hit the press but the Soviet government denied any responsibility and accused the Nazis of the crime. Two years later the war ended, the communists took power in Poland and Katyń became a taboo word for decades, even though most Poles were aware of the tragic events.

It wasn't until 1990 that the Soviets admitted their 'mistake', without revealing details. In October 1992 the Russian government finally made public secret documents showing that Stalin's Politburo was responsible for the massacre at Katyń. Meanwhile, in the summer of 1991, further mass graves of Polish soldiers were discovered in Myednoye and Kharkov, both in central Russia.

Over the past decade the picture has become more complete. Soon after their invasion of Poland in September 1939, the Soviets took an estimated 180,000 prisoners comprising Polish soldiers, police officers, judges, politicians, intellectuals, scientists, teachers, professors, writers and priests, and crammed them into various camps throughout the Soviet Union and the invaded territories. On Stalin's order, signed in March 1940, about 21,800 of these prisoners, including many high-ranking officers and intellectuals, were transported from the camps to the forests of Katyń, Myednoye and Kharkov, shot dead and buried.

Much like the Nazis, the Soviets aimed to exterminate the intellectual elite of Polish society, to eliminate the driving power and the leadership of the nation. Statistics confirm that in WWII Poland lost 21% of its prewar judges, 30% of university teachers, 40% of physicians and 57% of lawyers, some of them in Katyń and the other two massacre sites.

Meanwhile, outside Poland, the warring nations jockeyed for position. Once the Germans had attacked the Soviets, Stalin did an about-face and turned to Poland for help in the war against Germany, promising in exchange to form a Polish army. Diplomatic relations were established with the Polish government-in-exile.

This chumming-up with Stalin elicited mixed feelings in Poland, but at the time it seemed the most pragmatic course of action and certainly the only way to re-establish the Polish armed forces. The army was founded anew late in 1941 under General Władysław Anders but it soon became apparent that the military would have to operate on Soviet terms. Anders tactically removed the majority of his troops to North Africa, where they joined the British fighting forces. The Poles distinguished themselves at Tobruk, Monte Cassino and in other Allied campaigns.

Having failed to control Anders' army, Stalin began to organise a new Polish fighting force in 1943; in order to assure full Soviet control, most of the officers were taken from the Red Army. This army set about liberating German-occupied Poland during the last stage of the war.

As a result of Stalin's efforts to spread communism in Poland, the new Polish communist party, the Polish Workers' Party (PPR), was formed in Warsaw in 1942. It in turn organised its own military forces, the Armia Ludowa (AL) or People's Army, a counterpart to the already existing noncommunist force, the Armia Krajowa.

Hitler's defeat at Stalingrad in 1943 marked the turning point of the war on the eastern front, and from then on the Red Army successfully pushed westwards. After the Soviets liberated the Polish city of Lublin, the pro-communist Polish Committee of National Liberation (PKWN) was installed on 22 July 1944 and assumed the functions of a provisional government. A week later the Red Army reached the outskirts of Warsaw.

Warsaw at that time remained under Nazi occupation. In a last-ditch attempt to establish an independent Polish administration, the resistance forces decided to gain control of the city before the arrival of the Soviet troops. On 1 August 1944, the orders for a general anti-German uprising, sanctioned by the government-in-exile, were given by General Tadeusz Bór Komorowski, then commander of the Home Army. For 63 days the struggle dragged on with unprecedented savagery, but the insurgents were ultimately forced to surrender. Approximately 200,000 Poles were killed in the Warsaw Uprising and all survivors were expelled from the city. Immediately afterwards, on Hitler's order, Warsaw was literally razed to the ground.

During these appalling events, the Red Army, which was sitting just across the Vistula River, didn't lift a finger. Upon learning of the uprising, Stalin halted the offensive and ordered his generals not to intervene or provide assistance in the fighting. Nor were the Soviets to do anything to prevent the destruction that followed. It wasn't until 17 January 1945 that the Soviet army finally marched in to 'liberate' Warsaw, which by that time was little more than a heap of empty ruins.

For the Poles, the Warsaw Uprising was one of the most heroic and simultaneously most tragic engagements of the war. Ironically, the Germans had done the Soviets' work for them by eliminating the best of the Polish nation, the only obstacle standing in the way of a communist takeover of the country.

Through the winter, the Red Army continued its westward advance across Poland, and after a few months reached Berlin. The Nazi Reich capitulated on 8 May 1945.

The impact of the war on Poland was staggering. The country had lost over six million people, about 20% of its prewar population. Of three million Polish Jews in 1939, only 80,000 to 90,000 survived the war. The country and its cities lay in ruins; only 15% of Warsaw's buildings had survived. Many Poles who had seen out the war in foreign countries opted not to return to the new political order.

Communist Rule

At the Yalta Conference in February 1945, Roosevelt, Churchill and Stalin decided to leave Poland under Soviet control. They agreed that Poland's eastern frontier would roughly follow the Nazi-Soviet demarcation line of 1939. In effect, the Soviet Union annexed 180,000 sq km of prewar Polish territory. In August 1945 at Potsdam, Allied leaders established Poland's western boundary along the Odra (Oder) and the Nysa (Neisse) rivers, thereby reinstating about 100,000 sq km of Poland's western provinces after centuries of German rule.

The radical boundary changes were followed by population transfers of some 10 million people: Poles were moved into the newly defined Poland while Germans, Ukrainians and Belarusians were resettled outside its boundaries. In the end, 98% of Poland's population was ethnically Polish.

As soon as Poland formally fell under Soviet control, Stalin launched an intensive Sovietisation campaign. Wartime resistance leaders were charged with Nazi collaboration, tried in Moscow and summarily shot or sentenced to arbitrary prison terms. A provisional Polish government was set up in Moscow in June 1945 and then transferred to Warsaw. General elections were postponed until 1947 to allow time for the arrest of prominent Polish political figures by the secret police. Even so, Stanisław Mikołajczyk, the government-in-exile's only representative to return to Poland, received over 80% of the popular vote.

The 'official' figures, however, revealed a majority vote for the communists. The new Sejm elected Bolesław Bierut president; Mikołajczyk, accused of espionage, fled back to England.

In 1948 the Polish United Workers' Party (PZPR), henceforth referred to as 'the Party', was formed to monopolise power. In 1952 a Soviet-style constitution was adopted. The office of president was abolished and effective power passed to the First Secretary of the Party Central Committee. Poland became an affiliate of the Warsaw Pact, the Soviet bloc's version of NATO; and of the Council of Mutual Economic Assistance (Comecon), the communists' equivalent of the European Economic Community.

All commercial and industrial enterprises employing more than 50 workers were nationalised. In a forced march towards industrialisation, priority was given to heavy industry, particularly coal mining and steel manufacturing. Early attempts at agricultural collectivisation were later abandoned and about 80% of cultivated land remained in the hands of individual farmers. In the arts, socialist realism became the dominant style, and was to leave behind an abominable body of painting, sculpture, architecture, literature and music. Meanwhile, the citizenry united to rebuild Polish cities.

Despite all its horrors, Stalinist fanaticism never gained as much influence in Poland as in neighbouring countries and it subsided fairly soon after Stalin's death in 1953. The powers of the secret police were eroded and some concessions were made to popular demands. The press was liberalised and Polish cultural values were resuscitated. In 1956, when Nikita Khrushchev denounced Stalin at the Soviet 20th Party Congress, Bierut died of a heart attack!

In June 1956, a massive industrial strike demanding 'bread and freedom' broke out in Poznań. Tanks rolled in and crushed the revolt, leaving 76 dead and over 900 wounded. Soon afterward, Władysław Gomułka, an ex-political prisoner of the Stalin era, was appointed first secretary of the Party. At first he commanded popular support, primarily because he'd managed to reduce Soviet meddling in Polish affairs and offered some concessions to the Church and peasantry. Later in his term, however, he displayed an increasingly rigid and authoritarian attitude, putting pressure on the Church and intensifying persecution of the intelligentsia. But it was ultimately an economic crisis that brought about his downfall; when he announced official price increases in 1970, a wave of mass strikes erupted in Gdańsk, Gdynia and Szczecin. Again, the violence was put down by force, resulting in 44 deaths. The Party, to save face, ejected Gomułka from office and replaced him with Edward Gierek.

On assuming power, Gierek launched an extensive program of modernisation of the heavy industrial sector. Polish labour, energy and raw materials were cheaper than those in the West, and his strategy was to acquire modern technology abroad which would be paid for from profits made by selling products of the new industry on the international market. Despite some initial growth, however, the poorly conceived factories, inefficiency due to lack of individual worker incentives, the inferior quality of Polish products and, finally, the world market recession of the mid-1970s combined to spell failure for the scheme.

An attempt to raise prices in 1976 incited labour protests, and again workers walked off the job, this time in Radom and Warsaw. Caught in a downward spiral, Gierek took out more foreign loans, but to earn hard currency with which to pay the interest, he was forced to divert consumer goods away from the domestic market and sell them abroad. By 1980 the external debt stood at US$21 billion and the economy had slumped disastrously.

By then, the opposition had grown into a significant force, backed by numerous advisers from the intellectual circles. The election of Karol Wojtyła, the archbishop of Kraków, as Pope John Paul II in 1978 and his triumphal visit to his homeland a year later dramatically increased political ferment. When in July 1980 the government again announced food-price increases, the results were predictable: fervent and well-organised strikes and riots broke out and spread like wildfire throughout the country. In August, they paralysed major ports, the Silesia coal mines and the Lenin Shipyard in Gdańsk.

Unlike most previous popular protests, the 1980 strikes were nonviolent; the strikers did not take to the streets, but stayed in their factories. Although the strikes started by demanding wage rises, they very soon took on more general economic and political overtones. Concerted protest by workers and their advisers from the intelligentsia had proved a successful and explosive combination. In contrast, the Party was weak, split and disorganised, and after a decade of mismanagement, the economy was in a state of virtual collapse. The government was no longer in a position to use force against its opponents.

Solidarity

After long, drawn-out negotiations in the Lenin Shipyard in Gdańsk an agreement was eventually reached on 31 August 1980. The government was forced to accept most of the strikers' demands. The most significant of these was recognition of the workers' right to organise independent trade unions, and to strike. In return, workers agreed to adhere to the constitution and to accept the Party's power as supreme.

Workers' delegations from around the country convened and founded Solidarność or 'Solidarity', a nation-wide independent and self-governing trade union. Lech Wałęsa, who led the Gdańsk strike, was elected chair. In November, the Solidarity movement, which by then had garnered nearly 10 million members (60% of the workforce), was formally recognised by the government. Amazingly, one million Solidarity members had come from the Party's ranks!

Gierek was ejected from office and his post taken over by Stanisław Kania; in October 1981 Kania was replaced by General Wojciech Jaruzelski, who continued to serve as prime minister and minister of defence, posts which he had held prior to his new appointment.

Solidarity had a dramatic effect on the whole of Polish society. After 35 years of restraint, the Poles launched themselves into a spontaneous and chaotic sort of democracy. Wide-ranging debates over the process of reform were led by Solidarity, and the independent press flourished. Such taboo historical subjects as the Stalin-Hitler pact and the Katyń massacre could for the first time be openly discussed.

Not surprisingly, the 10 million Solidarity members represented a wide range of attitudes: from confrontational to conciliatory. By and large, it was Wałęsa's charismatic authority that kept the union on a moderate and balanced course in its struggle to achieve some degree of political harmony with the government.

The government, however, under pressure from both the Soviets and local hardliners, became increasingly reluctant to introduce any significant reforms and systematically rejected Solidarity's proposals. This only led to further discontent, and, in the absence of other legal options, strikes became Solidarity's main political weapon. Amid fruitless wrangling, the economic crisis grew more severe. After the unsuccessful talks of November 1981 between the government, Solidarity and the Church, social tensions increased and led to a political stalemate.

Martial Law & its Aftermath

When General Jaruzelski unexpectedly appeared on television in the early hours of the morning of 13 December 1981 to declare martial law, tanks were already on the streets, army checkpoints had been set up on every corner, and paramilitary squads had been posted to possible trouble spots. Power was placed in the hands of the Military Council of National Salvation (WRON), a group of military officers under the command of Jaruzelski himself.

Solidarity was suspended and all public gatherings, demonstrations and strikes were banned. A night-time curfew was introduced and the principal industrial and communications enterprises were taken over by the army. Telephone conversations and mail were subject to recording and censorship, and the courts were allowed to carry out proceedings virtually without reference to the law, on the pretext of countering 'a threat to public order'. Several thousand people, including most Solidarity leaders and Wałęsa himself, were interned. The spontaneous demonstrations and strikes that followed were crushed, and military rule was effectively imposed all over Poland within two weeks of its declaration.

Whether the coup was a Soviet decision or simply Jaruzelski's attempt to prevent Soviet military intervention, it attained its goal: reform was crushed and life in the Soviet bloc returned to the pre-Solidarity norm.

As soon as Jaruzelski became confident in power, he had to turn to the economy, which throughout the period had continued to deteriorate. He started to implement economic reforms, but the results were far below expectations. Firstly, the Western countries, particularly the USA, imposed economic sanctions in protest against martial law. Secondly, Poland was unable to raise more loans. Lastly, Jaruzelski had no popular support as most Poles were hostile to the government. In October 1982 the government formally dissolved Solidarity and released Wałęsa from detention. Martial law was officially lifted in July 1983.

Solidarity continued underground on a much smaller scale, and enjoyed widespread sympathy and support. In July 1984 a limited amnesty was announced and some members of the political opposition were released from prison. However, further arrests continued, following every public protest, and it was not until 1986 that all political prisoners were freed.

In October 1984 the pro-Solidarity priest Jerzy Popiełuszko was brutally murdered by the security police. The crime aroused popular condemnation, and the funeral was attended by a crowd of over 200,000 people. In an unprecedented public trial the authorities sentenced the perpetrators to prison.

Collapse of Communism

The election of Gorbachev in the Soviet Union in 1985 and his *glasnost* and *perestroika* programs gave an important stimulus to democratic reforms all through Eastern Europe. Again, Poland undertook the role of a guinea pig. Jaruzelski softened his position and became willing to compromise over the democratisation of the system. In April 1989, in so-called round-table agreements between the government, the opposition and the Church, Solidarity was re-established and the opposition was allowed to stand for parliament.

In the consequent semi-free elections in June 1989, Solidarity succeeded in getting an overwhelming majority of its supporters elected to the Senat, the upper house of parliament. However, the communists reserved for themselves 65% of seats in the lower house, the Sejm. Jaruzelski was placed in the presidency as a stabilising guarantor of political changes for both Moscow and the local communists, but the noncommunist prime minister, Tadeusz Mazowiecki, was installed as a result of personal pressure from Wałęsa. This power-sharing deal, with the first noncommunist prime minister in Eastern Europe since WWII, paved the way for the domino-like collapse of communism throughout the Soviet bloc. The Party, losing members and confidence at the speed of light, dissolved itself in 1990.

In January 1990 the government introduced a package of reforms to change the centrally planned communist system into a free-market economy. The brain behind the radical plan was finance minister Leszek Balcerowicz. In a shock-therapy transition, all prices were permitted to move freely, subsidies were abolished, the money supply was tightened and the currency was sharply devalued and made fully convertible with Western currencies.

Within a few months the economy appeared to have stabilised, food shortages were no longer the norm and the shelves of shops filled up with goods. Meanwhile, however, prices skyrocketed and unemployment exploded. Not surprisingly, an initial wave of optimism and forbearance was turning into uncertainty and discontent, and the tough austerity measures caused the popularity of the government to decline.

In the mid-1990 differences over the pace of political reform emerged between Mazowiecki and Wałęsa. Wałęsa complained that the government was too slow in removing old communists, the ex-members of the already nonexistent Party, from their political and economic posts. Mazowiecki, on the other hand, wary of political purges during a period of intense hardship, preferred instead to concentrate on the economic program. A bitter rivalry continued until the presidential elections in November 1990. The first fully free elections were eventually won by Wałęsa. The Third Republic came into being.

Lech Wałęsa's Presidency

During Wałęsa's statutory five-year term in office, Poland witnessed no fewer than five governments with their corresponding five prime ministers, each struggling to put the newborn democracy on wheels and each doing it differently.

After his election, Wałęsa appointed Jan Krzysztof Bielecki, an economist and his former adviser, to serve as prime minister. His cabinet attempted to continue the austere economic policies introduced by the former government but was unable to retain parliamentary support and resigned after a year in office. The next government, under prime minister Jan Olszewski, was, like its predecessor, plagued by discord, and collapsed after only five months of existence.

In June 1992, Wałęsa gave his consent to the formation of a government led by Hanna Suchocka of the Democratic Union. An independent and articulate university professor specialising in constitutional law, she was the nation's first woman prime minister, and became known as the Polish Margaret Thatcher. Suchocka's coalition government managed to command parliamentary majority, but was in increasing discord over many issues, and failed to survive a vote of no confidence in June 1993.

The impatient Wałęsa stepped in. Instead of asking another Solidarity politician to form a government, he decided to dissolve the parliament and call a general election. This was a gross miscalculation. The postcommunist opposition parties accused the parties of the outgoing Solidarity-led coalition of mismanagement and indifference to the painful social cost of their radical reforms, and promised a more balanced program offering growth but focused on the people's needs. They succeeded in swaying public opinion and the pendulum swung to the left.

The election resulted in a leftist government based on two parties – the Democratic Left Alliance (SLD) and the Polish Peasant Party (PSL) – both of which were reformed communist parties from the pre-1989 era. The two parties commanded almost a two-thirds majority in the 460-strong Sejm. The new coalition government was headed by PSL leader Waldemar Pawlak. The general direction of transformation to a market economy slowed down, particularly in the area of privatisation and foreign investment.

The continuous tensions within the coalition and its running battles with the president brought about a change in February 1995, following Wałęsa's threats to dissolve the parliament again unless Pawlak was replaced by a more pro-reform leader. The parliament came up with Józef Oleksy, another former communist party official, yet the quarrels with the president continued unabated.

Wałęsa's presidential style and his accomplishments were repeatedly questioned by practically all political parties and the majority of the electorate. His quirky behaviour and his capricious use of power prompted a slide from the favour he had enjoyed in 1990 to his lowest-ever level of popular support in early 1995, when polls indicated that only 8% of Poles preferred him as president for the next term. Despite this, Wałęsa manoeuvred vigorously towards his goal of another five years in office and, in a miraculous comeback, went close to achieving it.

Aleksander Kwaśniewski's Presidency

The November 1995 election was essentially a duel between the anticommunist folk figure, Lech Wałęsa, and the much younger, smooth, one-time communist technocrat and the SLD leader, Aleksander Kwaśniewski. They finished nearly neck and neck: Wałęsa with 33% of the vote narrowly behind Kwaśniewski with 35%. As neither collected a clear half of the vote, a second round was held two weeks later. Again, Kwaśniewski won by a narrow margin (51.7% against 48.3%).

Włodzimierz Cimoszewicz, another former communist party official, took the post of prime minister. In effect, the postcommunists gained a stranglehold on power, controlling the presidency, government and parliament – a 'red triangle', as Wałęsa warned. The centre and the right – almost half of the political nation – effectively lost control over the decision-making process. Another loser was the Church, much favoured by Wałęsa during his term in the saddle. The Church didn't fail to caution the faithful against the danger of 'neopaganism' under the new regime.

By 1997, the electorate had apparently realised that the pendulum went too much to the left. The parliamentary elections, held in September 1997, were won by the alliance of about 40 small Solidarity offshoot parties, collectively named the Solidarity Electoral Action (AWS). The alliance formed a coalition with the centrist liberal Freedom Union (UW), pushing ex-communists into opposition. Jerzy Buzek of AWS, a professor in chemistry, became prime minister, and the new government accelerated the privatisation program.

A completely new constitution was finally passed in October 1997, to replace the Soviet-style document in force since 1952 (though it had been amended to correspond with the postcommunist status quo).

President Kwaśniewski's political style sharply contrasted with an abrasive and unpredictable style of his predecessor, Wałęsa, marked by constant quarrels and backroom manoeuvring. Kwaśniewski brought political calm to his term in post, and was able to cooperate successfully with both the left and right wings of the political establishment. This gained him a remarkable degree of popular support, and paved the way to another five-year term in office.

On the international front, in March 1999 Poland was granted full membership of NATO (along with the Czech Republic and Hungary), on the 50th anniversary of the organisation. In the late 1990s, Poland was also working hard on preparing for joining the European Union. The government put together a schedule in order to be ready to comply with the conditions required by EU by 2003, and thus would expect to join the union by 2005.

Recent Developments

As many as 13 contenders went into the presidential race in the October 2000 election, but this time there were few doubts about who would be the winner. Kwaśniewski, who consistently led the polls throughout the presidential campaign, won a sweeping victory, capturing 54% of the vote. The centrist businessman Andrzej Olechowski came a distant second, with 17% support. Wałęsa,

who again tried his luck, suffered a disastrous defeat, collecting just 1% of the vote. The political life of the legendary Solidarity leader ended in humiliation.

The September 2001 parliamentary election changed the political centre of gravity altogether. The major winner was the ex-communist Democratic Left Alliance (SLD), which staged its great second comeback, taking 216 seats in the Sejm (parliament's lower house), just 15 short of an outright majority. The party formed a coalition with the Polish Peasant Party (PSL), repeating the pattern of the shaky alliance of 1993. Ex-communist party senior official Leszek Miller became the prime minister. In effect, the pendulum went to the far left, resulting again in a 'red triangle' of a post communist president, parliament and government firmly back in place.

The Solidarity coalition that had led the previous government, failed to retain even a single seat in the Sejm, thus repeating a humiliating crash of its former leader, Lech Wałęsa, a year earlier. Instead, two new wild-card parties gained significant blocks of seats: Self-Defence, the peasants' party led by populist Andrzej Lepper, and the right-wing League of Polish Families. Both parties are opposed to Poland's accession to the European Union.

GEOGRAPHY

Poland covers an area of 312,677 sq km. It is approximately as big as the UK and Ireland put together, or less than half the size of Texas. Almost 25 Polands would fit on the Australian continent. The country is roughly square in shape, reaching a maximum of about 680km from west to east and 650km from north to south.

Poland is bordered by the Baltic Sea to the north-west along a 524km coastline; by Germany to the west (along a 460km border); both the Czech and Slovak republics to the south (1310km); and Ukraine, Belarus, Lithuania and Russia to the east and north-east (1244km).

A quick glance at the map suggests that Poland is a vast, flat, low-lying plain with mountains only along its southern frontier.

A closer look, however, reveals a more complex topography. The really flat part is the wide central belt – stretching from west to east across the middle of the country – which comprises the historically defined regions of Great Poland (Wielkopolska), Lower Silesia (Dolny Śląsk), Mazovia (Mazowsze) and Podlasie. This area is Poland's main granary and for the most part the land is agricultural.

The northern part of Poland, comprising Pomerania (Pomorze), Warmia and Masuria (Mazury), is varied and gently undulating, relatively well forested and covered by several thousand postglacial lakes, most of which are in Masuria. Poland has over 9000 lakes, more than any other country in Europe except Finland.

Towards the south of the central lowland belt, the terrain rises, forming the uplands of Little Poland (Małopolska) and Upper Silesia (Górny Śląsk). Still farther to the south, along the southern frontier, it concludes in the Sudeten Mountains (Sudety) and the Carpathian Mountains (Karpaty).

The Sudetes, to the west, are 250km long and geologically very old; their highest part, Karkonosze, is topped by Mt Śnieżka (1602m). The Carpathian Mountains, to the east, are fairly young and are made up of several ranges. The highest of these is the Tatra Mountains (Tatry), the only Alpine-style range in Poland, which is shared with Slovakia to the south. Here is Poland's tallest peak, Mt Rysy (2499m).

To the north of the Tatras lies the lower but much larger, densely forested range of the Beskids (Beskidy), with their highest peak being Mt Babia Góra (1725m). The south-eastern tip of Poland is taken up by the Bieszczady, part of the Carpathians; their tallest peak is Mt Tarnica (1343m).

All Poland's rivers run towards the north and drain into the Baltic Sea. The longest (1047km) is the Vistula (Wisła), which runs through the middle of the country. It is known as the mother river of Poland because it passes through the most historically important cities of Kraków and Warsaw, and its entire basin lies within the country's boundaries.

The second-longest is the Odra (Oder) which forms part of Poland's western border. In July 1997, it caused catastrophic floods (reputedly the largest in the country's history), which cost more than 50 lives and caused damages worth an estimated US$2 billion.

CLIMATE

The seasons are clearly differentiated. Spring starts in March and is initially cold and windy, later becoming pleasantly warm and often sunny. Summer, which begins in June, is predominantly warm but hot at times, with plenty of sunshine interlaced with heavy rains. July is the hottest month. Autumn comes in September and is at first warm and usually sunny, turning cold, damp and foggy in November. Winter lasts from December to March and includes

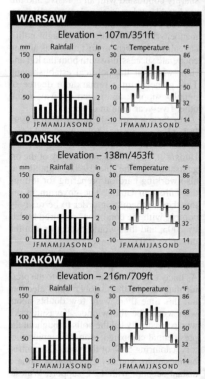

shorter or longer periods of snow. High up in the mountains, snow stays well into May. January and February are the coldest months. The temperature sometimes drops below -15°C or even -20°C.

Poland's climate is influenced by a continental climate from the east and a maritime climate from the west. As a result, the weather is changeable, with significant differences from day to day and from year to year. Winter one year can be almost without snow, whereas another year very heavy snows can paralyse transport for days on end. Summer can occasionally be cold, wet and disappointing.

The average annual rainfall is around 600mm, with the greatest falls in the summer months. The central part of Poland is the driest, receiving about 450mm a year, while the mountains receive more rain (or snow in winter) – around 1000mm annually.

ECOLOGY & ENVIRONMENT

The communist regime in Poland spent virtually nothing on protecting the country's environment. Decades of intensive industrialisation without even the most elementary protection have turned rivers into sewers and air into smog. It wasn't until 1990, after the regime crumbled, that the Ministry of Environmental Protection was founded and began to develop an environmental policy to try to clean up the mess left by the communists. Today, a decade down the track, Poland's environment is a bit better off yet still in an unenviable state.

Poland has a number of seriously polluted urban and industrial areas (the 'ecological hazard zones'), which account for about 10% of the country's territory. They are a priority of the government's current environmental policy.

Air

Air pollution continues to be one of Poland's most serious problems. The major pollutant is the energy sector, which uses outdated technologies and highly polluting fuels, such as coal and lignite. The situation is worst in large industrial cities, and especially in Upper Silesia, which occupies just 2% of the country's territory but produces nearly 20% of the sulphur dioxide emissions.

With the sixth highest level of carbon dioxide emissions in Europe, Poland is a significant contributor to global warming. Its goal to diminish emissions is still a way ahead. So far the country has managed to stabilise them at the (alarmingly high) 1990 level, which is already a significant achievement. Poland now receives World Bank assistance to reduce carbon dioxide emissions. Ironically, the main benefactors are the major polluters themselves, the huge, belching plants which have been going bankrupt and closing.

Transportation is currently less of a culprit but a massive rise in the number of cars has worsened the situation over the past years.

Water

Poland's natural water supplies are limited, with the available water per capita figures being among Europe's lowest. At the same time, the use of water in Poland is inefficient, with high per capita consumption. To make matters worse, a great deal of the water available – that received by over half the population – is polluted, largely because of poor waste water treatment. Poland has upgraded or constructed about 350 waste water treatment plants over the past decade, yet many more are needed. Another aspect of the problem is that virtually all Polish rivers flow into the Baltic Sea, a shallow and tideless body of water with weak circulation, and highly sensitive to pollution.

Waste

Poland is one of Europe's largest sources of industrial waste (mainly from coal mining and heavy industry), and only about 1% of it is treated. Treatment of municipal waste is also minimal, and it virtually all ends up in landfills without sorting.

Nature Conservation

About 23% of the country's territory is currently under some sort of protection (in national or landscape parks or other protected areas), and the goal is to achieve a total of 30%. Remarkably, Poland has succeeded in extending its forested area (mostly by reforestation) from about 21% of the land just after WWII, to about 28% today. Yet it's still well behind Europe's average of approximately 32%.

Significant parts of forested areas have survived in a remarkably good, natural state, even though the wildlife has decreased. The best-preserved forests, with much of their primeval flora and fauna, are in eastern Poland, mainly along the eastern border, and in the Carpathians, though the latter are endangered by the ski lobby.

Environmental Policies

Although the Ministry of Environmental Protection remains the major player in the environmental management, strategy and conservation field, there are also a number of other government and nongovernment environmental agencies, plus various green groups.

Poland's major goal now is to adjust its internal environmental indicators to comply with EU requirements – a necessary condition for integration with the EU. The process requires an improvement of domestic environmental quality by enforcing strict standards in a number of fields, including air and water pollution, energy and material consumption, waste management, radiation protection and nature conservation. Other related issues are forestry, organic farming and ecotourism.

FLORA & FAUNA

The last ice age ended only about 10,000 years ago in Poland, and depleted the country's vegetation and wildlife, destroying a number of plant and animal species. Consequently, the flora and fauna in Poland, like elsewhere in Europe, is not abundant or extremely diverse.

Flora

Forests cover roughly 28% of Poland's territory – nearly 90,000 sq km. This area is increasing – every year some 100 to 130 sq km of new forest is planted, with a goal of achieving 30% forest coverage by 2025. Over 80% of the forest area is administered by the state, about 2% of which is protected by national parks.

By far the most common species is pine (over 60% of the total area), but the share of deciduous species, such as oak, beech, birch and linden is on the increase, enriching the forest's biological diversity and its natural resistance.

Forests provide timber (about 20 million cubic metres a year), wild mushrooms and fruit, habitat for wildlife, a playground for hunting (now largely restricted) and a base for recreation and activities.

Fauna

Poland's fauna numbers some 90 species of mammals, of which the most common ones include the hare, red deer and wild boar. Wolves and foxes inhabit various regions, but they have been largely decimated. Some elk live in the woods of the far north-east, while occasional brown bears and wildcats can be found in the mountain forests. Several hundred European bison live in the Białowieża National Park and some other limited areas. These massive animals once inhabited the continent in large numbers but were brought to the brink of extinction early in the 20th century.

One animal with more than merely symbolic importance is the horse. Poland has a long tradition of breeding Arabian horses, which are much appreciated on world markets. Many important international championships have been won by Polish-bred Arabians. There are a number of stud farms and horse riding is popular.

With some 420 species, birds are reasonably well represented. Some of them migrate south in autumn to return in spring. The most common species are the sparrow, crow, magpie, skylark, nightingale and the swallow. Storks, which build their nests on the roofs and chimneys of houses in the countryside, are much loved. In the lake regions, there are plenty of water birds, such as mallards, swans and herons. A small community of cormorants lives in the Masurian Lakes. The eagle, though not very common today, is Poland's national bird and appears in the Polish emblem.

The White Stork – a Bird of Good Luck

Everybody knows that storks bring babies, right? In many countries, including Poland, it's also believed that storks drop off not only little bundles of joy but healthy doses of good luck. Consequently, storks are much loved and attract special attention, and this is particularly true in Poland, which is home to a large population of storks.

Of the 17 existing stork species, the one most commonly seen in Poland is the white stork (*Ciconia ciconia*). It's a large bird, about 1m tall and with a wingspan of up to 2m, white with black flight feathers, it has a red bill and long red legs. It is voiceless but is capable of clattering its bill loudly.

Each summer, Poland becomes home to one in three of the European white stork population and attracts some 30,000 stork couples. The regions where they are most numerous include Masuria and Podlasie in north-eastern Poland.

Storks will come from as far away as South Africa every spring and return to their old nests, built many years back. Favourite locations for nests include rooftops of countryside cottages, particularly chimneys, tops of churches and castle towers, and posts including phone and power line posts.

The white stork population in Poland is diminishing, mostly because of human impact on its habitat. Many storks die by attempting to perch on power lines and towers. In some areas their numbers have dropped drastically, as evidenced by the many abandoned nests. Strong measures are needed to help prevent their extinction.

National Parks

As of 2001, Poland had 23 national parks (*parki narodowe*), which covered about 3200 sq km, a mere 1% of the country's area. Some new parks have been planned. The parks are scattered roughly, yet evenly, throughout the country, other than in the Carpathian Mountains where there are six. One Polish national park, Białowieża, is on the Unesco World Heritage list.

About 85% of the area of all parks is state owned, whereas the remaining 15% is in private hands. The state is gradually acquiring the private land, a process which will take a decade or two to complete. The parks are administered by a special department of the Ministry of Environment; park maintenance is financed from the state budget.

No permit is necessary to visit the parks, but most have introduced entry fees (of about US$1), which you pay at the park office or an entry point. Camping in the parks is not allowed except on specified sites.

Apart from the national parks, a network of other, not so strictly preserved, areas called *parki krajobrazowe*, or landscape parks, has been established. As the name suggests, their scenery was the major factor in selecting them and, accordingly, they are usually picturesque. The first landscape park was created in 1976 and today there are 105 of them. They are found in all regions and together cover about 20,000 sq km, or 6% of the country's area.

There are also the *rezerwaty*, or reserves. These are usually small areas that contain a particular natural feature such as a cluster of old trees, a lake with valuable flora or an interesting rock formation.

GOVERNMENT & POLITICS

Poland is a parliamentary republic. The president is elected in a direct vote for a five-year term as head of state and is subsequently empowered to nominate the prime minister.

The parliament consists of two houses, the 460-seat lower house, the Sejm or Diet, and the 100-seat upper house, the Senat or senate. The senate was only created in 1989; before that there was just the one-house parliament based on the Sejm. Both the senate and the president have the power

POLAND'S NATIONAL PARKS

of veto over the Sejm, but these vetoes can be overridden by a two-thirds majority vote in the Sejm.

Administratively, the country is divided into 16 provinces called *województwa*, which are further split into 373 *powiaty* – 308 rural and 65 urban districts. This division only came into force in 1999, replacing the old 49-province system.

The Polish flag is divided horizontally into two equal belts: white above and red below. The national emblem is a white eagle, which has regained its crown since the fall of communism.

ECONOMY

Bituminous coal has traditionally been Poland's chief mineral resource, with the largest deposits concentrated in Upper Silesia. Coal supplies a large part of the domestic demand for electricity. Poland possesses considerable reserves of sulphur, believed to be among the largest in the world, but large scale exploitation creates daunting ecological problems. Among other mineral resources, there are significant deposits of zinc and lead, and smaller ones of copper and nickel. The country's oil resources are insignificant.

Hydroelectric power is responsible for only a small fraction of electricity production, and the potential is not great. A nuclear reactor based on Soviet technology was started in the early 1980s near Gdańsk but construction was abandoned in 1990.

Approximately half of Poland's territory is arable. Among the main agricultural crops are rye, potatoes, wheat, sugar beet, barley and oats. Over 80% of farmland in Poland, unlike that in the rest of the former communist bloc, remained in the hands of individual farmers even in Soviet times. Collective farms, known as cooperatives, occupied only about 2% of the land.

Many of Poland's huge state-owned factories dating from the period of the postwar rush towards industrialisation are still in operation. Their major products include steel, chemicals (fertilisers, sulphuric acid), industrial machinery and transport equipment (ships, railway cars and motor vehicles). Yet, in a decade since the fall of communism, the situation has changed dramatically. While the old state-owned industries have been falling apart, a plethora of new, mostly small, private enterprises have sprung up.

Today's Poland has the well-established foundations of a market economy and a dynamic, new private sector. Trade has shifted towards the West, yet Poland wisely maintains and expands economic links with the countries of the ex-Soviet bloc, to preserve its position as a bridge between West and East.

The huge inflation of the early 1990s dropped to 32% in 1994 and came down to 7% in 2001. Average monthly wages stood at about US$225 in 1993 and reached around US$400 by 2000.

More than 60% of Poland's GDP is now produced by the private sector, which employs about 60% of the workforce. GDP growth averaged 5.5% in the past decade, peaking at 7% in 1995. However, it dropped below 5% in 1999 and ended up at 4% in 2000. In 2001 it went down to 2%, the lowest figure in 10 years. The level of unemployment reached a low of about 10% by the end of 1998, but went up to a dangerous 16% by mid-2001.

POPULATION & PEOPLE

Poland's population in 2001 stood at about 39 million. The rate of demographic increase, which was pretty high in the postwar period, has dropped gradually over the last two decades to stabilise at about 0.7%, a figure comparable to those of Western European countries.

There were massive migratory movements in Poland in the aftermath of WWII, and the ethnic composition of the nation is now almost entirely homogeneous. According to the official statistics, Poles make up 98% of the population, Ukrainians and Belarusians about 1%, and the remaining 1% is composed of all other minorities – Jews, Germans, Lithuanians, Tatars, Roma (Gypsies), Lemks, Boyks and a dozen other groups.

Today's ethnic composition differs significantly from that before the war. Poland was for centuries one of the most cosmopolitan countries, and had the largest community of Jews in Europe. Just before the outbreak of WWII they numbered around three million. Only about 5000 to 10,000 Jews remain in Poland today.

Population density varies considerably throughout the country, with Upper Silesia being the most densely inhabited area while the north-eastern border regions remain the least populated. Over 70% of the country's inhabitants live in towns and cities. Warsaw is by far the largest Polish city (1,750,000), and is followed by Łódź (840,000) and Kraków (770,000). Approximate population figures (as of 2001) are given for all cities, towns and major villages described in this book.

According to rough estimates, between five and 10 million Poles live abroad. This is basically the result of two huge migrations, at the beginning of the 20th century and during WWII. Postwar emigration, particularly in the two last decades, has sent additional large numbers of Poles all over the world. The largest Polish emigre community lives in the USA, with the biggest group being in Chicago. Poles joke that Chicago is the second-largest Polish city, as nearly a million of them live there.

EDUCATION

The educational system is well developed and comprehensive at all levels. Education is compulsory between the ages of seven and 18, and the literacy rate stands at 98%. Nearly a fifth of the population have completed secondary and post-secondary education. Education at all levels was free in communist Poland, but this has changed after 1990. School and university programs have been thoroughly revised and adapted to the new Poland.

Private education was almost nonexistent before 1990, only a handful of religious orders having the right to run schools. The only semi-private tertiary facility was KUL, the Lublin Catholic University, supported to a great extent by the Catholic Church.

The law on education has been changed and private schools at all levels have sprung up from nowhere. As of late 2001, there were 216 private tertiary education facilities, mainly in the areas of high demand, such as business, computer science and languages. They teach half a million students, or a third of all students.

The number of university-level schools has gone up by almost 50% in recent years, mainly because of the introduction of courses that enable people who work to study at the same time. These are provided by both private and public universities. The higher demand for education reflects the situation in the job market, where people who have a degree in certain areas find it much easier to obtain a well-paid job. About 8% of Poles have completed tertiary education.

ARTS
Music

Though music has always been an integral part of human life, the first written records mentioning Polish music date only from the 12th century. Music in Poland was centred around the Church and the court, included both vocal and instrumental forms, followed mostly Western patterns and used the Latin language. Folk music certainly contained more native elements but there's very little information available about it.

The Renaissance marked some developments in the musical culture but it was not until the Romantic period that Polish music reached its peak. The foremost figure was, without doubt, Frédéric Chopin (1810–49), who crystallised the national style, taking inspiration from folk or court dances and tunes such as *polonez* (polonaise), *mazurek* (mazurka), *oberek* and *kujawiak*. No one else in the history of Polish music has so creatively used folk rhythms for concert pieces and no one else has achieved such international recognition. Chopin has become the very symbol of Polish music.

Overshadowed by Chopin's fame, another composer inspired by folk dances, Stanisław Moniuszko (1819–72), created Polish national opera. Two of his best known operas, *Halka* and *Straszny Dwór*, are staples of the national opera houses. Also shaded by Chopin's achievements was Henryk Wieniawski (1835–80), another remarkable 19th-century composer, who also was a great violinist.

By the beginning of the 20th century, Polish artists were starting to make their way onto the world stage. The first to do so were the piano virtuosi Ignacy Paderewski (1860–1941) and Artur Rubinstein (1886–1982), the latter performing right up until his death.

The premier musical personality of the first half of the 20th century was Karol Szymanowski (1882–1937), and his best-known composition, the ballet *Harnasie*, was influenced by folk music from the Tatra Mountains, which he transformed into the contemporary musical idiom.

In the composition of contemporary music, Poland has been up there with the world's best. In the 1950s and 1960s a wealth of talent emerged, including Witold Lutosławski, with his *Musique Funèbre* and *Jeux Vénitiens*, and Krzysztof Penderecki, with his monumental dramatic forms such as *Dies Irae*, *Devils of Loudun*, *Ubu Rex*, *Seven Gates of Jerusalem* and *Credo*.

Originally eclipsed by the aforementioned masters, Henryk Górecki developed his own musical language. His Symphony No 3 was written in 1976, but it wasn't until the early 1990s that the second recording of this work hit musical audiences worldwide. The phenomenal success of the Third Symphony shed light on the other compositions of Górecki, notably his String Quartets Nos 1 and 2, written for, and exquisitely performed by, the Kronos Quartet.

Another composer whose name has entered international music dictionaries is Zbigniew Preisner, the author of music for Krzysztof Kieślowski's major films, including *Decalogue, The Double Life of Veronique* and *Three Colours*. His first non-film musical piece, *Requiem for my Friend*, dedicated to Kieślowski, saw its much celebrated premiere in October 1998.

Folk music is cultivated and propagated by two national song and dance ensembles, Mazowsze and Śląsk, as well as many other smaller, mostly amateur bands.

Jazz took off in the 1950s, at that time underground, around the legendary pianist Krzysztof Komeda, who later composed the music to most of the early Polański films before his tragic death. Komeda inspired and influenced many jazz musicians, such as Michał Urbaniak (violin, saxophone), Zbigniew Namysłowski (saxophone) and Tomasz Stańko (trumpet), all of whom became pillars of Polish jazz in the 1960s and remain pretty active today. Urbaniak opted to pursue his career in the USA, and is the best known Polish jazzman on the international scene.

Of the younger generation, Leszek Możdżer (piano) is possibly the biggest revelation thus far, followed by several other exceptionally skilled pianists such as Andrzej Jagodziński and Włodzimierz Pawlik. Other young jazz talents to watch out for include Piotr Wojtasik (trumpet), Maciej Sikała (saxophone), Adam Pierończyk (saxophone), Piotr Baron (saxophone) and Cazary Konrad (drums).

Like elsewhere, popular music has a huge following. While Polish pop has mirrored the major Western fashions, it has added local colour and language. The best known rock/pop veteran groups include Lady Punk, Republika, Budka Suflera, Manaam and Bajm. Recent years have seen a rash of productions covering just about

every musical genre and style from salsa to rap. Brathanki and Golec uOrkiestra, popular new groups, creatively mix folk and pop rhythms. Fans of hip-hop should check for gigs of Kaliber 44, Molesta, Warszawski Deszcz and Paktofonika.

Literature

Literature began to develop after the introduction of Christianity in the 10th century, and for nearly half a millennium it consisted mostly of chronicles and political treatises, written almost exclusively in Latin. Not many written records from that period are left. The oldest surviving document is a chronicle from around the 12th century written by Gall Anonim, a foreigner of unknown origin. As for native historians, Jan Długosz (1415–80) was the most outstanding figure and his monumental 12-volume chronicle (in Latin), narrating Polish history from the very beginnings right up till the author's death, is an invaluable source of information. The oldest text in Polish, the song *Mother of God (Bogurodzica)*, was written in the 13th century and became the national anthem until the 18th century.

During the Renaissance the Polish language was commonly used, and the invention of printing meant that books in Polish became widespread; the first Polish printed text appeared in 1475. In the course of the 16th century Latin was completely dominated by the mother tongue and a wide range of Polish-language literature was published, of which the most brilliant was the poetry of Jan Kochanowski (1530–84).

Although the baroque period witnessed a wealth of literary creativity and the subsequent Enlightenment epoch produced some fine poetry by Ignacy Krasicki (1735–1801), it wasn't actually until Romanticism, the period when Poland formally didn't exist, that Polish poetry really blossomed. Three poets, Adam Mickiewicz (1798–1855), Juliusz Słowacki (1809–49) and Zygmunt Krasiński (1812–59), all working in exile, executed some of the greatest masterpieces of Polish poetry ever written and have since been known to every single Pole. It comes as no surprise that their work is strong in patriotic feelings and prophetic visions. One more noteworthy representative of Romantic poetry, Cyprian Kamil Norwid (1821–83), was not properly recognised until well into the 20th century because of the innovative form and language he used.

In the period of Positivism that followed, the central stage was dominated by the prose writers, and their approach was based on different foundations: in contrast to the Romantic visions, they worked from science, empiricism and realism. The leading writers of this time include Eliza Orzeszkowa (1841–1910), Bolesław Prus (1847–1912) and particularly, Henryk Sienkiewicz (1846–1916), who was awarded the Nobel Prize in 1905 for *Quo Vadis?*.

Good times for the novel continued well into the period known as Young Poland, a major movement in Polish art and literature between about 1890 and the outbreak of WWI. During this time, writers such as Stefan Żeromski (1864–1925) and Władysław Reymont (1867–1925), the latter winning another Nobel Prize in literature, for *The Peasants (Chłopi)*, in 1924, made their mark. Outsiders, however, will probably know better the work of Joseph Conrad (1857–1924). The author of classic novels such as *Heart of Darkness* and *Lord Jim*, he was born in Poland as Józef Konrad Korzeniowski. Conrad left the country in 1874 and, after 20 years travelling the world as a sailor, settled in England and dedicated himself to writing (in English).

The period of Young Poland also marked the revival of poetry and one of the greatest Polish dramas, *The Wedding (Wesele)* by Stanisław Wyspiański, was published in this time. Wyspiański also practised painting and other forms of decorative art.

Between the wars several brilliant avantgarde writers emerged who were only fully appreciated after WWII. They include Bruno Schulz (1892–1942), Witold Gombrowicz (1904–69) and Stanisław Ignacy Witkiewicz, or Witkacy (1885–1939).

Witkacy, an unusual talent in many fields, including painting, literature and photography, was the originator of unconventional philosophical concepts, the most notable being the 'theory of pure form', as well as creating the theatre of the absurd long before Ionesco made it famous. Only in the 1960s were Witkacy's plays, such as *Mother (Matka)*, *Cobblers (Szewcy)* and *New Deliverance (Nowe Wyzwolenie)*, discovered internationally. He committed suicide soon after the outbreak of WWII as an expression of his belief in 'catastrophism', the disintegration of civilisation.

The postwar period presented writers with a conundrum: adopt communism and effectively 'sell-out' or take a more independent path and risk persecution. Czesław Miłosz, who broke with the communist regime, gives an analysis of the problem in *The Captive Mind (Zniewolony Umysł)*. Miłosz occupies the prime position in Polish postwar literature, and the Nobel Prize awarded to him in 1980 was recognition of his achievements. He started his career in the 1930s and expresses himself equally brilliantly in poetry and prose, dividing his time between writing, translating and lecturing.

Other internationally known Polish emigres include Witold Gombrowicz, who published *Ferdydurke* before WWII but most of whose work, which includes *The Wedding (Ślub)*, *Operetta (Operetka)* and *Pornography (Pornografia)*, was written during the postwar period; Jerzy Kosiński, known particularly for his novel *The Painted Bird (Malowany Ptak)*; and Sławomir Mrożek, the foremost dramatist who, by means of burlesque and satire, parodies sociopolitical goings on.

Literary life in Poland has been pretty active since WWII and still has a high profile. One of the most remarkable figures, Tadeusz Konwicki, was initially a follower of official dogma but gradually moved away, which has resulted in two brilliant novels, *A Minor Apocalypse (Mała Apokalipsa)* and *The Polish Complex (Kompleks Polski)*. The work of another judge of Polish reality, Kazimierz Brandys, gives an accurate insight into complex sociopolitical issues, as in his *Warsaw Diary 1977–81 (Pamiętnik Warszawski 1977–81)*.

Polish postwar literature was honoured for a second time with a Nobel Prize in

Wisława Szymborska – 1996 Nobel Prize Winner

Polish postwar literature has twice been awarded the Nobel Prize: in 1980 it went to Czesław Miłosz and in 1996 to Wisława Szymborska. While Miłosz, a longtime emigre based in the USA, is familiar to international readers due to his extensive literary output and numerous translations, Szymborska is little known outside Poland, or at least she was until 1996.

A poet, translator and literary critic, Szymborska was born in 1923 in a small village near Poznań. In 1931 her family moved to Kraków, where she studied Polish literature and sociology at the Jagiellonian University in 1945–48. Her early literary works, which she later disclaimed, were products of a climate of socialist realism, the official artistic doctrine in postwar Poland.

It wasn't until 1955 that censorship subsided and artists began to create with increasing freedom. Her 1957 collection of poems titled *Calling Out to Yeti (Wołanie Yeti)* was probably Szymborska's first autonomous work. Next was *Salt (Sól)*, in 1962. She was a dissident in the 1970s, and later, in the period of martial law and its aftermath, she wrote under a pen name for the local underground press and for the magazine *Kultura* published in Paris by Polish emigres. She has also translated some French poetry into Polish.

Szymborska's literary output is relatively modest – no more than just 10 slim poetry collections – yet it's powerful stuff. The Swedish Academy described her as 'the Mozart of poetry' with 'something of the fury of Beethoven', and awarded her the Nobel Prize for 'poetry that with ironic precision allows the historical and biological context to come to light in fragments of human reality'.

The Academy also admitted that 'the stylistic variety in her poetry makes it extremely difficult to translate', which is one of the reasons why she has been so little known outside Poland. For those intending to sample her work, a good introduction is the volume entitled *View with a Grain of Sand*, published in 1995. It's a selection of 100 of Szymborska's poems translated into English, spanning nearly 40 years of her work. Szymborska currently lives in Kraków.

1996, this time to Wisława Szymborska, a Kraków poet who by the time of the award was little known beyond the boundaries of her motherland. Among other renowned poets are Tadeusz Różewicz (also a playwright), Zbigniew Herbert and Stanisław Barańczak. A number of younger talents are currently making their mark also.

Stanisław Lem is no doubt Poland's premier science fiction writer, while Ryszard Kapuściński's journalism is internationally known. Kapuściński has always had a good nose for being in the right place at the right time: he has witnessed 26 coups and revolutions. His books have been translated into 20 languages.

Almost all the authors listed in this section have been translated into English.

Architecture

The earliest dwellings were made of perishable materials, and almost nothing has survived of them. The only important example of early wooden architecture in Poland is the pre-Slavic fortified town in Biskupin, which dates from about 730 BC.

Stone as a construction material was only introduced in Poland with the coming of Christianity in the 10th century. From then on, durable materials – first stone, then brick – were used, and some of that architectural heritage has been preserved to this day.

Poland has followed the main Western European architectural styles, with some local variations. The first, the Romanesque style, which dominated from the late 10th century to the mid-13th century, used mainly stone and was austere, functional and simple. Round-headed arches, semicircular apses and symmetrical layouts were almost universal. The remnants of the Romanesque style in Poland are few but there are some precious examples, mostly churches.

The Gothic style made its way into Poland in the first half of the 13th century but it was not until the early 14th century that the so-called High Gothic became universally adopted. Elongated, pointed arches and ribbed vaults are characteristic of the style. Brick came into common use instead of stone, and the buildings, particularly churches, tended to reach impressive loftiness and monumental size. Gothic established itself for a long time in Poland and left behind countless churches, castles, town halls and burghers' houses.

In the 16th century a new fashion transplanted from Italy started to supersede Gothic as the dominant style. More delicate and decorative, Renaissance architecture didn't go for verticality and large volume but instead focused on perfect proportions and a handsome visual appearance. In contrast to Gothic, brickwork was almost never allowed to go uncovered. Much attention was paid to both detail and decoration, with bas-reliefs, gables, parapets, galleries, round arches and stucco work. There are a number of Renaissance buildings in Poland, though many of them were later 'adorned' by the subsequent architectural fashion, the baroque.

Baroque appeared on Polish soil in the 17th century and soon became ubiquitous. A lavish, highly decorative style, it placed a strong imprint on existing architecture by adding its sumptuous decor, which is particularly evident in church interiors and the palaces of the aristocracy. The most prominent figure of the baroque period in Poland was Tylman van Gameren, a Dutch architect who settled in Poland and designed countless buildings. In the 18th century baroque culminated in French-originated rococo, but it didn't make much of a mark on Poland, which by then was swiftly sliding into economic and political chaos.

At the beginning of the 19th century, a more complex phase of architectural development started in Poland which might be characterised as a period of the 'neo', or a general turn back towards the past. This phrase comprised neo-Renaissance, neo-Gothic and even neo-Romanesque styles. The most important of all the 'neo' fashions, though, was neoclassicism, which used ancient Greek and Roman elements as an antidote to the overloaded baroque and rococo

opulence. Monumental palaces adorned with columned porticoes were erected in this period, as well as churches that looked like Roman pantheons. Italian architect Antonio Corazzi was very active in Poland in this period, and designed several massive neoclassical buildings, including the Grand Theatre in Warsaw. Neoclassicism left its strongest mark in Warsaw.

The second half of the 19th century was dominated by eclecticism – the style which profited from all the previous trends – but it didn't produce any architectural gems. More innovative was Art Nouveau, which developed in England, France, Austria and Germany, and made its entrance into Poland (still under partition) at the beginning of the 20th century. It left behind some fresh decorative marks, especially in Kraków and Łódź. After WWI, neoclassicism took over again but lost out to functionalism just before WWII.

The postwar period started with a heroic effort to reconstruct destroyed towns and cities, and the result, given the level of destruction, is really impressive. Meanwhile, one more architectural style, socialist realism, was imposed by the regime. The most spectacular building in this style is the Palace of Culture and Science in Warsaw, a gift from the Soviet Union.

Since the 1960s, Polish architecture has followed more general European styles, though with one important local distinction: almost all major cities have been ringed by vast suburbs of anonymous concrete apartment blocks, a sad consequence of massive urbanisation and the lack of imagination of architects. In Poland's defence, it didn't have the necessary cash flow to accommodate aesthetic values. Nor did Poland receive external assistance such as the Marshall Plan, which helped other Western European nations to rebuild after the war. Only after the fall of communism has there been a trend towards the construction of homes on a more human scale.

Painting & Sculpture

Almost nothing is left of Romanesque mural painting but sculpture from that period survives in church doorways and tombs. Gothic sculpture reached an outstanding beauty and impeccable realism in wooden statues and intricate carved altarpieces, of which the most famous is the work by the German Veit Stoss in St Mary's Church in Kraków. Painting, too, was extremely realistic and was of a high standard. Both forms were almost exclusively religious in character, and most works were anonymous.

Sculpture during the Renaissance period achieved a mastery in the decoration of church chapels and tombs (eg, the Wawel Cathedral in Kraków), and bas-reliefs on the facades of houses (such as those in Kazimierz Dolny). Paintings gradually began to depart from religious themes, taking as their subjects members of distinguished families or scenes from their lives.

Baroque was not only a matter of ornate forms and luxuriant decoration – it brought expression and motion to the visual arts. Baroque works are distinguished by dynamic, often dramatic, expression of the figures. Baroque also introduced *trompe l'œil* wall-painting, seemingly three-dimensional. Finally, baroque was extremely generous in the use of gold as an adornment.

Two Italian painters working in Poland distinguished themselves during the reign of Stanisław August Poniatowski, the last Polish king: Marcello Bacciarelli, the king's favourite portraitist, who also produced a set of paintings depicting important moments in Polish history; and Bernardo Bellotto, commonly known in Poland as Canaletto, who executed a series of paintings that depict with astonishing accuracy Warsaw's major architectural monuments.

As for Polish painters, the first of significance was perhaps Piotr Michałowski (1800–55), whose favourite subject was horses; he also painted numerous portraits.

The second half of the 19th century saw a proliferation of monumental historical paintings. The works of Jan Matejko (1838–93), the greatest artist in this genre, showed the glorious moments of Polish history, presumably in an attempt to strengthen the national spirit during the period of partition. Today, they are the pride of Poland's mu-

seums. Other painters of the period who documented Polish history, especially battle scenes, include Józef Brandt (1841–1915) and Wojciech Kossak (1857–1942), the latter particularly remembered as co-creator of the colossal *Panorama Racławicka*, which is on display in Wrocław.

The closing decades of the 19th century saw the development of Impressionism in Europe, but it was met with much reserve by Polish artists. Even though many of the first-rank national painters of this period such as Aleksander Gierymski (1850–1901), Władysław Podkowiński (1866–95), Józef Chełmoński (1849–1914), Leon Wyczółkowski (1852–1936) and Julian Fałat (1853–1929) were in some way, or for some time, influenced by the new style, they preferred to express themselves in traditional forms and never completely gave up realism. This is particularly true of their Polish landscapes, an important part of their work.

On the other hand, the revolution in European painting influenced those Polish artists who lived and worked outside Poland, particularly those in Paris. Among them are Olga Boznańska (1865–1940), whose delicate portraits were painted with notable hints of Impressionism, and Tadeusz Makowski (1882–1932), who adopted elements of cubism and developed an individual, easily recognisable style.

In the visual arts, the dominant style was the Secesja, highly decorative and characterised by flowing curves and lines, which originated in England, and was known in Austria, Germany and France as Sezessionstil, Jugendstil and Art Nouveau, respectively. (As the last of these terms is most used in English, it has therefore been used in this book regardless of the source of influence.)

The most outstanding figure of the Young Poland movement was Stanisław Wyspiański (1869–1907). A painter, dramatist and poet, he is as much known for his literary achievements as for his pastels. Other artists from that movement include Józef Mehoffer (1869–1946), renowned mainly for his stained-glass designs, and Jacek Malczewski (1854–1929), Poland's best symbolic painter of the era.

The interwar years resulted in a diversity of trends ranging from realism to the avant-garde. The graphic arts began to develop, and colourism, rooted in Paris, attracted some Polish painters, the best known being Jan Cybis (1897–1973).

Stanisław Ignacy Witkiewicz, commonly known as Witkacy, executed a series of expressionist portraits (the largest collection is in the museum in Słupsk), as well as a number of colourful abstract compositions. Read more about him under Literature, earlier in this section.

After WWII and up till 1955, the visual arts were dominated by socialist realism, but later they developed with increasing freedom, expanding in a variety of forms, trends and techniques. Among the outstanding figures of the older generation are: Tadeusz Kulisiewicz (1899–1988), who started his career before WWII but reached mastery in his delicate drawings in the postwar period; Tadeusz Kantor (1915–90), renowned mainly for his famous Cricot 2 Theatre but also very creative in painting, drawing and other experimental forms; Jerzy Nowosielski, whose painting is strongly inspired by the iconography of the Orthodox Church and who has also carried out internal decorations in churches; and Zdzisław Beksiński, considered one of the best contemporary painters Poland has produced, who created a unique, mysterious and striking world of dreams.

Other important postwar painters whose works now adorn museum collections include Jan Tarasin, Leszek Sobocki, Jacek Waltoś, Zbylut Grzywacz, Jerzy Duda-Gracz, Jan Dobkowski, Henryk Waniek and Edward Dwurnik.

Artists who have achieved remarkable success in the graphic arts include Mieczysław Weiman, Janina Kraupe, Antoni Starczewski, Leszek Rózga, Jacek Sienicki, Jan Lebenstein, Józef Gielniak, Andrzej Pietsch, Jacek Gaj, Stanisław Weiman, Krzysztof Skórczewski and Henryk Ożóg.

Among the more prominent creators of modern sculpture (including related fields such as assemblages, installations etc) are Bronisław Chromy, Marian Kruczek, Władysław Hasior, Magdalena Abakanowicz, Gustaw Zemła and Adam Myjak.

There's a great deal of activity among the younger generation in painting, sculpture and the graphic arts alike. Their works are presented in temporary exhibitions put on by museums and commercial art galleries.

Folk Arts & Crafts

Poland has long and rich traditions in folk arts and crafts, and there are significant regional distinctions. Folk culture is strongest in the mountainous regions, especially in the Podhale at the foot of the Tatras, but other relatively small enclaves such as Kurpie and Łowicz (both in Mazovia) help to keep traditions alive.

Industrialisation and urbanisation increasingly encroach on traditional customs. People no longer wear folk-dress except for special occasions, and the artefacts they make are mostly for sale as either tourist souvenirs or museum pieces; in any case, not for their original purposes. The growing number of ethnographic museums is an indicator of the decline of traditional folk art; these museums are the best places to see what is left. One interesting type of ethnographic museum is the *skansen*, or open-air

Poster Art

Posters in Poland are taken very seriously and since the 1960s have gained international recognition as an art form. There is a museum of posters in Warsaw, and plenty of poster exhibitions, from local to international level.

Among the great Polish poster artists one cannot avoid mentioning names such as Henryk Tomaszewski, Wiktor Górka, Jan Lenica, Jan Młodożeniec, Franciszek Starowieyski, Roman Cieślewicz and Waldemar Świerzy.

Poster art has found many followers who successfully continue this genre today. The most creative artists of the younger generation include Mieczysław Górowski, Jerzy Czerniawski, Wiesław Rosocha, Stasys Eidrigevicius, Wiktor Sadowski, Piotr Młodożeniec, Wiesław Wałkuski, Roman Kalarus, Andrzej Pągowski and Wiesław Grzegorczyk.

museum, created to preserve traditional rural architecture.

Despite the decline there's still a lot to see outside the museums and skansens. The Polish rural population is conservative and religious, which means that traditions don't die overnight. The farther off the beaten track you get, the more you'll see. Traditions periodically spring to life around religious feasts and folk festivals, and these events offer the best opportunity to get a feel for how deep the folk roots remain.

Cinema

Though the invention of the cinema is attributed to the Lumière brothers, some sources claim that a Pole, Piotr Lebiedziński, should take some of the credit, having built a film camera in 1893, two years before the movie craze took off.

The first Polish film was shot in 1908, but it was only after WWI that film production began on a larger scale. Until the mid-1930s Polish films were largely banal comedies or adaptations of the more popular novels, and were hardly recognised beyond the country's borders. The biggest Polish contribution to international film in that period was that of the actress Pola Negri, who was born in Poland and made her debut in Polish film before gaining worldwide fame.

During the first 10 years after WWII, Polish cinematography didn't register many significant achievements apart from some semi-documentaries depicting the cruelties of the war. One such remarkable example is *The Last Stage (Ostatni Etap)*, a moving documentary-drama directed by Wanda Jakubowska, an Auschwitz survivor.

The period that followed (1955–63) was unprecedentedly fruitful, so much so that it's referred to as the Polish School. Beginning with the debut of Andrzej Wajda, the school heavily drew on literature and dealt with moral evaluations of the war, and its common denominator was heroism. A dozen remarkable films were made in that period, including Wajda's famous trilogy: *A Generation (Pokolenie)*, *Canal (Kanał)* and *Ashes and Diamonds (Popiół i Diament)*. Since then, the tireless Wajda has produced a film every

couple of years; the ones that have gained possibly the widest recognition are *Man of Marble (Człowiek z Marmuru)*, its sequel, *Man of Iron (Człowiek z Żelaza)*, and *Danton*.

In the early 1960s two young talents, Roman Polański and Jerzy Skolimowski, appeared on the scene. The former made only one feature film in Poland, *Knife in the Water (Nóż w Wodzie)*, and then decided to continue his career in the West. The latter shot four films, of which the last, *Hands Up (Ręce do Góry)*, made in 1967, was kept on the shelf until 1985, and he also left Poland. Whereas Skolimowski's work abroad has not gained widespread recognition, Polański has made it to the top. His career includes such remarkable films as *Cul-de-Sac*, *Rosemary's Baby*, *Chinatown*, *Macbeth*, *Bitter Moon* and *Death and the Maiden*.

Another ambassador of Polish cinema, Krzysztof Kieślowski, started in 1977 with *Scar (Blizna)* but his first widely acclaimed feature was *Amateur (Amator)*. After several mature films, he undertook the challenge of making the *Decalogue (Dekalog)*, a 10 part TV series that was broadcast all over the world. He then made another noteworthy production, *The Double Life of Veronique*, and confirmed his extraordinary abilities as a film maker with the trilogy *Three Colours: Blue/White/Red*. The last project won him important international film awards and critics' acclaim as one of Europe's best directors. He died during heart surgery in March 1996.

Other important directors who started their careers during communist times include Krzysztof Zanussi, Andrzej Żuławski and Agnieszka Holland. The postcommunist period has witnessed a rash of young directors, but one still waits for talent of the class of Polański or Wajda.

Poland has produced a number of world-class cinematographers, including Janusz Kamiński, awarded with two Oscars for his work on Steven Spielberg's *Schindler's List* and *Saving Private Ryan*. He also directed photography in *Jurassic Park: The Lost World*.

Less known but perhaps no less talented are several other Polish cinematographers responsible for various acclaimed Hollywood

Poland's Skansens

'Skansen' is a Scandinavian word referring to an open-air ethnographic museum. Aimed at preserving traditional folk culture and architecture, a skansen gathers together a selection of typical, mostly wooden rural buildings such as dwelling houses, barns, churches, mills etc, collected from the region, and often reassembled to look like a natural village. The buildings are furnished and decorated in their original style, incorporating a variety of historical household equipment, tools, crafts and artefacts, giving an insight into ancestors' lives, work and customs.

The concept of open-air museums emerged in the late 19th century in Scandinavia. Their originator was reputedly Swedish ethnographer Artur Hazelius, who bought some peasant cottages in 1885, reassembled them on Djurgården Island in Stockholm and opened them as a museum named 'skansen'. Several similar museums emerged in the following years around Sweden.

It didn't take long for neighbouring countries to follow the example, with Norway opening its first open-air museum in 1902. By the outbreak of WWI, Norway already had 16 of them, more than a third of Europe's total of 44 open-air museums.

Interest in skansens spread further afield in the interwar period, all over Europe and beyond, including Austria, Germany, the UK and the USA. After WWII, during which many museums were damaged or destroyed, development continued apace, and today there are over 500 open-air museums worldwide. Although a good part of them are in Scandinavia and Central Europe, they now exist on most continents, including Asia, Africa and Australia. The largest existing open-air museum is the Muzeul Satului in Bucharest.

Poland's first skansen was established in 1906 in Wdzydze Kiszewskie, near Gdańsk, and displayed Kashubian folk culture. The next one was founded in 1927 in Nowogród in northern Mazovia, showing traditional Kurpie culture. Both were almost totally destroyed during WWII but were later reconstructed.

There are currently about 35 museums of this kind in Poland, scattered over most regions and featuring distinctive regional traits. They are called museums of folk architecture (muzeum budownictwa ludowego), museums of the village (muzeum wsi) or ethnographic parks (park etnograficzny), but the term 'skansen' is universally applied to all of them.

Most skansens have been established by collecting the buildings from the region, but there are also some small in-situ skansens, including those in Kluki and Osiek. Skansens usually focus on general aspects of local culture, but there are also some specialist ones, notably the oil industry skansen in Bóbrka and the beekeeping skansen in Swarzędz. Poland's largest skansens include those in Sanok, Ciechanowiec, Lublin, Tokarnia, Nowy Sącz and Dziekanowice. It's hard to list any hard-and-fast 'top 10' but at the very least you shouldn't miss the skansens in Sanok and Nowy Sącz.

productions, including Adam Holender (*Midnight Cowboy*), Andrzej Bartkowiak (*Verdict, Jade, Terms of Endearment, Prizzi's Honor*), Andrzej Sekuła (*Pulp Fiction*) and Piotr Sobociński (*Marvin's Room, Ransom*).

Theatre

Although theatrical traditions in Poland go back to the Middle Ages, theatre in the proper sense of the word didn't develop until the Renaissance period and initially followed the styles of major centres in France and Italy. By the 17th century the

first original Polish plays were being performed on stage. In 1765 the first permanent theatre company was founded in Warsaw and its later director, Wojciech Bogusławski, came to be known as the father of the national theatre.

Theatre development was hindered during partition. Only the Kraków and Lviv theatres enjoyed relative freedom, but even they were unable to stage the great Romantic dramas, which were not performed until the beginning of the 20th century. By the outbreak of WWI, 10 permanent Polish theatres were operating. The interwar period witnessed a lively theatrical scene with the main centres in Warsaw and Kraków.

After WWII Polish theatre acquired an international reputation. Some of the highest international recognition was gained by the Teatr Laboratorium (Laboratory Theatre) created (in 1965) and led by Jerzy Grotowski in Wrocław. This unique experimental theatre, remembered particularly for *Apocalypsis cum Figuris*, was dissolved in 1984, and Grotowski concentrated on conducting theatrical classes abroad until his death in early 1999. Another remarkable international success was Tadeusz Kantor's Cricot 2 Theatre of Kraków, formed in 1956. Unfortunately, his best creations, *The Dead Class (Umarła Klasa)* and *Wielopole, Wielopole*, will never be seen again; Kantor died in 1990 and the theatre was dissolved a few years later.

Among existing experimental theatres, the most powerful and expressive include the Gardzienice, based in the village of the same name near Lublin, the Teatr Witkacego (Witkacy Theatre) in Zakopane, and the Wierszalin in Białystok.

In the mainstream, the most outstanding theatre company in Kraków is the Teatr Stary (Old Theatre). In Warsaw there are several top-ranking theatres, including the Centrum Sztuki Studio (Studio Art Centre), Teatr Polski (Polish Theatre), Teatr Ateneum, Teatr Powszechny and Teatr Współczesny.

Theatre directors to watch out for include Jerzy Jarocki, Andrzej Wajda, Jerzy Grzegorzewski, Kazimierz Dejmek, Krystian Lupa and Maciej Prus.

Prominent among other forms of theatre are Wrocławski Teatr Pantomimy (Pantomime Theatre of Wrocław) and Polski Teatr Tańca (Polish Dance Theatre) based in Poznań.

SOCIETY & CONDUCT

By and large, Poles are more conservative and traditional than Westerners and there's a palpable difference between the city and the village. While the way of life in large urban centres increasingly mimics Western European and, especially, North American patterns, the traditional spiritual culture is still very much in evidence in the remote rural areas. Religion plays an important role in this conservatism, the other factor being the still limited and antiquated infrastructure of services and communications. All in all, travelling in some rural areas can be like going back a century in time.

Poles are friendly and hospitable, and there's even a traditional saying, 'a guest in the house is God in the house'. If you happen to befriend Polish people, they may be extremely open-handed and generous, reflecting another popular unwritten rule, 'get in debt but show your best'.

Poles are remarkable individuals, each of them with their own solution for any dilemma within the family or the nation, and history proves well enough that there has never been a consensus over crucial national questions. On the other hand, they possess an amazing ability to mobilise themselves at critical moments. Not always realistic, Poles are sometimes charmingly irrational and romantic. While they love jokes and are easy-going, they may suddenly turn serious and hot-blooded when it comes to argument.

Poles don't keep as strictly to the clock as people do in the West. You may have to wait a bit until your friend arrives for an appointed meeting. Likewise, if you are invited to dinner or a party in someone's home, don't be exactly on time.

In greetings, Polish men are passionate about hand-shaking. Women, too, often shake hands with men, but the man should always wait for the woman to extend her hand first. You may often see the traditional polite way of greeting when a man kisses the hand of a woman. Here, again, it's the woman who suggests such a form by a perceptible rise of her hand.

Polish men are also passionate about giving flowers to women. The rose was traditionally the flower reserved for special occasions, but there's no strict rules these days. What does still seem to be largely observed, however, is the superstition of presenting an odd, not even, number of flowers.

RELIGION

Poland is a strongly religious country and over 80% of the population are practising Roman Catholics. Needless to say, the 'Polish pope', John Paul II, has strengthened the position of the Church in his motherland.

Since its introduction in 966, the Catholic Church (Kościół Katolicki) has always been powerful, as it is today. However, in contrast to the present day, for centuries it had to share power with other creeds, particularly with the Eastern Orthodox Church (Kościół Prawosławny). Always on the borderline between Rome and Byzantium, Poland has had both faiths present for most of its history.

With the Union in Brest (1596), the Polish Orthodox hierarchy split off and accepted the supremacy of the pope in Rome. It became the so-called Uniate Church (Kościół Unicki), often referred to as the Greek-Catholic Church (Kościół Greko-Katolicki). Despite the doctrinal change, the Uniate Church retained its Eastern rites, its traditional practices and liturgic language.

After WWII, Poland's borders shifted towards the west, and consequently the Orthodox Church is now present only along a narrow strip on the eastern frontier. Its adherents number a bit over 1% of the country's population, yet it is the second-largest creed after Roman Catholicism.

Poland's Catholic Church Today

A characteristic feature of Poland's current sociopolitical life is a remarkable expansion of the Catholic Church, which has swiftly filled the vacuum left behind by the communists, claiming land, power and the role of moral arbiter of the nation. Lech Wałęsa, when president, was the Church's most prominent supporter, and never went anywhere without a priest at his side.

The interference of the Church in politics notably changed political priorities. In the early 1990s, the crusade against abortion soared to the top of the agenda and pushed economic issues into the background. Abortion had been legalised since 1956 – during the communist era – and was, in practice, a common form of birth control. Even though only about 10% of the population supported a total ban on abortion, the Church achieved its aim and the parliament duly voted for a ban. An anti-abortion law was introduced in 1993. Moderates did manage to have amendments attached to the law requiring that contraceptives be made available and that Polish schools begin providing sex education for the first time.

The Church has also turned its attention to the rising generation. Voluntary religious education was introduced in primary schools in 1990 and became mandatory in 1992. Priests have become a new export item and many Catholic priests in Europe today are Polish.

Since around 1994, the Church has begun to lose popular support. Ironically, it has become the victim of its own victories. Compulsory religious instruction in public schools, the strong anti-abortion law and numerous privileges such as special treatment in the process of granting electronic media licences began to breed resentment among segments of the population, damaging the people's good opinion of the Church.

Perhaps even more ironically, the Church contributed to the 1995 return to power of the former communists, its archenemy. It alienated quite a number of voters, who rebelled against the clerical militancy backed by Lech Wałęsa and instead opted for Aleksander Kwaśniewski. Yet despite losing some adherents, the Church remains extremely powerful.

LPP

The liturgy of the Orthodox Church uses the Old Church Slavonic language, though sermons are usually either in Belarusian or Ukrainian, depending on the ethnic composition of the region. As for their places of worship, the Orthodox churches – *cerkwie* (*cerkiew* in the singular) – are recognisable by their characteristic onion-shaped domes. Inside is the iconostasis, a partition or screen covered with icons, which separates the sanctuary from the main part of the church.

The Uniate Church has an even smaller number of believers (at most 0.5%), mostly Ukrainians and Lemks scattered throughout the country as a result of the forced resettlement imposed by the communist authorities in the aftermath of WWII. The architecture and decoration of Uniate churches are similar to those of their Orthodox counterparts, and they are also referred to as cerkwie.

A small bunch of Protestant churches exist mostly in the regions which were German before WWII, particularly in Silesia. They represent at most another 0.5% of the population. The remaining creeds are insignificant: Poland's three mosques serve the tiny Muslim population, and a handful of functioning synagogues hold religious services for the Jewish believers.

LANGUAGE

Polish belongs to the group of West Slavonic languages, together with Czech and Slovak. Today it's the official language of Poland and is spoken by over 99% of the population.

In medieval Poland, Latin was the lingua franca and the language used by the Crown's state offices, administration and the Church. The Latin alphabet was adapted to write the Polish language, but in order to write down the complex sounds of the Polish tongue a number of consonant clusters and diacritical marks had to be applied. The visual appearance of Polish is pretty fearsome for people outside the Slavonic circle, and it's no doubt a difficult language to master. It has a complicated grammar, with word endings changing depending on case, number and gender, and the rules abound in exceptions.

As for Western languages, English and German are the best known in Poland though by no means are they commonly spoken or understood. English is most often heard in larger urban centres among the better educated youth, while German is largely a heritage of prewar territorial divisions and the war itself, and as such is mainly spoken by the older generation, particularly in the regions that were once German. Taking that as a rough rule, you may have some English conversations in major cities, but when travelling in remote parts of Masuria or Silesia, the German language will be a better tool of communication.

This said, remember that most ordinary Poles don't speak any other language than Polish. This includes attendants of public services such as shops, post offices, banks, bus and train stations, restaurants and hotels (except for some top-end ones), and you may even encounter language problems at tourist offices. It is also true of phone emergency lines, including police, ambulance and fire brigade.

See the Language chapter near the end of the book for a practical guide to the pronunciation of Polish, and some vocabulary essentials.

Facts for the Visitor

HIGHLIGHTS
Nature

Poland's mountains, lakes and sea coast are superb. In terms of height and popularity, the Tatras are the uncontested winners among the mountain ranges. Far less known but also magnificent are the Góry Stołowe (Table Mountains) in the Sudetes. The Bieszczady and the Pieniny are quite different though just as picturesque.

There are several lake districts in Poland, of which the Great Masurian Lakes are the largest and most popular. The sea coast has sandy beaches along almost its entire length; one of the most beautiful and least polluted stretches is near Łeba, with its shifting dunes.

Primeval Białowieża Forest on Poland's eastern border is home to the largest remaining herd of European bison, and other wildlife. Each of these environments is distinct and equally worth experiencing.

Historic Towns

Of all Poland's large cities, only Kraków has a fully authentic old centre, almost untouched by WWII. The damaged historic cores of Poznań, Toruń and Wrocław have been masterfully restored. The old towns in Gdańsk and Warsaw were destroyed almost completely and rebuilt from scratch, with surprisingly good results. All are well worth visiting. Among the smaller urban centres, Zamość in south-east Poland is a picturesque 16th-century Renaissance town.

Museums

Warsaw's National Museum holds Poland's largest art collection, though the national museums in Kraków, Wrocław, Poznań and Gdańsk also have extensive collections and are worth visiting. The Modern Art Museum in Łódź houses Poland's largest collection of modern painting, while Płock has the most representative collection of Art Nouveau. The small town of Jędrzejów has a unique set of over 300 sundials, but if icons are what you like, go to Sanok and Przemyśl. The

Auschwitz museum at Oświęcim is perhaps the most touching and meaningful.

Anyone interested in traditional rural architecture and crafts should visit some of Poland's *skansens* (open-air museums), in particular those at Sanok and Nowy Sącz.

Castles

There are over 100 castles in Poland of many different kinds. The imposing Malbork castle, one-time seat of the Teutonic Knights, is reputedly the largest surviving medieval castle in Europe. Other remarkable castles built by the knights include those in Lidzbark Warmiński and Kwidzyn.

For hundreds of years the mighty Wawel castle in Kraków sheltered Polish royalty, most of whom are buried in the adjacent cathedral. True castle lovers will also seek out castles in Pieskowa Skała, Baranów Sandomierski, Niedzica, Książ and Gołuchów. All these castles are now museums.

Among ruined castles, the Krzyżtopór in the tiny village of Ujazd is possibly the most impressive, and the charming ruin in Ogrodzieniec is also worth a trip.

Palaces

Warsaw contains Poland's two most magnificent royal palaces: the 17th-century Wilanów palace and the 18th-century Łazienki palace. In the countryside feudal magnates constructed some splendid Renaissance, baroque and rococo palaces, the best of which include those in Łańcut, Nieborów, Kozłówka, Rogalin and Pszczyna, all open as museums.

Churches

In a country as staunchly Catholic as Poland, churches are everywhere from the smallest villages to the largest cities. Kraków alone has several dozen of them. Plenty of old churches are of great historic and often artistic value. It's hard to name highlights here but any list should include the cathedrals in Kraków, Toruń and Gniezno; St Mary's churches in Kraków and Gdańsk; and the Monastery of Jasna Góra in Częstochowa.

These famous buildings apart, there's a galaxy of other churches, ranging in size from minuscule to colossal, and often of amazing artistic beauty. The Carpathian foothills are dotted with rustic timber Catholic churches and roadside chapels, which deserve to be explored.

The heritage of the Orthodox and Uniate churches includes over 100 charming wooden churches in the Carpathian Mountains alone, not to mention another hundred scattered along the eastern Polish border.

Unesco World Heritage List

The list includes eight sites in Poland: the historic quarters of Kraków, Toruń, Warsaw and Zamość, Auschwitz concentration camp, Wieliczka salt mine, Malbork castle and Białowieża National Park.

SUGGESTED ITINERARIES

Your itinerary will depend on a number of factors, including your particular interests, the amount of time you have, the season and your method of transport, but some very rough guidelines can be given.

The following suggestions have been made assuming you arrive at Warsaw and plan on visiting a mix of cultural and natural highlights of the country, but various options are given to suit personal interests. Regardless of how short your visit is try not to miss Kraków. For more suggestions, see the preceding Highlights section, and the Highlights box at the beginning of each chapter.

One week

Spend one to three days in Warsaw, the rest of the week in Kraków; include a short trip to Auschwitz, and, if time allows, the Tatra Mountains.

Two weeks

To the above, add any of the four following options, depending on your taste: the cultural trip to Gdańsk, Malbork and Toruń; wildlife watching in Białowieża and Biebrza national parks; the pleasant eastern route between Warsaw and Kraków visiting Lublin, Zamość and Sandomierz; hiking in the Tatras and the Pieniny.

One month

You'll be able to fit in most of the options listed above.

Two months

To the above, add Wrocław and the Sudeten Mountains, plus the Beskids and Bieszczady in the Carpathian Mountains – both these ranges provide a good mix of local culture and nature; beach-goers might like to relax in some of the Baltic coastal resorts including Łeba and its environs, while lake-lovers may fancy a week or two of kayaking or sailing in Masuria.

PLANNING
When to Go

The tourist season runs roughly from May to September, that is, from mid-spring to early autumn. Its peak is in July and August, the months of school and university holidays, and also the time when most Polish workers and employees take their annual leave. The Baltic beaches are taken over by swarms of holiday makers, resorts and spas are invaded by tourists, Masurian lakes are crowded with hundreds of sailing boats, and mountains can hardly be seen for walkers.

In that period, transport becomes more crowded than usual, and can get booked out in advance. Accommodation may be harder to find, and sometimes more expensive. Fortunately, a lot of schools, which are empty during the holidays, double as youth hostels, and student dormitories in major cities open as student hostels. This roughly meets the demand for budget accommodation. Most theatres are closed in July and August.

If you want to escape the crowds, the best time to come is either late spring (mid-May to June) or the turn of summer and autumn (September to mid-October), when tourism is under way but not in full flood. These are pleasantly warm periods, ideal for general sightseeing and outdoor activities such as walking, biking, horse riding and canoeing. Many cultural events take place in both these periods.

The rest of the year, from mid-autumn to mid-spring, is colder, darker and perhaps less attractive for visitors. However, this doesn't mean that it's a bad time for visiting city sights and enjoying the cultural life as it's not much less active than during the tourist season. Understandably, hiking and other outdoor activities are less prominent in this period, except for skiing in winter. Most camp sites and youth hostels are closed at this time.

The ski season goes from December to March. The Polish mountains are spectacular, but the infrastructure (hotels and chalets, lifts and tows, cable cars, transport etc) is still not well developed. Zakopane, Poland's winter capital, and the nearby Tatra Mountains have some of the best ski facilities.

Maps

Poland produces plenty of maps, and they are generally of good quality, inexpensive and easily available. The situation has improved greatly in recent years. Apart from the state-run map producer, the PPWK, there are now a number of private map publishers.

There's a wide range of general maps of Poland to choose from. You can buy either a single map covering the whole country or a set of four or eight sheets (sold separately) that feature fragments of the country on a larger scale and provide greater detail. Two different kinds of the book-format *Atlas Samochodowy* (Road Atlas) are available, and they are particularly convenient for motorists. They differ in scale (1:300,000 or 1:250,000) and price (US$10 or US$12, respectively) but both are very accurate and readable, and include sketch maps of major cities, Polish road signs and a full index.

All cities and most large towns have their own city maps, which are a good supplement to the maps contained in this book. The maps have a lot of useful information including tram and bus routes, alphabetical lists of streets, post offices, hotels, hospitals, pharmacies etc.

Other very useful maps are the large-scale tourist maps (usually between 1:50,000 and 1:75,000) of the most attractive tourist areas. They cover a relatively small sector, a single mountain range or a group of lakes, and are very detailed. These maps show marked hiking routes and practically everything else you might be interested in when hiking, driving, biking etc. They are a must if you plan on walking.

All the maps listed above are easy to buy in the larger urban centres; buy them there (at bookshops and/or tourist offices), as they may still be hard to come by in the smaller localities. Maps (including city maps) cost somewhere between US$1 and US$3 each.

Polish maps are easy to decipher. Most symbols are based on international standards, and they are explained in the key in three foreign languages, English included.

On the city maps, the word for street, *ulica* or its abbreviated version *ul*, is omitted, but *Aleje* or *Aleja*, more often shortened to *Al*, is placed before the names of avenues to distinguish them from streets.

What to Bring

The first and most important rule is to bring as little as possible – a large, heavy backpack can soon become a nightmare. The times of empty shelves in Poland are long over and you can now buy almost everything you might need. Things such as clothes, footwear, toiletries, stationery, sports and camping equipment etc, both locally produced and imported, are easily available in shops and markets, and they can be cheaper than those you've brought along.

When preparing for the trip, concentrate on the most important things, such as a good backpack, comfortable shoes, reliable camera equipment and any medicines you might need. If you plan on hiking, give some thought to trekking gear such as a tent, sleeping bag, waterproof jacket etc. These things are available in Poland but you may prefer to bring your own. Disposable gas cartridges for Camping Gaz International stoves can be bought at local sports stores. Winter can be cold, so a good warm jacket is essential at that time of year.

RESPONSIBLE TOURISM

A responsible tourist is, perhaps, one who treats the visited place as if it were home. Would you wander into your hometown church during a service and start taking flash photos? Would you bluntly point your camera at your friends while they go about their daily business? Would you leave rubbish scattered in your favourite park?

Respect rituals and ceremonies, traditions and beliefs. Be aware that some customs can challenge your own belief system, and avoid trying to impose on the locals your own view of the world.

In some popular destinations (such as Kraków or Tatra Mountains), the summer influx of tourists puts a real strain on local infrastructure, ancient buildings and the environment. One way to minimise your own impact – and probably enjoy yourself more – is to avoid visiting in the high season.

Spending your pounds or dollars in less-visited areas is another way to even out tourism's financial impact, while simultaneously broadening your enjoyment and understanding of the country. Encourage ecotourism projects that aim to preserve or restore local environments.

Wherever you are, littering is irresponsible and offensive. Mountain areas have fragile ecosystems, so stick to the marked trails whenever possible, and always carry your rubbish away with you. Don't use detergents or toothpaste in or near watercourses, even if they are biodegradable.

Remember that plastic bags, aliminium cans, silver foil, tampons or condoms you leave behind can endanger wildlife. Burying your rubbish won't solve the problem – it disturbs soil and ground cover and encourages erosion. It can also be dug up by animals who may be injured or poisoned by it.

TOURIST OFFICES
Local Tourist Offices

Most larger cities have local tourist offices, which are usually good sources of information and most sell maps and tourist publications. The situation has largely improved over recent years, in terms of both quality of information and the publications the offices provide. Also, an increasing number of attendants speak English and/or German.

In smaller localities, where there are no genuine tourist offices, look for PTTK, or the Polish Tourists Association. PTTK was once a helpful organisation, focusing on outdoor activities such as hiking, sailing, cycling and camping. Today it's just another travel agency, yet some offices are well stocked with maps and trekking brochures, can arrange guides and may provide some information. PTTK also has information regarding accommodation (usually cheap).

Tourist Offices Abroad

Polish tourist offices abroad include:

France (☎ 01 47 42 07 42, fax 01 42 66 35 88, W www.tourisme.pologne.net) 49 av. de l'Opéra, 75002 Paris
Germany (☎ 30-210 09 211, fax 210 09 214, W www.polen-info.de) Marburger Strasse 1, 10789 Berlin
Netherlands (☎ 20-625 35 70, fax 623 09 29, W www.members.tripod.com/~poleninfo) Leidsestraat 64, 1017 PD Amsterdam
UK (☎ 020-7580 8811, fax 7580 8866) 1st Floor, Remo House, 310–312 Regent St, London W1R 5AJ
USA (☎ 212-338 9412, fax 338 9283, W www.polandtour.org) 275 Madison Ave, Suite 1711, New York, NY 10016

VISAS & DOCUMENTS
Passport

A valid passport is essential, and it must be stamped with a visa if you need one. Theoretically, the expiry date of your passport shouldn't be less than six months after the date of your departure from Poland. Make sure that your passport has a few blank pages for visas and entry and exit stamps.

Visas

Bilateral conventions allowing visa-free visits have been signed with over 50 countries, including most of Eastern Europe, the Commonwealth of Independent States and the three Baltic republics. Among other countries whose citizens don't need visas for Poland are Argentina, Austria, Belgium, Bolivia, Chile, Costa Rica, Cuba, Cyprus, Denmark, Finland, France, Germany, Greece, Honduras, Iceland, Ireland, Italy, Japan, Liechtenstein, Luxembourg, Malta, Monaco, the Netherlands, Nicaragua, Norway, Portugal, South Korea, Spain, Sweden, Switzerland, Uruguay, the UK and the USA. Stays of up to 90 days are allowed, except for Britons who are allowed to stay in Poland without a visa for up to 180 days.

Nationals of other countries should check with a Polish consulate and apply for a visa if they need one. Canadians, Australians, New Zealanders, South Africans and Israelis still required a visa at the time of writing.

Visas are issued for a period of up to 180 days, and the price is the same regardless of the visa's duration – about US$40 to US$60, varying from country to country. Some consulates may give shorter visas if you apply by mail. You can stay in Poland only within the period specified in the visa, which you have to indicate in the application form. You normally cannot extend your tourist visa once you are in Poland, so ask for a sufficiently long period while applying for it at home. There are also 48-hour transit visas (onward visa required) if you just need to pass through Poland. Visas are generally issued in a few days, with an express same-day service available in some consulates if you pay 50% more.

Travel Insurance

Ideally, all travellers should have a travel insurance policy, which will provide some sense of security in the case of a medical emergency or the loss or theft of your belongings. It may seem an expensive luxury, but if you can't afford a travel health insurance policy, you probably can't afford medical emergency charges abroad either, if something goes wrong.

You may prefer a policy that pays doctors or hospitals directly rather than you having to pay on the spot and claim later. If you have to claim later, make sure you keep all documentation. Some policies ask you to call back (reverse charges) to a centre in your home country where an immediate assessment of your problem is made. Check that the policy covers ambulances or an emergency flight home.

For claims involving loss or theft, you must produce a police report detailing the situation (refer to the Dangers & Annoyances section later in this chapter). You also need proof of the value of any items lost or stolen. Purchase receipts are the best, so if you buy a new camera for your trip, for example, hang onto the receipt.

Driving Licence

If you plan on driving in Poland, make sure you bring your driving licence. Your licence from home will normally be sufficient if it bears a photograph, but if not, or if you want to play it absolutely safe, bring an International Driving Licence together with your local one. If you're bringing your own vehicle, car insurance (the so-called Green Card) is required.

Hostel Cards

An HI membership card can gain you 10% to 25% discount on youth hostel prices, though some hostels don't give discounts to foreigners. Bring the card with you, or get one issued in Poland at the provincial branch offices of the Polish Youth Hostel Association (PTSM) in the main cities.

Student Cards

If you are a student, bring along your International Student Identity Card (ISIC card). You can also get one in Poland if you have your local student card or any document stating that you're a full-time student. The Almatur Student Bureau (which has offices in most major cities) issues ISIC cards for around US$7 (bring a photo). The card gives reductions on museum admissions (normally by 50%), Polferry ferries (20%), LOT domestic flights (10%) and urban transport in Warsaw (50%), plus discounts on international transport tickets. There are no ISIC discounts on domestic trains and buses.

Vaccination Certificates

No vaccinations are necessary for Poland, though if you come from an area infected with yellow fever or cholera you may be asked for an International Health Certificate with these inoculations. For your own safety, you are advised to have the vaccination for hepatitis or at least a gamma globulin jab. See Health, later in this chapter, for more information.

Copies

Make copies of your important documents such as passport (data pages plus visas), credit cards, airline tickets, travel insurance policy and travellers cheque receipt slips. Take notes of the serial numbers on your cameras, lenses, camcorder, notebook and any other pieces of high-tech stuff you'll be taking on the trip. Make a list of phone numbers of the emergency assistance services (credit cards, insurance, your bank etc). Leave a copy of everything with someone at home and keep another with you, separate from the originals. Slip US$50 or US$100 into an unlikely place to use as an emergency stash.

EMBASSIES & CONSULATES
Polish Embassies & Consulates

Poland has embassies in the capitals of about 90 countries. The consulates are usually at the same address as the embassy. In some countries there are additional consulates in other cities. The list includes:

Australia
(☎ 02-6273 1208) 7 Turrana St, Yarralumla, Canberra ACT 2600
(☎ 02-9363 9816) 10 Trelawney St, Woollahra, Sydney NSW 2025
Belarus
(☎ 172-13 43 13) ul Rumiancewa 6, 220034 Minsk
Canada
(☎ 613-789 0468) 443 Daly Av, Ottawa 2, Ont K1N 6H3
(☎ 514-937 9481) 1500 Avenue des Pins Ouest, Montreal, PQ H3G 1B4
(☎ 416-252 5471) 2603 Lakeshore Blvd West, Toronto, Ont M8V 1G5
(☎ 604-688 3530) 1177 West Hastings St, Suite 1600, Vancouver, BC V6E 2K3
Czech Republic
(☎ 2-2422 8722) Václavské Námestí 49, Nové Mesto, Prague 1
(☎ 69-611 80 74) ul Blahoslavová 4, 70100 Ostrava 1
France
(☎ 1-43 17 34 22) 5 rue de Talleyrand, 75007 Paris
(☎ 3-20 06 50 30) 45 Boulevard Carnot, 59800 Lille
(☎ 4-78 93 14 85) 79 rue Crillon, 69006 Lyons
Germany
(☎ 30-22 31 30) Lassenstrasse 19–21, 14193 Berlin
(☎ 221-38 70 13) Leyboldstrasse 74, 50968 Cologne

(☎ 40-631 20 91) Gründgensstrasse 20, 22309 Hamburg
Japan
(☎ 3-5794 7020) 2-13-5 Mita, Meguro-ku, Tokyo 153
Latvia
(☎ 2-732 16 17) Elizabetes iela 2, 1340 Riga
Lithuania
(☎ 2-709 001) Smelio gatve 20 A, Vilnius
Netherlands
(☎ 70-360 28 06) Alexanderstraat 25, 2514 JM The Hague
Russia
(☎ 095-231 15 00) ulitsa Klimashkina 4, 123557 Moscow
(☎ 812-274 41 70) ulitsa 5 Sovietskaya 12/14, 193130 St Petersburg
(☎ 0112-27 33 77) ulitsa Kashtanova 51, 236000 Kaliningrad
Slovakia
(☎ 7-544 13 175) ul Hummelova 4, 81491 Bratislava
UK
(☎ 020-7580 0475) 73 New Cavendish St, London W1N 7RB
(☎ 0131-552 0301) 2 Kinnear Rd, Edinburgh E3H 5PE
Ukraine
(☎ 44-224 80 40) vulitsya Yaroslaviv 12, 252034 Kyiv
(☎ 322-97 08 61) vulitsya Ivana Franko 110, 290000 Lviv
USA
(☎ 202-234 3800) 2640 16th St NW, Washington, DC 20009
(☎ 312-337 8166) 1530 North Lake Shore Drive, Chicago, IL 60610
(☎ 212-889 8360) 233 Madison Ave, New York, NY 10016
(☎ 310-442 8500) 12400 Wilshire Blvd, Suite 555, Los Angeles, CA 90025

Embassies & Consulates in Poland

All countries that maintain diplomatic relations with Poland have their embassies in Warsaw. Consulates are usually at the same address as the embassies. Embassies and consulates (in Warsaw unless otherwise stated) include:

Australia
(☎ 22-521 34 44) ul Nowogrodzka 11
Belarus
(☎ 22-617 39 54) ul Ateńska 67
(☎ 85-744 66 61) ul Waryńskiego 4, Białystok

Your Own Embassy

It's important to realise what your own embassy – the embassy of the country of which you are a citizen – can and can't do to help you if you get into trouble. Generally speaking, it won't be much help in emergencies if the trouble you're in is remotely your own fault. Remember that you are bound by the laws of the country you are in. Your embassy will not be sympathetic if you end up in jail after committing a crime locally, even if such actions are legal in your own country.

In genuine emergencies you might get some assistance, but only if other channels have been exhausted. For example, if you need to get home urgently, a free ticket home is exceedingly unlikely – the embassy would expect you to have insurance. If you have all your money and documents stolen, it might assist with getting a new passport, but a loan for onward travel is out of the question.

(☎ 58-341 00 26) ul Jaśkowa Dolina 50, Gdańsk
Canada
(☎ 22-584 31 00) Al Jerozolimskie 123
Czech Republic
(☎ 22-628 72 21) ul Koszykowa 18
(☎ 32-251 85 76) ul Stalmacha 21, Katowice
France
(☎ 22-529 30 00) ul Puławska 17
(☎ 12-422 18 64) ul Stolarska 15, Kraków
(☎ 61-851 61 40) ul Miełżyńskiego 27, Poznań (honorary)
(☎ 58-550 32 49) ul Kościuszki 16, Sopot (honorary)
(☎ 71-360 51 31) ul Powstańców Śląskich 95, Wrocław (honorary)
Germany
(☎ 22-617 30 11) ul Dąbrowiecka 30
(☎ 58-341 43 66) Al Zwycięstwa 23, Gdańsk
(☎ 12-421 84 73) ul Stolarska 7, Kraków
(☎ 61-852 24 33) ul Paderewskiego 7, Poznań (honorary)
(☎ 91-422 52 12) ul Królowej Korony Polskiej 31, Szczecin
(☎ 71-342 52 52) ul Podwale 76, Wrocław
Ireland
(☎ 22-849 66 55) ul Humańska 10
Japan
(☎ 22-696 50 00) ul Swoleżerów 8
Latvia
(☎ 22-848 98 05) ul Rejtana 15

Lithuania
(☎ 22-625 34 10) Al Szucha 5
(☎ 87-516 22 73) ul 22 Lipca 9, Sejny
Netherlands
(☎ 22-849 23 51) ul Chocimska 6
(☎ 58-346 76 18) Al Jana Pawła II 20, Gdańsk (honorary)
(☎ 61-852 78 84) ul Gwarna 7, Poznań (honorary)
(☎ 71-344 49 85) Rynek 39/40, Wrocław (honorary)
New Zealand
(☎ 22-645 14 07) ul Migdałowa 4
Russia
(☎ 22-621 34 53) ul Belwederska 49
(☎ 58-341 10 88) ul Batorego 15, Gdańsk
(☎ 12-422 83 88) ul Westerplatte 11, Kraków
(☎ 61-841 75 23) ul Bukowska 55A, Poznań
(☎ 91-422 48 77) ul Piotra Skargi 14, Szczecin
Slovakia
(☎ 22-628 40 51) ul Litewska 6
UK
(☎ 22-628 10 01) Al Róż 1
(☎ 58-341 43 65) ul Grunwaldzka 100/102, Gdańsk (honorary)
(☎ 32-206 98 01) ul PCK 10, Katowice (honorary)
(☎ 61-853 29 19) ul Kramarska 26, Poznań (honorary)
(☎ 71-344 89 61) ul Oławska 2, Wrocław (honorary)
Ukraine
(☎ 22-629 34 46) Al Szucha 7
(☎ 58-346 06 09) ul Jaśkowa Dolina 44, Gdańsk
(☎ 12-656 23 36) ul Krakowska 41, Kraków
USA
(☎ 22-628 30 41) Al Ujazdowskie 29/31
(☎ 12-422 14 00) ul Stolarska 9, Kraków
(☎ 61-851 85 16) ul Paderewskiego 7, Poznań (honorary)

CUSTOMS

When entering Poland, you're allowed to bring duty-free articles for your personal use while you travel and stay there. They include still, cine and video cameras plus accessories; portable self-powered electronic goods such as a personal computer, video recorder, radio, CD player and the like, together with accessories; a portable musical instrument; sports and tourist equipment such as a sailboard, kayak (up to 5.5m in length), bicycle, tent, skis etc; and medicines and medical instruments for your own use. You'll rarely be asked to declare these things.

Unlimited amounts of foreign currency and travellers cheques can be brought into the country, but only up to the equivalent of €5000 can be taken out by a foreigner without a declaration. If you enter with more than the equivalent of €5000 and want to take it all back out of Poland, you need to fill in a currency-declaration form upon your arrival and have it stamped by customs officials. You are allowed to import or export Polish currency.

The duty-free allowance on arrival is up to 250 cigarettes or 50 cigars or 250g of pipe tobacco and up to two litres of alcoholic drinks (not allowed for people aged under 17). Narcotics are forbidden and you'd be asking for big trouble smuggling them across the border.

When leaving the country, you may take out gifts and souvenirs of a total value not exceeding €90, free of duty. The export of items manufactured before 9 May 1945 is strictly prohibited, unless you first get an authorisation.

MONEY
Currency
The official Polish currency is the złoty (literally, gold), abbreviated to zł. Złoty is pronounced 'zwo-ti'. It is divided into 100 units called the grosz, abbreviated to gr. New notes and coins were introduced in 1995, and include five paper bills (10, 20, 50, 100 and 200zł) and nine coins (one, two, five, 10, 20 and 50 gr, and one, two and 5 zł). The bills feature Polish kings, have different sizes and are easily recognisable.

Exchange Rates
Polish currency is convertible and easy to change either way. There's no longer a black market in Poland and the official exchange rate roughly represents the currency's actual value. The złoty's rate of depreciation against hard currencies has slowed down significantly over the past few years, to about 7% per year in 2001.

At the time we went to press the approximate rates were:

country	unit		złoty
Australia	A$1	=	2.18 zł
Canada	C$1	=	2.63 zł
Czech Republic	1K	=	0.11 zł
euro	€1	=	3.64 zł
Japan	¥100	=	3.16 zł
New Zealand	NZ$1	=	1.78 zł
Slovakia	SK10	=	0.86 zł
UK	UK£1	=	5.95 zł
USA	US$1	=	4.22 zł

Exchanging Money
An essential question for many travellers is what to bring: cash, travellers cheques or a credit card? Any of the three forms is OK in Poland, though it's probably best to bring a combination of two or even three to allow more flexibility. Travelling in Poland is generally safe, so there are no major problems in carrying cash, which is easiest to change. Travellers cheques are safer but harder to change and you pay about 2% to 3% commission.

Finally, with the recent rash of Automatic Teller Machines (ATMs), credit cards have become the most convenient option of getting local currency.

Cash The place to exchange cash is the *kantor*, the private currency-exchange office. They are ubiquitous; there are actually so many of them that we haven't bothered to mark them on the maps. They're easy to find, but if you can't, just ask anybody for a kantor.

The kantors are either self-contained offices or just desks in travel agencies, train stations, post offices, department stores and the more upmarket hotels etc. The farther out from the cities you go, the less numerous they are, but you can be pretty sure that every medium-sized town has at least a few of them. Kantors are usually open between 9am and 6pm on weekdays and till around 2pm on Saturday, but some open longer and a few stay open 24 hours.

Kantors change cash only (no travellers cheques) and accept many major world currencies. The most common and thus the most easily changed are US dollars. Australian dollars and Japanese yen are somewhat exotic to Poles and not all kantors will change them. There's no commission on transaction – you get what is written on the board (every kantor has a board displaying the exchange rates of the currencies it changes). The whole operation takes a few seconds and there's no paperwork involved. You don't need to present your passport or fill out any forms.

Kantors buy and sell foreign currencies, and the difference between the buying and selling rates is usually not larger than 2%. Exchange rates differ slightly from city to city and from kantor to kantor (about 1%). Smaller towns may offer up to 2% less, so it's advisable to change money in large urban centres.

Travellers Cheques Changing travellers cheques is not as straightforward as changing cash, and is more time-consuming. The usual place to change travellers cheques is a bank, but not all banks handle these transactions. The best known bank which offers this facility is the Bank Polska Kasa Opieki SA, commonly known as the Bank Pekao. It has a dozen offices in Warsaw and branches in all major cities.

Several other banks, including the Bank Gdański, Bank Zachodni, Bank Śląski, Powszechny Bank Kredytowy and Powszechny Bank Gospodarczy, also provide this service, and they too have many regional branches.

Banks in the larger cities are usually open 8am to 5pm or 6pm weekdays (some also open till 2pm on Saturday), but in smaller towns they tend to close earlier. They change most major brands of cheque, of which American Express is the most widely known and accepted.

The exchange rate is roughly similar to, or marginally lower than, that for cash in kantors, but banks charge a commission *(prowizja)* on transactions, which varies from bank to bank (somewhere between 1% to 2.5%). Banks also have a set minimum charge of US$2 to US$3. For example, the Bank Pekao commission on cashing cheques is 1.5% with a minimum charge of US$2.50.

Banks can be crowded and inefficient; you'll probably have to queue a while and then wait until they complete the paperwork. It may take anything from 10 minutes to an hour. You'll need your passport in any transaction. Some provincial banks may insist on seeing the original receipt from the purchase of your travellers cheques.

You can also cash travellers cheques in an American Express office, but there are only two offices in Warsaw. They are efficient, speak English and change most major brands of cheque, and their rates are a bit lower than those of the banks.

Cash a sufficient amount of travellers cheques in a big city to last until you set foot in another big city before setting off for a trip into remote countryside.

In case of theft or loss of AmEx cheques, call American Express Travellers Cheques

Some Tips about Changing Money

To avoid hassles exchanging currency, one important thing to remember before you set off from home is that any banknotes you take to Poland must be in good condition, without any marks or seals. Kantors can refuse to accept banknotes that have numbers written on them (a common practice of bank cashiers totalling bundles of notes) even if they are in an otherwise perfect condition.

Kantors that trade on Sunday and at night usually give poor rates – try to avoid these times by changing enough money on Friday or Saturday to last you until Monday.

Don't forget to change your extra złotys back to hard currency before you leave Poland, but don't leave it to the last minute as exchange facilities at the land border crossings and airports tend to offer poor rates. If you are leaving from an airport, change your złotys in the city centre beforehand.

There are still a few street moneychangers hanging around touristy places (most notably in Gdańsk) but give them a miss. They won't offer you a better rate than that in a kantor, and if one does, you may be pretty sure that you're being conned.

Refund Centre in the UK, toll-free ☎ 00 800 44 11 200. They will ask you for the missing cheque numbers, date and place of their purchase etc, and will give you a code which you have to present at one of the AmEx offices in Warsaw (in the Marriott Hotel at Al Jerozolimskie 65/79; or ul Sienna 39) while applying for a refund.

Credit Cards & ATMs Credit cards are increasingly popular for buying goods and services, though their use is still limited to upmarket establishments, mainly in major cities. Among the most popular cards accepted in Poland are Visa, MasterCard, American Express, Diners Club, Eurocard and Access.

Credit cards are also useful for getting cash advances in banks, and the procedure is faster than changing travellers cheques. The best card to bring is Visa, because it's honoured by the largest number of banks, including the Bank Pekao and all the other banks listed in the previous section. Bank Pekao will also give cash advances on MasterCard.

Still faster and more convenient is to get an advance from a *bankomat*, or an ATM. They first appeared in Poland in 1996 and spread like wildfire. Today most major banks have their own ATMs, and there are also a lot of ATMs operated by Euronet, the largest ATM network in Poland, with dozens of outfits across city centres. Euronet ATMs accept 17 different credit cards, including Visa and MasterCard.

International Transfers A credit card solves the problem of transferring money, provided you are prepared to carry the credit charge or have someone back at home pay your expenses for you. Be aware of your credit limit.

If you don't have a credit card, you can have money sent to you through some major banks, but the transfer may take a while. If you need money urgently, you can use the Western Union Money Transfer. You will receive the money within 15 minutes from the moment your sender pays it (along with the transaction fee) at any of the 30,000 Western Union agents scattered

worldwide. Transaction charges are: US$50 for a transfer of US$1000; US$90 for US$2000; and US$22 for every additional US$500 above US$2000.

Western Union's outlets can be found in all Polish cities and most large towns. Information on locations and conditions can be obtained on the toll-free ☎ 0800 120 224.

Costs

Though not the bargain it used to be, Poland is still a cheap country for travellers. Just how cheap, of course, depends largely on what degree of comfort you need, what hotel standards you are used to, what kind of food you eat, where you go, how fast you travel and the means of transport you use. If, for example, you are accustomed to rental cars and plush hotels, you can spend as much as you would in the West.

However, if you are a budget traveller, prepared for basic conditions and willing to endure some discomfort on the road, a daily average of around US$30 should be sufficient. This amount would cover accommodation in cheap hotels and hostels, food in budget restaurants, travel at a reasonable pace by train or bus, and would still leave you a margin for some cultural events, a few beers and occasional taxis. If you plan on camping or staying in youth hostels, and eating in cheap bistros and other self-services, it's feasible to cut this average down to US$20 per day, without experiencing too much discomfort. It's important to remember that cities are more expensive than the rural areas, with Warsaw being the most expensive.

Tipping & Bargaining

In restaurants, service is included in the price so you just pay what's on the bill. Tipping is up to you and there doesn't seem to be any hard and fast rules about it. In low-priced eateries guests rarely leave a tip; they might, at most, round the total up to the nearest whole figure. In upmarket establishments it's customary to tip up to 10% of the bill.

Tipping in hotels is essentially restricted to the top-end establishments, which usually have decent room service and porters, who all expect to be tipped. Taxi drivers are normally not tipped, unless you want to reward someone for their effort.

Bargaining is not common in Poland, and is limited to some informal places such as flea markets, fruit bazaars and street vendors.

Taxes

Value-added tax (VAT) is calculated at three levels: 0% (books, press, some basic food products); 7% (most food); and 22% (fine food, hotels, restaurants, petrol, luxury items). The tax is normally included in the price, so you won't really feel it directly, and in most cases you won't even realise you're paying it.

POST & COMMUNICATIONS

Postal services are operated by the Poczta Polska, while communications facilities are provided by the Telekomunikacja Polska. Both these companies usually share one office, called the *poczta* (post office), although

recently the Telekomunikacja has been opening its own communications-only offices.

In the large cities there will be a dozen or more post offices, of which the *Poczta Główna* (main post office) will usually have the widest range of facilities, including poste restante and fax. Larger post offices in the cities are normally open 8am to 8pm weekdays, and one will usually stay open 24 hours. In the smaller localities business hours may only be till 4pm on weekdays.

Post

Airmail letters sent from Poland take about a week to reach a European destination and up to two weeks if mailed to other continents. The rates for a 20g letter or a postcard are: US$0.50 to Europe, US$0.60 to the USA and Canada, and US$0.80 elsewhere. Packages and parcels are reasonably cheap if sent by surface mail but they can take up to three months to reach their destination.

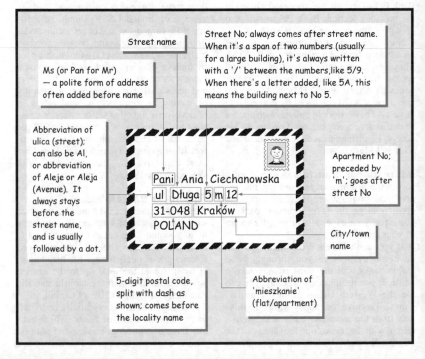

Street name

Street No; always comes after street name. When it's a span of two numbers (usually for a large building), it's always written with a '/' between the numbers, like 5/9. When there's a letter added, like 5A, this means the building next to No 5.

Ms (or Pan for Mr) — a polite form of address often added before name

Abbreviation of ulica (street); can also be Al, or abbreviation of Aleje or Aleja (Avenue). It always stays before the street name, and is usually followed by a dot.

Pani Ania Ciechanowska
ul Długa 5 m 12
31-048 Kraków
POLAND

Apartment No; preceded by 'm'; goes after street No

City/town name

5-digit postal code, split with dash as shown; comes before the locality name

Abbreviation of 'mieszkanie' (flat/apartment)

Airmail packages are expensive, with prices comparable to those in Western Europe.

If you want mail sent to you, use the poste restante in the large cities, such as Warsaw, Kraków and Gdańsk (see these sections for details). Mail is held for 14 working days, then returned to the sender. American Express customers can receive poste restante mail via the Warsaw AmEx offices.

Telephone

The Polish telephone system is antiquated and unreliable. Modernisation was minimal until the mid-1990s, when progress in telecommunications really took off and some more adequate telephone exchanges were installed.

Public Phones Public telephones are few and far between by Western standards, and not infrequently out of order. If you can't find one that works, go to a post office – each should have at least one functioning public phone. Old phones, that operate on tokens (żetony), have almost disappeared, and virtually all phones nowadays only operate on phonecards. There are two types of card: the more common magnetic cards (used in rectangular-shaped phones) and chip cards (used in egg-shaped phones).

It's well worth buying a phonecard (at the post office or newsagency kiosks) if you think you'll be using public phones from time to time. Cards come in three kinds: a 25-unit card (US$3), a 50-unit card (US$6) and a 100-unit card (US$11). One unit represents one three-minute local call. Cards can be used for domestic and international calls.

Mobile Phones Apart from the regular, cable phone network, there are three cellular phone providers: the analogue Centertel and the digital Era and Plus. All three cover most of Poland's territory. Cellular phone numbers begin with 0501/2/3 (Centertel), 0601 (Plus) and 0602 (Era), and don't require you to dial the area code. Mobile phones have quickly become popular, both as a status symbol and a more reliable alternative to the jammed stationary lines and scarce and often inoperable public phones.

Domestic Calls Intercity direct dialling is possible to just about anywhere in the country. The telephone system has been upgraded and now all the area codes are two-digits long, while local numbers are seven-digits long country-wide. Telephone area codes are listed in this book just below the heading of the relevant town or city, but you must first dial the operator's code (see the boxed text 'How to Dial Intercity').

International Calls You can now dial directly to just about anywhere in the world. When dialling direct, a minute will cost around US$0.75 within Europe, US$1.50 to the USA and Canada, and US$2 elsewhere. If you place the call through the operator at the post office, the minimum charge is for a three minute call which will cost about US$2.50 within Europe, US$5 to the USA and Canada, and US$7 elsewhere. Every extra minute costs a third more. For a direct person-to-person call, add an extra minute's charge.

How to Dial Intercity

Since July 2001 Telekomunikacja Polska (TP) is no longer a monopolist on the Polish telecommunications network market. It now has three competitors (NOM, Netia1 and Energis), which have got licences to operate long-distance domestic calls.

While calling outside your local area code, you now have to choose which operator you are going to use by dialling its four-digit code:

TP	☎ 1033
NOM	☎ 1044
Netia1	☎ 1055
Energis	☎ 1066

You first dial '0', then the operator's code, then the area code and the local number. For example, calling Kraków (area code ☎ 12) using NOM you dial ☎ 0 1044 12 and the local number.

The new system doesn't affect international calls (neither incoming nor outgoing ones) – you don't dial any four-digit codes.

Collect calls are possible to most major countries. Inquire at any Telekomunikacja Polska office for the toll-free number to the operator in the country you want to call, then call from any public or private telephone. These numbers include:

Australia	☎ 00 800 61 111 61
France	☎ 00 800 33 111 33
Germany	☎ 00 800 49 111 49
UK	☎ 00 800 44 111 44
USA (AT&T)	☎ 00 800 1 1111 11

To call a telephone number in Poland from abroad, dial the international access code of the country you're calling from, the country code for Poland (☎ 48), the two-digit area code (don't dial '0' or the operator's code) and the seven-digit local phone number.

To call direct abroad from Poland, dial ☎ 00 (the Polish international access code) before the country code of the country you are calling, area code and the local number.

eKno Communication Service Lonely Planet's eKno global communication service provides low-cost international calls – for local calls you're usually better off with a local phonecard. eKno also offers free messaging services, email, travel information and an online travel vault, where you can securely store all your important documents. You can join online at **W** www.ekno.lonely planet.com, where you will find local-access numbers for the 24-hour customer-service centre. Once you have joined, always check the eKno Web site for the latest access numbers and updates on new features.

Fax

Faxes can be sent from most larger post and communications offices. The service is priced similarly to phone calls placed through the operator, with a three-minute minimum charge applying.

Email & Internet Access

The Internet has become popular in Poland (though it's still way behind Western Europe) and there are a number of service providers. Internet cafes have mushroomed in the big cities and sizable towns. An hour of surfing the Web or emailing costs about US$1 to US$2 (up to US$3 in Warsaw).

DIGITAL RESOURCES

The World Wide Web is a rich resource for travellers. You can research your trip, hunt down bargain air fares, book hotels, check on weather conditions or chat with locals and other travellers about the best places to visit (or avoid!).

A good place to start your Web explorations is the Lonely Planet Web site (**W** www.lonelyplanet.com). Here you'll find succinct summaries on travelling to most places on earth, postcards from other travellers as well as the Thorn Tree bulletin board, where you can ask questions before you go or dispense advice when you get back. You can also find travel news and updates to the Poland guidebook, and the sub-WWWay section links you to the most useful travel resources elsewhere on the Web.

Polish Computer Jargon

If you surf the Web at a Polish Internet cafe you may have to do it in Polish. Following is a bit of useful Polish cyber-speak:

Bookmark	Zakładka
Close	Zamknij
Copy	Kopiuj
Cut	Wytnij
Delete	Usuń
Edit	Edycja
Exit	Zakończ
File	Plik
Help	Pomoc
Insert	Wstaw
New	Nowy
Open	Otwórz
Paste	Wklej
Print	Drukuj
Save	Zapisz
Save As	Zapisz Jako
Search	Szukaj
View	Widok

There are quite a few specific Web sites concerning Poland. Some useful sources of general and tourist information on Poland include:

W www.explore-poland.pl
W www.polandtour.org
W www.insidepoland.pl
W www.polishworld.com

Specific sites covering accommodation in Poland include:

W www.hotelspoland.com
W www.poltravel.com
W www.meteor.ipl.net

BOOKS
You will get far more out of your visit if you read up on the country before you go. There is no shortage of English-language books written about Poland as well as translations of the best of Polish writers and poets. There is also a choice of travel guides.

Check good travel bookshops for tourist guides. For background literature, look for bookshops specialising in Eastern Europe or Poland in particular. They exist in major cities around the world where significant Polish communities live. You can also contact Hippocrene Books (☎ 212-685 4371, fax 779 9338, e contact@hippocrenebooks .com, W www.hippocrenebooks.com), 171 Madison Ave, New York, NY 10016, USA, for its catalogue. It has a variety of books on Poland ranging from guidebooks and dictionaries to various translations of Polish literature.

In Poland itself there is an increasing number of foreign-language guidebooks about the country. These are more often than not English and/or German translations of Polish-language guidebooks.

Most books around the world are published in different editions by different publishers in different countries. As a result, a book might be a hardcover rarity in one country while it's readily available in paperback in another. Fortunately, bookshops and libraries search by title or author, so your local bookshop or library is best placed to advise you on the availability of the following recommendations.

Lonely Planet
If you're planning a wider journey than just Poland, consider taking LP's *Eastern Europe*, *Central Europe* or *Europe on a shoestring*, depending on which region you're going to travel around. Also note that LP has individual guidebooks to most European countries, including some of Poland's neighbours. See the back of this book for a complete rundown. Look out also for the *Kraków* city guide.

For some language help, get a copy of LP's *Polish Phrasebook*. If you plan to visit several Eastern European countries, the *Eastern Europe Phrasebook* may also be useful. It contains many essential words and phrases in Polish, Czech, Slovak, Hungarian, Romanian and Bulgarian, together with phonetic transcriptions.

History & Politics
God's Playground: A History of Poland by Norman Davies is one of the best accounts of Polish history. This two-volume work is beautifully written, easy to read and has, at the same time, a rare analytical depth, which makes it a perfect key to understanding a thousand years of the Polish nation.

The Heart of Europe: A Short History of Poland by Norman Davies is a more condensed account, with a greater emphasis on the 20th century. This is also an excellent work, highly recommended.

Jews in Poland: A Documentary History by Iwo Cyprian Pogonowski, provides a comprehensive record of half a millennium of Polish-Jewish relations in Poland.

The theme of the Holocaust has an extensive bibliography. *A Surplus of Memory: Chronicle of the Warsaw Ghetto Uprising* by Yitzhak Zuckerman is a detailed narrative on this heroic act of Jewish resistance. *Mila 18* by Leon Uris is another moving account of the same events.

Primo Levi, an Italian Jew who survived the horrors of Auschwitz, has contributed several chilling works, including *If this is a Man* and *The Drowned and the Saved*. The latter was published shortly before his suicide in 1987.

Turning to more recent history, *The Polish Revolution: Solidarity 1980–82* by Timothy Garton Ash is an insight into the Solidarity era, a 16-month period that undermined the whole communist system. Entertainingly written, the book explains how it all happened. *The Polish Challenge* by Kevin Ruane documents the same events and is a factual supplement to Garton Ash's book.

Mad Dreams, Saving Graces: Poland, a Nation in Conspiracy by Michael T Kaufman is a trip through the dark times of martial law and the gloomy period up till 1988 – as readable as it is informative. *Unquiet Days: At Home in Poland* by Thomas Swick is yet another vivid account of those events, told by an American who lived in Poland during the crucial period of Solidarity and later returned several times.

The Naked President: A Political Life of Lech Wałęsa by Roger Boyes, Eastern Europe correspondent for the *Times*, traces the life of the charismatic leader of Solidarity.

General

The Polish Way: A Thousand-Year History of the Poles and their Culture by Adam Zamoyski is one of the best accounts of the culture of Poland from its birth to the recent past. Fully illustrated and exquisitely written, the book is an excellent introduction to the subject.

Art, Architecture and Design in Poland 966–1990 by Stefan Muthesius is a compact yet comprehensive history of Polish art.

The History of Polish Literature by Czesław Miłosz is an encyclopaedic anthology covering everything from medieval Latin texts to contemporary poetry and prose.

It's a good idea to get a copy of a small English-Polish/Polish-English dictionary. Among the best is the one from the well-known yellow series published by Langenscheidt, easy to find in large bookshops both in and outside Poland.

There is a choice of audio systems for language learning that consists of cassettes or CDs as well as a textbook. VocabuLearn, Language/30 and Berlitz all have Polish courses. Check what's available in your local library.

NEWSPAPERS & MAGAZINES

Each large city has at least one local newspaper and there are nine papers with country-wide distribution. The *Gazeta Wyborcza* was the first independent daily in postwar Eastern Europe and is now the major national paper. The *Rzeczpospolita* is the main business daily.

Among weekly magazines, the biggest is *Wprost*. The long-lived *Polityka* is still an opinion-forming paper and retains some of its serious, in-depth character. In 2001, the Polish-language *Newsweek* appeared, but it covers mostly local affairs.

Some big foreign magazines – *Elle* and *Burda* among others – have established themselves on the local market. German publishers have been especially active in flooding Poland with their gossipy weekly and monthly women's magazines.

The major foreign newspapers, including *The Financial Times*, *The Wall Street Journal*, *The International Herald Tribune*, *The Times*, *Le Monde* and *Der Spiegel*, are sold in the major cities. Traditionally, *Time* and *Newsweek* have been very widely distributed. The best places to look for foreign publications are EMPiK stores, foreign-language bookshops and newsstands in the lobbies of upmarket hotels.

The major Polish publication in English is *The Warsaw Voice* – a well-edited and interesting weekly which is available from major newsagents (US$2). Despite its name suggesting a narrow city profile, it actually covers country-wide politics, business and culture, making it a good insight into Polish current affairs.

RADIO & TV

The state-run Polish Radio (Polskie Radio) is the main broadcaster. It operates on the AM long and medium-wave bands and on FM, and is received in every corner of the country. In early 1994, two previously local private broadcasters became nationwide networks: the Warsaw-based Radio Zet and the Kraków-based RFM. Plenty of other private competitors operate on FM. Apart from headline news in English broadcast by some of the private stations, all programs are in Polish.

Poland has two state-owned, country-wide TV channels: the general program I and the more educational and culture-focused program II. Both have commercial advertisements (up to 8% of transmission time), which were previously unknown. Some of the larger cities also have state-owned local programs. There are also several private channels, including the country-wide PolSat.

Individual satellite TV dishes have become hugely popular, allowing Poles to have direct access to the Western media. Most major hotels have also installed them. Rough estimates indicate that Poland owns more satellite dishes than any other country in Europe except for France and the UK. Experts reckon that every fourth household has either its own dish or access to one.

The indiscriminate installation of dishes and unauthorised reception of diverse broadcasting networks have been under scrutiny, meaning that Poland has entered the era of pay TV. There are already a number of coded cable TV channels and a queue of operators waiting for licences.

VIDEO SYSTEMS

If you want to record or buy video tapes to play back home, you won't get a picture if the image registration system is different. The French SECAM used to be the standard image registration system in communist Poland, but it has been replaced by PAL, the same as in most of Western Europe. VHS is the standard format for recording from TV and viewing rented films at home, although DVD is steadily making inroads.

PHOTOGRAPHY & VIDEO

Except for the usual restrictions on photographing military, industrial, transport and telecommunications installations, you can take pictures or videos of just about anything. You can take photos in most churches, but keep in mind that the interiors are usually pretty dim and a tripod or a flash

may be necessary. Many museums don't allow photography inside, or will charge extra (sometimes a lot) for the permit.

Skansens are good places for photographing the traditional rural architecture. As for people shots, the best places are regional folk festivals and religious feasts. It's here that you're most likely to see locals decked out in their traditional costumes. Markets, on the other hand, are usually colourless and dull. Needless to say, you should be very discreet and respectful when photographing people.

Film & Equipment

Kodak is the most popular film in Poland, with Fuji and Agfa not far behind. You can buy both slide and negative film in several commonly used speeds. For those who are more demanding, high-quality Ilford B&W film is available as well as Fujichrome professional series film including Velvia and Provia. Sample prices for film are: US$4 for a roll of Kodacolor, US$6 for Fujichrome 100; US$9 for Velvia. The prices are for a roll of 36 exposures and do not include processing.

As for processing, you can easily have your prints done, often within an hour, in any of the numerous photo minilabs. There's also an increasing number of laboratories which handle E6 slide processing.

You can buy Nikon, Canon, Minolta and other popular Japanese cameras, but the choice is limited and the prices are rather high. Bring along your own reliable gear. Getting your camera repaired in Poland can be a problem if you have an uncommon make and if any original spare parts are necessary. General mechanical faults can usually be fixed quite easily.

Poland is sufficiently safe for a tourist to carry a camera or a Handycam. If you bring the latter, don't forget to also bring along a conversion plug to fit electric sockets (the two-round-pin type) if you have a different system.

TIME

All of Poland lies within the same time zone, GMT/UTC+1. When it is noon in

Warsaw, the time in other cities around the world is:

Auckland	11pm
Berlin	noon
Hong Kong	7pm
London	11am
Los Angeles	3am
Moscow	2pm
New York	6am
Paris	noon
Prague	noon
San Francisco	3am
Stockholm	noon
Sydney	9pm
Tokyo	8pm
Toronto	6am
Vancouver	3am

Poland pushes the clocks forward an hour in late March and back again in late September.

A 24-hour clock is applied in Poland for official purposes, including all transport schedules. In everyday conversations, however, people commonly use the 2 x 12 hour system.

ELECTRICITY
Electricity is 220V, 50Hz. Plugs with two round pins are used, the same as in the rest of Continental Europe.

WEIGHTS & MEASURES
Poland uses the metric system. There's a conversion table at the back of this book.

LAUNDRY
Dry cleaners (pralnia) exist in the larger cities but are expensive and it will take them several days to clean your clothes. A more expensive express service can cut this time by half. Top-class hotels offer laundry facilities and are faster. Self-service laundrettes are unheard of so far, and there are still very few which offer service washes.

TOILETS
Self-contained public toilets in the cities are few and far between. If you're really desperate, look for a restaurant. Hotels, museums and train stations are other emergency options. Toilets are labelled 'Toaleta' or simply 'WC'. The gents will be labelled 'Dla Panów' or 'Męski' and/or marked with a triangle (an inverted pyramid), and the ladies will be labelled 'Dla Pań' or 'Damski' and/or marked with a circle.

The use of a public toilet (including those in restaurants and train stations) is almost never free. While it costs from US$0.10 to US$0.50, the price doesn't necessarily reflect the cleanliness of the establishment. Charges are posted on the door and collected by the toilet attendant sitting at the door, who will give you a piece of toilet paper. It's a good idea to carry a roll of paper, though, just in case.

HEALTH
Poland is not the most disease-ridden place on earth, but sanitary conditions still leave much to be desired and pollution contaminates water and air. Medical service and the availability of medications are not as good as in the West.

Travel health depends on your predeparture preparations, your daily health care while travelling and how you handle any medical problem that does develop.

Predeparture Planning
Immunisations While no vaccinations are required for travel to Poland, there are some routine vaccinations that are recommended. You are advised to get vaccinated against hepatitis A or at least have a gamma globulin jab. Hepatitis A vaccine (eg, Avaxim, Havrix 1440 or VAQTA) provides long-term immunity (possibly more than 10 years) after an initial injection and a booster at six to 12 months.

Alternatively, an injection of gamma globulin can provide short-term protection against hepatitis A – two to six months, depending on the dose. It is not a vaccine, but a ready-made antibody collected from blood donations. It is reasonably effective and, unlike the vaccine, it is protective immediately, but because it's a blood product, there are currently long-term safety concerns.

Make sure your vaccinations against tetanus, diphtheria and polio are up to date.

Health Insurance Make sure you have adequate health insurance. See Travel Insurance in the Visas & Documents section.

Other Preparations Make sure you're healthy before you start travelling. If you are going on a long trip make sure your teeth are OK. If you wear glasses take a spare pair and your prescription.

Take an adequate supply of any medication required, as it may not be available locally. Taking part of the packaging showing the generic name rather than the brand will make getting replacements easier. A legible prescription or letter from your doctor to show that you legally use the medication is a good idea.

A basic medical kit is useful, although most items you'll need are readily available.

Water

Tap water is usually safe to drink in Poland but, for reasons of taste, you may prefer to stick to bottled water; it's readily available.

Medical Problems & Treatment

Most minor problems can be solved by a visit to the pharmacy *(apteka)*. There's quite a number of them and they have qualified staff, some of whom speak English. They may help you with advice on buying the right medication or even on treating small wounds. Condoms, tampons and syringes are readily available.

In the event of a more serious illness or injury you should seek out a specialised doctor. Your embassy or consulate should be able to advise a good place to go. If you can't find help, just ask anybody for the nearest outpatient clinic *(przychodnia)*. These clinics have physicians of various specialities and are the places Poles go when they get ill. Charges are relatively low.

The country-wide emergency phone number for the ambulance service is ☎ 999 but don't expect the operator to speak English. Ask any Pole around to call them for you.

Infectious Diseases

Diarrhoea Simple things like a change of water, food or climate can all cause a mild bout of diarrhoea, but a few rushed toilet trips with no other symptoms is not indicative of a major problem.

Dehydration is the main danger with diarrhoea, and can occur quite quickly in children or the elderly. Under all circumstances fluid replacement (at least equal to the volume being lost) is the most important thing to remember. Weak black tea with a little sugar, soda water, or soft drinks allowed to go flat and diluted 50% with clean water are all good. With severe diarrhoea a rehydrating solution is preferable to replace minerals and salts lost. Commercially available oral rehydration salts (ORS) are very useful; add them to boiled or bottled water. Keep drinking small amounts often. Stick to a bland diet as you recover.

Hepatitis There are several different viruses that cause hepatitis, and they differ in the way that they are transmitted. The symptoms are similar in all forms of the illness, and include fever, chills, headache, fatigue, feelings of weakness and aches and pains, followed by loss of appetite, nausea, vomiting, abdominal pain, dark urine, light-coloured faeces, jaundiced (yellow) skin and yellowing of the whites of the eyes. People who have had hepatitis should avoid alcohol for some time after the illness, as the liver needs time to recover.

Hepatitis A is transmitted by contaminated food and drinking water. You should seek medical advice, but there is not much you can do apart from rest, drink lots of fluids, eat lightly and avoid fatty foods.

HIV & AIDS Infection with the human immunodeficiency virus (HIV) may lead to acquired immune deficiency syndrome (AIDS), which is a fatal disease. Any exposure to blood, blood products or body fluids may put the individual at risk. The disease is often transmitted through sexual contact or dirty needles – vaccinations, acupuncture, tattooing and body piercing can be potentially as dangerous as intravenous drug use.

Fear of contracting the HIV infection should never preclude treatment for serious medical conditions.

Bites & Stings

Bee and wasp stings are usually painful rather than dangerous. However, in people who are allergic to them severe breathing difficulties may occur and require urgent medical care. Mosquitoes can drive you almost insane during the late summer months, especially around the Great Masurian Lakes. Most people get used to mosquito bites after a few days as their bodies adjust, and the itching and swelling will be less severe. Calamine lotion or Stingose spray will give relief and ice packs will reduce the pain and swelling.

Ticks

You should check all over your body if you have been walking through a potentially tick-infested area as ticks can cause skin infections and other more serious diseases, including tick-borne encephalitis. You might want to consider a vaccination against tick-borne encephalitis if you plan to do extensive hiking between May and September.

If a tick is found attached, press down around the tick's head with tweezers, grab the head and gently pull upwards. Avoid pulling the rear of the body as this may squeeze the tick's gut contents through the attached mouth parts into the skin, increasing the risk of infection and disease. Smearing chemicals on the tick will not make it let go and is not recommended.

WOMEN TRAVELLERS

Travel for women in Poland is pretty much hassle-free except for occasional encounters with drunken local males. Harassment of this kind is not usually dangerous, but can be annoying. Steer clear of the drunks and avoid places considered male territory, particularly cheap drink bars.

On the other hand, a woman travelling alone, especially in remote rural areas, may expect to receive more help, hospitality and generosity from the locals than would a man on his own.

GAY & LESBIAN TRAVELLERS

Homosexuality isn't illegal in Poland, but the overwhelmingly Catholic society tends to both deny and suppress it. Many Poles,

particularly in the more traditional, rural communities, still consider sexual attraction to members of the same sex unnatural. To be openly gay in Poland can often limit vocational and social opportunities and may cause family ostracism. Consequently, few gays, and still fewer lesbians, voice their attitudes in a family or workplace forum, opting instead for discretion.

The Polish gay and lesbian movement is still very much underground. Warsaw has the largest gay and lesbian community and the most open gay life, and therefore is the best place to make contacts and get to know what's going on.

Warsaw's Rainbow gay and lesbian organisation (☎ 22-628 52 22), ul Czerniakowska 178 m 16, conducts meetings on Tuesday, Wednesday and Friday 6pm to 9pm; there may be someone around speaking English.

DISABLED TRAVELLERS

Poland is not well set up for people with disabilities, even though there has been a significant improvement over recent years. Wheelchair ramps are available only at some upmarket hotels and restaurants, and public transport will be a challenge for anyone with mobility problems. Few offices, museums or banks provide special facilities for the disabled traveller, and wheelchair-accessible toilets are few and far between.

Organisations

Disabled travellers in the USA might like to contact the Society for Accessible Travel & Hospitality (☎ 212-447 SATH, fax 725 8253, W www.sath.org), 347 Fifth Ave, Suite 610, New York, NY 10016. In the UK, a useful contact is the Royal Association for Disability & Rehabilitation (☎ 020-7242 3882, W www.radar.org.uk), 25 Mortimer St, London W1N 8AB.

SENIOR TRAVELLERS

There are few discounts for senior Poles and still fewer for senior visitors. Senior travellers (both nationals and foreigners) can expect a 20% reduction on LOT domestic flights and the Baltic ferries but that's about it. So far, there are no discounts for senior citizens on train and bus fares, accommodation rates, cinema and theatre tickets etc, though this may be slowly changing. Legally, senior Poles get discounts on admission fees for museums and other sights, but this doesn't apply to foreigners.

TRAVEL WITH CHILDREN

If you plan on taking along your offspring on a trip to Poland you shouldn't encounter any particular problems. Children enjoy privileges on local transport, accommodation and entertainment. Age limits for particular freebies or discounts vary from place to place, but are not often rigidly enforced. Basic supplies are easily available in the cities. There are quite a few shops devoted to kids' clothes, shoes and toys, and you can buy disposable nappies (diapers) and baby food in supermarkets and pharmacies. For general suggestions on how to make a trip with kids easier, pick up the current edition of Lonely Planet's *Travel with Children*.

DANGERS & ANNOYANCES

Poland is a relatively safe country to travel in, even though there has been a steady increase in crime since the fall of communism. Always keep your eyes open and use common sense. Problems mostly occur in big cities, with Warsaw being perhaps the least safe place in Poland. Take care when walking alone at night, particularly in the centre and the Praga suburb, and be alert at Warsaw central train station, the favourite playground for thieves and pickpockets. Other large cities appear to be quieter, but keep your wits about you. By and large, the smaller the town, the safer it is.

Don't venture into any rundown areas, dubious-looking suburbs and desolate parks, especially after dark. Use taxis if you feel uncertain about an area. Try and stay away from groups of suspicious-looking male characters hanging around markets, shady bars and bus and train stations. Stay at a safe distance from dogs. Poles are keen on big dogs, many of which roam without leads and not all are muzzled. Some are bigger and uglier than others.

Keep a sharp eye on your pockets and your bag in crowded places such as markets or city buses and trams. Beware of short-changing at train stations, taxis, restaurants etc. Always have some smaller bills in order to make change more easily. Hotels are generally safe, though it's better not to leave valuables in your room; in most places you can deposit them at the reception desk.

Theft from cars has become widespread – refer to Security & Hazards under Car & Motorcycle in the Getting Around chapter for information. Pirate or 'mafia' taxis are a problem in Warsaw and some other large cities – see the boxed text 'Welcome to the Land of Pirate Taxis' in the Warsaw chapter. Theft and robbery in trains has also been on the increase – see the boxed aside 'Train Theft Warning' in the Getting Around chapter.

If your passport, valuables and/or other belongings are lost or stolen, report it to the police. They will give you a copy of the statement which serves as a temporary identity document; if you have insurance, you'll need to present the statement to your insurer in order to make a claim. English-speaking police are rare, so it's best to take along an interpreter if you can. Don't hold out high hopes of having your possessions returned to you, for the police earn next to nothing and can be rather cynical about a 'rich' foreigner complaining about losing a few dollars.

Heavy drinking is a way of life in Poland and drunks may at times be disturbing. Poles smoke a lot and so far there has been little serious anti-tobacco campaigning. Polish cigarettes are of low quality and the smoke they produce is hardly tolerable for anyone unused to them, let alone a nonsmoker.

Slow and impolite service in shops, offices and restaurants is slowly being eradicated by the competitive market economy, though you can still occasionally experience it. Cheating is not common but there are some areas, especially those connected with foreign tourism, where you should be alert.

Since WWII Poland has been ethnically an almost entirely homogeneous nation and Poles, particularly those living in rural areas, have had little contact with foreigners.

That's why travellers looking racially different, eg, of African or Asian background, may attract some stares from the locals. In most cases, this is just a curiosity, without any hostility in mind. On the other hand, there have been some acts of racism in the cities, though it's still not a social problem by any definition.

LEGAL MATTERS

Foreigners in Poland, as elsewhere, are subject to the laws of the host country. While your embassy or consulate is the best stop in any emergency, bear in mind that there are some things it can't do for you, like getting local laws or regulations waived because you're a foreigner, investigating a crime, providing legal advice or representation in civil or criminal cases, getting you out of jail, and lending you money.

A consul can, however, issue emergency passports, contact relatives and friends, advise on how to transfer funds, provide lists of reliable local doctors, lawyers and interpreters, and visit you if you've been arrested or jailed.

BUSINESS HOURS

Most grocery shops are open from 7am or 8am to 6pm or 7pm on weekdays and till around 2pm on Saturday. Delicatessens and supermarkets usually stay open longer, until 8pm or 9pm, and there's at least one food shop in every major town and every district of the city which is open 24 hours. All such night shops have a section selling beer, wine and spirits, which is what keeps them going. General stores (selling clothing, books, stationery, household appliances, photo and sports stuff etc) normally open at 10am or 11am and close at 6pm or 7pm (at 2pm or 3pm on Saturday). The office working day is theoretically eight hours long, Monday to Friday, and there's usually no lunch break.

Consider this as a rough guide only; hours can vary considerably from shop to shop (or office to office) and from the city to the village.

The opening hours of museums and other tourist sights vary greatly. Most museums are closed on Monday; some of them also

> ## Emergency
>
> The nationwide toll-free 24-hour emergency phone numbers include:
>
> | | |
> |---|---|
> | Police | ☎ 997 |
> | Fire Brigade | ☎ 998 |
> | Ambulance | ☎ 999 |
> | Roadside Assistance | ☎ 981 |
>
> Don't expect the attendants of any of these services to speak English, so try to get a local to call on your behalf.

stay closed on the day following a public holiday. Many museums close one or two hours earlier in the off season. Museums usually cease selling tickets half an hour (sometimes even one hour) before their official closing time.

Churches are a bigger puzzle. The major churches in the main cities are often open all day long. On the other hand, rural churches in small villages will almost always be locked except during Mass, which may be only on Sunday morning.

PUBLIC HOLIDAYS

Official public holidays in Poland include New Year's Day (1 January), Easter Monday (March or April), Labour Day (1 May), Constitution Day (3 May), Corpus Christi (May or June), Assumption Day (15 August), All Saints' Day (1 November), Independence Day (11 November), and Christmas (25 and 26 December).

SPECIAL EVENTS

Apart from some well established national or international festivals of film, theatre and music, there are plenty of small local feasts, fairs, contests, meetings, competitions etc, some of which involve local folklore. Add to this a lot of religious celebrations.

Cultural Events

Among the classical music highlights, you should be in Łańcut in May for the Old Music Festival, in Warsaw in June/July for the Mozart Festival, in Kraków in August for the Music in Old Kraków Festival, and in Wrocław in September for Wratislavia Cantans with its oratorios and cantatas.

The best of contemporary music is presented at the Warsaw Autumn International Festival in September. If you are a jazz fan there's nothing better than the Warsaw Summer Jazz Days in June/July and the Jazz Jamboree, also in Warsaw, in late October.

Major theatre festivals take place in Warsaw (January), Kalisz (May), Toruń (May/June) and Poznań (June). Film festivals take place in Kraków (May/June), Gdynia (October), Warsaw (October) and Łódź (November/December).

The last week of June in Kazimierz Dolny is a must if you want to listen to genuine folk bands and singers from all over the country, but if you are interested in international folk songs and dances of highlanders, you should try to be in Zakopane in late August. Kraków hosts the prestigious Jewish Culture Festival in June/July.

You'll find more details on some of these events in the main text of the book. For further information, contact local tourist offices. Check the dates when you come as some festivals can move to neighbouring months.

Catholic Events

Given the strong Catholic character of the nation, religious feasts are much celebrated, especially among the more traditional rural population. The Church calendar is marked by two major cycles which culminate in Christmas and Easter, and both cycles include set periods before and after the proper ceremonies take place. There are also a number of feast days devoted to particular saints, of whom the Virgin Mary is the most widely celebrated.

Christmas The Christmas cycle begins with Advent (Adwent), a four-week-long period preceding Christmas, which is characterised by the preparation of Nativity scenes in churches. Kraków is particularly notable for this; a competition is held there and the winning examples are rewarded.

As for Christmas (Boże Narodzenie) itself, Christmas Eve (Wigilia) is the day most celebrated in Polish homes, culminating in a solemn supper which should start when the first star appears in the sky. Before the meal the family shares holy bread (opłatek), wishing each other all the best for the future. Then the supper begins which traditionally consists of 12 courses, including some of the best of traditional Polish cuisine. An extra seat and a place setting are left prepared for an unexpected guest. Kids will find their gifts under the Christmas tree (choinka), or sometimes they will be handed out by Santa Claus (Święty Mikołaj).

In the more traditional rural homes there will still be much magic and witchcraft involved in the ceremony, the forms differing from region to region. It's believed, for example, that animals speak with human voices on that one night, and that at midnight the water in wells turns into wine.

After the supper is finished, the family will set off for church for the specially celebrated Christmas Mass (Pasterka) at midnight. The service is held by almost all churches, and all are packed.

Christmas Day is, like the previous day, essentially a family day, with Mass, eating and relaxing. The holiday atmosphere continues for the remaining days of the year up until New Year's Eve (Sylwester), when the action starts with a variety of formal balls and private parties, principally among urban communities.

On 6 January comes Epiphany (Dzień Trzech Króli), marked by carol singers, usually armed with a small portable crib or other religious images, who go in groups from door to door. On this day people have a piece of chalk consecrated in church, then use it to write 'K+M+B' (the initials of the three Magi) on their front doors, to insure Heaven's care over the home.

Easter Just as important as Christmas, Easter (Wielkanoc) is a moveable feast falling on the Sunday past the first full moon after 21 March (any day between 22 March and 25 April). It's preceded by Lent (Wielki Post), the season of fasting and penitence which begins on Ash Wednesday (Środa Popielcowa), 40 weekdays prior to Easter.

Poland's Major Cultural Events

January
Warsaw Theatre Meetings – Warsaw

February
Shanties – Festival of Sailors' Songs – Kraków
Musica Polonica Nova – Contemporary Music
Festival – Wrocław

March
Poznań Jazz Festival – Poznań

March/April
Organ Music Festival – Kraków

April
Stanisław Moniuszko International Vocal
Competition – Warsaw

April/May
Warsaw Ballet Days – Warsaw

May
Student Song Festival – Kraków
Gaude Mater – International Festival of
Religious Music – Częstochowa
Kalisz Theatre Meetings – Kalisz
Jazz on the Odra River – International Jazz
Festival – Wrocław
Old Music Festival – Łańcut
International Book Fair – Warsaw
Łódź Ballet Meetings – Łódź

May/June
Contact – International Theatre Festival –
Toruń
International Festival of Orthodox Church
Music – Hajnówka
Polish & International Short Film Festival –
Kraków

June
Festival of Polish Song – Opole
Malta – International Theatre Festival – Poznań
Festival of Folk Bands & Singers – Kazimierz
Dolny

June/July
Jewish Culture Festival – Kraków
Mozart Festival – Warsaw

Zamość Theatre Summer – Zamość
Warsaw Summer Jazz Days – Warsaw

June–August
International Organ Music Festival – Gdańsk

June–September
Festival of Organ & Chamber Music – Kamień
Pomorski

July
Summer Jazz Festival – Kraków
International Festival of Street Theatre –
Kraków
Gdynia Summer Jazz Days – Gdynia
Art of the Street – International Festival –
Warsaw

August
International Song Festival – Sopot
Music in Old Kraków – International Festival –
Kraków
Tatra Autumn – International Festival of
Mountain Folklore – Zakopane

September
Wratislavia Cantans – International Oratorio &
Cantata Festival – Wrocław
Festival of Piano Music – Słupsk
Warsaw Autumn – International Festival of
Contemporary Music – Warsaw
Festival of Polish Feature Film – Gdynia

October
Warsaw International Film Festival – Warsaw
Mediaschool – International Film & Television
Schools' Festival – Łódź
Jazz Jamboree – International Jazz Festival –
Warsaw
Chopin International Piano Competition –
Warsaw, every five years (next in 2005)
Wieniawski International Violin Competition –
Poznań, every five years (next in 2006)

November/December
International Piano Jazz Festival – Kalisz
Camerimage – International Film Photography
Festival – Łódź

Holy Week (Wielki Tydzień) begins with Palm Sunday (Niedziela Palmowa), a reminder of the triumphal entry of Christ into Jerusalem, where he was welcomed with date-palm branches. Today the most common substitutes are willow branches overspread with white catkins. However, there are still some villages, notably Rabka, Tokarnia (near Rabka) and Łyse (in the Kurpie region), where the tradition is taken quite seriously: the 'palms' made there are elaborate works of art stretching up to 10m in height.

Palm Sunday also marks the beginning of the famous ceremony in Kalwaria Zebrzydowska near Kraków, which reaches its zenith on Maundy Thursday (Wielki Czwartek) and Good Friday (Wielki Piątek) when a Passion play is performed, re-enacting the last days of the life of Christ. In a blend of religious rite and popular theatre, local amateur actors take the roles of Roman soldiers, apostles, Jewish priests and Christ himself, and circle 20-odd Calvary chapels representing the stages of the Way of the Cross, accompanied by a crowd of pilgrims and spectators.

On Good Friday people visit the Holy Sepulchres set up in churches, while on Holy Saturday (Wielka Sobota) the faithful go to church with baskets filled with food such as bread, sausage, cake and eggs to have them blessed. The eggs are particularly characteristic for Easter as they are decoratively painted, sometimes with very elaborate patterns. Inspired by this tradition, the eggs are also made of wood, painted and sold as souvenirs.

Easter Day (Niedziela Wielkanocna) begins with Mass, usually accompanied by a procession, after which the faithful come back home to have a solemn breakfast, when the consecrated food is eaten. Before breakfast, family members share eggs while wishing each other the best.

Easter Monday (Lany Poniedziałek) is when people sprinkle each other with water, which can mean anything from a symbolic drop of perfumed water to a bucket of water over the head, or even a dousing from a fire engine.

Pentecost (Zielone Święta) falls on the 50th day after Easter Day (hence its name), and a further 10 days on comes Corpus Christi (Boże Ciało). The latter is characterised by processions held all over the country, of which the best known is that in Łowicz.

Other Feasts Among the Marian feasts, the most important is the Assumption (Święto Wniebowzięcia NMP) on 15 August, celebrated in many places throughout Poland but nowhere as elaborately as in the Monastery of Jasna Góra in Częstochowa, where pilgrims from all corners of the country arrive on that very day, sometimes after a journey of several days on foot.

All Saints' Day (Dzień Wszystkich Świętych) on 1 November is a time of remembrance and prayers for the souls of the dead. On no other day do cemeteries witness so many people leaving flowers, wreaths and candles on the graves of their relatives, and they look most spectacular at night. The celebrations continue to a lesser extent on the following day.

ACTIVITIES
Hiking
This is probably the most popular outdoor activity in Poland, and not without reason. Thousands of kilometres of marked trails run through the most attractive areas of the countryside, particularly in the mountains. Trails are usually well marked and easy to follow and don't present great difficulties even for beginners. The most popular hiking routes are those in the Tatra Mountains (see the special section 'Hiking in the Tatra Mountains' in the Carpathian Mountains chapter) but there are many other amazing trails in the Pieniny, the Bieszczady and the Karkonosze, to list just a few. Hiking is basically a summer activity; the season does not really start until May.

Cycling
Having your own two wheels gives you an opportunity to explore remote areas rarely visited by tourists. Don't worry about the state of the roads – most are in acceptable

shape – and most of the country is comfortably flat for biking. Bike-rental businesses are finally opening in some touristy areas; inquire at the local tourist offices about where to hire a bike.

Kayaking

There are some almost virgin regions which offer fabulous conditions for kayakers. The Krutynia and Czarna Hańcza Rivers, both in Masuria, have some of the best kayaking in the country (see the Olsztyn and Augustów sections for details).

Sailing

The Masurian lakes are ideal for sailing and get crowded with hundreds of boats in summer. It's possible to hire sailing boats in Giżycko, Mikołajki (see these sections) and several other Masurian resorts. Some travel agencies organise sailing holidays. Sea sailing is much less popular in Poland.

Windsurfing

This is becoming popular along the Baltic coast, with the main centre in the Gulf of Gdańsk between Władysławowo and Chałupy (see the Hel Peninsula section in the Pomerania chapter for details).

Rafting

Probably the only rafting trip you will be able to find is the well organised tourist run down the Dunajec River. The Dunajec Gorge section in the Carpathian Mountains chapter has all the details.

Horse Riding

Horse riding is popular in Poland and there are a lot of stud farms. Many of them have riding courses for beginners and will rent horses to experienced riders.

Caving

There are over 1000 caves of various kinds in Poland, most of which are found in the Kraków-Częstochowa Upland and in the Tatra Mountains. However, only a handful of caves are adapted for ordinary tourists and open to all. The most spectacular of these are arguably the Bear's Cave near

Kłodzko and the Paradise Cave near Kielce, both detailed in the book.

Bird-Watching

Poland offers good bird-watching opportunities, particularly in the north-eastern part of the country. Bird Service in Kraków (see the Kraków chapter for details) is the best specialist agency.

Skiing

Skiing is fairly popular and is mostly concentrated in the Carpathians. Zakopane at the foot of the Tatra Mountains is Poland's No 1 ski centre, and the second is probably Szczyrk in the Beskid Śląski. There are plenty of other, smaller ski resorts though their facilities are usually more modest.

Hang-Gliding & Paragliding

These are relatively new sports but are developing, particularly in the mountain regions, which offer the best conditions. There are several centres (in Bielsko-Biała and Zakopane, among others) which provide equipment and training. Inquire at Zakopane's tourist office for more information.

LANGUAGE COURSES

Courses of Polish language are available in most major cities. See under Language Courses in the Warsaw, Kraków and Gdańsk sections for further information.

WORK

Travellers hoping to find paid work on the spot in Poland will probably be disappointed. First of all, to work legally you need a work visa, and getting one involves complex and lengthy paperwork. Secondly, wages are low in Poland (an average monthly salary is about US$400), so unless you are a highly qualified specialist in a particular area it's not a great deal. Lastly, forget about casual manual jobs as there are armies of 'tourists' from beyond Poland's eastern border, and most will be eager to work for much less than you would ever expect to be paid.

Qualified English teachers have the best chance of getting a job, yet it's not that easy. Try the English-teaching institutions, linguistic departments at universities, and private language schools. If you don't have bona fide teaching credentials, you may still try to organise some informal arrangements, like for example giving private language lessons.

ACCOMMODATION

The choice of accommodation has grown and diversified considerably over the past decade. Unfortunately, prices have risen as well, though they are still well below those in Western Europe. Budget accommodation is still cheap but the standard is usually low.

Warsaw is the most expensive place to stay, followed by Kraków, Poznań and other major cities. The farther away from the big cities you go, the cheaper. The summer resorts, particularly those on the Baltic coast, on the Masurian Lakes and in the mountains, have higher prices in the high season. Similarly, the mountain ski centres put their prices up in winter. The price of accommodation is the same for foreigners as for Poles, except in some youth hostels, which charge foreigners marginally more.

Accommodation listed in the Places to Stay sections of this book is ordered according to price, from the bottom to the top. Where sections are broken down into price brackets, the budget accommodation includes anything costing less than about US$25 a double; the mid-range bracket covers hotels priced from approximately US$25 to US$50 a double, and anything over US$50 is considered top end. Warsaw and Kraków have higher price brackets – see these chapters for details.

Room prices are usually displayed at the reception desk. You are most likely to find listings there for a single room (pokój 1-osobowy) and a double room (pokój 2-osobowy). They can be with bath (z łazienką) or without bath (bez łazienki), or with basin only (z umywalką). The prices normally include VAT, so you just pay what is written, unless indicated otherwise.

Camping

Poland has over 500 camping and bivouac sites registered at the Polish Federation of Camping & Caravanning. They are distributed throughout the country, and can be found in all the major cities (usually on the outskirts), in many towns and in the countryside, particularly in attractive tourist areas.

About 40% of them are genuine camping grounds as understood by this term in the West. They are fenced around and lit, and have electricity, running water, showers, kitchen and caravan facilities. They often have cabins, though it may be hard to come by one in July and August. They are identified by numbers and/or by names.

The remaining 60% are bivouac sites, or just open grounds for camping, usually equipped with toilets but not much more. The Campingi w Polsce map available in large bookshops (approximately US$2) has details of registered camping and bivouac sites.

Over recent years, a number of private camp sites have sprung up all over Poland. They range from small back gardens with a bath in the owner's house to large grounds with bungalows, cafes, shops, bike and boat rental etc. These sites are not included on the camping map.

Most camp sites are open from May to September, but some run only from June to August. The opening and closing dates given here are a rough guide only: they may open and close earlier or later in the season, depending on the weather, flow of tourists etc.

The usual way of charging is per tent site (US$1.50 to US$3) plus per person (US$2 to US$4). Cabins, where available, go for US$4 to US$10 per person, though in most cases you will have to take the whole room, which may sometimes be a double but is more often a triple or quad.

Youth Hostels

The youth hostels in Poland (schroniska młodzieżowe) are operated by the Polskie Towarzystwo Schronisk Młodzieżowych (PTSM), a member of Hostelling International. PTSM has its main office in Warsaw and branch offices in all provincial capitals. Founded in 1926, PTSM was the world's third youth hostel organisation (after Germany and Switzerland) and managed to operate throughout the period of communist rule as the only such institution in Eastern Europe. What's more, the network expanded during those days to nearly 1000 youth hostels, more than any other country in the world!

By 2001, there were about 580 hostels, including about 130 all-year hostels and 450 seasonal ones open in July and August only. They are distributed more or less evenly throughout the country, and there's at least one in every major city. PTSM publishes the *Informator PTSM*, a guidebook containing the full list of youth hostels in Poland. It's updated biennially and is available in the central and regional offices and in some of the major youth hostels for approximately US$3.

The all-year hostels are more reliable and have more facilities, including showers, a place to cook and a dining room. Some hostels are in pretty poor shape, while others have good, modern facilities.

The seasonal hostels are usually installed in schools, while the pupils are off for their holidays. These schools are in no way adapted to being hostels – they hardly ever have showers or kitchens, and hot water is a rare occurrence. The seasonal hostels are highly unreliable; only about 80% of them will actually be open at any one time, while the remaining ones can be under renovation, or simply stay closed.

Many previously strict hostel rules have been relaxed or abandoned. Youth hostels are now open to all, members and non-members alike, and there is no age limit. Curfew is 10pm, but some hostel staff may be flexible about this. Almost all hostels are closed between 10am and 5pm. Check-in time is usually until 9pm or 10pm, but may be 8pm in some minor seasonal hostels. It's best to check in reasonably early after 5pm.

Hostels cost US$4 to US$9 (depending on the hostel's category) per bed in a dorm. Singles, doubles and triples, if there are any, cost about 20% to 50% more. The youth hostel card gives a 10% to 25% discount off these prices for nationals and, in some places, for foreigners. If you think you'll be using youth hostels regularly, bring along a membership card or buy one at any branch office of the PTSM in Poland. If you don't have your own bed sheets, the staff will provide sheets for US$1 to US$1.50 (not available in some seasonal hostels).

Youth hostels are the cheapest form of accommodation after camping, but do be prepared for basic conditions. Given the low prices, hostels are popular with travellers and are often full. A particularly busy time is early-May to mid-June when hostels are crowded with Polish school groups.

Youth hostels are marked with a green triangle with the PTSM logo inside, placed over the entrance door.

PTTK & Mountain Hostels

Over decades PTTK (Polish Tourists Association) has build up an array of its own hostels, called Dom Turysty or Dom Wycieckowy. They are aimed at budget travellers, providing a simple shelter for the night. They are in some cities, towns, villages and the countryside, often at attractive locations.

PTTK hostels rarely have singles, but always have a choice of three and four-bed rooms, usually with shared facilities, where you can often take just a bed (not the whole room) for US$5 and US$10. Some PTTK hostels, particularly those in the large cities, are now under private management and are more expensive.

PTTK also runs an array of mountain hostels *(schroniska górskie)*, which are an essential resource for trekkers. They are often wonderfully located and are charming buildings in themselves. Conditions are usually simple but you don't pay much and

Polish symbol for youth hostels

the atmosphere can be great. They also serve cheap hot meals. The more isolated mountain hostels are obliged to take in all comers, regardless of how crowded they get, which means that in the high season (summer and/or winter) it can sometimes be hard to find even a space on the floor. These hostels are open all year though you'd better check at the nearest regional PTTK office before setting off.

Student Hostels

These are the hostels set up in student dormitories during the summer holiday period (July to late September) when students are away on holiday. Each major university city has at least a few student dorms, some of which are open as student hostels in summer, and the picture may change from year to year. Some student dorms have a limited number of rooms available year-round. Student hostels cost US$8 to US$18 single, US$15 to US$30 double. Facilities are usually shared but some hostels have rooms with private baths.

Hotels

This is the most voluminous category and is growing fast. It is also the most diverse group, encompassing an immense variety of old and new places ranging from ultra-basic to extra-plush.

The old-generation hotels, dating from before the Berlin Wall went down, were split into classes and given from one to five stars, intended to reflect their quality and price. The rudimentary one-star places are mostly confined to the smaller provincial towns, whereas the upmarket five-star establishments, monopolised by Orbis, dot the central areas of big cities.

The arrival of the market economy has changed the picture altogether. On the one hand, plenty of small, mostly private hotels have sprung up. Many of them cater to the middle-priced market, thus nicely filling the gap between PTTK and Orbis. On the other hand, various international hotel chains have arrived to provide luxury for those who were not satisfied with Orbis' services. Lastly, various state-run lodging networks,

previously accessible to only a few, have now opened to all. The latter category includes the sports and workers' hotels (detailed in the following sections), both of which fall into the bottom price bracket.

Most hotels provide single and double rooms, and some also offer triples. As a rule, single rooms work out proportionally more expensive than the doubles. A double usually costs only 20% to 40% more than a single. A triple often costs only slightly more than a double. Rooms with private bath can be considerably more expensive than those with shared facilities.

If possible, check the room before accepting. Don't be fooled by the hotel reception areas, which may look great in contrast to the rest of the establishment. If you ask to see a room, you can be pretty sure that they won't give you the worst one, which might happen otherwise.

Workers' Hotels During the postwar industrial development, large factories and other enterprises had to provide lodging facilities for their workers, many of whom came from other regions. An extensive network of workers' dormitories had been built up over the communist period, each dorm exclusively for the employees of a given company. Most of these places are now open to the general public.

These hotels mostly exist in the cities, particularly industrial ones. They are almost always large, hardly inspiring blocks, often a long way from the city centre. They are called Hotel Pracowniczy or Hotel Robotniczy, though most have disguised themselves under a proper name. Their standards are usually low, but so is the price, US$5 to US$10 per bed in a double, triple or quad. Singles are rare, as are private baths. They are just about the cheapest hotels you can find and, judging by their facilities, they might well be classified as hostels.

Sports Hotels Sports hotels were built within sports centres in order to create facilities for local and visiting teams. For a long time, most of them accepted athletes only but now almost all are open to the general public. In many aspects they are similar to the PTTK hostels and workers' hotels: they seldom have singles, offer mostly shared facilities and you can usually pay just for your bed, not the whole room. Expect to pay US$5 to US$12 per head. They are usually located next to the local stadium, often well away from the town or city centre. Most commonly, they are called Hotel Sportowy, Hotel OSiR or Hotel MOSiR, and some of them run camp sites in summer.

Orbis & Other Upmarket Hotels Orbis (**W** www.orbis.pl) runs the largest hotel chain in Poland – 55 hotels with a total of over 10,000 rooms. They are found in most of the major cities and smaller places of tourist interest. Focusing on moneyed tourists and business people from abroad as well as the more affluent Poles, Orbis hotels keep their prices high, about US$40 to US$80 a single and US$60 to US$120 a double, or even more in some establishments in Warsaw, Kraków and Wrocław.

Until recently a monopolist of hotel luxury, Orbis now faces increasing competition from various joint ventures with international hotel chains, which have moved in to build some even ritzier venues, mostly in the bigger cities. Predictably, the prices are out of the range of average travellers, but guests can enjoy most of the luxuries they'd find in top-class hotels in the West.

Holiday Homes

In popular holiday areas such as the mountains or the coast, you'll come across workers' holiday homes, known to Poles as Domy Wczasowe or Domy Wypoczynkowe. In the communist times, these large establishments either served the employees of a company or were directed centrally by the FWP (Workers' Holiday Fund), but were off limits to individual tourists. Nowadays they welcome everybody. Most are open in summer only, but some run year-round. They tend to be pretty full in July and August, but it's relatively easy to get a room in June or September. Their standard varies but on the whole it's not bad, and prices are usually reasonable. Almost all have their own dining

rooms, where they serve meals for guests. Full board is usually optional but in some homes it can be compulsory.

Pensions

Also concentrated in the attractive summertime resorts, pensions or *pensjonaty* are small, privately run guesthouses that provide bed and board (half or full). By and large, pensions are clean, comfortable and friendly, and prices are not astronomic – for singles/doubles it's roughly US$20/30. Some of them focus directly on Westerners, particularly Germans, and may have higher prices.

Private Rooms

These are rooms in private homes rented out to tourists. They are available in some major cities and many smaller touristy places. They are arranged through specialist agencies or directly with owners. They are not expensive and can be good value.

In the large cities (eg, Warsaw or Kraków), rooms cost US$15 to US$20 for singles, US$25 to US$30 for doubles. The staff in the office show you what's available, you then decide, pay and go to the address they give you. The most important thing is to choose the right location, taking into consideration both distance and transport. Some places are a hell of a long way from the centre and you'd do better paying more for a central hotel and saving hours travelling on public transport.

Private rooms are a lottery: you don't know what sort of room you'll get or who your hosts will happen to be. It's therefore a good idea to take the room for a night or two and then extend if you decide to stay longer.

In popular holiday resorts, you'll find plenty of signs at the entrances to private homes saying *pokoje* (rooms) or *noclegi* (lodging), which indicate where to knock and ask for a room. They are usually cheaper than in the cities – US$6 to US$10 a head in most cases.

Agrotourist Accommodation

Known as *kwatery agroturystyczne*, this refers to accommodation in farms, country houses and cottages, where owners rent some of their rooms to tourists. They can normally provide meals if requested, and sometimes offer other facilities such as horse riding, angling, canoes, bikes etc. In most cases, rooms are simple and rarely have private baths, but prices are reasonable – usually between US$5 and US$10 per bed.

The owners of these places are affiliated with the agrotourist associations (*stowarzyszenia agroturystyczne*), which have 30-plus regional offices around the country, and a central office in Warsaw.

This is the most dynamic accommodation sector in the country. In 1995 agrotourism was hardly heard of; by the time of writing, there were well over 1000 farms providing such accommodation scattered all over the country.

Agrotourist lodging can be an interesting proposition for those who want to relax for a while somewhere in the countryside. It's easy to enjoy the slow beat of life, local folklore and traditions and healthy regional food – all for a reasonable price. It can also be alternative accommodation for those who have their own means of transport and can easily roam along the back roads and rural areas.

This accommodation is not included throughout this book, but information is pretty easy to get from the tourist offices, which will either give you the relevant information or direct you to the regional agrotourist association office. Most offices have published their regional catalogues, and there's also a thick general catalogue.

FOOD

Poland was for centuries a cosmopolitan country and its food has been influenced by various cuisines. The Jewish, Lithuanian, Belarusian, Ukrainian, Russian, Hungarian and German traditions have all made their mark. Polish food is hearty and filling, with thick soups and sauces, abundant in potatoes and dumplings, and rich in meat.

Poland's most internationally known dishes are *bigos* (sauerkraut with a variety of meats), *pierogi* (ravioli-like dumplings stuffed with cottage cheese or minced meat or cabbage and wild mushrooms) and *barszcz* (red beetroot soup, originating from

Russian borsch). Favourite Polish ingredients and herbs include dill, marjoram, caraway seeds and wild mushrooms.

Eating Habits

Poles start off their day with breakfast (*śniadanie*) which is roughly similar to its Western counterpart and may include bread and butter (*chleb z masłem*), cheese (*ser*), ham (*szynka*), eggs (*jajka*), and tea (*herbata*) or coffee (*kawa*).

The most important and substantial meal of the day, the *obiad*, is normally eaten somewhere between 1pm and 5pm. It's usually prepared at home, but those who don't cook have it in the workplace canteen (*stołówka*) or in a cafeteria. Obiad has no direct equivalent in English: judging by its contents, it's closer to Western dinner, but timing is closer to lunch. Put simply, it's a dinner at lunch time.

The third meal is supper (*kolacja*). The time and contents vary greatly: occasionally it can be nearly as substantial as the obiad;

Bring on the Bigos

If there's a genuine traditional Polish dish, it's bigos. It's made of sauerkraut, fresh chopped cabbage and a variety of meats including pork, beef, game, sausage and bacon. All this is cooked on a low flame for several hours and put aside to be reheated a few times, a process which allegedly enhances its flavour. The whole operation takes a couple of days but the effect can be impressive – a well-cooked, several-days-old bigos is mouthwatering. Everybody has their own mysterious recipe as far as the ingredients, spices and cooking time are concerned and you will never find two identical dishes.

Because it's so time-consuming, bigos does not often appear on a restaurant menu and the dish you encounter under this name in cheap bars and other seedy eateries is a very far cry from the real thing. The best place to try bigos is a private home and if you ever happen to get such an invitation, don't miss it. Bigos tastes most delicious when it's washed down, so bring along a bottle of good clear vodka.

more often it's similar to breakfast, or even as light as just a croissant and a glass of tea.

Etiquette and table manners are more or less the same as in the West. When beginning a meal, whether it's in a restaurant or at home, it's good manners to wish your fellow diners *smacznego*, or 'bon appetit'. When drinking a toast, the Polish equivalent of 'cheers' is *na zdrowie* (literally, to the health).

Places to Eat

With the move towards capitalism, there has been a dramatic development on the gastronomic scene. Western-style eating outlets (almost nonexistent in communist Poland) such as bistros, snack bars, pizza houses, salad bars and fast-food joints have sprung up to serve things which were previously uncommon or unobtainable. Most of the large international fast-food chains, including McDonald's, Burger King, KFC and Pizza Hut, have conquered Polish cities, and a myriad Polish imitations have also settled in.

There has also been an explosion of ethnic restaurants. Oddly enough, despite having such long and deeply rooted Jewish, Lithuanian, Ukrainian, Belarusian and Russian traditions, Poland ignores their cuisines almost totally. Instead, a variety of restaurants serving culturally exotic food – from Greek and Spanish to Vietnamese and Japanese – have opened.

For some reason, pizzerias have found a particularly fertile soil and have settled in astonishing numbers. Be warned though: not all pizzas are what you normally associate with this term. Some establishments think that any round pancake covered with a thick layer of tomato sauce (ketchup) is a pizza.

Most old drab restaurants have either closed down or been renovated, and the footpaths have filled with food stalls and open-air cafe-bars. The prices have obviously gone up in the process, but you now have a decent choice, can eat and drink till late, and it's all still a cheaper experience than in the West.

Following is an outline of the main types of eating establishments. Note that in Poland, the word 'bar' is used to describe a variety of gastronomic venues, not only those for drinking as traditionally understood by the term in the West.

Restaurants A restaurant *(restauracja)* is the main place for a meal with table service. They range from unpretentious cheap eateries where you can have a filling meal for less than US$5 all the way up to luxurious establishments that may leave a sizable hole in your wallet.

The former class is mostly to be found in smaller towns and the back streets of city suburbs, while the latter kind is almost exclusively confined to the largest cities. The menus of most top-class restaurants are in Polish with English and/or German translations, but don't expect foreign-language listings in cheaper eateries, nor waiters speaking anything but Polish.

Restaurants generally open around 9am or 10am (usually with a breakfast menu) or at about noon. Closing time varies greatly from place to place and from city to province. In smaller towns it may be pretty hard to find somewhere to eat after 9pm, whereas in big cities there are always places that stay open until 11pm or midnight.

Milk Bars A Polish milk bar *(bar mleczny)* is a no-frills, self-service cafeteria that serves mostly vegetarian dishes at ultra-low prices. The 'milk' part of the name reflects the fact that a good part of the menu is based on dairy products. You can fill up completely for about US$2 to US$3.

Milk bars were created to provide cheap food for the less affluent, and were subsidised by the state. The free-market economy forced many to close, but a number have survived by introducing meat dishes, upgrading standards and raising their prices. They are no longer genuine milk bars but remain budget places to eat. They wisely left most of their vegetarian fare (including some Polish specialities) on the menu, and the cost of this hasn't gone up too much.

There are still some archetypal milk bars that have somehow managed to survive in virtually unchanged form and they remain extremely cheap. A word of warning, in some of these places, the food quality may not be worth the dirt cheap price. It looks like these soup kitchens may become extinct over the next few years.

Milk bars open around 7am to 8am and close at 6pm to 8pm (earlier on Saturday); only a handful are open on Sunday. The menu is posted on the wall. You choose, then pay the cashier who gives you a receipt which you hand to the person dispensing the food. Once you've finished your meal, carry your dirty dishes to a designated place, as you'll see others doing. Milk bars are popular and there are usually lines to the counter, but they move quickly. Smoking is not permitted and no alcoholic beverages are served.

Cafes A cafe *(kawiarnia)* in communist Poland was essentially a meeting place rather than an eating place. They offered coffee, tea, sweets and a choice of drinks, but hardly anything more substantial. Now most cafes have introduced meals, which can be more attractive and cheaper than those of some restaurants. Generally speaking, the borderline between a cafe and a restaurant has become blurred.

Cafes tend to open around 10am and close at any time between 9pm and midnight. Most cafes are smokers' territory and, given Polish smoking habits, the atmosphere can be really dense.

Starters & Buffet Meals

Starters and buffet meals have traditionally been the favourite (and sometimes the only) accompaniment to a glass or a bottle of vodka. The most popular include:

befsztyk tatarski or simply *tatar* – raw minced beef accompanied by chopped onion, raw egg yolk and often chopped dill cucumber; eat it only in reputable restaurants
karp w galarecie – jellied carp
łosoś wędzony – smoked salmon
nóżki w galarecie – jellied pigs' knuckles
sałatka jarzynowa – vegetable salad commonly known as Russian salad
śledź w oleju – herring in oil accompanied by chopped onion
śledź w śmietanie – herring in sour cream

Soups

Soup *(zupa)* is an essential part of a meal, not just a starter, and for most Poles the *obiad* without soup is unthinkable. Polish soups are usually rich and substantial and some of them can be a filling meal in themselves. The average menu will include some of the following:

barszcz czerwony – beetroot broth; very typical Polish soup; can be served clear *(barszcz czysty)*, with tiny ravioli-type dumplings stuffed with meat *(barszcz z uszkami)*, or accompanied by a hot pastry filled with meat *(barszcz z pasztecikiem)*
botwinka – another summertime soup, but this one is hot and made from the stems and leaves of baby beetroots; often includes a hard-boiled egg
chłodnik – cold beetroot soup with sour cream and fresh vegetables; served in summer only
flaki – seasoned tripe cooked in bouillon with vegetables
grochówka – pea soup, sometimes served with croutons *(z grzankami)*
kapuśniak – sauerkraut soup with potatoes
krupnik – a thick barley soup containing a variety of vegetables and occasionally small chunks of meat
rosół – beef or chicken bouillon, usually served with noodles *(z makaronem)*
(zupa) grzybowa – mushroom soup
(zupa) jarzynowa – mixed vegetable soup
(zupa) ogórkowa – dill cucumber soup, usually with potatoes and other vegetables
(zupa) pomidorowa – tomato soup, usually served with either noodles *(z makaronem)* or rice *(z ryżem)*
(zupa) szczawiowa – sorrel soup, most likely to appear with hard-boiled egg
żurek – another Polish speciality: rye-flour soup thickened with sour cream; most likely to be served with hard-boiled egg *(z jajkiem)*, with sausage *(z kiełbasą)* or both, and sometimes accompanied by potatoes

Main Courses

A Pole doesn't usually consider a dish a serious meal if it comes without a piece of meat *(mięso)*. The most commonly consumed meat is pork *(wieprzowina)*, followed by beef *(wołowina)* and veal *(cielęcina)*. Chicken is pretty popular but game and fish tend to be linked to upmarket or specialised restaurants.

Pork, Beef & Veal Among the most common dishes are the following:

befsztyk – beef steak
bryzol – grilled beef steak
golonka – boiled pigs' knuckle served with horse-radish; a favourite dish for many Poles
gołąbki – cabbage leaves stuffed with minced beef and rice, sometimes also with mushrooms
kotlet schabowy – a fried pork cutlet coated in breadcrumbs, flour and egg, found on every menu
pieczeń wołowa/wieprzowa – roast beef/pork
polędwica pieczona – roast fillet of beef
rumsztyk – rump steak
schab pieczony – roast loin of pork seasoned with prunes and herbs
stek – steak
sztuka mięsa – boiled beef with horse-radish
zraz zawijany – stewed beef rolls stuffed with mushrooms and/or bacon and served in sour cream sauce

Fish Fish dishes don't abound on the menus of average restaurants, but there are specialist fish restaurants in big cities. The most common sea fish is cod *(dorsz)*; of the freshwater varieties, you're most likely to encounter carp *(karp)* and trout *(pstrąg)*. Seafood is rare and to be found only in top-end establishments at high prices.

Poultry The most common bird on the table is chicken *(kurczak)*, which is usually roasted or grilled and is more or less the same as all over the world. Some upmarket places may have duck *(kaczka)*, turkey *(indyk)* and goose *(gęś)*, almost always roasted; duck is often stuffed with apples *(kaczka z jabłkami)*.

Game Although game is no longer common in the country's forests, you may still have a chance to eat some. The animals that you're most likely to find on menus are wild boar *(dzik)*, hare *(zając)*, pheasant *(bażant)* and roe-deer *(sarna)*.

Vegetarian Dishes Vegetarians won't starve in Poland – the cheapest place to look is a milk bar, but many of the new restaurants and bistros will have some vegetarian

The Art of Reading Polish Menus

The menu is normally split into several sections, including starters *(przekąski)*, soups *(zupy)*, main courses *(dania drugie)*, accompaniments *(dodatki)*, desserts *(desery)* and drinks *(napoje)*. The main courses are often further split into meat dishes *(dania mięsne)*, fish dishes *(dania rybne)*, poultry *(drób)* and vegetarian dishes *(dania jarskie)*.

The name of the dish on the menu is accompanied by its price and, usually, by its weight or other quantity. The price of the main course doesn't normally include the accompaniments such as potatoes, chips, salads etc, which you choose from the dodatki section. You then have to tally up the price of the components to get the complete cost of the dish. Only when all these items are listed together is the price which follows for the whole plate of food.

Also note that the weight of a portion of some dishes such as fish or poultry is hard to determine beforehand so the price given in the menu is usually for 100g. Don't expect them, however, to cut 100g of fish for you: if you're not precise when ordering, they'll most probably serve you the whole fish, which will weigh much more than 100g, and cost accordingly. To avoid surprises in the bill *(rachunek)*, study the menu carefully and make things clear to the waiter.

dishes. On the whole, vegetarian food is cheaper than meat; it's varied and usually well prepared. Typical Polish vegetarian fare includes:

knedle – dumplings stuffed with plums or apples
kopytka – Polish gnocchi; noodles made from flour and boiled potatoes
leniwe pierogi – boiled noodles served with cottage cheese
naleśniki – crepes; fried pancakes, most commonly with cottage cheese (*z serem*) or jam (*z dżemem*), served with sour cream and sugar
pierogi – dumplings made from noodle dough, stuffed and boiled; the most popular are those with cottage cheese (*z serem*), with blueberries (*z jagodami*), with cabbage and wild mushrooms (*z kapustą i grzybami*)
placki ziemniaczane – fried pancakes made from grated raw potatoes with egg and flour; served with sour cream (*ze śmietaną*) or sugar (*z cukrem*)
pyzy – ball-shaped steamed dumplings made of potato flour

Accompaniments & Salads

Potatoes (*ziemniaki*) are the most common accompaniment to the main course and they are usually boiled or mashed. Chips (*frytki*) are also popular, as are *kasza gryczana*, steamed buckwheat groats, which go perfectly with some dishes, especially with *zrazy*. Rice (*ryż*) is not common.

Salads (*surówki* or *sałatki*) can come as a light dish on their own or as a side dish to the main course. The latter variety includes:

ćwikła z chrzanem – boiled and grated beetroot with horseradish
mizeria ze śmietaną – sliced fresh cucumber in sour cream
ogórek kiszony – dill cucumber
sałatka z pomidorów – tomato salad, often served with onion
surówka z kiszonej kapusty – sauerkraut, sometimes served with apple and onion

Desserts

Some of the common desserts include:

budyń – milk pudding
ciastko – pastry, cake
lody – ice cream
melba – ice cream with whipped cream and fruit

DRINKS
Nonalcoholic Drinks

Tea & Coffee Poles are passionate tea drinkers. Tea (*herbata*) is served in a glass, rarely in a cup, and is never drunk with milk. Instead, a slice of lemon is a fairly popular addition, plus a lot of sugar. In restaurants you usually get a glass of boiling water and a tea bag on the side.

Coffee (*kawa*) is another popular drink, and here too the Polish way of preparing it probably differs from what you are used to. The most common form is *kawa parzona*, a concoction made by putting a couple of teaspoons of ground coffee beans directly into a glass and topping it with boiling water. An increasing number of cafes serve espresso coffee (*kawa z ekspresu*) and cappuccino.

Soft Drinks All the big name soft drinks, either bottled or canned, are readily available everywhere.

Mineral water (*woda mineralna*) comes from springs in different parts of the country, and is good and cheap.

Alcoholic Drinks

Beer Polish beer (*piwo*) comes in a number of local brands, the best of which includes Żywiec, Okocim and EB. Beer is readily available in shops, cafes, bars, pubs and restaurants – virtually everywhere. Depending on the class of the establishment, a half-litre bottle of Polish beer will cost anything from US$1 to around US$2.50. Not all cheap establishments serve it cold, so ask for *zimne piwo* (cold beer) when ordering.

Wine Poland doesn't have much of a wine tradition, and consumption is limited. The country doesn't produce wine (*wino*), apart from a suspicious alcoholic liquid made on the basis of apples and who knows what else, nicknamed by Poles *wino-wino* or *bełt* and consumed by those on the dark margins of society who either can't afford or can't find a bottle of vodka.

Imported wines have traditionally come from the ex-eastern bloc, mostly from Hungary and Bulgaria, and if you're not too fussy they're acceptable and cheap. Western

European wines, particularly French, German and Spanish, are now widely available in shops and restaurants, though some of them are fairly expensive.

Spirits Vodka *(wódka)* is the No 1 Polish brew and is consumed in large quantities. Commonly associated with Russia, vodka is as much the Polish national drink as it is Russian, and the Poles claim it was they who invented it.

These days drinking habits in the cities are changing, with Poles increasingly turning to beer instead of vodka. Yet, as soon as you go to a small town and enter the only local restaurant, you'll see those same tipsy folk debating jovially over bottles of vodka. Old habits die hard.

Polish vodka comes in a number of colours and flavours. Clear vodka is not, as is commonly thought in the West, the only species of the family. Though it does form the basic 'fuel' for seasoned drinkers, there's a variety of other kinds, from very sweet to extra dry, including *myśliwska* (vodka flavoured with juniper berries), *wiśniówka* (flavoured with cherries), *żubrówka* ('bison vodka', which is flavoured with grass from the Białowieża forest on which the bison feed) and *jarzębiak* (flavoured with rowanberry). Other notable spirits include *krupnik* (honey liqueur), *śliwowica* (plum brandy), *winiak* (grape brandy) and Goldwasser (thick liqueur with flakes of gold). Finally, there's *bimber* – home-made spirit, which ranges in quality from very poor to excellent.

A half-litre bottle of vodka costs US$5 to US$10 in a shop, but in restaurants it can double or even triple in price. Clear vodka should be served well chilled though this does not always happen in lower-class establishments. Coloured vodkas don't need much cooling and some are best drunk at room temperature.

ENTERTAINMENT
Pubs & Bars
The fashion for all things Western has brought pubs to Poland. They first appeared around 1990 in Warsaw and spread like wildfire to other cities and farther on out into

---

Drinking Vodka Polish-Style

Some basic information about drinking vodka may be useful. To begin with, forget about using vodka in cocktails. In Poland vodka is drunk neat, not diluted or mixed, in glasses usually of 50mL but ranging from 25mL to 100mL. Regardless of the size of the glass, though, it's drunk in one gulp, or *do dna* ('to the bottom'), as Poles say. A piece of a snack or a sip of mineral water is consumed just after drinking to give some relief to the throat, and the glasses are immediately refilled for the next drink.

As you might expect, at such a rate you won't be able to keep up with your fellow drinkers for long, and will soon end up well out of touch with the real world. Go easy and either miss a few turns or sip your drink in stages. Though this seems to be beyond comprehension to a 'normal' Polish drinker, you, as a foreigner and guest, will be treated with due indulgence. Whatever you do, don't try to outdrink a Pole. Na Zdrowie (Cheers)!

---

the provinces. Warsaw already has well over a hundred of them and is closely followed by Kraków, Łódź and other large cities. Some pubs tend to mimic their English or Irish siblings, including the brands of beer on offer, while others follow local style and serve mostly Polish beer. Some pubs are amazing artistic creations – we've tried to point out some good examples in this book.

Until not long ago, most pubs and bars were strictly drinking venues, but in recent years many of them have introduced a food menu, which may be an interesting proposition. Virtually all pubs and bars are smoking establishments, and in some places the smoke can be heavy. Pubs and bars usually close anywhere between midnight and 2am, but some don't close until the wee hours of the morning.

Clubs & Discos
A lot of new clubs and discos have opened in recent years. Many new venues have plenty of bells and whistles, large dance floors and several bars around the place to

keep you conveniently close to the tap. The music is usually a ragbag of everything from rock to reggae, though some discos focus on specific musical genres such as techno, hip-hop or golden oldies. Most discos spring into action Thursday to Saturday nights, but some open nightly. Sunday and Monday are the slowest days and many clubs are closed. Some discos charge an admission fee on weekends.

Jazz & Rock

Polish jazz is of a high standard, and the big international jazz names visit the country quite frequently. Warsaw and Kraków have the liveliest jazz life and quite a few jazz clubs.

Big rock stars play concerts in large auditoriums and stadiums, while their followers have gigs in pubs, clubs, cultural centres, cafes etc.

Classical Music

The Filharmonia (Philharmonic) is the place to head for. Most larger cities have their philharmonic halls, and concerts are usually held on Friday and Saturday, for next to nothing.

You might occasionally come upon some of the greatest virtuosi, both national and international. The repertoire ranges from medieval music to the latest works from the pillars of Polish contemporary music, though most of the fare ranges from somewhere between Bach and Stravinsky.

Cinema

Cinemas run the usual Western fare with several months' delay. The majority of films come from the USA while the number of Polish films is minimal. All films are screened with original soundtrack and Polish subtitles. The admission fee is around US$4 to US$6.

Theatre

Polish theatre has long been well-known both locally and abroad and it continues to fly high. Language is obviously an obstacle for foreigners, but some plays are based more on the visual than on language and

these are particularly recommended for non-Polish speakers. Productions range from Greek drama to recent avant-garde with room for great classics from Shakespeare to Beckett.

Theatres run usually one show nightly from Tuesday to Sunday. Theatre tickets cost US$5 to US$10. Almost all theatres close in July and August as the actors go on holiday.

Opera & Ballet

Only some of the largest cities have proper opera houses. You'll probably find the best productions in Warsaw and Łódź and they're usually well worth the money – about US$15 at most.

SPECTATOR SPORTS

Soccer is Poland's most popular spectator sport. The country had quite a strong national team in the 1970s, but its fortunes later fell and are only recently on the way up. The matches of the national league invariably fill the stadiums.

Soccer apart, there doesn't seem to be any particular sport that drives the nation crazy. Cycling is reasonably popular in some circles, as is basketball. Poland has had some international successes in athletics, and occasionally kayaking and rowing, and was once strong in speedway racing, boxing, wrestling and fencing.

Recently, tennis and skiing are becoming popular, as both spectator and participator sports, though Poland has no international stars in either. With a few racetracks in the country, including ones in both Warsaw and Sopot, horse racing has its small group of devotees.

Interestingly, some of the hugely popular sports in some Western countries, including cricket, baseball, rugby, football and golf, are almost unknown in Poland.

SHOPPING

For local handicrafts, try Cepelia shops, which exist in all large cities. The most common Polish crafts include paper cutouts, woodcarving, tapestries, embroidery, paintings on glass, pottery and hand-painted wooden boxes and chests.

Amber is typically Polish. It's a fossil resin of vegetable origin, which appears in earthy hues from pale yellow to reddish brown. You can buy amber necklaces in Cepelia shops, but if you want it in a more artistic form, look for jewellery shops or commercial art galleries. Prices vary with the quality of the amber and the level of craftwork. Possibly the best choice of amber jewellery is in Gdańsk.

Polish contemporary painting, original prints and sculpture are renowned internationally and sold by private commercial art galleries. The galleries in Warsaw and Kraków have the biggest and the most representative choice. Polish posters are among the world's best – a tempting souvenir. The best selection of them is, again, in Warsaw and Kraków.

The main seller of old art and antiques is a state-owned chain of shops called Desa. Large Desa shops may have an amazing variety of old jewellery, watches, furniture and whatever else you could imagine. Remember that it's officially forbidden to export any item manufactured before 9 May 1945, works of art and books included, unless you've got permission.

Poland publishes quite an assortment of well-edited and lavishly illustrated coffee-table books about the country, many of which are also available in English and German. Check the large bookshops in the main cities.

Polish music (pop, folk, jazz, classical and contemporary) is easily available on CD. Polish CDs cost about US$10 to US$15; imported CDs are US$15 to US$20.

Getting There & Away

Poland is certainly not the world's major tourist destination, but sitting in the middle of Europe it does have plenty of air and overland transport links with the rest of the continent. It is also relatively well connected by air with the rest of the world.

There are sizable Polish communities living abroad (USA, Canada, Australia, UK, France, Germany) and their own Polish-run travel agencies will be happy to sell you tickets. They are likely to be familiar with all possible routes to the motherland and organise tours, and they may be able to offer attractive deals.

AIR
Airports & Airlines
Poland's major international hub is Warsaw, but other large cities, including Gdańsk, Katowice, Kraków, Poznań and Wrocław, also handle international flights. Poland is serviced by most major European carriers, including Air France, Alitalia, British Airways and KLM, plus the national carrier LOT Polish Airlines.

LOT links Warsaw with most major European cities, and outside Europe it has direct flights to/from Chicago, Istanbul, New York, Tel Aviv and Toronto. LOT no longer operates Russian planes; it now flies smoothly on Boeings, and has a remarkably young fleet. However, despite its modern stock and friendly in-flight service, LOT doesn't always run on time. Keep this in mind if you have connections with other carriers, and allow sufficient time between flights.

Furthermore, LOT is no longer cheap. It operates in the same free market as other airlines and is just one more competitor; it can be cheaper on some routes but more expensive on others.

Fares vary greatly depending on what route you're flying and what time of the year it is. Poland's high season (and that of Europe in general) is in summer and a short period around Christmas, with the rest of the year being quieter and cheaper.

Buying Tickets
World aviation is competitive, so you have to research the options carefully to make sure you get the best deal.

Full-time students and people under 26 years (under 30 in some countries) have access to better deals than other travellers. You have to show a document proving your date of birth or a valid International Student Identity Card (ISIC) when buying your ticket and boarding the plane.

Generally, there's nothing to be gained by buying tickets direct from airlines. Discounted tickets are released to selected travel agencies and specialist discount agencies, and these are usually the cheapest deals.

One exception to this rule is the expanding number of 'no-frills' carriers, which mostly sell only direct to travellers. Unlike the 'full-service' airlines, no-frills carriers often make one-way tickets available at around half the return fare, meaning that it is easy to put together an open-jaw ticket when you fly to one place but leave from another.

The other exception is booking on the Internet. Many airlines, full-service and no-frills, offer some excellent fares to Web surfers. They may sell seats by auction, or simply cut prices to reflect the reduced cost of electronic selling.

Many travel agencies around the world have Web sites, which can make the Internet a quick and easy way to compare prices. There is also an increasing number of online agencies that operate only on the Internet.

Online ticket sales work well if you are doing a simple one-way or return trip on specified dates. However, online superfast fare generators are no substitute for a travel agent who knows all about special deals, has strategies for avoiding layovers and can offer advice on everything from which airline has the best vegetarian food to the best travel insurance to bundle with your ticket.

You may find the cheapest flights are advertised by obscure agencies. Most such firms are honest and solvent, but there are some rogue fly-by-night outfits around. If you feel suspicious about a firm, go somewhere else.

You may decide to pay a bit more than the rock-bottom fare by opting for the safety of a better-known travel agency. Firms such as STA Travel, who have offices worldwide, Council Travel in the USA or Travel CUTS in Canada offer good prices to most destinations and are not going to disappear overnight, leaving you clutching a receipt for a nonexistent ticket.

Paying by credit card generally offers protection, as most card issuers provide refunds if you can prove you didn't get what you paid for. Similar protection can be obtained by buying a ticket from a bonded agent, such as one covered by the Air Travel Organiser's Licence (ATOL) scheme in the UK (W www.atol.org.uk).

If you purchase a ticket and later want to make changes to your route or get a refund, you need to contact the original travel agent. Airlines issue refunds only to the purchaser of a ticket – usually the travel agent who bought the ticket on your behalf.

Travellers with Specific Needs

If they're warned early enough, airlines can often make special arrangements for travellers, such as wheelchair assistance at airports or vegetarian meals on the flight. Children under two years travel for 10% of the standard fare (or free on some airlines) as long as they don't occupy a seat. They don't get a baggage allowance. 'Skycots', baby food and nappies should be provided by the airline if requested in advance. Children aged between two and 12 can usually occupy a seat for half to two-thirds of the full fare, and do get a baggage allowance.

The disability-friendly Web site W www .everybody.co.uk has an airline directory that provides information on the facilities offered by various airlines.

Departure Tax

The airport tax is US$10 for international departures from Warsaw, and around US$8 for departures from other Polish airports servicing international flights. You don't pay the tax at the airport itself, as it is automatically added to the price of your air ticket when you buy it.

The USA & Canada

There are direct, nonstop LOT flights from New York, Chicago and Toronto to Warsaw, but they are not necessarily the cheapest. Inquire at LOT on its toll-free number (USA ☎ 800-223 0593 and Canada ☎ 800-668 5928).

Agents often use indirect connections with other carriers such as British Airways, Lufthansa, KLM or Air France. Not only may these work out cheaper, but they can also let you break the journey in Western Europe for the same price or a little extra – a bonus if you want to stop en route in London, Paris or Amsterdam.

In the USA, two reputable discount travel agencies are STA Travel (toll-free ☎ 800-777 0112, W www.statravel.com) and Council Travel (toll-free ☎ 800-226 8624, W www.counciltravel.com). Canada's leading bargain ticket agency is Travel Cuts (toll-free ☎ 800-667 2887, W www.travel cuts.com). All three have offices throughout

Air Travel Glossary

Alliances Many of the world's leading airlines are now intimately involved with each other, sharing everything from reservations systems and check-in to aircraft and frequent-flyer schemes. Opponents say that alliances restrict competition. Whatever the arguments, there is no doubt that big alliances are the way of the future.

Courier Fares Businesses often need to send urgent documents or freight securely and quickly. Courier companies hire people to accompany the package through customs and, in return, offer a discount ticket which is sometimes a bargain. However, you may have to surrender all your baggage allowance and take only carry-on luggage.

Fares Airlines traditionally offer 1st class (coded F), business class (coded J) and economy class (coded Y) tickets. These days there are so many promotional and discounted fares available that few passengers pay full fare.

Lost Tickets If you lose your airline ticket, an airline will usually treat it like a travellers cheque and, after inquiries, issue you with another one. Legally, however, an airline is entitled to treat it like cash and if you lose it then it's gone forever. Take very good care of your tickets.

Onward Tickets An entry requirement for many countries is that you have a ticket out of the country. If you're unsure of your next move, the easiest solution is to buy the cheapest onward ticket to a neighbouring country or a ticket from a reliable airline which can later be refunded if you do not use it.

Open-Jaw Tickets These are return tickets where you fly out to one place but return from another. If available, this can save you backtracking to your arrival point.

Overbooking Since every flight has some passengers who fail to show up, airlines often book more passengers than they have seats. Usually excess passengers make up for the no-shows, but occasionally somebody gets 'bumped' onto the next available flight. Guess who it is most likely to be? The passengers who check in late. If you do get 'bumped', you are normally offered some form of compensation.

Reconfirmation Some airlines require you to reconfirm your flight at least 72 hours prior to departure. Check your travel documents to see if this is the case.

Restrictions Discounted tickets often have various restrictions on them – such as needing to be paid for in advance and incurring a penalty to be altered or cancelled. Others are restrictions on the minimum and maximum period you must be away.

Round-the-World Tickets RTW tickets give you a limited period (usually a year) in which to circumnavigate the globe. You can go anywhere the carrying airlines go, as long as you don't backtrack. The number of stopovers or total number of separate flights is decided before you set off and they usually cost a bit more than a basic return flight.

Ticketless Travel Airlines are gradually waking up to the realisation that paper tickets are unnecessary encumbrances. On simple one-way or return trips, reservation details can be held on computer and the passenger merely shows ID to claim their seat.

Transferred Tickets Airline tickets cannot be transferred from one person to another. Travellers sometimes try to sell the return half of their ticket, but officials can ask you to prove that you are the person named on the ticket. On an international flight, tickets are compared with passports.

their respective countries. Although they all specialise in student travel, they also offer discount tickets to nonstudents of all ages.

Ticket Planet (W www.ticketplanet.com) is a leading ticket consolidator in the USA and is recommended.

Expect return air fares to Poland to start at around US$500 from the USA and C$900 from Canada. If money is more of a concern to you than comfort or time, fly with any of the hotly competing airlines to one of the main European destinations such as London or Amsterdam, and then continue overland by bus. Also check the air fares to Berlin, which may be a reasonable compromise. Berlin is just 100km from the Polish border and 6½ hours by train from Warsaw.

Australia

Australia and Poland are a hell of a long way apart. The distance between Sydney and Warsaw is over 17,000km – nearly half the circumference of the earth. The journey will take at least 20 hours in the air, not to mention stopovers on the way. It won't be the cheapest trip of your life.

There are no direct scheduled flights between Australia and Poland, so any journey will involve a change of flight. You can fly with one of the European carriers such as British Airways, Lufthansa, KLM or Lauda, to London, Frankfurt, Amsterdam or Vienna respectively, from where the same airline or one of its associates will take you to Warsaw. The return fares from Sydney/ Melbourne to Warsaw will be somewhere between A$1600 and A$2300, depending on the season and where you buy your ticket.

Another way of getting from Australia to Poland can be a Round-the-World (RTW) ticket. Since Australia is pretty much on the other side of the world from Europe or North America, it can sometimes work out cheaper to keep going right round the world on a RTW ticket than do a U-turn on a return ticket.

Two well-known agencies for cheap fares are STA Travel (☎ 131 776 Australia-wide, W www.statravel.com.au) and Flight

Centre (☎ 131 600 Australia-wide, W www .flightcentre.com.au). Both have offices throughout Australia.

There are also a number of Polish travel agencies in Australia. Magna Carta Travel is possibly the largest, with offices in Sydney, Melbourne and other major Australian cities. Others operate locally but can be marginally cheaper. The Polish agencies include:

All Tours & Travel (☎ 02-9328 4555) 110 New South Head Rd, Edgecliff, NSW 2027

Magna Carta Travel (☎ 02-9746 9964) 1 Albert Rd, Strathfield, NSW 2135; (☎ 03-9523 6981) 387 Glenhuntly Rd, Elsternwick, Vic 3185

Mekina Travel (☎ 03-9663 4022) 5th floor, 277 Flinders Lane, Melbourne, Vic 3000

Orbis Express (☎ 02-9737 8099) 296 Parramatta Rd, Auburn, NSW 2144

Tatra Travel (☎ 03-9576 2444) 8 Glenferrie Rd, Malvern, Vic 3144

The UK

The London-Warsaw route is operated once daily by both British Airways and LOT, with several more LOT flights in summer. There are also direct weekly London-Gdańsk and London-Kraków flights year-round (with additional flights in summer), both routes being serviced by LOT. Also, LOT has Manchester-Warsaw direct flights in summer.

The travel market is very busy in London and there are countless agencies offering cheap fares. Poland is not a best seller but it does appear on the agencies' menus. Pick up the Sunday edition of local papers or, better still, *Time Out* magazine, where you should find some bargains. London's major operators, which may offer competitive deals for both students and nonstudents, include:

STA Travel (☎ 020-7581 4132, 0870-160 0599, W www.statravel.co.uk) 86 Old Brompton Rd, London, SW7 3LQ

Trailfinders (☎ 020-7628 7628, W www.trail finders.co.uk) 1 Threadneedle St, London EC2R 8JX

Travel Cuts (☎ 020-7255 1944, W www.travel cuts.co.uk) 295a Regents St, London W1B 2HN

It may also be worthwhile checking Polish-run agencies. These include:

Fregata Travel (☎ 020-7247 8484,
W www.fregatatravel.co.uk) 83 White Chapel
High St, London E1 7QX
Gem Tazab Travel (☎ 020-7341 2600,
W www.gemtazab.co.uk) 273 Old Brompton
Rd, London SW5 9JB
New Millennium (☎ 0156-477 0750) 1665 High
St, Knowle, Solihull, Birmingham B93 0LL
Polorbis (☎ 020-7636 4701,
W www.polorbis.co.uk) Suite 530-532 Walmar
House, 288/300 Regent St, London W1B 3AL
Travelines (☎ 020-8741 5541, W www.travelines
.com) 246a King St, Hammersmith, London
W6 0RA

Expect a London-Warsaw return ticket to
cost between UK£160 and UK£240, but it
may be cheaper if you are under the age of
26. You may also check for cheap flights to
Berlin and continue overland by train (a
three-hour trip to Poznań or a bit more than
six hours to Warsaw).

Continental Europe
There are a number of flights to Warsaw
from all major European capitals, with both
LOT and Western carriers, but regular one-
way fares are high. Cheaper Apex fares are
available and travel agents can beat the
price down further.

As a pointer, the fare from Paris is
roughly comparable to that from London,
and that from Amsterdam only marginally
cheaper. The closer to Poland you are, the
more attractive the train and coach become
as they guarantee a considerable saving
over the cost of an air fare.

France Recommended travel agencies include Usit Connect Voyages (☎ 01 42 44 14
00), 14 rue de Vaugirard, 75006 Paris, with
branches across the country; and OTU Voyages (☎ 01 40 29 12 12, French-language
W www.otu.fr), 39 Ave Georges-Bernanos,
75005 Paris, also with branches across the
country. Both companies are student and
youth-specialist agencies.

Other recommendations include Voya-
geurs du Monde (☎ 01 42 86 16 00), 55 rue
Ste-Anne, 75002 Paris, and Nouvelles Frontières (nationwide number ☎ 08 25 00 08 25,
Paris ☎ 01 45 68 70 00, French-language

W www.nouvelles-frontieres.fr), 87 blvd de
Grenelle, 75015 Paris, with branches across
the country.

Germany STA Travel (☎ 030-311 0950)
at Goethesttrasse 73, 10625 Berlin, has
branches in major cities across the country.

Italy Recommended travel agencies in-
clude CTS Viaggi (06-462 0431), 16 Via
Genova, Rome, a student and youth spe-
cialist with branches in major cities, and
Passagi (☎ 06-474 0923), Stazione Termini
FS, Galleria Di Tesla, Rome.

The Netherlands Agencies include Budget
Air (☎ 020-627 1251), 34 Rokin, Amsterdam
and Holland International (☎ 070-307 6307),
with offices in most cities.

Spain The recommended agencies include
Usit Unlimited (☎ 91-225 25 75, Spanish-
language W www.unlimited.es), 3 Plaza de
Callao, 28013 Madrid, with branches in
other major cities; and Barcelo Viajes
(☎ 91-559 1819), Princesa 3, 28008 Madrid,
also with branches in major cities. Nouvelles Frontières (☎ 91-547 42 00, Spanish-
speaking W www.nouvelles-frontieres.es)
has an office at Plaza de España 18, 28008
Madrid, plus branches in other major cities.

Switzerland Useful agencies include SSR
(☎ 022-818 02 02, W www.ssr.ch), 8 rue de
la Rive, Geneva, with branches throughout
the country, and also Nouvelles Frontières
(☎ 022-906 80 80), 10 rue Chante Poulet,
Geneva.

LAND
Border Crossings
Sitting in the middle of Europe and sharing
its borders with seven countries, Poland has
plenty of rail and road crossings with its
neighbours. Border crossings are more numerous with Germany to the west and the
Czech and Slovak republics to the south,
than they are with Ukraine, Belarus, Lithuania and Russia to the east and north-east. For
further details about road crossings, see
under Car & Motorcycle later in this chapter.

Train

Quite a number of international trains link Poland with other European countries. On the whole, train travel is not cheap and, on longer routes, the price of an ordinary train ticket can be almost as much as that of a discounted air fare.

Fortunately, there's a choice of special train tickets and rail passes: the InterRail pass, which gives European residents unlimited 2nd class travel for a month on most of the state railways of Western and Central Europe (including Poland); and the Euro-Domino pass (or Freedom pass), which can be used for a number of days within a specified month, and also gives substantial discounts off the ordinary fares. Those aged under 26 years get the best deal.

US residents can learn more about European rail travel from Rail Europe (toll-free ☎ 800-4 EURAIL), while Canadians can call their local office of Rail Europe (toll-free ☎ 800-361 RAIL). The Rail Europe's Web site (⚋ www.raileurope.com) has information about the rail passes and where to buy them.

International trains to Poland, as well as those to other Central European countries, have become notorious for theft. Keep a grip on your bags, particularly on the Berlin-Warsaw overnight trains. For more advice on security, see Train in the Getting Around chapter.

The UK From London, you can travel to Warsaw via either the Channel Tunnel or Ostend. The ordinary return fares in high season are around UK£300 and UK£260 respectively (UK£260 and UK£220 in low season). People under 26 can get a return fare to Warsaw for below UK£180. Contact Rail Europe (☎ 0990-848 848) for information. Tickets can be bought from British Rail ticket offices or travel centres. Agencies that specialise in travel to Poland, such as Fregata and Polorbis (see the earlier Air section for the full list), may offer cheaper fares.

Germany A number of German cities are linked by train (direct or indirect) with the major Polish cities. Direct connections with Warsaw include Berlin, Cologne, Dresden and Leipzig. There are also direct trains between Berlin and Kraków (via Wrocław).

The Warsaw-Berlin route (via Frankfurt/Oder and Poznań) is serviced by six trains a day in each direction, including three EuroCity express trains which cover the 569km distance in 6½ hours.

Czech Republic & Austria Trains between Prague and Warsaw (four daily) travel via either Wrocław (740km, 12 hours) or Katowice (10 hours). Four trains a day run between Prague and Wrocław (339km, seven hours). There are also trains between Prague and Kraków (via Katowice).

Two trains per day travel between Vienna and Warsaw (753km, eight to 10 hours) via Katowice.

Slovakia & Hungary There are two trains daily operating between Budapest and Warsaw (837km, 10 to 12 hours) via Bratislava and Katowice. They are routed through a short stretch of the Czech Republic, so make sure you have a Czech transit visa if required.

A different route through Košice in eastern Slovakia is followed by trains between Budapest and Kraków (598km, 11 hours).

Ukraine, Belarus, Lithuania & Russia Warsaw has direct train links with Kyiv in Ukraine, Minsk and Hrodna in Belarus, Vilnius in Lithuania, and Moscow and St Petersburg in Russia. These trains only have sleeping cars and you'll be automatically sold a sleeper when buying your ticket.

Remember that you need transit visas for the countries you will be passing through en route. The Warsaw-Vilnius-St Petersburg rail line, for example, passes via Hrodna in Belarus, and the Belarusian border guards come aboard and slap unsuspecting tourists with a US$30 Belarusian transit visa fee if discovered without a visa. According to some recent reports, the guards no longer issue transit visas but put you on the next train back to where you've just come from. Be warned. You may avoid this by taking a bus from Poland directly to Lithuania. Also note that a Belarusian transit visa doesn't allow you to break the journey in Hrodna, even just to look around for a few hours before continuing the trip.

Bus

Bus is the cheapest means of public transport to Poland from most of Europe. There are some reputable international bus companies servicing Poland, of which Eurolines is the best known. It's a consortium of coach lines with offices all over Europe. Its coaches are comfortable, air-conditioned and often as fast as the train. Eurolines also has flexible two-month 'Euro Explorer' itineraries with unlimited stopovers en route.

Apart from the Western bus carriers, there are also a number of Polish bus companies or companies operated by Polish emigres. These mostly cater to the Polish communities scattered over Europe and are cheaper, though their standards vary.

Most coach companies will give a 10% discount to people aged under 26 and senior citizens, and children will usually get still bigger reductions.

The UK Quite a few bus companies operate services between the UK and Poland. They include Eurolines and several Polish companies that call at the UK (eg, Pekaes Bus).

Eurolines (☎ 0990-808 080, **W** www .eurolines.co.uk) runs buses from London to Warsaw (via Ostend, Brussels and Poznań) and to Kraków (the same route as far as Poznań, and then via Wrocław and Katowice). The frequency of the service varies depending on the season: it's as often as daily in summer and slows down to twice weekly the rest of the year. The fare for each route is around UK£70 one way and UK£110 return. Tickets are can be bought from any National Express office and from a number of travel agencies.

Information about other bus carriers is available from the Polish expatriate-run agencies, some of which operate their own buses. Their addresses are listed in the Air section earlier in this chapter.

Western Europe As mentioned earlier, Eurolines operates an extensive coach network all around Europe and maintains plenty of offices, many of which are located at bus terminals in the major cities. Eurolines outlets include:

Amsterdam (☎ 20-560 87 87) Amstel Bus Station, Julianaplein 5
Berlin (☎ 30-860 0960) Bayern Express, Mannheimerstrasse 33–34
Brussels (☎ 2-217 00 25) 50 Place de Brouckere
Frankfurt (☎ 69-790 353) Am Romerhof 17
Paris (☎ 1-49 72 51 51) Gare Routière Internationale, 28 Ave du Général de Gaulle, Bagnolet
Vienna (☎ 1-712 04 53) Blaguss Reisen, Bahnhof Wien-mitte, Top 7, Landstrasser Hauptstrasse 1b

Apart from Eurolines, plenty of Polish companies operate buses that run to and from most mainland European destinations (servicing altogether over 200 cities) across the border.

Standards, reliability and comfort may vary from bus to bus, but on the whole are not too bad. Most buses are from the modern generation, and come equipped with air-conditioning, toilet facilities and a video. Information and bookings are available from travel agencies that are run by Polish emigres.

As a rough guide only, average one-way and return fares and journey times between Warsaw and some Western cities are as follows:

to	one way (US$)	return (US$)	time (hours)
Amsterdam	70	100	21
Brussels	70	100	22
Cologne	55	85	20
Frankfurt	50	85	19
Hamburg	45	70	16
Munich	55	85	20
Paris	80	120	27
Rome	90	140	27

Hungary There are a few buses a week between Budapest and Kraków (US$30, 10 hours).

Ukraine, Belarus & Lithuania The Polish PKS bus company runs daily buses from Warsaw to Lviv (US$16), Minsk (US$20) and Vilnius (US$18). These routes shouldn't normally take more than 12 hours, though the actual time depends on traffic lines at the border and customs. There are also regular buses between Przemyśl and Lviv (US$4, three hours), and one bus a week between Suwałki and Vilnius (US$5, 5½ hours).

Car & Motorcycle

Travelling by car or motorcycle, you'll pass the frontier via one of the designated road border crossings. Following is the list of road border crossings open 24 hours. The localities listed are the settlements on the Polish side of the border and you can find them on road maps.

Belarusian border (south to north): Terespol, Kuźnica Białostocka
Czech border (west to east): Porajów, Zawidów, Jakuszyce, Lubawka, Kudowa-Słone, Boboszów, Głuchołazy, Pietrowice, Chałupki, Cieszyn
German border (from north to south): Lubieszyn, Kołbaskowo, Krajnik Dolny, Osinów Dolny, Kostrzyn, Słubice, Świecko, Gubin, Olszyna, Łęknica, Zgorzelec, Sieniawka
Lithuanian border (east to west): Ogrodniki, Budzisko
Russian border (east to west): Bezledy, Gronowo
Slovak border (west to east): Chyżne, Chochołów, Łysa Polana, Niedzica, Piwniczna, Konieczna, Barwinek
Ukrainian border (south to north): Medyka, Hrebenne, Dorohusk, Zosin

Travellers bringing their vehicles to Poland need their driving licence, vehicle registration and insurance policy. Normally your domestic licence will do, but it's advisable to bring an International Driving Permit as well. If you're arriving in someone else's car, carry a notarised letter from the owner saying you're allowed to drive it.

A certificate of insurance, commonly known as a Green Card, is available from your insurer. If you haven't already bought it at home, you'll be required to buy one at the border from the PZM office. PZM, the Polish Motoring Association, has offices at most road border crossings.

Read the Car & Motorcycle section in the Getting Around chapter for more about driving in Poland, local traffic rules, compulsory car accessories, fuel etc.

SEA

Poland has a regular ferry service to/from Denmark and Sweden, operated by the Unity Line, Stena Line and Polferries. The Unity Line (W www.unityline.pl) covers the Ystad-Świnoujście route (US$50, nine hours, daily). The Stena Line (W www.stenaline.com) runs between Karlskrona and Gdynia (US$50, 11 hours, six days a week), whereas Polferries (W www.polferries.pl) runs the Copenhagen-Świnoujście route (US$50, 10 hours, five times a week), the Ystad-Świnoujście route (US$60, nine hours, daily) and Nynäshamn-Gdańsk (US$65, 18 hours, daily). All routes operate year-round.

The prices given are the deck fares, which normally don't need to be booked. Cabins of different classes are available and reservations are recommended in summer. Book early, but don't pay until you're sure you'll be going; there may be hefty cancellation fees. You can bring along your car (it will cost roughly an equivalent of another deck fare) but book in advance. Bicycles go free. A return ticket costs about 20% less than two singles and is valid for six months. Students and senior citizens get a 20% discount. There's a variety of other discounts for families, larger parties, groups plus car etc, which vary from route to route. Any travel agency throughout Scandinavia will have tickets; in Poland inquire at any of the numerous Orbis Travel offices.

ORGANISED TOURS

Various tours to Poland can be arranged from abroad. Some US and Britain-based tour operators that include Poland in their programs are specified in the following sections. Also see Organised Tours in the Getting Around chapter for what kind of tours can be organised from within Poland.

The USA

Affordable Poland, a division of Sophisticated Traveler, (☎ 408-871 3290 or toll-free

☎ 800-801 1055, W www.s-traveler.com), Suite 609, 1600 Saratoga Ave, San Jose, CA 95129 has various tours covering Poland's highlights, and offers a range of independent packages, so you can build your own tour and explore destinations of your choice at your own pace.

Walking Softly Adventures (☎ 503-788 9017 or toll-free ☎ 888-743 0723, W www .wsadventures.com), PO Box 86 250, Portland, OR 97 286, organises hiking tours in small groups to Poland's mountainous regions in the south of the country.

Pat Tours (☎ 413-747 77 02, toll-free ☎ 800-388 0988, W www.polandtours.com), 1285 Riverdale St, West Springfield, MA 01089, has plenty of tours, including many cultural trips covering historic cities, castles and palaces.

Adventures Abroad (☎ 360-775 9926, toll-free ☎ 800-665 3998, W www.adventures-abroad.com), 1123 Fir Ave, Blaine, WA 98230, offers one- to two-week tours to Poland's popular destinations, including Warsaw and Kraków, as well as tours to the other countries in the region.

The American Travel Abroad (AMTA; W www.amta.com) company organises tours to Poland and Central Europe. The agency has two offices in the USA: (☎ 212-586 5230 or toll-free ☎ 800-228 0877) 250 West 57th St, New York, NY 10107; and (☎ 773-467 0700 or toll-free ☎ 800-342 5315) 5316 N Milwaukee Ave, Chicago, IL 60630.

The UK

Most of the UK-based Polish travel agencies, including the Fregata and Polorbis (full listing in the Air section earlier in this chapter), offer package tours to Poland, usually one to two weeks long, ranging from sightseeing in historic cities to skiing or horse-riding holidays. Other UK operators worth checking include:

Sherpa Expeditions (☎ 020-8577 2717, W www.sherpa-walking-holidays.co.uk), which offers 15-day hiking tours in the Polish and Slovak Tatras, with accommodation in mountain huts.

Bogdan Travel (☎ 020-8992 8866, W www.bogdantravel.com), 5 The Broadway, Gunnerbury Lane, London W3 8HR, has plenty of tours to Poland, including sightseing in the great historic cities, taking it easy in spas and walking in the mountains.

Martin Randall Travel (☎ 020-8742 3355, W www.martinrandall.com), 10 Barley Mow Passage, London W4 4PH, offers tours to Poland which cover major cities and their cultural attractions.

Exodus Expeditions (☎ 020-8675 5550, W www.exodus.co.uk), 9 Weir Rd, London SW12 0LT, has a 14-day 'Historic Poland' tour, which includes Warsaw, Gdańsk, Poznań, the Masurian Lakes and Białowieża National Park. Exodus also offers a 14-day hiking trip in the Tatras and Beskids, with accommodation in mountain hostels.

Getting Around

AIR

LOT Polish Airlines ([W] www.slot.com), Poland's only commercial carrier, services both international and domestic routes. Within the country, it has regular flights from Warsaw to Gdańsk, Katowice, Kraków, Poznań, Rzeszów, Szczecin and Wrocław. There are no direct flights between these cities; all go via Warsaw, and connections aren't always convenient. On domestic routes, LOT uses French-Italian new-generation ATR 72 turbo aircraft.

From late March to late October, there are at least three scheduled flights a day from Warsaw to each of the above destinations except Katowice and Rzeszów, which are serviced by one or two flights a day. In the remainder of the year, there are fewer flights, usually one or two per day, and still fewer to Katowice and Rzeszów.

The regular one-way fare on any of the direct flights to/from Warsaw is around US$125, except for Szczecin (US$140). Any combined flight via Warsaw (eg, Szczecin-Kraków or Gdańsk-Wrocław) will cost around US$150. Tickets can be booked and bought at any LOT and Orbis office, and from some travel agencies.

Senior citizens over 60 years of age pay 80% of the full fare on all domestic flights. Foreign students holding an ISIC card get a 10% discount. There are attractive stand-by fares (about 25% of the regular fare) for young people below 20 and students below 26; tickets have to be bought right before scheduled departure. There are also some promotional fares on selected flights in certain periods (eg, early or late flights, selected weekend flights etc); they can be just a third of the ordinary fares and are applicable to everybody.

Most airports are a manageable distance – between 10km and 20km – from city centres and are linked to them by public transport. Only Szczecin and Katowice airports are farther out. You must check in at least 30 minutes before departure. Have your passport at hand – you'll be asked to show it. There's no airport tax on domestic flights.

You probably won't be flying a lot in Poland. First, it's expensive compared with taking the train; second, it doesn't save much time except on long, across-country routes.

TRAIN

Trains will be your main means of transport around the country, especially when travelling long distances. Trains in Poland are relatively inexpensive, pretty reliable and usually run on time. They are normally not overcrowded, except for occasional peaks in July and August.

Railways are administered by the Polskie Koleje Państwowe (Polish State Railways), commonly known by the abbreviation PKP. With over 27,000km of lines, the railway network is fairly extensive and covers most places you might wish to go to. Most of the important lines have been electrified and steam has virtually disappeared save for a handful of narrow-gauge lines. Predictably, the network covers less of the mountainous parts of Poland, and trains are slower there.

Types of Train

There are three main types of train: express, fast and ordinary. The express train (*pociąg ekspresowy* or *ekspres*) is the fastest and the most comfortable of them. These trains cover long intercity routes and only stop at major cities en route. They carry only bookable seats; you can't travel standing if all the seats are sold out. Express trains tend to run during the daytime, rather than overnight. Their average speed is 80 km/h to 100km/h.

A more luxurious version of the express train, the InterCity train, began operating in the early 1990s. InterCity trains are even faster and more comfortable than regular express trains, and a light snack is included in the price. These trains run on some major routes out of Warsaw and they don't stop en route at all. The main destinations (along with distances and approximate travelling times) include: Gdańsk (three hours 20 minutes, 333km), Katowice (two hours 40 minutes, 303km), Kraków (two hours and 35 minutes, 297km), Poznań (three hours 10 minutes, 311km) and Szczecin (five hours 40 minutes, 525km).

The fast train *(pociąg pospieszny)* stops at more intermediate stations. Usually not all carriages require booking; some will take passengers regardless of how crowded they get. At an average speed of between 60km/h and 80km/h, fast trains are still a convenient way to get around the country and are one-third cheaper than express trains. They often travel at night, and if the distance justifies it they carry couchettes *(kuszetki)* or sleepers *(miejsca sypialne)* – a good way to avoid hotel costs and reach your destination early in the morning. Book as soon as you decide to go, as there are usually only a couple of sleeping cars and beds may run out fast.

An ordinary or local train *(pociąg osobowy)* is far slower as it stops at all stations along the way. These trains mostly cover shorter distances, but they do run on long routes as well. You can assume that their average speed is between 30km/h and 40km/h. They are less comfortable than express or fast trains and don't require reservations. It's OK to travel a short distance, but a longer journey can be tiring and is not recommended.

Almost all trains carry two classes: 2nd class *(druga klasa)*, and 1st class *(pierwsza klasa)*, which is 50% more expensive. The carriages of long-distance trains are usually divided into compartments: the 1st-class compartments have six seats, while the 2nd-class ones contain eight seats. Smoking is allowed in some compartments and the part of the corridor facing them, but many Poles are chain smokers and a journey in such company is almost unbearable. It's better to book a seat in a nonsmoking compartment and go into the smoking corridor if you wish to smoke.

The 2nd-class couchette compartments have six beds, three to a side; the 1st-class compartments have four beds, two to a side. Sleepers come in both 2nd and 1st class; the former sleep three to a compartment, the latter only two, and both have a washbasin, sheets and blankets.

Train Stations

Most larger train stations are purpose-built and of a reasonable standard. They have a range of facilities, including waiting rooms, snack bars, newsstands, left-luggage rooms and toilets. The biggest stations in the major cities may also have a restaurant, a *kantor* (money exchange office) and a post office. In some small villages, on the other hand, the station can be just a sort of shed without facilities except for a ticket window, which will be open for a short time before trains arrive. If there's more than one train station in a city, the main one is identified by the name 'Główny' and is the one which handles most of the traffic and usually the only one to operate express trains.

Some train stations – even major ones – are poorly marked, and, unless you're familiar with the route, it's easy to miss your stop. If in doubt, asking fellow passengers is probably the best plan of action.

All large stations have left-luggage rooms *(przechowalnia bagażu)*, which are usually open round the clock. You can store your luggage there for up to 10 days. There's a low basic daily storage charge per item (about US$0.50), plus 1% of the declared value of the luggage as insurance. These cloakrooms seem to be secure. One thing to remember is that they usually close once or twice a day for an hour or so. The times of these breaks are displayed over the counter. If you've put your baggage in storage, be sure to arrive at least half an hour before your departure time to allow time for some queuing and paperwork. You pay the charge when you pick up your luggage, not when you deposit it.

Timetables

Train timetables *(rozkład jazdy)* are displayed in all stations, with departures *(odjazdy)* usually on yellow boards and arrivals *(przyjazdy)* usually on white ones.

The ordinary trains are marked in black print, fast trains in red, and if you spot an additional 'Ex', this means an express train.

POLISH RAILWAYS

InterCity trains are identified by the letters 'IC'. The letter 'R' in a square indicates a train with compulsory seat reservation. There will be some letters and/or numbers following the departure time; always check them in the key below. They usually say that the train runs *(kursuje)* or doesn't run *(nie kursuje)* in particular periods or days. The timetables also indicate which platform *(peron)* the train departs from.

Tickets

Since most of the large stations have been computerised, buying tickets *(bilety)* is now less of a hassle than it used to be, but queuing is still a way of life. Be at the station at least half an hour before the departure time of your train and make sure you are queuing at the right ticket window. As cashiers rarely speak English, the easiest way of buying a ticket is to have all relevant details written down on a piece of paper. These should include the destination, the departure time and the class *(pierwsza klasa* or *druga klasa)*. If seat reservation is compulsory on your train, you'll automatically be sold a reserved seat ticket *(miejscówka)*; if it's optional, you must state whether you want a miejscówka or not.

Baltic beach life in Poland

Puppets join the parade in Wrocław, Lower Silesia

Musician in traditional Polish folk costume

Fishy business in Darłowo, Pomerania

Pedestrians at the entrance to Sopot pier

KRZYSZTOF DYDYŃSKI

Baroque facade of Wilanów Palace, Warsaw

MARK DAFFEY

Quirky shop front in Warsaw's Old Town

KRZYSZTOF DYDYŃSKI

Soviet-style building on Plac Konstytucji, Warsaw

BRETT WINERBRENNER

Architectural gems in Park Łazienkowski, Warsaw

If you are forced to get on a train without a ticket, you can buy one directly from the conductor for a small supplement, but you should find him/her right away. If the conductor finds you first, you'll be fined for travelling without a ticket.

Couchettes and sleepers can be booked at special counters at the larger stations; it's advisable to reserve them in advance. Advance tickets for journeys of over 100km and tickets for couchettes and sleepers can also be bought at any Orbis Travel office and some other agencies, which may be quicker.

Fares

Fast-train tickets are about 60% dearer than those for ordinary trains, and an express train costs 50% more than a fast train. First class is 50% more expensive than 2nd class. Following are approximate prices of 2nd-class tickets.

distance (km)	ordinary (US$)	fast (US$)	express (US$)
50	1.80	3.00	4.50
100	3.10	5.10	7.70
150	4.10	6.70	10.10
200	4.80	7.80	11.70
250	5.30	8.60	12.90
300	5.70	9.30	13.90
350	6.00	9.80	14.70
400	6.30	10.30	15.40
450	6.50	10.60	15.90
500	6.70	10.90	16.40

A reserved-seat ticket costs an additional US$2 (US$3 on IC trains) regardless of distance. A 2nd/1st-class couchette costs an additional US$12/15, while a sleeper costs an additional US$22/33.

The approximate fares on InterCity trains (including the compulsory seat reservation) from Warsaw to any one of Gdańsk, Katowice, Kraków and Poznań are US$20/29 in 2nd/1st class, and those to Szczecin are US$22/32.

There are no discounts for ISIC card holders on domestic trains, even though there are reduced fares for Polish students.

Rail Passes

The Eurotrain Explorer pass is available to people under 26 years of age, ISIC card holders, teachers and their spouses and children. Individual Explorer passes for Poland, Hungary, the Czech and Slovak republics and several other countries allow for a week's unlimited 2nd-class travel within the respective country. You must buy these passes outside the country where they are to be used.

You may also be interested in the internal Polrail Pass offered by PKP, which allows for unlimited travel on the entire domestic rail network. The pass comes in durations of eight days (US$68), 15 days (US$78), 21 days (US$88) and 30 days (US$115). Prices are given for 2nd class; add 60% if you want to travel in 1st class. Persons aged under 26 years can buy a Junior pass for about 25% less. Seat reservation fees are included. The pass is available from North American travel agencies through Rail Europe or Orbis

Train Theft Warning

Theft on international trains is becoming a problem, mainly on the Berlin-Warsaw trains, which are notorious for gangs of thieves who unlock compartments and rob the valuables of the sleeping passengers. There have been some recent reports of armed assaults in these trains. Most cases of theft occur between the German/Polish border and Poznań. You should also be on guard in the Berlin-Kraków and Prague-Warsaw trains, though theft here hasn't reached alarming proportions so far.

Some travellers have been robbed at knife-point in slow local trains while sitting by themselves in a compartment. They were easy prey for robbers, who could do their job inconspicuously, then get off at the next tiny station and disappear without a trace. Don't sit in a cabin alone; join other passengers.

Watch your luggage and your pockets closely when you are getting on or off the train, as these are the most convenient moments for muggers to distract your attention. Warsaw central train station is the favourite playground for robbers, and is therefore a place in which to exercise particular care.

Travel or Polorbis offices abroad, and it also can be bought in Poland.

BUS

Buses are often more convenient than trains over a short distance. On longer routes, too, you may sometimes find a bus better and faster when, for instance, the train route involves a long detour.

You'll often travel by bus in the mountains, where trains are slow and few. Ordinary buses on short routes are cheaper than the 2nd class of ordinary trains.

Most bus transport is operated by the state bus company, Państwowa Komunikacja Samochodowa, or PKS. The total network of bus routes is much more comprehensive than that of trains, and buses go to most villages that are accessible by road. The frequency of service varies a great deal: on the main routes there may be a bus leaving every quarter of an hour or so, whereas some small, remote villages may be visited by only one bus per day. Almost all buses run during the daytime, sometimes starting very early in the morning.

Unlike PKP, which monopolises the whole train service, PKS is experiencing increasing competition. There are a number of small private operators which run vans, minibuses and buses on regional routes, mostly short distance. The biggest competitor, though, is Polski Express (**W** www.polskiexpress.pl), a joint venture with Eurolines National Express based in the UK. It runs several major long-distance routes out of Warsaw, including Białystok, Gdańsk (via Ostróda and Elbląg), Kraków (via Łódź and Katowice), Rzeszów (via Puławy and Lublin) and Bydgoszcz (via Płock and Toruń). It is faster and more comfortable than PKS, and costs much the same.

Types of Bus

There are two types of PKS bus service, ordinary and fast. The ordinary or local buses (*autobusy zwykłe*) stop at all stops on the route and their average speed hardly exceeds 35km/h. The standard of these buses leaves a little to be desired. Their departure and arrival times are written in black on timetable boards. The fast buses (*autobusy pospieszne*), marked in red, cover mainly long-distance routes and run as fast as 45km/h to 55km/h. As a rule, they take only as many passengers as they have seats. Their standards tend to be better than that of the ordinary buses.

Bus Terminals

The PKS bus terminal (*dworzec autobusowy PKS*) is usually found alongside the train station. Save for the large terminals in the major cities, bus terminals don't normally provide a left-luggage service and have few other facilities. They are closed at night. Polski Express uses PKS terminals in some cities.

Timetables

Timetables are posted on boards either inside or outside PKS bus-terminal buildings. There are also notice boards on all bus stops along the route (if vandals haven't damaged or removed them). The timetable of departures (*odjazdy*) lists destinations (*kierunek*), the places passed en route (*przez*) and departure times.

Keep in mind that there may be more buses to the particular town you want to go to than those that are mentioned in the destination column of the timetable under the town's name. You therefore need to check whether your town doesn't appear in the przez (via) column on the way to more distant destinations.

Also check any additional symbols that accompany the departure time, which can mean that the bus runs only on certain days or in certain seasons. They're explained in the key at the end of the timetable.

Tickets

The only place to buy PKS tickets is the terminal itself; Orbis Travel doesn't handle this service. Tickets on long routes serviced by fast buses can be bought up to 30 days in advance but those for short, local routes are only available the same day.

Tickets are numbered, and buying one at the counter at the terminal assures you of a seat. If you get on the bus somewhere along the route, you buy the ticket directly from the driver and you won't necessarily have a seat.

Tickets for Polski Express buses can be bought at the terminals where they arrive/depart from (PKS or the company's own), and from some Orbis Travel offices.

Fares

The approximate fares for ordinary and fast PKS buses are as follows:

distance (km)	ordinary (US$)	fast (US$)
20	0.75	1.20
40	1.30	1.70
60	1.75	2.30
80	2.20	3.00
100	2.75	3.50
120	3.20	4.10
140	3.70	4.60
160	4.20	5.10
180	4.70	5.60
200	5.20	6.10
220	5.70	6.60
240	6.20	7.10

Polski Express may be an interesting alternative to both PKS bus and PKP train on some of its routes. Following are some of its destinations out of Warsaw:

destination	fare (US$)	time (hrs)	distance (km)	frequency (daily)
Białystok	5.75	3½	188	3
Bydgoszcz	8.25	4½	255	15
Gdańsk	10.50	5¾	339	2
Lublin	6.00	3	161	7
Łódź	5.25	2½	134	7
Rzeszów	10.00	6½	303	1
Toruń	7.25	3¾	209	15

Students below 26 (ISIC cards accepted) and senior citizens over 60 get a 30% discount on all fares from Tuesday to Thursday.

CAR & MOTORCYCLE

Travelling with your own vehicle is a far more comfortable way to visit Poland than by using the public trains and buses. The biggest bonus, though, is the opportunity to get far away from the cities, exploring obscure villages and distant countryside, stopping on the way when you wish. With the relatively low price of petrol and the reasonable roads, travelling by car in Poland really does have lots of advantages.

Atlas Samochodowy, the book-format road map of Poland, is helpful. Two kinds are available, differing in format and scale (1:250,000 or 1:300,000). Apart from detailed maps, they both contain a full index of localities, sketch maps of major towns and cities complete with locations of filling stations, and a table of the traffic signs used in Poland.

Roads

Poland has a dense network of sealed roads that total 220,000km. The massive increase in traffic over recent years, along with extreme climatic conditions, have led to deterioration in road surfaces, with some in better shape than others.

There are only a few motorways in the proper sense of the word, but an array of two and four-lane highways crisscross the country; some of these roads are quite crowded. Secondary roads are narrower but they usually carry less traffic and are OK for leisurely travel. The sealed minor roads, which are even narrower, are also often in acceptable condition, though driving is harder work as they tend to twist and turn, are not so well signposted and pass through every single village along the way.

Road Rules

As in the rest of continental Europe, you drive on the right-hand side of the road in Poland. Also as in most countries, traffic coming from the right has priority unless indicated otherwise by signs. Driving rules and traffic signs are similar to those in the West, although with some local variations.

Unless signs state otherwise, cars and motorcycles can be parked on pavements, as long as a minimum 1.5m-wide walkway is left for pedestrians. Parking in the opposite direction to the flow of traffic is allowed. Some traffic signs that may be unfamiliar to Britons and non-European visitors include:

Blue disc with red border and red slash: no parking on the road, but you still can park on the footpath; if the sign is accompanied by a white board below saying 'dotyczy również chodnika' or 'dotyczy także chodnika' ('it also refers to the footpath'), you can't park on either the road or the footpath

Blue disc with red border and crossed red slashes: no stopping

White disc with red border: no vehicles allowed

Red disc with horizontal white line: no entry

Yellow triangle (point down) with red border: give way to crossing or merging traffic

Yellow diamond with white border: you have right of way; a black slash through it means you no longer have right of way

The permitted blood alcohol level is 0.02%, so it's best not to drink at all before driving. Seat belts must be worn by the driver and front-seat passengers at all times. From October to February, car and motorbike lights must be on at all times while driving, even during a sunny day. Cars must be equipped with a first-aid kit, a left-hand outside rear mirror and a red warning triangle that has to be placed behind the car in the event of accident or breakdown. Motorcyclists should remember that both rider and passenger must wear crash helmets.

Following are the maximum speed limits on Polish roads:

60km/h (37mph) for all vehicles throughout built-up areas

80km/h (50mph) for all vehicles pulling caravans or trailers outside built-up areas, the motorways included

90km/h (56mph) for cars and motorbikes on roads outside built-up areas

100km/h (62mph) for cars and motorbikes on two-lane express highways

110km/h (69mph) for cars and motorbikes on four-lane express highways

130km/h (81mph) for cars and motorbikes on the motorways

Traffic signs may override the general rules and sometimes they impose ridiculously low speed limits. Don't ignore them, however, as these are favourite spots for the police's well hidden radar speed traps.

In the cities, be careful with trams, especially if you haven't been used to driving

alongside them before. Special care should be taken when crossing the tramway, particularly while turning left and on roundabouts; in both cases you have to give way to trams. If you see a tram halting at a stop in the middle of the street, you are obliged to stop behind it and let all passengers get off and on. However, if there's a pedestrian island, you don't have to stop.

Petrol

Petrol is now readily available at hundreds of petrol stations, which have mushroomed throughout Poland. They sell several different kinds and grades of petrol, including 94-octane leaded (US$0.80 per litre), 95-octane unleaded (US$0.80), 98-octane unleaded (US$0.90) and diesel (US$0.70). The price of fuel can differ between the petrol stations by up to 10%. An increasing number of petrol stations accept credit cards.

Virtually all petrol stations have adopted a self-service system, which was almost unknown previously. Air and water are usually available, as well as oil, lubricants and basic spare parts such as light bulbs, fuses etc. An increasing number of new stations also offer food. Many stations located along main roads and in the large cities are open round the clock.

Rental

Avis (toll-free ☎ 0800-120 010, Ⓦ www.avis.pl), Budget (☎ 22-650 40 62, Ⓦ www.budget.com), Hertz (toll-free ☎ 08 00-143 789, Ⓦ www.hertz.com) and other international agencies are now well represented in Poland, and there are also plenty of local operators. Check Ⓦ www.amta.com/cars.htm for more information. Most rental vehicles are European makes, such as Peugeot, Renault, Opel, Fiat, VW, BMW, Audi, Mercedes and Volvo.

One-way rentals within Poland are possible with most companies (usually for an additional fee), but most will insist on keeping the car within Poland. In any case, no company is likely to allow you to take its car beyond the eastern border.

Rental agencies will require you to produce your passport, a driving licence held

Road Distances (km)

	Białystok	Bydgoszcz	Częstochowa	Gdańsk	Katowice	Kielce	Kraków	Lublin	Łódź	Olsztyn	Opole	Poznań	Rzeszów	Szczecin	Toruń	Warsaw	Wrocław	Zielona Góra
Białystok	---																	
Bydgoszcz	389	---																
Częstochowa	410	316	---															
Gdańsk	379	167	470	---														
Katowice	485	391	75	545	---													
Kielce	363	348	124	483	156	---												
Kraków	477	430	114	565	75	114	---											
Lublin	260	421	288	500	323	167	269	---										
Łódź	322	205	121	340	196	143	220	242	---									
Olsztyn	223	217	404	156	479	394	500	370	281	---								
Opole	507	318	98	485	113	220	182	382	244	452	---							
Poznań	491	129	289	296	335	354	403	465	212	323	261	---						
Rzeszów	430	516	272	642	244	163	165	170	306	516	347	517	---					
Szczecin	656	267	520	348	561	585	634	683	446	484	459	234	751	---				
Toruń	347	46	289	181	364	307	384	375	159	172	312	151	470	313	---			
Warsaw	188	255	222	339	297	181	295	161	134	213	319	310	303	524	209	---		
Wrocław	532	265	176	432	199	221	268	428	204	442	86	178	433	371	279	344	---	
Zielona Góra	601	259	328	411	356	422	427	542	303	453	245	130	585	214	281	413	157	---

for at least one year, and a credit card. You need to be at least 21 or 23 years of age to rent a car, although renting some cars, particularly luxury models and 4WDs, may require a higher age.

Car rental is not cheap in Poland – the prices are comparable to full-price rental in Western Europe – and there are seldom any promotional discounts. As a rough guide only, economy models offered by reputable companies begin at around US$60 to US$70 (including insurance and unlimited mileage) a day. Expect cheaper fares if you are going to use the car for a longer time, a week being the usual minimum period. The local operators are cheaper, but their cars and rental conditions may leave something to be desired.

It's usually cheaper to pre-book your car from abroad rather than to front up at an agency inside Poland. Furthermore, this will ensure that you have the car you need upon arrival in Poland; otherwise you may wait for a few days or, sometimes, a few weeks.

It would be cheaper to rent a car in the West, say in Berlin, and drive it into Poland, but few rental companies will allow you to take their car to the east.

When renting a car, read the contract carefully before signing it. Pay close attention to any theft clause, as it may load a large percentage of any loss onto the hirer. Check the car carefully before you drive off.

It's next to impossible to hire a motorcycle in Poland.

Bringing Your Own Vehicle

Many Western tourists, mainly Germans, bring their own vehicles with them into Poland. There are no special formalities: all you need at the border is your passport with a valid visa if necessary, your driving licence and vehicle insurance for Poland (the so-called Green Card). If your insurance isn't valid for Poland, you must buy an additional policy at the border. The car registration number will be entered in your passport. A nationality plate or sticker has to be displayed on the back of the car.

If you decide to bring your own vehicle to Poland, remember that life will be easier for you if it's not brand-new or a fancy recent model. A more modest vehicle won't draw crowds of curious peasants – or gangs of thieves in large cities. The shabbier your car looks, the better. Don't wash it too often.

There's a widespread network of garages that specialise in fixing Western cars (though not many for motorcycles), but they mostly deal with older, traditional models with mechanical technology. The more electronics and computer-controlled bits your car has, the more problems you'll face having something fixed if it goes wrong. These parts can be ordered for you, but they'll usually take a while to arrive, and you'll pay inflated Western prices.

Security & Hazards

Bring along a good insurance policy from a reliable company for both the car and your possessions. Car theft is well established in Poland, with several gangs operating in the large cities. Some of them cooperate with Russians in smuggling stolen vehicles across the eastern border, never to be seen again.

Even if the car itself doesn't get stolen, you might lose some of its accessories, most likely the radio/cassette player, as well as any personal belongings you've left inside. Hide your gear, if you must leave it inside; try to make the car look empty. Preferably, take your luggage to the hotel you stay in. If possible, always park your car in a guarded car park (*parking strzeżony*). If your hotel doesn't have its own, the staff will tell you where the nearest one is, probably within walking distance.

In the cities, it may be more convenient and safer to leave your vehicle in a secure place (eg, your hotel car park), and get around by taxi or public transport.

Drive carefully on country roads, particularly at night. There are still a lot of horse-drawn carts on Polish roads, and the farther off the main routes you wander, the more carts, tractors and other agricultural machinery you'll encounter. They are lit poorly

or not at all. The same applies to bicycles – you'll hardly ever see a properly lit bike. Pedestrians are another problem, drunks staggering along the middle of the road being the biggest danger.

And while driving around the countryside roads, take note that scarcely dressed young women – sometimes in just a bra and a miniskirt – waving cars and trucks on the roadsides are not hitchhikers.

BICYCLE

Poland is not a bad place for cycling. Most of the country is fairly flat, so riding is easy and any ordinary bike is OK. If you plan on travelling in the mountainous southern regions, you'll do much better with a multispeed bike. Camping equipment isn't essential, as hotels and hostels are usually no more than an easy day's ride apart, but carrying your own camping gear does give you more flexibility.

Major roads can carry pretty heavy traffic and are best avoided. Instead, you can easily plan your route along secondary and other minor roads, which are usually much less crowded and in fair shape. Stock up with detailed tourist maps, which feature all minor roads, specifying which are sealed and which are not, and also show marked walking trails. Some of these trails are easily travelled by bike, which gives you still more itinerary options.

On a less optimistic note, the standard of driving in Poland may not exactly be what you've been used to at home. Some vehicles may drive along the middle of the road and fail to move over for you. The number of up-market Western cars has soared in recent years (Poland is believed to have Europe's largest population of Mercedes outside Germany). Some drivers may relentlessly overtake anything in their path – particularly cyclists – regardless of oncoming traffic. Note that in Poland cyclists are not allowed to ride two abreast.

Cities are not pleasant for cyclists either, as separate bike tracks are few and far between, and some car drivers are not particularly polite to cyclists. Furthermore, city roads are often in poor shape, and cobbled streets are not uncommon.

Hotel staff will usually let you put your bike indoors for the night, sometimes in your room; it's often better to leave it in the hotel during the day as well, and get around city sights on foot or by public transport. Bikes, especially Western ones, are attractive to thieves, so it's a good idea to carry a solid lock and chain, for the frame and both wheels, and always use them when you leave the bike outdoors, even if only for a moment.

If you want to skip part of Poland to visit another region, you can take your bike on the train. Some long-distance trains have a freight carriage. If this is the case, you should normally take your bike to the railway luggage office, fill out a tag and pay a small fee. They will then load the bike and drop it off at your destination. It's a good idea to strip the bike of anything easily removable and keep an eye out to be sure they've actually loaded it on your train. You could also take your bike straight to the freight carriage (which is usually attached at the front or the rear of the train), but this can be hard to do at intermediate stations where the train may only stop for a few minutes. Collect the bike as soon as you arrive.

Bikes are not allowed on express trains or on those that take reservations, since these trains don't carry baggage cars. Many ordinary trains don't have baggage cars either, but you can try to take the bike into the passenger car with you as some Poles do. Check at the baggage window in the station before you do so. Buses don't normally take bikes.

Cycling shops and repair centres are popping up in large cities, and in some of the major tourist resorts. You can now buy various makes of Western bikes and some popular spare parts – at Western prices, of course. For rural riding, you should carry all essential spare parts, for it's unlikely there'll be a bike shop around. In particular, spare nuts and bolts should be carried. Given the jolting from Poland's numerous cobbled roads, cyclists should check their bikes frequently.

Bike-rental outlets are still few and far between. They seldom offer anything other than ordinary Polish bikes, and their condition may leave a bit to be desired.

HITCHING

Hitching (autostop) is never entirely safe anywhere in the world. Travellers who decide to hitch should understand that they are taking a small but potentially serious risk. Those who choose to hitch will be safer travelling in pairs, and letting someone know where they are planning to go.

That said, hitching does take place in Poland, though it's not very popular. Car drivers rarely stop to pick up hitchers, and large commercial vehicles (which are easier to wave down) expect to be paid the equivalent of a bus fare.

BOAT

Poland has a long coastline and lots of rivers and canals, but the passenger-boat service is pretty limited and operates only in summer. There are no regular boats running along the main rivers or along the coast. Several cities, including Szczecin, Gdańsk, Toruń, Wrocław and Kraków, have local river cruises during the summer, and a few coastal ports (Kołobrzeg and Gdańsk) offer sea excursions.

On the Masurian Lakes, excursion boats run in summer between Giżycko, Mikołajki, Węgorzewo and Ruciane-Nida. Tourist boats are also available in the Augustów area where they ply a part of the Augustów Canal. The most unusual canal trip is the full-day cruise along the Elbląg-Ostróda Canal. There is also a spectacular raft trip through the Dunajec Gorge in the Pieniny Mountains.

LOCAL TRANSPORT
Bus, Tram & Trolleybus

Most cities have both buses (autobus) and trams (tramwaj), and some also have trolleybuses (trolejbus). Public transport operates from around 5am to 11pm and may be crowded during the rush hours. The largest cities also have night-time services, on either bus or tram. Timetables are usually posted at stops, but don't rely too much on their accuracy.

In many cities there's a flat-rate fare for local transport so the duration of the ride and the distance make no difference. If you change vehicles, however, you need another ticket. The ordinary fare is around US$0.50. In some cities the fare depends on how long you travel, with the ticket valid for a certain period of time, such as 30 minutes and one hour. Night services are more expensive than daytime fares. An ISIC card gives a 48% discount in Warsaw only.

Each piece of bulky luggage (legally anything measuring more than 60cm x 40cm x 20cm) is an additional ordinary fare.

There are no conductors on board; you buy tickets beforehand and punch or stamp them upon boarding in one of the little machines installed near the doors. You can buy tickets from Ruch kiosks or, in some cities, from street stalls around the central stops, recognisable by the *bilety* (tickets) boards they display. Buy a bunch of them at once if you are going to use public transport. Buy enough tickets on Saturday morning to last you until Monday, as few kiosks are open on Sunday. Tickets purchased in one city cannot be used in another. Make sure you punch or stamp the correct ticket value, or a couple of tickets.

The plain-clothed ticket inspectors control tickets more often today than they did before and foreign backpackers are their favourite targets. These inspectors tend to be officious, dogged and singularly unpleasant to deal with.

If you are caught without a ticket, it's best to pay the fine straight away. Never give an inspector your passport, even if they threaten you with police intervention if you don't.

Taxi

Taxis are easily available and not too expensive by Western standards. As a rough guide, a 5km taxi trip will cost around US$3, and a 10km ride shouldn't cost more than US$5. Taxi fares are 50% higher at night (10pm to 6am), on Sunday and outside the city limits. The number of passengers (usually up to four) and the amount of luggage doesn't affect the fare.

There are plenty of taxi companies, including the once monopolist state-run Radio Taxi (☎ 919), which is the largest and operates in most cities. Taxis are recognisable by large boards on the roof with the company's name and its phone number. There are also pirate taxis (called the 'mafia' by Poles), which usually have just a small 'taxi' label on the roof without any name or phone number. Mafia taxis are a plague in Warsaw and exist in some other large cities (see the boxed text 'Welcome to the Land of Pirate Taxis' in the Warsaw chapter).

Taxis can be waved down on the street, but it can be easier to go to a taxi stand (*postój taksówek*), where you'll almost always find a line of them. There are plenty of such stands and everybody will tell you where the nearest one is. Taxis can also be ordered by phone, and there's usually no extra charge for this service. Taxis should normally arrive within 10 minutes unless you request one at a specified time later on.

When you get into a taxi, make sure the driver turns on the meter. Also check whether the meter has been switched to the proper rate: '1' identifies the daytime rate, and '2' is the night-time rate. A typical drivers' scam for foreigners is to drop the flag to the higher night-time rate throughout the daytime.

Remember to carry small bills, so you'll be able to pay the right fare. If you don't, it's virtually impossible to get change back from the driver who's intent on charging you more. It's always a good idea to find out beforehand how much the right fare should be by asking the hotel staff or an attendant at the airport.

ORGANISED TOURS

For tours organised from outside Poland, see Organised Tours in the Getting There & Away chapter. Included below are tours organised in Poland by Polish agencies and you'll normally arrange them after coming to Poland. See the relevant regional sections for further information about the agencies, their tours, prices etc.

City tours are organised by several companies in Warsaw and Kraków. The same agencies offer various regional tours.

Jewish tourism is run by some specialised operators, including Our Roots (☎/fax 22-620 05 56) in Warsaw and Jarden

Jewish Bookshop (☎ 12-421 71 66) in Kraków.

Almatur (with its offices in Poland's larger cities, including Warsaw, Kraków, Gdańsk and Wrocław) offers two-week sailing, kayaking and horse-riding holidays in July and August. These trips are intended principally for students and are priced very reasonably.

Mazury travel agency (☎/fax 89-527 40 59) in Olsztyn runs regular 10-day kayak tours along the Krutynia River from late June to mid-August. Similar kayak trips

along Czarna Hańcza River are available from several agencies in Augustów. Various operators in Masuria (principally in Giżycko and Mikołajki) handle yacht rental.

Some new-generation 'green' tour operators, including Kampio (☎ 22-823 70 70) in Warsaw and Bird Service (☎ 12-292 14 60) in Kraków, organise nature tours (birdwatching, kayaking, biking etc) in out-of-the-way areas. It may be a good idea to get in contact them before you set off from home to see what their programs and schedules are.

Warsaw

☎ 22 • pop 1,750,000

The capital of Poland, Warsaw (Warszawa in Polish, pronounced 'var-**shah**-vah') is set roughly in the centre of the country and is twice as populous as the nation's second-largest city, Łódź. Its size and status make it the major focus of political, scientific and educational life.

Annihilated during WWII then emerging like a phoenix from the ashes, Warsaw is essentially a postwar city. Its handful of historic precincts have been meticulously reconstructed, but most of its urban landscape is modern, including everything from dull products of the Stalin era to more creative accomplishments of recent years. The war also changed Warsaw's social structure; vast numbers of its citizens perished and the city was repopulated with newcomers, thus weakening its centuries-old cultural traditions.

A decade after the fall of communism, Warsaw has turned into a thrilling, busy city swiftly catching up with the West. It's Poland's most cosmopolitan, dynamic and progressive urban centre, dotted with luxury hotels, elegant shops and diverse services. Whether you are interested in plush accommodation, fine dining, shopping, museums, theatre or bazaars, you will find more to choose from here than in any other Polish city.

In a way, Warsaw epitomises the Polish nation. It's a blend of old and new, in both appearance and spirit – respecting tradition but racing towards the future. Warsaw is an interesting layered cake which will take several days to digest.

HISTORY

By Polish standards, Warsaw is a young city. When other towns such as Kraków, Poznań, Wrocław or Gdańsk were about to celebrate their quincentenaries, the present-day capital was just beginning to emerge from obscurity in the middle of the Mazovian forests.

Though traces of settlement in the area date from the 10th century, it was not until

Highlights

- Admire the Old Town, the historic core meticulously rebuilt from scratch
- Stroll through the charming park-and-palace complex of Łazienki
- Explore Wilanów, another lovely park-and-palace complex
- Discover a treasure trove of art at the National Museum
- Visit the Royal Castle to learn how kings once lived
- Treat yourself to an evening of opera at the Grand Theatre
- Browse around the gigantic bazaar at the 10th Anniversary Stadium

RUSSIA

✪ Warsaw p108
Central Warsaw p110
Warsaw – Old Town & Around p118

CZECH REPUBLIC

SLOVAKIA

the beginning of the 14th century that the dukes of Mazovia built a stronghold on the site where the Royal Castle stands today, thus giving birth to a township. Like most medieval Polish towns, it was planned on a grid around a central square and surrounded with fortified walls. In 1413 the dukes made Warsaw their seat, and it began to develop more quickly. By then, the New Town had begun to emerge to the north outside the Old Town's walls. In 1526, after the last duke died without an heir, Warsaw and the whole of Mazovia came under the direct rule of the king in Kraków.

The turning point of Warsaw's fortunes came in 1569, when the Sejm, which had convened in Lublin, unified Poland and Lithuania and voted to make Warsaw the seat of the Sejm's debates, because of its central position. Four years later, Warsaw also became the seat of royal elections, though kings continued to reside in Kraków. The final ennoblement came in 1596 when King Zygmunt III Waza decided to move the capital from Kraków to Warsaw. Reasons of state apart, the king seemed to have a personal motivation for the change – Warsaw was closer to Sweden, his motherland.

Like the rest of Poland, Warsaw fell prey to the Swedish invasion of 1655–60. The city suffered severe damage, but soon recovered and continued to develop. Paradoxically, the 18th century – a period of catastrophic decline for the Polish state – witnessed Warsaw's greatest ever prosperity. It was then that a wealth of great palaces

and churches was erected. Cultural and artistic life flourished, particularly during the reign of the last Polish king, Stanisław August Poniatowski. In 1791, the first constitution in Europe was signed in Warsaw. By then, the city had 120,000 inhabitants.

When Poland was partitioned in 1795, Warsaw found itself under Prussian domination and was reduced to the status of a provincial town. It became a capital once more in 1807 when Napoleon created the Duchy of Warsaw, and it continued as capital of the Congress Kingdom of Poland. In 1830, however, Poland fell under Russian rule and remained so until WWI broke out.

Steady urban development and industrialisation took place in the second half of the 19th century. A railway linking Warsaw with Vienna and St Petersburg was built. By 1900, there were 690,000 people living in Warsaw.

After WWI Warsaw was reinstated as the capital of independent Poland and within 20 years made considerable advances in the fields of industry, education, science and

Warsaw in the 16th century, a thriving town on the Vistula River

WARSAW

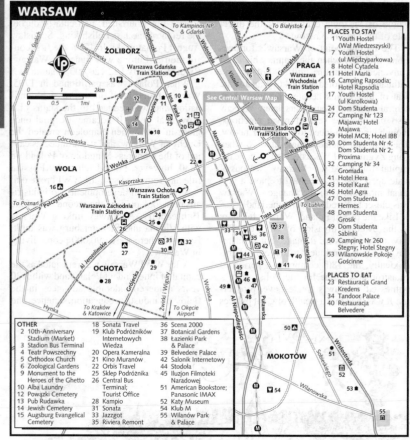

WARSAW

To Kampinos NP & Gdańsk
To Białystok

ŻOLIBORZ

PRAGA

Warszawa Gdańska Train Station

Warszawa Wschodnia Train Station

See Central Warsaw Map

Warszawa Stadion Train Station

WOLA

Warszawa Ochota Train Station

Warszawa Zachodnia Train Station

To Poznań

To Lublin

Trasa Łazienkowska

OCHOTA

To Kraków & Katowice

To Okęcie Airport

MOKOTÓW

PLACES TO STAY
1 Youth Hostel (Wał Miedzeszyński)
7 Youth Hostel (ul Międzyparkowa)
8 Hotel Cytadela
11 Hotel Maria
16 Camping Rapsodia; Hotel Rapsodia
17 Youth Hostel (ul Karolkowa)
24 Dom Studenta
27 Camping Nr 123 Majawa; Hotel Majawa
29 Hotel MCB; Hotel IBB
30 Dom Studenta Nr 4; Dom Studenta Nr 2; Proxima
32 Camping Nr 34 Gromada
41 Hotel Hera
43 Hotel Karat
46 Hotel Agra
47 Dom Studenta Hermes
48 Dom Studenta Grosik
49 Dom Studenta Sabinki
50 Camping Nr 260 Stegny; Hotel Stegny
53 Wilanowskie Pokoje Gościnne

PLACES TO EAT
23 Restauracja Grand Kredens
34 Tandoor Palace
40 Restauracja Belvedere

OTHER
2 10th-Anniversary Stadium (Market)
3 Stadion Bus Terminal
4 Teatr Powszechny
5 Orthodox Church
6 Zoological Gardens
9 Monument to the Heroes of the Ghetto
10 Alba Laundry
12 Powązki Cemetery
13 Pub Rudawka
14 Jewish Cemetery
15 Augsburg Evangelical Cemetery
18 Sonata Travel
19 Klub Podróżników Internetowych Wiedza
20 Opera Kameralna
21 Kino Muranów
22 Orbis Travel
25 Sklep Podróżnika
26 Central Bus Terminal; Tourist Office
28 Kampio
31 Sonata
33 Jazzgot
35 Riviera Remont
36 Scena 2000
37 Botanical Gardens
38 Łazienki Park & Palace
39 Belvedere Palace
42 Salonik Internetowy
44 Stodoła
45 Iluzjon Filmoteki Narodowej
51 American Bookstore; Panasonic IMAX
52 Katy Museum
54 Klub M
55 Wilanów Park & Palace

culture. The population increased from about 750,000 in 1918 to nearly 1.3 million in 1939. About 380,000 of the latter figure were Jews, who had traditionally made up a significant part of Warsaw's community.

Nazi bombs began to fall on 1 September 1939 and a week later the city was besieged. Despite brave resistance, Warsaw was forced to capitulate on 28 September. This, however, turned out to be only the beginning of the tragedy. The five-year Nazi occupation, marked by constant arrests, executions and deportations, triggered two acts of heroic armed resistance, both cruelly crushed.

The first was the Ghetto Uprising in April 1943, when heavily outnumbered and almost unarmed Jews fought fiercely for almost a month against massive Nazi forces. See the boxed text 'The Warsaw Ghetto & the Ghetto Uprising' later in this chapter for more about this tragic event.

The second Warsaw Uprising aimed to liberate the capital and set up an independent government before the arrival of the Red Army (which was already on the opposite bank of the Vistula River). Street fighting began on 1 August 1944, but after 63 days the insurgents were forced to capitulate. For the next three months the Nazis methodically razed Warsaw to the ground. Only on 17 January 1945 did the Soviet army cross the river to 'liberate' the city.

According to postwar estimates, about 85% of Warsaw's buildings were destroyed and 700,000 people, over half of the city's prewar population, perished. No other Polish city suffered such immense loss of life and such devastation in the war. Given the level of destruction, there were even suggestions that the capital should move elsewhere.

After some consideration it was decided to rebuild parts of the prewar urban fabric. According to the plan, the most valuable historic monuments, most notably the Old Town, would be restored to their previous appearance based on original drawings which had survived the war. With the help of the citizenry, this gigantic task was carried out for over a decade and the result is truly spectacular.

Apart from historic monuments, the authorities had to build from scratch a whole new city capable of providing housing and services to its inhabitants. This communist legacy is less impressive. The city centre was, until recently, a blend of bunker-like Stalinist structures and equally boring edifices of a later era, while the outer suburbs, home to the majority of Warsaw's inhabitants, were composed almost exclusively of anonymous prefabricated concrete blocks.

With the arrival of the market economy, the face of Warsaw started changing rapidly. Newly constructed steel-and-glass towers are increasingly breaking the monotony of the grey landscape, the shop windows are catching the eye with innovative designs and colour, and the city outskirts are steadily filling up with villas and family houses on a more human scale than the monstrous slabs of yesterday.

ORIENTATION

The city is divided by the Vistula (Wisła) River into two very different parts. The western left-bank sector is much larger and features the city centre including the Old Town, the historic nucleus of Warsaw. Almost all tourist attractions, as well as the lion's share of tourist facilities, are on this side of the river. The eastern right-bank part of Warsaw, the suburb of Praga, has no major sights and sees few tourists.

The main focus of tourist interest is the Old Town area. To the south stretches the new city centre with the monstrous Palace of Culture and Science; this is not a place to go for historic monuments but for the bustling commercial atmosphere of contemporary Warsaw. A few kilometres south-east is the beautiful Łazienki park-and-palace complex, linked to the Old Town by the 4km-long Royal Way. Many tourist sights are along this route. Another attraction is Wilanów Palace, on the southern outskirts of the city.

Finding your way around is relatively easy. The major inconvenience is that budget and mid-range accommodation is scattered over the city centre and beyond without a clearly defined 'hotel area', but cooperative tourist offices (including the ones at the airport and train station) are likely to find somewhere for you to crash.

If you arrive by air at Okęcie airport, you can easily get to the city centre by urban bus or taxi. Coming by train, you arrive at the central train station right in the city centre. When arriving by bus at the central bus terminal, you can get to the city centre by commuter train from adjoining Warszawa Zachodnia station or by urban bus. By whichever means you come, consider buying a city map, available from newsagents and tourist offices, or rely on one in publications distributed free of charge.

If you arrive by your own means of transport, just follow the signs saying 'Centrum'. Should you have any doubts, simply steer towards the spire of the giant Palace of Culture and Science, visible from everywhere, which marks the city centre.

INFORMATION
Tourist Offices

The city tourist office, Stołeczne Biuro Informacji i Promocji Turystycznej (☎ 94 31, ⓔ info@warsawtour.pl, ⓦ www.warsaw tour.pl) has several information outlets around town (all open 8am to 6pm daily,

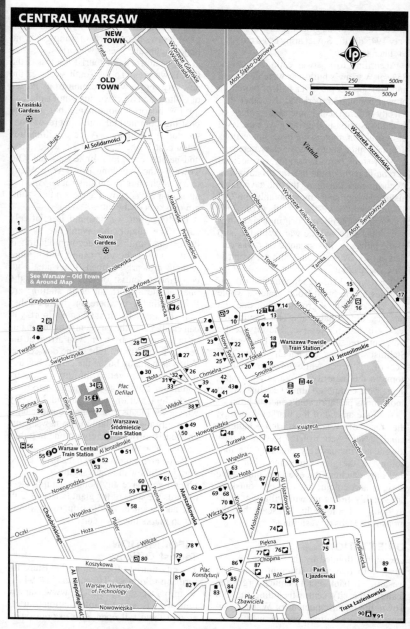

CENTRAL WARSAW

NEW TOWN

OLD TOWN

Krasiński Gardens

Al Solidarności

Saxon Gardens

See Warsaw – Old Town & Around Map

Vistula

Wybrzeże Gdańskie (Wisłostrada)

Most Śląsko-Dąbrowski

Wybrzeże Szczecińskie

Wybrzeże Kościuszkowskie

Most Świętokrzyski

0 250 500m
0 250 500yd

Grzybowska

Twarda

Świętokrzyska

Sienna

Złota

Chałubińskiego

Nowogrodzka

Wspólna

Hoża

Oczki

Koszykowa

Al Niepodległości

Warsaw University of Technology

Nowowiejska

Emilii Plater

Plac Defilad

Warszawa Śródmieście Train Station

Warsaw Central Train Station

Al Jerozolimskie

Poznańska

Marszałkowska

Wilcza

Piękna

Plac Konstytucji

Plac Zbawiciela

Al Róż

Park Ujazdowski

Myśliwiecka

Trasa Łazienkowska

Warszawa Powiśle Train Station

Al Jerozolimskie

Książęca

Wiejska

Chopina

Długa
Freta
Kredytowa
Jasna
Mazowiecka
Królewska
Krakowskie Przedmieście
Nowy Świat
Chmielna
Złota
Widok
Nowogrodzka
Żurawia
Wspólna
Hoża
Krucza
Mokotowska
Al Ujazdowskie
Rozbrat
Dobra
Browarna
Topiel
Tamka
Solec
Jaracza
Kruczkowskiego
Dobra
Smolna
Foksal
Kopernika
Zielna
Emilii Plater

CENTRAL WARSAW

PLACES TO STAY
5 Hotel Mazowiecki
15 Hotel Belfer
17 Hotel Na Wodzie
19 Youth Hostel
27 Hotel Gromada
54 Marriott Hotel
63 Grand Hotel
65 Sheraton Hotel; Someplace Else
70 Biuro Kwater Prywatnych Syrena Univel (Private Rooms)
83 Hotel MDM
89 Youth Hostel Agrykola

PLACES TO EAT
14 Salad Bar Tukan
20 Restauracja Soma
21 Tam Tam
22 Mata Hari
24 Bar Mleczny Familijny
25 Café Blikle
26 Wedel
31 Bar Turecki
32 Grill Bar Zgoda
33 Bar Krokiecik
38 London Steak House
39 TriBeCa Coffee
40 Między Nami
42 Restauracja Polska
47 Bar Mleczny Szwajcarski
58 Bar Aysza Tripolis
59 Warsaw Tortilla Factory
61 Antykwariat Cafe

66 Café Ejlat
67 Restauracja Adler
68 Bar Mleczny Bambino
78 Bar Mleczny Złota Kurka
79 Salad Bar Tukan
82 Bar Hoa Lan
86 Słodki... Słony...
91 Qchnia Artystyczna

OTHER
1 Mazowieckie Centrum Kultury
2 Jewish Theatre
3 Nożyk Synagogue
4 Our Roots Jewish Travel Agency
6 Klub Tygmont
7 American Bookstore
8 Leksykon
9 studio.tpi
10 Almatur Student Travel Agency
11 Akademia Muzyczana
12 Ostrogski Palace; Chopin Museum
13 Morgan's Irish Pub
16 Teatr Ateneum
18 Cul-de-Sac
23 Desa
28 Main Post Office
29 Philharmonic Hall
30 EMPiK Megastore
34 Centrum Sztuki Studio
35 Tourist Office
36 AmEx Office

37 Palace of Culture & Science
41 Orbis Travel
43 EMPiK Megastore
44 Former Communist Party Headquarters
45 National Museum
46 Polish Army Museum
48 Australian Embassy
49 Kasy ZASP
50 Western Union
51 Fotoplastikon
52 British Council
53 Bookland
55 Tourist Office
56 Polski Express Bus Stop
57 LOT Office
60 Ground Zero
62 Galeria Grafiki I Plakatu
64 St Alexander's Church
69 Księgarmia Muzyczna Odeon
71 American Medical Centre
72 Bulgarian Embassy
73 Parliament House
74 US Embassy
75 French Embassy
76 Hungarian Embassy
77 Romanian Embassy
80 Pub Internetowy Piękna
81 American Bookstore
84 Desa
85 Orbis Travel
87 Czech Embassy
88 UK Embassy
90 Ujazdów Castle; Centre for Contemporary Art

longer in summer), including at Plac Zamkowy (Royal Square), the Warsaw central train station (main hall), the central bus terminal and at Okęcie airport (arrival hall).

Another state-run tourist office, Warszawska Informacja Turystyczna i Kulturalna (☎ 656 68 54, fax 656 71 36, msitur@msiwarszawa.com.pl, W www.msiwarszawa.com.pl) is in the Palace of Culture and Science (the main entrance is from ul Marszałkowska), and is open 9am to 6pm daily.

The private tourist office (☎/fax 635 18 81, e mit@mufa.pl), Plac Zamkowy 1/13 opposite the Royal Castle, is open 9am to 6pm weekdays, 10am to 6pm Saturday, 11am to 6pm Sunday (may stay open until 8pm daily in July and August).

Staff at all three tourist offices are knowledgeable and helpful, all speak English, and all sell maps and tourist publications.

Tourist Publications
Pick up a copy of the free monthly magazines *Warszawa: What, Where, When* and *Welcome to Warsaw* at the tourist offices or at luxury hotels. Both include a map of central Warsaw and current information about tourist facilities. Far better is the comprehensive monthly *Warsaw Insider* (US$1.50), which also comes with a map of the central area. Also excellent is the bi-monthly *Warsaw in Your Pocket* (US$1.50).

A booklet listing youth hostels in Poland is available (US$4) from Polskie Towarzystwo Schronisk Młodzieżowych

WARSAW

(PTSM; ☎ 849 81 28), ul Chocimska 28, room 20 (open 8am to 3pm weekdays).

Money

Kantors are easy to find around the centre. Some of them open 24 hours, but they lower the exchange rate at night, so try to plan ahead and avoid large night-time transactions.

The Bank Pekao, which cashes travellers cheques, has a dozen offices in the city, including those at Plac Bankowy 2, ul Mazowiecka 14, ul Czackiego 21/23, ul Grójecka 1/3 and Al Jerozolimskie 65/79. You can also get cash advances on Visa and MasterCard here, either from the cashier or the bank's ATM. There has also been a rash of ATMs installed, independent of the banks, around the city centre.

Travellers cheques can also be cashed at the American Express office (☎ 581 51 15), ul Sienna 39 (open 9am to 6pm weekdays), which exchanges its own cheques as well as those of other major banks, but the rate may be lower than that at Bank Pekao. However, staff speak English and there are no long lines, unlike in the banks. It's here that you apply for a refund of lost or stolen AmEx cheques. AmEx also provides a poste restante service – see the following section.

There's another AmEx outlet (☎ 630 69 52) in the Marriott Hotel at Al Jerozolimskie 65/79, open 8am to 8pm weekdays, 10am to 6pm weekends. It changes travellers cheques but doesn't have a poste restante service.

Western Union Money Transfer (general information on ☎ 636 56 88 or toll-free ☎ 0800 120 224) can be found at a number of locations, including its main central office at Al Jerozolimskie 27.

Post & Communications

Warsaw has over 100 post offices, the main one being at ul Świętokrzyska 31/33. It's open 8am to 8pm for mail and round the clock for telephones. You can also send faxes from here. If you're going to send parcels abroad, there is a packing service and you don't have to worry about customs.

Poste restante is at window No 12. If you want letters sent to you, the address is c/o

Poste Restante, Poczta Główna, ul Świętokrzyska 31/33, 00–001 Warszawa 1. The mail is kept for 14 working days.

AmEx card holders can also receive poste restante mail through the AmEx office. Letters should be addressed c/o American Express Poland, ul Sienna 39, 00–121 Warszawa. Mail is kept for three months.

Public telephones are still in short supply and some are out of order. Virtually all public phones these days only operate on magnetic or electronic phonecards.

Email & Internet Access

Places providing email and Internet facilities include:

Casablanca (☎ 828 14 47) ul Krakowskie Przedmieście 4/6
EMPiK (☎ 551 44 55) in Junior Department Store, 2nd floor, ul Marszałkowska 104
Klub Podróżników Internetowych Wiedza (☎ 838 44 27) Al Jana Pawła II 57
Pub Internetowy Piękna (☎ 622 33 77) ul Piękna 68A
Salonik Internetowy (☎ 628 64 35) in Salon Prasowy Ruch, ul Bagatela 14
Sonata (☎ 824 27 08) in Kino Ochota, ul Grójecka 65
studio.tpi (☎ 826 59 53) ul Świętokrzyska 3
W Sieci (☎ 831 04 95) ul Freta 49/51

All the listed places are open daily and charge between US$1.50 and US$3 per hour. Sonata and Wiedza are open 24 hours and may have discounted night-time fees. The British Council (☎ 695 59 00), Al Jerozolimskie 59, provides free Internet access for its library members (US$12 for a half-year membership).

Travel Agencies

Orbis Travel is the largest agency, with offices all over town, including ones at ul Bracka 16 (☎ 827 72 65), ul Świętokrzyska 20 (☎ 826 20 16) and Plac Konstytucji 4 (☎ 629 92 01).

Student travel is handled by Almatur (☎ 826 35 12, 826 26 39, ☒ www.almatur.com.pl), ul Kopernika 23. It organises cheap sailing, kayaking and horse-riding summer holidays, sells international air, bus and ferry tickets, and may have attractive discounts for students and people under 26 years. It also issues ISIC cards (US$7).

Sonata Travel (☎ 636 06 48), ul Bellottiego 1, represents STA Travel and has various cheap international air fares for particular age groups and for students.

Trakt (☎ 827 80 68, e trakt@trakt .com.pl, W www.trakt.com.pl), ul Kredytowa 6, offers guides in several major languages, English included (US$90 per group for up to five hours plus US$15 for each extra hour). The private tourist office (☎ 635 18 81), Plac Zamkowy 1/13, arranges foreign-language guides for a similar price.

Our Roots (☎/fax 620 05 56), ul Twarda 6, next to the Nożyk Synagogue, is the Jewish travel bureau. The agency stocks some guidebooks and general publications referring to Jewish issues, and offers daily tours around Jewish monuments in Warsaw (US$25 per person). Other tours can be organised on request.

Bookshops
Some of the widest selection of maps and guidebooks (including Lonely Planet guidebooks) can be found in Sklep Podróżnika (☎ 822 54 87), ul Kaliska 8/10.

The American Bookstore (W www .americanbookstore.pl) is one of the best places for English-language publications, including contemporary and classic literature, coffee-table books, magazines and specialist fares. It also has a choice of guidebooks, including most Lonely Planet titles. It can be found at three locations: (☎ 827 48 52), ul Nowy Świat 61; (☎ 660 56 37), ul Koszykowa 55; and in Sadyba Best Mall (☎ 550 31 73), ul Powsińska 31.

Other places for English-language stuff include Co Liber (☎ 828 05 88), Plac Bankowy 4; Leksykon (☎ 826 45 33), ul Nowy Świat 41; and Bookland (☎ 625 41 46), Al Jerozolimskie 61.

The best bookshop with French-language literature is Marianne (☎ 826 62 71) in the French Institute at ul Senatorska 38. It also has a decent selection of French press.

Foreign newspapers and magazines are available from some larger newsagencies,

or you can try the foyers of top-class hotels. The widest selection, however, is to be found in two EMPiK Megastores, at ul Nowy Świat 15/17 (☎ 827 06 50) and ul Marszałkowska 116/122 (☎ 827 82 96).

Cultural Centres
All of the foreign cultural centres have their own libraries with a selection of books and press from their country.

Austrian Institute of Culture (☎ 620 96 20) ul Próżna 8
British Council (☎ 695 59 00) Al Jerozolimskie 59
Cervantes Institute (Spanish) (☎ 622 54 19) ul Myśliwiecka 4
French Institute (☎ 827 76 40) ul Senatorska 38
Goethe Institute (German) (☎ 656 60 50) Palace of Culture and Science
Italian Institute of Culture (☎ 826 62 88) ul Foksal 11
Russian Culture and Information Centre (☎ 827 76 21) ul Foksal 10

Laundry
Alba laundry, ul Karmelicka 17, corner of ul Anielewicza (open 9am to 5pm weekdays, 9am to 1pm Saturday), charges US$7 to wash and dry up to 6kg. You're asked to call ☎ 831 73 17 a couple of days ahead to make a reservation. Bring your own detergent or buy some in the laundry.

Medical Services
There's a wide network of pharmacies in Warsaw; ask for an *apteka*. There are always several of them that stay open all night; a list is given in the *Gazeta Wyborcza* daily (its Supermarket section).

If you happen to get sick, look for an outpatient clinic *(przychodnia)*. There are plenty of them and you can get general information on ☎ 827 89 62 (8am to 8pm weekdays, 8am to 3pm Saturday, English sometimes spoken). If possible, ring your embassy for recommendations.

One of the best (but most expensive) places to try is the American Medical Center (☎ 622 04 89, emergency 24-hour mobile ☎ 0602 24 30 24, W www.amcenters.pl), ul Wilcza 23 m 29. This small private outpatient clinic has English-speaking staff that handle some services in-house; if they can't, they will refer you to other providers.

Also reliable is the CM Medical Center (☎ 458 70 00, 630 30 30, W www.cm-lim .com.pl) in the Marriott Hotel building. It has English-speaking specialist doctors, its own ambulance service, carries out laboratory tests and attends house calls. It's open 7am to 9pm weekdays, 8am to 8pm Saturday, 9am to 1pm Sunday.

The Damian Medical Centre (☎ 847 33 13, 853 16 44, W www.damian.com.pl), ul Wałbrzyska 46, is another reputable institution, which has an outpatient clinic and hospital facilities.

The Danish company Falck (☎ 96 75), staffed with English-speaking attendants, has no clinic but will provide free information on where to go in case of emergency. It has its own 24-hour ambulance service and makes house calls. Falck has branch offices in Gdańsk, Katowice, Kraków, Poznań, Szczecin and Wrocław, contactable on the same local number (☎ 96 75) in each city.

The city ambulance service can be contacted on ☎ 999 and ☎ 628 24 24, but don't count on staff speaking English.

Avoid drinking Warsaw's tap water. Its quality is so bad that half the city's population doesn't drink it either, opting instead for Oligocene water taken from wells several hundred metres deep. This water has undergone centuries of natural filtration and is drinkable without any treatment. There are about 150 wells in Warsaw, 50 of which are accessible to the public. City dwellers carrying water home from them in bottles, buckets, jerry cans etc is a typical Warsaw street scene. Bottled water is easily available from shops and supermarkets.

Emergency
See the boxed text 'Emergency' in the Facts for the Visitor chapter.

Dangers & Annoyances
Warsaw is perhaps the least safe Polish city, so you should take precautions while strolling about streets at night, and watch your possessions on public transport and in other crowded places. Beware of 'mafia' taxis (see the boxed text 'Welcome to the Land of Pirate Taxis' later in this chapter), and be on guard in and around the central train station (see the boxed text 'Train Theft Warning' in the Getting Around chapter, and Train under Getting There & Away later in this chapter).

ROYAL CASTLE & AROUND
Like most visitors, you'll probably start your sightseeing from the Old Town area or, more precisely, from **Castle Square** (Plac Zamkowy), which is the usual gateway to the Old Town. The square got its present shape in the 19th century when the fortified walls were pulled down. Remnants of the fortifications, most notably a 14th-century Gothic bridge on the western edge of the square, were excavated and subsequently restored.

In the centre of the square stands the 22m-high **Monument to Sigismund III Vasa** (Kolumna Zygmunta III Wazy), the king who moved the capital from Kraków to Warsaw. It's Poland's second-oldest secular monument (after Gdańsk's Neptune), erected by the king's son in 1644. The bronze statue, once gilded, represents the king in a coronation cloak over a suit of armour, a sabre and a cross in his hands. The column was knocked down during WWII, but the statue survived and was placed on a new column four years after the war.

The eastern side of the square is occupied by the **Royal Castle** (*Zamek Królewski;* ☎ *657 21 70, Plac Zamkowy 4; adult/ student US$2-4/1-2, free Sun; open 10am-6pm Tues-Sat, 11am-6pm Sun & Mon mid-May–mid-Sept;   10am-3pm   Tues-Sun mid-Sept–mid-May).*

You visit some rooms on the ground floor, but it's the king's apartments on the upper level that really demonstrate the castle's splendour. The **Ballroom** there is the largest and most impressive of all the castle's chambers. Built in the 1740s, it had many uses, serving as an audience room, concert hall and a place for important court meetings. The enormous ceiling painting, *The Dissolution of Chaos*, is a postwar re-creation of a work by Marcello Bacciarelli.

Behold, a Castle Reborn

The Royal Castle's history goes back to the 14th century, when a wooden stronghold was built by the dukes of Mazovia and later rebuilt in brick. Greatly extended when the capital was moved to Warsaw, the castle became the seat of the king and the Sejm and remained so until the fall of the Republic in 1795. It then served the tsars, and in 1918, after Poland had regained its independence, it became the residence of the president. The castle survived most of WWII without major damage, but after the Warsaw Uprising in 1944 it was blown up by the Nazis and virtually nothing was left.

It wasn't until 1971 that reconstruction began, and by 1984 the splendid baroque castle stood again as if nothing had happened. Given its spiritual importance as the very symbol of Warsaw, no wonder thousands of Poles living all over the world donated funds for the castle's rebirth, and plenty of volunteers participated in the building's re-creation. Although the brick structure is a copy, many original architectural pieces have been incorporated into the walls. The castle's 300 rooms have been filled with period furniture and works of art, some of which had been hidden elsewhere and survived WWII, while most have been collected from other historic buildings.

A good part of the castle's interior is now a museum, providing an insight into how royalty once lived. The rooms are crammed with *objets d'art*, as they were two centuries ago, and you wouldn't think anything is missing. It's particularly remarkable, keeping in mind that there was nothing here just 30 years ago.

Next to the Ballroom is a magnificent **Knight's Hall** adorned with six large paintings by Bacciarelli, which depict important events from Polish history. The **Marble Room** to one side boasts 22 portraits of Polish kings, from Bolesław Chrobry to Stanisław August Poniatowski, who himself ordered the collection. In the same area is the lavishly decorated **Throne Room**.

Another of the castle's highlights is the **Canaletto Room**, with 23 paintings by Bernardo Bellotto (who used the name of his famous uncle and therefore is commonly known in Poland as Canaletto). Bellotto (1721–80) documented with amazing detail the best of Warsaw's architecture of the time. These paintings, which survived WWII, were of great help in reconstructing the city's historic monuments.

You'll also see a collection of paintings by Jan Matejko, including one of his most famous works, *The Constitution of the 3rd of May*, the act itself having been proclaimed from the castle in 1791.

There are two routes of the castle interior visited by guided tours. Route 1 includes the ground-level rooms, the parliament chambers and Matejko's paintings, and costs US$2 (US$1 for students). Route 2 covers most of the castle's highlights, principally the great and king's apartments, for US$4 (US$2 for students). The tour ticket allows you to visit other rooms and exhibitions not included in the two routes, including the castle's cellars.

Guided tours in English and other major languages are available for US$18 extra per group; call in advance on ☎ 657 21 78, though English and German-speaking guides can usually be obtained at short notice.

Admission is free on Sunday, but come early as plenty of people take advantage of this fact and the number of tickets is limited. Visitors go around the castle rooms on their own on a special route which includes selected parts of routes 1 and 2, and there's no guide service on that day. The detailed captions in Polish and English are a good help, and you can also buy guidebooks on the castle published in several major languages.

OLD TOWN

Warsaw's Old Town (Stare Miasto) was rebuilt from the foundations up on what, after WWII, was nothing but a heap of rubble. Official records put the level of the quarter's destruction at 90%. The monumental reconstruction took place between 1949 and 1963 and aimed to restore the town to its 17th- and 18th-century appearance, eliminating all accretions from later periods. There's now not a single building in the area that looks younger than 200 years. Every authentic architectural fragment found among the ruins was incorporated in the restoration. Unesco's decision to include Warsaw's Old Town on the World Heritage List is proof of its value and recognition of the work done by Polish restorers.

Entering the Old Town from Plac Zamkowy through ul Świętojańska, historically its main artery, you'll soon come to **St John's Cathedral** (*Katedra Św Jana;* ☎ *831 02 89, ul Świętojańska 8; open to visitors 10am-1pm & 3pm-6pm Mon-Sat, 3pm-6pm Sun*). The oldest of Warsaw's churches, it was built at the beginning of the 15th century on the site of a wooden church, and subsequently remodelled several times. Razed during WWII, it regained its Gothic shape through postwar reconstruction, except for the facade, which is a new design in a mock-Gothic style.

Roofed in by a gracious Gothic vault, the interior is modestly decorated; only a couple of tombstones survived out of about 200. Look for the red-marble Renaissance tomb of the last Mazovian dukes, which is in the right-hand aisle. Go downstairs to the crypt (the entrance is from the left-hand aisle) to see more tombstones, including that of Nobel prizewinning writer Henryk Sienkiewicz.

Just a few steps north along ul Świętojańska is the **Old Town Square**

(Rynek Starego Miasta), the loveliest square in Warsaw and one of the most amazing in Poland. If you had been here in 1945 you would have seen a sea of rubble with the walls of two houses (Nos 34 and 36) sticking up out of it. Today, the Rynek is a fine blend of Renaissance and baroque with Gothic and neoclassical elements. There used to be a town hall in the middle of the square but it was pulled down in 1817 and never rebuilt. Today, you'll find the **Mermaid** (Syrena) here, the symbol of Warsaw, cast in 1855.

The Rynek is harmonious if diverse in style and decoration and, more importantly, doesn't give the impression of being a replica. It's alive and atmospheric, particularly in summer, when it fills up with a dozen open-air cafes and stalls selling paintings and drawings.

The **Historical Museum of Warsaw** (*Muzeum Historyczne Warszawy;* ☎ *635 16 25, Rynek Starego Miasta 42; adult/student US$1.50/0.75, free Sun; open 11am-6pm Tues & Thur, 10am-3.30pm Wed & Fri, 10.30am-4pm Sat & Sun*) occupies the entire northern side of the Rynek. In 60 rooms on four storeys, you'll find an extensive collection which illustrates the history of Warsaw from its beginnings until the present day. Documents, maps, drawings, paintings, armour, crafts and other *Varsoviana*, all displayed in period interiors, make this one of the city's most charming museums. Don't miss a startling documentary, screened a few times daily, about the destruction and reconstruction of the city; the English version is usually at noon.

The **Museum of Literature** (*Muzeum Literatury;* ☎ *831 40 61, Rynek Starego Miasta 20; admission US$1.50; open 10am-3pm Mon, Tues & Fri, 11am-6pm Wed & Thur, 11am-5pm Sun*) features a permanent exhibition dedicated to Adam Mickiewicz and temporary shows related to mostly Polish, sometimes foreign, writers.

From the Rynek it's worth strolling about the neighbouring streets. Wander to the picturesque, triangular Kanonia square behind the cathedral which, until the 19th century, served as a church graveyard. Note the

Marie Curie – Discoverer of Radium & Polonium

One of the major contributors to modern physics, Marie Curie laid the foundations for radiography, nuclear physics and cancer therapy. This Polish-born French physicist won numerous awards and distinctions, including two Nobel prizes. Determined, tireless and compassionate, she paid the highest price for her scientific work – it cost her her life. Albert Einstein, her friend, once wrote that 'she was the only person that had not been corrupted by fame'. She is the first (and so far the only) female of merit buried (in 1995) in the crypt of the famous Panthéon of Paris, among such luminaries as Voltaire, Émile Zola and Victor Hugo.

Born in 1867 in Warsaw (then under Russian partition) into a family of Polish teachers, Maria Skłodowska lived here for the first 24 years of her life. She completed her education at a local state lyceum with a gold medal, by which time she had developed a strong fascination for science and had decided to pursue a scientific career. Under Russian rule, however, women were not allowed to enter institutions of higher education.

Therefore, Skłodowska went to Paris in 1891 to study. Living a humble, almost Spartan, life, she studied physics and mathematics at the Sorbonne, earning degrees in both subjects. In 1895 she married French physical chemist Pierre Curie (1859–1906), and their scientific partnership proved to be extremely fruitful, even though their living conditions were deplorable. Their laboratory was not much more than a barn.

Their investigation of the radiation of uranium ore resulted in the discovery in 1898 of two new radioactive chemical elements, polonium (named after Marie's motherland) and radium. In 1903, they both, together with Henri Becquerel, were awarded the Nobel prize for physics, for the discovery of natural radioactivity.

After Pierre's tragic death in a traffic accident in 1906, Marie devoted all her energy to the research work they had begun together. She succeeded him as lecturer and head of the physics department at the Sorbonne – the first woman ever to teach in this 650-year-old university. Two years later she became titular professor and in 1911 was awarded the Nobel prize for chemistry, for the isolation of pure radium.

Marie Curie was instrumental in founding the Radium Institute in Paris in 1914, which later became a universal centre for nuclear physics and chemistry. She also helped establish the Radium Institute in Warsaw in 1932, in the country of her birth, with which she always maintained close links. She died in a sanatorium in southern France in 1934 of leukaemia caused by prolonged exposure to radiation. By that time she was almost blind, her fingers burnt with 'her dear radium'.

Marie Curie was the first woman ever to be awarded a Nobel prize and the first person to be awarded twice. She is also the only woman to date with two Nobel prizes in science; the only other scientists with two Nobel prizes are US physicist John Bardeen and English biochemist Frederick Sanger.

Her example inspired scientists of a younger generation, including her own daughter Irène who, with her husband, physicist Jean-Frédéric Joliot-Curie, conducted experiments which led to the discovery of artificial radioactivity. This earned them the Nobel prize for chemistry in 1935 – only the second in history for a female scientist, the first having been won by Irène's mother. And like her mother, Irène also died of leukaemia.

KN

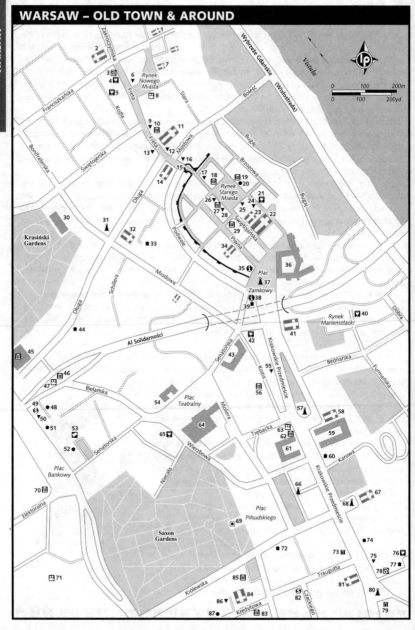

WARSAW – OLD TOWN & AROUND

PLACES TO STAY
33 Bursa Szkolnictwa Artystycznego
39 Dom Literatury
44 Pokoje Gościnne Federacji Metalowcy
60 Le Royal Méridien Bristol Hotel
72 Hotel Sofitel Victoria
77 Hotel Harenda

PLACES TO EAT
6 Restauracja Ekologiczna Nove Miasto
9 Café Galerie Belle Epoque
12 Pożegnanie Z Afryką
13 Restauracja Pod Samsonem
16 Bar Mleczny Pod Barbakanem
17 Same Fusy
24 Restauracja Tsarina
25 Restauracja Bazyliszek
26 Restauracja U Fukiera
28 Dom Restauracyjny Gessler
50 Salad Bar Tukan
55 Restauracja Siedem Grzechów
75 Bar Mleczny Uniwersytecki
86 Salad Bar Tukan

OTHER
1 Church of the Visitation of the Virgin
2 Franciscan Church
3 W Sieci
4 Jazz Café Helicon
5 Pub Koźla

7 Church of the Nuns of the Holy Sacrament
8 Kino Wars
10 Maria Skłodowska-Curie Museum
11 St Hyacinthus' Church
14 Church of the Holy Spirit
15 Barbican
18 Historical Museum of Warsaw
19 Museum of Literature
20 Dom Sztuki Ludowej
21 John Bull Pub
22 St John's Cathedral
23 Jesuit Church
27 Galeria Plakatu
29 Zapiecek Art Gallery
30 Krasiński Palace
31 Monument to the Warsaw Uprising
32 Polish Army's Field Cathedral
34 St Martin's Church
35 Tourist Office
36 Royal Castle
37 Monument to Sigismund III Vasa
38 Tourist Office
40 Pub Pod Baryłka
41 St Anne's Church
42 Irish Pub
43 Primate's Palace
45 Archaeological Museum
46 Museum of Independence
47 Cinema Paradiso
48 Jewish Historical Institute
49 Bank Pekao
51 Co Liber

52 French Institute
53 Belgian Embassy
54 Jabłonowski Palace
56 Museum of Caricature
57 Monument to Adam Mickiewicz
58 Carmelite Church
59 Radziwiłł Palace
61 Potocki Palace
62 Art Gallery
63 Kino Kultura & Rejs
64 Grand Theatre
65 Barbados
66 Monument to Marshal Józef Piłsudski
67 Church of the Nuns of the Visitation
68 Monument to Cardinal Stefan Wyszyński
69 Tomb of the Unknown Soldier
70 John Paul II Collection
71 Kino Feliks
73 Czapski Palace; Academy of Fine Arts
74 Warsaw University
76 Pub Harenda
78 Casablanca
79 Staszic Palace
80 Monument to Nicolaus Copernicus
81 Holy Cross Church
82 Bank Pekao
83 Ethnographic Museum
84 Evangelical Church
85 Zachęta Modern Art Gallery
87 Trakt Guide Service

gallery at the southern end, which once gave Poland's kings direct access from the castle to the cathedral. Go to the viewpoint on ul Brzozowa which looks over the Vistula, then continue north along this street and return to the Rynek through a long, narrow stone stairway, the Kamienne Schodki (Stone Steps). Visit the Zapiecek Art Gallery, just south of the Rynek, which often holds interesting exhibitions of modern art.

Going north along ul Nowomiejska you'll get to the **Barbican** (Barbakan), a powerful, semicircular Gothic structure topped with a decorative Renaissance parapet, built on a bridge over a moat as a reinforcement of the medieval fortifications. It was partially dismantled in the 19th century, but reconstructed after WWII, giving more authenticity and atmosphere to the Old Town.

NEW TOWN

The New Town (Nowe Miasto) was founded at the end of the 14th century, not long after the Old Town, and in 1408 was granted a ducal privilege which allowed it to have its own jurisdiction and administration. Since then, there have been two towns half a kilometre apart, each with its own main square, town hall and parish church. The New Town was inhabited mostly by people of lower social standing. Consequently, its buildings were simpler and made of wood and there were never fortifications like those around the prosperous Old Town.

Heading north from the Barbican along ul Freta, the New Town's main street, you'll soon get to the house at No 16 which was the family home of Marie Curie, discoverer of radium and polonium and twice Nobel prizewinner, for physics in 1903 and chemistry in 1911. The **Museum of Maria Skłodowska-Curie** (☎ 831 80 92, ul Freta 16; adult/student US$1.50/0.75; open 10am-4pm Tues-Sun) has a modest exhibition on the life and work of this distinguished scientist, who was born here in 1867 but spent her adult life in France.

Continue along ul Freta to the **New Town Square** (Rynek Nowego Miasta). Like its Old Town counterpart, this square also boasted a town hall, but it was pulled down at the beginning of the 19th century. A cast-iron well marks the place where the town hall once stood.

The **Church of the Nuns of the Holy Sacrament** (Kościół Sakramentek; ☎ 635 71 13, Rynek Nowego Miasta 2) at the square is the work of the most prominent architect of the baroque period in Poland, Tylman van Gameren. Dutch by birth, he settled in Poland and designed countless churches, palaces and the like all over the country. Laid out on the plan of a Greek cross and topped by a dome on an octagonal drum, the church was an exquisite example of baroque sacral architecture, with a richly decorated interior. During the 1944 Warsaw Uprising the church was used as a hospital, and several hundred people died inside it when it was bombed.

Just north of the square is the **Church of the Visitation of the Virgin Mary** (Kościół Nawiedzenia NMP; ☎ 831 24 73, ul Przyrynek 2). Built in the 15th century as the parish church of the New Town, it was later enlarged several times and got a freestanding belfry in 1581. Its interior has some fine Gothic vaulting.

WEST OF THE OLD TOWN

The route suggested below will allow you to see some of the sights to the west and south-west of the Old Town. All are within easy walking distance and are shown on the Warsaw – Old Town & Around map.

Take ul Długa off the Barbican to the corner of ul Miodowa, where you'll find the fair-sized 17th-century Piarist Church, today doing the honours as the **Polish Army's Field Cathedral** (Katedra Polowa Wojska Polskiego; ul Długa 13/15), the soldiers' place of worship. A large anchor and aeroplane propeller, in front of the church, pay homage to the sailors of the Navy and pilots of the Air Force, respectively, who lost their lives fighting for the motherland. The church's main door features bas-reliefs of the major battles fought by the Polish forces. Do go inside to see numerous commemorative plaques in memory of Polish soldiers who perished on various fronts all over the world.

Across the street from the church is the **Monument to the Warsaw Uprising** (Pomnik Powstania Warszawskiego). Only in the late 1980s did the government pay tribute to the heroes of one of the most heroic and tragic acts in the nation's history. The monument was unveiled on 1 August 1989 on the 45th anniversary of the uprising.

Slightly farther west on the opposite side of ul Bonifraterska is the large **Krasiński Palace** (Pałac Krasińskich), considered one of the most splendid baroque palaces in Warsaw. Designed by the ubiquitous Tylman van Gameren, the palace was built in 1677–83, and though it was later remodelled several times, postwar reconstruction gave it back its original decor. An elaborate triangular tympanum on the front facade is worth a closer look, as is the other tympanum on the garden elevation. The garden itself, also designed by van Gameren, was reputedly one of the most fashionable in the city, but not much of the original layout remains.

Turn back and continue south-west along ul Długa to the former **Arsenal** (Arsenał), a massive 17th-century building which now houses the **Archaeological Museum** (Muzeum Archeologiczne; ☎ 831 15 37, ul Długa 52; adult/student US$1.50/0.75, free Sun; open 9am-4pm Mon-Fri, 10am-4pm Sun). The permanent exhibition on the prehistory of Poland is periodically enlivened by temporary displays.

A short walk south-east will bring you to the Radziwiłł Palace, which houses the **Museum of Independence** (*Muzeum Niepodległości;* ☎ 826 90 91, Al Solidarności 62; *adult/student US$1.50/0.75, free Sun; open 10am-5pm Tues-Fri, 10am-4pm Sat & Sun*). The museum stages temporary exhibitions related to Poland's struggles for independence.

The nearby blue skyscraper marks Plac Bankowy (Bank Square). Just behind it is the **Jewish Historical Institute** (*Żydowski Instytut Historyczny;* ☎ 827 92 21, ul Tłomackie 3/5; *adult/student US$2.50/1.25; open 9am-4pm Mon-Wed & Fri, 11am-6pm Thur*). Located in what, before WWII, was the main Judaic library, the museum features a collection of paintings, sculptures and old religious objects related to Jewish culture, and photos from the Warsaw Ghetto of 1940–43.

The western side of Plac Bankowy is lined by two massive neoclassical palaces, now the seat of the city municipal authorities. At the southern end of the square is the building of the former stock exchange and the Bank of Poland. It's now home to the **John Paul II Collection** (*Kolekcja im Jana Pawła II;* ☎ 620 27 25, Plac Bankowy 1; *adult/student US$1.50/0.75; open 10am-4pm Tues-Sun*). Here you'll find works by some of the best European painters, including Cranach, Rubens, Velázquez, Goya, Renoir, Sisley, Van Gogh and Chirico. The core of the collection was assembled by the Carrol-Porczyński family of Polish emigres and donated to the Polish Church – that's why the pope's name is included in the name of the museum and his portraits adorn the collection.

Cross the square and take ul Senatorska to Plac Teatralny (Theatre Square), bordered on the south by the colossal **Grand Theatre** (*Teatr Wielki;* ☎ 826 50 19, Plac Teatralny 1*). This neoclassical edifice, thought to be the largest theatre building in Europe, was designed by Antonio Corazzi and erected in 1825–33. After it was burnt out during WWII, only the facade was restored; the rest was reshaped to suit modern needs. Inside is an opera auditorium capable of seating 1900 spectators, and two smaller stages. Opposite the theatre is the

Jabłonowski Palace (Pałac Jabłonowskich), rebuilt in 1997 to its pre-WWII shape.

From Plac Teatralny, proceed along ul Senatorska towards the Old Town. The right-hand side of the street is dominated by the **Primate's Palace** (Pałac Prymasowski), yet another neoclassical affair, adorned with a colonnaded portico and semicircular wings. If you still have an appetite for palaces, take ul Miodowa to the left where, 400m along, you'll find no less than seven of them.

ALONG THE ROYAL WAY

The Royal Way (Trakt Królewski) refers to a 4km-long route from the Royal Castle to Łazienki Palace, the royal summer residence. The route follows Krakowskie Przedmieście, Nowy Świat and Aleje Ujazdowskie, and includes a number of sights on and near the Way. It's best to do the whole stretch on foot and allow a full day for sightseeing. The time you need will depend largely on how long you spend in museums.

Beginning from Castle Square, the first stop is **St Anne's Church** (*Kościół Św Anny;* ☎ 826 89 91, ul Krakowskie Przedmieście 68*). One of the most attractive city churches, it was erected in 1454 but was burnt down by the Swedes and rebuilt in the 1660s in baroque style. Further alterations gave it a neoclassical facade, while the freestanding belfry acquired a neo-Renaissance form. The church miraculously escaped major damage in the war. Its interior boasts an 18th-century trompe l'œil painting on the vault, a baroque high altar, pulpit and organ. You can go up to the terrace on top of the belfry for a good view over Castle Square.

Continuing south, you'll pass the **Monument to Adam Mickiewicz**, the most renowned Polish Romantic poet, just before reaching the former **Carmelite Church** (*Kościół Karmelitów;* ☎ 826 05 31, ul Krakowskie Przedmieście 52/54*). This church, too, escaped the ravages of war and, like St Anne's, has 18th-century fittings, including the high altar designed by Tylman van Gameren.

A short detour along ul Kozia will bring you to the **Museum of Caricature** (*Muzeum Karykatury;* ☎ 827 88 95, ul Kozia 11;

adult/student US$1.50/0.75; open 11am-5pm Tues-Sun). It has a collection of some 15,000 original works by Polish and foreign caricaturists plus satirical and humorous books, magazines etc.

Next along the Royal Way, two grand palaces face each other on opposite sides of the street. To the west stands the baroque **Potocki Palace** (Pałac Potockich), now the headquarters of the Ministry of Culture and Art, its courtyard guarded by two wrought-iron gates. The Guardhouse *(Kordegarda; ☎ 620 02 31, Krakowskie Przedmieście 15/17; admission free; open 10am-6pm Tues-Sun)* houses a gallery of modern art.

Across the road, the even larger neoclassical **Radziwiłł Palace** (Pałac Radziwiłłów) is the Polish equivalent of the White House. The palace is guarded by four stone lions, reinforced by an equestrian **Statue of Prince Józef Poniatowski**, sword in hand, in the palace forecourt. The prince was the nephew of the last Polish king, Stanisław August, and commander in chief of the Polish army of the Duchy of Warsaw created by Napoleon. The 1832 statue, based on antique models, is the work of Danish sculptor Bertel Thorvaldsen.

Continuing south, you'll pass between two neo-Renaissance-style hotels, the Europejski (1877) and the Bristol (1901), and soon get to the **Church of the Nuns of the Visitation** *(Kościół Wizytek; ul Krakowskie Przedmieście 34)*, with its elegant baroque facade. The highlight of its interior is an ebony tabernacle (1654), lavishly ornamented with silver, at the high altar. Also note the boat-shaped rococo pulpit (1760), looking as if it's sailing in particularly heavy weather.

In front of the church stands the **Monument to Cardinal Stefan Wyszyński**, unveiled in 1987. The Primate of Poland for three decades (1951–81) and a tireless defender of human rights during the communist regime, he came to be known as the 'Primate of the Millennium'.

At this point it's worth taking a short detour off the Royal Way. Take ul Królewska, which opens onto Plac Piłsudskiego (Piłsudski Square) with the **Tomb of the Unknown Soldier** (Grób Nieznanego Żołnierza) on its western side. In the 18th century the mighty Saxon Palace (Pałac Saski) here served the king as a residence, with the magnificent French-style Saxon Gardens (Ogród Saski) stretching behind it. The tomb is actually the only surviving fragment of the former palace, while the gardens were turned into an English landscape park in the 19th century. The only reminder of the original layout is the central alley shaded by old chestnut trees. Be at the tomb on Sunday at noon when the ceremonial changing of the guard is held.

South of the tomb across ul Królewska is the **Zachęta Modern Art Gallery** *(☎ 827 58 54, Plac Małachowskiego 3; adult/student US$2.50/2, free Fri; open 10am-6pm Tues-Sun)*, the leading venue for temporary exhibitions, where you'll always find something interesting.

To the south is the 18th-century **Evangelical Church** *(☎ 827 68 17, Plac Małachowskiego 3)*. A circular edifice topped with the largest dome in Warsaw, the church is renowned for its excellent acoustics and is the venue for a variety of musical events.

Across the street is the **Ethnographic Museum** *(Muzeum Etnograficzne; ☎ 827 76 41, ul Kredytowa 1; adult/student US$1/0.50; open 9am-4pm Tues, Thur & Fri, 11am-6pm Wed, 10am-5pm Sat & Sun)*, which provides an insight into Polish folklore and crafts. It also has a collection of tribal art from Africa, Oceania and Latin America.

If you follow ul Traugutta eastwards you'll return to the Royal Way next to the late baroque **Czapski Palace** (Pałac Czapskich), now home to the Academy of Fine Arts.

Directly opposite the academy, behind a decorative entry gate with the Polish eagle on top, is **Warsaw University** *(Uniwersytet Warszawski; ☎ 620 03 81, ul Krakowskie Przedmieście 26/28)*, which occupies a whole complex of buildings. The oldest one (1634) is the **Kazimierz Palace** (Pałac Kazimierzowski) at the far eastern end of the campus, now the office of the rector. Since its founding in 1816, Warsaw University has always been a focus for independent political thinking – a child unloved first by tsars and later by communist governments. In the postwar period, most student protests started here. It's also pretty active culturally – go onto campus to see what's happening.

Because it's so close to the university, the **Holy Cross Church** (*Kościół Św Krzyża;* ☎ 826 89 10, ul Krakowskie Przedmieście 3) has witnessed more student demonstrations and tear gas than any other church in Poland. Earlier, during the Warsaw Uprising, it was the site of heavy fighting between the insurgents and the Nazis. It was seriously damaged, but some original baroque altarpieces have survived and adorn its interior; the high altar is a replica of the original made in 1700. Note the epitaph to Frédéric Chopin on the second pillar on the left-hand side of the nave. It covers an urn containing the composer's heart, brought from Paris after Chopin's death and placed here in accordance with his will.

The southern end of Krakowskie Przedmieście is bordered by **Staszic Palace** (Pałac Staszica), designed by Antonio Corazzi (also responsible for the Grand Theatre) and built in the 1820s for the Society of Friends of Sciences. Following that tradition, the palace is today the headquarters of the Polish Academy of Sciences.

A contemplative figure sitting on a plinth in front of the palace is the **Monument to Nicolaus Copernicus** (Pomnik Mikołaja Kopernika), the great Polish astronomer who, as Poles often say, 'stopped the sun and moved the earth'. The statue is another of Bertel Thorvaldsen's works, unveiled in 1830. During WWII, the Nazis replaced the Polish plaque with a German one and later took the whole statue away for scrap. It was found after the war on a scrapheap in Silesia, and was returned to its site.

At this point, Krakowskie Przedmieście turns into Nowy Świat (literally, New World). In the 19th century and up until WWII it was the main shopping street, with fashionable cafes occupying the houses' ground floors. Though the destruction of 1944 was almost total, the reconstruction here was as meticulous as in the Old Town and gave the street back its 19th-century

neoclassical appearance, characterised by a remarkable stylistic unity. Architecture apart, it's also one of the busiest commercial streets in the city, lined with shops, boutiques, bookshops and cafes.

When strolling down Nowy Świat, take a short detour east into ul Ordynacka, which will lead you to the **Ostrogski Palace**. Placed on a high fortified platform on the Vistula escarpment, the small baroque palace (again, designed by Tylman van Gameren) is today the seat of the Chopin Society, which runs recitals and chamber music concerts in a lovely concert hall inside. There is also a small **Chopin Museum** (☎ 827 54 71, ul Okólnik 1; adult/student US$2/1; open 10am-5pm Mon, Wed & Fri, noon-6pm Thur, 10am-2pm Sat & Sun) related to the artist's life and work.

Back on the Royal Way, proceeding south, you'll get to the junction with the busy Al Jerozolimskie. The large, squat block in front of you is the former headquarters of the Polish Communist Party (Dom Partii), today the seat of the Polish stock exchange.

A little farther east towards the Vistula is the huge building of the **National Museum** (*Muzeum Narodowe;* ☎ 621 10 31, Al Jerozolimskie 3; adult/student US$2.50/1.25, free Sat; open 10am-4pm Tues, Wed & Fri, noon-5pm Thur, 10am-5pm Sat & Sun). The museum has several permanent sections, and stages various temporary exhibitions.

The ancient art, displayed on the ground floor, includes Roman, Greek, and Egyptian pieces, plus a collection of over 60 frescoes from an early Christian cathedral in Pharos, Sudan. These date from between the 8th and 12th centuries, and were discovered by a Polish archaeological team. At the far end of the exhibition hall, hidden behind the frescoed slabs, is a display of amazing Coptic crosses.

The Polish medieval art section features an excellent collection of religious painting and sculpture from all over Poland, including some of the best Gothic altarpieces you'll see anywhere in the country.

The upper floors are given over to Polish painting from the 16th century until the mid-20th century, and it's one of the most representative selections in Poland. There's also a collection of European painting, including French, Italian, German, Flemish and Dutch works, mainly from the 16th to the 18th centuries.

Next door (in the same building), the **Polish Army Museum** *(Muzeum Wojska Polskiego;* ☎ *629 52 71, Al Jerozolimslie 3; open 10am-4pm Wed-Sun)* presents the history of the Polish army from the beginning of the state until WWII. There's also a small collection of tribal weapons from Asia, Africa and Australia. Heavy armour, tanks and fighter planes used by the Polish Army during WWII are displayed in the park adjoining the museum building.

Return to Nowy Świat and follow it south to Plac Trzech Krzyży (Three Crosses Square) to have a look at the 19th-century **St Alexander's Church** (Kościół Św Aleksandra), modelled on the Roman Pantheon, in the middle of the square.

From here, the Royal Way leads down Aleje Ujazdowskie, a pleasant avenue bordered by old mansions, embassies and parks. An oasis of greenery close to the city centre, the area has long been popular with the locals for a stroll or a rest.

Go down Aleje Ujazdowskie and turn left just past a busy motorway, Trasa Łazienkowska. There, surrounded by trees, stands **Ujazdów Castle** (Zamek Ujazdowski), a stately square building adorned with four corner towers. Erected in the 1620s for King Zygmunt III Waza as his summer residence, it was burned by the Nazis in 1944, blown up by the communists in 1954 and rebuilt in the 1970s. It houses the **Centre for Contemporary Art** *(Centrum Sztuki Współczesnej;* ☎ *628 12 71, Al Ujazdowskie 6; adult/student US$2.50/1.25, free Thur; open 11am-5pm Tues-Sun, 11am-9pm Fri)*, which features temporary exhibitions.

Nearby to the south are the **Botanical Gardens** *(Ogród Botaniczny;* ☎ *628 75 14, Al Ujazdowskie 4; admission US$1; open 9am-6pm daily Apr-Oct)*, established in 1818. About 400m farther down Al Ujazdowskie is 18th-century **Belvedere Palace** *(*☎ *849 48 39, ul Belwederska 52)*. It changed owners

and appearance several times before becoming the residence of the presidents after WWI, as it was until 1994. A new exhibition dedicated to Marshal Piłsudski (who was one of the palace's residents) is to be opened here (possibly in 2002).

Between the Botanical Gardens and the Belvedere Palace stretches Łazienki Park.

ŁAZIENKI

A former summer residence of King Stanisław August Poniatowski, Łazienki *(*☎ *625 79 44, ul Agrykola 1)* is a park-and-palace complex, one of the most beautiful in the country. Once a hunting ground attached to Ujazdów Castle, the area was acquired by the king in 1776 and within a short time transformed into a splendid park complete with a palace, an amphitheatre and a number of buildings scattered around. Despite various ups and downs the complex has retained its original shape and architecture and is a good place for a leisurely stroll.

The large, 74-hectare **park** *(admission free; open to sunset)* can be entered from different sides but the most popular ways in are from Al Ujazdowskie. The **Chopin Monument** (Pomnik Chopina), just behind the middle entrance, was unveiled in 1926 and is the latest addition to the park's historic structures. Open-air Chopin concerts are held here on summer Sundays, invariably drawing crowds of music lovers and casual passers-by.

Wandering down the hill into the park, you'll come upon the **Water Reservoir** *(Wodozbiór; admission free; open 9am-4pm Tues-Sun)*, a circular structure which served to collect underground water for distribution, through wooden pipes, to the palace and its fountain. It's now an art gallery.

The nearby glazed building with a garden guarded by lions is the **Old Orangery** *(Stara Pomarańczarnia; adult/student US$1.50/1; open 9am-4pm Tues-Sun)*. It features a gallery of Polish sculpture and the Royal Theatre (Teatr Stanisławowski), one of the few theatres of its type in Europe which preserved its original 18th-century decor.

Continue downhill to the **Little White House** (Biały Domek), the first building erected in the park (1776) and a temporary residence of the king until the proper palace was built. This square wood-and-plaster structure, with four identical facades, has retained most of its 18th-century interior decoration.

From here, the King's Promenade (Promenada Królewska) will take you to the **Palace on the Isle** (Pałac Na Wyspie) the former residence of the king. Like most other Łazienki buildings, the palace was designed by the court architect Domenico Merlini. It was constructed on an islet in the middle of an elongated lake, using an existing bathhouse (in Polish, *łazienki*, hence the name of the whole complex, pronounced 'wah-**zhen**-kee'), which had been built on this site 100 years before by the former owners. A fine neoclassical palace was decorated and crammed with *objets d'art*. Not long after, the king had to abdicate and the building has never been inhabited since. During WWII the Nazis set the palace alight, partly destroying the 1st floor, but they didn't manage to blow it up as they had planned.

Renovated and refurbished, the palace is open as a museum (☎ 625 79 44; adult/student US$3/2, free Thur; open 9am-4pm Tues-Sun). While visiting it, note the rooms adapted from the former baths, the Bacchus Room lined with Dutch tiles, and the Bathroom decorated with bas-reliefs.

The **Myślewice Palace** (Pałac Myślewicki), a few paces east, survived the war unscathed, which is why it has even more authentic, if more modest, interiors. In the same area is the **Museum of Hunting and Horsemanship** (Muzeum Łowiectwa i Jeździectwa; ☎ 628 42 05; adult/student US$1.50/1; open 10am-3pm Tues-Fri).

The **Amphitheatre** (Amfiteatr) has been constructed on the bank of the lake in such a way that its stage is on the islet separated by a narrow channel, thus allowing part of the action to take place on the water. Plays are occasionally performed here in summer.

There are a dozen other buildings and pavilions within the grounds, including the **New Orangery** (Nowa Pomarańczarnia) farther south, which houses a posh restaurant.

WILANÓW

On the city limits, 6km south of Łazienki, is another park-and-palace complex, Wilanów (☎ 842 07 95, ul Wiertnicza 1), easily accessible on bus No 116 or 180 from anywhere on the Royal Way. Wilanów served as the royal summer residence for Jan III Sobieski, remembered for his victory over the Turks in the Battle of Vienna in 1683.

The king acquired the land in 1677 for his rural residence, calling it in Italian 'villa nuova' (which is where the Polish name came from, pronounced 'vee-**lah**-noof'), and within 20 years managed to transform the existing simple manor house into a splendid Italian baroque villa. After the king's death, Wilanów changed hands several times, with each new owner extending and remodelling it. The palace grew considerably, acquiring a range of styles from baroque to neoclassical. During WWII the Nazis plundered it, but the building itself didn't suffer major damage. Most of the furnishings and art were retrieved after the war, and after a decade-long restoration the palace regained its former splendour. It is now open to the public.

There's a lot to see in the **palace** (visits by guided tours, adult/student US$4/2 per person guided in Polish, US$20 for a group up to 5 in English, French, German, Russian, or Spanish; open 9.30am-4pm Wed-Mon, last entry 2.30pm). You proceed through dozens of rooms fitted out with period furniture and decoration in various styles. Highlights include the two-storey Grand Entrance Hall and the Grand Dining Room. Some of the upper-floor rooms accommodate the **Gallery of Polish Portraits**, featuring a collection of paintings from the 16th to 19th centuries. Note the so-called coffin portraits – a very Polish feature – which are images of noble persons painted on a piece of tin or copper plate, then attached to the coffin during the funeral, personifying the deceased. See the boxed text 'Coffin Portraits – Funerals Polish-style' under Poznań in the Wielkopolska chapter.

In summer, come early and be prepared to queue. There are short descriptions of the rooms' contents in English and French. If you want to know more about the site, brochures in English and other major languages are available at a small shop in the palace's wing.

The side gate beside the northern wing of the palace leads to the **gardens** and **parks** *(adult/student US$2/1, free Thur; open 9.30am-sunset daily)*, which, like the palace itself, include a variety of styles. The central part is taken by a manicured, two-level baroque Italian garden, which extends from the back facade of the palace down to the lake. South of it is the Anglo-Chinese park, and in the northern part of the grounds is the English landscape park. Don't miss a 17th-century sundial with a figure of Chronos, the god of time, on the garden facade of the palace.

The **Orangery** *(Oranżeria; open 9.30am-3.30pm Wed-Mon)*, off the northern wing of the palace, features decorative art and sculpture from the 16th to 19th centuries.

Just outside the main gateway to the palace grounds is the **Poster Museum** *(Muzeum Plakatu; ☎ 842 26 06, ul Kostki Potockiego 10/16; adult/student US$2/1.50, free Wed; open 10am-4pm Tues-Sun)*, the only institution of its kind in Poland and probably one of the few in the world. It displays just what it says – posters – and the exhibits are changed regularly. The International Poster Biennial (established in 1966) is held here for a few summer months in even-numbered years.

If you take a trip to Wilanów, you can visit the **Katyń Museum** *(Muzeum Katyńskie; ☎ 842 66 11, ul Powsińska 13, Sadyba district; bus No 180; admission free; open 11am-5pm Wed-Sun 15 May-30 Sep, 10am-4pm Wed-Sun 1 Oct-14 May)* en route. Opened in 1993, the museum reveals details of the massacre of Polish officers and intellectuals by the Soviets in 1940 at Katyń and two other camps (see the boxed text 'Massacre at Katyń' in the Facts about Poland chapter). The moving exhibition includes maps, photographs, documents, letters, press cuttings, personal belongings unearthed during exhumations, and family memorabilia. Video documentaries can be watched on request. Unfortunately, all the captions and video commentaries are in Polish.

The museum has been set in the casemates of a brick fort built in 1883. The other part of the fort houses exhibitions dedicated to the Polish Army and Air Force. There's an extensive outdoor exhibition of tanks, heavy guns, armoured vehicles, war planes, helicopters, radiolocation (radar) stations, missiles and other WWII and postwar junk.

NEW CITY CENTRE

The new centre is almost entirely a postwar creature and has few significant tourist attractions. Chaotic, crowded and flooded with cars parked virtually everywhere, it's essentially a shopping area, with trade going on both indoors and outdoors.

The focal point is the **Palace of Culture and Science** *(Pałac Kultury i Nauki; Plac Defilad 1)*, a blackened edifice which is hard to miss as it's the largest and tallest city building. A gift of friendship from the Soviet Union to the Polish nation, the palace was built in the early 1950s and briefly named after Stalin. The monster has attracted countless nicknames and insults, from 'the Russian wedding cake' to 'the vertical barracks'.

On the palace's 30th floor (115m up) there's a **viewing terrace** *(☎ 656 71 36; adult/student US$4/2.50; open 9am-6pm daily, often longer in summer)*, which gives a bird's-eye view of the city. Poles often joke that this is the best view of the city because it's the only one that doesn't include the Palace of Culture itself! Enter the palace through the main entrance from ul Marszałkowska and continue straight ahead up the stairs to the ticket office.

Just south of the palace is the **Fotoplastikon** *(☎ 625 35 52, Al Jerozolimskie 51; US$2 per session; open noon-5pm Mon-Fri, 11am-2pm Sat)*. This is reputedly the last working example in Europe of a once popular apparatus. It's a great revolving drum; 22 people can sit around it and look through individual eyepieces at 3D photos dating from the beginning of the 20th century, some in colour. It is amazingly lifelike. There's a varied selection of programs, and special performances are available upon request. Each session consists of 48

Palace of Culture & Science – a Defiant Monster

'That enormous, spired building has inspired fear, hatred, and magical horror. A monument to arrogance, a statue to slavery, a stone layer cake of abomination. But now it is only a large, upended barracks, corroded by fungus and mildew, an old chalet forgotten at some Central European crossroad.'

Tadeusz Konwicki (from A Minor Apocalypse**)**

Stalin, it seems, must have been envious of New York's famous skyscrapers. Just after WWII, he ordered eight palace-like high-rise towers to be built in Moscow, apparently as counterparts of the Chrysler and Empire State buildings and the like. He altered his plan at the last minute, however, and decided that the eighth tower would be built in Warsaw, presumably to emphasis a Soviet presence on the Vistula River. When it was finished it just happened to be the largest 'palace' of the lot.

The building was erected in 1952–55 right in Warsaw's centre, using 40 million bricks. It stands on a vast 30-hectare square, Plac Defilad, reputedly Europe's largest, created for the palace by indiscriminately bulldozing the partly ruined central sector. The sandstone monster occupies an area of 3.32 hectares and has 3288 rooms. It shelters a huge congress hall for 3000 people, three theatres, a multiplex cinema and two museums; the upper floors house offices. At 231m, it was Europe's second-highest building when erected, and the highest in Poland.

A solitary giant amid ruins, the palace aroused mixed feelings from the moment of its construction. Predictably, it was fêted by official propaganda and hated by most of the city's residents. No-one could remain indifferent, for the palace was visible from almost any point in the city and beyond. And it looked clearly out of place.

Stalinist city planners put height limits on any constructions around the palace, so that it would remain a dominant landmark. It wasn't until the 1980s that the first skyscrapers went up in the area. The Marriott Hotel, erected in 1989, was the nearest competitor, yet at 140m it was still a long way behind.

Once communism collapsed and borders opened, Warsaw experienced an avalanche of 'tourist-traders' from beyond the eastern frontier, who – irony of ironies – chose the Plac Defilad as their trading ground. The square became a huge Russian bazaar, with the blackened palace overlooking the action. No longer a dead piece of Soviet architecture, it was now alive, surrounded with its people, language, merchandise and atmosphere.

Meanwhile, Poles discussed what to do with the 'wedding cake' colossus, and ideas ranged from pulling it down to turning it into a communist skansen. An international competition was held in 1992; the winning design (from 300-odd entries) proposed constructing a ring of high-rise buildings around the palace, vaguely suggesting a crown, to make the palace less conspicuous, yet still visible. The project immediately attracted a storm of criticism from virtually everyone, including architects, historians, business lobbies, local government and the public.

A decade has passed and still nothing has happened. One reason is that city authorities apparently didn't want to go ahead with the highly controversial project. Meanwhile, a more prosaic reason has appeared – the unsolved issue of the real estate titles of pre-WWII landowners. Nobody had been able to challenge the Stalinist bulldozers, but now, in the new regime, the legitimate owners and their descendants began to claim their land and rights. So, until this issue is resolved you can enjoy an unobstructed view of the palace from every side and just about any perspective – something you certainly can't say about the Chrysler or Empire State buildings. Nearly 50 years after its construction, it is still Poland's highest building. And it remains a distinctly alien sight.

stereoscopic pictures and takes about 20 minutes. This family-run business has been operating here since 1901.

To get a feel for today's Warsaw, wander through the busy commercial area to the east of the Palace of Culture, behind the large Centrum department stores, or set off south along ul Marszałkowska. The early postwar architecture that lines this major thoroughfare reaches its peak at Plac Konstytucji, another showpiece of socialist realism adorned with huge stone candelabras.

FORMER JEWISH DISTRICT

The vast area of the Mirów and Muranów districts stretching to the north-west of the Palace of Culture was once inhabited predominantly by Jews. During WWII the Nazis established a ghetto there and after crushing the 1943 Ghetto Uprising they razed the quarter to the ground. Few remnants of the Jewish legacy are left.

A five-minute walk north-west of the Palace of Culture, right behind the Jewish Theatre, is the **Nożyk Synagogue** (☎ 620 43 24, ul Twarda 6; admission US$1.50; open to visitors 9am-5pm Sun-Fri). Built in 1902 in neo-Romanesque style and named after its founder, it was the only one of Warsaw's synagogues to survive WWII, albeit in a sorry state. It was restored and today is open for religious services.

Some of the important places related to the ghetto's history have been included in the **Memorial Route to the Struggle and Martyrdom of the Jews 1940–43**. The route begins at the Monument to the Heroes of the Ghetto, ul Zamenhofa, and goes along ul Zamenhofa and ul Stawki to the Umschlagplatz Wall Monument, which marks the point from which Jews were deported to the death camps. The route, which takes 15 minutes to complete, is marked by 16 black granite blocks commemorating events and people from those tragic days. A museum of Polish Jewry is to be built in the area.

CEMETERIES

Warsaw has plenty of graveyards of various denominations, of which the oldest ones are grouped in the Wola district, about 3km north-west of the centre. There are several cemeteries here next to each other, which give a good idea of the religious and cultural diversity of Warsaw's past.

The largest and most significant to Poles is the Catholic **Powązki Cemetery** (Cmentarz Powązkowski; ☎ 633 21 40, ul Powązkowska; open 7am-dusk daily), consecrated in 1792. The final resting place of many prominent Poles (including composers Henryk Wieniawski and Stanisław Moniuszko), the 45-hectare graveyard boasts some amazingly ornate old tombstones, intricate sepulchral chapels and mausoleums. Be sure to visit the cemetery on All Saints' Day (1 November) if you happen to be in Warsaw. Thousands of lit candles on the graves make an impressive sight, especially in the evening (the cemetery is open longer on this day).

Just south of the Powązki, and almost as large, is the **Jewish Cemetery** (Cmentarz Żydowski; ☎ 838 26 22, ul Okopowa 49/51; open 9am-4pm Sun-Fri May-Sept, 9am-3pm Sun-Fri Oct-Apr). Founded in 1806, it suffered little during the war and still boasts over 100,000 tombstones – the largest collection of its kind in Europe. However, since almost the whole of Warsaw's Jewish community perished in the war, and the communist authorities took no responsibility for the cemetery's preservation, it stayed largely neglected for over 40 years and many tombstones are dilapidated. Yet there's a wealth of remarkable examples, some topping the graves of eminent Polish Jews, including Ludwik Zamenhof, the creator of Esperanto.

Just south of here is the smaller **Augsburg Evangelical Cemetery** (Cmentarz Ewangelicko-Augsburgski; ☎ 632 10 14, ul Młynarska 56/58; open 8am-dusk daily). A visit to this tranquil, tree-shaded Lutheran graveyard will illustrate the social status of the German minority in the Warsaw area during the Partition years. The graves date back to the late 18th century, but most are from the 19th and early 20th. Most of the people buried here belonged to the learned professions or the merchant class; many tombs of the latter are opulently lavish. The inscriptions and the spelling of the surnames indicate the degree to which many of

The Palace of Culture and Science, Warsaw

Tourist-friendly signs in Warsaw

Cover stars adorn a magazine kiosk in Warsaw

The changing face of Poland's capital city

Zachęta Modern Art Gallery, Warsaw

The cosmopolitan streetscape of Nowy Świat, in Warsaw, is lined with cafes

10th Anniversary Stadium bazaar, Warsaw

Monument to the Warsaw Uprising, Warsaw

St Anne's Church at Wilanów, Warsaw

The Warsaw Ghetto & the Ghetto Uprising

At the outbreak of WWII Warsaw was home to about 380,000 Jews (almost 30% of the city's total population), more than any other city in the world except New York.

The Warsaw ghetto was established by the Nazis in November 1940 and the whole district was sealed off by a 3m-high brick wall. Over the following months, about 450,000 Jews from the city and its environs were crammed into an area of 307 hectares within the walls, thus forming the largest and most populous ghetto in Europe. Living in inhuman conditions, by mid-1942 as many as 100,000 Jews had died of starvation and epidemic diseases, even before deportation to concentration camps had begun.

In a massive liquidation campaign in summer 1942, about 300,000 Jews were taken from the ghetto to the death camp in Treblinka. Only 50,000 people were left in the ghetto and its area was diminished. In April 1943 the Nazis began the final liquidation of the ghetto, but the remaining Jews took up arms in a desperate act of protest.

From the outbreak of the 19 April uprising it was clear that the Jews had little chance of victory against the heavily armed Nazis. German planes soon began dropping incendiary bombs, turning the entire quarter into a sea of burning ruins.

Fierce fighting lasted for almost three weeks until, on 8 May, the Nazis surrounded the Jewish command bunker and tossed in a gas bomb. The members of the command, including the commander-in-chief Mordechaj Anielewicz, took their own lives instead of surrendering to the Nazis. Without leadership the uprising was soon over, even though the last Jewish fighters defended themselves until mid-July.

In total, about 7000 Jews were killed in the uprising and another 6000 perished in fires and under ruins. The Nazis lost 300 men with another 1000 injured. What little remained of the ghetto was razed to the ground.

these expats had become Polonised. An odd reminder of Russian occupation is a large sepulchre in the form of an Orthodox church and with Cyrillic inscriptions.

PRAGA

Praga is the part of Warsaw that lies on the right bank of the Vistula. Founded in the 15th century, Praga gradually developed from the original village and was incorporated into Warsaw in 1791. By the outbreak of WWII, it was a large, working-class suburb. As it was not directly involved in the battles of 1944, Praga didn't suffer much damage and retained some of its prewar architecture and atmosphere. However, since it had no architectural marvels in the first place, there's not much to see. If you decide to set foot in Praga, the most interesting area lies just across the Vistula from the Old Town. It's a short trip by any tram heading east over the Śląsko-Dąbrowski Bridge, or a 15-minute walk.

Past the bridge are the **Zoological Gardens** (*Ogród Zoologiczny;* ☎ *619 40 41, ul Ratuszowa 1/3; adult/student US$2/1; open 9am-5pm daily*). Established in 1928, the zoo stretches north behind a park and has some 3000 animals representing 280 species from around the world. Farther down Al Solidarności, at the intersection with ul Targowa, is the **Orthodox Church** (*Cerkiew Prawosławna;* ☎ *619 08 86, Al Solidarności 52*), topped with five onion-shaped domes. Built in the 1860s in Russo-Byzantine style, it retains its original interior decoration. It's best to coincide your visit with Mass (at 9am weekdays, 10am Sunday). This is one of two Orthodox churches functioning in Warsaw (the other one is in the Wola district).

WHAT'S FREE

It's easy to spend a fortune on sightseeing, tours and entertainment, but some of the most enjoyable things cost nothing. Consider the following:

- Admire the ornate interiors of the Royal Castle on Sunday
- Discover the National Museum's treasure-trove of art on Saturday
- Stroll about the meticulously rebuilt Old Town with its lovely market square
- Explore the city churches, all of which are free to visit
- Enjoy a piano recital near Chopin's Monument in the Łazienki Park on Sunday
- Browse around the huge bazaar at the 10th-Anniversary Stadium
- Visit the Centre for Contemporary Art on Thursday and the Zachęta Modern Art Gallery on Friday, both of which are known for excellent exhibitions

LANGUAGE COURSES

There's quite a choice if you want to learn or practise Polish. The 'Polonicum' Institute of Polish Language and Culture for Foreigners (☎/fax 826 54 16) at Warsaw University, ul Krakowskie Przedmieście 26/28, has the longest tradition. It runs a one-year extensive course and a one-month intensive course in August (four hours a day). Polonicum's courses are the cheapest you'll find (about US$5.50 per hour), but groups may be large (up to 15 students) and methods seem to be quite traditional.

Private schools which have appeared on the market over recent years are more flexible about clients' needs, but they are more expensive. Warsaw's private schools include:

Academia Polonica (☎ 629 93 11, ☎/fax 629 62 11, **W** www.academia-polonica.com.pl) Al Jerozolimskie 55 m 14
IKO (☎ 826 31 08, fax 828 52 68, **W** www.iko.com.pl) ul Nowy Świat 26
Linguae Mundi (☎ 654 22 18, fax 654 22 19, **W** www.centrumlm.com.pl) ul Złota 61
Meritum (☎/fax 625 29 16, **W** www.meritum .com.pl) ul Wspólna 63A m 10
Schola Polonica (☎ 625 26 52, fax 625 08 17, **W** www.schola.pl) ul Jaracza 3 m 19

They all can organise courses to suit your language level (costing roughly US$8 to US$15 per hour) and can provide teachers for individual classes (about US$12 to US$25 per hour). Note that the 'hour' usually means a 45-minute lesson.

Check the Web sites then contact the schools in advance for details, but even if you turn up without warning, many will try to snap you up before a competitor does.

You may also try Berlitz (**W** www.ber litz.com) which has no regular courses but can provide teachers for individual classes. Berlitz has four schools in Warsaw and branches in Gdańsk, Katowice, Kraków, Poznań and Wrocław.

ORGANISED TOURS

Mazurkas Travel (☎/fax 629 18 78, 629 12 49, **e** mazurkastravel@wp.pl, ul Nowo-grodzka 24/26) five-hour city tour US$30 per person, full-day Warsaw environs tour US$55. Warsaw's major tour operator is situated in the lobby of the Hotel Forum. It can organise longer trips (eg, to Kraków and Gdańsk) on request.

Kampio (☎ 823 70 70, fax 823 71 44, **e** kampio@it.com.pl, **W** www.kampio.com .pl, ul Maszynowa 9 m 2) focuses on eco-tourism, organising kayaking, biking and bird-watching trips to out-of-the-way areas. Biking trips in Masuria and bird-watching in Białowieża and Biebrza National Parks are on the tour list.

For information on tours organised by Almatur and Our Roots, see Travel Agencies earlier in this chapter.

SPECIAL EVENTS

Warsaw hosts a number of important cultural events. January witnesses the **Warsaw Theatre Meetings**, a fortnight-long presentation of recent productions by some of the best theatre companies from all over the country – a good opportunity to get an idea of what's new on the Polish scene.

The **Witold Lutosławski International Composers Competition** is organised by the National Philharmonic in February. The **Stanisław Moniuszko International Vocal Competition** is held for one week in late April.

Warsaw Ballet Days takes place in the Grand Theatre at the end of April and beginning of May. This week-long event usually includes invited international ballet groups.

The **International Book Fair** has been held annually in May for over 40 years in the Palace of Culture and Science. May also sees the 10-day **International Festival of Sacred Music**.

The **Mozart Festival**, organised by the Warsaw Chamber Opera in June and July, is an increasingly important and popular cultural event. It features a presentation of most of Mozart's major works.

Late June or early July brings the four-day **Warsaw Summer Jazz Days** to town. It's worth checking the program if you're a jazz fan, as there may be some leading international jazz stars taking part.

The relatively young but interesting **'Art of the Street' International Festival** in July features street theatre, open-air art installations and happenings.

The **Festival of Organ Music**, which goes from July to mid-September, includes Sunday organ recitals in the cathedral.

With a tradition nearly 40 years old, the **'Warsaw Autumn' International Festival of Contemporary Music**, held for 10 days in September, is the city's pride and joy and offers a chance to hear the world's best avant-garde music, including new works by major Polish composers.

In October, there's the **Warsaw Film Festival**. The much-acclaimed **Chopin International Piano Competition** takes place every five years in October (the next one is in 2005).

The **'Jazz Jamboree' International Jazz Festival** is one of the most prestigious festivals in Europe and has already played host to most of the jazz greats, from Dizzy Gillespie to Miles Davis and Wynton Marsalis. It takes place in late October and lasts four days.

PLACES TO STAY

Warsaw is the most expensive Polish city to stay in. It has an increasing collection of up-market hotels, whereas cheaper places are not that numerous. Furthermore, the latter are scattered throughout the city, sometimes a long way from the centre, and there isn't any obvious 'budget hotel area' to head for upon arrival. If you don't book in advance, try to arrive in the city early in the day in order to track down a room. The city tourist offices (including the two convenient outlets at the airport and the central train station) will help you to find and book somewhere free of charge. The private tourist office will also help but will charge a US$2.50 service fee per booking.

Places to Stay – Budget

If your budget is up to about US$30 a double per night, you have a choice between youth hostels, camp sites, student hostels and private rooms. There are very few other hostels or hotels which fall into this price bracket.

Camping Warsaw has several camping grounds, most of which have cabins and/or budget all-year hotels. The ones listed below are within reasonable distance of the centre and are accessible by public transport.

Camping Nr 34 Gromada (☎ 825 43 91, ul Żwirki i Wigury 32) Tent site US$3 plus US$3 per person, bed in cabins US$6. Open May-Sept. Gromada is the most central and popular camp site among Westerners, and is easily accessible from both the airport (bus Nos 175 and 188) and the central train station (bus Nos 136 and 175).

Camping Nr 123 Majawa & Hotel Majawa (☎ 823 37 48, ☎/fax 822 91 21, ul Bitwy Warszawskiej 1920r 15/17) Tent site US$2.50 plus US$3 per person, double cabins with bath US$35, double/triple hotel rooms without bath US$30/38. Located in Ochota, close to the central bus terminal, Majawa has heated cabins and a hotel open year-round.

Camping Nr 260 Stegny & Hotel Stegny (☎ 842 41 64, ul Inspektowa 1) Tent site US$2 plus US$3 per person, double/triple hotel rooms without bath US$18/30. This place is in the Stegny suburb on the way to Wilanów. It has a shadeless tent area and no cabins, but has an all-year hotel.

Camping Rapsodia & Hotel Rapsodia (☎ 634 41 64, ul Fort Wola 22) Tent site US$2 plus US$3 per person, double/triple hotel rooms without bath US$25/28, with bath US$30/34. Set in the Wola suburb, Rapsodia camp site is open from roughly June to September, but the associated hotel is an all-year facility.

Youth Hostels Warsaw has three all-year youth hostels and two seasonal hostels. Altogether, they provide about 350 beds, which is not much for a capital city, so keep in mind that they can be full.

Youth hostel (☎/fax 827 89 52, ul Smolna 30) Beds US$7-15. This is the most central hostel, located close to the National Museum. Its 110 beds are distributed in a variety of rooms and dorms from singles and doubles to 12-bed dorms. Curfew is at 11pm. The hostel is accessible by bus No 175 from the airport and by any eastbound tram from the main train station.

Youth hostel (☎ 632 88 29, ☎/fax 632 97 46, ul Karolkowa 53A) Beds US$8-16. This 140-bed hostel in Wola, 2km west of the train station, is accessible by tram Nos 12, 22 and 24. There's no direct transport from the airport. The hostel also has a variety of rooms ranging from singles to 14-bed dorms. It has a cafe, Internet access and an 11pm curfew.

Youth hostel Agrykola (☎ 622 91 10, fax 622 91 05, ul Myśliwiecka 9) Beds US$10. This is the smallest, youngest and best of Warsaw's youth hostels. Its 30 beds are in rooms of three or four beds, and there's no curfew.

Youth hostel (☎/fax 831 17 66, ul Międzyparkowa 4/6) Beds US$5-8. Open 1 Apr-31 Oct. This hostel is more basic than the all-year hostels, but cheaper. Its 44 beds are distributed in six- to eight-bed dorms. It's on the northern outskirts of the New Town, accessible by bus No 175 from both the train station and the airport.

Youth hostel (☎/fax 617 88 51, Wał Miedzeszyński 397) Beds US$5-7. Open 15 Apr-15 Oct. This is the least convenient and reliable hostel. It's on the eastern side of the Vistula close to the Trasa Łazienkowska (the main west-east city motorway). You can get there by bus No 501 from the train station, or No 188 from the airport.

Student Hostels The tourist offices should know which student dorms are open as hostels (normally from early July to late September). Of those that have opened each summer over the past few years, you could try *Dom Studenta Nr 1 (☎ 668 63 07, ul*

Żwirki i Wigury 95/97); *Dom Studenta Nr 2 (☎ 554 80 00, ul Żwirki i Wigury 95)*; *Dom Studenta (☎ 822 18 69, ul Spiska 16)*; *Dom Studenta Hermes (☎ 849 67 22, ul Madalińskiego 6/8)*; *Dom Studenta Grosik (☎ 849 23 02, ul Madalińskiego 31/33)*; and *Dom Studenta Sabinki (☎ 646 32 00, Al Niepodległości 147)*. All are in Ochota or Mokotów, reasonably close to the centre. It costs US$7 to US$10 per bed in doubles or triples with shared facilities, and some may offer a limited number of rooms year-round.

Other Hostels & Hotels *Bursa Szkolnictwa Artystycznego (☎ 635 41 74, 635 79 05, ul Miodowa 24A)* Bed in double or triple rooms without bath US$12. This art school dorm is possibly the cheapest place to stay in the immediate vicinity of the Old Town, and it's clean and quiet. It's normally open in July and August but may also have some vacancies on weekends in other months. The entrance is from ul Kilińskiego – follow the 'Bursa' arrows.

Pokoje Gościnne Federacji Metalowcy (☎ 831 40 21, fax 635 31 38, ul Długa 29) Singles/doubles/quads without bath US$15/ 24/44. This is probably the cheapest all-year hotel so close to the Old Town, and it's not bad value.

Hotel Na Wodzie (☎/fax 628 58 83) Single/double cabins without bath US$18/ 24. Open Apr-Nov. This hotel is in two boats, *Anita* and *Aldona*, anchored by the Vistula shore between the railway and Poniatowski bridges.

Wilanowskie Pokoje Gościnne (☎ 642 90 68, ul Rumiana 87) Doubles without/with bath US$30/40. Located in Wilanów, this small quiet hotel is reasonable value even though it's away from the centre.

Private Rooms *Biuro Kwater Prywatnych Syrena Univel (☎ 628 75 40, ☎/fax 629 49 78, ul Krucza 17)* Singles/doubles US$20/28 per night, studio apartments (sleeping up to three) US$65. Open 9am-7pm Mon-Fri, 11am-7pm Sat & 2pm-7pm Sun. This organisation rents out rooms in private apartments, as well as whole apartments. All the accommodation it offers is in the city centre and one-night rental is OK. If you can't arrive before 7pm (when they close the office), let them know in advance by phone and inquire in the Bar Lokomotywa, next door, before 8pm.

Places to Stay – Mid-Range

This section includes hotels that cost between US$30 and US$60 a double. There are few central hotels in this price bracket and they tend to fill up fast, despite the fact that they aren't anything special. Hotels farther from the city centre are more likely to have vacancies.

Hotel Hera (☎ 553 10 00, fax 553 10 03, ul Belwederska 26/30) Singles/doubles without bath US$28/40, with bath US$50/60, all include breakfast. Located in Mokotów close to Łazienki Park, Hera is an affordable proposition, with frequent transport to the city centre.

Hotel Belfer (☎ 625 51 85, Wybrzeże Kościuszkowskie 31/33) Singles/doubles without bath US$34/45, with bath US$45/60, all include breakfast. Belfer is a large former teachers' hotel on the Vistula bank. Rooms on the upper floors provide good views.

Hotel Mazowiecki (☎/fax 827 23 65, ul Mazowiecka 10) Singles/doubles/triples without bath US$35/50/65, doubles with bath US$70, all include breakfast. Mazowiecki is a former army dorm once reserved for military officers, but now open to all. It's nothing remarkable but is centrally located.

Hotel Agra (☎/fax 849 38 81, ul Falęcka 9/11) Doubles with shared bathroom US$34. One of the cheapest options in this price bracket, Agra is a reasonable option in Mokotów. One bathroom is shared between two adjacent rooms.

Hotel MCB (☎/fax 668 50 17, ul Trojdena 4) Singles/doubles with bath & breakfast US$44/50. In a quiet location in Ochota, this small hotel of the International Centre of Biocybernetics is neat and comfortable.

Hotel IBB (☎ 658 47 94, fax 658 47 89, ul Pawińskiego 5A) Singles/doubles with bath & breakfast US$45/50. Located in the same complex of buildings as the MCB,

IBB is another small scholarly facility. It offers similar standards.

Places to Stay – Top End

This section includes hotels that cost more than about US$60 a double, but if you really need some luxury be prepared to pay well above US$100. Orbis and Syrena own some of the best locations, but many of their hotels date from early communist days and completely lack style. The newest and poshest establishments will cost from US$200 upwards. All hotels listed in this section have rooms with private baths and serve breakfast, which is included in the room price. They all have their own restaurants. Many offer discounted rates at weekends – make sure to ask while booking.

Dom Literatury (☎ 635 04 04, ☎/fax 828 39 20, ul Krakowskie Przedmieście 87/89) Bed in singles/doubles/triples with bath US$55. Ideally located just opposite the Royal Castle, Dom Literatury has 12 rooms on its top floor. Most rooms provide a superb view over Castle Square.

Hotel Cytadela (☎/fax 687 77 15, Krajewskiego 3/5) Doubles/triples US$65/85. A 10-minute walk north-west of the New Town, this army-run hotel opened in 1993 and is not bad value.

Hotel Harenda (☎/fax 826 26 25, ul Krakowskie Przedmieście 4/6) Singles/doubles US$80/90. This 50-bed hotel is well located on the Royal Way. Rooms are acceptable but don't expect too much.

Hotel Karat (☎ 601 44 11, fax 849 52 94, ul Słoneczna 37) Singles/doubles US$80/100. Another reasonable option close to the city centre, Karat is a 60-bed hotel in Mokotów.

Hotel Maria (☎ 838 40 62, fax 838 38 40, Al Jana Pawła II 71) Singles/doubles US$85/100. This 22-room hotel in the northern suburb of Muranów has a family atmosphere and a good restaurant.

Hotel Gromada (☎ 625 15 45, fax 625 21 40, Plac Powstańców Warszawy 2) Singles/doubles US$100/120. Formerly called Dom Chłopa, the 300-bed Gromada is not very inspiring but is comfortable and conveniently located.

WARSAW

Grand Hotel (☎ 583 21 00, fax 621 97 24, ul Krucza 28) Singles/doubles US$120/140. This 560-bed hotel from the early communist years has recently undergone a well-deserved refit and now has a new feel and satisfactory facilities.

Hotel MDM (☎ 621 62 11, fax 621 41 73, Plac Konstytucji 1) Singles/doubles US$120/150. Another refurbished early communist relic, MDM has spacious rooms, grand candelabras out front and a lot of weird social-ist-realism statues.

Sheraton Hotel (☎ 657 68 00, fax 657 69 20, ul Prusa 2) Doubles US$200. The 350-room Sheraton is pretty new and reasonably priced for what it offers.

Hotel Sofitel Victoria (☎ 827 57 64, fax 657 80 57, ul Królewska 11) Doubles US$275. Wholly refurbished, Victoria is one of the finest hotels in the city centre, with arguably the best hotel swimming pool in town.

Le Royal Méridien Bristol Hotel (☎ 551 10 00, fax 625 25 77, ul Krakowskie Przedmieście 42/44) Singles/doubles US$360/400. For a splurge, you may try this classy, old-style hotel, reputedly the best in town. Built in 1901, it reopened in 1993 after a US$36 million renovation and provides much of what you'd expect, including a gym, sauna and swimming pool.

PLACES TO EAT

Warsaw has more eating places than any other Polish city, in every price bracket. The capital has some of Poland's classiest restaurants, and is the city that offers the greatest choice of ethnic cuisines. Yet, Warsaw is also the most expensive city in which to dine out, particularly in upmarket restaurants.

Places to Eat – Budget

This section includes milk bars, bistros and other cheap eateries where a filling meal shouldn't cost more than US$5 to US$6.

Bar Mleczny Pod Barbakanem (☎ 831 47 37, ul Mostowa 27/29) Mains US$1-3. Sitting next to the Barbican, this small milk bar has successfully survived the fall of the Iron Curtain and is perhaps the cheapest place to eat in the Old/New Town area.

Bar Mleczny Uniwersytecki (☎ 826 07 93, ul Krakowskie Przedmieście 20) Mains US$1-3. Next to Warsaw University, Uniwersytecki is invariably packed with students – a sign that it's not a bad place to eat.

Bar Mleczny Familijny (☎ 826 45 79, ul Nowy Świat 39) Mains US$1-2.50. Conveniently set in the middle of Nowy Świat, Familijny also provides big helpings for little money.

Mata Hari (☎ 620 98 29, ul Nowy Świat 52) Mains US$2-3. Hidden off the street, this tiny three-table place is one of Warsaw's few exclusively vegetarian and vegan eateries. Eat inside or take away.

Bar Mleczny Szwajcarski (☎ 621 45 81, ul Nowy Świat 5) Mains US$1-2.50. Szwajcarski is another useful rock-bottom eating outlet on the Royal Way.

Bar Mleczny Bambino (☎ 625 16 75, ul Krucza 21) Mains US$1-2.50. This is another central milk bar that serves very cheap, unpretentious food.

Bar Mleczny Złota Kurka (☎ 621 32 80, ul Marszałkowska 55/73) Mains US$1-2.50. Close to Plac Konstytucji, Złota Kurka is yet another milk bar that serves straightforward Polish fare at proletarian prices.

Warsaw Tortilla Factory (ul Wspólna 62) Mains US$2-4. This is perhaps the cheapest and one of the most authentic Mexican restaurants in town.

Bar Aysza Tripolis (☎ 524 17 18, ul Wspólna 65A) Mains US$2-3. This tiny shop-cum-cafe serves some of the cheapest Middle-Eastern fare in town. The food is fresh, tasty and authentic.

Bar Turecki (☎ 826 66 14, ul Zgoda 3) Mains US$2-3. Open 24hr. Bar Turecki is another tiny Middle-Eastern eatery, marginally more expensive than the Aysza.

Bar Krokiecik (☎ 827 30 37, ul Zgoda 1) Mains US$2-4. The self-service Krokiecik is deservedly popular thanks to its excellent food at very moderate prices.

Grill Bar Zgoda (☎ 827 99 34, ul Zgoda 4) Mains US$4-6. Across the street from the Krokiecik, Zgoda is a bit more expensive but worth it.

Bar Hoa Lan (☎ 626 81 66, ul Śniadeckich 12) Mains US$2-3. Hoa Lan is one of numerous Vietnamese budget eateries which have populated Warsaw streets over recent years.

Salad Bar Tukan (☎ *531 25 20, Plac Bankowy 2)* Salads US$2-5. In the blue skyscraper, Tukan offers one of the better selections of salads in town. It has several other outlets around the city, including at ul Tamka 37, ul Kredytowa 2 and ul Koszykowa 54.

Między Nami (☎ *827 94 41, ul Bracka 20)* Set lunches US$4. Między Nami has good vegetarian set lunches on weekdays, different each day. The place is popular with local youth. There's no sign over the door; look for the Gauloises Blondes awnings.

Places to Eat – Mid-Range

This section covers restaurant where an average meal will cost somewhere between US$8 and US$16.

Restauracja Pod Samsonem (☎ *831 17 88, ul Freta 3/5)* Mains US$5-7. Open 10am-11pm. Pod Samsonem is one of the best inexpensive restaurants in the area of the Old/New Town. The interior is rather simple, but the food – a mix of Polish and Jewish cuisine – is decent and tasty.

Restauracja Ekologiczna Nove Miasto (☎ *831 43 79, Rynek Nowego Miasta 13/15)* Mains US$6-8, salads US$5-7. This was the first natural-food restaurant in town. In bright, cheery surroundings it serves vegetarian dishes and salads, reputedly prepared from organically grown vegetables.

Tam Tam (☎ *828 26 22, ul Foksal 18)* Mains US$6-8. Tam Tam is Warsaw's first African restaurant, and has become a trendy place. The food is not purely African but is good and reasonable.

Restauracja Soma (☎ *828 21 33, ul Foksal 19)* Mains US$7-10, salads US$5-7. This new chic place offers an inventive menu in spacious colourful surroundings.

Słodki... Słony... (☎ *622 49 34, ul Mokotowska 45)* Mains US$6-8. Beautifully decorated, this cosy restaurant-cafe offers some wonderful salads, soups and main courses plus some of the best cakes and pies in town.

London Steak House (☎ *827 00 20, Al Jerozolimskie 42)* Mains US$8-12. Well

established and maintaining good standards, this place is known for its steaks.

Restauracja Adler (☎ *628 73 84, ul Mokotowska 69)* Mains US$8-12. This restaurant serves copious plates of hearty Polish and Bavarian food (plus good salads) in a cosy, warm interior (or at outdoor tables in summer).

Cafe Ejlat (☎ *628 54 72, Al Ujazdowskie 47)* Mains US$6-10. This small restaurant has innovative Jewish food, a good atmosphere and occasional klezmer (Jewish folk music).

Qchnia Artystyczna (☎ *625 76 27, Al Ujazdowskie 6)* Mains US$6-12, salads US$5-6. Open noon-midnight. Located in Ujazdów Castle, which houses the Centre for Contemporary Art, the Qchnia has an artistic touch to it. The interior is arranged in – as the owners say – 'postmodernist' style, and there's an arty atmosphere. The menu – an artistic creation in itself – includes a choice of vegetarian dishes and some good salads.

Places to Eat – Top End

There's an extensive and swiftly growing array of upmarket restaurants all over the city centre and beyond. They include some of Poland's finest (and most expensive) eateries serving exquisite Polish and international food. Larger parties are advised to make reservations in summer, particularly for dinner. You can assume that most upmarket restaurants have foreign-language menus and accept credit cards. Check the prices of drinks before ordering – in some posh restaurants they can be extraordinarily expensive.

Restauracja U Fukiera (☎ *831 10 13, Rynek Starego Miasta 27)* Mains US$12-25. U Fukiera is one of the highlights of Warsaw's gastronomic scene. It offers a creative menu, based on old Polish cuisine enriched with French and Spanish elements, served in beautifully arranged surroundings. Reservations are essential.

Restauracja Bazyliszek (☎ *831 18 41, Rynek Starego Miasta 3/9)* Mains US$10-20. This is one of the best-established restaurants in town, and it maintains high standards. Bazyliszek serves traditional

Polish food (including game) in appropriately old-fashioned surroundings.

Dom Restauracyjny Gessler (☎ 831 44 27, Rynek Starego Miasta 21/21A) Mains US$12-25. The Dom (literally 'house') actually has two eateries: an elegant, formal restaurant on the 1st floor, and the Karczma, a traditional country inn, arranged in amazing labyrinthine vaulted cellars (among the best in town), and serving typical old-Polish peasant food. Don't miss going there if only to have a look around.

Restauracja Tsarina (☎ 635 74 74, ul Jezuicka 1/3) Mains US$10-25. This exclusive place, with its opulent furnishing and decor and traditional Russian fare, will take you back to prerevolutionary Russia.

Restauracja Polska (☎ 826 38 77, ul Nowy Świat 21) Mains US$10-20. Polska is in an elegant basement and specialises in traditional Polish cuisine. The food tastes as if it was cooked by your mum and is good value. The restaurant is 100m back from the street – enter gate No 21 and walk straight ahead until you see it on your right.

Restauracja Grand Kredens (☎ 629 80 08, Al Jerozolimskie 111) Mains US$10-25. Kredens is an artistic creation with a bold decor, and good food – a combination of Polish and international cuisines.

Restauracja Siedem Grzechów (☎ 826 47 70, ul Krakowskie Przedmieście 45) Mains US$10-20. This re-creation of a typical interwar Warsaw restaurant provides good typical local food in an intimate basement interior decorated with 1920s memorabilia.

Restauracja Belvedere (☎ 841 48 06, Łazienki Park) Mains US$15-30. Accommodated in the glazed New Orangery full of plants and trees, the Belvedere has, no doubt, a fabulous setting. Tables are scattered around the interior amid lush greenery, and you'll feel as though you're dining in an exotic garden. The fare, which combines elements of Polish, French and Mediterranean cuisines, is prepared in the manner of nouvelle cuisine, so portions are not that copious. It's all exquisite but quite pricey.

Tandoor Palace (☎ 825 23 75, ul Marszałkowska 21/25) Mains US$10-16. This is arguably the best Indian restaurant in town, if not in Poland, with food prepared by experienced Indian chefs.

Le Royal Méridien Bristol Hotel (☎ 551 10 00, fax 625 25 77, ul Krakowskie Przedmieście 42/44) Sunday brunch US$36. Open 12.30pm-4pm. The brunch here is superb, with unlimited sparkling wine and a buffet that includes smoked salmon, caviar, salads, cheeses, meats, several main dishes, sweets and coffee. Reservations are required a couple of days in advance.

Cafes

Pożegnanie z Afryką (ul Freta 4/6) Coffee US$2. This tiny coffee shop, one of about 20 similar places scattered around Poland's major cities, offers nothing but coffee – but what coffee! There are about 50 flavours to choose from.

Café Galerie Belle Epoque (☎ 635 41 05, ul Freta 18) Coffee US$3-4. This is a magical place with a fairy-tale decor, and unique in that you can buy everything you see there. Don't miss going downstairs to sample another atmospheric interior.

Café Blikle (☎ 826 66 19, ul Nowy Świat 33) Breakfast US$8-10, salads US$7-8. Open 7.30am-11pm. A landmark of the Royal Way, the cafe began operating in 1869, and gained a reputation for cooking the best doughnuts (pączki) in town. Destroyed in 1945, it reopened in 1994 and continues to serve its famous doughnuts and a range of other pastries, but its menu goes beyond that, offering set breakfasts (Polish, French, English, Viennese, Russian and American), light lunches, salads, ice creams, coffee etc. It's not cheap but it's trendy.

Antykwariat Cafe (☎ 629 99 29, ul Żurawia 45) This place has a lovely antiquarian atmosphere. You can have tea, coffee and pastries, and read any of the hundreds of books on the shelves lining the walls.

TriBeCa Coffee (ul Bracka 22) Coffee US$2-3. This modern cafe is a good port of call for a quick espresso, cappuccino or caffe latte, plus a snack or a pastry.

Wedel (ul Szpitalna 8) On the corner of ul Górskiego adjacent to the Wedel chocolate shop, this is the place for a cup of hot chocolate and chocolate waffles.

Same Fusy (☎ *635 90 14, ul Nowomiejska 10*) Tea US$2-4. Open 1pm-11pm. This cellar teahouse, just off the Old Town Square, offers 150 tea flavours, including exotic varieties such as Argentinian *yerba mate*.

ENTERTAINMENT

Warsaw has a thrilling cultural life, particularly classical music, opera and theatre. The city also offers a lot of lighter entertainment, confined to bars, pubs, jazz clubs, discos and nightspots.

Museums, art galleries, theatre performances and cinema shows are listed in local papers, including *Gazeta Wyborcza*. Its Friday edition has the comprehensive *Co Jest Grane* section on cultural events. The city cultural monthly *IKS* has detailed listings of museums, art galleries, cinemas, theatres, musical events and festivals. Pick up copies of two useful and free what's-on monthlies, *Aktivist* and *City Magazine*, distributed through plenty of restaurants, bars, clubs etc. Posters are a good source of information too, so keep your eyes open.

As for some English-language help, the monthly *Warsaw Insider* provides good information on cultural events as well as on bars, pubs and other nightspots. Also check the entertainment columns of *Warsaw Voice*.

The Kasy ZASP (☎ 621 94 54, 621 93 83), Al Jerozolimskie 25, sells tickets for some of the city's theatres, opera, musical events and visiting shows. The office is open 11am to 6pm weekdays, 11am to 2pm Saturday. You can also buy tickets for some major events at the Bileteria of the two EMPiK Megastores: at ul Marszałkowska 116/122 (☎ 551 44 37) and ul Nowy Świat 15/17 (☎ 625 12 19); both are open 9am to 10pm daily. Tickets for particular events can also be bought directly from the box offices of the respective theatres and other venues that stage them.

Bars & Pubs

Warsaw is flooded with bars and pubs these days. Central options include:

Irish Pub (☎ *826 25 33, ul Miodowa 3*) This is one of the popular drinking haunts in the Old Town area, and stages live music most nights (Irish, folk, country etc).

Morgan's Irish Pub (☎ *826 81 38, ul Okólnik 1*) Possibly the most authentic Irish pub in town, this is a friendly place for meeting expats and enjoying a Guinness. It regularly has live music and offers some hearty food. Enter from ul Tamka.

Pub Pod Baryłką (☎ *826 62 39, ul Garbarska 5/7*) If you prefer something more local, go to this Polish pub on Mariensztat Square. It serves a number of Polish beers – a good testing ground for visiting beer connoisseurs – and prices are reasonable.

John Bull Pub (☎ *831 03 67, ul Jezuicka 4*) This was one of the first pubs to open in Warsaw and perhaps the first genuine English watering hole to cross the Iron Curtain. It's elegant and comfortable but unfortunately tends to follow its motherland's prices and closing times (at 11pm). There's another outlet at ul Zielna 37.

Pub Harenda (☎ *826 29 00, ul Krakowskie Przedmieście 4/6*) Next to Hotel Harenda, this is a trendy and lively spot and is open longer than most other places of its kind.

Someplace Else (☎ *657 67 10, ul Prusa 2*) The Sheraton Hotel's upscale pub is among the most popular expat hang-outs in Warsaw, particularly on Friday night. It has live music, Tex-Mex food, classy decor and prices to match.

Clubs & Discos

Warsaw's main student clubs include *Riviera Remont* (☎ *660 91 11, ul Waryńskiego 12*), *Stodoła* (☎ *825 60 31, ul Batorego 10*) and *Proxima* (☎ *822 87 02, ul Żwirki i Wigury 99*). They all have discotheques on weekend nights. In the summer holiday period, all the clubs run discos several days a week or even nightly, with occasional live bands. A student card will get you in cheaply. Other places for some night dancing include:

Ground Zero (☎ *625 43 80, ul Wspólna 62*) Open Wed-Sat. This is one of Warsaw's hippest discos and is popular with foreigners. On weekends it's often full.

Barbados (☎ *827 71 61, ul Wierzbowa 9*) Open Wed-Sat. Next to the Grand Theatre, this trendy upmarket club is frequented by the beautiful people.

Scena 2000 (☎ *625 60 07, Al Armii Ludowej 3/5)* Open Wed, Fri & Sat. This large bar/disco attracts some local artist and journalist types.

Cul-de-Sac (☎ *827 87 07, ul Foksal 2)* Open Wed, Fri & Sat. Located at the dead end of the street, this nice new place has good music and atmosphere.

Gay & Lesbian Venues

Warsaw's gay and lesbian haunts include:

Pub Koźla (*ul Koźla 10/12)* This is one of the central spots for a drink, located in a small back street of the New Town.

Pub Rudawka (☎ *633 19 99, ul Elbląska 53)* Rudawka is another gay pub, but a way out of the city centre, beyond the Powązki Cemetery. Check for the Friday discos.

Klub M (☎ *549 92 92, ul Wałbrzyska 11)* Another gay haunt, this one is in Mokotów. It can have discos on weekends also.

Między Nami (☎ *827 94 41, ul Bracka 20)* This pleasant cafe-cum-art gallery is essentially a straight place but it's gay-friendly.

Centrum Fanton (☎ *630 54 16, ul Bracka 20)* Behind the Między Nami, this is a fitness club and sauna.

Jazz

Jazz Café Helicon (☎ *635 00 77, ul Freta 45/47)* This small cafe has live jazz usually on Tuesday, Thursday and Sunday (admission free). It has a short food menu, reasonably cheap beer and an attached CD shop specialising in jazz.

Klub Tygmont (☎ *828 34 09, ul Mazowiecka 6/8)* Tygmont is a new place which has jazz almost daily. Depending on what's on, there's usually an admission fee of US$3 to US$5, but sometimes it's free.

Jazzgot (☎ *579 68 19, Al Armii Ludowej 26)* This young but active jazz club is one of Warsaw's major jazz venues. International stars often have their gigs here.

Desant Jazz Club (☎ *628 24 02, ul Nowogrodzka 31)* The most recent addition to the city's jazz scene, Desant has live music on most nights.

Mazowieckie Centrum Kultury (☎ *544 07 40, ul Elektoralna 12)* This cultural centre has monthly jazz concerts, aiming at presenting some of the leading Polish jazz groups.

Pub Harenda (☎ *826 29 00, ul Krakowskie Przedmieście 4/6)* One of Warsaw's more popular pubs, Harenda has jazz concerts in its cellar from time to time.

Riviera Remont (☎ *660 91 11, ul Waryńskiego 12)* This student club has live jazz every Thursday, except during student holidays from July to September.

In July and August, there are free open-air jazz concerts in the Old Town Square at 7pm every Saturday.

Classical Music

Filharmonia Narodowa (*National Philharmonic;* ☎ *826 72 81, ul Jasna 5)* This venue has a concert hall (enter from ul Sienkiewicza 10) and a chamber hall (enter from ul Moniuszki 5). Regular concerts are held in both halls, usually on Friday and Saturday, by the brilliant Warsaw Orchestra and visiting ensembles.

Akademia Muzyczna (*Music High School; ul Okólnik 2)* The school has its own concert hall on the premises, where student presentations take place.

Chopin Society (☎ *827 54 71, ul Okólnik 1)* The society organises piano recitals in its beautiful historic auditorium in Ostrogski Palace.

Piano recitals are also held next to the Chopin monument in Łazienki Park every Sunday from May to September, and in Żelazowa Wola, Chopin's birthplace, 53km from Warsaw (see the Mazovia & Podlasie chapter).

Evangelical Church (☎ *827 68 17, Plac Małachowskiego 3)* The church opposite the Ethnographic Museum hosts some musical events, including chamber concerts and organ recitals.

Chamber concerts are also staged in summer in the Old Orangery in Łazienki Park.

Cinema

There are about 40 cinemas in Warsaw, most of which are in the greater central area. A number of modern multiplex cinemas have been built over recent years, which match Western standards. You also have the 3D *Panasonic IMAX* (☎ 550 33 33, ul Powsińska 31), the first of the chain built in Eastern Europe.

About three-quarters of the films that are shown are US productions, which arrive in Poland within a few months to a year of their release at home. The remaining quarter is mainly Western European films garnished with occasional productions from Australia, New Zealand and some developing countries. Polish films are infrequently screened, as are Russian films, which accounted for up to half the fare during the communist era.

Iluzjon Filmoteki Narodowej (☎ 646 12 60, ul Narbutta 50A) This is Warsaw's main art cinema and it's worth checking what's on here.

Other cinemas which tend to screen more thought-provoking films include *Cinema Paradiso* (Al Solidarności 62), *Kino Feliks* (☎ 687 90 26, Plac Żelaznej Bramy 2), *Kino Kultura & Rejs* (☎ 826 33 35, ul Krakowskie Przedmieście 21/23), *Kino Muranów* (☎ 831 03 58, ul Andersa 1) and *Kino Wars* (☎ 831 44 88, Rynek Nowego Miasta 5/7).

Almost all foreign films (except for children's films) have original soundtracks and Polish subtitles. Cinema tickets cost from about US$4 to US$6.

Theatre

Polish theatre has long had a high profile and continues to do so. Warsaw has about 20 theatres, some of which are among the best in the country. The leading playhouses include *Centrum Sztuki Studio* (☎ 620 21 02, Palace of Culture & Science, Plac Defilad), *Teatr Ateneum* (☎ 625 73 30, ul Jaracza 2) and *Teatr Powszechny* (☎ 818 25 16, ul Zamoyskiego 20), all of which tend towards contemporary productions. Most theatres close in July and August for their annual holidays.

Teatr Żydowski (Jewish Theatre; ☎ 620 70 25, Plac Grzybowski 12/16) This theatre derives its inspiration from Jewish culture and traditions, and some of its productions are performed in Yiddish, with Polish and English translations provided through headphones.

Opera & Ballet

Teatr Wielki (Grand Theatre; ☎ 826 32 88, Plac Teatralny 1) This is the main setting for opera and ballet performances. The theatre stages operas from the international repertoire and some by Polish composers, mainly Moniuszko. Tickets can be bought from the box office or booked by phone. Advance booking is recommended.

Opera Kameralna (Chamber Opera; ☎ 831 22 40, Al Solidarności 76B) This company performs operas in a more intimate but splendid setting.

SHOPPING

Warsaw's shopping scene has changed enormously over the past decade and is now lively, colourful and varied. Shops are well stocked and the assistants are more polite than they used to be. Supermarkets tend to follow Western fashions and the old rundown establishments of the communist era have almost completely disappeared.

Markets

For most of the 1990s much trading took place outdoors on the street. Many streets and squares became bazaars, with traders selling their goods from plastic sheets, folding beds or makeshift stalls. Over recent years, this trade has returned to the shops and proper markets. By far the largest and arguably the cheapest is the *market* at the main city stadium, Stadion Dziesięciolecia (10th-Anniversary Stadium), overlooking the Vistula from the Praga side.

Giełda Foto (☎ 825 60 31, ul Batorego 10) Open 10am-2pm Sun. This photo market, in the Stodoła student club, is a good place to look for photo equipment and film. There's always an amazing variety of cameras and accessories on offer ranging from prewar to the newest equipment, and people from other cities come here to buy and sell photo gear. Film, cameras and accessories can be bought here more cheaply than in shops. If you are a camera buff it's worth visiting even if only to have a look.

Bric-a-brac and antiques bazaar (ul Obozowa) Open early morning-2pm Sat & Sun. This bazaar is located at the far end of

Eastern Europe's Largest Bazaar

Accommodating more than 3000 regular stalls, plus a constellation of part-time and casual vendors, the bazaar at Warsaw's 10th Anniversary Stadium is thought to be the largest in Eastern Europe. Its average daily turnover is estimated to be around US$2 million. It's a town within a town. The market sells just about every everyday product, though you won't find quality goods here. Apart from dozens of stalls selling clothing, footwear, toiletries, electrical appliances, watches, hardware, computer software, CDs, cigarettes and alcohol, you can also buy Soviet military uniforms, gas masks, Lenin busts, handcuffs, pets, carpets etc. It's a good place to get a feel of contemporary Warsaw and its cosmopolitan community, since many vendors are foreigners, coming from the former Soviet Union, Mongolia, Romania, Vietnam and even Africa. The bazaar is open from dawn until around noon daily; it's busiest days are Saturday and Sunday.

the suburb of Wola. Trams Nos 1, 13, 20 and 24, and buses Nos 159 and 167 will take you there from the centre.

Crafts

There's an extensive chain of Cepelia shops, which include outlets at Rynek Starego Miasta 10 ('Dom Sztuki Ludowej'), ul Nowy Świat 35, ul Krucza 6/14, ul Krucza 23/31, Chmielna 8, Plac Konstytucji 5 and ul Marszałkowska 99/101 opposite Hotel Forum.

Antiques

Antiques are sold by Desa outlets and by a variety of small antique shops, most of which are in the Old Town and along the Royal Way. Among the best Desa stores are those at ul Nowy Świat 51 (on the corner of ul Warecka) and at ul Marszałkowska 34/50 (near Plac Zbawiciela); both have a range of old furniture, silverware, watches, paintings etc. Note that it's officially forbidden to export products manufactured before 1945.

Contemporary Art

If you are serious about buying Polish modern art, shop around in Warsaw and Kraków, as the choice is limited and rather unpredictable elsewhere.

There are plenty of commercial art galleries in Warsaw though their standard varies greatly. The galleries nestling in the lobbies of top-class hotels are predictably targeted at hotel guests – moneyed tourists who are not necessarily connoisseurs – so they may have a good supply of genteel daubs.

Zapiecek Art Gallery (☎ 831 99 18, ul Zapiecek 1) In the heart of the Old Town, Zapiecek is one of the most prestigious city showrooms and offers good-quality works of art for sale.

Art Gallery (☎ 828 51 70, ul Krakowskie Przedmieście 17) Near the corner of ul Trębacka, this gallery often has interesting prints and paintings.

Centrum Sztuki Współczesnej (☎ 628 12 71, Al Ujazdowskie 6) The Centre for Contemporary Art has a shop that features quality works of art, including sculpture, glass and painting.

Galeria Grafiki i Plakatu (☎ 621 40 77, ul Hoża 40) This art gallery has unquestionably the best selection of original prints and graphic art in Poland. It also has a good choice of posters.

Galeria Plakatu (☎ 831 93 06, Rynek Starego Miasta 23) This is another good address for posters.

Books & CDs

There's a number of well-edited coffee-table books (in English) about Polish art, architecture and nature – nice souvenirs to take home. The Galeria Plakatu (Poster Gallery), Rynek Starego Miasta 23, is a good point to start looking for such books. You'll find more bookshops around the Old Town as well as along the Royal Way. Two EMPiK Megastores (listed in the Bookshops section earlier in this chapter) have extensive collections of such books. They also have large music sections, with a good choice of Polish classical, contemporary, rock, folk and jazz music on CDs. For jazz, you can also try the Jazz Café Helicon (listed in the Jazz section earlier).

Księgarnia Muzyczna Odeon (☎ 621 80 69, ul Hoża 19) This CD shop stocks reasonable selections of national composers from Chopin to Penderecki, and also has some Polish jazz.

GETTING THERE & AWAY
Air
Airport Okęcie airport is on the southern end of ul Żwirki i Wigury, 10km south of the city centre, and it's named after the suburb in which it is located. It's Warsaw's only commercial airport, handling all domestic and international flights. The small but functional airport terminal has international arrivals on the ground level and departures upstairs. The domestic section occupies a small separate part of the same building.

The international section houses the tourist office (on the arrivals level), which has good information, sells city maps and can help to find a place to stay. A few ATMs on the same level accept most major credit cards. Orbis Travel has a kantor that cashes travellers cheques at very low rates. There are several more kantors, distributed over both levels, which change cash only, but they all give low rates. Probably the best is the kantor of the Powszechny Bank Kredytowy (upper level), but it doesn't give high rates either. It's advisable to change only a small amount, enough to get to the city where any of the numerous kantors will pay you more for your cash. By the same token, if you are leaving Poland from here, you should change your extra złotys back to a hard currency in the city, not at the airport.

The arrivals level has several car-rental companies, a left-luggage room and a newsagency (the place to buy public transport tickets). Buses and taxis depart from this level.

Flights You'll find information about domestic routes and fares in the Air section of the Getting Around chapter. Tickets can be booked and bought from the main LOT office in the building of the Marriott Hotel, or from any Orbis Travel office and many other travel agencies.

LOT and foreign carriers link Warsaw with Europe and beyond. Pick up the LOT timetable, which lists international flights to/from Poland on the airlines that land here, along with domestic flights.

Train
Warsaw has several train stations, of which Warszawa Centralna, or Warsaw central station, opposite the Marriott Hotel in the city centre, handles the overwhelming majority of traffic including all international trains. When you arrive, get off the train quickly as the central station is not the terminus.

The station includes a spacious main hall at street level (which houses ticket counters, a post office, newsagency, the helpful tourist office and an ATM) and a subterranean level with tracks and platforms, right underneath the hall. On an intermediate level between the hall and the platforms is an extensive array of passageways. Here you'll find fast-food outlets, half a dozen kantors (one of which is open 24 hours), a left-luggage office (open 7am to 9pm), lockers (almost always occupied), several Ruch kiosks (for city transport tickets and city maps), a bookshop (well stocked with regional and city maps) and plenty of shops selling food, clothing etc. The taxi stand is also on this level, right outside the station on its northern side.

Watch your belongings closely on all levels, and particularly in the passageways which are usually crowded. Be alert on platforms and while boarding the train – pickpocketing and theft are on the increase here.

Warsaw central station is Poland's busiest railway junction, from where trains run to just about every corner of the country. Read the section in this book that deals with your destination and assume that there are roughly the same number of trains in the opposite direction. For details on InterCity trains originating from Warsaw, see the Train section in the Getting Around chapter.

International destinations include Berlin, Bratislava, Brussels, Bucharest, Budapest, Cologne, Dresden, Hrodna, Kyiv, Leipzig, Minsk, Moscow, Odesa, Prague, St Petersburg, Vienna and Vilnius. For details, see Land in the Getting There & Away chapter.

Both domestic and international train tickets are available either directly from the counters at the station or from any Orbis Travel office. Some other travel agencies also sell train tickets.

You can buy tickets at the station from any of 16 windows (all sell all types of tickets). The lines during holiday periods may be long and sometimes keep you queuing for an hour or more. No English is spoken, it may help to write down your requests in Polish on paper – see Train in the Getting Around chapter for details. In that section you will also find information about types of trains and fares.

Other major train stations include Warszawa Zachodnia (West Warsaw), next to the central bus terminal; and Warszawa Wschodnia (East Warsaw), in the suburb of Praga. Warszawa Śródmieście station, about 200m east of Warsaw central, handles local trains.

Bus

Warsaw has two PKS bus terminals. The Dworzec Centralny PKS (the central bus terminal) operates all domestic buses that head towards the south and west. The terminal is west of the city centre, adjoining Warszawa Zachodnia train station. To get there from the centre, take the commuter train from Warszawa Śródmieście station (two stops).

The Dworzec PKS Stadion (Stadium bus terminal), behind the main city stadium, adjoining the Warszawa Stadion train station (and also easily accessible by commuter train from Warszawa Śródmieście), handles all domestic bus traffic to the north, east and south-east. Bus tickets are sold at the respective terminals.

The Polski Express bus company (see Bus in the Getting Around chapter) runs its coaches from Okęcie airport. They all call (and can be boarded) at the carrier's bus stop on Al Jana Pawła II, next to the central train station. Tickets for Polski Express routes are available from either of its offices and from selected Orbis Travel outlets, but they cannot be bought at PKS terminals. Information about Polski Express services can be obtained on ☎ 620 03 30.

Using PKS services, you might be interested in taking the bus if you're going to Płock, Kazimierz Dolny, Hajnówka (for Białowieża) and some of the Masurian destinations (Ruciane-Nida, Mikołajki and Giżycko). Otherwise, it's perhaps more convenient to travel by train. With Polski Express, you may consider travelling by bus to such destinations as Białystok, Lublin, Rzeszów, Łódź, Płock, Toruń, Bydgoszcz, Ostróda and Elbląg. All these cities are serviced by train, but bus travel will be cheaper, and in most cases is almost as fast as the train.

International buses are operated by a few dozen bus companies and depart from either the central PKS bus terminal or Warsaw central train station. Tickets are available from the companies' offices, selected Orbis Travel offices, Almatur and a number of other travel agencies. Shop around, as the carriers and prices vary. A wide range of options for travel to Western Europe is offered by Anna Travel (☎ 825 53 89) at Warsaw central train station and the Aura Travel Centre (☎ 628 62 53) at Al Jerozolimskie 63. The 'Turystyka' section of the Saturday edition of Gazeta Wyborcza lists most of the bus companies along with their routes, schedules, bus standards, fares and details of where to buy tickets. PKS has daily departures to Vilnius (US$18), Minsk (US$20) and Lviv (US$16). For more information on international routes, see Land in the Getting There & Away chapter.

GETTING AROUND
To/From the Airport

The cheapest way of getting from the airport to the city (and vice versa) is by bus No 175, which will take you right into the centre and up to the Old Town, passing en route Warsaw central train station and the youth hostel at ul Smolna. Watch your bags and pockets closely – this line has become a favourite playground for thieves. Don't forget to buy tickets for yourself and your luggage at the airport's newsagency, and to validate them in one of the ticket machines upon boarding the bus.

Since the AirportCity bus no longer operates, the only other option of getting to the city is by taxi. The taxi stand is right at the door of the arrivals hall and handles taxis by three companies – Radio Taxi, Sawa Taxi and Taxi Merc. They all have stands inside the terminal, so you can ask about the fare to your destination if in doubt – it shouldn't be more than about US$7 to the central train station and US$10 to the Old Town.

The 'mafia' taxis have eventually been pushed away from the taxi stand, though some mafia drivers still come to the airport, park outside the official rank and then hunt for tourists inside the terminal – just ignore them.

Bus & Tram

There are about 30 tram routes and over 100 bus routes, which are clearly marked on city maps (tram routes in red, bus routes in blue) and at the stops.

Public transport operates from about 5am to about 11pm. After 11pm several night bus lines link major suburbs to the city centre. The night 'terminal' is at ul Emilii Plater next to the Palace of Culture, from where buses depart every half-hour. Warsaw's public transport is frequent and pretty reliable, though it's often crowded in rush hours and may be trapped in traffic jams.

In late 2001 a new complex ticket system was introduced, which includes no less than 75 different types of tickets – a mess for the locals, let alone for foreigners. The types that you may use include a single-ride ticket (US$0.60), a 10-ride ticket (US$5.40), a 60/90/120-minute ticket (US$0.90/1.20/1.50), a 24-hour ticket (US$1.80), a three-day ticket (US$3) and a weekly ticket (US$6). You use the same tickets for all means of public transport – bus, tram and metro.

Foreign students below 26 years of age with an ISIC card have a concession of 48% in Warsaw (no other Polish city gives ISIC student concessions). A night-bus ride is US$1.20. Bulky luggage (according to the regulations, any that exceeds 60 x 40 x 20cm) costs an extra single-ride fare.

There are no conductors on board; you buy tickets beforehand from Ruch kiosks, then board the tram or bus and validate the ticket in one of the yellow machines inside. Inspections are not unusual and fines are high: US$25 for travel without a validated ticket and US$10 for luggage. There's a new breed of tough and rude plain-clothes inspectors, who literally hunt for foreign tourists.

Watch out for pickpockets on crowded city buses and trams (especially the notorious bus No 175 and trams running along Al Jerozolimskie). Some are highly skilled and can easily zip open a bag you thought was right in front of you. Don't become separated from your companion by people reaching between you to grab hold of the handrail. The pleasant-looking young man who says hello may only be trying to distract you.

Metro

The construction of a metro consisting of a single north-south line began in 1983, and more than half of the line, from the southern suburb of Ursynów (Kabaty station) to Plac Bankowy (Ratusz station), is in operation. Plans are to open Dworzec Gdański station by mid-2003, and to finish the remaining part of the northern stretch up to Młociny by 2005. There are also plans to build another, east-west line.

The 14km bit in operation includes 14 stations and is serviced by trains which run every eight minutes (every four minutes in rush hours), carrying 140,000 passengers a day. The Kabaty-Ratusz ride takes 22 minutes.

Yellow signs with a big red letter 'M' indicate the entrances to metro stations. Every station has a public toilet and there are lifts for disabled passengers. You use the same tickets as on trams and buses, with the difference that you validate the ticket at the gate at the entrance to the platform, not inside the vehicle.

Welcome to the Land of Pirate Taxis

Beware of pirate taxis which Poles call 'mafia' taxis. These taxis are not associated with legal taxi companies. They exist in some major cities, but are most numerous in Warsaw.

Many pirate taxis don't have meters, but even if they have they may not show the correct fare. The drivers have been known to overcharge up to several times the normal fare, while being rude and aggressive towards passengers who question such absurd fares.

Pirate taxis are easily recognisable because their roof 'taxi' signs are small and don't show any phone number or company name. They park at some central taxi ranks, including at the Rotunda (on the corner of ul Marszałkowska and Al Jerozolimskie), at Plac Zamkowy and in the vicinity of some luxury hotels and tourist sights. Local authorities have managed to push the cab mafia out of some places (eg, the airport), but they simply moved elsewhere and continue to operate.

Car & Motorcycle

The condition of Warsaw's road surfaces is disgraceful. Streets are full of potholes – some more dangerous than others – so driving demands constant attention and may be tiring. The city transport authorities estimate that 70% of the road surface needs repair or replacement. However, there are no funds for it.

The local government has introduced paid parking on central streets (US$0.70 per hour). You pay by coins in the nearest parking machine (*parkomat*) and get a receipt which you display in the windscreen. For security, try to park your car in a guarded car park (*parking strzeżony*). There are some in central Warsaw, including one on ul Parkingowa behind Hotel Forum.

Car Rental Warsaw has more than 20 car rental operators. Most companies need advance booking, sometimes as far ahead as one or two weeks. The major international companies such as Avis, Budget or Hertz are pricey and rarely offer any discounts. It's probably cheaper to arrange rental through the company office at home before your trip. Polish operators tend to be cheaper, sometimes considerably so. Among them, you can try the Auto Plaza Rent-a-Car (☎ 863 27 00, W www.autoplaza.com.pl) and the Ann Rent-a-Car (☎ 840 84 30, W www.ann-rent -a-car.com.pl).

Car Problems PZM operates a 24-hour road breakdown service (*pomoc drogowa*) from its office at ul Kaszubska 2 (☎ 981, ☎ 96 37). A host of private operators advertise in the local press and you'll find their ads under the *autoholowanie* heading in the *Gazeta Wyborcza* and *Życie Warszawy* papers.

Taxi

Taxis in Warsaw are easily available and not very expensive by Western standards. There are about 20 taxi companies, including Radio Taxi (☎ 919), Super Taxi (☎ 96 22), Lux Taxi (☎ 96 66), Tele Taxi (☎ 96 27) and OK! Taxi (☎ 96 28), all of which are pretty reliable. All are recognisable by big signs on top of the car with their name and phone number.

The daytime charge (from 6am to 10pm) is US$1.50 for the first kilometre plus US$0.50 per each additional kilometre; night-time fares are US$1.50 and US$0.75 respectively. All official taxis in Warsaw have their meters adjusted to the appropriate tariff, so you just pay what the meter says. When you board a taxi, make sure the meter is turned on in your presence, which ensures you don't have the previous passenger's fare added to yours.

Taxis can be waved down on the street, but it can be faster to walk to the nearest taxi stand, which are plentiful. You can also order a taxi by phone and there's no extra charge for this service.

Mazovia & Podlasie

Mazovia (Mazowsze in Polish, pronounced 'Mah-**zof**-sheh') was incorporated into Poland in the early days of Piast rule. It became of central importance to the Crown when two consecutive Polish kings, Władysław Herman and Bolesław Krzywousty, resided in the Mazovian town of Płock (1079–1138). When the latter divided the country between his sons, Mazovia became one of several rival principalities. Kazimierz Wielki regained suzerainty over the region, though it was ruled by Mazovian dukes until the last of the line died without an heir in 1526. Mazovia again came to the fore in 1596 when Poland's capital was transferred from Kraków to Warsaw.

Despite its political role, however, it was never a rich region – its soil being infertile – so it was not densely populated. Old Mazovian towns are few and far between. Nonetheless, there are some attractions in the region that are well worth exploring. Some sights can be conveniently visited on day trips from Warsaw (the Kampinos National Park, Żelazowa Wola, Łowicz, Nieborów and Arkadia), while others are probably better seen on the way to other regions, unless you have your own transport.

To the east of Mazovia, stretching along the Polish-Belarusian border, lies the Podlasie plain. Culturally quite different but geographically similar, it's usually tacked onto Mazovia in studies of Poland.

Western Mazovia

KAMPINOS NATIONAL PARK
☎ 22

The Kampinos National Park (Kampinoski Park Narodowy or, as it's popularly called, the Puszcza Kampinoska) begins just outside Warsaw's north-western administrative boundaries and stretches west for about 40km. Occupying an area of 357 sq km, it's one of the largest national parks in Poland. About 75% of its area is covered by forest,

Highlights

- Experience the colourful Corpus Christi procession in Łowicz
- Wander through the aristocratic palace in Nieborów
- Wander around the grounds of the romantic Arkadia Park
- Relive history at the skansen in Ciechanowiec
- Go bird-watching in Biebrza National Park
- Explore the unique Białowieża National Park

mainly pine and oak. The park has wooded dunes up to 30m high, and some barely accessible swamps and bogs, which shelter much of its animal life.

Elk live in the park but are hard to spot; you are more likely to see other animals such as hares, foxes, deer and occasionally wild boar. Among birds, there are black storks, cranes, herons and marsh harriers.

Orientation
The park is popular among hikers from the capital. There are about 300km of marked walking trails running through the most

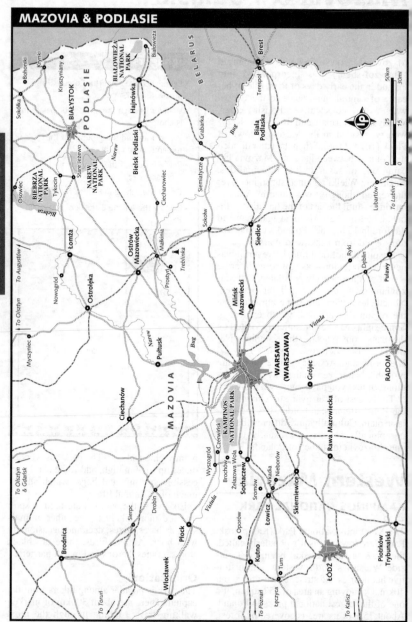

MAZOVIA & PODLASIE

attractive parts of the park, and some trails are good for cycling as well. The eastern part of the park, closer to the city, is more favoured by walkers as it's accessible by public transport. The western part is less visited, though it also provides a variety of one-day hikes. For those who want to spend longer in the forest, there are two long trails, marked in red and green, which cross the whole length of the park from east to west. Both start from Dziekanów Leśny on the eastern edge of the park and wind westwards, crossing each other several times on the way. The red trail (54km) ends in Brochów, and the green one (51km) in Żelazowa Wola.

If you plan on hiking in the park, buy a copy of the detailed *Kampinoski Park Narodowy* map (scale 1:50,000), readily available from bookshops in Warsaw (see Bookshops in the Warsaw chapter).

Accommodation

There are no hotels within the park but you can camp in several bivouac sites designated for camping. There are hotels just outside the park's boundaries, including in Czosnów, Laski, Leszno, Tułowice and Zaborów. Inquire at Warsaw's tourist office (☎ 94 31) for a full list of places to stay in the park.

There are also some agrotourist farms in the region. Details of these can be obtained from the Wojewódzki Ośrodek Doradztwa Rolniczego (☎ 843 84 51) in Warsaw and the Ośrodek Doradztwa Rolniczego (☎ 725 01 35) in Kampinos.

Getting There & Away

There are buses from Warsaw to towns and villages on the outskirts of the park and within its borders. The most popular jumping-off point for walks in the eastern part of the park is the village of Truskaw. Warsaw suburban bus No 708 goes there from Plac Wilsona in the Żoliborz district. Alternatively, you can take bus No 701, also from Plac Wilsona, to Dąbrowa Leśna, but this is a less convenient starting point.

If you plan to hike in the western part of the park, one of the good points to start from is Kampinos, 41km from Warsaw, serviced

by PKS buses from Warsaw's central bus station.

ŻELAZOWA WOLA
☎ 46

Żelazowa Wola ('Zheh-lah-**zo**-vah **Vo**-lah') is a tiny village 53km west of Warsaw, on the edge of the Kampinos National Park. It owes its fame to Frédéric Chopin, who was born here on 22 February 1810. The house where the event took place has been restored and furnished in a style reminiscent of the composer's era, and is now a **museum** (*☎ 863 33 00; museum & park ticket adult/student US$2.50/1.25, park-only adult/student US$1/0.50; open 9.30am-5.30pm Tues-Sun May-Sept, 10am-4pm Tues-Sun Oct-Apr*). The exhibition is modest and doesn't include much of Chopin's original memorabilia, but the tranquillity and charm of the place make for a pleasant stop.

The major attraction of the place is the Sunday **piano recitals**, often performed by top-rank virtuosi. These are held from the first Sunday of May to the last Sunday before 17 October, the anniversary of Chopin's death (in Paris in 1849). There are usually two concerts, up to an hour long, on each Sunday, at 11am and 3pm. The music is played in the parlour while the audience is seated on the terrace in front of the house. There's no fee for these recitals other than the park-only entrance ticket. Check the program and times in Warsaw (in the tourist offices or the Chopin Society in the Ostrogski Palace) before setting off.

There's a restaurant opposite the entrance to the park in Żelazowa Wola but nowhere to stay for the night. The nearest accommodation is in Sochaczew, 6km away.

Getting There & Away

There are two ways of getting to Żelazowa Wola from Warsaw. One is to take a train from Warszawa Śródmieście station to Sochaczew. From there, catch the local urban bus No 6, which goes every hour to Żelazowa Wola (6km), or take a taxi.

The other way is to go directly by PKS bus; there are one or two morning buses from the Warsaw central bus terminal to the town of Wyszogród, which go via Leszno and Kampinos and will drop you off at Żelazowa Wola.

Several travel agencies in Warsaw put together organised tours for the Sunday concerts – a more comfortable but more expensive option.

ŁOWICZ
☎ 46 • pop 32,000
After its founding in the 12th century, Łowicz ('Wo-veech') was the seat of the archbishops of Gniezno – the supreme church authority in Poland – for over 600 years. Consequently the town has a number of churches and other ecclesiastical buildings, including the massive cathedral overlooking the central square. Łowicz has also become known as a regional centre for folk arts and crafts, which is best seen during the elaborate celebrations of Corpus Christi.

Information
The PTTK office (☎ 837 32 69) is at Stary Rynek 3 (the main square). Bank Pekao, ul Długa 27, exchanges travellers cheques, but if all you want is a cash advance on a credit card, there's a useful ATM on Stary Rynek 11. For changing cash, you have kantors on Stary Rynek 12 and 15.

Things to See
The Łowicz Museum (☎ 837 39 28, Stary Rynek 5/7; adult/student US$1.50/1, free Sat; open 10am-4pm Tues-Sun, closed days following public holidays) is in the old missionary college, which was designed by prolific Dutch architect Tylman van Gameren and built at the end of the 17th century. The best-preserved part of the college's interior is the former priests' chapel, with its vault decorated with baroque frescoes (1695) by Italian artist Michelangelo Palloni. The chapel is part of the museum and houses the baroque art section.

The historical section (1st floor) is devoted to the archaeology of the region and the history of Łowicz. The ethnographic section (2nd floor) boasts a collection of local folk costumes, decorated wooden

furniture, coloured paper cut-outs, painted Easter eggs, pottery and woodcarving.

In the back garden of the museum are two old farmsteads from the region, complete with original furnishings, implements and decoration.

Among churches, the most interesting is the vast 15th-century Łowicz Cathedral in the middle of Stary Rynek. Originally Gothic, it underwent several renovations and reflects a mishmash of styles including Renaissance, baroque and rococo. Twelve archbishops of Gniezno and primates of Poland are buried in the church.

Corpus Christi
Łowicz's main religious event is Corpus Christi (on a Thursday in May or June), during which a procession circles the main square and the cathedral, with most of its participants dressed in traditional costumes. Arguably the most solemnly celebrated Corpus Christi in the country, this is the best time to come to Łowicz to see the brightly coloured and embroidered dresses and get a taste of the Catholic fervour of the Polish countryside. The procession starts about noon and takes roughly two hours to do the whole loop.

Places to Stay & Eat
Youth hostel (☎ 837 37 03, ul Grunwaldzka 9) Dorm beds US$3-4. Open July-Aug. This basic summer hostel opens in a primary school next to the Warsaw-Poznań highway, 1.5km north of Stary Rynek.

Hotel Aneta (☎ 837 04 48, ul Powstańców 1863r 12) Doubles/triples without bath US$13/16, doubles with bath US$22. Aneta is a former workers' dorm, about 1.5km south of the centre. It's Łowicz's cheapest all-year accommodation.

Hotel Akademicki (☎/fax 837 43 38, ul Warszawska 9A) Doubles/triples with bath US$28/34, beds in quads US$12. This hotel, near the train station, is good value, and also has some comfortable suites.

Hotel Zacisze (☎/fax 837 33 26, ul Kaliska 5) Singles/doubles/triples with bath & breakfast US$25/30/35. Located 300m south of the Rynek, Zacisze is a comfortable and convenient place and has its own, reasonably priced restaurant.

Bar U Błażeja (☎ 837 64 73, ul 11 Listopada 7) Mains US$3-4. Just off Stary Rynek, this is one of the best budget restaurants, serving tasty meals till 6pm.

Getting There & Away

The bus and train stations are side by side, a five-minute walk east from the main square. There are regular trains to Warsaw (82km), Łódź (63km) and Kutno (45km). There are also regular buses to Łódź (52km) and several daily to Płock (58km). For Arkadia (5km) and Nieborów (10km), take any bus heading for Bolimów or Skierniewice via Bolimów.

NIEBORÓW

☎ 46 • pop 1500

The small village of Nieborów ('Nyeh-**bo**-roof'), 10km south-east of Łowicz, is noted for its magnificent palace. Designed by Tylman van Gameren for Cardinal Radziejowski, the archbishop of Gniezno and Primate of Poland residing in Łowicz, the baroque palace was built in the last decade of the 17th century. Shortly afterwards, a French garden was laid out directly behind the palace.

After changing hands several times, the palace was eventually bought by Prince Michał Hieronim Radziwiłł in 1774. He and his wife Helena lavishly crammed it with valuable furniture and works of art, including paintings and antique sculptures, and an imposing library.

The English-style informal landscaped park, designed by Szymon Bogumił Zug, was laid out next to the old baroque garden. A majolica (a type of porous pottery) factory, the only one in Poland at the time, was established on and off until 1906.

In the 1920s the palace underwent its last important transformation when a mansard storey was added to the building. The palace remained in the possession of the Radziwiłł family right up till WWII, after which, fortunately undamaged, it was taken over by the state and converted into a museum.

Things to See

The **Nieborów Museum** *(☎ 838 56 35; adult/student U$2/1, free Mon; open 10am-4pm daily 16 Jan-30 Apr & 1 July-30 Oct, 10am-6pm daily May & June, closed days following public holidays & 1 Nov-15 Jan)* occupies over half of the building's rooms. Part of the ground floor features Roman sculpture and pieces of bas-relief, most of which date from the first centuries AD. You then go upstairs by an unusual staircase clad, both walls and ceiling, with ornamental Dutch tiles dating from around 1700.

The whole 1st floor was restored and furnished according to the original style and contains a wealth of *objets d'art*. Note the tiled stoves, each one different, made in the local majolica factory, and don't miss the two late-17th-century globes in the library, the work of Venetian geographer Vincenzo Coronelli.

The **French garden** *(open 10am-dusk daily)* on the southern side of the palace, with a wide central alley lined with old lime trees, is dotted with sculptures, statues, tombstones, sarcophagi, pillars, columns and other stone fragments dating from various periods. Many of them were brought from the Arkadia park (see the following section on Arkadia). The **English landscape park** *(open 10am-dusk daily)*, complete with a stream, lake and a couple of ponds, is to the west of the garden, behind an L-shaped reservoir.

Places to Stay & Eat

There are no hotels in Nieborów, only a camp site and a youth hostel.

Camping Nr 77 (☎ 838 56 92) Tent site US$2 plus US$2 per person, cabins for singles/doubles/triples US$12/15/18. Open May-Oct. The camping ground is west of the palace park, off the Skierniewice road (a 10-minute walk from the park's main gate). It has 16 cabins, each containing two triple rooms and a bath. There is a snack bar in the grounds, which also offers some meals.

Youth hostel (☎/fax 838 56 94, Al Legionów Polskich 92) Dorm beds US$3-5. Open July & Aug. The hostel is in the local school, 1.5km north of the palace on the road towards Bednary.

MAZOVIA & PODLASIE

Day trippers to Nieborów can use a *cafe* in the palace complex that serves light meals.

Getting There & Away

There are no direct buses to/from Warsaw (80km), but about six buses daily run to Łowicz (10km), from where hourly trains will take you on to Warsaw. An alternative way to get to Warsaw is by walking to Bednary (4km), where the Łowicz-Warsaw trains stop. See the following section for more about transport.

ARKADIA

Laid out by Princess Helena Radziwiłł, the lady of the Nieborów palace, this **romantic park** *(admission US$1, free Mon; open 10am-dusk daily)* was, in the words of its creator, to be an 'idyllic land of peace and happiness'.

The park is just by the Łowicz-Nieborów road and there's a map at the entrance showing the location of the surviving structures. They include the Diana's Temple (Świątynia Diany), Archpriest's Sanctuary (Przybytek Arcykapłana), Margrave's House (Dom Margrabiego), the Gothic House (Domek Gotycki) and the Aqueduct (Akwedukt). The Diana's Temple and Archpriest's Sanctuary may shelter some exhibitions.

Discover for yourself the charm of the pavilions, temples and other structures, by wandering at your leisure amid tall trees and abandoned bits and pieces of carved stone, some of them 2000 years old. Look for curious details, read the peculiar inscriptions, and feel the poetry of the ruins and tombs.

The Unusual Romantic Park of Arkadia

The design of Arkadia was a product of new philosophical and aesthetic trends that had emerged in the second half of the 18th century in Western Europe, originally in Britain and France. Taking their inspiration from the traditions of the classical world and the Middle Ages, the authors of the new philosophy called for a return to the past and to nature.

These fashionable ideas did not take long to inspire the leisured ladies of the foremost Polish clans, including the Czartoryski, Lubomirski, Ogiński and Radziwiłł families. They all rushed to design their own parks in the closing decades of the 18th century. Of these, Arkadia, created by Princess Helena Radziwiłł of Nieborów, was probably the most original and unusual.

Begun around 1780, the park was developed, enlarged and improved until the death of the princess in 1821. During her frequent foreign travels, she collected and sent home decorative elements, tombstones and statues, fragments of antique sculptures and rare and exotic works of art. She also brought to Arkadia architectural details from the parish church and the ruined castle in Łowicz. All these bits and pieces were then fitted into the park's design, either as freestanding elements or incorporated into buildings (most evident in the Archpriest's Sanctuary, an amazingly haphazard composition).

In the first stage, up till 1800, Szymon Bogumił Zug, the court architect of King Stanisław August Poniatowski, was the chief designer of the park. Most of the structures built during that period have survived in better or worse shape to this day. After 1800, a new architect of Italian origin, Enrico Ittar, introduced innovative and bold solutions and, returning to a Roman vision, built the Amphitheatre (patterned upon the theatre of Pompeii), the Roman Circus and the Tomb of Illusions. Unfortunately, almost nothing of his work survives.

After the princess's death, the park fell into decay. Most of the works of art have been taken to Nieborów's palace and can be seen today either in its museum or the garden, and the abandoned buildings fell gradually into ruin. Only recently some conservation work was carried out and led to restoration of Diana's Temple and Archpriest's Sanctuary, while most other structures and the park itself have been left virtually untouched. Paradoxically, the air of decay adds to the charm and the romantic atmosphere of the place.

Getting There & Away

Arkadia is conveniently accessible from Warsaw. Take a train to Łowicz (departing roughly every hour from Warszawa Śródmieście station), get off at the obscure station of Mysłaków (the last one before reaching Łowicz) and walk seven minutes to the park. Note that fast trains don't stop in Mysłaków.

There are five or six buses daily passing through Arkadia on their way to Łowicz (5km) and, in the opposite direction, to Nieborów (5km).

It's hard to 'do' Łowicz, Arkadia and Nieborów within a one-day round trip from Warsaw. If you exclude Łowicz, it's relatively easy. Probably the best way to do it is to go by train to Arkadia (as described earlier) and to check the bus schedule to Nieborów before visiting the park. If there is a bus due, take it and visit Arkadia on your way back. When you arrive at Nieborów, again, first check when the buses return to Arkadia (they go through to Łowicz).

SROMÓW
☎ 46 • pop 800

Sromów ('**Sro**-moof') is a small, unremarkable village 10km north-east of Łowicz, which you can hardly find even on detailed, large scale maps. Yet it does have one great attraction – the private **Folk Museum** (*Muzeum Ludowe;* ☎ *838 44 72, admission US$1.50; open daily*), founded by skilled artisan and passionate crafts collector Julian Brzozowski.

Set in a garden full of folksy statues, the museum is housed in four buildings, two of which feature animated tableaux of historic scenes and village life – a country wedding, a pageant of kings, a Corpus Christi procession, the four seasons on the farm etc. The figures are all carved from wood and painstakingly painted and costumed. The animation, with synchronised music, is by concealed rods and shafts driven by 28 electric motors. All this is the result of 50 years of work by Mr Brzozowski and his family. Although a little kitsch, it is unique and fascinating.

The other buildings house a collection of about 30 old horse carts and carriages assembled by the owner from the people living in the surrounding villages. Other exhibits include typical paper cut-outs, regional costumes, folk paintings, decorated wooden chests and embroidery. The most recent achievement of Mr Brzozowski is a chapel featuring a dozen life-sized figures, built next to the museum to commemorate the 1999 visit of the Pope to the region.

The museum is on the village's main road. It's open 'daily from the morning till the evening', as the board says. If it's locked, inquire at Mr Brzozowski's house across the road from the museum, and he or someone from the family will open it and guide you around.

Getting There & Away

Sromów is 7km from Łowicz along the main highway to Warsaw, then 2km north along the side road towards Rybno, and finally 1km west to the village itself. Sporadic buses from Łowicz to Rybno will let you off at the second turn-off, 1km from the museum. The museum is signposted from the main Łowicz-Warsaw highway. Motorists can easily visit the museum in conjunction with Nieborów palace, only 10 minutes drive away.

ŁÓDŹ
☎ 42 • pop 840,000

Łódź ('Woodge') is a young city, but after rapid industrial development it has surpassed much older towns and is today Poland's largest urban centre after Warsaw. Although the first account of its existence dates from the 14th century, it remained an obscure settlement until the beginning of the 19th century. In the 1820s the government of the Congress Kingdom of Poland embarked on a program to industrialise the country, and Łódź was selected to be a new textile centre. It subsequently underwent an unprecedented economic boom.

Enterprising industrialists – Jews, Germans and Poles alike – rushed in to build textile mills, closely followed by workers flooding into the city. The arrival of the steam engine in 1838 and the abolition of customs barriers to Russia in 1850 were two

MAZOVIA & PODLASIE

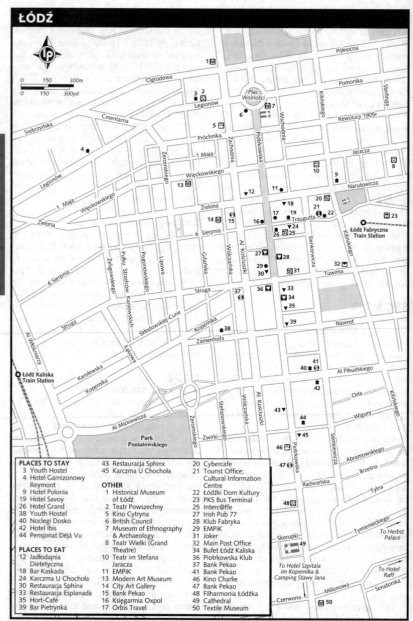

ŁÓDŹ

0   150   300m
0   150   300yd

PLACES TO STAY
3 Youth Hostel
4 Hotel Garnizonowy
   Reymont
9 Hotel Polonia
19 Hotel Savoy
26 Hotel Grand
38 Youth Hostel
40 Noclegi Dosko
42 Hotel Ibis
44 Pensjonat Déjà Vu

PLACES TO EAT
12 Jadłodajnia
   Dietetyczna
18 Bar Kaskada
24 Karczma U Chochoła
30 Restauracja Sphinx
33 Restauracja Esplanada
35 Hort-Café
39 Bar Pietrynka

43 Restauracja Sphinx
45 Karczma U Chochoła

OTHER
1 Historical Museum
   of Łódź
2 Teatr Powszechny
5 Kino Cytryna
6 British Council
7 Museum of Ethnography
   & Archaeology
8 Teatr Wielki (Grand
   Theatre)
10 Teatr im Stefana
   Jaracza
11 EMPiK
13 Modern Art Museum
14 City Art Gallery
15 Bank Pekao
16 Księgarmia Oxpol
17 Orbis Travel

20 Cybercafe
21 Tourist Office;
   Cultural Information
   Centre
22 Łódzki Dom Kultury
23 PKS Bus Terminal
25 Interc@ffe
27 Irish Pub 77
28 Klub Fabryka
29 EMPiK
31 Joker
32 Main Post Office
34 Bufet Łódź Kaliska
36 Piotrkowska Klub
37 Bank Pekao
41 Bank Pekao
46 Kino Charlie
47 Bank Pekao
48 Filharmonia Łódźka
49 Cathedral
50 Textile Museum

milestones in the city's growth. Opulent palaces of the mill owners mushroomed, as did drab proletarian suburbs. By the outbreak of WWI, Łódź had grown a thousandfold, reaching a population of half a million.

After WWI the city's growth slowed, mainly because of the loss of the huge eastern market, but industrial sectors such as machinery and chemistry continued to expand. In the 1930s ethnic Poles made up only half the population; the rest were mostly Jews and Germans. Having escaped major destruction during WWII, Łódź continued as Poland's textile capital – the Polish Manchester – responsible for nearly half of Poland's textile production, though this figure has dropped over recent years.

Łódź is also the Polish Hollywood. As a result of a film school and film studios being established here, the city became the national centre for cinematography. Most of the great figures of Polish cinema, such as Polański, Skolimowski, Wajda and Kieślowski, started out in Łódź.

At first sight, Łódź looks sprawling, grubby and unpleasant, but this is only half the real picture. Although there isn't a single city building older than 200 years, there is an enormous wealth of 19th-century architecture, including the mill owners' residences, in a hotchpotch of styles. Look for some amazing examples of Art Nouveau, for which Łódź is known nationally.

Orientation

Łódź has developed around ul Piotrkowska, its nearly 4km-long north-south backbone, extensively restored over the past decade. It is in this area that most of the surviving 19th-century architecture (including some fine Art Nouveau buildings) can be seen. Most museums, too, are on or near this street, and in some cases they are installed in old palaces (one in an old mill).

Most tourist attractions are within walking distance from each other, but if you prefer, use pedal rickshaws that have appeared en masse over recent years in the car-free section of ul Piotrkowska, moving locals and visitors for around US$0.50 per passenger. Łódź is the only Polish city that has

managed to apply this 'exotic' means of transport successfully.

Information

Tourist Offices The Centrum Informacji Turystycznej (☎/fax 633 71 69), ul Traugutta 18, is the city's main tourist office, open 8.30am to 4.30pm weekdays, 10am to 2pm Saturday. It's well-run and the staff are helpful and knowledgeable. The cultural information centre is also here (see Entertainment later in this section). Pick up the free *Welcome to Łódź*, a practical tourist magazine.

Money There are plenty of kantors along ul Piotrkowska and in the adjacent streets. There are also several useful ATMs at ul Piotrkowska 81 and 126, and ul Narutowicza 8/10. Travellers cheques can be exchanged in Bank Pekao, which has a dozen branch offices around town, including ones at ul Piotrkowska 215, Al Piłsudskiego 12, and Al Kościuszki 3 and 47.

Post & Communications The main post office is at ul Tuwima 38.

Email & Internet Access There are perhaps a dozen cybercafes on ul Piotrkowska itself, including the ones at Nos 79, 91, 101, 107, 122 and 143. Other nearby facilities include Interc@ffe (☎ 632 31 05), ul Moniuszki 4A; Joker (☎ 630 34 89), ul Tuwima 6; and Cybercafe (☎ 632 37 23), ul Kilińskiego 59/63.

Most of the listed places are open daily, often till late or even 24 hours, and cost around US$1 per hour.

Bookshops The Księgarnia Oxpol (☎ 630 20 13), ul Piotrkowska 63, has a choice of English-language publications. For foreign press, check the two central EMPiKs, at ul Piotrkowska 81 and ul Narutowicza 8/10.

Things to See

A good point to start is the **Historical Museum of Łódź** (*Muzeum Historii Miasta Łodzi;* ☎ 654 03 23, ul Ogrodowa 15; adult/student US$1.50/0.75, free Sun; open 10am-2pm Tues & Thur-Sun, 2pm-6pm

Piotrkowska Street – Łódź's Microcosmos

What Broadway is to New York or the Champs Élysées to Paris, Piotrkowska is to Łódź – a well-known street that acts as a city symbol. Cutting right through the heart of the city, the 3623m-long Piotrkowska street is Łódź's commercial and gastronomic nerve centre. It's a favourite rendezvous site and point of reference, similar to the Rynek in Kraków. There's something magical about Piotrkowska.

Piotrkowska street started its life in the 19th century as the beginning of the road to Piotrków Trybunalski (hence the name of the street), then the major town of the region. By the beginning of the 20th century Piotrkowska was already a trendy boulevard, lined with mighty Art Nouveau buildings. Post-WWII it ended up as a grey, gloomy and badly-lit street with darkened facades and a few empty shops, much like most streets all over communist Poland. Its phenomenal revival came in the 1990s, after the Piotrkowska Street Foundation was created by a group of local artists and architects in order to turn the derelict street into a lively European city mall.

Ten years on, it's a vibrant avenue dotted with restaurants, open-air cafes, art galleries and elegant shops. The street hosts various cultural activities, feasts, festivals, happenings, buskers and street theatre. Many facades have been restored, making Piotrkowska Poland's best Art Nouveau street. Hidden in the backyards behind the facades are reputedly 105 pubs.

The famous Grand Hotel (at No 72), the city's oldest existing hotel, has been serving punters since 1888. In front of the hotel is the 'Avenue of the Stars', made by installing stars in the pavement, each dedicated to a star of Polish film. Nearby is 'Rubinstein's Piano', a monument to Artur Rubinstein, presenting him at the grand piano. It's in front of the house where the pianist once lived (No 78). A few paces down the street is 'Tuwim's Bench' (No 104), another unusual monument, this one created in memory of local poet Julian Tuwim. Touch his nose – it's supposed to bring good luck. The last of the series is 'Reymont's Chest' (No 135), a monument presenting the Nobel Prizewinner in literature, Władysław Reymont, sitting on a large travel chest.

Another unusual recent challenge for the street is the project to create the world's largest graffiti, which should be ready by the time you read this. Measuring 40m x 24m, it's to be painted on the wall at No 152. The authors are convinced that their huge work of art will be acknowledged in the *Guinness Book of Records*.

Part of Piotrkowska street is a no-car or bus area, but locals came up with the idea of using pedal rikshas, and it worked phenomenally, unlike in any other Polish city. The rikshas ply the street for a small fee back and forth year-round, and you can even request one by phone, as you would a taxi!

Wed). It's located in the opulent palace of the Poznański family, who were among the wealthiest Jewish clans in the city. The museum features exhibitions dedicated to Łódź's history and its famous citizens, including pianist Artur Rubinstein, writer Jerzy Kosiński and poet Julian Tuwim. All three were of Jewish origin born in Łódź.

The **Museum of Ethnography and Archaeology** (☎ 632 84 40, Plac Wolności 14; adult/student US$1.50/0.75, free Tues; open 10am-5pm Tues, Thur & Fri, 9am-4pm Wed, 9am-3pm Sat, 10am-3pm Sun) has archaeological finds from central Poland from the Stone Age to the Middle Ages and changing ethnographic exhibitions from the region.

The **Modern Art Museum** (Muzeum Sztuki; ☎ 633 97 90, ul Więckowskiego 36; adult/student US$1.50/1, free Thur; open 10am-5pm Tues, 11am-5pm Wed & Fri, noon-7pm Thur, 10am-4pm Sat & Sun) contains an extensive collection of 20th-century Polish and international paintings, including many by contemporary artists. There are works by Picasso, Chagall and Ernst (not always on display).

Nearby is the **City Art Gallery** (Miejska Galeria Sztuki; ☎ 632 24 16, ul Wólczańska 31/33; adult/student US$1/0.50; open noon-5pm Tues-Fri, noon-4pm Sat & Sun) in the old residence of Kindermann, a German industrialist. There are temporary exhibitions so you never know what you will see, but the building itself is well worth a look. Built in 1903, it is a handsome Art Nouveau villa.

Near the southern end of ul Piotrkowska is the **Textile Museum** *(Centralne Muzeum Włókiennictwa;* ☎ *683 26 84, ul Piotrkowska 282; adult/student US$1.50/0.75, free Fri; open 9am-4pm Tues-Fri, 11am-4pm Sat & Sun).* Located inside one of the oldest mills, dating from the 1830s, it houses a collection of textile machinery ranging from the early looms to contemporary devices. Fabrics, clothing and other objects related to the industry are on the 1st floor. The upper floors have temporary exhibitions.

The **Herbst Palace** *(Księży Młyn;* ☎ *674 96 98, ul Przędzalniana 72; adult/student US$1.50/0.75; open 10am-5pm Tues, noon-5pm Wed & Fri, noon-7pm Thur, 11am-4pm Sat & Sun)* is the former residence of the Herbst family. It's 1.5km east of the Textile Museum (a 20-minute walk along ul Tymienieckiego, or take bus No 55). The building (from 1875) is now a museum and gives some insight into how the barons of industry lived up till WWII. Although the owners fled abroad, taking all the furnishings and works of art with them, the interior has been restored and furnished like the original.

Łódź's **Jewish Cemetery** *(Cmentarz Żydowski;* ☎ *656 70 19, ul Bracka 40; admission US$1; open 9am-5pm Sun-Thur, 9am-3pm Fri)* was founded in 1892 to provide a final resting place for members of the large and steadily growing Jewish community. Covering an area of about 40 hectares, this is the largest Jewish graveyard in Europe. There are around 68,000 surviving tombstones, some of which are very beautiful. You'll need a head cover to get in. The cemetery is about 3km north-east of the centre. You can get there from the centre by tram No 1 from ul Kilińskiego or No 6 from Al Kościuszki. The cemetery's entrance is from ul Zmienna, close to the tram terminus.

Special Events

The Festival of Theatre Schools takes place in April. It's a presentation of the best productions by students of the major theatre schools in Poland.

The **Łódź Ballet Meetings** is a dance and ballet festival that includes both Polish and foreign groups. Performances are staged in the Grand Theatre, and the event runs for two weeks in May of every odd year.

The **International Artistic Textile Triennial** gathers together a collection of artistic creations involving textiles. The main exhibition is in the Textile Museum from early June to late October, and is accompanied by other displays in the private art galleries. The 11th Triennial will be held in 2004.

Mediaschool, or the **International Film and Television Schools' Festival**, is held every October and displays film achievements by students from all over the world. In November or December, Łódź hosts the **Camerimage International Film Photography Festival**, which was previously held in Toruń. In December, there's the modest **Łódź Theatre Meetings**, which features various productions by Polish amateur theatres.

Places to Stay

As with most large cities, Łódź has plenty of hotels in every price bracket. The tourist office keeps an eye on local accommodation and prices, and may help you to find a room if asked.

Places to Stay – Budget

Camping Łódź has two camping grounds.

Camping Nr 167 Na Rogach (☎ *659 70 13, ul Łupkowa 10/16)* Double cabins without/with bath US$18/30. Na Rogach camp site is about 5km north-east of the city centre on the Łowicz road. It has all-year heated cabins. It's accessible by bus No 56 or 60 from ul Narutowicza near Łódź Fabryczna train station.

Camping Stawy Jana (☎ *646 15 51, ul Rzgowska 247)* Double cabins without/with shower US$20/25. Stawy Jana also has heated cabins year-round. It's 5km south of the centre on the Piotrków Trybunalski road. Take tram No 5 from ul Kilińskiego near Łódź Fabryczna station to the end of the line and continue walking south the remaining 500m.

Hostels & Hotels The city has two youth hostels, both centrally located and both open year-round.

Youth hostel (☎ 630 66 80, fax 630 66 83, ul Legionów 27) Beds US$7-15. With a cafe and a gym, and some rooms equipped with radio, TV and private bath, this place is one of Poland's best youth hostels. It's often full so it pays to book ahead.

Youth hostel (☎ 636 65 99, ul Zamenhofa 13) Beds US$6-10. This is also a good hostel, with rooms ranging from singles to a maximum of quads, even though they only have shared facilities. It's normally open Thursday to Monday unless booked in advance by groups or if the other youth hostel is full.

Hotel Raff (☎/fax 684 75 10, ul Milionowa 25) Singles/doubles/triples without bath US$12/18/22. Nothing special, but this is one of the cheapest hotels close to the city centre.

Noclegi Dosko (☎ 636 04 28, fax 636 86 72, Al Piłsudskiego 8) Singles US$15-20, doubles US$20-30, beds in triples or quads US$10-12. This very central place is a former workers' dorm. It occupies the top three floors of a 16-storey tower, providing good views over the city centre. Rooms don't have private baths and vary in standards and rates, so ask to see the room before booking in.

Hotel Szpitala im Kopernika (☎ 681 15 77, ul Paderewskiego 13) Singles/doubles/triples without bath US$11/14/20. This small hospital hostel is 3km south of the city centre but is easily accessible by bus No 57 from Łódź Fabryczna station.

Places to Stay – Mid-Range

Hotel Urzędu Miasta (☎ 640 66 09, fax 640 66 45, ul Bojowników Getta Warszawskiego 9) Singles/doubles/triples with bath US$25/35/42. Just 500m north of Plac Wolności, this hotel, run by the city authorities, provides decent facilities close to the centre – good value.

Hotel Garnizonowy Reymont (☎/fax 633 80 23, ul Legionów 81) Singles/doubles/triples with bath US$35/45/55. Extensively refurbished, Garnizonowy is a former army dorm. It has no great style but is relatively close to the city centre.

Hotel Polonia (☎ 632 87 73, fax 633 18 96, ul Narutowicza 38) Singles with bath US$20-24, doubles with bath US$32-40. Close to the train and bus stations, Polonia is not a classy place but it's not very expensive either.

Places to Stay – Top End

Hotel Savoy (☎ 632 93 60, fax 632 93 68, ul Traugutta 6) Singles with bath US$40-45, doubles with bath US$55-85. The cheapest central option in this price bracket, Savoy is a five-minute walk from the Łódź Fabryczna station and just off ul Piotrkowska – a great location, though don't expect great luxury. Breakfast is included in the room price.

Hotel Ibis (☎ 638 67 00, fax 638 67 77, Al Piłsudskiego 11) Doubles with bath US$60 Mon-Thur, US$40 Fri-Sun. Much the same as others in the Ibis chain, this new 209-room hotel is OK and reasonable, though nothing atmospheric. Optional buffet breakfast is US$6.

Pensjonat Déjà Vu (☎ 636 20 60, fax 636 70 83, ul Wigury 4/6) Doubles with bath & breakfast US$60. This small guesthouse, set in a fine villa dating from 1925, has preserved its style and interior decoration, and has a lot of charm and character. The hotel has just six spacious rooms, each different. Advance booking is essential.

Hotel Grand (☎ 633 99 20, fax 633 78 76, ul Piotrkowska 72) Singles US$65-90, doubles US$80-120, suites US$150-220, all including breakfast. The old-style, Orbis-run Hotel Grand is the city's oldest existing hotel. Opened in 1888 at the peak of the textile boom, it was for a long time the city's top hotel, with such distinctive guests as Pablo Casals and Isadora Duncan. Today it doesn't fly so high, but nonetheless is still comfortable and convenient.

Places to Eat

The city's main culinary artery is ul Piotrkowska and its environs. There's still an array of the milk bar-style places in central Łódź, which provide some of the cheapest meals in town.

Jadłodajnia Dietetyczna (☎ 633 90 91, ul Zielona 5/7) Mains US$2.50-4. Very popular with locals, this well-established budget restaurant serves hearty meals, including some dietetic dishes. If you have any dietetic conditions, this is the place to go. If not, it's still worthwhile coming for a straightforward, tasty meal.

Bar Kaskada (ul Narutowicza 7/9) Mains US$2-3.50. One of the cheapest eateries in the centre, the self-service Kaskada has acceptable food, though don't expect too much.

Bar Pietrynka (ul Piotrkowska 72) Mains US$3-4. Pietrynka is another option for a budget lunch, conveniently set in the middle of the central mall.

Hort-Café (☎ 636 63 77, ul Piotrkowska 106/110) Mains US$2-4. Formerly called Hortex, it's a complex of several eateries, each with a different style and menu. Some focus on sweets such as pastries, cream cakes and milk shakes, while others serve meals, salads, crepes etc.

Restauracja Sphinx (☎ 632 23 68, ul Piotrkowska 93, ul Piotrkowska 175A & ul Piotrkowska 270) Mains US$3-5. Part of a chain that was born in Łódź and is now swiftly expanding across Poland, this agreeable and good value place offers tasty food (a combination of Middle-Eastern and Polish cuisine), generous portions and fast service.

Karczma U Chochoła (☎ 632 51 38, ul Traugutta 3; ul Piotrkowska 200) Mains US$8-10. Arranged in the style of a traditional country inn, U Chochoła serves typical old-Polish fare.

Restauracja Esplanada (☎ 630 59 89, ul Piotrkowska 100) Mains US$8-12. Esplanada is an upmarket trendy place that offers respectable Polish and international food in fine, stylish surroundings, with good service, prices to match and live music on some evenings.

Entertainment

The Ośrodek Informacji Kulturalnej (Cultural Information Centre; ☎ 633 72 99), ul Traugutta 18, open 8.30am to 4.30pm weekdays, 10am to 2pm Saturday, shares premises with the tourist office and is the best place to find out what's on. It also sells tickets for some shows.

The city publishes a good cultural monthly, *Kalejdoskop*, which details (in Polish) what's going on in local theatres, cinemas, art galleries and museums. It can be bought from Ruch kiosks and the cultural centre for US$0.60.

Bars & Pubs There has been an explosion of pubs appearing over recent years – there are now reputedly more than 100 of them on ul Piotrkowska alone. Many are hidden in back alleys with an entrance gate on the main street.

Klub Fabryka (☎ 630 16 44, ul Piotrkowska 80) A very trendy drinking hole established in an old mill hall, Fabryka is a large pub with high-volume music that attracts mostly younger folk. It's well off the street in one of the backyards – ask around to find out how to get there.

Bufet Łódź Kaliska (☎ 630 69 55, ul Piotrkowska 102) A spacious two-level pub with a balcony and occasional live music, Łódź Kaliska has long been popular with locals, both the younger and older clientele.

Piotrkowska Klub (☎ 632 24 78, ul Piotrkowska 97) This place is easily recognisable by its unique, double-level outdoor drinking area. Inside, it's an enjoyable place that includes a pub and restaurant.

Irish Pub 77 (☎ 632 48 76, ul Piotrkowska 77) One of Łódź's oldest pubs, and invariably popular, it occupies a large basement, and opens into an outdoor area in summer. It often has live music.

Cinema Łódź has a dozen commercial cinemas screening the same fare as elsewhere in the country, but if you need something more thought-provoking, try the following:

Łódzki Dom Kultury (Łódź Cultural Centre; ☎ 633 98 00, ul Traugutta 18) The centre runs its own arthouse cinema with often interesting programming.

Two other interesting options for arthouse films are *Kino Charlie (☎ 636 00 92, ul Piotrkowska 203/205)* and *Kino Cytryna (☎ 632 18 59, ul Zachodnia 81/83)*.

Opera, Theatre & Classical Music With a philharmonic hall, an opera house and eight theatres, Łódź has fairly diverse cultural and artistic offerings.

Teatr Wielki *(Grand Theatre;* ☎ *633 99 60, 633 31 86, Plac Dąbrowskiego)* This is the main venue for opera and ballet, plus important visiting shows.

Teatr Muzyczny *(Music Theatre;* ☎ *678 19 68, ul Północna 47/51)* This theatre stages mostly operetta and musicals.

Teatr im Stefana Jaracza *(*☎ *632 66 18, ul Jaracza 27)* This is among the most respected drama theatres.

Teatr Powszechny *(*☎ *633 50 36, ul Legionów 21)* Powszechny is another good drama theatre.

Filharmonia Łódzka *(Łódź Philharmonic;* ☎ *637 14 82, ul Piotrkowska 243)* The philharmonic stages regular concerts of classical music on Friday and, irregularly, on some other days of the week.

Getting There & Away

Train The city has two main train stations: Łódź Kaliska to the west of the centre and Łódź Fabryczna to the east. They are not directly linked by rail, so trains for different destinations depart from either one or the other station (in some cases, from both).

Łódź Kaliska handles trains to Wrocław (263km, four daily), Poznań (251km, three daily) and Łowicz (63km, nine daily). You'll also use this station when going to Toruń, Bydgoszcz, Kalisz and Gdańsk.

For Warsaw (138km), it's better to take the train from Łódź Fabryczna (about 15 daily) rather than from Łódź Kaliska (three daily and they take longer). Also use Łódź Fabryczna when going to Katowice (237km, four daily) and Częstochowa (151km, four daily).

For Kraków, there's one morning train from Łódź Fabryczna, and one evening train from Łódź Kaliska. Both take 3¼ hours to get there.

Bus The PKS bus terminal is next to the Łódź Fabryczna train station. There are fast buses to Kielce (143km, eight daily), Radom (137km, eight daily) and Płock (104km, 10 daily). Polski Express runs buses to Warsaw (134km, seven daily), and

Kraków (271km, three daily) via Częstochowa (121km) and Katowice (196km).

ŁĘCZYCA & TUM
☎ 24 • pop 17,000 & 500

Set amid the marshes in the valley of the Bzura River, Łęczyca ('Wen-**chi**-tsah') is an ordinary small town with a 1500-year history. It began in the 6th century when a stronghold was built 2km east of the present town site. By the 10th century a Benedictine abbey was established, and one of the first Christian churches in Poland was built. In the 12th century a monumental Romanesque collegiate church replaced the former one, and the settlement expanded. It was burnt down by the Teutonic Knights in the early 14th century, and the town was then moved to its present location, where a castle and defensive walls were erected.

During the next two centuries Łęczyca prospered, becoming the regional centre and the seat of numerous ecclesiastical synods. Later on, however, due to wars, fires and plagues, the town lost its importance. In the 19th century the defensive walls and most of the castle were sold for building material. The surviving part of the castle was restored after WWII and turned into a museum.

The original site of the town grew into an independent village and was named Tum. The stronghold fell into ruin but the collegiate church was rebuilt. It's Poland's largest Romanesque church and a fine example of the architecture from that period.

Things to See

Łęczyca The focus of interest here is the **Łęczyca Museum** *(*☎ *721 24 49, ul Zamkowa 1; adult/student US$1/0.50; open 10am-4pm Tues-Fri, 10am-3pm Sat & Sun)* set in what is left of the castle. There are modest archaeological and historical collections, and an ethnographic section that features regional artefacts, mostly woodcarving.

The mid-17th-century **Bernardine Church** is a two-minute walk from the Rynek. It has an opulent rococo interior with a frescoed vault from the 18th century.

Tum Although rebuilt several times, the collegiate church has essentially preserved its original 12th-century form. It's a sizable defensive construction with two circular and two square towers, and two semicircular apses on each end, all built from granite and sandstone. The interior retains Romanesque features but is influenced by later Gothic remodelling, especially in the aisles. The Romanesque portal in the porch (the entrance to the church) is one of the finest in Poland. From the same period are the fragments of the frescoes in the western apse. If the church is locked, get the keys from the priest's house, 100m east of the church, on the opposite side of the road.

The remains of the original stronghold are still visible about 400m to the southwest from the church but it's just a grass-covered hill.

Places to Stay & Eat

Zajazd Senator (☎/fax 721 24 04, ul Ozorkowskie Przedmieście 47, Łęczyca) Doubles/triples with bath $25/32. Probably the only reliable place to stay in town, the Zajazd is on the Łódź road, some distance from the centre. It has its own restaurant, or you can eat at more basic restaurants in the town centre. There's nowhere to stay or eat in Tum.

Getting There & Away

The train station is on the southern outskirts of Łęczyca. Several trains daily run north to Kutno (24km) and south to Łódź (44km).

The bus terminal is near the castle. There are plenty of buses to Łódź (35km), and several to Kutno (25km). To Tum (2.5km), take any bus to Leśmierz (three daily) or to Łódź via Leśmierz (three more), or walk.

OPORÓW

☎ 24 • pop 1000

Lying off the main tourist routes, the village of Oporów ('O-**po**-roof') is rarely visited, even though it may be worth a detour for its Gothic **castle**. Although it's a fairly small and not particularly elaborate construction, this is one of the few castles in Poland that have survived in almost their original form.

The fortified residence was built in the mid-15th century for Władysław Oporowski, the archbishop of Gniezno. Though it changed owners several times during its history, it underwent only a few alterations. The more important changes are the 17th-century wooden ceilings on the 1st floor, covered with Renaissance decoration, the enlargement of the windows and the construction of the terrace at the entrance.

Restored after WWII, today it contains the **Oporów Museum** (☎ 285 91 22, adult/student US$1/0.50, free Sat; open 10am-4pm Tues-Sun) featuring a collection of furniture, paintings, weapons and other objects dating from the 15th to the 19th century. The majority of the exhibits are not directly connected with the castle's history – they were acquired from old palaces and residences of the region.

The castle is surrounded by a moat and a fine **park** (admission free; open 8am-6pm daily).

Getting There & Away

Unless you have your own transport, the most convenient starting point in the area is Kutno, 15km from Oporów. There are buses between Kutno and Oporów running every hour or two. Kutno has frequent bus or train transport to/from Warsaw, Łowicz, Płock, Łódź and Poznań.

PŁOCK

☎ 24 • pop 130,000

Perched on a cliff high over the Vistula, Płock ('Pwotsk') still evokes its illustrious past, its skyline being marked with half a dozen old church towers. One of the oldest settlements in Poland, it was the residence of kings between 1079 and 1138 and the first Mazovian town to get its municipal charter (in 1237). A castle and fortified walls were built in the 14th century and the town developed until the 16th century as a wealthy trading centre.

An omen of disasters to come was the flooding of the Vistula in 1532, when half the castle and part of the defensive walls slid into the river. The wars, fires and plagues which tormented the town during the following centuries brought its prosperity to an end. Płock never regained its former glory and failed to develop into a major city.

After WWII the new regime made Płock an industrial centre by building a large oil refinery and a petrochemical plant just 2km north of the historic centre. This altered the town's character and brought heavy pollution. While local authorities focused their attention on the city's industries, the old town was for a long time largely neglected. This has finally changed in recent years. There has been much restoration work and parts of the quarter have recovered their former appearance. This, together with some museums and the cathedral, make the city a worthwhile stop on the tourist path.

Information

The Centrum Informacji Turystycznej (☎ 262 94 97) is at ul Tumska 4, just a stone's throw from the cathedral.

Bank Pekao, with branches at several central locations including ul Kwiatka 6, ul Kolegialna 14A and on the corner of Al Jachowicza and ul Kochanowskiego, handles travellers cheque transactions and has useful ATMs. Kantors can be found throughout

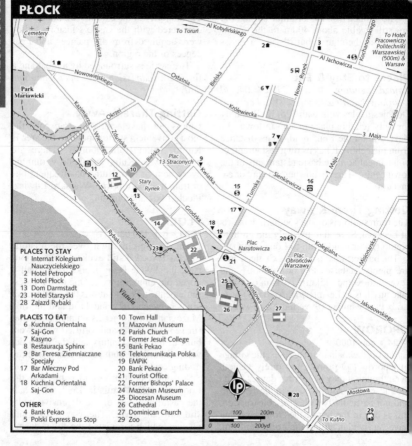

PŁOCK

PLACES TO STAY
1 Internat Kolegium Nauczycielskiego
2 Hotel Petropol
3 Hotel Płock
13 Dom Darmstadt
23 Hotel Starzyski
28 Zajazd Rybaki

PLACES TO EAT
6 Kuchnia Orientalna Saj-Gon
7 Kasyno
8 Restauracja Sphinx
9 Bar Teresa Ziemniaczane Specjały
17 Bar Mleczny Pod Arkadami
18 Kuchnia Orientalna Saj-Gon

OTHER
4 Bank Pekao
5 Polski Express Bus Stop

10 Town Hall
11 Mazovian Museum
12 Parish Church
14 Former Jesuit College
15 Bank Pekao
16 Telekomunikacja Polska
19 EMPiK
20 Bank Pekao
21 Tourist Office
22 Former Bishops' Palace
24 Mazovian Museum
25 Diocesan Museum
26 Cathedral
27 Dominican Church
29 Zoo

the centre, mostly on ul Tumska and adjacent streets.

EMPiK is on Plac Narutowicza and Telekomunikacja Polska has its office on ul Sienkiewicza.

Things to See
The only substantial vestiges of the original Gothic castle are its two brick towers: the Clock Tower (Wieża Zegarowa) and the Noblemen's Tower (Wieża Szlachecka). The adjacent 16th-century Benedictine abbey has been extensively reconstructed and houses the **Mazovian Museum** (*Muzeum Mazowieckie;* ☎ *262 44 91, ul Tumska 2; adult/student US$1.50/0.75, free Thur; open 9am-4pm Tues-Thur & Sun, 10am-5pm Fri & Sat 15 May-30 Sept; open 9am-3pm Wed-Fri, 9am-4pm Sat & Sun 1 Oct-14 May).* It features exhibits on the history of the town and the castle, and the Art Nouveau (Secesja) exhibition. It's Poland's best Art Nouveau collection, which includes furniture, painting, sculpture, glass, ceramics, everyday utensils etc, from Poland and beyond.

The mighty **cathedral** (*open 10am-5pm Mon-Sat, 2pm-5.30pm Sun & public holidays),* facing the museum, was built in the 12th century, and although it lost its original Romanesque character during numerous transformations, it remains an imposing structure dominating the area. Note the sculptured main doors made of bronze – they're a copy of the original 12th-century doors, commissioned by the local bishops. These doors disappeared in mysterious circumstances and reappeared in Novgorod, Russia, where they are now.

The interior, topped with a Renaissance dome added in the mid-16th century, boasts a number of tombstones and altarpieces from various periods. The wall paintings date from the early 20th century. The royal chapel (at the back of the left aisle) holds the sarcophagus of two Polish kings, Władysław Herman and his son Bolesław Krzywousty, who resided in Płock during their reigns.

Next to the cathedral is the **Diocesan Museum** (*Muzeum Diecezjalne;* ☎ *262 26 23, ul Tumska 3A; adult/student US$1/0.50; open 10am-3pm Tues-Sat & 11am-4pm Sun May-*
Sept, 10am-1pm Wed-Sat & 11am-2pm Sun Oct-Apr) which has a collection of paintings, religious art and folk woodcarving.

To the north-west of the castle and the cathedral stretches the Old Town. Although the street layout has been preserved largely unmodified, the architecture changed over the centuries. Today it's the neoclassical style that is the most noticeable, particularly on the facades of houses lining ul Grodzka, the old quarter's thoroughfare.

Stary Rynek, the old market square, was the heart of the 14th-century township. The trees on the square give a refreshing air to the 18th- and 19th-century renovated houses standing around it. The Rynek's western side is occupied by the neoclassical **town hall** (Ratusz), built in the 1820s after an old Gothic town hall, once in the middle of the square, was pulled down in 1816.

Farther to the west are two large 19th-century granaries, recently restored. One of them is an extension of the **Mazovian Museum** (☎ *262 25 95, ul Kazimierza Wielkiego 11B; admission US$0.50; opening hours the same as the museum's main location).* It features temporary exhibitions of ethnographic and folk art.

You can return to the cathedral by the path skirting the cliff top – a pleasant walk providing wide views over the Vistula all the way along. Continuing farther down the riverside park you'll get to the picturesquely located **zoo** (*Ogród Zoologiczny;* ☎ *262 32 72, ul Norbertańska 2; adult/student US$1.50/0.75; open 9am-dusk daily),* which has about 3300 animals belonging to 430 species, including Poland's largest snake collection.

Places to Stay
Płock has a reasonable choice of places to stay to suit every budget.

Internat Kolegium Nauczycielskiego (☎ *262 43 40, 262 43 58, ul Nowowiejskiego 6)* Beds in triples without bath US$7. This all-year Internat (boarding school) is one of the most convenient and cheapest of several dorms of that type scattered across town (most others are seasonal and/or a long way from the centre).

MAZOVIA & PODLASIE

Hotel Pracowniczy Politechniki Warszawskiej (☎ 367 59 96, Al Jachowicza 2) Beds in triples/quads without bath US$7/6. Another low-budget place, though a little less convenient, this 19-room hostel is midway between the centre and the train station.

Dom Darmstadt (☎ 264 11 11, fax 262 20 00, Stary Rynek 8) Doubles with breakfast US$30. Ideally located on the top floor of a historic townhouse facing the Rynek, Dom Darmstadt is a quiet, cosy place that has just three double rooms plus one bathroom and a kitchen – excellent value. Book well in advance.

Hotel Płock (☎ 262 93 93, ☎/fax 268 54 77, Al Jachowicza 38) Doubles with bath US$32. Located close to the centre, Płock is one of the cheapest regular hotels, with impressive brand-new carpets throughout.

Zajazd Rybaki (☎/fax 264 56 58, ul Mostowa 5/7) Singles/doubles/triples with bath & breakfast US$35/40/50. The Zajazd is in a 19th-century house near the bridge over the Vistula, which once served as an inn. Restored and refurbished, it provides satisfactory accommodation, and has its own restaurant.

Hotel Starzyński (☎/fax 262 40 61, ul Piekarska 1) Singles US$50-70, doubles US$60-80, all with bath & breakfast. This attractively situated hotel on the edge of the cliff offers reasonable standards. Rooms facing the river provide good views, as does the hotel restaurant.

Hotel Petropol (☎ 262 44 51, fax 262 44 50, Al Jachowicza 49) Singles/doubles with bath & breakfast US$55/75. The Orbis-run Petropol has recently been revamped and is arguably the best place in town, though stylish it is not.

Places to Eat

Płock's main eating artery is its central pedestrian mall, ul Tumska, though more and more places are appearing on and around Stary Rynek.

Bar Mleczny Pod Arkadami (☎ 262 95 21, ul Tumska 5) Mains US$1-2. Very basic and extra cheap, this survivor of all the political and economic changes of recent decades has hardly ever been renovated, and

therefore provides a rare insight into an archetypal milk bar of the communist era, with its food, decor and clientele.

Kasyno (☎ 262 26 52, ul Tumska 13) Mains US$2-3. Slightly more expensive than the milk bar but much better, Kasyno is a modest restaurant that serves tasty, unpretentious meals. It's in the backyard off the street – enter the gate and you'll see it on your right.

Kuchnia Orientalna Saj-Gon (☎ 268 77 00, Plac Narutowicza 1; Nowy Rynek 9) Mains US$2-3. Saj-Gon is probably the best of several new Oriental budget eateries. The second shop at Nowy Rynek 9 is a smaller outlet.

Bar Teresa Ziemniaczane Specjały (☎ 268 61 68, ul Kwiatka 22) Snacks US$1-2. This small unusual snack bar serves just about everything that can be made from potato, all reputedly prepared according to old Polish recipes.

Restauracja Sphinx (☎ 262 84 81, ul Tumska 13) Mains US$3-5. Occupying a spacious locale with an open-air area in front, Sphinx is pleasant, good and cheap, like any other in the chain around Poland. Come hungry – the portions are huge.

Płock's upmarket eating establishments include restaurants in *Zajazd Rybaki*, *Hotel Starzyński* and *Hotel Petropol*.

Getting There & Away

The train station is nearly 2km north-east of the centre. There are no direct trains to Toruń and only one to Warsaw.

The bus terminal is in front of the train station. There are regular PKS buses to Warsaw (111km) and to Toruń (103km). Polski Express also plies these routes, with hourly departures to both destinations. This service is faster and more comfortable, and is approximately the same price as PKS. Polski Express has its bus stop at Nowy Rynek in the centre.

SIERPC

☎ 24 • pop 20,000

The town of Sierpc ('Shehrpts') has an interesting **skansen** (*Muzeum Wsi Mazowieckiej; ☎ 275 28 83, ul Narutowicza 64;*

adult/student US$2/1.50; open 10am-5pm Tues-Sun May-Sept, 9am-3pm Tues-Sun Oct-Apr). It's 3km west of town on the Lipno road. Buses ply this route regularly and can let you off near the entrance.

A typical north Mazovian village of a dozen farms was reproduced in the grounds using old buildings collected from the region. As in most skansens, the cottages have traditional furnishings, implements and decoration, and can be visited.

CZERWIŃSK
☎ 24 • pop 1700
Set on the bank of the Vistula River off the Warsaw-Płock road, the village of Czerwińsk ('**Chehr**-veensk') boasts the Romanesque **Church of the Annunciation of the Virgin Mary** (☎ 231 50 88, 231 50 35, ul Klasztorna 23). The stone basilica, perched on a cliff overlooking the river, was built in 1129–48, and is one of the oldest examples of Romanesque architecture in Poland. Though it has been remodelled several times, the main structure, complete with its twin towers, is close to the original.

Inside, frescoes were found and uncovered in the 1950s; the oldest ones, from the beginning of the 13th century, can be seen at the head of the right-hand aisle. Note also the Romanesque portal at the entrance to the church from the vestibule.

The church is usually locked, but someone from the monastery at the back will open it for you and show you around. They will also show you a small museum.

The church is 1km off the main road where buses pass regularly on their way to Płock (48km) and Warsaw (63km).

Northern & Eastern Mazovia

PUŁTUSK
☎ 23 • pop 19,000
With a history going back to the 10th century, Pułtusk ('**Poow**-toosk') is one of Mazovia's oldest towns. It enjoyed its golden age in the 15th and 16th centuries when it

was the residence of the bishops of Płock and an important trade and cultural centre. Later on, however, serious fires devastated the town several times, as did repeated invasions, for Pułtusk often found itself at the centre of conflict. In 1806 Napoleon's army fought one of its toughest battles here in the campaign against Russia, and in 1944 Pułtusk was in the front line for several months during which time 80% of its buildings were destroyed.

Things to See
The town's historic core, set on an island, is laid out around a 400m-long cobbled **Rynek**, the longest old market square in the country. In its middle stands the 15th-century brick tower of the town hall, today a **Regional Museum** (☎ 692 51 32, Rynek; adult/student US$1.25/0.75; open 10am-4pm Tues-Sat, 10am-2pm Sun), which features the history of the town and archaeology of the region, plus temporary exhibitions.

The northern end of the square is bordered by the **collegiate church** (kolegiata). Erected in the 1440s, the church received a Renaissance touch a century later. Its interior, crammed with a dozen baroque altars, has Renaissance stucco decoration on the nave's vault but the aisles have retained their original Gothic features. Note the 16th-century wall paintings in the chapel at the head of the right-hand aisle.

At the opposite end of the square stands the **castle**. Built in the late 14th century as an abode for bishops, it was rebuilt several times in later periods. It's now a plush hotel and conference centre. A small Renaissance church in front of the hotel was once the castle's chapel.

Places to Stay & Eat
Zajazd Zalewski (☎ 692 05 23, ul Jana Pawła II 19) Singles/doubles with bath US$25/30. One of the cheaper places in town, Zalewski offers simple rooms and is conveniently close to the bus terminal.

Hotel Baltazar (☎ 692 04 77, ul Baltazara 41) Doubles/triples with bath & breakfast US$30/38. Another affordable hotel, Baltazar is off the Ostrołęka road.

Dom Polonii (☎ 692 90 00, fax 692 05 24, *ul Szkolna 11*) Singles/doubles/triples with bath & breakfast US$60/75/90; cheaper rooms in other buildings: singles US$30-40, doubles US$40-60. Situated in the castle, Dom Polonii is the best hotel in town. Literally, the Polonia Home (Polonia is a general term referring to all Poles living abroad), the hotel mainly serves Polish emigrants but is open to the general public. It has two restaurants that offer a traditional Polish menu, as well as a cafe and nightclub. The hotel also provides other facilities, including a tennis court, horses, kayaks and rowing boats.

Getting There & Away
Pułtusk lies on the route from Warsaw to the Great Masurian Lakes. There's no railway in town, but bus transport is busy, including half-hourly buses to Warsaw (60km).

NOWOGRÓD
☎ 86 • pop 1800
Nowogród ('No-**vo**-groot') is a small town on the Narew River, on the eastern edge of the Puszcza Zielona (Green Forest). It was one of the early strongholds of the Mazovian dukes and traditionally one of the craft centres of the Kurpie, as this part of northern Mazovia is called. Its inhabitants, the Kurpie, have developed their own culture recognisable by their style of dress, music and decoration of their houses. Perhaps the best known are their paper cut-outs and weaving.

During the Nazi offensive of September 1939 Nowogród literally ceased to exist. Slowly rebuilt after the war, it's now just another small town, which wouldn't normally warrant a visit if not for its skansen.

Kurpie Skansen
Founded in 1927, the Skansen Kurpiowski (☎ 217 55 62, *ul Zamkowa 25; adult/ student US$1.25/0.75; open 9am-4pm Tues-Fri, 10am-5pm Sat & Sun May-Sept, 9am-2pm Mon-Fri Oct-Apr*) is the second-oldest museum of its kind in Poland. Like the rest of the town, it was completely destroyed during the war and rebuilt from scratch. It's not, however, a replica; most of the buildings are 19th-century pieces of rural wooden architecture collected from all over the Kurpie region, dismantled, brought to the skansen and reassembled.

There are about 30 buildings including cottages, barns, granaries and mills, and some are open for visits. Although they are mostly small and modest – reflecting living standards in this relatively poor region – the architectural detail is often fine and elaborate, revealing high levels of skill. A collection of charming beehives, including old hollow tree trunks, suggests that honey must have been important to the Kurpie.

The skansen is spectacularly located on a steep bank of the Narew, which gives it an additional charm and provides a good vista over the river.

Places to Stay & Eat
Youth hostel (☎ 217 55 17, *ul 11 Listopada 12*) Beds US$3-4. Open July & Aug. This basic hostel is in the local school two blocks south of the Rynek.

Hotel Zbyszko (☎/fax 217 55 18, *ul Obrońców Nowogrodu 2*) Singles/doubles/ triples with bath & breakfast US$30/40/50. The best accommodation in town, Zbyszko provides neat rooms and has its own restaurant – the only eating place in town to speak of. It's 2km from the town centre, off the Olsztyn road.

The *skansen* (☎ 217 55 62) offers accommodation in summer in a small cottage in the grounds (for up to four people) for US$8 per person.

Getting There & Away
Buses run regularly to Łomża (16km) and several times a day to Myszyniec (42km). To other destinations, transport is sporadic. The bus stop is on the Rynek, a few minutes walk from the skansen.

TREBLINKA
☎ 25
Treblinka, about 100km north-east of Warsaw, is the site of the second-largest extermination camp after Auschwitz. Initially, a penal labour camp was established here, with prisoners forced to work in the local gravel pit. The camp came into being in

summer 1941 and operated until July 1944. More than 20,000 inmates, mainly Poles, passed through it; half of them died of exhaustion, starvation or torture, or were shot.

In spring 1942, the Nazis set up a second camp 2km north of the existing one. Known as Treblinka II, this was strictly a death camp destined to exterminate Jews. During its 16-month operation, about 800,000 Jews from 10 European countries were murdered here.

Things to See

The camp's site is now the **Museum of Struggle & Martyrdom** (*Muzeum Walki i Męczeństwa;* ☎ 787 90 76; *admission free; site open all hours, kiosk open 9am-7pm Apr-Oct, 9am-4pm Nov-Mar*). It's essentially a memorial place, with a monument erected on the site of each camp to commemorate its victims. Access is by a short road that branches off the Małkinia-Sokołów

The Death Camp of Treblinka

Established amid Mazovian forests near the obscure village of Treblinka, the camp received its first transports of Jews from the Warsaw Ghetto in July 1942. From then on, Jews were brought here from all over Europe, including Austria, Czechoslovakia, France, Germany, Greece, Yugoslavia and the Soviet Union.

The 17-hectare camp had 10 gas chambers where victims were gassed with exhaust fumes. There were no crematoria, as the Nazis anticipated that they wouldn't cope with the number of bodies. Instead, the dead were placed on specially constructed open-air grates, doused with a flammable liquid and burned. The fire and smoke continued day and night.

On average, about five to six thousand people were murdered daily, but this went up to 17,000 victims a day during the camp's 'heyday'. In all, around 800,000 Jews, as well as some Gypsies (Roma), died at Treblinka, before the camp was closed down in November 1943. The gas chambers and barracks were demolished and the whole area was ploughed and sown with lupin. Nothing has remained, except for the ashes of nearly a million people.

Podlaski road and leads to the car park and a kiosk, which provides information and sells guidebooks.

It's a 10-minute walk from the car park to the memorial of **Treblinka II**. The path leads through woods until you reach the mock-up railway ramp, an artistic vision created on the site where the transports of Jews arrived. The monument, just 200m east of the ramp, stands on the site where gas chambers were located. Around it is a vast symbolic cemetery in the form of a forest of granite stones – 17,000 of them – reputedly representing the top daily 'output' of the camp. It's one of the most impressive memorials of its kind and will probably live long in your memory.

The monument dedicated to the victims of the penal labour camp of **Treblinka I** is 2km south, accessible by a road paved with massive cobblestones, the so-called 'black road'. Remains of the camp, including the foundations of the demolished barracks, have been preserved. A lookout provides an impressive view over what once was the gravel pit.

Getting There & Away

Unless you have your own wheels, Treblinka is not that easy to get to by public transport. Consequently, there aren't many visitors, which only adds to the poignancy of the place.

The Treblinka memorial site is off the Małkinia-Sokołów Podlaski road, 8km south of Małkinia (4km past the Treblinka village). However, there's no public transport on this stretch of the road.

Probably the easiest way to get to the memorial site is to go by train to the village of Prostyń, on the Warsaw-Białystok line next west of Małkinia. From Prostyń, there are half a dozen buses daily going to Sokołów Podlaski, passing near the Treblinka site. Alternatively, go to Małkinia and negotiate a taxi.

CIECHANOWIEC

☎ 86 • pop 4800

The small old town of Ciechanowiec ('Cheh-hah-**no**-vyets'), on the borderland between Mazovia and Podlasie, has a good museum, worth a visit if you're in the area.

MAZOVIA & PODLASIE

Museum of Agriculture

The Muzeum Rolnictwa (☎ 277 13 28, ul Pałacowa 5; adult/student US$1.50/0.75; open 9am-4pm Mon-Sat & 9am-6pm Sun May-Sept, 9am-4pm daily Oct-Apr) has been established on the grounds of a former estate, consisting of an early 19th-century palace, stables, coach house and some other outbuildings, all set in a park. The buildings have been turned into exhibition halls and the park now gives grounds to a skansen, with a good range of wooden architecture from Mazovia and Podlasie. The collection includes dwellings representing different social classes, from simple peasant cottages to manor houses of the nobility, and has a variety of granaries, barns and mills. There's a 19th-century water mill in working order, and plenty of old beehives.

You'll be guided through the skansen, visiting several interiors. You'll also be shown exhibitions featuring old agricultural machinery, archaic tractors, primitive steam engines, peasants' horse-drawn carts, rudimentary tools etc. There's also a small botanical garden with medicinal plants and a veterinary exhibition. The tour takes about two hours.

English and German-speaking guides (US$10 per group) may be available on the spot but if you want to be sure call the museum in advance and book.

Places to Stay & Eat

The *museum* (☎ 277 13 28) offers accommodation, about 45 beds altogether, distributed in the palace and several other buildings on the grounds. They include some attractive places, such as the hunting lodge from 1858 and the water mill, both of which are part of the skansen's collection. The standard varies depending on where you are staying, but the price is the same, US$6 per person.

Restauracja Astoria (☎ 277 21 38, Plac 3 Maja) Mains US$3-4. This is the best of the few eating options in town.

Getting There & Away

The bus station is a few minutes walk from the museum. Half a dozen buses run daily to Białystok (84km or 100km depending on the route), Bielsk Podlaski (48km), Siemiatycze (38km) and Łomża (60km). To Warsaw (138km), there are two fast buses in the morning and two ordinary buses in the early afternoon. Trains don't call at Ciechanowiec.

Podlasie

Podlasie (pronounced 'Pod-**lah**-sheh', literally 'the land close to the forest') owes its name to the vicinity of the vast forests that once covered much of that part of Poland. The best preserved of these, the Białowieża Forest, now boasts the Białowieża National Park, which is the major tourist sight in the region. There's much more to see and do here, however.

Stretching along the border of Poland and Belarus, Podlasie has for centuries been influenced by these two cultures. With its blend of West and East, Catholicism and Orthodoxy, you will, at times, feel as though you're travelling in a completely different country. The farther off the main track you go, the more onion-shaped domes of Orthodox churches you'll see and the more Belarusian language you'll hear.

The Tatars settled in Podlasie in the 17th century, giving the region a Muslim touch, and their legacy survives to this day (see Kruszyniany & Bohoniki later in this chapter). There were also Jews living here and they too have left traces of their presence (see Tykocin later in this chapter).

Other attractions of the region include the national parks of the Biebrza and Narew Rivers. They both protect extensive lowland marshes of the river valleys. Refer to the specific sections later in this chapter for more details.

Except for the Białowieża National Park, Podlasie is not a touristy area and seldom sees foreign visitors. The only city is Białystok; everything else, particularly the countryside, seems to be half asleep, enjoying the unhurried life of bygone days, as it has for centuries.

BIAŁYSTOK
☎ 85 • pop 280,000

Founded in the 16th century, Białystok ('Byah-**wis**-tok') really began to develop in the mid-18th century, when Jan Klemens Branicki, the commander of the Polish armed forces and owner of vast estates including the town, established his residence here and built a palace. A century later the town received a new impetus from the textile industry, and eventually became Poland's largest textile centre after Łódź.

During the textile boom, Białystok attracted an ethnic mosaic of entrepreneurs, including Poles, Jews, Russians, Belarusians and Germans, and simultaneously drew in a sizable urban proletariat. The town grew in a spontaneous and chaotic manner (still visible today) and by the outbreak of WWI had some 80,000 inhabitants and over 250 textile factories.

In 1920, during the Polish-Soviet war, the Bolsheviks installed a provisional communist government in the Branicki palace, but it didn't survive a month. Its leaders, Julian Marchlewski and Feliks Dzierżyński, called for the formation of a Polish Soviet Republic.

WWII was not kind to Białystok. The Nazis murdered half of the city's population, including almost all the Jews, destroyed most of the industrial base and razed the central district. Postwar reconstruction concentrated on tangible issues such as the recovery of industry, infrastructure and state administration, together with the provision of basic necessities. Historical and aesthetic values receded into the background, as you can see today.

Białystok doesn't have many great attractions and is not a prime tourist destination. However, the mix of Polish and Belarusian cultures gives it a special feel not found in other Polish cities. Białystok is also the starting point for excursions to Tykocin, Kruszyniany and Bohoniki (see the relevant sections).

Information
Tourist Offices The Punkt Informacji Turystycznej (☎ 653 79 50) is in the Holiday Travel office, ul Sienkiewicza 3 (1st floor). It's open 10am to 6pm weekdays.

Money Bank Pekao has branch offices at ul Sienkiewicza 40 and Al Piłsudskiego 11. Other useful banks include Bank Gdański, Al Piłsudskiego 13 and Powszechny Bank Kredytowy, Rynek Kościuszki 7. Kantors are easy to find throughout the centre, as are ATMs.

Post & Communications There are a few post offices in the centre of town. The main post office is at ul Warszawska 10.

Email & Internet Access Central Internet facilities include Oxford (☎ 744 19 58), ul Brukowa 9, Local 1; Netcraft (☎ 742 26 97), ul Legionowa 9/1, Local 028 (in the basement under Savona Pizza Club); and Cyber net (☎ 742 33 11), ul Grochowa 2.

Things to See
Most attractions are along the city's main thoroughfare, ul Lipowa. Starting from its western end, **St Roch's Church** (Kościół Św Rocha), overlooking the centre, was built between 1927–40, and was very modern for its times. It has an 83m tower and an octagonal interior, covered with a glass dome.

Walking eastward, you get to **St Nicholas' Orthodox Church** (Cerkiew Św Mikołaja, ul Lipowa 15). Built in neoclassical style in the mid-19th century, it has an iconostasis from that period, but the frescoes, copied from a Kyiv church, date from the early 1900s.

One block east of the church is a triangular Rynek. The 18th-century **town hall**, in the middle, was reconstructed from scratch after the war and is now home to the **Podlasie Museum** (Muzeum Podlaskie; ☎ 742 14 73, Rynek Kościuszki 10; adult/student US$1/0.50; open 10am-5pm Tues-Sun). It features a modest collection of Polish painting, including some important names such as Malczewski and Witkacy, and temporary exhibitions.

Farther east is a strange merger of two churches: a small 17th-century **old parish church** and, attached to it, a huge mock-Gothic **cathedral**. The latter was constructed

MAZOVIA & PODLASIE

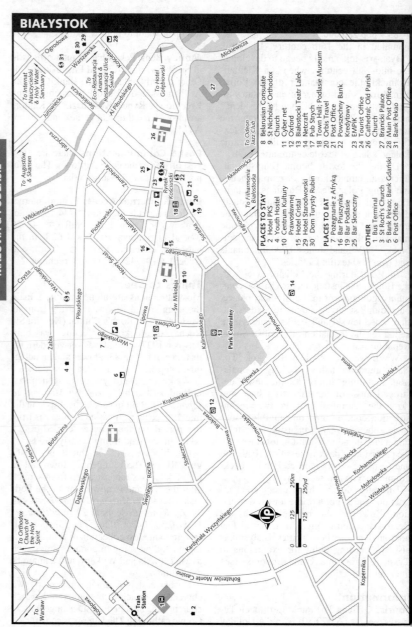

BIAŁYSTOK

PLACES TO STAY
2 Hotel PKS
4 Youth Hostel
10 Centrum Kultury
    Prawosławnej
15 Hotel Cristal
29 Hotel Starodworski
30 Dom Turysty Rubin

PLACES TO EAT
7 Pożegnanie z Afryką
16 Bar Pruszynka
19 Bar Podlasie
25 Bar Słoneczny

OTHER
1 Bus Terminal
3 St Roch's Church
5 Bank Pekao; Bank Gdański
6 Post Office
8 Belarusian Consulate
9 St Nicholas' Orthodox
   Church
11 Oxford
12 Cyber net
13 Białostocki Teatr Lalek
14 Netcraft
17 Pub Strych
18 Town Hall; Podlasie Museum
20 Orbis Travel
21 Post Office
22 Powszechny Bank
   Kredytowy
23 EMPIK
24 Tourist Office
26 Cathedral; Old Parish
   Church
27 Branicki Palace
28 Main Post Office
31 Bank Pekao

at the beginning of this century as an 'extension' of the former, the only way to bypass the tsarist bureaucracy that officially forbade Poles to build Catholic churches.

In the park across the street stands the **Branicki Palace** (Pałac Branickich). Eminent in Polish political life, Branicki was a contender for the Polish crown, but after Stanisław August Poniatowski was elected, Branicki left the court, moved to Białystok and set about building a residence that would rival the king's in importance and luxury. The mighty, horseshoe-shaped baroque palace that was erected used to be referred to as the Versailles of the North.

The palace was burnt down in 1944 by the retreating Nazis. After the war, its exterior was restored to its original 18th-century shape, but the interior, except for the central ballroom, was largely modernised. Today it's the seat of the Academy of Medicine and is not open to tourists. The park around is open to all and consists of a formal French garden and an English landscaped park.

Outside the central area, it's worth seeing the modern **Orthodox Church of the Holy Spirit** (Cerkiew Św Ducha; ☎ 653 28 54, ul Antoniuk Fabryczny 13), 3km north-west of the centre (bus No 5 from ul Lipowa in the centre will let you off nearby). Begun in the early 1980s, the construction of this monumental building, the largest Orthodox church in Poland, is complete, though the interior still needs some work.

The architects took the best of the traditional forms, added modern shapes and lines, and produced a truly impressive church. The huge central onion-shaped dome is topped with a large cross (weighing 1500kg) symbolising Christ, while 12 smaller crosses represent the apostles. The spacious interior boasts a spectacular main iconostasis and two other smaller ones on both sides, and a fantastic giant chandelier. The church is locked, except for daily morning services and the Sunday Mass, but inquire at the Kancelaria (open 8am to 11am and 3pm to 5pm weekdays) in the house behind the church, and somebody may open it for you.

Białystok has a **skansen** (Białostockie Muzeum Wsi; ☎ 743 60 82, Szosa do Jurowiec; adult/student US$1.25/0.75, free Sun; open 8am-3pm Tues-Fri, 9am-5pm Sat, 11am-6pm Sun May-Oct), which features a collection of about 20 old timber buildings representing traditional architecture of the region. It's on the Augustów road, near the village of Jurowce, 5km north of Białystok's centre; bus No 102 from Rynek Kościuszki will take you there.

Searchers of Polish Catholic fervour may want to take a trip to the **Holy Water Sanctuary** (Sanktuarium Święta Woda), near the town of Wasilków, about 10km north of Białystok. Thanks to its miraculous spring, the site has been drawing in the faithful since the early 18th century, but it wasn't until 1997 that the nearby hill was declared the Monument to the 3rd Millennium, or the Mountain of Crosses, and the place began to change dramatically. Since then, crowds of pilgrims rushed to visit the site, bringing and leaving crosses of every shape and size. By the time of writing, there were already more than 10,000 crosses and the number was growing quickly every day. The place is next to the road to Sokółka, 2km past Wasilków. To get there, take bus No 100 from ul Bohaterów Monte Cassino opposite the PKS bus terminal in Białystok.

Places to Stay

Białystok has reasonable accommodation on offer, but there's no longer a camp site in the city.

Youth hostel (☎ 652 42 50, fax 652 60 69, Al Piłsudskiego 7B) Beds US$4-6. Open year-round. The hostel is in an old timber villa, oddly set between dull apartment blocks (it's tucked away from the street behind block No 7). It can sleep about 45 guests, all in bunk beds in dormitories of six to 16 beds. It's simple but well kept, and is within easy walking distance of the train station and the centre.

Internat Nauczycielski (☎ 732 36 64, fax 732 98 65, ul Sienkiewicza 86) Doubles/triples/quins US$7/7/6. This is probably the cheapest place near the city centre after the youth hostel. It offers fairly reasonable room standards, though only with shared facilities.

Hotel PKS (☎ 742 76 14, fax 742 76 45, ul Bohaterów Monte Cassino) Doubles/triples without bath US$10/8. Located on the top floor of the building next to the PKS bus terminal and surrounded by hordes of buses, this is not an atmospheric place by any definition, but it's clean and convenient, especially if you're arriving late or are in transit to another destination.

Dom Turysty Rubin (☎ 677 23 35, fax 732 12 39, ul Warszawska 7) Doubles/triples without bath US$18/24, with bath US$32/40. Nothing special but a cheap option close to the city centre.

Hotel Starodworski (☎/fax 653 74 18, ul Warszawska 7A) Singles/doubles/triples with bath US$32/50/64, breakfast included. Next door to the Rubin, Starodworski is a small, pleasant place run by a Macedonian couple.

Centrum Kultury Prawosławnej (☎ 744 30 10, fax 742 40 88, ul Św Mikołaja 5) Singles/doubles with bath US$22/36. One of the best affordable options right in the city centre, this small, neat, quiet, non-smoking place is run by the Orthodox Church community – recommended.

Hotel Cristal (☎ 742 50 61, fax 742 58 00, ul Lipowa 3) Singles US$50-60, doubles US$60-70, all with bath & breakfast, 20-40% cheaper on weekends. Located in the very centre, Cristal has had its much-needed revamp and is now one of the best places in town, providing particularly good value on weekends. Guests have free access to the hotel's sauna, jacuzzi and gym.

Hotel Gołębiewski (☎ 743 54 35, fax 653 73 99, ul Pałacowa 7) Singles/doubles US$50/60, 30% cheaper on weekends. Another centrally located top-end choice, this relatively new hotel offers decent facilities, including a swimming pool and sauna.

Places to Eat

Bar Podlasie (☎ 742 25 04, Rynek Kościuszki 15) Mains US$1.50-2.50. Open 8am-8pm. Podlasie is a modernised milk bar which serves tasty meals at ultra-low prices.

Bar Słoneczny (☎ 743 58 15, ul Sienkiewicza 5) Mains US$1.50-2.50. Słoneczny is another rock-bottom option for a straightforward meal.

Bar Pruszynka (☎ 742 60 42, ul Malmeda 1) Mains US$2-4. Open 8am-1am. Slightly more expensive than the above, but a bit more agreeable and open longer. It also serves beer and drinks.

Eco-Restauracja Ananda (☎ 741 33 36, ul Warszawska 30) Mains US$3-4. Open 11am-10pm. Behind Hotel Gołębiewski, Ananda is a pleasant place that offers vegetarian food at very reasonable prices.

Restauracja Ulice Świata (☎ 740 41 61, ul Warszawska 30B) Mains US$3-6. Next door to the Ananda, this is an attractive two-level place that serves varied food from around the world, and is open till late.

Upmarket hotels have their own eating facilities, of which the restaurants in **Hotel Cristal** and **Hotel Gołębiewski** are the best though the most expensive.

Pożegnanie Z Afryką (ul Waryńskiego 3/5) Coffee US$2. Open 10am-8pm. This is the place for a cup of coffee (30-odd blends to choose from).

Entertainment

Pub Strych (☎ 653 72 39, Rynek Kościuszki 22) Strych means 'loft', and that's exactly where this pub is. It's one of the more popular watering holes in town.

Odeon Jazz Club (☎ 742 49 88, ul Akademicka 10/1) Odeon is one of the very few places where you can listen to live jazz and blues, mostly on weekends.

Białostocki Teatr Lalek (☎ 742 50 31, ul Kalinowskiego 1) This is one of Poland's best puppet theatres.

Filharmonia Białostocka (☎ 732 23 31, ul Podleśna 2) There are concerts on Friday and sometimes on other days as well.

Getting There & Away

The bus and train stations are adjacent to each other, about 1km west of the central area. You can walk to the centre in 15 minutes or get there by bus No 10.

Train Trains to Warsaw (184km) and Sokółka (41km) leave regularly throughout the day, and there are also couple of departures to Olsztyn (250km) and Gdańsk (429km).

International trains to Vilnius in Lithuania (241km) and St Petersburg in Russia (948km) stop at Białystok. If you plan on taking this route, check in advance whether you need a Belarusian transit visa, because the railway cuts through a short stretch of Belarus, passing through Hrodna. Orbis Travel sells tickets.

Bus About 14 buses daily run north to Augustów (91km), of which half continue up to Suwałki (122km). There are only two buses directly to Białowieża (85km or 98km), at 6.30am and 3pm. Alternatively, go by any of the frequent buses to Hajnówka (66km), then continue by another bus to Białowieża, but check the connections before you set off. Buses to Tykocin (27km or 38km) run roughly every hour. For connections to Kruszyniany (56km) and Bohoniki (46km), see Kruszyniany & Bohoniki later in this chapter.

Polski Express operates three buses a day to Warsaw (188km). They run the distance in 3½ hours (only marginally longer than the fast train) and cost US$5.75 (cheaper than 2nd class in the fast train).

On the international routes, there's one departure a day to Minsk (US$12, 10 hours) and one a week (on Friday) to Vilnius (US$10, eight hours).

TYKOCIN
☎ 85 • pop 2100

Tykocin ('Ti-**ko**-cheen') came into being in the 13th century as one of the strongholds of the Mazovian dukes. Its real growth began in the 15th century and was further accelerated after the town became the property of King Zygmunt August in 1543. It was during this period that Jews started to settle in Tykocin, their community growing rapidly to define the town's character for the next four centuries.

Located on the Warsaw-Vilnius trade route and enjoying numerous royal privileges, Tykocin developed into the commercial centre of the region, to be surpassed by Białystok only at the end of the 18th century. This marked the turning point of Tykocin's fortunes and from then on the town gradually

slid into decline. During WWII it lost all its Jews – half of the town's population – and in 1950 it was deprived of its town charter to become an ordinary village. It recovered its charter in 1994, but otherwise nothing has changed; it remains a small, sleepy place, where not much goes on. Yet several surviving historic buildings are evidence of the town's illustrious past.

Things to See
The star of the Tykocin sights is the **synagogue**, one of the best preserved buildings of its kind in Poland. It dominates the western part of town, which was traditionally inhabited by Jews. This sober-looking edifice, erected in 1642, was used for religious services right up till WWII.

Renovated after the war, the synagogue is now the **Tykocin Museum** (☎ 718 16 13, ul Kozia 2; adult/student US$1.50/0.75; open 10am-5pm Tues-Sun). The interior, with a massive Bimah in the centre and an elaborate Aron Kodesh (the Holy Ark where the Torah scrolls are kept) in the eastern wall, has preserved many of the original wall paintings including Hebraic inscriptions. The exhibition features Talmudic books, liturgical equipment and other objects related to religious ritual. The extension of the museum is in the Talmudic house, right behind the synagogue, which is used mostly for temporary exhibitions.

At the opposite end of the town stands the 18th-century baroque **Holy Trinity Church** (Kościół Św Trójcy). With two symmetrical towers linked to the main building by arcaded galleries, the whole facade looks a little like a palace. It has a baroque and rococo interior.

The church overlooks the spacious **Rynek** (called Plac Czanieckiego). In its middle stands the **Monument to Stefan Czarniecki**, a national hero who distinguished himself in battles against the Swedes. The statue, from the 1760s, is one of the oldest secular monuments in Poland.

Places to Stay & Eat
Youth hostel (☎ 718 16 85, ul Kochanowskiego 1) Open July & Aug. This

basic summer hostel opens in the local school.

Dom Pod Czarnym Bocianem (☎ *718 74 08, ul Poświętna 16*) Beds in doubles with bath US$10. This pleasant new place, on the bank of the Narew River, near the Holy Trinity Church, offers just five double rooms. Guests can use kayaks free of charge.

Restauracja Tejsza (☎ *718 77 50, ul Kozia 2*) Mains US$3-4. Tejsza is a modest, agreeable place, in the basement of the Talmudic house (enter from the back), which serves inexpensive local and Jewish dishes.

Dworek Nad Łąkami & Karczma Rzym (☎ *718 70 79, Kiermusy; information & booking ☎/fax 742 16 02, ul Legionowa 30, Białystok*) Doubles US$50-80. Mains US$7. This impressive-looking complex of manor house and countryside inn was recently built and decorated in a traditional old-Polish style in the tiny hamlet of Kiermusy, 3km west of Tykocin. It can be an attractive proposition for the night or for lunch or dinner, particularly for motorists since public transport on the access road is sporadic.

Getting There & Away
There are about 20 buses daily between Tykocin and Białystok. They either take a short cut via Siekierki (27km) or go by the main road via Stare Jeżewo (38km). If you don't plan on returning to Białystok and want to head west, take any bus to Stare Jeżewo (8km), from where there's regular transport to Łomża, Zambrów and farther on. Stare Jeżewo is also the jumping-off point for Kurowo in the Narew Landscape Park (see Narew National Park later in this chapter). In Tykocin, buses stop at Stary Rynek, 100m from the synagogue.

BIEBRZA NATIONAL PARK
☎ 86

The Biebrza National Park (Biebrzański Park Narodowy) came into being in 1994 and, with its area of about 592 sq km, is Poland's largest park. It embraces the basin of the Biebrza ('**Byehb**-zhah') River along almost its entire course of more than 100km, from its source next to the Belarusian border to its mouth at the Narew River.

The Biebrza Valley is Central Europe's largest natural bog area. The varied landscape consists of river sprawls, peat bogs, marshes and damp forests. Typical local flora includes numerous species of moss, reed-grass and plenty of medicinal herbs. The fauna is rich and diverse and features a variety of mammals such as wolf, wild boar, fox, roe deer, otter and beaver. The king of the park, however, is the elk; there are about 500 specimens living in the valley.

With a total of about 270 species (more than half of all species recorded in Poland), birds are particularly well represented, and the park has become a favourite destination for bird-watchers. You'll find storks, cranes, hawks, curlews, snipes, ruffs, egrets, harriers, crakes, sandpipers, owls, shrikes and at least half a dozen species of warblers. Among some less common varieties are the great snipe, the white-winged black tern and the aquatic warbler.

Orientation
The park can be broadly divided into three geographical entities corresponding to three stretches of the Biebrza River's course. The northern part, in the upper course of the river, known as the Northern Basin (Basen Północny), is the smallest and least visited area of the park.

The Middle Basin (Basen Środkowy), stretching along the river's middle course, is wide and features a combination of wet forests and boglands. The showpiece here is the Red Marsh (Czerwone Bagno), a strict nature reserve encompassing a wet alder forest inhabited by about 400 elk.

The Southern Basin (Basen Południowy) is equally extensive, but here most of the terrain is taken up by marshes and peat bogs. The river here reaches a width of up to 35m before it flows into the Narew. This basin is the best for bird-watching, as it's the favourite habitat of many species, including two of the park's highlights – the great snipe and the aquatic warbler.

Information
The place to visit before any exploration of the park is the visitors information centre

(☎ 272 06 20, 272 08 02, W www.bie brza.org.pl) at the park's headquarters in Osowiec. The office is open 7.30am to 7.30pm daily May to September, 7.30am to 3.30pm weekdays October to April. You pay the admission fee to the park here – US$1 (US$0.50 for students) per day.

The helpful English-speaking staff will provide information about the park and its facilities. They'll give you details of where to stay and eat (or to buy food), and will advise on the best watching spots for different bird species and tell you how to get there. They provide information where to find guides (US$10 an hour per group) and rent out kayaks (US$1 an hour or US$6 a day). The office is stocked with maps and brochures on the park, some of which are in English.

Exploring the Park

Despite its overall marshy character, large parts of the park can be explored relatively easily on foot. About 200km of signposted trails have been tracked through the park's most interesting areas, including nearly 50km through the Red Marsh alone. Dikes, boulders and dunes among the bogs provide access to some splendid bird-watching sites. Several viewing towers on the edge of the marshland allow for more general views of the park.

Another way of exploring the park is by boat. The principal water route in the park goes from the town of Lipsk downstream along the Biebrza to the village of Wizna. This 139km stretch can be paddled at a leisurely pace in seven to nine days. Bivouac sites along the rivers allow for overnight stops and food is available in towns on the way. The visitors office in Osowiec can provide kayaks, maps and information. You can also take the kayak for just a few hours or a day and sail part of the route; the staff will tell you which part to go to.

Places to Stay

There are several bivouac sites within the park and more outside its boundaries. The three most strategically located sites are in Osowiec (2km from the office), Grzędy (a gateway to the Red Marsh) and Barwik

(close to the great snipe's habitat). All three are accessible by road and have car parks. You'll pay about US$1 per person a night to pitch your tent. There are also five rooms (for up to 16 people) in the hunting lodge in Grzędy (US$7 per person).

The nearest hotels to the park are in Goniądz, Mońki and Rajgród. Youth hostels in the region include ones in Goniądz, Grajewo, Osowiec and Wizna; all are open in July and August only. There are also about 70 agrotourist farms in the region – the park's information office has the details.

Getting There & Away

Osowiec sits on the railway between Białystok (58km) and Ełk (46km), with trains in each direction going every two to three hours. The park office is 200m from Osowiec station.

Other regional destinations can be reached by bus, but the service is infrequent. Having your own transport is a huge advantage, as you can easily access most of the park's major attractions.

NAREW NATIONAL PARK

The Narew ('**Nah**-ref') National Park (Narwiański Park Narodowy) is another marshland nature reserve, just as interesting as the Biebrza park, though of a slightly different character. The park protects the unusual stretch of the Narew River. Nicknamed the 'Polish Amazon', the river here splits into dozens of channels that spread across a 2km-wide valley, forming a constellation of swampy islets in between. This is said to be the last place of its kind in Central Europe.

The park encompasses an area of about 73 sq km, 25% of which is bog and a further 3% water. Predictably, the most abundant flora and fauna species are those accustomed to aquatic conditions, including the omnipresent white and yellow water lilies. Among mammals, the beaver is the most characteristic inhabitant, numbering at least 250 individuals living in about 70 lodges. The area is a favourite ground for birds, with as many as 200 species identified in the park, including about 150 species that breed here.

Orientation

The park lies about 20km west of Białystok, to the south of the Białystok-Warsaw highway. The most interesting area is the northwestern part of the park, where the watery labyrinth of channels is most extensive.

The best way to get a taste of the marshland is by boat. While paddling along narrow, snaking canals and ponds, you'll enjoy the lush, green carpets formed by the flora and will spot many birds living here. The water is so crystal clear that you can see fish and plants to a depth of 2m.

The array of the river's arms is so complex and extensive that you may tour around for hours without passing through the same channel twice. The best time for a bird-watching trip is either early morning or late afternoon, when the water birds are most active.

The starting points for exploration of the park include Kurowo, Waniewo and Rogowo. All are just tiny villages sitting on the riverbank and all provide accommodation and boats.

Kurowo

Kurowo sits on the left (western) bank of the Narew, somewhat in the middle of nowhere. It's connected to the outer world only by a rough road, which rarely sees a passing car. The central point of this tiny hamlet is a late-19th-century country mansion surrounded by a 10-hectare park. The building houses the headquarters of the Narew National Park (☎ 85-718 14 17, 86-476 48 12) and a small exhibition (open weekdays) related to the park. You can camp near the building in your tent and use the toilets but there are no showers. There's no restaurant so bring your own food. Kayaks are available for US$1 an hour.

Waniewo

Farther south, Waniewo is larger and has a sealed access road linking it to civilisation. Midway along its main street is the office of 'Sołtys' (village administrator), where you'll find Eugeniusz Sokół (☎ 86-476 47 80), a local tour operator who speaks English and German. As well as offering accommodation (singles/doubles with bath US$15/20), he runs boat excursions around the nearby Narew channels (US$5 per person for a two-hour trip). The trips are in small boats powered by a wooden pole.

Rogowo

Another hamlet on the Narew, Rogowo lies farther to the north-east, where the array of waterways is slightly less developed. The 24-bed Dwór Nad Narwią in the village provides accommodation (singles/doubles with bath US$20/30) plus meals on request. Boat excursions can be arranged with the locals. There's no phone in the Dwór; you need to arrange the accommodation with the owner in Białystok (☎ 85-743 55 95, 85-675 33 93).

Getting There & Away

Rogowo is accessible by a few buses a day from Białystok. Alternatively, take a bus to Kruszewo, get off at the turn-off to Rogowo and walk 2.5km to the Dwór.

There's no public transport to Kurowo or Waniewo, so you'll have a bit of a walk. The usual starting point for Kurowo is the village of Stare Jeżewo on the Warsaw-Białystok highway, 28km west of Białystok. It's frequently serviced by buses from Białystok and Tykocin, and there are also some buses passing through from Warsaw and Łomża.

From Stare Jeżewo, walk 500m south on the road to Sokoły, until you get to an unsigned crossroad. Take the sealed side road to the left for 3km until you reach a T-junction where the seal ends. Take the road to the right (south) for another 1km until you see a large brick granary where the road divides. Take the left-hand fork for the last 1km to Kurowo. It all takes a bit over an hour, and it's a pleasant walk through a bucolic landscape.

From Kurowo, you can walk to Waniewo by the red-signed trail. It leads along an unsealed country road for the first 2km, then goes on the sealed road towards Łapy for another 3km, and finally branches off to the left to Waniewo, 1km away.

Another way of getting to both Waniewo and Kurowo is from the south, from the

Łupianka-Pszczółczyn road, but it's serviced by only two or three daily buses from Białystok. For Waniewo, get off at the Waniewo bus stop, and walk about 1km to the village. For Kurowo, get off in the village of Pszczółczyn and walk the remaining 3km to the park's headquarters.

KRUSZYNIANY & BOHONIKI
☎ 85

These two small villages, close to the Belarusian border to the east of Białystok, are noted for their timber mosques, the only historic mosques surviving in Poland. They were built by the Muslim Tatars, who settled here at the end of the 17th century.

Kruszyniany

Spreading for over 2km along the road, Kruszyniany looks much larger than it really is. The **mosque**, hidden in a cluster of trees back from the main road, is in the central part of the village. It is an 18th-century rustic wooden construction, in many ways similar to old timber Christian churches.

The mosque's modest interior, made entirely from pine, is divided into two rooms, the smaller one designed for women, who are not allowed into the main prayer hall. The latter, with carpets covering the floor, has a small recess in the wall, the Mihrab, in the direction of Mecca. Next to it is the Mimbar, a sort of pulpit from which the

MAZOVIA & PODLASIE

The Tatars of Poland

In the 13th century large parts of Eastern Europe were ravaged by hordes of fierce Mongol horsemen from Central Asia. These savage nomadic warriors (commonly, though confusingly, referred to in all Europe as the Tatars) came from the great Mongol empire of Genghis Khan, which at its peak stretched from the Black Sea to the Pacific. They first invaded Poland in 1241 and repeatedly overran and destroyed most of Silesia and Małopolska, the royal city of Kraków included. They withdrew from Europe as fast as they came, leaving few traces other than some folk stories (such as Kraków's Lajkonik). Not long after, the empire broke up into various independent khanates.

By the end of the 14th century Poland and Lithuania faced an increasing threat from the north, from where the Teutonic Order swiftly expanded southwards and eastwards over their territories. As a measure of protection, Lithuania (which soon was to enter into a political alliance with Poland) began looking for migrants eager to settle its almost uninhabited borderland fringes. It welcomed the refugees and prisoners of war from the Crimean and Volgan khanates, offspring of the once powerful Golden Horde state ruled by the inheritors of Genghis Khan. The new settlers were Muslim Tatars of a different tribal background.

Tatars' military involvement in Polish affairs began in 1410 at the battle of Grunwald, where King Jagiełło defeated the Teutonic Knights; in this battle a small unit of Tatar horsemen fought alongside the Polish-Lithuanian forces. From that time the numbers of Tatar settlers grew, and so did their participation in battles in defence of their adopted homeland. By the 17th century, they had several cavalry formations reinforcing Polish troops in the wars, which were particularly frequent at that time.

In 1683, after the victory over the Turks at the battle of Vienna, King Jan Sobieski granted land in the eastern strip of Poland to those who had fought under the Polish flag. The Tatars founded new settlements here and built their mosques. Of all these villages, Kruszyniany and Bohoniki are the ones that have preserved some of the Tatar inheritance, though apart from their mosques and cemeteries not much else remains. The original population either integrated or left, and there are only a few families living here today that are true descendants of the Tatars.

Of a total of some 3000 people of Tatar origin in Poland, the majority found homes in large cities such as Warsaw, Białystok and Gdańsk. Nonetheless, they flock together in Kruszyniany and Bohoniki for important holy days, as Poland's only mosques are here (apart from one built in Gdańsk in the 1990s). And they usually end up here at local Tatar graveyards, two of only three still in use in the country (the other is in Warsaw).

imam says prayers. The painted texts hanging on the walls, the Muhirs, are verses from the Koran.

The mosque is used for worship, and on the most solemn holy days there may not be enough room inside for all the congregation. At other times it's locked, but go to house No 57, next to the mosque on the same side of the road, and someone will open it for you. Be properly dressed (no bare legs) and take off your shoes before entering the prayer hall.

The Mizar, or **Muslim cemetery**, is in the patch of woodland 300m beyond the mosque. The recent gravestones are Christian in style, showing the extent of cultural assimilation that has taken place, and are on the edge of the graveyard. Go deeper into the wood, where you'll find old tombstones hidden in the undergrowth. Some of them are inscribed in Russian, a legacy of tsarist times.

Bohoniki

This village is smaller and so is its **mosque**. Its interior is similar in its decoration and atmosphere to that of Kruszyniany, though it's more modest. It, too, can be visited and the keys are kept at the house across the road from the mosque.

The **Muslim cemetery** is about 1km north of the mosque. Walk to the outskirts of the village then turn left up to a small forested area. As in Kruszyniany, the old tombstones are farther afield, overgrown by bushes and grass.

Places to Stay & Eat

There's nothing in Bohoniki and only a sort of shabby bar in Kruszyniany. In the vicinity, there's a summer *youth hostel* (☎ 711 18 14, ul Szkolna 10) and a basic restaurant in Krynki, and two budget *hotels* in Sokółka (☎ 711 27 93, ul Mickiewicza 2 & ☎ 711 25 67, ul Wodna 20) along with a few places to eat.

Getting There & Away

The two villages are 37km apart, each about 50km from Białystok. If you plan on visiting only one village, go to Kruszyniany. A visit

to both in one day from Białystok is possible but would involve an early start, several changes of bus and a fair bit of a walk. There are no direct buses from Białystok to Bohoniki, and only a few to Kruszyniany.

The best way to do the trip is to go first to Kruszyniany by the 8am bus. After visiting the village take a bus to Sokółka, but if there's no bus on its way, go to Krynki and change, as there are more buses from there. Get off at Drahle Skrzyżowanie, the last stop before arriving at Sokółka, and walk 3.5km east along the side road to Bohoniki. There's virtually no traffic on this road and only a couple of buses. If you're lucky, you might catch the afternoon bus from Bohoniki to Sokółka, but if not, walk the same way back to the main road, where buses to Sokółka run until around 8pm. From Sokółka, trains go to Białystok till about 10pm.

HAJNÓWKA
☎ 85 • pop 25,000

Set on the edge of the Białowieża Forest, Hajnówka ('Hahy-**noof**-kah') is the main gateway for the Białowieża National Park. The town was founded in the 18th century as a guard post to protect the Białowieża Forest, which was used as a hunting ground by the Polish kings, and later by the tsars. Early this century, when the tsars were busy with domestic problems, the exploitation of the forest began in earnest, which is how the town came to grow. Today, Hajnówka is a local centre of the timber industry, with a mixed Polish-Belarusian population.

Information

The tourist office (☎ 682 51 41) is at ul Parkowa 3. You can also try the PTTK office (☎ 682 27 85) at ul 3 Maja 37. There are two banks in town (PBK and PKO BP) that may change travellers cheques and service credit cards.

Orthodox Church of the Holy Trinity

This church (*Cerkiew Św Trójcy*, ☎ 873 29 71, ul Dziewiatowskiego 13), is the town's major sight and arguably one of the most beautiful modern Orthodox churches in Poland. Begun in the early 1970s and fully completed two decades later, the irregular structure, covered by an undulating roof, supports two slender towers, the main one 50m high. The bold, unconventional design, the work of Polish architect Aleksander Grygorowicz, has resulted in a powerful and impressive building.

Its creators have also done a good job inside. The icons and frescoes were painted by a Greek artist whereas the stained-glass windows came from a Kraków workshop. Look for the chandelier and the iconostasis.

The *Kancelaria* (church office) is in the house next to the church. If you inquire there during its opening hours (10am to 1pm and 2pm to 5pm Monday to Saturday) one of the priests will to show you around the church. Otherwise coincide with the services (Sunday at 10am, weekdays at 8am).

Lovers of Orthodox churches may be interested in another impressive piece of architecture, the **Orthodox Church of St John the Baptist** (*Cerkiew Św Jana Chrzciciela, ul Reja 12*), on Hajnówka's outskirts, off the road to Białowieża. Its structure is completed but the interior still lacks furnishings and decoration.

Special Events
The Church of the Holy Trinity is the scene for the **International Festival of Orthodox Church Music**, which takes place annually in May/June and attracts a score of choirs from all over the world. The week-long event is organised by the Fundacja Muzyka Cerkiewna (☎ 682 32 02), ul Białostocka 2, just a few steps from the church.

Places to Stay & Eat
Dom Nauczyciela (☎/*fax 682 25 85, ul Piłsudskiego 6*) Singles/doubles/triples without bath US$15/20/25. Dom Nauczyciela is a clean, but simple, year-round budget choice.

Zajazd Orzechowski (☎ 682 27 58, fax 682 23 94, ul Piłsudskiego 14) Singles/doubles/triples with bath & breakfast US$40/60/75. This relatively new hotel is good and has a reasonable restaurant.

Entertainment
Bar U Wołodzi (☎ 682 46 26, ul 3 Maja 34A) Pop into this bar, known countrywide, for a beer amid a bizarre collection of communist memorabilia. Ask to be let into the VIP room, where you can try on any of the dozens of Soviet uniforms and take as many snaps as you wish.

Getting There & Away
The train and bus stations are next to each other, about 1km south of the Orthodox church.

There are about eight buses daily to Białowieża. They go by two routes, either directly (19km) or via Budy (25km); both these trips go through the splendid forest and are spectacular. Trains to Białowieża have been suspended due to the poor shape of the rail lines, but PKP is planning to introduce a type of bus that runs on rail tracks.

There are only a couple of trains to Białystok (76km) but buses ply this route fairly regularly. One train and one bus daily go straight to Warsaw (214km and 233km, respectively).

BIAŁOWIEŻA NATIONAL PARK
☎ 85
Lying on Poland's border with Belarus, the Białowieża National Park (Białowieski Park Narodowy) is the oldest national park in the country and the only Polish one included on Unesco's World Heritage list. The park is a small section of a vast forest known as the Puszcza Białowieska, or Białowieża ('Byah-wo-**vyeh**-zhah') Forest.

Today encompassing about 1200 sq km, distributed roughly evenly between Poland and Belarus, the puszcza was once an immense and barely accessible forest stretching for hundreds of kilometres. In the 15th century it became a private hunting ground for the Polish monarchs and continued to be so for the tsars in the 19th century after Poland's partition. During WWI the Germans exploited it intensively, cutting some five million cu metres of timber, and depleting animal life. The inevitable gradual colonisation and exploitation of its margins has also diminished the forest area

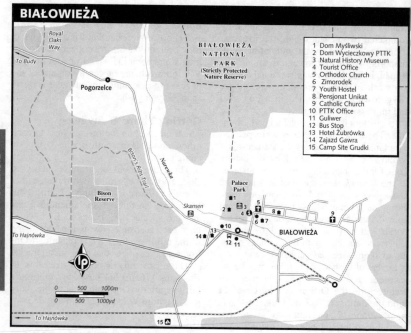

BIAŁOWIEŻA

Royal Oaks Way

To Budy

Pogorzelce

BIAŁOWIEŻA
NATIONAL
PARK
(Strictly Protected
Nature Reserve)

1 Dom Myśliwski
2 Dom Wycieczkowy PTTK
3 Natural History Museum
4 Tourist Office
5 Orthodox Church
6 Zimorodek
7 Youth Hostel
8 Pensjonat Unikat
9 Catholic Church
10 PTTK Office
11 Guliwer
12 Bus Stop
13 Hotel Żubrówka
14 Zajazd Gawra
15 Camp Site Grudki

Narewka

Bison's Ribs Trail

Bison
Reserve

Palace
Park

Skansen

To Hajnówka

BIAŁOWIEŻA

0   500   1000m
0   500   1000yd

To Hajnówka

15

and altered the ecosystem. Even so, this vast forest, protected for so long by the royal guards, has kept its centre largely untouched. It's the largest original lowland forest in Europe, and retains much of its primeval landscape and plant and animal life.

Soon after WWI the central part of the puszcza was made a nature reserve, and in 1932 it was formally converted into a national park. Today the total area of the park is 105 sq km, of which 47 sq km is completely protected, making it the largest strictly conserved forest in Europe.

The park is relatively flat, in parts swampy, and covered with mixed forest, with oak, hornbeam, spruce and pine being the predominant species. Trees reach spectacular sizes uncommon elsewhere, with spruce 50m high and oak trunks 2m in diameter. Some of the oak trees are more than 500 years old.

The forest is home to a variety of animals. There are about 120 species of birds including owls, cranes, storks, hazel-hens and nine species of woodpecker. Among the mammals are elk, stag, roe deer, wild boar, lynx, wolf, beaver and the uncontested king of the puszcza, the bison.

Orientation

The starting point for the excursions into the park is the village of Białowieża. It has accommodation, food and several travel agencies, whom you'll need if you want to visit the strictly protected natural reserve.

Coming by bus from Hajnówka, you can get off at the entrance to the 48-hectare Palace Park (Park Pałacowy) at the western end of the village. You'll find four hotels within a five-minute walk from the bus stop (two in the park and two on the main access road). The Palace Park itself was laid out at the end of the 19th century after a splendid tsarist palace was built in 1894. The palace was destroyed by the Nazis during WWII.

If you plan on staying in the youth hostel, continue by bus to the next stop, opposite the Orthodox church.

Once you've found a place to stay, check the travel agents about visiting the strictly protected nature reserve. Do this soon after your arrival, as all visits must be accompanied by a guide, and it may take a while to arrange one or to collect a group to share the costs. If you have some time before your tour, visit the museum, which will introduce you to the local habitat and its wildlife.

Information

Tourist Offices The tourist office (☎ 681 29 01) is at the eastern entrance to the Palace Park. It's open 9am to 5pm daily.

Money There's a kantor in Białowieża, in the Hotel Żubrówka, but it gives poor rates, so it's better to change in a bigger urban centre beforehand.

Travel Agencies There are half a dozen agencies that organise trips to the strictly protected nature reserve (see the following section in this chapter). The major operator is PTTK (☎ 681 22 95) at the southern entrance to the Palace Park. Alternatively try Guliwer (☎ 681 23 66), ul Kolejowa 3, or Zimorodek, ul Waszkiewicza 2.

Some agencies (including Zimorodek) and hotels (Zajazd Gawra, Dom Wycieczkowy PTTK, Hotel Żubrówka) handle bike rental, which may be a convenient and enjoyable form of visiting some more distant sites, eg, the Bison Reserve. Many walking trails in the area are suitable for bikes. A bike will cost about US$0.70 to US$1 per hour or US$5 to US$8 for the whole day.

Natural History Museum

The museum *(Muzeum Przyrodniczo-Leśne;* ☎ *681 22 75, Park Pałacowy; adult/student US$1.50/0.75; open 9am-4pm Tues-Sun, closed days following public holidays)* features exhibitions devoted to the park's history, the archaeology and ethnography of the region, and a collection of plants and animals that grow or live in the puszcza, including the famous bison.

Strictly Protected Nature Reserve

The reserve *(Rezerwat Ścisły)* can only be entered with a guide. Visits can be organised through any of the travel agencies, which can provide English-speaking guides (as well as German and occasionally French).

The most comfortable way to visit the reserve is by horse-drawn cart. The standard tour takes about three hours, but longer routes including some more remote areas are also available. The cart takes four people and costs about US$28 for a regular tour. A foreign-language guide will cost another US$30 per group. Add to it an admission fee to the reserve per adult/student US$1.50/0.75. In effect, it comes to about US$16 per adult if the cart is fully occupied.

Another way of exploring the reserve is by bike, though this requires special permission from the park's management, which can be hard to get. The standard bike route is 8km long, but again, there is no obstacle to longer rides. Bikes can be rented from some agencies and hotels (see Information earlier), and you need a guide, which will cost US$30 per group. The US$1.50/0.75 admission fee applies here as well.

Finally, you can set off for the reserve on foot, and this is probably the best way to get a close feel for the forest, and the most popular with visitors. You normally walk along the usual 8km trail, which takes about four hours and costs US$30 for a guide per group (plus an adult/student US$1.50/0.75 admission fee).

The reserve gets pretty swampy in spring (March to April) and may at times be closed to visitors.

Bison Reserve

The Bison Reserve *(Rezerwat Pokazowy Żubrów;* ☎ *681 23 98; adult/student US$1.50/0.75; open 9am-4pm daily)* is a wildlife park where the animals typical of the puszcza, including bison, elk, wild boar, stag and roe deer, are kept in large enclosures. You can also see the *żubroń,* a cross between a bison and cow, which has been bred in Białowieża so successfully that the progeny are even larger than the bison itself, reaching weights of up to 1200kg.

MAZOVIA & PODLASIE

The Bison – Back from the Brink

The European bison *(Bison bonasus)*, żubr in Polish, is the biggest European mammal, its weight occasionally exceeding 1000kg. These large cattle, which live for as long as 25 years, look pretty clumsy but can move at 50km/h when they need to.

Bison were once found all over the continent, but the increasing exploitation of forests in Western Europe began to push them eastwards. In the 19th century the last few hundred bison lived in freedom in the Białowieża Forest. In 1916 there were still 150 of them here but three years later they were totally wiped out. By then, there were only about 50 animals of the species kept in zoos throughout the world.

It was in Białowieża that an attempt to prevent the extinction of the bison began in 1929, by bringing several animals from zoos and breeding them in their natural habitat. The result is that today there are about 250 bison living in freedom in the Białowieża Forest alone and about 350 more have been sent to a dozen other places in Poland. Many bison from Białowieża have been distributed among European zoos and forests, and their total current population is estimated at about 2500.

BISONS SVM POLONIS SVBER, GERMANIS BI SONT: IGNARI, VRI NOMEN DEDERANT

Another peculiarity is the tarpan *(Equus caballus gmelini)*, a small, stumpy, mouse-coloured horse with a dark stripe running along its back from head to tail. The tarpan is a Polish cousin of the wild horse *(Equus ferus silvestris)* that once populated the Ukrainian steppes but became extinct in the 19th century. The horse you see is the product of selective breeding in the 1930s, which preserved the creature's original traits.

The reserve is 3km west of the Palace Park (by road it's 4.5km). You can get there on foot by the green- or yellow-marked trails, both starting from the PTTK office, or by the trail called Żebra Żubra (Bison's Ribs). Buses to Hajnówka that go down the main road (not via Budy) will let you off at the Białowieża Skrzyżowanie bus stop, a 10-minute walk from the reserve. You can also get there by horse-drawn cart – ask in the travel agencies for details.

The Royal Oaks Way

About 3km north of the Bison Reserve is the Royal Oaks Way (Szlak Dębów Królewskich), a path traced among a score of ancient oak trees, some over four centuries old. Each of the trees is named after a Lithuanian or Polish monarch. To get there, take the blue trail from Białowieża or the yellow trail from the Bison Reserve. If you take a cart to the Bison Reserve, you can visit the Oaks on the same trip.

Białowieża Village

Apart from the natural attractions, you might like to stroll about the village of Białowieża. This sleepy little place, which today has some 2500 inhabitants (70% of whom are Orthodox church believers), still has some of its 19th-century wooden houses. Near the Palace Park is the late-19th-century Orthodox church, which features a rare ceramic iconostasis. There's a small private skansen on ul Zastawa – inquire at the PTTK agency about the possibility of visiting it.

Places to Stay & Eat

Białowieża has quite a choice of accommodation options, most of which are inexpensive. Apart from the places listed here there are rooms rented out by locals in their homes – inquire at the tourist office.

Youth hostel (☎/fax 681 25 60, ul Waszkiewicza 6) Beds US$4-7. Open year-round. The cheapest place in town, this friendly hostel is hidden behind a mustard-coloured wooden school building. It has 48 beds distributed in a few small rooms and several dormitories of six to 12 beds each.

Pensjonat Unikat (☎/fax 681 27 74, ul Waszkiewicza 39) Singles/doubles with bath US$14/26. Mains US$3-5. About 300m beyond the youth hostel, Unikat is a reasonable small and quiet guesthouse with its own restaurant – possibly the best budget place for a meal.

Dom Wycieczkowy PTTK (☎/fax 681 25 05, Park Pałacowy) Singles/doubles without bath US$9/15, doubles/triples/quads with bath US$20/25/30. The cheapest place to stay after the youth hostel, the 82-bed PTTK is popular with school and student groups, so it can be busy and noisy. It has a bistro that serves budget meals.

Dom Myśliwski (☎ 681 25 84, fax 681 23 23, Park Pałacowy) Singles/doubles/triples /quads with bath US$18/25/30/35. Another Palace Park option, this is much better and quieter than the PTTK.

Hotel Żubrówka (☎ 681 23 03, fax 681 25 70, ul Olgi Gabiec 6) Doubles/triples with bath US$25/30. Mains US$5-10. Room standards are pretty regular, but a large upmarket extension is being constructed and may provide some of the best luxuries in town with singles/doubles at US$60/75, with breakfast. The hotel restaurant is OK but twice as expensive as that in the Unikat.

Zajazd Gawra (☎ 681 28 04, ul Polecha 2) Doubles without/with bath US$18/26. Just behind the Hotel Żubrówka, the Gawra has rooms of differing standards, but generally it's not bad value. Gawra also runs a simple *camp site* in Grudki, 2km southwest of the village.

Getting There & Away

The only gateway to Białowieża is Hajnówka. You have to go through it and, more often than not, change your bus or train.

About eight PKS buses daily run to Hajnówka, either via the main road (19km) or via the village of Budy (25km), providing a spectacular trip through the forest. Trains no longer operate, but PKP plans to introduce a bus that runs on rails.

There are only two direct buses from Białowieża to Białystok (82km or 98km), or go to Hajnówka and change.

GRABARKA

The Holy Mountain of Grabarka hardly means a thing to the average Pole, yet it's the major place of pilgrimage for the Orthodox Church community. Remote from important urban centres and main roads, the mountain, which is actually a small forested hill, lies 1km from the obscure village of Grabarka. The only town of any size in the region is Siemiatycze, 9km to the west.

A convent and a church are hidden among woods on top of the hill. The 18th-century timber church went up in flames in 1990, but it was rebuilt in a similar shape to the previous one. The convent was established in the aftermath of WWII, to gather all the nuns scattered throughout the country from the five convents that had existed before the war. Since then Grabarka has become the largest Orthodox pilgrimage centre in Poland.

The most striking thing about the place is that the hill is covered with thousands of crosses of different shapes and sizes ranging from 5cm miniatures to structures several metres tall.

Transfiguration

Grabarka's biggest feast is the Spas, or the day of Transfiguration of the Saviour, on 19 August. The ceremony begins the day before at 6pm and continues with Masses and prayers throughout the night, culminating at 10am with the Great Liturgy, celebrated by

MAZOVIA & PODLASIE

The Crosses of Grabarka

The story of the Grabarka crosses goes back to 1710, when an epidemic of cholera broke out in the region and decimated the population. Amid utter despair, a mysterious sign came from the heavens, which indicated that a cross should be built and carried to a nearby hill. Those who reached the top escaped death, and soon afterwards the epidemic disappeared. The hill became a miraculous site and the thanksgiving church was erected. Since then people have been carrying crosses to place alongside the first one.

Apart from the thanksgiving crosses, pilgrims have been bringing crosses for various other intentions such as healing or penance. The size of the cross is supposed to represent either the gravity of the disease or the seriousness of the sins of its maker. No matter the reason or the size, however, the forest of perhaps 20,000 crosses makes for a very unusual and powerful sight.

the metropolitan of the Orthodox Church in Poland. Up to 50,000 people may come from all over the country to participate.

Before climbing the Holy Mountain, the pilgrims perform ritual ablutions in the stream at the foot of the hill and drink water from the holy well, which supposedly has miraculous properties. The more fervent of them fill large bottles with the wonder-working liquid to take back home to prevent misfortune or heal the ill. Those who bring crosses have them blessed before adding them to the spectacular collection.

On that night, the surrounding forest turns into a vast car park and camp site, with cars and tents tightly filling the spaces between the trees. Yet, despite this wave of modernity, the older, more traditional generation comes on foot without any camping gear and keeps watch all night. The light of the familiar thin candles adds to the mysterious atmosphere.

If you wish to come on this magical night, you have the same options – to pitch your tent or to stay awake. The commercial community is well represented with plenty of stalls selling food and drink and a variety of religious goods, including CDs and cassettes with Orthodox church music.

Getting There & Away

Transport is basically by train, the Sycze station being a short walk from the hill. Trains run regularly to/from Siedlce (63km) and semi-regularly to/from Hajnówka (58km). There is only one train directly to/from Warsaw (156km) and Lublin (202km), and three trains to/from Białystok (106km).

From the Sycze train platform, it's a little over a kilometre to the Holy Mountain. There are no obvious signs to indicate the direction but the yellow trail heading south will get you there. If you are coming from Hajnówka, go left from the platform down the road. From there the road veers right, but follow the track straight into the forest – you'll come across the trail and signs as you go.

Only one or two buses link Grabarka to Siemiatycze (9km) and it's better not to rely on them at the time of the celebrations.

Kraków

☎ 12 • pop 770,000

The royal capital for half a millennium, Kraków has witnessed and absorbed more of Poland's history than any other city in the country. Moreover, unlike most other Polish cities, it came through the last war unscathed, so it has retained much of this history, guarded in its walls, works of art and traditions. The postwar period seems to have had little impact: the tallest structures on Kraków's skyline are not skyscrapers but the spires of old churches.

No other city in Poland has so many historic buildings and monuments (about 6000), and nowhere else will you encounter such a vast collection of works of art (2.5 million). In appreciation of the town's exceptional historic and artistic values, in 1978 Unesco included the centre of Kraków on its first World Heritage list.

Yet there's more to see than ancient walls. Kraków is alive and vibrant, with the past and present mingling harmoniously. The continuity of its traditions has created its own peculiar atmosphere, and countless legends have added their aura. Kraków is a city with character and soul.

Kraków has traditionally been one of the major centres of Polish culture, and its cultural status remains very high. Many leading figures of contemporary arts and culture – Andrzej Wajda, Roman Polański and Krzysztof Penderecki, to name just a few – are associated with Kraków. The two Nobel prizewinners in literature, Czesław Miłosz (1980) and Wisława Szymborska (1996), live here. The city also gave the world its first Polish pope.

Kraków is Poland's best-educated city. With its renowned 14th-century Jagiellonian University and 12 other institutions of higher education, it has over 70,000 students, nearly a tenth of the city's population.

Give yourself at least several days or even a full week for Kraków. This is not a place to rush through. The longer you stay, the more captivating you'll find it and

Highlights

- Stroll around the magnificent Main Market Square
- Visit Wawel castle and cathedral, possibly the most important historic sights in Poland
- Admire Veit Stoss' Gothic altarpiece in St Mary's Church
- Explore the Czartoryski Museum's rich collection including Leonardo da Vinci's *Lady with the Ermine*
- Take in an evening of live entertainment, listening to *klezmer* music in one of Kazimierz's cafes
- Tour the labyrinthine 700-year-old salt mine in Wieliczka
- Soak up some atmosphere and taste a couple of local ales in the fabulous cellar-vaulted pubs

RUSSIA

Greater Kraków p186
Kraków – Old Town & Wawel p190
Kraków – Kazimierz p202

CZECH REPUBLIC

SLOVAKIA

there's almost always a festival or some other special event going on.

HISTORY

The first traces of the town's existence date from around the 7th century. In the 8th and

183

The seperate walled cities of Kraków and Kazimierz in the late 15th century

9th centuries Kraków was one of the main settlements of the Vistulans or Wiślanie, the tribe which several centuries earlier had spread around the region known as Little Poland or Małopolska. The earliest written record of Kraków dates from 965, when an Arabian traveller and merchant of Jewish descent, Ibrahim ibn Yaqub from Cordova, visited the town and referred to it in his account as a trade centre called Krakwa.

In 1000 the bishopric of Kraków was established, and in 1038 Kraków became the capital of the Piast kingdom. The Wawel castle and several churches were built in the 11th century and the town, initially centred around the Wawel hill, grew in size and power.

In 1241 the Tatars overran Kraków and burned down the town, which was mostly made of timber. In 1257 the new town's centre was designed on a grid pattern, with a market square in the middle. Brick and stone largely replaced wood, and Gothic became the dominant architectural style. Fortifications were gradually built.

Good times came with the reign of King Kazimierz Wielki, a generous patron of art and scholarship. In 1364 he founded the Kraków Academy (later renamed the Jagiellonian University), the second university in central Europe after Prague's. Nicolaus Copernicus, who would later develop his heliocentric theory, studied here in the 1490s.

Kraków's economic and cultural expansion reached a peak in the 16th century. The Renaissance period, Poland's golden age, saw the city flourish as never before. The medieval Wawel castle gave way to a mighty palace, learning and science prospered, and the population passed the 30,000 mark.

It was not to last, however. The transfer of the capital to Warsaw in 1596–1609 brought an end to Kraków's good fortune. Though the city remained the place of coronations and burials, the king and the court resided in Warsaw and political and cultural life was centred there. The Swedish invasion of 1655 did a lot of damage, and the 18th century, with its numerous invasions, accelerated the decline. By the end of the century the city population had dropped to 10,000. Following the final Third Partition of Poland, Kraków fell under Austrian rule.

Austria proved to be the least oppressive of the three occupants, and the city enjoyed a reasonable and steadily increasing cultural and political freedom. By the closing decades of the 19th century it had become a major centre for Polish culture and the spiritual capital of the formally nonexistent country, a focus for intellectual life and theatre. The avant-garde artistic and literary movement known as Młoda Polska (Young Poland) was born here in the 1890s. It was also here that a national independence movement originated, which later produced the Polish Legions under the command of Józef Piłsudski.

After Poland's independence was restored in 1918, Warsaw took over most political and administrative functions but Kraków retained much of its status as a cultural and artistic centre. By the outbreak of WWII the city had 260,000 inhabitants, 65,000 of whom were Jews.

During the war, Kraków, like all other Polish cities, witnessed the silent departures of Jews who were never to be seen again. The city was thoroughly looted by Nazis but didn't experience major combat or bombing. As such, Kraków is virtually the only large Polish city that has its old architecture almost intact.

After the liberation, the communist government was quick to present the city with a huge steelworks at Nowa Huta, just a few miles away from the historic quarter, in an attempt to break the traditional intellectual and religious framework of the city. The social engineering proved less successful than its unanticipated by-product – ecological disaster. Monuments that had somehow survived Tatars, Swedes and Nazis plus numerous natural misfortunes have been gradually and methodically eaten away by acid rain and toxic gas.

With the creation of Nowa Huta and other new suburbs after the war, Kraków trebled in size to become the country's third-largest city, after Warsaw and Łódź. However, the historic core has changed little and continues to be the political, administrative and cultural centre.

ORIENTATION

The great thing about Kraków is that almost all you need is at hand, conveniently squeezed into the compact area of the Old Town. Even consulates, which normally prefer quiet, residential districts outside central areas, have gathered right in the heart of the historic quarter.

The Old Town, about 800m wide and 1200m long, has the Main Market Square in the middle, and is encircled by the green park of the Planty, which was once a moat. On the southern tip of the Old Town sits the Wawel castle, and farther south stretches the district of Kazimierz.

The bus and train stations – where you're most likely to arrive – are next to each other on the north-eastern rim of the Old Town. Rynek Główny, the heart of the city, is a 10-minute walk from the station.

INFORMATION
Tourist Offices

The Małopolskie Centrum Informacji Turystycznej (☎ 421 77 06, 421 30 51, W www.mcit.pl, W www.krakow.pl), strategically located in the Cloth Hall in the middle of the Rynek Główny, is open 9am to 6pm weekdays, 9am to 2pm Saturday.

The Punkt Informacji o Mieście (☎ 432 00 60, 432 01 10), in a free-standing kiosk at ul Szpitalna 25 near the train station, is open 8am to 4pm weekdays (from May to September until 8pm and also 9am to 5pm on Saturday and Sunday). There's another Punkt Informacji o Mieście (☎ 432 08 41) at ul Józefa 7 in Kazimierz, open 10am to 4pm weekdays.

Kraków also has a knowledgeable Culture Information Centre (see the Entertainment section later in this chapter).

Tourist Publications

A number of locally produced guidebooks to Kraków have been published in English and German, with some of them in other languages, including French. Many larger bookshops will stock a selection of these guidebooks.

Watch out for two free monthly tourist magazines: *Welcome to Cracow* and *Kraków: What, Where, When*. They can be picked up from tourist offices, some upmarket hotels, travel agencies etc. The best practical guidebook to the city is *Kraków In Your Pocket*, which has just about all the useful information you would possibly need, and is particularly comprehensive on where to eat and drink.

KRAKÓW

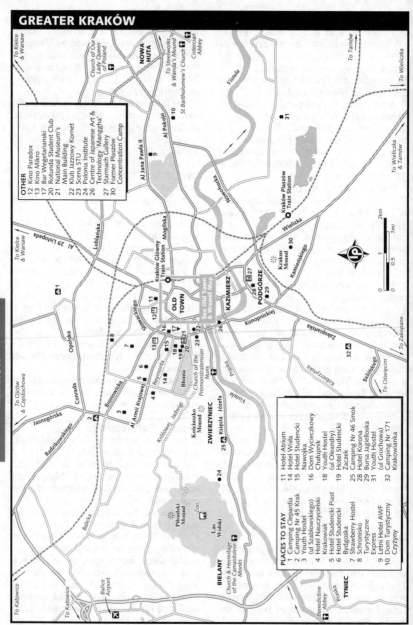

GREATER KRAKÓW

See Old Town & Wawel Map

OTHER
12 Kino Paradox
13 Kino Mikro
17 Bar Wegetariański
20 Rotunda Student Club
21 National Museum's Main Building
22 Scena STU
23 Klub Jazzowy Kornet
24 Polonia Institute
26 Centre of Japanese Art & Technology 'Manggha'
27 Starmach Gallery
30 Former Płaszów Concentration Camp

PLACES TO STAY
1 Camping Clepardia
2 Camping Nr 45 Krak (ul Szablowskiego)
3 Youth Hostel
4 Hotel Nauczycielski Krakowiak
5 Hotel Studencki Piast
6 Hotel Studencki Bydgoska
7 Strawberry Hostel
8 Schronisko Turystyczne Express
9 Letni Hotel AWF
10 Dom Turystyczny Czyżyny
11 Hotel Atrium
14 Hotel Wisła
15 Hotel Studencki Nawojka
16 Dom Wycieczkowy Chałupnik
18 Youth Hostel (ul Oleandry)
19 Hotel Studencki Żaczek
25 Camping Nr 46 Smok
28 Hotel Korona
29 Bursa Jagiellońska
31 Youth Hostel (ul Grochowa)
32 Camping Nr 171 Krakowianka

Money
Cash can be exchanged in any of the numerous kantors scattered throughout Old Town. Some trade on Sunday, but the rates are usually poorer; change enough money on Saturday to last you until Monday.

Travellers cheques are probably best to change at Bank Pekao at Rynek Główny 31. Cash advances on Visa and MasterCard are obtainable at Bank Pekao, either from the cashier inside or the ATM outside, and there are many more ATMs throughout the central area.

Post & Communications
The main post office at ul Westerplatte 20 has a poste-restante service. Mail should be addressed c/o Poste Restante, Poczta Główna, ul Westerplatte 20, 31-045 Kraków 1, Poland, and can be collected at window No 1. The mail is kept for 14 working days only.

There's a telephone centre next to the main post office (open 24 hours). There's also a post/phone office (with a 24-hour telephone service) at ul Lubicz 4, opposite the central train station.

Email & Internet Access
The oldest and possibly best-known place in town is the Cyber Café U Luisa (☎ 431 18 22), set in spectacular vaulted cellars at Rynek Główny 13. While checking your mail or surfing the Web, you can smoke and drink and listen to the music from the other vaults of the cafe. Other central Internet facilities include:

Cafe Internet br@cka (☎ 421 78 52)
  ul Bracka 3–5
Cafe Internet Citiplex Ars (☎ 421 41 99)
  ul Św Jana 6
Cafe Internet e-network (☎ 431 23 94)
  ul Sienna 14
Centrum Internetowe CafeTera (☎ 431 21 84)
  Rynek Główny 9, Pasaż Bielaka
InterMark Internet Club (☎ 422 03 19)
  ul Floriańska 30
Klub Internetowy pl@net (☎ 292 76 85)
  Rynek Główny 24
Klub Garinet (☎ 423 22 33) ul Floriańska 18
Looz Internet Café (☎ 428 42 10)
  ul Mikołajska 13

All the listed places are no farther than two-minutes' walk from the main square. They all are open until 10pm or longer daily, and cost from US$1 to US$1.50 per hour.

Travel Agencies
Orbis Travel (☎ 422 40 35), Rynek Główny 41, sells transportation tickets (air, train, ferry) and organises tours – see the Organised Tours section later in this chapter for details.

Sonata Travel (☎ 429 51 65), ul Św Tomasza 4, represents STA Travel and has cheap international air fares for young people and students.

Bookshops
English-language literature can be found at EMPiK (☎ 429 45 77), Rynek Główny 5; English Book Centre (☎ 422 62 00); Plac Matejki 5; Inter Book (☎ 632 10 08), ul Karmelicka 27; Columbus (☎ 431 20 98), ul Grodzka 60; and Szawal (☎ 421 53 61), ul Długa 1. Księgarnia Edukator (☎ 421 53 17) in the French Institute, ul Św Jana 15, has the best selection of books in French.

The widest choice of publications related to Jewish issues is to be found at the Jarden Jewish Bookshop (☎ 421 71 66), ul Szeroka 2 in Kazimierz.

Some of the best selection of regional and city maps is in Sklep Podróżnika at ul Jagiellońska 6 (☎ 429 14 85) and ul Szujskiego 2 (☎ 421 89 22); the latter sells Lonely Planet guidebooks. EMPiK (see earlier in this section) also has a good map section.

Cultural Centres
Foreign cultural centres in Kraków include:

British Council (☎ 422 94 55)
  Rynek Główny 26
Center for Jewish Culture (☎ 423 55 95)
  ul Meiselsa 17
Centre of Japanese Art and Technology 'Manggha' (☎ 267 27 03) ul Konopnickiej 26
French Institute (☎ 422 09 82) ul Św Jana 15
Goethe Institute (German) (☎ 422 69 02)
  Rynek Główny 20
Italian Institute of Culture (☎ 421 89 46)
  ul Grodzka 49

KRAKÓW

'Manggha' – Centre of Japanese Art and Technology

'Manggha' centre is the brainchild of the Polish film director Andrzej Wajda. In 1987 he donated US$340,000, his entire Kyoto Prize Money that he received from the Inamori Foundation for his artistic achievements. The building was designed by the Japanese architect Arata Isozaki, and the centre was opened in 1994.

The centre's main aim is to exhibit the art collection of old Japanese weapons, ceramics, fabrics, scrolls and woodcuts. Numbering about 6000 pieces, this valuable collection was assembled by Feliks Jasieński (1861–1929), an avid traveller, art collector, literary critic and essayist, known by his pen name of Manggha (which is where the centre's name comes from). He donated the collection to Kraków's National Museum, before it had the facilities to exhibit it. Part of the collection is now finally presented in the centre's exhibition rooms. The centre also has a multifunctional high-tech auditorium where events presenting Japanese culture (film, theatre, traditional music) are held.

Medical Services

Pharmacies are everywhere – the city has more than 200 of them. You will find one pharmacy at Rynek Główny 13, and more in the adjacent streets.

Medicover (☎ 422 76 33; 24-hour hotline ☎ 96 77), ul Krótka 1, has English-speaking specialist doctors and does lab tests. Mediprof (☎ 421 79 97), ul Szpitalna 38, also has doctors of various specialities, many of whom speak English. Dent America (☎ 421 89 48), Plac Szczepański 3, is a Polish-American dental clinic. Falck (☎ 96 75), ul Racławicka 26, attends house calls and has its own ambulance service. The US consulate department of citizen services (☎ 429 66 55) can provide a list of doctors speaking English. The city ambulance emergency phone number is ☎ 999.

OLD TOWN

The Old Town developed gradually throughout the centuries. Its plan was drawn up in 1257 after the Tatar invasions, and has survived more or less in its original form. The construction of the fortifications began in the 13th century, and it took almost two centuries to envelop the town with a powerful, 3km-long chain of double defensive walls complete with 47 towers and eight main entrance gates, plus a wide moat.

With the development of military technology, the system lost its defensive capability and, apart from a small section to the north, was demolished at the beginning of the 19th century. The moat was filled up and a ring-shaped park, the Planty, was laid out on the site, surrounding the Old Town with parkland.

The Old Town has plenty of historical monuments, enough to keep you exploring for at least several days. There are a dozen museums and nearly 20 churches here, not to mention scores of other important sights.

Noble, harmonious and elegant, Kraków's Old Town has a unique atmosphere, felt as much in its busy street life during the daytime, as in its majestic silence late at night. Except for some enclaves, the sector is car-free or a car limited-access area, so you can stroll largely undisturbed by traffic noise and pollution. It's best explored casually without a particular plan, savouring its architectural details and the old-time air, while dropping into art galleries, trendy boutiques and cosy cafes and bars along the way.

Main Market Square

Measuring 200m x 200m, Kraków's Main Market Square (Rynek Główny) is the largest medieval town square in Poland and reputedly in all of Europe. It's considered to be one of the finest urban designs of its kind. Its layout was drawn up in 1257 and has been retained to this day, though the buildings have changed over the centuries. Today most of them look neoclassical, but don't let the facades confuse you – the basic structures are older, sometimes considerably so, as can be seen in their doorways, architectural details and interiors. Their cellars date from medieval times.

When strolling around the Rynek, pop into the Krzysztofory Palace at the northern corner, which is home to the **Historical Museum of Kraków** (*Muzeum Historyczne Krakowa;* ☎ *422 99 22, Rynek Główny 35; adult/student US$1/0.50, free Sat; open 9am-3.30pm Wed & Fri-Sun, 11am-6pm Thur*). It features a bit of everything related to the city's past, including old clocks, armour, paintings, *szopki* (Nativity scenes), and the costume of the Lajkonik (see Special Events later in this chapter).

In the past, the square was the marketplace and was crammed with vendors' stalls and houses. All that went in the 19th century, leaving behind three important buildings of which the largest is the centrally positioned **Cloth Hall** (Sukiennice). It was built in the 14th century as a centre for the cloth trade, but was gutted by fire in 1555 and rebuilt in Renaissance style. In the late 19th century arcades were added, giving the hall a more decorative appearance. The ground floor is still a trading centre, today for crafts and souvenirs, while the upper floor is taken over by the **Gallery of 19th-Century Polish Painting** (☎ *422 11 66, Rynek Główny 1; adult/student US$2/1, free Sun; open 10am-3.30pm Tues, Wed, Fri, Sat & Sun, 10am-5.30pm Thur*). It displays works by painters of the period, including Józef Chełmoński, Jacek Malczewski, Aleksander Gierymski and the leader of monumental historic painting, Jan Matejko.

The gallery is a branch of the National Museum, which has seven other outlets in the city, including Matejko House, Czartoryski Museum, Wyspiański Museum and the Gallery of 20th-Century Polish Painting. All these are described separately in the following sections. On the entrance door of each branch you'll find a board displaying the opening hours of all branches. The National Museum offers special US$5 tickets (US$3 for students), which warrant admission to all the permanent exhibitions of all its branches at any time. The ticket is cheaper than a total of individual admission fees, and you can buy it at any of the branch museums.

The **Town Hall Tower** (Wieża Ratuszowa) next to the Cloth Hall is all that is left of the 15th-century town hall dismantled in the 1820s. It has been extensively renovated over the past years and is open to visitors in summer.

In the southern corner of the square is the small, domed **St Adalbert's Church** (Kościół Św Wojciecha). One of the oldest churches in the town, its origins date from the 10th century. You can see the original foundations in the basement, where a small exhibition also presents archaeological finds excavated from the Rynek.

A few steps north from the church is the **Statue of Adam Mickiewicz** surrounded by four allegorical figures: the Motherland, Learning, Poetry and Valour. It's here that the szopki competition (see Special Events later in this chapter for more information) is held in early December.

The flower stalls just to the north of the statue have reputedly been trading on this site from time immemorial. This area is also the 'pasture' for Kraków's population of pigeons, thought to be the second-largest in Europe after that of Venice.

St Mary's Church

Overlooking the square from the east is St Mary's Church (Kościół Mariacki). The first church on this site was built in the 1220s and, typically for the period, was 'oriented' – that is, its presbytery pointed east. Following its destruction during the Tatar raids the construction of a mighty basilica started, using the foundations of the previous church. That's why the church stands at an angle to the square.

The facade is dominated by two unequal towers. The lower one, 69m high and topped by a Renaissance dome, serves as a bell tower and holds five bells, while the taller one, 81m high, has traditionally been the city's property and functioned as a watchtower. It's topped with a spire surrounded by turrets – a good example of medieval craftsmanship – and in 1666 was given a 350kg gilded crown, about 2.5m in diameter. The gilded ball higher up contains Kraków's written history.

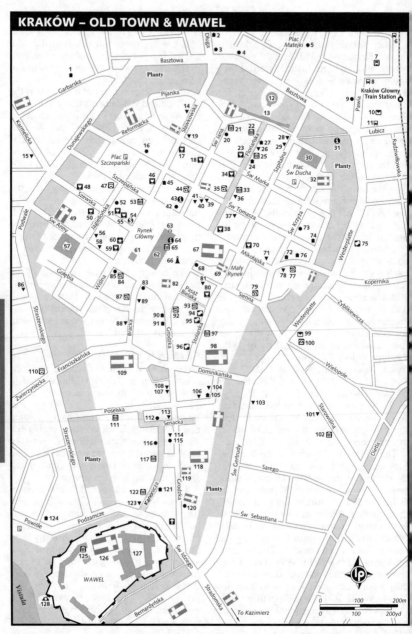

KRAKÓW – OLD TOWN & WAWEL

KRAKÓW - OLD TOWN & WAWEL

PLACES TO STAY
1 Bursa im St Pigonia
2 Pokoje Gościnne Jordan
24 Pokoje Gościnne SARPu
27 Dom Gościnny UJ
45 Hotel Saski
72 Hotel Amadeus
74 Hotel Campanile
76 Hotel Wit Stwosz
90 Dom Polonii
91 Hotel Rezydent
105 Hotel Wawel-Tourist
121 Hotel Copernicus
124 Pensjonat i Restauracja
    Rycerska

PLACES TO EAT
14 Restauracja Cyrano de
    Bergerac
15 TriBeCa Coffee
19 Kuchnia Staropolska U Babci
    Maliny
26 Jama Michalika
28 Restauracja Sąsiedzi
29 Różowy Słoń
36 Bar Mleczny Dworzanin
37 Pożegnanie Z Afryką
39 Café Camelot
40 Restauracja Cherubino
41 Restauracja Chłopskie Jadło
56 Jadłodajnia Kuchcik
58 Salad Bar Chimera
71 Jadłodajnia U Stasi
78 Restauracja Bombaj Tandoori
81 Różowy Słoń
86 Różowy Słoń
88 Café Botanica
89 Gospoda CK Dezerter
101 Taco Mexicano
103 Bar Wegetariański Vega
104 Restauracja Korsykańska
    Paese
106 Taco Mexicano
107 Restauracja Pod Aniołami
108 Wiśniowy Sad
113 Bar Mleczny Pod Temidą
114 Bar Grodzki
123 Demmers Teehaus

OTHER
3 Szawal
4 LOT Office
5 English Book Centre
6 Bus No 208 to Airport;
    Minibuses to Wieliczka
7 PKS Bus Terminal
8 Centrum Turystyki
9 Waweltur (Private Rooms)
10 Post/phone Office
11 Bus No 152 to Airport
12 Barbican
13 Florian Gate
16 Sonata Travel
17 Equinox
18 Irish Pub Pod Papugami
20 French Institute
21 Czartoryski Museum
22 Labirynt
23 Piwnica Pod Złotą Pipą;
    InterMark Internet Club
25 Matejko House
30 Teatr im Slowackiego
31 Tourist Office
32 Church of the Holy Cross
33 Museum of Pharmacy
34 Indigo Jazz Club
35 Klub Garinet
38 Jazz Club U Muniaka
42 Orbis Travel
43 Culture Information Centre
44 Cafe Internet Citiplex Ars
46 Free Pub
47 Stary Teatr
48 Klub Kulturalny
49 St Anne's Church
50 Piec Art
51 Music Bar 9
52 Sklep Podróżnika; Piwnica
    Pod Ogródkiem
53 Historical Museum of
    Kraków
54 Bank Pekao
55 Klub Pasja
57 Collegium Maius
59 Harris Piano Jazz Bar
60 Police Station
61 Town Hall Tower

62 Cloth Hall
63 Public Toilet
64 Tourist Office
65 Gallery of 19th-Century
    Polish Painting
66 Statue of Adam
    Mickiewicz
67 St Mary's Church
68 EMPiK
69 St Barbara's Church
70 Klub Pod Papugami
73 Bird Service
75 Russian Consulate
77 Looz Internet Café
79 Cafe Internet e-network
80 Pub Bastylia
82 St Adalbert's Church
83 Goethe Institute
84 Klub Internetowy pl@net
85 British Council
87 Cafe Internet br@cka
92 Cyber Café U Luisa
93 Centrum Internetowe
    CafeTera
94 German Consulate
95 US Consulate
96 French Consulate
97 Poster Gallery
98 Dominican Church
99 Main Post Office
100 Main Telecommunication
    Office
102 Artemia
109 Franciscan Church
110 Kraków Philharmonic
111 Archaeological Museum
112 Salon Muzyczny
115 Italian Institute of Culture
116 Cricoteka
117 Wyspiański Museum
118 Church of SS Peter & Paul
119 St Andrew's Church
120 Columbus
122 Archdiocesan Museum
125 Wawel Cathedral Museum
126 Wawel Cathedral
127 Wawel Castle
128 Dragon's Cave

KRAKÓW

The main church entrance, through a baroque porch added to the facade in the 1750s, is used by the faithful only; tourists enter through the side, southern door (where a small admission fee is charged), which gives access to the chancel. The chancel is illuminated by the magnificent stained-glass windows dating from the late 14th century. On the opposite side of the church, above the organ loft, is a fine Art Nouveau stained-glass window by Stanisław Wyspiański and Józef Mehoffer. The colourful wall paintings designed by Jan Matejko harmonise beautifully with the

Kraków's Musical Symbol

Every hour the *hejnał* (bugle call) is played on a trumpet from the higher tower of St Mary's Church to the four quarters of the world in turn. today a musical symbol of the city, this simple melody, based on five notes only, was played in medieval times as a warning call. Intriguingly, it breaks off abruptly in mid-bar. Legend links it to the Tatar invasions; when the watchman on duty spotted the enemy and sounded the alarm, a Tatar arrow pierced his throat in mid-phrase, the tune has stayed this way thereafter. Since 1927, the *hejnał* has been broadcast on Polish Radio every day at noon.

medieval architecture and make an appropriate background for the grand high altar, which is acclaimed as the greatest masterpiece of Gothic art in Poland.

The altarpiece is a pentaptych (like a triptych, but consisting of a central panel and two pairs of side wings), intricately carved in limewood, painted and gilded. The main scene represents the Dormition of the Virgin, while the wings portray scenes from the life of Christ and the Virgin. The altarpiece is topped with the Coronation of the Virgin and, on both sides, the statues of the patron saints of Poland, St Stanislaus and St Adalbert.

Measuring about 13m high and 11m wide, the pentaptych is the largest piece of medieval art of its kind. It took 12 years for its maker, the Nuremberg sculptor Veit Stoss (known to Poles as Wit Stwosz), to complete this monumental work before it was solemnly consecrated and revealed in 1489.

The pentaptych is opened daily at 11.50am and closed after the evening Mass, except for Saturday when it's left open for the Sunday morning Mass. The altarpiece apart, don't miss the stone crucifix on the

baroque altar in the head of the right-hand aisle, another work by Veit Stoss, and the still larger crucifix placed on the rood screen, attributed to pupils of the master.

To the south of the church is the small charming **St Mary's Square** (Plac Mariacki) which until the early 19th century was a parish cemetery. The 14th-century **St Barbara's Church** (Kościół Św Barbary) bordering the square on the east was the cemetery chapel. Next to its entrance, there's an open chapel featuring stone sculptures of Christ and three apostles, also attributed to the Stoss school.

A passage adjoining the church will take you straight onto the **Little Market Square** (Mały Rynek), which was once the second largest marketplace in town and traded mainly in meat.

North of the Market Square

The area to the north of Rynek Główny is noted for its regular chessboard layout. Its main commercial street, ul Floriańska, is part of the traditional Royal Way that leads from the Barbican to the Wawel castle. A suggested walking tour might take in the following attractions.

Museum of Pharmacy The Museum of Pharmacy *(Muzeum Farmacji;* ☎ *421 92 79, ul Floriańska 25; adult/student US$1.50/ 0.75; open 2pm-7pm Tues, 11am-2pm Wed-Sun)* is one of Europe's largest museums of its kind, and one of the best. Accommodated in a beautiful historic townhouse, it features the 22,000-piece collection which includes old laboratory equipment, rare pharmaceutical instruments, heaps of glassware, stoneware, mortars, jars, barrels, medical books, documents, prescriptions etc. This is a fascinating museum, worth visiting not only by specialists in the subject, and there are detailed descriptions of the contents in four languages.

Matejko House The Matejko House *(Dom Matejki;* ☎ *422 59 26, ul Floriańska 41; adult/student US$1.50/0.75, free Sun; open 10am-3.30pm Tues-Thur, Sat & Sun, 10am-5.30pm Fri)* is the place where, for

Art Nouveau building in central Łódź

'Tuwim Bench', Łódź

The Art Nouveau City Art Gallery, Łódź

The stunning 15th-century Łowicz cathedral

Statue of the Polish-born Pope John Paul II, Płock

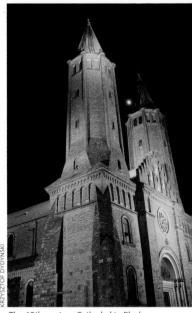

The 12th-century Cathedral in Płock

Dappled light on the aqueduct of Arkadia Park

Treblinka II memorial site, Mazovia

the 20 most fruitful years of his life (1873–93), Jan Matejko lived and worked. Matejko, the uncontested leader of national historical painting, was renowned for his powerful canvases documenting Polish history. Today, his house is a museum displaying memorabilia of the artist and some of his paintings and drawings (his larger paintings are in the Cloth Hall gallery). The house itself is a 16th-century structure, but was remodelled according to a design by Matejko himself.

Florian Gate The Florian Gate (Brama Floriańska) is the only one of the original eight gates that was not dismantled during the 19th-century 'modernisation'. It was built around 1300, although the top is a later addition. The adjoining walls together with two towers have also been left and today host an outdoor art gallery, where you can buy some charming kitsch paintings.

Barbican The most intriguing remnant of the medieval fortifications, the Barbican (Barbakan; adult/student US$1.25/0.75; open 9am-5pm daily in summer) is a powerful, circular brick bastion adorned with seven turrets. There are 130 loopholes in its 3m-thick walls. This curious piece of defensive art was built around 1498 as an additional protection of the Florian Gate and was once connected to it by a narrow passage running over a moat. It's one of the very few surviving structures of its kind in Europe, the largest and perhaps the most beautiful.

Church of the Holy Cross Undistinguished from the outside, the small 15th-century Church of the Holy Cross (Kościół Św Krzyża; ul Św Krzyża 23) deserves a visit for its Gothic vaulting, one of the most beautiful in the city. An unusual design with the palm-like vault supported on a single central column, it was constructed in 1528 and was recently thoroughly renovated.

Czartoryski Museum The Czartoryski Museum (Muzeum Czartoryskich; ☎ 422 55 56, ul Św Jana 19; adult/student US$2/1.25; open 10am-3.30pm Tues-Thur, Sat & Sun,

10am-5.30pm Fri) is one of the best in town. Originally established in 1800 in Puławy by Princess Izabela Czartoryska as the first historical museum in Poland, the collection was secretly moved to Paris after the November Insurrection of 1830 (in which the family was implicated) and in the 1870s brought to Kraków. The collection experienced another 'excursion' during WWII when the Nazis seized it and took it to Germany, and not all the exhibits were recovered. Even so, there's a lot to see, including Greek, Roman, Egyptian and Etruscan ancient art, Oriental armour, artistic handicrafts from Europe and Asia, and old European painting, mainly Italian, Dutch and Flemish. The star pieces of the collection are Leonardo da Vinci's Lady with the Ermine (about 1485) and Rembrandt's Landscape with the Good Samaritan, also known as Landscape before a Storm (1638).

West of the Market Square

A good part of this sector was once inhabited by Jews, who were moved out when the Kraków Academy was founded here in 1364. Since then it has traditionally been the university quarter, which still has its own particular atmosphere during the academic year. Apart from the two major sights listed below, it's worth looking over the other university buildings.

Collegium Maius The Collegium Maius (☎ 422 05 49, ul Jagiellońska 15; adult/student US$2/1, free Sat; open 11am-2.30pm Mon-Fri, 11am-1.30pm Sat), built as part of the Kraków Academy, is the oldest surviving university building in Poland, and one of the best examples of 15th-century Gothic architecture in the city. It has a magnificent arcaded courtyard and a fascinating university collection kept inside.

You will be shown around historic interiors where you'll find rare 16th-century astronomic instruments, supposedly used by Copernicus, a bizarre alchemy room, old rectors' sceptres and, the highlight of the show, the oldest existing globe (from about 1510) that has the American continent marked on it. You'll also visit an impressive Aula, a hall with an original Renaissance ceiling, crammed with portraits of kings, benefactors and professors of the university. It was here that Pope John Paul II and Czesław Miłosz received honorary doctorates.

All visits are guided in groups; tours begin every half-hour and there's usually one tour daily in English. Tours in French and German can be arranged on request. In summer it's advisable to reserve in advance, either personally in the museum office (2nd floor) or by phone. The courtyard is open 7am until dusk and can be entered free of charge.

St Anne's Church Just round the corner from the Collegium Maius is the baroque St Anne's Church (*Kościół Św Anny; ul Św Anny 11*). Designed by the omnipresent Tylman van Gameren, and built in the late 17th century as a university church, it was long the site of inaugurations of the academic year, doctoral promotions, and a resting place for many eminent university professors. A spacious, bright interior fitted out with fine furnishings, gravestones and epitaphs, and embellished with superb stucco work and murals – all stylistically homogeneous – puts the church among the best classical baroque buildings in Poland.

South of the Market Square

The southern part of the Old Town has no regular layout. The main artery here is ul Grodzka, dotted with several churches, while the parallel ul Kanonicza is perhaps the most picturesque of Kraków's streets.

Franciscan Church The mighty Franciscan Church (*Kościół Franciszkanów; ul Franciszkańska*) was erected in the second half of the 13th century but repeatedly rebuilt and refurnished after at least four fires, the last and the most destructive being in 1850 when almost all the interior was burnt out. Of the present decorations, the most interesting are the Art Nouveau stained-glass windows in the chancel and above the organ loft, the latter regarded among the greatest in Poland. All were designed by Stanisław Wyspiański, who also executed most of the frescoes in the presbytery and the transept.

Adjoining the church from the south is the monastery which preserved its original Gothic cloister complete with fragments of 15th-century frescoes. There's a valuable collection of portraits of Kraków's bishops on the cloister walls. The entrance to the cloister is from the transept of the church or from the outside next to the chancel.

Dominican Church The equally powerful Dominican Church (*Kościół Dominikanów; ul Stolarska 12*) was also built in the 13th century and badly damaged in the 1850 fire, though its side chapels, dating mainly from the 16th and 17th centuries, have been preserved in reasonably good shape. Monumental neo-Gothic confessionals and stalls are a later adornment. Note the original 14th-century doorway at the main entrance to the church.

The monastery, just behind the northern wall of the church, is accessible from the street. The cloister there has retained its Gothic shape pretty well and boasts a number of fine epitaphs, tombs and paintings.

Archaeological Museum The Archaeological Museum (*Muzeum Archeologiczne;* ☎ 422 71 00, ul Poselska 3; adult/student US$2/1, free Thur; open 9am-2pm Mon-Wed, 2pm-5pm Thur, 10am-2pm Fri & Sun) presents Małopolska's history from the Palaeolithic period up until the early Middle Ages.

Wyspiański Museum Dedicated to one of Kraków's most beloved sons and the key figure of the Młoda Polska (Young Poland) movement, the Wyspiański Museum (*Muzeum Wyspiańskiego;* ☎ 422 83 37, ul Kanonicza 9; adult/student US$1.50/1; open 10am-3.30pm Tues, Wed, Fri, Sat, Sun, 10am-5.30pm Thur), reveals how many diverse branches of art Stanisław Wyspiański explored. A painter, poet and playwright, he was also a designer, particularly renowned for his stained-glass designs, some of which are in the exhibition.

His most unusual proposal, though, is the 'Acropolis', a project to reconstruct the Wawel as Poland's political, religious and cultural centre. There's a model made according to his design – an amazing mix of epochs and styles, a Greek amphitheatre and a Roman circus included. Wyspiański's vision has never been realised. Later calculations proved that the hill wouldn't support so many buildings squeezed onto its top.

Church of SS Peter & Paul The first baroque building in Kraków, the Church of SS Peter and Paul *(Kościół Św Piotra i Pawła; ul Grodzka)* was erected by the Jesuits who had been brought to the city in 1583 to fight the Reformation. Designed on the Latin cross layout and topped with a large dome, the church has a refreshingly sober interior, apart from some fine stucco decoration on the vault. The figures of the Twelve Apostles standing on columns in front of the church are copies of the statues from 1723.

St Andrew's Church Built towards the end of the 11th century, St Andrew's Church *(Kościół Św Andrzeja; ul Grodzka)* is one of Kraków's oldest, and has preserved much of its austere Romanesque stone exterior. As soon as you enter, though, you're in a totally different world; its small interior was subjected to a radical baroque overhaul in the 18th century.

Archdiocesan Museum Located in the 14th-century townhouse, the Archdiocesan Museum *(Muzeum Archidiecezjalne; ☎ 421 89 63, ul Kanonicza 19; adult/student US$1.50/0.75; open 10am-3pm Tues-Sun)* presents a collection of religious sculpture and painting, dating mostly from the 14th to 16th centuries. Also on exhibition is the room where Karol Wojtyła (today's Pope John Paul II) lived in 1951–58, complete with furniture and belongings, including his skis.

WAWEL
The very symbol of Poland, the Wawel ('Vah-vel') is saturated with Polish history as no other place in the country. It was the seat of the kings for over 500 years from the early days of the Polish state, and even after the centre of power moved to Warsaw, it retained much of its symbolic and almost

magical power. Today a silent guardian of a millennium of national history, Wawel is about the most visited sight in Poland.

The way up the Wawel hill begins at the end of ul Kanonicza, from where a lane leads uphill. Past the equestrian statue of Tadeusz Kościuszko, it turns to the left leading to a vast open central square surrounded by several buildings, of which the cathedral and the castle are the major attractions.

Reserve at least three hours if you want anything more than just a general glance over the place. Note the different opening hours of the cathedral and the castle exhibitions (see the following sections). In summer, it's best to come early as there may be long queues for tickets later in the day. Avoid weekends, when Wawel is besieged by visitors.

Wawel Cathedral
The national temple, the Wawel royal cathedral *(cathedral admission free, combined ticket to the bell tower & crypts adult/student US$1.50/1; open 9am-5.15pm Mon-Sat, 12.15pm-5.15pm Sun & public holidays June-Sept; until 3pm Oct-May)* has witnessed most of the royal coronations and funerals and is the last resting place for most of the Polish monarchs. Many outstanding artists had a hand in the gradual creation of the cathedral, and have left behind a wealth of magnificent works of art and craft. It's both an extraordinary artistic achievement and Poland's spiritual sanctuary.

The building you see is the third church on this site, erected in 1320–64. The original cathedral (known as St Gereon's Church) was founded around 1020 by the first Polish king, Bolesław Chrobry, and was replaced with a considerably larger Romanesque construction some 100 years later. It was burnt down in 1305 and only a crypt, known as St Leonard's Crypt, survived.

The present-day cathedral is basically a Gothic structure but chapels in different styles were later built all round it. Before you enter, note the massive iron door and, hanging on a chain to the left, prehistoric animal bones. They are believed to have magical powers; as long as they are here,

KRAKÓW

Wawel Chakra

Once upon a time Lord Shiva threw seven magic stones towards seven parts of the world, and one of these landed in Kraków. The places that had been hit began to radiate the god's energy. That's what legend says, but according to Hindu esoteric thinkers, these seven sites are indeed centres of supernatural energy, which is reputed to give exceptional spiritual strengths. The centres, known as chakras (also spelt chakrams), are related to seven celestial bodies and include Delhi (Moon), Delphi (Venus), Jerusalem (Sun), Kraków (Jupiter), Mecca (Mercury), Rome (Mars) and Velehrad (Saturn). The seven earth chakras have their seven equivalent spiritual centres of power in the human body.

Kraków's chakra resides at Wawel, in the north-western corner of the royal castle's courtyard. It's believed to be centred in the chancel of St Gereon's Church, considered Wawel's first cathedral, founded around 1020. Only the foundations and crypt of this church have survived, but are off-limits to tourists. The holy stone which, as the legend has it, lies here is said not only to produce energy that revives life-giving forces, but also protects the city from misfortunes (as it did by saving it from destruction in WWII).

The history of the Wawel chakra is as esoteric as the chakra itself. It's not known whether the kings had any idea about what they were living on – at least there are no historic records about it. In the 19th century, Wawel was becoming a legendary place, often compared to the Acropolis or Zion, but this was more due to its significance as a spiritual symbol of Poland in the time when the country formally didn't exist, rather than as a source of a supernatural energy.

This Pandora's box of controversy was probably opened by a Hindu traveller who visited Kraków in the early 1920s and, for some reason, expressed particular interest in the remains of St Gereon's Church. The following years witnessed a number of other Hindu visitors, all of whom came specifically to the ruined church where they meditated for hours in deep silence, to the increasing astonishment of the Wawel management. The management was perhaps in for an even bigger shock when the Indian government delegation led by Prime Minister Nehru kindly asked if they could include the ruin into their official Wawel tour and be left alone inside.

The chakra has drawn in all sorts of dowsers who came with divining rods and wands. According to their measurements, Wawel radiates stronger energy than any other known site in Poland (the far second strongest is Częstochowa). They also confirmed that the main source of radiation lies underneath the chancel of St Gereon's Church. The studies published by them after a complex research of Wawel are full of diagrams, figures and comments, all of which seem to confirm the uniqueness of the place and its supernatural properties.

Predictably, the Wawel chakra has been drawing people in. They flock to this particular corner of the courtyard and stand immobile for minutes or hours, attracting curiosity of unaware passers-by and some ironic smiles from those who don't believe in such things. No matter which side you take, Wawel has yet another attraction, even though the Wawel management flatly denies the existence of any chakra.

the cathedral will remain too. The bones were excavated on the grounds at the beginning of the 20th century.

Once inside, you'll get lost in a maze of sarcophagi, tombstones and altarpieces scattered throughout the nave, chancel and ambulatory. Among a score of chapels, the showpiece is the **Sigismund Chapel** (Kaplica Zygmuntowska) on the southern wall, often referred to in tourist brochures as 'the most beautiful Renaissance chapel north of the Alps'. From the outside, it's easily recognised by its gilded dome. Another highlight is the **Holy Cross Chapel** (Kaplica Świętokrzyska) in the south-western corner of the church, distinguished by the unique 1470 Byzantine frescoes and marble sarcophagus from 1492 by Veit Stoss.

Right in the middle of the church stands the laboriously decorated baroque **Shrine of St Stanislaus** (Mauzoleum Św Stanisława), dedicated to the bishop of Kraków who was canonised in 1253 to become the patron saint of Poland (see the boxed text 'St Stanislaus – Patron Saint of Poland' later in this chapter). The silver coffin, adorned with 12 relief scenes from the saint's life, was made in Gdańsk around 1670; the ornamented baldachin over it is about 50 years older.

Ascend the **Sigismund Tower** (accessible through the sacristy) to see the Sigismund Bell, popularly called 'Zygmunt'. Cast in 1520, it's 2m high and 2.5m in diameter, and weighs 11 tonnes, making it the largest historic bell in Poland. Its clapper weighs 350kg, and six strong men are needed to ring the bell, which happens only on the most important church holidays and for significant state events.

Back down in the church, go downstairs (from the left-hand aisle) to the **Poets' Crypt** where three great Romantic poets, Adam Mickiewicz, Juliusz Słowacki and Cyprian Kamil Norwid, are buried.

Farther towards the back of the church in the same aisle you'll find the entrance to **St Leonard's Crypt**, the only remnant of the 12th century Romanesque cathedral. Follow through and you will get to the **Royal Crypts** where, apart from kings, several national heroes including Tadeusz Kościuszko and Józef Piłsudski are buried. Visit the Royal Crypts at the end of your cathedral tour, because the exit is outside the cathedral.

Diagonally opposite the cathedral is the **Cathedral Museum** (*Muzeum Katedralne; adult/student US$1/0.50; open 10am-3pm Tues-Sun*), which holds historical and religious objects from the cathedral. There are plenty of exhibits but not a single crown. They were all stolen from the treasury by the Prussians in 1795 and reputedly melted down. Each crown could easily contain 1kg of pure gold, not to mention their artistic value.

Wawel Castle

The political and cultural centre of Poland until the early 17th century, the Wawel royal castle is, like the cathedral, the very symbol of Poland's national identity.

The original small residence was built in the early 11th century by King Bolesław Chrobry, beside the chapel dedicated to the Virgin Mary (known as the Rotunda of SS Felix and Adauctus). King Kazimierz Wielki turned it into a formidable Gothic castle. It was burnt down in 1499, and King Zygmunt Stary commissioned a new residence. Within 30 years a splendid Renaissance palace, designed by Italian architects, had been built. Despite further extensions and alterations, the Renaissance structure, complete with a spacious arcaded courtyard, has been preserved to this day.

Repeatedly sacked and devastated by Swedes and Prussians, the castle was occupied after the last Partition by the Austrians, who intended to make Wawel a citadel. Their plan included turning the castle into barracks, and the cathedral into a garrison church, moving the royal tombs elsewhere. They succeeded in realising some of their projects. They turned the royal kitchen and the coach house into a military hospital, and razed two churches standing at the outer courtyard to make room for a parade ground. During the work, they stumbled upon a perfectly preserved pre-Romanesque Rotunda of SS Felix and Adauctus and pulled down a good part of it. They also enveloped the whole hill with a new ring of

KRAKÓW

massive brick walls, largely ruining the original Gothic fortifications.

Only in 1918 was the castle recovered by Poles and restoration work begun. It was continued after WWII and succeeded in recovering a good deal of the castle's earlier external form and its interior decoration.

The castle is now a museum containing five separate sections in different parts of the building. The ticket office, on the access lane to the Wawel hill, opposite the statue of Kościuszko, sells separate tickets to all sections. For further information on all the exhibitions and a foreign-language guide service call ☎ 422 16 97. Free entry to all the castle exhibitions (except for the Royal Private Apartments) is on Wednesday (June to September) and Sunday (other months). The number of visitors per day is limited, so you should be early for your free tickets, especially in summer.

The **Royal Chambers** (*Komnaty Królewskie; adult/student US$3/2; open 9.30am-3pm Tues-Thur & Sat, 9.30am-4pm Fri, 10am-3pm Sun*) is the largest and most impressive exhibition; the entrance is in the south-eastern corner of the courtyard. Proceed through the apparently never-ending chain of rooms and chambers of the castle, restored in their original Renaissance and early baroque style and crammed with period furnishings and works of art.

The two biggest (and probably most spectacular) interiors you'll pass on your way are the **Senators' Hall**, originally used for the senate sessions, court ceremonies, balls and theatre performances, and the **Throne Hall**. Look at the coffered ceiling of the latter, with 30 wooden heads, each different (known as Wawel heads). The heads are all that have survived from a total of 194 heads, which were carved and painted around 1540 and once adorned the place.

Another of the castle's showpieces is the **Royal Private Apartments** (*Prywatne Apartamenty Królewskie; adult/student US$3/2.50; open 9.30am-3pm Tues-Thur & Sat, 9.30am-4pm Fri, 10am-3pm Sun*) – the entrance is in the middle of the eastern side of the courtyard. In a way, it's a continuation of the previous trip, but leading through

some more intimate interiors, and thus giving an insight into how the royalty once lived. The apartments are visited with a guide (included in the ticket price) – groups guided in English depart on the full hour.

In both the Royal Chambers and Private Apartments you'll see plenty of magnificent old tapestries hanging on the walls. The collection, largely assembled by King Zygmunt August, once numbered over 350 pieces but only 138 survive. Even so, this is probably the largest collection of its kind in Europe, and one of Wawel's most precious possessions.

The **Crown Treasury and Armoury** (*Skarbiec Koronny i Zbrojownia; adult/student US$3/2; open 9.30am-3pm Tues-Thur & Sat, 9.30am-4pm Fri, 10am-3pm Sun*) are housed in vaulted Gothic rooms surviving from the 14th-century castle, in the north-eastern part of the castle. The most famous object in the treasury is the Szczerbiec or Jagged Sword from around 1250, which was used at all Polish coronations from 1320 onwards. The adjacent armoury features a collection of old weapons from various epochs (mainly from the 15th to 17th centuries), as well as replicas of the banners of the Teutonic Knights captured at the battle of Grunwald in 1410.

The **Oriental Art** (*Sztuka Wschodu, adult/student US$1.50/1; open 9.30am-3pm Tues-Thur & Sat, 9.30am-4pm Fri, 10am-3pm Sun*) features a collection of 17th-century Turkish banners and weaponry captured after the Battle of Vienna, displayed along with a variety of old Persian carpets, Chinese and Japanese ceramics and other Oriental objects. The entrance is from the north-western corner of the courtyard.

The **Lost Wawel** (*Wawel Zaginiony, adult/student US$1.50/1; open 9.30am-3pm Mon, Wed, Thur & Sat, 9.30am-4pm Fri, 10am-3pm Sun*) exhibition is accommodated in the old royal kitchen. Apart from the remnants of the late 10th-century Rotunda of SS Felix and Adauctus, which is reputedly the first church in Poland, you can see various archaeological finds (including amazing old ceramic tiles from the castle's stoves), as well as models of the previous Wawel churches. The entrance to the exhibition is from the outer side of the castle.

Dragon's Cave

You can complete your Wawel trip with a visit to the Dragon's Cave (Smocza Jama; admission US$1; open 10am-5pm daily May-Oct), former home of the legendary Wawel Dragon (Smok Wawelski). The entrance to the cave is next to the Thieves' Tower (Baszta Złodziejska) at the western edge of the hill. From here you'll get a good panorama over the Vistula and the suburbs farther to the west, including the Centre of Japanese Art on the opposite bank of the river, and the Kościuszko Mound far away on the horizon.

You descend 135 steps to the cave, then walk some 70m through its interior and emerge onto the bank of the Vistula next to the fire-spitting bronze dragon, the work of renowned contemporary sculptor Bronisław Chromy.

KAZIMIERZ

Today, one of Kraków's inner suburbs located within walking distance south-east of the Wawel, Kazimierz was for a long time an independent town with its own municipal charter and laws. Its colourful history was determined by its mixed Jewish/Polish population, and though the ethnic structure is now wholly different, the architecture gives a good picture of its past, with clearly distinguishable sectors of what were Christian and Jewish quarters. The suburb boasts some important tourist sights, including churches, synagogues and museums.

Western Kazimierz

The western part of Kazimierz was traditionally Catholic, and although many Jews settled here from the early 19th century until WWII, the quarter preserved much of its original character complete with its churches.

Beginning from the Wawel hill, walk south along the river bank. Shortly past the bridge you'll find the **Pauline Church**

Kraków's Dragon

According to legend, once upon a time there lived a powerful prince, Krak or Krakus, who built a castle on a hill named Wawel on the banks of the Vistula and founded a town named after himself. It would have been paradise if not for a dragon living in a cave underneath the castle. This fearsome and ever-hungry huge lizard decimated cattle and sheep, and was not averse to human beings, especially pretty maidens.

The wise prince ordered a sheep's hide to be filled with sulphur, which was set alight, and the whole thing was hurled into the cave. The voracious beast devoured the bait in one gulp, only then feeling the sulphur burning in its stomach. The dragon rushed to the river, and drank and drank and finally exploded, giving the citizens a spectacular fireworks display. The town was saved. The dragon has become the symbol of the city, immortalised in countless images, and the dragon's monument has been placed where the beast once lived.

Kraków's Dragon (woodcut by Sebastian Münster, in Cosmogaphia, 1550)

Kazimierz's Chequered Jewish-Polish History

Kazimierz was founded in 1335 by King Kazimierz Wielki (hence its name) just on the southern outskirts of Kraków. Thanks to numerous privileges granted by the king, it developed swiftly and soon had its own town hall and a market square almost as large as that of Kraków, and two huge churches. The town was encircled with defensive walls and by the end of the 14th century came to be Małopolska's most important and wealthiest city after Kraków.

The first Jews came to settle in Kazimierz soon after its foundation, but it wasn't until the end of the 15th century that their numbers began to grow quickly, following their expulsion from Kraków in 1494 by King Jan Olbracht. They settled in a relatively small prescribed area of Kazimierz, northeast of the Christian quarter, and the two sectors were separated by a wall.

The subsequent history of Kazimierz was punctuated by fires, floods and plagues, with both communities living side by side, confined to their own sectors. The Jewish quarter became home to Jews fleeing persecution from all corners of Europe, and it grew particularly quickly, gradually determining the character of the whole town.

At the end of the 18th century Kazimierz was administratively incorporated into Kraków and in the 1820s the walls were pulled down. At the outbreak of WWII Kazimierz was a predominantly Jewish suburb, with a distinctive culture and atmosphere. However, most Jews were exterminated by the Nazis in the death camps. Of 65,000 Kraków Jews (most of whom lived in Kazimierz) in 1939, only about 6000 survived the war. The current Jewish population in the city is estimated at between 100 and 150.

During the communist rule, Kazimierz was largely a forgotten place on Kraków's map, partly because the government didn't want to touch the sensitive Jewish question. In the early 1990s, the suburb slowly made its way onto the pages of tourist publications but its grubby appearance didn't help much to promote it. Then came Steven Spielberg to shoot *Schindler's List* and everything changed overnight.

Actually, Kazimierz was not the setting of the movie's plot – most of the events portrayed in the film took place in the Płaszów death camp, the Podgórze ghetto and Schindler's factory, all of which were farther to the south-east, beyond the Vistula. Yet the film turned the world's attention to Kraków's Jewry as a whole, and since Kazimierz is the only substantial visual relic of Jewish heritage, it has benefited the most. 'Schindler's Tourism' now draws in crowds of visitors – Poles and foreigners alike – to the place which hardly saw any tourists a decade ago. Isn't it a bitter irony that a couple of hours on screen can mean more than half a millennium of history?

As a result of the state's long neglect, the quarter still looks dilapidated, except for some of its small enclaves that have been restored and revitalised by private entrepreneurs. A more comprehensive development program is hindered by limited funds and, particularly, unsettled titles of real estate once belonging to Jews.

(*Kościół Paulinów; ul Skałeczna 15*), commonly known to Poles as the Skałka (the Rock) due to its location, for it was built on a rocky promontory (which is no longer pronounced). Today's mid-18th-century baroque church is the third building on the site, previously occupied by a Romanesque rotunda and later a Gothic church. The place is associated with Bishop Stanisław (Stanislaus), canonised in 1253 and made patron saint of Poland.

The memory of the saint lives on in the church's dim interior. You can even see the tree trunk (on the altar to the left) believed to be the same one on which the king beheaded the bishop. The body is then supposed to have been dumped into the pond in front of the church. The pond was later transformed into a pool, with a sculpture of St Stanislaus placed in the middle. It's a common held belief that the water holds miraculous powers.

The cult of the saint has turned the place into sort of a national pantheon. The crypt underneath the church shelters the tombs of 12 eminent Poles including medieval historian Jan Długosz, composer Karol Szymanowski, and painters Jacek Malczewski and Stanisław Wyspiański.

About 200m east is **St Catherine's Church** (*Kościół Św Katarzyny; ul Augustiańska 7*). One of the most monumental churches in the city and possibly the one that has best retained its original Gothic shape, it was founded in 1363 and completed 35 years later, though the towers have never been built. The church was once on the corner of Kazimierz's market square but the area was built up in the 19th century. The lofty and spacious whitewashed interior boasts the imposing, richly gilded baroque high altar from 1634.

Continue east on ul Skałeczna, turn right into ul Krakowska, and you'll see the former **town hall** of Kazimierz in front of you. Built in the late 14th century in the middle of a vast market square (Plac Wolnica is all that's left), it was significantly extended in the 16th century, at which time it acquired its Renaissance appearance. The

Ethnographic Museum (*Muzeum Etnograficzne;* ☎ *430 55 63, Plac Wolnica 1; adult/student US$1.25/0.75; open 10am-6pm Mon, 10am-3pm Wed-Fri, 10am-2pm Sat & Sun*) accommodated here after WWII has one of the largest collections in Poland but only a small part of it is on display. The permanent exhibition features the reconstructed interiors of traditional peasant cottages (ground floor), folk costumes from all over Poland and some extraordinary Nativity scenes (1st floor), and folk and religious painting and woodcarving (2nd floor).

In the north-eastern corner of Plac Wolnica is the **Corpus Christi Church** (*Kościół Bożego Ciała; ul Bożego Ciała*). Founded in 1340, it was the first church in Kazimierz and for a long time the parish church. Its interior has been almost totally fitted out with baroque furnishings, including the huge high altar, extraordinary massive stalls in the chancel and a boat-shaped pulpit. Note the surviving early 15th-century stained-glass window in the presbytery.

Jewish Quarter

A tiny area of about 300m x 300m northeast of Corpus Christi Church, the Jewish

---

St Stanislaus – The Patron Saint of Poland

St Stanislaus, Poland's first saint, was Kraków's bishop Stanisław Szczepanowski in his real life. In 1079 he was condemned to death by King Bolesław Śmiały (Boleslaus the Bold) for joining the opposition against the king and excommunicating him. According to the legend, the king himself carried out the sentence by beheading the bishop.

The murder not only got the bishop canonised as patron saint of Poland, but it also cast a curse on the whole royal line. The first victim was the executioner himself, who was forced into exile. Successive kings built a commemorative church on the site of the crime (known as Skałka Church) and made penitential pilgrimages to it, but it didn't seem to help. In another effort, a sumptuous mausoleum to the saint was erected in the very centre of the Wawel Cathedral, yet the curse continued to hang over the throne. It was believed, for example, that no king named Stanisław could be crowned and buried at Wawel, and indeed, two Polish monarchs bearing this name, Stanisław Leszczyński and Stanisław August Poniatowski, were crowned and buried elsewhere.

The curse went even further: no clergyman named Stanisław could become Kraków's bishop. The only one of that name in the town's history, Stanisław Dąbski, was elected in 1699, but fell ill and died just a few months later. The Church authorities apparently didn't risk election of another Stanisław since. Meanwhile, they have desperately tried to conciliate the saint. Every year, on the Sunday following 8 May (the saint's holy day), a procession attended by the Church's top hierarchy, with almost all the episcopate present, proceeds from the Wawel Cathedral to the Skałka Church.

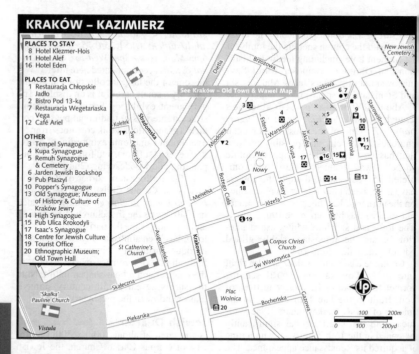

KRAKÓW – KAZIMIERZ

PLACES TO STAY
8 Hotel Klezmer-Hois
11 Hotel Alef
16 Hotel Eden

PLACES TO EAT
1 Restauracja Chłopskie Jadło
2 Bistro Pod 13-ką
7 Restauracja Wegetariaska Vega
12 Café Ariel

OTHER
3 Tempel Synagogue
4 Kupa Synagogue
5 Remuh Synagogue & Cemetery
6 Jarden Jewish Bookshop
9 Pub Ptaszyl
10 Popper's Synagogue
13 Old Synagogue; Museum of History & Culture of Kraków Jewry
14 High Synagogue
15 Pub Ulica Krokodyli
17 Isaac's Synagogue
18 Centre for Jewish Culture
19 Tourist Office
20 Ethnographic Museum; Old Town Hall

See Kraków – Old Town & Wawel Map

KRAKÓW

sector of Kazimierz became, over the centuries, a centre of Jewish culture like nowhere else in the country. In WWII, the Jewish people were slaughtered by the Nazis and with them disappeared all the folklore, life and atmosphere of the quarter. Today only the architecture reveals that this was once the Jewish town. Miraculously, all seven synagogues survived the war in better or worse shape, but only one of them continues to function as a regular place of worship, and two more have been turned into museums.

Beginning your tour from the Corpus Christi Church, walk north and then eastward along ul Józefa (historically the main entry to the Jewish town) to **Isaac's Synagogue** (*Synagoga Izaaka;* ☎ *430 55 77, ul Kupa 18; adult/student US$2/1.50; open 9am-7pm Sun-Fri, closed Jewish holidays*). Kraków's largest synagogue, built in 1640-44, it's today open as a museum. You can see the remains of the original stucco and

wall-painting decoration, and watch historic documentaries about Kraków's Jewry.

One block east is the **Old Synagogue** (Stara Synagoga). The name refers to the fact that this is the oldest Jewish religious building in Poland, dating back to the end of the 15th century. Damaged by fire in 1557, it was reconstructed in Renaissance style by the Italian architect Matteo Gucci. It was plundered and partly destroyed by the Nazis, but later restored and today houses the **Museum of History and Culture of Kraków Jewry** (*☎ 422 09 62, ul Szeroka 24; adult/student US$1.50/1; open 9am-3pm Wed, Thur, Sat & Sun, 11am-6pm Fri, closed 1st Sat & Sun of each month, in which case it opens on the following Mon & Tues 10am-3.30pm*). The prayer hall, complete with a reconstructed Bimah (raised platform at the centre of the synagogue where the Torah is read) and the original Aron Kodesh (the niche in the eastern wall where Torah scrolls are kept), houses an exhibition of liturgical objects related to Jewish culture. The adjacent rooms are dedicated to Jewish traditions and art, and on the upper floor you can see old photographs depicting Jewish martyrdom during WWII.

To the north of the Old Synagogue stretches ul Szeroka, the central street of the Jewish quarter. Short and wide, it looks more like an elongated square than a street, now packed with tourist coaches and cars. Near its northern end are the **Remuh Synagogue and Cemetery** (☎ 422 12 64, ul Szeroka 46; adult/student US$1.25/0.75; open 9am-4pm Mon-Fri). This is the smallest synagogue in Kazimierz and the only one regularly used for religious services. The synagogue was established in 1553 by a rich merchant, Israel Isserles, but associated with his son Rabbi Moses Isserles, a philosopher and scholar.

The cemetery is just behind the synagogue. Founded at the same time as the synagogue itself, it was closed for burials in the early 19th century, when a new, larger cemetery was established. During WWII Nazis razed the tombstones to the ground. However, during postwar conservation work, workers discovered some old tombstones under the layer of earth. Further systematic work uncovered about 700 gravestones, some of them outstanding Renaissance examples four centuries old. It seems that the Jews themselves buried the stones to avoid their desecration by the foreign armies which repeatedly invaded Kraków in the 18th century. The tombstones have been meticulously restored, making up one of the best preserved Renaissance Jewish cemeteries anywhere in Europe. The tombstone of Rabbi Moses, dating from 1572, is right behind the synagogue. You can recognise it by the stones placed on top in an expression of respect.

The neo-Romanesque **Tempel Synagogue** (ul Miodowa 24; adult/student US$1.25/0.75; open 10am-4pm Mon-Fri) is Kazimierz's youngest synagogue, dating from 1862. The large prayer hall, with a balcony running all around it, has walls and ceiling decorated with colourful floral and geometric patterns, and beautiful stained-glass windows.

Much larger than the old Remuh graveyard is the **New Jewish Cemetery** (ul Miodowa 55), behind the railway bridge. It was established around 1800 and is the only current burial place for Jews in Kraków. Its size gives an idea of how large the Jewish population must have been. There are still about 9000 surviving tombstones – the oldest dating from the 1840s – some of which are of great beauty. In contrast to the manicured Remuh cemetery, the newer one is completely unkempt, which makes it an eerie sight. The entrance to the cemetery is through the funeral building you'll see to your right or through the gate in the fence – whichever you find open.

You can return to the Old Town by tram from ul Starowiślna, or just walk. If you want to continue exploring the Jewish heritage, you can contact the Jarden Jewish Bookshop at ul Szeroka 2 which offers a variety of tours, including their showpiece, the Schindler's List tour (see the Organised Tours section).

KRAKÓW'S SUBURBS & OUTSKIRTS
Zwierzyniec
Zwierzyniec's prime attraction is the **Kościuszko Mound** (Kopiec Kościuszki; adult/student US$1.50/1; open 10am-5pm, to dusk in summer), erected in 1820–23 soon after Kościuszko's death, to pay tribute to the man who had embodied the dreams of independent Poland in times of foreign occupation. It measures 34m and sits on a natural hill, so it commands a spectacular view over the city.

The entrance is through a small neo-Gothic chapel which has a small display of memorabilia related to Kościuszko. The large brick fortification at the mound's foothill is a fortress built by the Austrians in the 1840s (now a hotel).

Bus No 100 will take you (every hour or so) directly to the mound from Plac Matejki opposite the Barbican. Otherwise you can take tram No 1, 6 or 32 to the end of the line in Zwierzyniec and continue on foot along the tree-shaded, car-free Al Waszyngtona (a 25-minute walk).

KRAKÓW

Kraków Mounds

Kraków is exceptional among Polish cities in having mounds. These are cone-shaped hills of earth erected by human hands, of which the two oldest, the Krakus' Mound in Podgórze and Wanda's Mound in Nowa Huta, are both approximately 16m high and date back to about the 7th century. Little is known about what they were raised for.

A third mound was erected in Zwierzyniec in the early 1820s, and here the purpose was absolutely clear: to pay tribute to Tadeusz Kościuszko, a widely venerated national hero. He first distinguished himself in the American War of Independence before returning to Poland to lead the nationwide insurrection of 1794 aimed at saving Poland's sovereignty, which nonetheless was lost a year later. A

defender of liberty and independence – two values that Poles hold deep in their hearts – Kościuszko has always been highly respected, even by the communist regime. No wonder then that the mound was raised with the enthusiastic participation of thousands of volunteers, and eventually reached a height of 34m.

Continuing the tradition, a fourth mound went up in the woodland park of Las Wolski in the mid-1930s, to honour Marshal Józef Piłsudski, the man who brought about Poland's independence after WWI.

MH

When taking trip to Zwierzyniec, you may visit the **National Museum's Main Building** (*Gmach Główny;* ☎ *634 33 77, Al 3 Maja 1; adult/student US$2/1; open 10am-3.30pm Tues & Thur-Sun, 10am-5.30pm Wed*) on the way. It houses three permanent exhibitions: the Gallery of 20th-Century Polish Painting, the Decorative Art and Polish Arms and Uniforms – plus various temporary exhibitions. The painting gallery features an extensive collection of Polish painting (and some sculpture) covering the period from 1890 until the present day. There are several stained-glass designs (including the ones for Wawel Cathedral) by Stanisław Wyspiański, and an impressive selection of Witkacy's paintings. Jacek Malczewski and Olga Boznańska are both well represented also. Of the postwar artists, take particular note of the works by Tadeusz Kantor, Jerzy Nowosielski and Władysław Hasior, to name just a few.

Las Wolski

The 485-hectare Las Wolski (Wolski Forest), west of the city centre, beyond Zwierzyniec, is the largest forested area within the city limits. It's a popular weekend destination among the city dwellers, thanks to the beauty of the forest and the attractions it shelters.

The forest's hilly southern part facing the Vistula, known as Srebrna Góra (Silver Mountain), is topped with the mighty **Church and Hermitage of the Camaldolese Monks** (Kościół i Erem Kamedułów). The order was brought to Poland from Italy in 1603 and in time founded a dozen monasteries throughout the country; today only two survive (the other is in Masuria).

The order with very strict monastic rules, it attracts curiosity – and a few ironic smiles – for its 'Memento Mori' motto ('remember you must die'), and for the ascetic way of life of its members. The monks live in seclusion in hermitages and contact each other only during prayers, and some have no contact with the outer world at all. They are vegetarian and have solitary meals in their 'homes', with only five common meals a year. There's no TV or radio, and the conditions of life are austere. The hermits don't sleep in coffins as rumoured, but they do keep the skulls of their predecessors in the hermitages.

Kraków was the first of the Camaldolese seats in Poland; a church and 20 hermitages were built in 1603–42 and the whole complex was walled in. Not much has changed since. The place is spectacularly located and can be visited.

You approach it through a long walled alley that leads to the main gate. Once inside, you come face to face with the massive white limestone facade of the church, 50m high and 40m wide. A spacious, single-nave interior is covered by a barrel-shaped vault and lined on both sides with ornate baroque chapels.

Underneath the chancel of the church is a large chapel used for prayers and, to its right, the crypt of the hermits. Bodies are placed into niches without coffins and then sealed. Latin inscriptions state the age of the deceased and the period spent in the hermitage. The niches are opened after 80 years and the remains moved to a place of permanent rest. It's then that the hermits take the skulls to keep in their shelters.

In the garden behind the church are 14 surviving hermitages where several monks live (others live in the building next to the church), but the area is off-limits to tourists. You may occasionally see hermits in the church, wearing fine cream gowns.

Men can visit the church and the crypt any day from 8am to 11am and 3pm to 5pm (until 4pm in autumn and winter), but women are allowed inside only on major holidays. There are 12 such days during the year: 7 February, 25 March, Easter Sunday, Sunday and Monday of the Pentecost, Corpus Christi, 19 June, the Sunday after 19 June, 15 August, 8 September, 8 December and 25 December.

The hermitage is 7km west of the city centre. Take tram No 1, 6 or 32 to the end of the line in Zwierzyniec and change for any westbound bus except No 100. The bus will let you off at the foot of Srebrna Góra, from where it's a 10-minute walk up the hill to the church.

After visiting the church you can walk north for 20 minutes through the forest to the **Zoological Gardens** (*Ogród Zoologiczny;* ☎ 425 35 51; open 9am-dusk daily). The 20-hectare zoo is home to about 2000 animals representing 300 species from around the world.

About 1km farther north is the **Piłsudski Mound** (Kopiec Piłsudskiego), the youngest and largest of the four city mounds, erected in honour of the marshal after his death in 1935. Bus No 134 from the zoo will bring you back to the city.

Tyniec

A distant suburb of Kraków, 10km southwest of the centre, Tyniec is the site of the **Benedictine Abbey** (Klasztor Benedyktynów) perched on a cliff above the Vistula. The Benedictines were brought to Poland in the second half of the 11th century, and it was in Tyniec that they established their first home. The original Romanesque church and the monastery were destroyed and rebuilt several times. Today, the church is essentially a baroque building though the stone foundations and the lower parts of the walls, partly uncovered, show its earlier origins.

You enter the complex through a pair of defensive gates, resembling the entrance to a castle, and find yourself in a large courtyard. At its far end is an octagonal wooden pavilion, which protects a stone well dating from 1620.

The monastery cannot be visited but the church is open to all. Behind a sober facade, the dark interior is fitted out with a mix of baroque and rococo furnishings. The organ is plain but has a beautiful tone, and concerts are held here in summer. Check the current program with the Cultural Information Centre and try to make your trip coincide with a concert – a much more attractive bet than just visiting the building. To get to the abbey take bus No 112 from Rynek Dębnicki, near Rondo Grunwaldzkie.

KRAKÓW

Nowa Huta

The youngest and largest of Kraków's suburbs, Nowa Huta (New Steelworks) is a result of the postwar rush towards industrialisation. In the early 1950s a gigantic steelworks and a new town to serve as a dormitory for the workforce, were built 10km east of the city centre. The steel mill accounted for nearly half the national iron and steel output and the suburb has become a vast urban sprawl populated by over 200,000 people.

Because of increasing awareness of environmental issues, the industrial management was forced to cut production and reduce the workforce, yet the mammoth plant is still working despite the fact that it's unprofitable.

The steelworks can't be visited, but you might still want to have a look around the suburb. Nowa Huta is a shock after the medieval streets of the Old Town. Tram No 4 or 15 from the central train station will drop you at Plac Centralny, the suburb's central square. It actually doesn't matter where you start your sightseeing as the landscape varies little throughout the district. Most of it is just a grey concrete sea of Stalinist architecture, but fortunately, there are a few interesting sights in that sea.

In the north-western part of the suburb, is the **Church of Our Lady Queen of Poland** *(ul Obrońców Krzyża)*, commonly known as the Arka Pana (Lord's Ark). This interesting though rather heavy, boat-shaped construction was the first new church permitted in Nowa Huta after WWII, and was completed in 1977. Up to that year, the inhabitants used the two historic churches which somehow escaped the avalanche of concrete. They are both on the south-eastern outskirts of Nowa Huta, in the Mogiła suburb, and are worth a visit if you are in the area. The small, shingled **St Bartholomew's Church** *(Kościół Św Bartłomieja; ul Klasztorna)* dates from the mid-15th century, which makes it Poland's oldest surviving three-naved timber church. It's open only for the Sunday religious service. At other times, inquire in the house at the back, and a nun may open it for you.

Just across the street is the **Cistercian Abbey** (Opactwo Cystersów), which consists of a church and a monastery with a large garden-park behind. The Cistercians came to Poland in 1140 and founded their first monastery in Jędrzejów. They later established several other abbeys throughout the country, including this one in Mogiła, in 1222.

The church, open most of the day, has a large three-naved interior with a balanced mix of Gothic, Renaissance and baroque furnishings and decoration. Have a look at the Chapel of the Crucified Christ (in the left transept), the polyptych in the high altar, and beautiful stained-glass windows behind it.

Nowa Huta – A Communist Fantasy

The postwar communist regime deliberately built Nowa Huta steelworks in Kraków to give a 'healthy' working-class and industrial injection to the strong aristocratic, cultural and religious traditions of the city. Other, more rational reasons counted less. It was not of any importance, for example, that Kraków had neither ores nor coal deposits and that virtually all raw materials had to be transported from often distant locations. The project didn't take into account that the site boasted one of the most fertile soils in the region, nor that construction of the complex would destroy villages with histories going back to the early Middle Ages.

The communist dream hasn't materialised exactly as planned. Nowa Huta hasn't in fact threatened the deep traditional roots of the city. Worse, it actually became a threat to its creators, with strikes breaking out here as frequently as anywhere else, paving the way for the eventual fall of communism. The steelworks did, however, affect the city in another way: it brought catastrophic environmental pollution that threatened people's health, the natural environment and the city's historical monuments.

Wieliczka

Just outside the administrative boundaries of Kraków, 15km south-east of the city centre, Wieliczka ('Vyeh-**leech**-kah') is famous for its **Salt Mine** *(Kopalnia Soli;* ☎ *278 73 02,* W *www.kopalnia.pl, ul Daniłowicza 10; open 7.30am-6.30pm daily 16 Apr-15 Oct, 8am-4pm rest of year),* which has been operating uninterrupted for at least 700 years, making it the oldest Polish industrial plant in continuous operation. Polish/English tours of the salt mine cost US$7/8.

The mine is renowned for the preservative qualities of its microclimate, as well as for its health-giving properties. An underground sanatorium has been established at a depth of 211m, where chronic allergic diseases are treated.

The mine has a labyrinth of tunnels, about 300km of them, distributed over nine levels, the deepest being 327m underground. A section of the mine is open to the public as a museum, and it's a fascinating trip. The Wieliczka mine is on Unesco's World Heritage list.

You visit three upper levels of the mine, from 64m to 135m below the ground, walking through an eerie world of pits and chambers, all hewn out by hand from solid salt. Some have been made into chapels, with altarpieces and figures included, others are adorned with statues and monuments – all carved out of salt – and there are even underground lakes.

The highlight is the ornamented **Chapel of the Blessed Kinga** (Kaplica Błogosławionej Kingi), which is actually a fair-sized church measuring 54m x 17m and 12m high. Every single element here, from chandeliers to altarpieces, is of salt. It took over 30 years (1895–1927) to complete this underground temple, and about 20,000 tonnes of rock salt had to be removed. Occasional Masses and concerts are held here.

All visitors are guided in groups and the tour takes about two hours. You have about 2km to walk through the mine – wear comfortable shoes. The temperature in the mine is 14°C. In summer, when the mine is often overrun by visitors, tours start every five minutes or so, but in winter tours depart every half-hour to an hour, when enough tourists have turned up.

Tours are in Polish, but from June to September there are English-language tours a few times a day (at the time of writing they started at 10am, 12.30pm and 3pm, with additional tours in July and August at 11.30am and 1.45pm – check the times beforehand with the tourist offices or call the mine). Alternatively, you can hire an English guide (US$45 per group plus US$6 entry ticket per person). English-language brochures are available at the souvenir kiosk by the mine entrance.

There's a **museum** *(*☎ *278 32 66; adult/ student US$3/1.50; open same hours as the mine)* accommodated in 16 worked-out chambers on the 3rd level of the mine, where the tour ends. It features a collection of objects related to the mine. You need a separate ticket if you want to visit it. From here a lift takes you back up to the outer world.

There's another **museum** *(adult/student US$1/0.50; open 9am-4pm Wed-Mon)* in Wieliczka, in the local castle near the mine, which has exhibits on the archaeology and history of the region, and a collection of some 200 old saltcellars.

The easiest way of getting to Wieliczka from Kraków's centre is by Lux-Bus minibus – they depart every six to 12 minutes from near the PKS bus terminal, and will let you off close to the mine (US$0.50). There are also trains from the Kraków Główny station, but they are not as frequent and will leave you farther away from the mine.

WHAT'S FREE

You can enjoy quite a few freebies in Kraków, here are some suggestions:

• Go to Wawel castle on Sunday (Wednesday in summer) to see how the kings once lived
• Stroll about the narrow cobbled streets of the Old Town and the Main Market Square
• Visit the National Museum on Sunday, the day all its sections are free to visit
• Watch out for Kraków's colourful buskers, often performing on the main square and the adjacent streets
• Tour private art galleries to keep yourself up to date on Polish contemporary art

KRAKÓW

- Explore the city churches, all of which (except for the chancel of St Mary's Church) are free to visit
- Catch a free concert, show or exhibition going on around the centre (check the program with the cultural centre)

LANGUAGE COURSES

The most reputable institution in this matter is the **Instytut Polonijny Uniwersytetu Jagiellońskiego** (*Polonia Institute of the Jagiellonian University;* ☎ *429 76 32, fax 429 93 51, ul Jodłowa 13*). The institute conducts a variety of lectures on Polish issues (history, culture, literature etc) throughout the year, and regular one- and two-semester classes of Polish language (US$1800 per semester).

In July and August, the institute runs the Szkoła Letnia Kultury i Języka Polskiego (Summer School of Polish Language and Culture). The school offers a choice of three/four/six-week language courses, conducted on eight levels, from 'survival' to 'native speaker', and provides accommodation and board. The courses cost, depending on length, US$960/1260/1670 respectively, including bed and full board. Contact the school office well in advance for details (☎ 421 36 92, fax 422 77 01, e plschool@ jetta.if.uj.edu.pl), ul Garbarska 7A.

Kraków has several other language schools, which are not as renowned but cheaper and more flexible to the tourists' needs. If they're not running a course when you arrive, they can arrange teachers for individual classes (US$14 to US$18 per hour). The schools include:

Berlitz (☎ 632 90 75, fax 632 90 73, W www .berlitz.com) Al Słowackiego 64
Poliglota (☎ 430 21 85, W www.poliglota.pl) Plac Szczepański 3

ORGANISED TOURS

Three travel agencies – **Orbis Travel** (☎ *422 40 35, Rynek Główny 41*), **Jan-Pol** (☎ *421 42 06, ul Westerplatte 15/16*) and **Intercrac Travel** (☎ *422 58 40, ul Krupnicza 3*) – jointly operate a set program of tours in and outside Kraków. They include city sightseeing by coach (US$28), the traces of Jewish culture (US$28), the Wieliczka salt mine (US$30) and the Auschwitz-Birkenau death camps (US$30). Students under 25 get 25% discount on the Wieliczka and Auschwitz tours. Contact any of the three operators for their free *Cracow Tours* brochure with full descriptions.

Jarden Jewish Bookshop (☎ *421 71 66, ul Szeroka 2*) in Kazimierz's Jewish quarter is the best-known agency offering a choice of tours discovering Jewish heritage, including its famous Schindler's List tour. This two-hour tour, which includes the film's locations and other sites related to local Jewry, is conducted daily in summer (at other times on request) in a car or minibus and costs US$12 per person. Alternatively, buy the *Schindler's List* guidebook (US$2) in the bookshop, and set off for the tour on your own. Jarden's other popular tour is a three-hour walking tour around Jewish sites in Kazimierz and Podgórze (US$8). Jarden also does an Auschwitz-Birkenau tour (US$24).

Bird Service (☎ *292 14 60, fax 292 11 53,* e *bird@bird.pl,* W *www.bird.pl, ul Św Krzyża 17*) is one of Poland's best specialists in bird-watching tours. It organises birding trips in eastern Poland, including the Białowieża and Biebrza national parks. It also offers week-long bicycle tours along the Dunajec River in the Carpathian Mountains.

Bird Service organises the Polish Bird Festival, held annually in the second week of May in north-eastern Poland. This is a holiday package that covers eight nights accommodation in an optimal bird-watching location, half board and information.

SPECIAL EVENTS

Kraków has one of the richest cycles of annual events in Poland. The Cultural Information Centre (see Entertainment later in this chapter) will give you program details.

The **Festival of Sailors' Songs 'Shanties'** takes place in February. With a tradition of over 30 years, the **Organ Music Festival** in March/April gives people a chance to listen to organ recitals, which take place in several city churches.

May sees the **Student Song Festival**, an event organised annually since the mid-1960s. Some concerts are staged on the Main Market Square. In the same month is the **Juvenalia**, a student carnival, when students receive symbolic keys to the town's gates and 'take power' over the city for four days and three nights. There's street dancing, fancy dress parades, masquerades and lots of fun. The **Polish and International Short Film Festivals** take place in May/June.

Seven days after Corpus Christi (a Thursday in May or June), a colourful **pageant** headed by the Lajkonik, a funny figure disguised as a Tatar riding a horse, parades from Zwierzyniec to the main square.

The **Jewish Culture Festival** in June/July features a variety of cultural events including theatre, film, music and art exhibitions, and concludes with a grand open-air *klezmer* (Jewish folk music) concert on Szeroka Street. It's reputedly the biggest festival of its kind in Europe.

From late June to late August, **organ recitals** are held on Sunday in the Benedictine Abbey, Tyniec. There are also organ recitals in July and August in St Mary's Church.

The highlights of July include the **International Festival of Street Theatre**, taking place on the Main Market Square, and the **Summer Jazz Festival**, featuring the best of Polish modern jazz. Another jazz event, **Old Jazz in Kraków Festival**, is held throughout July and August and focuses on traditional jazz forms.

The most important musical event of August is the **Music in Old Kraków International Festival**. This two-week event spans five centuries of musical tradition, from medieval to contemporary, presented in concert halls, churches and other historic interiors.

On the first Thursday of December, a **competition of szopki** is held on the main square beside the statue of Adam Mickiewicz and attracts crowds of spectators. A sort of Nativity scene, but very different from those elsewhere in the world, Kraków's szopki are elaborate compositions built in an architectural, usually church-like form, made in astonishing detail from cardboard, wood, tinfoil and the like, and sometimes even mechanised. The prizewinning specimens are put on display until mid-February at a special exhibition in the Historical Museum of Kraków. You can see some of the old Nativity scenes in the Ethnographic Museum.

There are some important events near Kraków, particularly the famous **Passion Play** on Maundy Thursday and Good Friday during Easter week in Kalwaria Zebrzydowska (see the Carpathian Mountains chapter for details).

Lajkonik – Kraków's Legendary Figure

Lajkonik is a fairy-tale figure looking like a Tatar riding a little horse, decked out in embroidered garments, performed by a disguised man. He comes to life on the Thursday, seven days after Corpus Christi, and heads a joyful pageant from the Premonstratensian Convent in the suburb of Zwierzyniec to the Rynek Główny.

The pageant, accompanied by a musical band, takes at least six hours to complete the trip, while Lajkonik takes to dancing, jumping and running, greeting passers-by, popping into cafes en route, collecting donations and striking people with his mace, which is said to bring them good luck. Once the pageant reaches the main square, Lajkonik is greeted by the city mayor and presented with a symbolic ransom and a goblet of wine.

The event is believed to stem from the Tatar invasions of the 13th century. Legend has it that the headman of the local raftsmen defeated a Tatar khan, then put his robes on and triumphantly rode into the city. The Lajkonik festivities have taken place for at least two hundred years.

The horse's structure and garb used in the event were designed by Stanisław Wyspiański and the original is kept in the Historical Museum of Kraków. It consists of a wooden frame covered with leather and caparison, embroidered with nearly a thousand pearls and coral breads. The whole outfit weighs about 40kg.

PLACES TO STAY

Kraków is Poland's premier tourist destination, so finding a reasonable room in the summer tourist season can sometimes be tricky and may involve a bit of legwork. Fortunately, several large student hostels open during that time, which normally meets the demand for budget lodging. Hotels in Kraków are generally cheaper than in Warsaw, but a bit more expensive than in other large Polish cities. Most hotels increase their rates for the summer season by 10% to 20% (prices listed here are for the high season).

The tourist offices are likely to help you find somewhere to stay. If they can't find anything at a reasonable distance from the centre, they can send you to some less appealing hostels in Nowa Huta or other outer suburbs which almost never fill up. If you know beforehand which specific place or area you'll be likely to stay in, consider booking in advance. If you don't, try to arrive at the city reasonably early in the day to allow time for possible hotel hunting.

Places to Stay – Budget

Kraków has a good supply of budget places, though few of these are anywhere close to the centre and will need to do some commuting. Included in this section are places to stay where you normally shouldn't pay more than around US$30 per double.

Camping Kraków has several camping grounds, all of which are pretty distant from the centre but are linked to it by public transport.

Camping Nr 46 Smok (☎ 421 02 55, ul Kamedulska 18) Tent site US$2 plus US$4/person. Open June-Sept. Smok is 4km west of the centre, 1km beyond the Kościuszko Mound. It's small, quiet and pleasantly located. From Kraków Główny train station, take tram No 2 to the end of the line in Zwierzyniec and change for any westbound bus except No 100.

Camping Clepardia (☎ 415 96 72, ul Pachońskiego 28A) Tent site US$2 plus US$4/person, double/triple cabin US$26/34. Open June-Sept. Clepardia has tent space and several cabins with a bathroom.

Guests have free access to the outdoor swimming pool next to the camp site. It's 4km north of the centre, accessible by bus No 115 from the main train station; get off at Billa Supermarket.

Camping Nr 171 Krakowianka (☎ 266 41 91, ul Żywiecka Boczna 4) Tent site US$2 plus US$3.50 per person, 6-bed cabin US$32, triple hotel room without bath US$30. Open May-Sept, hotel open year-round. This camping ground is on the road to Zakopane, 6km south of the centre. It's simple and clean. You can get there from the train station by tram No 19 or bus No 119.

Camping Nr 45 Krak (☎ 637 21 22, ul Radzikowskiego 99) Tent site US$2.50 plus US$4/person. Open June–mid-Sept. The camp site is next to Motel Krak on the Katowice road, about 5km north-west of the centre. Take bus No 501 from the station. It's the city's largest and most expensive camping ground.

Youth Hostels Kraków has three regular PTSM youth hostels, but only one is near the Old Town.

Youth hostel (☎ 633 88 22, fax 633 89 20, ul Oleandry 4) Beds US$5-8. Open year-round. With its 380 beds, this is Poland's largest youth hostel but it nonetheless fills up at times. It has some doubles, triples and quads, but if anything's available it's more likely to be a bed in one of the large dorms sleeping 14 to 16 guests. The curfew is at midnight. This is the most central youth hostel, 1km west of the Old Town. To get there from the train station, take tram No 15 and get off just past the Hotel Cracovia, or walk the whole way (20 minutes).

Youth hostel (☎/fax 653 24 32, ul Grochowa 21) Beds US$6-8. Open year-round. This new and good, but inconvenient hostel, has dorms that sleep two to eight people. It's in the Płaszów suburb, 5km south-east of the centre, accessible by bus No 115 from the train station.

Youth hostel (☎ 637 24 41, fax 638 49 15, ul Szablowskiego 1C) Beds US$3-6. This hostel has 40 all-year beds (difficult to find unoccupied) and an additional 200 seasonal beds in July and August (which are not as hard to come by). It's 4km north-west of the Old Town; tram No 4 or 13 from the train station will let you off nearby. Check by phone for vacancies before you go.

Student Hostels There are a number of student dorms that open as student hostels in summer (July to late September), though some have a limited number of rooms available year-round. The picture may change from year to year, so inquire at the tourist offices to check which dorms are currently open. They are most likely to include the following:

Hotel Studencki Żaczek (☎ 633 19 14, fax 632 87 35, Al 3 Maja 5) Doubles without/with bath US$20/32. Żaczek is the most central student hostel, 1km west of the Old Town, a 10-minute walk. It has plenty of rooms during summer and also a few the rest of the year.

Hotel Studencki Nawojka (☎ 633 52 05, fax 633 55 48, ul Reymonta 11) Doubles without/with bath US$18/28. Located 2km west of the centre, Nawojka has a dozen all-year rooms and many more in summer.

Hotel Studencki Bydgoska (☎ 637 44 33, ul Bydgoska 19) Doubles without/with bath US$18/28. A bit farther away from the centre, Bydgoska offers about 70 beds year-round (but only in rooms without baths) plus 250 seasonal beds in summer.

Hotel Studencki Piast (☎ 637 49 33, fax 637 21 76, ul Piastowska 47) Doubles US$25-30, with bath US$30-40. Probably the biggest of the lot, Piast is also the most expensive student hostel and is farther away from the centre.

Bursa Jagiellońska (☎ 656 12 66, ul Śliska 14) Singles/doubles/triples US$15/25/35. Located in Podgórze, 2.5km south of the Old Town (and linked to it by tram No 10), Bursa is a good, neat and well-equipped place, open July to September.

Letni Hotel AWF (☎ 648 02 07, Al Jana Pawła II 82) Singles/doubles with bath US$15/20. AWF is a large 320-bed hostel, 4km east of the train station, midway to Nowa Huta, which can be easily reached by trams Nos 4, 5, 10 and 15. The hostel has its own cafeteria serving inexpensive meals.

Other Hostels There are a number of other hostels scattered throughout the city.

Dom Wycieczkowy Chałupnik (☎ 633 47 21, ☎/fax 633 75 01, ul Kochanowskiego 12) Doubles US$18, beds in quads US$8. This is about the most central all-year hostel. It's not a Sheraton and has only shared facilities, but you probably won't find a cheaper shelter within just a 10-minute walk from the main square.

Strawberry Hostel (☎ 636 15 00, ul Racławicka 9) Beds in doubles, triples or quads US$10. Open July & Aug. Well run and popular with travellers, this 200-bed hostel is 2km north-west of the Old Town and easily accessible by several tram lines.

Schronisko Turystyczne Express (☎/fax 633 88 62, ul Wrocławska 91) Beds in doubles/triples/6-bed dorms US$9/8/7. Open year-round. Express is a neat 100-bed hostel, a cross between a private guesthouse and a youth hostel, and is good value. Advance bookings are recommended. It's 2.5km north-west of the centre; bus No 130 from the train station will get you there (get off at the fifth stop).

Dom Turystyczny Czyżyny (☎ 644 67 00, fax 643 65 66, ul Centralna 32) Singles/doubles/triples with bath US$20/28/35. Located in Nowa Huta, this large 300-bed hostel is not particularly inspiring (nor is the area) but has private facilities and may have vacancies when most other places don't.

Private Rooms *Waweltur* (☎ 422 19 21, 422 16 40, ul Pawia 8; open 8am-8pm Mon-Fri, 8am-2pm Sat) arranges accommodation in private rooms for singles (US$18), and doubles (US$26 to US$32). Rooms are scattered around the city so check the location carefully before deciding.

You may also be offered a private room by someone on the street. The tourist offices don't recommend these services, but if you decide to use them, ask to see the location on the map first, and pay only after you have seen the room and accepted it.

Places to Stay – Mid-Range

This section includes places where a double room costs between US$30 and US$60.

Unfortunately, there are not that many reasonable hotels in this price bracket. The ones that fall into this category are often overrated or located well away from the centre, or both. Generally speaking, Kraków lacks decent mid-range accommodation, in contrast to an extensive offering of both budget and upmarket hotels.

Hotel Saski (☎ 421 42 22, fax 421 48 30, ul Sławkowska 3) Singles/doubles/triples US$40/50/60, with bath US$65/90/100. Ideally located in a historic townhouse just one block off Rynek Główny, Saski is a place with tradition, style and atmosphere, though the rooms with shared facilities won't let you feel that too much. Note the century-old lift, still in working order.

Pokoje Gościnne SARPu (☎/fax 429 17 78, ul Floriańska 39) Singles/doubles US$40/60. SARP is a small former architects' dorm that offers six rooms only, one single and five doubles. They are on the 3rd floor of a historic building, just two blocks from the main square. Two adjacent rooms share one bath, cooking facilities and fridge.

Hotel Wawel-Tourist (☎ 422 67 65, ul Poselska 22) Singles/doubles US$40/50, with bath US$50/70, breakfast included. This place is also in a good, central location, but its rooms with shared facilities are pretty average.

Dom Polonii (☎/fax 422 43 55, Rynek Główny 14) Doubles/suite with bath US$60/110. You couldn't ask for a more central location than this. The Dom has just two doubles (overlooking the Rynek) and one double suite, all on the top floor.

Pensjonat i Restauracja Rycerska (☎ 422 60 82, fax 422 33 99, Plac Na Groblach 22) Doubles without/with bath US$50/70, breakfast included. Sitting at the foot of Wawel hill, this 16-room pension offers acceptable if quite simple rooms.

Pokoje Gościnne Jordan (☎ 421 21 25, fax 422 82 26, ul Długa 9) Singles/doubles/triples with bath & breakfast US$35/ 55/70. Jordan is a small, reasonable place on the northern edge of the Old Town. The rooms are on the upper floors but you book through the travel agency downstairs.

Hotel Korona (☎/fax 656 15 66, ul Kalwaryjska 9/15) Singles/doubles/triples with bath & breakfast US$35/50/60. This 23-room sports hotel in Podgórze, 2km south of the Old Town (and easily accessible by tram No 10 from the train station), is OK.

Hotel Wisła (☎/fax 633 49 22, ul Reymonta 22) Singles/doubles/triples with bath US$30/40/45. Another affordable sports accommodation, Wisła is 2km west of the Old Town. Tram No 15 from the train station will let you off nearby.

Hotel Nauczycielski Krakowiak (☎ 637 73 04, fax 637 73 25, Al Armii Krajowej 9) Singles/doubles with bath US$30/34. This 150-room former teachers' dorm is a reasonable choice even though it's quite far from the centre. Take bus No 501 or 511 from the train station to get there.

Places to Stay – Top End

There are plenty of upmarket accommodation options in the Old Town and around, which is certainly Kraków's most atmospheric area in which to stay. Yet, most of these hotels are pretty costly and not always good value. The hotels listed below all have rooms with private baths and the prices include breakfast.

Dom Gościnny UJ (Jagiellonian University Guest House; ☎/fax 421 12 25, ul Floriańska 49) Singles/doubles US$55/85. Dom is a good and central place, but it's often full. It has 15 singles and eight doubles. Rooms are spacious, quiet and clean, and have large beds, desks and telephones.

Bursa im St Pigonia (☎ 422 30 08, ☎/fax 422 67 66, ul Garbarska 7A) Singles/doubles US$55/85. Another guesthouse of the Jagiellonian University, Bursa is just north-west of the Old Town and provides similar standards. It's quiet and has a cheap car park in the grounds – a great bonus in central Kraków.

Hotel Campanile (☎ 424 26 00, fax 424 26 01, ul Św Tomasza 34) Doubles US$80. Kraków's outlet of the French hotel chain, this new, large (105 rooms) and modern hotel has somehow succeeded in nestling in the Old Town, just a few blocks from the Rynek. It has good rooms and facilities, including air-conditioning and its own car park in the basement.

Hotel Atrium (☎ 430 02 03, fax 430 01 96, ul Krzywa 7) Singles/doubles/triples US$70/90/110. Another brand-new hotel, Atrium offers 40 spacious and comfortable rooms close to the train station.

Hotel Rezydent (☎ 429 54 95, fax 429 55 76, ul Grodzka 9) Singles/doubles/triples US$85/120/150, suites US$130-230. Just a stone's throw of the Rynek, Rezydent is a fairly new place which provides good standards and amenities.

Hotel Wit Stwosz (☎ 429 60 26, fax 429 61 39, ul Mikołajska 28) Doubles US$70-90, triples US$100-110. Accommodated in a historic townhouse in a quiet street, Wit Stwosz is very comfortable and stylish, with spacious rooms and remarkably reasonable rates.

Hotel Amadeus (☎ 429 60 70, fax 429 60 62, ul Mikołajska 20) Doubles/suites US$170/220. One of the newest and classiest city hotels, Amadeus provides excellent service and adequate amenities, including air-con, fitness club and sauna.

Hotel Copernicus (☎ 424 34 00, fax 431 11 40, ul Kanonicza 16) Singles/doubles US$160/200, suites US$270-350. Nestled in two beautifully restored buildings in one of Kraków's most picturesque and atmospheric streets, Copernicus is arguably the city's finest and most luxurious offering. The rooftop bar with spectacular views over Wawel and the swimming pool accommodated in medieval vaulted brick cellar add to the hotel's class.

There are more upmarket hotels in the Old Town; the tourist offices will give you information if you need it. There are also an increasing number of hotels in Kazimierz, including:

Hotel Klezmer-Hois (☎/fax 411 12 45, ul Szeroka 6) Singles/doubles US$70/85. This stylish historic place has 10 good, spacious rooms, each differently decorated.

Hotel Alef (☎/fax 421 38 70, ul Szeroka 17) Suites for 2/3/4 guests US$90/110/125. Alef offers four huge, charming suites, furnished with genuine antique furniture and adorned in old-world style. None of the rooms has a TV but all provide a great view over the street.

Hotel Eden (☎ 430 65 65, fax 430 67 67, ul Ciemna 15) Singles/doubles/triples US$75/100/120. Located in three meticulously restored 15th-century townhouses, Eden has 27 comfortable rooms and comes complete with a pub, sauna and the only mikvah (traditional Jewish bath) in Poland. Kosher meals are available on request in advance.

PLACES TO EAT

By Polish standards, Kraków is a food paradise – the Old Town is tightly packed with gastronomic venues, reputedly 400 of them – catering for every pocket, from rock bottom to top-notch. Privatisation has eliminated most of the old proletarian eateries, whereas many excellent places have popped up in their place offering superior fare at affordable prices. Pushcart vendors sell obwarzanki, ring-shaped pretzels powdered with poppy seeds, a local speciality.

Places to Eat – Budget

There are still several milk bars in the centre, which provide some of the cheapest meals in town. The most central and popular of these include:

Bar Mleczny Pod Temidą (☎ 422 08 74, ul Grodzka 43) Mains US$1-2. The place looks rather drab but the food is OK and unbelievably cheap, and has one of the cheapest salad bars in town. There are long queues at lunch time.

Bar Mleczny Dworzanin (☎ 422 76 21, ul Floriańska 19) Mains US$1-2. Another rock-bottom cafeteria, Dworzanin is also often full due to its tasty food and low prices, and it also has a very cheap salad bar.

Apart from milk bars, Kraków has plenty of budget eateries called jadłodajnia. These small places offer hearty Polish meals tasting as if they were cooked at home, and you can be perfectly full for US$2 to US$4. Following is a list of some eateries on offer.

Jadłodajnia U Stasi (☎ 421 50 84, ul Mikołajska 16) Mains US$1.50-3. One of the oldest and best-known jadłodajnias, this extremely simple place is invariably popular among the locals for its food, particularly a variety of the *pierogi* (stuffed dumplings), for which they are famous. The place is open weekdays from 12.30pm until 'the meals run out', which usually happens at around 4pm though the most attractive dishes run out much earlier. The jadłodajnia is off the street; enter the gate, head for the backyard and join the queue – which may give some indication of the popularity of the place.

Jadłodajnia Kuchcik (☎ 422 26 07, ul Jagiellońska 12) Mains US$1.50-3. Another tiny place providing home-cooked meals, Kuchcik is also very popular and fills up at lunch time.

Kuchnia Staropolska U Babci Maliny (☎ 422 76 01, ul Sławkowska 17) Mains US$2-3.50. Accommodated in the basement of the building of the Polska Akademia Umiejętności, and recently extensively refurbished, Kuchnia is one of the best jadłodajnias, offering long menu, excellent food, generous portions and pleasant surroundings – recommended.

Restauracja Sąsiedzi (☎ 421 41 46, ul Szpitalna 40) Mains US$2-4. Marginally more expensive than most other jadłodajnias, but open longer, this two-level place has a beautiful cellar and good food.

Bar Grodzki (☎ 422 68 07, ul Grodzka 47) Mains US$2-3.50. Grodzki is yet another good address for a hearty meal, particularly its delicious *placek po myśliwsku* (potato pancake with goulash).

Bistro Pod 13-ką (ul Miodowa 13, Kazimierz) Mains US$2-3.50. This is arguably the best jadłodajnia in Kazimierz.

Bar Wegetariański Vega (☎ 422 34 94, ul Św Gertrudy 7; ul Krupnicza 22) Mains US$1-3. Vega is an excellent, cheap, exclusively vegetarian place, serving tasty pierogi, crepes, tofu, salads etc. The second outlet at ul Krupnicza 22 has the same menu. The same people have recently opened *Restauracja Wegetariańska Vega* (☎ 431 01 29, ul Szeroka 3), in Kazimierz, which is a bit more expensive yet still modestly priced, and is beautifully decorated.

Różowy Słoń (Pink Elephant; ☎ 421 83 22, ul Sienna 1; ul Szpitalna 38; ul Straszewskiego 24) Mains US$1.50-3. This modern bistro is popular thanks to a varied menu (including salads, spaghetti, pierogi, barszcz and 20-odd flavours of crepes) and low prices.

Salad Bar Chimera (☎ 429 11 68, ul Św Anny 3) Salads US$2-3. Chimera is Kraków's best budget salad bar, nestled in attractive cellars consisting of several vaults, each with its own distinctive atmosphere. It offers an amazing array of fresh, good, cheap salads. In summer, there is an umbrella-shaded open-air section in the backyard of the building.

Piwnica Pod Ogródkiem (☎ 292 07 63, ul Jagiellońska 6) Galettes US$3. This basement creperie-cum-pub offers delicious *galletes* (typical French savoury pancakes) with a variety of fillings, each of which provides a substantial meal.

Taco Mexicano (☎ 421 54 41, ul Poselska 20; ul Starowiślna 15A) Mains US$2-5. Opened in 1993, Taco has quickly became popular among locals and visitors for its fairly authentic Mexican food at reasonable prices. You can have enchiladas, burritos and tacos and wash them down with cafe carajillo or tequila.

Places to Eat – Mid-Range & Top End

Gospoda CK Dezerter (☎ 422 79 31, ul Bracka 6) Mains US$5-8. Dezerter is a pleasantly decorated place that focuses on traditional regional food, including Austro-Hungarian cuisine from the old recipes.

Restauracja Cherubino (☎ 429 40 07, ul Św Tomasza 15) Mains US$5-8. Cherubino offers hearty Tuscan and Polish cuisine in its charming, artsy interior, which features antique carriages and boats.

Restauracja Bombaj Tandoori (☎ 422 37 97, ul Mikołajska 11) Mains US$4-7. This agreeable Indian establishment, one of the very few in Kraków, brings some Indian specialities to town, including curry, tandoori and marsala.

Café Ariel (☎ 421 79 20, ul Szeroka 18, Kazimierz) Mains US$5-8. Located in the heart of Kazimierz, Ariel serves traditional Jewish dishes, cakes and desserts, and a hearty kosher beer. Its cosy and intimate interior is furnished in a manner reminiscent of the 19th century. You'll find similar food, decor and atmosphere next door at **Hotel Alef** (☎ *421 38 70, ul Szeroka 17)* and a few paces down the street at **Hotel Klezmer-Hois** (☎ *411 12 45, ul Szeroka 6)*.

Restauracja Chłopskie Jadło (☎ *421 85 20, ul Św Agnieszki 1, Kazimierz;* ☎ *429 51 57, ul Św Jana 3)* Mains US$5-12. This place, a short walk south of Wawel, looks like a rustic country inn somewhere at the crossroads in medieval Poland, and serves up traditional Polish 'peasant grub', as its name says. Live folk music is performed here on some evenings, adding to the rustic atmosphere. It's one of Kraków's most unusual culinary adventures, and has very reasonable prices. A smaller outlet of the same chain has recently opened its doors in the Old Town.

Restauracja Korsykańska Paese (☎ *421 62 73, ul Poselska 24)* Mains US$7-10. Paese offers Corsican and some mainland French cuisine, including fine seafood. The food is good, the prices acceptable and the interior bright and cheerful.

Restauracja Pod Aniołami (☎ *421 39 99, ul Grodzka 35)*. Mains US$8-12. Literally, 'Under the Angels' offers excellent typical Polish food in some of the most amazing surroundings. It's in fantastic vaulted cellars, beautifully decorated with traditional household implements and old crafts. It's easily one of the most attractive options for that special dinner in the city.

Restauracja Cyrano de Bergerac (☎ *411 72 88, ul Sławkowska 26)* Mains US$8-18. Another marvellous place, this restaurant serves fine, authentic French food in one of the city's loveliest cellars. It's not exactly a budget eatery, and the portions are not overly copious, but the quality matches the price and it's certainly less that you'll pay in Paris.

Cafes

Kraków has traditionally had a wealth of cafes, a good number of them located in historic buildings and their medieval cellars. Until not long ago they served mainly coffee and sweets and were predominantly meeting places rather than eating places. Now most have introduced food menus, and some have even changed their sign, replacing 'Cafe' with 'Restaurant'. And they've all extended their once limited drink repertoire. In effect, the distinction between cafe, restaurant and bar has become blurred.

Jama Michalika (☎ *422 15 61, ul Floriańska 45)* Jama is perhaps Kraków's most famous cafe. Established in 1895, it was traditionally a hang-out for painters, writers and all sorts of artists. Decorated with artworks of the period, it gives the impression of a small *fin-de-siècle* museum. It's nonsmoking – one of few such cafes in the city.

Pożegnanie Z Afryką (Farewell to Africa; ul Św Tomasza 21) Coffee US$2. This place offers the best choice of coffee in town. It is a nonsmoking shop-cum-cafe that sells about 70 kinds of coffee, half of which is on offer inside at the tables. Coffee is prepared in sophisticated coffee makers and spring water is used, not tap water which is pretty bad in Kraków.

Café Camelot ☎ *421 01 23, ul Św Tomasza 17)* Salads US$4-5. Camelot is an amazing, bohemian cafe, decorated with beautiful pieces of folk art, which apart from coffee and drinks has a short menu of light dishes and snacks, including delicious salads.

Café Botanica (☎ *422 89 80, ul Bracka 9)* This little place feels like a greenhouse or garden, filled with potted plants, and even the chairs and tables are designed to match the whole interior design.

TriBeCa Coffee (☎ *421 30 85, ul Karmelicka 8)* Coffee US$1.50-2.50. TriBeCa is a warm and inviting place, which offers excellent coffee plus a fine choice of sandwiches and pastries.

Wiśniowy Sad (☎ *430 21 11, ul Grodzka 33)* With its old furniture, piano, lace tablecloths and period bits and pieces, Wiśniowy Sad has a nostalgic air of Chekhov's days.

Demmers Teehaus (ul Kanonicza 21) An outlet of the famous Viennese teahouse, this is possibly the best place in Kraków for a cup of tea. It sells heaps of tea varieties, many of which can be tried in an intimate tearoom in the cellar.

KRAKÓW

ENTERTAINMENT

Kraków has a very lively cultural life, particularly in the theatre, music and visual arts, and there are numerous annual festivals. The Centrum Informacji Kulturalnej (Culture Information Centre; ☎ 421 77 87, fax 421 77 31, W www.karnet.krakow2000 .pl), ul Św Jana 2, just off the main square, will provide detailed information on what's on. It publishes a comprehensive Polish/English monthly magazine, *Karnet*, listing cultural events, and sells tickets for some of them. The office is open 10am to 6pm weekdays, 10am to 4pm Saturday.

Another local what's-on monthly magazine, *Miesiąc w Krakowie* (This Month in Kraków), is detailed and helpful but is mostly in Polish. For some English-language help, get a copy of *Kraków In Your Pocket*, which has excellent coverage of entertainment, including bars, pubs and discos. The two leading local papers, *Gazeta Krakowska* and *Gazeta Wyborcza*, list programs of cinemas, theatres, concerts etc. The Friday edition of the latter has a more comprehensive what's-on section which includes information on museums, art galleries and activities.

Bars & Pubs

There are more than 100 of these in the Old Town alone. Some offer snacks but most serve just drinks, mainly beer. Many are in vaulted cellars, often very attractive. All are smoking venues, so in some places those sensitive to cigarette smoke might find an oxygen mask essential. Some pubs are open until midnight, but many don't close until the wee hours of the morning. Here are a few places to help you start your exploration.

Irish Pub Pod Papugami (☎ 422 82 99, ul Św Jana 18) Recently wholly refurbished, the 'Under the Parrots' pub is a charming cellar watering hole, decorated with old motorcycles, radios, cameras, brass instruments etc.

Klub Kulturalny (☎ 429 67 39, ul Szewska 25) Set in a labyrinthine array of beautiful medieval brick vaults, the 'Cultural Club' has long been a popular haunt, with its good music and atmosphere.

Piwnica Pod Złotą Pipą (☎ 421 94 66, ul Floriańska 30) Enjoying another spectacular cellar location, this pub-cum-restaurant is pleasant, quiet and comfortable, suitable for a quiet chat, perhaps even accompanied by a light dinner.

Free Pub (☎ 413 03 63, ul Sławkowska 4) Another cellar affair, the Free Pub is open longer than most, so you may include it towards the end of your night during your pub expedition.

Pub Bastylia (☎ 431 00 09, ul Stolarska 3) A new kid on the block, Bastylia is an amazing, spacious five-level place with a barbecue restaurant downstairs and the upper levels arranged as the infamous French jail.

Should you need a good watering hole in Kazimierz, try *Pub Ulica Krokodyli* (☎ 431 05 16, ul Szeroka 30) or *Pub Ptaszyl* (☎ 429 65 67, ul Szeroka 10).

Clubs & Discos

There are quite a number of night clubs and discos in the Old Town. The following are recommended.

Klub Pasja (☎ 423 04 83, ul Szewska 5) Occupying vast brick cellars, Pasja is trendy and attractive and is frequented by foreigners. It's open daily and has a billiard section.

Music Bar 9 (☎ 422 25 46, ul Szewska 9) Close to Pasja, this complex of a large bar in a covered courtyard and a disco in the cellar, attracts mostly younger folk and operates Tuesday to Saturday.

Equinox (☎ 421 17 71, ul Sławkowska 13/15) Equinox has long been one of the most popular haunts, with discos nightly.

Klub Pod Papugami (☎ 422 08 06, ul Szpitalna 1) Another popular disco (not to be confused with the pub of the same name), Pod Papugami has discos nightly except Monday.

Jazz

Kraków has a lively jazz life and a number of jazz clubs.

Jazz Club U Muniaka (☎ 423 12 05, ul Floriańska 3) Housed in a fine cellar, this is one of the best-known jazz outlets, founded by the veteran saxophonist Janusz Muniak who often performs here. Live jazz is usually on Thursday to Saturday nights.

Harris Piano Jazz Bar *(☎ 421 57 41, Rynek Główny 28)* Another active jazz haunt, Harris hosts bands mainly on weekends.

Indigo Jazz Club *(☎ 429 17 43, ul Floriańska 26)* Positioned in amazing vaulted cellars with beautiful acoustics, Indigo doesn't seem to have a strict concert schedule, but does host live jazz once or twice a week.

Piec Art *(☎ 429 64 25, ul Szewska 12)* This cosy cellar club tends to stage jazz on Wednesday with irregular gigs on other days.

Rotunda Student Club *(☎ 634 34 12, ul Oleandry 1)* Rotunda goes jazzy on Tuesday.

Klub Jazzowy Kornet *(☎ 427 02 44, Al Krasińskiego 19)* A bit out of the centre, Kornet has concerts and/or jam sessions on Wednesday and Friday.

Jewish Music

In recent years, Kraków has become an active centre of klezmer music, regularly played live by various klezmer bands in the cafes of Kazimierz, including the Ariel, Alef and Klezmer-Hois (see earlier in Places to Eat). Concerts normally start at 8pm and there's a US$5 admission fee.

Classical Music

Filharmonia Krakowska *(☎ 422 09 58, ul Zwierzyniecka 1)* The Kraków Philharmonic is home to one of the best orchestras in the country. Concerts are held on Friday and Saturday and irregularly on other days.

Cinema

Kraków has about 20 movie houses, half of them in the centre. The cinemas that may have some arthouse and quality mainstream movies on their program include ***Kino Mikro*** *(☎ 634 28 97, ul Lea 5)*, ***Kino Paradox*** *(☎ 430 00 25, ul Krowoderska 8)* and the cinema club in the ***Rotunda Student Club*** *(☎ 634 34 12, ul Oleandry 1)*.

Theatre

Kraków has a dozen theatres (more than any other Polish city, except Warsaw), including some of Poland's best playhouses.

Cricoteka *(☎ 422 83 32, ul Kanonicza 5)* Cricoteka is the centre that documents the avant-garde Cricot 2 theatre created in 1955 by Tadeusz Kantor. Kraków's best-known theatre outside the national borders, Cricot 2 was dissolved after Kantor died in 1990. Theatre buffs may be interested in visiting this place.

Stary Teatr *(Old Theatre; main stage ☎ 422 40 40, ul Jagiellońska 1; 2 small stages ☎ 428 47 00, ul Starowiślna 21 & ☎ 421 59 76, ul Sławkowska 14)* This is the best-known city theatre and has attracted the cream of the city's actors.

Teatr im Słowackiego *(Słowacki Theatre; ☎ 422 45 75, Plac Św Ducha 1)* The theatre focuses on Polish classics and large-scale productions. It's in a large and opulent building – a historical monument in itself – patterned on the Paris Opera and built in 1893. It was totally renovated in 1991 and its interior is spectacular. Opera and ballet performances are also staged here, as there's no proper opera house in Kraków.

Scena STU *(☎ 422 27 44, Al Krasińskiego 16)* STU started in the 1970s as an 'angry', politically involved, avant-garde student theatre and was immediately successful. Today, it no longer deserves any of those adjectives, but nonetheless it's a solid professional troupe.

SHOPPING
Crafts

There are several Cepelia shops scattered around the central area, but the obvious place to go is the Cloth Hall in the middle of the main square, where several dozen stands sell every imaginable Polish craft. Some of them sell jewellery, particularly of semiprecious stones and amber set in silver, which may be good value.

Antiques

Kraków has a number of antique shops, including the ones at ul Grodzka 8, ul Mikołajska 10, ul Stolarska 17 and ul Floriańska 13.

Antykwariat *(ul Sławkowska 10)* This shop sells a variety of old books, prints, maps, drawings and etchings.

KRAKÓW

In the summer season, an antique and bric-a-brac fair is held for one weekend a month at the main square. For the rest of the year, it's every second and fourth Saturday of the month at ul Siemiradzkiego 13.

Contemporary Art

Kraków is a good place to get an insight into what's currently happening in Polish art and, if you wish, to buy some. There are plenty of commercial art galleries in town.

Starmach Gallery (☎ 656 43 17, ul Węgierska 5) One of the most prestigious art galleries in town, Starmach has renowned contemporary painting, though perhaps not for everyone's pocket.

Labirynt (☎ 292 60 80, ul Floriańska 36) A more affordable place for art, Labirynt has a decent mix of painting and sculpture.

Artemis (☎ 422, ul Starowiślna 21) This is another place for contemporary painting.

Jan Fejkiel Gallery (☎ 429 15 53, ul Grodzka 25) Fejkiel has the best collection of original prints in town.

Andrzej Mleczko Gallery (☎ 421 71 04, ul Św Jana 14) The gallery displays and sells comic drawings by one of the most popular Polish satirical cartoonists.

Galeria Plakatu (*Poster Gallery;* ☎ 421 26 40, ul Stolarska 8-10) Without any doubt, this is Kraków's best choice of posters, created by Poland's most prominent poster makers.

Books & Records

EMPiK (☎ 429 45 77, Rynek Główny 5) Like elsewhere, EMPiK has well-stocked sections with attractive coffee-table books, including some alluring photographic accounts of Kraków (English-language versions are available). It also has a good music section, with a choice of Polish rock, contemporary, folk, classical and jazz music on CDs.

Jarden Jewish Bookshop (☎ 421 71 66, ul Szeroka 2, Kazimierz) The bookshop has the best selection of books referring to Jewish issues.

Salon Muzyczny (*ul Senacka 6*) The Salon has a lot of CDs with classical and contemporary music.

Jazz Compact (☎ 422 26 53, Rynek Główny 28) This tiny shop has an extensive selection of jazz, including Polish jazz.

GETTING THERE & AWAY
Air

The airport is in Balice, about 12km west of the city, and is accessible by bus No 208 from just north of the PKS bus terminal and by the more frequent bus No 152 from the bus stop at ul Lubicz south of the train station. A taxi between the airport and the city centre shouldn't cost more than US$10. The LOT office (☎ 411 67 00), ul Basztowa 15, deals with tickets and reservations.

Within Poland, the only flights are to Warsaw, but you can get there much more cheaply, centre-to-centre, by train in 2¾ hours. Kraków has direct flight connections with Copenhagen, Frankfurt/Main, London, Paris, Rome, Vienna and Zurich.

Train

The central train station, Kraków Główny, on the north-eastern outskirts of the Old Town, handles all international and most domestic trains. The only other station of any significance is Kraków Płaszów, 4km south-east of the city centre, which operates some trains that don't call at Kraków Główny. Local trains between the two stations run every 15 to 30 minutes. All trains listed in this section depart from the central station.

There are two morning, two afternoon and one evening InterCity trains to Warsaw (297km) and the trip takes about 2¾ hours. There are also several express and fast trains to Warsaw which take a bit longer.

To Częstochowa (132km), there are two morning fast trains as well as several afternoon/evening trains. Trains to Katowice (78km) run every half-hour to an hour, and there's also good transport farther on to Wrocław (268km), with a dozen departures a day. A dozen trains run daily to Zakopane (147km) but it's much faster by bus.

There are plenty of trains daily to Tarnów (78km) that pass through Bośnia (a gateway to Nowy Wiśnicz). A dozen of these trains continue to Rzeszów (158km).

To Oświęcim (65km), you have a couple of trains early in the morning and then nothing until the afternoon. There are more trains to Oświęcim from Kraków Płaszów station, though they don't depart regularly either; check the bus schedule before going to Płaszów.

Internationally, there's one or two direct trains daily to Berlin, Bratislava, Bucharest, Budapest, Hamburg, Kyiv, Odesa, Prague and Vienna.

Tickets and couchettes can be bought directly at Kraków Główny station or at the Orbis Travel at Rynek Główny 41.

Bus

The PKS bus terminal is next to Kraków Główny train station. Travel by bus is particularly advisable to Zakopane (104km) as it's considerably shorter and faster than by train. Fast PKS buses go there every hour (US$3, 2½ hours). Two private companies, Trans-Frej and Szwagropol, also run buses to Zakopane, which are marginally faster. They depart from the front of the terminal. Tickets for Trans-Frej are available from Wawelturi (☎ 422 19 21), ul Pawia 8. For Szwagropol, tickets are sold by Centrum Turystyki (☎ 422 29 04), ul Worcella 1.

There are three morning PKS departures to Częstochowa (114km) and three morning buses to Oświęcim (64km). Other destinations include two buses a day to Lublin (269km), two to Zamość (318km) and eight to Cieszyn (Czech border, 121km). You will also use buses while going to Kalwaria Zebrzydowska (33km) and Ojców (26km). To other destinations, it is better to go by train. Tickets are available directly from the bus terminal. Note that buses to Oświęcim don't depart from the terminal but from the bus stop on the opposite side of the train station, accessible by a passageway under the platforms.

There are plenty of international bus routes originating in Kraków, going to Amsterdam (US$75), Budapest (US$30), London (US$90), Munich (US$55), Paris (US$85), Prague (US$35), Rome (US$80), Vienna (US$30) and other destinations. Information and tickets are available from travel agencies throughout town, including Sindbad (☎ 421 02 40) in the bus terminal.

GETTING AROUND

Most tourist attractions are in the Old Town or within easy walking distance, so you won't need buses or trams unless you're staying outside the centre. Should you need a taxi, some of the better known companies include Radio Taxi (☎ 919), Tele Taxi (☎ 962), Wawel Taxi (☎ 96 66), Royal Taxi (☎ 96 23) and Express Taxi (☎ 96 29).

If you're travelling by car, note that the Old Town is closed to traffic except for access to two guarded car parks, on Plac Szczepański and Plac Św Ducha – the most convenient places to park (US$2.50 per hour), if you can find space. If not, use one of the guarded car parks in the surrounding area. Street parking in the belt around the Old Town area requires special tickets (karta postojowa) which you buy in a Ruch kiosk, mark with the correct month, day and time, and then display on your windscreen.

AROUND KRAKÓW

Kraków is a convenient jumping-off point for day trips to some nearby places of interest, of which the Ojców National Park and Oświęcim (Auschwitz-Birkenau death camps) are two obvious destinations. Kalwaria Zebrzydowska is one more example, especially if you happen to be here during Easter. You could also consider Nowy Wiśnicz and Dębno if you are not heading farther east. You'll find all these places detailed elsewhere in this book.

KRAKÓW

Małopolska

Małopolska (literally, Little Poland) is in south-eastern Poland with Mazovia to the north and the Carpathian Mountains to the south. Historically, together with Wielkopolska (Great Poland), it was the cradle of the Polish state. Settled by Slavs from the early Middle Ages, Małopolska became of prime importance after the kings chose Kraków as the royal seat in 1038. As a royal province, the region enjoyed the special attention of the kings, who built an array of castles to protect it. Małopolska was always one of the most 'Polish' regions of the country, and retains much of that traditional flavour to this day.

It's a land of softly rolling hills and green valleys, sprinkled with villages and towns, and much of it still bears a bucolic air of bygone times. You'll see long, wooden horse carts on the roads and people working the fields as they have for centuries.

Geographically speaking, Małopolska encompasses the Małopolska Upland and its two bordering areas – the Kraków-Częstochowa Upland to the west and the Sandomierz Valley to the east. The Lublin Upland, which is similar in both geography and history, is generally included in Małopolska as well. Also included in this chapter is the Radom Plain, on the borderline with Mazovia.

The Kraków-Częstochowa Upland

The Kraków-Częstochowa Upland (Wyżyna Krakowsko-Częstochowska) is a picturesque belt of land, roughly 20km to 40km wide, that stretches for over 100km from Kraków to Częstochowa. It was formed of limestone some 150 million years ago in the Jurassic period (the name comes from the Jura mountains in France, and this Polish upland region is also popularly known as the Jura).

Highlights

- Make a pilgrimage to Jasna Góra in Częstochowa, Poland's national shrine
- Check out the unique Sundial Museum in Jędrzejów
- Stroll about the fantastic ruin of Krzyżtopór castle in Ujazd
- Explore the lethargic old town of Sandomierz
- Visit the extraordinary Chapel of the Holy Trinity in Lublin Castle
- See Kozłówka's sumptuous palace and the stunning socialist-realist gallery
- Wander around the lovely Renaissance town of Zamość

Erosion of the upland has left behind a variety of strange rock formations, taking the shapes of freestanding pillars, clubs and gates, for example. There are also between 500 and 1000 caves, the overwhelming majority of all those in Poland. The largest concentrations are in the Ojców area and around the village of Olsztyn near Częstochowa. They are largely unexplored – the haunt of speleologists and other adventurers.

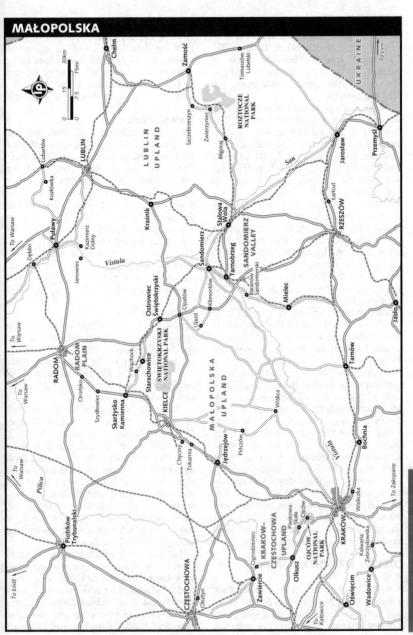

The flora and fauna of the upland is diverse. A good part of the region is covered by forest, mostly beech, pine and fir. There are 17 species of bat – the symbol of the Jura – living in the local caves, and you can occasionally come across hares, roe deer and even elk.

The region's great cultural attractions are the numerous castles. When Silesia fell to Bohemia in the mid-14th century, leaving the Jura a natural border between the two countries, King Kazimierz Wielki set about fortifying the frontier, and a chain of castles was built all the way from Kraków to Częstochowa. Taking advantage of the topography, they were built on the hill tops along the ridge and, like the Great Wall of China, were meant to form an impregnable barrier against the enemy. They were indeed never breached by the Bohemians, with whom there were simply no more major conflicts. It was the Swedish invasion of 1655 that brought destruction to the castles and successive invasions during the 18th century reduced most of them to ruins. Apart from the Pieskowa Skała, the castles were not rebuilt. Today there are a dozen ruined castles scattered around the upland; the most impressive are at Ogrodzieniec and Olsztyn.

An excellent way to explore the upland is the Trail of the Eagles' Nests (*Szlak Orlich Gniazd*) hike. The trail, signposted in red, winds for 164km from Kraków to Częstochowa and passes through the most interesting parts of the Jura, including a dozen ruined castles. Total walking time is about 42 hours. Accommodation, in youth hostels (July and August only), hotels or agrotourist farms, is within a day's walking distance, so you don't need camping gear. There are regional maps that give details of the route and tourist facilities. The tourist offices in Kraków and Częstochowa should have these maps and other information.

OJCÓW NATIONAL PARK
☎ 12

At only 21 sq km, the Ojców National Park (Ojcowski Park Narodowy) is Poland's second smallest national park, yet it's very picturesque and varied. The park encompasses some of the most beautiful parts of the Kraków-Częstochowa Upland. In its small area you'll find two castles, a number of caves, impressive rock formations and a wide variety of plant life. Most of the park is beech, fir, oak and hornbeam forest which is particularly photogenic in autumn.

Orientation

Most tourist attractions are along the road that runs through the park beside the Prądnik River with Ojców and Pieskowa Skała, about 7km apart, being the main points of interest. Though buses run between these two localities, it's best to walk the whole stretch, enjoying the sights and scenery. The Trail of the Eagles' Nests also follows this road.

Give yourself plenty of time in the park – it's a captivating place. Buy the *Ojcowski Park Narodowy* map (scale 1:22,500) in Kraków before setting off. The map includes all the marked trails, rocks, caves, gorges and the like.

Things to See

Ojców is the only village in the park. Its predominantly wooden houses are scattered across a slope above the river. The hill at the northern end of the village is crowned with the ruins of **Ojców Castle**, with its original 14th-century entrance gate and an octagonal tower.

One of the two long buildings just south of the castle houses the **Natural History Museum** (*Muzeum Przyrodnicze;* ☎ 389 20 40, adult/student US$1/0.50; open 9am-4pm Tues-Sun*), which focuses on the geology, archaeology and flora and fauna of the park. A wooden mansion a few paces farther south accommodates the **Regional Museum** (*Muzeum Regionalne;* ☎ 389 20 10, adult/student US$1/0.50; open 9am-3pm Tues-Sun*) which features the history and ethnography of the region.

The black trail which heads southwards from Ojców Castle takes you to the **Łokietek Cave** (*Jaskinia Łokietka; admission US$1.50; open 9am-5pm June-Aug, 9am-4pm May & Sept*). About 250m long, this cave consists of one small and two large chambers. Guided tours take half an hour.

More interesting and larger is the **Wierzchowska Górna Cave** (☎ *411 07 21; adult/student US$2.50/2; open 9am-5pm May-Aug, 9am-4pm Apr, Sept & Oct)*, in the village of Wierzchowie outside the park boundaries, 5km south-west of Ojców; the yellow trail will take you there. It's the longest cave in the whole region – 1km long – and about 370m of its length can be visited. The 50-minute tours begin on the hour. The temperature inside is 7.5°C year-round.

Other caves open to the public (in summer) include the **Dark Cave** (Jaskinia Ciemna), close to Ojców and easily reached by the green trail, and the **Bat Cave** (Jaskinia Nietoperzowa), farther away and accessible by the blue trail.

About 200m north of Ojców Castle is the **Chapel upon the Water** (Kaplica na Wodzie), positioned above the river bed where it was rebuilt from the former public baths. The chapel is open only for religious services on Sunday morning.

In the hamlet of Grodzisko, about 2km to the north, the road divides: take the left-hand fork skirting the river and look for the red trail that branches off the road to the right and heads uphill. It will take you to the small baroque **Church of the Blessed Salomea**, erected in the 17th century on the site of the former convent of Poor Clares. The stone wall encircling the church is adorned with statues representing Salomea and her family. Behind the church is an unusual carved stone elephant (1686) supporting an obelisk on its back.

Follow the red trail, which brings you back down to the road. Walk for several kilometres to an 18m-tall limestone pillar known as **Hercules' Club** (Maczuga Herkulesa). A short distance beyond it is the **Pieskowa Skała Castle**. The castle was erected in the 14th century but the mighty fortress you see is the result of major rebuilding in the 16th century. It's the best-preserved castle in the upland and it houses a **museum** (☎ *389 60 04; adult/student US$2.50/2; open 10am-3.30pm Tues-Sun)*.

You first enter a large outer courtyard which is accessible free of charge. From here you get to the arcaded inner courtyard and the museum. On display is European art from the Middle Ages to the mid-19th century, including furniture, tapestries, sculpture, painting and ceramics.

There's a restaurant-cafe in the outer courtyard of the castle, a good place to finish your sightseeing with a beer, coffee or a meal. In summer they open the terrace on the roof, providing a good view over the castle and the surrounding forest.

Places to Stay & Eat

Local people in Ojców rent out *rooms* in their homes for around US$6 to US$8 per person. The rooms can be arranged through the Ojcowianin travel agency (☎ 389 20 89) or the PTTK office (☎ 389 20 10), both in the building of the regional museum.

Camping Złota Góra (☎ *389 20 14, Złota Góra)* Bed in on-site tent US$3. Open May-Sept. This camping ground has six large military tents with beds and a restaurant.

Dom Wycieczkowy Zosia (☎ *389 20 08, Złota Góra)* Beds in doubles, triples or quads without/with bath US$6/8. About 500m down the road from the camping ground, this place is one of the few regular all-year hostels around. Zosia is 1km west of Ojców Castle.

Getting There & Away

There are a few morning buses from Kraków to Ojców (22km, daily). You can then walk to Pieskowa Skała, from where you can take a bus back to Kraków (29km), or continue to Olkusz (16km) and from there farther north to Ogrodzieniec and Częstochowa.

OGRODZIENIEC

☎ 32 • pop 4500

Perched on top of the highest hill of the whole upland (504m), the fairy-tale ruin of the **Ogrodzieniec Castle** (☎ *673 22 20; adult/student US$1.50/1; open 9am-dusk Apr-Oct)* is among the most picturesque in the country. Using natural rock for the foundations and some parts of the walls – a feature typical of castles in the region – the fortress was built during the reign of King Kazimierz Wielki but enlarged and remodelled in the mid-16th century. The owner at

MAŁOPOLSKA

the time, the wealthy Kraków banker Seweryn Boner, employed the best Italian masters from the royal court, who turned the Gothic castle into a Renaissance residence, said to be almost as splendid as the Wawel castle. The castle fell prey to the Swedes in 1655 and never regained its grandeur. The last owners abandoned it in the 1810s, and since then the ruin has been untouched. It's now a tourist sight.

Getting There & Away

The castle is in the small village of Podzamcze, 2km east of Ogrodzieniec; the two places are linked by local buses. Ogrodzieniec lies on the Zawiercie-Olkusz road and buses run regularly between these towns. From Zawiercie, you can continue north on one of the frequent trains to Częstochowa, while buses from Olkusz can take you to Pieskowa Skała, Ojców or directly to Kraków.

CZĘSTOCHOWA

☎34 • pop 260,000

Częstochowa (pronounced 'Chen-sto-**ho**-vah') is the spiritual heart of Poland and the country's national shrine. It owes its fame to the miraculous icon of the Black Madonna, kept in the Monastery of Jasna Góra (literally, Bright Mountain), which has been pulling in pilgrims from all corners of the country and beyond for centuries.

Today, Częstochowa attracts some of the largest pilgrimages in the world (local sources put it fifth, after Varanasi, Mecca, Lourdes and Rome). Tourists and the faithful alike flock in large numbers throughout the year, with significant peaks on Marian feasts, particularly on the day of the Assumption on 15August. You're likely to find yourself drawn to the city, whether through devotion or curiosity.

History

Though the earliest document mentioning Częstochowa's existence dates from 1220, the town's development really began with the arrival of the Paulite Order from Hungary in 1382. The monks founded a monastery atop a hill known as Jasna Góra.

The monastery probably would not have gained its exceptional fame if not for a painting of the Virgin Mary, commonly referred to as the Black Madonna, which was presented to the order in 1384 and soon began to attract crowds of believers, thanks to numerous miracles attributed to the image.

Growing in wealth and importance, the monastery was gradually extended and turned into a fortress surrounded by stout defensive walls with massive bastions. It was one of the few places in the country to withstand the Swedish sieges of 1655–56, the 'miracle' naturally being attributed to the Black Madonna and contributing to still larger floods of pilgrims. Interestingly, before the siege the Madonna was transferred to Silesia for safekeeping, yet somehow she was still able to save the monastery.

The town of Częstochowa grew as a centre providing facilities for the pilgrims visiting the monastery. In the second half of the 19th century, the construction of the Warsaw-Vienna railway line stimulated the development of commerce and industry. By the outbreak of WWII the city had 140,000 inhabitants.

After the war, in an attempt to overshadow the town's religious status, the communists intensified the development of industry. Today Częstochowa has a large steelworks and a number of other factories complete with a forest of smoky chimneys. Amid them, however, the tower of the Paulite monastery still proudly overlooks the city, showing pilgrims the way to the end of their journey.

Orientation

The main thoroughfare in the city centre is Al Najświętszej Marii Panny (referred to in addresses as Al NMP), a wide, tree-lined avenue with the Monastery of Jasna Góra at its western end and St Sigismund's Church at the eastern end. The train and bus stations are just south of the eastern part of Al NMP, a 20-minute walk from the monastery. Most places to stay are near the monastery, whereas many places to eat are either on or just off Al NMP.

centre for the cloth trade in the 14th century, Kraków's Cloth Hall now plays host to the tourist trade

t Mary's Church, Kraków

'Krakowiacy', Kraków's famous folk musicians

Kraków's main market square

The 14th-century Wawel Castle, Kraków

Folk dancers in traditional costume twirl on Kraków's old market square

Church of SS Peter and Paul, Kraków

Gateway to the medieval Great Barbican, Kraków

The Black Madonna of Częstochowa

The Black Madonna is a painting on a lime-tree timber panel measuring 122cm x 82cm that depicts the Virgin Mary with the Christ child. The picture looks like a Byzantine icon, but it's not known when and where the original was created: the time of its creation is put somewhere between the 6th and 14th centuries, and theories of its provenance range from Byzantium and Red Ruthenia to Italy and Hungary. What is known is that the icon was brought from Ruthenia in 1382 and offered to the Paulite Order a couple of years later.

In 1430 the icon was damaged by the Hussites, who slashed the face of the Madonna and broke the panel. The picture was repainted afterwards in a workshop in Kraków, but the scars on the face of the Virgin Mary were left as a reminder of the sacrilege.

In 1717 the Black Madonna was crowned 'Queen of Poland' in a ceremony attended by 200,000 of the faithful. This was the first ever painting crowned outside Italy. Since then the image has traditionally been crowned and dressed with richly ornamented robes, and these days the Madonna has a wardrobe of robes and crowns which are changed on special occasions.

TW

Information

Tourist Office The Centrum Informacji Turystycznej (☎ 368 22 50, ☎/fax 368 22 60), Al NMP 65, is open 9am to 5pm Monday to Friday, 9am to 2pm Saturday.

The Monastery of Jasna Góra has its own information centre, the Jasnogórskie Centrum Informacji (☎ 365 38 88, fax 365 43 43, ⓌW www.jasnagora.pl) inside the compound. It's open 7.30am to 7pm daily from May to mid-October, 8am to 5pm the rest of the year.

Money There are a number of kantors and ATMs on Al NMP. The Bank Pekao at ul Kopernika 19 will change your travellers cheques and also gives cash advances on Visa and MasterCard.

Email & Internet Access Częstochowa's Internet services are among the cheapest in Poland – usually not more than US$1 an hour. Central facilities include Centrum Internetowe in Dom Handlowy Seka, Al NMP 12D; Strefa, Al NMP 29; Need for PSX, Al NMP 35; Klub Internetowy, Al Wolności 11; and Xtreme, Al NMP 65A.

Monastery of Jasna Góra

A vibrant symbol of Catholicism in a secular sea, the monastery retains the appearance of a fortress. It's on the top of a hill, west of the city centre, and is clearly recognisable from a distance by its slender tower. The main entrance is from the southern side through four successive gates. There's also a gate from the western side. Gates are open 5.30am to 9.30pm daily.

Inside the walls are a number of buildings including a chapel, a church and the monastery. The **Chapel of the Miraculous Picture** (Kaplica Cudownego Obrazu) is the oldest part of the complex and is where the Black Madonna is kept. The picture is placed on the high altar and covered with a silver screen at night (9.30pm to 6am) and from noon to 1.30pm (1pm to 2pm on Saturday, Sunday and public holidays). It may be hard to get close to the picture as the chapel is usually packed with pilgrims.

MAŁOPOLSKA

CZĘSTOCHOWA

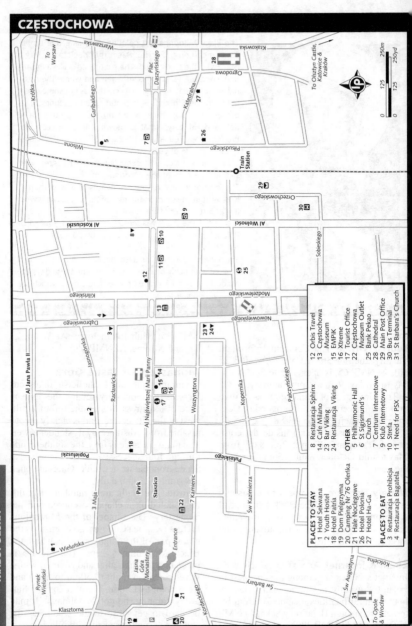

PLACES TO STAY
1 Hotel Sekwana
2 Youth Hostel
18 Hotel Patria
19 Dom Pielgrzyma
20 Camping Nr 76 Olenka
21 Hale Noclegowe
26 Hotel Polonia
27 Hotel Ha-Ga

PLACES TO EAT
3 Restauracja Prohibicja
4 Restauracja Bagatela

8 Restauracja Sphinx
14 Cafe Milano
23 Bar Viking
24 Restauracja Viking

OTHER
5 Philharmonic Hall
6 St Sigismund's
   Church
7 Centrum Internetowe
9 Klub Internetowy
10 Strefa
11 Need for PSX

12 Orbis Travel
13 Częstochowa
   Museum
15 EMPiK
16 Xtreme
17 Tourist Office
22 Częstochowa
   Museum Outlet
25 Bank Pekao
28 Cathedral
29 Main Post Office
30 Bus Terminal
31 St Barbara's Church

The sizable **basilica** (*bazylika*), adjoining the chapel to the south, was initially a single-nave Gothic construction. Its present shape dates from the 17th century and the interior has opulent baroque furnishings and decoration.

On the opposite, northern side of the chapel is the monastery, where you can visit the 17th-century **Knights' Hall** (Sala Rycerska) on the 1st floor. The hall boasts a series of nine paintings that depict major events from the monastery's history, including the Hussite raid of 1430 and the Swedish siege of 1655. An exact copy of the Black Madonna, not embellished with robes, is placed in the corner of the hall, allowing for a closer inspection of the icon.

The monastery has three museums, all open 9am to 5pm daily April to September (till 4pm the rest of the year). Admission is free, or you can leave a donation in the box placed at the entrance to each museum.

The **600th-Anniversary Museum** (Muzeum Sześćsetlecia), on the western side of the complex, displays liturgical vessels and vestments, old musical instruments, painted scenes from monastic life and portraits of the founders and superiors, plus a number of votive offerings including Lech Wałęsa's 1983 Nobel Peace Prize. Next door, the **arsenal** contains old weapons and one of the robes for the Madonna.

The **treasury** (*skarbiec*) is above the sacristy and displays votive offerings presented by the faithful. Among a variety of exhibits you'll find old reliquaries, monstrances, home altars, drawings by Matejko and yet another robe for the Madonna.

To complete your visit, climb up the **tower** (*wieża; open 8am-4pm daily Apr-Sept*). It has been destroyed and rebuilt several times and the present one only dates from 1906. Over 106m high, it's the tallest historic church tower in Poland. Note the crow with a loaf of bread on the very top. The tower houses a set of 36 bells which play a Marian melody every quarter of an hour.

Other City Attractions

The monastery is obviously Częstochowa's biggest drawcard, but if you have got a leisurely itinerary, you may want to visit other sights. **St Barbara's Church** (Kościół Św Barbary), about 1km south of the monastery, was built in the 17th century on the spot where the Hussites were thought to have slashed the icon and thrown it away. The monks who found the panel wanted to clean the mud off it, and a spring miraculously bubbled from the ground. The spring exists to this day in the chapel behind the church and the water is supposed to have health-giving properties. The painting on the vault of the chapel depicts the story.

The **Częstochowa Museum** (*Muzeum Częstochowskie;* ☎ *324 32 75, Plac Biegańskiego; admission US$0.50; open 10.30am-4pm Tues-Sun*), in the late neoclassical town hall dating from 1828, features an ethnographic collection and modern Polish paintings, plus some temporary exhibitions. The museum has an outlet in the Park Staszica (same opening hours) which stages temporary exhibitions.

Olsztyn Castle

A visit to the Olsztyn castle, 11km east of Częstochowa, is a refreshing trip out of the city. The castle is in ruins, but what a charming ruin it is. You can get to Olsztyn by city bus No 58 or 67 from ul Piłsudskiego opposite the train station. Alternatively, you can walk along the Trail of the Eagles' Nests, which starts from Plac Daszyńskiego and leads via Olsztyn up to Kraków.

Special Events

The major **Marian feasts** at Jasna Góra are on 3 May, 16 July, 15 August, 26 August, 8 September, 12 September and 8 December, and on these days the monastery is packed with pilgrims. The celebration of **Assumption** (15 August) is particularly important, with pilgrims from all over Poland travelling to Jasna Góra on foot. The Warsaw pilgrims leave the capital on 6 August every year for the 250km trip. Up to 250,000 of the faithful flock to the monastery for this feast.

On a more artistic front, the city's main event is the **'Gaude Mater' International Festival of Religious Music**, held in May.

Places to Stay

Bear in mind that Częstochowa gets lots of pilgrims, so finding a place to stay, especially a cheap one, may not be easy – particularly on and around Marian feast days. It may be best to avoid these periods or make a day trip to the city.

Camping Nr 76 Oleńka (☎ *324 74 95, fax 365 14 79, ul Oleńki 10/30*) Tent site US$2 plus US$3 per person; singles/doubles in cabins without bath US$7/14; triples/quads/quins in cabins with bath US$22/28/34. Just behind the monastery, the Oleńka camping ground has clean bungalows containing rooms of different sizes, with a total capacity of 80 guests. There's an inexpensive snack bar on the grounds.

Youth hostel (☎ *324 31 21, ul Jasnogórska 84/90*) Dorm beds US$3-5. Open July & Aug. This 90-bed hostel is also close to the monastery, but it's only open during summer holidays.

Hale Noclegowe (☎ *377 72 24, ul Klasztorna 1*) Beds in 2- to 9-bed dorms US$4. Open May-mid Oct. This Church-run place, just next to the monastery, provides some of the cheapest accommodation in town. It's clean but basic; rooms have shared facilities and there's no hot water. There's a 10pm curfew.

Dom Pielgrzyma (*Pilgrim's Home;* ☎ *377 75 64, fax 365 18 70, ul Wyszyńskiego 1/31*) Singles/doubles/triples with bath US$16/22/28, beds in quads without bath US$6. Dom is another Church-operated lodging facility, right behind the monastery. Curfew here is also at 10pm. There's a cheap cafeteria on the premises.

Hotel Ha-Ga (☎/fax *324 61 73, ul Katedralna 9*) Singles/doubles/triples/quads without bath US$14/16/20/24, with bath US$20/24/28/30. One of the cheapest options close to the train station, Ha-Ga is basic but acceptable.

Hotel Polonia (☎ *324 23 88, fax 365 11 05, ul Piłsudskiego 9*) Singles/doubles/triples/quads with bath US$28/35/40/48. Better than Ha-Ga but nothing particularly special, Polonia is opposite the station.

Hotel Sekwana (☎ *324 89 54, ☎/fax 324 63 67, ul Wieluńska 24*) Singles/doubles with bath & breakfast US$40/55. A comfortable place to stay in the monastery area, Sekwana has 20 rooms and its own restaurant specialising in Polish and French cuisine.

Hotel Patria (☎ *324 70 01, fax 324 63 32, ul Popiełuszki 2*) Singles/doubles with bath & breakfast US$90/120. This Orbis-owned hotel is the top-end option in the monastery area. Like most Orbis stock, it's hardly an inspiring place but provides a decent level of comfort. It may have attractive weekend discounts.

Places to Eat

As might be expected, there are plenty of budget eating outlets in the monastery area, apart from the above-mentioned cafeteria of Dom Pielgrzyma and the snack bar at the camping ground. There are also quite a number of eateries on and off Al NMP.

Bar Viking (☎ *324 57 68, ul Nowowiejskiego 10*) Mains US$2-4. One of the cheapest eateries in the centre, Bar Viking serves tasty meals and has outdoor tables in summer. The adjacent restaurant of the same name is a more upmarket proposition.

Cafe Milano (☎ *365 49 29, Al NMP 57/59*) Open 7am-11pm daily. This Spanish-run cafe serves up the best espresso, cappuccino and ice cream in town – warmly recommended.

Restauracja Sphinx (☎ *366 41 85, ul Al Kościuszki 1*) Mains US$3-5. Like elsewhere, Sphinx is a worthwhile addition to the city culinary scene, with its tasty food, copious portions, efficient service and low prices.

Restauracja Bagatela (☎ *324 06 21, ul Dąbrowskiego 6*) Mains US$6-9. Bagatela is a quiet, cosy restaurant which offers good Polish food.

Restauracja Prohibicja (☎ *368 18 19, ul Dąbrowskiego 7*) Mains US$6-10. One of the outlets of another attractive restaurant chain expanding across Poland, Prohibicja offers fine international food in surroundings that recall the US prohibition era.

Getting There & Away

Train The new train station (the main entrance is from Al Wolności) handles half a dozen fast trains to Warsaw daily (235km) and about the same number of fast trains to Kraków (132km). Łódź (153km) is serviced by four trains daily and there are a couple of trains running to Wrocław (177km). Trains to Katowice (86km) run every hour or so, from where there are connections to Kraków and Wrocław.

Bus The bus terminal is close to the central train station and operates plenty of buses in the region. You may use it if going to Jędrzejów (93km) or Opole (98km). There's one direct bus to Ogrodzieniec at 2pm (59km); if you don't want to wait for it, take any of the frequent trains to Katowice, get off in Zawiercie and change for a bus.

There are half a dozen buses to Kraków, going different ways and taking up to three hours. Alternatively, take the faster Polski Express bus which has three departures a day and takes two hours.

The Małopolska Upland

Occupying an area skirted by the Vistula and Pilica rivers, the Małopolska Upland (Wyżyna Małopolska) culminates in the Holy Cross Mountains (Góry Świętokrzyskie), at the foot of which sits Kielce, the main urban centre of the region. The upland offers a number of varied cultural attractions and wide stretches of beautiful landscape.

KIELCE
☎ 41 • pop 220,000
Kielce ('**Kyel**-tseh') is set in a valley amid gentle hills and consists of a compact centre with predominantly 19th-century architecture, and a ring of postwar suburbs perched on the surrounding slopes.

The city doesn't have many tourist attractions, but it lies close to a fine mountain range (see under Świętokrzyski National Park later in this section) and might be a stopover before or after visiting the park. There are also some interesting places in Kielce's vicinity (see the Around Kielce section).

Information
Tourist Office The Miejski Ośrodek Informacji Turystycznej (☎ 367 60 11), in the building of the city's municipal office at Rynek 1, is open 7.30am to 5pm weekdays (April to October till 7pm and also on Saturday 10am to 3pm).

Money Travellers cheques can be cashed at the Bank Pekao, ul Sienkiewicza 18, which also gives advances on Visa and MasterCard and has an ATM. For changing cash, there are plenty of kantors on ul Sienkiewicza.

Email & Internet Access Internet facilities in the city centre include Arena (☎ 344 22 47), ul Piotrkowska 6; Euro Trade, ul Mała 9; Małpka (☎ 343 86 81), ul Słowackiego 8; Planetka (☎ 344 87 92), ul Planty 12; and Strefa 51 (☎ 366 09 89), ul Paderewskiego 34.

Things to See
The most important city sight is the **Palace of the Kraków Bishops** (Pałac Biskupów Krakowskich), a sumptuous 17th-century baroque structure reflecting Kraków's wealth and prosperity. Yes, Kraków – because Kielce and its surroundings were the property of the Kraków bishops from the 12th century up to 1789, and they built the palace as one of their seats.

Today, the palace houses the **National Museum** (☎ 344 40 14, Plac Zamkowy 1; adult/student US$2.50/1.25, free Sun; open 10am-6pm Tues, 9am-4pm Wed-Sun) where you can see authentic interiors from the 17th and 18th centuries. Of unique value are the three elaborate plafonds (ornamented ceilings) from around 1641, painted in the workshop of the Venetian Tommaso Dolabella. The whole clan of Kraków bishops look down on you from the murals in their former dining hall, the largest room in the palace: the upper strip was painted in the 1640s, the lower one added two centuries later.

The palace's side wing features a gallery of Polish painting from the 17th century to WWII, while the ground floor houses a collection of historic armour and temporary exhibitions.

MAŁOPOLSKA

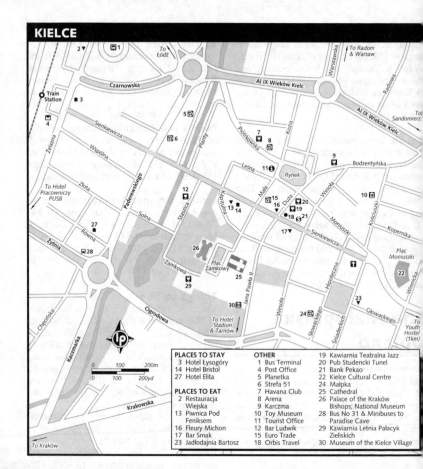

KIELCE

PLACES TO STAY	OTHER	19 Kawiarnia Teatralna Jazz
3 Hotel Łysogóry	1 Bus Terminal	20 Pub Studencki Tunel
14 Hotel Bristol	4 Post Office	21 Bank Pekao
27 Hotel Elita	5 Planetka	22 Kielce Cultural Centre
	6 Strefa 51	24 Małpka
PLACES TO EAT	7 Havana Club	25 Cathedral
2 Restauracja	8 Arena	26 Palace of the Kraków
Wiejska	9 Karczma	Bishops; National Museum
13 Piwnica Pod	10 Toy Museum	28 Bus No 31 & Minibuses to
Feniksem	11 Tourist Office	Paradise Cave
16 Fleury Michon	12 Bar Ludwik	29 Kawiarnia Letnia Pałacyk
17 Bar Smak	15 Euro Trade	Zieliskich
23 Jadłodajnia Bartosz	18 Orbis Travel	30 Museum of the Kielce Village

The **cathedral** facing the palace was originally Romanesque, but the present-day building dates from the 17th century and has been altered several times since then; the opulent interior fittings reflect these transformations, though baroque decoration predominates.

Nearby is the **Museum of the Kielce Village** (*Muzeum Wsi Kieleckiej;* ☎ 344 92 97, *ul Jana Pawła II 6; admission US$0.50; open 10am-3pm Mon-Fri & Sun*). Accommodated in an 18th-century thatched country manor, the museum stages temporary ethnographic exhibitions.

The **Toy Museum** (*Muzeum Zabawkarstwa;* ☎ 344 40 78, *ul Kościuszki 11; admission US$0.75; open 10am-5pm Tues-Sun*) is one of only two toy museums in Poland (the other is in Karpacz).

Places to Stay

Youth hostel (☎/fax 344 73 93, *ul Szymanowskiego 5*) Beds US$5-8. Open year round. This well-run 67-bed hostel is a 15-minute walk east of the city centre.

Hotel Pracowniczy PUSB (☎ 345 51 50, *ul Urzędnicza 13*) Singles/doubles/triples/quads without bath US$12/14/18/24. An other budget place near the centre, this huge 350-bed basic hotel is about 1km south-west of the train station.

Hotel Stadion (*☎/fax 368 77 15, ul Ściegiennego 8)* Singles/doubles/triples with bath US$30/35/40. Stadion offers reasonable standards and is within walking distance from the centre.

Hotel Bristol (*☎ 366 24 66, ☎/fax 366 30 65, ul Sienkiewicza 21)* Singles/doubles/triples with bath & breakfast US$50/60/70. Central and convenient, the 45-bed Bristol has recently been superficially revamped, but it's not great value. The entrance is from ul Kapitulna, not ul Sienkiewicza.

Hotel Łysogóry (*☎ 366 25 11, fax 366 29 48, ul Sienkiewicza 78)* Singles/doubles/triples with bath & breakfast US$75/80/100. Another very central but overpriced option.

Hotel Elita (*☎ 344 17 64, fax 344 33 37, ul Równa 4A)* Singles/doubles/triples with bath & breakfast US$50/70/80. This 13-room hotel is possibly the best central option.

Places to Eat
Bar Ludwik (*☎ 368 18 75, ul Staszica 6/8)* Mains US$1-3. This new, efficient, self-service place is one of the best options for a budget meal.

Bar Smak (*☎ 344 49 27, ul Sienkiewicza 13)* Mains US$1-2.50. A refurbished milk bar, Smak is one of the cheapest places around and has a salad bar attached.

Fleury Michon (*☎ 344 63 11, ul Sienkiewicza 28)* With fresh rolls, croissants and pastries, and a few tables to sit at, this is a good place for breakfast or just a snack.

Jadłodajnia Bartosz (*☎ 344 52 85, ul Głowackiego 1)*. Mains US$2-3. Another budget place that serves solid Polish food.

Piwnica Pod Feniksem (*☎ 343 19 20, ul Sienkiewicza 25)* Mains US$6-8. This basement restaurant serves good food, though the decor is plain. The speciality is *tatar* (raw minced beef).

Restauracja Wiejska (*☎ 366 05 45, ul Czarnowska 22)* Mains US$6-8. This split-level restaurant offers traditional old-Polish peasant food in what looks like an old timber country inn, decked out with folksy decor.

Entertainment
Karczma (*☎ 368 22 87, ul Bodzentyńska 9)* and *Pub Studencki Tunel* (*☎ 344 52 00, ul Duża 7)* are among the best places for a beer or two. In summer, you can also try the open-air *Kawiarnia Letnia Pałacyk Zielińskich* (*☎ 368 20 55, ul Zamkowa 5)*.

Havana Club (*☎ 343 80 04, ul Piotrkowska 12)* is one of the city's hippest discos. *Kawiarnia Teatralna Jazz* (*ul Duża 9)* is Kielce's leading jazz club.

Getting There & Away
Train The train station is in the centre, at the western end of ul Sienkiewicza. Two dozen trains run to Radom (85km, daily) and half of them continue on to Warsaw (187km). There are about 10 trains to Kraków daily (132km), six to Lublin (213km), three to Częstochowa (113km) and eight to Katowice (173km).

Bus The strange UFO-shaped bus terminal, close to the train station, is relatively well organised. There are seven fast buses to Łódź daily (143km) and five to Kraków (114km). Five buses go to Święty Krzyż daily (32km), and six go to Sandomierz (90km). For Święta Katarzyna (21km), take a bus going to Bodzentyn or Starachowice; and for Nowa Słupia (36km), board a bus to Ostrowiec Świętokrzyski. For Tokarnia (20km), there are buses every one to two hours – inquire at the information desk.

AROUND KIELCE
☎ 41
Paradise Cave
Discovered in 1964, the Paradise Cave (*Jaskinia Raj;* ☎ *346 55 18; tours US$3; open 10am-5pm Tues-Sun May-Aug, 10am-4pm Tues-Sun Mar-Apr & Sept-Nov)* is one of the better caves in Poland (the best one is arguably the Bear's Cave in the Sudeten Mountains – see the Kletno section in the Silesia chapter for more information). Although relatively small – only 8m high at its highest point – the cave has a couple of spectacular chambers complete with stalactites, stalagmites and columns.

A building at the entrance to the cave shelters a ticket office, a cafe and a museum. Some finds from the cave which are on display in the museum show that it was once used by animals and primitive humans as a shelter. You enter the cave and do a 180m-long loop through its chambers. All visits are guided (in Polish only) in groups of up to 15 people; the tour takes around half an hour. No photography is allowed inside.

The cave has become a major tourist attraction for school groups, with the result that, at times (particularly in May and June), little room is left for individual tourists. Owing to environmental factors, a limited number of people are allowed inside each day, so some days may be fully booked out. In order to be assured of a tour, book in advance on ☎ 346 55 18. Bring some warm clothes, as the temperature inside the cave is only 9°C year-round.

The cave is 600m off the Kraków road, about 10km from central Kielce. You can get close on city bus No 31, which runs through to Chęciny every half-hour (every hour on Sunday). It departs from near the corner of ul Żytnia and ul Paderewskiego in Kielce. Ask to be let off at the bus stop just before the turn-off to the cave; the next bus stop is a long way off. There are also private minibuses departing from the same place as buses, as soon as they fill up with passengers.

Zajazd Raj (☎ 346 51 27) Singles/doubles/triples with bath US$25/32/44. Near the cave beside the car park, Zajazd offers rooms and has a restaurant which serves budget meals.

Tokarnia

The village of Tokarnia is home to the **Open-Air Museum of the Kielce Village** (*Muzeum Wsi Kieleckiej;* ☎ 315 41 71; *adult/student US$2/1; open 10am-5pm Tues-Sun Apr-Sept, 10am-4pm Tues-Sun Oct, 10am-2pm Mon-Fri Nov-Mar (interiors locked in that period)*). Covering an area of 80 hectares (including 20 hectares of woodland), this is one of Poland's largest skansens. About 30 structures have been completed, including interiors. A number of fine implements have been collected, some are amazing (note the huge barrels

carved out of a single tree trunk). Give yourself about two hours to see it all at a leisurely pace. In summer, a cafe opens in the house at the entrance to the museum.

The skansen is 20km from Kielce; buses ply this route roughly every hour. Get off at the bus stop in the village of Tokarnia and walk for 10 minutes up the road to the skansen's entrance.

JĘDRZEJÓW
☎ 41 • pop 18,000

The pride of Jędrzejów ('Yend-**zheh**-yoof') is its **Sundial Museum** (*Muzeum Zegarów Słonecznych;* ☎ 386 24 45, *Rynek 7/8, adult/student US$1.50/0.75; open 8am-4pm Tues-Sun 16 Apr-15 Oct, 8am-3pm Tues-Sun rest of year, closed day following public holidays*). With more than 300 specimens, it's reputedly the world's third-largest sundial collection after Oxford and Chicago. Among the exhibits are the 16th and 17th-century pocket sundials made of ivory that are adjustable depending on the latitude; two intricate instruments capable of measuring time to within half a minute; and a range of sundials from the Far East. Strangest of all is the 18th-century apparatus equipped with a cannon which used to fire at noon. The oldest instrument in the collection, dating from 1524, was designed for measuring time at night from the position of the stars. The museum also has an extensive gnomonics (the science of sundials) library, old clocks and watches, furniture and household implements.

All visitors are guided in groups; 50-minute tours begin on the hour. The last tour departs one hour before closing time.

Church buffs might be interested in visiting the **Cistercian Abbey** (*Opactwo Cystersów; ul 11 Listopada*) on the western outskirts of town, 2km from the Rynek, on the road to Katowice. Founded in 1140, this was the first Cistercian abbey in Poland. For the Poles, the place is associated with Wincenty Kadłubek (1161–1223), Kraków's bishop and the first known Polish chronicler, author of *Chronica Polonorum*. He spent the last years of his life in the monastery and was buried here.

The original Romanesque church was repeatedly modified, most recently in the 18th century, when the twin towers were added and the interior acquired its baroque decor. The stucco walls resemble marble, and the rich interior furnishings include opulent altarpieces, stalls in the presbytery and a splendid organ. Kadłubek's remains repose in a small 17th-century baroque coffin in the side chapel off the left-hand aisle. The monastery adjoining the church has a courtyard lined with 15th-century Gothic cloisters.

Places to Stay & Eat

Noclegi Zacisze (☎ 386 18 26, Al Piłsudskiego 4) Singles/doubles/quads without bath US$9/15/24. Apparently the only regular accommodation in town, Zacisze is a large, uninspiring block, 800m west of the Rynek along ul 11 Listopada, that offers basic rooms and has its own restaurant. There are more places to eat in the town centre.

Getting There & Away

The bus and train stations are next to each other, 2km west of the Rynek and linked to it by urban buses. Since Jędrzejów lies on the Kraków-Kielce highway and railway line, there's sufficient transport to either destination and you shouldn't have to wait more than an hour for a bus or train.

ŚWIĘTOKRZYSKI NATIONAL PARK
☎ 41

The Góry Świętokrzyskie (literally, Holy Cross Mountains) run for 70km east-west across the Małopolska Upland. This is Poland's oldest mountainous geological formation, and consequently the lowest, due to gradual erosion for over 300 million years. The highest peak is just 612m, and the whole outcrop is more a collection of gently rolling wooded hills rather than mountains in the real sense of the word. The region retains some of its primeval nature, and a national park has been set up to protect the best of what is left.

The Świętokrzyski ('Shfyen-to-**kshis**-kee') National Park protects the highest, 15km-long central range, known as the

Łysogóry, or Bald Mountains. It has a peak at each end: Mt Łysica (612m) in the west and Mt Łysa Góra (595m) in the east. Between them is a belt of forest, mostly fir and beech, which covers almost all the 60 sq km of the park. Watch out for the unusual *gołoborza*: heaps of broken quartzite rock on parts of the northern slopes below the two peaks.

Apart from these natural attractions, there's the **Święty Krzyż abbey** and adjacent museum on top of Mt Łysa Góra, and another museum at the foothill village of Nowa Słupia. The mountains make a pleasant half or full-day trip.

Getting There & Around

The park is about 20km east of Kielce. You can get there by bus from the city to three different access points: the village of Święta Katarzyna on the western end, at the foot of Mt Łysica; the Święty Krzyż abbey on the top of Mt Łysa Góra; and the village of Nowa Słupia, 2km east from Święty Krzyż.

If you're not enthusiastic about walking, it's best to go by bus directly to Święty Krzyż, visit the place, then go down to Nowa Słupia to see the museum and take a bus back to Kielce or wherever else you want to go.

If you plan on hiking, there's an 18km marked trail between Święta Katarzyna and Nowa Słupia, via Święty Krzyż. It's best to set off from Nowa Słupia, as there are museums here and in nearby Święty Krzyż; if you started from the opposite end of the trail, you would have to get moving early to reach the museums before they close. The following description includes the whole route from Nowa Słupia to Święta Katarzyna.

Nowa Słupia

The village of Nowa Słupia is known for its **Museum of the Holy Cross Ancient Metallurgy** (*Muzeum Starożytnego Hutnictwa Świętokrzyskiego;* ☎ 317 70 18, ul Świętokrzyska 59; adult/student US$1/0.50; open 9am-4pm Tues-Sun), on the road to Święty Krzyż. The museum has been established on the site where primitive smelting furnaces, or *dymarki*, dating from the 2nd century AD,

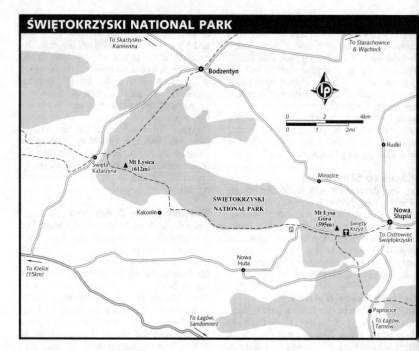

ŚWIĘTOKRZYSKI NATIONAL PARK

were unearthed in 1955. A huge number of furnaces have been found in the surrounding area, indicating that the region was an important ancient metallurgical centre, the largest so far discovered in Europe.

From the museum, a 2km path called King Way (Droga Królewska) leads up to Święty Krzyż (by car, it's a 16km detour).

Nowa Słupia has some budget accommodation options, and locals rent out rooms in their homes.

Camping Pod Skałką (☎ 317 70 85, ul Świętokrzyska 57) Tent site US$1.50 plus US$1.50 per person, beds in cabins US$5. Open May-Sept. The camp site offers tent space, basic cabins without bath and a budget restaurant.

Youth hostel (☎ 317 70 16, ul Świętokrzyska 61) Beds US$3-6. Open year-round. This hostel, next to the museum, offers 60 beds in doubles, quads and large dorms.

Buses from Nowa Słupia can take you to Kielce (36km). For Sandomierz, you have to change buses in either Ostrowiec Świętokrzyski or Łagów.

Święty Krzyż

Giving its name to the mountains, Święty Krzyż (Holy Cross) is a Benedictine abbey built on top of Mt Łysa Góra. The abbey was built in the early 12th century, on the site of a pagan place of worship which existed here in the 8th and 9th centuries. The abbey's **Holy Cross Church** (*open 9am-5pm Mon-Sat, noon-5pm Sun & holidays*) was rebuilt several times over the years and the present-day church is a product of the late 18th century with a mainly neoclassical interior.

The monastery has retained more of its original shape, including its Gothic vaulted cloister. It shelters a small **Missionary Museum** (*Muzeum Misyjne;* ☎ 317 70 21; *open 9am-noon & 1pm-4pm Mon-Sat, noon-4pm Sun*) featuring some objects collected by the missionaries.

The **Natural History Museum** (*Muzeum Przyrodniczo-Leśne;* ☎ 317 70 87; admission US$1; open 10am-4pm Tues-Sun Apr-Oct, 9am-3pm Tues-Sun Nov-Mar, closed days following public holidays) is on the western side of the abbey, facing a huge TV mast. It focuses on the geology and the plant and animal life of the park.

The *gołoborze* is just past the TV mast to the right; a short side path will lead you there.

There are two budget places to stay next to each other, near the car park on the access road, 2km before Święty Krzyż.

Jodłowy Dwór (☎ 302 50 28, fax 302 61 46) Doubles/triples with bath & breakfast US$28/34. This large 160-bed hotel doesn't offer much luxury, but is reasonable and has a cheap restaurant.

Almatur Jodłowy (☎ 302 50 97) Beds in rooms without/with bath US$7/8. Basic but acceptable, the Almatur hostel has 50 beds and simple meals.

From Święty Krzyż you can take the bus straight to Kielce (32km, every three hours) or walk along the red trail to Święta Katarzyna.

The Trail

The 16km trail from Święty Krzyż to Święta Katarzyna provides an easy four-hour walk in the park. The trail follows the road for the first 2km to the car park (where the Jodłowy Dwór and Almatur hostel are), then branches off and runs west along the edge of the forest for about 9km. It then enters the woods, ascends the peak of Mt Łysica and winds down for 2km to Święta Katarzyna.

Święta Katarzyna

This small village is developing into a local holiday centre with several simple places to stay and eat including:

Youth hostel (☎ 311 22 06, ul Kielecka 45) Beds US$4-6. Open all-year. The hostel provides simple lodging in four- to eight-bed dorms for 45 guests.

Zajazd Baba Jaga (☎ 311 22 26, ul Kielecka 18) Doubles/quads without bath US$16/26, doubles/triples with bath US$28/40. Zajazd is a simple, budget option with its own restaurant.

Ośrodek Wypoczynkowy Jodełka (☎ 311 21 11, fax 311 21 12, ul Kielecka 3) Doubles/triples/quads without bath US$24/30/38, with bath US$34/46/54. This former Dom Wycieczkowy PTTK has been extensively revamped and now offers reasonable standards and its own restaurant.

Buses go regularly to Kielce (21km), if you don't want to stay here after the trek.

The Sandomierz Valley

The Sandomierz Valley (Kotlina Sandomierska) covers an extensive area in and around the fork of the Vistula and San rivers. The region's major historic centre – and today its main tourist destination – is the town of Sandomierz. There are also some impressive castles in the region.

SANDOMIERZ
☎ 15 • pop 27,000

Sandomierz is a small, pleasant town overlooking the Vistula River from a 40m hill. It preserves the yesteryear atmosphere typical of old country towns, and shelters some fine historic buildings, remnants of its illustrious past. Both its atmosphere and architecture make a visit worthwhile.

History

It's not exactly clear when the town sprang to life, but at the end of the 11th century the chronicler Gall Anonim classified Sandomierz along with Kraków and Wrocław as *sedes regni principales*, or major settlements of the realm. Destroyed by Tatar raids in 1259, the town was moved uphill to its present location and fortified in the 14th century. A busy river port and trade centre on the Kraków-Kyiv route, Sandomierz grew and prospered until the mid-17th century. Its glory came to an abrupt end with the Swedish Deluge, after which the town never really revived. By the outbreak of WWII it numbered 10,000 inhabitants, not many more than three centuries earlier.

MAŁOPOLSKA

Sandomierz was a prosperous port and trade centre during the late 16th century

The town came through the war unscathed and preserved its historic architecture intact, but ironically it nearly lost the lot in the 1960s when the soft loess soils on which Sandomierz sits began a dangerous slide down into the river. A rescue operation was launched, and the city was again 'fortified', this time with substantial injections of concrete and steel into the slopes. Today, safe and restored, the town still proudly boasts its historic gems.

Information

There's no genuine tourist office in town. Try the PTTK office (☎ 832 23 05, ☎/fax 832 26 82), at Rynek 26.

There are only a few kantors in the Old Town, including one in the post office at Rynek 10. The Kredyt Bank a few doors south of the post office also changes cash and may pay better than the kantor. There are also a few kantors on ul Mickiewicza close to the corner of ul 11 Listopada, about 1km north-west of the Old Town. One of the very few central ATMs is at Rynek 9.

Things to See

The 14th-century **Opatów Gate** (*Brama Opatowska; admission US$0.50; open 10am-5.30pm daily in summer*) is the main entrance to the Old Town and the only surviving gate of the four that were built as part of the fortification system. The decorative Renaissance parapets were added in the 16th century. You can go to the top to look

around, but the view of the Old Town is not that good.

The sloping **Rynek** is lined with houses dating from different periods, some of which were built after WWII. In the 16th century all the houses had arcades. Today only two of them, those at Nos 10 and 27, still have their arcades.

Right in the middle stands the **town hall**, the oldest building on the Rynek. Its main Gothic structure was adorned with decorative parapets and a tower in the Renaissance period. Its ground floor houses a section of the **Regional Museum – Town Hall** (*Muzeum Okręgowe – Ratusz; adult/student US$1/0.50; open 10am-5pm Tues-Sun May-Sept; 9am-4pm Tues-Fri, 10am-3pm Sat & Sun Oct-Apr*). It's related to the town's history and features a fine model of what the town looked like three centuries ago.

One of the town's star attractions is the **Underground Tourist Route** (*Podziemna Trasa Turystyczna; ☎ 832 30 88, ul Oleśnickich; adult/student US$2/1; open 10am-5.30pm May-Sept, 10am-4.30pm Apr & Oct, 10am-3.30pm Nov-Mar*). It leads through a chain of 30-odd cellars beneath the houses around the Rynek. Built mostly during the boom times in the 15th and 16th centuries, these storage cellars gradually fell into disuse and were abandoned when trade declined. Dug out of soft soil and lacking proper reinforcements, they effectively undermined the city and contributed to the postwar near-disaster. In the complex

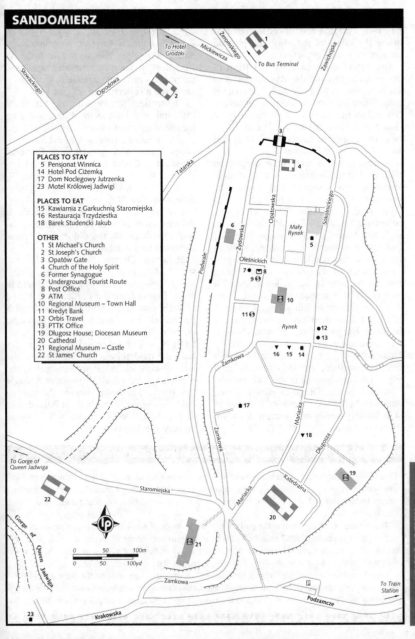

SANDOMIERZ

PLACES TO STAY
5 Pensjonat Winnica
14 Hotel Pod Ciżemką
17 Dom Noclegowy Jutrzenka
23 Motel Królowej Jadwigi

PLACES TO EAT
15 Kawiarnia z Garkuchnią Staromiejska
16 Restauracja Trzydziestka
18 Barek Studencki Jakub

OTHER
1 St Michael's Church
2 St Joseph's Church
3 Opatów Gate
4 Church of the Holy Spirit
6 Former Synagogue
7 Underground Tourist Route
8 Post Office
9 ATM
10 Regional Museum – Town Hall
11 Kredyt Bank
12 Orbis Travel
13 PTTK Office
19 Długosz House; Diocesan Museum
20 Cathedral
21 Regional Museum – Castle
22 St James' Church

To Hotel Grodzki
To Bus Terminal
Żeromskiego
Mickiewicza
Zawichojska
Słowackiego
Ogrodowa
Tatarska
Opatowska
Sokolnickiego
Podwale
Żydowska
Mały Rynek
Oleśnickich
Rynek
Zamkowa
Mariacka
Długosza
Zamkowa
Staromiejska
To Gorge of Queen Jadwiga
Gorge of Queen Jadwiga
Katedralna
Mariacka
Zamkowa
Podzamcze
Krakowska
To Train Station

0 50 100m
0 50 100yd

MAŁOPOLSKA

restoration program carried out in 1964–77 they were restored and linked together to ensure the safety of the town and provide yet another tourist attraction.

The entrance to the cellars is from ul Oleśnickich, just off the Rynek, and you finish the tour in the town hall. The route is about 500m long and the deepest cellars are 12m below the street level. It can only be visited on a guided tour (in Polish only); these leave approximately every hour and take 40 minutes to complete.

Nearby, the 18th-century **synagogue** on ul Żydowska retains the remains of its decoration on the inside, but it houses the town's registry and cannot be visited.

From the Rynek, take ul Mariacka to the **cathedral** (☎ 832 73 43, ul Mariacka; open to visitors 10am-2pm & 3pm-5pm Tues-Sat, 3pm-5pm Sun & public holidays). Built in the 1360s, this massive church has preserved much of its Gothic exterior, apart from the baroque facade added in the 17th century. The baroque took hold more strongly inside the building, though some of the earlier decoration has survived, notably the Russo-Byzantine frescoes in the chancel. One of the few examples of such frescoes in Poland, they were painted in the 1420s but later whitewashed, and only revealed and restored at the beginning of the 20th century.

Nearby is the **Długosz House** (Dom Długosza) built for the medieval historian in 1476. It today houses the **Diocesan Museum** (Muzeum Diecezjalne; ☎ 832 23 04, ul Długosza 9; adult/student US$1.50/0.75; open 9am-4pm Tues-Sat, 1.30pm-4pm Sun & public holidays Apr-Oct; 9am-3pm Tues-Sat, 1.30pm-3pm Sun & public holidays Nov-Mar). It features furniture, tapestries, ceramics, crafts and archaeological artefacts, and a collection of religious art.

The **castle**, a few steps downhill from the cathedral, was built in the 14th century on the site of a previous wooden stronghold and gradually extended during the next three centuries. It now accommodates the **Regional Museum – Castle** (Muzeum Okręgowe – Zamek; ☎ 644 57 57, ul Zamkowa 14; adult/student US$1.25/0.75; open 10am-5pm Tues-Sun May-Sept; 9am-4pm Tues-Fri, 10am-3pm Sat & Sun Oct-Apr). It features small ethnographic, archaeological and art collections, the old castle kitchen, and temporary exhibitions.

St James' Church (Kościół Św Jakuba; ☎ 832 73 43, ul Staromiejska; open to visitors 10am-4pm) is the oldest monument in town. Dating from the 1230s, it's believed to be the first brick church in Poland and is particularly renowned for its Romanesque doorway. The church retains the austere exterior typical of the period, but the interior has been modernised. Among the few historic objects left is the sarcophagus in the presbytery, carved in 1676 out of a single oak trunk. The belfry beside the church holds two of the oldest bells in Poland, cast in 1314 and 1389. They can only be heard on very special occasions.

Martyrologium Romanum of Sandomierz's Cathedral

One of the most unusual sights inside Sandomierz's cathedral is a series of 12 large paintings on the side walls, known as the *Martyrologium Romanum*. Look closely – they depict all imaginable methods of torture and just about all the horrific ways a human could die. You could spend hours examining the details.

This bizarre set of canvases is the early 18th-century work of Karol de Prevot. The paintings are supposed to symbolise the 12 months of the year. Next to each scene of torture on each painting is the ordinal number which reputedly represents the day of the month. Legend has it that if you find the month and the day on which you were born, you'll discover how you're going to die.

Prevot was also responsible for another four similarly macabre paintings on the back wall of the church under a sumptuous baroque organ. These pictures depict scenes from Sandomierz's history, including the Tatar massacre of 1259 and the blowing up of the castle by the Swedes in 1656.

Continue up ul Staromiejska as far as St Paul's Church and turn left downhill into the **Gorge of Queen Jadwiga** (Wąwóz Królowej Jadwigi), the best of the gorges around the town. It will lead you down to ul Krakowska, or you can take the first path to the left and back to St James' Church.

Places to Stay
Dom Noclegowy Jutrzenka (☎ 832 22 19, ul Zamkowa 1) Singles/doubles US$18/20, beds in triples and quads US$8. Jutrzenka is one of the cheapest places to stay in the Old Town. It only has six rooms, and all are with shared facilities, but it's clean and perfectly acceptable.

Pensjonat Winnica (☎ 832 31 30, Mały Rynek 2) Singles/doubles/triples/quads US$14/20/24/28. Another budget option with shared facilities, Winnica is pretty basic and has similarly basic restaurant.

Motel Królowej Jadwigi (☎/fax 832 29 88, ul Krakowska 24) Singles/doubles/triples/quads with bath & breakfast US$35/40/50/60. Located a little off the Old Town, this 13-room motel has reasonable rooms and a charming restaurant, all nicely decorated with antiques and paintings, and full of flowers.

Hotel Grodzki (☎ 832 24 23, fax 832 27 45, ul Mickiewicza 38) Doubles/triples with bath US$50/70, doubles without bath US$35, all prices include buffet breakfast. Grodzki is a large new hotel 1km northwest of the Old Town. It offers satisfactory standards and reasonable Polish food in its own restaurant. Doubles without bath are small yet it's not bad value for its price given an unlimited breakfast.

Hotel Pod Ciżemką (☎ 832 05 50, fax 832 05 52, Rynek 27) Doubles/suites with bath US$70/90. Extensively refurbished, Pod Ciżemką is the best place in the Old Town, offering six comfortable double rooms, three suites, and a good restaurant.

Places to Eat
Barek Studencki Jakub (☎ 832 72 30, ul Mariacka 9) Mains US$1.50-3. Jakub is a small basement cafeteria which serves some of the cheapest meals in town.

There are a few budget places to eat on the Rynek, including *Restauracja Trzydziestka (☎ 644 53 12, Rynek 30)* and *Kawiarnia z Garkuchnią Staromiejska (☎ 832 37 78, Rynek 28)*, both of which serve simple but acceptable food. For something more substantial, try the hotel restaurants listed in the Places to Stay section.

Getting There & Away
Train The train station, 3km south of the Old Town, on the other side of the Vistula, is served by city buses to/from Brama Opatowska. Three fast trains run to Warsaw daily (243km) and two to Przemyśl (153km).

Bus The bus terminal is more centrally located but it's still 1.5km north-west of the Old Town; frequent urban buses go there from Brama Opatowska.

There are a dozen fast buses to Warsaw (248km), which cost roughly the same as the train.

Buses to Tarnobrzeg (14km) depart roughly every half-hour but the suburban bus No 11 from Brama Opatowska is more convenient, and just as frequent. From Tarnobrzeg, frequent buses will take you on to Baranów Sandomierski (another 14km).

For Ujazd (39km), you need to go to Klimontów (buses roughly every hour) and change there. The staff at the terminal can work out the connection.

BARANÓW SANDOMIERSKI
☎ 15 • pop 1500
The village of Baranów Sandomierski lies on the edge of an area where huge sulphur deposits were discovered in the 1950s. Its fame, however, is based not on sulphur but on its **castle** (☎ 811 80 39, ul Zamkowa 20; adult/student US$2.50/1.25; exhibitions open 9am-3pm Tues-Fri, 9am-4pm Sat, 9am-5pm Sun, closes one hour earlier Sat & Sun Oct-Apr, closed days following public holidays).

The castle was built at the end of the 16th century for the Leszczyński family, the owners of large estates in Wielkopolska. It was encircled with powerful fortifications but they were dismantled in the 19th century.

MAŁOPOLSKA

The whole structure is thought to have been designed by the talented Italian architect Santi Gucci, who was responsible for many other projects in Poland.

In the late 17th century, the new owners, the Lubomirski family, commissioned Tylman van Gameren for an enlargement of the western wing. Although the castle suffered two major fires in the 19th century, it was refurbished both times and was inhabited almost continuously until WWII. Damaged during the war, it was handed over to the care of the Siarkopol, a state-owned sulphur enterprise, which restored it and maintained it until recently.

The castle is considered one of the most beautiful Renaissance residences in Poland. Set in a pleasant, well-kept park, it has four corner towers and a lovely arcaded courtyard. The two-storeyed arcades, with their slender columns supporting graceful arches, are very Italianesque. Look out for the fanciful masks on the column plinths, the vault decoration, and the superb carved-stone portals.

Some of the castle's original rooms, complete with period furnishings, paintings and decoration, are open to visitors. The former chapel on the west side of the building is used for temporary exhibitions.

Another exhibition, a reminder of the castle's former patron, is in the basement and shows the achievements of the sulphur industry, plus some archaeological finds that include the remains of the Gothic stronghold discovered after WWII during the process of the castle's restoration.

Places to Stay & Eat

Hotel Zamkowy (☎/*fax 811 80 39, ul Zamkowa 20*) Singles/doubles/suites with bath & breakfast US$45/55/100. Accommodated in the building just to the west of the castle, the hotel has been thoroughly renovated and now offers good standards, plus its own restaurant.

You can also stay in the *castle* itself: one side of it has been modified to provide accommodation for US$80/100 a single/double with bath and breakfast. There's a restaurant in the basement of the castle. Castle accom-

modation is arranged through the reception desk of Hotel Zamkowy.

Zajazd Wisła (☎ *811 03 80, Tarnobrzeg road*) Singles/doubles with bath US$22/28. This roadside hotel, about 1km from Baranów, has 14 rooms and a basic but very cheap restaurant.

Getting There & Away

The train station is well out of the village so it's much more convenient to travel by bus; the bus stop is close to the Rynek, a 10-minute walk from the castle.

There's no direct transport to Sandomierz (28km) but frequent buses run to Tarnobrzeg (14km), where you catch another, equally frequent bus. Some of the buses to Tarnobrzeg depart from the entrance to the castle.

There are four fast buses to Kraków (190km); the last one passes through just before 1pm. All Kraków-bound buses go via Tarnów (104km). Four buses a day run to Warsaw (223km) and one (around noon) to Zamość (143km). There are also two buses a day to Zakopane via Tarnów and Nowy Sącz.

UJAZD
☎ 15 • pop 600

The small village of Ujazd ('**Oo**-yahst') is known for the ruined **Krzyżtopór Castle** (☎ *860 11 33; admission US$1; open till dusk daily*) which dominates the area. Designed by Italian architect Lorenzo Muretto (Wawrzyniec Senes to the Poles) for the governor of the Sandomierz province, Krzysztof Ossoliński, this monumental building was erected between 1631 and 1644 and was one of the most unusual castles in Poland.

Ossoliński didn't enjoy his home for long; he died in 1645, a year after the castle was completed. Only 10 years later, the Swedes did significant damage to the castle, and took away some of the most precious treasures. Though the subsequent owners lived in part of the castle till 1770, it was only a shadow of its former self and swiftly declined thereafter.

After WWII, plans to transform the castle into a military school were discussed but rejected and the ruins were left to their fate for four decades. In the early 1990s, restora-

The Unusual Krzyżtopór Castle

Krzyżtopór is one of Poland's largest and strangest castles – a folly of its founder, Krzysztof Ossoliński, or perhaps a manifestation of his megalomania. In fact, he went down in history more for his castle than his political career or other achievements. The castle cost a fortune and employed hundreds of workers, carpenters and artists on its construction, furnishings and decoration.

Today it's just a ruin, but a ruin which arouses astonishment, admiration and reflection that few other castles in Poland can match.

Built inside massive stone walls with bastions at the five corners, the castle was designed to embody the structure of a calendar. It had four towers symbolising the four seasons and 12 big halls, one for each month. Exactly 52 rooms were built, one for each week in the year, and 365 windows. The designer didn't forget to provide an additional window which was only to be used during the leap year, and walled up the rest of the time.

The castle's great dining hall had a huge crystal aquarium built into its ceiling. An extensive system of cellars was built; some of them were used as stables for the owner's 370 white stallions, and are said to have been equipped with mirrors and black-marble mangers. Like every respectable castle, there was a tunnel, which linked Krzyżtopór to his brother's castle at Ossolin, 15km away. The tunnel's floor is said to have been covered with sugar, to allow the brothers to visit each other in horse-drawn sledges, at the same time enjoying an impression of travelling on snow.

Nothing is left of the mangers or aquariums, yet these and other stories, merging fact with legend, have given the castle an other-worldly reputation. Ossoliński's personal interest in astrology and magic may also have something to do with it.

The castle has long attracted interest and fascination. Pulitzer prizewinner, James A Michener mentions the castle in his novel *Poland*. In the 1960s a group of Swedes offered to completely refurbish it and make it into film studios. A Texan entrepreneur wanted to buy the lot, dismantle it piece by piece, take it to the US and reassemble it on his estate. So far the castle hasn't been sold or restored and can be found where it's always been.

tion work started, aiming to rebuild the castle and perhaps make it into a hotel, but the plan was abandoned. So, until a new program is launched, all you can see is a formidable ruin.

Miraculously, the entrance gate still proudly bears the two massive stone symbols of the castle – the Krzyż, or Cross, representing the religious devotion of the owner, and the Topór, or Axe, the coat of arms of the Ossoliński family, both still in good condition.

Don't miss this place: the longer you stay, the more it grows on you. The castle is off the beaten track so it doesn't get many tourists, particularly on weekdays. You may find you have the ruin all to yourself.

Places to Stay & Eat

There are no hotels around but if you have a tent, you can camp right at the foot of the castle or, perhaps, even in its courtyard – an idyllic location. There doesn't seem to be anywhere to eat, except for a *kiosk*, by the entrance to the castle, where you can buy some basic food and drink.

Getting There & Away

Ujazd lies on a side road and has no direct transport links with the major cities of the region. The only points of access are Opatów (16km) or Klimontów (13km), which are linked with Ujazd by several buses daily and also have onward transport to Sandomierz and Kielce.

The Radom Plain

The Radom Plain (Równina Radomska) stretches between Małopolska to the south and Mazovia to the north.

RADOM
☎ 48 • pop 250,000

Radom is an important industrial centre 100km south of Warsaw. Although it developed into a strong fortified town during the reign of King Kazimierz Wielki, little of its historical character is left. If you decide to stop here, visit the skansen.

Things to See

The Miasto Kazimierzowskie, or the historic town founded by Kazimierz Wielki in the mid-14th century, preserves its layout but not its urban fabric. Possibly the best reminder of those times is the Gothic **parish church**, built in the 1360s.

One block west is the Rynek, today lined with a hotchpotch of buildings, mostly from the 19th century. On its southern side is the **Radom Museum** *(Muzeum im Jacka Malczewskiego; ☎ 362 43 29, Rynek 11; adult/student US$2/1; open 10am-3pm Sun & Mon, 9am-3pm Tues-Thur, 10am-5pm Fri)*, which features a small permanent archaeological collection plus some temporary exhibitions.

East of the old quarter is Radom's new centre, stretched along its main nerve, the 1km-long ul Żeromskiego. Partly closed to the traffic, the street boasts some 19th-century neoclassical houses.

The most interesting city sight is the **skansen** *(Muzeum Wsi Radomskiej; ☎ 331 59 28, ul Szydłowiecka 30; adult/student US$2/1; open 9am-5pm Tues-Fri & 10am-6pm Sat & Sun May-Sept;10am-3pm Tues-Sun Oct-Apr)*, on the south-western outskirts of the city, 9km outside the centre and 1km off the Kielce road. Urban buses Nos 5, 17 & K from the city centre will let you off nearby.

The skansen features examples of traditional rural architecture brought together from all over the region. It has five charming windmills and a cluster of over 100 beehives. A couple of peasants' cottages have been furnished in the original style while other timber houses display exhibitions on local folklore.

Places to Stay & Eat

Youth hostel *(☎ 360 05 14, ul Kilińskiego 20)* Beds US$4-6. This is the more central

of Radom's two all-year youth hostels. It has 40 beds in six- to eight-bed dorms. Checking-in time is 5pm to 9pm. If it's full, try the other **hostel** *(☎ 331 10 06, ul Batalionów Chłopskich 16)*.

Hotel Iskra *(☎ 362 84 33, fax 363 87 45, ul Planty 4)* Doubles without/with bath US$20/32. Located opposite the train station, this is one of the cheapest central hotels.

Hotel TM *(☎/fax 363 27 08, ul Focha 12)* Doubles with bath & breakfast US$50. TM is a decent yet affordable hotel right in the city centre. It has its own, reasonably priced restaurant.

Getting There & Away

The train and bus stations are situated next to each other, a 15-minute walk south from the central city mall, ul Żeromskiego. A dozen trains and two dozen buses run to Warsaw (102km). To Lublin (105km) and Puławy (58km), take the bus (seven daily), while to Kielce (85km) it's better to travel by train (at least 15 daily). Buses to Szydłowiec (31km) run approximately every hour; the same buses, as well as the urban bus K, will take you to Orońsko (17km).

OROŃSKO
☎ 48 • pop 1200

A small roadside village near Radom, Orońsko is the home of the **Centre of Polish Sculpture** *(Centrum Rzeźby Polskiej; ☎/fax 618 45 16, ul Topolowa 1; adult/student US$1.50/0.75; indoor exhibitions & palace open 8am-4pm Tues-Fri, 10am-5pm Sat & Sun Apr-Oct; 8am-3pm Tues-Fri, 10am-3pm Sat & Sun Nov-Mar; park open till dusk daily)*, established in the grounds of a 19th-century estate complete with a palace, chapel, orangery, granary and coach house, all surrounded by a lovely landscaped park.

A spacious exhibition hall was constructed in 1993 to present changing displays of some of Poland's best modern art. Temporary exhibitions are also held in the orangery and outbuildings. Some of the sculptures have been scattered throughout the park to make an outdoor display. Additionally, you can visit the palace; it has been left in late 19th-century style, exactly as it was during the time the Polish painter Józef Brandt (1841–1915) lived and worked here.

Places to Stay & Eat

The centre has its own *hotel (☎/fax 618 45 16, ul Topolowa 1)* Singles/doubles/triples with bath for US$12/16/20. Rebuilt from a former granary, this hotel offers neat rooms and has a *cafe* that serves drinks and snacks. The centre's kitchen can provide meals for guests if requested, but you should let them know in advance.

Getting There & Away

Orońsko lies on the Radom-Kielce highway and the bus service is frequent (there's no railway at all). To Radom (17km), you can go either on the Radom urban bus K or the PKS bus coming through from Szydłowiec. The same buses will let you off close to Radom's skansen (roughly halfway to Radom; ask the driver). To Szydłowiec (14km), PKS buses run every hour or so. There are no direct buses to Kielce (58km); you will need to change in Skarżysko Kamienna.

SZYDŁOWIEC

☎ 48 • pop 14,000

Szydłowiec ('Shi-**dwo**-viets'), on the Radom-Kielce highway, is an old town which got its municipal charter in 1470. It passed through the hands of some great aristocratic families, including the Sapieha and Radziwiłł, who made it a prosperous urban centre. Just before WWII, 70% of its population was Jewish. The town has some important sights, justifying a visit.

Things to See

The **town hall**, in the middle of the Rynek, is a handsome, castle-like structure complete with towers and decorative parapets, whitewashed all over. Built in the early 17th century, it's a good example of Polish Renaissance architecture.

The **church**, shaded by tall trees on the southern side of the Rynek, dates from the end of the 15th century and its interior is living proof of its age. The original details include the wooden high altar, the polyptych in the presbytery, the panelled ceiling under the organ loft and the impressive flat wooden ceiling of the nave – all from the beginning of the 16th century.

A five-minute walk north-west of the Rynek is a large 16th-century **castle** encircled by a moat. It shelters the **Museum of Polish Folk Musical Instruments** *(Muzeum Polskich Ludowych Instrumentów Muzycznych; ☎ 617 12 43, ul Sowińskiego 2; adult/student US$1/0.50; open 9am-3.30pm Tues-Sun)*, the only one of its kind in the country. The museum has a collection of over 2000 instruments, but only a small selection is displayed due to limited space.

The town has a **Jewish cemetery**, one of the largest in Poland. What you see today is a quarter of the original graveyard – it was four times larger when founded in 1788 and right up to WWII. Over 2000 tombstones, mostly from the 19th century (the oldest dating from 1831), stand amid trees and undergrowth untouched for decades. To get there, take ul Kilińskiego east from the Rynek, turn left onto ul Kościuszki (the road to Radom) and after 250m turn right into ul Spółdzielcza. The cemetery is 100m ahead.

Places to Stay & Eat

Youth hostel (☎ 617 59 55, 617 41 46, ul Kolejowa 16) Beds US$4-6. Open year-round. Just about the only place to stay in town, the hostel is in a nice house beyond a colony of dull apartment blocks, 1km south-east of the Rynek. The reception is open 5pm to 9pm.

Piwnica Szydłowiecka (☎ 617 02 24, Rynek 5) Mains US$3-5. Sheltered in the cellars of the town hall, this is the most pleasant place to eat and drink in town.

Getting There & Away

The train station is 5km east of town – not worth the trip.

The bus terminal is a 10-minute walk north from the Rynek. There are plenty of buses to Radom (31km), passing Orońsko on their way. Only a few buses go straight to Kielce (44km); if you can't be bothered

MAŁOPOLSKA

waiting, take a half-hourly bus to Skarżysko Kamienna and continue on another bus, also frequent.

The Lublin Upland

The Lublin Upland (Wyżyna Lubelska) stretches to the east of the Vistula and San rivers, up to the Ukrainian border. The upland is largely unspoilt, the only city of any size being Lublin. The closer to the eastern border you get, the stronger the Eastern Orthodox Church influence. Having private transport is useful for exploring more remote areas. Otherwise, you'll probably visit the three important historic towns and the showpieces of the region – Lublin, Kazimierz Dolny and Zamość – and perhaps some of their environs.

LUBLIN
☎ 81 • pop 360,000

Lublin has always been one of Poland's most important cities. Interestingly, it often seemed to take the lead at crucial historical moments when the country's fate hung in the balance. In 1569 the so-called Lublin Union was signed here, uniting Poland and Lithuania into a single political entity, thus creating the largest European state of the time. In November 1918, the last days of WWI, it was in Lublin that the first government of independent Poland was formed, which soon handed power over to Józef Piłsudski. It was here again that the provisional communist government was installed by the Soviets during the last stages of WWII, in July 1944. Lublin is also considered by some to be the cradle of Solidarity; the avalanche of strikes that in 1980 spread throughout Poland and eventually led to the Gdańsk agreements began in Lublin.

Despite such historical prominence, Lublin usually came in second best, a poorer cousin of more illustrious, progressive or simply more attractive towns. Even today, when most of the great historical cities have their old quarters beautifully restored or rebuilt, Lublin is still grimly struggling with the task of restoration, and it will be a while before it's completed.

History

Lublin came to life as an outpost protecting Poland against repeated raids by Tatars, Lithuanians and Ruthenians, from the east. In the 12th century, a stronghold was built on the site where the castle stands today. In 1317 Lublin received a municipal charter and soon after the castle and fortified walls were built by Kazimierz Wielki. When the Polish kingdom expanded towards the southeast, Lublin became an important trading centre and continued to develop. In 1578 the Crown Tribunal, the highest law court of Małopolska, was established here. By the end of the 16th century the population passed the 10,000 mark and the town prospered.

The glorious times ended there. As elsewhere, from the mid-17th century Lublin slid into decline. It revived before WWI, and in 1918 the Lublin Catholic University (commonly known as KUL) was founded. It managed to operate throughout the period of communist rule. Right up until the collapse of communism in 1989, it was the only private university in Eastern Europe.

A Jewish community developed in Lublin in the mid-14th century, and grew so rapidly that some 200 years later the town had the third-largest Jewish population in Poland after Kraków and Lviv. In the mid-18th century Jews formed half of the city's inhabitants, and just before WWII made up about 30%. Over three dozen synagogues and prayer houses and four Jewish graveyards existed. A visit to the Majdanek death camp will help you to understand what happened later.

Since WWII Lublin has expanded threefold and today it is the largest and most important industrial and educational centre in eastern Poland. Vast, anonymous suburbs and factories have been built all around the historic town.

Luckily, Lublin didn't experience significant wartime damage, so its Old Town has retained much of its historic architectural fabric. Early postwar restoration was superficial, and unfortunately, the quarter looks dilapidated and untidy. A more thorough

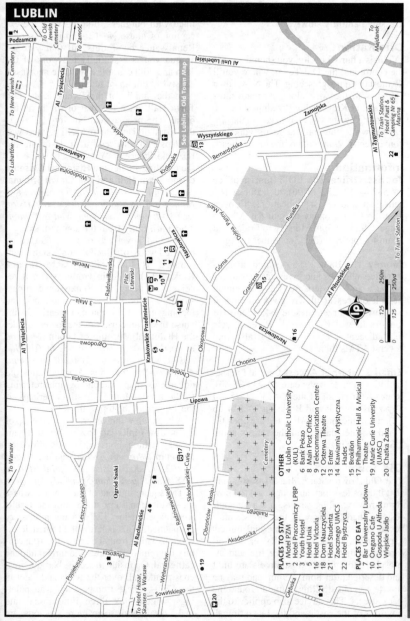

LUBLIN

To Old Jewish Cemetery
To Zamość
To New Jewish Cemetery
To Lubartów
To Warsaw
To Hotel Huzar, Skansen & Warsaw
To Majdanek
To Train Station, Hotel Piast & Camping Nr 65 Marina
To Train Station

Podzamcze

Al Tysiąclecia
Al Unii Lubelskiej
Zamojska
Wyszyńskiego
Bernardyńska
Rusałka
Al Zygmuntowskie
Al Piłsudskiego

See Lublin – Old Town Map

Grodzka
Królewska
Lubartowska
Wodopojna
Niecała
Radziwiłłowska
Plac Litewski
3 Maja
Chmielna
Ogrodowa
Spokojna
Al Tysiąclecia
Leszczyńskiego
Popiełuszki
Długosza
Ogród Saski

Narutowicza
Dolna Panny Marii
Górna
Graniczna
Narutowicza
Krakowskie Przedmieście
Okopowa
Chopina
Lipowa
Cemetery
Skłodowskiej-Curie
Obrońców Pokoju
Raabego
Akademicka
Radziszewskiego
Weteranów
Sowińskiego
Głęboka

250m
125
250yd
125
0

PLACES TO STAY
1 Motel PZM
2 Hotel Pracowniczy LPBP
3 Youth Hostel
5 Hotel Unia
16 Hotel Victoria
18 Dom Nauczyciela
21 Hotel Studenta Zaocznego UMCS
22 Hotel Bystrzyca

PLACES TO EAT
7 Bar Uniwersalny Ludowa
10 Oregano Cafe
11 Gospoda U Alfreda Wiejskie Jadło

OTHER
4 Lublin Catholic University (KUL)
6 Bank Pekao
8 Main Post Office
9 Telecommunication Centre
12 Osterwa Theatre
13 Enter
14 Kawiarnia Artystyczna Hades
15 Brokilon
17 Philharmonic Hall & Musical Theatre
19 Marie Curie University (UMCS)
20 Chatka Żaka

program is currently underway, but it's progressing painfully slowly.

Orientation

Lublin is a fairly big city, you should aim for the centre and the Old Town, where you'll do most of your sightseeing. The New Town stretches to the west along its main thoroughfare, ul Krakowskie Przedmieście.

Coming by bus you arrive right in the city centre, while the train deposits you, less conveniently, 2km south of the town's heart.

Information

Tourist Office The LOIT tourist office (☎ 532 44 12, 532 17 96), ul Jezuicka 1/3, sells maps and tourist publications. It's open 10am to 6pm Monday to Saturday May to August, 9am to 5pm Monday to Friday and 10am to 2pm Saturday September to April.

Money The Bank Pekao, which changes travellers cheques and gives cash advances on Visa and MasterCard, has convenient branch offices at ul Królewska 1 and ul Krakowskie Przedmieście 64. Plenty of kantors line ul Krakowskie Przedmieście and adjacent streets, and you'll also find several ATMs there.

Email & Internet Access Central Internet facilities include www cafe (☎ 442 35 80), Rynek 8 (3rd floor); Enter (☎ 743 60 25), ul Wyszyńskiego 3; and Brokilon (☎ 534 56 22), ul Graniczna 13. All listed are open till 10pm or later daily, and the rate is about US$1.50 per hour.

Old Town

The Old Town (Stare Miasto) is so small that it takes less than an hour to get to know its narrow, winding streets. It's a bit soulless, as there are few of the shops, cafes, restaurants and other commercial outlets (apart from some on the Rynek and ul Grodzka) that normally give life and atmosphere to a town. Most streets are unlit and deserted after 8pm or 9pm, and may be unsafe – avoid strolling at night around the back streets. This advice also applies to the environs of the castle and the bus terminal.

The **Rynek**, built on an irregular plan, is lined with burghers' houses. With the exception of house No 12 with its preserved Renaissance bas-reliefs, all that you see around you is essentially the work of the 19th and 20th centuries, with the neoclassical style a dominant feature.

In the middle of the Rynek is the **Old Town Hall**, once the seat of the royal tribunal. The neoclassical building (1781) is the work of Domenico Merlini, who was perhaps more successful in designing the Łazienki Palace in Warsaw. The cellars of the building shelter the **Historical Museum of the Town Hall and the Crown Tribunal** (*Muzeum Historii Ratusza i Trybunału Koronnego; ☎ 532 68 66, Rynek 1; admission US$0.50; open 9am-4pm Wed-Sat, 9am-5pm Sun*). Enter from the southern side.

The Old Town was once surrounded by fortified walls, of which the only significant remnant is the **Kraków Gate** (Brama Krakowska). Built in Gothic style, it received an octagonal Renaissance superstructure in the 16th century and a baroque topping in 1782 – you can clearly distinguish these three parts of the tower. Inside, the **Historical Museum of Lublin** (*Muzeum Historii Miasta Lublina; ☎ 532 60 01, Plac Łokietka 3; admission US$0.50; open 9am-4pm Wed-Sat, 9am-5pm Sun*) contains old documents, maps and photographs referring to the town. More interesting, perhaps, is the view from the top of the tower.

A better view, however, is from the top of the nearby **Trinitarian Tower** (Wieża Trynitarska), which houses the **Archdiocesan Museum** (*Muzeum Archiecezjalne; ☎ 743 73 92, ul Królewska 19; adult/student US$1/0.75; open 10am-5pm daily Apr-Oct*).

The square in front of the tower is where the Jesuit monastery stood until the Jesuits were expelled in 1773 and the monastery dismantled. What is left is the former Jesuit Church, dating from the end of the 16th century but remodelled later and turned into the **cathedral**. Go inside to see the baroque frescoes painted all over the walls and vault in the 1750s. These trompe l'œil wall paintings, which look three-dimensional and make the interior seem more spacious, are

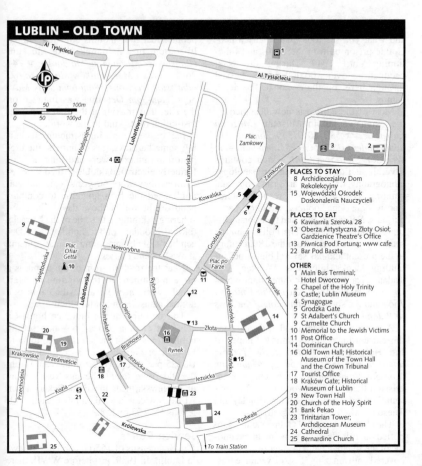

LUBLIN – OLD TOWN

PLACES TO STAY
8   Archidiecezjalny Dom
    Rekolekcyjny
15 Wojewódzki Ośrodek
    Doskonalenia Nauczycieli

PLACES TO EAT
6   Kawiarnia Szeroka 28
12 Oberża Artystyczna Złoty Osioł;
    Gardzienice Theatre's Office
13 Piwnica Pod Fortuną; www cafe
22 Bar Pod Basztą

OTHER
1   Main Bus Terminal;
    Hotel Dworcowy
2   Chapel of the Holy Trinity
3   Castle; Lublin Museum
4   Synagogue
5   Grodzka Gate
7   St Adalbert's Church
9   Carmelite Church
10 Memorial to the Jewish Victims
11 Post Office
14 Dominican Church
16 Old Town Hall; Historical
    Museum of the Town Hall
    and the Crown Tribunal
17 Tourist Office
18 Kraków Gate; Historical
    Museum of Lublin
19 New Town Hall
20 Church of the Holy Spirit
21 Bank Pekao
23 Trinitarian Tower;
    Archdiocesan Museum
24 Cathedral
25 Bernardine Church

the work of Moravian artist Józef Majer.
Visit the **acoustic chapel** *(kaplica akusty-
czna; open 10am-2pm & 3pm-5pm Tues-
Sun)*, so called because two people standing
in opposite corners can whisper and still be
heard. Behind the chapel is the treasury
(skarbiec; same opening hours), where you
can inspect trompe l'œil frescoes by Majer
in more detail (those in the chapel are copies).
The entrance to the chapel and the treasury
is through the far end of the right-hand aisle
of the cathedral.

Another remarkable religious building,
the **Dominican Church** (Kościół Dominikanów). It was founded by King Kazimierz Wielki in 1342 but was burnt down
twice, rebuilt in Renaissance style and most
of its internal fittings was later replaced by
baroque decoration. It was in this church
that the Lublin Union was signed in 1569.
Note the large historical painting by an unknown artist, which depicts the 1719 fire of
the city. The painting is in the chapel just to
the right as you enter the church.

Castle
Erected on a hill, north-east of the Old
Town, the original 14th-century castle was

destroyed (apart from its tower and chapel), and what you see today is actually a neo-Gothic prison built in the 1820s and functioning until 1944. During the Nazi occupation, over 100,000 people passed through here, on their way to the death camps.

Most of the edifice is now occupied by the extensive **Lublin Museum** (*Muzeum Lubelskie;* ☎ *532 50 01, ul Zamkowa 9; adult/student US$1.50/0.75; open 9am-4pm Wed-Sat, 9am-5pm Sun*), which contains several sections including archaeology, ethnography, decorative art, arms, coins and painting. The ethnographic section features fine woodcarving, pottery, basketry, paper cut-outs, Nativity scenes and traditional costumes from the region. The Polish painting section covers works from the 18th century to the present and has several big names including Jacek Malczewski, Witkacy and Tadeusz Kantor, plus two important works by Jan Matejko: the giant *Lublin Union of 1569* and the smaller *Admission of the Jews to Poland in 1096*.

Adjoining the eastern end of the castle is the extraordinary 14th-century **Chapel of the Holy Trinity** (*Kaplica Św Trójcy; adult/student US$2.50/1.50; open 9am-4pm Mon-Sat, 9am-5pm Sun*). The chapel's admission ticket entitles you to visit the museum's exhibitions (except for Monday and Tuesday, when they are closed).

The chapel's beautiful Gothic vault is supported on a single pillar standing in the middle of the square nave. The interior is entirely covered with amazing Russo-Byzantine frescoes painted in the 1410s, considered the finest medieval wall paintings in Poland. It's a real gem – don't miss it.

The frescoes were commissioned by King Władysław Jagiełło, who apparently preferred Eastern iconography over Western style. The frescoes were later plastered over and only discovered in 1897. The complex restoration took (with some breaks) exactly 100 years.

Majdanek

Majdanek, 4km south-east of Lublin's centre, was one of the Nazi's largest death camps, site of the death of about 235,000 people. Just four months after the camp's liberation, the **Majdanek State Museum** (*Państwowe Muzeum na Majdanku;* ☎ *744 26 47, Droga Męczenników Majdanka 67; admission free; open 8am-6pm daily May-Sept, 8am-3pm Oct-Apr*) was founded on the site, thus making it the first memorial institution of its kind in the world.

Part of the camp's infrastructure, including some barracks, gas chambers, the crematorium, guard towers and long lines of formerly electrified double barbed wire remain as they were 60 years ago, and you don't need much imagination to comprehend the horror of those days. There are sobering exhibitions in some of the barracks (closed Monday, public holidays and December to February), and a small cinema shows documentaries.

Near the road, in front of the camp, is a large monument to the victims of Majdanek, while at the rear of the camp is a domed mausoleum holding their ashes.

The building at the entrance houses a cafe, the cinema and a bookshop selling publications about the site. Guided tours in English or German can be organised for US$25 per group. To get to the camp from the Old Town, take trolleybus No 156 from ul Królewska near the Bank Pekao. From Al Racławickie and ul Lipowa, catch trolleybus No 153 or 158.

Jewish Relics

The first census of 1550 recorded 840 Jews in Lublin. In 1939, just before WWII, there were 42,830 Jews, about 8000 of whom survived the war. Today there are, at most, two dozen Jews living in the city.

There's only one surviving **synagogue** (☎ *532 09 22, ul Lubartowska 8; exhibition open 1pm-3pm Sun*) of the 38 which functioned before WWII. It's in an early 20th-century building, similar to many others on this street, without any apparent features of a synagogue. The synagogue occupies the 1st floor of the building, as it did before the war. Religious services are now sporadic. There's a modest exhibition of old photographs, books in Hebrew and ritual ob-

The Death Camp of Majdanek

Established on the south-eastern outskirts of Lublin, Majdanek was one of the Nazis easternmost camps, purposely located in accord with Hitler's plans of easternward expansion. At the same time, the camp was set in the region populated by a sizable Jewish population.

According to initial plans, the camp was to cover 516 hectares and hold 250,000 prisoners at a time, but the defeat of the German army on the eastern front led to a change of plan. Only about 20% of the initial project was eventually built, yet it still came to be one of the Nazis largest camps.

The camp began to operate in autumn 1941 and was gradually extended over the following years, using prisoners as a workforce. Gas chambers were built by mid-1942 and became the main means of extermination, along with mass executions, starvation and exhaustion. Cyklon B gas was the major factor used to put the victims to death – more than 7700kg of it was brought to the camp. The dead bodies were initially burned on open-air grates made of truck chassis, until a purpose-built crematorium, capable of cremating up to 1000 bodies a day, was completed in autumn 1943.

The Nazis kept anything of value that belonged to the victims. All the clothing, personal possessions, jewellery, money etc were taken away from the prisoners on entering the camp. As if this was not horrific enough, the prisoners' hair was cut and sold to a textile company to add in manufacturing the fabrics – a total of 730kg of hair was sent out of Majdanek. Gold and silver teeth were removed from the dead bodies. The Nazis even used the ashes of the cremated bodies as a fertiliser in the camp's gardens and fields.

Majdanek was liberated by the Soviet Army in July 1944. During its nearly three-year period in operation some 235,000 people, representing 50-odd nationalities, were exterminated. Jews were the dominant group – some 110,000 perished here. About 75,000 Poles also perished.

jects. Enter the gate from the street and you'll find the door leading upstairs to the synagogue on your right in the passageway.

The **old Jewish cemetery** was established in the first half of the 16th century and today has 30-odd readable tombstones. The oldest dates from 1641 and is the oldest Jewish tombstone in Poland in its original location. The graveyard is on a wooded hill between ul Sienna and ul Kalinowszczyzna, a short walk north-east from the castle. It is surrounded with a high brick wall so you cannot see anything from the outside, and the gate is locked. Contact Józef Honig (☎ 747 86 76) at his flat at ul Dembowskiego 4, apartment 17, 200m north of the cemetery. He has the keys and lets visitors in (leave a donation).

The **new Jewish cemetery** was founded in 1828, and about 52,000 Jews were buried here until 1942. The cemetery was devastated by the Nazis and there are no tombs except for a few very damaged ones. In 1991 a modern concrete mausoleum was erected behind the entrance, and it houses a small museum dedicated to the history of the Lublin Jewry. The new graveyard is on ul Walecznych, a 10-minute walk north from the old one. The graveyard and the museum can be visited daily at any time during daylight – there is a 24-hour guard on duty.

Skansen

Lublin has an interesting skansen (*Muzeum Wsi Lubelskiej*; ☎ 533 85 13, ul Warszawska 96; adult/student US$1.50/1; open 9am-6pm daily June-Aug, 9am-5pm daily Apr-May & Sept-Oct, 9am-3pm Fri-Sun Nov-Dec), about 5km west of the city centre, on the Warsaw road. Covering an undulating terrain of 25 hectares, it has half a dozen old farmsteads with fully equipped interiors, open to visitors. It all looks like a natural traditional village. There's also a fine manor house, a windmill, an Orthodox church and a carved timber gate (1903) designed by Stanisław Witkiewicz (refer to the Zakopane section in the Carpathian Mountains chapter).

To get to the skansen from the centre, take bus No 18 from ul Krakowskie Przedmieście anywhere west of Plac Litewski.

MAŁOPOLSKA

Places to Stay

Lublin has quite a choice of places to stay and many of them are inexpensive. The flip side of the coin is that most are pretty ordinary and at some distance from the centre, involving the use of public transport or at least a long walk.

Places to Stay – Budget

Camping *Camping Nr 65 Marina (☎/fax 744 10 70, ul Krężnicka 6)* Tent site US$2 plus US$2 per person, 5-person cabin US$15. Open May-Sept. Lublin's only camping facility, the site is on an artificial lake, the Zalew Zemborzycki, about 8km south of the centre. It's accessible by bus No 8 from ul Narutowicza opposite the Osterwa Theatre in the centre. From the main train station, take bus No 17, 20, 21, 27 or 29 to the Stadion Sygnał and change for bus No 25.

Hostels & Hotels *Youth hostel (☎/fax 533 06 28, ul Długosza 6)* Beds US$4-7. Open year-round. This simple but well-run 80-bed hostel is 2km west of the Old Town. It's accessible by trolleybus No 150 from the train station and buses Nos 5, 10, 18 and 57 from the bus terminal.

Wojewódzki Ośrodek Doskonalenia Nauczycieli (☎ 532 92 41, fax 534 46 34, ul Dominikańska 5) Beds in doubles, quads or quins with bath US$10. This 25-bed hostel, just one short block from the Rynek, is good value. It's often full – book ahead.

Archidiecezjalny Dom Rekolekcyjny (☎ 532 41 38, ul Podwale 15) Beds in doubles US$8; beds in 3- to 7-bed dorms (some with bath) US$7. Centrally located, this is one of the cheapest places you'll find in the Old Town. Be on your best behaviour – this is a Catholic Church institution – and don't be too late: they lock the door at 10pm.

Hotel Pracowniczy LPBP (☎ 747 44 07, fax 444 42 42, ul Podzamcze 7) Doubles/triples/quads without bath US$13/16/18, doubles with bath US$22. LPBP is the most central of the city's workers' hotels, 500m north-east of the bus terminal. Basic and located in a drab block, this isn't a particularly memorable place, yet it may serve as an emergency shelter if other, more savoury

central hostels are full. From the train station, take bus Nos 17 or 34.

Hotel Dworcowy (☎ 747 87 01, Al Tysiąclecia 6) Singles/doubles/triples without bath US$12/15/18. Another basic and unprepossessing option, this nine-room hotel in the PKS central bus terminal is convenient if you're coming late and don't feel like looking for a more decent place.

Hotel Piast (☎ 532 16 46, ul Pocztowa 2) Singles/doubles/triples without bath US$12/17/22, beds in a 4- or 5-bed dorm US$6. Again, a basic and ordinary facility, you may need this hotel, next to the train station, if you're arriving late.

Hotel Bystrzyca (☎ 532 30 03, fax 532 05 00, Al Zygmuntowskie 4) Singles/doubles/ triples US$16/22/25. Bystrzyca is a former sports dorm, 1km north of the train station. It's not very convenient but has reasonable standards. Some rooms have own bath, while others share one bathroom between two.

Hotel Studenta Zaocznego UMCS (☎/fax 525 10 81, ul Sowińskiego 17) Singles/doubles US$18/22. This is an acceptable all-year student hostel, providing similar standards as Bystrzyca. One bathroom is shared by two adjacent rooms.

Dom Nauczyciela (☎ 533 82 85, ul Akademicka 4) Singles/doubles without bath US$22/28. This small, simple teacher hostel is 2km out of the centre but is accessible by frequent public transport.

Places to Stay – Mid-Range & Top End

Motel PZM (☎ 533 42 32, ul Prusa 8) Singles/doubles with bath & breakfast US$32/42. Partly refurbished but nothing special, this motel is affordable and is within walking distance of the Old Town.

Hotel Huzar (☎/fax 533 05 36, ul Spadochroniarzy 7) Singles/doubles with bath & breakfast US$50/60. Huzar is quiet and has neat rooms. It's 3km west of the Old Town.

Hotel Victoria (☎ 532 70 11, fax 532 90 26, ul Narutowicza 58/60) Singles with bath US$60-70, doubles with bath US$90-110, breakfast included. Rooms here are fairly comfortable if a bit noisy. It's reasonably close to the centre.

Hotel Unia (☎ *533 20 61, fax 533 30 21, Al Racławickie 12)* Singles/doubles US$125/150, breakfast included. Despite being overpriced, this is the best place in town. Not surprisingly, it's often empty, so you can easily get a room here. Inquire about discount rates on the weekend.

Places to Eat

Bar Pod Basztą (☎ *532 96 78, ul Królewska 6)* Mains US$2-3. Open till 10pm. This is one of the cheapest places to eat in the Old Town area, as the camping-style plastic plates and cutlery will testify.

Bar Uniwersalny Ludowa (☎ *532 97 91, ul Krakowskie Przedmieście 60)* Mains US$1.50-2.50. Open till 7pm, closed Sunday. This rock-bottom eatery in the New Town has acceptable food and even has table service.

Gospoda U Alfreda Wiejskie Jadło (☎ *532 32 00, ul Peowiaków 3)* Mains US$4-6. Furnished and decorated like an old countryside inn, Gospoda serves traditional Polish food till late.

Oberża Artystyczna Złoty Osioł (☎ *532 90 42, ul Grodzka 5A)* Mains US$5-8, salads US$4-5. Oberża is a charming place in the heart of the Old Town. It has a pleasant outdoor eating area, and serves hearty Polish food.

Kawiarnia Szeroka 28 (☎ *534 61 09, ul Grodzka 21)* Mains US$5-7. Another lovely Old Town place, this cafe has several rooms, plus a terrace overlooking the castle, and a theatre upstairs. The decor features elements of traditional Polish and Jewish cultures, and so does the cuisine. There may be some live *klezmer* (jewish folk music) on some evenings.

Oregano Cafe (☎ *442 55 30, ul Kościuszki 7)* Mains US$7-12. This pleasant cafe serves up Mediterranean cuisine in its cosy interior.

Piwnica Pod Fortuną (☎ *534 03 34, Rynek 8)* Mains US$8-12. The Old Town's top-end venue is in an extensively restored establishment with vaulted cellars on different levels, it claims to be Lublin's oldest restaurant, serving up Polish fare since the late 16th century. The lowest level is 8m below the Rynek's surface, making it the deepest cellar in town. Make sure to see the 16th-century Renaissance frescoes featuring some risque scenes.

Entertainment

The major local daily paper, the *Kurier Lubelski*, has listings of what's on. The *Lublin w Pigułce* free monthly covers cultural events. The tourist office may also be able to tell you what's going on around town.

Pubs & Clubs There's a growing collection of watering holes in the Old Town (on the Rynek and ul Grodzka) and the New Town (mostly on ul Krakowskie Przedmieście). The previously mentioned *Oberża Artystyczna Złoty Osioł* and *Kawiarnia Szeroka 28* (see under Places to Eat) are as good for a drink only as they are for a lunch or dinner.

Kawiarnia Artystyczna Hades (☎ *532 56 41, ul Peowiaków 12)* Hades has live music (rock, jazz etc) on some nights and discos usually on Friday. The annual three-day-long Hades Jazz Festival takes place here in October.

Chatka Żaka (*ul Radziszewskiego 16)* This student club of Marie Curie University has a pool table and a beer garden, and live music events on some days.

Cultural Activities *Filharmonia Lubelska* (☎ *532 44 21, ul Skłodowskiej-Curie 5)* The Philharmonic has a new, huge auditorium, where it stages concerts of classical and contemporary music.

Teatr Muzyczny (☎ *532 25 21, ul Skłodowskiej-Curie 5)* Sharing the same building with the Philharmonic, the Musical Theatre presents operettas and various musical events.

Teatr im Osterwy (*Osterwa Theatre;* ☎ *532 42 44, ul Narutowicza 17)* This is the main city venue for drama, featuring mostly classical plays, with some emphasis on great national works.

Theatre buffs may be interested in the experimental *Gardzienice Theatre* (*office in Lublin* ☎ *532 98 40, 532 96 37, ul Grodzka 5A)*, one of the most outstanding

MAŁOPOLSKA

companies currently performing in Poland. Each of its productions is a whirl of sights and sounds performed barefoot by candlelight with reckless energy and at breakneck speed, accompanied by music and singing by the actors themselves. Established in 1977 in the small village of Gardzienice, 28km south-east of Lublin, the theatre is based and performs there. The theatre is often abroad and, when at home, only performs on weekends, to an audience small enough to be packed into its tiny theatre. You need to book well in advance.

Getting There & Away

Train The main train station, Lublin Główny, is linked to the Old Town by trolleybus No 160 and several buses including Nos 13 and 17. There are at least half a dozen fast trains to Warsaw daily (175km), Radom (128km) and Kielce (213km), and two fast trains to Kraków (345km). Tickets can be bought directly from the station or from the Orbis Travel at ul Narutowicza 33A. Ordinary trains to Chełm (75km) depart every one or two hours.

Bus The main bus terminal, Dworzec Główny PKS, is at the foot of the castle near the Old Town and handles most of the traffic. Buses to Kazimierz Dolny (44km) run every hour or so (look for the Puławy bus via Nałęczów and Kazimierz). To Zamość (89km), PKS buses run every half-hour, and there are also private minibuses departing every 20 minutes from just behind the terminal.

There are three buses to Sandomierz daily (110km) – look for the Tarnobrzeg bus in the timetable. Buses to Chełm (68km) run approximately every other hour. Every morning a fast bus goes directly to Kraków (269km). A Polski Express bus goes to Warsaw every other hour.

There are two morning buses to Kozłówka (38km), and then nothing until about 3pm. They are hard to find in the timetable – ask at the information counter.

Four buses a day to Przemyśl (185km) depart from the south terminal next to the train station.

KOZŁÓWKA
☎ 81

The hamlet of Kozłówka ('Koz-**woof**-kah'), 38km north of Lublin, is famous for its magnificent late-baroque palace. Built in the mid-18th century, the residence was acquired by the Zamoyski family in 1799. The palace was then extended and remodelled and its interior fitted out in sumptuous pseudo-rococo style. The new owner's collection of 1000 paintings proved difficult to accommodate, and pictures were placed on every spare bit of wall, bathrooms included. Much of the palace's original decoration has been preserved and is open to the public.

Things to See

The palace complex is now the **Zamoyski Museum** (☎ 852 70 91; adult/student US$3/1.50; open 10am-4pm Tues, Thur & Fri Mar-Nov; 10am-5pm Wed, Sat & Sun Mar-Nov). The opulent palace rooms are fitted out with period furnishings, ceramic stoves, crystal mirrors etc. However, the most striking thing about the palace is the number of paintings, each one complete with its own distinct ornate frame. The pictures date mostly from the 17th to 19th centuries (the oldest is from 1672) and aren't necessarily valuable pieces of art; many are copies. The sheer quantity, however – about 360 on display – makes for a very unusual sight.

All visits to the palace are guided in groups which depart on the hour and take 45 minutes, but there may be more tours if there is a demand. The last tour departs one hour before the museum's closing time. Commentary is in Polish. Call the museum in advance if you need a foreign-language guide. It will cost an extra US$10 per group.

Kozłówka is also known country-wide for its unique **Socialist-Realist Art Gallery** (Galeria Sztuki Socrealizmu; adult/student US$1/0.50; same opening hours as the palace) displayed in one of the palace's side wings. You'll find the whole pantheon of beloved comrades, including Stalin, Lenin, Marx and Mao Zedong, plus most Polish revolutionary communist leaders. There's also a collection of paintings depicting

Socialist Realism – Art as a Political Tool

Socialist realism originated in the 1920s in the Soviet Union and became the only accepted style in visual arts, architecture, film, music and literature by the mid-1930s. After WWII, it spread widely throughout the countries of the eastern bloc, by then controlled by the Soviet Union.

In Poland, the new regime initially allowed for some ideological and cultural pluralism. Only in 1949, when the communists felt themselves sufficiently strong and safe in the saddle, was socialist realism formally implemented, and it came to be the official artistic doctrine until 1955. A huge body of paintings, sculptures, monuments, poems and songs were produced in that short period.

According to its official credo, socialist realism was 'a creative way of transferring Marxism into the realm of art'. It was a doctrine that was designed to develop a 'socialist culture' by artistic means. Its creators aimed to find an artistic vehicle to promote the communist ideology. In effect, art was reduced to the role of communist propaganda tool. The artists could no longer express themselves but were obliged to just transmit the official dogma in a determined pseudo-artistic form.

Since the new 'art' was intended to target the masses, not just an intellectual elite, it had to be easily understood by ordinary people. It therefore employed 19th-century realism and academism as the easiest way to promote the new ideas in painting and sculpture. Modern styles and artistic experiments were out of question, as were any independent creative attempts. The new art had to be optimistic and motivating, promoting the new order.

Images of communist leaders were probably the most common in the visual arts of the new artistic creation. These apart, the apotheosis of labour was very popular – happy bricklayers at work, smiling young women drivers on tractors ploughing the fields, or dockyard workers enthusiastically building a ship. Other common subjects included important historical and social events, communist party meetings, congresses etc.

After Stalin's death in 1953, the lunacy began to subside fairly quickly in Poland. Socialist realism works were discreetly removed from public view and put into the confines of warehouses. Kozłówka, which was then the central storage facility of the Ministry of Culture and Art (the Kozłówka palace wasn't opened until 1977), was one of the major recipients. Today, it's all back on the walls and pedestals, but this time as museum pieces.

everyday scenes from communist life. The canvases are tightly packed all over the walls – a bizarre bridge to the Zamoyski painting collection in the palace.

The socialist-realist gallery can be visited individually, before or after the palace tour. There's a cafe beside the gallery, and statues of Lenin and Marchlewski behind it.

To round off your visit, take a stroll about the garden behind the palace. Look out for a huge statue of Bolesław Bierut standing among the trees near the palace.

Getting There & Away

The usual departure point for Kozłówka is Lublin – see Getting There & Away in that section for transport details. Returning to Lublin, there are only a few direct buses in the afternoon, so check the timetable before

visiting the museum, and plan your visit accordingly. There are more buses to Lubartów, from where buses and minibuses run regularly to Lublin. There are also a few afternoon buses from Kozłówka to Puławy.

PUŁAWY
☎ 81 • pop 55,000

The town of Puławy ('Poo-**wah**-vi') reached its golden age at the end of the 18th century when the Czartoryski family, one of the big aristocratic Polish clans, made it an important centre of political, cultural and intellectual life. Prince Adam Kazimierz Czartoryski and his wife Izabela accumulated a large library and art collection, and surrounded themselves with artists and writers.

After the failure of the November Insurrection of 1830, which was strongly backed

MAŁOPOLSKA

by the Czartoryskis, the whole estate was confiscated by the tsar, and the family had to flee the country. The art collection was secretly moved to Paris. In the 1870s it was brought back to Poland, but to Kraków, not Puławy, and today it constitutes the core of the Kraków Czartoryski Museum.

After WWII a huge nitrate combine was built near Puławy and the town become a badly polluted industrial centre.

Information

There's no genuine tourist office in Puławy. If in need, try the PTTK office (☎ 886 47 56), ul Czartoryskich 8A, at the entrance to the Czartoryski park-and-palace complex.

The Bank Pekao is at Al Królewska 11A, close to the palace. There are several kantors in the centre, including a few on ul Piłsudskiego.

Things to See

The **Czartoryski Palace**, designed by the ubiquitous Tylman van Gameren and erected in 1676–79, has been altered quite substantially over the years and has eventually ended up as a sober, late neoclassical building. It's now the home of an agricultural research institute, and is not a tourist sight but you can try to have a discreet look inside. Enter through the main central door, turn to the right and go up the staircase to the 1st floor to see the only two rooms worth a glimpse, the music hall and the Gothic hall.

The **landscape park** (admission free; open till dusk) that surrounds the palace was founded in the late 18th century by Princess Izabela. It is a typical romantic park of the era (similar to the Arkadia park in Mazovia) and incorporates several pavilions and buildings. The Temple of the Sybil (Świątynia Sybilli) and the Gothic House (Domek Gotycki) both date from the early 19th century and are used as exhibition grounds from May to October. A map of the park showing the location of important sights is displayed at the entrance.

The **Regional Museum** (☎ 887 86 74, ul Czartoryskich 6A; admission US$0.50; open 10am-2pm Tues-Sun), 200m north of the palace, features ethnographic and ar-

chaeological exhibits, plus temporary displays, some of which are related to the Czartoryski family.

About 200m to the west, on ul Piłsudskiego, is the **Czartoryski Chapel**, modelled on the Roman Pantheon and built in 1801–03. The circular, domed interior has lost its original furnishings and decoration. Today it's a parish church.

Places to Stay & Eat

Youth hostel (☎ 886 33 67, fax 888 36 56, ul Włostowicka 27) Beds US$4-6. Open year-round. This large, 118-bed hostel is 2km out of the centre on the Kazimierz Dolny road. Don't come back into the centre if you're heading for Kazimierz – catch the bus near the entrance of the hostel.

Wojewódzki Ośrodek Metodyczny (☎/fax 887 42 77, ul Kołłątaja 1) Singles with bath US$15, doubles without bath US$18. A simple but cheap option in the city centre, this teachers' hostel is opposite the Czartoryski Chapel.

Hotel Wisła (☎ 886 27 37, ☎/fax 886 46 15, ul Wróblewskiego 1) Doubles/triples with bath US$26/32. Another affordable central place, Wisła has airy rooms with bath and its own restaurant.

Centrum Szkoleniowo-Kongresowe Instytutu Uprawy, Nawożenia i Gleboznawstwa (☎/fax 887 73 06, 887 73 07, Al Królewska 17) Singles/doubles US$25/30. Optional breakfast US$5. Centrum is a good, quiet place just 200m from the Czartoryski Palace. It has its own restaurant.

Prima Hotel (☎ 886 38 24, 886 46 15, ul Partyzantów 44) Singles with bath US$20-25, doubles with bath US$30-40. Close to the train station, Prima is a new small hotel with its own restaurant.

If all you need is a straightforward lunch, go to the **Bufet** in the basement of the brick building of Rada Powiatu, Al Królewska 19, opposite the palace, which serves cheap, tasty meals 1pm to 2.30pm Monday to Friday.

Getting There & Away

Train The town has two train stations: Puławy and Puławy Miasto. The latter is the main one and is closer to the centre, yet it's still nearly 2km north-east of the central area. It is serviced by city buses; otherwise use taxis.

At least one train per hour leaves for Lublin (50km) but it's more convenient to travel by bus, which go centre-to-centre. Trains to Warsaw (125km) run roughly every other hour. For Kraków (294km), there is only one morning and one evening train, but several fast trains go to Radom (78km) and on to Kielce (157km), from where the transport to Kraków is regular.

Bus The PKS bus terminal is in the city centre. PKS buses to Lublin (47km) depart every half-hour, but the service to Warsaw (127km) is less frequent. Both these destinations are also serviced by Polski Express, with seven departures a day to each. Half a dozen PKS buses run to Radom (58km) and four to Łódź (193km). There are also three morning buses to Lubartów which will let you off at Kozłówka.

For Kazimierz Dolny (14km), PKS buses leave at least every hour, but also check the schedule of suburban bus No 12 in front of the terminal and take the one that goes first. Do the same if you head for Janowiec (choosing between PKS and city bus No 17).

KAZIMIERZ DOLNY
☎ 81 • pop 4000
Positioned on the bank of the Vistula at the foot of wooded hills, Kazimierz Dolny is a charming, picturesque town. It has some fine historic architecture, good museums and is nestled in attractive countryside. For many years Kazimierz has attracted artists and intellectuals, and you will almost always see painters setting up their easels outdoors.

Kazimierz has become a fashionable weekend and holiday spot for tourists, mainly from Warsaw, which gives it something of a split personality – from a quiet, sleepy, old-fashioned village on weekdays and off season, it turns into a hive of activity on summer weekends.

History
The town was founded in the 14th century by King Kazimierz Wielki (hence its name), who built the castle and gave it a municipal charter with numerous privileges attached. The town was called Dolny (lower), to distinguish it from upriver Kazimierz, which is today part of Kraków.

Kazimierz Dolny soon became a thriving commercial centre. Merchandise from the whole region, principally grain and salt, was shipped down to Gdańsk and farther on for export. Kazimierz enjoyed particularly good times between the mid-16th and mid-17th centuries. A large port, a number of splendid burghers' mansions and nearly 50 granaries were built in that period, and the population passed the 2500 mark by 1630.

The Swedish Deluge, then the Northern War and the cholera epidemic of 1708, brought an end to the town's prosperity, and the displacement of the Vistula bed towards the west, away from the town, accelerated its economic decline. By the 19th century, Puławy overshadowed Kazimierz as both a trade and a cultural centre. A small scale revival as a tourist spot began at the end of the 19th century, but then came WWI and WWII, both of which caused serious damage to Kazimierz. After WWII, a development plan aimed at preserving the town in line with its historical character was approved, and many old buildings have since been restored.

The history of Kazimierz, like that of the whole region, is intimately linked with Jewish culture. From the town's beginnings, Jews formed an important and expanding part of the community, becoming the majority during the 19th century. Before WWII they formed over half the town's population, but only a handful survived the war. About 3000 Jews from Kazimierz and its environs had their lives ended in the Nazi death camps.

Information
The PTTK office (☎ 881 00 46), Rynek 27, has information about the town and sells brochures and maps. The office is open 8am to 6pm Monday to Friday, 10am to 5.30pm Saturday from May to September. For the rest of the year it closes at 4pm on weekdays and 2.30pm on Saturday.

MAŁOPOLSKA

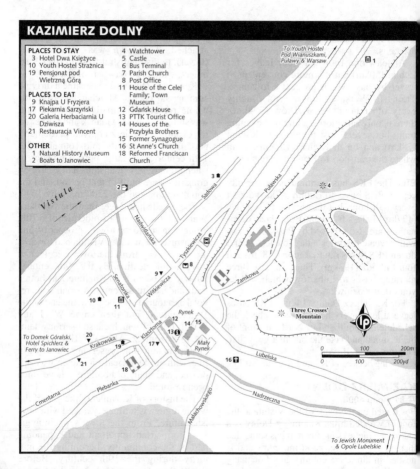

KAZIMIERZ DOLNY

PLACES TO STAY
3 Hotel Dwa Księżyce
10 Youth Hostel Strażnica
19 Pensjonat pod
  Wietrzną Górą

PLACES TO EAT
9 Knajpa U Fryzjera
17 Piekarnia Sarzyński
20 Galeria Herbaciarnia U
  Dziwisza
21 Restauracja Vincent

OTHER
1 Natural History Museum
2 Boats to Janowiec

4 Watchtower
5 Castle
6 Bus Terminal
7 Parish Church
8 Post Office
11 House of the Celej
  Family; Town
  Museum
12 Gdańsk House
13 PTTK Tourist Office
14 Houses of the
  Przybyła Brothers
15 Former Synagogue
16 St Anne's Church
18 Reformed Franciscan
  Church

To Youth Hostel
Pod Wianuszkami,
Puławy & Warsaw

Vistula

Three Crosses'
Mountain

To Domek Góralski,
Hotel Spichlerz &
Ferry to Janowiec

Rynek

Mały
Rynek

To Jewish Monument
& Opole Lubelskie

0   100   200m
0   100   200yd

MAŁOPOLSKA

There are no banks in town; the nearest
are in Puławy. There's a kantor in the post
office building at ul Tyszkiewicza 2, and an
ATM in the back wall of the same building.

Things to See
The **Rynek**, with an old wooden well in the
middle, is lined with merchants' houses, of
which the finest are the two arcaded **Houses
of the Przybyła Brothers** (Kamienice
Przybyłów). Built in 1615, both of them
have rich Renaissance facades, decorated
with bas-relief figures of the owners' patron
saints, St Nicholas and St Christopher, and

are topped by ornamented parapets. Also on
the Rynek are the baroque-style **Gdańsk
House** (Kamienica Gdańska) from 1795,
and several characteristic arcaded houses
with wooden-tiled roofs, dating from the
18th and 19th centuries.

There's another fine historic building, the
1630 **House of the Celej Family** (Kamienica
Celejowska), on ul Senatorska. It shelters
the **Town Museum** (☎ 881 01 04, ul Senatorska 11; adult/student US$1/0.50; open
10am-4pm Tues-Sun May-Sept, 10am-3pm
Tues-Sun Oct-Apr, closed days following
public holidays) which features paintings of

Kazimierz and its surroundings, and an exhibition on the town's history.

The museum also presents a collection of gold and silverwork, including Judaic cult silverware and jewellery, belonging to the **Museum of Goldsmithery** (Muzeum Sztuki Złotniczej), which is currently undergoing extensive reconstruction.

Set on the nearby hill is the **Reformed Franciscan Church** (Kościół Reformatów). It was built at the end of the 16th century but lost its original style with subsequent baroque and neoclassical decorations.

The Gothic **parish church** on the opposite side of the Rynek was built in the mid-14th century but was remodelled when the Renaissance style flooded Poland. Of interest in its interior is the ornate carved organ from 1620, which sounds as good as it looks; organ recitals are held here. Also note the Renaissance stalls in the chancel and the stucco decoration of the nave's vault, a classic example of the so-called Lublin-Renaissance style, typical of the region. Looking up, don't miss the unusual chandelier featuring the stag's antlers.

Farther along ul Zamkowa is the **castle** or, more precisely, what is left of it. Built in the 14th century, it was partly destroyed by the Swedes, and later gradually fell into ruin. Only fragments of the walls remain.

The **watchtower**, 200m up the hill, was built a century before the castle as a part of the wooden fortifications, which no longer exist. It's 20m high and its walls are 4m thick at the base. For security, the entrance was built 6m above the ground and access was by ladders, but wooden stairs were later built. There's a panoramic view once you reach the top.

From the watchtower, take the path to the left leading to **Three Crosses' Mountain** (Góra Trzech Krzyży). The crosses were erected in the early 18th century to commemorate the plague that decimated the town's population. The view over the town is even better than from the watchtower. The path down will lead you directly to the parish church and on to the Rynek.

Have a glimpse at the 18th-century **synagogue** on ul Lubelska, rebuilt after the war and turned into a cinema. Just behind it is the reconstructed wooden building which used to house the Jewish butchers' stalls. This area was once the Jewish quarter but not much is left of it.

Perhaps the most moving reminder of the Jewish legacy is the **Jewish monument,** raised in 1984 in homage to the Jews murdered in Kazimierz during WWII. It's a large concrete wall covered by several hundred tombstones and tombstone fragments from the old cemetery, which was just behind the wall. There are still some finely carved tombstones *in situ*, worth looking around. The monument is a little over 1km from the Rynek, on the road to Opole Lubelskie.

On the opposite side of town, on the Puławy road, is the **Natural History Museum** (*Muzeum Przyrodnicze;* ☎ *881 03 26, ul Puławska 54; adult/student US$1/0.50; open 10am-4pm Tues-Sun May-Sept, 10am-3pm Tues-Sun Oct-Apr, closed days following public holidays*). It is housed in a large, finely restored granary dating from 1591, and has mineralogy and flora and fauna sections. When you get to the top floor, look up at the intricate wooden structure supporting the roof – an exquisite example of 16th-century engineering. The massive beams have been joined by wooden pegs only – no nails were used.

Only a few **granaries** have survived out of a total of nearly 50. Most were built in the 16th and 17th centuries, during a boom in the grain trade. Apart from the one housing the National History Museum and its neighbour just 50m away, there's a good example on ul Krakowska, which is now the Hotel Spichlerz.

Hiking

The area around Kazimierz has been decreed the Kazimierz Landscape Park (Kazimierski Park Krajobrazowy). Many walking trails have been traced in the countryside, and in places they wind through the gorges which are a feature of the region.

There are three easy short trails known as *szlaki spacerowe* (walking routes) signposted in yellow, green and red, and three significantly longer treks called *szlaki turystyczne* (tourist routes) marked in blue, green and red.

Almost all these routes originate in the Rynek. The tourist office sells maps of the park, which have trails marked on them.

Special Events

The highly acclaimed **Festival of Folk Bands and Singers** takes place in the last week of June, from Friday to Sunday. Concerts are held on the Mały Rynek, while the main Rynek fills up with handicraft stalls. The festival offers an opportunity to listen to kinds of music you rarely hear nowadays. Dozens of amateur groups perform, ranging from soloists to large choirs, and they all wear the traditional costumes of their regions.

Kazimierz also hosts a more subdued **Film and Art Festival** in August, with classical music concerts, art exhibitions and outdoor film shows.

Places to Stay

Kazimierz has plenty of places to stay. Particularly numerous are *rooms* for rent in private houses. The PTTK office on the Rynek can arrange rooms (US$7 to US$9 per person) in some of the houses. Virtually every third house in town has some rooms for rent, and you'll easily recognise them by boards saying 'pokoje' (rooms) or 'noclegi' (accommodation). Aside from private rooms, there are heaps of regular hostels and hotels to choose from.

Youth Hostel Pod Wianuszkami (*☎/fax 881 03 27, ul Puławska 80*) Bed & breakfast US$7-8. Open year-round. Located in a granary, 1.5km from the Rynek, this 68-bed hostel is pleasant and well run.

Youth Hostel Strażnica (*☎ 881 04 27, ul Senatorska 25*) Bed & breakfast US$6-8. Open year-round. A bit smaller and more basic but very central, Strażnica hostel is in the building of the fire brigade station.

Domek Góralski (*☎ 881 02 63, ul Krakowska 47*) Beds in rooms without bath US$8. One of the cheapest places, Domek is a small 20-bed hostel in a charming house built in the style typical of the Tatra Mountain region. The in-house dining room serves budget meals.

Pensjonat Pod Wietrzną Górą (*☎ 881 05 43, ☎/fax 881 06 40, ul Krakowska 1*) Beds in doubles, triples or quads with bath & breakfast US$20 per person. Located in a historic house just 100m from the Rynek, this is a small five-room guesthouse with its own restaurant.

Hotel Dwa Księżyce (*☎ 881 08 33, ☎/fax 881 07 61, ul Sadowa 15*) Doubles/suites with bath & breakfast US$50/90. Another central place, 'Two Moons' is a good and pleasant hotel which has 16 stylish rooms and four suites, plus sauna and a restaurant.

Hotel Spichlerz (*☎/fax 881 00 36, ul Krakowska 59/61*) Doubles/triples US$40/60. Located in a 400-year-old granary, Spichlerz oozes character, though it doesn't exactly provide five-star standards. It has its own restaurant. The owners run another stylish hotel nearby and a *camp site* just behind the granary.

Places to Eat

Several cafes on and around the Rynek serve simple meals. The hotel restaurants listed under Places to Stay provide decent dining, and there are more eateries around town, including:

Piekarnia Sarzyński (*☎ 881 06 43, ul Nadrzeczna 6*) The Sarzyński bakery has delicious rolls and bread, including some unusual bread in the shape of roosters, crayfish and other animals. There's decent espresso to wash it all down too.

Galeria Herbaciarnia U Dziwisza (*☎ 881 02 87, ul Krakowska 6*) An art gallery-cum-tea room, this is a charming and cosy place. There are around 100-odd flavours of tea to choose from.

Knajpa U Fryzjera (*☎ 881 04 26, ul Witkiewicza 2*) Mains US$6-8. This agreeable place serves up Jewish specialities.

Restauracja Vincent (*☎ 881 08 76, ul Krakowska 11/13*) Mains US$7-12. Serving international food in pleasant surroundings, Vincent is one of Kazimierz's finest restaurants.

Getting There & Away

Kazimierz can be conveniently visited as a stop on your Lublin-Warsaw route, or as a day trip from Lublin. There's no railway in Kazimierz but the bus service is OK.

Bus The PKS bus terminal is a two-minute walk from the Rynek and has a service to Puławy (14km) every half-hour or so. The similarly frequent Puławy urban bus No 12 can take you directly to the Puławy train station. Buses to Lublin (44km) go roughly every hour, taking nearly two hours to get there. There are about five fast buses straight to Warsaw daily (3½ hours, 140km), or go to Puławy and change for the train.

Boat A pleasure boat to Janowiec, on the opposite side of the Vistula, runs in summer if there are passengers interested – ask at the wharf at the end of ul Nadwiślańska.

There's also a car/passenger ferry from May to September. Its departure point is 1km west of Hotel Spichlerz.

JANOWIEC
☎ 81 • pop 1200

The village of Janowiec ('Yah-**no**-vyets'), 2km upstream on the other side of the Vistula from Kazimierz Dolny, is known for its **castle**, now part of the **Janowiec Museum** (☎ 881 52 28; adult/student US$1.50/0.75; open 10am-5pm Tues-Sun May-Sept, 10am-3pm Tues-Sun Oct-Apr).

Built at the beginning of the 16th century by the Firlej family and gradually extended during the next century by the subsequent owners, the castle grew to have over 100 rooms and became one of the largest and most splendid castles in Poland. Many prominent architects, including Santi Gucci and Tylman van Gameren, had a hand in the castle's development.

The castle went into decline in the 19th century and was largely destroyed during WWI and WWII. It was the only private castle in Poland under communist rule until its owner donated it to the state in 1975. By then, it was a genuine ruin.

While it's still a ruin, much has changed over recent years. Intensive work has been going on and has given the castle back some of its rooms and portions of the walls, complete with vaults, arcades and external painted decoration. The latter is possibly its most striking feature; the walls have been painted with horizontal white and red strips

and grotesque human figures. It all looks like a modern-art joke, but reputedly isn't; historians say that's how the original castle was adorned. Some of the restored rooms house an exhibition related to the castle.

In the park beside the castle is a **manor house** from the 1760s (another part of the museum), fitted out with period furnishings and decoration, and giving an insight into how Polish nobility once lived. Among the outbuildings surrounding the manor is an old two-storey granary, which has an interesting **ethnographic exhibition** that features old fishing boats, ceramics, tools and household implements.

It's also worth going downhill to the village of Janowiec, at the foot of the castle, to visit its mid-14th-century Gothic **parish church**, extensively rebuilt in Renaissance style in the 1530s. Inside is the tomb of the Firlej family, carved in the workshop of Santi Gucci in 1586–87.

Places to Stay & Eat
There are seven double rooms with bath in the **manor house** (☎ 881 52 28), rented out for US$9 a head. Hotel guests can visit all the museum exhibitions free of charge. For a meal, go to the **Restauracja Serokomla** (☎ 881 52 77, ul Sandomierska 24) or **Maćkowa Chata** (☎ 881 54 62, ul Sandomierska 2) both close to Janowiec's Rynek.

Getting There & Away
You can visit Janowiec from Kazimierz Dolny, by pleasure boat or ferry. Alternatively, there is a regular service to/from Puławy (13km) by urban bus No 17 and PKS buses.

CHEŁM
☎ 82 • pop 70,000

Chełm ('Hewm') is a mid-sized town about 70km east of Lublin, not far from the Ukrainian border. It's off the popular tourist track, but won't take you far off the Lublin-Zamość route. One of the most interesting things about Chełm is that it sits on a layer of almost pure chalk 800m thick. Over the centuries Chełm's economic development

MAŁOPOLSKA

has relied on rich chalk deposits. The old tunnels, below the ground, are the town's primary tourist attraction.

History

Chełm was founded in the 10th century and, like most towns along the eastern border, it shifted between the Polish Piast crown and the Kyivan duchy on various occasions. King Kazimierz Wielki eventually got hold of the area in 1366 and King Władysław Jagiełło established a bishopric here some 50 years later.

Around this time Jews began to settle in the town. Swiftly growing in strength and numbers – by the end of the 18th century Jews accounted for 60% of the town's population. At that time there were 49 houses lining the market square, and 47 of them belonged to Jews.

As happened elsewhere in the country, Chełm's good times ended in the 17th century – the period of wars, ravages and Poland's general decline. Later came the Partitions, and the town fell under first Austrian then Russian occupation.

It wasn't until WWI that Chełm began to recover as part of independent Poland, only to experience the horrors of WWII two decades later, including the mass execution of Jews, whose population had grown by that time to about 17,000.

Information

The Chełmski Ośrodek Informacji Turystycznej (☎ 565 36 67, fax 565 41 85), ul Lubelska 63, is open 8am to 4pm weekdays, and 9am to 2pm Saturday.

The Bank Pekao is at ul I Armii WP 41, some distance from the centre, but there are several central ATMs, including ones at Lwowska 1 and 11D and ul Lubelska 65 and 69. Kantors are in reasonable supply, including some on ul Lwowska.

Internet facilities include Imelus ic, ul Lubelska 8, and Adyton, ul Lwowska 11P.

Things to See

Chełm lies on a plain with a conspicuous hill right in the middle. The first settlement and stronghold were on top of the hill.

Nothing is left of this apart from a distinctly recognisable man-made elevation.

Today, the hill is crowned with the large **St Mary's Basilica** (Bazylika Mariacka) surrounded by a complex of religious buildings that were once a bishops' palace and a monastery. The late baroque basilica was remodelled from a Uniate church built here in the mid-18th century. The interior is sober and lacks much decoration, except for the silver antependium at the high altar, which shows Polish knights paying homage to Our Lady of Chełm. The picture of the lady herself overlooks the altar. It's a replica; the original hasn't survived.

More impressive is the former **Piarist Church** (Kościół Pijarski), off Plac Łuczkowskiego. This twin-towered late baroque church was built on an oval plan in the mid-18th century. Once you enter through the massive ornamented doors, you'll find yourself enveloped in a colourful interior, with wall paintings covering every square centimetre of the walls and vaults. This trompe l'œil decoration was executed in 1758 by Józef Mayer, the same artist who embellished Lublin's cathedral. The furnishing are all in rococo style. Today it's the parish church.

The former monastery next door houses the **Chełm Museum** (Muzeum Chełmskie; ☎ 565 26 93, ul Lubelska 55; adult/student US$1/0.50, free Sat; open 10am-4pm Tues-Fri, 11am-3pm Sat & Sun), which features a collection of modern Polish painting plus temporary exhibitions. The museum has three other outlets (open the same hours). The branch at ul Lubelska 57 has sections on archaeology, history and natural history. The section at ul Lubelska 56A stages ethnography and temporary exhibitions. The third one, in the St Nicholas' Chapel at ul Św Mikołaja 4, only has temporary exhibitions. Concerts of classical music are held here at times. Admission fee is due to each outlet, or you can buy a combined entry ticket to all four sites for US$2/1.

The city's star attraction is the **Chełm Chalk Tunnels** (Chełmskie Podziemia Kredowe; ☎ 565 25 30, ul Lubelska 55A; adult/student US$2.50/1.50), an array of old

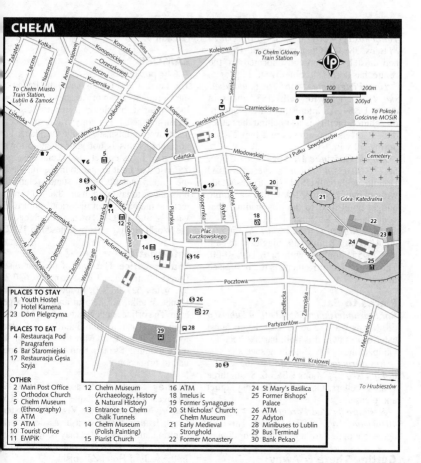

CHEŁM

To Chełm Główny Train Station

To Chełm Miasto Train Station, Lublin & Zamość

To Pokoje Gościnne MOSiR

Góra Katedralna

Cemetery

Plac Łuczkowskiego

To Hrubieszów

PLACES TO STAY
1 Youth Hostel
7 Hotel Kamena
23 Dom Pielgrzyma

PLACES TO EAT
4 Restauracja Pod Paragrafem
6 Bar Staromiejski
17 Restauracja Gęsia Szyja

OTHER
2 Main Post Office
3 Orthodox Church
5 Chełm Museum (Ethnography)
8 ATM
9 ATM
10 Tourist Office
11 EMPiK
12 Chełm Museum (Archaeology, History & Natural History)
13 Entrance to Chełm Chalk Tunnels
14 Chełm Museum (Polish Painting)
15 Piarist Church
16 ATM
18 Imelus ic
19 Former Synagogue
20 St Nicholas' Church; Chełm Museum
21 Early Medieval Stronghold
22 Former Monastery
24 St Mary's Basilica
25 Former Bishops' Palace
26 ATM
27 Adyton
28 Minibuses to Lublin
29 Bus Terminal
30 Bank Pekao

chalk passages hewn out by hand about 12m below ground level. Reputedly the world's only underground chalk mine, it started in medieval times, and by the 16th century was known nationally for the excellent quality of the local chalk. By 1939 a multilevel labyrinth of corridors grew to a total length of 15km. They effectively undermined the town and became a real danger. Following the collapse of a building and part of a street in 1965, the mine was closed and the voids were silted up, except for an 1800m stretch which was strengthened and opened as a tourist attraction.

All visits are guided (in Polish only) in groups. Tours normally depart at 11am, 1pm and 4pm daily and take about 45 minutes. The temperature in the tunnels is 9°C year-round, so come prepared.

Of the scarce relics of the Jewish legacy, you may want to have a look at the **synagogue** of 1914, on the corner of ul Kopernika and ul Krzywa. It now houses a cafe and a bank. A few steps north, on Plac Kościuszki, is the neoclassical **Orthodox church** built under tsarist rule in the mid-19th century. Services are held on Sunday morning.

Places to Stay

Youth hostel (☎ 564 00 22, ul Czarnieckiego 8) Beds US$3-5. Open year-round. This 50-bed hostel, conveniently located in the centre, has dorms sleeping five to 14 people.

Dom Pielgrzyma (☎ 565 36 56, ul Lubelska 2) Singles with bath US$7, beds in dorms US$4. An interesting budget option, this church facility is just behind the cathedral. It offers two singles and two 25-bed dorms, all with bath.

Pokoje Gościnne MOSiR (☎ 563 02 86, fax 563 00 03, ul I Pułku Szwoleżerów 15A) Doubles with bath US$15-18, triples/quads without bath US$16/22. MOSiR is a simple budget hotel next to the city stadium, beyond the Góra Katedralna.

Hotel Kamena (☎ 565 64 01, fax 565 64 00, Al Armii Krajowej 50) Singles with bath US$25-55, doubles with bath US$30-60. The central Hotel Kamena is the best place in town.

Places to Eat

Bar Staromiejski (☎ 565 43 40, ul Lubelska 68) Mains US$1-2.50. One of the cheapest eateries in town, this milk bar has been revamped and is OK if nothing special.

Restauracja Gęsia Szyja (☎ 565 23 21, ul Lubelska 27) Mains US$3-6. Set in three vaulted cellars, Gęsia Szyja is cosy, quiet and pleasant.

Restauracja Pod Paragrafem (☎ 564 06 10, ul Gdańska 13) Mains US$3-6. This is an agreeable option for a tasty lunch or dinner.

Getting There & Away

Train The town has two train stations: Chełm Miasto 1km west of the Old Town, and Chełm Główny 2km to the north-east. Both are serviced by urban buses. Trains to Lublin (75km) run every hour or two, and there are three fast trains per day to Warsaw; all these trains stop at both stations.

Bus The bus terminal is on ul Lwowska 300m south of the Rynek. PKS buses to Lublin (68km) go roughly every two hours, and there are also private minibuses departing from just outside the terminal. Half a dozen buses a day run to Zamość (62km).

Two fast buses go straight to Warsaw daily (229km).

ZAMOŚĆ

☎ 84 • pop 65,000

The Pearl of the Renaissance, the Padua of the North, the Town of Arcades – that's how local tourist brochures refer to Zamość ('Zah-moshch'). The copywriters may seem a bit over-enthusiastic about the place, but nonetheless this is not your average town. Designed in its entirety four centuries ago, Zamość was built in one go in the middle of the Lublin Upland, and it stands relatively unchanged today. With more than 100 architectural monuments of historical and artistic value, Zamość's Old Town was included on the World Heritage list by Unesco in 1992.

Information

Tourist Office The staff at the Zamojski Ośrodek Informacji Turystycznej (☎ 639 22 92; ☎/fax 627 08 13), in the town hall or Rynek Wielki, are helpful and knowledgeable. The office is open 8am to 6pm Monday to Friday, 10am to 4pm Saturday and 10am to 3pm Sunday from May to September. In other months, it's open 8am to 4.30pm Monday to Friday only.

Money The Bank Pekao, ul Grodzka 2 changes travellers cheques, has an ATM and gives advances on Visa and MasterCard. It also changes cash, as do several central kantors, but rates may be lower than in large cities. There's another useful ATM in the wall of Hotel Zamojski.

Internet & Email Access There are several facilities close to the north of the Old Town (and close to each other), including NetSystem (☎ 639 34 75), ul Peowiaków 9 Optimus (☎ 639 20 56), ul Peowiaków 6 and Kafejka Internetowa (☎ 639 25 21), ul Peowiaków 8. In the Old Town, you can use the computer at the public library in the former synagogue.

Things to See

Zamość is one of those towns in which strolling aimlessly is more fun than walking

Zamość – Zamoyski's Perfect City

Zamość was the brain child of Jan Zamoyski (1542–1605), who was the chancellor of Poland and the commander-in-chief of the armed forces. A Renaissance man, Zamoyski intended to create a perfect city which would at the same time be a great cultural and trading centre and an impregnable fortress.

Having studied in Padua, Zamoyski – like virtually all the Polish aristocracy of the period – was looking for artistic inspiration and models in Italy, not in neighbouring Russia. For his great plan, he commissioned an Italian architect from Padua, Bernardo Morando, who followed the best Italian theories of urban planning of the day in putting Zamoyski's ideas into practice.

The whole project started in 1580 and within 11 years there were already 217 houses built and only 26 plots still empty. Soon afterwards most of the public buildings, including the palace, church, town hall and university, were completed, and the city was encircled with a formidable system of fortifications.

The experiment proved as successful as its founder hoped. The location of the town on the crossroads of the Lublin-Lviv and Kraków-Kyiv trading routes attracted foreign merchants including Armenians, Jews, Greeks, Germans, Scots and Italians, who came to settle here. The Zamoyski Academy, founded in 1594 as the third institution of higher education in Poland, after Kraków and Vilnius, soon became one of the main centres of learning.

The first military test of the fortress came in 1648, when Cossacks raided, the city had no problems defending itself. The town's defensive capabilities were confirmed during the Swedish invasion of 1656, when Zamość was one of only three Polish cities to withstand the Swedish siege (Częstochowa and Gdańsk were the other survivors).

During the partitions, Zamość fell first to Austria but later came under tsarist rule. In the 1820s the Russians further fortified the town, at considerable aesthetic cost. It was then that many of the previously splendid buildings (the palace, academy and the town hall among others) were adapted for military purposes and accordingly were given a uniform, barracks-like appearance. Much of the Renaissance decoration was destroyed during that period and replaced with a dry neoclassical overlay. The defences were abandoned in 1866 and partly dismantled soon afterwards.

During WWII Zamość, renamed by the Germans 'Himmlerstadt', became the centre of Nazi colonisation, the first of its kind on Polish territory. After the brutal expulsion of the Polish population, Germans settled in their place to create what Hitler planned would become the eastern bulwark of the Third Reich. However, they had to flee the Red Army and fortunately didn't manage to destroy the city.

A thorough restoration plan, aimed at bringing back the Renaissance appearance of the town, was launched in 1963 and is ongoing.

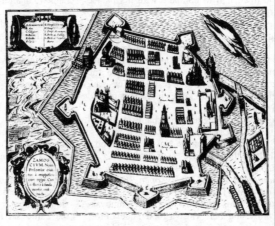

The fortified city of Zamość in approximately 1602

MAŁOPOLSKA

map in hand from one sight to the next. The Old Town is partly a car-free area and only 600m long by 400m wide. It's centred around the square, which is likely to be your starting point.

The original fortifications were altered beyond recognition by the Russians; those on the eastern side of town survived in part, including one of the bastions, and the position of the rest can still be traced by the mound surrounding the Old Town.

Old Town Square Measuring 100m x 100m, the spectacular Renaissance Rynek Wielki is lined with old arcaded burghers' houses, dominated by a lofty **town hall**, built into the northern side of the square. Constructed soon after the town's foundation, it was extended around the mid-17th century and got its curving exterior stairway in 1768.

Each side of the Rynek has eight houses (except for the northern one where half the space is taken by the town hall) and each is bisected by streets designed as the two main axes of the town: one running west-east from the palace to the most important bastion, and the other one oriented north-south, linking three market squares. The town's founder, Jan Zamoyski didn't want the town hall to compete with his palace and interrupt the view, and that's why it doesn't sit, as is usual, in the middle of the square.

Originally, all the houses had decorative parapets on their tops but these were removed in the 1820s; only those on the northern side have been restored. These are the most beautiful houses in the square, and probably always were. As they once belonged to Armenian merchants, you will find some Oriental motifs on their facades.

Two of these houses, Nos 24 and 26, now shelter the **Zamość Museum** (*Muzeum Zamojskie;* ☎ 638 64 94, *ul Ormiańska 30; adult/student US$1/0.50; open 10am-4pm Tues-Sun*). The collection includes archaeological finds and portraits of the Zamoyski family, and there's also a good model of fortified Zamość from the end of the 17th century. Note the original wooden ceilings and decoration around the windows and doors.

Walk through the arcades around the square to see some fine doorways (eg Nos 21 and 25) and the stucco work on the vaults in the vestibules (eg No 10). Go into the old pharmacy of 1609 (No 2). Walk round the square outside the arcades to see the facades.

Around the Old Town The **cathedral**, just south-west of the Rynek, took about 40 years (1587–1628) to complete. The outside form was largely changed in the early 19th century, but the interior has preserved many original features. Note the authentic Lublin-Renaissance-style vault, some good stone and stucco work, and the unusual arcaded organ loft. In the high altar is the rococo silver tabernacle of 1745. The Zamoyski chapel at the head of the right-hand aisle shelters the tomb of the founder. The stairs next to the chapel will take you down to the family crypt (for a nominal entry fee).

Back outside the church, you can go up to the top of the freestanding **bell tower** for a panoramic view, though the terrace is not high enough to provide a good vista over the Old Town and the Rynek. The original tower was made of timber and went up in flames. The present one was built in 1755–75. There are three bells inside, of which the largest, named Jan after the founder, weighs 4300kg and is over three centuries old.

Behind the church is the former vicarage from the 1610s, known as the Infułatka, with its splendid ornate doorway. It leads to the **Religious Museum** (*Muzeum Sakralne; ul Kolegiacka 2; admission US$0.50; open Sun & public holidays 10am-1pm year-round, 10am-4pm Mon-Sat May-Sept*) which features a collection of religious art accumulated by the church.

West from the collegiate church is the old arsenal, which now houses the **Arsenal Museum** (*Muzeum Arsenał;* ☎ 638 40 76, *ul Zamkowa 2; adult/student US$1/0.75; open 10am-4pm Tues-Sun*). There's a lot of old weaponry on permanent display plus occasional temporary exhibitions. To the north is the **Zamoyski Palace** (Pałac Zamoyskich), which was reputedly a splendid residence until it was turned into a military hospital in the 1830s. It's not a tourist sight.

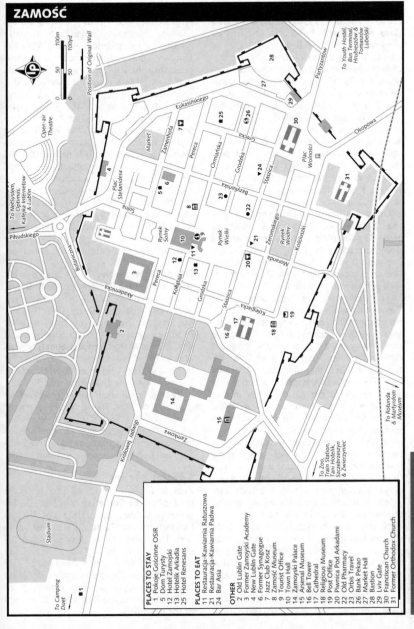

ZAMOŚĆ

PLACES TO STAY
1 Pokoje Gościnne OSiR
5 Dom Turysty
12 Hotel Zamojski
13 Hotelik Arkadia
25 Hotel Renesans

PLACES TO EAT
11 Restauracja-Kawiarnia Ratuszowa
21 Restauracja-Kawiarnia Padwa
24 Bar Asia

OTHER
2 Old Lublin Gate
3 Former Zamoyski Academy
4 New Lublin Gate
6 Former Synagogue
7 Jazz Club Kosz
8 Zamość Museum
9 Tourist Office
10 Town Hall
14 Zamoyski Palace
15 Arsenal Museum
16 Bell Tower
17 Cathedral
18 Religious Museum
19 Post Office
20 Piwnica Pod Arkadami
22 Old Pharmacy
23 Orbis Travel
26 Bank Pekao
27 Market Hall
28 Bastion
29 Lviv Gate
30 Franciscan Church
31 Former Orthodox Church

A partly ruined brick structure just north across ul Królowej Jadwigi is the **Old Lublin Gate** (Stara Brama Lubelska). Just after its construction in 1588 it was walled up to commemorate the victorious battle at Byczyna in which the Austrian Archduke Maximilian, a claimant to the Polish throne, was taken prisoner and triumphantly led under guard into the town through the gate. He was the last person to walk through.

To the east of the gate is the famous **Academy** (Akademia) which, again, lost its style in tsarist times. Behind it you'll find the Rynek Solny, the Salt Market Square. You are now at the back of the town hall. Have a look at the symbol of justice over the gate; there was once a jail inside.

One block east from the Rynek Solny is the Renaissance **synagogue** built in 1610–18, complete with its reconstructed decorative parapets. Today it's a public library; go inside to see the partly surviving stucco decoration and some fragments of wall paintings on the vault.

The area around the Rynek Solny and ul Zamenhofa was once the heart of the Jewish quarter. The Jews were granted permission to settle in Zamość in 1588, and by the mid-19th century they accounted for about 60% of the town's population of 4000. By the eve of WWII their numbers had grown to 12,000 (45% of the total population). In 1941 they were moved to the ghetto that was formed to the west of the Old Town, and by the following year most had been murdered in death camps.

On the eastern edge of the Old Town is the best surviving **bastion** of the seven the town originally had. Guided tours take you through the array of underground passageways. The entrance is from the Hala Targowa Nadszaniec, the building adjacent to the bastion, now an indoor market.

Next to the market is the **Lviv Gate** (Brama Lwowska). It was one of three gateways to the city and, despite later changes, it has kept some of its original decoration including an inscription about the foundation of the town (from its eastern side).

Opposite the gate is the massive **Franciscan Church** (Kościół Franciszkanów).

When built in 1637–65, it was reputedly the largest and one of the most beautiful baroque churches in Poland, yet virtually nothing of its splendour is left. After the Partitions, the Austrians turned it into a hospital; then the Russians used it as an arms depot until 1840, when they remodelled it for barracks, pulling down its magnificent twin baroque towers in the process. Between the wars, the building housed a museum and cinema, and after WWII an art college moved in as soon as the museum found a new location. It wasn't until 1994 that the Franciscans eventually reclaimed the building and made it a church again.

Farther south is the former **Orthodox church**, built in the 1620s by Greek merchants and complemented with a fortified tower half a century later. The church was rebuilt several times but the original stucco decoration of the vault has been preserved.

Other Attractions A 10-minute walk south-west of the Old Town is the **Rotunda**, a ring-shaped fort built in the 1820s as part of the city's defence. During WWII it was used by the Nazis for executions (8000 local residents were executed here), and now it is the **Martyrdom Museum** (*Muzeum Martyrologii; ul Męczenników Rotundy; admission free; open 9am-5pm May-Oct*). It's more a shrine than a museum.

Zamość has a small **zoo** (*Ogród Zoologiczny; ☎ 639 34 70, ul Szczebrzeska 8; adult/student US$1/0.50; open 9am-dusk daily*), which features popular local species and some exotic attractions, including monkeys and tigers. It's opposite the train station.

Special Events

Zamość hosts three annual jazz festivals: the **Jazz on the Borderlands** in June, the **International Meeting of Jazz Vocalists** in October, and the **Zamość Blues Festival** in early December. All the three events are organised by, and take place at, Jazz Club Kosz (☎ 638 60 41), ul Zamenhofa 3.

The Zamość Theatre Summer takes place from mid-June to mid-July with open-air performances on the Rynek Wielki in front of the town hall.

Places to Stay

Camping Duet (*☎/fax 639 24 99, ul Królowej Jadwigi 14*) Tent site US$2 plus US$1.50 per person; singles/doubles/triples/quads in bungalows with bath US$18/22/28/32. The camp site is 800m west of the Old Town. It has all-year bungalows, a restaurant, snack bar, gym, sauna, three tennis courts and a covered swimming pool.

Youth hostel (*☎ 627 91 25, ul Zamoyskiego 4*) Beds US$4-6; open July & Aug. The 50-bed seasonal hostel opens in summer in a school, about 1.5km east of the Old Town, not far from the bus terminal.

Dom Turysty (*☎ 639 26 39, ul Zamenhofa 11*) Doubles without bath US$14; beds in 3- to 6-bed dorms US$6. Very simple and very central, Dom Turysty is the cheapest place to stay in the Old Town, and is good value for the price.

Tani Hotelik (*☎ 639 21 89, ul Śląska 3*) Beds in singles, doubles or triples without bath US$7. Another budget option, but farther away from the centre, Tani Hotelik (literally, Cheap Small Hotel) is 1.5km west of the Old Town, accessible by frequent buses.

Pokoje Gościnne OSiR (*☎/fax 638 60 11, ul Królowej Jadwigi 8*) Singles/doubles/triples/quads with bath US$22/28/32/36, beds in 5- or 6-bed dorm without bath US$7. Another budget option within walking distance of the Old Town, OSiR is a sports hostel and is sometimes full with sports groups.

Hotelik Arkadia (*☎ 638 65 07, Rynek Wielki 9*) Singles/doubles/triples/suites with bath & breakfast US$28/34/40/50. A small hotel in a historic house right on the main plaza, Arkadia has just six rooms, two of which overlook the Rynek. It has a restaurant on the 1st floor.

Hotel Renesans (*☎ 639 20 01, fax 638 51 74, ul Grecka 6*) Singles/doubles with bath & breakfast US$35/48. Less attractive than the Arkadia, Renesans is in an ordinary modern building (why on earth they built it in the Old Town?), yet it's affordable and central, and is more likely to have vacancies. Ask about discount rates on weekends.

Hotel Zamojski (*☎ 639 25 16, fax 639 28 86, ul Kołłątaja 2/4/6*) Singles/doubles/suites with bath & breakfast US$55/75/125. The most recent and posh addition to Zamość's lodging scene, the Orbis-run Hotel Zamojski occupies six restored 16th-century burgher houses next to the Old Town Square. It has two restaurants, which, like the hotel itself, are the finest and most expensive in town.

Places to Eat

There's an increasing number of simple eating outlets appearing around the main plaza and nearby streets, which put tables outside in summer. They serve the usual set of popular dishes such as *flaki*, *barszcz*, sausage, pizza, *pierogi* etc, plus lots of beer. There are also some fancier places, including the hotel restaurants listed above.

Bar Asia (*☎ 639 23 04, ul Staszica 10*) Mains US$1.50-3. This superficially refurbished old-time milk bar continues to serve basic meals at some of the lowest prices around.

Restauracja-Kawiarnia Ratuszowa (*☎ 627 15 57, Rynek Wielki 13*) Mains US$3-5. Located in the town hall, Ratuszowa is one of the cheaper restaurants in the main plaza.

Restauracja-Kawiarnia Padwa (*ul Staszica 23*) Mains US$3-6. Enjoying a pleasant cellar location opposite the town hall, Padwa is one of the more decent places for lunch or dinner.

Entertainment

Piwnica Pod Arkadami (*ul Staszica 25*) One of the first pubs in Zamość, this cellar watering hole with pool tables continues to be a popular haunt often full with the locals.

Jazz Club Kosz (*☎ 638 60 41, ul Zamenhofa 3*) Apart from the jazz festivals (see Special Events earlier in this section), Kosz stages unscheduled jazz concerts and jam sessions if somebody turns up in town. Entrance is from the back of the building.

Getting There & Away

Train The train station is about 1km southwest of the Old Town; walk or take the city bus. There are several slow trains to Lublin (118km) but give them a miss – they take a long, roundabout route. It's much faster to go by bus.

Three ordinary trains go directly to Warsaw (293km), but they take over six hours to get there. Go by bus direct to Warsaw or to Lublin and there change for train. Inquire at the tourist office for timetables.

Bus The bus terminal is 2km east of the centre; frequent city buses link it with the Old Town. Buses to Lublin (89km), either fast or ordinary ones, run roughly every half-hour till about 6pm, and there are also plenty of private minibuses, which are cheaper and faster. There are two morning buses to Rzeszów (148km), passing Łańcut on the way, and one to Przemyśl (148km). Two morning fast buses goes directly to Kraków (318km), one to Sandomierz (157km) and four to Warsaw (247km).

ZWIERZYNIEC
☎ 84 • pop 3800
Zwierzyniec ('Zvyeh-**zhi**-nyets'), 32km south-west of Zamość, developed at the end of the 16th century, when Jan Zamoyski created a game reserve in the area (see the following Roztocze National Park section). Soon afterwards the family's summer residence, complete with a palatial larch-wood villa and a spacious park, was established here. Later a chapel was built on an island on the lake opposite the palace. Meanwhile, a hamlet grew around the residence, eventually developing into a small town. The palace itself was pulled down in 1833.

Things to See
Today Zwierzyniec is essentially the gateway to the Roztocze National Park, housing the park's headquarters and the **Natural History Museum** (*Muzeum Przyrodnicze;* ☎ 687 20 66, ul Plażowa 3; adult/student US$1/0.50; open 9am-5pm Tues-Sun May-Oct, 9am-4pm Tues-Sun Nov-Apr) related to the park. It's on the southern edge of the town, a 10-minute walk from the bus stop.

The only significant structure left of Zamoyski's residential complex is the chapel. Known as the **Chapel upon the Water** (Kaplica na Wodzie), this charming, small baroque church enjoys a spectacular location: it sits on one of the four tiny islets

on the small lake named the Staw Kościelny (Church Pond), and is linked to the mainland by a bridge. The lake is halfway between the bus stop and the museum.

Near the church is the **Zwierzyniec Brewery**, established here in 1806 and producing an excellent beer named – yes, you've guessed it – Zwierzyniec. You probably won't be allowed to visit the facility, but you can at least try their brew, served in the bar at the entrance to the brewery. Don't miss it, as it's almost impossible to find it elsewhere (virtually all the production goes for export).

Places to Stay & Eat
Apart from the places listed below, the town has several holiday centres and plenty of locals rent rooms in their homes – ask around.

Camping Echo (☎ 687 23 14, ul Biłgorajska 3) Tent site US$1.50 plus US$1.50 per person, beds in cabins US$3-4. Open May-Sept. Echo camp site has basic cabins with three and six-bed rooms and a snack bar serving simple meals.

Youth hostel (☎ 687 21 75, ul Partyzantów 3B) Beds US$3. Open July & Aug. The 40-bed summer hostel, in the local school, is basic but cheap.

Hotel Jodła (☎ 687 20 12, fax 687 21 24, ul Parkowa 3A) Beds in doubles, triples or quads without/with bath US$8/9. Jodła is near the bus stop, in a large timber villa, with two side buildings. It's a simple but pleasant place and has a cafe. Meals are available only if requested in advance.

Karczma Młyn (☎ 687 25 27, ul Wachniewskiej 1A) Mains US$3-5. Pleasant and inexpensive, Karczma is possibly the best place around for a lunch or dinner.

Getting There & Away
The bus stop is on ul Zamojska, in the centre of the town. There's a large town map posted beside it, which has the tourist attractions and facilities marked on it. Buses to Zamość (32km) pass pretty regularly, and there are infrequent buses to more distant destinations, including Sandomierz and Rzeszów. The train station is about 1km east of town.

ROZTOCZE NATIONAL PARK
☎ 84

Decreed in 1974, the Roztocze National Park *(Roztoczański Park Narodowy; park's office in Zwierzyniec; ☎ 687 20 70, ul Plażowa 2; admission US$0.50)* covers an area of 79 sq km to the south and east of Zwierzyniec. The site was actually a nature reserve for over 350 years as part of the estates owned by the Zamoyski family. Following the purchase of a vast stretch of land complete with six towns, 149 villages and about 1600 sq km of forest in 1589, Jan Zamoyski created an enclosed game reserve named Zwierzyniec (hence the name of the town). A remarkable achievement at that time, as this was not a hunting ground but a protected area where various species of animals roamed in relative freedom. It was here that the world's last specimens of the original tarpan (see Białowieża National Park in the Mazovia & Podlasie chapter) were kept in the 19th century, until they were given away to the locals when the estate fell into disarray under tsarist rule.

Today's national park includes much of Zamoyski's original reserve. Occupying undulating terrain, 93% of which is covered with forest, the park retains much of its primeval character, with rich and varied flora and fauna. The park is crossed from east to west by the Wieprz, one of the least polluted rivers in the region.

The forest features an interesting mix of plant species typical of the valley as well as of the mountain. A product of different soil types, topography, climate and water sources, it contains a wide variety of trees, including fir, spruce, pine, beech, sycamore, hornbeam, oak, elm and lime. Fir trees in the park reach heights of up to 50m – the tallest in Poland – and beech trees are not much shorter.

The park's fauna is just as diverse. Almost all species of forest animals, including stag, roe deer, boar, fox, marten and badger, live here, and elk, wolves and lynxes show up from time to time. In 1969 beavers were reintroduced, and in 1982 a refuge for tarpans was created.

There are approximately 190 bird species, about 130 of which nest regularly in the park. There is also a rich world of insects, the beetles alone numbering approximately 2000 different species.

Walking Trails

The normal starting point for walks in the park is the town of Zwierzyniec, or more specifically the museum (see the preceding Zwierzyniec section). Here you can buy booklets and maps on the park, and the staff can provide further information. Tarpans can be seen beyond the museum – ask the staff to point out where they are.

The most popular walking path begins from the museum and goes south up to the top of the Bukowa Góra (Beech Mountain) at 306m (a 75m ascent). Just 1.5km long, the path (which is actually a former palace's park lane) gives a good idea of the park's different forest habitats, passing from pine to fir to beech woods at 500m intervals.

There are some side paths branching off from the main one and allowing for a return by a different way. There are also some longer trails, called tourist trails, crossing various parts of the park and providing access to selected areas; they are marked on tourist maps. Inquire at the museum information desk for advice and information.

MAŁOPOLSKA

The Carpathian Mountains

The Carpathian Mountains (Karpaty in Polish) are the highest and largest mountain system in Central Europe, stretching from southern Poland to central Romania. The Polish portion of the Carpathians occupies a 50km to 70km-wide belt along the southern border from Upper Silesia to Ukraine.

Geographically, the Polish Carpathians are made up of rugged mountain ranges that run east-west along the frontier, and a vast stretch of undulating terrain to the north, known as the Pogórze Karpackie, or the Carpathian Foothills. This chapter deals with all the territory lying south of the Kraków-Tarnów-Rzeszów-Przemyśl road.

This is one of the most attractive regions for tourists. Not only is it largely unspoilt, with wooded hills and mountains (a favourite haunt of hikers), but the culture and rural architecture here has preserved more of the traditional forms than seen in other regions. Travelling around you'll still see plenty of old-style timber houses and rustic shingled churches as well as hundreds of tiny roadside chapels and shrines dotting every winding country lane. Here is a Poland to be savoured.

Highlights

- Watch the mysterious Passion play at Easter in Kalwaria Zebrzydowska
- Visit the Łańcut palace with its fabulous art collection
- Examine the splendid icon collection and perhaps Poland's best skansen at Sanok
- Go for a relaxing hike in the Bieszczady
- Tour around charming Catholic, Orthodox and Uniate timber churches scattered about the region
- Explore Nowy Sącz's lovely skansen
- Take a walk through the picturesque Pieniny and an enjoy a raft trip down the Dunajec Gorge
- Hike among the dramatic alpine scenery of the Tatra Mountains

The Carpathian Foothills

The Carpathian Foothills are a green, hilly belt sloping from the true mountains in the south to the valleys of the Vistula and San Rivers to the north. Except for Kalwaria Zebrzydowska, which is usually a round trip from Kraków, most sights in the region are located along the Kraków-Tarnów-Rzeszów-Przemyśl road (and are ordered accordingly, west to east, in this chapter).

KALWARIA ZEBRZYDOWSKA
☎ 33 • pop 4800
One of Poland's major pilgrimage destinations, Kalwaria Zebrzydowska (pronounced

'Kahl-**vah**-ryah Zeb-zhi-**dof**-skah') is set amid hills about 30km south-west of Kraków. The town owes its existence and subsequent fame to the squire of Kraków, Mikołaj Zebrzydowski, who commissioned the church and monastery for the Bernardine Order in 1600. Having seen the resemblance of the area to the site of Jerusalem, he set

THE CARPATHIAN MOUNTAINS

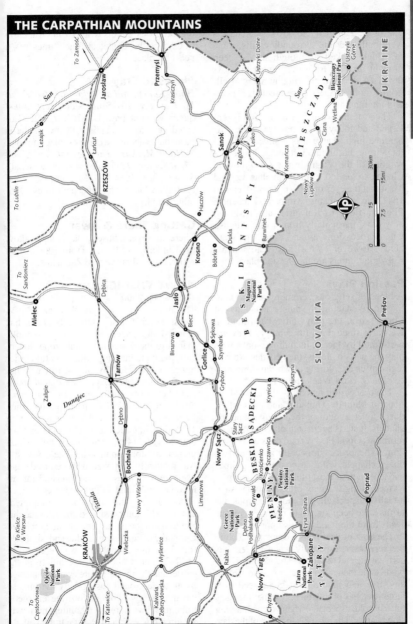

about creating a place of worship similar to that in the Holy City. By 1617, 24 chapels were built over the surrounding hills, some of which looked as though they'd been brought directly from the mother city. As the place attracted growing numbers of pilgrims, more chapels were erected, eventually totalling 40.

The original **church** was gradually enlarged and today it's a massive edifice. Its baroque high altar boasts a silver figure of the Virgin, but the holiest image inside is a painting of the Virgin in the Zebrzydowski Chapel, to the left of the high altar. Legend has it that the eyes of the Virgin shed tears in 1641, and from that time miracles happened. Pilgrims flock to Kalwaria on all Marian holy days, particularly from 13–15 August, when processions around the chapels are held. However, what has really made Kalwaria famous are the Passion plays.

Passion Plays

A blend of religious ceremony and popular theatre, re-enacting the most crucial days of Christ's life, the plays have been held in Kalwaria since the 17th century. They are performed by locals, including monks who play the parts of Jesus, the apostles, Roman legionaries etc, during a two-day-long procession in Holy Week (Easter).

The procession sets off in the early afternoon of Maundy Thursday and goes on till dusk, covering half of the circuit round the chapels. It starts again at about 6am the next morning (Good Friday) and ends at roughly 2pm. The procession calls at about two dozen chapels, with various stopping times and a sermon in most of them. The play performed along the way often becomes such a realistic spectacle that more vigorous pilgrims have been known to rush in to rescue Jesus from the hands of his oppressors.

The time of year adds a dramatic touch to the ceremony, especially when Easter falls early, at the end of winter. The weather is unpredictable then, with snow or rain possible at any time and mud almost guaranteed over large stretches of the route. It sometimes gets bitterly cold, especially when you are moving slowly around the chapels for most of the day.

If your visit coincides with one of the two big religious events you'll find Kalwaria flooded with people; at other times it's a peaceful place.

Places to Stay

Hotel Kalwarianka (☎/fax 876 64 92, ul Mickiewicza 16) Singles/doubles/triples/quads without bath US$10/14/18/22. Located next to the stadium, Kalwarianka is basic but is about the cheapest place around.

Hotel Merkury Tatarscy (☎/fax 867 62 77, ul Sądowa 11) Doubles/triples with bath & breakfast US$40/50. Merkury is a good central option and has cheaper rooms in another building.

Getting There & Away

There are several buses a day from Kraków to Kalwaria (33km). Trains also pass Kalwaria on their way to Zakopane.

NOWY WIŚNICZ
☎ 14 • pop 2500

The little town of Nowy Wiśnicz ('**No**-vi **Veesh**-neech'), just south of Bochnia, has reached the pages of tourist guidebooks thanks to its castle. This well proportioned, early baroque building with graceful corner towers surrounded by massive pentagonal fortifications was designed by Italian architect Matteo Trapola for one of the most powerful men in Poland at the time, Stanisław Lubomirski (1583–1649). It was built in 1615–21 using the foundations and parts of the walls of a 14th-century stronghold which previously stood on this site. The new castle was reputedly very well prepared to defend itself from enemies – it had food and ammunition to withstand a three-year siege.

As soon as the castle was completed, Lubomirski commissioned the same architect to build the monastery for the Discalced Carmelites. Equally splendid and similarly fortified, the monastery was erected in 1622–35 about 500m up the hill from the castle, and the two structures were connected by an underground passage. By the time of the monastery's completion, the energetic Lubomirski was already rebuilding his newly acquired possession, the castle in Łańcut.

Neither the castle nor the monastery enjoyed their beauty and splendour for long. Despite its defensive capabilities, the castle surrendered to the Swedes in 1655 in exchange for the promise that they would not destroy it. They indeed kept their word, but nonetheless thoroughly plundered the interior, taking away some 150 wagonloads of treasure. The castle suffered a series of further misfortunes, including a fire in 1831, which left it in ruins. Only after WWII was restoration undertaken, and this is ongoing. The exterior has already been renovated, but there is still a long way to go on the inside.

The monastery hasn't had a glorious history either. After the Carmelites were expelled in the 1780s, the monastery was turned into a prison and remains so to this day. It's designed for particularly dangerous criminals and is among the best guarded in the country.

Things to See

The **castle** (☎ 612 83 41; adult/student US$1.50/0.75; open 9am-2pm Mon-Fri Sept-Apr, 9am-2pm Mon, 9am-4pm Tues-Thur, 9am-5pm Fri, 10am-5pm Sat, 10am-6pm Sun & public holidays May-Sept) is a 10-minute walk uphill from the town's centre.

All visitors are guided around in groups, so you may have to wait a while for the next tour to depart. The 45-minute tour covers the courtyard and rooms on the two upper floors including the domed chapel, a large hall with a splendid ornate ceiling, and a huge ballroom measuring 30m x 9m and 9m high. There's also the sarcophagus of Stanisław Lubomirski, a small exhibition displaying three models of the castle from different periods and photographic documentation of postwar reconstruction.

The road up the hill from the castle goes to the prison. Halfway along you'll find a fine wooden house called Koryznówka in which Jan Matejko was once a frequent guest. Today it's a modest **museum** (☎ 612 83 47; admission US$0.50; open 10am-2pm Wed-Sun) which features some memorabilia of this most famous Polish history painter.

Famous Polish painter, Jan Matejko, was a regular visitor to Nowy Wiśnicz

In the town centre, near the Rynek, you can visit the **parish church**, also the work of Trapola.

Places to Stay & Eat

Hotel Kmita (☎/fax 612 88 25) Singles/doubles/suites with bath & breakfast US$35/65/100. Installed in the reconstructed building placed on the castle's defensive walls, the Kmita offers 22 beds in good, comfortable rooms and suites. It has its own restaurant, but meals have to be requested in advance.

Hotel Atlas (☎ 612 91 25, ☎/fax 685 59 50) Singles/doubles/triples with bath US$25/34/40. An alternative option to the Kmita, the small Atlas offers 10 neat rooms and also has its own restaurant. Optional breakfast is US$4. The place is 2.5km from Nowy Wiśnicz (3km from the castle), on the road to Bochnia.

There are a few basic eating outlets in the town centre, on and around the Rynek.

Getting There & Away

Nowy Wiśnicz is well serviced from Bochnia (7km) by either hourly suburban Bochnia bus No 12, or the PKS buses running every quarter of an hour or so. Bochnia is on the main Kraków-Tarnów route, with frequent buses and trains to both destinations.

DĘBNO
☎ 014 • pop 1200

Halfway between Bochnia and Tarnów is the small village of Dębno. Though little known and rarely visited, the **castle** here is a good example of a small defensive residence. It was built in the 1470s on the foundations of a previous knights' stronghold, and gradually extended until the 1630s. It was plundered several times since, but the structure survived without major damage. Postwar restoration took more than three decades and the result is admirable – the castle looks much as it would have done 350 years ago.

The castle consists of four two-storey buildings joined at the corners to form a small rectangular courtyard, all surrounded by a moat and ponds, now dry. The structure is adorned with fine corner towers, oriels, bay windows and doorways, which have survived almost intact.

The castle is now a **museum** (☎ 665 85 82; *adult/student US$1/0.50; open 10am-5pm Tues & Thur, 9am-3pm Wed & Fri, 11am-3pm Sat, 11am-5pm Sun Apr-Sept, 10am-4.30pm Tues & Thur, 9am-3pm Wed & Fri, 11am-3pm Sat & Sun Oct-Mar, closed Sat & Sun Dec-Feb*). You can visit a good part of the interior including the cellars. The rooms have been refurnished and have some exhibitions (weapons, paintings, the castle's history). Its small size gives you the refreshing feeling that you are visiting a modest private home, the only two larger rooms being the knights' room and the concert room, the latter serving for occasional piano recitals.

Places to Stay & Eat
Restauracja Agawa (☎ 665 83 17), 1km down the highway toward Tarnów, offers budget food and has 10 rooms upstairs (US$25/34 a double without/with bath). There's another budget eatery, *Restauracja Pod Jesionami*, close to the castle.

Getting There & Away
The castle is an easy stopover on the Kraków-Tarnów highway. There are regular buses on this road, which will let you off at the village centre, from which the castle is just a five-minute walk.

TARNÓW
☎ 14 • pop 125,000

Tarnów ('**Tar**-noof') is an important regional industrial centre, yet you wouldn't notice this while strolling about its pleasant, finely restored Old Town. The city has some attractions and can be a worthwhile stop if you are travelling around the region.

The city map reveals a familiar layout – an oval centre with a large square in its middle – suggesting that the town was planned in medieval times. Tarnów is indeed an old city, its municipal charter was granted in 1330. Developing as a trade centre on the busy Kraków-Kyiv route, the town enjoyed good times in the Renaissance period, and a branch of the Kraków Academy was opened here.

Not uncommonly for the region, Tarnów had a sizable Jewish community, which by the 19th century accounted for half the city's population. Of 20,000 Jews living here in 1939, only a handful survived the war.

Today the city is considered to be one of the major centres for Polish Gypsies. However, Gypsies (or Roma) never settled in Poland in such numbers as they did elsewhere in Europe, say in Spain or Romania, and their total current population in the whole country is thought to be no more than about 20,000. Before WWII there were over 50,000 Roma in Poland but the Nazis treated them the same way as they did the Jews. Of a total of a million Roma living in Europe before the war, the Nazis exterminated over half.

Information
Tourist Offices The Tarnowskie Regionalne Centrum Koordynacji i Obsługi Turystyki (☎ 637 87 35, W www.turystyka.tarnow.pl), Rynek 7, is open 8am to 6pm weekdays (also 9am to 5pm Saturday May to September).

Money Central ATMs include those on Plac Katedralny and Plac Sobieskiego. Travellers cheques can be cashed at Bank Przemysłowo Handlowy at ul Wałowa 10 (note the ornate facade of the building) or Bank Pekao at Plac Kościuszki 4. Kantors are easy to find in the central area.

Email & Internet Access Central facilities include Café Internet Forum (☎ 627 43 46), ul Wekslarska 9, and Salon Multimedialny Maestro, Plac Kazimierza Wielkiego 5.

Things to See

The **Rynek** retains much of its former appearance. The **town hall** in the middle is a familiar combination of Gothic walls and a tower, with Renaissance parapets topping the roof. The Renaissance doorway at the southern side leads to the **Regional Museum** (*Muzeum Okręgowe; ☎ 621 21 49, Rynek 1; adult/student US$1/0.50; open 10am-5pm Tues & Thur, 9am-3pm Wed & Fri, 10am-2pm Sat & Sun*). It features a collection of historic paintings, armoury, furniture, glass and ceramics. The museum's extension, in the arcaded houses on the northern side of the square, Rynek 20/21, has temporary exhibitions.

The **cathedral**, just off the Rynek, dates from the 14th century but it was thoroughly remodelled in the 1890s, eventually mutating into a neo-Gothic edifice. The interior shelters several Renaissance and baroque tombs, of which two in the chancel are among the largest in the country. Also of interest are the 15th-century stalls under the choir loft and two original stone portals – at the southern and western porches – both dating from the early 16th century.

Right behind the cathedral, in a lovely house from 1524, is the **Diocesan Museum** (*Muzeum Diecezjalne; ☎ 621 99 93, Plac Katedralny 6; admission free; open 10am-noon & 1pm-3pm Tues-Sat, 9am-noon & 1pm-2pm Sun & public holidays*). It has a good collection of Gothic sacred art, including some marvellous Madonnas and altarpieces, and an extensive display of folk and religious painting on glass, reputedly the best in the country.

The area east of the Rynek was traditionally inhabited by Jews, but not much original architecture has survived. Of the 17th-century **synagogue** off ul Żydowska, only the brick bimah is left. A more moving sign of the Jewish legacy is the **Jewish Cemetery** (Cmentarz Żydowski), which is a short walk north along ul Nowodąbrowska,

then to the right into ul Słoneczna. The cemetery dates from the 17th century and boasts about 3000 tombstones (the oldest surviving one is from 1734), many fallen or leaning perilously. The original cemetery gate is now on display at the United States Holocaust Memorial Museum in Washington. The cemetery is locked but you can look over the fence from ul Słoneczna. For a closer inspection, ask for the key at the guard desk of the Regional Museum, Rynek 20/21.

Back in the Old Town, stroll along the restored ul Wałowa, lined with fine neoclassical buildings. Closed to traffic, it's a popular rendezvous among the locals. Its curved course follows the line where the medieval moat once was.

The **Ethnographic Museum** (*Muzeum Etnograficzne; ☎ 622 06 25, ul Krakowska 10; adult/student US$1/0.50; open 10am-5pm Tues & Thur, 9am-3pm Wed & Fri, 10am-2pm Sat & Sun*) has a collection of exhibits related to Roma culture. Six Roma caravans can be seen at the back of the museum.

There are two beautiful small wooden churches south of the Old Town. The shingled **St Mary's Church** (Kościół NMP) on ul Konarskiego dates from the 1440s, making it one of the oldest surviving wooden churches in Poland. The interior has charming folk decoration including a fine rococo high altar.

Half a kilometre farther south, behind the cemetery (take ul Tuchowska to get there), is the **Church of the Holy Trinity** (Kościół Św Trójcy), built in 1562, with a similar naively charming rustic interior including an early baroque high altar.

Places to Stay

Camping Nr 202 (*☎ 621 51 24, ul Piłsudskiego 28A*) Tent site US$1 plus US$3 per person; doubles/triples/quads in 4-bed cabins US$14/18/20. Open May-Sept. The camp site is 1km north of the Old Town. It has simple, cheap cabins without bath.

Youth hostel (*☎ 621 69 16, ul Konarskiego 17*) Dorm beds US$4-5. Open year-round. The youth hostel, a five-minute walk south of the Rynek, is simple but clean and well run. It only has large dormitories (for 12 and 16 people). You need to check in before

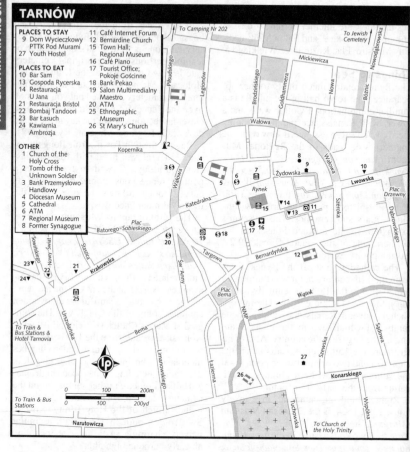

TARNÓW

PLACES TO STAY
9 Dom Wycieczkowy
   PTTK Pod Murami
27 Youth Hostel

PLACES TO EAT
10 Bar Sam
13 Gospoda Rycerska
14 Restauracja
   U Jana
21 Restauracja Bristol
22 Bombaj Tandoori
23 Bar Łasuch
24 Kawiarnia
   Ambrozja

11 Café Internet Forum
12 Bernardine Church
15 Town Hall;
   Regional Museum
16 Café Piano
17 Tourist Office;
   Pokoje Gościnne
18 Bank Pekao
19 Salon Multimedialny
   Maestro
20 ATM
25 Ethnographic
   Museum
26 St Mary's Church

OTHER
1 Church of the
  Holy Cross
2 Tomb of the
  Unknown Soldier
3 Bank Przemysłowo
  Handlowy
4 Diocesan Museum
5 Cathedral
6 ATM
7 Regional Museum
8 Former Synagogue

9pm. From the train station it's a 20-minute walk, or take bus No 1, 8 or 26.

Dom Wycieczkowy PTTK Pod Murami (☎/fax 621 62 29, ul Żydowska 16) Doubles/triples/quads without bath US$20/25 /30, beds in 5- or 6-bed dorms US$7. This simple but acceptable place is in the heart of the Old Town.

Pokoje Gościnne (☎ 627 87 35, fax 627 87 38, Rynek 7) Singles/doubles with bath US$15/22. Rented out by the tourist office, all four rooms are on the top floor and are excellent value. You can book in at reception which is open 24 hours.

Hotel Tarnovia (☎ 621 26 71, fax 621 27 44, ul Kościuszki 10) Singles/doubles with bath & breakfast US$40/55. The three-star Tarnovia, in a modern suburb near the bus and train stations, is one of the best places to stay in the city.

Places to Eat

Bar Łasuch (☎ 627 71 23, ul Sowińskiego 4) Mains US$1-2.50. Łasuch is a modernised milk bar which is nothing particularly special but the food is OK and dirt cheap.

Bar Sam (☎ 627 71 19, ul Lwowska 12) Mains US$1-2.50. Another refurbished milk bar, Sam is conveniently located close to the Old Town.

Kawiarnia Ambrozja (☎ 627 39 32, ul Mościckiego 6) Mains US$3-4. One of the more recent budget eateries, the Ambrozja has an inner patio for dining and drinking in summer.

Gospoda Rycerska (☎ 627 59 80, ul Wekslarska 1) Mains US$3-5. This new pleasant place, just off the Rynek, serves hearty Polish meals.

Restauracja Bristol (☎ 621 22 79, ul Krakowska 9) Mains US$4-6. This intact survivor of the communist era, with its old decor and atmosphere, serves unsophisticated but tasty food at budget prices.

Bombaj Tandoori (☎ 627 38 41, ul Nowy Świat 2) Mains US$4-8. An interesting new addition to the local culinary picture, this fine restaurant offers Indian and Oriental cuisine in elegant surroundings.

Restauracja U Jana (☎ 628 62 80, Rynek 14) Mains US$5-8. A brand-new restaurant in a prime location, U Jana has reasonable food and CK Browar draught beer from Kraków. By the time you read this, there may also be an upmarket hotel here.

Entertainment
Café Piano (☎ 621 92 48, Rynek 9) Set in beautifully decorated cellars, this charming place offers plenty of drinks, a few budget dishes and live jazz on some Friday nights.

Getting There & Away
The train and bus stations are next to each other, south-west of the centre. It's a 20-minute walk to the Old Town, or you can take bus No 2, 9, 30, 32, 35, 37 or 41.

Train Trains to Kraków (78km) run every hour or so; get off in Bochnia if you plan on visiting Nowy Wiśnicz castle. There are regular departures to Rzeszów (80km) and Nowy Sącz (89km), and several trains to Warsaw (396km).

Bus There are frequent buses west to Kraków (86km) and regular departures south-east to both Jasło (58km) and Krosno (83km). For Sandomierz (104km), take any

of the Tarnobrzeg buses which depart every two hours and then change; there is frequent transport between Tarnobrzeg and Sandomierz.

ZALIPIE
☎ 14 • pop 800
The village of Zalipie has been known as a centre for folk painting for almost a century, since its inhabitants started to decorate their houses with colourful floral designs. Actually, they used to adorn almost everything possible: cottages, barns, wells, stoves, tools and furniture.

The best-known painter was Felicja Curyłowa (1904–74), and since her death her farm has been open to the public as a **museum** (☎ 641 19 12; admission US$1; open 10am-4pm Tues-Sun). If you find it locked, ask for the keys in the house across the road.

In order to help maintain the tradition, the 'Painted Cottage' contest for the best decorated house has been held annually since 1948. It takes place just after Corpus Christi (Friday to Sunday), but it's not a tourist event. It's better to visit Zalipie after the contest rather than before, as you'll see fresh paintings.

The **House of Women Painters** (Dom Malarek; ☎ 641 19 38) was opened in 1978 to serve as a centre for the village's artists. A large board in front of the house features a map of the village which shows the location of the decorated houses and the so-called 'trail of the painted farms'. Obviously, don't expect every house to be painted over – there are perhaps a dozen decorated cottages in the whole village.

There are only a few buses from Tarnów daily (31km), and the village spreads over a large area. It's very useful to have your own transport, instead of having to walk around the place. Before setting off, inquire at Tarnów's tourist office and Ethnographic Museum for current information about Zalipie.

RZESZÓW
☎ 17 • pop 155,000
The chief city of south-eastern Poland, Rzeszów ('**Zheh**-shoof') started its life in

the 13th century as an obscure Ruthenian settlement. When in the mid-14th century Kazimierz Wielki captured vast territories of Ruthenia, the town became Polish and acquired its present name. It grew rapidly in the 16th century when Mikołaj Spytek Ligęza, the local ruler, commissioned a castle and a church, and built fortifications. It later fell into the hands of the powerful Lubomirski clan but this couldn't save the town from subsequent gradual decline experienced throughout Poland.

After WWII the new government tried to revive the region and crammed the city with industry and new residential suburbs. The hurried building program increased the size of the town but with little aesthetic consideration. Fortunately, a handful of surviving historic buildings have been restored to their original form, which may give you a reason to visit if you are passing this way.

Information

Tourist Offices The tourist office, ul Asnyka 6, closed down in 2001, but it may reopen (in this or another location) if city authorities arrange funding.

Money Bank Pekao at Al Cieplińskiego 1, opposite Hotel Rzeszów, cashes travellers cheques, gives advances on Visa and MasterCard and also has an ATM. There are several Euronet ATMs around the centre, including ones at Al Piłsudskiego 34, ul Grottgera 10 and on the corner of ul Kościuszki and ul 3 Maja. Cash can be exchanged in kantors, which are in plentiful supply in the centre.

Email & Internet Access Internet access is cheap in Rzeszów (up to US$1 an hour) but connections are rather slow. Central facilities include Kawiarnetka (☎ 852 69 14), ul Bardowskiego 5; Matrix (☎ 853 70 70), ul Mickiewicza 4; Quatro, ul Matejki 2; Net Computers (☎ 852 99 11), ul Zygmuntowska 7; and Tio Media (☎ 852 82 21), Plac Śreniawitów 6. Kawiarnetka is probably the fastest, is open 24 hours, and is no more expensive than the others.

Things to See

Most of the **Rynek** has been restored over recent years, though it will still be a while before the remaining part is completed. In the middle of the square is a monument to Tadeusz Kościuszko. The 16th-century **town hall**, in the corner of the Rynek, was wholly remodelled a century ago in pseudo-Gothic style and looks a bit like a wedding cake.

The city's most recent attraction is the **Underground Tourist Route** (*Podziemna Trasa Turystyczna;* ☎ *862 95 16, Rynek 12, entrance from ul Króla Kazimierza; admission US$1; open 9am-5pm Tues-Thur, 10am-4pm Fri & Sat, noon-5pm Sun*). It took 17 years to link 34 old cellars into a 213m-long route which opened in 2001. The cellars date from various periods (from the 15th to 20th centuries) and are on different levels (the deepest one is nearly 10m below the Rynek's surface). Visits are by half-hour-long guided tours.

The **Ethnographic Museum** (*Muzeum Etnograficzne;* ☎ *862 02 17, Rynek 6; adult/student US$1/0.50; open 9am-2pm Tues-Thur & Sun, 9am-5pm Fri*) has traditional folk costumes and old woodcarvings from the region on permanent display and puts on occasional temporary exhibitions.

The Ethnographic Museum is part of the **Regional Museum** (*Muzeum Okręgowe;* ☎ *853 52 78, ul 3 Maja 19; adult/student US$1.50/1, free Sun; open 10am-5pm Tues & Fri, 10am-3pm Wed & Thur, 9am-2pm Sun*). Housed in the former Piarist monastery, the museum has permanent exhibitions featuring Polish painting from the 18th to 20th centuries, European painting from the 16th to 19th centuries, glass, faïence, and furniture. A bonus attraction is the surviving 17th-century frescoed vaults.

A short walk south, on ul Dekerta, is the early 18th-century baroque **Lubomirski Palace**, the work of Tylman van Gameren, today home to the Academy of Music.

Nearby to the south-west stands the **castle**. Begun at the end of the 16th century, the building has changed a lot since then but the entrance tower and the bastions have retained their original shape. From the 19th century until 1981 the castle served as a

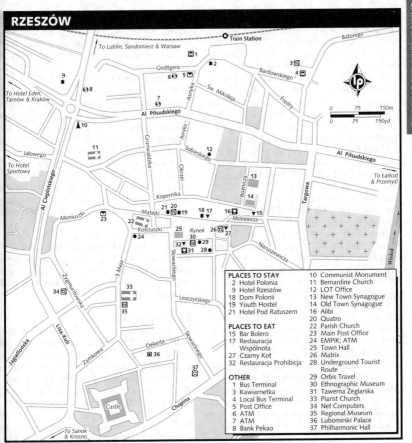

RZESZÓW

PLACES TO STAY
2 Hotel Polonia
9 Hotel Rzeszów
18 Dom Polonii
19 Youth Hostel
21 Hotel Pod Ratuszem

PLACES TO EAT
15 Bar Bolero
17 Restauracja
   Wspólnota
27 Czarny Kot
32 Restauracja Prohibicja

OTHER
1 Bus Terminal
3 Kawiarnetka
4 Local Bus Terminal
5 Post Office
6 ATM
7 ATM
8 Bank Pekao

10 Communist Monument
11 Bernardine Church
12 LOT Office
13 New Town Synagogue
14 Old Town Synagogue
16 Alibi
20 Quatro
22 Parish Church
23 Main Post Office
24 EMPiK; ATM
25 Town Hall
26 Matrix
28 Underground Tourist
   Route
29 Orbis Travel
30 Ethnographic Museum
31 Tawerna Żeglarska
33 Piarist Church
34 Net Computers
35 Regional Museum
36 Lubomirski Palace
37 Philharmonic Hall

jail, among its inmates were several political prisoners. It was solidly renovated in the '90s and houses the law court.

Return north to the **Bernardine Church** (Kościół Bernardynów), with its opulent furnishing and decoration. It was built for Ligęza as his mausoleum, and there are life-size alabaster effigies of his family in the side walls of the chancel. In the gilded chapel to the right is the early 16th-century statue of the Virgin Mary to whom numerous miracles have been attributed; intriguing wall paintings on both sides depict a hundred people who were cured.

Go eastwards to ul Bożnicza where two synagogues stand close to each other. Though less attractive from the outside, the 18th-century **New Town Synagogue** (*Synagoga Nowomiejska; ☎ 853 38 11, ul Sobieskiego 18*) has more to offer on the inside as it holds an art gallery. Note the entrance to its cafe on the 1st floor, it's the work of the contemporary sculptor Marian Kruczek. The 17th-century **Old Town Synagogue** (*Synagoga Staromiejska; ul Bożnicza 4*) now houses the city's registry and is also a centre for studies on the history of local Jews.

Places to Stay

Youth hostel (☎ 853 44 30, Rynek 25) Beds US$5-8. Open year-round. This is the cheapest and most central option – right on the main square. It has some doubles and triples but most beds are in larger dorms.

Hotel Sportowy (☎ 853 40 77, ul Jałowego 23A) Doubles without/with bath US$14/20. Located in a sports complex a short, 10-minute walk west of the Rynek, Sportowy is a good budget choice.

Hotel Eden (☎ 852 56 83, ul Krakowska 150) Beds in doubles, triples or quads without/with bath US$7/11. Open year-round. Eden is a student hostel which offers reasonable standards, but it's a long way from the centre. Westbound bus No 1 or 22 from Al Piłsudskiego will take you there.

Hotel Polonia (☎ 852 03 12, fax 862 46 03, ul Grottgera 16) Singles/doubles/triples with bath US$28/36/40. Polonia has been revamped and is OK, though its location right opposite the train station is not the most picturesque or quiet.

Hotel Pod Ratuszem (☎ 852 97 80, ☎/fax 852 97 70, ul Matejki 8) Singles/doubles with bath & breakfast US$35/50. This new, perfectly central hotel offers 13 neat, if rather small, rooms.

Dom Polonii (☎ 862 14 51, ☎/fax 862 14 52, Rynek 19) Singles/doubles US$35/60. Another very central option, Dom Polonii has just two single rooms and two double suites (the suites overlook the Rynek). It's good value, though it's not easy to find a vacancy here.

Hotel Rzeszów (☎ 852 34 41, fax 853 33 89, Al Cieplińskiego 2) Singles/doubles with bath & breakfast US$50/70. Although located in a drab building, this hotel offers possibly the best facilities in the town centre. If you take a front room, you'll have a good view from your window of the huge monument erected 'in memory of the heroes of the revolutionary struggles for the People's Poland', a legacy of the communist fantasy, but now a dilemma for the authorities.

Places to Eat

Bar Bolero (☎ 852 02 49, ul Mickiewicza 19) Mains US$1.50-3.50. One of the best addresses for a tasty budget meal in the centre, Bolero is a pleasant place offering an extensive menu including salads, and has a nonsmoking area downstairs in a vaulted cellar.

Restauracja Prohibicja (☎ 852 79 80, Rynek 5) Mains US$7-12. One in a new chain expanding across Poland, the Prohibicja has a mostly European menu, though there are some exotic additions such as genuine imported Argentinian beef. The restaurant has a pleasant basement pub section.

Czarny Kot (Black Cat; ☎ 852 31 79, ul Mickiewicza 4) Mains US$7-12. Another attractive restaurant-cum-pub, this large, two-level labyrinthine place with many tiny cosy rooms offers an exceptionally long, 25-page menu.

Restauracja Wspólnota (☎ 862 92 29, Rynek 18) Mains US$6-10. Not as trendy or attractive as the Black Cat, the Wspólnota also has a spacious interior split into several rooms, long menu, generous portions and reasonable prices.

Entertainment

The pub sections of the previously listed **Restauracja Prohibicja** and **Czarny Kot** are among the most attractive places for a drink. Particularly amazing is the latter – fantastic brick vaulted cellars, quite possibly the best in town. Discos are held here most nights till late. You can also try:

Alibi (☎ 852 93 33, ul Mickiewicza 13) This modern restaurant-cum-nightclub has discos on most nights and can be an alternative place to the Black Cat for some night dancing.

Tawerna Żeglarska (☎ 862 02 39, Rynek 6, entrance from ul Króla Kazimierza) Frequented by students, this 'Sailors' Tavern' often hosts musical evenings.

Getting There & Away

The train and bus stations are next to each other and only about 500m from the Rynek. Rzeszów is an important transport hub and there are a lot of buses and trains in all directions. The airport is in Jasionka, 11km north of the city, accessible by bus No 14 from Al Piłsudskiego.

Air From late March to late October, there are flights to Warsaw daily, Rzeszów's only direct air link. In the remaining period, there may be only a few flights per week. The LOT office (☎ 862 03 47), Plac Ofiar Getta 6, will book and sell tickets.

Train There are about 20 trains to Przemyśl daily (87km) and the same number to Tarnów (80km). A dozen trains a day leave for Kraków (158km) and eight for Jasło (71km). To Warsaw (326km), there are two morning express trains and one evening fast train. There's also one train to Lviv which continues to Kyiv.

Bus PKS buses leave regularly throughout the day to Sanok (76km), Krosno (59km), Przemyśl (84km) and Lublin (170km). Six buses go to Ustrzyki Dolne daily (116km) and two of them continue up to Ustrzyki Górne (163km). There are two fast buses to Zamość (163km). Buses to Łańcut (17km) run roughly every half-hour and are more convenient than trains, as they deposit you near the palace.

ŁAŃCUT
☎ 17 • pop 18,000

Łańcut ('**Wine**-tsoot') is famous for its castle, which is arguably the best-known aristocratic home to be found anywhere in Poland. It's one of the largest residences of its kind and holds an extensive and diverse collection of art.

The building started life in the 15th century but it was Stanisław Lubomirski who made it a great residence, a palace rather than a castle. Soon after he had successfully completed his beautiful Nowy Wiśnicz castle, he came into possession of the large property of Łańcut and commissioned Matteo Trapola to design a new home even more spectacular than the old one. It was built in 1629–41 and surrounded with a system of fortifications laid out in the shape of a five-pointed star, modelled on the latest Italian theories of the day.

Some 150 years later the fortifications were partly demolished while the castle was reshaped in rococo and neoclassical style.

The last important alteration, executed at the end of the 19th century, gave the building its neobaroque facades, basically the form which survives today.

A fabulous collection of art was accumulated in the castle over the centuries. The last private owner, Alfred Potocki, was regarded as one of the richest men in prewar Poland. Shortly before the arrival of the Red Army in July 1944, he loaded 11 railway carriages with the most valuable objects and fled with the collection to Liechtenstein.

Things to See
Just after WWII, the castle was taken over by the state and opened as a **castle museum** (☎ 225 20 08, ul Zamkowa 1; adult/student US$4/2.50; open 9am-4pm Tues-Sun Feb-Mar & Oct-Nov, 9am-4pm Tues-Sat, 9am-5pm Sun Apr-Sept), which suggests that there must have been enough works of art left to put on display. The collection has systematically been enlarged and supplemented, and today it conveys the impression of being bigger than before the war. In fact the rooms are so crammed that it's virtually impossible to take it all in on one visit.

The castle is visited in groups accompanied by a guide, and the tour takes from 1½ to two hours. The last tours depart one hour before closing times, but try to avoid them as they tend to rush at breakneck speed to visit the complex in an hour. Guides speaking English, French and German are available for US$25 per group (plus tickets). Book your guide a day or two in advance. In summer, there are many individual foreign visitors and package bus excursions, and you can often tag along with one of these groups and share costs.

You'll be shown around the whole 1st floor and the western side of the ground floor, altogether about 50 castle rooms. In the carefully restored original interiors – representing various styles and periods – you will find heaps of paintings, sculptures and *objets d'art* of all description. The 18th-century theatre (reshaped later), the ballroom, and the dining room with a table that seats 80 people are among the highlights. Brochures in English are available.

After viewing the castle's rooms, you'll be shown around the **orangery** adjoining the castle, and then will go to see Potocki's collection of 55 **carriages**, in the coach house, south of the castle. A further 75 old, horse-drawn vehicles have been acquired by the museum since WWII, making this one of the largest collections of its kind. Both the orangery and carriages are visited on the same ticket as the castle, with the same guided tour.

You can then individually visit a **collection of icons** *(adult/student US$0.75/0.50; same opening hours as the castle museum)*. There are over 1000 icons here, from the 15th century onwards, but this is essentially a storage facility and only a small portion is on display.

The castle is surrounded by a well-kept **park** *(admission free; open 7am-dusk)*.

Just outside the park to the west is the **synagogue** *(admission US$1; open 10.30am-4.30pm Tues-Sun 15 June-30 Sept)*. Built in the 1760s, the synagogue has retained much of its original decoration. It can be visited in other months but you will need to request this a few days in advance by faxing 225 20 12.

Special Events
In May, the **Old Music Festival** is held in Łańcut for about 10 days, with chamber music concerts performed in the castle ballroom. The festival has gained a high reputation and, given the limited capacity of the auditorium, tickets sell out fast. The castle is closed to visitors during the festival.

Places to Stay & Eat
Hotel Zamkowy *(☎ 225 26 71, ☎/fax 225 26 72, ul Zamkowa 1)* Doubles/triples without bath US$16/24, with bath US$45/50. Located in the castle, the hotel is quite simple but OK and cheap, unless you need a room with bath. It may be hard to find a vacancy here in summer. The hotel's *Restauracja Zamkowa*, across the small courtyard, has acceptable food at reasonable prices.

Dom Wycieczkowy PTTK *(☎ 225 45 12, ☎/fax 225 31 84, ul Dominikańska 1)* Bed US$7 per person in doubles, US$6 in triples or quads, US$5 in larger rooms. This 50-bed hostel, in the former Dominican monastery just off Łańcut's Rynek, offers simple rooms without bath to sleep from two to 10 people. It has its own restaurant.

Hotelik Pałacyk *(☎/fax 225 20 43, ul Paderewskiego 18)* Doubles with bath US$34, suite US$50. About 200m south of the synagogue, the Pałacyk (literally, small palace) is set in a small palace-like mansion and is a pleasant place to stay. It has six doubles and a suite, plus its own restaurant.

Hotelik Szwadron *(☎/fax 225 60 42, ul Mickiewicza 16)* Singles/doubles/triples with bath & breakfast US$35/40/55. About 300m beyond the Pałacyk and housed in another historic mansion (from 1784), the Szwadron has 10 rooms and a restaurant – another agreeable family-run place for the night.

Getting There & Away
The bus terminal is 500m north-east of the castle while the train station is about 2km north; it's therefore more convenient to arrive and depart by bus.

Buses and trains to Rzeszów (17km) run roughly every half-hour, and to Przemyśl (67km) every hour or two. Three buses a day go to Zamość (157km).

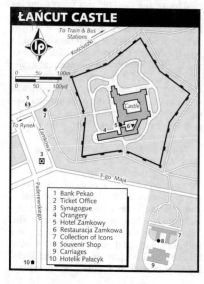

ŁAŃCUT CASTLE

To Train & Bus Stations
Kościuszki
0   50   100m
0   50   100yd
To Rynek
Zamkowa
Castle
3-go Maja
Paderewskiego

1 Bank Pekao
2 Ticket Office
3 Synagogue
4 Orangery
5 Hotel Zamkowy
6 Restauracja Zamkowa
7 Collection of Icons
8 Souvenir Shop
9 Carriages
10 Hotelik Pałacyk

PRZEMYŚL

☎ 16 • pop 70,000

Founded in the 10th century on terrain long fought over by Poland and Ruthenia, Przemyśl ('**Psheh**-mishl') changed hands several times before being annexed by the Polish Crown in 1340. It experienced its golden period in the 16th century, and declined afterwards. During the Partitions it fell under Austrian administration.

Around 1850 the Austrians began to fortify Przemyśl. This work continued right up till the outbreak of WWI, producing one of the largest fortresses in Europe, perhaps the second-biggest after Verdun. It consisted of a double ring of earth ramparts, including a 15km-long inner circle and an outer girdle three times longer, with over 60 forts placed at strategic points. This formidable system played an important role during WWI but nevertheless the garrison surrendered to the Russians in 1915 due to lack of provisions.

At the end of WWII, only 60% of Przemyśl's buildings were left. The major historic monuments in the Old Town were restored, while new districts sprang up on the opposite (northern) side of the San River.

Information

Tourist Offices The Centrum Informacji Turystycznej (☎/fax 675 16 64, **W** www.um .przemysl.pl), Rynek 26, is open 9am to 5pm weekdays, 9am to 1pm Saturday.

Money Bank Pekao branches at ul Jagiellońska 7 and ul Mickiewicza 6 handle travellers cheque transactions and have useful ATMs, and you'll find more ATMs around the Old Town. There are several kantors in the centre, some of which may offer poor exchange rates; shop around.

Email & Internet Access Try the Internet Game Cafe, ul Ratuszowa 8, though it's not very fast. Alternatively check the Internet service in the Miejska Biblioteka Publiczna (City Public Library) in the old synagogue at ul Słowackiego 15. If you're staying in the youth hostel, the Portal cybercafe in the Archiwum (Registry) building at ul Lelewela 4, is just a few paces away.

Things to See

Perched on a hillside and dominated by four mighty churches, the Old Town is a picturesque place, pleasant for leisurely strolls. The sloping **Rynek** has preserved some of its old arcaded houses, mostly on its southern and northern sides.

The **Franciscan Church** (Kościół Franciszkański), just off the Rynek, was built in 1754–78 in late baroque style, but its monumental facade was remade later. The church has a beautiful interior with florid baroque decoration of both the altars and vault.

Just up the hill behind it stands the former **Jesuit Church** (Kościół Pojezuicki). Built in 1627–59, it's also a baroque construction, and it has its original facade. The church now serves the Uniate congregation. All the Catholic fittings have been removed and replaced with decoration related to the Eastern rite, principally the heavily gilded iconostasis.

The adjacent former Jesuit college shelters the **Archdiocesan Museum** (*Muzeum Archidiecezjalne; ☎ 678 27 92, Plac Czackiego 2; admission free; open 10am-3pm daily May-Oct*), which contains religious art.

Up the hill is one more house of worship, the **Carmelite Church** (Kościół Karmelitów). Designed by Italian architect Galeazzo Appiani (who also built Krasiczyn castle – see later in this section), the church has preserved some of its original features, including the main doorway and stucco work on the vaulting. Note the large wooden pulpit in the shape of a boat complete with mast, sail and rigging.

A few steps down from the church is the **Regional Museum** (*Muzeum Ziemi Przemyskiej; ☎ 678 33 25, Plac Czackiego 3; adult/student US$1/0.50, free Sun; open 10.30am-5.30pm Tues & Fri, 10am-2pm Wed, Thur, Sat & Sun*). It displays a fine selection of about 80 Ruthenian icons (of over 500 pieces in the museum's collection assembled from the region). You'll also come across ethnographic and archaeological galleries.

A short walk west along ul Katedralna is the **cathedral** with its 71m-high freestanding bell tower. Originally a Gothic building

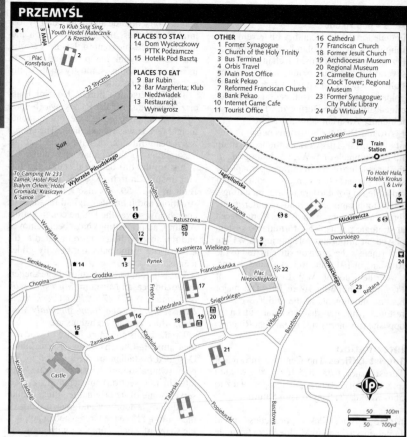

PRZEMYŚL

PLACES TO STAY
14 Dom Wycieczkowy PTTK Podzamcze
15 Hotelik Pod Basztą

PLACES TO EAT
9 Bar Rubin
12 Bar Margherita; Klub Niedźwiadek
13 Restauracja Wyrwigrosz

OTHER
1 Former Synagogue
2 Church of the Holy Trinity
3 Bus Terminal
4 Orbis Travel
5 Main Post Office
6 Bank Pekao
7 Reformed Franciscan Church
8 Bank Pekao
10 Internet Game Cafe
11 Tourist Office

16 Cathedral
17 Franciscan Church
18 Former Jesuit Church
19 Archdiocesan Museum
20 Regional Museum
21 Carmelite Church
22 Clock Tower; Regional Museum
23 Former Synagogue; City Public Library
24 Pub Wirtualny

(still visible in the vault in the chancel), the church was remodelled on various occasions and is now predominantly baroque.

Continue up the same street to the **castle**, or rather what is left of it. Built by Kazimierz Wielki in the 1340s, it mutated into a Renaissance building two centuries later when it got its four corner towers. Two of them have been repaired along with one side of the castle. A local theatre, Teatr Fredreum, and a cafe now occupy the restored rooms. One of the towers is open to visitors in summer, but the view over the Old Town is obscured by trees.

A much better view is from the top of the **Clock Tower** (*Wieża Zegarowa;* ☎ 678 96 66, ul Władycze 3; adult/student US$1/0.50; open 10.30am-5.30pm Tues & Fri, 10am-2pm Wed, Thur, Sat & Sun). Built in 1775–77, this solitary baroque structure was used from 1905 to 1983 as a watchtower by the local fire brigade. Now it's part of the Regional Museum, which, apart from splendid vistas over the Old Town, has interesting collections of bells and pipes, both unique in Poland.

Those interested in war matters may want to see the famous **fortifications**. However, as these were mostly earth ramparts, they are overgrown with grass and bushes and now resemble natural rather than artificial bulwarks. If you want to see what's left anyway, perhaps the best places to go are Siedliska (Fort I), Łętownia (Fort VIII) and Bolestraszyce (Fort XIII). The tourist office can give you information about these sites and transport details.

The only significant relics of the Jewish legacy are two synagogues (of four existing before WWII), both dating from the turn of the 19th/20th centuries, renovated after the war and given other uses. One is off the Plac Konstytucji on the northern side of the San River; the other (now the city public library) is on ul Słowackiego.

Places to Stay

Camping Nr 233 Zamek (*☎/fax 675 02 65, Wybrzeże Piłsudskiego 8A)* Tent site US$3 plus US$2 per person; doubles/triples/ quads in all-year cabins with bath US$18/ 20/24, beds in seasonal cabins without bath US$5. The camp site is reasonably close to the centre. Seasonal cabins are open May to September.

Youth Hostel Matecznik (*☎/fax 670 61 45, ul Lelewela 6)* Beds US$4-6. Open year-round. This good hostel is a 15-minute walk from the Old Town, or take one of the frequent city buses.

Dom Wycieczkowy PTTK Podzamcze (*☎ 678 53 74, ☎/fax 678 32 74, ul Waygarta 3)* Doubles without bath US$15, dorm beds US$5-6. Conveniently located just one block from the Rynek, the PTTK hostel has rooms with bunks and shared facilities only.

Hotelik Pod Basztą (*☎ 678 82 68, ul Królowej Jadwigi 4)* Singles/doubles/triples without bath US$14/18/24. Enjoying a quiet, central location, this small hotel offers one single, five doubles and one triple. Rooms don't have private facilities.

Hotel Hala (*☎/fax 678 38 49, ul Mickiewicza 30)* Singles/doubles/triples/quads without bath US$14/16/20/24, with bath US$18/22/26/30. The 92-bed sports hotel Hala has fairly simple facilities. It's a 10-minute walk east from the train station, away from the Old Town.

Hotelik Krokus (*☎/fax 678 51 27, ul Mickiewicza 47)* Singles/doubles/triples/quads with bath US$18/24/28/32. Some 200m farther east from the Hala, the Hotel Krokus provides reasonable standards in rooms private facilities.

Hotel Pod Białym Orłem (*☎/fax 678 61 07, ul Sanocka 13)* Doubles/triples with bath & breakfast US$34/38. Located about 1km west of the Old Town, this 16-room hotel is an affordable option with private facilities within an easy walking distance from the Old Town.

Hotel Gromada (*☎ 676 11 11, fax 676 11 13, Wybrzeże Piłsudskiego 4)* Singles/ doubles/triples with bath & breakfast US$45/70/85. A top-end central addition to the city's accommodation scene, the three-star Gromada has 116 comfortable rooms and its own restaurant.

Places to Eat

Bar Margherita (*☎ 678 49 94, Rynek 1)* Mains US$1.50-3. This inviting place has a long and interesting menu and is one of the cheapest eateries around.

Bar Rubin (*☎ 678 25 78, ul Kazimierza Wielkiego 19)* Mains US$2-5. This small and friendly family restaurant is one of the best places to grab a bite to eat in the Old Town, with tasty Polish food at very affordable prices. There are only seven tables, so you may well have to wait a few minutes in the mid-afternoon, but it's definitely worth it.

Restauracja Wyrwigrosz (*☎ 678 58 58, Rynek 20)* Mains US$3-5. For a break from Polish cuisine, this restaurant-cum-pub offers budget Oriental-style food. It has a pleasant outdoor eating/drinking area in summer, with comfortable wicker chairs and a view over the Rynek.

Entertainment

As mentioned above, the *Restauracja Wyrwigrosz* is a good place for a drink. Alternatively, you may try the new, modern *Pub Wirtualny* (*☎ 676 04 70, ul Dworskiego 12)*, which also has an outdoor section.

Klub Niedźwiadek (*☎ 678 32 85, Rynek 1)* Sharing the locale with Bar Margherita, this cafe-bar may have occasional live music, mostly jazz.

Klub Sing Sing (☎ *677 05 00, ul 3 Maja 19*) Occupying a spacious basement of the Dom Handlowy Szpak, a shopping centre 200m past Plac Konstytucji, Sing Sing has a restaurant, bar, pizzeria, pool tables and one of the trendiest discos in town.

Getting There & Away

The train and bus stations are next to each other, on the north-eastern edge of the centre.

Train Trains to Rzeszów (87km) depart regularly throughout the day. There are half a dozen fast trains and two express trains a day to Kraków (245km). One express and two fast trains go to Warsaw daily (414km), and one fast train to Lublin (241km). International trains to Lviv, Odesa and Kyiv pass via Przemyśl. There are no trains to Ustrzyki Dolne any more.

Have a look at the station building, a neo-baroque piece of architecture, now a historic monument. Built in 1895, it retains some of its decoration, both inside and out.

Bus At least five buses run to Sanok daily (63km) and three to Ustrzyki Dolne (77km). There are about 10 buses a day to Rzeszów (84km). Half a dozen buses go to Lviv daily (95km, US$4, three hours).

KRASICZYN
☎ 16 • pop 1000

No-one would notice the small village of Krasiczyn ('Krah-**shee**-chin') if not for its **castle** (☎ *671 83 16; adult/student US$1.50/ 1; open for tours only*), a late Renaissance construction acclaimed as one of the finest of its kind in the country. It's in a spacious landscaped **park** *(open dawn-dusk daily)* abounding with a variety of trees and shrubs.

The castle was designed by an Italian, Galleazzo Appiani, and built between 1592 and 1618 for the rich Krasicki family. Despite numerous wars and fires it has somehow retained most of its original features though not in good shape. It was partly restored over recent decades.

The castle is more or less square, built around a spacious, partly arcaded courtyard with four different cylindrical corner towers. They were supposed to reflect the social order of the period and were named (clockwise from the south-western corner) after God, the pope, the king and the nobility. The God tower, topped with a dome, houses a chapel. The fifth, square tower, in the middle of the western side, served as the main entrance to the castle and is accessible by a long arcaded bridge over a wide moat.

Tourists can visit the courtyard and three of the corner towers in summer. Visits are in groups with a guide, which depart a few times a day (at 9am, 11am, 1pm and 3pm at the time of writing).

Places to Stay & Eat

Hotel Zamkowy (☎ *671 83 21, ☎/fax 671 8. 16*) Singles US$30-50, doubles US$50-70, triples US$60-80, suites US$60-150. The Hotel Zamkowy, next to the castle, offers comfortable rooms with bath. Discount weekend rates may be available outside the summer season. The hotel has a gym, sauna and a restaurant, located in the castle itself.

Getting There & Away

The castle is a short round trip from Przemyśl (10km) on one of the regular suburban No 40 or PKS buses. You can continue from Krasiczyn to Sanok (55km, four daily) or Ustrzyki Dolne (67km, three daily).

The Bieszczady

The Bieszczady ('Byesh-**chah**-di') is a wild, scantily populated mountain region of thick forests and open meadows. It's in the far south-eastern corner of Poland, sandwiched between the Ukrainian and Slovakian borders. Largely unspoilt and unpolluted, it's one of the most attractive areas in the country. As tourist facilities are modest, roads sparse and public transport limited, the Bieszczady retains its relative isolation and makes for an off-the-beaten-track destination. It's popular with nature lovers and hikers. Large scale tourism hasn't yet arrived

In geographical terms, the Bieszczady is a mountain system running east-west for some 50km along Poland's southern frontier, and lower hills to the north, referred to as the Przedgórze Bieszczadzkie, or the foothills. In practical terms, the Bieszczady is the whole area to the south-east of the Nowy Łupków-Zagórz-Ustrzyki Dolne railway line, up to the national borders: approximately 2100 sq km, about 60% of which is forest, largely fir and beech. Trees survive only to an altitude of about 1200m, above which you find the *połoniny*, steppe-like pastures that are particularly lush in June.

The highest and most spectacular part has been decreed the Bieszczady National Park (Bieszczadzki Park Narodowy), and at 271 sq km it's Poland's third-largest national park after Biebrza and Kampinos. The highest peak is Mt Tarnica (1346m).

The region was once much more densely populated than it is today – and not by Poles, but by ethnic groups known as Boyks and Lemks. See the boxed text 'The Boyks & the Lemks – Variations on a Theme' for more about them. Visit the skansen in Sanok, which has some good examples of Boyk and Lemk architecture.

SANOK
☎ 13 • pop 40,000

For the average Pole, Sanok brings to mind the *Autosan* – the locally produced bus. It's the type used in intercity and urban transport throughout the country. The bus factory, along with several other plants, make the town an important regional industrial centre. Don't let this put you off, however. Sanok has some important attractions well worth visiting.

Information
Tourist Offices In the absence of a municipal tourist office, the PTTK office (☎ 463 21 71, ☎/fax 463 25 12), ul 3 Maja 2, performs this role. It's open 8am to 4pm weekdays.

Money Bank Pekao's branches at ul Mickiewicza 29 and ul Kościuszki 4 change travellers cheques and have ATMs. There are half a dozen kantors on ul Kościuszki in the vicinity of the latter Pekao branch, and more in the centre.

Things to See
One of Sanok's star attractions is the **Historical Museum** *(Muzeum Historyczne; ☎ 464 13 66, ul Zamkowa 2; adult/student US$1.50/1; open noon-3pm Mon, 9am-5pm Tues-Sun 16 June-15 Sept, noon-3pm Mon, 9am-5pm Tues & Wed, 9am-3pm Thur-Sun 16 Sept-15 Jun)*. Housed in a 16th-century castle, thoroughly refurbished over recent years, the museum has several sections, of which the highlight is a 700-piece collection of Ruthenian icons, the best in Poland. The selection on display consists of about 450 pieces, dating from the 15th to 18th centuries. They are displayed in roughly chronological order, so you can study the evolution of the style: the pure, somewhat unreal early images gradually giving way to the greater realism of later icons showing the Roman Catholic influence. Most icons were acquired after WWII from abandoned Uniate churches. If you are particularly interested in icons, note that there are also collections in Przemyśl, Łańcut, Nowy Sącz and in Sanok's skansen.

The museum's other treasure is the collection of paintings by Zdzisław Beksiński, presented on the castle's top floor. Beksiński is one of Poland's most remarkable contemporary painters, who was born in and lived in Sanok. The exhibition features 90-odd paintings, including some of his best works.

Another place you shouldn't miss is the local skansen, the **Museum of Folk Architecture** *(Muzeum Budownictwa Ludowego; ☎ 463 16 72, ul Rybickiego 3; admission US$2/1; open 9am-4pm daily Apr & Oct, 8am-6pm daily May-Sept, 9am-2pm daily Nov-Mar)*, 1.5km north of the centre.

Poland's largest open-air museum, it has gathered about 120 traditional buildings from the south-east of the country and provides an insight into the culture of the Boyks and Lemks. Among the buildings, there are four beautiful timber churches (one Catholic and three Orthodox/Uniate ones), an inn, a school and even a fire brigade station. The

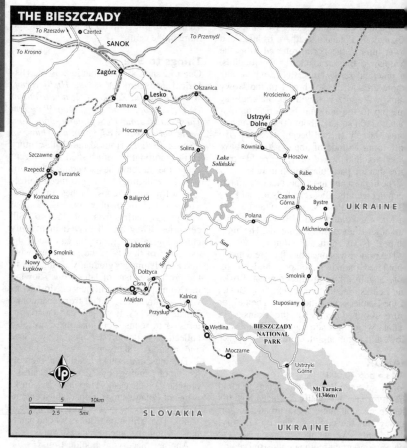

THE BIESZCZADY

To Rzeszów • Czertez
To Przemyśl
SANOK
To Krosno
Zagórz
Olszanica
Lesko
Krościenko
Tarnawa
San
Ustrzyki Dolne
Hoczew
Solina
Równia
Hoszów
Szczawne
Lake Solińskie
Rzepedź • Turzańsk
Rabe
Komańcza
Baligród
Czarna Górna
Żłobek
Bystre
UKRAINE
Polana
San
Michniowiec
Jabłonki
Solinka
Smolnik
Smolnik
Nowy Łupków
Dołżyca
Cisna
Stuposiany
Majdan
Kalnica
Przysłup
BIESZCZADY NATIONAL PARK
Wetlina
Moczarne
Ustrzyki Górne
▲ Mt Tarnica (1346m)

0   5   10km
0   2.5   5mi

SLOVAKIA
UKRAINE

interiors of many cottages are furnished and decorated as they once were, while some buildings house exhibitions; one of these features a collection of 200 icons. It's arguably Poland's best skansen.

Visits are in guided groups of up to 20 people (in Polish), and the tour takes about two hours. In summer, there may be some English-speaking guides – inquire at the ticket office, or preferably call in advance on ☎ 463 16 72. They cost US$10 per group, in addition to the entry ticket. You can buy a leaflet in English or German with a short description of selected objects. There's a cafe

at the entrance serving the usual fare of snacks and light dishes. Bus No 1 or 3 from the Rynek will let you off by the bridge leading across the San River to the skansen.

Of the town's churches, the oldest (built in the 1630s) is the **Franciscan Church** but it was reshaped several times after its construction. In the left-side altar is the venerated painting of the Virgin Mary. The neo-Romanesque **parish church** dating from 1874–86 has Art Nouveau wall paintings. The neoclassical **Orthodox Church of the Holy Trinity** was built in 1784 and initially served the Uniate congregation; it's open a

10.30am and 5pm for Sunday Mass, but can be opened on request for visitors – inquire at the building next door.

Places to Stay

Camp Biała Góra (☎ 463 28 18, *Biała Góra*) Beds in 2- to 5-bed room in bungalow US$4-7. Open June-Sept. Located close to the skansen, Biała Góra is one of the cheapest places to stay in town. It has 15 rustic tent-like bungalows, some with bath. A few tents can be pitched at the back.

Youth hostel (☎ 463 09 25, *ul Konarskiego 10*) Dorm beds US$3-5. Open July & August. Another basic and cheap place to stay, the 60-bed youth hostel is between the bus terminal and the centre.

Dom Turysty PTTK (☎ 463 10 13, ☎/fax 463 14 39, *ul Mickiewicza 29*) Singles with bath US$8-12, doubles with bath US$10-25. This large all-year PTTK hostel offers plenty of beds. Private baths and low prices may seem an attractive option, but be warned that some rooms are in poor shape. Make sure to

The Boyks & the Lemks – Variations on a Theme

The Bieszczady, as well as the Beskid Niski and Beskid Sądecki farther west, were settled from about the 13th century by various nomadic groups migrating from the south and east. Most notable among them were the Wołosi from the Balkans and the Rusini from Ruthenia. Living in the same areas and intermarrying for centuries, they slowly developed into distinct ethnic groups known as the Bojkowie and Łemkowie.

The Bojkowie, or the Boyks, inhabited the eastern part of the Bieszczady, roughly east of Cisna, while the Łemkowie, or the Lemks, populated mountainous regions stretching from western Bieszczady up to the Beskid Sądecki. The two groups had much in common culturally, though there were noticeable differences in dialects, dress and architecture. They shared the Orthodox creed with their Ukrainian neighbours.

After the Union of Brest in 1596, most Lemks and Boyks turned to the Uniate Church, which accepted the supremacy of Rome but retained old Eastern rites and religious practices. From the end of the 19th century, however, the Roman Catholic hierarchy slowly but systematically imposed Latin rites. In response, many locals opted for a return to the Orthodox Church. By WWII both creeds were practised in the region, coexisting with varying degrees of harmony and conflict. By that time the total population of Boyks and Lemks was estimated at 200,000 to 300,000. Ethnic Poles were a minority in the region and consequently the Roman Catholic Church was insignificant.

All this changed dramatically in the aftermath of WWII when the borders were moved and the new government was installed. Not everyone was satisfied with the new status quo and some of its opponents didn't lay down their arms. One such armed faction was the Ukrainian Resistance Army which operated in the Bieszczady. Civil war continued in the region for almost two years.

In order to destroy the rebel base, the government decided to expel the inhabitants of all the villages in the region and resettle the entire area. In the so-called Operation Vistula (Operacja Wisła) in 1947, most of the population was brutally deported either to the Soviet Union or to the northern and western Polish territories just regained from Germany. Ironically, the main victims of the action were the Boyks and the Lemks, who had little to do with the conflict apart from the fact that they happened to live there. Moreover, Lemks were also deported from areas farther west where there was no partisan activity. Their villages were abandoned or destroyed, and those that survived were resettled with new inhabitants from other regions. Only some 20,000 Lemks were left in the whole region, and very few Boyks.

Today, the most evident survivors of their tragic history are the Orthodox or Uniate churches. These dilapidated wooden buildings still dot the countryside and add to the region's natural beauty. When hiking on remote trails, especially along the Ukrainian border, you'll find traces of destroyed villages, including ruined houses and orchards.

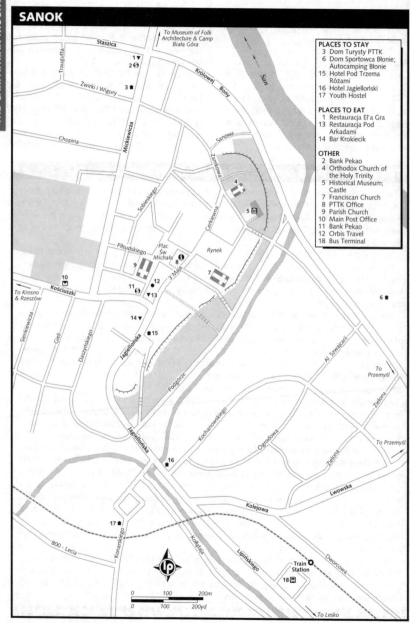

SANOK

PLACES TO STAY
3 Dom Turysty PTTK
6 Dom Sportowca Błonie;
  Autocamping Błonie
15 Hotel Pod Trzema
  Różami
16 Hotel Jagielloński
17 Youth Hostel

PLACES TO EAT
1 Restauracja El'a Gra
13 Restauracja Pod
  Arkadami
14 Bar Krokiecik

OTHER
2 Bank Pekao
4 Orthodox Church of
  the Holy Trinity
5 Historical Museum;
  Castle
7 Franciscan Church
8 PTTK Office
9 Parish Church
10 Main Post Office
11 Bank Pekao
12 Orbis Travel
18 Bus Terminal

To Museum of Folk
Architecture & Camp
Biała Góra

Staszica
Traugutta
Żwirki i Wigury
Chopina
Mickiewicza
Królowej Bony
San
Sanowa
Zamkowa
Sobieskiego
Cerkiewna
Piłsudskiego
Plac
Św
Michała
Rynek
Kościuszki
3 Maja
Sienkiewicza
Grzeg
Daszyńskiego
Jagiellońska
Podgórze
To Krosno
& Rzeszów
Al. Szwalcarni
To
Przemyśl
Zelona
Kochanowskiego
Ogrodowa
Zelona
To Przemyśl
Lwowska
Kolejowa
Konarskiego
Kolejija
Lipińskiego
Dworcowa
800 - Lecia
Train
Station
To Lesko

0   100   200m
0   100   200yd

THE CARPATHIAN MOUNTAINS

inspect the room before you decide. The hostel has its own restaurant which is basic but very cheap.

Dom Sportowca Błonie (☎ *463 02 57, fax 463 14 93, ul Królowej Bony 4)* Singles/doubles/triples with bath US$15/20/24; July-Aug dorm beds US$6. Dom Sportowca, in the sports centre, is yet another budget option and is a reasonable option. In July and August it opens an additional building, which has dorms without bath. From June to September, it also runs ***Autocamping Błonie*** Tent site US$2 plus US$2 per person.

Hotel Pod Trzema Różami (☎/fax 463 09 22, ul Jagiellońska 13)* Singles/doubles/triples with bath US$20/28/34. 'Under Three Roses' is a small place that offers acceptable facilities and is conveniently set in the city centre. It also has a pizzeria in the basement.

Hotel Jagielloński (☎/fax 463 12 08, ul Jagiellońska 49)* Singles US$20-28, doubles US$25-32, triples US$30-35. Jagielloński is the best place to stay in town, and is excellent value. Rooms are spacious and have private facilities. It has its own restaurant which, like the hotel itself, is probably the best eatery in town.

Places to Eat
Most of the places to stay have their own eating facilities (see above). Other eating options worthy of mention include:

Bar Krokiecik (ul Jagiellońska 2)* Mains US$1-3. Krokiecik is one of the cheapest acceptable options for a meal.

Restauracja Pod Arkadami (☎ *464 44 54, ul Grzegorza 2)* Mains US$3-6. This basement restaurant is not particularly memorable, but it provides solid Polish food that doesn't cost much.

Restauracja El'a Gra (☎ *464 31 01, ul Mickiewicza 29)* Mains US$4-8. A culinary curiosity, this basement restaurant serves Egyptian food which, as the menu puts it, is prepared according to traditional recipes that recall times of the Pharaohs. Well, it's not exactly clear what Pharaohs had for dinner, yet the food is tasty and reasonably priced.

Getting There & Away
The train and bus stations are next to each other, a bit over 1km south-east of the centre.

Two fast trains run to Warsaw daily (460km) and two to Kraków (244km). A dozen ordinary trains go to Jasło (62km) via Krosno.

There's regular bus transport to Rzeszów (76km) and Lesko (15km). About 10 buses run to Ustrzyki Dolne daily (40km) and six to Ustrzyki Górne (87km). There are several buses to Cisna (54km) and Wetlina (73km) plus additional buses in summer. A couple of buses go to Komańcza (38km). Five fast buses go directly to Kraków (205km) and two to Warsaw (379km).

AROUND SANOK
Icon Trail
The environs of Sanok are sprinkled with small villages, many of which still boast old Orthodox or Uniate churches, a reminder of the prewar ethnic and religious fabric of the region. In 1993, an idea emerged to include some of the churches in a tourist route, and by 1998 a walking trail, called the Szlak Ikon (Icon Trail), was traced and marked. It's a 70km loop path which begins and ends in Sanok and winds along the San River valley north of the city. The net walking time is about 15 hours, and it's also suitable for bicycles.

The route covers about 10 churches, most of which are charming small timber structures typical of the region. Most date from the 18th and 19th centuries, but the route also includes the oldest Orthodox timber church in Poland, in Ulucz, built in 1510. You can visit all the churches on the way; arrangements have been made with each of the church's hosts to let visitors in and show them around. A small donation is appreciated.

A large board in front of Sanok's castle has the route's sketch map and general description (in Polish). Inquire at Sanok's PTTK office for further information and a brochure with the trail's description (published in Polish and English). It includes details of where to ask to have the church opened for you. Also inquire at the office about accommodation and eating options along the route.

Czerteż

Czerteż is a small village 5km north-west of Sanok on the Rzeszów road. It has a beautiful wooden Uniate church from 1772 with the original iconostasis. It's not included in the Icon Trail, but it's one of the best churches in the region and is worth a short trip. Sanok urban buses will drop you nearby. The church is hidden in the cluster of tall trees behind an agricultural cooperative. It can be visited under the same arrangements as churches on the Icon Trail. The keys are kept by Mr Jan Hałajcio (☎ 463 20 15), Zabłotce 61, about 600m from the church. The PTTK office may provide further information.

LESKO

☎ 13 • pop 6200

Founded in 1470, Lesko had a mixed Polish-Ruthenian population, a reflection of the region's history. From the 16th century onwards, a lot of Jews arrived, initially from Spain, trying to escape the Inquisition. Their migration continued to such an extent that by the 18th century Jews made up half of the town's population.

WWII and the years that followed changed the ethnic picture altogether. The Jews were slaughtered by the Nazis, the Ukrainians were defeated by the Polish military and the Lemks were deported. The town was rebuilt, and without having developed any significant industry, is now a small tourist centre, a stopover on the way south into the Bieszczady.

Information

The Bieszczadzkie Centrum Informacji Turystycznej (☎ 469 66 95) is in a pavilion next to the town hall on the Rynek. It's open 8am to 4pm weekdays. A large town map, posted on a board next to the office, is useful for orientation.

Things to See

Lesko is notable for its Jewish heritage. The 17th-century **synagogue**, on ul Joselewicza

just off the Rynek, has a Spanish flavour and its tower is a sure sign that it was once part of the town's defensive system. The interior houses an art gallery but little of its original decoration has survived. At the front is what looks like a row of small houses built on to the main structure; these served as a prayer hall for women.

Follow ul Moniuszki downhill from the synagogue and you'll see stairs on the right leading up to the old **Jewish cemetery**. More than a thousand gravestones, the oldest ones dating back to the mid-16th century, are scattered amid trees and high grass. Some of them have amazingly rich decoration. Left in total isolation, in different stages of decay, they're a very impressive sight.

Go back to the Rynek, passing the 19th-century **town hall** in the middle, and head 200m north to the **parish church** on ul Kościuszki. It was built in 1539 and its exterior still retains many Gothic features. The freestanding baroque bell tower was added in 1725. At that time the church's interior got its baroque overlay, including the high altar and ornate pulpit.

Lesko has a **castle** – it's on the Sanok road 200m downhill from the Rynek. Built at the beginning of the 16th century, it lost most of its original form with extensive neoclassical alterations. Postwar restoration converted it into a hotel.

Places to Stay & Eat

Camping Nad Sanem (☎ 469 66 89, *ul Turystyczna 1*) Tent site US$1.50 plus US$1 per person, beds in bungalows US$5. Open May-Sept. The camp site is on the riverside beneath the castle. It has a dozen bungalows with rooms of different sizes, an area where you can pitch your tent and a restaurant.

Motel Fux (☎ 469 67 81, *ul Bieszczadzka 4*) Open May-Sept. Beds in doubles or triples without bath US$6. Fux, just behind the petrol station, is basic but cheap.

Hotelik Relax (☎/fax 469 85 73, *ul Piłsudskiego 11*) Singles/doubles/triples without bath US$10/14/22, suites with bath US$30. Sitting across the road from the bus terminal, this simple 96-bed hotel is clean and well kept, and better than the Fux.

Pensjonat Zamek (☎ *469 62 68, fax 469 58 78, ul Piłsudskiego 7*) Singles/doubles/triples with bath & breakfast US$28/35/45. Open year-round. Located in the castle (but don't expect stylish castle chambers), the Zamek was once a holiday centre for miners. It's now is a regular hotel with 87 beds.

There are half a dozen basic eateries on or near the Rynek.

Getting There & Away
There's no railway in Lesko. The bus terminal is on ul Piłsudskiego (the road to Sanok), about 1km from the Rynek. It's convenient to all the places to stay listed above.

There are plenty of buses to Sanok (15km), a dozen of which continue to Krosno (55km). About 10 buses run to Rzeszów daily (91km) and one goes directly to Kraków (220km).

For the Bieszczady, there are several buses to Cisna daily (39km), and some wind up as far as Wetlina (58km). Three or four buses to Ustrzyki Górne (72km) go via Ustrzyki Dolne. In summer, there are a couple of extra buses to each of these destinations.

USTRZYKI DOLNE
☎ 13 • pop 8800
An uninspiring town in the south-eastern corner of Poland, Ustrzyki Dolne ('Oost-**shi**-kee **Dol**-neh') is really only an overnight stop for those heading south into the Bieszczady. There's not much to see or do here except for the **Natural History Museum** (*Muzeum Przyrodnicze;* ☎ *461 10 91, ul Bełska 7; adult/student US$1/0.75; open 9am-5pm Tues-Sat also 9am-2pm Sun July & Aug*), just off the Rynek, which is a good introduction to the geology, flora and fauna of the Bieszczady National Park.

If you plan on independent trekking up to the mountains, Ustrzyki Dolne is the last reliable place to stock up on a decent range of provisions and exchange money. Farther south, food supplies will be more limited.

Information
Tourist Offices The Bieszczadzkie Centrum Informacji i Promocji (☎ 471 11 30), Rynek 16, is open 8am to 5pm weekdays.

The museum has an information desk (open same hours as the museum) for Bieszczady National Park.

Money There are a few kantors, including one in the tourist office. Bank Pekao is next door, at Rynek 17, and has an ATM in the Dom Handlowy Halicz, a shopping centre just east of the Rynek. There's another ATM opposite the museum.

Places to Stay & Eat
There are half a dozen regular places to stay in town and many locals rent out rooms in their homes.

Hotelik Bieszczadzki (☎ *461 10 71, fax 461 10 74, Rynek 19*) Singles/doubles/triples without bath US$10/15/20, doubles/triples with bath US$22/28. Open year-round. The most central place, the Bieszczadzki is quite simple and has a similarly simple budget restaurant.

Hotelik Strwiąż (☎/*fax 461 14 68, ul Sikorskiego 1*) Doubles/triples without bath US$15/20, doubles with bath US$22. Just off the Rynek, Strwiąż is another hotel on the basic side.

Dom Wycieczkowy Laworta (☎ *461 11 78,* ☎/*fax 461 11 77, ul Nadgórna 107*) Singles/doubles/triples/quads with bath US$12/14/20/26. In the northern suburb, high on the mountain slope, a 10-minute walk uphill from the train and bus stations, Laworta is a large (170-bed) place with its own restaurant.

Getting There & Away
The train and bus stations are in one building. You won't get far by train (trains to Przemyśl and on to Warsaw no longer operate, and there are only a few to Zagórz and Jasło), but bus traffic is reasonable. Two dozens buses run to Sanok daily (40km) and pass Lesko (25km) on the way. Five buses (several more in summer) go to Ustrzyki Górne daily (47km). Most come through from Przemyśl or Sanok. There are also bus services to farther destinations, including five buses a day to Przemyśl, five to Rzeszów, one to Kraków and one to Warsaw.

HIKING IN THE BIESZCZADY

The Bieszczady is one of the best places in Poland to go hiking. The region is beautiful and easy to walk, and you don't need a tent or cooking equipment, as hostels and mountain hostels are a day's walk apart and provide food. The main area for trekking is the national park, with Ustrzyki Górne and Wetlina being the most popular starting points. You can also use Cisna as a base.

Once in the mountains, things become easier than you might expect. There are plenty of well-marked trails giving a good choice of shorter and longer walks. All three jumping-off points have PTTK hostels and friendly staff can give you information. All have boards depicting marked trails complete with walking times, uphill and downhill, on all routes. The mountain hostels will put you up for the night and feed you regardless of how crowded they get. In July and August the floor will most likely be your bed, as these places are pretty small. Take a sleeping bag with you.

Get a copy of the *Bieszczady* map (scale 1:75,000) which covers the whole region, not just the national park. The map is also helpful if you plan to explore the region using private transport.

USTRZYKI GÓRNE

☎ 13 • pop 500

Ustrzyki Górne is just a string of houses loosely scattered along the road, rather than a village in the proper sense of the word. Yet, it's Bieszczady's major hiking base. Thanks to its location in the heart of these beautiful mountains (now a national park), the place has long attracted trekkers curious for something new and prepared for basic facilities.

Since the Bieszczady loop road was built in 1955–62, the mountains have become more accessible and fashionable. The region is changing but the process is slow. It's still remote country and Ustrzyki Górne is a good example – there are a few mostly rudimentary places to stay and eat, a shop and not much else. The village springs to life in summer, then sinks into a deep sleep for most of the rest of the year, only stirring a little in winter when cross-country skiers arrive.

Places to Stay & Eat

Accommodation doesn't seem to be much of a problem. Apart from the regular places listed below, many locals rent out rooms in their homes, and even the priest provides beds for tourists in a large house next to the church.

Camping Nr 150 PTTK (☎ 461 06 04) Tent site US$1.50 plus US$2 per person, beds in old/new cabins US$5/10. Open May-Sept. The camp site is in the northern part of the village. It has some old triple cabins without bath and newer double cabins with bath.

Schronisko PTTK Kremenaros (mobile ☎ 0502 234 501) Dorm beds US$5-6. Open year-round. Kremenaros is in the last house of the village on the Cisna road. It's old and basic, but staff are friendly and the atmosphere is good. Their ***Gospoda Kremenaros*** has a very short menu but the food is cheap and OK.

Hotelik Biały (☎ 461 06 41) Beds in 4- or 5-bed dorms US$5-6. Open year-round. This 63-bed hostel is run by the management of the Bieszczady National Park. It's on a side road, about 500m from the turn-off next to the shop. It has slightly better standards than the Kremenaros. Linen is US$1.25 extra.

Hotel Górski (☎ 461 06 04, fax 461 06 20) Beds in rooms with bath & breakfast US$24 July & Aug, US$20 Sept-June. The new PTTK-run hotel, at the end of the village, on the Ustrzyki Dolne road, is significantly better and larger than anything else around. It has 64 rooms – singles, doubles, triples, quads and suites – all clean, comfortable and modern, and all have their own baths. The hotel has a swimming pool, gym and sauna, and its own restaurant with reasonable prices, though much higher than the Kremenaros.

Apart from the two all-year PTTK eateries listed above, more places open in summer along the main road.

Getting There & Away

There are four buses to Ustrzyki Dolne (47km), two to Krosno (117km) and one to Rzeszów (163km). A couple more buses

...un in July and August to the above destinations, as well as several buses to Wetlina (15km) and Cisna (34km).

WETLINA
☎ 13 • pop 400

Wetlina is another popular jumping-off spot for hiking in the Bieszczady. In many ways it's similar to Ustrzyki Górne – it also has a choice of simple places to sleep and eat, and attracts a similar genre of people.

Places to Stay & Eat
Dom Wycieczkowy PTTK (☎/fax 468 46 15) Dorm beds US$4-7. This old and basic hostel offers beds year-round in doubles/triples and larger dorms. In summer you can also stay in cabins and pitch your tent on the grounds. There's a basic restaurant here.

Hotel Górski Wetlina (☎ 468 46 34) Camping US$5 per tent, singles/doubles/triples with bath US$20/28/40, beds in bungalows US$8. Run by the PTTK, the place has all-year rooms, summer bungalows, a camp site and a restaurant.

Youth hostel Dorm beds US$4-7. Open year-round. The 50-bed hostel has some triples but most beds are in large dorms.

Zajazd Pod Połoniną (☎ 468 46 11) Beds in doubles, triples or quads US$6-8. The 48-bed Zajazd has rooms with and without bath and a budget *restaurant*. It may have bikes for rent.

Locals also offer private *rooms* for rent. In summer, a number of places to eat open along the main road.

Getting There & Away
Wetlina is accessible from Sanok (73km) and Lesko (58km) by a few buses a day year-round. Several buses a day run in summer east to Ustrzyki Górne (15km).

CISNA
☎ 13 • pop 700

Cisna sits on the borderland between the territories once inhabited by Boyks to the east and Lemks to the west. The region was quite densely populated before WWII. Today Cisna and its environs have no more than 1000 inhabitants, yet it's still the largest village in the central part of the Bieszczady. The village is not attractive in itself but it has a choice of accommodation and can therefore be used as a base for hiking. It is also the place from which to take the narrow-gauge tourist train.

Places to Stay & Eat
Noclegi Okrąglik (☎ 468 63 49) Beds in doubles, triples or quads US$4. Centrally located on the crossroads, the Okrąglik operates as long as there's demand. It has basic rooms with shared facilities, and you pay US$1.25 extra if you need bedsheets.

Ośrodek Wypoczynkowy Wołosań (☎ 468 63 73, fax 468 63 01) Beds in doubles or triples with bath US$8-10. Open year-round. The 70-bed Wołosań provides satisfactory standards and has a reasonable eatery, *Restauracja Partyja* (☎ 468 63 65).

Bacówka PTTK Pod Honem (mobile ☎ 0503 137 279) Beds US$4-6. Open year-round. The 44-bed PTTK mountain hostel is beautifully located high on the mountain slope above Cisna (a 20-minute walk up the hill from the centre along a steep dirt track). It's basic, friendly and cheap and will let you sleep on the floor if all the rooms are taken. It also serves simple meals. You can book a bed through Restauracja Partyja.

Ośrodek Wypoczynkowy Perełka (☎/fax 468 63 25) Beds in rooms with bath US$15. Possibly the best place to stay in Cisna, the Perełka has 34 beds in singles and doubles plus seasonal cabins. Meals are served on request.

Half a dozen budget eateries open in summer near the crossroads. Among them, *Bar Troll* (☎ 468 63 16) rents out bikes.

Getting There & Away
Train The narrow-gauge train known as Bieszczadzka Kolejka Leśna (Bieszczady Forest Train) was built for transporting timber and had its main station in Majdan, 2km west of Cisna. The first stretch of the railway between Majdan and Nowy Łupków was built at the end of the 19th century and subsequently extended north to Rzepedź and east to Moczarne beyond Wetlina. The train on

the Majdan-Rzepedź route was used until 1993 for the transport of timber. Additionally, a tourist train was put into operation on this line in summer. Though the trip lost some of its charm after steam was replaced by diesel in 1980, it was still a spectacular ride.

Both the freight and tourist trains were suspended in 1993 due to the dangerous condition of the railway. After several seasons out of operation, the tourist train now operates the 12km stretch from Majdan to Przysłup (midway between Cisna and Wetlina), and in the opposite direction the 18km stretch from Majdan to Wola Michowa. Check at Majdan station (☎ 468 63 35, fax 468 63 01) or a regional tourist office for periods of operation, schedules and fares.

Bus Several buses run to Sanok daily (57km) and Wetlina (19km). There are more seasonal buses in summer, including a few to Ustrzyki Górne (34km).

KOMAŃCZA
☎ 13 • pop 600
A village nestled in the valley between the Bieszczady and Beskid Niski, Komańcza is yet another base for hikers. Though not as popular as Ustrzyki Górne, Wetlina or Cisna, it offers something different. As it somehow escaped Operation Vistula in 1947, there's more of an ethnic and religious mix here than elsewhere in the region. There's a sizable community of Lemks living in the village and around, and old Uniate and Orthodox rites have not been pushed out by Catholicism.

Information
The Centrum Informacji Turystycznej (☎ 467 70 76) in the village's municipal office, is open 7am to 3pm weekdays.

Things to See
Small as Komańcza is, it boasts three churches – Uniate, Orthodox and Roman Catholic – and all three are in use. The oldest is a beautiful wooden **Orthodox church** from 1805, tucked away on the outskirts of the village, on the Dukla road. It's only open for Sunday morning Mass and attracts

a small congregation. If you can't make it at that time, the local Orthodox priest (☎ 467 72 24), Komańcza 216, may open it for you.

The Uniates make up a significant part of the village's population. In the late 1980s, they built a fair-sized **Uniate church** in the centre of the village. In the basement of the church is the **Lemk Museum** featuring a small collection of objects (household items, tools, crafts) referring to the Lemk culture. The museum is normally locked – you need to go to the Plebania (☎ 467 72 24) and ask to have it open.

The **Roman Catholic church**, a modest wooden structure, was built in the early 1950s for newly settled worshippers of the creed, which was virtually nonexistent in the region before WWII. The church is opposite the train station on the road to Sanok.

Continuing north along this road for about 1km and taking a narrow track which branches off to the left under the railway bridge, you'll get to the **Convent of the Nazarene Sisters**. Known to Poles as the site of the house arrest (in 1955–56) of Cardinal Stefan Wyszyński, Primate of Poland until 1981, this fine timber mansion is now a sort of shrine, though there's nothing special to look at inside.

Places to Stay & Eat
Schronisko PTTK (☎ 467 70 13) Beds in doubles/quads US$8/7, beds in cabins US$6. Fully refurbished, the all-year 20-bed Schronisko, close to the convent, has all its rooms with private baths and offers good standards. It serves simple hot meals. In summer it also operates cabins.

Otherwise, you have a summer *youth hostel*, a *camp site*, and a dozen agrotourist farms – just watch out for 'Agroturystyka' boards along the main road.

Getting There & Away
The standard-gauge railway links Komańcza with Zagórz via Rzepedź, with four trains daily in each direction. From Zagórz, you have frequent bus transport to Sanok and Lesko.

There are half a dozen buses to Sanok daily (49km). One bus goes to Cisna daily

(30km) and there is also sporadic transport to Dukla (42km).

AROUND KOMAŃCZA

Avid church visitors would not want to miss some fine Uniate and Orthodox churches scattered around the Komańcza region. You'll find the first good specimen in the village of **Rzepedź**, 5km north of Komańcza. It's 750m west of the main road. Extensively restored over recent years, this wooden structure, dating from 1824, with a bell tower in front of the entrance, is today the Uniate church. The key is kept by Mr Sławomir Jurkowski, Rzepedź 26, about 500m from the church.

A bit different in shape, and perhaps even nicer, is the church in **Turzańsk**, 1.5km east of Rzepedź. Topped with graceful onion domes and with a freestanding belfry, the church was built in 1838 and has preserved its internal decoration complete with rococo iconostasis. Today the church serves the Orthodox community and holds Mass at 10am every second Sunday. If you want to visit at other times, the keys are kept at the house of Mr Teodor Tchoryk, Turzańsk 63, at the opposite end of the village, about 2km from the church.

One more *cerkiew*, also following the Orthodox rite, is in the village of **Szczawne**, 3km north of Rzepedź by the main road, just before crossing the railway track. Watch out to the left as it's well hidden in a cluster of trees. Masses are held every second Sunday. The keys are kept by Mr Jan Walorny, Szczawne 20, in the large white house near the train station, 2km from the church.

The Beskid Niski

The Beskid Niski (literally, the Low Beskid) is a mountain range that runs for about 85km west-east along the Slovakian frontier. It's bordered on the west by the Beskid Sądecki and on the east by the Bieszczady. As its name suggests, it is not a high outcrop, its highest point not exceeding 1000m. Made up of gently undulating and densely forested hills, the Beskid Niski is easier for walking than its taller neighbours. It offers perhaps less spectacular vistas than the Bieszczady, but dozens of small Orthodox and Uniate churches add to its charm. Most of them are in the western half of the region.

KROSNO
☎ 13 • pop 49,000

Founded in the 14th century and prospering during the Renaissance – even referred to as 'little Kraków' – Krosno, like the rest of Poland, slid into decay later on. It revived in the mid-19th century with the development of the oil industry in the region and since then has slowly grown to become a regional petroleum centre. Krosno is also well known for its glassworks.

Today it is a rather ordinary city except for its tiny historic core perched on a hill, a remnant of its glorious past. There are some interesting sights nearby, notably the church in Haczów and the skansen in Bóbrka.

Information
Tourist Offices The tourist office (☎/fax 432 77 07) is at ul Pużaka 49, close to the train station, but is expected to move closer to the centre.

Money Bank Pekao is pretty far from the centre at ul Bieszczadzka 5, but you can try Bank Śląski at Rynek 8. There are several kantors in the Old Town and a convenient ATM at ul Słowackiego 4.

Email & Internet Access Central facilities include Internet Expo, Rynek 10, and Internet Imex, Plac Konstytucji 3 Maja 3.

Things to See
The Old Town is the focal point for the visitor. The spacious **Rynek** has retained some of its former appearance, notably in the houses fronted by wide arcaded passageways that line the south and half of the north side of the square.

A few steps east of the Rynek is the large 15th-century **Franciscan Church** (Kościół Franciszkanów), today filled with neo-Gothic furnishings. The showpiece here is the Oświęcim Family Chapel (Kaplica

THE BESKID NISKI

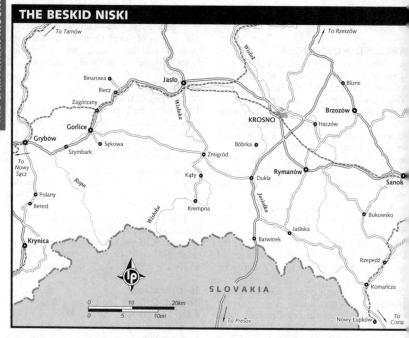

To Tarnów · To Rzeszów · Binarowa · Biecz · Jasło · Blizne · Zagórzany · Brzozów · KROSNO · Haczów · Gorlice · Grybów · Sękowa · Bóbrka · Szymbark · Żmigród · To Nowy Sącz · Rymanów · Ropa · Kąty · Dukla · Sanok · Polany · Berest · Krempna · Bukowsko · Jaśliska · Barwinek · Jaśliska · Krynica · Rzepedź · Komańcza · SLOVAKIA · 0 10 20km · 0 5 10mi · To Prešov · Nowy Łupków · To Cisna

Oświęcimów), just to the left as you enter the church. Built in 1647 by Italian architect Wincenty Petroni, and embellished with stucco work by another Italian master, Jan Falconi, the chapel has been preserved with virtually no changes and is considered one of the best early baroque chapels in Poland.

Another huge brick structure, the **parish church**, is 100m north-west of the Rynek. Built in the 15th century, it was almost entirely consumed by fire in 1638 – only the chancel survived – and reconstructed in an altered style. In contrast to its quite sober exterior, the church's interior is exuberant. The powerful gilded high altar is 350 years old, as is the elaborate pulpit. The organ looks a bit more modest, yet it's acclaimed for its excellent sound, reputedly the best in the region.

One block north-west of the church is the **Regional Museum** (*Muzeum Podkarpackie;* ☎ 432 13 76, ul Piłsudskiego 16; adult/ student US$1/0.50, free Sun; open 10am-

4pm Tues-Sun May-Oct, 10am-2pm Tues-Sun Nov-Apr). Installed in the 15th-century former Bishops' Palace, the museum has the usual historical, archaeological and ar[t] sections but the highlight is an extensive collection of decorative old kerosene lamps reputedly the largest in Europe. Also worth seeing is the collection of contemporary artistic glass from regional glassworks.

Directly opposite is the **Craft Museum** (*Muzeum Rzemiosła;* ☎ 432 41 88, ul Piłsudskiego 17; adult/student US$1/0.50, open 9am-3pm Mon-Sat), featuring old objects of everyday use and tools and workshops used to manufacture them.

Places to Stay

Reshotel (☎ 432 19 54, ul Okulickiego 13A, Singles/doubles/triples without bath US$7/ 10/15. This former workers' hostel in an industrial suburb 1km west of the train station, now welcomes everybody and is one of the cheapest all-year places to stay in Krosno.

Mini Hotelik (☎/*fax 436 36 76, ul Kletówka 14)* Singles/doubles/triples US$16/24/28. Conveniently set in a quiet suburb between the train station and the centre (and within easy walking distance from both), the Mini Hotelik offers 20 beds in simple but perfectly acceptable rooms. One bathroom is shared between two rooms.

Motel Skorpion (☎/*fax 436 21 74, ul Podkarpacka 38)* Singles/doubles/triples with bath US$22/28/34. Conveniently for motorists, the Skorpion is next to the petrol station, 4km out of the centre on the Rzeszów road. It has one single, three doubles and one triple room, and its own restaurant.

Hotel Krosno-Nafta (☎ *436 62 12, fax 436 87 31, ul Lwowska 21)* Singles/doubles with bath & breakfast US$60/90. The city's top-end accommodation, this 92-bed hotel, a bit over 1km from the centre on the Sanok road, has been refurbished and offers satisfactory conditions and its own upmarket restaurant. It may have discount rates on weekends.

Places to Eat

Marhaba Bar (☎ *420 24 92, ul Sienkiewicza 2)* Dishes US$3-4. A new and popular outlet on the Rynek, Marhaba offers some Middle-Eastern standards such as kebab, felafel, kufta and the like.

Piwnica Wójtowska (☎ *432 15 32, Rynek 7)* Mains US$5-8. Located in a pleasant vaulted cellar on the Rynek, the Piwnica offers Polish cuisine.

Restauracja Royal (☎ *436 12 25, Rynek 5)* Mains US$5-7. Probably not as attractive as the Piwnica, the Royal is another option for some Polish food.

Getting There & Away

The train and bus stations are next to each other, 1.5km west of the Old Town; it's a 15-minute walk to the centre, or you can take the urban bus.

Most trains cover the Zagórz-Jasło route which can be used for Sanok but not much else. There are two trains a day to Warsaw and two to Kraków.

Bus traffic is busier and will take you all around the region. There are a dozen buses eastwards to Sanok (40km), of which four

continue to Ustrzyki Dolne (83km) and two go as far as Ustrzyki Górne (130km). A dozen fast buses depart to Kraków daily (165km), and even more buses go to Rzeszów (59km). To the south, there are around 15 buses a day to Dukla (21km) and about 10 to Bóbrka (10km). Buses to Haczów (13km) depart roughly every hour (on the timetable, watch out for Brzozów buses via Haczów).

HACZÓW

The village of Haczów ('**Hah**-choof'), 13km east of Krosno, boasts what is considered the largest timber Gothic church in Europe. Built around the mid-15th century on the site of a previous church founded by Władysław Jagiełło in 1388, it is also one of Europe's oldest timber churches. What's more, it has beautiful interior wall paintings, dating from approximately 1494, discovered in 1955 and restored in the '90s. There are also five baroque side altars, but the main altar complete with its singularly impressive original pietà from around 1400, is now in the new church, built in 1935–39 right next to the old one.

Both churches are open during the day, but if you find them locked, ask the friendly priest, who lives in the house next to the churches, to let you have a look inside. There's another excellent old timber church in Blizne, 5km north of Brzozów.

Getting There & Away

You shouldn't wait more than an hour for a bus to Krosno. They go either via Krościenko Wyżne or Miejsce Piastowe, and both are OK. Buses to Brzozów (15km) run regularly throughout the day.

BÓBRKA
☎ 13 • pop 800

The small village of Bóbrka, 10km south of Krosno, was the cradle of the oil industry. It was here that the world's first oil well was sunk by Ignacy Łukasiewicz in 1854. Today, the site where the oil business was born is a skansen, the **Museum of the Oil Industry** (*Muzeum Przemysłu Naftowego;* ☎ *433 34 78; adult/student US$1/0.50;*

Bóbrka – Birthplace of World Oil Industry

Natural oil was known in the Krosno region for centuries. It oozed to the earth's surface out of crannies in the rock and was used by locals for domestic and medicinal purposes. However, it was in 1854 in Bóbrka that Ignacy Łukasiewicz sank what is thought to be the world's first oil well, giving birth to commercial oil exploitation.

Łukasiewicz, a pharmacy graduate from universities in Lviv, Kraków and Vienna, studied the properties of crude oil, and he was the first to obtain paraffin oil from petroleum. In 1853 he constructed the world's first kerosene lamp, which was first used in the Lviv hospital to light a surgical operation which had to be carried out urgently at night. A year later in Gorlice, the world's first street kerosene lamp was lit by Łukasiewicz. It was then that a local landlord pointed out a site in the Bóbrka forest, where substantial amounts of oil accumulated in natural hollows in the land.

The first approach to get oil out of the soil was by means of a ditch. A 120m-long, 1.2m-deep ditch was dug and oil was collected by bucket, but there was not that much to collect. This led to experiments with vertical shafts, which proved to be much more effective. By 1858, four years after initial trials, the new Małgorzata shaft yielded about 4000L of oil a day, a milestone which fostered further exploitation.

More shafts were immediately sunk all over the place, followed by the opening of primitive refineries. The region prospered, reaching its peak before WWI. Later on, when larger deposits were discovered elsewhere, the importance of the local oil fields diminished. Rudimentary exploitation continues, and even though output today is insignificant, the site preserves the memory of what happened here 150 years ago, introducing a product which changed the world.

open 9am-5pm Tues-Sun May-Sept, 7am-3pm Tues-Sun Oct-Apr).

Established in 1961, this interesting open-air museum is unique – it doesn't feature old peasant architecture, but old oil machinery. It's based on a group of early oil wells, complemented by their old drilling derricks and other machinery collected elsewhere. The first surviving oil shaft from 1860, Franek, can be seen with oil still bubbling inside. The other shaft nearby, Janina, is over 100 years old and still used commercially.

The building, which was at one time Łukasiewicz's office, now houses a small museum. The collection of kerosene lamps includes decorative and industrial examples. Note the original map of the Bóbrka oil field with the shafts marked on it; the deepest went down as far as 319m. A copy of the lamp invented by Łukasiewicz can also be seen. Łukasiewicz also invented a method of refining oil.

Places to Stay & Eat
Youth hostel (☎ 431 30 97) Dorm beds US$4-5. Open May-Oct. This 30-bed hostel is the only place to stay in Bóbrka. It's in the local school and its opening times are somewhat erratic – check in advance. Bring some food with you as there's nowhere to eat out.

Getting There & Away
The usual jumping-off point for Bóbrka is Krosno. There are about 10 buses daily (fewer on weekends) to the village of Bóbrka. The skansen is 2km away, linked by road but not by bus. This road leads through the forest and makes a pleasant walk. Alternatively, take a bus from Krosno to Kobylany or Makowiska (at least a dozen daily), get off in Równe Skrzyżowanie and walk 600m uphill to the skansen. One or two buses from Równe run south to Dukla, or you can walk 1.5km east to the main road where buses to Dukla pass by every hour.

DUKLA
☎ 13 • pop 2200
Dukla is close to the Dukla Pass (Przełęcz Dukielska), the lowest and most easily accessible passage over the Western Carpathians. In the 16th century this strategic location brought prosperity to the town, which became a centre of the wine trade on

the route from Hungary. In autumn 1944, on the other hand, the town's position led to its destruction. One of the fiercest mountain battles of WWII was fought nearby, in which the combined Soviet and Czechoslovakian armies crushed the German defence, leaving over 100,000 soldiers dead.

Things to See

Dukla's large **Rynek** boasts a squat town hall in the middle. Across the Krosno road is the mighty **parish church** built in 1764–65, a good example of late baroque architecture.

Diagonally opposite the church is the **Historical Museum** *(Muzeum Historyczne; ☎ 433 00 85, Trakt Węgierski 5; adult/ student US$1.50/1; open 10am-6pm Tues-Sun May-Sept, 10am-3.30pm Tues-Sun Oct-Apr).* Accommodated in an 18th-century palace, it has a permanent display related to the battle of 1944 and some temporary exhibitions. In the palace park, there are some heavy weapons from WWII.

Places to Stay & Eat

Dom Wycieczkowy PTTK (☎ 433 00 46, Rynek 25) Beds in dorms without bath US$6, doubles with bath US$20. This is a basic place and has an equally basic restaurant.

Youth hostel (☎ 433 08 86, Rynek 9) Beds in 6- to 10-bed dorms US$3-5. Open year-round. Another basic option on the Rynek, this youth hostel has 40 beds.

Getting There & Away

There are regular buses north to Krosno (21km) and several buses south to Barwinek (16km) near the border. Crossing the border is fast and easy, but get rid of złotys in Barwinek's kantor – it will be hard to trade them in Svidnik or Bardejov in Slovakia.

One seasonal bus runs the backwoods route from Dukla to Komańcza (42km) and on to Cisna (72km), which is a short cut to the Bieszczady. Westwards, one bus plies the Dukla-Gorlice road daily (43km).

BIECZ

☎ 13 • pop 5100

One of the oldest settlements in Poland, Biecz ('Byech') was for a long time a busy commercial centre benefiting from the trading route heading south over the Carpathians to Hungary. In the 17th century its prosperity came to an end and Biecz found itself in the doldrums, left only with its memories. This sleepy atmosphere seems to have remained to this day, however, some important historic monuments and a good museum, make the town a worthwhile stop on your route.

Things to See

The town's landmark is the **town hall** in the Rynek or, more precisely, its huge 66m-high octagonal **tower**, looking a bit like a lighthouse. It was built in 1569–81, except for the top which is a later, baroque addition. It was recently thoroughly restored, including its original Renaissance decoration and the unusual 24-hour clock face on its eastern side. The town hall now houses the local municipal office – inquire there during office hours and you may be let up to the top of the tower.

West of the Rynek is a monumental **parish church**. This mighty Gothic brick structure, evidence of former wealth but now looking too large for the town's needs, dates from the late 15th/early 16th centuries. Inside, the chancel holds most of the church's treasures, most notably the late Renaissance Flemish high altar and massive stalls, all from the early 17th century. Less conspicuous but worthy of attention is a gilded woodcarving depicting the genealogical tree of the Virgin Mary, standing to the side of the high altar. Farther up, is an impressive crucifix from 1639.

The church is only open for visits immediately before or after Mass. There are several Masses on Sunday, but on weekdays they are only held early in the morning and late in the afternoon.

Biecz has a good **Regional Museum** *(☎ 447 10 93; ul Węgierska & ul Kromera 3; adult/student US$1/0.50; open 8am-3pm Tues-Sat Oct-Apr, also 9am-2pm Sun May-Sept).* It's housed in two 16th-century buildings, both close to the church. The one at ul Węgierska holds the complete contents of an ancient pharmacy including its laboratory, musical instruments, traditional household utensils and equipment from old craft workshops. The other part of the museum, at ul Kromera, has more historical exhibits on the town's past, plus archaeological and numismatic collections.

Places to Stay & Eat
Youth hostel (☎/fax 447 10 14, ul Parkowa 1) Beds US$3-6. Open year-round. The 60-bed youth hostel is in a large school building a 10-minute walk from the Rynek. The hostel is on the top floor and only has doubles and quads, so it provides more privacy than most.

Hotel Restauracja Grodzka (☎/fax 447 11 21, ul Kazimierza Wielkiego 35) Singles/doubles with bath US$15/18, double suite US$25. This is an acceptable budget option, close to the youth hostel. It has its own restaurant which is OK.

Hotel Centennial (☎/fax 447 15 76, Rynek 6) Suites with bath & breakfast US$125-250. Probably the most expensive accommodation in the region, this new small posh hotel offers suites of different size and design in two historic burgher houses. The hotel has three restaurants, one of which, *Restauracja Ogród*, serves solid Polish food at surprisingly low prices – excellent value.

Getting There & Away
The train station, 1km west of the centre, handles 10 trains a day to Jasło (15km), two to Nowy Sącz (59km), two to Kraków (164km) and one to Warsaw (484km).

There's no bus terminal in Biecz; all buses pass through and stop on the Rynek. Buses to Jasło (18km) run regularly but only a few buses continue to Krosno (43km). Plenty of buses, both the PKS and No 1 suburban buses, run to Gorlice (15km). A couple of buses go to Nowy Sącz daily (56km), Nowy Targ (132km) and Zakopane (156km).

BINAROWA
The village of Binarowa, 5km north-west of Biecz, has a beautiful wooden Catholic church. Built around 1500, its interior is entirely covered with paintings which have remained in remarkably good shape. Those on the ceiling were produced shortly after the church's construction, while the wall decoration, in quite a different style, dates from the mid-17th century. Though the church is open only for Mass (early in the morning on weekdays, all morning till noon on Sunday) the priest who lives in the house behind it will probably open it for you.

Binarowa is accessible by buses from Gorlice via Biecz. They go every hour or so on weekdays, less frequently on weekends.

GORLICE
☎ 18 • pop 31,000
Gorlice's name was made, along with Bóbrka, for being the cradle of the Polish oil industry. In 1853, in the local chemist shop in Gorlice, Ignacy Łukasiewicz obtained paraffin from crude oil. Gorlice was also the site of a great 1915 battle, fought for 126 days, which ended with the Austrians breaking through the Russian Carpathian front, leaving 20,000 dead.

Gorlice has little to entice tourists but the region to the south was once Lemk land and still shelters some amazing old Orthodox and Uniate churches. The town is a major transportation hub for the region, and the helpful tourist office can provide information.

Gorlice can be used as a starting point for hiking into the Beskid Niski. Two marked trails, blue and green, wind south-east from the town up the mountains, joining the main west-east red trail which crosses the range.

Information
The Gorlickie Centrum Informacji (☎ 353 50 91), ul Legionów 3, is open 8am to 6pm weekdays, 9am to 3pm Saturday. Bank Pekao is at ul Legionów 12, and there are a few kantors and ATMs in the centre. There's an Internet cafe at ul Piekarska 6.

Things to See
The **Regional Museum** (☎ 352 26 15, ul Wąska 7/9; admission US$0.50; open 9am-4pm Tues-Fri, 10am-2pm Sat, also 10am-2pm Sun May-Sept), just off the Rynek, has exhibitions on Lemk ethnography, the oil industry and the Gorlice battle of 1915.

Gorlice claims to have the world's first street kerosene lamp. It's attached to the chapel topped by a figure of a contemplating Christ, on the corner of ul Kościuszki and ul Węgierska, a short walk south from the centre.

Places to Stay

Dom Nauczyciela (☎ 353 52 31, *ul Wróblewskiego 10)* Doubles without/with bath US$15/24. This is the simplest and cheapest of the central places. It's 100m from the Rynek.

Dwór Karwacjanów (☎ 353 56 18, *fax 353 56 01, ul Wróblewskiego 10A)* Doubles with bath US$24. Next door to the Dom Nauczyciela, the Dwór is an attractive fortified mansion whose roots reputedly go back to 1417. Extensively renovated, the building now houses an art gallery, a pub, and four double rooms with private bath on the top floor – good value.

Hotel Max (☎/fax 352 16 28, *ul Legionów 6D)* Doubles with bath & breakfast US$32-44. This small six-room hotel is yet another central option and may offer discount rates at weekends.

Getting There & Away

Train Gorlice has no train station as such. The main railway track is 5km north, through the village of Zagórzany which is linked with Gorlice by a shuttle train, running back and forth every two or three hours. From Zagórzany, there's transport to Jasło, and two trains a day to Kraków.

Bus Travelling by bus is the more convenient option. Six fast buses go to Kraków (140km) and double that number to Nowy Sącz (41km). Nowy Targ (117km) is serviced by at least five buses daily, as is Krosno (57km). For Biecz (15km), buses run every half-hour or so.

There's also a reasonable service southwards to Łosie, Ujście Gorlickie, Hańczowa and Wysowa, plus occasional buses to Izby, Kwiatoń, Smerekowiec and Gładyszów.

The bus terminal is next to the shuttle train station, a 10-minute walk from the Rynek.

SĘKOWA

Sitting in the prewar ethnic borderland between the Poles and the Lemks, Sękowa was one of the southernmost outposts of Roman Catholicism. Farther south, the Orthodox and Uniate faith predominated and you won't find old Catholic churches beyond this point.

The small wooden **church** in Sękowa is an exquisite example of timber architecture. The main part of the building dates back to the 1520s, though the bell tower and the *soboty*, which look like verandahs around the church, were added in the 17th century. The soboty – the word means 'Saturdays' – were built to shelter churchgoers from distant villages arriving late on Saturday night in time for early Sunday morning Mass. You will see many soboty on churches in the region.

The church passed through particularly hard times during WWI when the Austro-Hungarian army took part of it away to reinforce the trenches and for firewood, but careful reconstruction has restored its gracious outline. The interior lacks some furnishings but it's worth seeing anyway – the nuns who live in the house next to the church will give you the key.

Getting There & Away

The church is 5km south-east of Gorlice. To get there, take the suburban bus No 6 (to Ropica), No 7 (to Owczary) or No 17 (to Sękowa), get off in Siary and continue in the same direction for 50m until the road divides. Take the left-hand fork, cross the bridge 300m ahead and you'll see the church to your right.

SZYMBARK
☎ 18 • pop 2800

Szymbark is just a scattering of houses that spreads along the Gorlice-Grybów road for over 3km. You'd hardly notice you were passing through it if not for the road signs with the village's name. Roughly halfway through is a large modern church and it's here that the buses stop.

The old peasant cottages in the orchard next to the church constitute a skansen, the

Centre of Folk Architecture (*Ośrodek Budownictwa Ludowego;* ☎ *351 31 14; adult/student US$1/0.50; open 9am-4pm Tues-Fri, 10am-4pm Sat & Sun May-Sept, 9am-3pm Mon-Fri Oct-Apr).* The skansen is pretty small but nonetheless has some curiosities, the biggest being a fortified castle-like manor house from the 16th century, adorned with characteristic Renaissance parapets. It's being renovated and is off-limits to visitors. Of a dozen old timber cottages in the grounds, some have been furnished and decorated and can be visited.

Places to Stay & Eat

Pensjonat Perełka (☎ *351 30 11)* Beds in doubles, triples or quads without bath US$7. This simple guesthouse, in an 80-year-old timber villa, is across the road from the skansen. Meals can be provided if requested in advance.

Restauracja Watra (☎ *801 00 14)* Doubles with bath & breakfast US$28. Warta, 500m from the skansen towards Gorlice, is a roadside restaurant which serves reasonable food and has six double rooms with bath.

Getting There & Away

Buses on the main east-west road run regularly throughout the day to both Gorlice (7km) and Nowy Sącz (34km).

HIKING IN THE BESKID NISKI

Two main trails wind through the whole length of the range. The trail marked blue originates in Grybów, goes south-east to the border and winds eastwards all along the frontier to bring you eventually to Nowy Łupków near Komańcza. The red trail begins in Krynica, crosses the blue trail around Hańczowa, continues east along the northern slopes of the Beskid, and arrives at Komańcza. Both these trails head farther east into the Bieszczady.

You need four to six days to do the whole of the Beskid Niski on either of these routes, but there are other trails as well as a number of rough roads that link the two main trails.

A dozen youth hostels scattered in small villages throughout the region provide

shelter but most are open only in July and August. There are also a number of agro-tourist farms, and these are open longer or even year-round. If you plan on more ambitious trekking, camping gear may be useful. You can buy some elementary supplies in the villages you pass but you're better off stocking up on essentials before you start.

The major starting points for the Beskid Niski are Krynica, Grybów and Gorlice from the west; Komańcza and Sanok from the east; and Krosno, Dukla and Barwinek for the central part. Most of these places are described in separate sections later in this chapter.

The *Beskid Niski i Pogórze* map (scale 1:125,000) will give you all the information you need for hiking. It's usually available in larger cities, but not always in the region itself. The map is also very useful for those exploring the region using private transport.

The Beskid Sądecki

Lying south of Nowy Sącz, the Beskid Sądecki ('**Bes**-keed Son-**dets**-kee') is yet another attractive mountain range where you can hike, sightsee or simply have a rest in one of the mountain spas, the most popular being Krynica. The mountains are easily accessible from Nowy Sącz by two roads that head south along the river valleys, joining up to form a convenient loop; public transport is good on this route.

The Beskid Sądecki consists of two ranges, the Pasmo Jaworzyny and the Pasmo Radziejowej, separated by the valley of the Poprad River. There are a number of peaks over 1000m, the highest being Mt Radziejowa (1262m). It's good hiking country and you don't need a tent or cooking gear as mountain hostels dot the trails.

The Beskid Sądecki was the westernmost territory populated by the Lemks, and a dozen of their charming rustic churches survive, particularly around Krynica and Muszyna. The *Beskid Sądecki* map (scale 1:75,000) is helpful for both hikers and cerkiew-seekers.

THE BESKID SĄDECKI

NOWY SĄCZ
☎ 18 • pop 81,000

Founded in 1292 and fortified in the 1350s by King Kazimierz Wielki, Nowy Sącz ('**No**-vi Sonch') developed rapidly until the 16th century thanks to its strategic position on trading crossroads. Between 1430 and 1480 the town was the centre of the renowned Sącz school (Szkoła Sądecka) of painting. The works of art created here in that period now adorn a number of collections, including that of the royal seat of Wawel in Kraków.

As elsewhere, the 17th-century decline gave way to a partial revival at the close of the 19th century. Nowy Sącz grew considerably after WWII, and its historic district has been largely restored over recent years. It's a pleasant place and has some attractions, notably a good museum and a skansen. The town has an array of hotels and restaurants and as such can be a good base for further exploration.

Information
Tourist Offices The Centrum Informacji Turystycznej (☎/fax 443 55 97, 444 24 22), ul Piotra Skargi 2, off the Rynek, is open 9am to 5pm weekdays, 9am to 2pm Saturday.

Money Bank Pekao at ul Jagiellońska 50A (which changes travellers cheques and gives advances on Visa and MasterCard) is outside the centre, but it has a useful ATM at ul Jagiellońska 15, near the Rynek. Even more central is an ATM on the western wall of the town hall.

Email & Internet Access In the centre, you have Internet facilities in the Kawiarnia Cechowa (☎ 443 88 47), Rynek 11, and C@ffe Internet (☎ 443 84 33), ul Kościuszki 22.

Things to See
At 160m x 120m, the **Rynek** is one of the largest in Poland and is lined on all sides

with a harmonious collection of historic houses. The eclectic **town hall**, plonked in the middle in 1897, is quite large but it fortunately doesn't look oversized on this spacious square.

St Margaret's Church (Kościół Św Małgorzaty), a block east of the Rynek, is the oldest church in town, dating from the 17th century, yet it has undergone many additions and changes. The eclectic interior goes from Gothic to contemporary. A largish Renaissance high altar has a small 15th-century image of Christ at its centre, recalling the Byzantine influence.

The building to the south of the church houses the **Regional Museum** *(Muzeum Okręgowe; ☎ 443 77 08, ul Lwowska 3; adult/student US$1/0.50; open 10am-3pm Tues-Thur, 10am-5.30pm Fri, 9am-2.30pm Sat & Sun)*. The ground floor features religious paintings and woodcarvings dating from the 14th to 19th centuries. On the 1st floor, you'll find works of religious folk art collected from rural churches, domestic altars and roadside chapels throughout the region. The woodcarvings and paintings on show are mostly the work of anonymous local artists from the 18th to the early 20th centuries.

Next comes the collection of icons from the 15th to 19th centuries, a sign of the Lemks' presence. As this region was the westernmost outpost of the Orthodox church, the Roman Catholic influence is noticeable, particularly in icons dating from the 17th century on.

Two blocks north of the Rynek is the former **synagogue** *(☎ 444 23 70, ul Joselewicza 12; adult/student US$1.50/1; open 10am-3pm Wed & Thur, 10am-5.30pm Fri, 9am-2.30pm Sat & Sun)*, built in the first half of the 18th century in baroque style but remodelled in the 1920s. Partly destroyed in WWII, it was restored and now houses an art gallery, presenting changing exhibitions, plus a small permanent display of Jewish memorabilia.

The remains of the **Royal Castle** (Zamek Królewski), built by King Kazimierz Wielki in the 1350s, are 100m farther north. The castle often hosted Polish kings but

after a fire in 1616 and subsequent misfortunes of nature it never revived.

A five-minute walk farther north on ul Rybacka is the **Jewish cemetery**. It's a moving sight: a couple of hundred destroyed tombstones amid overgrown grass. This can be seen from over the fence but if you want a closer inspection, the keys to the cemetery gate are kept in the house at ul Rybacka 3, directly opposite the gate.

The **Sącz Ethnographic Park** *(Sądecki Park Etnograficzny; ☎ 441 44 12, ul Długoszowskiego 83B; adult/student US$1.50/1; open 10am-5pm Tues-Sun May-Sept, 10am-2pm Mon-Fri Oct-Apr)* is one of the best skansens in the country. It's about 3.5km south-east of the centre (1.5km beyond the camp site). Infrequent urban bus Nos 14 and 15 go there from the train station, passing the bus terminal on their way and skirting the edge of the central area.

The skansen gives an insight into the typical rural architecture of the region. The buildings of several ethnic cultures from the Carpathian Mountains and the foothills are displayed in groups. About 55 buildings have been assembled, of which a dozen can be visited. The interiors have all been carefully decorated, furnished and filled with household implements. The collection is steadily growing – an Orthodox church has recently been reassembled.

Visits are in groups guided in Polish. You can buy a booklet in English or German which describes the skansen's contents.

Places to Stay

Youth hostel (☎/fax 442 38 97, ul Reytana 18) Beds US$4-7. Open year-round. The 50-bed youth hostel is about the cheapest place to stay in town. It has two triples but most beds are in larger dorms (six to 10 beds). It's a bit hard to find – take the small ul Konopnickiej and follow the signs.

Dom Akademicki (☎ 443 56 90, ul Długosza 61) Beds in quads without bath US$6, doubles with bath US$24. This student/teacher dorm, near the bus terminal, is essentially open to the public in July and August, but there are a few rooms available year-round.

NOWY SĄCZ

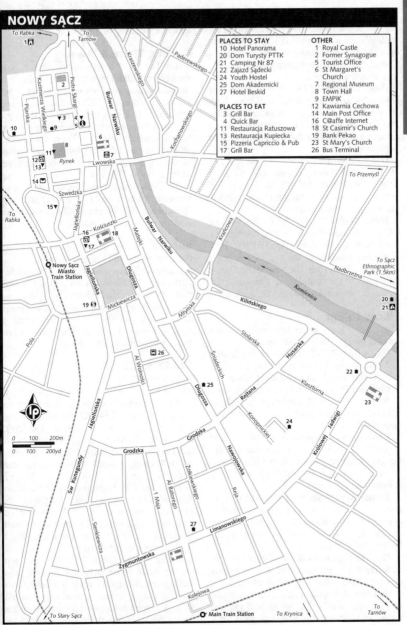

To Rabka →
To Tarnów

Paderewskiego
Kraszewskiego
Piotra Skargi
Bulwar Narwiku
Kochanowskiego
Kazimierza Wielkiego
Pijarska
Rynek
Lwowska
Szwedzka
Jagiellońska – Kościuszki
Matejki
Bulwar Narwiku
Krańcowa
To Przemyśl
To Rabka →
Nowy Sącz Miasto Train Station
Jagiellońska
Długosza
Mickiewicza
Młyńska
Kilińskiego
Kamienica
Nadbrzeżna
To Sącz Ethnographic Park (1.5km)
Al Wolności
Długosza
Stolarska
Śniadeckich
Husarska
Klasztorna
Jagiellońska
Grodzka
Grodzka
Rejtana
Konopnickiej
Nawojowska
Reja
Królowej Jadwigi
Św. Kunegundy
Sienkiewicza
1 Maja
Żółkiewskiego
Limanowskiego
Zygmuntowska
Kolejowa
Pola
Al Batorego
→ To Stary Sącz
Main Train Station
To Krynica
To Tarnów

0   100   200m
0   100   200yd

PLACES TO STAY
10 Hotel Panorama
20 Dom Turysty PTTK
21 Camping Nr 87
22 Zajazd Sądecki
24 Youth Hostel
25 Dom Akademicki
27 Hotel Beskid

PLACES TO EAT
3 Grill Bar
4 Quick Bar
11 Restauracja Ratuszowa
13 Restauracja Kupiecka
15 Pizzeria Capriccio & Pub
17 Grill Bar

OTHER
1 Royal Castle
2 Former Synagogue
5 Tourist Office
6 St Margaret's Church
7 Regional Museum
8 Town Hall
9 EMPiK
12 Kawiarnia Cechowa
14 Main Post Office
16 C@affe Internet
18 St Casimir's Church
19 Bank Pekao
23 St Mary's Church
26 Bus Terminal

Zajazd Sądecki (☎ 443 67 17, fax 443 83 36, ul Królowej Jadwigi 67) Doubles/triples/quads with bath US$22/24/26. Sitting opposite the impressive modern St Mary's Church, the Zajazd has simple rooms and its own restaurant.

Dom Turysty PTTK (☎ 441 50 12, ul Jamnicka 2) Doubles/triples without bath US$18/20, doubles/quads with bath US$20/36. This all-year PTTK hostel operates a camp site, *Camping Nr 87*, from May to September.

Hotel Panorama (☎ 443 71 10, fax 442 36 00, ul Romanowskiego 4A) Singles/doubles with bath US$25/38. This is the only place to stay in the Old Town, and it has a reasonable restaurant.

Hotel Beskid (☎ 443 57 70, fax 443 51 44, ul Limanowskiego 1) Singles/doubles with bath & breakfast US$70/80. This Orbis-run hotel is at the top of the price scale. It's 300m from the train station but a long walk to the centre (take a bus or taxi). Discount weekend rates may be available.

Places to Eat

There are plenty of small eating outlets serving budget meals. They include:

Quick Bar (☎ 442 14 48, ul Piotra Skargi 4) Mains US$1-3. Next to the tourist office just off the Rynek, this is a good place.

Grill Bar (☎ 443 89 77, ul Franciszkańska 7; ☎ 443 66 91, ul Jagiellońska 31) Mains US$1-3. These are good places for a quick tasty meal.

Restauracja Ratuszowa (☎ 443 56 15, Rynek 1) Mains US$3-7. Located in the cellar vaults of the town hall, the Ratuszowa has reasonable prices and food, including some budget dishes.

Restauracja Kupiecka (☎ 442 08 31, Rynek 10) Mains US$7-12. Another vaulted cellar affair, the Kupiecka offers European cuisine. It's not that cheap but is one of the better places in town.

Pizzeria Capriccio & Pub (☎ 442 01 16, ul Szwedzka 3) Pizzas US$2-4. Don't miss this pizzeria, lodged in fabulous vaults – enter from ul Wąsowiczów 2. It's popular with young locals, has good background music and atmosphere, and is as good for a

budget pizza, salad or spaghetti as it is for an espresso, beer or a stronger drink.

Getting There & Away

Train The main train station is over 2km south of the Old Town but urban buses run frequently between the two. There are some trains to Kraków (167km) but buses are more useful. Trains to Krynica (61km) go regularly throughout the day and pass Stary Sącz (7km) on their way. There's a reasonable service to Tarnów (89km), with trains departing every hour or two, and three trains a day to Warsaw.

The Nowy Sącz Miasto station is close to the centre but trains (six a day) only go from here to Chabówka (halfway along the Kraków-Zakopane route).

Bus The bus terminal is midway between the city centre and the train station. Buses to Kraków (99km) and Krynica (34km) depart every half-hour or so and are much faster than the trains. There's a regular service to Gorlice (41km), Szczawnica (48km) and Zakopane (100km or 116km depending on the route). Frequent PKS and urban buses run to Stary Sącz (8km).

STARY SĄCZ
☎ 18 • pop 8500

The oldest town in the region, Stary Sącz ('**Stah**-ri Sonch') owes its existence to Princess Kinga (1234–92), the wife of King Bolesław Wstydliwy (Boleslaus the Shy), who in the 1270s founded the convent of the Poor Clares (Klasztor Klarysek) here. After the king's death, Kinga entered the convent, where she lived for the last 13 years of her life, becoming its first abbess. This, together with various charitable acts and donations she made to the town, gave birth to the cult of the Blessed Kinga which spread through the region. The name Kinga is ubiquitous in the town.

On the secular front, the town's position on the trade route between Kraków and Buda (now Budapest) made it a busy commercial centre, though it gradually lost out to its younger but more progressive sister, Nowy Sącz. Today there's no comparison between the two – Stary Sącz is just a small satellite town. However, it has preserved much of its old atmosphere and architecture.

Things to See

There are not many genuine cobbled market squares left in Poland but the **Rynek** in Stary Sącz is definitely one of them. A solitary cluster of trees in its centre shades an old well. The town hall that was once here burnt down in 1795. The neat houses lining the square are almost all one-storey buildings. The oldest, No 6, dates from the 17th century and now holds the **Regional Museum** (☎ 446 00 94, Rynek 6; admission US$0.75; open 10am-1pm Tues-Sun, may close later in summer). Its collection of objects related to the town is reminiscent of a charming antique shop.

Enter the gate at Rynek 21 and have a look at the decoration on the vault above your head. Then walk to the backyard to see a dilapidated house guarded by folksy figures. Until 1990 this was a centre for local naive artists, complete with a folk art gallery. It was run by Józef Raczek, an amateur painter, sculptor and writer, but since his death the house has gradually fallen into ruin. Hopefully, you'll still be able to see some of the decoration left in this unique place.

The **parish church**, one block south of the Rynek, dates from the town's beginnings but has been changed considerably and is now a textbook example of unbridled baroque, with its five large florid altars fitted into the small interior. The elaborate pulpit, organ and, particularly, the unique stalls under the choir loft, complete the decoration.

Equally splendid is the **Church of the Poor Clares** (Kościół Klarysek), a short walk east. Surrounded by a high defensive wall, this was the birthplace of the town. Originally a Gothic building, completed in 1332, this church also ended up with opulent baroque fittings. The traces of its creator are clearly visible: the baroque frescoes in the nave depict scenes from the life of the Blessed Kinga, and her chapel (in front of you as you enter the church) boasts a 1470

statue of her on the altar. On the opposite wall, the pulpit from 1671 is an extraordinary piece of art.

Places to Stay & Eat

Zajazd Szałas (☎ 446 00 77, ul Jana Pawła II 77) Doubles/quads with bath & breakfast US$25/45. The only year-round accommodation in the area, the Zajazd is 1.5km outside the town on the Nowy Sącz road. It has only two doubles and two quads. Its restaurant serves inexpensive meals. Just behind the Zajazd is a camp site with tent sites and a collection of bungalows, but it was closed for refurbishing at the time of writing.

Restauracja Marysieńka (☎ 446 00 72, Rynek 12) Mains US$2-5. Established on the 1st floor of the tallest house in the square, the Marysieńka is probably the most pleasant place to eat in town. If the weather is fine, the balcony is the right place to grab a table and enjoy the vista over the square while having a lunch or a beer.

Getting There & Away

Train The train station is a 15-minute walk east of the centre and has a regular service south to Krynica (54km) and north to Nowy Sącz (7km). Several trains to Kraków daily (174km) and Tarnów (96km) depart mostly in the afternoon and evening.

Bus Buses stop in the Rynek. A continuous service to Nowy Sącz (8km) is provided by both the PKS and several lines of urban buses (Nos 8, 9, 10, 11, 24 and 43). About nine buses run to Szczawnica daily (48km) and six to Zakopane (100km); all come from Nowy Sącz.

KRYNICA

☎ 18 • pop 13,500

Set in attractive countryside amid the wooded hills of the Beskid Sądecki, Krynica ('Kri-**nee**-tsah') is possibly Poland's most popular mountain health resort. Though the healing properties of the local mineral springs had been known for centuries, the town only really began to develop in the 1850s. By the end of the century it was a fashionable hang-out for the artistic and intellectual elite, and continued to be so right up till WWII. Splendid villas and pensions were built in that period, blending into the wooded landscape. Development continued after the war but priorities shifted towards the needs of the working class rather than the artists. Massive concrete holiday homes and sanatoria came to occupy the slopes of surrounding hills, some of them less than sympathetic to their environment.

Information

Tourist Offices Information is provided by the Jaworzyna tourist bureau (☎ 471 56 54, ☎/fax 471 55 13, ⓦ www.krynica.pl), ul Piłsudskiego 8. The office is open 8am to 4pm Monday to Saturday. In the summer and winter high seasons it closes at 8pm.

Money You'll find useful ATMs at ul Piłsudskiego 3 and 19, ul Zdrojowa 35 and ul Kraszewskiego 1. There are also some kantors, including ones at ul Piłsudskiego 9 and in the post office at ul Zdrojowa 1.

Things to See & Do

About 20 mineral springs are exploited and roughly half of them feed the public pump rooms where, for a token fee, the waters can be tried by anybody. The largest of all is the **Main Pump Room** (*Pijalnia Główna;* ☎ 471 22 23, Al Nowotarskiego 9; open 6.30am-6pm daily). It's in a large modern building in the middle of Al Nowotarskiego, the central pedestrian promenade (called *deptak*) where the life of the town is concentrated.

There are a number of different waters to choose from in the Pijalnia and displays list the chemical composition of each. By far the heaviest, as you'll notice, is the Zuber, which has over 21g of soluble solid components per litre – a record for all liquids of that type in Europe. It won't be the best tasting brew you've ever tried, and the smell is appalling.

You'll need your own drinking vessel; a bottle or a plastic cup will do, but if you want to follow local style, buy one of a striking collection of small porcelain tankards from downstairs in the Pijalnia or in the

shops nearby. Local practice is to drink the water slowly while walking up and down the promenade. If you want to kill the taste, there's a good supply of places serving beer, coffee etc.

On a more cultural front, there's the interesting **Nikifor Museum** (*Muzeum Nikifora;* ☎ 471 53 03, Bulwary Dietla 19; adult/student US$1/0.50; open 10am-1pm, 2pm-5pm Tues-Sun). Located just west of the promenade, the museum displays about 50 works by Nikifor (1895–1968), possibly the best-known Polish naive painter. Lemk by origin, he produced hundreds of watercolours and drawings and is referred to as the Matejko of Krynica, the town of his birth. There are also various temporary exhibitions.

You can take a short trip on the **Funicular to Góra Parkowa** (*Kolej Linowa na Górę Parkową;* ☎ 471 22 62, ul Nowotarskiego 1; US$2/1.25 return/one way). The bottom station is near the northern end of the promenade. The car departs every half-hour (more often in high season) till 9pm or 10pm, depending on the season and the demand. The ascent of 142m takes less than three minutes. You can walk down or take the funicular back.

A longer trip can be taken by the modern **Cable Car to Mt Jaworzyna** (*Kolej Gondolowa na Jaworzynę;* ☎ 471 38 68, ul Czarny Potok 75; US$4.50/4 return/one way). Finished in 1997, the Austrian-made cable car system consists of 55 six-person cars that run from the bottom station in the Czarny Potok Valley (about 5km from Krynica's centre) up to the top of Mt Jaworzyna (1114m). The route is 2210m long and you climb 465m in seven minutes.

Places to Stay & Eat

Krynica has lots of holiday homes, hotels and pensions – approximately 120 in all – and there are also plenty of private rooms waiting for tourists. Like all resorts of this sort, the supply of accommodation changes notably throughout the year, peaking in summer, particularly in July and August, and in winter, mostly in January and February. Prices fluctuate depending on the season, weather, annual events etc, and are sometimes negotiable in the off-season.

Many places – particularly holiday homes, but also some pensions – will offer you full board, not just a bed, which can be convenient and cheaper than dining out.

It's best to start off at the Jaworzyna office, which deals with accommodation as well as tourist information. The staff will help you find and book a place – they claim they won't leave anybody on the street no matter how busy the season might be.

Expect to pay somewhere between US$5 and US$12 per bed in most places with shared facilities, US$8 to US$25 with baths. Add another US$8 to US$20 for full board.

Jaworzyna also arranges *private rooms* (US$5 to US$10 per person), though in the high season few owners will be interested in travellers intending to stay just a night or two (less hassle in the off-season).

Just in case you are arriving late when Jaworzyna is closed, here are a few options:

Dom Wypoczynkowy PTTK Rzymianka (☎ 471 22 27, ul Dąbrowskiego 17) Beds US$6. The PTTK is one of the cheapest places, but only offers shared facilities. It's pretty central, just 300m from the Jaworzyna office.

Hotel Rapsodia (☎/fax 471 27 85, ul Ebersa 5) Beds US$10-15. This is a typical middle-range option, with private facilities and a reasonable standard of comfort, plus its own restaurant. Rapsodia is close to the train and bus stations, convenient for late arrivals.

Pensjonat Zamek (☎/fax 471 55 01, ul Piękna 11) Beds US$10-15. The castle-like Zamek is roughly in the same class as the Rapsodia, but is closer to the centre.

Ośrodek Panorama (☎/fax 471 28 85, ul Wysoka 15) Singles with bath US$25-30, doubles with bath US$40-50. This large 140-bed holiday home, high up the wooded slope, offers quite good standards, though it's lacking in atmosphere.

Like accommodation, the culinary scene is also heavily influenced by the seasons. In the high season heaps of eating establishments open, including dining rooms and

cafes in holiday homes and pensions, and small bistros and snack bars along the central streets.

Getting There & Away

The train and bus stations are next to each other in the southern part of town; it's a 10-minute walk to the promenade from there.

Train There's a regular service to Nowy Sącz (61km) by a roundabout but pleasant route via Muszyna and Stary Sącz. Half a dozen trains continue to Tarnów (150km) and some of these go up to Kraków (228km).

Bus Buses to Nowy Sącz (34km) take a different, much shorter route to the train and run every half-hour to hour. The buses to Grybów (25km) depart regularly, passing through Berest and Polany. There are plenty of buses (both PKS and suburban) south to Muszyna (11km) via Powroźnik, and a fairly regular service to Mochnaczka, Tylicz and Muszyna (see later in this chapter).

AROUND KRYNICA
☎ 18

Krynica is a good base for hiking into the surrounding countryside, with its beautiful wooded valleys, hills and charming small villages. Some of these, once populated by the Lemks, have their old churches preserved to this day. An essential aid for exploring the region (whether you're interested in hiking or in churches) is the *Beskid Sądecki* map (scale 1:75,000), which is readily available.

Things to See

Most of the churches are accessible by bus. All churches listed below were originally the Uniate churches of the Lemks, but were taken over by the Roman Catholics after WWII. All are wooden structures, characteristic of the region.

To the north of Krynica, on the road to Grybów, there are good cerkwie in **Berest** and **Polany**, both with some of the old interior fittings including the iconostasis. Buses ply this route every hour or so and you shouldn't have problems coming back to

Krynica or continuing to Grybów, from where there's frequent transport west to Nowy Sącz or east to Szymbark and Gorlice.

The loop via Mochnaczka, Tylicz and Powroźnik is an interesting trip. The 1846 church in **Mochnaczka Niżna** still has its old iconostasis, although it's disfigured by a central altar. You can also see the old small cerkiew, 600m down the road towards Tylicz on the other side. Built in 1787, it holds a beautiful tiny iconostasis complete with original icons. If you find the church locked, ask the nuns living in the nearby house. There are several buses from Krynica to Mochnaczka daily but take an early one if you want to continue along the route.

The next village, **Tylicz**, boasts two churches, a Catholic one and the Uniate cerkiew. The latter is only used for funerals. The priest is not eager to open the churches for visitors but in July and August he runs a guided tour around their interiors (at 10am Monday at the time of writing). Call ☎ 471 13 10 for information on current times.

From Tylicz, a spectacular road skirts the Muszyna River valley to **Powroźnik** which features yet another cerkiew. This one is the oldest in the region (1643) and the best known. The exterior is beautiful, and inside is an 18th-century iconostasis and several older icons on the side walls. The church can only be visited just before or after Mass which is held at 7am and 11am on Sunday, and once a day on weekdays: at 6pm on Wednesday and Friday, at 6.30am on remaining days.

If you have your own means of transport, you can include Muszyna and Wojkowa in your loop, both of which have old churches (bus transport is infrequent on these side roads). St Mary's Church in Krynica (the town's main church) displays the times of religious services in all churches in the region, which could help you plan your trip.

Hiking

Two marked trails, green and red, head westward from Krynica up to the top of Mt Jaworzyna (1114m). It's two to three hours to walk there by either trail (or you can also get there faster by cable car). At the top, you'll get some good views, and may even spot the Tatras on clear days. There's a **PTTK mountain hostel** (☎ 471 54 09) just below the summit where you can stay overnight (in good doubles or cheap dorms) and eat, or you can go back down to Krynica the same day. You can also continue on the red trail west to Hala Łabowska (2½ hours from Mt Jaworzyna) where you'll find another **PTTK mountain hostel** (☎ 442 07 80) providing cheap beds and food. The red trail continues west to Rytro (five hours). This route, leading mostly through the forest along the ridge of the main chain of the Beskid Sądecki, is spectacular and easy, and because of the accommodation on the way you can travel light. From Rytro, you can go back to Krynica by train or bus.

MUSZYNA
☎ 18 • pop 4900

Much smaller than Krynica, Muszyna is also geared to tourism. Here, too, mineral springs have been discovered and exploited and a number of sanatoria have sprung up. There's a small **Regional Museum** (☎ 471 41 40, ul Kity 26; admission US$0.50; open 9am-4pm Wed-Fri, 9am-1.30pm Sat & Sun) in the old inn, which displays artefacts and old household implements collected from the region. Otherwise, Muszyna has no remarkable sights, though it can be a convenient starting point for trips into the surrounding region (see the following section), which is every bit as interesting as the area around Krynica.

Information

The Vector travel agency (☎ 471 80 03, fax 471 80 04), Rynek 32, can provide tourist information, help in finding accommodation, organise a tour and find an English-speaking guide. The office is open 8am to 6pm Monday to Saturday, and (in summer only) 8am to 3pm on Sunday.

Places to Stay

There are perhaps as many as 30 holiday homes in the area and plenty of *private rooms*. It's best to go directly to the Vector agency instead of going hotel-hunting on your own. In case you are late in town and haven't contacted the agency in advance, here are some options:

Ośrodek Wczasowy Kraśniczanka (☎ *471 42 25, fax 471 41 64, ul Piłsudskiego 110*) Beds US$6-7. This place, 800m south of the Rynek, is one of the cheapest options and only has shared facilities.

Dom Profilaktyczno-Wypoczynkowy Wiarus (☎/*fax 471 42 81, Złockie 79*) Beds in doubles or triples with bath US$10-12. Wiarus, in Złockie, 3km north of Muszyna, offers reasonable standards.

Ośrodek Sanatoryjno-Wczasowy Geovita (☎/*fax 471 41 83, Złockie 80*) Bed & meals US$30 a day. Another option in Złockie, this is one of the best places around, with its own swimming pool, sauna and tennis courts.

If you just need a simple place somewhere close in Muszyna, contact Mr Stanisław Hans (☎ 471 42 27, 471 80 60, ul Piłsudskiego 80A) who rents out *rooms* for US$4 to US$7.

Getting There & Away

Muszyna is on the Nowy Sącz-Krynica railway line and trains go regularly to either destination. Buses to Krynica. (11km) run frequently, and there's also an adequate service to Nowy Sącz (52km).

AROUND MUSZYNA

Having belonged to the bishops of Kraków for nearly 500 years (from 1288 to 1772), Muszyna was traditionally a Polish town so, not surprisingly, it has a Catholic church but not a cerkiew. But the surrounding villages were populated predominantly by Lemks, whose wooden Uniate churches still dot the region, and there are at least five within 5km of Muszyna.

Three of them are north of the town, in **Szczawnik**, **Złockie** and **Jastrzębik**. All three were built in the 19th century – the 1860s one in Złockie being the youngest and different in style – and each boasts the original iconostasis. Krynica suburban buses go via Muszyna to these villages several times a day and can shorten the walk.

Two more wooden churches, in **Milik** and **Andrzejówka**, are west of Muszyna, and have their original iconostases; you can get there by the regular buses or trains heading for Nowy Sącz. In Andrzejówka, ask for the key in the mustard-coloured house 50m down the road from the church; in Milik, the priest lives in the house at the foot of the cerkiew.

Two **hiking trails** originate in Muszyna and wind north up the mountains. The green one will take you to Mt Jaworzyna (1114m), while the yellow one goes to the peak of Mt Pusta Wielka (1061m). You can get to either in three to four hours, then continue to Krynica, Żegiestów or Rytro – the Beskid Sądecki map has all the details.

The Pieniny

The Pieniny, the mountain range between the Beskid Sądecki and the Tatras, is famous for the raft trip down the spectacular Dunajec Gorge, which has become one of Poland's major tourist highlights. Yet there's much more to see and do here. Walkers won't be disappointed with the hiking paths, which offer more dramatic vistas than the Beskid Sądecki or Bieszczady, while lovers of architecture will find some amazing old wooden Catholic churches here. There's also a picturesque mountain castle in Niedzica, or you can just take it easy in the pleasant spa resort of Szczawnica.

The Pieniny consists of three separate ranges divided by the Dunajec River, the whole chain stretching east-west for about 35km. The highest and most popular is the central range topped by Mt Trzy Korony (Three Crowns; 982m), overlooking the Dunajec Gorge. Almost all this area is now the Pieniny National Park (Pieniński Park Narodowy). To the east, behind the Dunajec River, lies the Małe Pieniny (Small Pieniny), while to the west extends the Pieniny Spiskie. The latter outcrop is the lowest and the least spectacular, though the region around it, known as the Spisz, has an interesting blend of Polish and Slovakian cultures.

THE CARPATHIAN MOUNTAINS

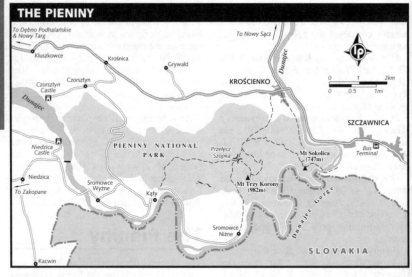

HIKING IN THE PIENINY

Almost all hiking concentrates on the central Pieniny range, a compact area of 10km x 4km decreed a national park. Trails are well marked and short and no trekking equipment is necessary. There are three starting points on the outskirts of the park, all providing accommodation and food. The most popular is Krościenko at the northern edge, then Szczawnica on the eastern rim and Sromowce Niżne to the south. Buy the *Pieniński Park Narodowy* map, which shows all hiking routes.

Most walkers start from Krościenko. They follow the yellow trail as far as the pass, the Przełęcz Szopka, then switch to the blue trail branching off to the left and head up to the top of Mt Trzy Korony (982m), the highest summit of the central range. The reward for this two-hour walk is a breathtaking panorama which includes the Tatras, 35km to the south-west, if the weather is clear. You are now about 520m above the level of the Dunajec River.

Another excellent view is from Mt Sokolica (747m), 2km east as the crow flies from Mt Trzy Korony, or a 1½-hour walk along the blue trail. From Mt Sokolica, you can go back down to Krościenko by the green trail, or to Szczawnica by the blue one, in less than an hour to either.

If you plan on taking the raft trip through the Dunajec Gorge, you can hike all the way to Kąty. There are several ways of getting there and the map mentioned shows all of them. The shortest way is to take the blue trail heading west from the Przełęcz Szopka and winding up along the ridge. After 30 to 40 minutes, watch for the red trail branching off to the left (south) and leading downhill. It will take you directly to the wharf in about half an hour.

Alternatively, take the yellow trail descending south from the Przełęcz Szopka into a gorge. In half an hour or so you'll get to the beautifully located PTTK hostel. You can stay here for the night, or continue 1km downhill to the village of Sromowce Niżne (where there is a basic camp site and some private rooms for rent) and go by bus (nine daily) or foot to Kąty (5km).

SZCZAWNICA
☎ 18 • pop 6800
Szczawnica ('Shchahv-**nee**-tsah') is the major tourist hub in the region. Picturesquely

located along the Grajcarek River, the town has developed into a popular summer resort, while its mineral springs have made it an important spa. It's also the finishing point for Dunajec Gorge raft trips.

The town spreads over 4km along the main road, ul Główna, and is divided into two suburbs, the Niżna (Lower) to the west and Wyżna (Upper) to the east, with the bus terminal between the two. A good part of the tourist and spa facilities are in the upper part, which also boasts most of the fine old timber houses.

Szczawnica is a good starting point for hiking in the Pieniny or the Beskid Sądecki. Three trails originate from the town and two more begin from Jaworki, 8km east.

Places to Stay & Eat

Accommodation in Szczawnica is the same as in many other mountain resorts: plentiful, cheap and highly varied depending on the season. There are few regular all-year hotels as well as a number of small pensions and holiday homes (most only open in summer). Plenty of locals also rent out rooms.

Travel agencies which arrange accommodation include Orbis Travel (☎ 262 22 57, ☎/fax 262 22 37), ul Główna 32, 150m east of the bus terminal; Podhale Tour (☎ 262 23 70, ☎/fax 262 27 27), ul Główna 20, 150m farther east; and PTTK (☎ 262 23 32, ☎/fax 262 22 95), ul Główna 1, another 150m farther east along the same road. One more agency, the Pieniny (☎ 262 14 79, ☎/fax 262 21 74), is at ul Skotnicka 8, 400m west of the bus terminal.

All the offices tend to close around 4pm or 5pm, but don't panic if you arrive later – just ask for a bed where you spot the signs 'noclegi', 'pokoje' or 'kwatery', indicating private rooms. There are plenty of these signs along ul Główna and the side streets. Expect to pay US$5 to US$10 a bed.

There are plenty of small eateries on or just off ul Główna, most of which trade in season only.

Getting There & Away

Buses to Nowy Targ (38km) depart roughly every hour. There are also regular buses to Nowy Sącz (48km) which pass via Stary Sącz (40km). Six fast buses run straight to Kraków daily (118km).

For the Dunajec Gorge, take a bus (four daily in season) to Sromowce Niżne and get off in Kąty (21km) – the driver will set you down at the right place. There are also private minibuses which depart when full. Also, check the PTTK, which organises tours if it can assemble 10 or more people; this may work out much the same price that you'd pay if doing the trip on your own.

KROŚCIENKO
☎ 18 • pop 4500

A small town (founded in 1348) at the northern foot of the Pieniny, Krościenko is today a local holiday resort that fills with tourists in summer. Rich mineral springs were discovered here in the 19th century, but the town didn't exploit them and the title of spa went to nearby Szczawnica, which did take advantage of the curative waters. With time Szczawnica overshadowed Krościenko in popularity, yet Krościenko remains No 1 as a hiking base for the Pieniny.

While in town, you can drop into the local church to see the surviving fragments of 15th-century frescoes depicting scenes from the life of Christ, and look over the pleasant Rynek in front of the church.

Information

The tourist office (☎ 262 33 04), Rynek 32, is open 8am to 4pm weekdays.

Places to Stay & Eat

There are half a dozen small pensions, including *Pensjonat Granit* (☎ 262 57 07, ul Jagiellońska 70), *Pensjonat Leśnik* (☎ 262 30 22, ul Jagiellońska 102), *Pensjonat Hanka* (☎ 262 32 98, ul Jagiellońska 55) and *Pensjonat U Gerwazego* (☎ 262 34 52, ul Zdrojowa 23). They all are simple but acceptable and will set you back about US$6 to US$8 per bed.

If you need something cheaper, the PTTK office (☎ 262 30 59, ul Jagiellońska 28), right in the centre, has a list of private rooms for rent, at around US$5 to US$7 per head. If you arrive after 3pm (the time they close the office) or on Saturday or Sunday, just look for signs that read 'noclegi' or 'kwatery' outside the houses.

Restauracja U Walusia (☎ 262 30 95, *ul Jagiellońska*) Mains US$3-6. This is the best of Krościenko's restaurants. It's 800m from the Rynek along the Nowy Targ road. Its specialities include the *placki po góralsku* (potato pancakes with goulash).

Getting There & Away

Lying on the Nowy Sącz-Nowy Targ route, Krościenko has a regular bus service to both these destinations. To Szczawnica (5km), buses run every 20 minutes or so. Four buses go to Sromowce Niżne daily (21km), which is the way to the raft wharf in Kąty (16km), and there are also private minibuses to Kąty in summer. You can also walk to Kąty (see Getting There & Away in the following section). Five fast buses run directly to Zakopane. Krościenko's main bus stop is at the Rynek.

DUNAJEC GORGE
☎ 18

The Dunajec Gorge (Przełom Dunajca) is a spectacular stretch of the Dunajec ('Doonah-yets') River, which snakes for about 8km between steep cliffs, some of which are over 300m high. The river is narrow, in one instance funnelling through a 12m-wide bottleneck, and changes constantly from majestically quiet, deep stretches to shallow mountain rapids.

The place has been a tourist attraction since the mid-19th century, when primitive rafts did the honours for guests of the Szczawnica spa. Today the raft trip through the gorge attracts some 200,000 people annually, not counting those in their own kayaks. Take note though that this is not a white-water experience but a leisurely pleasure trip; the rapids are gentle and you won't get wet.

The raft itself is a set of five narrow, 6m-long, coffin-like canoes lashed together with rope. Until the 1960s they were genuine dugouts but now they are made of spruce planks. The raft takes 10 passengers

and is steered by two raftsmen, each decked out in embroidered folk costume and armed with a long pole used to navigate.

The trip begins in the small village of Kąty, at the **Raft Landing Place** (*Przystań Flisacka;* ☎ 262 97 21, ☎/fax 262 97 93; *US$9 per person; 8.30am-5pm May-Aug, 8.30am-4pm Sept, 9am-2pm Oct*). You take a 17km trip and disembark in Szczawnica. It takes two to three hours, depending on the level of the river. Some rafts go farther downstream to Krościenko for US$2 more, but there's not much to see on that stretch of the river.

There are about 250 rafts in operation and they depart as soon as 10 passengers are ready to go. In general you won't have to wait long to get on the raft.

Rafts normally operate from 1 May to 31 Oct though both dates can change if it snows. There may also be some trips in late April and/or early November if the weather is fine. The trips may be suspended occasionally for a day or two when the river level is high.

Getting There & Away

Kąty is serviced by five buses from Nowy Targ daily (33km) and four from Szczawnica (21km). There's also a seasonal private minibus service from Szczawnica and Krościenko, and two PKS buses a day from Zakopane. Another way of getting to Kąty is to hike from Krościenko or Szczawnica. Travel agencies in Kraków, Zakopane, Szczawnica, Krynica and other touristy places in the region organise tours.

If you have private transport, you either have to leave your vehicle in Kąty and come back for it after completing the raft trip in Szczawnica, or you can drive to Szczawnica and leave your vehicle there, so you'll have it as soon as you complete the trip. There are car parks in both Kąty and Szczawnica, and the raft operator provides a bus service between the two locations.

NIEDZICA
☎ 18 • pop 3000

Niedzica, 5km west of Kąty, is known for its **castle**. Perched on a rocky hill above the Dunajec reservoir, the castle was built in the first half of the 14th century as one of the Hungarian border strongholds and was extended in the early 1600s. Since then it has altered little and has retained its graceful Renaissance shape.

The castle shelters a **museum** (☎ 262 94 89; adult/student US$1.50/1; open 9am-5pm daily May-Sept, 9am-4pm Tues-Sun Oct-Apr) featuring small collections on the archaeology and history of the region. You'll also get fine views over the surrounding area, including the reservoir of a hydroelectric project, just at the foot of the castle. An ethnographic section of the museum is presented (in summer only) in an old timber granary, 150m from the castle.

Places to Stay & Eat

Zespół Zamkowy (☎ 262 94 89, fax 262 94 80) Doubles with bath US$45-65, triple suites US$100. Open year-round. Part of the castle has been adapted for hotel needs, providing 32 beds, some of which are in the historic castle chambers. The castle management also offers cheaper *rooms* (some without bath) in the Celnica, a fine timber house built in the local style, 200m up the road from the castle. The castle restaurant provides meals. Some snack bars open in the tourist season near the castle entrance.

There are some accommodation options farther away from the castle, including:

Pensjonat Pieniny (☎/fax 262 94 08, ul 3 Maja 12) Beds in rooms/cabins without bath US$7/3. This large pensjonat is in the village of Niedzica, 2km south of the castle. It offers 100 budget beds in all-year rooms, plus another 50 beds in basic seasonal cabins. Meals are available.

Hotel Pieniny (☎/fax 262 94 74, ul Kanada 38) Singles/doubles with bath & breakfast US$14/24. Located halfway between Niedzica village and the castle, this is another budget option.

Getting There & Away

There are half a dozen buses a day from Nowy Targ (25km) to Niedzica castle. The village of Niedzica is better serviced from Nowy Targ, with about 10 buses per day, but not all go via the castle. When buying your ticket, make sure to specify 'Niedzica-Zamek' (castle). Bus links between the castle and other towns in the region are sporadic.

CZORSZTYN
☎ 18 • pop 2500

The village of Czorsztyn ('**Chor**-shtin'), across the Dunajec from Niedzica, boasts another **castle** (admission US$1; open 9am-6pm daily May-Sept, 10am-3pm Tues-Sun Oct-Apr). It was built as the Polish counterpart to the Hungarian Niedzica stronghold. It's now just a ruin, but a picturesque one, and provides some fine views over the Dunajec valley and the Tatras. There's a small exhibition featuring the castle's history.

The castle is 2km west of the new village of Czorsztyn (no public transport). The village was built in the 1990s to accommodate residents of old Czorsztyn, farther west, now flooded by the waters of the hydroelectric scheme. The village is just off the Krośnica-Kąty road, accessible by the same buses you take for the Dunajec raft trip at Kąty.

DĘBNO PODHALAŃSKIE
☎ 18 • pop 3000

This small village boasts one of the oldest and most highly rated timber churches in Poland. It was built in the 1490s on the site of a former church and, like most others, the larch-wood construction was put together without a single nail. The paintings that cover all the ceiling and most of the walls date from around 1500 and have not been renovated since; despite that, the colours are still brilliant.

A triptych from the late 15th century adorns the high altar, whereas the crucifix that stands on the rood beam dates from 1380 and was probably transferred from the previous church. There are some antique objects on the side walls, including a wooden tabernacle from the 14th century.

Another curiosity is a small musical instrument, a sort of primitive dulcimer from the 15th century, which is used during Mass instead of the bell. The seemingly illogical thing about it is that the thicker the bars, the higher the notes they produce.

The priest living just across the road takes visitors through the church. He expects tourists 8.30am to noon and 2pm to 4.30pm weekdays (until 3.30pm in autumn and winter). He will wait until about 10 people turn up, so you may have to wait as well.

GRYWAŁD
☎ 18 • pop 1500

Far less known than that in Dębno, the **church** in Grywałd is another small and quite amazing rustic construction, and it too has an interesting interior. The original wall paintings from 1618 adorn a good part of the walls and the ceiling. To see inside, ask the priest living in the house just north of the church.

Grywałd lies 1km north of the main Krościenko-Nowy Targ road, serviced regularly by buses daily. Get off at the turn-off and walk for 15 minutes to the church.

The Tatras

The Tatras are the highest range of the Carpathians and the only alpine type, with towering peaks and steep rocky sides dropping hundreds of metres to icy lakes. There are no glaciers in the Tatras but patches of snow remain all year. Winters are long, summers short and the weather erratic.

The vegetation changes with altitude, from mixed forest in the lower parts (below 1200m) to evergreen spruce woods higher up (to 1500m), then to dwarf mountain shrubs and highland pastures (up to 2300m) and finally moss. The wildlife is similarly stratified, with deer, roe deer and wildcats living in the lower forests, and the marmot and chamois in the upper parts.

The whole range, roughly 60km long and 15km wide, stretches across the Polish-Slovakian border. A quarter of it is Polish territory and is now the Tatra National Park (Tatrzański Park Narodowy), encompassing 212 sq km. The Polish Tatras boast two dozen peaks exceeding 2000m, the highest of which is Mt Rysy (2499m).

At the northern foot of the Tatras lies the Podhale region, which spreads from Zakopane to Nowy Targ. The Podhale, dotted with small villages populated by the *górale* (literally, highlanders), is one of the few Polish regions where old folk traditions are still observed in everyday life.

NOWY TARG
☎ 18 • pop 34,000

One of the oldest settlements at the foot of the Tatras, Nowy Targ started life around the 13th century, but in 1784 it was almost entirely consumed by fire and little of its old architecture has survived. Comfortably sitting in the fork of the Czarny (Black) and Biały (White) Dunajec Rivers, today it is a busy commercial town and a transport hub on the crossroads between the Tatras, Gorce, Pieniny, Spisz and Orawa. Nowy Targ is also known as a gliding centre; the airfield is on the south-eastern outskirts of the town.

The town is a possible jumping-off point for the surrounding countryside, though accommodation offerings are poor. You'll find a better selection of lodging options in Zakopane and Szczawnica.

Information
There's no tourist office to speak of. Bank Pekao is at Al Tysiąclecia 44. There are several kantors and ATMs in the central area.

Things to See
The town hall on the Rynek shelters the **Regional Museum** (*Muzeum Podhalańskie* ☎ 266 94 99, Rynek 1; admission US$1 open 9am-2pm Mon-Fri*) featuring local folk art and history of the region.

One block north of the Rynek is **St Catherine's Church** (Kościół Św Katarzyny), built in the mid-14th century (the presbytery still has Gothic features) but extensively reformed in the early 1600s. The interior boasts the usual baroque overlay.

Farther north, beyond the River, is the cemetery. At its entrance is the 16th-century shingled **St Anne's Church** (Kościół Św Anny). The interior is embellished with wall paintings from 1866. The church is open for Sunday services, at 10.30am and 4pm.

[Continued on page 329]

Hiking in the Tatra Mountains

W ith a huge variety of trails, totalling about 250km, the Tatras are ideal for walking. No other area in Poland is so densely crisscrossed with hiking paths and nowhere else will you find such a diversity of landscapes.

Warning

Like all alpine ranges, the Tatras can be dangerous, particularly during the snowy period, roughly from November to May. There's a real danger of avalanches in some areas, so check carefully the conditions of your planned route before setting off. Use common sense and go easy. Remember that the weather can be tricky, with snow or rain, thunderstorms, fog, strong wind etc occurring frequently and unpredictably. Bring good footwear, warm clothing and rain gear.

Planning

When to Go The Tatras are beautiful in every season, and there is no one time when they are at their best. If you don't appreciate crowds, it's probably best to avoid the mountains in July and August, when they may be overrun by tourists. Late spring and early autumn seem to be the best times for visits. Theoretically at least, you can expect better weather in autumn (September to October) when rainfall is lower than in spring.

Orientation

Although marked trails go all across the region, the most popular area for hiking is Tatra National Park, which begins just south of Zakopane. Its northern boundary goes along the service road known as Droga Pod Reglami, and it stretches south up to the national border.

Geographically, the Tatras are divided into Tatry Zachodnie (West Tatras) to the west and the Tatry Wysokie (High Tatras) to the east. Both areas are attractive for hiking, though they offer quite different scenery. West Tatras are lower and gentler, and don't actually provide much of alpine-type landscape. By and large, they are greener, easier to walk and safer.

The High Tatras, in the south-eastern part of the park, are a different story; it's a land of bare granite peaks with alpine lakes at their feet. Trekkers will face more challenges here, but they will also enjoy more dramatic views, and will find themselves in a true mountain environment.

Maps The *Tatrzański Park Narodowy* map (scale 1:25,000) published by Sygnatura is probably the best general map. It shows all the trails in the area, complete with walking times both uphill and downhill. It also has the Zakopane city map on the reverse side, a nice bonus.

Previous page: A winter scene in May at Lake Morskie Oko, in the Tatra Mountains (photographer: Craig Pershouse)

Hiker taking in the High Tatras in the Tatra National Park, on the Poland/Slovakia border

Snow-covered Tatra mountains in Southern Poland

Spruce forest, Tatra foothills

Polish lakes, Tatra Mountains

Chochołowska Valley, Tatra Mountains

Town Hall's Tower, Biecz

A hirsute Easter passion play near Kraków

River rafts ready for the trip along Dunajec Gorge in the Pieniny Mountains

The Gothic/renaissance town hall in Tarnów

Hay bales, Pieniny Mountains

TATRA NATIONAL PARK

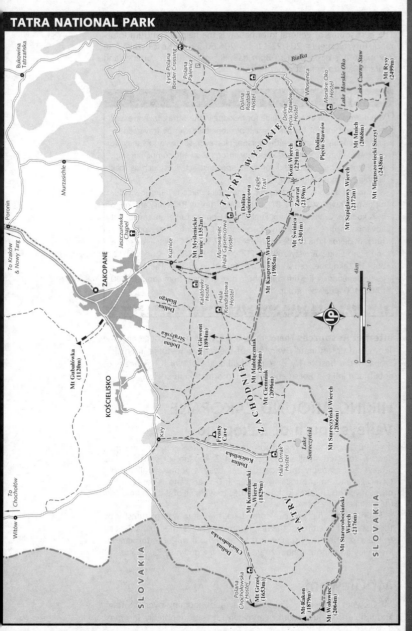

Information

The best source of general information is the helpful Centrum Informacji Turystycznej (☎ 201 22 11, fax 206 60 51), ul Kościuszki 17, in Zakopane. It's open 8am to 8pm daily in season (both summer and winter), 9am to 5pm at other times.

Guides

You normally don't need a guide for trekking in the Tatras; trails are well marked and except for some small portions they can be traversed by any reasonably fit and healthy person. However, some visitors may be interested in guide services, for safety, information and companionship. Also, guides may be useful for more specialist activities such as rock climbing or mountaineering.

A useful address for arranging a mountain guide is Biuro Przewodnickie Mr Travel (☎ 206 32 81), in the Dom Turysty PTTK, ul Zaruskiego 5, Zakopane. Guides speaking English and German can be arranged, but advance notice is usually necessary. Centrum Przewodnictwa Tatrzańskiego (Tatra Guide Centre; ☎ 206 37 99), ul Chałubińskiego 44, and Biuro Usług Turystycznych PTTK (☎ 201 58 48), ul Krupówki 12, both in Zakopane, can also arrange mountain guides. The cost of a guide depends on the difficulty of the hike or climb; from about US$40 to US$100 a day per group.

Internet Resources There are quite a few Web sites concerning the Tatras, but unfortunately very few of them have anything in English. Probably the best to try is ⓦ www.zakopane.pl which has heaps of details and links in Polish and general information in English.

HIKING AROUND ZAKOPANE
Valleys South of Zakopane

If you just want to go for a short walk, there are several picturesque, densely forested small valleys south of Zakopane, of which Dolina Strążyska is arguably the nicest. It has been a popular walking and picnic ground among locals for over 150 years, and it continues to draw in visitors. It takes just 40 minutes to walk all of it by the red trail up to Polana Strążyska.

From the Polana, you can come back the same way or transfer by the black trail to either of the neighbouring valleys, the Dolina Białego to the east being the usual way. It takes an hour to get to this charming valley and another hour to go all the way down to Zakopane.

Mt Giewont

Mt Giewont (1894m) is Zakopane's symbol, looming over the town and visible from just about everywhere. It's also reputedly the most popular mountain top climbed on foot in the Tatras (and apparently in Poland for that matter). Part of that drawing power seems to be due to the huge cross on the top, which has made the site a shrine.

There are basically two ways to the top of Mt Giewont. One is via the Dolina Strążyska mentioned earlier. Once you've reached Polana Strążyska, you continue by the red trail for 2½ hours to the cross. Altogether it's 3½ hours from Zakopane.

Another slightly easier way is from Kuźnice by the blue trail (about 2¼ hours). Kuźnice is easily accessible by frequent bus/minibus services. Whichever way you ascend, try to go down the other way, to enjoy more varied landscape. It's a good half- to full-day walk from Zakopane, but should you like to linger longer on the hills, note that you have two mountain hostels on the way, at Kalatówki and Hala Kondratowa.

Mt Giewont's Cross

Mt Giewont is topped with a cross. Appearing quite small while looking at it from a distance, the cross is actually 15m high and weighs 1819kg. The brainchild of a local vicar, the cross was erected in 1901, and the work took just six days. The elements of the cross were transported up the Hala Kondratowa by horse, then carried uphill by porters.

Predictably, the cross has become a pilgrimage attraction, with the faithful gathering at the summit on 19 August and 14 September. On these days there may be long queues to the top.

In 1997, shortly before the visit of Pope John Paul II, local authorities changed Zakopane's coat of arms. It now features Mt Giewont's cross placed above the insignia of papal power, the crossed St Peter's keys.

HIKING IN THE WEST TATRAS

There are two long and beautiful valleys, the Dolina Chochołowska and the Dolina Kościeliska, in the western part of the park. You can switch from one to the other, either by the black trail called the Ścieżka nad Reglami, or by the more demanding yellow trail higher up, via the Iwaniacka Przełęcz, a pass at 1459m. Each valley has a mountain hostel if you want to eat or stay overnight.

Dolina Kościeliska

By far the most popular valley in the West Tatras, the Kościeliska is easily accessible from Zakopane by frequent PKS buses and private minibuses to its gateway at Kiry. From here, take a dirt road going south along the valley's bed on almost flat terrain. After a 35-minute walk, you'll find a black trail that branches off to the left and goes up (20 minutes) to Jaskinia Mroźna (Frosty Cave), Tatra's most popular cave, lit and open to tourists 10am to 4pm daily (longer in summer).

It's about 500m long, with the usual world of stalactites and stalagmites, and is visited in groups with a guide. The tour takes 45 minutes and costs US$1 per person.

Back on the road, you can continue gently uphill for 25 minutes to the site of several more caves, including Jaskinia Mylna. Here lies the impressive Wąwóz Kraków (Kraków Gorge) which you can visit along the yellow trail designed as a loop (one hour).

You can then continue up the road to the Hala Ornak Hostel (30 minutes), from where you have various options for further exploration. You can either take the yellow trail west to the Dolina Chochołowska, or head east along the green trail to the Czerwone Wierchy, but this is a long haul.

Dolina Chochołowska

The westernmost valley in the Polish Tatras, the Chochołowska is overshadowed by the Kościeliska, even though it's also beautiful, particularly so in late March/early April when it gets covered with thousands of flowering crocuses. Long, wide and flat, the valley is easy to walk, and there's a road going along its bed beside a creek. It's a two-hour walk up to the Polana Chochołowska Hostel.

Several trails depart from the hostel, allowing for some shorter and longer walks. One possible excursion is a loop via the mountain tops along the Slovakian border. Take the yellow trail going west up to Mt Grześ (1653m), continue south by the blue trail to Mt Rakon (1879m) and on to Mt Wołowiec (2064m), and return by the green trail north to the hostel. It will take roughly five hours to do the whole loop.

Instead of returning down the Dolina Chochołowska, you can switch by the yellow trail east to Dolina Kościeliska (three hours to get to Hala Ornak Hostel).

HIKING IN THE HIGH TATRAS

The High Tatras offer the widest choice of walks and the most dramatic views, and they are easily and conveniently accessible from two different sides: by cable car to Mt Kasprowy Wierch; and by bus to Lake Morskie Oko. Both these ways are hugely popular with visitors.

Mt Kasprowy Wierch

The cable-car is an easy way to get into the heart of the mountains, and is an excellent way to enjoy splendid views during the journey itself (clouds permitting). Once at the top, you have several options. The first and easiest one is to go back the same way by cable car. If you bought a return ticket, you have one hour and 40 minutes at the summit, which only allows for a short walk around the top. If you need more time, you'll have to buy a one-way ticket up, and then another one down.

Mt Kasprowy Wierch to Kuźnice Many people don't return by cable car, opting instead to walk. There are several marked trails from Mt Kasprowy Wierch that can take you either back to Kuźnice or to other parts of the Tatras. To go down, the most popular way is by the yellow trail via Dolina Gąsienicowa to Murowaniec Hala Gąsienicowa Hostel (1¼ hours), and on, initially by the blue then by the yellow trail via Dolina Jaworzynka to Kuźnice (1¾ hours). In other words, in three hours you are back after an easy, all-the-way-down pleasant walk, unless you decide to stop for lunch or the night in Murowaniec.

MH

Mt Kasprowy Wierch to Lake Morskie Oko Many trekkers use Mt Kasprowy Wierch as a launching pad for Lake Morskie Oko via Dolina Pięciu Stawów, either as a full-day hike (six hours net walking time to Morskie Oko), or with an overnight stop at the Dolina Pięciu Stawów Hostel. Either way, it's a fascinating, extremely scenic walk, one of the best in the High Tatras. From Mt Kasprowy Wierch, you head eastwards along the red trail to Mt Świnica (2301m), and on to the Zawrat Pass (2¾ hours from Mt Kasprowy). It's a spectacular walk along the ridge. From Zawrat you descend south by the blue trail to the wonderful Dolina Pięciu Stawów (Five Lakes' Valley) where you'll find a mountain hostel (1½ hours from Zawrat). The blue trail continues west from the hostel to Lake Morskie Oko (1¾ hours).

Orla Perć

The most intrepid hikers don't descend from Zawrat Pass but head on up the ridges of the Orla Perć (Eagle Trail), just about the most adventurous and breathtaking route you can find in the Tatras, which follows a rocky ridge marked by the red trail from Zawrat Pass to Krzyżne Pass (six to seven hours). The Eagle Trail is very difficult and shouldn't be undertaken by inexperienced trekkers. The terrain is such that chains, foot holes and ladders have been put in place to help you – great if you're into that, but a bit daunting for some.

Lake Morskie Oko

The emerald-green Lake Morskie Oko (Eye of the Sea), acclaimed as being among the loveliest in the Tatras, is the most popular tourist destination in this part of Poland. You can get there on foot from the Dolina Pięciu Stawów as described above, but the lake is much easier to get to by road from Zakopane. As the trip involves little walking, it's extremely popular with tourists of all ages and is done by every second visitor to Zakopane. Hence, the lake is swamped with people in the high season, particularly in July and August. Try to avoid these months, but do come – this really is one of the most amazing corners of the Tatras.

Morskie Oko – Eye of the Sea

Morskie Oko is Tatras' largest lake and one of the most beautiful. It's 862m long, 566m wide and has an area of 34.5 hectares. It's 50.8m deep and 2613m in circumference. From November to May, the lake is covered with ice which can be more than 1.5m thick. Morskie Oko is the Polish Tatras' only lake with naturally stocked trout. The neighbouring peaks loom about 1000m above the lake's level, and include Poland's tallest peak, Mt Rysy (2499m). The lake's name comes from an old legend which says that it had an underground connection with the Adriatic.

PKS buses from Zakopane depart for the lake regularly, as do private minibuses from across the road from the bus terminal. They go as far as the car park at the Polana Palenica (US$1.25, 30 minutes). The 9km road continues uphill to the lake, but no cars, bikes or buses are allowed beyond the car park. You can walk the distance in two hours or take a horse-drawn carriage which will bring you to Włosienica, 2km from the lake. Between the car park and Włosienica, the road climbs 339m.

Horse-drawn carriages leave as soon as they collect about 15 people. The trip takes about 1¼ hours uphill and costs US$7; downhill it takes 45 minutes and costs US$4. In summer, carriages go up until about 4pm or 5pm and return up to around 8pm. In winter, transport is by horse-drawn four-seater sledges, which are more expensive than the carriages.

From the carriage stop at Włosienica, it's a 20-minute walk to the lake shore, where you'll get amazing vistas over the lake and the mountains behind it. Morskie Oko Hostel, spectacularly set at the lakeside, serves hearty meals and drinks.

Lake Morskie Oko to Lake Czarny Staw A stone walking path circles Lake Morskie Oko, and you can do the loop in 45 minutes, but break it at the far end and climb to Lake Czarny Staw (Black Pond), 187m higher up, in half an hour (50 minutes from the hostel). Czarny Staw is smaller than Morskie Oko but deeper and its water has a dark blue tone.

Lake Czarny Staw to Mt Rysy The trail continues steeply up to the top of Mt Rysy (2499m), Poland's highest peak. In return for your 3½-hour climb from Czarny Staw, you will get a view of over 100 peaks and a dozen lakes. This trek is difficult, and is only recommended for people with trekking experience. The trip is best done in late summer. There's a border crossing here to Slovakia, open in summer only.

PLACES TO STAY & EAT

Camping is not allowed in the park but there are eight PTTK mountain hostels which provide accommodation, costing about US$4 to US$10 per person. Hostels are not that big and fill up fast. In both midsummer and midwinter they may be packed far beyond capacity. No one is ever turned away, though you may have to crash on the floor if all the beds are taken. Don't arrive late and bring along a bed mat and sleeping bag.

All hostels serve simple hot meals, but their kitchens and dining rooms close early, in some places at 7pm. Hot water is usually available free of charge. The hostels are open year-round but some may be temporarily closed for repairs, usually in November. Before you set off, check the current situation at the tourist office in Zakopane. Following is basic information about all eight hostels, from west to east (including altitude):

Polana Chochołowska Hostel (Schronisko na Polanie Chochołowskiej; 1148m; ☎ 207 05 10) Beds US$5-8, floor US$3.50. Tatra's westernmost mountain hostel has 133 beds. It's nestled at the upper part of the Dolina Chochołowska, and is the largest of the eight hostels with rooms ranging from doubles to large dorms. Built in 1953, the hostel is accessible by road and you can get there by bike.

Hala Ornak Hostel (Schronisko na Hali Ornak; 1108m; ☎ 207 05 20) Beds US$4-6, floor US$2.50. This fine stone chalet dating from 1948 has 85 beds. It's in the upper end of the Dolina Kościeliska and is accessible by road, but bikes are not permitted here. The hostel has some doubles but most rooms are in larger dorms.

Hala Kondratowa Hostel (Schronisko na Hali Kondratowej; 1333m; ☎ 201 52 14) Beds US$5. Delightfully situated on the trail to Mt Giewont, this 20-bed timber hostel is one of the most charming, but note the size – it's the smallest of the eight hostels.

Kalatówki Hostel (Hotel Górski na Kalatówkach; 1198m; ☎ 206 36 44) Doubles with bath US$32, doubles/triples without bath US$25/32, beds in dorms US$8. An 84-bed hotel rather than a hostel, Kalatówki provides more comfort than any other hostel and is the only one which has rooms with private baths. It's accessible by road from the Kuźnice cable-car station (a 40-minute walk).

Murowaniec Hala Gąsienicowa Hostel (Schronisko Murowaniec na Hali Gąsienicowej; 1505m; ☎ 201 26 33) Beds in 3- to 10-bed dorms US$7, 14-bed dorms US$6, floor US$4. This large (120 beds) fortress-like granite hostel built in 1925 sits at the crossroads of several popular trails, so it's often busy. Bikes are allowed to come here along the Dolina Suchej Wody.

Right: Mountain ridge from Rysy (2499m) marking the Slovakia-Poland border, Tatra Mountains (photographer: Mark Daffey)

Dolina Pięciu Stawów Hostel *(Schronisko w Dolinie Pięciu Stawów; 1672m;* ☎ *207 76 07)* Beds US$5-7, floor US$4. This is the highest and most scenically located hostel in the Polish Tatras. It has 70 beds and is crucial for hikers as it's located on one of the most spectacular and popular trails. Consequently, it can often fill up well beyond capacity. At times, the floor may not be big enough to accommodate all the guests.

Morskie Oko Hostel *(Schronisko nad Morskim Okiem; 1406m;* ☎ *207 76 09)* Beds in 3- to 6-bed dorms US$10, 13- to 16-bed dorms US$7, floor US$7. This 77-bed place is also extremely popular and it's hard to get a bed. There are actually two hostels here. The famous postcard chalet overlooking Lake Morskie Oko, known as the new hostel (built in 1908), has 34 beds in small dorms and is fine. The other one, from 1874, is a bit dilapidated and has 43 beds in large dorms.

Roztoka Hostel *(Schronisko w Roztoce; 1031m;* ☎ *207 74 42)* Beds US$5-7. A relatively small hostel (64 beds) dating back to 1876, it's the lowest-altitude hostel overlooking a wide valley, and is accessible by the Morskie Oko bus. It's an hour's walk from Polana Palenica. It's not the most popular hostel – most hikers go farther up the mountains.

GETTING THERE & AWAY
Funicular to Mt Gubałówka

Mt Gubałówka (1120m) offers an excellent view over the Tatras and is a favourite destination for those tourists who don't feel like exercising their legs too much. The funicular, built in 1938, provides comfortable access to the top. It covers the 1388m-long route in less than five minutes, climbing 300m. In summer, it operates every 10 minutes from 7am to 9pm. Return/one-way tickets cost US$3.50/2.

Cable Car to Mt Kasprowy Wierch

Since it opened in 1935, the cable-car trip from Kuźnice to the summit of Mt Kasprowy Wierch (1985m) – where you can stand with one foot in Poland and the other in Slovakia – has become almost a must for tourists to Poland. The route is 4290m long with an intermediate station midway at Mt Myślenickie Turnie (1352m). The one-way journey takes 20 minutes and climbs 936m.

The cable car operates year-round but shuts down for a few weeks in May/June, and again in November. Dates can vary from year to year. In midsummer it runs from 7.30am to 6pm; in winter 7.30am to 4pm.

Return/ascent/descent tickets cost US$7/4.50/2.50. If you buy a return, your trip back is automatically reserved two hours after departure time. Tickets can be bought at the Kuźnice cableway station (for the same day only). You can also buy them in advance from Orbis and some other travel agencies, but they charge a fee. At peak tourist times (both summer and winter), there are long lines in Kuźnice; get there early. PKS buses go to Kuźnice frequently from the bus terminal, as do the private minibuses that park across the street.

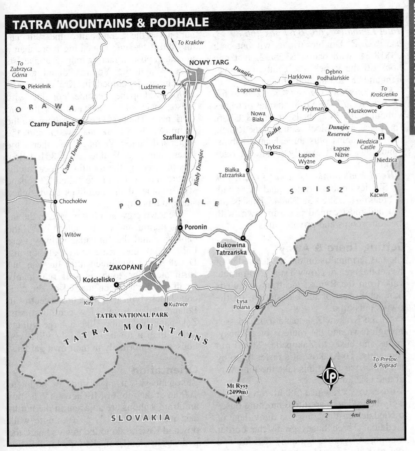

TATRA MOUNTAINS & PODHALE

[Continued from page 318]

The town's best-known attraction is the **Thursday market**, which has traditionally been held here for over half a millennium, following the king's privilege granted in 1487. However, since mass-produced consumer goods have become the dominant fare in recent years, the market has lost much of its former character and atmosphere. If you're thinking about buying hand-knitted sweaters, typical hats or other handicrafts, you're more likely to find what you're looking for in Zakopane. The market is held on the Plac Targowy, a few blocks east of the Rynek. These days, an equally big market is also held on the same square on Saturday. There have been some reports of pickpockets at the markets, so watch your belongings closely.

If you happen to be in the area on 15 August (the Assumption), try not to miss visiting the small village of **Ludźmierz**, only 5km from Nowy Targ, where the holy statue of the Virgin Mary in the local church attracts large numbers of the górale, most of them dressed up in their traditional costumes.

Places to Stay

Hotel Limba (☎ 266 70 64, fax 266 89 43, ul Sokoła 8) Doubles/triples without bath US$18/24, with bath US$28/32. Just one block off the Rynek, the Limba is convenient and cheap but pretty basic.

Klub Sportowy Gorce (☎/fax 266 26 61, Al Tysiąclecia 74) Beds in doubles or triples without bath US$6, beds in cabins US$6. This place, a few blocks south of the Rynek, has hotel rooms plus three heated cabins. Conditions aren't exactly plush but rates aren't high.

Hotel Podhalanka (☎ 266 63 66, Rynek 39) Singles/doubles/triples/quads with bath & breakfast US$24/32/36/44. This is the best and most central place in town, with spacious rooms and private baths.

Getting There & Away

The bus terminal is on the western edge of the central area of Nowy Targ, a 10-minute walk from the Rynek; the train station is 1km south-west of the bus station, on the town's outskirts.

All the Kraków-Zakopane traffic passes through town and the route is pretty busy. Trains and buses to Zakopane (24km) run frequently. To Kraków, it's faster to go by bus (80km) as the trains take the long way around (126km).

Buses to Szczawnica (38km) run roughly every hour. There are three morning buses to Niedzica castle, going via the village of Niedzica. Three buses go to the border crossing at Łysa Polana daily (37km), and five to Kąty (33km), where the raft trips through the Dunajec Gorge begin.

ZAKOPANE

☎ 18 • pop 30,000

Nestled at the foot of the Tatras, Zakopane is the most famous mountain resort in Poland and the winter sports capital. The town attracts a couple of million tourists a year, with peaks in summer and winter. Although Zakopane is essentially a base for either skiing or hiking in the Tatras, the town itself is an enjoyable enough place to hang about for a while, and it has lots of tourist facilities.

Zakopane came to life in the 17th century, but only in the second half of the 19th century did it become something more than a mountain post, attracting tourists and artists alike. When the Young Poland artistic movement developed in Kraków in the 1890s, Zakopane became popular with artists, many of whom came to settle and work here. The best known of these are the composer Karol Szymanowski and the writer and painter Witkacy. The father of the latter, Stanisław Witkiewicz (1851–1915), was inspired by the traditional local architecture and created the so-called 'Zakopane style'; some of the buildings he designed stand to this day.

The town grew at a faster pace in the interwar period, and shortly before WWII the cableway and the funicular railway were built, today the prime tourist attractions. Development continued after the war but fortunately the town is still reasonably small and hasn't been marred by the concrete blocks typical of most urban centres in Poland. Apart from a few central streets, Zakopane feels more like a large village rather than a town, its mainly villa-type houses set informally in their own gardens.

Orientation

Zakopane sits at an altitude of 800m to 1000m at the foot of Mt Giewont. The bus and train stations are adjacent in the north-east part of town. It's a 10-minute walk down ul Kościuszki to the town's heart, the pedestrian mall of Krupówki, always jammed with tourists.

The funicular to Mt Gubałówka is off the north-western end of Krupówki. The cable car to Mt Kasprowy Wierch is at Kuźnice, 3km to the south-east.

Information

Tourist Offices The helpful Centrum Informacji Turystycznej (☎ 201 22 11, fax 206 60 51), ul Kościuszki 17, is open 8am to 8pm daily in season (both summer and winter), 9am to 5pm at other times.

Money Bank Pekao, Al 3 Maja 5, changes most major brands of travellers cheques and pays złoty advances on Visa and Master-Card. Bank Przemysłowo Handlowy, ul Krupówki 19, will change cheques and accepts Visa card. Kantors dot ul Krupówki every 50m or so, and there are also a number of ATMs.

Email & Internet Access Internet facilities include Top Net (☎ 206 42 31), ul Krupówki 2, and Internet Club Mikrokomputery (☎ 201 33 10), Krupówki 54.

Travel Agencies Orbis Travel (☎ 201 50 51), ul Krupówki 22, sells domestic and international train tickets, arranges accommodation in private houses and selected holiday homes and organises tours.

Other useful travel agencies include Trip (☎ 202 02 00), ul Tetmajera 18; Teresa (☎ 201 43 01), ul Kościuszki 7; and Infotour (☎ 206 42 64), ul Kościeliska 11B. They arrange accommodation in private rooms, sell transportation tickets and may have tours to popular regional tourist destinations, including the Dunajec Gorge (US$15 to US$18 per person).

Bookshops You'll find the best choice of maps and guidebooks on the Tatras and other mountain regions at Księgarnia Górska (☎ 201 24 81), in the Dom Turysty PTTK.

Things to See

You'll probably start your sightseeing at Krupówki, the trendy central mall, lined with restaurants, cafes, boutiques and souvenir shops. After wandering up and down once or twice you should have a good feel for the local atmosphere. Krupówki is the place to be, and some tourists seem to do nothing but parade up and down this mall for days on end.

Your first stop might be the **Tatra Museum** (*Muzeum Tatrzańskie; ☎ 201 52 05, ul Krupówki 10; adult/student US$1.50/1; open 9am-4pm Tues-Sat, 9am-3pm Sun*), which has sections on history, ethnography, geology and flora and fauna and is thus a good introduction to the region.

At the lower end of Krupówki is the large stone neo-Romanesque **parish church**,

which looks as though it had been imported from a completely different culture. It was built at the end of the 19th century when the much smaller **old parish church** couldn't cope any longer with the numbers of worshippers. The latter, 100m away on ul Kościeliska, is a rustic wooden construction dating from 1847. It has charming folksy decorations inside.

The **stone chapel** standing beside it is about 30 years older and is in fact the first place of worship and the oldest surviving building in Zakopane. Just behind it is the **old cemetery** with a number of amazing wooden tombs.

West on ul Kościeliska is the **Villa Koliba**, the first design (1892) of Witkiewicz in the Zakopane style. It now accommodates the **Museum of Zakopane Style** (*Muzeum Stylu Zakopiańskiego; ☎ 201 36 02, ul Kościeliska 18; adult/student US$1.50/1; open 9am-4pm Wed-Sat, 9am-3pm Sun*).

About 500m south-east is **Villa Atma**, once the home of Karol Szymanowski. Today it's a museum (*☎ 201 34 93, ul Kasprusie 19; adult/student US$1.50/1; open 10am-3.30pm Tues-Sun*) dedicated to the composer. Summer piano recitals are held here.

Don't miss the **Władysław Hasior Art Gallery** (*☎ 206 68 71, ul Jagiellońska 18C; adult/student US$1.50/1; open 11am-6pm Wed-Sat, 9am-3pm Sun*), displaying striking assemblages by this avant-garde artist, who was also closely associated with Zakopane until his recent death.

A 20-minute walk south of here, next to the roundabout called Rondo, is the **Tatra National Park Museum** (*Muzeum TPN; ☎ 201 41 92, ul Chałubińskiego 42A; adult/student US$1/0.50; open 9am-2pm Mon-Sat*) with an exhibition on the natural history of the park.

A short walk east up the hill will lead you to the **Villa Pod Jedlami**, another splendid house in the Zakopane style (the interior cannot be visited). Perhaps Witkiewicz's greatest achievement is the **Jaszczurówka Chapel**, about 1.5km farther east on the road to Morskie Oko.

THE CARPATHIAN MOUNTAINS

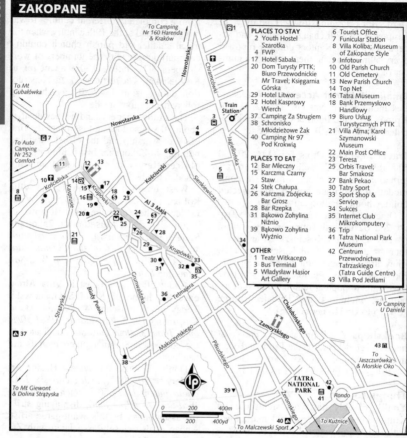

ZAKOPANE

PLACES TO STAY
2 Youth Hostel Szarotka
4 FWP
17 Hotel Sabała
20 Dom Turysty PTTK; Biuro Przewodnickie Mr Travel; Księgarnia Górska
29 Hotel Litwor
32 Hotel Kasprowy Wierch
37 Camping Za Strugiem
38 Schronisko Młodzieżowe Żak
40 Camping Nr 97 Pod Krokwią

PLACES TO EAT
12 Bar Mleczny
15 Karczma Czarny Staw
24 Stek Chałupa
26 Karczma Zbójecka; Bar Grosz
28 Bar Rzepka
31 Bąkowo Zohylina Niźnio
39 Bąkowo Zohylina Wyźnio

OTHER
1 Teatr Witkacego
3 Bus Terminal
5 Władysław Hasior Art Gallery

6 Tourist Office
7 Funicular Station
8 Villa Koliba; Museum of Zakopane Style
9 Infotour
10 Old Parish Church
11 Old Cemetery
13 New Parish Church
14 Top Net
16 Tatra Museum
18 Bank Przemysłowo Handlowy
19 Biuro Usług Turystycznych PTTK
21 Villa Atma; Karol Szymanowski Museum
22 Main Post Office
23 Teresa
25 Orbis Travel; Bar Smakosz
27 Bank Pekao
30 Tatry Sport
33 Sport Shop & Service
34 Sukces
35 Internet Club Mikrokomputery
36 Trip
41 Tatra National Park Museum
42 Centrum Przewodnictwa Tatrzaskiego (Tatra Guide Centre)
43 Villa Pod Jedlami

Cycling

Cycling can be a pleasant and convenient means of getting around the Zakopane region, including some of the less steep parts of the Tatras. Bikes are permitted in certain areas of Tatra National Park, but only on designated routes. These include the Dolina Chochołowska and Dolina Suchej Wody, both picturesque and attractive for biking. Droga Pod Reglami, the service road which marks the northern boundary of the park, also offers some good rides. Check when you arrive which routes are open for bikes, because this tends to

change. Note that the access road to Lake Morskie Oko is no longer open for bikes. They can go only as far as the car park at Polana Palenica.

Bicycles are available for rental from a number of companies in Zakopane, including Sukces (☎ 201 48 44), ul Sienkiewicza 39; Sport Shop & Service (☎ 201 58 71), ul Krupówki 52A; Tatry Sport (☎ 201 44 23), ul Piłsudskiego 4; and Malczewski Sport (☎ 201 20 05), ul Bronisława Czecha. Expect a bike to cost US$2 per hour (with a possible three-hour minimum charge), and US$10 per day.

Skiing

Zakopane is known as Poland's winter sports capital. The town's environs have a number of ski areas, ranging from flat surfaces to steep slopes – suitable for everyone from beginners to ski masters – dotted with about 50 ski lifts in all.

Mt Kasprowy Wierch offers some of the most challenging ski slopes in the area, as well as the best conditions, with the ski season extending right up until early May. You can get to the top by cable car then stay up the mountains and use the two chair lifts, in the Goryczkowa and Gąsienicowa valleys, on both sides of Mt Kasprowy Wierch. Lift tickets are approximately US$1 per ride, or alternatively, purchase an all-day pass.

Mt Gubałówka is another popular skiing area and it too, offers some steep slopes and good conditions. It's easily accessible by the funicular from central Zakopane, and there are some T-bar lifts up there. Nearby, 2km to the west, is **Mt Butorowski Wierch**, with its 1.6km long chair lift, making it yet another good skiing area.

One more major ski area is at the slopes of **Mt Nosal**, on the south-eastern outskirts of Zakopane. Facilities include a chair lift and a dozen T-bars. Mt Nosal is also very popular for paragliding.

Ski equipment rental is available at most facilities and also from a number of rental companies in Zakopane. See the Cycling section earlier in this section for some useful addresses – companies which rent out bikes in summer, also rent out ski equipment in winter.

Skiing the slopes of the High Tatras

Special Events

The **International Festival of Mountain Folklore** in late August is the town's leading cultural event. In July, a series of concerts presenting music by Karol Szymanowski and also other composers is held in the Villa Atma.

Places to Stay

Zakopane has no shortage of places to stay and, except for occasional peaks, finding a bed is no problem. Even if hotels and hostels are full, there will generally be some private rooms around – in fact, private rooms provide some of the cheapest and best accommodation in town.

As with all seasonal resorts, accommodation prices in Zakopane fluctuate (sometimes considerably) between high and low seasons, peaking in late December, January and February, and then in July and August. Prices given are for the high season.

Camping *Camping Nr 97 Pod Krokwią* (☎ 201 22 56, ul Żeromskiego 34) Beds in bungalows US$8-10. Open year-round. The camping ground has large heated bungalows, each containing several double and triple rooms. They are often full in the July-August period. To get to the camping grounds from the bus/train stations, take any bus to Kuźnice or Jaszczurówka and get off at Rondo.

Zakopane has several more camping grounds, including *Camping Nr 160 Harenda* (☎ 201 47 00) on the Kraków road; *Camping Za Strugiem* (☎ 201 45 66, ul Za Strugiem 39); *Camping U Daniela* (☎ 206 12 96) in Oberconiówka; and *Auto Camping Nr 252 Comfort* (☎ 201 49 42, ul Kaszelewskiego 7) on the Kościelisko road.

Hostels *Youth Hostel Szarotka* (☎ 206 62 03, ul Nowotarska 45) Beds US$4-8. Open year-round. Zakopane's youth hostel is a 10-minute walk from both the centre and the stations. With some 250 beds (mostly in eight- to 12-bed dorms), this is one of the largest hostels in the country, but this may change. Just before we went to press, the hostel was considering a major revamp, aimed at cutting down the number of beds while improving the standards.

Schronisko Młodzieżowe Żak (☎ 201 57 06, ul Marusarzówny 15) Dorm beds US$5, beds in doubles US$6. Open year-round. This place is in a quiet, verdant southwestern suburb of town. Run by Almatur, it's not a regular PTSM youth hostel, but it works on similar principles and costs much the same.

Dom Turysty PTTK (☎ 206 32 07, fax 206 32 84, ul Zaruskiego 5) Doubles/triples with bath US$30/35, with shower only US$26/32, without bath US$22/28, beds in 4-/8-/14-bed dorms US$8/6/5. The very central PTTK hostel has 470 beds in heaps of rooms of different sizes, mostly dormitories. The place can often be swamped with school excursion groups.

Private Rooms The business of private rooms for hire is flourishing in Zakopane. It's run by the tourist office and most travel agencies (see the Information section earlier). In the peak season, they probably won't want to fix up accommodation for a period shorter than three nights, but in the off season, this shouldn't apply. You can expect a bed in a double room to cost US$6 to US$10 in the peak season. Check the location before deciding.

In the high season, there are usually quite a few locals hanging around the bus and train stations, who approach arriving passengers to offer them rooms in their homes. As a rule, you shouldn't pay more than when renting a room through an agency. Again, check the location first before setting off for the place.

Also look for signs reading 'pokoje', 'noclegi' or 'zimmer frei' outside private homes. There are plenty of them in town.

Holiday Homes There are many holiday homes in Zakopane and most of them are open to the general public, renting rooms either directly or through travel agencies. The major agent is FWP (☎ 201 27 63), ul Kościuszki 19, in the DW Podhale. It's open 8am to 5pm weekdays and Saturday in the busy season.

The office rents rooms in nine FWP holiday homes around the town. Rooms range from doubles to quads, some with baths. You can take just a room or room with board (three meals). As a rough guide, in July and August a bed in rooms without/with bath will cost around US$10/18, and US$6/10 in the off season; add US$10 for full board. One-night stays are OK.

Hotels Given the number of private rooms, holiday homes and other cheap options, few travellers bother with a hotel, which is more expensive and isn't always good value. However, if you fancy somewhere upmarket in the centre, here are a few good options:

Hotel Kasprowy Wierch (☎/fax 201 27 38, ul Krupówki 50B) Doubles/triples with bath & breakfast US$50/70. One of the cheaper upscale options, the Kasprowy Wierch is neat and decent and its restaurant serves copious portions of solid Polish fare.

Hotel Sabała (☎/fax 201 50 93, ul Krupówki 11) Doubles with bath & breakfast US$70-110. Situated in a beautiful typical local villa from 1894, which has been meticulously restored over recent years, Sabała provides some of the best and most atmospheric accommodation in town, and has an excellent restaurant.

Hotel Litwor (☎/fax 201 71 90, ul Krupówki 40) Doubles with bath & breakfast US$100-120. Another top-end option, the 55-room Litwor combines elements of traditional style with modern facilities. It has two restaurants, a swimming pool, fitness centre and sauna.

Places to Eat

The central mall, ul Krupówki, boasts heaps of eateries, everything from hamburger stands to well-appointed establishments. Eating cheaply is not a problem in Zakopane – the proliferation of small fast-food outlets around town is astonishing, and there are also plenty of informal places in private homes in back streets, displaying boards saying 'obiady domowe' (home-cooked lunches). Don't miss trying the smoked sheep's-milk cheese sold at street stands all along ul Krupówki.

Among the cheapest places to eat are the basic *Bar Mleczny* (*ul Krupówki 1*); *Bar Grosz* (*Krupówki 28*); and *Bar Smakosz* (*ul Krupówki 22*). It's less than US$3 a meal in any of them.

Bar Rzepka (☎ *201 54 16, ul Krupówki 43*) Mains US$3-4. Extensively refurbished, Rzepka serves tasty typical Polish fare – good value.

Stek Chałupa (☎ *201 59 18, ul Krupówki 33*) Mains US$4-6. With rustic timber tables and benches, plus a folksy decor, Chałupa is a pleasant place for grilled sausages, steaks, baked potatoes and other local specialities.

Karczma Zbójecka (☎ *201 38 56, ul Krupówki 28*) Mains US$4-6. An attractive basement brick-and-timber inn, the Karczma has typical regional food and a good atmosphere, plus local folk music on some evenings.

Karczma Czarny Staw (☎ *201 38 56, ul Krupówki 2*) Mains US$5-8. Run by the same people as Zbójecka, this is quite similar, if a bit more upmarket. It's equally trendy and charming.

Bąkowo Zohylina Niźnio (☎ *206 62 16, ul Piłsudskiego 6*) Mains US$5-10. This is another amazing creation with typical local decor, food and live music, and it has an equally amazing sibling named 'Wyźnio' (Upper), 1km up the same street.

Entertainment

Teatr Witkacego (*Witkacy Theatre;* ☎ *206 82 97, ul Chramcówki 15*) This is one of the best theatres in Poland.

Getting There & Away

Most regional routes are covered by bus, while the train is better for long-distance travel – to the bigger cities like Warsaw, for example.

Train There are a number of trains to Kraków (147km), but buses are faster and run more frequently. One train (a few more in season) runs to Warsaw daily (439km). Tickets are available from the station or from Orbis Travel, ul Krupówki 22.

Bus The PKS fast buses run to Kraków every hour (US$3, 2½ hours, 104km). There are also two private companies, Linia Frej and Szwagropol, which run regularly to Kraków, departing from the front of DW Podhale, ul Kościuszki 19. They may be marginally cheaper and a bit faster than PKS. There are several PKS buses to Nowy Sącz daily and single buses to Tarnów, Przemyśl, Rzeszów and Krynica. PKS has two direct buses to Kąty (for the Dunajec raft trip) in summer.

In the region around Zakopane, bus transport is relatively frequent. PKS buses can take you to the foot of the Kościeliska and Chochołowska valleys as well as to Polana Palenica, the gateway to Lake Morskie Oko. There are also private minibuses which ply the most popular tourist routes, departing from across the road from the PKS terminal.

There are a couple of buses per week to Budapest (US$24, nine hours), and three or four buses a day to Poprad in Slovakia (US$3.50); if you take the first one around 7am, you can catch the express train to Prague departing from Poprad around 11am.

You can also take any of the Polana Palenica PKS buses or private minibuses, get off at Łysa Polana (22km), cross the border on foot and continue by bus (regular transport) to Tatranská Lomnica (30km).

Silesia

Occupying the whole of south-western Poland, Silesia (Śląsk in Polish; pronounced 'Shlonsk') is made up of three geographically distinct regions. Its eastern part is the Silesian Upland (Wyżyna Śląska), or Upper Silesia (Górny Śląsk). This relatively small area is Poland's most industrialised and densely populated region.

To the north-west lies the Silesian Lowland (Nizina Śląska), known as Lower Silesia (Dolny Śląsk), which stretches along the Odra River for over 300km. The main city, Wrocław, is also the main tourist attraction of the region.

The lowland is bordered on the south-west by the Sudetes (Sudety), a mountain range running along the Czech border. This is probably the most interesting area for travellers, for both its natural beauty and its picturesque towns.

Silesia has had quite a chequered history. The region was settled gradually during the second half of the 1st millennium AD by Slavonic tribes known collectively as the Ślężanie or Silesians. It became part of Poland during the rule of Duke Mieszko I shortly before the year 1000. When Poland split into principalities in the 12th century, Silesia was divided into independent duchies ruled by Silesian Piasts, a branch of the first Polish dynasty.

During the second quarter of the 14th century the region was gradually annexed by Bohemia. In 1526 it fell under Habsburg administration, and in 1741 it passed to Prussia. Part of Upper Silesia returned to Poland after WWI but the rest of the region, including the whole of Lower Silesia, joined Poland only in the aftermath of WWII. The Germans were repatriated into the new Germany soon after the end of the war, and their place was taken by Poles resettled from Poland's eastern provinces lost to the Soviet Union. Evidence of this dynamic and complex history can be detected in the local architecture, the people and the atmosphere.

Highlights

- Browse around Wrocław's old market square, museums and churches
- Hike to the summit of Mt Ślężia and marvel at the mysterious stone statues, still standing from centuries ago
- Pop into the hillside town of Kłodzko
- Visit the impressive Bear's Cave
- Wonder at the bizarre Chapel of Skulls near Kudowa-Zdrój
- Trek in the fairy-tale rocky world of the Góry Stołowe
- Explore the baroque churches of Krzeszów
- Take some invigorating walks in the Karkonosze Mountains

Upper Silesia

Upper Silesia occupies only about 2% of Poland's territory, yet it's home to over 10% of the country's population. It's the nation's main centre of heavy industry thanks to large deposits of coal. The bulk of the industry – principally coal and steel – is

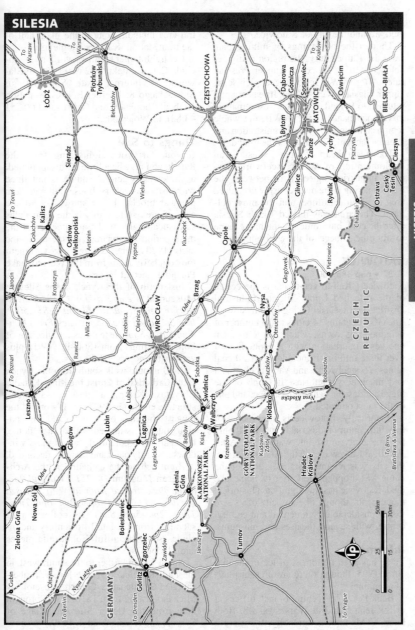

concentrated in the central part of the upland, around the city of Katowice.

Though the beginnings of mining date from the 12th century, the region really developed in the 19th century under Prussian rule. After WWI, following a plebiscite, Upper Silesia was cut in two. Its eastern part returned to Poland, while the west remained in German hands. After WWII, the whole region came under Polish administration and became the nation's industrial heartland.

Today, the heart of Upper Silesia is an agglomeration of mines, steelworks and other industries squeezed in between the cities, making it the most densely urbanised area in Central Europe, and the most polluted. The area was named Black Silesia after the coal, but ironically the name came to suit other aspects of the environment.

KATOWICE
☎ 32 • pop 385,000

Katowice ('Kah-to-**vee**-tseh') is the centre of the so-called Upper Silesian Industrial District (Górnośląski Okręg Przemysłowy). The GOP contains 14 cities and a number of neighbouring towns, which merge to form one vast conurbation with a population of over three million. It includes over 50 coal mines, 16 steelworks and various chemical and machinery factories. It's one of the biggest industrial centres in Europe, and one of the most outdated.

Historically, Katowice is the product of the 19th-century industrial boom, but it only became a city in the interwar period. After WWII, on the wave of the Stalinist craze, the city was renamed Stalinogród, but the name was dropped soon after its namesake died. Katowice has few significant historical monuments, though like any city of its size it's a considerable commercial and cultural centre, with several theatres and museums.

Information
There has been no tourist office in the city since 1995, though there are present plans to open one.

Bank Pekao has central branch offices at ul Św Jana 5 and ul Warszawska 8. Both have ATMs and, additionally, there are a number of Euronet ATMs around the central area including one in the main hall of the train station. Kantors are plentiful.

Central Internet facilities worth trying include Cafe Kontakt (☎ 259 93 50), ul Stawowa 3; Internet Cafe Supernet, ul Słowackiego 8; Internet Bob Cafe in Bob Klub, ul Chopina 8; and Cafe Eranet (☎ 251 43 83), ul Wojewódzka 7.

Things to See
If you start your sightseeing from the **Rynek**, you may be a little bit disappointed, as Katowice's central square is not lined with historic burghers' houses but with drab postwar blocks. It's a showpiece of the early Gierek style – this is the term Poles sarcastically give to the architecture of the brisk period of apparent prosperity in the early 1970s, when Gierek's government took out hefty loans from the West to make Poland a 'second Japan'.

Just north of the Rynek is the **Silesian Museum** (Muzeum Śląskie; ☎ 258 56 61, Al Korfantego 3; adult/student US$1.50/1, free Sat; open 10am-5pm Tues-Fri, 11am-4pm Sat & Sun). It features a collection of Polish paintings from 1800 till WWII, plus various temporary exhibitions.

A 10-minute walk south from the Rynek is the **Cathedral of Christ the King** (Katedra Chrystusa Króla), a massive sandstone structure erected in 1927–55. It's one of the biggest churches built in Poland. Its spacious interior is topped with a large dome, but apart from colourful stained-glass windows it's fairly plain and scarcely decorated.

Right behind the cathedral is the **Archdiocesan Museum** (☎ 251 67 03, ul Jordana 39, entrance from ul Wita Stwosza 16; admission US$1; open 2pm-6pm Tues-Thur, 2pm-5pm Sun). Its collection of sacral art from the late 14th century and includes some beautiful Gothic altarpieces and Madonnas.

About 1.5km farther to the south-west, in the Park Kościuszki, is the lovely, timber-shingled **St Michael's Church** (Kościół Św Michała), dating from 1510. It was brought here from the Upper Silesian village of Syrynia and reassembled in 1939.

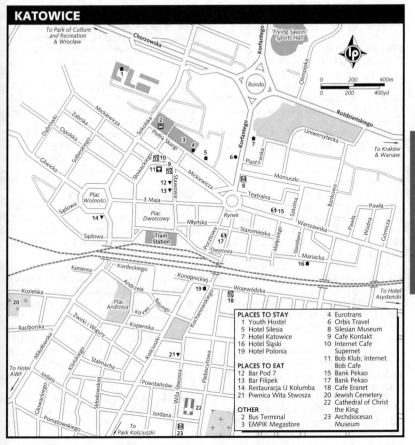

KATOWICE

PLACES TO STAY		4	Eurotrans
1	Youth Hostel	6	Orbis Travel
5	Hotel Silesia	8	Silesian Museum
7	Hotel Katowice	9	Cafe Kontakt
16	Hotel Śląski	10	Internet Cafe
19	Hotel Polonia		Supernet
		11	Bob Klub; Internet
PLACES TO EAT			Bob Cafe
12	Bar Pod 7	15	Bank Pekao
13	Bar Filipek	17	Bank Pekao
14	Restauracja U Kolumba	18	Cafe Eranet
21	Piwnica Wita Stwosza	20	Jewish Cemetery
		22	Cathedral of Christ
OTHER			the King
2	Bus Terminal	23	Archdiocesan
3	EMPiK Megastore		Museum

Katowice has the region's best-preserved **Jewish Cemetery** *(Cmentarz Żydowski; ☎ 251 28 26, ul Kozielska 16; open 8am-5pm Sun-Thur, 8am-noon Fri)*. Established in 1869, it's divided into two parts, of which the front one is older. Amid trees and thick undergrowth are several hundred tombstones, many of which are in remarkably good shape. Inscriptions on most older tombstones are in Hebrew and German, while those on the younger ones are in Hebrew and Polish – a reflection of the city's chequered history. The graveyard is 500m south-west of the train station. If you want

to take photos, you have to go first to the Gmina Żydowska at ul Młyńska 13 and ask for a permit.

The **Park of Culture and Recreation** (Wojewódzki Park Kultury i Wypoczynku) is possibly Katowice's most popular attraction (though administratively it belongs to the neighbouring city of Chorzów). This vast park, over five sq km, is the conurbation's major recreation area. It includes a stadium, zoo, amusement grounds, planetarium and a skansen, the Upper Silesian Ethnographic Park (Górnośląski Park Etnograficzny). The park is about 3km north-west of Katowice's centre; bus and tram lines going to Chorzów will take you there.

Places to Stay

Camping Nr 215 (☎ 256 59 39, fax 253 87 33, ul Murckowska 6) Tent site US$2 plus US$2.50 per person. Open May-Sept. The camp site is 2.5km south-east of the centre in the Dolina Trzech Stawów (Valley of Three Ponds).

Youth hostel (☎/fax 259 64 87, ul Sokolska 26) Beds US$5-10. Open year-round. This 50-bed hostel is a 10-minute walk north of the train station.

Hotel Asystencki (☎/fax 255 44 17, ul Paderewskiego 32) Seasonal doubles without bath US$18, doubles without/with bath & breakfast year-round US$34/55. This student dorm, 1.5km east of the centre, offers budget beds from July to mid-September. It also has better all-year rooms.

Hotel AWF (☎ 251 02 25, fax 251 02 26, ul Mikołowska 72C) Doubles/triples without bath US$25/34, doubles with bath US$40. Open year-round. Another student facility, this hotel is 1.5km south-west of the centre.

Hotel Polonia (☎/fax 251 87 18, ul Kochanowskiego 3) Singles/doubles without bath US$30/45, with bath US$35/50, all prices include breakfast. Just a five-minute walk from the train station, this very central hotel is not particularly special.

Hotel Śląski (☎ 253 70 11, fax 253 85 02, ul Mariacka 15) Singles/doubles without bath US$25/40, with bath US$33/48, all prices include breakfast. Another affordable central facility, the Śląski is not great value either, but slightly cheaper than the Polonia.

Hotel Katowice (☎ 258 82 81, fax 259 75 26, Al Korfantego 9) Singles/doubles with bath & breakfast US$60/90. A typical communist-era product, this 308-bed block has little character but acceptable standards and a central location.

Hotel Silesia (☎ 259 62 11, fax 259 61 40, ul Piotra Skargi 2) Singles/doubles US$90/ 120. Another uninspiring upmarket facility, this large Orbis-run hotel is roughly similar to the Katowice, but more expensive. Check weekend discounts, which may justify staying here.

Places to Eat

The 200m-long pedestrian ul Stawowa, just north of the train station, is packed with eating outlets, including two budget places for straightforward Polish food: *Bar Pod 7* at No 7, and *Bar Filipek* at No 9.

Restauracja U Kolumba (☎ 253 08 64, Plac Wolności 12A) Mains US$10-15. This elegant basement restaurant offers a long menu of Polish and European dishes.

Piwnica Wita Stwosza (☎ 257 11 61, ul Wita Stwosza 5) Mains US$10-15. Another upmarket central option, this restaurant also serves Polish and international food.

Getting There & Away

Air The airport is in Pyrzowice, 33km north of Katowice. The LOT office (☎ 206 24 60), Al Korfantego 36, takes bookings and sells tickets. Orbis Travel (☎ 258 64 84), Al Korfantego 2, does the same.

Train Trains are the main means of transport in the region and beyond. The train station is in the city centre and trains depart regularly in all directions, including Oświęcim (33km), Pszczyna (36km), Kraków (78km), Opole (98km), Wrocław (180km), Częstochowa (86km) and Warsaw (303km). International destinations include Berlin, Bratislava, Budapest, Hamburg, Kyiv, Prague and Vienna.

Bus The PKS bus terminal is on ul Piotra Skargi, 500m north of the train station, and handles buses around the region and beyond. International PKS connections include Bratislava (US$11) and Lviv (US$15). Eurotrans (☎ 259 64 43), next door to EMPiK Megastore, sells international bus tickets to just about anywhere in Europe.

Polski Express buses depart from the front of Orbis Travel, Al Korfantego 2. There are three buses a day to Kraków and three to Warsaw via Częstochowa and Łódź.

OŚWIĘCIM

☎ 33 • pop 48,000

Oświęcim ('Osh-**fyen**-cheem') is a medium-sized industrial town on the borderline between Silesia and Małopolska, about 30km south of Katowice and 60km west of

Kraków. The Polish name may be unfamiliar to outsiders, but the German one – Auschwitz – is not; the largest Nazi death camp was here. This is the scene of the largest experiment in genocide in the history of humankind and the world's largest cemetery. It is possibly the most moving sight in Poland.

The Auschwitz camp was established in April 1940 in the prewar Polish army barracks on the outskirts of Oświęcim. It was originally destined to hold Polish political prisoners but it eventually came to be a gigantic centre for the extermination of European Jews. For this purpose, in 1941–42 the much larger Birkenau (Brzezinka) camp, also referred to as Auschwitz II, was built 2km west of Auschwitz, followed by another one in Monowitz (Monowice), several kilometres to the west of town. About 40 smaller camps, branches of Auschwitz, were subsequently established all over the region. This death factory eliminated some 1.5 million people of 27 nationalities, including 1.3 million Jews, 150,000 Russians, 75,000 Poles and 21,000 Roma.

The name Auschwitz is commonly used for the whole Auschwitz-Birkenau complex, both of which are open to the public as the **State Museum Auschwitz-Birkenau** (☎ 843 21 33, W www.auschwitz-muzeum.oswiecim .pl, ul Więźniów Oświęcimia 20; admission free; open daily: 8am-7pm June-Aug, 8am-6pm May & Sept, 8am-5pm Apr & Oct, 8am-4pm Mar & Nov, 8am-3pm Dec-Feb).

Auschwitz

Auschwitz was only partially destroyed by the fleeing Nazis, and many of the original buildings stand to this day as a bleak testament to the camp's history. A dozen of the 30 surviving prison blocks now house museum exhibitions, either general ones or dedicated to victims from particular countries which lost citizens at Auschwitz.

During the communist era, the museum was conceived as an anti-fascist exhibition – the fact that most of the victims were Jewish was played down, and undue prominence was given to the Poles killed here. This approach has changed; block No 27, dedicated to the 'suffering and struggle of the Jews', now presents Auschwitz more correctly as a place of martyrdom of European Jewry.

From the visitors centre in the entrance building, you enter the barbed-wire encampment through the gate with the cynical inscription 'Arbeit Macht Frei' (Work Makes Free), then visit exhibitions in the prison blocks and finally see the gas chamber and crematorium. You don't need much imagination to take in what happened here.

A 15-minute documentary about the liberation of the camp by Soviet troops on 27 January 1945 is screened in the cinema in the visitors centre every half-hour, and a few times a day it is shown with a foreign-language soundtrack (English version is normally at 11am and 1pm). Before you set off for the camp check with the information desk at the visitors centre for screening times of the different language versions – although the film's message is clear in any language. An admission fee of US$0.50 is charged to enter the cinema.

Photos, film and video are permitted throughout the camp. Anyone under 14 is advised by the museum management not to visit the camp, but the final decision is left to the accompanying adults. There's a cheap, self-service Bar Smak by the entrance, facing the car park. There's also a kantor, a free left-luggage room and several bookshops stocked with publications about the place.

Get a copy of a small brochure (available in 17 languages, including Polish, English, French and German) which has plans of both Auschwitz and Birkenau camps and is quite enough to get you round the grounds. In the summer season, English-language tours of both camps are organised daily at 11am (US$5 per person), and sometimes also at 1pm if there's a demand. Otherwise you can hire a foreign-language guide for your party at the information desk; they cost US$45 for Auschwitz-Birkenau (three hours).

From 15 April to late October, there is a special bus from Auschwitz to Birkenau (US$0.50). It departs hourly, 11.30am to 4.30pm, from outside the entrance to the visitors centre, opposite Bar Smak. Alternatively, you can walk (2km) or take a taxi (US$4).

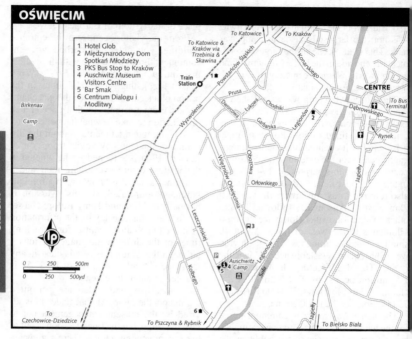

OŚWIĘCIM

1 Hotel Glob
2 Międzynarodowy Dom Spotkań Młodzieży
3 PKS Bus Stop to Kraków
4 Auschwitz Museum Visitors Centre
5 Bar Smak
6 Centrum Dialogu i Modlitwy

Birkenau

It was actually at Birkenau, not Auschwitz, that the extermination of larger numbers of Jews took place. Massive (175 hectares), purpose-built and 'efficient', the camp had over 300 prison barracks and four huge gas chambers complete with crematoria. Each gas chamber accommodated 2000 people and there were electric lifts to raise the bodies to the ovens. The camp could hold 200,000 inmates at a time.

Though much of Birkenau was destroyed by the retreating Nazis, the size of the place, fenced off with long lines of barbed wire and watchtowers stretching almost as far as the eye can see, will give you some idea of the scale of the crime. Don't miss going to the top of the entrance gate-tower for the view. Some of the surviving barracks are open to visitors.

At the back of the complex is the monument to the dead, flanked on each side by the sinister remains of gas chambers and crematoria. In the far north-western corner of the compound is a pond into which the ashes of the victims were dumped. It is still a distinctive grey colour – a chilling sight.

In many ways, Birkenau is an even more shocking sight than Auschwitz. It has the same opening hours as Auschwitz and entry is free. Make sure to leave enough time (at least an hour) to walk around the camp – it is really vast.

There are no buses from Birkenau to the train station; walk (2km) or go by taxi. Alternatively, take the same special bus back to Auschwitz (departing noon to 5pm on the hour) and change there for one of the frequent buses to the station.

Places to Stay & Eat

For most visitors, the Auschwitz-Birkenau camp is a day trip, in most cases from Kraków, and the previously mentioned *Bar Smak* probably has all you need to keep you going. However, if you want to linger longer, Oświęcim has a choice of places to stay and eat.

Centrum Dialogu i Modlitwy *(Centre of Dialogue and Prayer;* ☎ *843 10 00, fax 43 10 01, ul Kolbego 1)* Camping US$5 per person, bed & breakfast US$16/12 adult/ student. The 45-bed Centre is a Catholic Church-built facility, 700m south-west of the Auschwitz camp, which provides comfortable and quiet accommodation in rooms of two to 10 beds (most with bath) and a restaurant.

Międzynarodowy Dom Spotkań Młodzieży *(International Meeting House for Youth;* ☎ *843 21 07, fax 843 23 77, ul Legionów 11)* Camping US$4 per person, singles/doubles/triples/quads with bath US$24/32/36/40, students US$15/22/25/28. Another good place, 1km east of the train station, it was built in 1986 by the Germans. It essentially provides lodging for groups coming for longer stays but will take anyone if there are vacancies. Meals are available in the dining room on the premises.

Hotel Glob *(☎/fax 843 06 43, ul Powstańców Śląskich 16)* Singles/doubles/triples with bath US$25/36/44. Glob, outside the train station, has decent (if noisy) rooms and its own restaurant.

Hotel Olimpijski *(☎ 842 38 41, fax 847 41 94, ul Chemików 2A)* Singles/doubles/triples with bath & breakfast US$30/36/50. Located diagonally opposite the bus terminal, the Olimpijski has been refurbished, offers reasonable standards and has its own restaurant.

Getting There & Away

For most tourists, the jumping-off point for Oświęcim is Kraków, from where you can come by train or bus, or take a tour. Many tours to the camp are organised from Kraków (see that chapter for details), though even the cheapest tour will cost you much more than you'd spend taking public transport.

Buses can be a more convenient option than trains, because they will drop you off close to the Auschwitz museum. There are about 10 buses per day from Kraków to Oświęcim (64km). They pass by Oświęcim train station, then go along ul Więźniów Oświęcimia and stop near Auschwitz

museum before reaching the terminal on the far eastern outskirts of town. Don't miss the Auschwitz stop, otherwise you'll have to backtrack 4km by local bus which is infrequent.

You can go back to Kraków by bus, but take note that the last bus departs about 6pm, so if you want to return later, you need to take the train (which runs till about 9pm).

If Katowice is your starting point for Oświęcim, there are frequent trains between the two (33km).

If you want to go to Pszczyna from Oświęcim, take the train to Czechowice-Dziedzice (21km, regular departures) and change there for another one (8km, also frequent); or go directly by bus (25km), though there are only a couple a day.

PSZCZYNA
☎ 32 • pop 38,000

In heavily industrialised and urbanised Upper Silesia, Pszczyna comes as a surprise, for it feels like a small market town surrounded by wooded countryside. And it has the best palace-and-park complex in Silesia.

Pszczyna ('**Pshchi**-nah') is one of the oldest towns in the region, its origins going back to the 11th century when it was a Piast settlement. It came under the rule of the Opole dukes following the division of the kingdom, but later changed hands several times. In 1847 it became the property of the Hochberg family, powerful Prussian magnates and owners of huge estates which they ruled from Książ castle near Wałbrzych. In the last months of WWI, Pszczyna was the cradle of the first of three consecutive Silesian uprisings, in which Polish peasants took up arms and demanded that the region be incorporated into Poland. Their wishes were granted in 1921, following a plebiscite held by the League of Nations.

Information

There's no tourist office here; you may try the PTTK office (☎ 210 35 30) at Rynek 16. Travellers cheques can be cashed in Bank Śląski on the Rynek, which also has an ATM. Cash can be exchanged in the kantor at ul Piastowska 14.

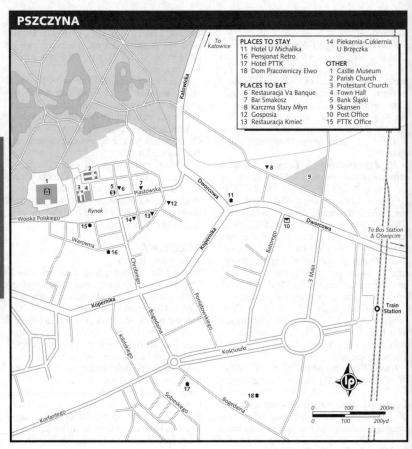

PSZCZYNA

PLACES TO STAY
11 Hotel U Michalika
16 Pensjonat Retro
17 Hotel PTTK
18 Dom Pracowniczy Elwo

PLACES TO EAT
6 Restauracja Va Banque
7 Bar Smakosz
8 Karczma Stary Młyn
12 Gosposia
13 Restauracja Kmieć

14 Piekarnia-Cukiernia
   U Brzęczka

OTHER
1 Castle Museum
2 Parish Church
3 Protestant Church
4 Town Hall
5 Bank Śląski
9 Skansen
10 Post Office
15 PTTK Office

Things to See

The elongated **Rynek** is lined with old burghers' houses dating mostly from the 18th and 19th centuries. On its northern side is the Protestant church and, next to it, the town hall, both remodelled early this century. Behind the town hall is the 14th-century parish church, much changed later.

Just west of the Rynek is the town's prime attraction, the **castle**. Its origins date from the 12th century, when the Opole dukes built a hunting lodge here, but the building has been enlarged and remodelled several times, most recently at the end of the 19th century. The

simple medieval castle gradually became a magnificent palace, incorporating various styles from Gothic to neoclassical. The Hochbergs, who owned it until 1945, furnished their home according to their status (they were among the richest families in Europe), and embellished it with numerous works of art.

After WWII the palace – which had been plundered but not destroyed – was taken over by the state, restored and turned into the **Castle Museum** (*Muzeum Zamkowe;* ☎ *210 30 37; adult/student US$2.50/1.25; open 9am-4pm Wed, 9am-3pm Thur & Fri,*

10am-3pm Sat, 10am-4pm Sun Feb-June & Sept–mid-Dec, 9am-4pm Wed, 9am-3pm Thur & Fri, 10am-4pm Sat, 10am-6pm Sun July & Aug, also 10am-3pm Tues Apr-Oct). Last visitors are permitted to enter an hour before closing time. You can buy a guide-book (in English and German) on the cas-tle's history and the museum's contents.

The furnished and decorated interiors, representing different periods of the castle's existence, feature some splendid rooms, such as the Mirror Hall; chamber music concerts are held here occasionally. Some of the palace's rooms shelter exhibitions, including the collection of armoury on the ground floor and hunting trophies on the 2nd floor.

Right behind the castle is an extensive, 84-hectare English-style **park**. With its lakes, streams, arched bridges, pavilions and a variety of exotic trees and shrubs, it's regarded as the most picturesque landscape park in Silesia.

A five-minute walk east of the Rynek is a small but interesting **skansen** *(Zagroda Wsi Pszczyńskiej; ul Parkowa; admission US$1; open 10am-3pm Tues-Sun Apr-Nov),* which features half a dozen old timber houses collected from the region. Most of the buildings are about 200 years old and feature ethnographic exhibitions.

Places to Stay
Hotel PTTK (☎ 210 38 33, fax 210 35 30, ul Bogedaina 16) Singles/doubles without bath US$14/25, doubles with bath US$30, beds in triples/quads US$9/7. The PTTK hotel, south of the Rynek, is in a former prison building which operated from 1902 to 1975.

Dom Pracowniczy Elwo (☎/fax 210 38 93, ul Bogedaina 23) Singles with bath US$18, doubles without bath US$15. Oc-cupying an ordinary apartment block, the Elwo offers 90 beds. It's not a classy place but it's not expensive either.

Pensjonat Retro (☎/fax 210 12 63, ul Warowna 31) Singles/doubles with bath & breakfast US$30/40. Retro is a small central guesthouse which has 44 beds and its own restaurant.

Hotel U Michalika (☎ 210 13 88, ul Dworcowa 11) Singles/doubles with bath & breakfast US$35/45. This new hotel offers 16 comfortable rooms and its own restaurant.

Places to Eat
Gosposia (ul Warowna 3) Meals US$2-3. This simple tiny place serves tasty lunches on weekdays.

Bar Smakosz (☎ 210 37 42, ul Pias-towska 7) Mains US$1.50-2.50. A mod-ernised milk bar, Smakosz can be an alternative choice for a budget meal, espe-cially on weekends when the Gosposia is closed.

Piekarnia-Cukiernia U Brzęczka (☎ 210 52 02, ul Piekarska 4) This bakery-cum-cake shop has fresh bread, pastries and de-cent espresso, plus a few tables to dine in, and is a good place for breakfast or a light snack.

Karczma Stary Młyn (☎ 210 57 77, ul Parkowa 2) Mains US$3-6. Situated in a historic timber country house, the Karczma serves traditional Polish food.

Restauracja Kmieć (☎ 210 36 38, ul Piekarska 10) Mains US$5-7. Set in a his-toric townhouse dating from 1756, this long-established restaurant has solid Polish food at reasonable prices.

Restauracja Va Banque (☎ 210 34 72, ul Bankowa 2) Mains US$7-10. The newest addition to the local gastronomic scene, Va Banque is a pleasant place and one of the best restaurants in town.

Getting There & Away
The bus and train stations are to the east of the centre, 200m apart. Trains to Katowice (36km) run roughly every hour. To Oświęcim, take any of the frequent Żywiec or Bielsko-Biała trains to Czechowice-Dziedzice (8km) and change for one to Oświęcim (21km). There are only two buses to Oświęcim (25km), and both continue to Kraków. If you want to get to Kraków and there's no bus due, go by train to Katowice, from where trains go to Kraków every hour or so. There are no direct trains between Pszczyna and Kraków.

Wrocław

☎ 71 • pop 675,000

Wrocław ('**Vrots**-wahf'), on the Odra River in the middle of Lower Silesia, is the major industrial, commercial, educational and cultural centre for the whole of south-western Poland. It's the provincial capital and Poland's fourth-largest city after Warsaw, Łódź and Kraków.

After six centuries in foreign hands – Bohemian, Austrian and Prussian – Wrocław only returned to Poland in the aftermath of WWII. The city has preserved some of these different historic layers overlapping each other, which makes an interesting architectural and cultural mosaic. The city has a magnificent old market square, a number of good museums and a memorable cluster of churches by the river. A bonus attraction is the city's location on the Odra banks, with its 12 islands, 112 bridges and large park stretching along the river.

Wrocław is also a lively cultural centre, with five theatres, an opera house, a concert hall, several festivals, and a large student community based in 13 institutions of higher education. And like any urban centre of this size, the city has a developed tourist infrastructure.

HISTORY

Wrocław was originally founded on the island of Ostrów Tumski – which is no longer an island since an arm of the Odra was filled in during the 19th century. The first recorded Polish ruler, Duke Mieszko I, brought the town, together with most of Silesia, into the Polish state. It must have already been a fair-sized stronghold by the year 1000, as it was chosen as one of Piast Poland's three bishoprics, along with Kraków and Kołobrzeg, all three being ruled from the archbishopric in Gniezno.

During the period of division in the 12th and 13th centuries, Wrocław was the capital of one of the principalities of the Silesian Piasts. Like most settlements in southern Poland, Wrocław was burned down by the Tatars. The town centre was then moved to the left bank of the river and laid out on the

chessboard plan which survives to this day. It was surrounded by defensive walls, and though they have gone, their position can be seen on the map, running along Grodzka, Nowy Świat, Kazimierza Wielkiego, Janickiego and Kraińskiego streets.

Wrocław continued to grow under Bohemian administration (1335–1526), reaching perhaps the height of its prosperity in the 15th century, and maintaining trade and cultural links with the Polish Crown. This speedy development led to the construction of new fortifications at the beginning of the 16th century, and the wide moat of the Fosa Miejska shows where they were once positioned.

The Habsburgs, who ruled the city for the next two centuries, were less tolerant of the Polish and Czech communities, and things got even worse after 1741 when Wrocław fell into the hands of Prussia and was increasingly Germanised for the subsequent two centuries; its name was changed to Breslau.

In the last stages of WWII, the city was besieged by the Red Army for nearly three months, the Nazis defending their last bastion to the end. During the battle, 70% of the city was razed to the ground. Of the prewar population of over 600,000 (mainly German), most were evacuated before the siege and those who were left either died or fled with the retreating German army.

A handful of Germans who remained were expelled to Germany, and the ruined city was resettled with people from Poland's prewar eastern regions, mostly from Lviv, which had been lost to the Soviet Union.

The reconstruction was painful and difficult, and continued well into the 1980s. There's a lot of postwar concrete, but the most important historic buildings have been faithfully reconstructed. Only in the late 1980s did the city surpass its prewar population level.

ORIENTATION

The train and bus stations are near to each other 1km south of the Old Town. Hotels are conveniently close to the city centre and the train station, and almost all major tourist attractions are within walking distance in the central area.

INFORMATION
Tourist Offices
The municipal tourist office (☎ 344 31 11, ☎/fax 344 29 62, ☒ www.tur-info.wroc.pl), Rynek 14, is open 9am to 5pm weekdays, 10am to 2pm Saturday. In summer, it can be open longer and also on Sunday.

Money
Bank Pekao, ul Oławska 2, changes travellers cheques and gives advances on Visa and MasterCard. For changing cash, there are plenty of kantors throughout the central area, including two or three in the train station which trade 24 hours a day. There are also a number of ATMs in the centre, including Euronet outlets in Orbis Travel at Rynek 29 and in the tourist office at Rynek 14.

Email & Internet Access
There are plenty of cybercafes in the centre, including Adan (☎ 781 86 69), ul Ruska 60/61; Cyber Tea Tavern (☎ 372 35 71), ul Kuźnicza 29A; Dziwne Dni (☎ 788 91 07), ul Kazimierza Wielkiego 39; Galaxy (☎ 374 61 14), ul Kazimierza Wielkiego 55; and W Sercu Miasta, Przejście Żelaźnicze in the middle of the Rynek.

Travel Agencies
Virgo (☎ 343 18 18), ul Oławska 16, represents STA Travel and may have attractive international airfares for students under 34 and nonstudents under 26. PTTK (☎ 343 03 44, 343 83 56), Rynek-Ratusz 11/12, can arrange foreign-language guides, but it usually needs to be notified well in advance. Almatur (☎ 343 41 35, 781 84 54), ul Kościuszki 34, sells ISIC cards and deals with both students and nonstudents.

Bookshops
English-language books are available from PolAnglo (☎ 341 97 60), ul Kuźnicza 49A; Columbus (☎ 342 41 74), ul Kuźnicza 57/58; Vademecum bookshop of the English Philology Department of Wrocław University, ul Kuźnicza 22; and EMPiK (☎ 343 39 72), Rynek 50 (top floor). EMPiK also has a large map/guidebook section (1st floor) and a choice of foreign-language papers and magazines (ground floor). There's another EMPiK (☎ 341 70 15) at Plac Kościuszki 21/23. Another good place for maps and guidebooks is Księgarnia Podróżnika (☎ 346 00 71), ul Wita Stwosza 19/20.

RYNEK
At 173m x 208m, Wrocław's Rynek is the second-largest old market square in the country, surpassed only by that in Kraków. A large area in the middle is occupied by a block of buildings so big that it incorporates three internal streets. Recently wholly refurbished, the Rynek is lively and architecturally mixed; the most immediately conspicuous building is the town hall on the southern side of the central block.

Town Hall
This is certainly one of the most beautiful historic city halls in Poland. The main structure took almost two centuries (1327–1504) to complete, and work on the tower and decoration continued for another century. Since then, it hasn't changed much; amazingly, it came through WWII without major damage.

The eastern facade, looking like a group of three different buildings, reflects the stages of the town hall's development. The northern segment, with its austere early Gothic features, is the oldest, while the southern part is the most recent and shows elements of the early Renaissance style. The central and most impressive section is topped by an ornamented triangular roof adorned with pinnacles – a favourite cover picture for local tourist brochures. The astronomical clock, made of larch wood, was incorporated in 1580.

The decorative post in front of the facade is the **whipping post** (pręgierz), marking the site where public floggings were carried out in medieval times. It's an exact replica of the 1492 original which stood here until WWII.

The southern facade of the town hall, dating from the early 16th century, is the most elaborate, with bay windows, carved stone figures and two elaborate friezes.

WROCŁAW

SILESIA

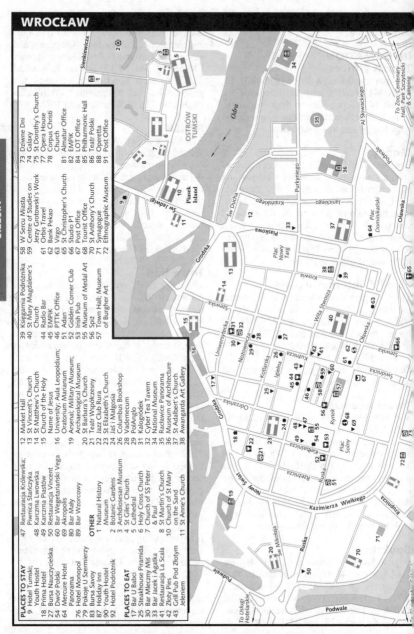

PLACES TO STAY
9 Hotel Tumski;
  Youth Hostel
18 Prima Hotel
27 Bursa Nauczycielska
54 Dwór Polski
64 Mercure Hotel
  Panorama
76 Hotel Monopol
79 Pokoje U Szermierzy
83 Bursa Savoy
87 Holiday Inn
90 Youth Hostel
92 Hotel Podróżnik

PLACES TO EAT
17 Bar U Babci
25 Steakhouse Piramida
30 Bar Mleczny Miś
33 Bar Jacek i Agatka
41 Restauracja La Scala
42 Złoty Pies
43 Grill Pub Pod Złotym
  Jeleniem

47 Restauracja Królewska;
  Piwnica Stańczyka
48 Karczma Lwowska
49 Karczma Piastów
50 Restauracja Vincent
60 Bar Wegetariański Vega
69 Akropolis
80 Bar Mały
89 Bar Wzorcowy

OTHER
1 Natural History
  Museum
2 Botanic Gardens
3 Archidiecesan Museum
4 St Giles' Church
5 Cathedral
6 Holy Cross Church
7 Church of SS Peter
  & Paul
8 St Martin's Church
10 Church of St Mary
  on the Sand
11 St Anne's Church

12 Market Hall
13 St Vincent's Church
14 St Matthew's Church
15 Church of the Holy
  Name of Jesus
16 University; Aula Leopoldium;
  Oratorium Marianum
19 Arsenal; Military Museum;
  Archaeological Museum
20 St Barbara's Church
21 Teatr Współczesny
22 Jazz Club Rura
23 St Elizabeth's Church
24 Jaś i Małgosia
26 Columbus Bookshop
28 Vademecum
29 PolAnglo
31 Kalogrodek
32 Cyber Tea Tavern
34 National Museum
35 Racławice Panorama
36 Museum of Architecture
37 St Adalbert's Church
38 Awangarda Art Gallery

39 Księgarnia Podróżnika
40 St Mary Magdalene's
  Church
44 Radio Bar
45 EMPiK
46 PTTK Office
51 Adan
52 Golden Corner Club
53 Irish Pub
55 Museum of Medal Art
56 Spiż
57 Town Hall; Museum
  of Burgher Art

58 W Sercu Miasta
59 Centre of Studies on
  Jerzy Grotowski's Work
61 Orbis Travel
62 Bank Pekao
63 Virgo
65 St Christopher's Church
66 Studio P1
67 Post Office
68 Tourist Office
70 St Anthony's Church
71 Synagogue
72 Ethnographic Museum

73 Dziwne Dni
74 Galaxy
75 St Dorothy's Church
77 Opera House
78 Corpus Christi
  Church
81 Almatur Office
82 EMPiK
84 LOT Office
85 Philharmonic Hall
86 Teatr Polski
88 Operetta
91 Post Office

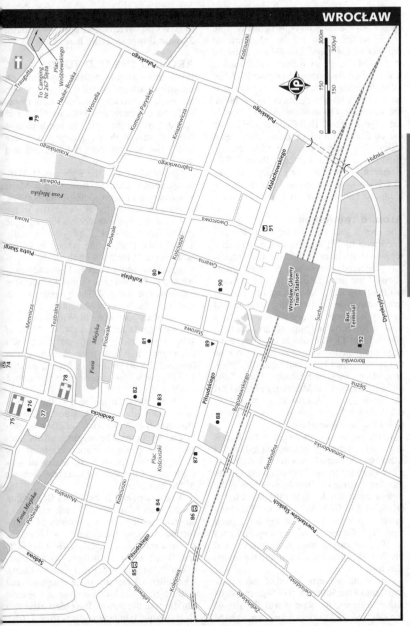

WROCŁAW

SILESIA

The western elevation is the most austere, apart from the early baroque doorway from 1615, which leads to the **Museum of Burgher Art** (*Muzeum Sztuki Mieszczańskiej; ☎ 344 14 34, Rynek-Ratusz; adult/student US$2/1, free Wed; open 11am-5pm Wed-Sat, 10am-6pm Sun*). The museum period interiors are every bit as magnificent as the building's exterior. The most amazing is probably the huge Knights' Hall (Sala Rycerska) on the 1st floor, with the original carved decorations from the end of the 15th century. Next to it is the Princes' Room (Sala Książęca), which was originally a chapel. The historic rooms house exhibitions, including a collection of gold and silverware.

Around the Rynek

The Rynek was laid out in the 1240s and lined with timber houses, which were later replaced with brick structures. They gradually changed over the centuries; some adopted the architectural style of the day, while others kept closer to tradition. After the wartime destruction, they were rebuilt as they had been before the war, so they now offer an amalgam of architectural styles from Gothic onwards. They have been renovated over recent years, so now the Rynek looks fresh and beautiful. Walk around and view the facades. One of the buildings houses the **Museum of Medal Art** (*Muzeum Sztuki Medalierskiej; ☎ 344 39 83, Rynek 6; admission free; open 11am-5pm Wed-Sat, 10am-6pm Sun*).

In the north-western corner of the Rynek are two charming houses called **Jaś i Małgosia**, or Hansel and Gretel, linked with a baroque gate from 1728, which once led to the church cemetery. Just behind them is the monumental brick **St Elizabeth's Church** (Kościół Św Elżbiety) with its 83m-high tower – you can go to the top for a good view. This Gothic church went up in flames in 1975 in suspicious circumstances, and much of the furnishing, including the organ, was lost.

The south-western corner of the Rynek spills into **Plac Solny**, or Salt Square. As its name suggests, the square was the site of the salt trade, a business which was carried on for over five centuries until 1815, when the last stalls were closed down. Nowadays, 24-hour flower stalls are here.

AROUND THE OLD TOWN

If you are on a tight schedule, concentrate on the areas north and east of the Rynek, where the most important historical monuments and best museums are. With more time to spend, you might visit the southern and western parts of the city centre too, where you'll find several more old churches and museums.

One block east of the Rynek is **St Mary Magdalene's Church** (Kościół Św Marii Magdaleny), a mighty Gothic brick building constructed during the city's heyday in the 14th century. Its showpiece is a Romanesque portal from around 1280. It originally adorned the Benedictine Abbey in Ołbin, now one of Wrocław's northern inner suburbs, but was moved here in 1546 and incorporated in the southern external wall after the abbey was demolished. The tympanum is on display in the National Museum.

One block east along ul Wita Stwosza is the **Awangarda Art Gallery** (*☎ 344 10 56, ul Wita Stwosza 32; admission free; open 11am-7pm Tues-Thur, noon-8pm Fri, noon-6pm Sat & Sun*) housed in a historic palatial building, which has temporary exhibitions of modern art.

About 100m farther east is the single-naved Dominican **St Adalbert's Church** (Kościół Św Wojciecha), another largish Gothic structure. The highlight of its interior is the baroque chapel adjoining the southern transept, with its alabaster sarcophagus of the Blessed Czesław, founder of the monastery.

A few steps east is the former Bernardine church and monastery, which provide a splendid setting for the **Museum of Architecture** (*Muzeum Architektury; ☎ 344 82 78, ul Bernardyńska 5; adult/student US$2/1, free Wed; open 10am-4pm Wed & Sat, 10am-3.30pm Thur & Fri, 10am-5pm Sun*). The collection features stone sculptures and stained-glass windows from various historic buildings of the region. The oldest exhibit, a Romanesque tympanum, dates from 1165.

Racławice Panorama

Panorama Racławicka (☎ 344 23 44, ul Purkyniego 11; adult/student US$$4/2.50; open 9am-5pm Tues-Sun) is Wrocław's most visited sight. Accommodated in a cylindrical building in the park behind the Museum of Architecture, it's a giant painting wrapped around the internal walls of the rotunda in the form of an unbroken circle and is viewed from an elevated central balcony. The painting shows one of the important episodes in Polish history, the Battle of Racławice of 1894.

Visits are by tours, which depart every half-hour and take just that. You are moving around the balcony to inspect each scene in turn while a recorded commentary provides you with explanations. Foreign-language versions including English, German and French are available; ask for headphones in your language from the stand at the balcony.

Buy your ticket early, as the place tends to be overrun by tourists, including endless school excursions. You may have some time to spare before your tour, which you can spend in the waiting room watching videos of the painting's restoration or visiting the exhibition in the 'small rotunda', just behind the ticket office, which features a model of the battlefield and the uniforms of forces engaged in the battle. With some more time, you can visit the nearby National Museum with the same-day Panorama ticket, without paying the museum ticket. By the way, have a look at the Katyń Monument, just behind the rotunda.

National Museum

Muzeum Narodowe (☎ 343 88 39, Plac Powstańców Warszawy 5; adult/student $2/1, free with same-day ticket to Panorama, also free Thur; open 10am-4pm Tues, Wed, Fri-Sun, 9am-4pm Thur) is a treasure-trove of art.

The museum's medieval Silesian art section is one of the highlights of the collection. Medieval stone sculpture is displayed in the central ground-floor hall, and exhibits include the Romanesque tympanum from

---

Racławice Panorama – Poland's Largest Painting

Panorama Racławicka is a cyclorama, or a 360° unbroken painting viewed from the centre. It's a canvas painting 15m high and 114m long – about half the area of a soccer field – and weighing 3500kg.

The picture depicts the battle of Racławice (a village about 40km north-east of Kraków) fought on 4 April 1794 between the Polish insurrectionist peasant army, led by Tadeusz Kościuszko, and Russian troops. One of the last attempts to defend Poland's independence, the battle was won by the Poles, but seven months later the nationwide insurrection was crushed by the tsarist army and the Third Partition was effected. Poland formally ceased to exist until WWI, yet the battle lived in the hearts of Poles as the most glorious engagement of the rebellion.

One hundred years after the battle, a group of patriots in Lviv set about commemorating the event and the idea of the panorama emerged. The project successfully got through the Austrian bureaucracy.

The painting is essentially the work of two artists, Jan Styka and Wojciech Kossak, with the help of seven painters commissioned for background scenes and details. They completed the monumental canvas in an amazingly short time – nine months and two days – while a specially designed rotunda was erected. The picture became one of Lviv's favourite attractions and was on display until 1944, when a bomb hit the building and damaged the canvas.

After the war, the painting, along with most of Lviv's legacy, was moved to Wrocław, but since it depicted a defeat of the Russians – Poland's official friend and liberator – the communist authorities were reluctant to put it on display. The rolled-up picture was kept in storage for 35 years. Only in 1980, after the Solidarity movement had brought the beginnings of democracy, was the decision taken to renovate the canvas and put it on public view. The work took five years and was regarded as the most difficult conservation operation of its kind in Poland.

the portal of St Mary Magdalene's Church, depicting the Dormition of the Virgin Mary. Medieval wooden sculpture is on the 1st floor and features some powerful Gothic triptychs and statues of saints. Also on this floor are European paintings from the 15th to 19th centuries.

The 2nd floor has Polish art, mainly painting, from the 17th century to the present. The collection covers most of the big names, including Jacek Malczewski, Stanisław Wyspiański, Witkacy and Jan Matejko. Among contemporary artists, Jerzy Nowosielski, Władysław Hasior and Tadeusz Brzozowski are particularly well represented. Wrocław's collection of modern Polish painting is considered one of the best in the country.

University Quarter

The quarter occupies the northern part of the Old Town, between the riverfront and ul Uniwersytecka. Coming from the museum, the first important historic building you'll see will be the Gothic **St Vincent's Church** (Kościół Św Wincentego), originally a Romanesque basilica founded before 1240. The largest church in the city after the cathedral, it was burned out in 1945 and only reconstructed in the 1990s. It's now used by the Uniate congregation as their cathedral.

The baroque **Church of the Holy Name of Jesus** (Kościół Najświętszego Imienia Jezus) was built in the 1690s on the site of the former Piast castle. Its spacious interior, adorned with fine illusionistic frescoes on its vault and crammed with ornate fittings, is spectacular.

The monumental building adjoining the church is the **university**. It was founded by Emperor Leopold I in 1702 as the Jesuit Academy and was built in 1728–42. Enter the central gate and go up to the 1st floor to see the **Aula Leopoldinum** (☎ 375 22 45, Plac Uniwersytecki; adult/student US$1/0.50; open 10am-3.30pm Thur-Tues). Embellished with elaborate stucco work, sculptures, paintings and a trompe l'œil ceiling fresco, it's the best baroque interior in the city. It's used for special university ceremonies but at other times can be visited at the hours listed here.

Classical music concerts are occasionally held here. The slightly more modest **Oratorium Marianum**, on the ground floor, is open the same hours.

West & South of the Old Town

Walk west for five-minutes along ul Grodzka and you'll arrive at the **Arsenal** (Arsenał), the most significant remnant of the 15th-century fortifications. It now houses the **Military Museum** (Muzeum Militariów; ☎ 344 15 71, ul Cieszyńskiego 9; adult/student US$1/0.50, free Wed; open 11am-5pm Wed-Sat, 10am-6pm Sun) featuring old weapons, uniforms and one of Europe's largest collections of helmets and tin hats.

The arsenal is also home to the **Archaeological Museum** (Muzeum Archeologiczne; ☎ 344 28 29, ul Cieszyńskiego 9; adult/student US$1/0.50, free Wed; open 11am-5pm Wed-Sat, 10am-6pm Sun) which displays the usual collection of archaeological finds, emphasising the Polish and Slavic roots of the region.

A short walk south-east from the arsenal will take you to the **Ethnographic Museum** (☎ 344 33 13, ul Kazimierza Wielkiego 34; adult/student US$1/0.50, free Sat; open 10am-4pm Tues-Sun). Part of the collection features old artefacts and household implements brought from the East by postwar settlers.

One block south-east is **St Dorothy's Church** (Kościół Św Doroty), another massive Gothic affair. It was founded in 1351 to commemorate the meeting between Polish King Kazimierz Wielki and his Bohemian counterpart, Charles IV, at which it was agreed to leave Silesia in Bohemia's hands. The lofty, whitewashed interior is filled with large baroque altars, and there's a sizable rococo tomb in the right-hand (southern) aisle.

To the south of the church is the Monopol, Wrocław's oldest hotel, and facing it, the neoclassical Opera House.

OSTRÓW TUMSKI & PIASEK ISLAND

Once an island, Ostrów Tumski was the cradle of Wrocław. It was here that the Ślężanie constructed their stronghold in the 7th or 8th

Church of SS Peter and Paul, Legnica

Outdoor dining in the Old Town, Wrocław

Colourful building facade, Wrocław

Entrance to Auschwitz Concentration Camp

Prison wall painting by Jewish inmate, Birkenau

KRZYSZTOF DYDYŃSKI

KRZYSZTOF DYDYŃSKI

KRZYSZTOF DYDYŃSKI

CRAIG PERSHOUSE

CRAIG PERSHOUSE

Old Town Square, Wrocław

The Baroque St Hedwig's Church, Legnickie Pole

Historic buildings, Old Town Square, Wrocław

Gothic decoration on Wrocław's Town Hall

Town Hall, Opole

century. After the town was incorporated into the Polish state and a bishopric established in 1000, Wrocław's first church was built here and was followed by other ecclesiastical buildings which gradually expanded onto the neighbouring island, the Piasek (literally, the Sand). Towards the 13th century the centre of town moved to the left bank of the Odra, but Ostrów retained its role as the seat of the church authorities. Over time a number of churches, monasteries and other religious buildings were constructed on both islands, and despite all further misfortunes, many of them are still standing today, giving a distinctive, markedly ecclesiastical character to the district.

Piasek Island is just north-east of the Old Town, over the Most Piaskowy (Piasek Bridge). The main monument here is the **Church of St Mary on the Sand** (Kościół NMP na Piasku), a lofty 14th-century building which dominates this tiny islet. The church was badly damaged during WWII but carefully reconstructed, including its magnificent ribbed vault.

Almost all the prewar fitments were burned out and the old triptychs you see inside have been collected from other Silesian churches. The Romanesque tympanum in the right-hand aisle is the only remnant of the first church built on this site in the 12th century. There's a mechanised *szopka* (Nativity scene) in the first chapel to the right.

The bridge behind the church will put you on Ostrów Tumski. The small 15th-century **Church of SS Peter and Paul** (Kościół Św Piotra i Pawła) to your left has a fine Gothic vault supported by a single central column. It's open only for Mass in the morning and evening. The entrance is through the adjoining building, a former orphanage. Opposite is the much larger **Holy Cross Church** (Kościół Św Krzyża), built between 1288 and 1350.

The monumental, two-towered structure farther east is the **cathedral**. This three-aisled 100m-long Gothic basilica was built between the 13th and 15th centuries and is the fourth church on this site. Seriously damaged during WWII, it was reconstructed in its previous Gothic form, and its

dim interior was refurbished with works of art collected from other churches. The high altar boasts a triptych from 1522 depicting the Dormition of the Virgin Mary, attributed to the school of Veit Stoss. You can go up to the top of the tower, and it's easy – this is Poland's only historic church which has a lift.

Directly north of the cathedral is the little **St Giles' Church** (Kościół Św Idziego). Built in 1218–30, this is the oldest surviving church in Wrocław, and has an original Romanesque doorway at the entrance.

A few steps east is the **Archdiocesan Museum** *(Muzeum Archidiecezjalne; ☎ 327 11 78, Plac Katedralny 16; admission US$0.50; open 9am-3pm Tues-Sun)*. It has a collection of Silesian sacred art, including some exquisite Gothic altarpieces.

The green area to the north is the **Botanic Gardens** *(Ogród Botaniczny; ☎ 322 59 57, ul Sienkiewicza 23; adult/student US$1/0.50; open 8am-6pm daily Apr-Oct)*.

EASTERN SUBURBS

There are some attractions in the eastern districts. Take tram No 2 or 10 from Plac Dominikański in the centre (or from behind the cathedral), and go to the **zoo** *(☎ 348 30 25, ul Wróblewskiego 1; adult/student US$2/1; open 9am-6pm daily, till dusk in winter)*. With about 3000 animals representing over 500 species, this is Poland's largest zoo and supposedly the best. It's also Poland's oldest zoo, founded in 1865.

Across the street from the zoo is the **Centenary Hall** (Hala Ludowa), a huge, round auditorium capable of accommodating 6000 people. It was designed by German architect Max Berg, and built in 1913 to commemorate Napoleon's defeat in 1813. The hall is topped with a huge dome, 65m in diameter, regarded as a great achievement in its day. Today it's a place for large scale performances, exhibitions and sporting events. At other times it is locked, but the guards may let you in to have a look.

The 96m-high steel **spire** *(iglica)* in front of the entrance was built in 1948 on the occasion of the Exhibition of the Regained Territories.

SILESIA

Behind the hall is **Park Szczytnicki**, Wrocław's oldest and largest wooded area, encompassing 112 hectares. A short walk north along the pergola will bring you to a small Japanese Garden, while farther east is a fine 16th-century larch church, brought here from the Opole region and reassembled in 1914. Temporary exhibitions are held in the church in summer.

At the north-eastern end of the park is a large sports complex with an Olympic stadium, all built before WWII in the expectation of holding the Olympic Games in 1940. Tram No 9 or 12 will take you back to the city centre.

SPECIAL EVENTS
Wrocław's major annual events include the **Musica Polonica Nova Contemporary Music Festival** in February, the **Jazz on the Odra River International Festival** in May and the **Wratislavia Cantans International Oratorio and Cantata Festival** in September.

PLACES TO STAY
Wrocław has a reasonable choice of accommodation. Many hotels are either near the train station or the Old Town, and these are the most convenient places to stay. Predictably, they tend to fill up first, so you may occasionally have to stay outside the centre, particularly if you arrive late.

Places to Stay – Budget
Camping Wrocław has two camping grounds and both have cabins:

Camping Nr 267 Ślęża (☎/fax 343 44 42, ul Na Grobli 16/18) Tent site US$2 plus US$2 per person, double/triple cabins without bath US$18/24, triple cabins with bath US$36. Open year-round. This camp site is on the bank of the Odra, 2km east of the Old Town. There's no urban transport all the way there; go to Plac Wróblewskiego (tram No 4 from the train station) and walk 1km east.

Camping Nr 117 Olimpijski (☎ 348 46 51, ul Paderewskiego 35) Tent site US$2 plus US$2 per person, double cabins US$12. Open May-Sept. This camp site, near the Olympic stadium in Park Szczytnicki, is about 4km east of the city centre –

take tram No 9 from the train station. It has more cabins than the other camp site.

Youth Hostels Wrocław has three all-year youth hostels.

Youth hostel (☎ 343 88 56, fax 343 88 57, ul Kołłątaja 20) Beds US$4-7. Located just a few paces from the main train station, this 53-bed hostel is often full due to its central position. It has mostly large dorms.

Youth hostel (☎ 322 60 99, fax 322 61 13, Wyspa Słodowa 10) Beds US$6-9. This new 50-bed hostel is the best of the three and enjoys the best location – quiet, pleasant and convenient for sightseeing.

Youth hostel (☎/fax 345 73 96, ul Kiełczowska 43) Beds US$4-7. This is the largest hostel (100 beds) and the least convenient – it's in the distant suburb of Psie Pole, about 10km north-east of the train station. Take bus N from its terminus on ul Sucha between the train station and bus terminal.

Other Hostels & Hotels *Bursa Nauczycielska (☎/fax 344 37 81, ul Kotlarska 42)* Singles/doubles US$14/24, beds in triples/quads US$8/7. Bursa is a 70-bed teachers' hostel, ideally located just a block north-east of the Rynek. Rooms don't have baths, but they are clean, well kept and quiet. The location, standard and prices make the Bursa one of the best budget bets in town.

Pokoje U Szermierzy (☎ 342 96 54, ul Krasińskiego 30B) Singles/doubles/triples without bath US$12/15/18. Not as good or central as the Bursa but cheaper, this sports dorm has 29 beds within easy walking distance of the Old Town. The hostel is in a free-standing building off the street – enter gate No 30 and you'll see it in front of you.

Usługi Hotelarskie (☎/fax 355 94 46, ul Trzemeska 4) Doubles without bath US$16. This is another basic but cheap option reasonably close to the Old Town – about 1300m west of the Rynek. This one has more than 120 beds, so it's usually easier to find a vacancy here than elsewhere.

Places to Stay – Mid-Range
Hotel Podróżnik (☎/fax 373 28 45, ul Sucha 1) Doubles/triples/quads with bath &

breakfast US$34/42/50. Podróżnik (literally, traveller), on the 1st floor of the bus terminal, isn't really anything special but is one of the cheapest options providing rooms with private baths.

Bursa Savoy (☎ *340 32 19, fax 372 53 79, Plac Kościuszki 19*) Singles/doubles/triples with bath US$30/36/44. The Savoy, within easy walking distance from both the train station and the Old Town, is a reasonable, quiet place and may have weekend discount rates. It's good value and, predictably, is often full.

Hotel Monopol (☎ *343 70 41, fax 343 51 03, ul Modrzejewskiej 2*) Singles/doubles without bath US$30/40, with bath US$45/65, breakfast included. Operating since 1892, the Monopol is the city's oldest hotel. Hitler stayed here whenever he visited Breslau (Wrocław's German name) and addressed the crowds from the balcony. It's not a classy place today, but it doesn't cost a fortune either, and sits opposite the Opera House, just a few minutes walk from the Rynek.

Places to Stay – Top End

All hotels listed in this section have rooms with bath and breakfast included, and all have their own restaurants.

Hotel Tumski (☎ *322 60 99, fax 322 61 13, Wyspa Słodowa 10*) Singles/doubles/triples US$50/65/75. Located on one of the islands on the Odra River, yet within walking distance of the Old Town, this new 100-bed hotel offers reasonable standards. Part of the hotel building is taken by one of the youth hostels listed earlier.

Dwór Polski (☎/*fax 372 34 15, ul Kiełbaśnicza 2*) Doubles US$60-80. Housed in a finely restored historic building, the 52-bed Dwór Polski is a stylish place and a very central one. Rates vary depending on room size and quality.

Prima Hotel (☎ *782 55 55, fax 342 67 32, ul Kiełbaśnicza 16-19*) Singles/doubles US$100/110. Poland's first of the Best Western hotel chain, the 78-room Prima is new, central and comfortable.

Mercure Hotel Panorama (☎ *323 27 00, fax 344 36 81, Plac Dominikański 1*) Singles/doubles US$100/110. The 300-bed Panorama is a new posh modern central

hotel, built as part of a large commercial centre. It may offer weekend discount rates.

Holiday Inn (☎ *787 00 00, fax 787 00 01, ul Piłsudskiego 49/57*) Singles/doubles US$130/150. Another large and brand-new upmarket hotel, Holiday Inn is one of Wrocław's dearest options and one of the best.

PLACES TO EAT

Budget eating is no problem in Wrocław. There are a number of cheap places scattered throughout the central area. Some of these are modernised milk bars, while others are establishments of the newer generation. You are likely to find a budget meal for usually no more than US$3 within a few minutes walk.

Bar Wegetariański Vega (☎ *344 39 34, Sukiennice 1/2*) Mains US$2-3. The most central and one of the most pleasant budget eateries, the Vega is also one of the very few exclusively vegetarian places.

Bar Mleczny Miś (☎ *343 49 63, ul Kuźnicza 48*) Mains US$1-2. One of the cheapest places, this old milk bar continues to draw in crowds of people at lunch time, mostly students from the nearby university quarter.

Other milk-bar-style budget eateries in the centre include **Bar Jacek i Agatka** (☎ *344 24 55, Plac Nowy Targ 27*), **Bar U Babci** (☎ *344 17 12, ul Więzienna 16*), **Bar Mały** (☎ *344 42 73, ul Kołłątaja 27/28*) and **Bar Wzorcowy** (☎ *343 33 65, ul Piłsudskiego 86*) near the train station.

Steakhouse Piramida (☎ *344 40 40, ul Więzienna 30*) Mains US$3-5. A new place which immediately became popular among locals, Piramida has an interesting combination of Middle-Eastern and Mediterranean food, including kebabs, gyros and shwarma, plus some steaks.

Akropolis (☎ *343 14 13, Plac Solny 18/19*) Mains US$4-6. Another pleasant place offering some Mediterranean fare, this time mostly from Greece.

Złoty Pies (☎ *372 37 60, Rynek 41*) Mains US$4-8. One of the cheapest eateries on the Rynek, the Golden Dog has a pleasant split-level setting with fabulous vaulted cellars, where it serves solid Polish and European food and cheap beer.

Grill Pub Pod Złotym Jeleniem *(☎ 372 39 51, Rynek 44)* Mains US$8-16. Another place with fine cellars, the Golden Stag specialises in game and is an upmarket option.

Karczma Lwowska *(☎ 343 98 87, Rynek 4)* Mains US$7-10. This enjoyable 1st-floor restaurant brings some Lviv cuisine to town.

Dwór Polski ☎ *372 48 96, Rynek 5)* Literally, the Polish Court, this is a gastronomic complex which includes two restaurants and a cafe. The posh ***Restauracja Królewska*** (King Restaurant) is one of Wrocław's top spots for traditional Polish cuisine in a historic interior. The more informal ***Karczma Piastów*** (Piast Inn), at the back of the same complex, has more popular Polish food.

Restauracja La Scala *(☎ 372 53 94, Rynek 38)* Mains US$5-12. La Scala is one of the best Italian eateries around. Occupying an elegant 1st-floor room, it has relatively inexpensive pastas and some pricier meat mains.

Restauracja Vincent *(☎ 341 05 20, ul Ruska 39)* Mains US$8-12. Situated in a historic building with several beautiful interiors, Vincent is a quiet, charming place with good international food and atmosphere.

ENTERTAINMENT

Wrocław is an important cultural centre, and there's much cultural activity year-round. Local papers have listings of what's on, or pick up copies of two free cultural monthlies, *Co Jest Grane* and *Aktivist*. Both are in Polish only, but some of the content can be deciphered. The tourist office may provide more information. *Aktivist* also covers bars, discos, clubs etc.

Bars & Pubs

Spiż (☎ 344 72 25, Rynek-Ratusz 2) Possibly Wrocław's most unusual drinking spot, this subterranean restaurant/bar beside the town hall serves beer straight from its own brewery. The restaurant is upmarket but a mug of its rich brew in the wood-panelled bar should fit into almost anyone's budget and belly, and you can see brass vats used in the production process behind the buffet.

There's a beer garden in summer on the square outside.

Kalogródek *(ul Kuźnicza 29B)* One of the cheapest watering holes in town, the open-air Kalogródek is an informal place with an amphitheatre-like patio, always full with young folks, including students from the nearby university.

Christopher Columbus *(☎ 369 37 39, Plac Orląt Lwowskich 20)* Installed in what was Świebodzki train station, this attractive pub-cum-restaurant has an amazing large central bar made in the form of the 15th-century Columbus' boat. It's an enjoyable place for a drink, a meal and for some dancing (discos are run nightly except Sunday).

Piwnica Stańczyka *(☎ 372 48 96, Rynek 5)* This bar is in fabulous cellars beneath the Dwór Polski.

Irish Pub *(☎ 344 60 15, Plac Solny 5)* This is rather an upmarket pub, but it has live music on some nights.

Discos

Radio Bar *(☎ 372 50 13, Rynek 48)* Radio Bar is a vast, attractive basement disco with several bars, invariably popular with locals and visitors.

Golden Corner Club *(☎ 341 02 17, ul Kiełbaśnicza 32)* Another large basement affair, Golden Corner Club is also good, reasonably cheap and popular.

Studio P1 *(☎ 370 69 41, ul Szewska 3A)* The Studio is a new, gigantic (1200 sq metres) disco with all the bells and whistles. This is the most expensive place for both admission and drinks.

You can also have a good time at the disco in ***Christopher Columbus***, mentioned under Bars & Pubs earlier.

Jazz

Jazz Club Rura *(☎ 344 33 20, ul Łazienna 4)* This long-standing venue is one of the very few places to stage live jazz.

Opera & Classical Music

Opera *(☎ 341 07 38, ul Świdnicka 35)* The opera house is the traditional venue for opera and ballet performances.

Filharmonia (Philharmonic Hall; ☎ *342 20 01, ul Piłsudskiego 19)* Classical music concerts are usually held here on Friday.

Theatre

Wrocław is internationally known for the avant-garde Teatr Laboratorium (Laboratory Theatre) of Jerzy Grotowski. He started out in 1959 in Opole's Theatre of 13 Rows but moved to Wrocław in 1965 and directed Laboratorium until 1984. The theatre was dissolved after Grotowski moved to Italy and established a theatre research centre in Pontedera. He died in 1999.

In 1990 the *Centre of Studies on Jerzy Grotowski's Work (*☎ *343 42 67, Rynek-Ratusz 27)* was founded in the theatre's former home. The centre has documentaries on the Laboratory Theatre and can present them on request. It also invites various experimental groups, often from abroad, to give performances in its small theatre.

Today, the main ambassador for Wrocław theatre is the Wrocławski Teatr Pantomimy created by Henryk Tomaszewski. The theatre is usually on tour somewhere. Check with the tourist office to see if it's in town.

Teatr Polski (☎ *343 86 53, ul Zapolskiej 3)* This is the major mainstream city venue, staging classic Polish and foreign drama.

Teatr Współczesny (☎ *343 87 73, ul Rzeźnicza 12)* Teatr Współczesny tends more towards contemporary productions.

GETTING THERE & AWAY
Air

The airport in Strachowice, 10km west of the city centre, is accessible by bus No 106 from near the former Wrocław Świebodzki train station, a 10-minute walk west of the Rynek. There are direct connections with Warsaw (six times a day), Frankfurt/Main (daily), Copenhagen (twice daily), Munich (daily) and Vienna (three times a week). The LOT office (☎ 343 63 76), ul Piłsudskiego 36, and Orbis Travel (☎ 344 41 09), Rynek 29, reserve seats and sell tickets.

Train

The main train station, Wrocław Główny, built in 1856, is a historical monument in itself. There are plenty of trains that will take you to most places in the region and beyond.

Fast trains to Katowice (190km) depart every two to three hours and pass via Opole (82km) on their way. Most of them continue to Kraków (268km). There are at least half a dozen fast trains plus three express trains to Warsaw (385km) and some call at Łódź (242km) en route. Wrocław also has regular train links with Poznań (165km), Wałbrzych (70km), Jelenia Góra (126km), Legnica (66km) and Kłodzko (96km).

International destinations include Berlin, Budapest, Dresden, Hamburg, Kyiv and Prague.

Bus

The bus terminal is on ul Sucha, just south of the train station. You probably won't need a bus to get out of Wrocław, except to Trzebnica (24km), Sobótka (34km), Świdnica (53km) and Nysa (83km), where trains don't go at all or require a change.

There are a number of international bus routes to places including Prague and plenty of cities in Western Europe. Tickets are available from Virgo (☎ 367 54 11, 367 73 77) at the terminal itself. Orbis Travel, Almatur and other travel agencies.

Around Wrocław

TRZEBNICA
☎ 71 • pop 12,000

A small town 24km north of Wrocław, Trzebnica ('Tsheb-**nee**-tsah') is noted for its former Cistercian Abbey (Opactwo Cysterskie). The order was brought to Poland in 1140 and established its first monastery in Jędrzejów, from where it swiftly expanded and set up nearly 40 abbeys all over the country. Among other places, the order had monasteries in Kraków, Gdańsk, Pelplin, Wąchock, Krzeszów, Henryków and Lubiąż, some of which are described in the appropriate sections of this book. Trzebnica was the site of the first Cistercian convent in Poland.

The convent was founded in 1202 by Princess Jadwiga (Hedwig), the wife of the

SILESIA

Duke of Wrocław, Henryk Brodaty (Henry the Bearded). After the duke's death, she entered the abbey and lived an ascetic life to the end of her days. Only 24 years later, in 1267, she was canonised and the abbey church where she had been buried has become a destination for pilgrims. She is regarded as the patron saint of Silesia.

Things to See
The **church** is thought to be one of the first brick buildings of its kind in Poland. Though it was rebuilt in later periods, the structure has preserved much of its initial austere Romanesque shape and, more importantly, still boasts two original **portals**. The one next to the main entrance, unfortunately partly hidden behind the baroque tower added in the 1780s, is particularly fine thanks to its tympanum from the 1220s, which depicts King David on his throne playing the harp to Queen Bathsheba.

Once inside, you are surrounded by ornate baroque decoration, including a lavishly ornamented high altar. At its foot is the very modest black-marble tomb of Henryk Brodaty.

The showpiece of the interior is **St Hedwig's Chapel** (Kaplica Św Jadwigi), to the right of the chancel. It was built soon after the canonisation of the princess, and the graceful, ribbed Gothic vault has been preserved unchanged, though the decoration dates from a later epoch. Its central feature is the large tomb of St Hedwig, an elaborate work in marble and alabaster created in stages between 1680 and 1750. Beside the sarcophagus is the entrance to the three-naved crypt, the oldest part of the church.

Places to Stay
Ośrodek Wypoczynkowy (☎/fax 312 07 47, ul Leśna 2) Seasonal double/triple/quad cabins US$14/20/22, all-year double/triple rooms US$16/22. Ośrodek provides the cheapest accommodation in town, though it's pretty basic. It features all-year rooms without bath, seasonal cabins (some with bath) and a tent area.

Hotel Pod Platanami (☎/fax 312 09 80, ul Kilińskiego 2) Doubles/triples US$22/28.

All the simple but acceptable 40-bed Platanami rooms have private baths.

Hotel Nowy Dwór (☎/fax 312 07 14, ul Prusicka 32) Singles/doubles/triples with bath & breakfast US$26/32/40. Hotel Nowy Dwór is another reasonable option with private facilities.

Getting There & Away
Buses from Wrocław to Trzebnica run frequently and will let you off near the church. Trains no longer ply this route.

LUBIĄŻ
☎ 71 • pop 1000
The small village of Lubiąż ('Loo-byonsh'), about 50km north-west of Wrocław, also owes its fame to the Cistercians. It boasts a gigantic **Cistercian Abbey** (Opactwo Cystersów), one of Europe's largest monastic complexes. Founded in 1175, the modest original abbey was gradually extended as the order grew. After the Thirty Years' War the monastery entered a period of prosperity, and it was then that a magnificent baroque complex was built – the work taking almost a century and finishing in 1739. It has a 223m-wide facade and 365 rooms. A team of distinguished artists, including the famous painter Michael Willmann, was commissioned for the monumental project.

In 1810 the abbey was closed down, and the buildings were subsequently occupied and devastated by a bizarre range of tenants: it was a horse stud, mental hospital, arsenal, Nazi military plant (during WWII), Soviet army hospital (1945–48), and finally a storehouse for the state book publisher. The postwar renovation was minimal and a large part of the complex is still unused.

It wasn't until 1991 that a Polish-German foundation took things in hand in order to restore the abbey. A few rooms have already been renovated and are open to the public as a small **museum** (☎ 389 71 66; adult/student US$1/0.50; 9am-6pm May-Sept, 10am-3pm Oct-Apr). The showpiece is the huge, 15m-high hall with its opulent baroque decoration from the 1730s.

The work on further interiors, including the refectory and library, is in progress, but

Michael Willmann – Silesian Baroque Painting at its Best

Michael Willmann (1630–1706) is regarded as the most outstanding painter of the Silesian baroque form. His art was initially influenced by the painting of Rubens and Rembrandt, but he soon developed his own style, noted for great expression and dynamism.

Willmann at first practised court art, until he met the abbot of the Cistercian Abbey of Lubiąż, in 1656, and dedicated himself to sacred painting. One of his greatest works is a series of 43 paintings depicting biblical scenes, made for the abbey. They are now scattered among 13 Warsaw churches and monasteries, and the national museums in Warsaw and Wrocław – none are in Lubiąż.

What is easier to see is Willmann's other remarkable achievement, the fresco decoration of St Joseph's Church in Krzeszów, a bravura work which covers the whole of the vault and walls of the spacious interior. You can even see the author of the painting himself, since Willmann couldn't resist leaving his own image on the wall in one of the scenes.

the mighty church and adjoining chapel will probably take longer to be restored. As yet they have no decoration apart from some surviving portals and fragments of frescoes by Willmann. The crypt beneath the church reputedly holds 98 mummified bodies, including that of Willmann himself, but cannot be visited.

Lubiąż lies off the main roads, and bus transport is infrequent, with only one bus to/from Legnica daily (28km) and several to/from Wrocław (51km). There's no railway here.

SOBÓTKA & MT ŚLĘŻA
☎ 71 • pop 6800

About 35km south-west of Wrocław, the solitary, forested, cone-shaped Mt Ślęża rises from an open plain to a height of 718m, about 500m above the surrounding plain. Mt Ślęża was one of the holy places of an ancient pagan tribe which, as in many other places around the world, used to set up its cult sites atop the mountains. It's not known for sure who they were – Celts, Scythians or one of the pre-Slavic tribes – though we do know that a centre of worship existed here from at least the 5th century BC till the 11th century AD, when it was overtaken by Christianity. The summit was circled by a stone wall marking off the sanctuary where rituals were held, and the remains of these ramparts survive to this day. Mysterious statues were carved out of granite, and several of them, in better or worse shape, are still scattered over the mountain's slopes.

At the northern foot of the mountain is the small town of Sobótka, a starting point for the hike to the top. The town's Rynek is dominated by the massive St Jacob's Church, originally Romanesque but repeatedly remodelled later. Nearby to the northwest, on Plac Wolności, is St Anne's Church, and beside it is one of the stone statues, known as the Mushroom (Grzyb).

About 200m south of the Rynek is the small **Regional Museum** (Muzeum Ślężańskie; ☎ 316 26 22, ul Św Jakuba 18; admission US$0.50; open 9am-4pm Wed-Sun), recognisable by a fine Renaissance doorway from 1568. The museum displays some of the finds of archaeological excavations in the region.

Proceed south along the same street for another 300m and take ul Garncarska to the right (west) and going uphill. About 500m on, you'll pass another stone statue, called the Monk (Mnich), the finest and best preserved of all. Another 500m up the road, you'll get to a hostel, the Schronisko Pod Wieżycą. The yellow trail from the hostel will take you up Mt Ślęża in about an hour. You'll find two more statues on the way, and a tall TV mast and a 19th-century church at the top.

Places to Stay & Eat
Gościniec Niedźwiadek (☎ 390 32 37, fax 316 22 52, Rynek 8) Doubles/triples/quads US$14/17/22. Niedźwiadek is a simple but acceptable budget place which has rooms with shared facilities. It also has a budget restaurant.

SILESIA

Zajazd Pod Misiem (☎ *316 20 35,* ☎*/fax 16 20 34, ul Mickiewicza 7/9)* Doubles/triples with bath US$24/26. The Zajazd, just off the Rynek, is nothing special but has private facilities, and it too has its own restaurant.

Schronisko Pod Wieżycą (☎ *316 28 57, ul Armii Krajowej 13)* Singles/doubles/triples/quads without bath US$14/16/18/22. The PTTK hostel, at the foot of Mt Ślęża, is very simple but pleasant and it also has a restaurant.

Hotel Zamek Górka (☎*/fax 316 21 33, ul Zamkowa 12)* Doubles/triples/quads without bath US$20/30/40, doubles & triples with bath US$30-60. This fairy-tale eclectic castle in Górka, a distant suburb of Sobótka, 3km west of the Rynek off the road to Świdnica, is possibly the most attractive accommodation around. It has rooms of different standards, without and with bath, and its own restaurant.

Getting There & Away
Sobótka is accessible by bus from Wrocław (32km) and Świdnica (21km). Buses run regularly and will deposit you in the town centre next to St Anne's Church.

Lower Silesia

A fertile lowland extending along the upper and middle course of the Odra River, Lower Silesia (Dolny Śląsk) was settled relatively early on, and is full of old towns and villages. Apart from Wrocław and its environs (detailed in the previous sections) there are other places in Lower Silesia which harbour interesting sights and warrant a stop. They have been organised in this section following the route downstream along the Odra.

OPOLE
☎ 77 • pop 132,000
Set halfway between Katowice and Wrocław, Opole lies on the border of Upper and Lower Silesia, and there's no consensus as to the region in which it belongs. Most locals don't feel part of either, but rather of their own Opolan Silesia (Śląsk Opolski). The region is known for an active German

minority, which is well represented in local government.

Opole has already passed its first millennium. The first stronghold was built in the 9th century, initially on Pasieka Island. In the 13th century the town became the capital of a principality, and it was ruled by a line of the Silesian Piasts until 1532, even though from 1327 it was part of Bohemia. Later on, Opole fell subsequently to Austria, then to Prussia, and after significant destruction during WWII returned to Poland in 1945. Today it's a fairly large regional industrial centre.

For most Poles, Opole is known for its Festival of Polish Song, which has taken place annually in late June since 1963 and is broadcast nationwide on TV. On these days the city sees crowds of visitors; the rest of the year few tourists bother to come here to explore the few attractions.

Information
The Miejska Informacja Turystyczna (☎ 451 19 87), ul Krakowska 15, is open 10am to 5pm weekdays, 10am to 1pm Saturday.

Useful banks include Bank Pekao, ul Osmańczyka 15, and Bank Zachodni, ul Ozimska 6, and both have ATMs. There are more ATMs in the centre, including one in Orbis Travel, ul Krakowska 31. Kantors are easy to find in the centre.

Central Internet facilities include HMS Computers (☎ 453 12 00), ul Krakowska 26, and ARCom (☎ 454 55 86), ul Kołłątaja 9.

Things to See
The **Rynek** was badly damaged during WWII but remarkably well rebuilt. The houses which line the square make up a coherent baroque-rococo composition. However, the oversized town hall in the middle looks as if it has been imported from another cultural sphere. Its 64m-tall tower was patterned on the Palazzo Vecchio in Florence and built in 1864. It collapsed in 1934 but was rebuilt in the same style.

The **Franciscan Church** (Kościół Franciszkanów), off the southern corner of the Rynek, was built around 1330, but the interior was reshaped later on various occasions. It boasts an ornate high altar, 18th-century

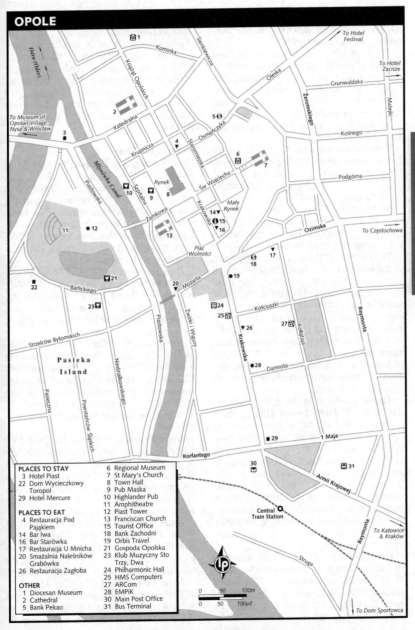

OPOLE

To Hotel Festival
To Hotel Zacisze

Odra (Oder)

To Museum of Opolan Village, Nysa & Wrocław

Kominka
Sienkiewicca
Oleska
Grunwaldzka
Matejki
Żeromskiego
Kośnego
Podgórna
Książąt Opolskich
Katedralna
Osmańczyka
Staromiejska
Krupnicza
Sw. Wojciecha
Młynówka Canal
Piastowska
Rynek
Szpitalna
Zamkowa
Kraków ska
Mały Rynek
Ozimska
To Częstochowa
Plac Wolności
Mozarta
Barlickiego
Kościuszki
Kolejala
ARCom
Reymonta
Strzelców Bytomskich
Piastowska
Żwirki i Wigury
Kraków ska
Damrota
Pasieka Island
Pasieczna
Powstańców Śląskich
Niedziałkowskiego
1 Maja
Korfantego
Armii Krajowej
Central Train Station
To Katowice & Kraków
Struga
To Dom Sportowca

SILESIA

PLACES TO STAY
3 Hotel Piast
22 Dom Wycieczkowy Toropol
29 Hotel Mercure

PLACES TO EAT
4 Restauracja Pod Pająkiem
14 Bar Iwa
16 Bar Starówka
17 Restauracja U Mnicha
20 Smażalnia Naleśników Grabówka
26 Restauracja Zagłoba

OTHER
1 Diocesan Museum
2 Cathedral
5 Bank Pekao
6 Regional Museum
7 St Mary's Church
8 Town Hall
9 Pub Maska
10 Highlander Pub
11 Amphitheatre
12 Piast Tower
13 Franciscan Church
15 Tourist Office
18 Bank Zachodni
19 Orbis Travel
21 Gospoda Opolska
23 Klub Muzyczny Sto Trzy, Dwa
24 Philharmonic Hall
25 HMS Computers
27 ARCom
28 EMPiK
30 Main Post Office
31 Bus Terminal

0   50   100m
0   50   100yd

organ, and domed Renaissance chapel in the left-hand aisle, separated by a fine late 16th-century wrought-iron grille.

The highlight of the church is the **Piast Chapel**, accessible from the right-hand aisle through a doorway with a tympanum. The Gothic-vaulted chapel houses a pair of massive double tombs of the local dukes, carved in sandstone in the 1380s. They were originally painted but the colour has almost disappeared.

Two blocks east of the Rynek, the former Jesuit college houses the **Regional Museum** (*Muzeum Śląska Opolskiego;* ☎ *453 66 77, Mały Rynek 7; adult/student US$1/0.50; open 9am-3pm Tues-Fri, 10am-3pm Sat, noon-5pm Sun*). The permanent display features the prehistory and history of the surrounding area and city, and there are always temporary exhibitions.

The Gothic **cathedral**, a short walk north of the Rynek, now features mostly baroque furnishing. The chapel in the right-hand aisle shelters the 1532 red-marble tombstone of the last of the Opole dukes. The only surviving Gothic triptych of the 26 that the church once had is also in this chapel.

A bit farther north, the **Diocesan Museum** (*Muzeum Diecezjalne;* ☎ *456 60 15, ul Kominka 1A; open 10am-noon, 2pm-5pm Tues & Thur*) boasts sacred sculpture collected from the region.

The only vestige of the dukes' castle is the 42m-tall **Piast Tower** (*Wieża Piastowska;* ☎ *452 42 24, ul Piastowska 14; adult/student US$1/0.50; open 10am-1pm, 2pm-5pm Tues-Sun May-Aug, 10am-1pm, 1.30pm-4pm Tues-Sun Sept & Oct*). Built in the 13th century on Pasieka Island, the castle was pulled down in the 1920s to make room for office buildings. The tower, which miraculously escaped 'modernisation', sticks up oddly from behind the drab blocks. You can climb to the top for a panoramic view over the city.

Opole has a good skansen, the **Museum of Opolan Village** (*Muzeum Wsi Opolskiej;* ☎ *474 30 21, ul Wrocławska 174; adult/student US$1.50/1, free Sat; open 10am-6pm Tues-Sun 16 Apr-15 Oct, 9am-2pm Mon-Fri 16 Oct-15 Apr*). Located in the

Bierkowice suburb, 5km west of the centre, and accessible by urban bus No 5, the skansen has a variety of rural architecture from the region. The shingled church of 1613, the water mill of 1832 and a couple of large granaries are among the showpieces. Several houses are fully furnished and decorated, and can be visited. From mid-October to mid-April the buildings stay locked.

Places to Stay

Dom Wycieczkowy Toropol (☎ *453 78 83, ul Barlickiego 13*) Beds in triples US$8. Toropol is a good budget bet. Well located on the 2nd floor of a freestanding building next to the amphitheatre on quiet Pasieka Island, it's only a five-minute walk from the Rynek and 10 minutes from the train station. Unfortunately, all of its 14 rooms can often be full up with groups.

Dom Sportowca (☎ *454 55 76, ul Kowalska 2*) Doubles without/with bath US$20/40, beds in 4- or 5-bed dorms US$10. This former sports dorm is a 10-minute walk south of the train station (twice that distance from the centre).

Hotel Zacisze (☎/fax *453 95 53, ul Grunwaldzka 28*) Singles/doubles/triples without bath US$18/34/40, singles/doubles with bath US$30/50, breakfast included. Located within reasonable walking distance of both the Rynek (10 minutes) and the station (15 minutes), the Zacisze has small but acceptable rooms.

Hotel Festival (☎ *455 60 11, fax 455 60 17, ul Oleska 86*) Singles/doubles with bath & breakfast US$65/70. The Hotel Festival, about 2km north-east of the centre, provides decent, spacious rooms complete with some other amenities such as gym, jacuzzi, sauna and a small swimming pool.

Hotel Mercure (☎ *451 81 00, fax 451 81 99, ul Krakowska 57-59*) Singles/doubles with bath & breakfast US$75/90. This strategically sited large 103-room hotel facing the train station has recently been renovated.

Hotel Piast (☎ *454 97 10, fax 454 97 17, ul Piastowska 1*) Singles/doubles with bath & breakfast US$75/90. Another top-end option, the Piast is located on the northern tip of Pasieka Island. It can be noisy due to heavy traffic, especially if you take a room facing the street.

Places to Eat

Bar Starówka (☎ 454 32 53, ul Krakowska 19) Mains US$1.50-3. A sort of an upgraded milk bar, the Starówka is one of the cheapest central places for a meal.

Smażalnia Naleśników Grabówka (☎ 454 17 96, ul Mozarta 2) Crepes US$1-2. Enjoying a waterfront location, this tiny place offers crepes with two dozen different fillings, including egg, cheese, ham, mushrooms and pineapple.

Bar Iwa (☎ 454 27 12, Mały Rynek 17) Mains US$4-5. Iwa is a tiny six-table establishment that serves typical Polish fare.

Restauracja Pod Pająkiem (ul Książąt Opolskich 2-6) Mains US$3-5. An agreeable new restaurant, Pod Pająkiem offers Hungarian and traditional Polish cuisine – good value.

Restauracja U Mnicha (☎ 454 52 34, ul Ozimska 10) Mains US$4-5. This modern basement restaurant serves up Polish and Middle-Eastern fare.

Restauracja Zagłoba (☎ 441 78 60, ul Krakowska 39) Mains US$6-8. Another new basement eatery, Zagłoba serves solid traditional Polish food in historic vaults.

Entertainment

Pub Maska (☎ 453 92 67, Rynek 4) Maska is a charming pub and a pleasant place for a drink. The Theatre of 13 Rows (Teatr 13-tu Rzędów) of Jerzy Grotowski operated in this house in 1959–64.

Highlander Pub (☎ 465 55 28, ul Szpitalna 3) An good alternative and central place for a beer, the Highlander hosts live music occasionally.

Gospoda Opolska (☎ 441 62 20, ul Barlickiego 2A) This waterfront inn with a pleasant outdoor sitting area overlooking a pond (formed from part of the old moat surrounding the castle), offers plenty of drinks and Polish food.

Klub Muzyczny Sto Trzy, Dwa (☎ 441 44 40, ul Niedziałkowskiego 1) Just across the road from the Gospoda, this music club also

has a pleasant outdoor drinking area in summer, and stages live music at times.

Getting There & Away

The train station and bus terminal face each other, not far south of the Old Town; you can walk to the Rynek in 10 minutes.

Opole is on the Katowice-Wrocław railway line and trains to both these destinations (98km and 82km, respectively) run regularly. Most Katowice trains continue to Kraków (176km). There are also several trains a day to Częstochowa (95km), as well as morning and late afternoon express trains to Warsaw (325km).

Buses go regularly to Nysa (53km) and Kłodzko (108km), a route not well serviced by trains.

BRZEG
☎ 77 • pop 40,000

A quiet, medium-sized town midway between Opole and Wrocław, Brzeg ('Bzhek') was founded in 1248 and became the capital of yet another Silesian Piast principality, the Duchy of Legnica-Brzeg. The princes initially set themselves up in Legnica but spent more and more of their time in Brzeg, which gradually took over many of the capital's functions.

During the town's heyday in the 16th century the existing Gothic castle was greatly extended and became a splendid Renaissance residence, modelled on Kraków's royal palace; it was even referred to as the 'Silesian Wawel'. In 1675 the last duke of the family died, marking the end of the Piast dynasty in Poland, and the town came under direct Habsburg rule and became known as Brieg. A century later, Prussia turned the town into a massive fortress, which nonetheless was seized by Napoleon, and the fortifications were later pulled down. In their place, a ring of parks is established, which now surrounds the historic core of the town, the ponds being the remains of the moat.

The town, like the whole region, was defended fiercely by the Germans in 1945, and half of its buildings were destroyed. The most important monuments have been reconstructed, and for these, principally the

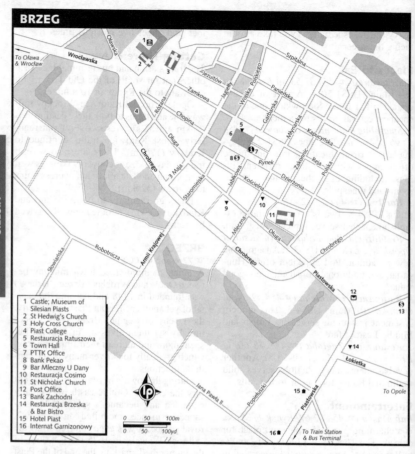

BRZEG

1 Castle; Museum of
   Silesian Piasts
2 St Hedwig's Church
3 Holy Cross Church
4 Piast College
5 Restauracja Ratuszowa
6 Town Hall
7 PTTK Office
8 Bank Pekao
9 Bar Mleczny U Dany
10 Restauracja Cosimo
11 St Nicholas' Church
12 Post Office
13 Bank Zachodni
14 Restauracja Brzeska
   & Bar Bistro
15 Hotel Piast
16 Internat Garnizonowy

castle, it's worth breaking your journey for
a couple of hours.

Information
There's no tourist office as such. The PTTK
office (☎ 416 21 00), Sukiennice 2, may answer some questions. Bank Pekao is at
Rynek 9 and Bank Zachodni at ul Powstańców Śląskich 6; both cash travellers
cheques and have ATMs.

Things to See
Coming from the station, you will enter the
Old Town by ul Długa. The monumental

14th-century **St Nicholas' Church** (Kościół
Św Mikołaja) to your right was partially
burned during WWII and the twin towers
were reconstructed – you can tell from the
different colour of the brick. The interior
has some burghers' epitaphs on the walls.

The Rynek was partly ruined during the
war and looks a bit plain, mainly because of
the substantial amount of postwar architecture. Yet the Renaissance **town hall**, from
the 1570s, was restored to a form close to
the original.

Two blocks west is the **Holy Cross
Church** built in the 1730s for the Jesuits. Its

ample, single-naved interior is decorated in exuberant baroque style throughout, including the trompe l'œil painted vault.

Next to the church is the **castle**, the pride of the town. It started as a stronghold built in the 13th century, but it was turned into a large Renaissance palace by Duke Jerzy II (George II). The richly decorated facade (c. 1552) of the central three-storey gateway gives some idea of the palace's former splendour. Immediately above the archway are the stone figures of Duke Jerzy and his wife Barbara. Farther up, the two-tier frieze depicts 24 busts of the Piast kings and princes, from the first legendary Piast to the father of Jerzy II, Duke Fryderyk II (Frederick II). In the middle of the balustrade at the top is the coat of arms of King Zygmunt August, with the Jagiellonian eagle at the centre.

The gate leads to a spacious arcaded courtyard, vaguely reminiscent of that of the Wawel except that one of the sides is missing. Note the Renaissance portals; the one at the main gate is particularly elaborate.

Part of the interior houses the **Museum of Silesian Piasts** (*Muzeum Piastów Śląskich;* ☎ 416 32 57, Plac Zamkowy 1; adult/ student US$1.50/0.75; open 10am-4pm Tues, Thur-Sun, 10am-6pm Wed), which traces the history of Silesia under the dynasty. The rooms upstairs shelter a collection of Silesian art from the 15th to 18th centuries, including some extraordinary altarpieces, retables and statues. The adjacent **St Hedwig's Church** (Kościół Św Jadwigi), formerly the castle's chapel, is sometimes opened for guided tours. It's also open to the faithful for Sunday Mass at 10am.

Places to Stay

Internat Garnizonowy (☎ 411 76 27, ul Piastowska 20) Singles/doubles without bath US$13/18. Located close to the bus and train stations, the Internat offers eight simple but cheap rooms.

Hotel Piast (☎/fax 416 20 27, ul Piastowska 14) Singles/doubles without bath US$20/30, with bath US$30/40. Also very close to the stations, the Piast provides reasonable facilities and has its own restaurant.

Places to Eat

Bar Mleczny U Dany (ul Długa 41) Mains US$1.50-2.50. U Dany is a basic milk bar and one of the cheapest eateries in town.

Restauracja Brzeska & Bar Bistro (☎ 416 76 11, ul Piastowska 15C) Mains US$2-6. Midway between the station and the Old Town, this is a reasonable option, especially the budget Bar Bistro, which is good value.

Restauracja Cosimo (☎ 444 29 24, ul Mleczna 2-3) Mains US$3-6. A new Italian restaurant, Cosimo has reasonably cheap pastas and slightly pricier meat dishes.

Restauracja Ratuszowa (☎ 416 52 67, Rynek-Ratusz) Mains US$4-7. The Ratuszowa, in the basement of the town hall, can be your choice for dinner as it closes later than most other places.

Getting There & Away

The train and bus stations are opposite each other, 1km south of the Old Town. Trains run every hour or two west to Wrocław (42km) and east to Opole (40km). A dozen fast trains continue east as far as Kraków (216km). Several trains and buses go south to Nysa (48km or 53km); choose whichever goes first.

AROUND BRZEG

There are several interesting Gothic churches in the villages near Brzeg, distinguished for their original wall paintings. The best examples are in Małujowice, Krzyżowice, Pogorzela and Strzelniki. The church in Małujowice, 5km west of Brzeg, is the largest, with amazing 15th-century frescoes. PKS buses from Brzeg's bus terminal will deposit you at the gate of the church.

LEGNICA
☎ 76 • pop 105,000

Legnica's origins go back to the 10th century, but it wasn't until the 13th century that its real development began when it became the co-capital of one of the Silesian Piast principalities, the Duchy of Legnica-Brzeg. In the 16th century the town – then under Bohemian rule – saw good times as an active centre of culture, with the first university established in Silesia. After the last duke of the Piast dynasty died in 1675, the town fell to the Habsburgs, and in 1741 to the Prussians. Badly damaged during WWII, the city revived as an industrial centre following the discovery of copper deposits in the region. For tourists, Legnica is not a particularly fascinating place, but you may want to see its few surviving historic buildings while passing this way.

Information

The municipal tourist office (☎ 851 22 80), Rynek 29, is open 9am to 5pm weekdays, 9am to 1pm Saturday. Bank Pekao is at ul Wrocławska 26/28, 500m south of the train station, while Bank Zachodni is at ul Gwarna 4A, 200m west of the Rynek. Both banks have ATMs and will cash travellers cheques.

Things to See

From the bus terminal, head south over a footbridge and then along ul Skarbowa to **St Mary's Church** (Kościół Mariacki), one of the oldest in Silesia but refurbished in mock-Gothic style in the 19th century. It's used today by the small Protestant community for infrequent services (Sunday only), and doubles as a stage for cultural events, such as organ and chamber music concerts.

Proceeding south-west by ul Najświętszej Marii Panny you'll get to the **Church of SS Peter and Paul**. This one also underwent a neo-Gothic metamorphosis, but its two original Gothic doorways survive. The one on the northern side (facing the Rynek) has a splendid tympanum depicting the Adoration of the Magi. The interior has the usual hotchpotch of furnishings, of which the oldest piece, the bas-reliefed bronze baptismal font (in the chapel off the left aisle), dates from the late 13th century and is reputedly the oldest metal font in Poland.

The **Rynek** is lined with ordinary modern buildings. The baroque **town hall** and a row of eight small arcaded houses known as the **herring stalls** (kramy śledziowe) are just about the only historic buildings on the square.

Just north of the Rynek is the **Museum of Copper** (Muzeum Miedzi; ☎ 862 49 49, ul Partyzantów 3; adult/student US$1/0.50; open 11am-5pm Wed-Sun). It focuses on the history of the town and the copper industry in the region, and also features temporary exhibitions.

Across the street from the museum is the baroque **St John's Church** (Kościół Św Jana). The chapel off the right-hand wall is actually the presbytery of the former Gothic church, set at right angles to the current one. The chapel is the mausoleum of the Legnica Piasts and houses their tombs. Inquire at the museum and they will open the chapel for you and show you around.

Back towards the station along ul Partyzantów, you'll pass the **castle**. Built in the 13th century, it was rebuilt in Gothic style (two brick towers from that period survive), then thoroughly modernised in the 1530s as a Renaissance residence, and again in 1835, when the noted German architect Karl Friedrich Schinkel gave it a neoclassical look. Enter through the main gate embellished with a Renaissance portal, the only significant remnant of the 16th-century renovation. A pavilion in the middle of the courtyard shelters the foundations of the 13th-century Romanesque chapel built here along with the original brick-and-stone castle by Henryk Brodaty. It should be open 10am to 4pm Tuesday to Saturday in summer.

Places to Stay

Youth hostel (☎ 862 54 12, ul Jordana 17) Beds US$4-6. Open year-round. The youth hostel, a 10-minute walk from the centre and about the same distance from the train station, offers 55 beds, most of which are in five- to 10-bed dorms.

Hotel Narol (☎ 866 95 78, ☎/fax 862 69 27, ul Gliwicka 1) Singles/doubles/triples without bath US$12/16/20. Narol, about 500m beyond the train station, is a former workers' dorm. It's on the basic side but OK and not bad value.

Hotel Tramp (☎ 862 00 10, fax 862 16 70, ul Kominka 7) Doubles/triples without bath US$24/34, doubles with bath US$28, including breakfast. Hotel Tramp, 500m north-west of the Rynek, has recently been refurbished and offers acceptable standards, yet most rooms have only shared facilities.

Hotel Cuprum (☎ 862 80 41, fax 862 85 44, ul Skarbowa 2) Singles US$50-70, doubles US$70-90, all with bath & breakfast. The Cuprum, diagonally opposite the bus terminal, is not a very classy place, yet it's the only upmarket accommodation in town.

Places to Eat

Bar Mleczny Ekspres (☎ 862 86 76, ul Dworcowa 8) Mains US$1-2. Sitting right opposite the train station, this basic milk bar has some of the cheapest meals in town.

Zakład Gastronomiczny Centrum (☎ 866 63 93, Plac Słowiański 1) Mains US$1.50-3. This large, drab, basic cafeteria, just a few paces south of the Rynek, provides acceptable if not memorable meals until 4pm.

Restauracja Tivoli (☎ 862 23 04, ul Złotoryjska 21) Mains US$4-7. The Tivoli, about 200m west of the Rynek, serves hearty traditional Polish fare, as it has since 1957.

Getting There & Away

The train and bus stations are next to each other on the north-eastern edge of the city centre and both offer regular services to Wrocław (75km). To other regional destinations such as Jelenia Góra (61km), Świdnica (56km) and Kłodzko (126km), take the bus. One bus a day (weekdays only) departs for Lubiąż (30km). There's one train to Warsaw daily.

LEGNICKIE POLE

☎ 76 • pop 2000

A small village 11km south-east of Legnica, Legnickie Pole (literally, the Legnica Field; 'Leg-**neets**-kyeh **Po**-leh') was the site of a great battle in 1241, in which Silesian troops under the command of Duke Henryk Pobożny (Henry the Pious) were defeated by the Tatars. The duke himself was killed and beheaded. The Tatars stuck his head on a spear and proceeded to Legnica but didn't manage to take the town. The duke's body was identified by his wife, Princess Anna, thanks to the fact that he had six toes on his left foot; this was confirmed in the 19th century when his tomb was opened.

Henryk's mother, Princess Hedwig (Księżna Jadwiga, the saint from Trzebnica), built a small commemorative chapel on the site of his decapitation, which was later replaced by a Gothic church. The church now shelters the **Museum of the Legnica Battle** (Muzeum Bitwy Legnickiej; ☎ 858 23 98; adult/student US$1/0.50; open 11am-5pm Wed-Sun). The modest exhibition features a hypothetical model of the battle (commentary in English and German available) and some related objects, including a copy of the duke's tomb (the original is in the National Museum in Wrocław).

Across the road from the museum is the former Benedictine Abbey. Its central part is occupied by **St Hedwig's Church**, a masterpiece of baroque art designed by Austrian architect Kilian Ignaz Dientzenhofer and built in the 1730s. Past the elaborate doorway you'll find yourself in a beautifully proportioned, bright and harmonious interior, with splendid frescoes on the vault, the work of Bavarian painter Cosmas Damian Asam. The fresco over the organ loft shows Princess Anna with the body of her husband after the battle, as does the painting on the high altar.

The church is locked except for religious services (it still serves as a parish church), but inquire in the museum and they will show you round once a few more tourists have arrived.

Places to Stay & Eat

Camping Nr 234 (☎ 858 23 97, ul Henryka Brodatego 7) Four-bed cabins US$12. Open May-Sept. This basic camp site has 10 cabins and a tent area.

Motel Legnickie Pole (☎/fax 858 20 94, ul Kossak-Szczuckiej 7) Doubles without/with bath US$20/28. This is the only all-year place to stay in Legnickie Pole and it also has a simple restaurant.

Getting There & Away

There's PKS service from Legnica, with buses every two to three hours. There are also private minibuses, leaving from next to Legnica's bus terminal.

ZIELONA GÓRA
☎ 68 • pop 118,000

If you are coming to Poland overland from Germany, then Zielona Góra, on the north-western edge of Silesia, may be the first place you stop on Polish soil. The town has no particularly notable historical monuments, but it's still an inviting place with a pleasant town centre and a decent range of accommodation.

The town was founded by the Silesian Piasts. It was part of the Głogów Duchy, one of the numerous regional principalities, before it passed to the Habsburgs in the 16th century and to Prussia two centuries later. Unlike most other Silesian towns, Zielona Góra came through the 1945 offensive with minimal damage, which is why prewar architecture is well represented, giving the town a refreshingly stylish appearance.

Zielona Góra is Poland's only wine producer. The tradition goes back to the 14th century, but the climate is less than ideal and business was never very profitable. It declined dramatically in the 19th century and never recovered. Today's output is merely symbolic, yet the city still holds the Feast of the Grape Harvest (Święto Winobrania) at the end of September, as it has for almost 150 years.

Information
Lubtour (☎ 320 27 00), ul Pod Filarami 1, on the southern side of the Rynek, is a travel agency but the staff provide tourist information. There may be a genuine tourist office by the time you read this.

Bank Pekao outlets at ul Chopina 21 and ul Pieniężnego 24 both have ATMs, as does Bank Zachodni at Al Konstytucji 3 Maja. There are more ATMs in the centre, as well as a good array of kantors.

Internet Pub Vadim (☎ 324 63 69), ul Kupiecka 28, is fast, very central and popular.

Things to See
The renovated **Rynek** (formally called Stary Rynek), lined with brightly painted houses, is a pleasant and harmonious place. The 17th-century **town hall**, complete with its slim 54m tower, has managed to escape being over-modernised in spite of changes over the years, and fits nicely on the square.

The **Church of the Virgin Mary of Częstochowa** (Kościół Matki Boskiej Częstochowskiej), just north of the Rynek, is the former Protestant church, as you can deduce from its half-timbered structure and the two-tiered galleries that line the interior. **St Hedwig's Church**, a block east of the Rynek, was built in the 13th century but completely destroyed by fire three times and rebuilt each time in the style of the day.

The **Regional Museum** (Muzeum Ziemi Lubuskiej; ☎ 320 26 78, Al Niepodległości 15; adult/student US$1.50/1, free Sat; open 11am-5pm Wed-Fri, 10am-3pm Sat, 10am-4pm Sun) features the history of wine in the region and an exhibition of works by Marian Kruczek (1927–83), the largest collection of his work in Poland. He used everyday objects – from buttons to spark plugs – to create striking assemblages. The museum also has temporary displays of items from its collections of Art Nouveau and modern art.

Next to the museum is the **BWA Art Gallery** (☎ 325 37 26, Al Niepodległości 19; admission US$1; open 10am-3pm Tues, 11am-5pm Wed-Fri & Sun, noon-6pm Sat), which hosts changing exhibitions of modern art.

There's a **skansen** (☎ 321 15 91; adult/student US$1.50/1; open 10am-5pm Wed-Sun May-Sept, 10am-3pm Oct-Apr) in Ochla, 7km south of the city, serviced by the regular bus No 27 (get off before arriving at the village; ask the driver to let you off near the entrance). Of about 20 buildings reassembled on the grounds, some are furnished and decorated and can be visited.

Places to Stay
Zielona Góra has two all-year youth hostels:

Youth hostel (☎/fax 320 22 37, ul Długa 13) Beds US$3-6. This new hostel, 700m west of the Rynek, offers 70 beds, most of which are in good six-bed dorms.

Youth hostel (☎/fax 327 08 40, ul Wyspiańskiego 58) Beds US$3-6. This older hostel is larger (130 beds) and also good but less convenient – it's 1km east of the train station and twice that distance from the Old

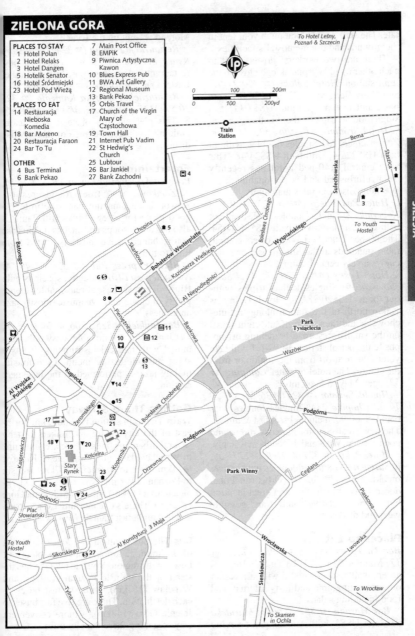

ZIELONA GÓRA

PLACES TO STAY
1 Hotel Polan
2 Hotel Relaks
3 Hotel Dangen
5 Hotelik Senator
16 Hotel Śródmiejski
23 Hotel Pod Wieżą

PLACES TO EAT
14 Restauracja Nieboska Komedia
18 Bar Moreno
20 Restauracja Faraon
24 Bar To Tu

OTHER
4 Bus Terminal
6 Bank Pekao

7 Main Post Office
8 EMPiK
9 Piwnica Artystyczna Kawon
10 Blues Express Pub
11 BWA Art Gallery
12 Regional Museum
13 Bank Pekao
15 Orbis Travel
17 Church of the Virgin Mary of Częstochowa
19 Town Hall
21 Internet Pub Vadim
22 St Hedwig's Church
25 Lubtour
26 Bar Jankiel
27 Bank Zachodni

Town. Reception closes at 9pm, so don't be late. The staff may let you pitch your tent in the grounds and use the hostel's facilities.

There are two workers' hostels next to each other on ul Wyspiańskiego close to the train station: *Hotel Relaks* (☎ 320 21 97) and *Hotel Dangen* (☎ 327 19 17). Both are basic but cheap – around US$7/11/15 a single/double/triple without bath.

Hotel Śródmiejski (☎/fax 325 44 71, ul Żeromskiego 23) Singles/doubles without bath US$22/34, with bath US$34/48. This very central, 140-bed hotel has recently been refurbished and is reasonable value. Weekend discount rates may apply.

Hotel Pod Wieżą (☎/fax 327 10 91, ul Kopernika 2) Singles/doubles/triples without bath US$24/34/46, with bath US$36/44/54. The 60-bed quiet Pod Wieżą offers comparable standards to the Śródmiejski and also enjoys a very central setting.

Hotel Leśny (☎/fax 320 27 94, ul Sulechowska 39) Singles/doubles/triples without bath US$20/28/32. Hotel Leśny is 1.5km north of the station along ul Sulechowska and then 500m to the right (east) on the small forest road branching off opposite the petrol station. Bus No 1 will take you to the turn-off from the station or from the centre. The hotel operates *Camping Nr 52*, open May to September.

Hotelik Senator (☎ 324 04 36, fax 324 79 10, ul Chopina 23A) Singles/doubles with bath US$60/90, includes breakfast & dinner. The new small Senator has cosy rooms and good service. Weekend discounts may apply.

Hotel Polan (☎ 327 00 91, fax 327 18 59, ul Staszica 9A) Singles/doubles with bath & breakfast US$70/90. The Orbis-run Polan doesn't have much style or a great location but provides relative comfort and possible weekend discounts.

Places to Eat
Bar To Tu (☎ 454 88 44, Plac Pocztowy 17) Mains US$3-4.50. To Tu (It's Here) is an enjoyable sort of bistro with a pleasant outdoor eating area and tasty international food including salads.

Bar Moreno (☎ 327 22 60, ul Mariacka 7) Mains US$3-4.50. Another place serving hearty, mainly Polish, budget meals. Moreno is right on the Rynek.

Restauracja Faraon (☎ 324 60 60, Stary Rynek 11) Mains US$3-5. This is a new restaurant serving large portions of Middle-Eastern and Polish food – good value.

Restauracja Nieboska Komedia (☎ 327 20 59, Al Niepodległości 3/5) Mains US$5-8. This pleasant arty place in the theatre building has a good choice of tasty Polish dishes.

Entertainment
Piwnica Artystyczna Kawon (☎ 324 43 86, ul Zamkowa 5) A true artistic creation. Kawon is an amazing bar – definitely a good place for a few drinks (till 2am). It also has a few soups and snacks just in case you're hungry. Live music is hosted from time to time.

Blues Express Pub (☎ 328 03 40, Al Niepodległości 10) A trendy, spacious pub. Blues Express has a reasonable menu, plenty of drinks and live music (mostly jazz and blues).

Bar Jankiel (☎ 325 35 06, ul Sobieskiego 14) Jankiel is an enjoyable, cosy pub, decorated with musical instruments. It has a short but interesting menu. Live music, mainly jazz, is performed in the basement section.

Getting There & Away
Train The train station is about 1km northeast of the city centre and linked to it by several urban bus lines. There are six trains to Wrocław daily (153km), one to Kraków (411km), five to Szczecin (207km) and six to Poznań (139km). Two trains run to Legnica daily (115km) and two to Jelenia Góra (172km). There's one morning express train and one night fast train to Warsaw (445km).

Bus The bus terminal is 200m south-west of the train station and operates plenty of buses in the region. You can take the bus instead of the train to Poznań (130km) and Wrocław (157km), with six fast buses to each destination. There are five fast buses to Jelenia Góra (148km), a more convenient way of getting there than by train.

The Sudeten Mountains

The Sudeten Mountains (Sudety in Polish) run for over 250km along the Czech-Polish border. The highest part of this old and eroded chain is the Karkonosze, reaching a maximum height of 1602m at Mt Śnieżka. Though the Sudetes don't offer much alpine scenery, they are amazingly varied and heavily cloaked in forest, and boast spectacular geological formations such as the Góry Stołowe (literally, the Table Mountains).

To the north, the Sudetes gradually decline into a belt of gently rolling foothills known as the Przedgórze Sudeckie. This area is more densely populated, and many of the towns and villages in the region still boast some of their centuries-old buildings. This section of the book covers both the mountains proper and the foothills; the information is organised from east to west.

The Sudetes and their foothills are well known for minerals and gem stones. This is Poland's richest region in precious and semiprecious stones, and reputedly has just about every jewel except for diamonds. You can find agate, amethyst, quartz, tourmaline, opal, chrysoprase, serpentine, morion and nephrite here, to name a few. While the variety is impressive, the quantity is modest. In most cases the size of the deposits is too small to be worth processing. But gem collectors will be in their element here among numerous old quarries (mostly no longer in use).

NYSA

☎ 77 • pop 48,000

Nysa ('Ni-sah') was for centuries one of the most important religious and educational centres in Silesia. In the 17th century it became a seat of the Catholic bishops, in flight from newly Protestant Wrocław. The bishops soon made Nysa a powerful bastion of the Counter-Reformation, so strong that it came to be known as the Silesian Rome. A number of churches were built in that time, some of which still survive.

Nysa experienced the pain of WWII with particular severity – 80% of its buildings were destroyed during the fierce battles of 1945, and it had to be rebuilt almost from the ground up. The reconstruction leaves a lot to be desired in aesthetic terms, yet amid the usual communist-style urban fabric there are a few surviving historic buildings.

Information

The PTTK office (☎ 433 41 71), ul Bracka 4, off the Rynek, is just about the only source of information. It's open 9am to 4pm weekdays. There are several kantors and ATMs in the centre. Internet facilities include Mikro System (☎ 448 10 10), ul Wałowa 7, and JTR (☎ 448 10 00), ul Bracka 1.

Things to See

The vast **Rynek** shows the extent of the war damage. Only the southern side of the square is anything like it used to be, with its restored houses originally dating from the 16th century. The freestanding building facing them, the 1604 **Town Weigh-House** (Dom Wagi Miejskiej), retains fragments of 19th-century wall painting on a side wall. Just round the corner, on ul Bracka, there are more historic houses and a 1701 baroque fountain.

The northern side of the Rynek is occupied by the powerful brick **cathedral** with a fine stone double doorway. It was built in the 1420s and remodelled after the fire of 1542, but it hasn't changed much since then. The cathedral's 4000-sq-metre roof is one of the steepest church roofs in Europe.

The vast interior is not crammed with the usual baroque furnishings and looks distinctly sober and noble, its loftiness being the most arresting feature. On closer inspection, however, you'll see that its side chapels (18 in all) boast a wealth of tombstones, funeral monuments and epitaphs, which together make up the largest collection of funerary sculpture in any Silesian church.

The construction of the cathedral's freestanding **bell tower** began 50 years after the church and it was supposed to be over 100m high. Despite 40 years work it only ever reached half that height, and as a result looks quite odd.

SILESIA

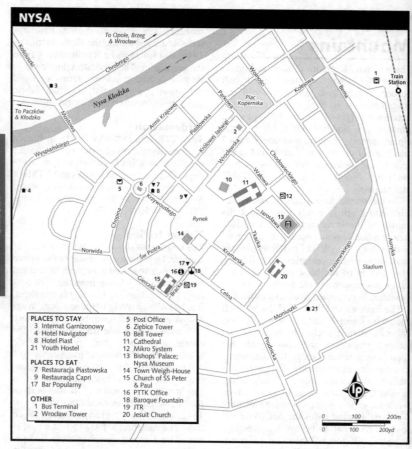

NYSA

PLACES TO STAY
3 Internat Garnizonowy
4 Hotel Navigator
8 Hotel Piast
21 Youth Hostel

PLACES TO EAT
7 Restauracja Piastowska
9 Restauracja Capri
17 Bar Popularny

OTHER
1 Bus Terminal
2 Wrocław Tower

5 Post Office
6 Ziębice Tower
10 Bell Tower
11 Cathedral
12 Mikro System
13 Bishops' Palace;
   Nysa Museum
14 Town Weigh-House
15 Church of SS Peter
   & Paul
16 PTTK Office
18 Baroque Fountain
19 JTR
20 Jesuit Church

To the east of the cathedral is the 17th-century **Bishops' Palace** (Pałac Biskupi), whose spacious interior is occupied by the **Nysa Museum** (☎ 433 20 83, ul Jarosława 11; adult/student US$1/0.50; open 9am-3pm Tues-Fri, 10am-3pm Sat & Sun). The collection related to the town's history includes exhibits ranging from archaeological finds to photos documenting war damage, plus a model of the town in its heyday. The museum also features European paintings from the 15th to the 19th centuries, mostly from the Flemish and Dutch schools.

To the south is the 17th-century **Jesuit Church** (Kościół Jezuitów) which has some interior stucco decoration and wall paintings.

More interesting is the twin-towered **Church of SS Peter and Paul**, built in the 1720s for the Hospitallers of the Holy Sepulchre. It has one of Silesia's best baroque interiors, complete with an opulent high altar, organ and trompe l'œil wall paintings. The church is locked except for services (8am or 6pm weekdays and 10am Sunday).

The only significant vestiges of the medieval defences are two 14th-century brick towers: the **Ziębice Tower** (Wieża Ziębicka) on ul Krzywoustego (you can go right up to the top from May to August), and the **Wrocław Tower** (Wieża Wrocławska) on ul Wrocławska.

Places to Stay

Youth hostel (☎ 433 37 31, ul Moniuszki 9) Beds US$4-6. Open year-round. Conveniently set just a few short blocks from the Rynek, the 54-bed youth hostel has small dorms of two to four beds, providing more privacy than most other hostels.

Internat Garnizonowy (☎ 433 10 35, fax 433 97 79, ul Kościuszki 4) Singles/doubles without bath US$8/14, with bath US$16/22. The Internat, just north across the river, is simple but acceptable and cheap.

Hotel Piast (☎ 433 40 84, fax 433 40 86, ul Krzywoustego 14) Singles/doubles/triples with bath & breakfast US$35/45/65. Piast is a decent central place providing reasonable standards and has its own restaurant.

Hotel Navigator (☎/fax 433 41 70, ul Wyspiańskiego 11) Singles US$25-45, doubles US$35-60, all with breakfast. Set in a spacious old mansion owned and run by a friendly German-speaking couple, the Navigator is a charming place full of antiques and has a family atmosphere. There are a dozen rooms, some of which have baths.

Places to Eat

Bar Popularny (☎ 433 30 15, Rynek 23/24) Mains 1.50-2.50. This unreformed old milk bar looks drab and basic but the food is acceptable and dirt cheap.

Restauracja Capri (☎ 431 52 40, Rynek 35) Mains US$3-5. The Capri, also at the Rynek, provides the usual assortment of popular Polish dishes.

Restauracja Piastowska Mains US$3-6. This hotel restaurant (in Hotel Piast – see Places to Stay earlier) offers reasonable Polish food at decent prices.

Getting There & Away

The bus and train stations face each other and are conveniently close to the Rynek, a 10-minute walk. Getting around the region is easier by bus – there's a fairly regular service to Paczków (26km), Kłodzko (55km),

Opole (53km) and Wrocław (83km). Trains are less frequent but may be useful when travelling to Brzeg (four trains daily) and Opole (six daily).

OTMUCHÓW

☎ 77 • pop 5500

If you are travelling the Nysa-Kłodzko route, you may want to stop in Otmuchów ('Ot-**moo**-hoof'). The town was the property of the Wrocław bishops for over 500 years and it came to be an important ecclesiastical centre. Some vestiges of its history can still be seen. Set between two lakes – Lake Otmuchowskie to the west and Lake Nyskie to the east – Otmuchów has become a local holiday spot.

Things to See

The sloping Rynek retains little of its former character apart from the 16th-century **town hall**, which has a Renaissance tower and a lovely double **sundial** built in 1575 around the corner of two walls. The baroque **parish church**, overlooking the Rynek, was built at the end of the 17th century and most of its internal decoration, including frescoes by Dankwart and paintings by Willmann, dates from that period.

Just south of the church, atop the hill, is a massive **castle**, erected in the 13th century but much extended and remodelled later. It's now a hotel, but its tower, which provides panoramic views, is open to nonguests in summer.

Places to Stay & Eat

Hotel Cukrowni Otmuchów (☎ 431 50 01 ext 330, ul Fabryczna 10) Beds in doubles or triples without bath US$5. This basic hotel, 1km east of Otmuchów's centre on the Nysa road, is the cheapest place to stay.

Hotel Zamek (☎ 431 46 91, ☎/fax 431 51 48, ul Zamkowa 4) Singles/doubles/triples with bath US$35/40/50. The Hotel Zamek, in the castle, has recently been revamped and is OK even though most rooms are pretty small.

There's the good *Restauracja Herbowa* in the castle, plus some more modest options to eat in the Rynek.

Getting There & Away

Otmuchów lies on the Nysa-Paczków road and buses ply this route regularly, stopping at the bus terminal just south of the castle.

PACZKÓW

☎ 77 • pop 8600

A small, sleepy town midway between Nysa and Kłodzko, the 750-year Paczków ('**Pach-koof**') has one of the most complete medieval fortifications in the country. Within the walls, the tiny Old Town has managed to retain some of its old appearance.

Information

The Eden travel agency (☎ 431 61 77), Rynek 14, may answer some queries. Bank Zachodni, Rynek 11, has a useful ATM.

Things to See

The oval ring of Paczków's **defensive walls** was built around 1350 and surrounded by a moat. This system protected the town for a time, but when firearms arrived in the 15th century, an additional, external ring of defences was erected outside the moat (it was pulled down in the 19th century). The original walls were fortunately retained and, as the town escaped major destruction during WWII, they still encircle the historic quarter. They were initially about 9m high for the whole of their 1200m length and had a wooden gallery for guards just below the top.

Four gateways were built, complete with towers and drawbridges (three towers are still in place), and there were 24 semicircular towers built into the walls themselves (19 have survived though most are incomplete). The best way to see the system is to walk along the walls, inside or outside. The oldest of the three main towers, the 14th-century **Wrocław Tower**, can be climbed (*admission US$0.75; open 10am-5pm May-Sept*).

The **Rynek** occupies a good part of the Old Town. The **town hall** was built in the mid-16th century but only its tower is original; the main building was largely modernised in the 1820s. You can climb to the top of the tower (*admission US$0.75; open 10am-5pm May-Sept*) for a good view (better than the one from the Wrocław Tower).

The **parish church**, just south of the Rynek, is a sturdy, squat structure built in the second half of the 14th century with an obvious defensive purpose in mind. Even the usually graceful Renaissance parapets are heavy and rather unattractive. Perhaps the best bit is the Gothic doorway.

Inside, the church now has predominantly neo-Gothic furnishings, and only a few fittings from earlier times remain. The most unusual is the well in the right-hand aisle, which provided water in time of siege.

A short walk north of the Rynek is the interesting **Museum of Gas Industry** (*Muzeum Gazownictwa; ☎ 431 68 34, ul Pocztowa 6; admission free; open 8am-2pm Mon-Fri*), installed in an old gas works from 1902 (closed in 1977). The museum gives an insight into the gas production process, featuring the machinery and various related products such as heaters, irons, lamps and stoves, plus Europe's largest collection of gas meters (over 500 items).

Places to Stay & Eat

Camping Nr 258 (☎ 431 65 09, ul Jagiellońska 8) Beds in cabins US$4. Open June-Sept. This camp site has a collection of rustic cabins and a tent area. It's in the local sports centre which has a swimming pool.

Youth hostel (☎ 431 64 41, ul Kołłątaja 9) Beds US$5-7. Open year-round. The hostel is on the 3rd floor of the school; the entrance is at the back of the building. It has three quads but the rest of its 50 beds are in large dorms.

Hotel Korona (☎/fax 431 62 77, ul Wojska Polskiego 31) Doubles/triples/quads with bath US$20/25/30. Korona is a small 10-room hotel with decent rooms and a homely atmosphere.

Hotel Energopol 7 (☎ 431 62 98, fax 431 68 77, ul Bolesława Chrobrego 1) Doubles/triples with bath US$20/25. Energopol provides reasonable standards, though it's a bit farther from the centre than the Korona. It has its own restaurant, which is good and cheap.

There are also a few simple places to eat in the Rynek.

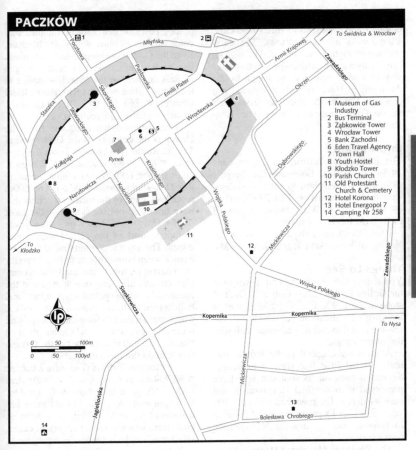

PACZKÓW

To Świdnica & Wrocław

1 Museum of Gas Industry
2 Bus Terminal
3 Ząbkowice Tower
4 Wrocław Tower
5 Bank Zachodni
6 Eden Travel Agency
7 Town Hall
8 Youth Hostel
9 Kłodzko Tower
10 Parish Church
11 Old Protestant Church & Cemetery
12 Hotel Korona
13 Hotel Energopol 7
14 Camping Nr 258

SILESIA

Getting There & Away

The bus terminal, on the edge of the Old Town, has services to Nysa (26km) every hour or so. In the opposite direction, to Kłodzko (29km), buses run every two to three hours. There are also buses (one or two departures a day) to Wrocław (88km), Opole (85km) and Kraków (273km).

KŁODZKO
☎ 74 • pop 32,000

Kłodzko ('**Kwots**-ko') sits on a hillside, and its steep winding streets, sloping main square, and houses overlooking each other give it a unique and special charm. Strolling about the place is an interesting up-and-down affair, through a rich architectural mix accumulated throughout the town's long history.

The first document mentioning Kłodzko's existence dates from 981, putting it among the oldest Silesian towns. From its beginning, it was a bone of contention between Bohemia and Poland, and changed hands several times. The Austrians took over in the 17th century, the Prussians a century later, and only after WWII did the town again become part of Poland.

Kłodzko was strategically placed on important trade routes, so its rulers paid close attention to its fortifications. The early wooden stronghold was replaced in the 14th century by a stone castle, which in turn gave way to a monstrous fortress begun by the Austrians in 1662 and only completed two centuries later by the Prussians. Today, it's the dominant, somewhat apocalyptic, landmark of the town.

Information

The Regionalna Informacja Turystyczna (☎ 865 89 70), Plac Bolesława Chrobrego 1 (Rynek), is open 9am to 6pm weekdays, 9am to 4pm Saturday. The PTTK office (☎ 867 37 40), ul Wita Stwosza 1, just off the Rynek, has lots of maps.

Bank Pekao, on the Rynek, and Bank Zachodni, ul Kościuszki 7, both have ATMs.

Things to See

You'll probably enter the Old Town over the **Gothic Bridge** (Most Gotycki). Built of stone in the 1390s, it was originally part of the town's fortifications but later lost its defensive function and was adorned with statues of the saints.

A short walk uphill is the **Rynek**, formally called Plac Bolesława Chrobrego. Several houses on its southern side have preserved their original Renaissance and baroque decor. The **town hall** was built 100 years ago after its predecessor had gone up in flames; nothing but the Renaissance tower survived.

The **Regional Museum** (*Muzeum Ziemi Kłodzkiej;* ☎ 867 35 70, *ul Łukasiewicza 4; admission US$0.75; open 10am-3.30pm Tues-Fri, 11am-4pm Sat & Sun*) has a display relating to the history of the town and the region, and a collection of contemporary glass by local artists (the region is noted for its glass production), plus temporary exhibitions.

The nearby **parish church** is the most imposing religious building in town. It took almost 150 years before the massive Gothic structure was eventually completed in 1490, and the overall shape hasn't changed much since. Inside, however, changes continued

for at least another 250 years. The altars, pulpit, pews, organ and 11 monumental confessionals all blaze with florid baroque. Even the Gothic vaulting, usually left plain, has been sumptuously decorated. Organ recitals are held in the church – inquire at the tourist office or in the Kłodzko Cultural Centre (☎ 867 33 64), Plac Jagiełły 1 (which organises the recitals).

A few steps down the stairs from the church is the entrance to the **Underground Tourist Route** (*Podziemna Trasa Turystyczna;* ☎ 867 30 48, *ul Zawiszy Czarnego 3; adult/student US$2/1; open 9am-5pm daily Apr-Oct, 10am-3pm Nov-Mar*). The 600m route uses some of the medieval cellars that were hollowed out for storage under most of the Old Town. Later on, when trade slumped, most of the cellars were abandoned. The town was reminded of their existence when houses began falling down for no apparent reason. In the late 1950s a complex conservation program started and the combined work of speleologists, miners and builders led to the restoration of the cellars, which were linked to form the underground route. You can walk the whole length in 10 minutes; the exit is at the foot of the fortress (you can do the route in reverse).

The **Kłodzko Fortress** (*Twierdza Kłodzka;* ☎ 867 34 68, *ul Grodzisko 1; adult/student US$3/1.50; open 9am-6pm daily Apr-Oct, 9am-5pm daily Nov-Mar*) offers more underground legwork, though of a different kind. Here you will see a network of defensive tunnels, which are less comfortable to walk through.

Guided 40-minute tours begin on the hour. You walk 1km or so, and some of the passageways are so low that you have to bend double. The average temperature is about 8°C and the humidity almost 100%. The corridors are now lit but the soldiers had to work here in complete darkness; the only source of light at that time was open flame, which was a little bit risky with all the gunpowder lying around.

After completing your underground trip, you can go to the top of the fortress for a bird's-eye view of town. There are also three exhibitions in the grounds: old fire-brigade

SILESIA

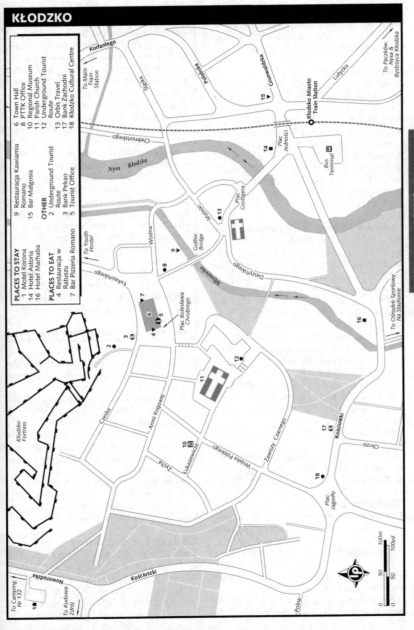

KŁODZKO

PLACES TO STAY
1 Motel Korona
14 Hotel Astoria
16 Hotel Marhaba

PLACES TO EAT
4 Restauracja w Ratuszu
7 Bar Pizzeria Romano

9 Restauracja Kawiarnia Romano
15 Bar Małgosia

OTHER
2 Underground Tourist Route
3 Bank Pekao
5 Tourist Office

6 Town Hall
8 PTTK Office
10 Regional Museum
11 Parish Church
12 Underground Tourist Route
13 Orbis Travel
17 Bank Zachodni
18 Kłodzko Cultural Centre

vehicles, contemporary glass from local factories, and bits and pieces of old stone sculptures (mostly tombstones) collected from historic buildings around the region.

Places to Stay

Camping Nr 132 (☎ *867 30 31, ul Nowy Świat 57*) All-year double/triple/quad rooms US$15/18/24, seasonal cabins US$20. This place, 1km north of the centre, offers 45 all-year rooms and another 30 beds in summer cabins. It also has tent space and a cafeteria.

Youth hostel (☎/fax *867 25 24, ul Nadrzeczna 5*) Beds US$4-6. Open year-round. The youth hostel, 1km north of the Rynek, offers 53 beds in doubles, triples, quads and larger dorms. The reception closes at 9pm.

Ośrodek Sportowy Na Stadionie (☎/fax *867 24 25, ul Kusocińskiego 1*) All-year double/triple rooms US$15/20, triple seasonal cabins US$18. The sports centre by the stadium, 1km south of the Old Town, offers simple but cheap accommodation and meals.

Hotel Astoria (☎/fax *867 30 35, Plac Jedności 1*) Singles/doubles/triples with bath US$20/26/32. Conveniently located opposite the bus and train stations, the Astoria is one of the cheapest options of those with rooms with private bath.

Hotel Marhaba (☎ *865 99 33, ul Daszyńskiego 16*) Singles/doubles with bath US$26/30. Another reasonable central option, the Marhaba is a bit more pleasant than the Astoria.

Motel Korona (☎ *867 37 37, fax 867 07 73, ul Noworudzka 1*) Doubles with bath US$32. Yet another affordable central option, the Korona is a five-minute walk from the Rynek and 10 minutes from the station.

Places to Eat

All the places to stay mentioned above (except for the youth hostel) have their own dining facilities. These apart, you may try:

Bar Małgosia (☎ *867 36 40, ul Połabska 2*) Mains US$2-3. Małgosia is a simple self-service bar that serves hearty Polish meals till 7pm – good value.

Bar Pizzeria Romano (☎ *867 09 35, Plac Bolesława Chrobrego 1*) Mains US$3-5.

Kłodzko Fortress

Kłodzko Fortress was patterned on Western systems of war architecture, principally on the Dutch school of fortification. It was begun in the mid-17th century and was extended, modernised and modified for the following 200 years. Covering 17 hectares, it became Poland's largest fortress of its kind, and the best preserved. The walls in the lower parts measured up to 11m thick, and at the top they were never thinner than 4m.

Altogether 40km of tunnels were drilled around the fortress, essentially for two purposes. Those under the fortifications were principally for communication, shelter and storage; the others ran up to 500m away from the fortress and were designed to destroy the enemy's artillery. They were divided into sectors, stuffed with gunpowder and when the enemy happened to move their guns directly above a particular sector, it was blown up. This bizarre minefield was initiated in 1743 by a Dutch engineer, and by 1807 an immense labyrinth of tunnels had been built. Today, part of the underground network is open to tourists.

Situated in the town hall on the Rynek, the Romano has, apart from its pizzas, a choice of Polish dishes.

Restauracja Kawiarnia Romano (☎ *867 73 24, ul Wodna 6*) Mains US$3-6. A younger and more elegant sister of Bar Pizzeria, the new Romano is only marginally more expensive but looks much better and has a large balcony overlooking the Gothic Bridge.

Restauracja w Ratuszu (☎ *865 81 45, Plac Bolesława Chrobrego 3*) Mains US$5-7. Located in the town hall, this restaurant has reasonable Polish food.

Getting There & Away

Train Kłodzko has two train stations. The centrally located Kłodzko Miasto station handles regional services, including trains to Bystrzyca Kłodzka (16km) and Wrocław (96km), and most (but not all) long-distance trains. You have more long-distance trains from the main Kłodzko Główne station, 2km north. Take either bus No 5 or the train which shuttles between the two stations every hour or two. Orbis Travel (☎ 867 27 75), Plac Grottgera 1, sells train tickets.

Bus The bus terminal, next to the Kłodzko Miasto train station, is the transport hub of the region. Buses to Duszniki-Zdrój (23km), Kudowa-Zdrój (39km) and Bystrzyca Kłodzka (16km) run roughly every hour. There's also a regular service to Wrocław (87km). There are no buses to Kletno; take the bus to Bolesławów (only one in the morning), get off in Stara Morawa and walk 5km to the Bear's Cave.

The Czech Republic There are two road border crossings in the region, both open 24 hours for both pedestrians and vehicles. One is at Kudowa-Zdrój (Poland)/Náchod (Czech Republic), 37km due west of Kłodzko on the way to Prague. The other one is at Boboszów/Králíky, 40km due south of Kłodzko on the Brno road.

One bus goes from Kłodzko to Náchod across the border daily (US$3). It departs 8am on weekdays and 7am on Saturday. Going through the spa towns of Polanica-Zdrój, Duszniki-Zdrój and Kudowa-Zdrój, stopping in each of them.

There are no buses direct to the Czech Republic via Boboszów. Take the bus to Boboszów (leaving at 6am weekdays only) and walk across the border 2km to Králíky, from where you have onward transport. There are more buses to Boboszów from Bystrzyca Kłodzka.

BYSTRZYCA KŁODZKA
☎ 74 • pop 14,000
Bystrzyca Kłodzka ('Bist-**shi**-tsah **Kwots**-kah') is the second-largest town in the region after Kłodzko. Perched on a hill above the Nysa Kłodzka River, it is also a picturesque place. Since the 13th century, when it was founded, the town has been destroyed and rebuilt several times, but it survived WWII virtually unscathed. It doesn't seem to have seen much fresh paint since, but it has some charm and a few attractions.

Information
The tourist office (☎ 811 37 31) is in the Knights' Tower at ul Rycerska 20.

Things to See
The houses lining the **Rynek** (formally called Plac Wolności) are a blend of styles of different epochs. The octagonal Renaissance tower of the **town hall**, in the middle of the square, gives the place an unusual, slightly Spanish feel. The tower, built in 1567, is the only really old part of the building, which assumed its current appearance in the 19th century. Next to the town hall is the elaborate baroque votive **Monument of the Holy Trinity**.

In the 14th century, the town was surrounded by fortified walls, some of which are still in place. The most substantial structures include the **Water Gate** (Brama Wodna) just south of the Rynek, and the **Kłodzko Tower** (Baszta Kłodzka) on the opposite side of the Old Town; the latter has access to the top from where there's a panoramic view.

The nearby **Knights' Tower** (Baszta Rycerska) was reshaped in the 19th century and turned into the belfry of a Protestant church which had been built alongside. After WWII the church was occupied by a **Philumenistic Museum** (*Muzeum Filumenistyczne;* ☎ 811 06 37, *Mały Rynek; admission US$0.75; open 9am-4.30pm Tues-Sun*) related to the match industry. A display of old cigarette lighters and matchbox labels from various countries forms the core of the museum's collection. On the square in front of the museum stands the old whipping post (*pręgierz*) from 1556; the Latin inscription on its top reads 'God punishes the impious'.

The **parish church** sits at the highest point of the Old Town, one block north-west of the Rynek. It has an unusual double-naved interior with a row of six Gothic columns running right across the middle.

Places to Stay
Hotel Piast (☎/fax 811 03 22, ul Okrzei 26) Singles/doubles without bath US$9/16, doubles with bath US$22, beds in triples &

SILESIA

quads US$7. The 60-bed Piast, on the edge of the Old Town, is basic.

Ośrodek Wypoczynkowy Energetyk (*☎/fax 811 15 54, ul Strażacka 28*) Beds in doubles or triples without bath US$7. This 80-bed hotel, on the Polanica-Zdrój road, about 1km from the centre, is a former workers' dorm.

Places to Eat
Bar Bistro Kasyno (*☎ 811 14 23, ul Słowackiego 8*) Mains US$2-3.50. Just round the corner from the bus terminal, the Kasyno serves good straightforward meals, including excellent *placek po węgiersku* (potato pancake with goulash).

Restauracja Regionalna (*☎ 811 31 50, Plac Wolności 5*) Mains US$3-5. This is probably the safest choice of the few undistinguished restaurants in town.

Getting There & Away
The train station is just east of the Old Town; several trains go from here to Kłodzko daily (16km), Międzylesie (18km) and Wrocław (112km). You can also get to Kłodzko by bus; it goes every hour from the terminal 200m north of the parish church. There are also reasonable bus connections to Międzygórze (13km), Polanica-Zdrój (18km) and Lądek-Zdrój (22km), and a few buses to Boboszów (24km). From early May to mid-October, one morning bus goes to Kletno (38km).

MIĘDZYGÓRZE
☎ 74 • pop 700
Międzygórze ('Myen-dzi-**goo**-zheh') is a small charming mountain village. Beautifully set in a deep valley surrounded by forested mountains, it was an exclusive German mountain resort in the late 19th/early 20th century. It still has some splendid (albeit run-down) historic villas, that look as if they have been brought from the Tyrol. The finest are on ul Sanatoryjna which heads north up the hill from the village centre. They are now used as holiday homes and will accommodate individual tourists.

Międzygórze boasts the lovely 21m-high Wilczki Waterfall. It's on the western edge of the village and there are paths all around, so you can see it from various angles including from a bridge right above.

Hiking
Międzygórze's countryside is attractive for hikers. North-west of the village is Mt Igliczna (845m), with a small baroque church on top. You can get there by any of three different routes – the trails waymarked red, green or yellow – in about an hour.

There are at least five longer trails originating in or passing through the village. The most popular is the hike to the top of Mt Śnieżnik (1425m), the highest peak in the region. It will take about three hours to get there by the red trail, and if you don't want to come back the same day, there's a 58-bed PTTK mountain hostel, *Na Śnieżniku* (*☎ 813 51 30*), half an hour before you reach the top. Take candles – there's no electricity there. If you plan on hiking in the area, get a copy of the *Ziemia Kłodzka* map (scale 1:90,000).

Places to Stay & Eat
Accommodation shouldn't be a problem. Some of the holiday homes are administered by the Centralna Recepcja or a central reception office (*☎ 813 51 09, ☎/fax 813 51 07*), ul Sanatoryjna 2, which does all the paperwork, charges the room fee (about US$7/12 per person in rooms without/with bath) and then gives you keys to the house. The office is open from 7am to 9pm daily, or even longer in summer.

Other accommodation options include pensions, hotels and private rooms.

Pokoje Gościnne Złoty Róg (*☎/fax 813 51 25, ul Wojska Polskiego 3*) Beds in doubles, triples or quads without bath US$4-7. Złoty Róg, opposite the church, is one of the cheapest options and has a cheap restaurant.

Dom Wczasowy Nad Wodospadem (*☎ 813 51 20, ☎/fax 813 51 92, ul Wojska Polskiego 12*) Doubles/triples with bath US$18/22. At the western end of the village, next to the waterfall, Nad Wodospadem offers reasonable rooms with bath and also has its own restaurant.

Pensjonat Millennium (*☎/fax 813 52 87, ul Wojska Polskiego 9*) Singles/doubles with bath & breakfast US$20/28. Millennium is a new 10-room guesthouse with its own restaurant, which is arguably the best place to stay and eat in Międzygórze.

Getting There & Away

The best connection is to Bystrzyca Kłodzka (13km), with buses running every couple of hours or so. Some of them continue to Kłodzko (29km).

For the Bear's Cave at Kletno (see below), take the ski trail marked black that goes east from the village along a rough road, and switch to the yellow one leading north. You should get to the cave in two hours.

KLETNO

☎ 74 • pop 300

Kletno is a tiny 'one-street' hamlet stretching along the road for over 3km. Its fame, however, is greater than its size would suggest, for Poland's most beautiful cave is near here. It was discovered accidentally in 1966 during marble quarrying. Bones of the cave bear, which lived here during the last ice age, were found and gave the place its name – the **Bear's Cave** (*Jaskinia Niedźwiedzia;* ☎ *814 12 50; adult/student US$4/3; open 10am-5.40pm Feb-Apr, 9am-4.40pm May-Aug, 10am-5.40pm Sept-Nov, closed Mon & Thur*).

A small 400m section of the 3km labyrinthine corridors and chambers, with stalactites and stalagmites, was opened in 1977. You enter the cave through a pavilion which houses a snack bar and a small exhibition focusing on the cave's history. The humidity inside the cave is nearly 100% and the temperature is 6°C all year – so come prepared.

Visits are by 40-minute tours (in Polish only), in groups of up to 15 people. The cave is popular and may be swamped with school excursions and individual visitors, especially in the late spring and summer. It's recommended to call the cave management in advance to check the situation and book if necessary.

There's an all-year 35-bed *youth hostel* (☎ *814 13 58*) at the lower end of Kletno, 4km down the road from the cave.

Getting There & Away

There is one seasonal bus (roughly May to mid-October) from Bystrzyca Kłodzka to Kletno (38km) via Lądek-Zdrój and Stronie Śląskie. The bus terminates at the upper end of Kletno, at the tourist car park (stalls sell snacks here in summer), about 1.5km below the cave.

There are no direct buses from Kłodzko to Kletno. If you don't mind walking, you can easily get by bus to Stronie Śląskie (regular transport) and walk 9km to the cave by the yellow trail (2½ hours). If this is too much for you, take the bus to Bolesławów (one morning departure only), get off at Stara Morawa and walk the remaining 5km.

You can also get to the cave by walking from Międzygórze (see Getting There & Away in that section for details).

KUDOWA-ZDRÓJ

☎ 74 • pop 11,000

There are three popular spas west of Kłodzko: Polanica-Zdrój, Duszniki-Zdrój and Kudowa-Zdrój. Kudowa is possibly the most popular and it's also the usual jumping-off point for the marvellous Góry Stołowe.

With a mild climate and several mineral springs, Kudowa-Zdrój is the biggest spa in the Kłodzko region. It's also one of the oldest, with well preserved spa architecture and a pleasant spa park.

Information

The tourist office (☎ 866 13 87), ul Zdrojowa 44, in the town's centre, is open 9am to 5pm weekdays, 9am to 2pm Saturday. The headquarters of the Góry Stołowe National Park (☎ 866 14 36) are at ul Słoneczna 31.

Things to See

Kudowa has an attractive **Spa Park** (Park Zdrojowy), which occupies 17 hectares, a substantial part of the town. The **pump room** *(Pijalnia)* is in the south-eastern corner of the park and serves several local waters.

Uphill to the north is an irregular landscaped park. Stroll about, then continue 1km farther north along ul Moniuszki to Czermna to see the bizarre **Chapel of Skulls** *(Kaplica Czaszek; adult/student US$1/0.75; open*

SILESIA

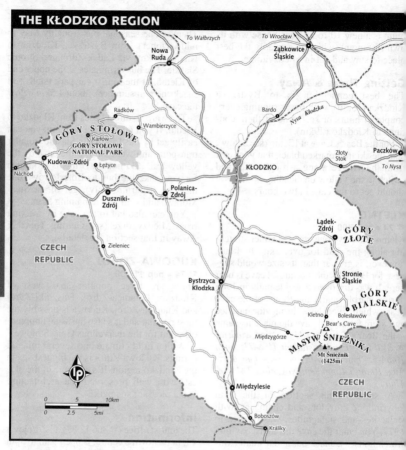

THE KŁODZKO REGION

9.30am-1pm & 2pm-5.30pm Tues-Sun May-Sept, 10am-1pm & 2pm-4pm Tues-Sun Oct-Apr). Inside, the whole length of its walls and ceiling are covered with human skulls and bones – about 3000 of them. The effect is stunning, but if this is not enough for you, the crypt beneath the chapel shelters another 21,000 skulls and bones (For more information see the boxed text 'Art of Skulls').

Places to Stay & Eat

Like most resorts of this kind, Kudowa has an extensive accommodation array, including seven hotels, a dozen holiday homes, another dozen pensions and a number of private rooms, providing more than 300 beds in all. The tourist office is likely to inform you about the options and their rates.

Recepcja FWP (☎ 866 12 61), at ul Zdrojowa 36, is open 7am to 10pm daily. This organisation will book a room in any of its seven budget holiday homes, which provide 580 beds for US$5 to US$12 per person.

Ośrodek Sportowy Na Stadionie (☎/fax 866 17 08, ul Łąkowa 12) All-year double rooms without/with bath US$16/22, beds in seasonal cabins US$6, beds in youth hostel US$4-6. This sports centre, 1km south of

Art of Skulls

The Chapel of Skulls in Czermna was built in 1776 and looks pretty modest and inconspicuous from the outside. Inside, however, it's a different story: it boasts thousands of skulls and bones crammed all over the walls and ceiling. It's the only chapel of its kind in Poland and reputedly one of just three in Europe (the others are in Rome and Kutná Hora in the Czech Republic).

The creator of this unusual 'Sanctuary of Silence' was Václav Tomášek, a Czech parish priest (Czermna belonged to the Prague Archdiocese at that time). He and the local grave-digger spent two decades collecting human skeletons, perhaps as many as 30,000 of them, which they then cleaned and conserved. The 'decoration' of the chapel wasn't completed until 1804. Skulls and bones which didn't fit on the walls and the ceiling were deposited in a 4m-deep crypt.

The skeletons came mostly from numerous mass graves scattered all over the fields and forests, as a result of two Silesian wars (1740–42 and 1744–45) and the Seven Years' War (1756–63). The cholera epidemic which plagued the region also contributed to such an impressive quantity of material.

Since the region was the borderland of the Polish, Czech and German cultures, and Catholic, Hussite and Protestant traditions, many of the collected bones are likely to have belonged to victims of nationalist and religious conflicts. Now their skulls can sit side by side in peace. Death reconciles everyone.

The chapel also shelters the skulls of the masterminds of the enterprise – the priest and the grave-digger. They were added after their death and are deposited in a glass case near the altar.

he town centre, has hotel rooms, cabins, a amp site, swimming pool, gym and a udget restaurant. A 46-bed all-year youth ostel is also here.

Dom Wycieczkowy Dunajec (☎/fax 866 8 66, ul Słoneczna 14) Beds in doubles or riples without bath US$5-7. The 50-bed unajec is one of the cheapest places close o the centre.

Pensjonat Sudety (☎ 866 37 56, fax 866 1 42, ul Zdrojowa 32) Beds in doubles or riples without bath US$5-7. Another acceptable budget option, the 70-bed Sudety s even more central than Dunajec.

Pensjonat Akacja (☎/fax 866 27 12, ul Kombatantów 5) Doubles/triples with bath & breakfast US$30/40. The 32-bed Akacja s central and comfortable.

Willa Sanssouci (☎/fax 866 13 50, ul Buczka 3) Singles/doubles/triples with bath & breakfast US$25/32/36. Located in one of the loveliest historic villas in town, the 48-bed Sanssouci has comfortable, ample rooms and good service.

Getting There & Away

Train The train station (the terminus of the line) is a long way south of the town and isn't much use unless you want to go a good distance, eg, to Warsaw (two trains daily). To Kłodzko and Wrocław it's better to go by bus.

Bus Buses depart from ul 1 Maja in the town centre. There's frequent transport to Kłodzko (39km) and regular services throughout the day to Wrocław (131km). Three buses go to Wałbrzych daily (101km).

For the Góry Stołowe, there are half a dozen buses a day to Karłów, which pass by the turn-off to Błędne Skały. In the high season, there are also private minibuses.

One morning bus (except Sunday) comes through from Kłodzko and goes across the Czech border to Náchod daily (see the Kłodzko section). Alternatively, go by local bus (or walk) to the border (3km), cross it on foot to Náchod, 2km behind the frontier, from where there are onward buses and trains.

GÓRY STOŁOWE
☎ 74

The Góry Stołowe (literally, the Table Mountains; 'Goo-ri Sto-wo-veh') are among the most spectacular ranges of all the Sudetes. Lying roughly 10km north-east of Kudowa-Zdrój, they are almost as flat-topped as their name suggests. However, from the main plateau rise smaller 'tables' which are remnants of the eroded upper layer of the mountains. Fantastic rock formations are scattered on the tops of these 'islands', as well as all over the main plateau. This magical landscape was created when soft sandstone, the dominant material of the formation, was eroded, leaving harder rocks behind. Lush vegetation adds colour to the rocks.

In 1994 the whole area became the Góry Stołowe National Park (Park Narodowy Gór Stołowych) which covers 63 sq km. The highlights of the park are the Szczeliniec Wielki and the Błędne Skały.

Information

The park's headquarters in Kudowa-Zdrój can provide information. Whether you hike in the mountains or explore them by car, the *Góry Stołowe* map is a great help. It has all the walking routes and the important rocks individually marked as well as plans of the Szczeliniec and the Błędne Skały. If you can't get this map, buy a copy of the more general *Ziemia Kłodzka* map, which covers the Góry Stołowe but in less detail.

Szczeliniec Wielki

The Szczeliniec Wielki is the highest outcrop of the whole range (919m). From a distance, it looks like a high plateau adorned with pinnacles, rising abruptly from fields and forests. The most popular way to the top is from Karłów, a small village about 1km south of the plateau from where a short road leads to the foothills. You then ascend 682 stone steps (built in 1790) to a PTTK hostel on the top – it takes about half an hour to get there. The hostel is not for overnight stays; it's only used during the day as a cafe.

From the hostel, a trail skirts the cliff (excellent views) before turning inland. The 'Long Steps' take you down to the 'Devils' Kitchen' from where, after passing 'Hell' and 'Purgatory', you go up to 'Heaven', which is another viewpoint. Whatever the nicknames say, however, it feels as though you are wandering through the ruins of a mysterious ancient castle, the rocks appearing to be artificially shaped into enormous geometrical blocks.

The trail continues to two more viewpoints on the opposite side of the plateau and winds back to the hostel, passing a string of rocks formed in a wild array of shapes.

The whole loop takes about an hour, including scenic stops. You can visit the place at any time; in summer a ticket desk opens and charges a small admission fee.

Błędne Skały

About 4km west as the crow flies, the Błędne Skały (literally, the Erratic Boulders) are another impressive sight. These are hundreds of monstrous boulders in vaguely geometric shapes that make a vast stone labyrinth. A trail runs between the rocks, which are so close together in places that you'll find you have to squeeze through sideways.

An hour is enough to do the loop, stopping to take pictures. As in Szczeliniec, a small entrance fee is charged in summer and there's a cafe by the entrance, but you can visit the place whenever you wish. Some adventurous trekkers come here in the middle of winter and dig their way through snow which in places can be chest-deep.

The Błędne Skały are 3.5km from the Kudowa-Karłów road, linked to it by a narrow, paved side road (no public transport). The turn-off is 7km from Kudowa (6km from Karłów). There's a red hiking trail between Szczeliniec and the Błędne Skały.

Places to Stay & Eat

The usual jumping-off point is Kudowa-Zdrój, but you can stay and eat closer to the mountains. Karłów, the closest village to Szczeliniec, has several places to stay, including ***Schronisko Pod Szczelińcem*** (☎ 871 21 90), ***Ośrodek Wypoczynkowy Pod Jesionami*** (☎ 871 22 28) and ***Domek w Lesie***. All have rooms with shared facilities that cost US$5 to US$6 per person. Numerous stalls open in summer and serve simple meals and snacks.

Getting There & Away

The Table Mountains cover a fairly small area, and a day trip would be enough time to cover the two highlights. There are half a dozen buses a day from Kudowa-Zdrój to

Karłów (13km), though some of these buses run in summer only and not on weekends. They go along the Road of the Hundred Bends, which snakes spectacularly through the forest and has virtually no straight sections. There are also private minibuses from Kudowa to the Table Mountains; they pick up passengers at the bus terminal.

WAMBIERZYCE
☎ 74 • pop 1200
A small village at the north-eastern foot of the Table Mountains, Wambierzyce ('Vahm-byeh-zhi-tseh') is an important pilgrimage site and one of the oldest. Legend has it that in 1218 a blind peasant recovered his sight after praying to a statue of the Virgin Mary, which had been placed in a hollow lime-tree trunk. A wooden chapel was constructed on the site of the miracle and was later replaced with a church. The fame of the place spread, and a large, two-towered basilica was subsequently erected in 1695–1711, but it collapsed shortly after its completion, except for its facade. Immediately afterwards a new sanctuary was built using the surviving Renaissance facade, and that's the church which stands to this day, more or less unchanged.

The largest numbers of pilgrims arrive on 8 July, 15 August and 8 September, and on the nearest Sunday to those dates.

Things to See
A wide flight of 33 steps (Christ was 33 when he was crucified) leads to the 50m-wide facade of the **church**, its palatial appearance emphasised by the absence of towers. The side entrance takes you into the square cloister running around the church, which is lined with chapels and Stations of the Cross, and adorned with paintings and votive offerings.

The church proper, in the centre of the complex, is laid out on two ellipses, with the main one being the nave and the other the chancel, each topped with a painted dome. The baroque decor includes an unusually elaborate pulpit. In the presbytery behind an ornamental grille of 1725, the florid high altar displays the miraculous

miniature figure (only 28cm high) of the Virgin Mary with Child.

The hill opposite the church is dotted with chapels, gates, grottoes, sculptures etc, representing the **Stations of the Cross**. The Calvary, established in the late 17th century, was modelled on the one in Jerusalem and was subsequently developed to include 79 stations.

East of the church you'll find the **Szopka** (*ul Objazdowa; admission US$0.75; open 10am-1pm, 2pm-4pm Tues-Sun*), a set of mechanised Nativity scenes. The main scene, representing Jesus' birth in Bethlehem, includes 800 tiny figurines (all carved of limewood), 300 of which can move. Other scenes portray the Crucifixion, the Last Supper and the Massacre of the Innocents. The Szopka was made by local artist Longinus Wittig (1824–95); it took him 28 years.

About 2.5km west of the church is the private **skansen** (*☎ 871 91 84, ul Wiejska 52; admission free, donation welcomed; open 9am till dusk*). The result of 10 years' work by the owner, this is a museum featuring just about everything you could think about, including antiques, old household implements, minerals, stuffed birds, miners' uniforms etc, plus a mini zoo. The skansen also offers budget accommodation and food.

Places to Stay & Eat
Hotel Wambierzyce (*☎ 871 91 86, fax 871 92 49, Plac NMP 1*) Singles/doubles/triples with bath US$30/45/60. This upmarket hotel, just next to the church, offers satisfactory standards and has a good restaurant.

For cheaper options, locals rent out rooms in their homes. The priests, too, offer budget accommodation – inquire at the Kancelaria Parafialna. Another budget place is the skansen.

There are a few simple places to eat around the main square.

Getting There & Away
There are regular buses to Kłodzko via Polanica-Zdrój, but only a few go direct to Kudowa Zdrój. Wambierzyce is not on a railway line.

SILESIA

WAŁBRZYCH
☎ 74 • pop 148,000

The largest city of Lower Silesia after Wrocław, Wałbrzych ('**Vahw**-bzhih') is an important industrial and mining centre. It's a heavily polluted city with few tourist attractions. If you are passing through, you may want to have a look at the arcaded baroque houses in the Rynek and visit the regional museum at ul 1 Maja 9 with its geology and porcelain collections. However, the major tourist sight is Książ castle (see the following section) on the northern outskirts of the city.

If you need more information, the tourist office (☎ 842 20 00) is at Rynek 9. If staying overnight, the cheapest place is the all-year *youth hostel* (☎ 847 79 42, ul Marconiego 1), while the top-end choice is *Hotel Sudety* (☎ 849 35 00, fax 847 64 50, ul Parkowa 15), and there are several options in between. Being the main city in the region, Wałbrzych has good transport connections by both train and bus.

KSIĄŻ
☎ 74

With its 415 rooms, Książ ('Kshonsh') is the largest **castle** in Silesia. It was built in the late 13th century by the Silesian Piast Prince Bolko I of Świdnica and continuously enlarged and remodelled until well into the 20th century. It's thus an amalgam of styles from Romanesque onwards.

During WWII Hitler planned to use the castle as one of his shelters and a huge bunker was hewn out of the rock directly beneath the courtyard. The castle itself was stripped of its valuable art collection. The Soviets used it as a barracks until 1949, after which it was more or less abandoned for 20 years. Finally, the authorities set about restoring it and turned it into a **museum** (☎ 843 28 40, ul Piastów Śląskich 1; adult/student US$3/2; open 10am-5pm daily May-Sept, 10am-4pm Tues-Sun Apr & Oct, 10am-3pm Tues-Sun Nov-Mar).

Approaching the castle from the car park, you will pass near the **viewpoint**; it's just to the left past a large, decorative, freestanding gate. Seen from the lookout, the castle, majestically perched on a steep hill amid lush woods, looks impressive. Its central portion with three massive arcades is the oldest. The eastern part (to the right) is an 18th-century baroque addition, while the western segment with two corner towers was built in 1908–23, in neo-Renaissance style. At about the same time the top of the main tower was added; it's open to visitors.

The castle's showpiece is the **Maximilian Hall**, built in the first half of the 18th century. It's the largest room in the castle and the only one restored to its original form, including the painted ceiling (1733) which depicts mythological scenes.

The 12 terraced **gardens** on the slopes around the castle were laid out gradually as the medieval fortifications were dismantled, from the 17th century on.

A five-minute walk east of the castle is a **stud farm** (Stadnina Koni; ☎ 840 58 67, ul Jeździecka 3; admission US$0.75; open 10am-5pm Tues-Sun), once the castle stables. It can be visited, and also offers riding lessons and has horses for hire.

Places to Stay & Eat
Hotel Książ (☎/fax 843 27 98, ul Piastów Śląskich 1) Doubles/triples without bath US$26/36, doubles with bath US$40-70, triples with bath US$45-80. The hotel occupies several outbuildings in the castle complex, providing different standards and facilities. There's also a restaurant.

Getting There & Away
The castle is on the northern administrative boundaries of Wałbrzych, about 8km from the centre. You can get to it from Wałbrzych by the No 8 city bus which runs every 30 to 50 minutes and will take you to the entrance. Alternatively, bus No 31 plies the Wałbrzych-Świdnica route every 20 minutes (every half-hour on Sunday), and will let you off on the main road near the car park, a 10-minute walk to the castle.

ŚWIDNICA
☎ 74 • pop 65,000

One of the wealthiest medieval towns in Silesia, Świdnica ('Shfeed-**nee**-tsah') was founded in the 12th century, and in 1290 became the capital of yet another of the myriad Silesian Piast principalities, the Duchy of Świdnica-Jawor. Unlike its neighbours, it didn't accept the sovereignty of Bohemia and only fell under its rule after the local Piast line died out in 1392. The Duchy of Świdnica-Jawor was one of the most powerful and largest, thanks essentially to its two gifted rulers: Bolko I, who founded it, and his grandson Bolko II, who significantly extended it.

The capital itself was a flourishing commercial centre, well known for its beer, which was served on the tables of Prague, Buda and Kraków. With 6000 inhabitants and 1000 houses by the end of the 14th century, it was one of the largest Polish towns, though in administrative terms it was by then part of Bohemia.

The town's heyday continued right up to the outbreak of the Thirty Years' War (1618–48). By 1648 the population of Świdnica had dropped to 200, the lowest in its history. It has never managed to become a city, remaining one of the many towns of its size in Silesia, way behind its former rival Wrocław. Świdnica escaped major damage

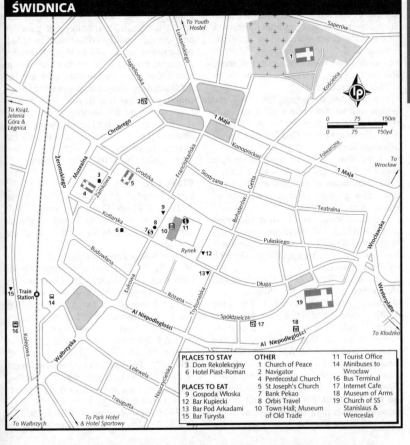

SILESIA

ŚWIDNICA

To Youth Hostel
Saperów
Łukasińskiego
Jagiellońska
Kościelna
To Książ, Jelenia Góra & Legnica
Chrobrego
Żeromskiego
1 Maja
0   75   150m
0   75   150yd
Konopnickiej
Folwarczna
To Wrocław
1 Maja
Muzealna
Grodzka
Franciszkańska
Siostrzana
Getta
Zamkowa
Bohaterów
Teatralna
Kotlarska
Wrocławska
Pułaskiego
Budowlana
Łukowa
Rynek
Westerplatte
Róźana
Trybunalska
Długa
Train Station
Al Niepodległości
Spółdzielcza
To Kłodzko
Wałbrzyska
Al Niepodległości
Kolejowa
Lelewela
Nauczycielska
Traugutta
To Park Hotel & Hotel Sportowy
To Wałbrzych

PLACES TO STAY
3 Dom Rekolekcyjny
6 Hotel Piast-Roman

PLACES TO EAT
9 Gospoda Włoska
12 Bar Kupiecki
13 Bar Pod Arkadami
15 Bar Turysta

OTHER
1 Church of Peace
2 Navigator
4 Pentecostal Church
5 St Joseph's Church
7 Bank Pekao
8 Orbis Travel
10 Town Hall; Museum of Old Trade

11 Tourist Office
14 Minibuses to Wrocław
16 Bus Terminal
17 Internet Cafe
18 Museum of Arms
19 Church of SS Stanislaus & Wenceslas

in WWII and has some important historic buildings. It's an agreeable place for a short stop, and a more pleasant jumping-off point for Książ castle than Wałbrzych.

Information

The tourist office (☎ 852 02 90), ul Wewnętrzna 2 (Rynek), is open 9am to 5pm weekdays, 8am to 4pm Saturday. Bank Pekao is also on the Rynek. Central Internet facilities include Navigator, ul Jagiellońska 1 and Internet Cafe in the Dom Handlowy Świdniczanin, ul Spółdzielcza 14.

Things to See

Świdnica's **Rynek** has everything from baroque to postwar architecture, the cumulative effect of rebuilding after successive fires and the damage caused by Austrian, Prussian and Napoleonic sieges. Most of the facades have been thoroughly revamped over recent years, giving the square an attractive appearance.

The **town hall** dates from the 1710s, and though well kept it looks a bit squat, lacking its tower which collapsed in 1967. Inside is the **Museum of Old Trade** (*Muzeum Dawnego Kupiectwa;* ☎ 852 12 91, Rynek 37; admission US$0.75; open 10am-3pm Tues-Fri, 11am-5pm Sat & Sun) which features re-creations of an old-time inn, pharmacy and grocery, and a collection of historic scales and balances.

The new **Museum of Arms** (*Muzeum Broni;* ☎ 852 52 34, ul Niepodległości 21; admission US$0.75; open 10am-2pm Tues-Sun) has arms and weapons from the 19th and 20th centuries.

The parish **Church of SS Stanislaus and Wenceslas** (Kościół Św Stanisława i Wacława), east of the Rynek, is a massive Gothic stone building whose facade is adorned with four elegant 15th-century doorways and an 18m-high window. The tower, completed in 1565, is 103m high, making it Poland's tallest historic church tower after that of the basilica in Częstochowa (106m). The spacious interior has the familiar Gothic structure and ornate baroque decoration and furnishings. Six huge paintings that hang high up in the nave seem thoroughly at home in this lofty interior.

The **Church of Peace** (*Kościół Pokoju;* ☎ 852 28 14, Plac Pokoju 6; adult/student US$1/0.50; open 9am-1pm, 3pm-5pm Mon-Sat, 3pm-5pm Sun), a short walk to the north, was erected in 1656–57 in just 10 months as a Protestant church following the Peace of Westphalia of 1648 (hence its name). It's a wood-and-clay shingled structure put up reputedly without a single nail, laid out in the form of a cross, and has no less than 28 doors. The 17th-century baroque decoration, with paintings covering the walls and ceiling, has been preserved intact. The large organ proved unreliable so another one was added above the high altar. Along the walls, two storeys of galleries and several small balconies were installed, reminiscent of an old-fashioned theatre. Arranged this way, the interior was able to seat 3500 people in comfort, plus another 4000 standing. However, if you attend Mass (Sunday only, at 10am), you're unlikely to find more than 50 worshippers. Classical music concerts are held here on some weekends. In the old cemetery surrounding the church, there are many decaying gravestones dating back 100 years or more.

Places to Stay

Youth hostel (☎ 852 26 45, ul Kanonierska 3) Beds US$4-6. Open year-round. This hostel, 700m north of the Rynek, offers acceptable accommodation in three- to seven-bed dorms.

Dom Rekolekcyjny (☎/fax 853 52 60, ul Muzealna 1) Singles/doubles/triples/quads with bath US$10/18/24/26. Conveniently positioned just one block off the Rynek, this 45-bed Pentecostal Church facility offers good, neat rooms, making it excellent value. Enter from ul Zamkowa 6.

Hotel Sportowy (☎/fax 852 25 32, ul Śląska 31) Doubles/triples without bath US$16/26. The Sportowy, about 1km south of the Old Town, is nothing very exciting but can be a shelter if other budget places can't accommodate you.

Hotel Piast-Roman (☎ 852 13 93, fax 852 30 76, ul Kotlarska 11) Singles/doubles with bath & breakfast US$36/46. The 60-bed Piast-Roman, just off the Rynek, is a reasonable compromise between the quality, location and price.

Park Hotel (☎/fax 853 70 98, ul Pionierów 20) Singles/doubles/triples with bath & breakfast US$40/55/70. A relatively new hotel within easy walking distance of the Old Town, the Park can be an alternative choice to Piast-Roman.

Places to Eat

Bar Kupiecki (☎ 852 03 48, Rynek 18) Mains US$1.50-2.50. Kupiecki is a good central address for a budget meal.

Bar Turysta (☎ 852 15 78, ul Kolejowa 3) Mains US$1.50-2.50. Another good place for a budget meal, Turysta is close to the bus terminal.

Bar Pod Arkadami (☎ 853 49 02, ul Trybunalska 2) This tiny snack bar is the place for a *barszcz* (beetroot broth) with a *pasztecik* (hot pastry filled with meat, cheese, or cabbage with mushrooms) – an excellent snack for US$1.

Gospoda Włoska (☎ 856 94 94, Rynek 35) Mains US$3-6. The lovely 'Italian Inn' offers affordable Italian food in amazing surroundings.

Getting There & Away

The train station and bus terminal are a convenient five-minute walk from the Rynek.

There are three trains a day to Nysa (87km), two to Legnica (57km), one to Jelenia Góra (87km) and one to Kraków (304km).

Hourly buses run to Wrocław (53km) and several a day depart for Kłodzko (63km). Private minibuses to Wrocław depart from the front of the train station. Urban bus No 31 goes every 20 minutes (every half-hour on Sunday) to Wałbrzych via Świebodzice and passes near Książ castle en route.

KRZESZÓW

☎ 75 • pop 1000

If you plan on visiting just a few of the best baroque churches in Poland, Krzeszów ('Ksheh-shoof') should be included on your list. This obscure village near the Czech border, well off the main roads and tourist routes, has not one but two extraordinary churches.

Krzeszów was founded in 1242 by Princess Anna, the widow of Henryk Pobożny (Henry the Pious), who was killed a year earlier in the Battle of Legnickie Pole. The princess donated the land to the Benedictine order from Bohemia, but the monks showed little interest and in 1289 relinquished the property to Prince Bolko I, the grandson of Henryk. Bolko, the wise ruler of the newly created Duchy of Świdnica-Jawor, granted the land to the Cistercians, who were by then well established in Poland and swiftly expanding. The monks soon built their monastery, and the donor of the land was buried in the newly constructed church in 1301. The church became the mausoleum of the Świdnica-Jawor dukes until the line died out in the late 14th century.

Repeatedly destroyed by various invaders, from the Hussites to the Swedes, the monastery was systematically rebuilt and extended. At the end of the 17th century a fair-sized church was raised and some 40 years later it was followed by another one, twice the size and even more splendid.

Despite the fact that the Cistercian order was secularised in 1810 and the abbey abandoned for over a century, the two churches survive today virtually unchanged.

Things to See

The older one, **St Joseph's Church** (Kościół Św Józefa), was built in 1690–96. From the outside, the building looks a bit plain, largely because its towers collapsed soon after they were built and were never reconstructed. The interior, in contrast, is impressive, with frescoes covering the whole of the vault, the chancel and 10 side chapels. These wall paintings are the work of Michael Willmann and are considered to be among his greatest achievements. In some 50 scenes, the life of St Joseph is portrayed, with the Holy Trinity on the vault of the chancel. Painted at the end of the 17th century, some of the frescoes are unusually free in their execution, strangely evocative of the Impressionist style of two centuries

SILESIA

later. Willmann left his own image on the walls – he is standing at the door of an inn painted on the wall in the right-hand chapel just before the chancel. Also note the elaborate rococo pulpit and a tiny organ.

The **Church of the Assumption** (Kościół Wniebowzięcia NMP) is much more developed architecturally, and at 118m in length is much bigger. Its twin-towered facade (70m high) is elaborately decorated from top to bottom and rich in detail. You can go up one of the towers for a view.

The lofty interior is exceptionally coherent stylistically, as the church was built (1728–35) from scratch and not adapted from an earlier structure as was usually the case. Furthermore, all the decoration and furnishings date from the short period of the church's construction and hardly anything was added later. The high altar, with the huge (7m x 3.5m) background painting by Peter Brandl depicting the Assumption of Virgin Mary, displays the miraculous icon of the Madonna, while at the opposite end of the church, the organ is regarded as the most splendid instrument in Silesia. The frescoes on the vault are the bravura work of George Wilhelm Neunhertz, the grandson and pupil of Willmann.

Behind the high altar is the **mausoleum** of the Świdnica Piasts, built as an integral part of the church (but you get in by a separate entrance from the outside). It's in the form of two circular chambers, each topped with a frescoed cupola and linked with a decorative arcade. The mausoleum holds the 14th-century tombstones of Prince Bolko I and his grandson Prince Bolko II, while the ashes of the two dukes and other rulers of the line have been deposited in the pillar in between. The frescoes, like those in the church, were executed by Neunhertz and show scenes from the abbey's history.

The abbey occupies the centre of the village, with the main church sitting in the middle of the grounds and the other one just 50m to the north. Between the two churches is the information office, which sells brochures about the place and tickets to the tower and mausoleum. The churches can be visited free of charge from 9am to 6pm (till dusk in winter) except during Mass. The monastic building (off limits) beside the larger church is now occupied by the Benedictines, who returned to Krzeszów in 1919.

There's also the **Way of the Cross** in Krzeszów, dating from the beginning of the 18th century, and consisting of a score of chapels scattered over the surrounding countryside to the west of the abbey.

Getting There & Away
The usual jumping-off point for Krzeszów is the town of Kamienna Góra, 8km to the north, with buses every hour or two on weekdays, but the service is poorer on weekends. Kamienna Góra has regular bus links with Jelenia Góra (38km), Bolków (19km) and Wałbrzych (19km).

JELENIA GÓRA
☎ 075 • pop 96,000
Set in a valley surrounded by mountain ranges, Jelenia Góra is a nice place with much historic character. Unlike many other towns in Silesia, it survived WWII pretty much undamaged; and as well as its architectural inheritance, it has the pleasant Cieplice spa (see the following section) at its southern end. Farther south are the Karkonosze Mountains, for which Jelenia Góra is a convenient starting point.

The town was founded in 1108 by King Bolesław Krzywousty (Boleslaus the Wry-Mouthed) as one of his fortified border strongholds, and came under the rule of the powerful Duchy of Świdnica-Jawor. Gold-mining in the region gave way to glass production around the 15th century, but it was weaving that gave the town a solid economic base from the 16th century on, and its high-quality linen was exported all over Europe.

After WWII the city was further industrialised with diverse branches of light industry, but fortunately, that side of things is well away from the historical centre.

Information
Tourist Offices The Centrum Informacji Turystycznej i Kulturalnej (☎ 767 69 25 ☎/fax 767 69 35, W www.sudety.it.pl), ul

Maja 42, is open 9am to 6pm weekdays, 10am to 2pm Saturday.

Money Bank Pekao, Plac Wyszyńskiego 35, and Bank Zachodni, Plac Niepodległości 4, both handle travellers cheque transactions and have useful ATMs. There's also a convenient ATM in the window of the Smok restaurant on the main square.

Email & Internet Access Central facilities include Nawigator, ul Bankowa 12; Wioska Internetowa, ul Grabowskiego 7; and Laboratorium Internetowe, ul 1 Maja 60.

Things to See

The elongated **Rynek**, formally called Plac Ratuszowy, is lined with a harmonious group of historic burghers' houses. Much of their charm is due to their ground-floor arcades, providing a covered passageway all around the square. The town hall on the square was built in the 1740s after its predecessor collapsed.

The **parish church**, off the central square, was erected in the 15th century, and the best-preserved relic from that time is the Gothic doorway in the southern entrance. The interior, with its powerful theatrical high altar, boasts mostly baroque furnishing and decoration.

Another outstanding ecclesiastical building, the massive **Holy Cross Church** is about 400m farther down the street. Designed by a Swede and modelled on St Catherine's Church in Stockholm, it was built in the 1710s for the Lutheran congregation and is thought to be the biggest Protestant church in Silesia (it now serves the Catholic community). The three-storeyed galleries plus the ground floor accommodate 4000 people. The ceiling is embellished with illusionistic baroque paintings of scenes from the Old and New Testaments, while the ornate 1720 organ over the high altar is a magnificent piece of craftwork and sounds as good as it looks.

The city has a good **Regional Museum** (*Muzeum Okręgowe*; ☎ 752 34 65, *ul Matejki 28; adult/student US$1/0.50; open 9am-3.30pm Tues, Thur & Fri, 9am-4.30pm Wed,* *Sat & Sun*), renowned for its extensive collection of glass, dating from medieval times to the present day. About 1200 pieces of the total of 7000 items (the largest collection in Poland) is on display. There are some amazing exhibits, including Art Nouveau pieces from the late 19th/early 20th centuries. The museum also has a large collection (over 1200 pieces) of old folk paintings on glass but it's not on permanent display.

Special Events

The **Festival of Street Theatre** is held during August/September. The **Theatre Festival** at the end of September has been taking place for over 20 years, and is the best established event in the city. Also in September is the **International Organ Music Festival** in the Holy Cross Church.

Places to Stay

Youth Hostel Bartek (☎/fax 752 57 46, *ul Bartka Zwycięzcy 10*) Beds US$3-5. Open year-round. Modest but pleasant, the youth hostel provides about 50 beds distributed in doubles, triples, quads, and six- and 10-bed dorms.

Bursa Szkolna Nr 1 (☎ 752 68 48, *ul Kilińskiego 5/7*) Beds in doubles, triples or quads US$5. Bursa is a basic school dorm facility which rents out its 130 beds in July and August, when students are away on their holidays. There may be some vacant beds in other months as well, mostly on weekends.

Bursa Szkolna Nr 2 (☎ 752 27 88, *ul Kilińskiego 38*) Beds in doubles, triples or quads US$5. This is another, smaller bursa, just 200m down the street, which offers much the same.

Dom Nauczyciela (☎ 752 93 00, ☎ 752 52 28, *ul Kilińskiego 22*) Beds in doubles, triples or quads US$5-8. In the same area as the bursas, Dom Nauczyciela is another simple budget option.

Hotel Park (☎ 752 69 42, *fax 752 60 21, ul Sudecka 42*) Doubles/triples with bath US$18/22. If you need a budget room with bath, Hotel Park is probably the cheapest option within walking distance of the centre. It also operates a *camp site* at the grounds in summer.

SILESIA

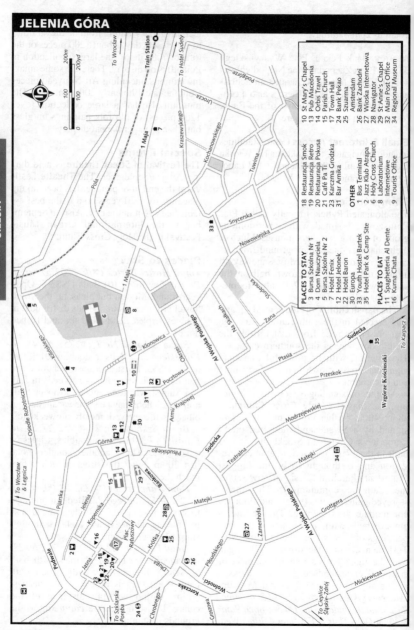

JELENIA GÓRA

Scale:
0   100   200m
0   100   200yd

To Wrocław → Train Station

To Hotel Sudety

PLACES TO STAY
3   Bursa Szkolna Nr 1
4   Dom Nauczyciela
5   Bursa Szkolna Nr 2
7   Hotel Fenix
12 Hotel Jelonek
22 Hotel Baron
30 Europa
33 Youth Hostel Bartek
35 Hotel Park & Camp Site

PLACES TO EAT
11 Spaghetteria Al Dente
16 Kurna Chata
18 Restauracja Smok
19 Restauracja Retro
20 Restauracja Pokusa
21 Café Pa Ti
23 Karczma Grodzka
31 Bar Arnika

OTHER
1   Bus Terminal
2   Jazz Klub Atrapa
6   Holy Cross Church
8   Laboratorium
    Internetowe
9   Tourist Office
10 St Mary's Chapel
13 Pub Macedonia
14 Orbis Travel
15 Parish Church
17 Town Hall
24 Bank Pekao
25 Szuarma
26 Bank Zachodni
27 Wioska Internetowa
28 Nawigator
29 St Anne's Chapel
32 Main Post Office
34 Regional Museum

To Wrocław & Legnica

To Szklarska Poręba

To Cieplice Śląskie-Zdrój

To Karpacz

Hotel Europa (☎ 764 72 31, fax 752 44 95, ul 1 Maja 16/18) Singles/doubles without bath US$16/22, with bath US$30/50. The Europa is right in the city centre, but its rooms with shared facilities are pretty simple.

Hotel Sudety (☎/fax 752 93 00, ul Krakowska 20) Singles/doubles without bath US$16/24, with bath US$30/45. Sudety offers reasonable standards but is not very convenient – a five-minute walk east of the train station, away from the centre.

Hotel Jelonek (☎ 764 65 41, fax 764 65 42, ul 1 Maja 5) Singles/doubles US$40/50, double suites US$60-80. Situated in a fine historic burgher's house, the 31-bed Jelonek is stylish, central and pleasant. Suites are more attractive than standard rooms. All rooms have private baths and rates include breakfast.

Hotel Baron (☎/fax 752 53 91, ul Grodzka 4) Singles/doubles with bath & breakfast US$45/55. Another charming and stylish small hotel, the Baron is ideally located just off the Rynek.

Hotel Fenix (☎ 641 66 00, fax 641 66 07, ul 1 Maja 88) Singles/doubles with bath & breakfast US$50/65. A new kid on the block, Fenix is comfortable and offers good facilities, including a restaurant, bar, sauna, gym and locked garage, although it's away from the centre.

Places to Eat
Bar Arnika (ul Pocztowa 8) Mains US$1.50-3. One of the cheapest central options, Arnika is a tiny place that serves basic Polish food. There's another, similar Arnika outlet in the Dom Nauczyciela.

Spaghetteria Al Dente (ul 1 Maja 31) Plates US$1-1.50. Nestled in the foyer of the local cinema, Spaghetteria offers cheap spaghetti, risotto and lasagne and is open till 10pm, ie, longer than most budget eateries.

Kurna Chata (☎ 642 58 50, Plac Ratuszowy 23/24) Mains US$2-3.50. A small cosy cafe with a folksy decor, Kurna Chata has good food, an inventive menu and is open till 10pm.

Restauracja Pokusa (☎ 752 53 47, Plac Ratuszowy 12) Mains US$4-6. With its outdoor tables in the arcaded passageway,

Pokusa is an agreeable place for lunch or dinner, and has reasonably priced, mostly Polish food, much like its two neighbours, *Restauracja Retro* and *Restauracja Smok*, also worth checking.

Karczma Grodzka (☎ 642 45 24, ul Grodzka 5) US$4-6. Next door to Hotel Baron, Karczma is a place for an affordable Polish lunch or dinner in a rustic timber interior, just as its 'inn' name suggests.

Café Pa Ti (☎ 752 53 91, ul Grodzka 4) Mains US$8-15. Also adjoining the Hotel Baron, Pa Ti offers international cuisine, but it's a more upmarket proposition.

Entertainment
Jazz Klub Atrapa (☎ 642 47 84, ul Forteczna 1) One of the most attractive haunts in the centre, Atrapa is a charming club with a dance floor, cheap beer and live music on some days.

Pub Macedonia (☎ 753 53 55, ul 1 Maja 3) A smoky basement bar with live music from time to time, Macedonia is another popular watering hole among local folks, and has a large outdoor terrace in summer.

Szuarma Amsterdam (☎ 752 39 66, ul Krótka 22) Run by two Dutch guys, Amsterdam is a good place for a beer or five. It has a cosy beer garden at the back.

Getting There & Away
The train station is about 1km east of the Old Town, a 15-minute walk to/from the Rynek, while the bus terminal is on the north-western edge of the town centre.

There's a regular train service to Szklarska Poręba (32km) and Wrocław (126km), and a couple of trains to Kraków daily (394km), Zielona Góra (191km) and Warsaw (516km). There are no trains to Karpacz.

Buses to Karpacz (24km) and Szklarska Poręba (20km) run every hour or so, and there's also reasonable bus transport to Kamienna Góra (38km) and Wrocław (117km). Buses to Karpacz and Szklarska Poręba also depart from the front of the train station.

There are buses in summer to Prague and Berlin. Contact the bus terminal for more information.

CIEPLICE ŚLĄSKIE-ZDRÓJ
☎ 75

As its suffix 'Zdrój' suggests, Cieplice ('Cheh-**plee**-tseh') is a spa, one of the oldest in the region. The local sulphur hot springs have probably been used for a millennium and the first spa house was established as early as the 13th century. Later on, the town developed as a weaving centre and glass producer. Only in the late 18th century were the curative properties of the springs recognised, paving the way for the building of the spa infrastructure. Set just 6km from Jelenia Góra, the spa was absorbed by the city in 1976 and is today a suburb within a single administrative area, yet it retains its distinctive atmosphere.

Information
The tourist office (☎ 755 88 44, ☎/fax 755 88 45) is on the central mall, Plac Piastowski 36. It's open 9am to 5pm weekdays, 10am to 2pm Saturday. It also opens 10am to 2pm Sunday in summer.

Things to See
The town's core is made up by a **Spa Park** (Park Zdrojowy) with a **Spa Theatre** (Teatr Zdrojowy) built on its grounds. The theatre hosts concerts and opera/operetta performances in summer.

The main mall, Plac Piastowski, is just to the north of the park. Roughly halfway along it stands the monumental **Schaffgotsch Palace**, built in the 1780s as a residence of the long-time owners of the town. These days it houses a high school.

At the western end of the mall is the 18th-century **parish church**, the interior of which has baroque furnishings. The painting on the large ornate high altar is by Michael Willmann. Should you wish to try the local waters, the **pump room** (pijalnia) is near the church on ul Ściegiennego and serves water from four of the eight springs that the town exploits.

South of the spa park is the Norwegian Park that holds the **Natural History Museum** (Muzeum Przyrodnicze; ☎ 755 15 06, ul Wolności 268; adult/student US$1/0.50; open 9am-4pm Tues-Sun). Its display of birds

and butterflies from all over the world stems from the collection of the Schaffgotsch family, who established the museum in 1876.

Places to Stay & Eat
Camping Słoneczna Polana (☎/fax 755 25 66, ul Rataja 9) Tent site US$3 plus US$2 per person, 5-bed cabin US$20/day. Open May-Sept. Run by a Dutch couple, Słoneczna Polana has 10 cabins and a tent/caravan area. It's well equipped with modern facilities and has a snack bar. Cabins are rented for a minimum of three days (US$60). The camp site is 1km west of the spa park. To get there from Jelenia Góra, take bus No 7, 9 or 17.

Ośrodek Wczasowo-Sanatoryjny Śnieżka (☎ 755 16 73, Plac Piastowski 28) Singles/doubles with bath US$12/15. Set directly opposite the Schaffgotsch Palace, Śnieżka offers 30 simple but perfectly acceptable rooms in the very centre of the spa.

You'll find a number of restaurants and snack bars within a few minutes' walk from the Śnieżka, as well as a tourist office which can provide information about other places to stay in the area.

Getting There & Away
Cieplice is served by frequent urban buses from Jelenia Góra, including Nos 4, 6, 7, 9, 14 and 17.

KARPACZ
☎ 75 • pop 5400

There are several mountain resorts along the foothills of the Karkonosze, of which Karpacz and Szklarska Poręba (see the following section in this chapter), on the eastern and western ends of the range, respectively, are the largest and have the best tourist facilities.

Karpacz sits on the slopes of Mt Śnieżka (1602m), the highest peak of the Sudetes. It's one of the most popular mountain resorts in Poland, as much for skiers in winter as for walkers in summer. This large village – it hardly has the appearance of a town – spreads over 3km along a winding road, with houses scattered across the slopes, without any obvious central area.

The eastern, lower part, known as Karpacz Dolny or Lower Karpacz, is more densely populated and has most of the accommodation and places to eat. At the far north-eastern end of this sector is the (inoperable) train station. The western part, the Karpacz Górny or Upper Karpacz, is just a collection of holiday homes. In the middle of the two districts is the bus terminal and Hotel Biały Jar. From this point several marked trails wind up the mountains. About 1km uphill from here is the lower station of the chairlift to Mt Kopa (1375m).

Information

The helpful Centrum Informacji Turystycznej (☎ 761 86 05, ☎/fax 761 97 16, Ⓦ www.karpacz.pl) is at ul Konstytucji 3 Maja 25A in Lower Karpacz. Off-season, it's open 8am to 6pm Monday to Saturday and 10am to 2pm Sunday. In the high season, it's open one or two hours longer. Bank Zachodni, ul Konstytucji 3 Maja 43, and Bank Pekao, ul Mickiewicza 6, have ATMs.

Things to See & Do

Like most resorts of this kind, Karpacz is not a place to look for historical relics, though it does happen to have a curious architectural gem – the **Wang Chapel** (*Świątynia Wang; ☎ 761 92 28, ul Na Śnieżkę 8; adult/student US$1.25/0.75; open 9am-5pm Mon-Sat, 11.30am-5pm Sun, till 6pm June-Aug)*, the only Nordic Romanesque building in Poland.

The chapel was originally built at the turn of the 12th century on the bank of Lake Wang in southern Norway as one of about 400 of its sort (23 survive today). By the 19th century it became too small for the local congregation, and was offered for sale, to make way for a larger and better building. It was bought in 1841 by the Prussian King Friedrich Wilhelm IV, carefully dismantled piece by piece and brought to Berlin. It was then transported to Karpacz, meticulously reassembled over a period of two years and consecrated in the presence of the king himself. Not only is it the oldest church in the Sudetes, it's also the most elevated, sitting at an altitude of 886m.

The church is made of hard Norwegian pine and put together without a single nail. It's surrounded by a cloister that helps to keep it warm. Part of the woodcarving is original and preserved in excellent shape, particularly the carved doorways and the capitals of the pillars. The freestanding stone belfry was added later.

The church is in Upper Karpacz, just off the main road. There is a taped commentary; German and English versions are available for groups of tourists.

Karpacz's other peculiar sight is the **Museum of Toys** (*Muzeum Zabawek; ☎ 761 85 23, ul Karkonoska 5; adult/student US$1/0.50; open 9am-3.30pm Tues-Fri, 10am-3.30pm Sat & Sun)*, one of only two in Poland (the other is in Kielce). It features a 2000-piece collection of puppets, dolls, teddy bears and other toys from all over the world. It's in a former holiday home in Upper Karpacz.

Karpacz is a good starting point for hiking. The village is bordered on the south by the Karkonosze National Park, an obvious destination for walkers. Most tourists aim for Mt Śnieżka, and there are half a dozen different trails leading there. The most popular routes originate from Hotel Biały Jar, and you can get to the top in three to four hours depending on the trail you choose. When planning a trip to Mt Śnieżka, try to include in your route two picturesque postglacial lakes bordered by rocky cliffs, Wielki Staw and Mały Staw. A couple of trails pass near the lakes.

The fastest and most comfortable way of getting to Mt Śnieżka is the **chairlift to Mt Kopa** (*Kolej Linowa na Kopę; ☎ 761 92 84, ul Turystyczna 4; US$4/5 one-way/return; operates 8.30am-5pm, stops earlier in winter)*, which will take you up 528m in 17 minutes. From Mt Kopa, you can get to the top of Mt Śnieżka in less than an hour by the trail signposted in black.

Places to Stay & Eat

There's plenty of accommodation in Karpacz and it's easy to find a room, even in the high season. The town offers tourists about 12,000 beds, more than twice the

SILESIA

number of its inhabitants. Apart from about 20 hotels, there are over 190 holiday homes and pensions, and they all will be eager to put you up for the night. Locals also offer rooms in their homes – look for boards reading 'pokoje', 'noclegi' or 'zimmer frei', the latter demonstrating the increase in German tourism in the region.

In season (summer or winter), most holiday homes and private houses will cost around US$5 to US$10 per bed in rooms without bath, US$7 to US$15 with bath; off season, it will be 20 to 40% cheaper. Hotels are usually more expensive.

The tourist office has a full list of accommodation options and will provide details and advice. Rooms in private houses and holiday homes can be arranged through local travel agencies, including Karpacz (☎ 761 95 47), ul Konstytucji 3 Maja 52; Edi-Tour (☎ 761 88 93), ul Karkonoska 1; Sudety (☎ 761 63 92), ul Konstytucji 3 Maja 31; and Śnieżka (☎ 761 64 14), ul Konstytucji 3 Maja 29. Zarząd Okręgu FWP (☎ 761 94 59, ul Obrońców Pokoju 1) can arrange rooms in any of its 10 holiday homes.

There are two camping grounds in Karpacz: *Camping Nr 165 Pod Lipami* (☎ 761 88 67, ul Konstytucji 3 Maja 8), near the train station, and *Camping Nr 211 Pod Brzozami* (☎ 761 88 67, ul Obrońców Pokoju 4), 1km up the road. Both are administered by one operator and open from around June to September.

Youth Hostel Liczyrzepa (☎ 761 92 90, ul Gimnazjalna 9) Beds US$3-5. Open year-round. As elsewhere, the youth hostel is one of the cheapest options, but most of Liczyrzepa's 60 beds are in large dorms.

Karpacz also offers an increasing choice of top-end accommodation. All the hotels listed below have rooms with private baths and the prices given (for high season) include breakfast. All of these places have their own restaurants.

Hotel Rezydencja (☎ 761 80 20, fax 761 95 13, ul Parkowa 6) Singles/doubles US$50/60. Situated in a beautiful large historic villa in the centre of Lower Karpacz, Rezydencja has 14 spacious and comfortable rooms.

Hotel Vivaldi (☎ 761 99 33, fax 761 99 35, ul Olimpijska 4) Singles/doubles US$50/60, suites US$80-100. Another finely restored historic building with wide vistas, Vivaldi is a new place that offers good facilities, including a small swimming pool, sauna and cybercafe.

Hotel Karkonosze (☎ 761 82 77, fax 761 80 33, ul Wolna 4) Doubles/triples US$60/80. With a gym, sauna, pool tables, and bike rental, the modern Karkonosze also boasts a good range of amenities.

As with accommodation, eating is no problem in Karpacz. A variety of places, ranging from rudimentary roadside stands selling sausages to the dining rooms of holiday homes, open during the tourist season.

Getting There & Away

Trains no longer call at Karpacz, but buses to Jelenia Góra run regularly. They go along Karpacz's main road, ul Konstytucji 3 Maja, and you can pick them up at different points.

SZKLARSKA PORĘBA
☎ 75 • pop 8700

Szklarska Poręba ('**Shklahr**-skah Po-**rem**-bah') is the other major Karkonosze resort, this one being at the foot of Mt Szrenica (1362m). It's also spread wide over the hills, but has a more definite centre along ul Jedności Narodowej, skirting the Kamienna River. At the lower end of this 500m street is the bus terminal, while off the upper end is the train station.

Information

The tourist office (☎/fax 717 24 49, Ⓦ www.szklarskaporeba.pl), ul Jedności Narodowej 3, is helpful and staff are knowledgeable. Off-season, it's open 8am to 4pm daily; in the high season, it opens 8am to 6pm weekdays, 10am-6pm weekends. Bank Zachodni is at ul Jedności Narodowej 16, and there are half a dozen kantors around the centre.

Things to See & Do

The town has a few small museums (the tourist office has details), but it's the natural beauty of the region and its activities that attract most visitors. There's a **chairlift to Mt Szrenica** (*Kolej Linowa na Szrenicę; ☎ 717 30 35, ul Turystyczna 25A; US$5/6 one-way/return; operates 8.30am-5pm*) which takes you up 603m and deposits you at the top in about 25 minutes. The lower chairlift station is about 1km south of the centre, uphill along ul Turystyczna.

There are some attractions within easy walking distance of Szklarska Poręba. The road to Jelenia Góra winds east in a beautiful valley along the Kamienna River. Some 3km down the road (or along the green trail on the opposite side of the river) is the 13m-high **Szklarka Waterfall** (Wodospad Szklarki). From here the blue trail heads up to the mountains and you can walk along it to Mt Szrenica in two to three hours.

The road that goes west from Szklarska Poręba to the Czech border in Jakuszyce passes the rocky cliffs called Krucze Skały (Ravens' Rocks). About 500m farther on, a red trail branches off to the left. It's a 25-minute walk up the hill along this trail to the **Kamieńczyk Waterfall** (Wodospad Kamieńczyka), the highest (27m) and one of the prettiest falls in the Polish part of Sudetes. Continuing on for about 1½ hours along the same trail you will get to Mt Szrenica.

Places to Stay

There are plenty of options, including 10 hotels, 90 holiday homes, 50 pensions and 60 registered private room owners, providing over 10,000 beds in all. The tourist office has all the listings and several local travel agents handle bookings. They include Karkonosze (☎ 717 23 93), ul 1 Maja 1; Korona (☎ 717 29 99), ul Jedności Narodowej 20; and WNT (☎ 717 21 00), ul Jedności Narodowej 22. Prices are much the same as in Karpacz (see that section earlier).

The town has several camp sites, including the very central *Camping Pod Mostem* (☎ 717 30 62, ul Gimnazjalna 5) and *Camping Pod Ponurą Małpą* (☎ 717 32 87, ul Jeleniogórska 2A), off the road to Jelenia Góra. Both tend to open in April/May and close in September.

Youth Hostel Wojtek (☎/fax 717 21 41, ul Piastowska 1) Beds US$3-5. Open year-round. The 80-bed youth hostel is pleasant and well-run but it's a long way north-east of the centre.

Among the finer hotels are:

Hotel Kryształ (☎/fax 717 44 30, ul 1 Maja 19) Singles/doubles US$35/45. Located in the wholly refurbished old timber villa, the Kryształ is central and stylish, and doesn't cost a fortune.

Hotel Bosman (☎/fax 717 22 20, ul Morcinka 2) Singles/doubles US$40/50. Also nestled in an old-style building close to the centre, Bosman provides good standards and fine vistas.

Hotel Bornit (☎ 753 95 03, fax 753 95 10, ul Mickiewicza 21) Singles/doubles US$50/80. New and modern, Bornit offers possibly the best facilities in town, including a swimming pool, sauna and gym, plus sweeping views.

Getting There & Away

Trains and buses run regularly to Jelenia Góra (20km). There are also four trains and six buses daily directly to Wrocław, plus one train to Warsaw.

For the Czech Republic, take the bus to Jakuszyce (6km) and cross the border to Harrachov, the first Czech village, from where there are buses onwards.

THE KARKONOSZE NATIONAL PARK

The Karkonosze National Park (Karkonoski Park Narodowy), just south of Karpacz and Szklarska Poręba, stretches up to the Czech border (which follows all the highest peaks of the Karkonosze). The 56 sq km park is a narrow belt that runs along the frontier for some 25km. On the other side, its Czech counterpart protects the southern part of the outcrop.

The range is divided by the Przełęcz Karkonoska (Karkonosze Pass; 1198m). The highest summit of the eastern section is Mt Śnieżka (1602m), while the western portion is crowned by Mt Wielki Szyszak (1509m).

Up to an altitude of about 1250m the park is predominantly spruce forest. Higher up

SILESIA

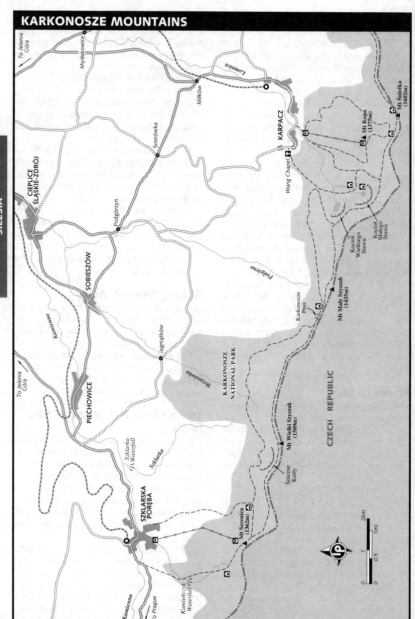

KARKONOSZE MOUNTAINS

are dwarf mountain pines and alpine vegetation, which fade away to leave only mosses on the highest peaks.

Characteristic of the Karkonosze are *kotły*, or cirques – huge hollows carved by glaciers during the ice age and bordered with steep cliffs. There are six cirques on the Polish side of the range; the most spectacular are Kocioł Małego Stawu and Kocioł Wielkiego Stawu near Mt Śnieżka, and Śnieżne Kotły at the foot of Mt Wielki Szyszak.

The Karkonosze is known for its harsh climate, with heavy rainfall (snow in winter) and highly variable weather, and strong winds and mists possible at any time. Statistically, the best chances of good weather are in January, February, May and September. Higher up, there's snow on the ground for six months of the year.

The Karkonosze National Park is the most popular hiking territory in the Sudetes. The two main gateways are Karpacz and Szklarska Poręba, from where most tourists ascend Mt Śnieżka and Mt Szrenica, respectively. There's a restaurant, a chapel and a meteorological observatory on the top of Mt Śnieżka.

For longer walks, probably the best idea is to take the red trail that runs right along the ridge between the two peaks, with excellent views on both sides. The trail also passes along the upper edges of the kotły. You can walk the whole stretch in six to seven hours. If you start early enough, it's possible to do the Karpacz-Szklarska Poręba (or vice versa) trip within a day, preferably by using the chairlift to speed up the initial ascent.

You can break the walk at the **Odrodzenie mountain hostel**, roughly halfway between the two peaks, or in any other of the half-dozen mountain hostels within the park. The **Samotnia hostel** at Kocioł Małego Stawu is possibly the most amazing place of all.

You can also shorten the trip by taking one of several trails that branch off downhill from the main red one at different points. Get a copy of the *Karkonoski Park Narodowy* or *Karkonosze* map. They come in different scales, produced by various map publishers. Take warm, waterproof clothes as the weather, as mentioned, is completely unpredictable.

Wielkopolska

Wielkopolska (literally, Great Poland) is the cradle of the Polish state, for it was here that the first recorded ruler, Duke Mieszko I, unified the scattered Slav tribes of the region into a single political unit in the second half of the 10th century. In 966 Mieszko was baptised, and Gniezno, where the event took place, became the capital.

Shortly after, the nearby town of Poznań took on a range of administrative and political functions, and came to be the main seat of Mieszko and his son and successor Bolesław Chrobry (Boleslaus the Brave). These two rulers succeeded in expanding the country's territory to an area not much smaller than that of present-day Poland, eventually incorporating in the regions of Wielkopolska, Pomerania, Mazovia, Silesia and Małopolska.

Despite the fact that the royal seat moved to Kraków in 1038, Wielkopolska remained an integral part of Poland during its often chequered history, even though it underwent intensive Germanisation under the Prussians during the 19th-century Partitions.

Wielkopolska shelters some of the valuable architectural legacy of the early Polish nation, which is one of the region's great tourist attractions. This apart, Wielkopolska boasts the 2700-year-old fortified town of Biskupin, the oldest surviving settlement in Poland, which shows that the region was settled by well organised social groups long before the birth of the state.

Poznań is the region's major city and an important tourist centre. From here many visitors set off along the so-called Piast Route (Szlak Piastowski) through the places where Poland was formed.

Poznań

☎ 61 • pop 610,000

A large industrial centre and the provincial capital, Poznań is also an important historic city and was the de facto capital of Poland

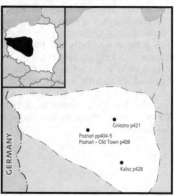

in the early years of the state. Most Poles, though, associate the city with the international trade fairs that have taken place regularly since WWI. These days there are two dozen different fairs throughout the year.

As you'd expect, during the fairs accommodation fills up with crowds of businesspeople and visitors, and prices rise. These are not good times for sightseeing. It's best to come at a quieter time, giving yourself two or three days to explore the city, and a few more for the environs.

Poznań has some important tourist attractions including the town hall and several museums, for which it's probably worth breaking a Berlin-Warsaw journey. If you

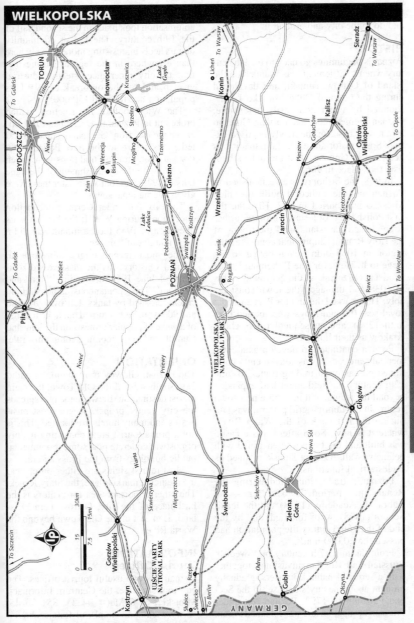

WIELKOPOLSKA

WIELKOPOLSKA

have more time, there's much more to see and do in the city and around it.

HISTORY

Poznań's beginnings go back to the 9th century when a settlement was founded on the island of Ostrów Tumski, and developed during the reign of Duke Mieszko I. Surrounded by water and easily defensible, Poznań seemed more secure than Gniezno as a power base for the newly baptised nation. Some historians even claim that it was here, not in Gniezno, that the duke's baptism took place in 966.

In 968, the bishopric was established in Poznań and the cathedral built, in which Mieszko was buried in 992. His son, the first Polish king, Bolesław Chrobry, further strengthened the island, and the troops of the Holy Roman Empire that conquered the region in 1005 didn't even bother to lay siege to it. However, the Bohemian Prince Bratislav (Brzetysław) did get round to this in 1038 and damaged the town considerably. This marked the end for Poznań as the royal seat (though kings were buried here until 1296), and subsequent rulers chose Kraków as their home.

Poznań continued to develop as a commercial centre, as it was conveniently positioned on east-west trading routes. By the 12th century the settlement had expanded beyond the island, and in 1253 a new town centre, in the familiar grid pattern, was laid out on the left bank of the Warta River, where it is now. Soon afterwards a castle was built and the town was encircled with defensive walls. Ostrów Tumski retained its ecclesiastical functions.

Poznań's trade flourished during the Renaissance period. Two colleges, the Lubrański Academy (1518) and the Jesuit School (1578), were founded, and by the end of the 16th century the population had passed the 20,000 mark.

From the mid-17th century on, Swedish, Prussian and Russian invasions, together with a series of natural disasters, gradually brought about the city's demise. In the Second Partition of 1793, Poznań fell under Prussian occupation and was renamed Posen.

Intensive Germanisation and German colonisation took place in the second half of the 19th century. The Polish community dug its heels in, resisting more actively here than elsewhere in the region. During that time the city experienced steady industrial growth and by the outbreak of WWI its population had reached 150,000.

The Wielkopolska Insurrection, which broke out in Poznań in December 1918, liberated the city from German occupation and led to its return to the new Polish state. Poznań's long trading traditions were given new life with the establishment of the trade fairs in 1921, and four years later these were given international status.

The city fell under German occupation once more during WWII; the battle for its liberation in 1945 took a month and did a huge amount of damage.

The most recent tragic milestone in Poznań's history was the massive workers' strike of June 1956, demanding 'bread and freedom'. This spontaneous demonstration, cruelly crushed by tanks, left over 70 dead and 900 wounded; it turned out to be the first of a wave of popular protests on the long and painful road to overcoming communist rule.

ORIENTATION

The Poznań Główny train station is about 2km south-west of the Old Town, the main tourist destination. Between the two spreads the city centre proper, where most businesses and many hotels are located. This is not a prime tourist area, consisting mainly of postwar concrete plus some monumental public buildings from the Prussian era.

Most tourist sights are either on or near the medieval marketplace, the Stary Rynek. The other important area for visitors is the birthplace of the city, Ostrów Tumski island, 1km east of the Old Town beyond the Warta River.

INFORMATION
Tourist Offices

Poznań has two useful tourist offices. The city tourist office, the Centrum Informacji Miejskiej or CIM (☎ 94 31, 851 96 45, W www.cim.poznan.pl), ul Ratajczaka 44,

Workers' Strike of June 1956

The June 1956 industrial strike in Poznań was the first mass protest in the Soviet bloc. Breaking out just three years after Stalin's death, it became the first milestone on Eastern Europe's road to democracy, and in some ways it served as an example and spawned a chain of revolts that broke out in Poland, Hungary and Czechoslovakia over the following decades. The massive Budapest strike came just four months later.

Poznań's protest originated in the city's largest industrial plant, the Cegielski metalworks (then named after Stalin), which produced railway stock. When the workers demanded the refund of an unfairly charged tax, factory management refused and simply threw the workers' delegates out of the meeting room. This sparked a spontaneous strike the next day (28 June), in which the workers of the Cegielski metalworks, joined by workers from other local industrial plants, headed for Mickiewicz Square (then named Stalin's Square).

The 100,000-strong crowd which gathered on the square (a quarter of the city's total population) demanded that changes be introduced to improve working conditions, and requested that authorities come and discuss the issue. However, the demonstration was disregarded by city officials.

Matters soon got out of hand. The angry crowd stormed the police headquarters and the communist party building, and released 257 prisoners from the local jail after disarming the guards. Shortly after, a battle for the secret police headquarters broke out, and it was there that the bloodshed began, when police started firing at people surrounding the building. Tanks were introduced into the action, and troops were hastily brought from Wrocław and told they were there to pacify a German riot.

Fierce street battles continued for the whole night and part of the next day, resulting in a total of at least 76 dead and 900 wounded. More than 300 people were arrested, 58 of whom were indicted.

Judging by the number of dead and wounded, this was the most tragic popular protest in communist Poland, yet it was little known and for a long time underestimated.

Only recently the historical importance of the revolt has been appreciated and given the status it deserves.

is open 10am to 7pm weekdays, and 10am to 5pm weekends. The provincial tourist office, the Centrum Informacji Turystycznej (☎ 852 61 56), Stary Rynek 59, is open 9am to 5pm weekdays, and 10am to 2pm Saturday (till 6pm on weekdays and till 4pm on Saturday from June to September).

If you are arriving at Poznań's main train station, you can inquire at the private agency Glob-Tour (☎ 866 06 67), in the station's main hall, which is open round the clock and provides tourist information.

Money

Useful banks include Bank Pekao at ul Św Marcin 52/56, ul Sieroca 7 and ul Masztalarska 8; Powszechny Bank Kredytowy at Stary Rynek 97/98 and Bank Gdański at ul Paderewskiego 10. Kantors are plentiful throughout the central area, and there are

also a number of ATMs. There's a 24-hour kantor at the main train station next to Glob-Tour.

Email & Internet Access

Central Internet facilities include Adax Internet Cafe, Półwiejska 28; Café Internet Klik, ul Szkolna 15 (entrance from ul Jaskółcza); Gallery & Internet Club (☎ 852 06 25), ul Wielka 18; Internet Cafe (☎ 852 79 33), Plac Wolno'ci 8 (1st floor); Internet C@fe (☎ 851 04 01), Plac Ratajskiego 4; Internet Club Vip Net (☎ 853 78 18), ul Garncarska 10; and Studio Internetowe Strong, ul 23 Lutego 7. Any of these charge about US$1.50 to US$2 an hour. Most are open till 10pm or later.

Bookshops

Księgarnia Omnibus (☎ 853 61 82), ul Św Marcin 39, is the best for English-language

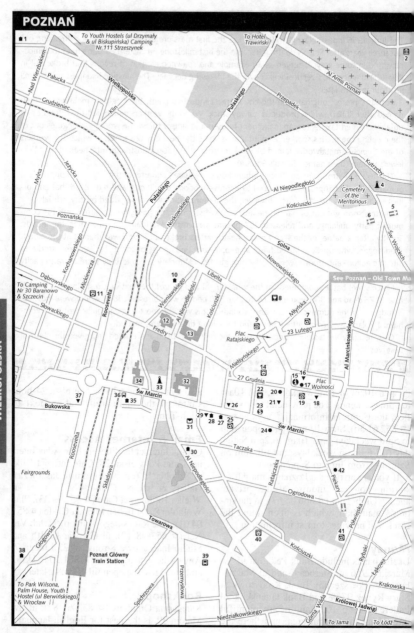

WIELKOPOLSKA

POZNAŃ

To Youth Hostels (ul Drzymały & ul Biskupińska) Camping Nr. 111 Strzeszynek

To Hotel Trawiński

Nad Wierzbakiem

Pałucka

Wielkopolska

Al Armii Poznań

Grudzieniec

Klin

Przepadek

Pułaskiego

Myńna

Jeżyca

Pułaskiego

Nieckowskiego

Al Niepodległości

Kościuszki

Kutrzeby

Cemetery of the Meritorious

4

5

6

Św Wojciech

Poznańska

Kochanowskiego

Solna

Nowowiejskiego

Dąbrowskiego

Mickiewicza

Roosevelta

Libelta

Młyńska

See Poznań – Old Town Ma

To Camping Nr 30 Baranowo & Szczecin

11

Słowackiego

Wieniawskiego

10

Kościuszki

8

Al Niepodległości

Fredry

12

13

9

7

23 Lutego

Plac Ratajskiego

Al Marcinkowskiego

Mielżyńskiego

14

34

33

32

27 Grudnia

15 16

17

Plac Wolności

Św Marcin

22

20

21

19 18

37

36 35

26

Bukowska

29 28 27 25

31

24

Św Marcin

30

Taczaka

Ratajczaka

Składowa

Al Niepodległości

42

Piekary

Ogrodowa

Połwiejska

Fairgrounds

Roosevelta

Głogowska

41

40

Rybaki

Łąkowa

Towarowa

Kościuszki

38

Poznań Główny Train Station

39

Przemysłowa

Spichrzowa

Krakowska

To Park Wilsona, Palm House, Youth Hostel (ul Berwińskiego) & Wrocław

Niedziałkowskiego

Górna Wilda

Królowej Jadwigi

To Jama

To Łódź

1

2

4

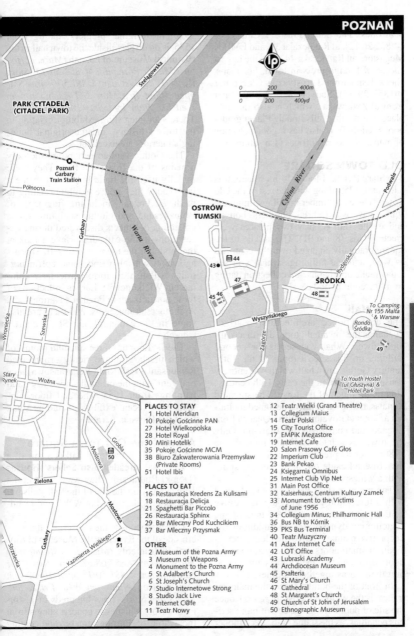

POZNAŃ

WIELKOPOLSKA

books, and also has some French and German ones. The Salon Prasowy Café Głos (☎ 852 26 12), ul Ratajczaka 39, and EMPiK Megastore, ul Ratajczaka 44, have the largest choice of foreign press in town. For maps, check Księgarnia Turystyczna Globtrotter (☎ 853 29 15), Stary Rynek 98/100 (enter from ul Żydowska), which is also the only place in town that sells Lonely Planet guidebooks. Glob-Tour also has a good selection of maps. The tourist offices also sell maps.

OLD TOWN SQUARE

The Stary Rynek, 140m x 140m square, was laid out in 1253 along with the rest of the Old Town. The early timber buildings lining the square gave way to brick burghers' houses, and in the 18th century two palaces were erected (Nos 78 and 91). The middle of the square gradually changed over the centuries as well, and the buildings which you see today make up a haphazard collection dating from different periods.

Town Hall

The unquestioned architectural pearl of Poznań is the town hall, topped with a 61m-high tower. What you see is the second building on this site; it replaced the 13th-century Gothic town hall which was entirely consumed by fire in the early 16th century, along with much of the town. The splendid Renaissance town hall was designed by Italian architect Giovanni Battista Quadro from Lugano and constructed in 1550–60. Only the tower is a later addition, built in the 1780s after its predecessor collapsed. Note the crowned eagle on the top of the spire, with a wingspan of 2m.

The main, eastern facade is embellished with a three-storey arcaded loggia. Above it, the painted frieze depicts kings of the Jagiellonian dynasty. In the middle of the decorative parapet, above the clock, there's a pair of small doors. Every day at noon the doors open and two metal goats appear and butt their horns together 12 times.

In front of the building, near the main entrance, is the **whipping post** (*pręgierz*), once the site of public floggings and of more serious penalties, as the statue of the executioner

on top suggests. This is a replica made in 1925; the original pręgierz, dating from 1535, is on display inside the town hall in the **Historical Museum of Poznań** (*Muzeum Historii Miasta Poznania;* ☎ 852 56 13, *Stary Rynek 1; adult/student US$1.50/1, free Sat; open 10am-4pm Mon & Tues, noon-6pm Wed-Fri, 9am-4pm Sat, 10am-3pm Sun).* There's an interesting exhibition relating to the town's history, and the original building's interiors are excellent.

The Gothic vaulted cellars are the only remains of the first town hall. They were initially used for trade but later became a jail. Today they house exhibits relating to medieval Poznań, including fragments of Romanesque and Gothic sculpture and a collection of objects discovered during excavations in the cathedral. Have a look at the model of the town as it was 1000 years ago. You will also find some coffin portraits, a Polish art form particularly common in Wielkopolska. Larger collections of these portraits are in Poznań's National and Archdiocesan museums, and there are also some in the cathedral and St Adalbert's Church.

The 1st floor has three splendid rooms, of which the largest, the richly ornamented **Renaissance Hall** (Sala Renesansowa), is a real gem, with the original stucco work and paintings from 1555. The 2nd floor contains more recent exhibits, including some from the Prussian period.

Around the Old Town Square

To the south of the town hall is a row of a dozen small arcaded **Fish Sellers' Houses** (Domki Budnicze). They were built in the 16th century on the site of the fish stalls but were largely destroyed in WWII and reconstructed later.

Directly opposite the houses, on the eastern side of the Rynek, is the **Museum of Musical Instruments** (*Muzeum Instrumentów Muzycznych;* ☎ 852 08 57, *Stary Rynek 45; adult/student US$1.50/1; open 10am-4pm Tues & Thur, 9am-5pm Wed, Fri & Sat, 11am-4pm Sun).* It has hundreds of instruments, from whistles to concert pianos from the whole of Europe and beyond, dating

Coffin Portraits – Funerals Polish-Style

A prerequisite for the funeral ceremonies of the Polish nobility and aristocracy in the baroque era, coffin portraits were paintings of deceased persons executed on a piece of copper or a tin plate. Designed to be attached to the coffin during the funeral, they were usually made in a hexagonal or octagonal shape to match the coffin's front. They were removed before the burial and placed in a tomb chapel of the deceased or left in the church as an epitaph.

A very Polish custom, virtually not found elsewhere in Europe, coffin portraits constituted an important element of a theatrical Castrum Doloris, a monumental decoration built in the church for a sumptuous funeral celebration. The paintings aimed at giving the impression that the deceased were participating actively in their own funeral.

In a grand par-theatrical spectacle, the image of the deceased formed an illusory bridge between life and death, or between mundaneness and transcendentality. While the portrait 'looked' at the audience, the orators performed speeches in the manner as if the deceased spoke themselves, thus making them the main actors of the ceremony.

Characteristic feature of the coffin portraits was that the subjects were usually presented frontally on a plain background, with eyes wide open to attract visual contact. Executed mostly by anonymous painters, the portrayed persons were often presented with great realism, sometimes showing their ugliness or facial defects.

While watching these paintings, one can notice that some aristocrats seem to have commissioned their portraits well before their death, sometimes when they were still pretty young, while others apparently forgot to immortalise their image before their death. In the latter case, the deceased person was painted just after the death, usually by any artist at hand.

Coffin portraits first appeared in the late 16th century but it wasn't until the 1640s that they became common in funeral ceremonies of the nobility. They began to disappear by the mid-17th century and were largely forgotten well into modern times, considered as a sub-art. Many were lost or destroyed during that period. Only after WWII has there been an increasing interest in coffin portraits and they have been lifted to the rank of works of art.

Coffin painting best developed in Wielkopolska and, accordingly, the region has today the largest number of such portraits. Some of the best collections are in the National Museum and Archdiocesan Museum in Poznań, and the Archdiocesan Museum in Gniezno. Outside the region, Wilanów Palace and the National Museum in Warsaw have reasonable collections.

from the 15th to 20th centuries, and including some intriguing folk specimens.

Behind the town hall is the **Weigh House** (Waga Miejska), a postwar replica of the 16th-century building designed by Quadro, which was dismantled in the 19th century. South of it are two large modern structures, strikingly out of harmony with the rest of the old Rynek. Unfortunately, the authorities put these nondescript blocks on the site of the old arsenal and the cloth hall, thus ruining the unity of the square. The one to the east houses the **Wielkopolska Military Museum** (*Wielkopolskie Muzeum Wojskowe; ☎ 852 67 39, Stary Rynek 9; adult/student US$1/0.50; open 9am-4pm Tues-Sat, 10am-*

3pm Sun). The other building houses the **Arsenal City Art Gallery** (*Galeria Miejska Arsenal; ☎ 852 95 01, Stary Rynek 3; adult/student US$1/0.50; open 11am-6pm Tues-Sat, 10am-3pm Sun*), which has temporary exhibitions of modern art, plus a restaurant and a bookshop.

In the south-western part of the square is the 19th-century neoclassical Guardhouse (Odwach).

SOUTH-EAST OF THE OLD TOWN SQUARE

Off the south-eastern corner of the Rynek, in the 16th-century Górka Palace (Pałac Górków), is the **Archaeological Museum**

WIELKOPOLSKA

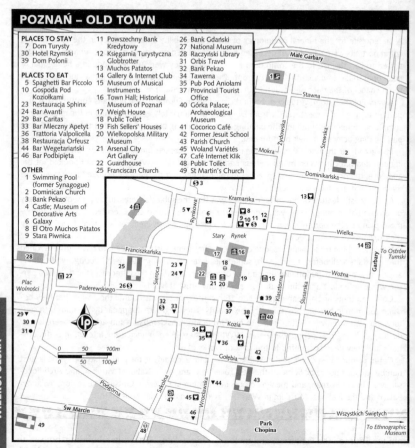

POZNAŃ – OLD TOWN

PLACES TO STAY
7 Dom Turysty
30 Hotel Rzymski
39 Dom Polonii

PLACES TO EAT
5 Spaghetti Bar Piccolo
10 Gospoda Pod Koziołkami
23 Restauracja Sphinx
24 Bar Avanti
29 Bar Caritas
33 Bar Mleczny Apetyt
36 Trattoria Valpolicella
38 Restauracja Orfeusz
44 Bar Wegetariański
46 Bar Podbipięta

OTHER
1 Swimming Pool (former Synagogue)
2 Dominican Church
3 Bank Pekao
4 Castle; Museum of Decorative Arts
6 Galaxy
8 El Otro Muchos Patatos
9 Stara Piwnica

11 Powszechny Bank Kredytowy
12 Księgarnia Turystyczna Globtrotter
13 Muchos Patatos
14 Gallery & Internet Club
15 Museum of Musical Instruments
16 Town Hall; Historical Museum of Poznań
17 Weigh House
18 Public Toilet
19 Fish Sellers' Houses
20 Wielkopolska Military Museum
21 Arsenal City Art Gallery
22 Guardhouse
25 Franciscan Church

26 Bank Gdański
27 National Museum
28 Raczyński Library
31 Orbis Travel
32 Bank Pekao
34 Tawerna
35 Pub Pod Aniołami
37 Provincial Tourist Office
40 Górka Palace; Archaeological Museum
41 Cocorico Café
42 Former Jesuit School
43 Parish Church
45 Woland Variétés
47 Café Internet Klik
48 Public Toilet
49 St Martin's Church

(*Muzeum Archeologiczne;* ☎ 852 82 51, *ul Wodna 27; adult/student US$1/0.50; open 10am-4pm Tues-Fri, 10am-6pm Sat, 10am-3pm Sun*). Before going in, stop and have a look at the fine Renaissance doorway on the building's eastern facade. The museum itself presents the prehistory of the region, from the Stone Age to the early medieval period. You'll also find a replica of the famous bronze doors from the Gniezno cathedral.

A few steps south of the museum is the **Parish Church** (Kościół Farny), originally built for the Jesuits by architects from Italy.

After more than 80 years of work (1651–1732), an impressive baroque church was created, with an ornamented facade and a spacious, lofty interior supported on massive columns and crammed with monumental altars.

Facing the church is the former **Jesuit School** (Szkoła Jezuicka), which was granted a college charter by King Zygmunt Waza, later annulled by the pope when the Kraków Academy protested. Today it's the Ballet School; in summer, plays are occasionally performed in the arcaded courtyard of the building.

WIELKOPOLSKA

A five-minute walk east from here is the **Ethnographic Museum** (*Muzeum Etnograficzne;* ☎ *852 30 06, ul Grobla 25; adult/student US$1.50/1, free Sat; open 10am-4pm Tues, Wed, Fri & Sat, 10am-3pm Sun*). It has a good collection of folk woodcarving, especially the large roadside posts and crosses, and the traditional costumes of the region. The entrance to the museum is from ul Mostowa 7, not from ul Grobla as may be assumed from the address and the location on the map.

WEST OF THE OLD TOWN SQUARE

If you head down ul Franciszkańska from the Rynek you'll come to the **Franciscan Church** (Kościół Franciszkanów). Built in 1674–1728, it has a complete baroque interior adorned with wall paintings and rich stucco work. Note the Chapel of the Virgin Mary (Kaplica NMP) in the left transept, with an altar carved in oak and a tiny miraculous image of St Mary.

On the hill opposite the church stands the **castle**, or what is left of it. The original 13th-century castle was repeatedly destroyed and rebuilt. What you see today is the postwar reconstruction of a late 18th-century building, hardly looking like a castle at all. It houses the **Museum of Decorative Arts** (*Muzeum Sztuk Użytkowych;* ☎ *852 20 35, Góra Przemysława 1; adult/student US$1.50/1, free Sat; open 10am-4pm Tues, Wed, Fri & Sat, 10am-3pm Sun*). The collection includes furniture, gold and silverware, glass, ceramics, weapons, clocks, watches and sundials from Europe and the Far East. Exhibits date from the 13th century to the present.

Go west to Plac Wolności, one of the main squares of contemporary Poznań. The finest (and oldest) building here is the neoclassical **Raczyński Library** (Biblioteka Raczyńskich), dating from the 1820s. However, the real interest lies inside the less appealing edifice of the **National Museum** (*Muzeum Narodowe;* ☎ *856 80 00, Al Marcinkowskiego 9; adult/student US$2.50/1.50, free Sat; open 11am-6pm Tues-Sun*), where an extensive collection of Polish and European art is displayed in countless rooms.

Polish painting of the last two centuries is represented by almost all the big names, including Jan Matejko, Stanisław Wyspiański and Jacek Malczewski. The museum also has a reasonable selection of Italian, Spanish, Flemish and Dutch painting.

A curiosity worth noticing is the collection of coffin portraits (see the boxed text 'Coffin Portraits – Funerals Polish-Style' earlier in this chapter). Medieval church woodcarving and painting are displayed in the basement.

The building itself was erected in the early years of the 20th century to serve as the Prussian museum.

There are more examples of Prussian architecture farther to the west, close to the train line. They include the Grand Theatre, the Collegium Maius, the Collegium Minus and, largest of all, the neo-Romanesque **Kaiserhaus** built in 1904–10 for German Emperor Wilhelm II. The castle-like building – gloomy and blackened – is today the Zamek Cultural Centre which houses several cultural institutions.

Next to the Kaiserhaus, on Plac Mickiewicza, stands the **Monument to the Victims of June 1956** (Pomnik Poznańskiego Czerwca 1956), commemorating the workers' tragic protest of 1956 (see the boxed text 'Worker's Strike of 1956' earlier in this chapter). The monument, consisting of two 20m-tall crosses bound together, was unveiled on 28 June 1981, the 25th anniversary, and the ceremony was attended by over 100,000 people.

Farther south, a five-minute walk from the main train station along ul Głogowska, is the Park Wilsona. Enter it and walk to its opposite, northern end to the **Palm House** (*Palmiarnia;* ☎ *865 89 07; adult/student US$1.50/1; open 9am-3pm or 5pm Tues-Sun depending on season*). Built in 1910 and occupying an area of over 4000 sq metres and a volume of 44,000 cu metres, this is one of the biggest greenhouses in Europe. Inside are 19,000 species of tropical and subtropical plants, including reputedly Europe's largest cactus collection and tallest bamboo trees. There's also a collection of exotic fish in the adjacent aquarium.

WIELKOPOLSKA

NORTH OF THE OLD TOWN SQUARE

Beginning from the Rynek, walk north along ul Żydowska. Before WWII this sector was populated mainly by Jews. Turn right into ul Dominikańska to look over the former **Dominican Church** (Kościół Podominikański), now belonging to the Jesuits. Built in the mid-13th century, it's the oldest monument on the left bank of the Warta River. It was repeatedly reshaped and redecorated in later periods but the fine early Gothic doorway at the main entrance is still in place.

Continue on ul Żydowska north to the end of the street, where you'll see a large building (from 1907) which was formerly the **synagogue**; now it's a swimming pool!

Cross the busy thoroughfare and take ul Św Wojciech uphill. You'll soon pass on your right the 15th-century **St Adalbert's Church** (Kościół Św Wojciecha). Its freestanding wooden belfry from the 16th century is the only substantial historic wooden building in Poznań. Inside the church, the Gothic vaulting is decorated with Art Nouveau wall paintings. The crypt beneath, open to visitors, has become a mausoleum for the most eminent Poles from Wielkopolska, among them Józef Wybicki, who wrote the lyrics of the national anthem.

During the Christmas period, the mechanised *szopka* (Nativity scene) is open in the church. It includes several dozen movable figures which depict the history of the region from Mieszko I to the present day.

A few steps up the street is the sloping **Cemetery of the Meritorious** (Cmentarz Zasłużonych), the oldest existing cemetery in the city (1810), with some 19th-century tombstones. Across the street is the modern **Monument to the Poznań Army** (Pomnik Armii Poznań) dedicated to the local armed force which resisted the German invasion of 1939 for almost two weeks.

Farther north is a large park laid out on what was the massive fortress known as the **Citadel** *(Cytadela)*. It was built by the Prussians in the 1830s on a hill once occupied by vineyards. The fortress was involved in one major battle, when the Germans defended themselves for four weeks in 1945. It was completely destroyed and only a few fragments have survived. Today it's the largest city park, and incorporates two museums: the **Museum of Weapons** (☎ 820 45 03; admission US$0.50; open 9am-4pm Tues-Sat, 10am-4pm Sun) and the **Museum of the Poznań Army** (☎ 820 45 03; admission US$0.50; open 9am-4pm Tues-Sat, 10am-4pm Sun). It also has cemeteries for Polish, Soviet and British and Commonwealth soldiers, all on the southern slopes of the hill.

OSTRÓW TUMSKI & BEYOND

The island of Ostrów Tumski is where Poznań and with it the Polish state took their first steps. The original 9th-century settlement was transformed in the mid-10th century into an oval stronghold surrounded by wood-and-earth ramparts, and an early stone palace was built. Mieszko I added a cathedral and further fortified the township. By the end of the 10th century Poznań was the most powerful stronghold in the country.

A couple of centuries later it spread beyond the island, first to the right, then to the left bank of the river. In the 13th century, when the newly designed town was laid out, Ostrów lost its trade and administrative importance but remained the residence of the Church authorities, which it still is.

Today it's a tiny, quiet ecclesiastical quarter, dominated by a monumental double-towered **cathedral**. Basically Gothic with additions from later periods, most notably the baroque tops of the towers, the cathedral was badly damaged in 1945 and its reconstruction took 11 years. Since little of the internal furnishing has survived, the present-day decoration has been collected from other churches, mostly from Silesia.

The aisles and the ambulatory are ringed with a dozen chapels containing numerous tombstones. The most famous of these is the **Golden Chapel** (Złota Kaplica) behind the high altar. Dating from the 15th century, it was completely rebuilt in the 1830s as the mausoleum of the first two Polish rulers, Mieszko I and Bolesław Chrobry. Enveloped in Byzantine-style decoration are the double tomb of the two monarchs on the one side and their bronze statues on the other.

The rulers' original burial site was the **crypt**, accessible from the back of the left-hand aisle. There, apart from the fragments of what are thought to have been their tombs, you can see the relics of the first pre-Romanesque cathedral from 968 and of the subsequent Romanesque building from the second half of the 11th century.

Opposite the cathedral is **St Mary's Church** (Kościół NMP), built in the mid-15th century and virtually unaltered since then. Its internal decoration, though, is modern. Just behind the church is the early 16th-century **Psałteria**, which was home to the choristers.

North of the cathedral is the **Lubrański Academy** (Akademia Lubrańskiego), also known as the Collegium Lubranscianum, the first high school in Poznań (1518). Across the street from it is the **Archdiocesan Museum** (*Muzeum Archidiecezjalne; ☎ 852 61 95, ul Posadzego 2; adult/student US$1/ 0.50; open 9am-3pm Mon-Sat*), which has a collection of sacred art.

Farther east, past the bridge over the Cybina River (a branch of the Warta), is the microscopic Śródka suburb. It was the main trade centre of Poznań in the 13th century, but lost its significance when the town moved to its present site. **St Margaret's Church** (Kościół Św Małgorzaty), originally a 14th-century structure but much altered later, is one of the few remainders of the heyday.

More interesting is the **Church of St John of Jerusalem** (Kościół Św Jana Jerozolimskiego) in the suburb of Komandoria, a five-minute walk farther east, behind the Rondo Śródka. The late 12th-century building (one of the oldest brick churches in the country) was extended in the Gothic period and later acquired a baroque chapel. The interior is an unusual combination of a nave with a single aisle to one side (both with beautiful Gothic star vaults) plus a chapel on the opposite side. Take note of the Romanesque doorway in the main western entrance.

South-east of the church is the 70-hectare artificial Lake Malta (Jezioro Maltańskie), and beyond it a zoo.

SPECIAL EVENTS

Poznań's trade fairs are its pride and joy, the main ones taking place in January, June, September and October, but there are two dozen other fairs throughout the year. July, August and December are fair-free months.

Culturally, major events include the **Poznań Jazz Festival** in March, the **Malta International Theatre Festival** in late June, and the **Wieniawski International Violin Competition** which takes place in October every five years (the next one will be in 2006).

St John's Fair (Jarmark Świętojański), which takes place at the Stary Rynek in June, is a handicraft and antiques fair, but it has been heavily commercialised over recent years.

PLACES TO STAY

Poznań's hotels and private rooms tend to double their prices when trade fairs are on. During major fairs all hotel rooms are likely to be fully booked, and private rooms may be scarce and at distant locations. The prices given in this section are for the 'off-fair' periods. Both tourist offices and Glob Tour are knowledgeable about the city's lodging options and are likely to help you find a bed.

Places to Stay – Budget

Camping Poznań has three camping grounds, and all have cabins.

Camping Nr 111 Strzeszynek (☎ 848 31 29, ul Koszalińska 15) Quad/quin cabins without bath US$35/40. Open May-Sept. This camping ground is in the Strzeszynek suburb, about 10km north-west of the centre.

Camping Nr 30 Baranowo (☎ 814 28 12) Quin cabins without bath US$40. Open May-Sept. Baranowo camp site is on Lake Kierskie, on the north-western outskirts of the city, about 11km from the centre.

Camping Nr 155 Malta (☎ 876 62 03, fax 867 62 83, ul Krańcowa 98) Double/triple/ quin cabins with private bath & kitchenette US$40/60/80. Open year-round. Malta is the best (but also the priciest) city camp site, and the closest one to the centre. It's on the north-eastern shore of Lake Malta, 3km east of the Old Town. It has 152 beds in 66 heated cabins, plus a restaurant.

Youth Hostels There are four all-year youth hostels in the city.

Youth hostel (*☎/fax 866 40 40, ul Berwińskiego 2/3)* Beds US$4-6. This is the closest youth hostel to the city centre; it's a 10-minute walk south-west from the train station along ul Głogowska. It's the smallest and the most basic of the lot and fills up fast. It has two doubles but most of its 52 beds are in eight- to 10-bed dorms.

Youth hostel (*☎/fax 848 58 36, ul Drzymały 3)* Beds US$5-8. This is the newest (and perhaps best) youth hostel. A good part of its nearly 100 beds are in small dorms. It's 3km north of the train station and 3km from the Old Town. To get there, take tram No 11 from the train station and tram No 9 from the Old Town.

Youth hostel (*☎/fax 822 10 63, ul Biskupińska 27)* Beds US$4-8. This 75-bed hostel is also good, with many small dorms, but it's a long way from the centre, about 7km north-west in the suburb of Strzeszyn. Bus No 60 from ul Solna on the northern edge of the centre will take you there.

Youth hostel (*☎/fax 878 84 61, ul Głuszyna 127)* Beds US$4-8. This is another reasonably good youth hostel, but it's still less convenient; it's on the southern city limits over 10km from the centre and there's no direct transport.

Private Rooms Rooms in private homes are arranged by several agencies, the largest of which is **Biuro Zakwaterowania Przemysław** (*☎ 866 35 60, ul Głogowska 16)*, opposite the train station. The office is open 8am to 6pm weekdays, 10am to 2pm Saturday (longer at fair times). Rooms normally go for US$12/18 a single/double, but it's roughly double that at fair times. Rooms are almost always available, but at fair times there may be less choice.

Places to Stay – Mid-Range

Mini Hotelik (*☎ 863 14 15, Al Niepodległości 8)* Singles/doubles without bath US$15/30, doubles with bath US$35. This new small hotel, with only eight rooms, is good value given its location, standards and rates.

Pokoje Gościnne MCM (*☎ 853 66 69, ul Skośna 1)* Doubles with bath US$35. This five-room place, near the June 1956 Monument, is also an interesting proposition due to its central location, acceptable standards and reasonable price – good value.

Hotel Wielkopolska (*☎ 852 76 31, fax 851 54 92, ul Św Marcin 67)* Singles/doubles without bath US$30/40, with bath US$45/55. This old hotel doesn't provide great luxuries but is affordable and well located. It's gradually being refurbished so the budget rooms without bath are likely to disappear in the future.

Dom Turysty (*☎/fax 852 88 93, Stary Rynek 91, enter from ul Wroniecka)* Singles/doubles/triples without bath US$30/ 42/48, with bath US$45/75/90; beds in 4-/5-bed dorms without bath US$15. Located in the 1798 former palace (destroyed in 1944 and reconstructed later) right on the market square, Dom Turysty is essentially a top-end place judging by its prices (not its standards) but has some cheaper dorms. Rooms are overpriced but you are paying for location and, apparently, the palatial appearance from the outside (nothing palatial inside).

Dom Polonii (*☎/fax 853 19 61, Stary Rynek 51)* Single/double with bath US$30/ 48. Ideally located on the old market square, the Dom Polonii has just two top-floor double rooms, one of which overlooks the Rynek. They usually need to be booked well in advance.

Pokoje Gościnne PAN (*☎ 851 68 41, ul Wieniawskiego 17/19)* Singles/doubles with bath & breakfast US$35/50. Well located in a quiet, leafy area behind the Grand Theatre, the PAN provides 48 beds in comfortable rooms.

Places to Stay – Top End

Hotel Rzymski (*☎ 852 81 21, fax 852 89 83, Al Marcinkowskiego 22)* Singles/doubles with bath & breakfast US$45/65. Within a short walking distance of the Rynek, this well-established 87-room hotel is not a bad choice, although don't expect Sheraton-type facilities.

Hotel Ibis (*☎ 858 44 00, fax 858 44 44, ul Kazimierza Wielkiego 23)* Doubles with bath & breakfast US$60. Similar to any other in the Ibis chain scattered all over Europe, this new Poznań outlet offers 145 air-conditioned rooms within an easy walk of the city's historic heart.

Hotel Royal (☎ 858 23 00, fax 853 78 84, ul Św Marcin 71) Singles/doubles with bath & breakfast US$70/100. The 27-room Royal has recently undergone a thorough refurbishing and now better befits its name. It's a comfortable central choice.

Hotel Park (☎ 879 40 81, fax 877 38 30, ul Majakowskiego 77) Singles/doubles with bath & breakfast US$90/120. For those who prefer to stay outside the downtown rush, the comfortable 100-room Park, on the southern bank of Lake Malta, may be a pleasant choice. Ask about attractive weekend discount rates.

Hotel Meridian (☎ 847 15 64, fax 847 34 41, ul Litewska 22) Singles/doubles with bath & breakfast US$70/100. With just 10 double rooms, the cosy Meridian also enjoys a quiet, waterfront location and is at the same time reasonably close to the centre.

Hotel Trawiński (☎ 827 58 00, fax 820 57 81, ul Żniwna 2) Singles/doubles with bath & breakfast US$100/125. A new, comfortable and tranquil accommodation option with most of the modern facilities such as air-conditioning, gym and sauna, Trawiński is one of the city's best hotels. It's on the western edge of Park Cytadela, 2.5km north of the centre.

PLACES TO EAT

Poznań has a wide range of eateries for every pocket, including a variety of fast-food outlets and posh restaurants. The majority of the places to eat are in the Old Town and west of it, particularly along ul Św Marcin and ul 27 Grudnia.

Bar Mleczny Apetyt (☎ 852 13 39, ul Szkolna 4) Mains US$1.50-2.50. Very central and open unusually long (till 10pm) for a milk bar, Apetyt has a choice of crepes and other popular Polish plates.

Bar Caritas (☎ 852 51 30, Plac Wolności 1) Mains US$1.50-2.50. Another popular milk-bar option, Caritas offers a long list of crepes and other dishes but it closes earlier.

Other convenient milk bars include *Bar Mleczny Przysmak* (☎ 847 48 47, ul Roosevelta 22); *Bar Mleczny Pod Kuchcikiem* (☎ 853 60 94, ul Św Marcin 75) and *Bar Podbipięta* (☎ 852 03 93, ul Podgórna 19).

Bar Wegetariański (☎ 852 12 55, ul Wrocławska 21) Mains US$1-2. This simple, tiny place is so far the only purely vegetarian eatery in town.

Bar Avanti (☎ 852 32 85, Stary Rynek 76) Spaghetti US$1-1.50. The very cheap and popular Avanti serves tasty platefuls of spaghetti, lasagna and a few salads. It has a 24-hour outlet at the main train station.

Spaghetti Bar Piccolo (☎ 851 72 51, ul Rynkowa 1) Spaghetti US$1-1.50. Another budget spaghetti affair, the tiny Piccolo, just off Stary Rynek, is even marginally cheaper than the Avanti. It also has some salads. There's another larger Piccolo outlet at ul Ratajczaka 37.

Gospoda Pod Koziołkami (☎ 851 78 68, Stary Rynek 95) Salads US$2-4, mains US$3-5. This pleasant place has a reasonable choice of salads and grilled meat and is open till late.

Restauracja Sphinx (☎ 852 07 02, ul Św Marcin 66/72) Mains US$3-5. As elsewhere, the Sphinx serves good-value grilled dishes and popular Middle-Eastern fare. Its new outlet at Stary Rynek 77 is even more popular and often full.

Trattoria Valpolicella (☎ 855 71 91, ul Wrocławska 7) Mains US$7-12. Valpolicella serves up a wide variety of pastas and other Italian specialities in finely decorated surroundings.

Restauracja Kredens Za Kulisami (☎ 855 32 60, ul Ratajczaka 44) Mains US$10-15. An amazing artistic creation, the Kredens serves European food in an interior crammed with old theatrical paraphernalia – it's certainly a memorable place. Enter from Plac Wolności.

Restauracja Delicja (☎ 852 11 28, Plac Wolności 5) Mains US$10-18. Another memorable place, though completely different to the Kredens, the Delicja is beautifully old-fashioned and elegant. It offers fine international cuisine, plus an imposing choice of wines.

WIELKOPOLSKA

Restauracja Orfeusz (☎ 851 98 44, ul Świętosławska 12) Mains US$10-15. Another possible address for fine dining in elegant traditional surroundings, the Orfeusz has Polish and European cuisine.

ENTERTAINMENT

Poznań has a comprehensive what's-on monthly, *iks* (US$1), containing listings and comments on everything from museums to outdoor activities, plus a useful city map. It's in Polish, but has a short summary of the most important events in English. It's available from Ruch kiosks and the tourist offices. The free monthly *City Magazine Poznań* can be an additional help, especially for lighter fare such as pubs, rock concerts etc.

Pubs & Bars

Poznań has plenty of these but the picture is pretty volatile. You're sure to find at least two dozen summer beer gardens on the main market square alone – just take your pick. Of other, less conspicuous, watering holes, you may try:

Muchos Patatos (☎ 851 91 73, ul Szewska 2) This was (maybe still is) one of the trendiest hang-outs among young locals when we were there, possibly due to a fine combination of hot Cuban rhythms, budget Mexican snacks and bright tropical colours on the walls, all accompanied by plenty of drinks headed by the legendary Cuba Libre. It was so successful that *El Otro Muchos Patatos* opened just off Stary Rynek, with much the same style and atmosphere.

Stara Piwnica (Stary Rynek 92) One of the cheapest pubs on the main square, the 'Old Cellar' occupies several pleasant cosy vaults.

Tawerna (☎ 851 69 36, ul Wrocławska 4, enter from ul Kozia) Another enjoyable brick vaulted place with cheap beer, Tawerna has comfortable armchairs and may have live music at times.

Pub Pod Aniołami (ul Wrocławska 4) Round the corner from the Taverna, 'Under the Angels' is a pleasant street-level pub that apart from drinks has a short food menu.

Woland Variétés (☎ 851 02 84, ul Wrocławska 18) This is sort of a music club

hosting different music genres (folk, blues, jazz) in its two-level locale, each level arranged in completely different style. Note the giant mirror.

Cocorico Café (☎ 665 84 67, ul Świętosławska 9) This pleasant, quiet cafe has a lovely decor and an amazing leafy back garden.

Discos

Galaxy (☎ 851 60 22, Stary Rynek 87/88) A vast basement establishment at the main square, Galaxy is the most central of the city discos. It's frequented mostly by students and young folk.

Imperium Club (ul Kantaka 2/4) Also large and reasonably cheap, this is another popular student haunt.

Studio Jack Live (☎ 852 05 22, ul Działyńskich 10) More expensive than Imperium and Galaxy, the double-level Jack Live has good lights and a lot of techno music.

Jama (☎ 833 25 90, ul Chwiałkowskiego 35/37) This is the most expensive and exclusive disco, attracting a more affluent clientele.

Zamek Cultural Centre

Centrum Kultury Zamek (☎ 852 32 38, ul Św Marcin 80/82) Located in the Kaiserhaus, this is an active cultural centre featuring art cinema, several art galleries, music and other events. In summer, concerts are staged in the building's courtyard.

Zamek is also home to two important music haunts:

Blue Note Jazz Club (☎ 851 04 08, enter from ul Kościuszki) Blue Note is arguably Poznań's major jazz spot, with pretty regular concerts and jam sessions by local groups and occasional gigs by big names passing through the city.

Dubliner Pub (☎ 851 01 69, enter from Al Niepodległości) The Dubliner is a rock haunt, with live music usually on Thursday to Saturday nights.

Classical Music

Filharmonia (☎ 852 47 08, ul Św Marcin 81) The Philharmonic Hall has concerts at least once a week on Friday, performed by the local symphony orchestra and often by visiting artists. Poznań has Poland's best boys' choir, the Polskie Słowiki (Polish Nightingales), which can be heard here.

Opera & Ballet

Teatr Wielki (Grand Theatre; ☎ 852 82 91, ul Fredry 9) This is the usual stage for opera, ballet and various visiting performances. Polski Teatr Tańca (Polish Dance Theatre; ☎ 852 42 41), ul Kozia 4, one of the best groups of its kind in Poland, also performs at the Teatr Wielki when it's in town.

Theatre

Teatr Polski (Polish Theatre; ☎ 852 56 27, ul 27 Grudnia 8/10) The Teatr Polski is Poznań's main repertory theatre, which often includes some classics in its repertoire.

Teatr Nowy (New Theatre; ☎ 848 48 85, ul Dąbrowskiego 5) Another important city theatre, this one tends more towards contemporary productions.

Teatr Muzyczny (Musical Theatre; ☎ 852 17 86, ul Niezłomnych 1) The Muzyczny features Broadway-style shows.

There are also two excellent performing groups worth mentioning. Teatr Ósmego Dnia (Theatre of the Eighth Day; ☎ 852 77 14), ul Ratajczaka 44, is one of Poland's best alternative groups. It started in the 1960s as an avant-garde, politically involved student theatre. It's still impressive and creative, performing more outdoor than indoor. Teatr Biuro Podróży (Travel Agency Theatre; ☎ 829 39 07), ul Madalińskiego 4/12, is another of Poznań's excellent street theatre groups which has gained acclaim country-wide and beyond.

GETTING THERE & AWAY
Air

The airport is in the western suburb of Ławica, 7km from the centre and accessible by several bus lines. Direct connections include six flights a day to Warsaw, one to Brussels, one to Copenhagen, one to Düsseldorf and one to Hanover. All are serviced by LOT, which has an office (☎ 858 55 00) at ul Piekary 6.

Train

Poznań is a busy railway hub. There are about 20 trains to Warsaw daily (311km), including the EuroCity and InterCity trains which take just over three hours. Almost equally frequent are services to Wrocław (165km) and Szczecin (214km), and there are also six fast trains direct to Kraków daily (398km).

Gdańsk (313km) is serviced by two express and five fast trains, and Toruń (142km) by two fast and two ordinary trains; all pass via Gniezno (51km). Six trains depart for Zielona Góra daily (139km).

Six international trains run to Berlin daily (261km), including four EuroCity trains which take just three hours to get there. There are also direct trains to Budapest, Cologne, Kyiv and Moscow.

Tickets and couchette reservations are handled by the train station or Orbis Travel (☎ 852 49 94) at Al Marcinkowskiego 21.

Bus

The PKS bus terminal is a 10-minute walk east of the train station. Buses run half-hourly to Kórnik (20km) and every couple of hours to Rogalin (24km or 31km, depending on the route). You can also get to Kórnik by hourly suburban bus NB from ul Św Marcin near the rail track. Buses to Gniezno (49km) depart hourly or so and go via either Kostrzyn or Pobiedziska; the latter pass Lake Lednica. On longer routes, you may use buses to get to Kalisz (130km) and Zielona Góra (130km), as they run more frequently than trains.

GETTING AROUND

Poznań's public transport system uses both time tickets (fare depends on how much time the journey takes) and distance tickets (fare depends on how many stops you travel). Time tickets cost US$0.25 for a 10-minute ride, US$0.50 for a half-hour trip, US$0.75 for a journey up to one hour, and US$4 for a 90-minute trip. Approximate times of rides are posted at bus and tram stops. Distance tickets cost US$0.50 for a ride up to 10 stops and US$0.70 for any longer trip.

WIELKOPOLSKA

Around Poznań

SWARZĘDZ
☎ 61 • pop 26,000

Swarzędz ('**Sfah**-zhents') is a satellite town of Poznań, 11km east of the city on the Warsaw road. It's widely known as one of Poland's main furniture producers, with a large factory and some 300 small carpentry workshops. Tourists, however, may be more interested in the **Open-Air Museum of Apiculture** (Skansen Pszczelarstwa; ☎ 651 18 17, ul Poznańska 35; adult/student US$1/0.75; open 9am-4pm Tues-Fri, 10am-3pm Sat & Sun).

Established in 1963, the skansen is in a small park squeezed between the busy Poznań-Warsaw highway and the equally busy railway line. It's devoted exclusively to bee-keeping and has the largest and most diverse collection of beehives in Poland – over 200 specimens. They range from simple hollow trunks (the oldest dating from the 14th century) to intriguing basket-like examples woven of straw. There are also beehives carved and painted in the shapes of people, animals, churches, houses, windmills – and even faithful copies of Poznań's town hall and cathedral.

Frequent city buses go to Swarzędz from Rondo Śródka in Poznań. The skansen is on the right-hand side of the road just before Swarzędz; ask the driver where to get off.

KÓRNIK
☎ 61 • pop 6000

An uninspiring small town 20km south-east of Poznań, Kórnik has found its way into the tourist brochures thanks to its **castle**. It was built by the powerful Górka family in the 15th century, but changed hands and was much altered in later periods. Its present-day appearance dates from the mid-19th century, when its owner at the time, Tytus Działyński, a fervent patriot and art collector, gave the castle a somewhat eccentric, fortified mock-Gothic character, partly based on a design by German architect Karl Friedrich Schinkel.

The interior was extensively remodelled as well, to provide a plush family home and accommodate the owner's collection. On the 1st floor a spectacular Moorish Hall was created, clearly influenced by the Alhambra in Granada, as a memorable setting for the display of armour and military accessories. The collection was expanded by Tytus' son Jan and his nephew Władysław Zamoyski; the latter donated the castle and its contents to the state in 1924.

The castle luckily survived the war and, miraculously, so did its contents. Part of it is now open as a **museum** (☎ 817 00 81, ul Zamkowa 5; adult/student US$2/1; open 9am-3pm Tues-Sun Mar-Nov, till 5pm June-Aug). You can wander through its fully furnished and decorated 19th-century interiors, some of which have family collections on display.

Behind the castle is a large, English-style park known as the **Arboretum** (☎ 817 01 55; adult/student US$1/0.50; open 9am-5pm daily May-Sept, 9am-3pm daily Oct-Apr), which was laid out during the castle's reconstruction. Numerous exotic species of trees and shrubs were imported from leading European nurseries, and Kórnik was considered to be the best stocked park in the country. Many species were later transplanted to Gołuchów where Jan Działyński was creating his new residence. Today the arboretum is run by a scientific research institute and has some 3000 plant species and varieties.

One more place to visit is the **coach house** (powozownia), 150m towards the town centre from the castle, on the opposite side of the road. Three London coaches, brought by Jan Działyński from Paris in 1856, can be seen here.

Getting There & Away

There's frequent bus transport from Poznań to Kórnik (20km). You can either take the PKS bus from the central bus terminal (departing every half-hour or so) or go by suburban bus NB from ul Św Marcin (hourly). Either bus will deposit you at the Rynek in Kórnik, a three-minute walk to the castle.

If you plan to continue on to Rogalin (13km), there are approximately five buses daily (check the timetable before visiting the castle).

ROGALIN
☎ 61 • pop 800

The tiny village of Rogalin, 13km west of Kórnik, was the seat of yet another Polish aristocratic clan, the Raczyński family, who built a **palace** here in the closing decades of the 18th century, and lived in it until WWII. Typically for such country residences of the period, the complex included a garden and park and some outbuildings complete with stables and coach house. Plundered but not damaged during WWII, the complex was taken over by the state and is today a branch of Poznań's National Museum (☎ 813 80 30; adult/student US$2/1.50; open 10am-4pm Tues-Sun).

Less visited than Kórnik's castle and quite different in its appearance, the Rogalin palace consists of a massive two-storey baroque central structure and two modest symmetrical wings linked to the main body by curving galleries, forming a giant horse-shoe enclosing a vast forecourt. The main house is closed due to snail-pace restoration, but the wings are open and used for temporary displays of some of the Raczyński collection.

Just beyond the left wing is the **Gallery of Painting** (Galeria Obrazów), with a display of Polish and European canvases from the 19th and early 20th centuries. The Polish collection has some first class work, with Jacek Malczewski best represented. The dominant work, though, is Jan Matejko's colossal *Joan of Arc*.

In the **coach house** by the front courtyard are a dozen old coaches, including Poznań's last horse-drawn cab.

Behind the palace is an unkempt **French garden** with a mound at the far end, which would have provided the owner with a fine view over his home.

West beyond the garden, the **English landscaped park** was laid out in primeval oak forest. Not much of the park's design can be deciphered today, but the ancient oak trees are still there. The three most imposing specimens have been fenced off and baptised with the names Lech, Czech and Rus, after the legendary founders of the Polish, Czech and Russian nations. The largest

– 9m in circumference – is Rus, and it also seems to be in the best health.

One more place to see is the **chapel** on the eastern outskirts of the village. It was built in the 1820s to serve as a mausoleum for the family and is a replica of the Roman temple known as Maison Carrée in Nîmes, southern France. The vaulted crypt beneath the church houses several dilapidated tombstones. The priest living in the house behind the church may open it for you.

Getting There & Away

There are several buses from Poznań to Rogalin going by various routes. Buses from Rogalin back to Poznań pass through every couple of hours till late afternoon; check the timetable before visiting the palace and plan accordingly.

WIELKOPOLSKA NATIONAL PARK
☎ 061

The 76-sq-km Wielkopolska National Park (Wielkopolski Park Narodowy) is just a few kilometres south-west of Poznań's administrative boundaries. About 80% of the park is forest – pine and oak being the dominant species – and its postglacial lakes give it a certain charm. It's reputedly one of the most interesting stretches of land in Wielkopolska, for its diversity and for the variety of flora and fauna concentrated in its small area. It can be a pleasant day away from the city rush.

Hiking

Getting to the park from Poznań is easy, and there are walking trails leading into it from different sides. If you plan on a day trip, a good point to start is the town of Mosina (21km from Poznań), served regularly by both train and bus from Poznań. From Mosina, follow the blue-marked trail heading north-west to Osowa Góra (3km). Once you reach the small round Lake Kociołek, switch to the red trail which winds south-westwards. After passing another miniature lake, the trail reaches Lake Góreckie, the most beautiful body of water in the park. The trail then skirts the eastern part of the lake and turns north-east to bring you eventually to the town of Puszczykowo, from where trains and buses can take you back to Poznań. It's about a 17km walk altogether, through what's probably the most attractive area of the park.

If you want to do more walking, there are four more trails to choose from. They cover most of the park and cross each other at several points. Get a copy of the *Wielkopolski Park Narodowy* map (scale 1:35,000), which has all the details.

Places to Stay & Eat

Both Puszczykowo and Mosina provide food and accommodation. They conveniently sit on the eastern edge of the park, just 4km apart, on the Poznań-Wrocław railway line (with regular transport in both directions).

Hotel Morena (☎ 813 27 46, fax 813 60 43, ul Konopnickiej 1, Mosina) Doubles without/with bath US$15/25. Morena is simple but cheap and acceptable and has its own *restaurant*.

Hotel Hubertus (☎/fax 813 22 60, ul Chopina 42, Mosina) Singles/doubles with bath US$25/30. Another option in Mosina, Hubertus is a small place which provides a bit more comfort than Morena.

Pensjonat Sadyba (☎ 813 31 28, ul Brzozowa 15A, Puszczykowo) Singles US$8, beds in doubles, triples or quads US$7. If you want a budget shelter in Puszczykowo, Sadyba is not a bad choice though rooms don't have private baths.

Motel Pod Kukułką (☎ 813 38 47, ul Reymonta 17, Puszczykowo) Beds in triples or larger dorms US$7. This is another inexpensive option with shared facilities, but has no singles or doubles.

The Piast Route

The Piast Route (Szlak Piastowski) is a popular tourist route winding from Poznań to Kruszwica. It covers places related to the early centuries of the Polish state, and historic monuments from that period, including the Iron Age village of Biskupin.

LAKE LEDNICA
☎ 61

Lake Lednica, 30km east of Poznań, is the first important point on the Piast Route. The 7km elongated postglacial lake has four islands, the largest of which, Ostrów Lednicki, was an important defensive and administrative outpost of the early Polish state.

Excavations have shown that Ostrów Lednicki was one of the major settlements of the first Piasts in the late 10th and early 11th centuries, rivalling Poznań and Gniezno. It was settled as early as the Stone Age, and in the 10th century a stronghold was built here along with a stone palace and a church. Two wooden bridges were constructed to link the island to the western and eastern shores of the lake, and it was over these bridges that the route between Poznań and Gniezno ran. The western bridge was 428m long and its foundations were nearly 12m under water at the deepest point.

The settlement was overrun and destroyed in 1038 by the Bohemians, and though the church and the defensive ramparts were rebuilt, the island never regained its previous importance. Between the 12th and 14th centuries a large part of it was used as a graveyard. Some 2000 tombs have been found here, making the site the largest cemetery from that period discovered in Central Europe.

Some of the finds of the excavations are on display in the museum established opposite the island. There is also an interesting skansen nearby.

Museum

The **Museum of the First Piasts** (*Muzeum Pierwszych Piastów;* ☎ 427 50 10, *Lednogóra; adult/student US$1.25/0.75; open 9am-3pm Tues-Sun 15 Feb-14 Apr & 1-15 Nov, 9am-5pm Tues-Sun 16-30 Apr & 1 July-31 Oct, 10am-6pm Tues-Sun 1 May-30 June, closed 16 Nov-14 Feb)* is on the lakeshore facing the island of Ostrów Lednicki. Among the buildings in the grounds is the oldest windmill in Poland (1585), and an 18th-century granary which has a display of human remains excavated on the island and at the cemetery behind the museum.

The main exhibition is in the church-like building, which has two floors of finds from excavations on and around the island. Among the exhibits, most of which date from the 10th and 11th centuries, are weapons, household items and implements, pottery and ornaments, and a dugout canoe which is one of the very few wooden objects to have survived for almost a millennium.

A small boat takes visitors (from mid-April to early November) from the museum's jetty to the island of Ostrów Lednicki, 175m away, where you can see what's left of the palace and the church. The foundations and lower parts of the walls are still in place and give a rough idea of how big the complex was. There are some helpful drawings in the museum of what the buildings might have looked like.

Skansen

Two kilometres south of the museum, also on the lakeshore, is the **Wielkopolska Ethnographic Park** (*Wielkopolski Park Etnograficzny;* ☎ *427 50 40, Dziekanowice; adult/student US$1.50/0.75; open 9am-3pm Tues-Sun 15 Feb-14 Apr & 1-15 Nov, 9am-5pm Tues-Sun 16-30 Apr & 1 July-31 Oct, 10am-6pm Tues-Sun 1 May-30 June, closed 16 Nov-14 Feb).* It's on the eastern side of the lake, 500m north of the Poznań-Gniezno road.

The skansen features a good selection of 19th-century rural architecture from Wielkopolska. About half of a typical village has been re-created so far and several houses can be visited. Just to the south is a manor house and its outbuildings, but they're occupied by the administration and can only be seen from the outside.

Getting There & Away

The lake lies on the Poznań-Gniezno road and there's a fairly regular bus service between the two cities. From whichever end you start, take the bus via Pobiedziska, not via Kostrzyn. If you are coming from Poznań, you'll see three old windmills on the hill to the left of the road, but don't get off there. Stay on the bus for another 2.5km and get off at the turn-off to Komorowo

(the bus stop is just by the turn-off). From here it's only a five-minute walk to the skansen. Another 25-minute walk north on a sealed road will bring you to the museum.

GNIEZNO
☎ 61 • pop 73,000

Gniezno ('**Gnyez**-no') is commonly considered to be the cradle of the Polish state, for it was probably the major stronghold of the Polanie, and the dispersed tribes of the region were unified from here in the 10th century.

Legend has it that Gniezno was founded by the mythical Lech, the grandson of the legendary Piast and the grandfather of Mieszko I, who, while hunting in the area, found the nest (*gniazdo*) of a white eagle, giving the town its name and the nation its emblem.

In historical terms, the settlement most likely existed since the 7th or 8th century, and was initially the centre of a pagan cult. Archaeological excavations have shown that by the end of the 8th century Gniezno was already fortified with wood and earth ramparts, and had regular trade links with commercial centres far outside the region.

This early development contributed to the key role that the town played. Duke Mieszko I is thought to have been baptised here in 966, thus raising Poland (at that time the region of Wielkopolska) from obscurity to the rank of Christianised nations. Gniezno was then made the capital of the newborn state.

Historical records from these early days are scarce, and don't show precisely where the capital was, though it's likely that Mieszko favoured Poznań over Gniezno. The first cathedral was, after all, built in Poznań, and the ruler was buried there.

Gniezno came to the fore in the year 1000, when the archbishopric was established here, and its position was further strengthened in 1025 when Bolesław Chrobry was crowned in the local cathedral as the first Polish king. Only 13 years later, the Bohemians invaded and devastated the region – Poznań, Gniezno and other strongholds alike – and the seat of power was shifted to the more secure Kraków in Małopolska.

WIELKOPOLSKA

This inevitably deprived the town of its importance, though kings were crowned in Gniezno until the end of the 13th century (but buried in Poznań). The town retained its status as the seat of the Church of Poland, and continues to be the formal ecclesiastical capital, even though archbishops are only occasional guests these days.

Information

The Biuro Informacji Turystycznej (☎ 428 41 00), ul Tumska 12, is open 9am to 6pm weekdays, 10am to 2pm Saturday. Bank Pekao is at ul Dąbrówki 14. Internet facilities include Centrum Internetowe Terabajt, ul Mieszka I 9, and Internet Pub Małpa, ul Tumska 15.

Cathedral

Gniezno's pride and joy is its cathedral, a large, double-towered brick Gothic structure, which looks pretty similar to the one in Poznań. The present church is already the third or fourth building on this site (the first was built in the 970s), and was constructed in the second half of the 14th century after the destruction of the Romanesque cathedral by the Teutonic Knights in 1331. It changed a lot in later periods: chapels sprouted all around it, and the interior was redecorated in successive styles. After considerable damage in WWII, it was rebuilt according to the original Gothic structure.

Inside, the focal point is the elaborate silver **sarcophagus of St Adalbert** in the chancel. The baroque coffin, topped with the reclining figure of the saint, is the work of Peter van der Rennen and was made in 1662 in Gdańsk.

St Adalbert was a Bohemian bishop who in 997 passed through Gniezno on a missionary trip to convert the Prussians, a heathen Baltic tribe which inhabited what is now Masuria in north-eastern Poland. The pagans were less than enthusiastic about accepting the new faith and terminated the bishop's efforts by cutting off his head. Bolesław Chrobry recovered the body, paying its weight in gold, then buried it in Gniezno's cathedral in 999. In the same year, Pope Sylvester canonised the martyr.

This contributed to Gniezno's elevation to an archbishopric a year later, and also led to the placing of several important memorials to the saint in the church.

One of these is the red marble **tombstone of St Adalbert**, made around 1480 by Hans Brandt. Unfortunately, it has been moved from the middle of the church to behind the high altar and it's impossible to get close to see it.

Easier to appreciate are two carved tombstones on the back wall of the church: to the left is the red marble **tomb of Primate Zbigniew Oleśnicki**, attributed to Veit Stoss; and to the right, the late 15th-century bronze **tomb of Archbishop Jakub** from Sienna. Also note an expressive wooden crucifix from around 1440, placed high on the rood beam at the entrance to the chancel.

The most precious possession of the church is the pair of Romanesque **bronze doors** from about 1175, in the back of the right-hand (southern) aisle, at the entrance from the porch. Undeniably one of the best examples of Romanesque art in Europe, the doors depict, in bas-relief, 18 scenes from the life of St Adalbert. They are ordered chronologically from the bottom side of the left-hand door – where the birth of the saint is portrayed – up to its top and then down the other door to the final scene of the burial in the cathedral.

Framing the doors is the exquisite 15th-century **Gothic portal** with the scene of the Last Judgment in its tympanum. In the opposite porch, right across the nave, is another elaborate **Gothic portal**, dating from the same period, this one with the scene of the Crucifixion in its tympanum.

The nearby entrance in the back wall of the church leads downstairs to the **basement** where the relics of the previous Romanesque cathedral can be seen, along with the Gothic tombstones of the bishops.

All along the aisles and the ambulatory are **chapels**, built from the 15th to 18th centuries, and separated from the aisles by decorative wrought-iron screens. There are 17 screens in all, ranging in style from Gothic via Renaissance to baroque, and they reputedly make for the most beautiful collection

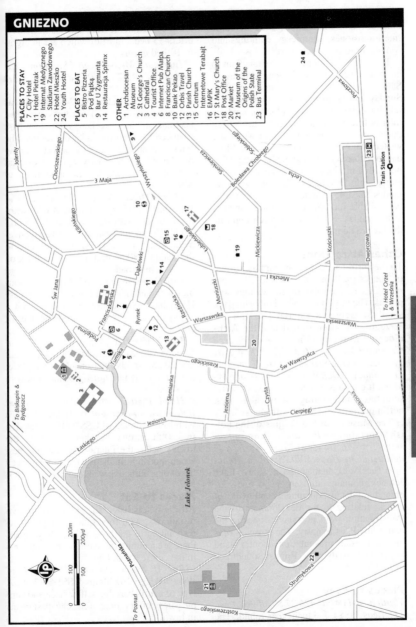

GNIEZNO

PLACES TO STAY
7 City Hotel
11 Hotel Pietrak
19 Internat Medycznego
22 Studium Zawodowego
Hotel Mieszko
24 Youth Hostel

PLACES TO EAT
5 Bistro Pizzeria
Pod Piątką
9 Bar U Zygmunta
14 Restauracja Sphinx

OTHER
1 Archdiocesan
Museum
2 St George's Church
3 Cathedral
4 Tourist Office
6 Internet Pub Małpa
8 Franciscan Church
10 Bank Pekao
12 Orbis Travel
13 Parish Church
15 Centrum
16 Internetowe Terabajt
EMPIK
17 St Mary's Church
18 Post Office
20 Market
21 Museum of the
Origins of the
Polish State
23 Bus Terminal

WIELKOPOLSKA

of its kind gathered in a single church in Poland. Inside the chapels, there are some fine tombstones, altarpieces, paintings and wall decorations – well worth a closer look.

The cathedral is open for visitors 9am to noon and 12.30pm to 5.30pm Monday to Saturday, 1pm to 3pm and 4pm to 5.30pm Sunday and holidays, unless there are any religious services. You can look around the interior free of charge, except for the bronze doors and the basement, both of which are visited (9am to noon and 1pm to 5pm Monday to Saturday) with a guide for a small fee, but with a minimum of US$3 per group for either sight. English or German-speaking guides for a 45-minute cathedral tour may be available for US$20 per group – inquire at the guides' office in the porch opposite the bronze doors.

Other Attractions

To the north-east of the cathedral is a group of houses built in the 18th and 19th centuries as residences for the canons and priests. The largest of them, right behind the small St George's Church (Kościół Św Jerzego), has been turned into the **Archdiocesan Museum** (*Muzeum Archidiecezji Gnieźnieńskiej;* ☎ 426 37 78, ul Kolegiaty 2; admission US$0.75; open 10am-4pm Tues-Sun Apr-Oct, 9am-3pm Tues-Sat Nov-Mar). It contains a rich collection of sacral sculpture and painting, liturgical fabrics, coffin portraits and votive offerings.

The **Museum of the Origins of the Polish State** (*Muzeum Początków Państwa Polskiego;* ☎ 426 46 41, ul Kostrzewskiego 1; adult/student US$1.50/0.75; open 10am-5pm Tues-Sun), on the opposite side of Lake Jelonek, contains archaeological finds, architectural details, documents and works of art, all relating to the development of the Polish nation from pre-Slavic times to the end of the Piast dynasty. The museum runs an audiovisual presentation about Poland under the Piast dynasty (English soundtrack available).

Places to Stay

Youth hostel (*☎/fax 426 27 80, ul Pocztowa 11*) Beds US$4-7. Open year-round. The youth hostel is just a five-minute walk north-east from the train and bus stations. It offers 55 beds, most of which are in eight-to 10-bed dorms.

Internat Medycznego Studium Zawodowego (*☎ 426 34 09, ul Mieszka I 27*) Beds in doubles US$8. This is a dorm of a medical college, but it rents 24 double rooms to the general public. The rooms are quiet, neat and ample – excellent value. One bath is shared between four adjacent rooms. The Internat is at the back of the corner building of Zespół Szkół Medycznych (Medical School); get there by the gate from ul Mieszka I.

Hotel Orzeł (*☎/fax 426 49 25, ul Wrzesińska 25*) Singles/doubles/triples without bath US$10/18/24, with bath US$16/28/34. Cheap but basic and not very convenient, Orzeł is a former sports dorm next to the stadium, 800m past the railway track on the Września road.

City Hotel (*☎ 425 35 35, Rynek 15*) Doubles without/with bath US$20/28. The City Hotel has seven double rooms. It's not a classy place, but is very central and doesn't cost a fortune.

Hotel Mieszko (*☎/fax 426 46 25, ul Strumykowa 2*) Singles/doubles with bath US$20/25. Another reasonably cheap place, the Mieszko is in a quiet green area next to the stadium.

Hotel Pietrak (*☎/fax 426 14 97, ul Bolesława Chrobrego 3*) Singles/doubles with bath & breakfast US$36/45. Located in two 18th-century burgher houses in the town's heart, the Pietrak provides the best accommodation in the town centre and may have some attractive weekend discount rates.

Places to Eat

All the hotels listed above have their own restaurants, with food quality roughly corresponding to the hotel price. These apart, there are a number of eating establishments in the centre, including:

Bar U Zygmunta (*☎ 426 37 74, ul Wyszyńskiego 20*) Mains US$1.50-2.50. A type of a milk bar, this self-service and simple eatery offers some of the cheapest meals in town.

WIELKOPOLSKA

Bistro Pizzeria Pod Piątką (☎ 426 18 00, ul Tumska 5) Mains US$3-4. Close to the cathedral, this is a convenient place for a simple budget meal, nothing more.

Restauracja Sphinx (☎ 426 13 73, ul Bolesława Chrobrego 4) Mains US$3-5. If you've already tried Sphinx elsewhere and you liked it, you'll also like this one, but come hungry as the portions are as generous as usual.

Getting There & Away
The train and bus stations are side by side 1km south-east of the cathedral.

Train Trains run regularly throughout the day to Poznań (51km), and in the opposite direction to Inowrocław (56km). There are also several departures to Bydgoszcz daily (102km), Toruń (91km), Gdańsk (261km) and Wrocław (216km).

Bus Buses go to Poznań (49km) via Kostrzyn hourly or so, but if you want to stop at Lake Lednica (18km), take the Poznań bus via Pobiedziska (eight daily but fewer on weekdays).

There are three or four morning buses to Żnin via Gąsawa (31km), where you can change for the narrow-gauge train to Biskupin or just walk 2km.

BISKUPIN
☎ 52

Biskupin is a fortified lake town built about 2730 years ago by a tribe of the Lusatian culture, which at that time lived in Central Europe. The settlement was accidentally discovered in 1933 and unearthed from beneath a thick layer of turf. It is the only known surviving Iron Age town in Poland, and proves that the region was already inhabited by well organised social groups over 1600 years before the Polish state was born. It has been partially reconstructed to make it more interesting for the casual visitor.

Things to See
The Iron Age town together with the park lying between the road and the lake shore form the **Archaeological Reserve** (*Rezerwat Archeologiczny;* ☎ 302 50 25, Biskupin; adult/student US$1.50/1; open 9am-6pm daily, closes at dusk in winter).

Entering the complex from the road, you'll find a car park, ticket office, half a dozen budget food outlets, and stalls that sell souvenirs and publications about the place (including some in English).

The **Iron Age town** lies on the peninsula in the northern end of the park, a five-minute walk from the entrance. The gateway, a fragment of the defensive wall and two rows of houses have been reconstructed to give some idea of what the town once looked like. The interiors of a few houses have been fitted out as they may have been 2700 years ago. From the wharf near the gateway, a pleasure boat departs several times a day for a short trip around the lake.

The **museum**, halfway between the peninsula and the park's entrance, shows the finds excavated on and around the island, together with background information about the place and the people. There's a model of the town as it once looked.

Getting There & Away
Bus From the bus stop at the entrance to the Archaeological Reserve, buses run every hour or two north to Żnin (7km) and south to Gąsawa (2km). There are no direct buses from Biskupin to Gniezno (33km); go to Żnin and change. You may also go via Gąsawa, but there are fewer buses from there to Gniezno than from Żnin.

Narrow-Gauge Train The narrow-gauge tourist train operates from May to September between Żnin and Gąsawa passing Biskupin and Wenecja on the way. There are five trains daily in either direction between around 10am and 4pm. In Żnin, the station is alongside the standard-gauge train station; in Gąsawa it's 700m south-west of the Rynek on the Gniezno road. In Biskupin, it's right by the entrance to the reserve.

The railway was built in 1894 and has a gauge of just 600mm, one of the narrowest in the world. Steam locomotives are no longer used, but you'll find many of them in Wenecja's museum.

WIELKOPOLSKA

Biskupin – Poland's Oldest Existing Town

The Iron Age settlement of Biskupin was built around 740–730 BC on a flat oval island measuring about 190m x 125m. The island was encircled by a 460m-long, 6m-high barricade consisting of a wooden framework filled with earth and sand. The island's shores were reinforced with a palisade of about 20,000 oak stakes lined up in several rows and driven into the lake bottom at an angle of 45 degrees to serve as a breakwater and a protection from potential invaders. The only access to the town was through a gateway topped with a watchtower and connected by a 250m bridge to the lake shore.

Within the defensive walls, 13 parallel rows of houses were laid out with streets between them, the whole encircled by a street running inside the ramparts. Over 100 almost identical houses were built, each inhabited by one family of seven to 10 members. The total population of the settlement was about 800 to 1000 people, which probably was a 'big city' for its inhabitants.

Recent investigations have confirmed that the whole town was built in just a few years, proving a high degree of engineering and organisation. Within that time thousands of oak trees were cut down in surrounding forests, pre-constructed on the mainland, then brought in ready-to-assemble elements onto the island over an iced lake in winter and put together. The earth and sand to fill the barricade were also brought from the mainland.

Farming, livestock breeding and fishing provided a steady, self-sufficient existence for the community, which also maintained trade ties with other settlements in the region and far beyond. Excavations revealed objects from places as distant as Egypt, Italy and the Black Sea coast.

Around 400 BC the town was destroyed, most likely by the Scythians, and it wasn't rebuilt. This was essentially because of climatic changes, which were causing the lake's level to rise, making the island uninhabitable. The remains of the wooden structure were preserved in mud and silt for 2300 years. Early in the 20th century the water level began to drop and the island re-emerged, eventually turning into a peninsula, as it is today.

The excavations have unearthed a variety of objects belonging to the tribe, including household utensils, tools, artefacts and weapons, thus giving a picture of the lifestyle, culture and religion of this ancient society.

WENECJA
☎ 52 • pop 1500

Wenecja ('Veh-**neh**-tsyah'), a small village across the lake from Biskupin, has the **Museum of Narrow-Gauge Railways** (*Muzeum Kolei Wąskotorowej;* ☎ *302 51 50; admission US$1; open 9am-6pm daily May-Aug, 9am-4pm daily Apr, Sept & Oct, 10am-2pm daily Nov-Mar*). It has plenty of old steam locomotives and carriages, some of which house uniforms, tools and other objects related to the railway. A convenient way to visit the museum is to break the Żnin-Biskupin train journey for an hour.

STRZELNO
☎ 52 • pop 6000

Strzelno ('**Stshel**-no') boasts two of the best Romanesque churches in the region and a museum. They are next to each other, about 200m east of the Rynek. Apart from infrequent religious services (mostly on Sunday) the churches are kept locked, but a local guide, Damian Rybak, is usually available between 9am and 5pm. If not, call him at home on ☎ 318 33 30. He lives nearby and will come and show you around.

St Procopius' Church
Kościół Św Prokopa was built of red stone around 1150 and has preserved its austere Romanesque form remarkably well, even though its upper part was rebuilt in brick after damage in the 18th century. It has a circular nave, with a square chancel on one side and a tower on the other, the whole adorned with typical semicircular apses on the northern side of the nave. The interior, almost free of decoration, looks admirably authentic. By the entrance is the original 12th-century font.

Church of the Holy Trinity

The larger church, Kościół Św Trójcy, was built a decade or two after its neighbour, but changed significantly later. It acquired a Gothic vault in the 14th century and a baroque facade four centuries later. The interior has mainly baroque furnishings, including the high altar and a decorative rood beam, which form a remarkably harmonious composition with Gothic vaulting supported on four original Romanesque columns. These columns, revealed only in 1946 during postwar restoration (they were previously plastered over in the walls which separated the nave from the aisles), are the most precious treasure of the church, particularly the two with elaborate figurative designs. There are 18 figures carved in each column; those on the left-hand column personify vices while those on the right are virtues.

The door at the head of the right-hand aisle leads to St Barbara's Chapel, its fine palm-like vault resting on yet another delicately carved Romanesque pillar.

Museum

Located in the building adjacent to the larger church, the museum presents some architectural remains (including a Romanesque portal with a tympanum depicting the scene of the Teaching of Christ) and archaeological finds.

Places to Stay & Eat

Strzelno's only hotel, *Dom Wycieczkowy* (☎ 318 92 37, Plac Daszyńskiego 1), was closed and for sale when we were researching. Check when you arrive. Alternatively, try the only other place to stay, the summer *youth hostel* (☎ 318 95 68, ul Parkowa 10), open July to August.

Gastronomy is not Strzelno's strong point either, with just one basic restaurant opposite the hotel and a couple of snack bars around the Rynek.

Getting There & Away

Passenger trains no longer call at Strzelno, but buses can take you to Gniezno, Inowrocław, Bydgoszcz and Toruń. The bus terminal is at the western end of town.

KRUSZWICA
☎ 52 • pop 9000

Set on the northern end of the 20km-long Lake Gopło, Kruszwica ('Kroosh-**fee**-tsah') existed from at least the 8th century as a fortified village of the Goplanie, one of the Slav tribes living in the area. The Polanie farther to the west and the Goplanie didn't get along particularly well, and the latter group was eventually subjugated. Today Kruszwica is an undistinguished small industrial town which boasts some remnants of the Piast legacy and legends about the region's early days.

Things to See

The early 12th-century stone Romanesque **collegiate church** was altered in later periods but returned more or less to its original form in the course of postwar restoration. The interior fittings include the 12th-century baptismal font at the entrance to the chancel. The church is on the north-eastern outskirts of town, a 10-minute walk from the Rynek.

The 32m-high octagonal **Mouse Tower** (Mysia Wieża), near the Rynek, is the only remainder of the 14th-century castle built by King Kazimierz Wielki. The name derives from a legend of the evil ruler of the Goplanie, Duke Popiel, who was eaten here by mice. You can go to the top of the tower (9am to 6pm May to September) for a view over the town and lake. From the foot of the tower a tourist boat departs several times a day in summer for an hour-long trip around Lake Gopło.

Places to Stay & Eat

Klub Sportowy Gopło (☎ 351 52 33, ul Poznańska 17) Doubles with bath US$25, beds in triples or quads without bath US$7. Gopło, next to the stadium (five minutes from the Rynek), offers acceptable standards and has a cheap bistro, or you can go for a budget meal to the *Zajazd U Piasta Kołodzieja* next to the Mouse Tower.

Pałac w Kobylnikach (☎ 351 54 21, fax 351 54 24) Beds in rooms without/with bath US$6/12. This hotel is in an eclectic Prussian-style brick palace built at the beginning of the 20th century by a German baron. It's

WIELKOPOLSKA

Legend of Duke Popiel

Once upon a time, a duke named Popiel lived in the castle of Kruszwica and ruled a vast country that was named Poland. The duke was a cruel and despotic ruler, and greedy for power. Not without reason, he was afraid that he could be overthrown by his countrymen, even by someone from his own family, and replaced by a more worthy person. In order to ensure there were no competitors to the throne he decided to kill all his kin and other distinctive members of the community.

To put his plan into effect, the duke organised a great party in the castle, to which all his family and other distinguished persons were invited. Once the initial toasts had relaxed the guests, a poisonous wine was discreetly served to selected invitees. All died in a great deal of pain. Popiel then threw the dead bodies out of the castle and refused to bury them as an example to others that they would suffer a similar fate for disobedience.

As weeks passed, the decomposing bodies attracted thousands of mice which rushed to the castle. Popiel sought refuge high up in the castle's tower but the mice cornered him and devoured him. Since then the tower has been known as the Mouse Tower.

Following Popiel's death, a modest peasant named Piast was chosen by the people and proclaimed the new ruler. He was the first leader of the Piast dynasty which ruled Poland for many many years and made it great and prosperous.

And the mice? Nobody has seen them since. Maybe they are still in the tower? Better watch your step!

pretty run down, yet still reasonable value at these rates. The palace is surrounded by a large wooded park. It's in Kobylniki, a village 1.5km north of Kruszwica on the Inowrocław road.

Getting There & Away

The main bus stop is on the Rynek. Buses to Strzelno (15km) depart every other hour or so. There are no trains to Inowrocław

(15km), but buses go there every half-hour. From Inowrocław trains run regularly to Bydgoszcz, Toruń and Gdańsk.

South-Eastern Wielkopolska

KALISZ

☎ 62 • pop 108,000

The main urban centre of south-eastern Wielkopolska, Kalisz ('**Kah**-leesh') is not a major tourist destination but can be a place to break your journey if you travel in the area. If you decide to stop here you may want to visit the two sights nearby, the castle at Gołuchów and the palace in Antonin (detailed in separate sections after Kalisz).

Kalisz has the longest documented history of any town in Poland; it was mentioned by Claudius Ptolemy in his renowned *Geography* of the 2nd century AD as Kalisia, a trading settlement on the Amber Route between the Roman Empire and the Baltic Sea. In the 9th century a stronghold was built (in the present-day suburb of Zawodzie) and the town continued to develop until the 13th century. Burnt down in 1233, it was rebuilt farther to the north, in its present location.

During the reign of Kazimierz Wielki the town acquired defensive walls with 15 watchtowers and a castle. It continued to grow steadily until the 16th century, from which point it began to decline. A huge fire in 1792 left only the churches standing, and almost all the fortifications were taken down in the early 19th century.

The greatest tragedy, sometimes compared to Warsaw's annihilation in 1944, came in WWI – in August 1914 Kalisz was razed to the ground by the invading Germans. Within a month, the population dropped from 70,000 to 5000 and most buildings lay in ruins, though the churches – as before – miraculously escaped destruction. The town was rebuilt on the old street plan, but in a new architectural style. Most of the buildings survived WWII without much damage, but the renovation process appears to be rather slow.

Information
The Centrum Informacji Turystycznej
(☎ 764 21 84), ul Garbarska 2, is open 10am
to 5pm weekdays, 10am to 2pm Saturday.

Bank Pekao branches at ul Grodzka 7 and
ul Śródmiejska 29 will exchange travellers
cheques and have ATMs. Cash can be easily changed at any of the kantors around the
Rynek.

Internet facilities worth trying include
Matrix (☎ 766 67 82), ul Pułaskiego 6; City
Jungle (☎ 767 67 00), Al Wolności 6; and
Abraxas (☎ 764 56 11), ul Sukiennicza 5A.

Things to See
The Old Town sits in the angle between the
Prosna and Bernardynka Rivers, with a
dozen small bridges and a park stretching to
the south-east. The best point to begin your
sightseeing is possibly the tower of the
town hall *(Rynek; admission US$0.50;
open 10am-2pm Mon-Fri, 10am-1pm Sat &
Sun)*. Apart from fine views from the top,
there's an exhibition related to Kalisz's and
the town hall's history.

The **Regional Museum** *(Muzeum Ziemi
Kaliskiej; ☎ 503 02 03, ul Kościuszki 12;
adult/student US$1/0.50; open 10am-2.30pm
Tues, Thur, Sat & Sun, noon-5.30pm Wed &
Fri)* features archaeological and historical
sections. The museum has a separate outlet in
the Jesuit college, the **Centre of Drawing &
Graphic Arts** *(Centrum Rysunku i Grafiki;
☎ 757 29 99 , ul Kolegialna 4, enter from ul
Łazienna; adult/student US$1/0.50; open
12.30pm-5pm 2nd & 4th Tues of month,
10am-2.30pm Wed & Fri, noon-5.30pm
Thur, 10am-2pm Sat, 10am-2pm 1st & 3rd
Sun of month)*. It displays temporary exhibitions of drawings and graphic arts, including
works by Tadeusz Kulisiewicz (1899–1988),
a Kalisz-born artist, known mainly for his
drawings.

Farther down ul Łazienna is the **Centre of
Culture and Arts** *(Centrum Kultury i Sztuki;
☎ 765 25 35, ul Łazienna 6)*, where various
cultural events take place.

Kalisz has some good churches. The oldest, **St Nicholas' Church** (Kościół Św Mikołaja), dates from the 13th century and was
originally Gothic, but has been modernised

several times. The interior today is mainly
baroque with a Renaissance-style vault. The
painting of the Descent from the Cross over
the high altar is a copy. The original, painted
in Rubens' workshop about 1617 and donated to the church, was burnt or stolen during a mysterious fire in 1973.

The former **Bernardine Church** (Kościół
Pobernardyński), built in 1607 and now
owned by the Jesuits, features a spectacular
interior. The church is somewhat unprepos-
sessing from the outside, but its wide nave
glows with amazing sumptuous baroque
decoration. Both the altars and the wall
paintings on the vault date from around the
mid-18th century.

Special Events
Kalisz's major annual events are the **Kalisz
Theatre Meetings** at the beginning of May
and the **International Piano Jazz Festival** in
late November. Both events have a tradition
of over 20 years and rank high on the national cultural map.

Places to Stay
Youth hostel *(☎ 757 24 04, Wał Piastowski
3)* Beds US$4-6. Open year-round. The 52-
bed youth hostel is pleasantly set in a park
on the riverbank, 200m off ul Często-
chowska. Book in before 9pm.

*Hotel Europa (☎ 767 20 31, fax 767 24
15, Al Wolności 5)* Singles/doubles without
bath US$14/20, with bath US$25/30. The
only really central option, the Europa has
long passed its best days and was actually
pretty run down when we were there, but
the new owner had plans to revamp the
place.

*Hotel Dyonizy (☎/fax 757 46 50, ul
Łódzka 29)* Singles/doubles/triples without
bath US$14/18/26, doubles/triples with bath
US$32/36. The former Dom Wycieczkowy
PTTK, now the Dyonizy, is better than Eu-
ropa, but less convenient. It's 1km east of
the centre; you can walk there through the
City Park in 15 minutes.

*Hotel Calisia (☎ 767 91 00, ☎/fax 767
91 14, ul Nowy Świat 1–3)* Singles/doubles/
triples with bath & breakfast US$44/
55/66. A good new addition to the city's

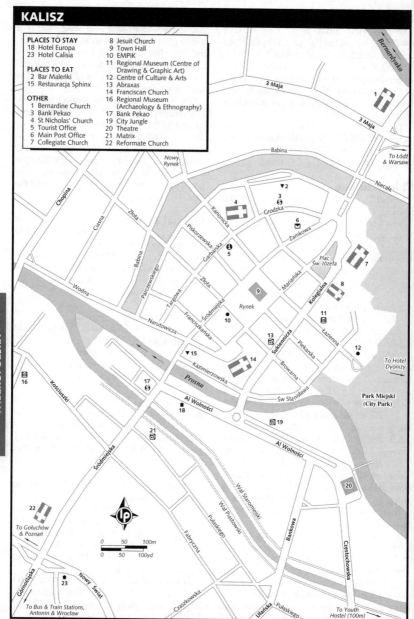

KALISZ

PLACES TO STAY
18 Hotel Europa
23 Hotel Calisia

PLACES TO EAT
2 Bar Maleński
15 Restauracja Sphinx

OTHER
1 Bernardine Church
3 Bank Pekao
4 St Nicholas' Church
5 Tourist Office
6 Main Post Office
7 Collegiate Church
8 Jesuit Church
9 Town Hall
10 EMPiK
11 Regional Museum (Centre of Drawing & Graphic Art)
12 Centre of Culture & Arts
13 Abraxas
14 Franciscan Church
16 Regional Museum (Archaeology & Ethnography)
17 Bank Pekao
19 City Jungle
20 Theatre
21 Matrix
22 Reformate Church

WIELKOPOLSKA

accommodation, the 80-bed Calisia is the best central hotel. Watch out for possible weekend discounts.

Places to Eat

Bar Maleńki (☎ 501 93 03, ul Parczewskiego 2–3) Mains US$1.50-2.50. This tiny cubbyhole ('maleńki' means 'tiny') serves excellent food, which makes it perhaps the best place for an ultra budget meal in town.

Restauracja Sphinx (☎ 501 94 01, ul Śródmiejska 16) Mains US$3-5. Since Kalisz hasn't a great choice of good, reasonably priced eateries, Sphinx fits particularly well on the local culinary scene.

Restauracja Calisia (☎ 767 91 00, ul Nowy Świat 1–3) Mains US$5-8. Located in the hotel of the same name, the Calisia serves fine Polish food, is open longer than most other eating establishments, and isn't overpriced.

Getting There & Away

The bus and train stations are close to each other, about 2km south-west of the centre. To get to the centre, take bus No 1 from the bus terminal and bus No 10 from the train station.

Train Trains to Łódź (113km) run regularly throughout the day. There are several fast trains and one express train to both Warsaw (256km) and Wrocław (130km). Three fast trains and two ordinary trains go to Poznań (138km).

Bus There are eight buses to Poznań daily (130km), and five to Wrocław (121km). The Wrocław buses can drop you off at Antonin (40km). To Gołuchów (17km), take the hourly suburban bus No 12A to Kowalew; it passes through the centre along ul Sukiennicza and ul Kolegialna.

GOŁUCHÓW

☎ 62 • pop 1200

The small village of Gołuchów ('Go-**woo**-hoof') boasts a castle looking a bit like those in the Loire Valley in France. It began around 1560 as a small fortified mansion with four octagonal towers at the corners,

built by the Leszczyński family. Some 50 years later it was enlarged and reshaped into a palatial residence in late Renaissance style. Abandoned at the end of the 17th century, it gradually fell into ruins until the Działyński family, the owners of Kórnik (see that section earlier in this chapter), bought it in 1856. It was completely rebuilt in 1872–85, and it was then that it acquired its French appearance.

The castle's stylistic mutation was essentially the brainchild of Izabela Czartoryska, daughter of the renowned Prince Adam Czartoryski and wife of Jan Działyński. She commissioned the French architect Viollet le Duc, and under his supervision many architectural bits and pieces were brought from abroad, mainly from France and Italy, and incorporated into the building.

Having acquired large numbers of works of art, Izabela crammed them into the castle (or rather the palace, by that stage), which became one of the largest private museums in Europe. During WWII the Nazis stole the works of art but the building itself survived relatively undamaged. Part of the collection was recovered and is now once more on display in the palace.

Things to See

The **castle** looks different from various sides; the best view is from the northern side. You enter the castle through a decorative 17th-century doorway which leads into a graceful arcaded courtyard.

Inside the building is the **museum** (☎ 761 50 90, ul Działyńskich 2; adult/student US$2/1.50; open 10am-4pm Tues-Sun). In its numerous rooms, a wealth of furniture, paintings, sculptures, weapons, tapestries, rugs and the like have been collected from Europe and beyond. One of the highlights is a collection of Greek vases from the 5th century BC.

To the south of the castle is the **oficyna**, which looks like a small palace. Initially a distillery, it was considerably extended in 1874 and adapted for a residence. It was here that the owners lived after the castle was turned into a museum. Today the building accommodates the **Museum of Forestry**

(Muzeum Leśnictwa; ☎ *761 50 36, ul Działyńskich 2; adult/student US$1.50/1; open 10am-3pm Tues-Sun),* which focuses on the history of Polish forestry and the timber industry. There's also a collection of contemporary art connected to forestry, either in subject matter or by means of the material used. The building has its original interior decoration. You can have a cup of coffee or a lunch in the cafe in the adjoining building before taking a stroll through the park.

The vast 160-hectare English-style **park** *(admission free; open 8am-8pm daily)* with several hundred species of trees and shrubs was laid out during the last quarter of the 19th century. Its oldest part is the 350m-long lime-tree alley planted in 1856.

The **Museum of Forest Techniques** *(Muzeum Techniki Leśnej;* ☎ *761 50 10; admission US$0.50; open 10am-3pm Tues-Sun),* in the far north of the park, 750m beyond the castle, features tools and machinery used in forestry.

A dozen bison live relatively freely in a large, fenced-off **bison enclosure** *(admission free; open 7am-dusk),* west of the park, 500m beyond the Museum of Forest Techniques (follow the signs).

Places to Stay & Eat

Dom Pracy Twórczej **(**☎ *761 50 45,* ☎*/fax 761 50 44, ul Borowskiego 2)* Doubles or triples with bath US$26. Open year-round. Located in a historic building just 250m from the castle, the Dom offers nine reasonable rooms and has a budget *restaurant*.

Kawiarnia Muzealna **(**☎ *761 50 27, ul Działyńskich 2)* Mains US$2-4. The Kawiarnia, adjoining the Museum of Forestry, has quite an extensive food menu. Its owner offers seven budget rooms in a pensjonat, 1km from the castle.

Gołuchowski Ośrodek Turystyki i Sportu **(**☎ *761 70 86, ul Leśna 1)* Cabins without/with bath US$25/34. Open May-Sept. Set in the forest on the lake shore, 1km from Gołuchów towards Kalisz, this summer recreational centre offers simple five-bed cabins (some with private baths) and tent sites.

Youth hostel **(**☎ *761 70 87, ul Czartoryskich 53)* Beds US$3-4. Open July & August. This small hostel is in the Gołuchów school.

Getting There & Away

Suburban bus No 12A goes roughly hourly (on Sunday every two hours) to/from Kalisz (17km). About eight buses run to Poznań daily (108km) and can drop you off in Kórnik (another castle; see the Kórnik section earlier).

ANTONIN

☎ 62 • pop 500

Today a local weekend/holiday resort, before WWII Antonin was the summer residence of the Radziwiłł family, one of the richest and best known aristocratic clans in Poland. In 1822–24 Prince Antoni Radziwiłł (after whom the place was named) built the **Hunting Palace** (Pałac Myśliwski). This handsome wooden structure was designed by Karl Friedrich Schinkel, one of the outstanding German architects of the period who was responsible for a number of monumental buildings in Berlin.

The palace is an unusual structure. The main body of the building is a large, octagonal, three-storey hall, called the Chimney Room, with a column in the middle supporting the roof and also functioning as a chimney for the central fireplace. There are four side wings, originally designed as living rooms for the owner and his guests. One such guest, Frédéric Chopin, stayed here a couple of times, performing concerts and composing.

Today the palace is a hotel. Its wings have been converted into hotel rooms and there's a stylish restaurant in the Chimney Room. The palace is surrounded by a forest which offers some pleasant walks.

Special Events

Piano recitals are held in the palace (normally on Sunday in July and August). A special bus is laid on for guests from Ostrów Wielkopolski and sometimes from Kalisz (inquire in the Centre of Culture and Arts). There's also a four-day **Chopin Festival** in September/October.

Places to Stay & Eat

Camping Nr 26 (☎ *734 81 94, ul Wrocławska 6)* Cabins US$16-24. Open May-Sept. The camping ground is adjacent to the Ośrodek. It also has cabins, or you can pitch your own tent; choose a place as far from the road as possible – the traffic noise can be annoying.

Pałac Myśliwski (☎ *734 81 14, ☎/fax 736 16 51)* Singles/doubles/triples with bath & breakfast US$32/42/48. Open year-round. By far the most romantic place to stay, the Hunting Palace offers reasonable rooms, and you can eat in its restaurant in the Chimney Room. Advance booking is recommended.

Motel Lido (☎/fax *734 81 91, ul Wrocławska 6)* Doubles with bath US$32. Sitting by the main road, the motel has eight double rooms with bath, and a restaurant.

Ośrodek Rekreacyjno-Wypoczynkowy Lido (☎/fax *734 81 27, ul Wrocławska 6)* Cabins US$10-25. Open May-Sept. This large lakeside holiday centre, right behind the motel, features a collection of double and triple cabins with and without bath. There are also two snack bars on the grounds.

Getting There & Away

The train station is about 1km from the palace, beyond the lake. Several trains run to Poznań daily (130km). There are no direct trains to Kalisz – you must change in Ostrów Wielkopolski.

There are five buses to Wrocław daily (81km), and five to Kalisz (40km). About eight buses run to Ostrów Wielkopolski (17km); from Ostrów suburban buses run regularly to Kalisz.

LICHEŃ
☎ 63 • pop 1500

Licheń ('Lee-hen'), a small village 13km north-east of Konin in the centre of Poland, is reputedly Poland's second most visited pilgrimage site after Częstochowa. The pilgrims' destination, a sizable ecclesiastical complex, occupies the village's centre and includes two churches, the Way of the Cross (Golgotha) in the form of a fairy-tale stone fortress, and chapels and statues scattered all over the grounds. The place attracts about 1.5 million pilgrims annually, who come to pay tribute to the miraculous image of the Virgin Mary, deposited in the

---

Licheń Basilica's Book of Records

Licheń's Basilica is Poland's longest church (120m), the seventh longest in Europe and 11th longest in the world. It's Poland's widest (77m) and highest (97m) church, and it also leads the league of Polish churches in its volume (268,800 cu metres) and floor area (8290 sq metres).

The church can comfortably sit 7000 faithful with another 10,000 standing – another record. More than 250,000 people can easily gather on the square in front of the church.

The basilica has Poland's highest church tower – 128m-high – well ahead of the second tallest, the Jasna Góra Monastery of Częstochowa (106m). Licheń also has Poland's largest bell (third largest in Europe) – the 14,770kg Maryja Bogurodzica – leaving the 11,000kg Zygmunt in Kraków's Wawel Cathedral well behind.

The basilica has 60 doors and 365 windows, some of which are 9m tall. There will be 50 confessionals. The 25m-diameter dome also holds some records, including one for the lightest construction of any dome in Europe.

In front of the church is the largest monument to Pope John Paul II ever built – a 9m-tall, 8-tonne bronze statue designed by Kraków sculptor Marian Konieczny.

The basilica possibly holds yet another record – the cost of its construction – but this one is harder to determine. It is said to have been financed exclusively by donations from the faithful, collected by the priest over 20 years. However, the priest won't give the figure, saying that one shouldn't look into God's pockets. Whatever can be said about the cost, it is enormous. The doors and windows alone cost US$3 million.

WIELKOPOLSKA

high altar of the main church. But things are changing.

Energetic local priest Eugeniusz Makulski decided to build a third church as a 'votive offering of the nation for the year 2000', to celebrate two millennia of Christianity. Construction began in 1994 and is close to conclusion. About 500 people work daily on the construction site.

This is not your average church. The gigantic basilica is Poland's largest church, exceeding anything that was built in the country over the past 1000 years. The structure is basically finished, except for the top of the tower, which is likely to be completed by the time you read this. The furnishing and decoration of the church's main hall will probably take longer to do, yet there have already been some Masses held inside. You can enter and see the interior.

Beneath the main hall is the round Golden Chapel, which is a good-sized church in itself. Completed in 1996, it's crammed with crystal chandeliers and golden stucco. The floor is of marble imported from all over the world to form a multicoloured design.

The design of the church, by Polish architect Barbara Bielecka, is nothing particularly bold, futuristic or stunning, except for the mammoth size of the building. It's a quite traditional, heavy edifice which 'combines the architectural style of the first centuries of Christianity with that of the 19th century'.

If you decide to come, give yourself sufficient time, at least half a day. There's really a lot to see, and crowds of pilgrims add to the atmosphere of the place. Local guidebooks (there are some in English) sold at various locations have all the details.

Places to Stay & Eat

Dom Pielgrzyma (☎ 270 81 62, fax 270 77 00, ul Klasztorna 4) Beds US$4-8. This is the main lodging facility built and operated by the church, located within the sanctuary complex. Together with the adjacent Dom Rekolekcyjny, there are around 500 beds, in two- to six-bed dorms, some with private bath, others without. A third dorm is being built, which will add another few hundred beds by the time you read this.

Church accommodation apart, most inhabitants of the village offer rooms in their homes for visitors.

Eating is not a problem either. There are three or four simple budget *cafeterias* within the sanctuary complex, plus another half a dozen just outside.

Getting There & Away

Konin, a fair-sized town 13km to the southwest, is the jumping-off point for Licheń. Konin sits on the busy Poznań-Warsaw rail line, with frequent connections in both directions. There are hourly buses linking Licheń with Konin.

Pomerania

Pomerania, or Pomorze, stretches along Poland's Baltic coast, from the German frontier in the west to the lower Vistula valley in the east. The region rests on two large urban pillars: Szczecin at its western end and Gdańsk to the east. Between them hangs the coastline and, farther inland, a wide belt of lake country.

Gdańsk is perhaps Poland's most attractive historic city after Kraków. Other cultural highlights of the region include the Gothic castles of the lower Vistula valley, with Malbork castle on the top of the list, and the charming Gothic town of Toruń. For those who prefer some sun and sand to castles, there's a long stretch of the beautiful Baltic coast densely dotted with seaside resorts.

Polish history has nowhere been more complex than in the north, where various areas have changed hands on numerous occasions. On balance, the north has spent more time outside the national borders than within them.

The Lower Vistula

The valley of the lower Vistula is a fertile land bisected by the wide, leisurely river. Flat, open and largely occupied by farms, the region shelters a rich cultural inheritance, even though much of it was lost in WWII.

The Vistula was an important waterway through which goods were shipped to the Baltic and abroad. In the 13th and 14th centuries many trading ports were established along the Vistula's banks all the way from Toruń down to Gdańsk. Most of these towns were founded by the Teutonic Order (see the boxed text 'Teutonic Order v the Polish Crown' later in this chapter), which by then occupied much of the valley. Remnants of the Teutonic Order now comprise some of the most important sights in the region.

Highlights

- Explore the Gothic town of Toruń with its mighty churches
- Wander around the lethargic old town of Chełmno
- Visit the exuberant 15th-century basilica in Pelplin
- Go for a tour of the giant Malbork castle
- Discover the little town of Frombork, the home of Copernicus
- Stroll about the streets of Gdańsk's meticulously reconstructed historic core and visit the colossal St Mary's Church
- View the unique shifting dunes in the Słowiński National Park

BYDGOSZCZ
☎ 52 • pop 390,000

Sitting on the border of Wielkopolska and Pomerania, Bydgoszcz ('**Bid**-goshch') was outside the territory of the Teutonic Order. Founded in 1346, the town developed unhurriedly as a trading centre and beer producer. During the wars with the Teutonic Order it served as a military base from where the Polish troops set off for battle.

POMERANIA

POMERANIA

Map labels:

BALTIC SEA
Gulf of Gdańsk

SŁOWIŃSKI NATIONAL PARK
BORY TUCHOLSKIE NATIONAL PARK
DRAWA NATIONAL PARK
WOLIN NATIONAL PARK

GERMANY

Hel
Władysławowo
Rozewie
Puck
Reda
Gdynia
Sopot
GDAŃSK
Wejherowo
Lębork
Łeba
Cewice
Ustka
Gardna
Słupsk
Sławno
Korzybie
Koszalin
Miastko
Bytów
Unciechowo
Czarna Dąbrówka
Sierakowice
Kartuzy
Kościerzyna
Wdzydze Kiszewskie
Starogard Gdański
Tczew
Malbork
Elbląg
Frombork
Krynica Morska
To Olsztyn
Nogat
Vistula
Kwidzyn
Pelplin
Gniew
Starogard Gdański
Świecie
Chełmno
Chełmża
Grudziądz
Radzyń Chełmiński
Wąbrzeźno
Golub-Dobrzyń
Kowalewo Pomorskie
TORUŃ
BYDGOSZCZ
Koronowo
Mąkowarsko
Więcbork
Nakło nad Notecią
Łobżenica
Złotów
Sępólno Krajeńskie
Chojnice
Człuchów
Tuchola
Szczecinek
Jastrowie
Piła
Wałcz
Czaplinek
Złocieniec
Drawsko Pomorskie
Kalisz Pomorski
Choszczno
Dobiegniew
Strzelce Krajeńskie
Barlinek
Gorzów Wielkopolski
Pyrzyce
Stargard Szczeciński
Maszewo
Nowogard
Goleniów
Kamień Pomorski
Świnoujście
Międzyzdroje
Kołbaskowo
SZCZECIN
To Berlin
Odra
Kołobrzeg
Trzebiatów
Gościno
Białogard
Karlino
Połczyn Zdrój
Świdwin
Łobez
Resko
Płoty
Dobra
Chociwel
Sławoborze
To Poznań
To Warsaw
Iława
Brodnica
Rypin
Sierpc
Lipno
Vistula
Inowrocław
Żnin
Noteć
Jabłonowo Pomorskie
To Olsztyn
Władysławowo

Scale bar:

0 15 30km
0 7.5 15mi

LP

The Lower Vistula – Bydgoszcz 435

Subjugated by the Prussians in the First Partition of 1773, Bydgoszcz returned to Poland in 1920 and underwent intensive industrial development. The rapid growth continued after WWII, and today it's a large and heavily industrialised city.

Despite its long history and considerable size, the city has little for tourists and ranks low on travel itineraries. Its historic quarter has largely lost its historic character, while the rest of the city is essentially a postwar product.

Information

The regional tourist office, the Regionalna Agencja Promocji Turystyki (☎ 322 84 32) is at ul Zygmunta Augusta 10, diagonally opposite the train station. The city tourist office, the Miejskie Centrum Informacji Turystycznej (☎ 322 44 62) is at ul Grodzka 12, in the Old Town.

Bank Pekao has central branches at ul Dworcowa 6 and ul Długa 57. Both have ATMs, and there are more ATMs throughout the central area.

Things to See

The Old Town is on the southern bank of the Brda River, a 20-minute walk from the train station. Its heart, the **Stary Rynek**, has recently been restored. The 15th-century brick **parish church**, just off the square, has preserved its Gothic form pretty well. The gilded baroque high altar boasts a 1466 painting of the Virgin Mary with a rose, and the stained-glass windows on both sides are fine replicas of medieval originals. The dark blue Gothic vault and the ornamental motifs on the walls (added in the 1920s) give the interior a pleasant touch.

West of the church, on a small island known as Wyspa Młyńska (Mill Island), is an 18th-century granary, the Biały Spichrz (White Granary). It houses a branch of the **Regional Museum** (☎ 327 03 93, ul Mennica 1; adult/student US$1/0.50; open 10am-6pm Tues-Fri, noon-4pm Sat & Sun) featuring the region's history and an art and craft collection.

Another branch of the **Regional Museum** (☎ 322 16 08, ul Gdańska 4; adult/student US$1/0.50; open 10am-6pm Tues-Fri, noon-4pm Sat & Sun) is on the other side of the river, in an old convent. It features temporary exhibitions.

Next door to the museum is the small Gothic-Renaissance **Church of the Poor Clares** (Kościół Klarysek). Its interior features some 17th-century paintings on the panelled ceiling and a fine decorative wrought-iron screen (1651) between the nave and the chancel with its heavily gilded high altar (1636).

Places to Stay

Youth hostel (☎/fax 322 75 70, ul Sowińskiego 5) Beds US$5-10. Open year-round. The 100-bed youth hostel, just a five-minute walk from the train station, has rooms ranging from singles to 10-bed dorms.

Hotel Asystenta (☎ 322 06 31, ul Dworcowa 79) Singles/doubles without bath US$24/26. One of the cheapest hotels in the train station area, this former teachers' dorm has 15 singles and four doubles, and is really nothing special.

Hotel Centralny (☎ 322 88 76, fax 322 88 70, ul Dworcowa 85) Singles/doubles/quads without bath US$28/44/80, singles/doubles/triples with bath US$36/56/80. Located just one short block from the station, the busy Centralny is not great value, yet it may be useful if you need an affordable room with bath near the trains (or a room without bath if the Hotel Asystenta is full).

Hotel Ratuszowy (☎ 322 88 61, fax 322 54 50, ul Długa 31) Singles/doubles with bath & breakfast US$40/60. Quiet and very central, the 28-room Ratuszowy is perhaps the only place to stay within the Old Town, just a block from the old market square.

Hotel Pod Orłem (☎ 583 05 30, fax 584 02 24, ul Gdańska 14) Singles/doubles US$100/120 (30% less on weekends), breakfast included. The Orbis-operated Pod Orłem, just north of the Old Town, is one of the city's fanciest hotels and a landmark. Built in 1896 and named 'Under the Eagle' (look up the facade to know why), it has hosted most visiting VIPs.

City Hotel (☎ 325 25 00, fax 325 25 05, ul 3 Maja 6) Singles/doubles US$100/120,

Teutonic Order v the Polish Crown

The Teutonic Order was a German religious and military organisation founded in the 1190s in Palestine during the Third Crusade. Initially overshadowed by two similar orders, the Templars and the Hospitallers, the Teutonic Knights came to the fore under their fourth Grand Master, Hermann von Salza, when they began spreading into Central Europe. They were backed by German feudal overlords, who saw this as an opportunity for territorial and political expansion to the east.

The order's involvement in Polish affairs began in 1226, when Duke Konrad of Mazovia sought its help against the Prussians, a pagan Baltic tribe which repeatedly invaded and laid waste to the northern provinces of the principality. The duke offered the order a stretch of land north of Toruń in exchange for protection of his duchy and the conversion to Christianity of the troublesome Prussians. The duke hoped to retain sovereignty over the Teutonic territory, but matters soon got out of hand and the agreement turned out to be one of Poland's worst political deals. The subsequent conflict punctuated the history of the two states for 250 years.

The order founded its first strongholds in Chełmno and Toruń, from where it swiftly expanded into the surrounding region. Following the loss of their base in Palestine, the knights began the construction of a new fortress in Malbork, into which the Grand Master moved from Venice in 1309. By that time, the order had conquered the region of Gdańsk, including the city itself (1308), and expanded to the east, swallowing up large areas of the Baltic provinces. In effect, the order cut Poland off from the sea. It also solved the problem of converting the native Prussians in the simplest possible way – by wiping them out. The name of the tribe survived, however; oddly enough, it passed to their exterminators (and descendants thereof), whose ethnic origin was quite different from the original tribe.

Apart from its military power, the order also grew in economic strength, taking advantage of its association with the Hanseatic League, or Hansa. Founded in the second half of the 13th century, the Hansa was an alliance of northern German towns which aimed to protect the trading interests of its members. It was soon joined by most of the ports of the North Sea and the Baltic, and inland cities of northern Europe. By the mid-14th century, the league numbered 100 towns and virtually monopolised north European trade. Many of the order's outposts such as Gdańsk, Toruń and Königsberg entered the league, as well as some major Polish cities including royal Kraków.

The conflict between the order and the Polish Crown intensified throughout the 14th century, culminating in the Battle of Grunwald of 1410, in which Władysław Jagiełło won a decisive victory over the knights. However, he was unable to capture Malbork, which was only seized in 1457 during the Thirteen Years' War (1454–66), presaging the eventual defeat of the order. The 1466 Treaty of Toruń gave Poland the western part of the knights' territory, which became known as Royal Prussia, while the remaining eastern part, Ducal (or East) Prussia, came under Polish rule in 1525, when the order converted to Lutheranism.

breakfast included. Another top-end accommodation, this Austrian built, owned and managed hotel is a modern establishment.

Places to Eat

Bar Mleczny Dworcowy (*ul Dworcowa 75*) Mains US$1-2.50. The cheapest place to eat in the train station area, this genuine milk bar serves tasty food for next to nothing.

Bar Kaskada (☎ *324 93 32, ul Mostowa 2*) Mains US$2-3.50. In a glass-and-steel building just off the Stary Rynek, Kaskada is one of the cheapest places to go for a meal in the Old Town.

Restauracja Sphinx (☎ *321 54 48, ul Magdzińskiego 18*) Mains US$3-5. Yes, Sphinx has already come to town, offering the same as elsewhere – copious plates of good Middle-Eastern and Polish food.

An upmarket option is the old-fashioned restaurant of the **Hotel Pod Orłem** which serves good Polish and European food.

Entertainment

Get a copy of *BIK – Bydgoski Informator Kulturalny*, a useful what's-on monthly which lists cultural events such as opera, theatre, art galleries, concerts etc. For some lighter fare try:

El Jazz Club (☎ 322 15 74, ul Kręta 3) Just a few steps from Stary Rynek, the Jazz Club hosts live music (not just jazz) most nights of the week.

Getting There & Away

The train station is 1.5km north-west of the Old Town, while the bus terminal is 1km east of the historic quarter; urban bus Nos 77 and 104 link the two stations, passing through the centre.

Both trains and PKS buses go frequently to Toruń (51km or 47km, respectively) and Inowrocław (46km or 43km). There are a dozen trains to Gdańsk daily (160km) and three to Warsaw (288km). Polski Express has hourly buses to Warsaw (US$8.25, 4½ hours, 255km) via Toruń and Płock.

TORUŃ

☎ 56 • pop 208,000

A wealthy Hanseatic port with a rich history, Toruń retains much of its old-time charm and character in its narrow streets, mighty churches, vaulted cellars and museums. The city has a well-preserved complex of Gothic architecture, which isn't common in this part of Europe. Toruń is also the birthplace of Nicolaus Copernicus (1473–1543). Though the famous astronomer only spent his youth here, the city is very proud of the man who 'stopped the sun and moved the earth', and his name (Mikołaj Kopernik for Poles) is all over town.

In 1997, Toruń's historic core was included on Unesco's World Heritage list. The city offers a chance to step briefly back in history without a lot of other tourists on your heels. It's certainly well worth coming here.

History

A Slav settlement is known to have existed on this site as early as the 11th century, but Toruń really came to life in 1233 when the Teutonic Knights set about transforming it into one of their early outposts, under the name of Thorn. The knights surrounded the town with a ring of walls and built a castle, and its position on the Vistula accelerated its development. So fast was its growth that the newly arriving merchants and craftspeople had to settle outside the city walls and soon built what became known as the New Town. It had its own square, town hall and church, and was also fortified. In the 1280s Toruń joined the Hanseatic League which gave further impetus to its development.

As the conflict between Poland and the Teutonic Order intensified, the town's internal affairs became explosive. In 1454, in a wave of protest against the economic restrictions imposed by the order, the inhabitants took up arms and destroyed the local castle. By then full-blown war had broken out between the order and Poland (the Thirteen Years' War) which concluded with the Treaty of Toruń in 1466. The treaty returned to Poland a large area of land stretching from Toruń to Gdańsk, and also presaged the military downfall of the Teutonic Order.

The period of prosperity which followed ended with the Swedish wars and since then the town's fortunes have been erratic. Following the Second Partition of Poland in 1793 the city fell under Prussian domination and didn't return to Poland until the Treaty of Versailles in the aftermath of WWI.

After WWII, which fortunately did relatively little damage to the city, Toruń expanded significantly, with vast new suburbs and industries. However, the medieval quarter was almost unaffected by the expansion and largely retains its old appearance. Much restoration has been carried out in recent decades, and there's still a lot to be done.

Orientation

The historic sector of Toruń sits on the northern bank of the Vistula. It is made up of the Old Town (Stare Miasto) to the west and the New Town (Nowe Miasto) to the east. Both towns, originally separated by walls and a moat, developed around their market squares, but gradually merged after the walls were taken down in the 15th century. All the major tourist attractions are in this area.

POMERANIA

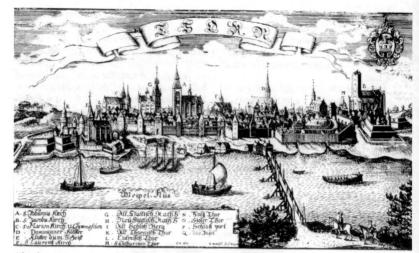

The thriving port city of Toruń in the 15th century; the main churches and many other stuctures are still visible today

The bus terminal is a five-minute walk north of the historic quarter, while the main train station is south across the river, a short bus ride. When coming from the station over the bridge, you'll get a fine view of the historic district, the impressive silhouette of the cathedral being the dominant landmark.

Information

Tourist Offices The friendly and knowledgeable Ośrodek Informacji Turystycznej (☎ 621 09 31, fax 621 09 30, Ⓦ www.it .torun.com.pl), Rynek Staromiejski 1 (in the Old Town Hall), is open 9am to 4pm Monday and Saturday, 9am to 6pm Tuesday to Friday and (May to August only) 9am to 1pm Sunday.

Money Bank Pekao, ul Wielkie Garbary 11 in the New Town, exchanges travellers cheques, gives advances on Visa and Master Card and has an ATM. There are more ATMs in the centre, as well as a satisfactory array of kantors.

Email & Internet Access Klub Internetowy Jeremi (☎ 633 51 00), at Rynek Staromiejski 33 (1st floor), was Toruń's first cybercafe and is now open 24 hours. Another popular central option is Klub Internetowy Hacker (☎ 663 54 21), ul Podmurna 28, open till midnight (longer on weekends). You can also try Klub Internetowy @ in the Telekomunikacja Polska office, ul Szeroka 40, but it's open shorter hours and not open at all on Sunday.

Old Town

The **Old Town Square** (Rynek Staromiejski) is the usual starting point for the visitor. The sizable brick building in the middle is the **Old Town Hall** (Ratusz Staromiejski). Built at the end of the 14th century, it hasn't changed much, save for some Renaissance additions giving a decorative touch to the sober Gothic structure. Apart from serving as the municipal seat, the town hall provided market facilities, but it lost them in the course of internal remodelling in the 19th century. After WWII, it also lost its administrative functions and today most of the building is occupied by the **Regional Museum** *(Muzeum Okręgowe; ☎ 622 70 38, Rynek Staromiejski 1; adult/student US$2/1, free Sun; open 10am-6pm Tues-Sun May-Sept, 10am-4pm Tues-Sun Oct-Apr).*

In the original interiors, you'll find several sections, including a collection of Gothic art (painting, woodcarving and stained glass), a display of the 17th- and 18th-centuries work of local craftspeople, and a gallery of Polish paintings from around 1800 to the present. You can also go to the top of the tower for a fine panoramic view.

A few steps from the entrance towards the museum is the **Statue of Copernicus**, one of the oldest monuments dedicated to the astronomer.

There are several fine buildings lining the Rynek. The most richly decorated is the house at No 35, known as the **House under the Star** (Kamienica Pod Gwiazdą). Its ornate baroque appearance is the result of the extensive modernisation of an original Gothic structure. It's part of the regional museum and may have exhibitions, but it was closed due to restoration work when we researched. Another outstanding mansion, the **Artus Court** (Dwór Artusa) at No 6, is now a cultural centre. On the western side of the square is the mid-18th-century **Church of the Holy Spirit** (Kościół Św Ducha), which was originally built for the Protestant congregation.

Between the church and the town hall is a small **fountain**, built here in 1914, with bronze-cast frogs sitting on its rim and topped with a statue of a boy playing violin, known as Janko Muzykant. Legend has it that a witch once came to the town, but wasn't welcomed by the locals. In revenge, she invoked a curse, and the town was invaded by frogs. The mayor offered a sackful of gold and his daughter to anyone who would rescue the town. A humble peasant boy then appeared and began to play his rustic violin. The frogs, enchanted by the touching melodies, followed him to the woods and the town was saved.

Just to the north-west of the square is the huge **St Mary's Church** (Kościół NMP), erected by the Franciscans at the end of the 13th century. Austere and plain from the outside, it has a lofty interior with tall, stained-glass windows and is pleasantly bright, particularly on a sunny day. The surviving fragments of late-14th-century frescoes can be seen in the right-hand nave. Note the impressive early-15th-century Gothic stalls in the chancel. The organ, placed unusually on a side wall, was added two centuries later.

Behind the church is the **Planetarium** (☎ 622 50 66, ul Franciszkańska 15/21; adult/student US$2/1.50). Installed in an old gas tank, the planetarium has a high-tech auditorium that can seat 160 spectators. Diverse shows are presented several times daily.

Take ul Piekary southwards to the end, where you'll find a few old **granaries** and the **Leaning Tower** (Krzywa Wieża) just round the corner. One block east is the **Monastery Gate** (Brama Klasztorna), one of three surviving medieval gates.

Walk north along ul Ducha Świętego, passing the **Wozownia Art Gallery** (☎ 622 63 39, ul Ducha Świętego 6; admission US$1; open 10am-6pm Tues-Fri, 11am-6pm Sat & Sun) which has changing displays of contemporary art.

Just round the corner from the gallery is the brick Gothic **House of Nicolaus Copernicus** (Dom Mikołaja Kopernika; ☎ 622 67 48, ul Kopernika 15/17; adult/student US$2.50/1.50, free Sun; open 10am-6pm Tues-Sun May-Sept, 10am-4pm Tues-Sun Oct-Apr), where he was born in 1473. Today it's another branch of the regional museum which features exhibits related to the great astronomer, including replicas of his astronomical instruments. The museum runs a short audiovisual presentation about Copernicus' times in Toruń, with a model of the town during that period. There are soundtracks in several languages, English included.

One block east of the museum is the largest and most impressive of the city's churches, the **Cathedral of SS John the Baptist and John the Evangelist** (Katedra Św Janów). Work started around 1260 and was only completed at the end of the 15th century, by which time the church dominated the town's skyline, as it does today. Its massive tower houses Poland's second-largest historic bell (after the one in the Wawel Cathedral of Kraków), the Tuba Dei (God's

POMERANIA

TORUŃ

NEW TOWN

OLD TOWN

POMERANIA

Vistula

To Toruń Miasto Train Station

To Hotel Kopernik

Wola Zamkowa

Warszawska

Szumana

Wysoka

Międzymurze

Wały Sikorskiego

Prosta

Sukiennicza

Zaszpitalna

Szczytna

Św Katarzyny

Piernikarska

Św Jakuba

Browarna

Sukiennicza

Rynek Nowomiejski

Królowej Jadwigi

Wielkie Garbary

Małe Garbary

Strumykowa

Podmurna

Dominikańska

Podmurna

Podmurna

Przedzamcze

Mostowa

Ciasna

Łazienna

Szeroka

Kopernika

Św Jana

Żeglarska

Rabiańska

Bankowa

Bulwar Filadelfijski

Szczytna

Szeroka

Chełmińska

Piekary

Panny Marii

Fosa Staromiejska

Rynek Staromiejski

Plac Teatralny

Franciszkańska

Łoża Staromiejska

Wały Sikorskiego

Różana

Ducha Świętego

Kopernika

Al Solidarności

Al 700-lecia Torunia

Al 700-lecia Torunia

Chopina

To Bus Terminal & Dom Wycieczkowy PTTK

To Youth Hostel

To Schronisko Turystyczne Fort IV

To Dom Studencki Nr 6 & Bursa Szkolna

To Train Station & Camping Nr 33 Tramp

To Central Park

0   50   100m
0   50   100yd

TORUŃ

PLACES TO STAY
4 Hotel Polonia
8 Hotel Trzy Korony
11 Hotel Heban
27 Hotel Petite Fleur
35 Hotel Pod Orłem
44 Hotel Gromada
46 Hotel Pod Czarną Różą

PLACES TO EAT
9 Bar Mleczny Małgośka
14 Restauracja Akropol
28 Bar Mleczny Pod Arkadami
31 Restauracja Sphinx
34 Karczma U Sołtysa

OTHER
1 Skansen
2 Ethnographic Museum
3 Polski Express Bus Stop
5 Teatr im Horzycy
6 Planetarium
7 St Mary's Church
10 Klub Internetowy Hacker
12 Former Protestant Church
13 St James' Church
15 Bank Pekao
16 Klub Internetowy @
17 House Under the Star
18 Klub Internetowy Jeremi
19 Statue of Copernicus
20 Piwnica Artystyczna Pod Aniołem
21 Tourist Office
22 Old Town Hall; Regional Museum
23 Public Toilet
24 Fountain
25 Main Post Office
26 Church of the Holy Spirit
29 Sklep Kopernik
30 Artus Court
32 Sklep Firmowy Katarzynka
33 ATM
36 Ruins of the Teutonic Castle
37 House of the Esken Family; Regional Museum
38 Cathedral of SS John the Baptist & John the Evangelist
39 House of Nicolaus Copernicus
40 Wozownia Art Gallery
41 Bridge Gate
42 Sailors' Gate
43 Former Bishops' Palace
45 Pub Czarna Oberża
47 Medieval Granaries
48 Monastery Gate
49 Leaning Tower

Trumpet). Cast in 1530, it weighs 7238kg and is rung for significant religious and national events. On the southern side of the tower, facing the Vistula, is a large 15th-century clock; its original face and hand (one only, as was the rule at the time) are still in working order.

Walking into the church with its once white, now blackened, walls and vault is like travelling back in time. The combination of Gothic vaulting high above and the maze of baroque altars and chapels at ground level is unusually harmonious. The walls and vaults were whitewashed by the Protestants, who used the church during the Reformation era and considered the brightly coloured medieval paintings unsuitable. Small fragments have been uncovered and can be seen in the chancel and the aisles. The most striking mural is the devil's figure high at the back of the right-hand aisle. The work of an unknown artist and dating from 1478, it's a startling monochrome, quite rare at the time.

The high altar, adorned with a Gothic triptych and topped with a crucifix, has as a background a superb stained-glass window in the best medieval style. The last chapel in the right-hand aisle holds the oldest object in the church, the font where Copernicus was baptised. To one side is his epitaph.

A few steps south of the church, at ul Żeglarska 8, is the beautifully renovated former **Bishops' Palace** (Pałac Biskupi), now part of the local university. A bit farther down the street is the plain **Sailors' Gate** (Brama Żeglarska).

The Gothic **House of the Esken Family** (*Dom Eskenów;* ☎ *622 86 80, ul Łazienna 16; adult/student US$1.50/1, free Sun; open 10am-4pm Wed-Sun*), at the back of the church, was converted into a granary in the 19th century and now is yet another branch of the regional museum. It features a collection of historic exhibits related to the city, a small display of old weapons and an archaeological section.

At the southern end of ul Mostowa is the third surviving city gate, **Bridge Gate** (Brama Mostowa), where the bridge across the river once was. The 700m-long bridge was built here in 1497–1500 and survived for over three centuries. It was the second-oldest bridge over the Vistula, but the first one, in Kraków, was much shorter. By comparison, the bridge in Warsaw was only built in 1568–73.

From the gate, take ul Podmurna, dotted with several dilapidated granaries. To the east, in a triangle squeezed between the Old and New Towns, is the **castle**, built by the

POMERANIA

Teutonic Knights. It was destroyed in 1454 and has remained in ruins to this day. The surviving cellars have been cleared out and are now used for some cultural events.

New Town

North of the castle lies the New Town centred around the **New Town Square** (Rynek Nowomiejski). It's not as spectacular as its older counterpart nor does it have a town hall. The building in the middle is the former Protestant church erected in the 19th century after the town hall was pulled down. Among the houses which line the Rynek, the best two are at opposite ends of the south-western side of the square.

St James' Church (Kościół Św Jakuba), just off the eastern corner of the square, dates from the same period as its Old Town brothers. It's also huge, though it's shaped like a basilica and is more elaborate from the outside, thanks to architectural details including a series of pinnacles adorning the rim of the roof. Its interior is filled with mostly baroque furnishings, but Gothic wall paintings have been uncovered in various places, notably under the organ loft. The high altar and the decorative rood-arch both date from the 1730s.

Around the Old & New Towns

In a park just to the north of the Old Town is the **Ethnographic Museum** (*Muzeum Etnograficzne;* ☎ 622 80 91, *Wały Sikorskiego 19; adult/student US$2/1.25; open 9am-4pm Mon, Wed & Fri, 10am-6pm Tues, Thur, Sat & Sun May-Sept, 9am-4pm Tues-Fri, 10am-4pm Sat & Sun Oct-Apr).* It focuses on traditional fishery, with all sorts of implements, boats and nets. In the grounds behind the museum building is a small but good **skansen** (open the same hours as the museum and visited with the same admission ticket), containing examples of traditional rural architecture of the region and beyond, including two farms, a blacksmith's shop, windmill and watermill.

Special Events

Major annual events include the **'Probaltica' Music and Art Festival of Baltic States** in May, the **'Contact' International Theatre Festival** in May/June, and the **'Music and Architecture' International Summer Festival** in July and August.

Places to Stay

Toruń has a reasonable array of places to stay and finding a room isn't usually difficult. The tourist office keeps an eye on local lodging options and is likely to help you track down a bed.

Places to Stay – Budget

Camping Nr 33 Tramp (☎/fax 654 71 87, ul Kujawska 14) Double/triple rooms without bath US$16/20, 4-/6-bed cabins without bath US$22/30. Open mid-May–mid-Sept. The Tramp camp site, a five-minute walk from the main train station, has basic hotel-style rooms, a collection of dilapidated cabins, and a tent/caravan area.

Youth hostel (☎ 654 45 80, ul Św Józefa 22/24) Beds US$4-6. Open year-round. The simple 30-bed youth hostel offers just five six-bed dorms. It's 2km north-west of the centre, accessible by bus No 11 from the train station and the Old Town.

Schronisko Turystyczne Fort IV (☎ 655 82 36, fax 655 81 34, ul Chrobrego) Beds US$4-6. Open year-round. Located in an old Prussian fort, this 100-bed hostel has dorms ranging from two to 18 beds and a budget cafeteria. It's a way off the centre but is linked by the direct No 14 bus with both the centre and the train station.

Bursa Szkolna (☎ 622 67 37, ul Słowackiego 47/49) Beds in 4- to 8- bed dorms with shared facilities US$4. The Bursa, 1km west of the Old Town, is a school dorm but has some rooms for the general public. It's basic but acceptable.

Dom Studencki Nr 6 (☎ 622 89 60, ul Słowackiego 1/3) Beds in doubles/triples without bath US$8/6. Open early July-late Sept. Just west of the Old Town, a mere five-minute walk to the Old Town Square, this is one of several student dorms of Copernicus University, which open in summer as student hostels. There may be different hostels open in different years but they are all next to each other and conditions are similar. The tourist office will know which ones are open the summer you come.

Dom Wycieczkowy PTTK (*☎/fax 622 38 55, ul Legionów 24*) Singles/doubles/triples/quads without bath US$18/22/28/32. The 65-bed PTTK hostel is a 10-minute walk north of the Old Town (five minutes from the bus terminal).

Hotel Trzy Korony (*☎/fax 622 60 31, Rynek Staromiejski 21*) Singles/doubles/triples/quads without bath US$22/24/30/36, singles/doubles/triples with bath & breakfast US$40/50/60. The Trzy Korony (Three Crowns) once hosted kings and tsars, but they probably wouldn't like to stay in it today. It's a rather simple place, yet it's ideally situated. Ask for a room facing the square.

Hotel Kopernik (*☎/fax 652 25 73, ul Wola Zamkowa 16*) Singles/doubles without bath US$20/22, with bath US$32/38. Located in the New Town, just two blocks off the New Town Square, the 75-bed Kopernik, formerly an army hotel, provides acceptable standards.

Places to Stay – Mid-Range & Top End

All the hotels listed in this section have rooms with private baths and are very central.

Hotel Pod Orłem (*☎/fax 622 50 24, ul Mostowa 17*) Singles/doubles/triples US$30/42/46. The Pod Orłem is one of Toruń's oldest hotels, with a history going back more than 100 years. It provides reasonable rooms at a reasonable price.

Hotel Polonia (*☎/fax 622 30 28, Plac Teatralny 5*) Singles/doubles/triples US$35/42/50. One block north of the Old Town Square, the Polonia has recently been refurbished and offers a fair compromise between its standards and rates.

Hotel Pod Czarną Różą (*☎/fax 621 96 37, ul Rabiańska 11*) Singles/doubles/triples US$44/55/66, breakfast included. Another well-located place, the 15-room 'Black Rose' is in a historic burgher's house in a quiet street.

Hotel Petite Fleur (*☎ 663 44 00, ☎/fax 663 54 54, ul Piekary 25*) Singles/doubles/triples US$46/58/66, breakfast included.

Yet another small hotel in a historic house at a very central location, Petite Fleur has just six rooms and a fine restaurant specialising in French cuisine.

Hotel Gromada (*☎ 622 60 60, fax 622 53 84, ul Żeglarska 10/14*) Singles/doubles US$50/80, breakfast included. Better known under its old name of Zajazd Staropolski, this tasteful hotel in a fine 14th-century townhouse offers reasonable rooms which are best enjoyed on weekends when rates drop by 20%.

Hotel Heban (*☎/fax 652 15 55, ul Małe Garbary 7*) Doubles US$60-90. The most luxurious central option, the Heban is in another historic central townhouse, meticulously restored and adapted for the hotel's needs. It has nine tastefully decorated rooms of various sizes and prices, plus an elegant restaurant serving Polish and European food.

Places to Eat

At the bottom budget end, there are two central milk bars, the basic ***Bar Mleczny Małgośka*** (*☎ 622 43 37, ul Szczytna 10/12*) and the better ***Bar Mleczny Pod Arkadami*** (*☎ 622 24 28, ul Różana 1*) just off the Old Town Square.

Restauracja Sphinx (*☎ 658 32 88, ul Żeglarska 31*) Mains US$3-5. Occupying a large two-level locale in a prestigious point on the corner of the Old Town Square, Sphinx does as good a job as elsewhere and, predictably, is often full.

Karczma U Sołtysa (*☎ 622 66 74, ul Mostowa 17*) Mains US$4-6. Styled as an old Polish inn, the restaurant serves solid traditional Polish fare at reasonable prices.

Restauracja Akropol (*☎ 652 16 15, Rynek Nowomiejski 10*) Mains US$4-6. As its name suggests, this place brings a Greek flavour to town.

If you are looking for fine dining, you won't go wrong if you choose the restaurants of ***Hotel Heban*** or ***Hotel Petite Fleur***, listed in the previous section.

Entertainment

Get a copy of *Toruńskie Vademecum Kultury*, a useful cultural monthly distributed free by the tourist office.

POMERANIA

Piwnica Artystyczna Pod Aniołem (☎ 622 70 39, Rynek Staromiejski 1) This splendid, spacious cellar in the town hall is one of the most popular drinking haunts among local youth. Live music such as rock, jazz, folk etc can be heard here from time to time.

Pub Czarna Oberża (Black Inn; ☎ 621 09 63, ul Rabiańska 9) This pub is another popular haunt among locals and has, apart from drinks, a modest food menu.

Central Park (☎ 622 67 63, Szosa Bydgoska 3) One of Poland's largest discotheques, the Central Park is Toruń's prime venue for night-time dancing.

Dwór Artusa (☎ 622 88 05, Rynek Staromiejski 6) The Artus Court has an auditorium used for presentation of musical events, including concerts and recitals of classical music.

Teatr im Horzycy (☎ 622 50 21, Plac Teatralny 1) The neobaroque town theatre, built in 1904, is the city's main stage for theatre performances.

Shopping
Toruń is famous for its gingerbread (*pierniki*), which has been produced here since the town was founded. It comes in a variety of shapes, including figures of Copernicus. The places to buy it are *Sklep Firmowy Katarzynka* (ul Żeglarska 25) and *Sklep Kopernik* (Rynek Staromiejski 6) in the Artus Court.

Getting There & Away
Train The Toruń Główny main train station is about 2km south of the Old Town, on the opposite side of the Vistula. Bus Nos 22 and 27 link the two. There's also the Toruń Miasto train station, 500m east of the New Town, but not all trains call in here.

It's easy to get around the region as trains to Grudziądz (62km), Bydgoszcz (51km), Inowrocław (35km) and Włocławek (55km) leave at least every other hour. As for longer routes, there are a few departures to Malbork daily (138km), Gdańsk (211km), Łódź (178km), Olsztyn (163km) and Poznań (142km). One express and four fast trains go to Warsaw (237km) in 3½ hours.

Bus The bus terminal, close to the northern edge of the Old Town, handles a regular bus service to Chełmno (41km), Golub-Dobrzyń (43km), Płock (103km) and Bydgoszcz (47km). Polski Express has a dozen departures daily (from Al Solidarności) to Warsaw (US$7.25, 3¾ hours, 209km).

GOLUB-DOBRZYŃ
☎ 56 • pop 12,500
The town of Golub-Dobrzyń, about 40km east of Toruń, was created in 1951 by unifying two settlements on opposite sides of the Drwęca River. Dobrzyń, on the southern bank, is newish and not worth a mention, but Golub was founded in the 13th century as a border outpost of the Teutonic Knights and still has their castle.

Castle
Overlooking the town from a hill, the castle consists of a massive Gothic brick base with a more refined Renaissance superstructure added in the 17th century, all extensively restored after WWII. There's a small **museum** (☎ 683 24 55; adult/student US$1.50/0.75; open 9am-4pm, longer in summer) inside the castle which is worth a look more so for the original Gothic interiors rather than for its modest ethnographic collection.

Every July the castle hosts the **International Knights' Tournament**; the program includes re-enactments of medieval jousting.

Places to Stay & Eat
Dom Wycieczkowy PTTK (☎ 683 24 55, fax 683 26 66, Zamek) Double rooms US$20. Dorm beds US$8. The castle's upper floor houses some of the cheapest 'castle accommodation' in Poland. A pleasant cafe in the vaulted cellar serves snacks and drinks.

Getting There & Away
The town has a regular bus service to Toruń (39km) and less frequent buses go to Grudziądz (52km). The bus stop is situated at the foot of the castle. The train station is on the opposite side, on the Grudziądz road, and operates several trains to Bydgoszcz daily (83km).

CHEŁMNO

☎ 56 • pop 22,000

The small town of Chełmno ('**Heum**-no'), 41km north of Toruń, is a bit of a surprise. Not only does it have almost its entire ring of medieval fortified walls – perhaps the most complete in Poland – but it also boasts half a dozen red-brick Gothic churches and a beautiful town hall.

Chełmno was a Polish settlement existing from the late 10th century, but it really began to develop as the first seat of the Teutonic Knights. They arrived in the late 1220s and immediately began to build a castle, which they completed by 1265. Naming the town Kulm, they initially planned to make it their capital but later opted for Malbork. Chełmno also did well out of the Vistula trade, benefiting from its affiliation to the Hanseatic League.

After the Treaty of Toruń, Chełmno returned to Poland, but despite its royal privileges it didn't shine as brightly as before. The Swedish invasion did considerable damage and a series of wars in the 18th century left the town an unimportant place with some 1600 inhabitants. Though it survived WWII without major damage, it never really revived. Today it's a lethargic town sealed within its walls, as it was six centuries ago.

Information

The Chełmińska Informacja Turystyczna (☎/fax 686 21 04) is in the town hall in the middle of the Rynek. It's open 8am to 3pm Monday and Saturday, 8am to 4pm Tuesday to Friday.

Bank Gdański at ul Dworcowa 3 will exchange travellers cheques and cash, and has an ATM. Kredyt Bank, ul Dworcowa 24A, also has a useful ATM.

Things to See

Coming from the bus terminal, you'll enter the Old Town through the **Grudziądz Gate** (Brama Grudziądzka), the only surviving medieval gateway. It was remodelled in the 17th century to incorporate a chapel. Note an expressive pietà in the niche in the gate's eastern facade.

Past the gate, you'll find yourself on a chessboard of streets, with the Rynek at its heart. In the middle stands the graceful Renaissance **town hall**, built around 1570 on the site of the previous Gothic structure and now home to the **Regional Museum** (*Muzeum Ziemi Chełmińskiej;* ☎ 686 16 41, *Ratusz; admission US$1; open 10am-4pm Tues-Fri, 10am-3pm Sat, 10am-1pm Sun*). The collection related to the town is exhibited in the original interiors, including a spectacular courtroom.

On the back wall of the town hall is the old Chełmno measure, the 4.35m-long *pręt chełmiński*. The entire town was laid out according to this measure, the streets all the same width apart. It is divided into 'feet' a little smaller than an English foot. The town also had its own weights. This unique system was used until the 19th century.

Just off the Rynek is the massive Gothic **parish church**, dating from the late 13th century. The magnificent interior is crammed with ornate baroque and rococo furnishings, including the high altar from 1710, the shell-shaped pulpit, the elaborate three-part organ from 1690 and numerous altarpieces throughout the nave and aisles. There are also some remnants from previous periods, notably the Romanesque stone baptismal font and fragments of Gothic frescoes.

The **Church of SS John the Baptist and John the Evangelist** (Kościół Św Jana Chrzciciela i Jana Ewangelisty), in the western end of the Old Town, was built in 1266–1325 next to the castle (which hasn't survived) as part of the Cistercian convent. Unusual for its two-level nave, it has a richly gilded high altar and an ornate organ to the side. Underneath the organ is a black-marble tombstone from 1275, one of the oldest in the region. The church is usually closed; enter the gate at ul Dominikańska 40 and ask to be let in.

Other churches are less spectacular and most of them are unused (after all, a town of this size doesn't need six houses of worship). Nevertheless you can have a look at them (particularly the Church of SS Peter and Paul) just for their original Gothic structures, all dating from the 13th and 14th centuries.

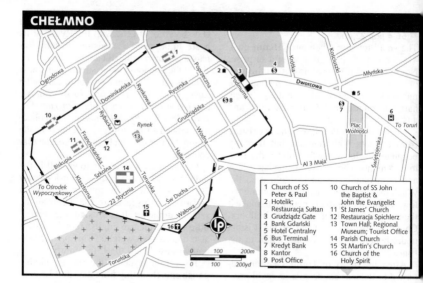

CHEŁMNO

1 Church of SS Peter & Paul
2 Hotelik; Restauracja Sułtan
3 Grudziądz Gate
4 Bank Gdański
5 Hotel Centralny
6 Bus Terminal
7 Kredyt Bank
8 Kantor
9 Post Office
10 Church of SS John the Baptist & John the Evangelist
11 St James' Church
12 Restauracja Spichlerz
13 Town Hall; Regional Museum; Tourist Office
14 Parish Church
15 St Martin's Church
16 Church of the Holy Spirit

Finally, you may want to inspect the 2.2km-long **fortified walls**, which are, together with those in Paczków in Silesia, the only examples in Poland to have survived almost in their entirety. There once were 23 defensive towers in the walls and some still exist though they're not all in good shape.

Places to Stay & Eat

Ośrodek Wypoczynkowy (☎ 686 12 56) Doubles/quads/quins in cabins US$8/15/20. Open May-Sept. On Lake Starogrodzkie, 2km west of the walled town, the Ośrodek has a colony of basic cabins and a camping ground.

Hotelik (☎ 676 20 30, ul Podmurna 3) Singles/doubles with bath & breakfast US$25/30. Located in a quiet corner of the Old Town, Hotelik offers eight good-sized neat rooms, all with private bath, making it good value for money. The *Restauracja Sułtan* downstairs serves tasty Middle-Eastern and Polish food at low prices till midnight.

Hotel Centralny (☎ 686 02 12, fax 686 44 21, ul Dworcowa 23) Singles/doubles/triples without bath US$18/24/28, with bath US$24/30/35. The Centralny is simple but

perfectly acceptable. It also has a good budget restaurant.

Restauracja Spichlerz (☎ 686 99 12, ul Biskupia 3) Mains US$3-5. Decked out in timber, Spichlerz is a warm and cosy place for a lunch or dinner, or just for a (very cheap) glass of beer.

Getting There & Away

Trains no longer come to town but buses leave pretty regularly to Bydgoszcz (49km), Toruń (41km) and Grudziądz (33km). There are also three buses a day direct to Gdańsk.

GRUDZIĄDZ
☎ 56 • pop 105,000

About 30km down the Vistula from Chełmno, Grudziądz ('**Groo**-dzyonts') is a large industrial town. It has some attractions, including a line of gigantic granaries, their size and location making them unique in Poland.

Grudziądz started life as an early Piast settlement. Repeatedly destroyed by the Prussians, it came under the rule of the Teutonic Knights as Graudenz in the 1230s, returning to the Crown in 1454 after an anti-Prussian rebellion. In the First Partition of 1773 it was swallowed by Prussia and went back to Poland once more in the aftermath of WWI.

Grudziądz was badly damaged in 1945 but the new authorities decided to make it an important regional industrial centre, as it had been before the war.

Information

Grudziądz doesn't seem to have a reliable tourist office. Useful banks include Bank Pekao, ul Chełmińska 68, and Bank Gdański, ul Sienkiewicza 19. Kantors are in good supply.

Things to See

Approaching the historic quarter from the south (eg, coming from the bus or train stations) you first get to the **museum** (☎ 465 90 63, ul Wodna 3/5; adult/student US$1.50/0.75; open 10am-3pm Tues-Fri, 10am-2pm Sat & Sun). The museum's main building, a former Benedictine convent, houses the gallery of contemporary paintings from the region and temporary exhibitions. The sections on local archaeology and history are in two old granaries just to the west.

From the museum, go down to the bank of the Vistula through the 14th-century **Water Gate** (Brama Wodna) to see the **granaries** (spichrze). They were built along the whole length of the town's waterfront to provide storage and protect the town from invaders. Begun in the 14th century, they were gradually rebuilt and extended until the 18th century, and some were later turned into apartment blocks by cutting windows in the walls. Decayed as they are, these massive buttressed brick buildings – most of them six storeys high – are an impressive and unusual sight. The best view is from the opposite bank of the Vistula but it's a long walk south and then over the bridge.

If this doesn't appeal, walk north along the shore and take the first stairs up to the right. They will lead you to the Gothic brick **cathedral**, which has a well-preserved original structure. Next to it is a small, former **Jesuit Church** (Kościół Pojezuicki), built in 1715, which has a beautiful mid-18th-century baroque high altar and unusual chinoiserie (particularly visible beneath the organ loft),

a decorative style almost unused in Polish churches. One block south is the **Rynek**, the historic centre of town, lined with houses built mainly at the end of the 19th century.

Places to Stay

Youth hostel (☎ 643 55 40, ul Hallera 37) Beds US$6. Open year-round. The 150-bed hostel is in a large nondescript 11-storey block of the Bursa Szkolna (school dorm), 1.5km south of the Old Town. It has doubles and triples only, no large dorms, so it provides more privacy than most other hostels.

Hotel Pomorzanin (☎ 462 61 41, ul Kwiatowa 28) Doubles/triples without bath US$12/18. Sitting midway between the train station and the Old Town, the Pomorzanin is convenient and cheap but basic.

Hotel Karolewicz (☎/fax 462 60 37, ul Toruńska 28) Singles/doubles with bath & breakfast US$25/32. Karolewicz is nothing out of the ordinary but relatively inexpensive and central, and has a budget restaurant.

Hotel Garnizonowy (☎ 458 23 92, ul Legionów 53) Singles/doubles/triples with bath US$20/30/40. Recently refurbished, the Garnizonowy offers reasonable standards but is away from the centre (take tram No 1 from the train station to get there).

Getting There & Away

The train station is about 1km south-east of the Old Town, a 15-minute walk. The bus terminal is near the station. Trains run regularly throughout the day south to Toruń (62km) and north to Kwidzyn (38km); most of the latter continue farther north to Malbork. Buses to Bydgoszcz (70km) leave every hour and to Chełmno (33km) every hour or two. There are also infrequent buses to Kwidzyn.

KWIDZYN

☎ 55 • pop 40,000

About 30km downriver from Grudziądz is Kwidzyn, another medieval Teutonic stronghold, noted for its castle and cathedral.

Things to See

The square **castle** with a central courtyard was built in the first half of the 14th century.

It experienced many ups and downs in subsequent periods and suffered a serious loss in 1798 when the Prussians pulled down two sides (eastern and southern) and the main tower. It passed unscathed through WWII.

After the war, the Polish authorities treated the castle with more respect than their predecessors, carefully restoring what was left. Most of the building from the cellars to the 2nd floor is now the **Kwidzyn Museum** (☎ 279 38 89, ul Katedralna 1; adult/student US$2/1; open 9am-3pm Tues-Sun), with several sections including medieval sacred art, regional folk crafts and natural history, particularly stuffed birds. Note the fine original interiors.

The most curious feature of the castle is the unusual tower standing some distance away from the western side and linked to it by a long arcaded bridge. This was the knights' toilet, later serving also as the execution ground. You can visit it while wandering around the interior, but it's also worth walking round the outside to see this peculiar construction.

The **cathedral** adjoining the castle from the east is a familiar Gothic brick blockbuster which has a somewhat defensive appearance with a 19th-century tower. Look for the interesting ceramic mosaic from around 1380 in the external wall above the southern porch. The spacious interior, supported on massive columns, has fragments of 14th-century frescoes while the furnishings are a combination of Gothic and neo-Gothic elements.

Places to Stay & Eat

Hotel Piastowsko-Słowiańska (☎ 279 34 33, ul Braterstwa Narodów 42) Doubles without/with bath US$16/24. Very central and close to the castle, this is the cheapest hotel in town, and has a basic restaurant.

Hotel Kaskada (☎ 279 37 31, fax 279 41 96, ul Chopina 42) Doubles without/with bath US$18/38. Opposite the train station, Kaskada also has a simple restaurant. Rooms with baths are much better than those without.

Pensjonat Miłosna (☎ 279 40 52, ul Miłosna 2) Doubles/triples with bath & breakfast US$40/50. Miłosna is a stylish villa set in the woods off the Grudziądz road, 4km from Kwidzyn, so it's basically a proposition for motorists. Rooms are cosy and comfortable, and there's also a good restaurant.

Getting There & Away

The bus and train stations are 200m apart, about a 10-minute walk to the castle. Trains north to Malbork (28km) and south to Grudziądz (38km) go fairly regularly throughout the day. Five direct trains run to Toruń daily (100km) and two to Gdańsk (89km). There are seven buses to Malbork daily (28km), three to Elbląg (58km) and three to Gdańsk (86km).

GNIEW
☎ 58 • pop 7200

Less known and visited than Kwidzyn, the town of Gniew ('Gnyef') on the other side of the Vistula also has a castle, which is more complete than that in Kwidzyn. The town has preserved its original medieval layout complete with the Rynek and church. It's a charming place to visit for a couple of hours.

Things to See

The first stronghold of the Teutonic Order on the left bank of the Vistula, the **castle** was built in the late 13th century on a square plan and is a massive multistorey brick structure with a deep courtyard. In 1464 it came under Polish rule and remained so until the First Partition of 1773. The Prussians remodelled it to accommodate a barracks, jail and ammunition depot. It was seriously burnt out in 1921, but the 2m-thick walls survived. Restoration work began in 1976 and is still in progress.

The castle now houses the **Archaeological Museum** (☎ 535 35 29, Plac Zamkowy 2; adult/student US$2/1.50; open 9am-5pm Tues-Sun May-Oct). The archaeological exhibition is in two rooms, but you will also be shown the chapel and temporary exhibitions in other rooms, and wander through most of the castle, up to the top floor (good views). All visits are guided and the tour takes up to 1½ hours.

View of historic Kalisz from the City Hall clock tower

Old Town Hall, Kalisz

Z. ZDJĘCIE Z KRZYŻ.
Way of the Cross, Licheń

Twin-towered Cathedral, Gniezno

Burger's houses, Poznań

1956
Metalworkers' Memorial, Poznań

Historic building facades on the Old Town Square, Poznań

Restored house facade, Gdańsk

View along the left bank of the Motława River, Gdańsk

Monument to the Fallen Shipyard Workers, Gdańsk

Bishop's Palace in Oliwa, Gdańsk

View over the old Gdańsk quarter from the Town Hall bell tower

Neptune Fountain, Gdańsk

The **Rynek** is a fine if dilapidated example of the old market square with the central town hall, even though most of the buildings were reshaped on various occasions. The **parish church**, off the square, has preserved its Gothic external shape and vaults.

Places to Stay & Eat

Dormitorium (*☎/fax 535 21 62*) Dorm beds US$7. Open year-round. Occupying part of the castle, the 90-bed Dormitorium offers bunk accommodation in spacious four- to 10-bed vaulted dorms, heated in winter. It's simple but clean and has character, and you'll hardly find a cheaper castle in which to sleep in Poland. The castle's vaulted cellars provide a great setting for the ***Piwnica Rycerska***, which serves budget meals.

Pałac Marysieński (*☎/fax 535 21 62*) Singles/doubles with bath & breakfast US$25/40. The Pałac is a large palatial building next to the castle. It has been fully renovated and provides comfortable accommodation. Its ***Restauracja Husarska*** is OK and affordable.

Getting There & Away

There's no railway in Gniew but the bus service is satisfactory. The bus terminal is about 200m north-west of the Rynek. There are over a dozen buses daily to Tczew (31km), nine to Gdańsk (65km), four to Grudziądz (48km) and one to Toruń. Buses to Pelplin leave every hour or two.

PELPLIN
☎ 58 • pop 8500

Pelplin, 14km north-west of Gniew, is another small town which hardly ever makes it into tourist brochures, yet it has one of Poland's best churches. There's nowhere to stay in Pelplin and only a few basic places to eat, but this is not a problem as bus and train transport is reasonable.

Things to See

Pelplin's church, which today acts as the **cathedral** (*☎ 536 16 64; Plac Mariacki 7; admission US$0.75*), owes its existence to the Cistercians who came in 1276 and founded their monastery. The construction of the church progressed until the mid-15th century, by which time it reached its monumental proportions. The 80m-long, 11-span basilica is one of the largest historic churches in the country.

The lofty interior, topped with an amazing Gothic vault, is a veritable treasury of sacred art, including 21 altars. The five-tier, 26m-tall, late Renaissance high altar (1629–40) is a masterpiece and reputedly the largest timber altar in Central Europe. The baroque organ (1677–79), Gothic stalls (1450–63) and pulpit (1682) are some of the other showpieces.

The cathedral is usually open during the daytime but if you find it locked, inquire at the seminary at the back. Visitors are guided around the church and the tour takes up to an hour. Tours in English, French, German and Italian can sometimes be arranged.

Another attraction is the **Diocesan Museum** (*Muzeum Diecezjalne; ☎ 536 12 21, ul Biskupa Dominika 11; adult/student US$1/0.50; open 11am-4pm Tues-Sat, 10am-5pm Sun*), 1km west of the cathedral, off the road to Starogard Gdański. It has a collection of religious objects, including paintings, sculptures and manuscripts. The highlight is a Gutenberg Bible, one of 47 worldwide and the only one in Poland.

Getting There & Away

The PKP and PKS stations are next to each other on the eastern edge of town, 1km from the church. Eight trains a day depart to Gdańsk, six to Bydgoszcz and one to Toruń. There are about 15 buses to Gniew daily and regular departures to Tczew and Starogard Gdański, from where you have good transport around the region and beyond.

MALBORK
☎ 55 • pop 42,000

Malbork is famous for its castle, reputedly Europe's largest Gothic castle. It's one of Poland's oldest castles and a splendid example of a classic medieval fortress, with multiple defensive walls, a labyrinth of rooms and chambers, and some exquisite architectural detail. In 1997, the castle was included on Unesco's World Heritage list.

POMERANIA

Information

The Centrum Informacji Turystycznej (☎ 272 92 46), ul Piastowska 15, is open 10am to 6pm Tuesday to Friday, 10am to 2pm Saturday and Sunday. Bank Pekao is at ul Piłsudskiego 9.

Castle

The castle sits on the bank of the Nogat River, an eastern arm of the Vistula, which was once the main bed of the river. The castle's enormous size is what hits you first. The best view of the complex is from the opposite side of the river (you can get there by footbridge), especially in the late afternoon when the brick turns an intense red-brown in the setting sun.

The castle is now a **Castle Museum** (*Muzeum Zamkowe;* ☎ 272 26 77, ul Starościńska 1; tours adult/student US$5/3; open 9am-5pm Tues-Sun May-Sept, 9am-3pm Oct-Apr). Most of the rooms and chambers are open for visitors, some of them housing exhibitions. The entrance to the complex is from the northern side, through what used to be the only way in. From the main gate, you walk over the drawbridge, then go through five iron-barred doors to the vast courtyard of the **Middle Castle** (Zamek Średni). On the western side (to your right) is the **Grand Masters' Palace** (Pałac Wielkich Mistrzów) with some splendid interiors. Alongside is the **Knights' Hall** (Sala Rycerska). Measuring 450 sq metres, it's the largest chamber in the castle. It has preserved its original palm vaulting in a remarkable shape, but the foundations of the building are subsiding. While the rescue work is in progress, it's

The Life & Times of Malbork Castle

Malbork castle was built by the Teutonic Knights, who named it Marienburg or the 'Fortress of Mary', made it their main seat and ruled their state from Malbork for almost 150 years.

The immense castle took shape in stages. First was the so-called High Castle, which was begun around 1276 and finished within three decades. It was a stronghold to be reckoned with, square with a central courtyard and surrounded by formidable fortifications.

When the capital of the order was moved from Venice to Malbork in 1309 and the castle became the home of the Grand Master, the fortress was expanded considerably, both to cope with its newly acquired functions and to provide adequate security. The Middle Castle was built to the side of the high one and followed by the Lower Castle still farther along. The whole complex was encircled by three rings of defensive walls and strengthened with dungeons and towers. The castle eventually spread over 21 hectares, making it the largest fortress built in the Middle Ages.

The castle was only seized in 1457 during the Thirteen Years' War, when the military power of the order had already been eroded, and the Grand Master had to retreat to Königsberg (present-day Kaliningrad in Russia). Malbork then became the residence of Polish kings visiting Pomerania, but from the Swedish invasions onwards it gradually went into decline. After the First Partition, the Prussians turned it into barracks, destroying much of the decoration and dismantling parts which were of no use for military purposes. They initially planned to take the castle down altogether and use its fabric to build new barracks. Only the enormous cost of the operation prevented the plan from being carried out.

A change in the castle's fortunes came with the 19th-century's increasing interest in old monuments. Marienburg was one of the first historic buildings taken under government protection to become a symbol of the glory of medieval Germany. It underwent a thorough restoration from the closing decades of the 19th century until the outbreak of WWI, regaining a shape close to the original. Not for long, however; during WWII, the eastern part of the fortress was shelled and the whole process had to start again, this time with Polish restorers. The bulk of the restoration was finished by the 1970s and the castle looks much the same as it did six centuries ago, dominating the town and the surrounding countryside.

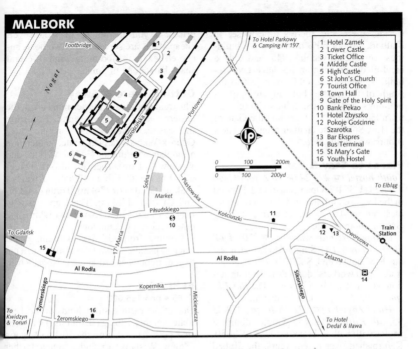

MALBORK

To Hotel Parkowy & Camping Nr 197

Footbridge

To Elbląg

1 Hotel Zamek
2 Lower Castle
3 Ticket Office
4 Middle Castle
5 High Castle
6 St John's Church
7 Tourist Office
8 Town Hall
9 Gate of the Holy Spirit
10 Bank Pekao
11 Hotel Zbyszko
12 Pokoje Gościnne Szarotka
13 Bar Ekspres
14 Bus Terminal
15 St Mary's Gate
16 Youth Hostel

Nogat

Starościńska
Portowa
Solna
Piastowska
Market
Pilsudskiego
17 Marca
Kościuszki
Dworcowa
Train Station
Al Rodła
Al Rodła
Żymierskiego
Kopernika
Mickiewicza
Sikorskiego
Żelazna
Żeromskiego

To Gdańsk
To Kwidzyn & Toruń
To Hotel Dedal & Iława

0 100 200m
0 100 200yd

closed to visitors and may not be open for several years. The building on the opposite side of the courtyard houses a collection of armour and an excellent exhibition of amber.

The tour proceeds to the **High Castle** (Zamek Wysoki), over another drawbridge and through a gate (note the 1280 doorway ornamented with a trefoil frieze in brick) to a spectacular arcaded courtyard with a well in the middle.

You'll then be taken round the rooms on three storeys, including the knights' dormitories, kitchen, bakery, chapterhouse and refectory. The entrance to the **castle church** is through a beautiful Gothic doorway, known as the Golden Gate. Underneath the church's presbytery is St Anne's Chapel with the Grand Masters' crypt below its floor.

Visitors can climb the castle's main square **tower** for an excellent view over the whole complex and the flat countryside

around. Finally, you'll visit the terraces which run around the High Castle between the castle itself and the fortified walls.

Visitors go round in groups, which set off as soon as enough people have arrived. The tour (in Polish) takes up to three hours. Late tours, which leave shortly before closing time, run at breakneck speed and miss some exhibitions.

German and English-speaking guides are available on request for US$30 per group (plus the US$4 entrance fee per person; US$2.50 for students). To be sure of one, book in advance (☎ 272 26 77). Individuals and parties which don't want to spend US$30 for a guide have two options: either wait until a tour group that speaks English (not very often) or German (much more frequent) arrives, then ask the tour guide/driver if you can join and give a tip to the guide; or get in with a Polish group, then 'lose' it and hang around a foreign-language tour (if you are lucky enough to come across one).

POMERANIA

Other Attractions

Besides the castle, there's little to see in Malbork. About 60% of the town's buildings were destroyed in 1945, and only a handful of old monuments have been rebuilt. There was an Old Town just to the south of the castle, but only four of its buildings survived (St John's Church, the town hall, St Mary's Gate and the Gate of the Holy Spirit) and an undistinguished new suburb was built there.

Places to Stay & Eat

Youth hostel (☎ 272 24 08, ul Żeromskiego 45) Beds US$4-7. Open year-round. Housed in the local school, the hostel has a few doubles, but most beds are in dorms sleeping eight or more people.

Pokoje Gościnne Szarotka (☎ 270 14 44, ul Dworcowa 1A) Singles/doubles/triples/quads without bath US$7/13/17/20. Szarotka is a 56-bed workers' dorm near the train station which offers basic rooms. The *Bar Ekspres* next door provides budget meals.

Hotel Zbyszko (☎ 272 26 40, fax 272 33 95, ul Kościuszki 43) Singles/doubles/triples with bath & breakfast US$30/44/50. Refurbished over recent years, the 50-bed Zbyszko is well located and reasonable value. The hotel has its own restaurant, which is OK and inexpensive.

Hotel Parkowy (☎ 272 24 13, ul Portowa 1) Doubles/triples US$30/40. The Parkowy, 1200m north of the castle, is less convenient and not good value, but you may need its summer *Camping Nr 197*, next to the hotel, though it's not good value either.

Hotel Dedal (☎ 272 68 50, ☎/fax 272 31 37, ul Charles de Gaulle'a 5) Singles/doubles/triples with bath & breakfast US$30/42/52. Dedal, 1km south of the centre along the Iława road, offers better standards than any earlier listing in this section. The hotel has its own restaurant.

Hotel Zamek (☎/fax 272 27 38, ☎/fax 272 33 67, ul Starościńska 14) Doubles with bath & breakfast US$80 in summer, US$60 at other times. Nestled in a restored medieval building of the Lower Castle, the 42-room Hotel Zamek is Malbork's top choice, as is the hotel restaurant – good food, fine surroundings and acceptable prices. If you are not up to it, however, cheap meals are served at the two boats anchored next to the footbridge, and at several snack bars along ul Solna.

Getting There & Away

The train station and bus terminal are at the eastern end of the town centre, 1km from the castle. Malbork sits on the busy Gdańsk-Warsaw railway route, so there are a number of trains to Gdańsk (51km) and Warsaw (278km). There are also fairly regular links with Elbląg (29km), Kwidzyn (38km), Grudziądz (76km), Toruń (138km) and Olsztyn (128km). There are buses to Elbląg (33km) and Kwidzyn (39km) and other regional destinations.

Coming from Gdańsk by train, you'll catch a splendid view of the castle; watch out to your right when crossing the Nogat River.

ELBLĄG

☎ 55 • pop 135,000

One of the earliest strongholds of the Teutonic Knights, Elbląg ('El-blonk') was their first port. At that time the Vistula Lagoon (Zalew Wiślany) extended much farther south than today and the town developed as a maritime port for several centuries.

When Elbląg came under Polish rule after the Toruń Treaty, it became one of the Crown's main gateways to the sea, taking much of the trade from the increasingly independent Gdańsk. It was in Elbląg that the first Polish galleon was built in the 1570s, when King Zygmunt August set about establishing a national navy. Later, the Swedish invasions and gradual silting up of the waterways eclipsed the town's prosperity, and a partial revival came only with industrial development in the late 19th century.

WWII turned Elbląg into a heap of rubble, particularly the Old Town. The recovery was hard and long, but it eventually made the town an important industrial centre. Not much of the old architecture has been recreated, but the new centre, currently being constructed, is an innovative design.

The city is a gateway to Frombork and the start of a trip along the Elbląg-Ostróda

Canal (see the Warmia & Masuria chapter). It's also a jumping-off point for the Russian region of Kaliningrad.

Information

The helpful Ośrodek Informacji Turystycznej (☎/fax 232 42 34, W www.umelblag .pl), ul Czerwonego Krzyża 2, is open 8am to 4pm weekdays (9am to 5pm weekdays, 10am to 2pm Saturday from mid-May to mid-September).

Useful banks include Bank Pekao, ul Hetmańska 3 and Stary Rynek 18A, and Bank Gdański, ul 1 Maja 16. There's no shortage of kantors throughout the centre.

Internet facilities include Gabo (☎ 230 48 20), ul Garbary 21; Virtual Cafe (☎ 239 73 33), ul Grunwaldzka 2; Syberiada (☎ 232 32 04), ul Brzozowa 14; and Nebit (☎ 236 72 02), ul Bema 55A.

Things to See

For a long time after the war, the Old Town area was not much more than a meadow with scattered remains of old buildings. It wasn't until the arrival of the market economy that work really started on a project combining elements of the old and new, a stylised **New Old Town**. There's still a long way to go, but many buildings have already been put up and the result is interesting. What's more, the quarter bustles with city life, with offices, banks, shops and bars springing up around the place.

In the middle of this construction site is the Gothic **St Nicholas' Church** (Kościół Św Mikołaja), noted for its 95m-high, carefully reconstructed tower. Less care was given to its interior and what was once a Gothic vault is now a flat concrete ceiling. Fortunately, part of the original woodcarving, including several triptychs, escaped war destruction.

Some 200m to the north is **St Mary's Church**, another massive Gothic brick temple. It houses a gallery of modern art and it's worth a look if only to see the imposing, spacious interior. A few steps from here is the only surviving gate of the medieval fortifications, the **Market Gate** (Brama Targowa).

A five minute walk south along the river bank is the **Elbląg Museum** (☎ 232 72 73,

Bulwar Zygmunta Augusta 11; adult/ student US$1.50/1; open 10am-4pm Tues, Wed, Fri & Sat, 10am-6pm Thur & Sun). Occupying two large buildings, the museum has sections on archaeology and the city's history, plus a photographic record of the town from the 19th century to WWII.

Places to Stay

Camping Nr 61 (☎/fax 232 43 07, ul Panieńska 14) 4-bed cabins US$22. Open May-Sept. The pleasantly shaded camp site is on the Elbląg River, close to the Old Town and about 1km west of the train and bus stations.

Hotel ZBK (☎ 239 84 34, fax 238 84 05, ul Związku Jaszczurczego 17) Doubles/ triples without bath US$10/12, singles/ doubles with bath US$14/20. Within easy walking distance from the Old Town, the ZBK is simple but OK, and one of the cheapest hotels in Elbląg.

Hotel Galeona (☎/fax 232 48 08, ul Krótka 5) Singles/doubles/triples without bath US$14/17/20, singles/doubles with bath US$20/30. Right in the city centre, Galeona is basic, particularly its rooms with shared facilities.

Pensjonat Boss (☎ 239 37 29, fax 239 37 28, ul Św Ducha 30) Singles/doubles with bath & breakfast US$45/60. One of the new small hotels in the Old Town, Boss offers 13 comfortable rooms.

Hotel Viwaldi (☎ 236 25 42, fax 236 25 41, Stary Rynek 16) Singles/doubles with bath & breakfast US$60/75. Another new addition to the Old Town's accommodation, Viwaldi is posher than Boss and has a fine but expensive restaurant.

Places to Eat

Bar Słoneczny (☎ 641 66 16, ul Hetmańska 16/22) Mains US$1-2. One of the cheapest places to eat in the centre, the Słoneczny has quite acceptable food and is open till 8pm.

Restauracja Pod Kogutem (☎ 641 28 82, ul Wigilijna 8/9) Mains US$3-4. This cosy place in the Old Town serves solid Polish food at low prices.

Restauracja U Bosmana (☎ 641 26 62, ul Św Ducha 27) Mains US$3-5. Another gastronomic outfit in the Old Town, U Bosmana is a good budget fish eatery.

Restauracja Pod Aniołami (☎ 236 17 26, *ul Rybacka 23/24A)* Mains US$3-5. The simpatico Pod Aniołami brings Latin American flavours to town, serving Mexican, Peruvian and Argentinian fare.

Steakhouse Casablanca (☎ 641 27 00, *ul Wigilijna 8/9)* Mains US$3-5. Yet another new Old Town eatery, Casablanca has straightforward Middle-Eastern fare.

Getting There & Away

Train The train station is 1km south-east of the centre. There are about 20 trains to Malbork daily (29km), 15 to Gdańsk (80km), seven to Olsztyn (99km) but only two to Frombork (40km).

Bus The bus terminal is next to the train station and handles regular buses to Gdańsk (61km) and Frombork (42km). Apart from PKS buses, there are private buses to Braniewo via Frombork.

Boat Boats for the Elbląg-Ostróda Canal (see that section in the Warmia & Masuria chapter) depart from the wharf next to the Old Town. Information and tickets are available at Camping Nr 61.

A bit farther south is the departure point for hydrofoils to Kaliningrad in Russia. They depart at 8am daily from May to September and return late in the afternoon, leaving five to six hours for visiting the city. Information and bookings in Elbląg are available from Elzam (☎ 230 61 91), Watur (☎ 641 26 12) and Lobos (☎ 642 17 72).

FROMBORK
☎ 55 • pop 2600

Although Kraków, Toruń and Olsztyn claim close links with Copernicus, it was actually in the tiny coastal town of Frombork that the astronomer spent the latter half of his life and conducted most of the observations and research for his heliocentric theory. By proving that the earth moves round the sun, he changed the course of astronomy, supplanting the old geocentric Ptolemaic system, which placed our planet at the centre of the universe. Copernicus was buried in the local cathedral, though the precise site is unknown.

The town owes its existence to the Warmian bishops (see the boxed text 'From Knight to Bishop – Warmia's History' in the Warmia & Masuria chapter), who arrived in the late 13th century in search of a new base after their previous seat in Braniewo had been ravaged by the Prussians. Within a century they had turned a local hill into a fortified ecclesiastical township, dominated by a huge cathedral and known since as Cathedral Hill. At the foot of the hill a town developed, but it lacked defensive walls and was invaded on several occasions. In 1626 Swedish troops plundered the town and cathedral complex and took most of the valuables, including the cathedral library and the Copernicus collection. The greatest disaster, though, came with WWII, when 80% of the town was destroyed. Today Frombork is a small, sleepy town, still dominated by the cathedral complex, which somehow survived the war unharmed.

Cathedral Hill

The Cathedral Hill (Wzgórze Katedralne) is today the **Nicolaus Copernicus Museum** *(Muzeum Mikołaja Kopernika;* ☎ 243 72 18, W *www.frombork.art.pl).* It covers several sights within the fortified complex, each visited on a separate ticket in its opening hours (differing from sight to sight). The entrance is from the southern side through the massive **Main Gate** (Brama Główna), where you'll find the ticket office.

The **cathedral** *(adult/student US$1/0.50; open 9.30am-5pm Mon-Sat May-Sept, 9am-4pm Mon-Sat Oct-Apr),* in the middle of the courtyard, is a huge brick Gothic construction embellished with a decorated main (western) facade and a slim octagonal tower at each corner. Built from 1329 to 1388, it was, and still is, the largest Warmian church and a model for most other churches put up by the bishops throughout the region.

Inside, the nave and chancel (95m long altogether) are topped with a Gothic star vault and crammed with predominantly baroque altars. The large marble high altar

FROMBORK

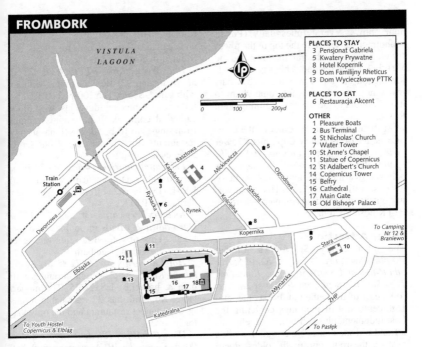

VISTULA LAGOON

PLACES TO STAY
3 Pensjonat Gabriela
5 Kwatery Prywatne
8 Hotel Kopernik
9 Dom Familijny Rheticus
13 Dom Wycieczkowy PTTK

PLACES TO EAT
6 Restauracja Akcent

OTHER
1 Pleasure Boats
2 Bus Terminal
4 St Nicholas' Church
7 Water Tower
10 St Anne's Chapel
11 Statue of Copernicus
12 St Adalbert's Church
14 Copernicus Tower
15 Belfry
16 Cathedral
17 Main Gate
18 Old Bishops' Palace

was made around 1750. Up to that year, a 1504 polyptych was here, which is now in the left-hand (northern) aisle.

The baroque organ, dating from 1683, is a replacement for the one looted by the Swedes in 1626. The organ is noted for its rich tone, best appreciated during Sunday recitals held annually in July and August since 1967. Ask about these at a tourist office before you set off for Frombork.

Note the large number of tombstones (97 in all), some of which are still set in the floor while others have been lifted and placed in the walls to preserve their carving. There's a particularly fine example (from around 1416) at the entrance to the chancel. Also look for the two intriguing baroque marble epitaphs, each with the image of a skeleton and a skull: one is on the first northern column (near the chancel), the other on the fifth southern column.

In the south-eastern corner of the courtyard is the **Old Bishops' Palace** (*Stary Pałac*

Biskupi; adult/student US$1/0.50; open 9am-4.30pm Tues-Sun May-Sept, 9am-4pm Tues-Sun Oct-Apr). On the ground floor are objects discovered during postwar archaeological excavations, while the 1st floor is devoted to the life and work of the astronomer.

Though Copernicus is essentially remembered for his astronomical achievements, his interests extended to many other fields, including medicine, economy and the law. Apart from the early edition of his famous *On the Revolutions of the Celestial Spheres (De Revolutionibus Orbium Coelestium)*, there are others of his treatises and manuscripts, together with astronomical instruments and a copy of Matejko's painting depicting the astronomer at work.

The high tower at the south-western corner of the defensive walls is the former cathedral **belfry** (*dzwonnica; admission US$0.50; open 9.30am-5pm daily May-Sept, 9am-4pm daily Oct-Apr*). There's a

POMERANIA

planetarium downstairs presenting half-hour shows several times daily (Polish soundtrack only). Go to the top of the tower for views of the cathedral, the town and the Vistula Lagoon beyond. This vast but shallow lagoon, separated from the sea by a narrow sandy belt, extends for some 90km to its only outlet to the sea near Kaliningrad in Russia.

At the north-western corner of the complex is the 14th-century **Copernicus Tower** (*Wieża Kopernika; admission US$0.50; open 9.30am-5pm Tues-Sat May-Sept*). It's believed that the astronomer took some of his observations from here. His home was just outside the fortified complex, where the PTTK hostel is today.

Other Attractions

The 15th-century **St Anne's Chapel** (*Kaplica Św Anny;* ☎ *243 75 62, ul Stara; adult/student US$1/0.50; open 10am-6pm Tues-Sat May-Sept, 9am-4pm Tues-Sat Oct-Apr*), east of the cathedral, boasts the late-15th-century wall paintings depicting the Last Judgment, plus exhibitions of religious art and old medicine. Note a giant stork's nest on the roof, one of the oldest documented in Poland.

The **Water Tower** (*Wieża Wodna;* ☎ *243 75 00, ul Elbląska 2; admission US$0.50; open 8am-6pm May-Aug, 8am-3pm Sept-Apr*), across the main road from the cathedral, was built in 1571 as part of one of the first water supply systems in Europe and was used for two centuries to provide Cathedral Hill with water through oak pipes. The water was taken from the Bauda River by a 5km-long canal built for this purpose. You can go to the top of the tower.

Places to Stay & Eat

Camping Nr 12 (☎ *243 73 68, ul Braniewska 14*) Doubles/triples in cabins US$9/14. Open mid-May–mid-Sept. The camp site is at the eastern end of town, on the Braniewo road. It has basic cabins and there is a snack bar on the grounds.

Youth Hostel Copernicus (☎ *243 74 53, ul Elbląska 11*) Dorm beds US$3-5. Open year-round. The hostel is 500m west of Cathedral Hill on the Elbląg road. It's good and neat and offers 120 beds for guests, distributed in dorms of three to 16 beds.

Dom Wycieczkowy PTTK (☎ *243 72 52, ul Krasickiego 2*) Beds in rooms without/with bath US$5/7. The 100-bed PTTK hostel occupies three buildings just west of the cathedral complex. It has rooms ranging from singles to 10-bed dorms. It has its own restaurant which looks shabby but serves acceptable cheap food.

Pensjonat Gabriela (☎/fax *243 78 19, ul Basztowa 2*) Doubles/triples with bath US$12/18. Gabriela offers a bit better standards than PTTK.

Kwatery Prywatne (☎ *243 77 31, ul Ogro-dowa 24*) Beds in doubles or triples US$8. This private villa rents out seven rooms, all with private bath.

Hotel Kopernik (☎ *243 72 85, fax 243 73 00, ul Kościelna 2*) Singles/doubles with bath & breakfast US$28/35. The modern Hotel Kopernik has 32 reasonable rooms, its own budget restaurant and the only kantor in town.

Dom Familijny Rheticus (☎/fax *243 78 00, ul Kopernika 10*) Apartments with bath & kitchen US$20-80. Located in a fine villa, Rheticus offers 10 apartments of one to three rooms to sleep up to five people.

Restauracja Akcent (☎ *243 72 75, ul Rybacka 4*) Mains US$3-5. Apart from the eateries listed above, this is a reasonable place.

Getting There & Away

The train and bus stations are next to each other near the waterfront. Buses run to Elbląg (42km) regularly, and four fast buses go direct to Gdańsk daily (112km). There are two or three buses to Lidzbark Warmiński daily (76km), providing an interesting backwoods route to the Great Masurian Lakes. Trains are of less interest – there are only two departures a day to Elbląg (40km).

Just north of the stations is the wharf from which boats go to Krynica Morska several times daily in summer (US$8, 1½ hours).

Gdańsk

☎ 58 • pop 475,000

Gdańsk is the largest city in northern Poland, even if you don't include Sopot and Gdynia, two urban centres which are merging with Gdańsk to form a single metropolis. The whole conurbation, known as the Tri-City (Trójmiasto), spreads for some 35km along the Gulf of Gdańsk (Zatoka Gdańska) and has a population of nearly 800,000.

Gdańsk is the biggest, oldest and by far the most interesting component of the Tri-City. Known as Danzig in German, it was the Hanseatic trading hub of the Teutonic Knights in medieval times, and evolved into the greatest port on the Baltic. Though it owed loyalty to the Polish kings for over 300 years, Poland had no more than nominal suzerainty and at times had to fight even for this. Demographically mostly German, architecturally reminiscent of Flanders rather than Poland, Gdańsk was effectively an independent city-state, yet it controlled most Polish trade. Wealthy, cultured and cosmopolitan, it was a city that forged its own history.

Napoleon was once heard to say that Gdańsk was the key to everything and Hitler seemed to share this opinion when he started WWII here. Not many European cities were devastated on the scale of Gdańsk, and nowhere on the continent was postwar reconstruction so extensive. Admirably – if somewhat surprisingly – the communist regime rebuilt, brick by brick, house by house, and street by street, the historic city from the ashes. Walking around central Gdańsk today is a bit like going back in time to a 16th century town – it's certainly worth coming here for this experience.

Though Gdańsk is known best to outsiders as the home of Solidarity, there are many other reasons to come here. This is a real city with a soul – a place to be savoured.

HISTORY

There was a fishing village here in the 9th century. It stood on the site of the present Main Town and had a population of around 300. In the closing decades of the 10th century Gdańsk, along with the rest of Pomerania, was annexed to the newborn Polish state and a stronghold was built where the Radunia canal flows into the Motława.

In 997 the Bohemian Bishop Adalbert arrived here from Gniezno and baptised the inhabitants before setting off eastwards on his ill-fated mission to convert the Prussians (see the Gniezno section in the Wielkopolska chapter). The story of his life, *Vita Sancti Adalberti*, written two years later by a monk from Rome, is the first historical document mentioning the town, under the name of Gyddanyzc. Accordingly, the year 997 in considered as the city's formal birth.

Gdańsk's Illustrious Sons

Over centuries, many artists and scholars came to Gdańsk from all over Europe, attracted by its lively cultural and intellectual life. The city also produced its own famous citizens. The astronomer Johannes Hevelius (1611–87), who produced one of the first detailed maps of the moon's surface, was born, lived and worked in Gdańsk. Also born here was Gabriel Daniel Fahrenheit (1686–1736), the inventor of the mercury thermometer whose name lives on, applied to his temperature scale.

Gdańsk was also the birthplace of pessimist philosopher Arthur Schopenhauer (1788–1860), notable for his unconventional view that will is the creative primary factor while idea is the secondary receptive factor. Of the city's prominant writers, Günter Grass (born in 1927) is no doubt Gdańsk's most famous son, perhaps best remembered for his first novel *The Tin Drum*. A novelist, dramatist and poet, Grass was awarded the Nobel Prize for literature in 1999.

Gdańsk's more recent great offsprings include the Solidarity trade union, born here in 1980, and its leader Lech Wałęsa. Together they made their contribution to the end of communism in Eastern Europe, an event that has dramatically changed the course of the continent's modern history.

POMERANIA

TRI-CITY AREA

To Reda, Wejherowo,
Hel, Łeba & Szczecin

Gdynia Chylonia
Gdynia Leszczynki 2
Gdynia Grabówek
Morska
Gdynia Stocznia
3
See Gdynia Map
Gdynia Główna

GDYNIA

Gdynia Wzgórze
Św Maksymiliana

Al Zwycięstwa
Wielkopolska
Obwodnica

Gdynia Redłowo

Gdynia Orłowo

GDYNIA
SOPOT

Sopot Kamienny Potok
4
5
6

7
8
Al Niepodległości
10
11
9
Sopot
12
SOPOT
13
Sopot Wyścigi
14

Spacerowa
SOPOT
GDAŃSK
JELITKOWO

15
Gdańsk Żabianka
16
Gdańsk
Oliwa
17 **BRZEŹNO**
WESTERPLATTE
OLIWA
18
19
Gdańsk Brzeźno
Gdańsk Nowy Port
Gdańsk Przymorze
Al Grunwaldzka
ZASPA
20
NOWY
PORT
Gdańsk Zaspa
Al Hallera
Suchackiego

21
Słowackiego
22
Gdańsk Wrzeszcz
Gdańsk Politechnika
23
24
WRZESZCZ
Obwodnica

GDAŃSK
25
28
OLD
TOWN
SUCHANINO
Gdańsk Główny
26
STOGI
MAIN
TOWN
29
Kartuska
27
Elbląska
See Gdańsk Map

To Kartuzy
& Kościerzyna

To
Tczew
To Toruń &
Bydgoszcz
To Camping Nr 69,
Elbląg, Frombork,
Olsztyn & Warsaw

GULF

OF

GDAŃSK

PLACES TO STAY
2 Youth Hostel
3 Studencki Dom Marynarza Nr 1
4 Hotel Miramar
5 Camping Nr 19
6 Ośrodek Wczasowy Magnolia
7 Grand Hotel
9 Pensjonat Eden
10 Hotel Rezydent
12 Villa Hestia
13 Camping Nr 67
17 Camping Nr 10
20 Youth Hostel
22 Domy Studenckie
   Politechniki Gdańskiej
23 Dom Nauczyciela
25 Camping Nr 218 Stogi
26 Dom Muzyka
27 Villa Akme
28 Pokoje Gościnne Mac-Tur;
   Pensjonat Angela
29 Youth Hostel

OTHER
1 Gdynia Ferry Terminal
   (Ferries to Nynäshamn)
8 Sopot Pier
11 Opera Leśna
14 Racecourse
15 Zoo
16 Oliwa Cathedral
18 Gdańsk Ferry Terminal
   (Ferries to Karlskrona)
19 Westerplatte Monument;
   Guardhouse No 1
21 Airport
24 State Baltic Opera

0   2   4km
0   1   2mi

POMERANIA

The settlement developed as a port over the next centuries, expanding northwards onto what is today the Old Town. Following Poland's fragmentation in 1138, the region of Gdańsk became an independent principality ruled by a local Slav dynasty, the East Pomeranian dukes. The German community arrived from Lübeck in the early 13th century, and from this point on the cosmopolitan character of the town developed, to determine the history of Gdańsk for over seven centuries.

The picture changed considerably after the Teutonic Knights, who were already comfortably established on the Lower Vistula, seized Gdańsk in 1308 and slaughtered the Polish population. Expansive and energetic, the knights swiftly turned Gdańsk into a fully fledged medieval town. A castle was built about 1340, replacing the existing ducal stronghold, and the Main Town was redesigned on a pattern which has survived unchanged to this day. The familiar ring of defensive walls enveloped the town to assure safety.

Joining the Hanseatic League in 1361, Gdańsk soon grew fat on trade and by 1400 had about 10,000 inhabitants. By then the knights had become involved in an armed struggle with Poland; they increased taxes from local merchants and recruited soldiers from the local population to fight their battles. The citizens weren't particularly happy about the order's militarism or its religious goals, so discontent and protests ensued. As in Toruń, tensions exploded in 1454 into a revolt in which the townspeople razed the knights' castle and soon afterwards pledged their loyalty to the Polish monarch. In turn, Gdańsk was rewarded with numerous privileges, including a monopoly on the grain trade and a greater degree of political independence than any other Polish city. The town continued to thrive for the next two centuries.

By the mid-16th century, Gdańsk had come to control three-quarters of Poland's foreign trade and its population reached 40,000. It was the largest Polish city, bigger than royal Kraków. Not only was it the Baltic's greatest port, but it was also the most important trading centre in Central and Eastern Europe. It attracted legions of international traders – Dutch people, Swedes, Scots, Italians and others – who joined the local German-Polish population.

The Reformation arrived in the 1520s, leaving a strong mark on the multinational community, and in 1580 the first academy, known as Athenae Gedanensis, was established. Splendid public buildings and burghers' houses were constructed, making the place reminiscent of northern European ports rather than of inland Polish towns. An outer ring of fortifications was built which, as it turned out, soon proved very useful; Gdańsk was one of the very few Polish cities which withstood the Swedish Deluge of the 1650s. However, since the rest of the country was devastated, the trade on which the town's prosperity stood declined drastically.

Prussia didn't try to seize Gdańsk in the First Partition of 1773, but it did take the area all around, separating the town from what was left of Poland. It imposed trade restrictions on the Vistula and blockaded the city from the sea. Twenty years later, in the Second Partition, Prussia annexed Gdańsk easily, for the port had already been weakened and its population had dropped to 36,000, half of that a century earlier.

The city was besieged in 1807, this time with the Prussians inside while the Napoleonic army, strengthened by Polish regiments, attacked it for two months. After taking it, Napoleon proclaimed it a free city under the supervision of a French governor. Not for long, though. Ironically enough, following Napoleon's retreat from Moscow in 1813, the French and the Poles in their turn were entrenched inside and held the fortress for 10 months against the combined Prussian and Russian troops.

In 1815 the Congress of Vienna gave Gdańsk back to Prussia. In the century that followed, the Polish minority was systematically Germanised, the city's defences reinforced and there was gradual but steady economic and industrial growth.

The next of numerous changes in control came in the aftermath of WWI. The Treaty of Versailles gave Poland the so-called Polish Corridor, a strip of land stretching from

POMERANIA

Toruń to Gdańsk, providing the country with an outlet to the sea. Gdańsk was excluded, however, and made the Free City of Danzig. It became virtually autonomous under the protection of the League of Nations represented by its high commissioner residing in the city. In the first elections to the 120-seat parliament, the Poles gained seven seats, which more or less represented their initial share of power. Step by step, the Germans further increased their control, particularly after Hitler came to power. The shipyard was then used for the production of German warships and the first German submarines.

WWII started in Gdańsk, at dawn on 1 September 1939, when the German battleship *Schleswig-Holstein* fired the first shots on the Polish military post in Westerplatte at the port entrance. During the occupation of the city, the Nazis continued to use the local shipyards for building warships (136 were made here), with Poles as forced labour.

The Russians arrived in March 1945; during the fierce battle the city virtually ceased to exist. The destruction of the historic quarter was comparable to that of Warsaw's Old Town – Polish authorities put it at 90%.

The social structure changed drastically after the war. The German majority either perished or fled, and those few who were left were expelled in 1946. Their place was taken by Polish newcomers, mainly from the territories lost to the Soviet Union.

After the initial shock, in 1949 the complex reconstruction of the Main Town began, firstly by removing two million cubic metres of rubble. The restoration took over 20 years, though work on some interiors continued well into the 1990s. Nowhere else in Europe was such a large area of a historic city reconstructed from the ground up.

In December 1970 a massive strike broke out in the shipyard and was 'pacified' by the authorities as soon as the workers left the gates, leaving 44 dead. This was the second important challenge to the communist regime after Poznań in 1956.

Gdańsk came to the fore again in 1980, when another popular protest paralysed the shipyard. This time, however, it culminated in negotiations with the government and the foundation of Solidarity. The electrician who led the strike and the subsequent talks, Lech Wałęsa, became the first freely elected president in postwar Poland.

ORIENTATION

You're most likely to arrive at the Gdańsk Główny main train station, from where it's just a 10-minute walk to the core of the historic quarter. If you come by bus, you arrive right next to the train station.

Sightseeing in Gdańsk is straightforward, for almost all the major attractions are in the city centre and a short walk apart. Buses and trams operate on the outskirts of the centre but don't go through it.

The city centre consists of three historic districts: the Main Town in the centre (part of it is a pedestrian precinct), the Old Town to the north, and the Old Suburb to the south. To the east of the Main Town, beyond the Stara Motława River, is the fourth integral part of the historic city, Spichlerze (Granary) Island, once crammed with over 300 granaries.

Besides sightseeing in the city centre, your itinerary might include a half-day trip to the suburb of Oliwa and a boat trip to the port and Westerplatte.

Gdynia is probably best done as a half-day visit from Gdańsk, but Sopot can be a destination in itself, particularly if you want to see how the Poles spend their holidays.

INFORMATION
Tourist Offices

The Gdańska Informacja Turystyczna (☎ 301 91 51), ul Długa 45, opposite the main town hall, is open 10am to 6pm Monday to Saturday. Open till 8pm and 10am to 8pm Sunday from June to mid-September. It's a good source of information and is well stocked with maps and brochures.

You can also use the helpful regional tourist office, the Stowarzyszenie Turystyczne Pomorze Gdańskie (☎ 301 43 55, ☎/fax 301 66 37), ul Heweliusza 27, on the northern edge of the Old Town. It's open 9am to 3pm weekdays (till 4pm in July and August).

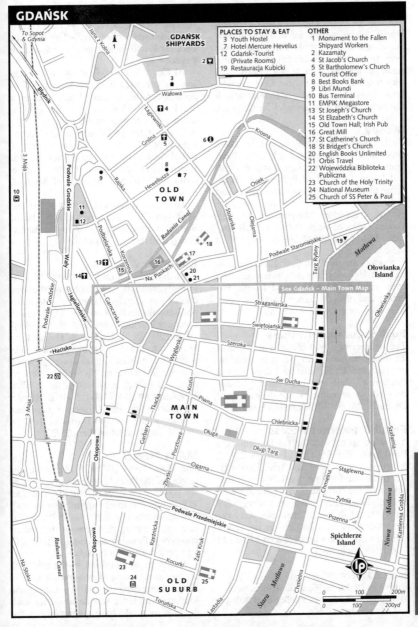

GDAŃSK

PLACES TO STAY & EAT
3 Youth Hostel
7 Hotel Mercure Hevelius
12 Gdańsk-Tourist (Private Rooms)
19 Restauracja Kubicki

OTHER
1 Monument to the Fallen Shipyard Workers
2 Kazamaty
4 St Jacob's Church
5 St Bartholomew's Church
6 Tourist Office
8 Best Books Bank
9 Libri Mundi
10 Bus Terminal
11 EMPiK Megastore
13 St Joseph's Church
14 St Elizabeth's Church
15 Old Town Hall; Irish Pub
16 Great Mill
17 St Catherine's Church
18 St Bridget's Church
20 English Books Unlimited
21 Orbis Travel
22 Wojewódzka Biblioteka Publiczna
23 Church of the Holy Trinity
24 National Museum
25 Church of SS Peter & Paul

POMERANIA

Pick up *Welcome to Gdańsk, Sopot, Gdynia* and *Gdańsk, Gdynia, Sopot: What, Where, When*, which are two free tourist magazines. If the tourist offices don't have them, try reception desks of upmarket hotels. Also, get a copy of the comprehensive and very helpful *Gdańsk in Your Pocket* guidebook, updated every three or four months. It can be bought in newsagencies for US$1.25.

Money

Bank Pekao is at ul Garncarska 23; Bank Gdański has offices at several central locations, including Wały Jagiellońskie 14/16 and Długi Targ 14/16; Powszechny Bank Kredytowy is at ul Ogarna 116. These and some other banks will exchange most major brands of travellers cheques and give advances on Visa; Bank Pekao will also accept MasterCard. ATMs are easy to find in the centre.

Kantors are plentiful throughout the central area. Beware of the moneychangers who hang around Długi Targ and Długie Pobrzeże and offer foreigners attractive rates. You may not get what you expect!

Post & Communications

The main central post office is at ul Długa 22. Poste restante is in the same building but you enter through the back door from ul Pocztowa. Mail sent here should be addressed: your name, Poste Restante, ul Długa 22/28, 80–801 Gdańsk 50, Poland.

Email & Internet Access

You can start off with the Telekomunikacja Polska (☎ 305 66 11), ul Długa 22/27, which is very central and free. However, it's open 10am to 6pm weekdays only and has just three computers. You usually need to book in advance, and access is normally limited to a half-hour. Otherwise, you have a number of payable facilities in the centre (which work longer hours and cost US$1 to US$1.50), including:

Jazz 'n' Java (☎ 305 36 16) ul Tkacka 17/18
Rudy Kot (☎ 301 39 86) ul Garncarska 18/20
Wojewódzka Biblioteka Publiczna (☎ 301 48 11) Targ Rakowy 5/6

Travel Agencies

Almatur (☎ 301 29 31), Długi Targ 11, provides its usual services, including ISIC student cards and international transportation tickets.

PTTK (☎ 301 60 96), ul Długa 45 (sharing the premises with the tourist office), arranges guides speaking English, German and French (US$50 per group for up to six hours plus US$8 for each extra hour).

Orbis (☎ 301 44 25), ul Podwale Staromiejskie 96/97, sells ferry tickets, international and domestic train tickets, and international bus tickets. It also organises tours in the city and beyond (Hel, Malbork, Frombork).

The Biuro Turystyki Lauer (☎ 301 16 19), ul Piwna 22/23, organises trips to Kaliningrad in Russia. Transport is by road to Elbląg and then by hydrofoil.

Bookshops

English Books Unlimited (☎ 301 33 73), ul Podmłyńska 10, has probably the best choice of English-language literature, phrasebooks and dictionaries. Other places to check include the Best Books Bank (☎ 346 20 33), ul Heweliusza 11, and Libri Mundi (☎ 305 15 74), ul Rajska 1. The widest selection of English-language newspapers and magazines (as well as the German and French press) is in the EMPiK Megastore (☎ 301 74 81), Podwale Grodzkie 8, across the street from the main train station. There's another smaller EMPiK (☎ 301 40 34) at Długi Targ 25/27.

MAIN TOWN

The Main Town (Główne Miasto) is the largest of the three historic quarters. It was always the richest architecturally, and after WWII was the most carefully restored. It now looks much as it did some 300 to 400 years ago, during the times of its greatest prosperity. Prussian accretions of the Partition period were not restored.

The town was laid out in the mid-14th century along a central axis consisting of ul Długa (Long Street) and Długi Targ (Long Market). The latter was designed for trading, which would have taken place in the

Gdańsk's Cultural Heritage Book of Records

Gdańsk did quite well over its 1000-year life as far as cultural and artistic achievements go. Furthermore, despite its almost total destruction in WWII, the city managed to preserve some of its historic treasures. Gdańsk would score quite a few top points in any European Cultural Heritage Book of Records. Here are some reasons why:

- Largest brick Gothic church (St Mary's Church, 105m long, 66m wide)
- Tallest Renaissance tiled stove (10.65m high, in Artus Court)
- Largest Gothic astronomical clock (14m high, in St Mary's Church)
- Largest medieval mill (seven-storey Great Mill, producing 200 tons of flour per day)
- Biggest medieval crane (Gdańsk Crane, capable of hoisting loads up to 2000kg)
- Largest church altar made of amber (6500kg of amber, in St Bridget's Church)

They all are detailed in this chapter, so simply go and see them for yourself.

Rynek or central market square. The axis came to be known as the Royal Way, for it was the thoroughfare through which the Polish kings traditionally paraded during their periodical visits.

Royal Way

Of the three Royal Ways in Poland (Warsaw, Kraków and Gdańsk), the Gdańsk one is the shortest – only 500m long – but it's architecturally perhaps the most refined.

The traditional entry point for kings was the **Upland Gate** (Brama Wyżynna) at the western end of the Royal Way. The gate was built in 1574 as part of the city's new fortifications, which were constructed outside the medieval walls to strengthen the system. The authorities weren't happy with the original structure, so in 1586 they commissioned a Flemish artist, Willem van den Block, to embellish it. It was covered with sandstone slabs and ornamented with three coats of arms: of Prussia (with unicorns), Poland (with angels) and Gdańsk (with lions). You'll find Gdańsk's shield, invariably with heraldic lions, on countless public buildings throughout the city.

Just behind the Upland Gate is a large 15th-century construction known as the **Foregate** (Przedbramie). It consists of the Torture House (Katownia) to the west and a high Prison Tower (Wieża Więzienna) to the east, linked to one another by two walls.

When the Upland Gate was built, the Foregate lost its defensive function and was turned into a jail. The Torture House then had an extra storey added as a court room and was topped with decorative Renaissance parapets. A gallows was built on the square to the north, where public executions of condemned foreigners were held. The locals had the 'privilege' of being hanged at the Long Market in front of the Artus Court. The Foregate was used as a jail till the mid-19th century. It was damaged during WWII and the restoration which began in 1951 has not yet been completed.

Next to the east is the **Golden Gate** (Złota Brama). Its function was not defensive but symbolic. Designed by Abraham van den Block, son of the decorator of the Upland Gate, and built in 1612, it's a sort of triumphal arch ornamented with a double-storey colonnade and topped with eight allegorical statues. The four figures on the side of the Prison Tower represent Peace, Liberty, Wealth and Fame, for which Gdańsk was always struggling against foreign powers, the Polish kings included. The sculptures on the opposite side symbolise the burghers' virtues: Wisdom, Piety, Justice and Concord. Today's figures are postwar copies of the 1648 originals.

Adjoining the gate to the north is the **Court of the Fraternity of St George** (Dwór Bractwa Św Jerzego), a good example of

POMERANIA

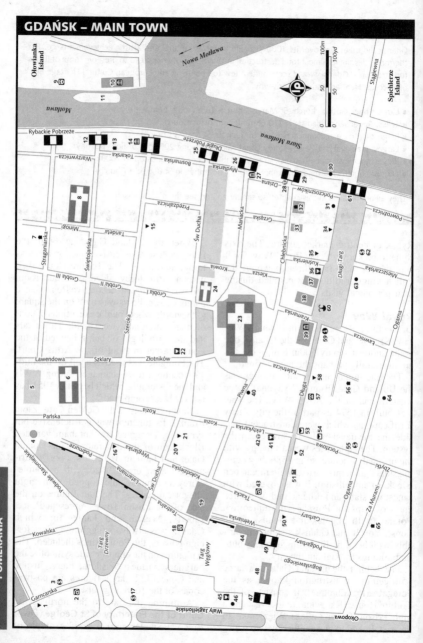

GDAŃSK - MAIN TOWN

PLACES TO STAY
7 Dom Aktora
13 Hotel Hanza
32 Dom Studenta ASP; House Under the Angels
56 Dom Wycieczkowy Zaułek
65 Dom Harcerza

PLACES TO EAT
1 Bar Green Way
15 Restauracja Pod Łososiem
16 Bar Mleczny Turystyczny
20 Bar Starówka
21 Restauracja Gdańska
34 Restauracja Sphinx
35 Bar Pod Rybą
50 Bar Pod Złotym Kurem
52 Karczma
58 Bar Mleczny Neptun

OTHER
2 Rudy Kot
3 Bank Pekao
4 Hyacinthus' Tower
5 Market Hall
6 St Nicholas' Church
8 St John's Church
9 Baltic Philharmonic Hall
10 Central Maritime Museum
11 Sołdek Museum Ship
12 St John's Gate
14 Gdańsk Crane; Central Maritime Museum
17 Bank Gdański
18 Teatr Wybrzeże
19 Great Arsenal
22 Cotton Club
23 St Mary's Church
24 Royal Chapel
25 Gate of the Holy Spirit
26 St Mary's Gate
27 Archaeological Museum
28 Public Toilet
29 Bread Gate
30 Pleasure Boats
31 EMPiK
33 Schlieff House
36 Jazz Club
37 Golden House
38 Artus Court
39 Town Hall; Historical Museum of Gdańsk
40 Biuro Turystyki Lauer
41 Celtic Pub
42 Public Toilet
43 Jazz 'n' Java
44 Court of the Fraternity of St George
45 Latający Holender
46 LOT Office
47 Upland Gate
48 Foregate
49 Golden Gate
51 Uphagen's House
53 Post Office
54 Poste Restante
55 Powszechny Bank Kredytowy
57 Telekomunikacja Polska
59 Tourist Office; PTTK Office
60 Neptune Fountain
61 Green Gate
62 Bank Gdański
63 Almatur
64 British Council's Library

late Gothic secular architecture, dating from the 1490s. The roof is topped with a 16th-century octagonal tower, with St George and the Dragon on the spire (the 1556 original is in Gdańsk's National Museum).

Once you pass the Golden Gate, you are on the gently curving **Long Street** (ul Długa), one of the loveliest streets in Poland, though despite its name it's only 300m long. In 1945 it was just a heap of smoking rubble. Stop at the **Uphagen's House** (*Dom Uphagena;* ☎ *301 23 71, ul Długa 12; adult/student US$1.50/0.75; open 10am-4pm Tues-Sun, to 5pm in summer*) to see the restored historic interior.

At the eastern end of the street is the **town hall**, with its tall slim tower, the highest in Gdańsk (81.5m). Look at the pinnacle; there's a life-sized gilded figure of King Zygmunt August on top – he was particularly generous in granting privileges to the city.

The town hall has both Gothic and Renaissance elements. The first building was reputedly put up in the 1330s, but it grew and changed until the end of the 16th century. In 1945 it was almost completely burnt

out and the authorities were on the point of demolishing the ruin, which was eventually saved thanks to local protests.

After serving as a municipal seat for over half a millennium, today it houses the **Historical Museum of Gdańsk** (*Muzeum Historii Miasta Gdańska;* ☎ *301 48 71, ul Długa 47; adult/student US$2/1; open 10am-4pm Tues-Sun, to 5pm in summer*). Enter the building by twin flights of balustraded stairs and go through an ornate baroque doorway (1766) topped by the city's coat of arms guarded by two lions which, unusually, are both looking towards the Golden Gate, supposedly awaiting the arrival of the king. The doorway was the final addition to the external decoration of the building.

Inside are several rooms with period decoration, either original or recreated from old drawings, engravings and photographs. The showpiece is the Red Room (Sala Czerwona) in the Dutch mannerist style from the end of the 16th century, which was once the setting for the Town Council's debates. There's a large, richly carved fireplace (1593) and a marvellous portal (1596) but

POMERANIA

Gdańsk's Long Market; once the city's major market place, it's now a major tourist attraction

your eyes will immediately be attracted to the ornamented ceiling, with 25 paintings dominated by the oval centrepiece entitled *The Glorification of the Unity of Gdańsk with Poland*. The painter, Isaac van den Block, yet another member of the Flemish family of artists, incorporated various themes in the painting, from everyday scenes to the panorama of Gdańsk on the top of the triumphal arch. All the decoration of the room is authentic; it was dismantled in 1942 and hidden outside Gdańsk.

The 2nd floor houses exhibitions related to Gdańsk's history, including photos of the destruction of 1945. From this floor you can enter the tower for a great view. To the east, just at your feet, is the **Long Market** (Długi Targ), once the main city market and now the major focus for tourists.

Next to the town hall is the **Neptune Fountain** (Fontana Neptuna), dominated by the sea god, trident in hand. The bronze statue is the work of another Flemish artist, Peter Husen; it was made in 1606–13 and is the oldest secular monument in Poland. In 1634 the fountain was fenced off with a wrought-iron barrier. This is linked to a legend that the Gdańsk vodka, Goldwasser, spurted out of the trident one merry night and

Neptune found himself endangered by crowds of drunken locals. A menagerie of stone sea creatures was added in the 1750s during the restoration of the fountain.

Behind the fountain is the **Artus Court** (*Dwór Artusa;* ☎ 346 33 58, *Długi Targ 43/44; adult/student US$2/1; open 10am-4pm Tues-Sun, to 5pm in summer*) where wealthy local merchants held meetings, banquets and general revelries. Built at the end of the 15th century, the court was given its monumental facade by Abraham van den Block in the 1610s. Inside, there's a huge hall, topped with a Gothic vault supported on four slim granite columns. The undisputed highlight of the interior is the giant Renaissance **tiled stove**, standing in the corner of the hall and almost touching the vault. It's reputedly the highest tiled stove in Europe, and it's truly wonderful.

The nearby 1618 **Golden House** (Złota Kamienica), designed by Johan Voigt, has the richest facade in the city. In the friezes between storeys are 12 elaborately carved scenes interspersed with busts of famous historical figures, including two Polish kings. The four statues waving to you from the balustrade at the top are Cleopatra, Oedipus, Achilles and Antigone.

Tiled Stove of Artus Court

Gdańsk's Artus Court shelters a rare gem – Europe's tallest Renaissance stove. Looking like a five-tier tower, 10.65m high, the stove is also amazingly beautiful, with a wealth of decoration in bas-relief and colour portraying rulers, allegorical figures, coats of arms etc. Built in 1546 by Georg Stelzener, the stove survived virtually unchanged until 1943, when local conservators dismantled the upper part and hid it outside the city. The lower tiers were badly damaged during fighting in 1945. All fragments were recollected after the war, and after a long and complex restoration, the stove was eventually put together and revealed to the public in 1995. It contains 520 tiles, 437 of which are original.

The Long Market is flanked from the east by the **Green Gate** (Zielona Brama), marking the end of the Royal Way. It was built in the 1560s on the site of a medieval defensive gate and was supposed to be the residence of the kings. But they never stayed in what turned out to be a cold and uncomfortable lodge; they preferred the houses nearby, particularly those opposite the Artus Court.

Waterfront

Just behind the Green Gate is the Motława River. There once was a busy quay along here, crowded with hundreds of sailing ships loading and unloading their cargo, which was stored either in the cellars of the burghers' houses in town or in the granaries on the other side of the river, on Granary Island. Today it's a popular tourist promenade lined with cafes, art galleries and souvenir shops.

In medieval times, the parallel east-west streets of the Main Town all had defensive gates at their riverfront ends. Some of them still exist, though most were altered in later periods. Walking north along the Długie Pobrzeże (literally, Long Waterfront), you first get to the **Bread Gate** (Brama Chlebnicka) at the end of ul Chlebnicka. It was built around 1450, still under the Teutonic Order, as shown by the original city coat of arms consisting of two crosses. The crown was added by King Kazimierz Jagiellończyk in 1457, when Gdańsk was incorporated into the kingdom.

Enter the gate and walk a few steps to see the palatial **House under the Angels** (Dom Pod Aniołami), also known as the English House (Dom Angielski) after the native country of the merchants who owned it in the 17th century. At that time it was the largest burgher's house in Gdańsk. Today it's a student dorm.

At No 14 stands the late Gothic **Schlieff House** of 1520. It's a replica built after the emperor of Prussia, Friedrich Wilhelm III, fell in love with its predecessor in the 1820s and had it taken apart brick by brick and rebuilt in Brandenburg. The original is in Potsdam, near Berlin.

The tiny ul Grząska will take you to **St Mary's street**, the most atmospheric of all the streets in Gdańsk and unique in Poland. It was reconstructed after the war almost from the ground up with the utmost piety on the basis of old documents and illustrations, and every detail found in the rubble was incorporated. It looks amazingly authentic. It's the only street with a complete row of terraces, which gives it enormous charm, and is a trendy place lined with shops selling amber jewellery.

The street ends at **St Mary's Gate** (Brama Mariacka), similar to the Bread Gate but constructed later as you'll see from its coats of arms. Next to it is the fair-sized Renaissance **House of the Naturalists' Society** (Dom Towarzystwa Przyrodniczego) with a tower and a five-storey oriel, unusual in Gdańsk. It now houses the **Archaeological Museum** (*Muzeum Archeologiczne;* ☎ *301 50 31, ul Mariacka 25/26; adult/student US$1.50/1; open 10am-4pm Tues-Sun*). The collection stresses the Polish cultural and ethnic roots of the region, and you can go to the top of the tower.

Back on the waterfront and a bit farther north is the modest **Gate of the Holy Spirit** (Brama Św Ducha) and, beyond it, the conspicuous **Gdańsk Crane** (Żuraw Gdański) at the end of ul Szeroka (Wide Street). Built in the mid-15th century as the biggest double-towered gate on the waterfront, it also served to move heavy cargoes directly onto or off the vessels. For this purpose two large wheels – 5m in diameter – were installed as a hoist with a rope wound around the axle; it was put in motion by people 'walking' along the inner circumference of the wheels which formed a treadmill. It could hoist loads of up to 2000kg, making it the biggest crane in medieval Europe. At the beginning of the 17th century another set of wheels was added higher up, for installing masts.

The crane suffered considerable damage in 1945 but was carefully rebuilt; it's the only fully restored relic of its kind in the world. It's now part of the **Central Maritime Museum** *(Centralne Muzeum Morskie; ☎ 301 53 11, ul Szeroka 67/68; admission to all sections of museum adult/student US$2.50/1.50; all open 10am-4pm Tues-Sun, to 6pm in summer)* which has exhibits relating to the history of shipping, plus a collection of shells, corals and other marine life from all over the world. You can also have a look at the hoisting gear of the crane. The modern building next to the crane is an extension of the museum, where traditional rowing and sailing boats from various non-European countries are on display.

The museum continues in three reconstructed granaries just across the Motława, on Ołowianka Island. The museum's boat shuttles between the crane and the island; otherwise it's a 15-minute walk around via the bridge facing the Green Gate. The exhibits, displayed in nine large halls in the granaries, illustrate the history of Polish seafaring from the earliest times to the present and include models of old sailing warships and ports, a 9th-century dugout, navigation instruments, ships' artillery, flags and the like.

Finally, there's the *Sołdek* museum-ship moored in front of the granaries. It was the first freighter built in Gdańsk after WWII (1948); it has now been withdrawn from service and is open to visitors.

Set apart three hours to visit all the sites – there's really a lot to see.

St Mary's Church

Set right in the middle of the Main Town, the Kościół Mariacki (Kościół NMP) is believed to be the largest old brick church in the world. It's 105m long and 66m wide at the transept, and its massive squat tower is 78m high. About 25,000 people can be easily accommodated in its half-hectare (5000-sq-metre) interior.

The church was begun in 1343 and reached its present gigantic size in 1502. It served as the parish church for the Catholic congregation until the Reformation gale blew into Gdańsk, and it passed to the Protestants in 1572, to be used by them until WWII.

The church didn't escape the destruction of 1945; half of the vault collapsed and the interior was largely burnt out. Fortunately, the most valuable works of art had been removed and hidden before the battle front arrived. They were brought back after a long and complex reconstruction.

The church's elephantine size is arresting and you feel even more ant-like when you enter the building. Illuminated with natural light passing through 37 large windows – the biggest is 127 sq metres in area – the three-naved, whitewashed interior topped with an intricate Gothic vault is astonishingly bright and spacious. It was originally covered with frescoes, the sparse remains of which are visible in the far right corner. Imagine the impact the church must have made on medieval worshippers.

On first sight, the church looks almost empty, but walk around its 30-odd chapels to discover how many outstanding works of art have been accumulated. In the floor alone, there are about 300 tombstones. In the chapel at the back of the left (northern) aisle is the replica of Memling's *The Last Judgment* – the original is in the National Museum. Note the extraordinary baroque organ.

The high altar boasts a Gothic polyptych from the 1510s, with the Coronation of the Virgin depicted in its central panel. Large as it is, it's a miniature in this vast space. The same applies to the 4m crucifix high up on the rood beam. Directly below it is a lofty wooden sacrarium from 1482, elaborately carved in the shape of a tower.

One object which does stand out, in terms both of size and rarity, is the 15th-century **astronomical clock** placed in the northern transept. Another great attraction of the church is its **tower** or, more precisely, the sweeping bird's-eye view which you get if you can climb 405 steps to the viewing platform at 82m above street level. The entrance is from the north-western corner of the church.

Royal Chapel

Just to the north of St Mary's Church, and completely overshadowed by the monster, sits the small Royal Chapel (Kaplica Królewska), squeezed between two houses. The only baroque church in old Gdańsk, it was built in 1678–81 to fulfil the last will of the Primate of Poland of the time, Andrzej Olszowski, which set aside funds for a house of worship for the Catholic minority in what was by then a predominantly Lutheran city. The local clergy felt obliged to respect the Primate's bequest and reluctantly allocated part of the upper floor of St Mary's vicarage to the chapel.

The chapel was designed by famous royal architect Tylman van Gameren. It was built on the 1st floor, though the facade was extended over the whole of the elevation to make the building look bigger and more impressive. Parts of the two adjoining houses were adapted as the chancel and the vestibule, and the nave was topped with a dome, typical of the baroque style and particularly of Gameren. The facade is more attractive than the bare interior. It has the coats of arms of Poland, Lithuania and King Jan Sobieski (the founder of the chapel) but, significantly, not that of Gdańsk.

Great Arsenal

To the west of St Mary's Church, ul Piwna (Beer Street) ends at the Great Arsenal (Wielka Zbrojownia). In Gdańsk, even such an apparently prosaic building as an armoury has evolved into an architectural gem. It's the work of Antoon van Opberghen, built at the beginning of the 17th century and, like most of Gdańsk's architecture, clearly shows the influence of the Low Countries. The main eastern facade, framed within two side towers, is floridly decorated and guarded by figures of soldiers on the top. Military motifs predominate, and the city's coat of arms guards the doorways. A small stone structure rather like a well, in the middle of the facade, is the lift which was used for hoisting heavy ammunition from the basement. Above it stands the goddess of warfare, Athena.

Astronomical Clock of St Mary's Church

The astronomical clock of St Mary's Church was constructed in the 1460s by Hans Düringer from Toruń and functioned until 1553. It's claimed that during that time it lost only three minutes. When made, it was the largest clock in the world, 14m tall. Legend has it that Düringer paid dearly for his masterpiece; his eyes were put out to prevent him from ever creating another clock that might compete with this one. He was probably buried under his clock.

Not only did the clock show the hour, day, month and year but also the phases of the moon, position of the sun and moon in the zodiac cycle and the calendar of the saints. It had six devices allowing figures of saints and the apostles to appear and disappear at certain times, and Adam and Eve rang the bells every hour.

The clock was neglected for centuries but stayed in its place until WWII. As the eastern front advanced in the late stage of the war, the clock was dismantled and stored outside Gdańsk in fear of its safety. In the mid-1980s, a long and costly reconstruction began, largely financed by various sponsoring institutions and private citizens.

About 70% of the clock's original housing that had survived – including its two amazing faces – were restored and complemented with missing elements and new mechanisms. It was mounted in its place and put back into work in 1990, after 437 years of quiescence. There are still some figures missing, but the clock shows the time and displays most of its puppet-theatre abilities. Be there at noon.

The armoury is now home to an indoor market but, even if you are not interested in shopping, walk through to the square on the opposite side, Targ Węglowy (Coal Market) to see the western facade. Though not as heavily ornamented as the other one, it's a fine composition looking like four burghers' houses.

Northern Main Town

The main attraction of this sector is **St Nicholas' Church**, one of the oldest in town. It was built by the Dominican Order which arrived from Kraków in 1227, but the church reached its final shape only at the end of the 15th century. Unlike most of the other Gothic churches in the city, this one has a rich interior decoration. The magnificent late Renaissance high altar of 1647 first catches the eye, followed by the imposing baroque organ made a century later. Among other highlights are the stalls in the chancel and an ornate baptismal chapel in the right-hand aisle, just as you enter the church. And don't miss the bronze rosary chandelier (1617) with the Virgin and Child carved in wood. It's hanging in the nave in front of the entrance to the chancel.

Just behind the church is the large and bustling **Market Hall** (Hala Targowa), constructed in the late 19th century after the Dominicans were expelled by the Prussian authorities and their monastery standing on this site was pulled down.

In front of the market hall is the tall octagonal **Hyacinthus' Tower** (Baszta Jacek), one of the remnants of the medieval fortifications. It was built around 1400 and apart from its defensive role also served as a watchtower.

About 200m east towards the river is the massive Gothic **St John's Church** (Kościół Św Jana). It was built during the 14th and 15th centuries on marshy ground and buttresses had to be added to support it. Note the crooked eastern wall. Damaged but not destroyed during the war, the church was locked for four decades. The internal decorations were removed; the organ and the pulpit, for instance, now adorn St Mary's Church. Only the monumental stone high altar was

left inside, simply because it was too large and heavy to be moved elsewhere. The interior has been partly restored and is used as an auditorium for some artistic events.

OLD TOWN

Despite its name, the Old Town was not the cradle of the city. The earliest inhabited site, according to archaeologists, was in what is now the Main Town area. Nonetheless, a settlement existed in the Old Town from the late 10th century and developed in parallel to the Main Town.

Under the Teutonic Order, the two parts merged into a single urban entity, but the Old Town was always poorer and had no defensive system of its own. One other difference was that the Main Town was more 'German' while the Old Town had a larger Polish population. During WWII it suffered as much as its wealthier cousin but, apart from a handful of buildings, mainly churches, it was not rebuilt in its previous shape. Today it's little more than an average postwar town, garnished here and there with reconstructed relics. The most interesting area is along the Radunia Canal, between Garncarska and Stolarska streets.

The largest monument of the Old Town is **St Catherine's Church** (Kościół Św Katarzyny), the oldest church in Gdańsk, begun in the 1220s. It was the parish church for the whole town until St Mary's was completed. As is common, the church evolved over centuries and only reached its final shape in the mid-15th century (save for the baroque top to the tower, added in 1634); since then it has remained unchanged.

The vaulted Gothic interior was originally covered with frescoes, fragments of which were discovered under a layer of plaster. Note the huge painting (11m long) depicting the entry of Christ to Jerusalem, placed under the organ loft in the left-hand aisle, and the richly carved enclosure of the baptismal font (1585) in the opposite aisle. The astronomer Johannes Hevelius was buried in the church's chancel and there is an 18th-century epitaph above the grave.

The church houses the **Tower Clocks Museum** (*Muzeum Zegarów Wieżowych;*

☎ *305 64 92, ul Wielkie Młyny; adult/student US$1/0.50; open 10am-4pm Wed-Sun May-Sept)*, which features a collection of old tower clocks from the 15th century onward. You can also go up the tower to see the carillon, a set of 49 bells which plays a melody every hour.

Immediately behind St Catherine's Church is **St Bridget's Church** (Kościół Św Brygidy). This was almost completely destroyed in 1945 and until 1970 only the walls were left standing. Once the authorities set about rebuilding it, it took five years for the whole structure, complete with a perfect Gothic vault and a Renaissance tower, to be returned to its original state. There's almost nothing left of the prewar furnishing and the interior has modern fittings. Lech Wałęsa attended Mass here when he was an unknown electrician in the nearby shipyard. With the wave of strikes in 1980 the church became a strong supporter of the dockyard workers and its priest, Henryk Jankowski, took every opportunity to express their views in his sermons.

The church remains a record of the Solidarity period, with several contemporary craftworks related to the trade union and to modern Polish history in general. You'll find the tombstone of murdered priest Jerzy Popiełuszko, the Katyń epitaph, a collection of crosses from the 1980 and 1988 strikes and a door with bas-reliefs of scenes from Solidarity's history – all in the right-hand (northern) aisle. In the same aisle, have a look at a spectacular 174cm-high Amber Monstrance depicting the tree of life. And don't miss the monumental high altar which is currently being built. It is being made entirely and exclusively from amber, and about 6500kg of amber is to be used.

The peculiar seven-storey building opposite St Catherine's Church is the **Great Mill** (Wielki Młyn). Built around 1350 by the Teutonic Knights, it was the largest mill in medieval Europe, over 40m long and 26m high, and equipped with a set of 18 millstones, each 5m in diameter. The mill operated until 1945 and just before WWII produced 200 tons of flour per day. It might still be working today if not for the war damage. The building was reconstructed but not its machinery. It now houses a modern shopping mall.

Behind the mill across a small park is the **Old Town Hall** (Ratusz Staromiejski), once the seat of the Old Town council. A Renaissance building, well proportioned and crowned with a high central tower typical of its Flemish provenance, it was designed at the end of the 16th century by Antoon van Opberghen, the architect later responsible for the Great Arsenal. The brick structure is delicately ornamented in stone, including the central doorway and a frieze with the shields of Poland, Prussia and Gdańsk.

The building now houses the Baltic Cultural Centre and an exhibition hall. Go upstairs to see the entrance hall, notable for its rich decoration, partly assembled from old burghers' houses. Note the arcaded stone wall (1560) with three Roman gods in bas-relief. This composition, older than the town hall itself, was moved here from one of the houses in the Main Town. One of the doors leads to the Great Hall, which can also be visited. Concerts are held here – check the program.

A 10-minute walk north is an important symbol of recent history, the **Monument to the Fallen Shipyard Workers** (Pomnik Poległych Stoczniowców), erected in memory of the workers killed in the riots of 1970. Placed in front of the Gdańsk shipyard where Solidarity was born, and unveiled on 16 December 1980, 10 years after the massacre, the monument is a set of three 42m-tall steel crosses, with a series of bronze bas-reliefs in their bases. One of the plates contains a fragment of a poem by Czesław Miłosz that reads:

You, who have wronged a simple man,
Bursting into laughter over his suffering,
DO NOT FEEL SAFE. The poet remembers.
You can kill him – another will be born.
Words and deeds will all be written down.

The first monument in a communist regime to commemorate the regime's victims, it immediately became a symbol and landmark of Gdańsk and a must for every visitor.

OLD SUBURB

The Old Suburb (Stare Przedmieście), south of the Main Town, was the product of the expansion of the city between the 15th and 17th centuries. Reduced to rubble in 1945 and rebuilt in the familiar bland postwar fashion, the suburb has little charm but boasts some important sights.

The most significant of these is the **National Museum** *(Muzeum Narodowe; ☎ 301 70 61, ul Toruńska 1; adult/student US$2/1; open 9am-4pm Tues-Fri, 10am-5pm Sat & Sun)* in the well-restored vaulted interiors of the former Franciscan Monastery. Ranking among the best museums in the country, it contains extensive collections of paintings and woodcarvings, gold and silverware, fabrics and embroidery, porcelain and faience, wrought iron and furniture. It has the original figure of St George from the spire of the Court of the Fraternity of St George, an assortment of huge, elaborately carved Gdańsk wardrobes (typical of the city from where they were sent all over the country) and several beautiful ceramic tiled stoves.

The 1st floor is given over to paintings, with a section devoted to Dutch and Flemish work. The jewel of the collection is Hans Memling's (1435–94) triptych of the *Last Judgment*, one of the earlier works of the artist, dating from 1472–73. You'll also find works by the younger Breughel and Van Dyck, and the beautiful macabre *Hell* by Jacob Swanenburgh, who was the master of the young Rembrandt.

Adjoining the museum from the north, and formerly belonging to the Franciscan monastery, is the **Church of the Holy Trinity** (Kościół Św Trójcy). It was built at the end of the 15th century, when the Gothic style had already reached its late decorative stage, best seen in the elaborate top of the western facade. After St Mary's Church it's the largest in town, with a spacious and lofty whitewashed interior topped with a superb, net-like vault. The chancel was badly damaged during the war and was separated from the nave by a wall.

The high altar has an assembly of panels from triptychs of different origins, while the filigree late Gothic pulpit from 1541 is topped with a Renaissance canopy. Note the floor paved almost entirely with old tombstones and the spidery baroque chandeliers of the mid-17th century.

To complete your picture of Gdańsk's Gothic churches, have a look at the **Church of SS Peter and Paul** (Kościół Św Piotra i Pawła) a block to the east, with its stepped gable on the tower. Once the parish church of the Old Suburb, it was destroyed in the war and reconstructed.

WESTERPLATTE

Westerplatte is a long peninsula at the entrance to the harbour, 7km north of the historic town. When Gdańsk became a free city after WWI, Westerplatte was the Polish tip of the port. It served both trading and military purposes and had a garrison to protect it.

WWII broke out here, when the German battleship *Schleswig-Holstein* began shelling the Polish post. The garrison, which numbered just 182 men, held out for seven days before surrendering. The site is now a memorial, with some of the ruins left as they were after the bombardment, plus a massive monument put up in memory of the defenders. The surviving **Guardhouse No 1** *(Wartownia Nr 1; ☎ 343 69 72, ul Sucharskiego; admission US$0.50; open 9am-4pm daily May-Oct)* houses a small exhibition related to the event, including a model of the battle with English labels.

Bus Nos 106 and 158 go to Westerplatte from the main train station, but a more attractive way to get there is by boat. Boats depart several times daily from the wharf next to the Green Gate. You can take the one which includes a visit to the port en route.

OLIWA

Oliwa, the north-westernmost suburb of Gdańsk, about 9km from the historic centre, boasts a fine cathedral set in a quiet park – an enjoyable half-day break after tramping the medieval streets of the Main Town. To get there, take the commuter train from central Gdańsk and get off at Gdańsk Oliwa station, from where it's a 10-minute walk.

The beginnings of Oliwa go back over 800 years, when the Pomeranian dukes who then ruled Gdańsk invited the Cistercians to settle here in 1186 and granted them land together with privileges, including the revenues of the port of Gdańsk.

The abbey didn't have an easy life. The original church from around 1200 was burnt out by the pagan Baltic Prussians, then by the Teutonic Knights. A new Gothic church, built in the mid-14th century, was surrounded by defensive walls, but that didn't save it from further misfortunes. When in 1577 the abbots supported King Stefan Batory in his attempts to reduce the city's independence, the citizens of Gdańsk burned the church down in revenge. The monks rebuilt their holy home once more, but then the Swedish wars began and the church fell prey to repeated looting, losing its organ and pulpit among other things. The monks' troubles came to an end in 1831, when the Prussian government decided to expel them from the city. The church was given to the local parish and, in 1925, raised to the rank of **cathedral**. It came through the war almost unscathed, and is an important, and unusual, example of ecclesiastical architecture.

The first surprise is its facade, a striking composition of two octagonal brick Gothic towers with a central baroque portion literally squeezed between them. You enter the church by going downstairs, for its floor is more than 1m below the external ground level. The interior looks extraordinarily long, mainly because of the unusual proportions of the building; the nave plus the chancel are 90m long but only 8.3m wide. At the far end of this 'tunnel' is a baroque high altar (1688), while the previous oak-carved Renaissance altar (from 1606) is now in the left-hand transept. Opposite, in the right transept, is the marble tombstone of the Pomeranian dukes (1613), placed on the site where the princes are supposed to have been buried.

The showpiece of the church is the **organ**. The instrument, begun in 1763 and completed 30 years later, is noted for its fine tone and the mechanised angels which blow trumpets and ring bells when the organ is played. In July and August, recitals take place on Tuesday and Friday evenings, but 20-minute performances are held daily

every hour or two between 10am and 3pm or 4pm (on Sunday in the afternoon only). Check the schedule with the tourist offices before setting off for Oliwa.

Behind the cathedral is the 18th-century abbots' palace which now accommodates the **Modern Art Gallery** *(Wystawa Sztuki Współczesnej;* ☎ *552 12 71, ul Cystersów 18; adult/student US$2/1; open 9am-4pm Tues-Sun)*, a branch of the National Museum of Gdańsk. The old granary opposite the palace houses the **Ethnographic Museum** *(Muzeum Etnograficzne;* ☎ *552 41 39, ul Cystersów 19; adult/student US$1.50/0.75; open 9am-4pm Tues-Sun)* with its collection of rural household implements and crafts from the region. The 18th-century **park**, with its lakes, old exotic trees, palm house, greenhouse and a small formal French garden, supplies a fine natural setting for the historic complex.

About 1.5km west of the cathedral (a 20-minute walk or take bus No 122) is a small **zoo** *(Ogród Zoologiczny;* ☎ *552 00 41, ul Karwieńska 3; adult/student US$1.50/0.75; open 9am-dusk)*, picturesquely sited on the wooded slopes of a valley.

LANGUAGE COURSES
There are several schools in the Tri-City area of which possibly the most specialised are two facilities in Sopot: the **Sopocka Szkoła Języka Polskiego** *(Sopot School of Polish Language;* ☎ *550 32 84, fax 550 06 96, Al Niepodległości 763)* and the **Centre for Polish Studies** *(*☎ *550 68 59,* W *www.learn polish.edu.pl, ul Podgórna 8)*. Both offer group courses on several levels and can organise individual tuition on request.

SPECIAL EVENTS
The **Dominican Fair** (Jarmark Dominikański) is the oldest city event, going back to 1260, when the Dominicans received the papal privilege of holding a fair on the feast day of their saint, 4 August. The fair was initially held on Plac Dominikański, the square next to St Nicholas' Church, but today it takes place on various sites in the Main Town during the first two weeks of August. It's become commercialised over recent years, but

there's still a lot of antiques, bric-a-brac and craftworks. The fair is accompanied by various cultural events, including street theatre, music concerts etc.

The **International Organ Music Festival** is held in the Oliwa cathedral, with twice weekly organ recitals from mid-June till the end of August. St Mary's Church is the stage for the **International Organ, Choir and Chamber Music Festival** (Fridays in July and August). St Nicholas' and St Bridget's churches are also used for organ recitals.

July hosts the **'Sounds of the North' Festival of Folklore Inspired Music**, featuring groups from such exotic locations as Greenland or Kamchatka. Also in this month is the **International Street and Open-Air Theatre Festival**.

Nearby, Sopot is famous for its **International Song Festival**, which has been held annually in August for over 30 years. Gdynia hosts the **Gdynia Summer Jazz Days** in July and the **Festival of Polish Feature Films** in September.

The unusual **International Championships in Amber Fishing** are held in August in the seaside village of Jantar, 20km east of Gdańsk, on the stretch of the coast prolific in amber.

PLACES TO STAY

Both tourist offices provide good information about accommodation options.

Places to Stay – Budget

Camping Gdańsk has three camping grounds, which open in May and close in September. All have budget cabins or you can pitch your own tent for about US$2.50 per tent site plus another US$2.50 per person.

Camping Nr 218 Stogi (☎ 307 39 15, fax 343 55 47, ul Wydmy 9) Beds in cabins US$5. Located in the Stogi suburb just 200m off the beach, this is the nearest camp site to the city centre, about 5.5km to the northeast. Here is possibly Gdańsk's best beach and the cleanest water. Tram No 8 from the main train station will take you there.

Camping Nr 69 (☎/fax 308 07 39, ul Lazurowa 5) Beds in cabins US$5-7. Another seaside facility, just a few minutes walk from the beach, this camp site is in Sobieszewo, 17km east of the city centre, accessible by half-hourly bus No 112 from the train station.

Camping Nr 10 (☎/fax 343 55 31, ul Hallera 234) Beds in cabins US$6-7. Located in the suburb of Brzeźno, about 1km from the beach, this is the closest camping ground to the ferry terminal, so it can be convenient if you arrive by ferry from Sweden – it's a short ride on tram No 15. From the main train station, the camp site is accessible by tram No 13.

Youth Hostels Gdańsk has three all-year youth hostels.

Youth hostel (☎/fax 301 23 13, ul Wałowa 21) Beds US$4-8. This is the most convenient hostel, a five-minute walk north-east from the main train station. Predictably, it's often full, particularly in summer. It has 96 beds distributed in dorms to sleep from two to eight people.

Youth hostel (☎ 302 60 44, fax 302 41 87, ul Kartuska 245B) Beds US$3-8. The next closest to the centre, this hostel is 3.5km west of the main train station. It has about 50 beds year-round plus another 70 beds in July and August. To get there, take bus No 161, 167 or 174 from ul 3 Maja at the back of the train station, or go by tram No 10 or 12 to the end of the line, then walk west along ul Kartuska for about 10 minutes.

Youth hostel (☎/fax 341 16 60, ul Grunwaldzka 240/244) Doubles without/with bath US$9/12, beds in quads without bath US$6. This is by far the best hostel, offering 208 beds in doubles (some with bath) and quads. It's in a sports complex next to the soccer field, 6km north-west of Gdańsk's centre. Take the commuter train to Gdańsk Zaspa station and walk northwest for five minutes along ul Grunwaldzka. The place can be identified by a large WMOSRiR board over the gate to the grounds.

Student Hostels *Domy Studenckie Politechniki Gdańskiej* (☎ 347 25 47, ul Wyspiańskiego 7A) Singles US$6-14, doubles US$10-24, triples US$12-30. Every year from July to late September, the Technical University opens about 10 of its student dorms as hostels, providing up to 3000 budget beds! Prices vary widely, depending on the standards of the rooms, some of which have private baths. All hostels are in Gdańsk Wrzeszcz, easily accessible by plenty of trams from the centre. All hostels have their own reception desks and phone numbers; call the information number given above and inquire.

Dom Studenta ASP (☎ 301 28 16, ul Chlebnicka 13/16) Beds US$7-15. Open July–mid-Sept. This is the dorm of the Academy of Fine Arts, ideally located in the historic English House in the Main Town. It's basic but look at the house and the location!

Other Hostels & Hotels There are some budget places conveniently based in the Main Town.

Dom Wycieczkowy Zaułek (☎ 301 41 69, ul Ogarna 107/108) Singles/doubles/ triples/quads/quins without bath US$16/20/ 25/29/32. Zaułek is a former workers' dorm that offers basic accommodation. It's just 100m from the town hall, in the five-storey, freestanding building between ul Długa and ul Ogarna.

Dom Harcerza (☎ 301 36 21, fax 301 36 21, ul Za Murami 2/10) Doubles/triples/ quads/quins without bath US$25/26/28/30. Much in the class of Zaułek, the equally basic Dom Harcerza is also perfectly central.

Dom Nauczyciela (☎ 341 55 87, fax 341 49 17, ul Uphagena 28) Singles/doubles/ triples without bath US$18/25/28, singles/ doubles with bath US$33/45, all with breakfast. Outside the central area, this teachers' hotel in Gdańsk Wrzeszcz offers simple but acceptable rooms. It's close to the Gdańsk Politechnika train station, accessible by frequent trams or commuter train.

Private Rooms *Gdańsk-Tourist (☎ 301 26 34, Podwale Grodzkie 8)*, opposite the train station, is the main agency handling private rooms. The office is open 8am to 7pm Monday to Saturday in summer, till 2pm on Saturday off-season. Expect rooms to cost

US$15/22 for singles/doubles in central area, US$12/18 for rooms farther out. You can book by phone but you must then go there to do the paperwork and pay. When making your choice, don't worry too much about the distance from the centre – work out how close the place is to the commuter train.

Places to Stay – Mid-Range
Dom Muzyka (☎ 300 92 60, fax 300 92 10, ul Łąkowa 1/2) Singles/doubles/triples with bath & breakfast US$25/38/48. A quiet, comfortable place within walking distance of the centre, Dom Muzyka is the Musical Academy facility that offers about 60 beds year-round plus another 80 beds from July to September.

Pokoje Gościnne Mac-Tur (☎/fax 302 41 70, ul Beethovena 8) Doubles with bath & breakfast US$35. In the suburb of Suchanino, 2km west of the main train station, Mac-Tur is a small guesthouse (English spoken) which offers cosy accommodation with a good breakfast. To get there, take bus No 184 from the train station, or alternatively, take a taxi (US$3).

Pensjonat Angela (☎/fax 302 23 15, ul Beethovena 12) Doubles with bath & breakfast US$35. Just a few paces from Mac-Tur, Angela is another friendly family home turned guesthouse, with similarly pleasant rooms and great breakfasts.

Villa Akme (☎/fax 302 40 21, ul Drwęca 1) Doubles with bath & breakfast US$35. Yet another small family-run place, 2km south-west of the station, Akme has 11 newly furnished rooms, and is easily accessible by bus No 155, 208 or 295 from the train station.

Places to Stay – Top End
Dom Aktora (☎/fax 301 59 01, ul Straganiarska 55/56) Apartments for 2/3/4 guests US$75/90/100. A cosy central option, Dom Aktora has seven small apartments, each with bath and kitchenette. It's a good place if you plan to stay for a while and want to feel at home, but book in advance.

Hotel Mercure Hevelius (☎ 321 00 00, fax 321 00 20, ul Heweliusza 22) Singles/ doubles with bath & breakfast US$100/130.

POMERANIA

The 17-storey, 281-room Hevelius has been refurbished and is a good place with great views over old Gdańsk if you get a room facing south on one of the upper floors.

Hotel Hanza (☎ 305 34 27, fax 305 33 86, ul Tokarska 6) Doubles US$150, suites up to US$250. If money is not a problem, then a stay at the Hanza is an option. It's a classy place attractively situated on the waterfront next to the Gdańsk Crane.

PLACES TO EAT

There are plenty of eateries throughout the centre catering to every budget. As you might expect, fish is better represented here than farther inland, though mainly in the more expensive establishments. Oddly enough for such an important port and cosmopolitan city, ethnic cuisines are poorly represented in central Gdańsk.

Ultra-budget dining is provided by two central milk bars: **Bar Mleczny Neptun** (☎ 301 49 88, ul Długa 33/34) and **Bar Mleczny Turystyczny** (☎ 301 60 13, ul Węglarska 1/4). Either will fill you up for no more than US$3. There are plenty of slightly more expensive budget eateries, including **Bar Pod Złotym Kurem** (☎ 301 61 63, ul Długa 4) and **Bar Pod Rybą** (☎ 305 13 07, Długi Targ 35/38). Other recommendations include:

Bar Starówka (☎ 301 03 13, ul Św Ducha 8/10) Mains US$2.50-4. A small, five-table cubbyhole, this is one of the best budget options for a hearty Polish meal, thanks to good food and a friendly atmosphere.

Bar Green Way (☎ 301 41 21, ul Garncarska 4/6) Mains US$2-4. This is a simple, modern place which serves tasty, exclusively vegetarian food. It's so good that even nonvegies come to eat here.

Karczma (☎ 346 37 29, ul Długa 18) Mains US$4-6. Well located on the main drag, Karczma is a good address for a tasty Polish meal at reasonable prices in pleasant surroundings.

Restauracja Sphinx (☎ 346 37 11, Długi Targ 31/32) Mains US$3-5. Strategically set on the Long Market, Sphinx does as good a job here as elsewhere, in its new large locale and summer garden.

Restauracja Kubicki (☎ 301 00 50, ul Wartka 5) Mains US$5-8. This waterfront restaurant has served solid, tasty Polish food at reasonable prices since 1918, making it Gdańsk's oldest restaurant in continuous operation.

Restauracja Gdańska (☎ 305 76 71, ul Św Ducha 16) Mains US$10-16. Gdańska provides well-prepared traditional Polish food, including game and fish, in ornate surroundings, and may be an option for fine dining.

Restauracja Pod Łososiem (☎ 301 76 52, ul Szeroka 54) Mains US$12-24. This is arguably Gdańsk's classiest and most famous restaurant. Founded in 1598, its strong point is fish, particularly the salmon after which the place is named, but it also has a list of meat dishes. Its typical drink is Goldwasser, a thick sweet vodka with flakes of gold floating in it. It was produced in its cellars from the end of the 16th century till the outbreak of WWII.

ENTERTAINMENT

Check the local press for listings of a cultural nature such as cinema and theatre. For bars and discos, *Gdańsk in Your Pocket* is very helpful.

Pubs, Discos & Jazz

The photogenic Mariacka street has several romantic little cafe-bars, which put tables on their charming front terraces. You'll find more open-air bars on the waterfront, Długie Pobrzeże. Other places you might want to try include:

Latający Holender (☎ 802 03 63, Wały Jagiellońskie 2/4) Nestled in the basement of the nondescript LOT building, the Flying Dutchman is a magical creation with strange creatures all over the place and a bar made in the shape of a boat.

Irish Pub (☎ 320 24 74, ul Korzenna 33/35) Set in the vast vaulted cellars of the old town hall, this is not an Irish pub by any definition, but it is a great place for a beer or 10, and has regularly live music or a DJ. In fact, it's one of the best central spots for dancing at night.

Celtic Pub (☎ 301 29 99, ul Lektykarska 3) Another cellar affair, Celtic Pub also hosts live music and sometimes discos as well. It's also a good place in which to linger over a bottle of beer.

Kazamaty (☎ 769 12 04, ul Doki 1) One of the hippest discos in town, accommodated in a gigantic warehouse, Kazamaty comes with half a dozen bars and a vast dance floor, and goes into action on Friday and Saturday night.

Jazz Club (☎ 301 54 33, Długi Targ 39/40) This is not a particularly atmospheric place but one of the very few that hosts live jazz from time to time.

Cotton Club (☎ 301 88 13, ul Złotników 25/29) Another place to check for occasional jazz gigs, and if there's no jazz at least there are three pool tables.

Opera, Classical Music & Theatre

State Baltic Opera (☎ 341 05 63, Al Zwycięstwa 15) The Opera House is in Gdańsk Wrzeszcz, just off the Gdańsk Politechnika station. Symphonic concerts are also held here.

Baltic Philharmonic Hall (☎ 305 20 40, ul Ołowianka 1) This is the usual home of chamber music concerts.

Teatr Wybrzeże (☎ 301 70 21, Targ Węglowy 1) The main city scene, next to the Arsenal in the Main Town, Wybrzeże features mostly mainstream fare, including some great Polish and foreign classics.

SHOPPING

Gdańsk is widely known for amber (see the boxed text 'Amber – the Baltic Gold'). It's sold either unset or, more often, in silver jewellery, some of which is of high quality. Most shops selling amber are on ul Mariacka, Długi Targ and Długie Pobrzeże. Although a selection of amber can also be found in Warsaw, Kraków and other major cities, Gdańsk has the best choice. Beware of overpriced jewellery and souvenir shops catering to Western visitors.

GETTING THERE & AWAY
Air

The airport is in Rębiechowo, 14km west of Gdańsk. Bus No 110 goes there from the Gdańsk Wrzeszcz train station, or you can take the infrequent bus B from the Gdańsk Główny station. The LOT office (☎ 301 11 61) is at ul Wały Jagiellońskie 2/4, next to the Upland Gate.

The only direct domestic flights are to Warsaw (seven times daily but fewer in the off season), while international flights go direct to Brussels (daily), Copenhagen (daily), Frankfurt (daily), Hamburg (daily) and London (three times a week).

Train

The main train station, Gdańsk Główny, on the western outskirts of the Old Town, handles all incoming and outgoing traffic. Note the station building itself; it's another historic monument which has been restored to its former glory.

Almost all long-distance trains coming from the south go to Gdynia (and usually appear under Gdynia in the timetables). Trains heading south originate not from Gdańsk but from Gdynia. On the other hand, most trains along the coast to western destinations such as Szczecin originate (and terminate) in Gdańsk and stop at Gdynia en route.

Gdańsk is a busy railway junction, with 18 trains to Warsaw daily (329km), including 10 express trains and five InterCity trains (which cover the distance in less than 3½ hours). All these trains go via Malbork (51km) but InterCity trains don't stop there (express trains do). There are six fast trains to Olsztyn daily (179km), which call at Malbork en route as well.

If you're travelling to Warsaw or Olsztyn and don't plan on stopping in Malbork, make sure your camera is ready as you pass the castle at Malbork.

There are two express and three fast trains to Wrocław (478km); they all go through Bydgoszcz (160km) and Poznań (313km). There are also six fast trains to Toruń (211km) and four to Szczecin (374km).

Bus

Gdańsk's PKS bus terminal is right behind the central train station and you can get there by an underground passageway. Buses will be handy for several regional

POMERANIA

Amber – the Baltic Gold

If there's a typically Polish 'precious stone', it's amber – with the distinction that amber is not a precious stone at all. It's actually an organic substance, a fossilised tree resin. Different kinds of amber have been found all over the world, including Canada, the USA, Mexico, Sicily, Myanmar, Japan, Tanzania and New Zealand, but the largest deposits are along the Baltic shores.

Baltic amber was formed roughly 40 to 60 million years ago, during the subtropical period of the early Cenozoic era. The vast forests of the region (which wasn't a sea by that time) produced thousands of tonnes of resin. Millions of years later the climate cooled and the forests were buried under a thick layer of ice. They surfaced again in a fossilised form with the climatic warming millions of years later. The melting of ice formed the Baltic Sea, which only reached its present-day size and shape around 6000 BC.

As a result of its complex evolution, amber is not a uniform material but can contain small air bubbles, sand grains, particles of minerals, carbonised wood and cones, insects and fragments of plants. Amber's chemical composition can vary greatly depending on the botanical source, as can its colour – from ivory through various shades of yellow and orange to reddish and brownish tints. The degree of transparency also varies, from perfectly clear to wholly opaque.

The majority of amber is on the Baltic's south-east shores, particularly on the Samland Peninsula in the Kaliningrad Region (between Lithuania and Poland). Smaller deposits are along the Polish, Lithuanian and Latvian coasts, and still smaller ones in other countries bordering the Baltic. The largest amber mine is in Yantarnyi near Kaliningrad; with an annual yield of around 750 tonnes, it produces over two-thirds of the world's amber and over 90% of Baltic amber. The largest existing lump of Baltic amber, kept in the Natural Museum of Humboldt University in Berlin, weighs 9.75kg and was found on the Polish coast in 1890.

Baltic amber was collected and traded for at least 12,000 years. It has been found in Egyptian tombs dating from 3200 BC, and in 4000-year-old burial sites near Stonehenge in England. It was carved into a variety of decorative and ritual objects, such as beads, rosaries, amulets and altarpieces. It wasn't until the 1860s that commercial exploitation, by dredging and mining, started. Until then amber was collected from the beaches.

Amber has long attracted interest for its delicacy, striking variations of colour and unusual properties, such as generating static electricity when rubbed, or the ability of some pieces to fluoresce. Often believed to hold special mystical powers, amber was named 'elektron' or 'substance of the sun' by the ancient Greeks.

Finds of extinct insects entombed inside, sometimes preserved in an exquisite state, have captured the imagination. They are usually small flies, mosquitoes, beetles or spiders, but butterflies and even lizards have also been found. They make fascinating material for DNA studies and for some (so far) fantasies like the one popularised by Steven Spielberg's film *Jurassic Park*.

Over recent years, amber has become one of the most popular 'stones' used in Polish jewellery-making. Manufacturers use 220 to 250 tonnes of amber a year, but only 10% to 20% is collected in Poland (mainly on the shores of the Gulf of Gdańsk); the rest comes from the Kaliningrad Region. About 85% of Polish amber jewellery is exported, earning roughly US$300 million annually. Of all Polish cities, Gdańsk has the longest and strongest traditions in amber jewellery.

destinations which seldom, or never, have trains.

There is one morning bus directly to Frombork (112km). Alternatively, you can take any of the half-hourly buses to Elbląg (61km), from where you have more buses to Frombork. Four fast buses go to Olsztyn daily (156km) and four to Lidzbark Warmiński (157km). For Łeba, go to Gdynia, from where four direct buses run to Łeba daily in summer, or take a bus or train to Lębork and change there.

For the Kaszuby region, you have hourly buses to Kartuzy (31km) and Kościerzyna (56km). In July and August there are five direct morning buses to Wdzydze Kiszewskie (72km), which is noted for its skansen.

There are plenty of connections to Western European cities; travel agencies (including Almatur and Orbis) have information and sell tickets. To the East, two PKS buses travel to Kaliningrad daily (US$8, five hours) and one to Vilnius via Olsztyn.

Ferry
Car ferries to Nynäshamn in Sweden depart from Gdańsk, while those to Karlskrona in Sweden start from Gdynia. Information, bookings and tickets can be obtained from Orbis Travel (☎ 301 44 25), Podwale Staromiejskie 96/97. See the introductory Getting There & Away chapter for ferry routes and prices.

GETTING AROUND
Commuter Train
A commuter train, known as SKM or Szybka Kolej Miejska (Fast City Train), runs constantly between Gdańsk Główny and Gdynia Główna (21km) from 4am till midnight, stopping at a dozen intermediate stations, including Sopot. The trains run every five to 10 minutes (not so frequently late in the evening) and the Gdańsk-Gdynia trip takes 35 minutes. You buy tickets in ticket offices in the stations or some Ruch kiosks and validate them in the machines at the platform entrance (not in the train itself).

Tram & Bus
These are slower means of transport than SKM and run between around 5am and 11pm. Fares depend on the duration of the journey: US$0.25 for up to a 10-minute trip, US$0.50 for up to a half-hour ride and US$0.80 for an hour's journey. A day ticket costs US$1.50. Remember to validate your ticket in the vehicle; it's stamped with the date and time you get on.

Boat
From mid-May to late September pleasure boats and hydrofoils go from Gdańsk's wharf near the Green Gate to Sopot (US$8/11 one way/return), Gdynia (US$10/14 one way/return) and across the Gulf of Gdańsk to the fishing village of Hel on the Hel Peninsula (US$11/15 one way/return). Students pay about two-thirds of the normal fare. The trip to Hel is a nice way to get in a sailing mood and do some sightseeing and beach bathing (see the Hel section later in this chapter).

Boats to Westerplatte run several times daily (hourly in summer) from April to October and most of them include a visit to the port (US$6/8 one way/return).

Around Gdańsk

SOPOT
☎ 58 • pop 43,000

Sopot, immediately north of Gdańsk, is one of Poland's most fashionable seaside resorts. A fishing village belonging to the Cistercians of Oliwa has existed here since the 13th century, yet Sopot was really discovered by Jean Georges Haffner, a former doctor of the Napoleonic armies, who established sea bathing here in 1823. Soon afterwards spa buildings went up, and a horse-drawn bus service from Gdańsk was introduced. In the course of the following decades an array of fine villas sprang up, some of which still exist.

After WWI, Sopot was attached to the Free City of Danzig and soon boomed, becoming a place where the filthy rich of the day rubbed shoulders. By the outbreak of WWII, Sopot was a vibrant resort with 30,000 residents.

In the postwar period, in Polish hands, Sopot was given a generous injection of 'new' architecture which happily hasn't managed to overpower what was built earlier. You can still get some of the feel of the past, even though the guest lists are somewhat different nowadays.

Orientation
From the train station, a few minutes walk will bring you to ul Bohaterów Monte Cassino, Sopot's attractive pedestrian mall

POMERANIA

which leads straight down to the 'molo', Poland's longest pier, built in 1928 and jutting 515m out into the Gulf of Gdańsk. North of the pier is the old-fashioned 1927 Grand Hotel and farther north stretches a long waterfront park. If you wander about the back streets in the centre, you'll find some fine villas from the end of the 19th century.

The western part of Sopot, behind the railway track and the Gdańsk-Gdynia thoroughfare, consists of newer suburbs, which ascend gradually, finally giving way to a wooded hilly area. Here is the Opera Leśna (Opera in the Woods), the amphitheatre that seats 5000 people, where the International Song Festival is held in the second half of August. On the southern outskirts of Sopot is the racecourse established in 1898.

Information

The tourist office (☎ 550 37 83), ul Dworcowa 4, diagonally opposite the train station, is open 8am to 4pm weekdays (in summer till 7pm and also 10am to 6pm on weekends).

Central Internet facilities include www .c@fe (☎ 555 14 24), ul Chmielewskiego 5A, and net cave (☎ 551 11 83), ul Pułaskiego 7A.

Places to Stay

As with all such resorts, accommodation varies largely in price and quantity between the high and low seasons. Year-round lodging facilities are supplemented by a variety of pensions and holiday homes in summer. Prices listed below are for the high season which peaks in July and August and can be very busy. The tourist office is knowledgeable about accommodation options and will help you find a place to stay.

Camping Nr 19 (☎ 550 04 45, ul Zamkowa Góra 25) Triples in cabins US$24. Open May-Sept. Located in the northern end of town (a five-minute walk from the Kamienny Potok train station), Camping Nr 19 is large, good and has cabins.

Camping Nr 67 (☎ 551 65 23, ul Bitwy pod Płowcami 69) Tent site US$2 plus US$2 per person. Open July-Aug. On the opposite, southern end of Sopot, near the beach, this camp site is more basic and has no cabins. It's far from the commuter train line.

Biuro Kwater Prywatnych (☎ 551 26 17, ul Dworcowa 4), which shares the locale with the tourist office, handles private rooms. Be prepared to pay about US$12/18/24 a single/double/triple in July and August, with a minimum rental period of three days. There may be some locals hanging around the office who will offer rooms.

From July to mid-September, several local student dorms open as *student hostels*, charging US$8 to US$10 a bed, but the picture can change from year to year. The tourist office should know which ones are open when you are there.

Ośrodek Wczasowy Magnolia (☎/fax 551 34 19, ul Haffnera 100) Singles/doubles/triples without bath US$15/20/28. One of the cheapest places in town, Magnolia is pretty basic but OK.

Hotel Miramar (☎ 550 00 11, ul Zamkowa Góra 25) Doubles/triples/quads without bath US$26/38/40, singles/doubles with bath US$40/60. Another all-year budget hotel, Miramar has plenty of rooms of different class, with and without bath, but is a bit away from the centre.

Pensjonat Eden (☎/fax 551 15 03, ul Kordeckiego 4/6) Doubles/triples without bath US$35/45, with bath US$50/70. Well located near the beach and the central drag, the cosy Eden is reasonable value.

Grand Hotel (☎ 551 00 41, fax 551 61 24, ul Powstańców Warszawy 12/14) Singles/doubles US$90/120. If you want to stay where the fashionable once flocked to, go to the Orbis-run Grand Hotel. The hotel lived up to its name more before the war than it does today, but a planned renovation should give it a fresher look.

Hotel Rezydent (☎ 555 58 00, fax 555 58 01, Plac Konstytucji 3 Maja 3) Doubles US$120-160. New, posh, central and stylish, the 74-room Rezydent is a worthy addition to Sopot's top-end accommodation options.

Villa Hestia (☎/fax 550 21 00, ul Władysława IV 3/5) Double/suite US$160/190. Ultra-top end of the scale, the 19th-century Villa Hestia is one of the most

Sun, surf and sand at Międzyzdroje

Trees half buried by sand dunes, Słowiński NP

Town Hall, Stargard Szczeciński

Medieval arch, Malbork Castle

'House under the Star', Toruń

Historic house on the Old Town Square, Szczecin

The Malbork Castle, a classic medieval fortress

Folk dancing competition, Olsztyn

Sailing boats on Lake Mikołajki, Masurian Lakes

Baroque church in Święta Lipka

14th-century Gothic castle in the village of Reszel

Boat jam, Masurian Lake District

amazing places to stay in Poland, for just nine guests, and has its own restaurant.

Places to Eat

Apart from a number of year-round eating outlets, plenty of bars, bistros, cafes, open-air restaurants and street stands open in summer throughout the town, particularly in the beach area. Good addresses include:

Bar Green Way (☎ 551 24 58, ul Powstańców Warszawy 2/4/6) Mains US$2-4. Similar to its sibling in Gdańsk, Green Way is a simple place with excellent budget vegetarian food.

Błękitny Pudel (☎ 551 16 72, ul Bohaterów Monte Cassino 44) Mains US$5-8. A cosy place in the middle of the main drag, the Blue Poodle is an amazing artistic creation, as good for a drink as it is for a dinner.

Klub Wieloryb (☎ 551 57 22, ul Podjazd 2) Mains US$7-10. Another charming pub-cum-restaurant, the Whale offers mostly Polish cuisine plus plenty of drinks.

For a more formal dinner, you won't go wrong if you try the restaurant of the **Hotel Rezydent** or **Villa Hestia**.

Getting There & Away

For details of long-distance trains, see the Gdańsk section, as all trains that service Gdańsk go to Gdynia and stop in Sopot. There are commuter trains to Gdańsk (12km) and Gdynia (9km) which run every five to 10 minutes.

Pleasure boats and hydrofoils, which operate from mid-May to the end of September, go to Gdańsk daily (US$8), Gdynia (US$5) and Hel (US$8 one way, US$11 return). The landing site is at the pier.

GDYNIA

☎ 58 • pop 260,000

North of Sopot is the third component of the Tri-City, Gdynia. It has nothing of the historic splendour of Gdańsk, nor of the relaxed beach atmosphere of Sopot. Gdynia is just a busy port city without much style or character.

Gdynia is a young city. Though a fishing village existed as early as the 14th century, it had hardly more than 1000 inhabitants by the outbreak of WWI. In the aftermath of that war, when Gdańsk became the Free City of Danzig and no longer represented Polish interests, the Polish government decided to build a new port in Gdynia to give Poland an outlet to the sea.

With the help of French finance, the construction of the port began in 1923 and 10 years later Gdynia had the largest and most modern port on the Baltic. By 1939 the population of the city had reached 120,000. The port was badly damaged during WWII, but was rebuilt and modernised and is now the base for much of Poland's merchant and fishing fleet.

Information

The Miejska Informacja Turystyczna (☎ 628 54 66) is at the main train station, where you are most likely to arrive in town. It's open 8am to 6pm weekdays, 9am to 4pm Saturday, 9am to 3pm Sunday from May to September; and 10am to 5pm weekdays, 10am to 3pm Saturday from October to April.

Directly opposite the office is the Kawiarnia Internetowa Tom, a fast, cheap and comfortable 24-hour cybercafe. Should you need Internet access near tourist attractions on the Southern Pier, try the Silver Screen (☎ 628 18 00) at the Centrum Gemini, ul Waszyngtona 21.

Things to See

The Southern Pier (Molo Południowe) has most of the sights. Near its tip is the **Oceanographic Museum and Aquarium** (*Muzeum Oceanograficzne i Akwarium Morskie; ☎ 621 70 21, Al Zjednoczenia 1; adult/student US$2.50/1.50; open 10am-5pm Tues-Sun Sept-Apr, 9am-7pm daily May-Aug*).

Moored on the northern side of the pier are two museum ships: the three-masted beautiful frigate **Dar Pomorza** (*☎ 620 23 71; adult/student US$1.50/1; open 10am-4pm Tues-Sun Oct-May, 10am-6pm daily June-Sept*), built in Hamburg in 1909; and the WWII destroyer **Błyskawica** (*☎ 626 36 58; adult/student US$1.50/1; open 10am-12.30pm & 2pm-3.30pm Tues-Sun May-Sept*). On the opposite side of the pier is the marina.

POMERANIA

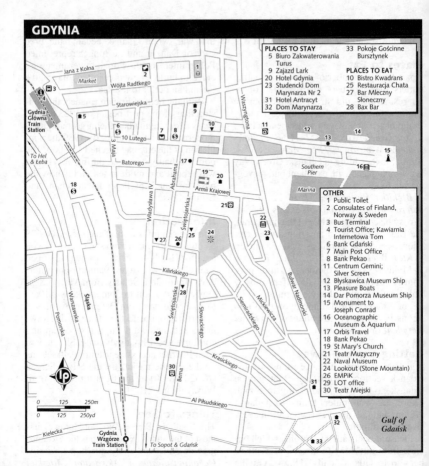

GDYNIA

PLACES TO STAY
5 Biuro Zakwaterowania Turus
9 Zajazd Lark
20 Hotel Gdynia
23 Studencki Dom Marynarza Nr 2
31 Hotel Antracyt
32 Dom Marynarza
33 Pokoje Gościnne Bursztynek

PLACES TO EAT
10 Bistro Kwadrans
25 Restauracja Chata
27 Bar Mleczny Słoneczny
28 Bax Bar

OTHER
1 Public Toilet
2 Consulates of Finland, Norway & Sweden
3 Bus Terminal
4 Tourist Office; Kawiarnia Internetowa Tom
6 Bank Gdański
7 Main Post Office
8 Bank Pekao
11 Centrum Gemini; Silver Screen
12 Błyskawica Museum Ship
13 Pleasure Boats
14 Dar Pomorza Museum Ship
15 Monument to Joseph Conrad
16 Oceanographic Museum & Aquarium
17 Orbis Travel
18 Bank Pekao
19 St Mary's Church
21 Teatr Muzyczny
22 Naval Museum
24 Lookout (Stone Mountain)
26 EMPiK
29 LOT office
30 Teatr Miejski

South of the pier, on Bulwar Nadmorski, is the **Naval Museum** (*Muzeum Marynarki Wojennej;* ☎ 626 39 84, ul Sędzickiego 3; *adult/student US$1/0.50; open 10am-4pm Tues-Sun*), which has an open-air display of guns, warplanes, helicopters and rockets.

Behind the museum there is a 52m-high hill called the **Stone Mountain** (Kamienna Góra), which provides views over the city centre and the harbour.

Places to Stay

Youth hostel (☎ 627 10 05, ul Energetyków 13A) Beds US$3-5. Open year-round. The hostel offers 48 beds in eight-bed dorms. It's 3km north-west of the centre, accessible by several bus lines including Nos 104, 150 and 170 from ul Jana z Kolna.

Biuro Zakwaterowań Turus (☎ 621 82 65, ul Starowiejska 47), opposite the main train station (enter from ul Dworcowa), arranges private rooms, mostly in the city centre, for around US$14/22 per single/double. Minimum stays of three nights are required.

Studencki Dom Marynarza Nr 2 (☎ 620 21 01, ul Sędzickiego 3) Beds in quads US$6. Open July–mid-Sept. Well located just behind the Naval Museum, this student dorm has up to 500 beds in summer.

Studencki Dom Marynarza Nr 1 (☎/fax 621 68 01, ul Beniowskiego 24/24A) Beds in doubles with bath US$14. Open year-round. Far better than No 2, but less convenient, this hostel is 2km north-west of the centre, accessible by trolleybus No 25 or 30, or by commuter train to Gdynia Stocznia station.

Zajazd Lark (☎/fax 621 80 47, ul Starowiejska 1) Singles/doubles/triples without bath US$20/30/33. Lark is on the basic side, but is very central.

Pokoje Gościnne Bursztynek (☎ 622 05 05, ul Wyspiańskiego 15) Singles/doubles/triples with bath US$24/28/30. Bursztynek is a family home, 200m from the beach, renting out eight good rooms – good value.

Dom Marynarza (☎ 622 00 25, fax 622 00 27, Al Piłsudskiego 1) Singles/doubles/triples with bath & breakfast US$35/45/55. Close to Bursztynek, the Sailor's Home has neat spacious rooms.

Hotel Antracyt (☎/fax 620 65 71, ul Korzeniowskiego 19) Singles/doubles/triples with bath & breakfast US$38/55/64. Another good option in the same area, the 77-bed Antracyt offers comfortable accommodation with views over the sea.

Hotel Gdynia (☎ 666 30 40, fax 620 86 51, ul Armii Krajowej 22) Singles/doubles US$80/100. Not much style but good facilities, Hotel Gdynia is the best place in town.

Places to Eat

Gdynia has plenty of eating outlets throughout the city centre.

Bar Mleczny Słoneczny (☎ 620 53 16, ul Władysława IV) Mains US$1-2. This is a genuine milk bar with exclusively vegetarian dishes that cost next to nothing. Efficient, clean and good, it's deservedly popular among the locals.

Bistro Kwadrans (☎ 620 15 92, Skwer Kościuszki 20) Mains US$2-3. Also hugely popular, Kwadrans serves generous portions of tasty Polish fare, and is open till 10pm.

Restauracja Chata (☎ 699 05 51, ul Świętojańska 49) Mains US$3-4. Another warmly recommended place, the Chata serves copious portions of home-cooked Polish food.

Bax Bar (☎ 620 64 32, ul Świętojańska 69) Mains US$3-4. Another good address, Bax Bar also has good budget food.

Getting There & Away

Train See the Gdańsk section earlier for information on long-distance trains. There are several trains daily to Hel (77km), and many more in summer. About 20 trains run to Lębork (where you change for the bus to Łeba).

Bus The bus terminal is next to the train station. Regional routes you may be interested in include Hel (78km) and Łeba (89km). Two fast buses run to Świnoujście daily (324km).

Boat Ferries to/from Karlskrona, Sweden, depart from and arrive at the Terminal Promowy (☎ 660 92 00), ul Kwiatkowskiego 60, 5km north-west of central Gdynia.

There are pleasure boats/hydrofoils to Gdańsk (US$10), Sopot (US$5) and Hel (US$8/11 one way/return) departing from the southern pier from mid-May to the end of September. One-hour boat excursions to Gdynia harbour go several times daily from April to October (US$5).

HEL PENINSULA
☎ 058

The Hel Peninsula (Mierzeja Helska) is a 34km-long, crescent-shaped sandbank to the north of the Tri-City. The peninsula is only 300m wide at the base and no wider than 500m for most of its length. Only close to the end does it widen out, reaching a width of about 3km. The highest point of the peninsula is 23m above sea level. Much of the landscape is covered with trees – picturesque, wind-deformed pines predominate – and there's also a number of typical coastal plant varieties including sand sedge and dune thistle.

The peninsula was formed in the course of about 8000 years by sea currents and winds, which gradually created an uninterrupted belt of sand. At the end of the 17th century, as old maps show, the sand bar was still cut by six inlets making it a chain of islands. In the present century the peninsula was cut several times by storms. The edges have been strengthened and the movement of the sand has been reduced by vegetation, but the sand bar continues to grow.

The peninsula is enclosed by two fishing ports: Hel at its tip and Władysławowo at its base. Between them is a third port, Jastarnia, and three villages: Chałupy, Kuźnica and Jurata. All are tourist resorts during the short summer season (July and August). There's a railway and a good road running the whole length of the peninsula.

All along the northern shore stretch beautiful sandy beaches and, except for small areas around the resorts (which are usually packed with holidaymakers), they are clean and deserted.

The Hel peninsula is easily accessible from the Tri-City by train, bus and boat. The bus and train can take you anywhere you want, while boats and hydrofoils sail from Gdańsk, Sopot and Gdynia to Hel. A boat trip is the most popular way of getting a feel for the peninsula.

Hel

Hel is a fishing port whose history is buried in the obscurity of the 9th century. The original village was founded 2km to the northwest from where it is today, not much later than Gdańsk, and benefited from its strategic location at the gateway of the developing port. By the 14th century Hel had a population of over 1200 and was a prosperous fishing port and trading centre.

The town never grew much bigger, however, as it was constantly threatened by storms and the shifting coastline, and was relatively isolated from the mainland because of the lack of overland links. Long belonging to Gdańsk, Hel followed the changes in power and religion of the big city, and, like Gdańsk, declined in the 18th century.

During the Nazi invasion of 1939, Hel was the last place in Poland to surrender; a garrison of some 3000 Polish soldiers defended the town until 2 October. The peninsula became a battlefield once more in 1945,

when about 60,000 Germans were caught in a bottleneck by the Red Army and didn't lay down their arms until 9 May; it was the last piece of Polish territory to be liberated.

Things to See A dozen 19th-century half-timbered **fishing houses** on the town's main street, ul Wiejska, managed to survive the various battles. The oldest building in town is the Gothic church from the 1420s, which is now the **Museum of Fishery** *(Muzeum Rybołówstwa; ☎ 675 05 52, Bulwar Nadmorski 2; adult/student US$1.50/1; open 10am-4pm Tues-Sun Sept-June, 10am-6pm daily July-Aug)*. It features exhibits related to fishing and boat-building techniques, plus a collection of old fishing boats. You can go up to the tower for good views.

The **Fokarium** *(☎ 675 08 36, ul Morska 2; admission US$0.50; open 8.30am-dusk)* is the place to see grey seals. It has three large tanks, which are home to half a dozen seals, and a museum is also being built. The grey seal is the largest and most populous seal species in the Baltic, numbering about 6500, but it's under threat.

There's a beautiful 100m-wide beach on the sea coast, 1km north of town, and a 42m-high brick **lighthouse**, which is open for visitors in summer.

Places to Stay & Eat The town has a reasonable array of places to stay and eat, most of which only open in summer when tourists come. Many locals rent out rooms in their homes – just ask around. The usual price is about US$15 per double room, but you'll probably find that few locals will want to rent out a room for just one night.

There are many restaurants on ul Wiejska which offer rooms. Try the *Tawerna Helska (☎/fax 675 12 05, ul Wiejska 82)*, *Captain Morgan Pub Hotel (☎ 675 00 91, ul Wiejska 21)* and *Pensjonat Nelson (☎/fax 675 11 55, ul Wiejska 62)*. All are small (five to eight rooms), and a double room with bath will cost US$25 to US$30 in any of them.

Getting There & Away Hel can be reached by road and railway (fairly regular services by both train and bus from Gdynia) and by pleasure boat/hydrofoils from mid-May to the end of September from Gdańsk, Sopot and Gdynia (see those earlier sections for fares). Note that a return ticket is considerably cheaper than two singles, so buy one if you plan on returning by boat. The boat schedule allows for up to seven hours at Hel.

Around the Peninsula

Instead of hanging around in Hel, you might like to walk along the beach to **Jurata** (12km) or 2km farther to **Jastarnia** and take the train from there, or stay for the night. Both are lively holiday resorts and have camp sites, places to eat and an array of holiday homes where you should be able to find a bed.

Farther north-west are two tiny ports, **Kuźnica** and **Chałupy**, which have retained their old atmosphere more than other places on the peninsula. Finally you get back to the base of the peninsula at **Władysławowo**, the largest fishing port and a town of some 13,000 people, with a good wide beach. The town has a number of accommodation options and an array of restaurants.

Between Chałupy and Władysławowo, there are eight camp sites which have windsurfing centres, providing equipment and instructors. This is one of the most popular **windsurfing** areas in Poland, especially recommended for beginners. The centres organise courses of different length and levels, and rent equipment. Some also offer kitesurfing.

About 8km west along the coast from Władysławowo is the **Rozewie Cape** (Przylądek Rozewie), the northernmost tip of Poland. Its 33m-high lighthouse set on a cliff houses a small museum dedicated to the lighthouse business; you can go to the top for sweeping views.

KASHUBIA
☎ 058

The region of Kashubia (Kaszuby in Polish) stretches for 100km to the south-west of Gdańsk. Hilly, well forested and dotted with many post-glacial lakes, it's a picturesque area garnished with small villages where people still seem to live close to nature. There are no cities, towns are few and

far between, and large scale industry hasn't arrived, leaving the lakes and rivers virtually unpolluted.

The original inhabitants, the Kashubians, were Slavs, once closely related to the Pomeranians. In contrast to most of the other groups which gradually merged to form one big family of Poles, the Kashubians have managed to retain some of their early ethnic identity, expressed in their distinctive culture, craft, architecture and language.

Far from the main trading routes and important urban centres, they lived as peacefully as frequent wars and shifting borders allowed. Interestingly, they were not displaced in the aftermath of WWII by the communist regime, which removed most other groups that didn't fit the ethnic picture.

The Kashubian language, still spoken by some of the old generation, is the most distinct dialect of Polish; other Poles have a hard time understanding it. It's thought to derive from the ancient Pomeranian language, which survived in its archaic form but which has assimilated words of foreign origin, mostly German during the Germanisation imposed by the Prussians.

The region between Kartuzy and Kościerzyna is the most diverse topographically and the highest point of Kashubia, Mt Wieżyca (329m), is here. This is also the most touristy area of Kashubia; an array of tourist facilities have already been built and others are in progress. Public transport between Kartuzy and Kościerzyna is fairly regular, with buses running every hour or two.

Unless you have your own transport – which is particularly useful in exploring Kashubia – you miss out on some of the region by being limited to the major routes. Public transport become less frequent the farther off the track you go. The two major regional destinations detailed below will give a taste of the culture of Kashubia, though less of its natural beauty.

Kartuzy
☎ 58 • pop 16,000

The town of Kartuzy, 30km west of Gdańsk, owes its birth and its name to the Carthusians, the order which was brought here from

POMERANIA

Bohemia in 1380. Originally founded in 1084 near Grenoble in France, the order was known for its austere monastic rules, its monks living an ascetic life in hermitages and, like another unusual congregation, the Camaldolese (see the Las Wolski section in the Kraków chapter for details of them), passing their days in the contemplation of death, their motto being 'Memento Mori'.

When they arrived in Kartuzy the monks built a church and, beside it, 18 hermitages laid out in the shape of a horseshoe. The order was dissolved by the Prussians in 1826 and the church is now a parish church. Of the hermitages, only one survives, still standing beside the church as does the refectory on the opposite side. The church is a 10-minute walk west of the bus and train stations across the town centre.

The **church** (☎ 681 20 85, ul Klasztorna 5) seems to be a declaration of the monks' philosophy; the original Gothic brick structure was topped in the 1730s with a baroque roof that looks like a huge coffin. On the outer wall of the chancel there's a sundial and, just beneath it, a skull with the 'Memento Mori' inscription.

The maxim is also tangibly manifested inside, on the clock on the balustrade of the organ loft. Its pendulum is in the form of the angel of death armed with a scythe. The clock is stopped periodically if there's an unusual number of funerals in town and it seems to help.

The interior fittings are mainly baroque, and the richly carved stalls deserve a closer look. There's some unusual cordovan (painting on goat leather) decoration (1685) in the chancel, while the oldest object, the extraordinary Gothic triptych from 1444 (only the central panel survives), is in the right-hand chapel.

Another attraction is the **Kashubian Museum** (Muzeum Kaszubskie; ☎ 681 14 42, ul Kościerska 1; adult/student US$2/1.50; open 8am-4pm Tues-Fri, 8am-3pm Sat, also 10am-2pm Sun May-Sept only), south of the train station near the railway track. It depicts the traditional culture of the region, with everything from curious folk musical instruments to typical household implements

and furniture. Tours in German are available for US$15 per group.

Hotel Korman (☎/fax 681 16 35, ul Maja 36) Singles/doubles with bath US$22/35. Korman is the only hotel in town, but you can easily leave on one of the hourly buses to Gdańsk (31km).

Wdzydze Kiszewskie
☎ 58 • pop 1000

The small village of Wdzydze Kiszewskie, 16km south of Kościerzyna, boasts an interesting **skansen** (Kaszubski Park Etnograficzny; ☎ 686 12 88; adult/student US$2/1.50; open 10am-3pm Tues-Sun 16 Oct-14 Apr, 9am-4pm Tues-Sun 15 Apr-15 Oct, till 6pm July & Aug) featuring typical Kashubian architecture. Established in 1906 by the local schoolmaster, this was Poland's first skansen. Pleasantly positioned on the lakeside, it now contains a score of buildings collected from central and southern Kashubia, including cottages, barns, a school, a windmill and an 18th-century church used for Sunday Mass. As elsewhere, some of the interiors are fitted with furnishings, implements and decorations, showing how the Kashubians lived a century or two ago.

Hotel Niedźwiadek (☎ 686 13 13, fax 686 13 33) Doubles/triples with bath & breakfast US$30/35. About 2km from the skansen, the Hotel Niedźwiadek is a reasonable place and has its own restaurant and camp site.

There are a few budget pensions in the village, which provide around 100 beds in all.

Wdzydze is linked to Kościerzyna by several buses daily. In summer, there are also five direct buses between Wdzydze and Gdańsk.

Central & Western Pomerania

To the west of Kashubia, the rolling, wooded countryside continues for about 150km; the lakes and forests only thin out as you descend to the Szczecin Lowland (Nizina Szczecińska), some 50km before reaching the Odra River and the border with

Germany. Like Kashubia, the region is essentially rural, sparsely populated, with only occasional towns and very little industry. Whether you're travelling by public transport, car, bicycle or kayak, it's a lovely region to explore. Some places, including Szczecinek, Czaplinek and Połczyn Zdrój, have developed into local holiday centres.

To the north of the lakeland is the coast. The Polish coastline is predominantly flat and straight, but its dunes, woods and coastal lakes give it a lot of charm. There are sandy beaches along almost the whole length, all the way from Hel to Świnoujście. Two particularly interesting portions of the coast have been made national parks.

The Baltic is considerably colder than the Mediterranean. The water temperature hardly ever goes above 20°C. Sea-bathing is a bit of a challenge except during a midsummer heatwave. On the whole, summers are not as hot on the coast as in central Poland. Conversely, winters are not as cold.

ŁEBA
☎ 59 • pop 4100

Łeba ('**Weh**-bah') is a small, old fishing port which these days is also a popular seaside resort. The wide sandy beach stretches in both directions as far as the eye can see and the water is reputedly the cleanest on the Polish coast. Nearby Słowiński National Park (see that section later in this chapter), with its unusual shifting dunes and relatively undisturbed nature, is well worth exploring. If you're looking to relax at a Baltic

A Short History of Pomerania

Pomerania has been an ethnic melting pot since time immemorial, providing a home for pre-Roman communities and subsequently for various Germanic tribes as they expanded eastwards. Goths from Scandinavia settled here early in the 1st millennium AD and some five centuries later the Slavs arrived from the south and gradually became dominant.

The first Polish monarch, Mieszko I, brought the whole of Pomerania, as far west as the Odra River and east to the Vistula, into the newborn Poland. However, typically for those early days, real power lay in the hands of local rulers rather than the king hundreds of kilometres away. For a time, Pomerania remained a largely independent dukedom ruled by Pomeranian Slavs.

The picture changed by the 14th century when the Teutonic Order conquered Gdańsk (in 1308) and the borderlands of Eastern Pomerania. Meanwhile, Western Pomerania was gradually turning towards its western neighbour, the Holy Roman Empire, both politically and economically. At that time Poland was expanding swiftly to the east and was more interested in keeping control of the vast, newly conquered territories stretching almost as far as the Black Sea, rather than in getting into wars with its strong western neighbour over its dubious western fringes. Economically too, Western Pomerania, and the coast in particular, was far more involved in trading with other western ports in the Hanseatic League than with Poland's inland towns. In 1521 the region formally pledged its loyalty to the Holy Roman Empire.

In 1621 the Swedes, who were by then a significant military power, conquered most of the Pomeranian coast. The Treaty of Westphalia of 1648 awarded them part of Pomerania, which became their strategic stronghold, a base for their devastating war against Poland. The Swedes were eventually forced out in the 1720s and the Brandenburgs (or by then the kingdom of Prussia, created in 1701) regained control over most of Pomerania, hanging on until the end of WWII. Only then did the region become part of Poland again.

Pomerania was the scene of particularly fierce fighting in 1945, and most of the urban fabric, from Gdańsk to Szczecin, was devastated. Most of the German population – the dominant group in the region – fled west before the Red Army came and all those who stayed were forcibly expelled in the aftermath of the war.

The ruined and deserted land was settled by a completely new population, people who in their turn had lost their homes in prewar Poland's eastern provinces, taken over by the Soviet Union.

POMERANIA

beach resort, Łeba is one of the best places to consider.

A settlement known as Old Łeba was founded on the western side of the mouth of the Łeba River, perhaps as early as the 12th century, but a catastrophic storm destroyed it almost completely in 1558. The inhabitants moved to a safer place farther inland on the opposite bank of the river and built a new village. In the course of time, the remains of the original settlement were buried by shifting dunes and the sole reminder of the tragedy is a fragment of the wall of a Gothic church.

Nature was not very kind to the new village either. The maritime trade was paralysed by the silting up of the port, and agriculture was unprofitable since fields were constantly covered by sand. At the end of the 19th century a new port was built and protected with breakwaters while the dunes were forested, slowing down the movement of the sands. This, together with the construction of the road and railway from Lębork, brought gradual economic growth. By then Łeba had also begun to develop as a seaside resort. Today it's still a large village rather than a town, but it attracts 10 times more visitors than it has permanent inhabitants.

Orientation

The train and bus stations are next to each other in the south-western part of Łeba, two blocks west of ul Kościuszki, the town's main drag. This shopping street runs north to the port, set on a brief stretch of the Łeba River which joins Lake Łebsko to the sea. The river divides Łeba's beach in two. The town is nestled behind the eastern beach, and this is also the main resort area. The beach on the western side of the river is less crowded and the broad white sands stretch back 75m to the dunes, making up some of the best beaches on the Baltic coast.

Information

The tourist office, the Biuro Promocji Miasta (☎/fax 866 25 65), ul 11 Listopada 5A, just round the corner from the train station, is open 8am to 4pm weekdays. Bank Pekao is at ul Kościuszki 85, and there are several kantors in town, including one at the post office.

Places to Stay & Eat

As in most seaside resorts, the lodging and culinary picture varies widely between the high season (July and August) and the rest of the year. Many holiday homes and pensions open their doors in summer. Most of them have their own eating facilities, apart from countless fish stalls and snack bars that mushroom all around town. Locals also rent out rooms in their homes.

By and large, expect a bed in high season to cost anywhere between US$6 and US$20, depending on standard, demand etc. In the off season rates drop to between US$4 and US$12 per head.

The helpful tourist office will give you full information of what's available and will advise where to go – it's certainly a good first stop in Łeba. Alternatively, you can inquire at agencies which arrange rooms in private homes, pensions and holiday homes. They include Centrum Turystyczne Łeba (☎ 866 22 77, ul Kościuszki 64) and Biuro Wczasów Przymorze (☎ 866 13 60, ul Dworcowa 1).

There are a dozen camping grounds in Łeba, including *Intercamp 84 (☎ 866 12 06, ul Turystyczna 10)*; *Camping Nr 275 Chaber (☎ 866 24 35, ul Turystyczna 1)*; *Camping Nr 51 Leśny (☎ 866 28 11, ul Brzozowa 16A)* and *Camping Nr 41 Ambré (☎ 866 24 72, ul Nadmorska 9A)*. Most camping grounds are open June to September and some have their own eating facilities. Some have cabins (eg, Intercamp and Chaber). Rates for pitching tents are US$2 to US$3 per tent site plus another US$2 to US$3 per person in any of the camp sites.

More permanent accommodation options (some operating year-round) are:

Ośrodek Wypoczynkowy Hutnik (☎/fax 866 13 41, ul Nadmorska 14) Beds in doubles, triples or quads with bath US$8-14. Nestled in the tourist resort area close to the beach, Hutnik is one of the cheaper holiday homes and is OK.

Hotel Marina (☎ 866 17 35, ul Jachtowa 1) Beds in doubles, triples or quads with bath US$8-12. Sitting next to the marina, out of town but close to the beach, this may be an option for those who want to stay away from holidaymakers.

Zespół Wypoczynkowo-Rehabilitacyjny Mazowsze (*☎/fax 866 18 70, ul Nadmorska 15*) Doubles/triples US$30/44. Just 150m from the beach, Mazowsze offers comfortable rooms and good facilities.

Hotel Gołąbek (*☎/fax 866 29 45, ul Wybrzeże 10*) Doubles/triples with bath & breakfast US$50/60. A new, decent accommodation option with a good restaurant, Gołąbek sits on the fishing wharf, with charming old fishing boats and port life to view from your window.

Hotel Neptun (*☎/fax 866 23 57, ul Sosnowa 1*) Doubles US$80-120. A spectacular historic villa right on the seashore, Hotel Neptun is Łeba's top option. It has a terrace overlooking the beach and great views of the sunset.

Getting There & Away

The usual transit point to/from Łeba is Lębork, a town 29km to the south, where you may need to change bus or train. Trains to Lębork depart every two to three hours in summer, but only two a day run the rest of the year. Buses ply the Łeba-Lębork route every hour or so. There are two direct buses between Łeba and Gdynia (94km) plus two extra ones in summer.

SŁOWIŃSKI NATIONAL PARK
☎ 59

The 186-sq-km Słowiński National Park (Słowiński Park Narodowy) includes the 33km stretch of coast between Łeba and the fishing-tourist village of Rowy, complete with two large lakes to the south, the Łebsko and the Gardno, and their surrounding belts of peatbogs, meadows and woods. The park is named after the Slav tribe of the Slovincians (Słowińcy), a western branch of the Kashubians who once inhabited this part of the coast. In the 19th century there were still several villages populated by the descendants of these aboriginal people. Today they're part of history.

The park contains a diversity of habitats, including forests, lakes, bogs, beaches and dunes. There's also a skansen and a natural history museum, and the lake wildlife is remarkably rich, particularly in birds. The park was included in Unesco's 1977 list of World Biosphere Reserves.

Shifting Dunes

The most unusual feature of the national park are shifting dunes (*wydmy ruchome*), which create a genuine desert landscape. They are on the sand bar separating the sea from Lake Łebsko, about 8km west of Łeba. It's actually a vast ridge of sand 40m high and…it's moving. During WWII, Rommel's Afrika Korps trained in this desert and the site was a secret German experimental missile testing ground from 1940 to 1945.

The dunes are easily reached from Łeba. Take the road west to the hamlet of Rąbka (2.5km), where there's a car park and the gate to the national park. Private minibuses ply this road in summer, or you can just walk. The sealed road continues into the park for another 3.5km to the site of the rocket launcher (which didn't survive), from where a wide path goes on through the

The Dunes that Walk

The shifting dunes in the Słowiński National Park are reputedly the world's only such phenomenon on such a scale. They consist of an accumulation of sand thrown up on the beach by waves. Dried by wind and sun, the grains of sand are then blown away to form dunes which are steadily moving inland. The 'white mountain' walks at a speed of 2m to 10m a year, depending on the particular area, burying everything it meets on its way. The main victim is the forest, which is gradually disappearing under the sand, to reappear several decades later as a field of skeletal trees, after the dune has passed.

The process started at least 5000 years ago, and by now the shifting dunes have covered an area of about 6 sq km and reached a height of 30m to 40m, with the highest peak of 42m. They apparently no longer grow higher but they do continue to spread inland over new areas. It all really gives a feel of being in a sort of mini-Sahara, with the distinction that the Sahara doesn't walk and you can't see the sea from it.

POMERANIA

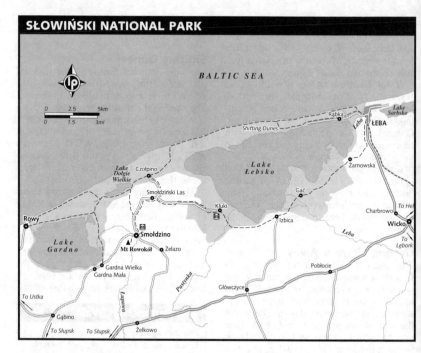

SŁOWIŃSKI NATIONAL PARK

forest for another 2km to the southern foot of the dunes, where trees can be seen half-buried in the sand.

No cars or buses are allowed beyond the car park. You can walk to the dunes (70 minutes), take one of the small electric trolleys (US$5 per three people), take a horse-drawn cart (US$14 per five people) or rent a bicycle (US$0.80 per hour). There are also large electric trolleys (US$0.75 per person) and boats (US$1), but both only go as far as the launcher, so you'll still have 2km to walk to the dunes. You then can climb a vast high dune for a sweeping view of desert, lake, beach, sea and forest. You can come back the same way, or walk to Łeba along the beach (8km), perhaps stopping for a swim – something you can't do in the Sahara!

Lakes

There are four lakes in the park, two large and two small. They are shallow lagoons which once were bays, gradually cut off from the sea by a sand bar. With densely overgrown, almost inaccessible marshy shores, they provide a habitat for about 250 species of birds which live here either permanently or seasonally. They include swans, mallard, gulls, geese and grebe, to list but a few. The white-tailed eagle, the largest bird found in Poland, with a wingspan of up to 2.5m, nests in the park, though nowadays it's very rare. Large parts of the lake shores have been made strict reserves, safe from human interference.

About 16km long and 71 sq km in area, Lake Łebsko is the biggest in Pomerania and the third-largest in Poland, after Śniardwy and Mamry in Masuria. It's steadily shrinking as a result of the movement of the dunes, the growth of weeds, and silting.

Kluki

Set on the south-western shore of Lake Łebsko, Kluki is a tiny hamlet of perhaps 200 souls. Isolated from the outer world, it was where local traditions survived longest. At the end of the 19th century, Kluki's population numbered over 500, mostly descendants of the Slovincians. The little that is left of their material culture can now be seen in the skansen.

Occupying the central part of the village, the skansen (*Muzeum Wsi Słowińskiej; ☎ 846 30 20; adult/student US$1.50/1; open 10am-3pm Tues-Sun Sept-May, 9am-5pm Tues-Sun June-Aug*) is modest but authentic, as most of the buildings are *in situ* and not collected from around the region as is the case in most other skansens. The long, two-family, whitewashed houses are fitted with traditional furniture and decorations.

Bus transport to Kluki is only from Słupsk (41km). In summer, half a dozen buses run in each direction, but fewer on Sunday; in winter, only a couple of buses ply this route. There are no direct bus links between Kluki and Łeba.

In summer, a tourist boat from Łeba goes to the skansen a few days a week, leaving in the morning and returning in the afternoon (US$8 return). You can also get to the skansen on bicycle (rented in Rąbka or Łeba).

Smołdzino

West of Kluki, outside the park's boundaries, Smołdzino boasts the **Natural History Museum** (*Muzeum Przyrodnicze; ☎ 811 72 04; adult/student US$1/050; open 7.30am-3.30pm Mon-Fri Oct-Apr, 9am-5pm daily May-Sept*), which features flora and fauna from the park. The park's headquarters are also here.

Just 1km south-west of the village is Mt Rowokół, the highest hill in the area, 115m above sea level. On its top is a 20m **observation tower**, providing sweeping views over the forest, the lakes and the sea. The path up the hill begins next to the petrol station and you can get to the top in 15 minutes.

Buses to Słupsk (30km) go fairly regularly till late afternoon. There are no buses to Łeba.

Places to Stay & Eat

Apart from accommodation in Łeba and Słupsk (see the relevant sections), there are some places to stay and eat in the region, including several agrotourist farms (inquire at the tourist office in Łeba or Słupsk). There are summer *youth hostels* in Smołdzino (*☎ 811 73 21*), Smołdziński Las (*no phone*) and Gardna Wielka (*☎ 811 72 52*). Gardna Wielka has more accommodation, including the basic *Dom Wycieczkowy PTTK* (*☎ 846 32 50*) and the better *Oberża Pod Diabelskim Kamieniem* (*☎ 846 32 69*), which also serves meals. There are also some options in Smołdzino, the best of which is the *Gościniec U Bernackich* (*☎ 811 73 64, ul Bohaterów Warszawy 26*), which provides rooms, meals and bikes for rent.

SŁUPSK
☎ 59 • pop 105,000

A large town 18km from the coast, Słupsk ('Swoopsk') is perhaps not a great tourist destination, yet it has some attractions, a good tourist office and a choice of places to stay and eat. It can be a jumping-off point for the coast or a stopover on the coastal route.

Słupsk's history is every bit as chequered as that of other Pomeranian settlements. After its birth in the 11th century as a Slav stronghold on the Gdańsk-Szczecin trading route, it came under the rule of the Gdańsk dukes in 1236, then passed into the hands of the Brandenburg margraves in 1307, but later became part of the West Pomeranian Duchy. In 1648 it reverted to the Brandenburgs and remained under Prussian administration until WWII. It was largely destroyed in 1945 and returned to Poland after the war.

Information

The tourist office (*☎ 842 07 91, ☎/fax 842 43 26*) is at Al Wojska Polskiego 16. It's open 8am to 4pm weekdays (till 6pm from June to August and also 9am to 3pm Saturday). Bank Pekao is at ul 9 Marca 6, while kantors are easy to track down in the centre.

Things to See

The most important sight is the 16th-century **castle** or, more precisely, the **Museum of Central Pomerania** (*Muzeum Pomorza Środkowego; ☎ 842 40 81, ul Dominikańska 5; adult/student US$1.50/1; open 10am-4pm*

POMERANIA

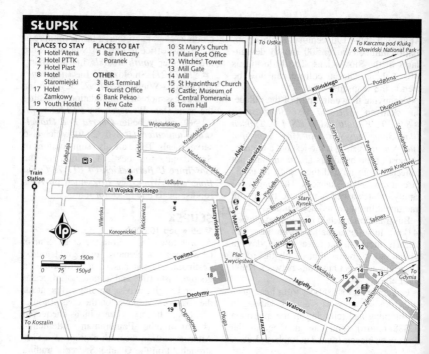

SŁUPSK

PLACES TO STAY	PLACES TO EAT	10 St Mary's Church
1 Hotel Atena	5 Bar Mleczny	11 Main Post Office
2 Hotel PTTK	Poranek	12 Witches' Tower
7 Hotel Piast		13 Mill Gate
8 Hotel	**OTHER**	14 Mill
Staromiejski	3 Bus Terminal	15 St Hyacinthus' Church
17 Hotel	4 Tourist Office	16 Castle; Museum of
Zamkowy	6 Bank Pekao	Central Pomerania
19 Youth Hostel	9 New Gate	18 Town Hall

Tues-Sun Sept-May, 10am-5pm daily June-Aug) which occupies its interior. Apart from sacral woodcarvings, historic furniture and other exhibits related to the town's history, the museum contains a 200-piece collection (the best in Poland) of portraits by Stanisław Ignacy Witkiewicz, commonly known as Witkacy. This controversial writer, photographer and painter was one of the foremost figures in interwar Polish art.

The building opposite the castle gate is the 14th-century **mill** *(młyn)*, which is today an extension of the museum and houses the regional ethnographical collection.

Next to the mill, the 15th-century **St Hyacinthus' Church** (Kościół Św Jacka) has had substantial later alterations and contains a late Renaissance high altar and pulpit, both from 1602. The organ has a fine tone which you can hear if your visit coincides with the summer concerts.

Almost nothing is left of the 15th-century fortified walls which once encircled the town. Two survivors, though, are the **Mill Gate** (Brama Młyńska), beside the mill, and the **Witches' Tower** (Baszta Czarownic), a bit farther north. In the 17th century the latter was turned into a jail for women suspected of witchcraft, and death sentences were often imposed; the last woman condemned to the stake was burned in 1701. One more remnant of the fortifications is the **New Gate** (Brama Nowa), facing the town hall.

Special Events

If you happen to be here in September, check out the **Polish Piano Festival**, which runs for a full week, with recitals held mainly in the castle. In July and August, concerts of organ and chamber music take place every Wednesday or Thursday night in St Hyacinthus' Church. In November, Słupsk has the **Komeda Jazz Festival**, dedicated to the father of Polish jazz, Krzysztof Komeda.

Places to Stay

Słupsk has a fair array of hotels and you shouldn't have problems finding a room. The hordes of holidaymakers who invade the coast in summer don't affect the city's accommodation.

Youth hostel (☎ 842 46 31, ul Deotymy 15) Dorm beds US$3-5. Open July & Aug. In the large school building close to the centre, the youth hostel is acceptable though it has large dorms only.

Hotel PTTK (☎ 842 29 02, ul Szarych Szeregów 1) Doubles without bath US$18, singles/doubles with bath US$16/22. Pretty simple but convenient, PTTK is perhaps the cheapest hotel in the central area.

Hotel Atena (☎/fax 842 88 14, ul Kilińskiego 7) Singles/doubles/triple with bath & breakfast US$25/35/45. Round the corner from PTTK, Atena has comfortable rooms and its own restaurant.

Hotel Zamkowy (☎/fax 842 52 94, ul Dominikańska 4) Singles with bath US$25-35, doubles with bath US$45-55, breakfast included. The refurbished Hotel Zamkowy is next to the castle.

Hotel Staromiejski (☎ 842 84 64, fax 42 50 19, ul Jedności Narodowej 4) Singles with bath US$30-45, doubles with bath US$40-60, breakfast included. This well-established central hotel is one of the best places in town, and comes complete with its own restaurant.

Hotel Piast (☎/fax 842 52 86, ul Jedności Narodowej 3) Doubles with bath US$40-60. Next door to the Staromiejski, Piast offers much the same and also has a restaurant.

Places to Eat

Apart from hotel restaurants already mentioned, you may want to check the following:

Bar Mleczny Poranek (☎ 842 50 24, Al Wojska Polskiego 46) Mains US$1-2.50. A basic milk bar, Poranek has tolerable food and is the only place in town for an early budget breakfast.

Karczma Pod Kluką (☎ 842 34 69, ul Kaszubska 22) Mains US$4-6. The best place for local cuisine, Pod Kluką serves regional specialities in appropriately folksy surroundings, and has an agreeable outdoor eating terraced area in summer. It's some distance from the centre but worth the walk.

Getting There & Away

The PKP train and PKS bus stations are close to each other and within easy walking distance of the centre.

Train The modern and functional station has regular services east to Gdańsk (132km) and west to Koszalin (67km); half a dozen trains continue west up to Szczecin (242km). Three trains go straight to Warsaw (461km), with three extras in summer.

Bus Five or six buses leave for Łeba daily (61km), Gdynia (110km), Koszalin (68km) and Darłowo (48km). Buses to Smołdzino (30km) go regularly throughout the day, and some continue as far as Kluki (41km). For Ustka (18km), PKS buses run regularly, or take the hourly suburban bus No 20.

USTKA
☎ 59 • pop 17,500

A fishing port and the gateway to the sea for Słupsk, Ustka is also an important seaside resort which swarms with holidaymakers in summer. It has a good tourist infrastructure and attractive beaches, even though they are narrower than those in Łeba.

Information

The helpful Biuro Promocji Miasta (☎ 814 71 70, ☎/fax 814 99 26) is at ul Marynarki Polskiej 87, 100m from the train station. The office is open 8am to 8pm Monday to Saturday and 10am to 6pm Sunday in July and August; at other times it opens 7.30am to 3.30pm weekdays. It has good information and can arrange accommodation.

Places to Stay

The tourist office will find you a place to stay in a hotel, pension, holiday home or private house, and you are warmly encouraged to visit it upon arrival. The cheapest lodging in summer shouldn't cost more than US$8 per person. In case you can't contact the tourist office, here's a brief selection for varying budgets:

There are two summer camp sites in town: **Camping Słoneczny** (☎ 814 42 10, ul Grunwaldzka 35), about 1200m away from the beach, and **Camping Nr 101 Morski** (☎ 814 44 26, ul Armii Krajowej), 1km farther back from the seaside. Both have cabins but forget about them in the high season.

Youth hostel (☎ 814 50 81, ul Jagiellońska 1) Beds US$4-6. Open year-round. Located in a large school 1.5km back from the beach, the youth hostel has about 40 beds in dorms sleeping four to 18 guests.

Pensjonat Sonata (☎/fax 814 68 03, ul Armii Krajowej 1) Singles/doubles with bath US$24/36. Close to Camping Morski, this is one of the cheapest pensions and is OK, but it's about a 20-minute walk to the beach.

Hotel Rejs (☎ 814 78 50, ☎/fax 814 78 51, ul Marynarki Polskiej 51) Singles/doubles with bath & breakfast US$40/45. A new, very central hotel, just minutes from the beach, the 14-room Rejs is good and has a fine restaurant.

Pensjonat Oleńka (☎/fax 814 85 22, ul Zaruskiego 1) Doubles/suites with bath & breakfast US$50/90. In a 19th-century granary, near the beach and port, Oleńka has just three rooms and four suites, and is one of the best and most stylish places to stay in town.

Getting There & Away

The only good connections are with Słupsk, 18km to the south. Ustka is the end of the railway line from Słupsk, serviced by trains roughly every other hour, but the bus service is much more frequent.

DARŁOWO

☎ 94 • pop 16,000

West of Ustka, the first place on the coast that's larger than a village is Darłowo ('Dar-wo-vo'). Once a prosperous medieval Hanseatic port, Darłowo is one of a handful of towns in Western Pomerania which has retained some of its original character. It still has the familiar chessboard of streets, as laid out in 1312, and several interesting historic buildings.

Darłowo isn't exactly on the coast but is 2.5km inland on the Wieprza River. The town's gateway to the sea is Darłówko, a waterfront suburb at the mouth of the river. It's a small fishing port which developed as a summer resort around its beaches and has a totally different atmosphere to the main town. Darłówko is linked to Darłowo by local buses which run regularly along both sides of the river.

Things to See

Darłowo The western side of the Rynek is occupied by the **town hall**, a largish baroque building, lacking a tower and fairly sober in decoration except for its original central doorway. Right behind it rises the massive brick **St Mary's Church**. Begun in the 1320s and enlarged later, it has preserved its Gothic shape pretty well (particularly the beautiful vaults), even though the fittings date from different periods.

A curiosity of the church are three tombs placed in the chapel under the tower. The one made of sandstone holds the ashes of Erik of Pomerania, king of Denmark, Sweden and Norway between 1396 and 1438. After his unwilling abdication, the king went into exile in the castle of Visby on Gotland, from where he commanded corsair raids on the Hansa's ships. Forced to flee, he found a refuge in Darłowo, where he died in 1459. His tombstone, commissioned in 1882 by the Prussian Emperor Wilhelm II, isn't as impressive as the two mid-17th-century, richly decorated tin tombs standing on both sides of it.

South of the Rynek is the 14th-century **castle**, the oldest and best preserved Gothic castle in Central and Western Pomerania. It was the residence of the Pomeranian dukes until the Swedes devastated it during the Thirty Years' War, and the Brandenburgs took it following the Treaty of Westphalia. The dethroned King Erik, the 'last Viking of the Baltic', lived in the castle for the last 10 years of his life and is believed to have hidden his enormous loot here; so far it remains undiscovered.

The castle is now a **museum** (*Muzeum Zamku Książąt Pomorskich*; ☎ 314 23 51, ul Zamkowa 4; adult/student US$2/1; open 10am-4pm daily). In the well-restored period interiors – an attraction in themselves

– you'll find a varied collection including folk woodcarving, portraits of Pomeranian princes, old furniture, sacred art, armour and even some exhibits from the Far East.

Of the town's medieval fortifications, only the **Stone Gate** (Brama Kamienna) survives which, despite its name, is made of brick. It's a block north of the Rynek. A few hundred metres beyond it is the marvellous **St Gertrude's Chapel** (Kaplica Św Gertrudy). The most unusual building in town, it is 12-sided and topped with a high, shingled central spire. It has been renovated and looks amazing, but is only open for Mass, 6pm on weekdays, with more Masses on Sunday.

Darłówko Darłówko is not a place for historic sights but a pleasant beach resort, packed with tourists in summer. It's cut in two by the Wieprza River, and linked by a pedestrian drawbridge which opens when boats go into or out of the bay, providing a spectacle for tourists. There are two breakwaters leading into the sea at the outlet of the river, which make for an enjoyable walk. At the base of the eastern mole is a lighthouse.

Places to Stay
Predictably, accommodation is highly seasonal, with all-year places scarce and summer lodgings operating mainly in Darłówko. There are plenty of small private *pensjonaty* (guesthouses) and many locals rent out rooms in their homes – watch out for signs saying *'pokoje'* or *'noclegi'*. Private rooms start at about US$6 per person.

Róża Wiatrów (☎ 314 21 27, ul Muchy 2, Darłówek) Tent site US$2 plus US$2 per person. Open July & Aug. This holiday complex has a large camp site and budget cabins.

Dom Rybaka (☎ 314 24 19, ul Wschodnia 2, Darłówko) Doubles/triples without bath US$16/24. Pretty basic but acceptable, Dom Rybaka is next to the drawbridge.

Pensjonat Bałtycki (☎ 314 29 75, ul Bałtycka 8, Darłówko) Beds in doubles, triples or quads with bath US$6-12. One of the cheaper pensions, the Bałtycki is close to the beach and can provide full board if requested.

Hotel Kubuś (☎ 314 29 19, Al Wojska Polskiego 63A, Darłowo) Doubles with bath US$24. One of the few options in Darłowo, Kubuś is small, simple and close to the Rynek.

Hotel Irena (☎ 314 36 92, Al Wojska Polskiego 64, Darłowo) Doubles/triples with bath US$22/32. Next door to Kubuś, Irena offers much the same.

Getting There & Away
The bus terminal is in the south-western end of Darłowo, a 10-minute walk from the Rynek. Buses run regularly to Sławno (21km) and Koszalin (34km) and – less often – to Ustka (38km) and Słupsk (48km). Trains no longer provide passenger service at Darłowo.

KOSZALIN
☎ 94 • pop 115,000
The largest city on the central coast, halfway between Szczecin and Gdańsk, Koszalin ('Ko-**shah**-leen') was once a wealthy Hanseatic port competing with Kołobrzeg for sea trade. The good times came to an end after its access to the sea through Lake Jamno silted up in the 17th century. WWII reduced the city to one big ruin with little left to be restored. Consequently, Koszalin is a postwar creation that offers few tourist attractions. Yet, if you're travelling along the coast, you'll almost inevitably pass through the city.

Information
The tourist office (☎ 342 73 99), ul Dworcowa 10, close to the train station, is open 8am to 4pm weekdays (till 5pm in July and August). Bank Pekao is nearby, at ul Jana z Kolna 11.

Things to See
The only historic relic of any substance in the centre is the **cathedral** just off the Rynek, which miraculously survived the 1945 shelling. It has finely restored Gothic vaults but otherwise little remains of the old fittings.

The **Regional Museum** (☎ 343 21 53, ul Piłsudskiego 53; adult/student US$1.50/1;

POMERANIA

open 10am-4pm Tues-Sun) about 1.5km north-east of the Rynek, focuses on the region's archaeology and the city history. The other branch of the museum at ul Młyńska 37/39, 300m north of the Rynek, has temporary exhibitions, plus a small ethnographic display in a 200-year-old cottage beside the museum building.

Places to Stay

Youth hostel (☎ 342 60 68, ul Gnieźnieńska 3) Beds US$3-6. Open year-round. The hostel has four large dorms plus six rooms (doubles to quads). It's about 2km southeast of the train station (1.5km from the Rynek) and is hard to find. Walk about 600m down ul Gnieźnieńska from the roundabout, and then 200m to the right into a small street, ul Kwiatowa, until you see a building with a large sign at the top saying 'Zespół Szkół Samochodowych'. It's here. Southbound bus No 13 from near the station will take you to the hostel.

Hotel PKS (☎ 342 78 51, ul Zwycięstwa 4) Singles/doubles/triples without bath US$12/18/24. One of the cheapest hotels in town, opposite the bus terminal, the PKS is probably all that budget travellers need while passing in transit and caught out for the night.

Hotel Arka (☎/fax 342 79 11, ul Zwycięstwa 20/24) Singles/doubles with bath & breakfast US$60/75. Arka is the best place to stay in town and is conveniently close to the station.

Getting There & Away

The train and bus stations are next to each other, 800m west of the Rynek, a 10-minute walk away. There's a fair number of buses to the seaside resorts as well as a regular train service on the Szczecin-Gdańsk route. Trains to Kołobrzeg leave every hour or two and there are five fast trains to Poznań.

KOŁOBRZEG

☎ 94 • pop 48,000

With 1300 years of history, Kołobrzeg ('Ko-**wob**-zhek') is one of the oldest settlements in Poland. It goes back to the 7th century, when salt springs were discovered

here, and their exploitation was the force behind the town's development. When in 972 it became part of the Polish state, Kołobrzeg was already a well-fortified and prosperous township, and as such gained the honour of becoming a seat of the bishopric in 1000. With this, it reached a position in the religious hierarchy equal to that of Kraków and Wrocław. Though in 1125 the seat was moved to Wolin, Kołobrzeg was by then a well-developed port town, with the fish and salt trades keeping it stable for centuries.

A wave of disasters began in the Thirty Years' War when Kołobrzeg was seized by the Swedes. In the aftermath of the war it fell under Brandenburg rule. The margraves set about making the town an impregnable fortress, but their elaborate fortifications didn't help much – Kołobrzeg (or Kolberg, as it was called then) was subsequently captured and destroyed by the Russians in 1761 and by Napoleon's army in 1807. The town recovered slowly, this time as a spa and seaside resort, but the worst was yet to come – in March 1945 the two-week battle over the city left it completely devastated.

Rebuilt, Kołobrzeg is once more a lively town and an important port, though it lacks any sense of history. For tourists, however, it's not history that pulls the hordes into town, but the beach and the array of holiday homes and sanatoria that have sprung up along the waterfront. This holidaymakers' area is separated by the railway track from the town centre farther inland, where a few remnants of the town's past can be found.

Information

The Centrum Informacji Turystycznej (☎ 352 79 39), ul Dworcowa 1, is in a kiosk diagonally opposite the train station. It's open 8am to 4pm weekdays (till 6pm daily in July and August).

Useful banks include Bank Pekao, ul Źródlana 5; Powszechny Bank Kredytowy, ul Łopuskiego 6; and Bank Gdański, ul Unii Lubelskiej 33B. All three have ATMs.

There are several Internet facilities in the centre, including Net Spin (☎ 354 73 66), Giełdowa 7C; InterNet Caffé (☎ 354 66 34), ul Giełdowa 7A; Matrix (☎ 354 43 50), ul Armii Krajowej 24/7; and Medicom Sas (☎ 354 62 95), ul Gierczak 26–27.

Things to See

The 14th-century **cathedral** is the most important historic sight in town. Though badly damaged in 1945, it has been rebuilt close to its original form. Its colossal two conjoined towers occupy the whole width of the building, and the facade is a striking composition of windows placed haphazardly – a bizarre folly of its medieval builders and rebuilders.

The five-naved interior is impressively spacious and still retains fragments of old frescoes. The most striking feature, however, is the leaning columns on the right side of the nave, which give the impression that the cathedral is on the point of collapsing. Don't worry – they have been leaning since the 16th century.

Old fittings include three 16th-century triptychs and the unique Gothic wooden chandelier from 1523 hanging in the central nave. There are some even older objects such as the bronze baptismal font (1355) featuring the scenes of Jesus Christ's life, a

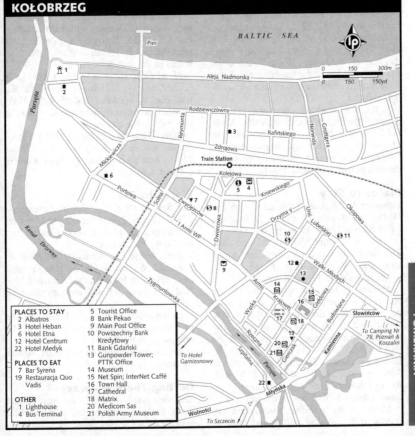

KOŁOBRZEG

BALTIC SEA

Pier

Aleja Nadmorska

Parzęta

Rodziewiczówny

Reymonta

Rafińskiego

Norwida

Grottgera

Mickiewicza

Zdrojowa

Train Station

Kolejowa

Kniewskiego

Portowa

Soľna

Zwycięzców

I Armii WP

Dworcowa

Drzymały

Uni Lubelskiej

Okopowa

Kanał Drzewny

Zygmuntowska

Wałki Młodych

Armii

Krajowej

Wąska

Giełdowa

Budowlana

Słowińców

To Camping Nr 78, Poznań & Koszalin

Rzeczna

Szpitalna

Gierczak

Parzęta

Kamienna

To Hotel Garnizonowy

To Szczecin

Młyńska

Wolności

PLACES TO STAY	5 Tourist Office
2 Albatros	8 Bank Pekao
3 Hotel Heban	9 Main Post Office
6 Hotel Etna	10 Powszechny Bank
12 Hotel Centrum	Kredytowy
22 Hotel Medyk	11 Bank Gdański
	13 Gunpowder Tower;
PLACES TO EAT	PTTK Office
7 Bar Syrena	14 Museum
19 Restauracja Quo	15 Net Spin; InterNet Caffé
Vadis	16 Town Hall
	17 Cathedral
OTHER	18 Matrix
1 Lighthouse	20 Medicom Sas
4 Bus Terminal	21 Polish Army Museum

POMERANIA

4m-high, seven-armed candelabra (1327) and the stalls in the chancel (1340).

The **town hall**, just east of the cathedral, is a neo-Gothic structure designed by Karl Friedrich Schinkel and erected in the 1830s after the previous 14th-century building was razed by Napoleon's forces in 1807. One of its wings houses a modern art gallery.

The area south of the town hall and the cathedral has been rebuilt as what you might call the **New Old Town** – an interesting architectural design, a blend of old and new, that adds some character to the otherwise gloomy landscape of monstrous tower blocks looming from behind.

If you are interested in military matters, the **Polish Army Museum** (*Muzeum Oręża Polskiego; ☎ 352 52 53, ul Gierczak 5; adult/student US$1/0.50; open 9am-3pm Tues-Sun Sept-May, 9am-5pm daily June-Aug*) covers the history of the Polish army. The other section of the museum at ul Armii Krajowej 13 contains history and archaeology exhibits.

In the seaside sector, there are no sights as such; the beach is the attraction. Walk out 200m over the sea on the pier (*molo*), an obligatory trip for all holidaymakers. Nearby to the west, by the harbour, stands the lighthouse; you can climb to its top.

Places to Stay

Camping Nr 78 Baltic (*☎/fax 352 45 69, ul IV Dywizji Wojska Polskiego 1*) Tent site US$1.50 plus US$2.50 per person. Doubles in cabins with bath US$35. Open June-Sept. The camp site has good cabins and a vast tent area, but despite its large size, it tends to get crowded in July and August.

Private rooms provide some of the cheapest accommodation, US$5 to US$10 per person, depending on the season and location, but don't even dream about the beach district. Rooms are arranged by PTTK (*☎ 352 32 87, ul Dubois 20*), in the Baszta Prochowa (Gunpowder Tower), and Albatros (*☎ 352 41 51, ul Morska 7A*), near the lighthouse. Both agencies usually require a three- to five-day minimum stay.

Many of the *holiday homes* rent out rooms to the general public and most of them are pleasantly located in the seaside area. They can be full with pre-booked groups in July and August but outside this period they usually have vacancies. The tourist office has a full list.

Hotel Garnizonowy (*☎/fax 357 46 85, ul Łopuskiego 43*) Doubles without bath US$15. One of the cheapest hotels in town, within walking distance of the centre, Garnizonowy is on the basic side.

Hotel Medyk (*☎ 352 34 50, fax 354 26 50, ul Szpitalna 7*) Doubles with bath US$22-34. Very close to the Old Town, the 10-storey Medyk is not a bad budget choice. Rooms vary in standard and price, but even the cheapest doubles are OK.

Hotel Heban (*☎/fax 352 48 41, ul Borzymowskiego 3*) Doubles with bath & breakfast US$45/55. Enjoying a quiet location near the beach, Heban is one of the nicer hotels in the seaside resort area.

Hotel Centrum (*☎ 354 55 60, fax 352 29 05, ul Katedralna 12*) Singles/doubles/triples with bath & breakfast US$35/50/55. Hotel Centrum provides comfortable accommodation right in the city centre.

Hotel Etna (*☎ 355 00 12, ☎/fax 355 01 26, ul Portowa 18*) Singles/doubles US$80/110. A new posh option, the Etna is one of the best hotels in town.

Places to Eat

Bar Syrena (*☎ 352 31 88, ul Zwycięzców 11*) Mains US$2-3. In the train station area, Syrena is a simple self-service eatery that does tasty Polish fare.

Restauracja Quo Vadis (*☎ 352 89 61, ul Gierczak 26A*) Mains US$5-7. Occupying a cosy basement locale in the Old Town, Quo Vadis serves solid Polish food at reasonable prices.

In the beach district, the holiday homes provide meals for their guests (and often for nonguests as well), and there are many seasonal fast-food outlets and cafes throughout the area.

Getting There & Away

The train and bus stations are next to each other, halfway between the beach and the historic centre (a 10-minute walk to either).

The harbour is 1km north-west of the train and bus stations.

Kołobrzeg lies off the main Szczecin-Gdańsk route so there are only a few trains to either destination. A regular service goes to Koszalin (43km). Two fast trains go to Warsaw nightly (571km).

The most frequent bus connection (every hour) is with Koszalin (44km). Three or four fast buses go to Świnoujście daily (106km) and Słupsk (112km).

KAMIEŃ POMORSKI
☎ 91 • pop 9500

Kamień Pomorski was founded in the 9th century as one of the strongholds of the Wolinians, a Slav tribe which had settled in the region a century earlier. In 1125 the West Pomeranian bishopric was established in the nearby village of Wolin, bringing Christianity to the locals, but in 1175 Wolin was destroyed by the Danes and the religious seat was moved to Kamień. The bishops immediately set about building a cathedral but took 100 years to complete the work. In the 14th century the town was circled with a ring of fortified walls and a town hall was erected in the Rynek.

Apart from its importance as a religious centre, the town was also a prosperous port and a trading centre – a tempting titbit for aggressive neighbours. The Swedes took it in 1630 and a few decades later it fell under Brandenburg rule. Not until 1945 was the town, which had been flattened as the battle front rolled over it, incorporated into Polish territory.

Facing the same dilemma as elsewhere, the new authorities restored what had partly survived but flooded the rest of the space with the usual nondescript apartment blocks. Yet it's still worth coming for what remains, particularly the cathedral.

Information

There's no tourist office in Kamień. Bank Pekao, just off the Rynek, changes travellers cheques and cash and has a useful ATM. There are several kantors in town (including one at the post office) but they will probably pay you less than the bank.

Cathedral

Begun in 1176 in a Romanesque style, the church was thoroughly revamped in the 14th century in Gothic fashion, which has basically survived to this day. Inside, the chancel has retained some of its old fitments, including an impressive triptych on the high altar, thought to derive from the school of Veit Stoss (the maker of the famous triptych in St Mary's Church in Kraków), the oak stalls and a large crucifix hanging from the vault. Up above the altar some of the 13th-century wall paintings have survived.

Baroque outfits were added in the second half of the 17th century and include a decorative wrought-iron screen separating the chancel from the nave, the pulpit and the organ. The latter deserves special attention for both its impressive appearance and excellent tone. The Festival of Organ and Chamber Music was started here in 1965 and takes place annually from mid-June to late August, with concerts held every Friday evening. If you can't turn up in Kamień on a Friday, there's a short performance on the organ twice daily, usually at 11am and 4pm.

While you're in the church, go up the steps from the left transept to the former treasury, now a small museum, and don't miss the cloister garth *(wirydarz)* – the entrance is through a door from the left-hand aisle. The 1124 baptismal font in the middle of the garth is the cathedral's oldest possession. The old tombstones on the walls of the cloister were moved here in 1890 from the church's floor. You can also go to the top of the tower but there's almost no view from there.

Other Attractions

The Rynek, a three-minute walk to the west, is a postwar production apart from its **town hall**, a 14th-century Gothic building with the familiar Renaissance additions. Going west you'll get to the **Wolin Gate** (Brama Wolińska), the only surviving medieval gate of the original five. It now houses the **Museum of Precious Stones** *(Muzeum Kamieni;* ☎ 382 42 43, ul Słowackiego 1; admission US$1.50; open 10am-6pm daily in summer)*, which features semiprecious stones from Silesia.

POMERANIA

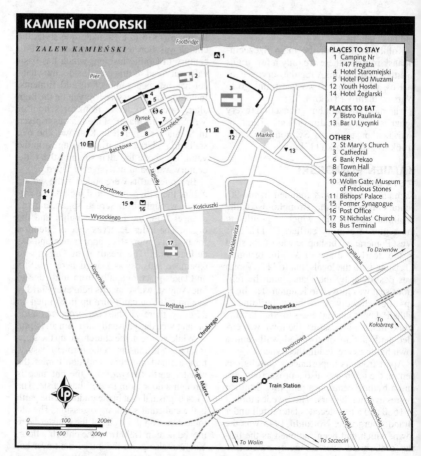

KAMIEŃ POMORSKI

ZALEW KAMIEŃSKI

Footbridge

Pier

Rynek

Strzelecka

Basztowa

Jagiełły

Pocztowa

Wysockiego

Kościuszki

Mickiewicza

Kopernika

Rejtana

Chrobrego

5-go Marca

Dworcowa

Szpitalna

Dziwnowska

Konopnickiej

Matejki

Market

To Dziwnów

To Kołobrzeg

To Wolin

To Szczecin

Train Station

0   100   200m
0   100   200yd

PLACES TO STAY
1 Camping Nr
   147 Fregata
4 Hotel Staromiejski
5 Hotel Pod Muzami
12 Youth Hostel
14 Hotel Żeglarski

PLACES TO EAT
7 Bistro Paulinka
13 Bar U Lycynki

OTHER
2 St Mary's Church
3 Cathedral
6 Bank Pekao
8 Town Hall
9 Kantor
10 Wolin Gate; Museum
   of Precious Stones
11 Bishops' Palace
15 Former Synagogue
16 Post Office
17 St Nicholas' Church
18 Bus Terminal

The former **synagogue** (hardly recognisable) on ul Pocztowa is just about the only legacy of the Jewish population. Nearby, tucked away amid trees, is **St Nicholas' Church**, built as the hospital's chapel in the 14th century (the tower was added later).

Places to Stay

Camping Nr 147 Fregata (☎ 382 00 76, ul Lipowa 1) Open June-Sept. On the waterfront at the foot of the cathedral, the Fregata is very basic and has no cabins.

Youth hostel (☎ 382 08 41, Plac Katedralny 5) Dorm beds US$3-5. Open July & Aug. In a school across the road from the cathedral, the 60-bed hostel has only large dorms.

Hotel Żeglarski (☎ 382 08 17, ul Wilków Morskich 4) Singles/doubles/triples/quads without bath US$11/15/18/22. The Żeglarski has a waterfront location on the marina but is basic and can be full with school groups.

Hotel Pod Muzami (☎ 382 22 40, fax 382 22 41, ul Gryfitów 1) Singles/doubles/triples with bath & breakfast US$24/34/42. In a beautiful historic house on the corner of the Rynek, the friendly Pod Muzami has 12 spacious rooms and a good budget restaurant.

POMERANIA

Hotel Staromiejski (☎ 382 26 44, fax 382 26 43, ul Rybacka 3) Singles/doubles/triples with bath US$28/38/48. Another pleasant place but more expensive than Pod Muzami and probably not such good value.

Places to Eat

Bar U Lucynki (☎ 382 41 27, ul Żwirki i Wigury 2) Mains US$2-3. This is possibly the best ultra-budget place to eat in town.

Bistro Paulinka (☎ 382 10 43, ul Strzelecka 1) Mains US$2-3. A milk-bar style establishment, Paulinka is central and acceptable, though perhaps not as good as U Lucynki.

The cosy restaurant in the *Hotel Pod Muzami*, listed earlier, is a pleasant place to eat and drink and is inexpensive.

Getting There & Away

The train station handles only local traffic and is pretty useless. The bus terminal next to it has regular services (every hour or two) to Szczecin (88km), Dziwnów (12km), Międzyzdroje (39km) and Świnoujście (52km). There are also four fast buses to Kołobrzeg daily (67km) and two to Gdynia (via Koszalin and Słupsk).

MIĘDZYZDROJE

☎ 91 • pop 6000

Międzyzdroje ('Myen-dzi-**zdro**-yeh') is one of Poland's most popular seaside resorts. It has good beaches and a picturesque sandy coastal cliff just to the north-east of town, and the attractive Wolin National Park stretching to the south-east. The sea here is warmer than on the eastern part of the coast and it's cleaner than around the resort's bigger western neighbour, the port of Świnoujście. Międzyzdroje lives almost entirely off summer tourism and is more or less dead for the rest of the year.

Międzyzdroje hosts the annual International Festival of Choral Music, usually at the end of June and beginning of July.

Natural History Museum

The Natural History Museum (*Muzeum Przyrodnicze*; ☎ 328 07 37, ul Niepodległości 3; adult/student US$1/0.50; 9am-3pm Mon-Fri Oct-Apr, 9am-5pm Tues-Sun May-Sept) features the flora and fauna of Wolin National Park. There's a good display of stuffed birds, including the white-tailed eagle, a symbol of the park and reputedly a model for Poland's national emblem. The museum also has an amazing collection of 150 ruffs, each different, which makes it one of the largest collections of this species in Europe.

Next to the museum building is a large cage with a live white-tailed eagle. The national park's headquarters are opposite the cage.

Places to Stay & Eat

Międzyzdroje has lots of holiday homes open to all comers. In addition, a plethora of pensions have sprung up everywhere. There are also plenty of *private rooms* offered by the locals. In all, Międzyzdroje has several thousand beds waiting for holidaymakers.

Instead of going room hunting by yourself, it's better to contact any of half a dozen specialised local travel agencies, which are able to do it for you. They include Viking Tour (☎ 328 07 68, ul Niepodległości 2A), Elmar (☎ 328 21 27, ul Traugutta 3), Bałtyk (☎ 328 15 18, ul Zwycięstwa 2A) and Wolin Travel (☎ 328 27 47, ul Turystyczna 2). Expect beds in private rooms to begin from US$7 in July and August, and from US$5 in other months. Beds in pensions/holiday homes will cost from US$9/7 upwards, respectively.

You can also try the Centralna Recepcja FWP Posejdon (☎ 328 05 67, ☎ 328 07 11, Promenada Gwiazd 4) which operates about 500 beds in its 33 holiday homes and rents them out for around US$8/13 per person in rooms without/with bath. Another address to check, PTTK (☎ 328 04 62, ul Kolejowa 2), can book beds in its own PTTK hostels, and may also offer private rooms.

Camping Nr 24 Gromada (☎ 328 02 75, ul Polna 10A) Tent site US$1.50 plus US$2.50 per person. Open June-Sept. At the south-western end of town, Gromada is the main camping facility, but there are two other camp sites in the same area closer to the beach.

POMERANIA

The Bird on Poland's National Emblem

The eagle has for millennia fascinated humans for its power, courage and dignity, so no wonder that it came to be the national emblem of dozens of countries, including the USA, Mexico, Germany, Egypt, Austria, Russia and Poland. The white eagle first appeared on heraldic seals of the Piast dukes in the early 13th century and it has been Poland's emblem ever since. It's not exactly clear which eagle species was the prototype for the national emblem, but most scholars agree that it was the white-tailed eagle (Haliaeetus albicilla), known to Poles by its popular name of the Bielik.

With a wingspan of up to 2.5m, the white-tailed eagle is the largest predatory bird species in Poland, and in Europe for that matter. It once populated all of Europe, but was pushed eastwards by the shrinking of its natural habitat due to demographic and industrial pressures. By the early 20th century, it was only found in north-eastern Europe and northern Asia, and it still inhabits these regions. Its global population is estimated at 9000 to 11,000 pairs, with the greatest single-country population in Norway (1700 pairs). Thanks to preservation measures of recent decades, its population is slowly growing and it seems to no longer be threatened with extinction.

The white-tailed eagle has wide wings and short wedge-shaped tail which is – you guessed it – white. The adult bird can weigh up to 6kg and live up to 30 years. It usually inhabits areas close to water, such as the sea or lakes, building its nests high on the trees, usually on pine, oak or beech. Nests which have been used for many seasons can reach monumental dimensions – 4m high and 2m in diameter – and can weigh up to 500kg. One pair can have more than one nest. The bird preys on open waters and its favourite diet includes fish and water birds, but in winter it doesn't mind carrion.

In Poland, the white-tailed eagle lives in the northern part of the country, mostly in Western Pomerania and Masuria. Its current population is put at roughly 450 pairs, which is Europe's second largest after Norway. There are four or five pairs living in the Wolin National Park.

Dom Turysty PTTK *(☎ 328 03 82, ul Kolejowa 2)* Beds in rooms without bath US$9 July-Aug, US$7 Sept-June. PTTK hostel is one of the cheapest places to stay, though neither its location nor the rooms are particularly impressive.

Dom Turysty PTTK Dąbrówka *(☎ 328 09 29, ul Dąbrówki 11)* Beds without/with bath US$12/16. Better located and closer to the beach, Dąbrówka is another PTTK facility. It has some rooms with bath but it's also on the basic side.

Hotel Amber Baltic *(☎ 328 10 00, fax 328 10 22, Promenada Gwiazd 1)* Singles/doubles/suites US$85/120/200, buffet breakfast included. If you fancy a splurge, you're in the right place – Amber Baltic is one of the best hotels on the coast. The US$15 buffet dinner (6pm to 10.30pm) is cheaper than an average three course a la carte meal.

Getting There & Away

The train station is at the southern end of town; the main bus stop is on ul Niepodległości opposite the museum.

Międzyzdroje is on the Szczecin-Świnoujście railway line and all trains stop here, providing regular transport to either destination. There are also some trains farther on to Gdynia, Poznań, Wrocław and Warsaw.

Frequent buses, both PKS and private, run to Świnoujście. Six fast buses go to Kołobrzeg daily and two as far as Gdynia. In summer there are several buses to Kamień Pomorski (42km), but fewer during the rest of the year.

WOLIN NATIONAL PARK

Set in the far north-western corner of the country, Wolin National Park (Woliński Park Narodowy) occupies the central part of Wolin Island, just south-east of Międzyzdroje. With a total area of about 50 sq km, it's one of the smaller Polish parks, yet it's picturesque enough to deserve a day or two's walking.

The park encompasses a coastal moraine left by a glacier, which reaches a maximum height of 115m on its northern edge and

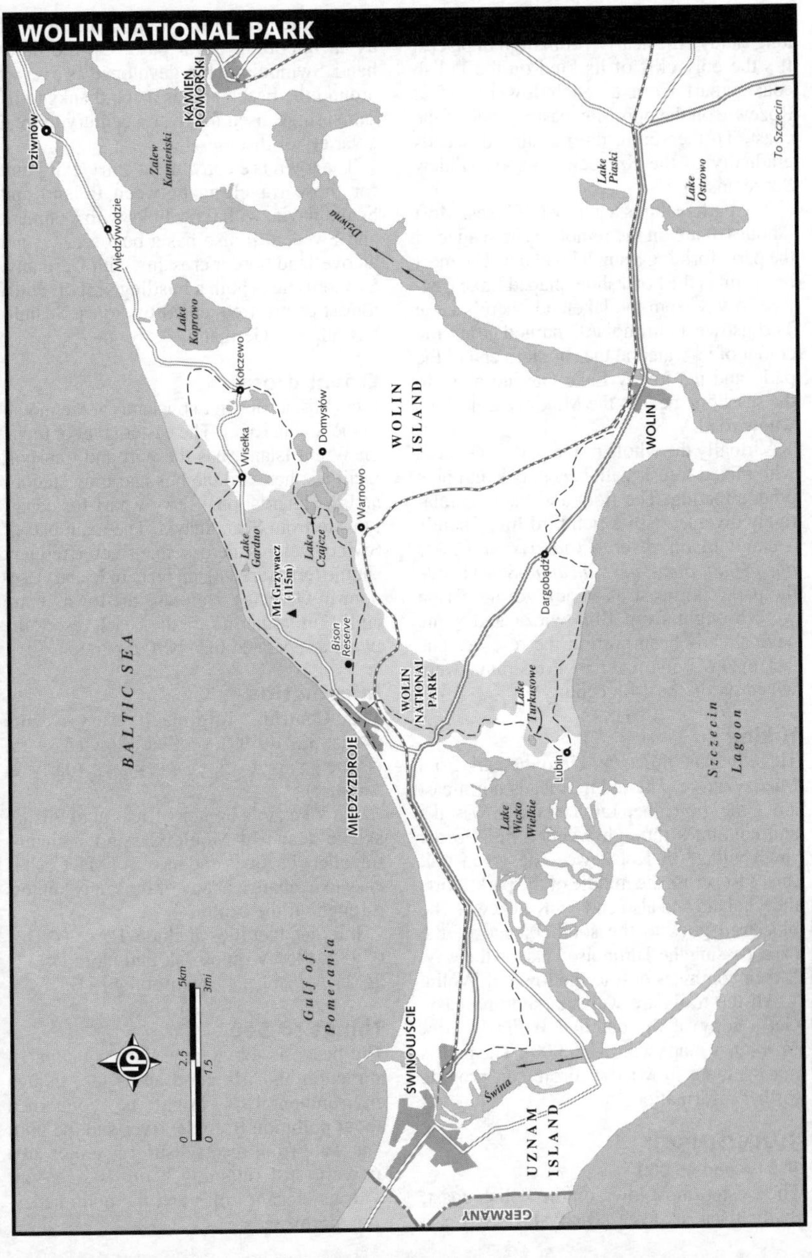

WOLIN NATIONAL PARK

Dziwnów

KAMIEŃ POMORSKI

Zalew Kamieński

Międzywodzie

Dziwna

Lake Piaski

Lake Ostrowo

To Szczecin

Lake Koprowo

Kołczewo

Wisełka

Domysłów

WOLIN ISLAND

WOLIN

BALTIC SEA

Lake Gardno

Lake Czajcze

Warnowo

Mt Grzywacz (115m)

Bison Reserve

Dargobądź

WOLIN NATIONAL PARK

Lake Turkusowe

MIĘDZYZDROJE

Lubin

Szczecin Lagoon

Lake Wicko Wielkie

Gulf of Pomerania

ŚWINOUJŚCIE

Świna

UZNAM ISLAND

GERMANY

0   2.5   5km
0   1.5   3mi

POMERANIA

drops sharply into the sea, forming a 11km-long sandy cliff nearly 100m high in places. It's the only cliff of its kind on the Polish coast, apart from a much lower cliff at Rozewie on the opposite, eastern side of the coast. To the south, the moraine descends gradually to the Szczecin Lagoon (Zalew Szczeciński).

The park features a number of lakes. Most (about 10) are on the remote eastern edge of the park, forming a small lakeland. The most beautiful is the horseshoe-shaped Lake Czajcze. Away from the lakeland, there's Lake Turkusowe (Turquoise), named after the colour of its water, at the southern end of the park, and the lovely Lake Gardno close to the seashore, next to the Międzyzdroje-Dziwnów road.

Virtually the whole of the park is covered with mixed forest, with beech, oak and pine predominating. The flora and fauna is relatively diverse, with a rich bird life. There's a small **bison reserve** *(admission US$1; open 10am-6pm Tues-Sun June-Sept)* inside the park, 2km east of Międzyzdroje. Bison were brought from Białowieża and some have already been born in the reserve. The last bison living wild in Pomerania were wiped out in the 14th century.

Hiking

Three marked trails wind into the park from Międzyzdroje. The red trail leads north-east along the shore, then turns inland to Wisełka and continues through wooded hills to the small village of Kołczewo. The green trail runs east across the middle of the park, skirts the lakeland and also ends in Kołczewo. The blue trail goes to the southern end of the park, passing the Turquoise Lake on the way. It then continues east to the town of Wolin.

All the trails are well marked and easy. Get a copy of the detailed *Woliński Park Narodowy* map (scale 1:30,000). The park's management in Międzyzdroje can provide further information.

ŚWINOUJŚCIE
☎ 91 • pop 45,000

The westernmost town on the Polish coast, Świnoujście ('Shvee-no-**ooysh**-cheh') is a fairly large fishing and trading port, as well as an important naval base. On the other hand, Świnoujście has developed as a resort around the beach and as a spa thanks to its salt springs, used for over a century to treat a variety of diseases.

The town is a convenient entry/exit point for those travelling between Poland and Scandinavia, with ferry links with Denmark and Sweden. It also has a boat service and an overland border crossing with Germany. Świnoujście is both a bustling seaport and a tourist centre frequented by Poles, Scandinavians and Germans.

Orientation

Świnoujście sits on two islands at the mouth of the Świna River. The eastern part of town, on Wolin Island, has the port and transport facilities; here are the bus and train stations and the international ferry wharf for departures to/from Scandinavia. The main part of Świnoujście is across the river (frequent shuttle ferry service), on Uznam Island (Usedom in German). Here are the town centre and, 1km farther north, the beach resort; the two are separated by a belt of parks.

Information

The Centrum Informacji Turystycznej (☎/fax 322 49 99), on Plac Słowiański 15, is open 9am to 5pm weekdays (daily in summer).

Bank Pekao's branch offices at ul Piłsudskiego 4 and ul Monte Cassino 7 change travellers cheques and have ATMs. Cash is easy to exchange at any of the many kantors throughout the centre.

Internet facilities include J@zz (☎ 321 03 09), Plac Wolności 4, and Nora (☎ 321 26 25), ul Bolesława Chrobrego 1B.

Things to See

The beach is, obviously, the major tourist attraction and it's good and wide, though environmentalists might be concerned about pollution from the river and the port. The waterfront resort district is a nice area as well, still retaining a *fin-de-siècle* air with its elegant villas and the main pedestrian promenade.

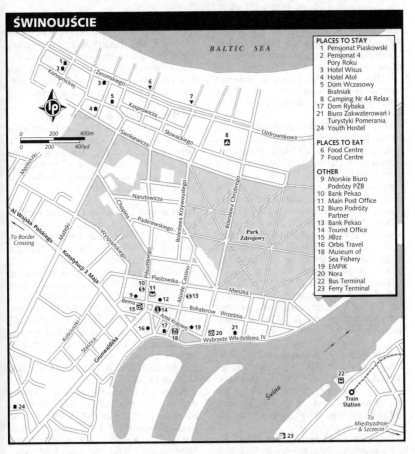

ŚWINOUJŚCIE

BALTIC SEA

PLACES TO STAY
1 Pensjonat Piaskowski
2 Pensjonat 4
  Pory Roku
3 Hotel Wisus
4 Hotel Atol
5 Dom Wczasowy
  Bratniak
8 Camping Nr 44 Relax
17 Dom Rybaka
21 Biuro Zakwaterowań i
  Turystyki Pomerania
24 Youth Hostel

PLACES TO EAT
6 Food Centre
7 Food Centre

OTHER
9 Morskie Biuro
  Podróży PŻB
10 Bank Pekao
11 Main Post Office
12 Biuro Podróży
  Partner
13 Bank Pekao
14 Tourist Office
15 J@zz
16 Orbis Travel
18 Museum of
  Sea Fishery
19 EMPiK
20 Nora
22 Bus Terminal
23 Ferry Terminal

In the town centre is the **Museum of Sea Fishery** *(Muzeum Rybołówstwa Morskiego; ☎ 321 23 26, Plac Rybaka 1; adult/student US$1/0.75; open 9am-4pm Tues-Fri, 11am-4pm Sat & Sun)*. It has collections of sea fauna, fishing equipment and navigation instruments, plus exhibits related to the town's history.

Places to Stay & Eat

As in other Baltic beach resorts, the high season is in July and August, and at times there may be few beds left vacant. The tourist office keeps an eye on what's available and should help. The prices given below are for the high season.

Camping Nr 44 Relax (☎/fax 321 39 12, ul Słowackiego 5) Tent site US$1.50 plus US$2 per person. Triples in cabins with bath US$40. Open June-Sept. The large camping ground is excellently located close to the beach and has cabins, but you're likely to need a miracle to get one in July or August.

Youth hostel (☎/fax 327 06 13, ul Gdyńska 26) Dorm beds US$5-6. Open year-round. The hostel offers 120 cheap dorm beds but is far from the beach.

POMERANIA

For private rooms, inquire at the *Biuro Zakwaterowań i Turystyki Pomerania* (☎/fax 321 37 66, Wybrzeże Władysława IV 12), opposite the ferry landing. The tourist office also has some rooms. Be prepared to pay US$7 to US$10 per person. Note that there are almost no private rooms in the beach area; they are mostly in the south-western suburbs.

Many *holiday homes* (almost all are near the beach) accept individual tourists, though some will insist on full board. Prices vary according to demand and standards, but count roughly US$20 to US$30 per bed with three meals, and not much less without. The tourist office has a detailed list of these homes and will help you to find somewhere.

Dom Rybaka (☎/fax 321 29 43, Wybrzeże Władysława IV 22) Singles/doubles/triples without bath US$11/18/24. If you need a budget option in the centre, the Dom Rybaka is perhaps the cheapest but it's basic.

Hotel Wisus (☎/fax 321 58 50, ul Żeromskiego 17) Beds in doubles/quads without bath US$10/8. In the seaside area, as close to the beach as you can get, Wisus is a basic student hostel which offers about 100 beds, most of which are in quads.

Dom Wczasowy Bratniak (☎ 321 28 46, ul Słowackiego 26) Beds in doubles, triples or quads without bath US$8. Another basic shelter near the beach, Bratniak also has only shared facilities. If it's full, the staff will probably send you to another hostel run by the same people.

Pensjonat Piaskowski (☎/fax 321 45 18, ul Żeromskiego 24) Doubles with bath & breakfast US$40-50. A more upmarket yet affordable option, the Piaskowski is a good choice and is right on the beach promenade.

Pensjonat 4 Pory Roku (☎ 321 16 94, ul Ujejskiego 8) Doubles with bath & breakfast US$50-70. In a fine villa just behind the Piaskowski, the Four Seasons offers 11 comfortable rooms.

Hotel Atol (☎ 321 30 10, fax 321 38 46, ul Orkana 3) Doubles with bath & breakfast US$60-70. Another upmarket option, the Atol is decent and has a good restaurant.

There are not many year-round restaurants (and these are mostly in the centre), but in summer a lot of seasonal venues open, including bistros, street stalls, bars and nightclubs (mainly in the beach area). There are two budget food centres on the beach promenade, ul Żeromskiego, which will keep you going. Some holiday homes serve lunch and dinner for nonguests.

Getting There & Away

The overland crossing to/from Germany is 2km west of town. The first town on the German side, Ahlbeck, handles bus transport farther into the country. The border is open to pedestrians only (bicycles can cross as well), of all nationalities.

Train & Bus The bus and train stations are next to each other on the right (eastern) bank of the Świna River. Passenger ferries shuttle constantly between the town centre and the stations (free, 10 minutes).

Ordinary trains go to Szczecin (116km) via Międzyzdroje (16km) every two or three hours (2¼ hours). There's one fast night train in summer directly to Warsaw (607km) and it has sleeping cars. To Kraków (729km), there are two year-round fast trains; they go via Poznań (301km) and Wrocław (466km). Tickets, sleepers and couchettes are available from Orbis Travel (☎ 321 44 11), Plac Słowiański 5/1.

Buses don't run to Szczecin, but do cover the coast, going as far as Gdynia (two fast buses daily). There are half a dozen buses to Kamień Pomorski (52km), and three or four fast buses to Kołobrzeg (98km); all go via Międzyzdroje. There are also half-hourly private buses to Międzyzdroje.

Car & Motorcycle If you're travelling by your own transport, you'll be crossing the Dźwina River 7km south of Świnoujście. Expect to wait during the peak season (usually no longer than a couple of hours). Passage for both vehicles and passengers is free.

Ferries to Scandinavia Polferries operates ferries to Ystad in Sweden and to Copenhagen. Information and tickets are handled by Morskie Biuro Podróży PŻB (☎ 322 43 96), ul Bema 9/2.

POMERANIA

Unity Line runs ferries to Ystad. Information and tickets are available from Biuro Podróży Partner (☎ 322 43 97), ul Bohaterów Września 83/14.

All ferries depart from the Ferry Terminal on Wolin Island. Refer to the introductory Getting There & Away chapter for general information.

Boats & Ferries to Germany Adler-Schiffe runs boats from Świnoujście to Ahlbeck, Heringsdorf, Bansin and Sassnitz. Information and tickets are available from Odratrans (☎ 322 42 88) in the port area on Wybrzeże Władysława IV.

Adler-Schiffe also runs daily car ferries to Altwarp; these depart from the Ferry Terminal on Wolin Island, across the Świna River. Adler-Shiffe's ticket office (☎ 321 68 90) at the terminal handles information and bookings.

SZCZECIN

☎ 91 • pop 425,000

Close to the German border, only 130km away from Berlin (and four times that distance from Warsaw), Szczecin ('**Shchehcheen**') is the main urban centre of northwestern Poland and the largest Polish port in terms of tonnage handled. Once Western Pomerania's capital, it has a colourful and stormy history. Most of the remnants of this history, however, were lost in the last war.

History

Szczecin's beginnings go back to the 8th century, when a Slav stronghold was built here. In 967, Mieszko I annexed the town, together with a large chunk of the coast, to the newborn Polish state. Mieszko didn't succeed in holding the region for long, however, nor was he able to Christianise it. It was Bolesław Krzywousty who recaptured the town in 1121 and brought the Catholic faith to the locals. Four years later, he moved the bishopric from Kołobrzeg to nearby Wolin, to have the priests and their gospel at hand.

Krzywousty died in 1138 and the Polish Crown crumbled; Pomerania formally became an independent principality. At that time, though, the Germans were expanding aggressively, and gradually took trade and decisive administrative posts into their own hands. In 1181 the Pomeranian Duke Bogusław I paid homage to the Holy Roman Emperor Frederick Barbarossa.

Three years later Denmark attacked and conquered Pomerania, taking control of vast parts of the Baltic coast as far as Estonia. In 1227, the Danes were defeated and forced out, and Szczecin, together with the surrounding region, came back under the rule of the Pomeranian princes, by then strongly dependent on the Brandenburg margraves.

In 1478 Western Pomerania was unified by Duke Bogusław X and Szczecin was chosen as the capital. Since the duke had been brought up at the Polish court and had married the daughter of the Polish King Kazimierz Jagiellończyk, he was keen to seek closer relations with Poland. This led to protests from the Brandenburgs and under pressure Western Pomerania acknowledged its allegiance to its western neighbour in 1521.

The next shift in power came in 1630. This time the Swedes conquered the city and occupied it until the Treaty of Westphalia of 1648 formally assigned it to them. After the Peace of Stockholm of 1720 concluded the Northern War, Sweden sold Szczecin to what was by then the kingdom of Prussia, which held the region until WWII. Under Prussian rule, Szczecin grew considerably, becoming the main port for Berlin, the two cities having been linked by a canal. By the outbreak of WWII the city had about 300,000 inhabitants.

In April 1945 the Red Army arrived on its way to Berlin and 60% of the urban area was left in ruins after the battle. Only 6000 souls remained of the former population, most of the others having fled.

With new inhabitants and new rulers, the battered city started a new life. However, there doesn't seem to have been the same enthusiasm and stamina in re-creating the former city as there were in some other big historic centres. Only individual buildings were restored and the rest of the ruins were replaced with the usual postwar creations.

POMERANIA

SZCZECIN

PLACES TO STAY
1 Youth Hostel
8 Radisson Hotel;
   Quo Vadis
9 Park Hotel
10 Porta Hotel
21 Dom Nauczyciela;
   Jadłodajnia U Lidki
29 Youth Hostel
31 Hotel Arkona
34 Hotel Podzamcze
40 Hotel Słowiaski
41 Hotel Rycerski
42 Hotel Piast
44 Hotelik Elka-Sen
45 Hotel Victoria;
   Night Club Tango
47 Pokoje Gościnne
   Pocztylion

PLACES TO EAT
5 Restauracja Chief
6 Kuchnia Wegetariaska
   Zielona Arka
15 Restauracja Chata
19 Bar Rybarex
20 Bar Mleczny Turysta
33 Pannekoekenrestaurant
   Haga
38 Steakhouse Piramida

OTHER
2 Philharmonic Hall
3 Pojcom
4 MediaNet
7 LOT Office
11 Maritime Museum
12 Christopher Columbus
13 Church of SS
   Peter & Paul
14 Royal Gate;
   Brama Jazz Cafe
16 Bank Pekao
17 National Museum
18 Bondi
22 Bank Pekao
23 EMPiK
24 Bank Pekao
25 Orbis Travel
26 Main Post Office
27 Bank Pekao
28 White Eagle's Fountain
30 Castle of the
   Pomeranian Princes;
   Tourist Office; Castle
   Museum; Restauracja
   Na Kuncu Korytarza
32 Town Hall; Historical
   Museum of Szczecin;
   Tawerna U Wyszaka
35 Polferries
36 Cathedral
37 Tourist Office
39 Harbour Gate
43 Portal
46 Bus Terminal
48 Post Office
49 St John's Church

Information

Tourist Offices The Centrum Informacji Turystycznej (☎ 434 04 40) is in a round pavilion at Al Niepodległości 1. It's open 9.30am to 5pm weekdays (also 10am to 2pm Saturday June to August). There's also a tourist office (☎ 489 16 30) in the castle, open 10am to 6pm daily.

Money Bank Pekao has several central branches, including Al Wojska Polskiego 1, ul Grodzka 9, Plac Żołnierza Polskiego16 and ul Obrońców Stalingradu 10/11. Kantors are plentiful all over the central area; the one at the train station is open 24 hours.

Email & Internet Access Central facilities include Bondi (☎ 812 20 28), ul Jedności Narodowej 1 and ul Wyzwolenia 1–3; Portal (☎ 488 40 66), ul Kaszubska 52; MediaNet (☎ 488 71 07), Al Wojska Polskiego 67; and Pojcom (☎ 433 51 46), Al Wojska Polskiego 69. They all are open till at least 10pm and cost US$1 to US$1.50 an hour.

Things to See

The most sizable city monument is the **Castle of the Pomeranian Princes** (Zamek Książąt Pomorskich). It was originally built in the mid-14th century but only in 1577 did it become a large residence with a square central courtyard. It was further enlarged and remodelled on various occasions. Badly damaged in 1945, the reconstruction gave it a predominantly Renaissance look, as it had been in the late 16th century. You can go to the top of its tower for a view of the town.

The castle now accommodates the opera auditorium, a restaurant and the **Castle Museum** (Muzeum Zamkowe; ☎ 434 22 62, ul Korsarzy 34; adult/student US$2/1; open 10am-4pm Tues-Sun, till 6pm in summer). The permanent exhibition on the castle's history includes six spectacular sarcophagi of the Pomeranian princes. They are large tin boxes decorated with a fine engraved ornamentation, made between 1606 and 1637 by artists from Königsburg. Following the death of the last Pomeranian duke, Bogusław XIV (whose sarcophagus is the most elaborate), the crypt, containing 14

sarcophagi, was walled up and only opened in 1946. The remains of the dukes were deposited in the cathedral, while the best preserved sarcophagi have been restored and are now the highlight of the display.

Various temporary exhibitions are presented in other rooms of the castle. In summer, concerts are held on Sunday at noon in the courtyard or in the former chapel of the castle, which occupies nearly half the northern side.

A short walk south will bring you to the 15th-century Gothic **town hall**, one of the finest buildings in the city. This is the only relic of the Old Town which was razed to the ground in 1945 and never rebuilt. A line of stylised burghers' houses has recently been put up right behind the town hall, in striking contrast to the line of communist blocks opposite.

The town hall accommodates the interesting **Historical Museum of Szczecin** (Muzeum Historii Miasta Szczecina; ☎ 488 02 49, Plac Rzepichy 1; adult/student US$1.50/0.75; open 10am-6pm Tues, 9am-3.30pm Wed & Fri, 10am-3.30pm Thur, 10am-4pm Sat & Sun).

There are two historic churches nearby. **St John's Church**, a typical 14th-century Gothic building, somehow managed to escape war destruction. Its interior is refreshingly devoid of decoration and has a perfect vault in the nave, supported on charmingly leaning columns. Vestiges of wall paintings from 1510 can still be seen in the right-hand aisle.

The **cathedral** is much larger, if similar in shape, but the interior is now fitted out with mostly modern decoration. On one side of the cathedral is the 15th-century vicarage and on the other a bell weighing almost six tonnes, dating from 1681.

Two blocks north is the **National Museum** (Muzeum Narodowe; ☎ 433 50 66, ul Staromłyńska 27; adult/student US$1.50/0.75; open 10am-6pm Tues, 9am-3.30pm Wed & Fri, 10am-3.30pm Thur, 10am-4pm Sat & Sun) in the 18th-century palace which formerly served as the Pomeranian parliament. It features a collection of religious art, mostly woodcarving from the 14th to 16th

POMERANIA

centuries, plus other historical exhibits related to Szczecin and Pomerania.

An extension of the museum, directly across the street, contains changing displays of modern art. Also part of the national museum is the **Maritime Museum** *(Muzeum Morskie;* ☎ *433 60 02, Wały Chrobrego 3; adult/student US$2/1; open 10am-6pm Tues, 9am-3.30pm Wed & Fri, 10am-3.30pm Thur, 10am-4pm Sat & Sun)* on the waterfront. Apart from an exhibition related to maritime matters, the museum has regional archaeological exhibits, and ethnography from Africa and Asia.

Places to Stay – Budget
Camping Nr 25 *(☎/fax 460 11 65, ul Przestrzenna 23)* Tent site US$2 plus US$2.50 per person, doubles/triples in cabins US$20/26. Open May-Sept. Szczecin has a good camping ground with cabins on the shore of Lake Dąbie in Szczecin Dąbie, about 7km south-east of the city centre. If you are coming by train and plan on staying there, get off in Szczecin Dąbie and continue by urban bus No 56 or walk 2km.

Youth hostel *(☎ 422 47 61, fax 423 56 96, ul Monte Cassino 19A)* Beds US$2-10. Open year-round. The hostel is friendly and well run, and has 130 beds reasonably distributed from double rooms to 14-bed dorms. It's 2km north-west of the centre – take tram No 3 from either the bus or train stations to Plac Rodła and change for the westbound tram No 1.

There are also two July-August **youth hostels** in the city: *(☎ 352 33 24, ul Jodłowa 21),* 2km west of the centre; and *(☎ 433 29 24, ul Grodzka 22).* The latter is basic but perfectly situated halfway between the castle and the cathedral in the city heart.

Porta Hotel *(☎ 459 13 11, fax 433 75 01, ul Starzyńskiego 3-4)* Singles/doubles without bath US$10/20, with bath US$20/30. One of the cheapest places in the centre, the Porta Hotel, close to the castle, is not bad value for these prices.

Hotel Piast *(☎ 433 66 62, Plac Zwycięstwa 3)* Singles/doubles without bath US$14/18, with bath US$18/25. Another central facility, the basic Piast haven't seen

new paint for ages, yet it has spacious rooms that don't cost a fortune.

Hotel Słowiański *(☎ 451 53 57, fax 433 77 45, ul Potulicka 1)* Singles/doubles without bath US$18/24, with bath US$28/34. A former police dorm, the Słowiański has modest but neat rooms.

Pokoje Gościnne Pocztylion *(☎ 440 12 11, ul Dworcowa 20B)* Beds in doubles, triples or quads without bath US$10, doubles with bath US$30-50. Near the bus and train stations, Pocztylion is a facility of Poczta Polska (Polish Post) and is a good option.

Places to Stay – Mid-Range & Top End
Dom Nauczyciela *(☎/fax 433 04 81, ul Śląska 4)* Singles/doubles/triples with bath & breakfast US$30/40/55. The 22-room Dom Nauczyciela is quiet, neat and central – good value.

Hotelik Elka-Sen *(☎ 433 56 04, fax 812 03 98, Al 3 Maja 1A)* Singles US$20-35, doubles US$25-45, triples US$45-65, quads US$50-60, all with bath & breakfast. Another quiet and neat place, Hotel Elka-Sen offers 13 reasonable rooms.

Hotel Rycerski *(☎/fax 488 81 64, ul Potulicka 2A)* Singles/doubles with bath & breakfast US$45/60. Extensively refurbished, this 54-bed army-run hotel is now a comfortable place, and is very central.

Hotel Podzamcze *(☎/fax 812 14 04, ul Sienna 1)* Singles/doubles with bath & breakfast US$45/60. Nestled in the reconstructed part of the Old Town, the small Podzamcze offers cosy rooms, plus a restaurant and pub downstairs.

Hotel Arkona *(☎ 488 02 61, fax 488 02 60, ul Panieńska 10)* Singles/doubles US$55/70. Also located in the Old Town area, Arkona is a communist relic and has not much style, but has been revamped and provides good standards. It may have attractive weekend rates.

Hotel Victoria *(☎ 434 38 55, fax 433 73 68, Plac Batorego 2)* Singles/doubles US$45/65. For those who need to stay close to transport, the 41-room Victoria is just a three-minute walk uphill from the bus terminal and not much more from the train tation. Rooms vary in size so it's best to have a look first.

Park Hotel (☎ *488 15 24, fax 434 45 03, ul Plantowa 1*) Singles/doubles with bath & breakfast US$80/90. Enjoying an attractive location in the park, this appropriately named option has 15 spacious rooms and a good restaurant.

Radisson Hotel (☎ *359 51 11, fax 359 50 15, Plac Rodła 10*) Singles/doubles US$120/130. As good as you can get in town, the 369-room Radisson is Szczecin's fanciest option, and comes complete with three restaurants, a swimming pool, sauna, gym, bar and disco.

Places to Eat

Bar Mleczny Turysta (☎ *434 22 01, ul Obrońców Stalingradu 6A*) Mains US$1.50-2.50. A refurbished milk bar, Turysta is acceptable, efficient and dirt cheap.

Bar Rybarex (*ul Obrońców Stalingradu 6*) Mains US$2-4. Next door to the Turysta, the Rybarex is a sort of budget fish and cheap eatery, and has a reasonable range of fish to choose from.

Jadłodajnia U Lidki (☎ *489 65 01, ul Śląska 4*) Mains US$2-3. In the Dom Nauczyciela, Jadłodajnia serves excellent home-made meals, which are great value. It's only open weekdays, noon to 5pm.

Kuchnia Wegetariańska Zielona Arka (☎ *434 48 08, ul Śląska 9*) Mains US$2-3. As its name suggests, Zielona Arka does vegetarian food, and it really does it well.

Steakhouse Piramida (☎ *488 16 63, Al Niepodległości 3*) Mains US$4-5. Next to the tourist office, Piramida serves generous portions of Middle-Eastern fare.

Pannekoekenrestaurant Haga (☎ *812 17 59, ul Sienna 10*) Crepes US$3-5. A new kid on the block, sitting next to the old town hall, Haga has Dutch crepes, 300 flavours in all, which you can have until 11pm.

Restauracja Chata (☎ *488 73 70, Plac Hołdu Pruskiego 8*) Mains US$6-8. The Chata (Hut) is a charming place that serves traditional Polish food in rustic timber countryside-style surrounds.

Restauracja Na Kuncu Korytarza (☎ *426 12 29, ul Korsarzy 34*) Mains US$5-10.

Nestled in the castle, this is another charming place for traditional Polish food.

Restauracja Chief (☎ *434 37 65, ul Rayskiego 16*) Mains US$8-18. On the corner of Plac Grunwaldzki, this is an upmarket fish restaurant with an extensive menu and some of the best fish in town.

Entertainment

Christopher Columbus (☎ *489 34 01, Wały Chrobrego 1*) An attractive bar-cum-restaurant overlooking the river, Columbus has a bar shaped like a boat, a large balcony above it, and a vast beer garden. It may have live music from time to time.

Colorado (☎ *488 19 21, Wały Chrobrego 1A*) In a similarly attractive location as Columbus, Colorado has a Wild West theme, and also has plenty of drinks till late.

Pub Nautilus (☎ *434 70 18, ul Jana z Kolna 7*) Decorated like its name, Nautilus has weekend discos and cheap beer.

Brama Jazz Cafe (☎ *804 62 95, Plac Hołdu Pruskiego 1*) Housed in the baroque Royal Gate, the Brama has live jazz, usually on Wednesday.

Night Club Tango (☎ *433 62 30, Plac Batorego 2*) The trendy Tango occupies large vaulted cellars deep underneath the Hotel Victoria and has discos/live music every night till 5am.

Tawerna U Wyszaka (*Plac Rzepichy 1*) If you want to dance in the best medieval interior in town, this is the place. Occupying a spacious, marvellous brick vaulted cellar of the town hall, Taverna operates as a restaurant-cum-bar during the day, and goes into a dancing frenzy later in the night.

Quo Vadis (☎ *359 55 95, Plac Rodła 10*) The trendy Quo Vadis is the disco of the Radisson Hotel, so you can quickly deduct that you may meet some beautiful people, but it's not exactly a budget establishment.

Getting There & Away

Air Szczecin has three to five flights a day to Warsaw and weekday direct flights to Copenhagen. The airport is in Goleniów, about 45km north-east of the city. The LOT office (☎ 433 50 58), ul Wyzwolenia 17, provides information and bookings.

Train The main train station, Szczecin Główny, is on the bank of the Odra River, 1km south of the centre. You can also buy tickets at Orbis Travel (☎ 434 26 18), Plac Zwycięstwa 1.

There are a dozen fast trains to Poznań daily (214km) and five to Gdańsk (374km). There are three express trains to Warsaw (525km), including one InterCity train which covers the distance in 5½ hours. A couple of trains leave for Kołobrzeg daily (138km) and five to Zielona Góra (207km). Trains to Stargard Szczeciński (40km) depart about every 30 minutes, and to Świnoujście (116km) every one to two hours.

Bus The bus terminal is uphill from the train station and handles regular summer departures to Kamień Pomorski (88km) but fewer buses off season. Buses to Stargard Szczeciński (32km) leave frequently. There are summer buses to beach resorts such as Dziwnów, Pobierowo and Niechorze, but almost nothing to Świnoujście and Międzyzdroje; go there by train.

There are minibuses to Berlin daily (US$12, 2½ hours). Inquire at Euro Ster (☎ 489 38 77), in the bus terminal building, or the Interglobus Tour (☎ 485 04 22), ul Kolumba 1, near the entrance to the train station.

Ferry There are ferries from Świnoujście to Copenhagen (Denmark) and Ystad (Sweden), both lines operated by Polferries (☎ 488 09 45), ul Wyszyńskiego 28. The route from Świnoujście to Ystad is also serviced by Unity Line (☎ 359 55 92), Plac Rodła 8. Orbis Travel also handles information and bookings.

STARGARD SZCZECIŃSKI
☎ 92 • pop 73,000

Stargard Szczeciński was once a flourishing port and trade centre with reputedly the most elaborate system of fortified walls in Pomerania. So prosperous was the town that it fought with Szczecin for the right to send merchandise down the Odra River to the sea. The fierce competition between the two ports led in 1454 to a virtual war, including regular battles complete with the ransacking and sinking of the enemy's ships. This, however, is history.

Today, Stargard has no port at all and is just a satellite town of Szczecin. It suffered badly in WWII when over 70% of its buildings were destroyed during the fighting. Now revived, it's a grey urban sprawl with a fair amount of industry.

The Old Town evokes mixed feelings: surrounded by medieval walls, partly preserved, it consists not of the old burghers' houses but of a mass of postwar drab blocks from which a few historic buildings stand out, with the two massive churches dominating. It's worth stopping here for the little that's left.

Things to See
The town's pride and joy is **St Mary's Church**, a mighty brick construction (one of the largest in Western Pomerania) begun in 1292 and extended successively until the end of the 15th century; since then, no major alterations have been made to its structure. It has a rich external decoration of glazed bricks and tiles and three different elaborate doorways.

Next to the church is the **Regional Museum** (☎ 577 25 56, *Rynek Staromiejski 2/4; adult/student US$2/1, free Sat; open 10am-4pm Tues-Sun*), which has exhibits on local history, archaeology and weights and measures. Adjoining the museum is the **town hall**, the late Gothic building with a beautifully ornamented Renaissance gable.

St John's Church, on the opposite side of the Old Town, was constructed in the 15th century but was later changed significantly; it has the highest tower in Western Pomerania (99m).

The **fortified walls** were begun in the late 13th century and completed at the beginning of the 16th century, by which time they were 2260m long. Roughly half of that length has survived, complete with several towers and gates. You can walk around the walls – you'll come across three gates and four towers; some of them may have exhibitions in summer.

Places to Stay

Hotel PTTK (☎/fax 578 31 91, ul Kuśnierzy 5) Singles/doubles/triples without bath US$12/16/22, with bath US$20/28/34. Just a few minutes walk from the cathedral, the very simple 37-bed PTTK is in a lovely old building, one of only a few to have survived in the area.

Hotel Staromiejski (☎ 577 22 23, fax 577 65 62, ul Spichrzowa 2) Singles/doubles without bath US$15/19, with bath US$20/25. An alternative budget option if the PTTK is full, just 200m to the north, the Staromiejski is much larger, but it's just a nondescript apartment block.

Getting There & Away

The train and bus stations are close to each other, 1km west of the Old Town. Urban buses ply this route if you feel lazy.

Transport to/from Szczecin is frequent by both bus (32km) and train (40km). For Świnoujście, take the train (five daily) as buses are scarce. Six trains go to Warsaw daily (some via Poznań) and five to Gdańsk; all come through from Szczecin.

Warmia & Masuria

Warmia and Masuria occupy north-eastern Poland, from the lower Vistula valley in the west to the Lithuanian border in the east. The region is gently undulating, forested and not densely populated. There's little industry and consequently pollution is minimal.

Masuria (Mazury in Polish) has a myriad postglacial lakes – perhaps as many as 3000. Most of them are concentrated in the Great Masurian Lake District (Kraina Wielkich Jezior Mazurskich), which is Poland's major destination for yachtspeople and canoeists. Warmia is more remarkable for its cultural heritage rather than lakes. Although its geography is roughly similar to that of Masuria, its history is quite distinct. The only significant urban centre in the whole region is Olsztyn, on the southern edge of Warmia.

Originally the region was inhabited by diverse pagan tribes, of which the non-Slavic Prussians and the Jatzvingians were the major ones. When the region was conquered by the Teutonic Knights in the second half of the 13th century, the native inhabitants were wiped out. Warmia came to Poland in the aftermath of the Toruń Treaty of 1466 but Masuria only paid fealty to the Polish king in 1525. Even then Masuria – known since then as Ducal Prussia – continued to be in the German sphere of influence, and in the mid-17th century it came under the rule of the Hohenzollerns of Brandenburg. Warmia was annexed to the kingdom of Prussia in the First Partition of 1773 and the whole region stayed this way until WWII (except for a small area around Suwałki, which joined Poland after WWI).

After WWII Stalin arbitrarily defined the Soviet-Polish border by drawing an almost straight line on the map, from east to west. The area to the south was given to Poland, while the land to the north, with the port of Kaliningrad (previously Prussian Königsberg), was taken over by the Soviet Union. The Russians didn't give this strategic territory to any of the republics but kept it for themselves, despite the fact that it is cut off

Highlights

- Paddle in a kayak down the lovely Krutynia River
- Take a boat trip along the unique Elbląg-Ostróda Canal
- Visit the Gothic castle in Lidzbark Warmiński
- Explore Święta Lipka, the best baroque church in northern Poland
- Sail around the Great Masurian Lakes
- Enjoy a kayak trip down the Czarna Hańcza River

geographically from its motherland by Lithuania, Latvia and Belarus.

The Olsztyn Region

The Olsztyn region covers Warmia and the land to the south of Olsztyn. There are several important architectural monuments in this area (particularly the castle in Lidzbark Warmiński and the church in Święta Lipka), a good skansen in Olsztynek, and the unique Elbląg-Ostróda Canal.

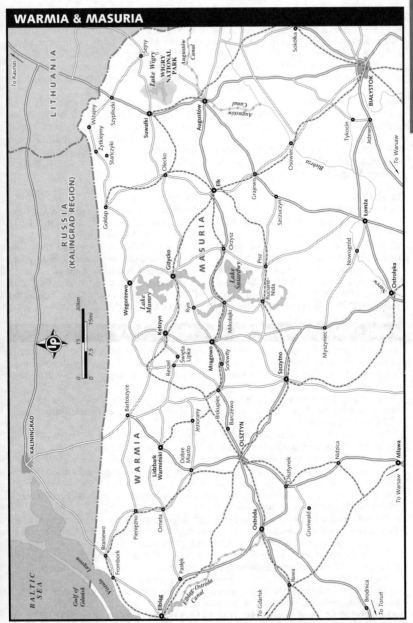

WARMIA & MASURIA

LITHUANIA

To Kaunas

RUSSIA
(KALININGRAD REGION)

KALININGRAD

BALTIC
SEA

Gulf of
Gdańsk

Vistula

Lagoon

Sejny

Lake Wigry

WIGRY NATIONAL PARK

Augustów Canal

Sokółka

Wizajny

Szypliszki

BIAŁYSTOK

Suwałki

Augustów

Augustów Canal

Żytkiejmy

Stańczyki

Olecko

Ełk

Grajewo

Osowiec

Tykocin

Jeżewo

To Warsaw

Biebrza

Łomża

Gołdap

Szczuczyn

Nowogród

Ostrołęka

MASURIA

Węgorzewo

Giżycko

Orzysz

Pisz

Lake
Mamry

Ryn

Lake
Śniardwy

Kucane-Nida

Myszyniec

Kętrzyn

Mikołajki

Święta Lipka

Reszel

Mrągowo

Sorkwity

Szczytno

Bartoszyce

Jeziorany

Biskupiec

Barczewo

OLSZTYN

Nidzica

Mława

To Warsaw

WARMIA

Dobre Miasto

Lidzbark Warmiński

Orneta

Olsztynek

Pieniężno

Braniewo

Frombork

Pasłęk

Ostróda

Grunwald

To Gdańsk

Iława

Brodnica

To Toruń

Elbląg

Elbląg-Ostróda Canal

30km
15mi
0 7.5 15

The Teutonic Knights arrived here in the mid-13th century, but it was the Warmian bishops who eventually converted and colonised the region, and controlled it for several centuries. Travelling around the region, you'll still come across relics of the bishops' great days, mostly to be found in their former district seats.

The so-called Copernicus Route (Szlak Kopernikowski) winds through places connected with the astronomer. It includes several Warmian towns with which Copernicus was closely related, among them Olsztyn, Lidzbark Warmiński and Frombork.

OLSZTYN
☎ 89 • pop 165,000

The history of Olsztyn ('Ol-shtin') has been a successive overlapping of Prussian and Polish influences, as in most of the region. Founded in the 14th century as the southernmost outpost of Warmia, Olsztyn came under Polish control following the Toruń Treaty of 1466. With the First Partition of Poland in 1773, Olsztyn became Prussian (renamed Allenstein) and remained so until WWII. Only in 1945 did the town, 40% of which was destroyed during the war, return to Poland. After massive rebuilding, the city is now the largest and most important urban centre in Warmia and Masuria – though little can be seen of its past.

For travellers, Olsztyn is probably more important as a jumping-off point for, or stopover between, attractions in the region rather than a destination in itself. Though the city has reasonable food and accommodation facilities, you can see its historic sites in a few hours.

Information
Tourist Offices The Wojewódzkie Centrum Informacji Turystycznej (☎/fax 535 35 66), at ul Staromiejska 1, is open 8am to 4pm weekdays (till 5pm and also 10am to 2pm Saturday and Sunday in July and August). It sells maps, although a much better selection can be found at the Sklep Podr-óżnika (Traveller's Shop), behind the High Gate.

From Knight to Bishop – Warmia's History

Warmia is one of Poland's historically determined regions, sitting in the far north of the country between Pomerania and Masuria. Its name derives from the original inhabitants of this land, the Warmians, who were wiped out by the Teutonic Knights in the 13th century, in much the same manner as other ethnic communities of the region.

Like most of Poland, Warmia has had a turbulent history, but what clearly differentiates it from the other provinces is that for over five centuries it was a largely autonomous ecclesiastical state. It was a citadel of Catholicism run by the Warmian bishops.

The Warmian diocese was brought into being by the papal bulls of 1243 as the largest (4250 sq km) of four, which were created in the territories conquered by the Teutonic Order. Though administratively within the Teutonic state, the bishops used papal protection to achieve a far-reaching autonomy. Their bishopric extended to the north of Olsztyn up to the present-day national border, and from the Vistula Lagoon in the west to the town of Reszel in the east. It was divided into 10 districts with regional seats in Frombork, Braniewo, Pieniężno, Orneta, Lidzbark Warmiński, Dobre Miasto, Olsztyn, Barczewo, Jeziorany and Reszel.

The first seat of the bishopric was founded around 1250 in Braniewo but was soon destroyed by the Prussians. The seat was then moved to the more defendable Frombork, and in 1350 was transferred to Lidzbark Warmiński, where it stayed for over four centuries.

Following the 1466 Treaty of Toruń, Warmia was incorporated into the kingdom of Poland, but the bishops retained much of their control over internal affairs. The bishopric was not subordinated to the archbishopric of Gniezno but was responsible directly to the pope. When the last Grand Master adopted Protestantism in 1525, Warmia became a bastion of the Counter-Reformation. In 1773 Warmia fell under Prussian rule and it wasn't until WWII that it returned to Poland.

Money Useful banks include Bank Pekao, ul 1 Maja 10, and Powszechny Bank Kredytowy, ul Mickiewicza 2, and both have their own ATMs. Kantors are easy to find in the centre.

Email & Internet Access Central facilities include Metropolis (☎ 535 01 92), ul Prosta 38/6, and Strefa, ul Skłodowskiej-Curie 7.

Things to See

The **High Gate**, the historic gateway to the Old Town, is all that remains of the 14th-century city walls. Just to the west is the branch of the **Museum of Warmia and Masuria** *(Muzeum Warmii i Mazur; ☎ 534 01 19, Targ Rybny 1; adult/student US$1.50/ 0.75; open 9am-5pm Tues-Sun June-Aug, 10am-4pm Tues-Sun Sept-May)*. It features exhibitions related to the city's and region's past. A block south is the **Rynek** (formally called ul Stare Miasto). It was destroyed during WWII and rebuilt in a style only superficially reverting to the past.

The most important historic building in town is the **castle**, a massive red-brick structure built in the 14th century. It now houses the main part of the **Museum of Warmia and Masuria** *(☎ 527 95 96, ul Zamkowa 2; adult/student US$2/1; open 9am-5pm Tues-Sun June-Aug, 10am-4pm Tues-Sun Sept-May)*. It features works of art from Warmia, including paintings and silverware. Part of the 1st floor is dedicated to Copernicus, who was the administrator of Warmia and lived in the castle for more than three years (1516–20). He also made some of his astronomical observations here, and you can still see the diagram he drew on the cloister wall to record the equinox and thereby calculate the exact length of the year. Models of the instruments he used for his observations are on display in his former living quarters. Note the original crystal-like vaulting of the ceiling.

The **cathedral** dates from the same period, though its huge 60m tower was only added in 1596. Here, too, crystal-like vaults can be seen in the aisles, but the nave has net-like vaulting dating from the 17th century.

Olsztyn's huge castle served as a home for Copernicus for three years

Among remarkable works of art is the 16th-century triptych at the head of the left aisle.

Outside the Old Town, there is a **planetarium** *(☎ 533 49 51, Al Piłsudskiego 38; adult/student US$2/1.50; open Tues-Sun)*, which has shows several times a day. A show with the English soundtrack is usually scheduled at noon.

The **astronomical observatory** *(☎ 527 67 03, ul Żołnierska 13; adult/student US$2/ 1.50)* is in the old water tower. It provides observations of the sun (several times a day except Monday), and of the stars (Tuesday to Friday twice nightly), provided the sky is clear.

Kayaking

The **Mazury travel agency** *(☎/fax 527 40 59, ul Staromiejska 1)* runs 10-day kayaking tours along the Krutynia River (known as Szlak Kajakowy Krutyni). The 103km route begins at Stanica Wodna PTTK (☎ 742 81 24) in Sorkwity, 50km east of Olsztyn, and goes down the Krutynia River and Lake Bełdany to Ruciane-Nida. The 10-kayak (20-people) tours go daily from late June to mid-August (US$200). The price includes kayak, food, lodging in cabins and a Polish-speaking guide.

You can also do the trip on your own, renting a kayak from the Stanica in Sorkwity (US$6 to US$7 per day), but check the kayak availability in advance. You can use the same overnight bases as the tours but you can't always count on cabins – be prepared

WARMIA & MASURIA

OLSZTYN

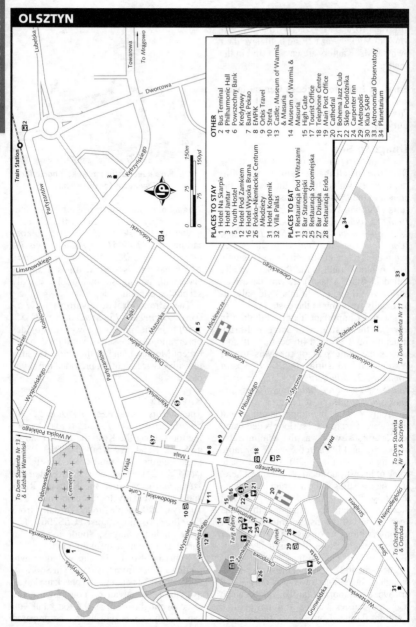

PLACES TO STAY
1 Hotel Na Skarpie
3 Hotel Jantar
5 Youth Hostel
12 Hotel Pod Zamkiem
16 Hotel Wysoka Brama
26 Polsko-Niemieckie Centrum Młodzieży
31 Hotel Kopernik
32 Villa Pallas

PLACES TO EAT
11 Restauracja Pod Witrażami
23 Bar Staromiejski
25 Restauracja Staromiejska
27 Bar Dziupla
28 Restauracja Eridu

OTHER
2 Bus Terminal
4 Philharmonic Hall
6 Powszechny Bank Kredytowy
7 Bank Pekao
8 EMPIK
9 Orbis Travel
10 Strefa
13 Castle; Museum of Warmia & Masuria
14 Museum of Warmia & Masuria
15 High Gate
17 Tourist Office
18 Telephone Centre
19 Main Post Office
20 Cathedral
21 Bohema Jazz Club
22 Sklep Podróżnika
24 Carpenter Inn
29 Metropolis
30 Klub SARP
33 Astronomical Observatory
34 Planetarium

to camp. It's much easier to get a kayak and a shelter in June or September, than in July and August.

Brochures in English and German with a detailed description and maps of the Krutynia route have been published – inquire at the Mazury office. The description in German is also available online (W www.masuren-online.de).

Places to Stay

Youth hostel (☎ 527 66 50, fax 527 68 70, ul Kopernika 45) Beds US$4-6. Open year-round. The youth hostel, halfway between the Old Town and the train station, is well-run and tidy, though most of its 71 beds are in large dorms with bunks.

Hotel Wysoka Brama (☎/fax 527 36 75, ul Staromiejska 1) Beds in dorms US$4, singles without bath US$12, doubles without/with bath US$15/20. The 70-bed PTTK hotel is excellently located on the edge of the Old Town. Its old section in the High Gate has dorms of four and six beds, whereas the adjacent new building houses singles and doubles. In summer the hotel is crammed with backpackers.

From July to mid-September, some student dorms open as hostels, but the picture can change each year. Check **Dom Studenta Nr 11** (☎ 527 60 34, ul Żołnierska 14B); **Dom Studenta Nr 12** (☎ 535 90 95, ul Niepodległości 57) and **Dom Studenta Nr 13** (☎ 535 81 51, Al Wojska Polskiego 14). These places cost US$5 to US$6 per bed in doubles, triples or quads with shared facilities.

Hotel Jantar (☎ 533 54 52, fax 539 13 62, ul Kętrzyńskiego 5) Singles/doubles/triples/quads without bath US$14/20/24/30. A former workers' dorm, Jantar is convenient for those who need to be close to the train station, but otherwise it's an uninspiring place.

Hotel Podgrodzie (☎ 527 27 80, fax 527 54 71, ul Osińskiego 12/13) Bed in a triple or quad US$8. Another central if unprepossessing place, the Podgrodzie is just 500m south of the Old Town.

Hotel Na Skarpie (☎/fax 526 93 81, ul Gietkowska 6A) Singles/doubles with bath & breakfast US$28/38. This large former army dorm, a 10-minute walk north of the Old Town, is a reasonable compromise between price and comfort.

Hotel Pod Zamkiem (☎ 525 12 87, ☎/fax 534 09 40, ul Nowowiejskiego 10) Singles/doubles/triples with bath US$35/45/55. Set in a large historic villa, this is a stylish place with character, and it's very close to the Old Town.

Polsko-Niemieckie Centrum Młodzieży (☎ 534 07 80, ☎/fax 527 69 33, ul Okopowa 25) Singles/doubles with bath & breakfast US$40/50. Ideally located next to the castle, this 20-room hotel is another comfortable central option.

Hotel Kopernik (☎ 522 99 29, fax 527 93 92, ul Warszawska 37) Singles/doubles with bath & breakfast US$45/65. The new 62-room Kopernik has no great style but does provide a reasonable standard close to the centre.

Villa Pallas (☎ 535 01 15, fax 535 99 15, ul Żołnierska 4) Singles/doubles with bath & breakfast US$60/70. Villa Pallas, in a large old villa, is one of the best places in town. When booking, ask for a room in the old section, which has more style and atmosphere than the hotel's new extension.

Places to Eat

Bar Dziupla (☎ 527 50 83, ul Stare Miasto 9/10) Mains US$2-3. The Dziupla provides some of the best cheap meals in the Old Town, including delicious pierogi and chłodnik.

Bar Staromiejski (☎ 527 34 87, ul Staromiejska 4/6) Mains US$2-4. Bar Staromiejski can be a central alternative, though it's not as good as the Dziupla.

Restauracja Staromiejska (☎ 527 58 83, ul Stare Miasto 4/6) Mains US$4-6. An upmarket cousin of the bar, the restauracja offers decent Polish fare at acceptable prices.

Restauracja Eridu (☎ 534 94 67, ul Prosta 3/4) Mains US$3-5. The Eridu has some popular Middle-Eastern fare, including the inevitable felafel.

Restauracja Pod Witrażami (☎ 543 05 85, ul 11 Listopada 7/1) Mains US$5-8. This cosy quiet place offers an imaginative Polish menu.

The restaurants of the *Polsko-Niemieckie Centrum Młodzieży* and *Villa Pallas* are about the best and most expensive hotel restaurants in the centre.

Entertainment

Bohema Jazz Club *(ul Lelewela 4)* The town's major jazz haunt, the Bohema is a two-level place with live jazz hosted irregularly on the lower level. Upstairs is an amazingly decorated bar with jazz CDs playing through the stereo.

Carpenter Inn *(Stare Miasto 3)* Another charming place, the Carpenter Inn also has a beautiful upper-level room. Old good rock, played from CDs, adds to the atmosphere.

Klub SARP *(☎ 535 96 49, ul Kołłątaja 14)* Located in an old granary, SARP is yet another double-level pleasant bar popular with local folks.

Getting There & Away

The bus and train stations are in one building, on ul Partyzantów, and are pretty busy. You can walk to the Old Town in 15 minutes or take one of the frequent city buses that drop you off in front of the High Gate.

Train About five fast trains leave for Gdańsk daily (179km) via Elbląg (99km). One express and two fast trains go to Warsaw (233km) all year, and there are a couple of more trains in summer. Half a dozen trains run to Toruń daily (163km), a route which is not covered by buses.

Bus Buses to Olsztynek (28km) and Lidzbark Warmiński (46km) go every hour. There are about 10 departures to Giżycko daily (104km), 14 to Kętrzyn (88km) and six to Elbląg (95km). Half a dozen fast PKS buses run to Warsaw (213km).

Among international destinations, PKS has daily departures to Kaliningrad (US$5, four hours) and Vilnius (US$13, nine hours).

OLSZTYNEK

☎ 89 • pop 8000

Olsztynek has an interesting skansen, the **Museum of Folk Architecture** *(Muzeum Budownictwa Ludowego; ☎ 519 21 64, ul Sportowa 21; adult/student US$1.50/1; open 9am-3pm Tues-Sun Apr & Oct, 9am-5pm daily May, 9am-5.30pm daily June-Aug, 9am-4.30pm Tues-Sun Sept, 9am-3pm Mon-Fri Nov-Mar but houses locked).* Tucked away on the north-eastern outskirts of town, the skansen features about 40 examples of regional timber architecture from Warmia and Masuria, and also has a cluster of Lithuanian houses. There's a variety of peasant cottages complete with outbuildings, various windmills and a thatch-roofed church. A number of buildings have been furnished and decorated inside, and it's been done really well.

The 14th-century Protestant church, on the Rynek, was rebuilt after WWII damage and is now an **art gallery** *(☎ 519 24 91, Rynek 1; adult/student US$1/0.50; open 9am-5pm Tues-Sun May-Sept, 9am-4pm Tues-Sun Oct-Apr)* displaying mostly crafts.

Places to Stay & Eat

Zajazd Mazurski *(☎ 519 28 85, ul Park 1)* Doubles/quads with bath & breakfast US$28/30. The Zajazd, 1km from the centre on the Gdańsk road, is the only place to stay. It has its own restaurant, or you can eat in one of a few simple eateries in the town centre.

Getting There & Away

The train station is 1km north-east of the centre, close to the skansen. Trains north to Olsztyn (31km) and south to Działdowo (53km) run every hour or two.

The bus terminal is 250m south of the Rynek, but many regional buses call in at the train station. You can go from either to Olsztyn (28km, buses every half an hour or so), Grunwald (19km, five daily) and Ostróda (29km, six daily).

GRUNWALD

☎ 89

Grunwald is hard to find even on detailed maps, yet the name is known to every Pole. Here, on 15 July 1410, the combined Polish and Lithuanian forces (supported by contingents of Ruthenians and Tatars) under King Władysław Jagiełło defeated the army of the Teutonic Knights. A crucial moment in Polish history, the 10 hours of carnage left the Grand Master of the Teutonic Order, Urlich von Jungingen, dead and his forces decimated. This was reputedly the largest medieval battle in Europe.

The battlefield is an open, gently rolling meadow adorned with three monuments. Built on the central hill is the **Museum of the Grunwald Battlefield** (*Muzeum Bitwy Grunwaldzkiej*; ☎ 647 22 27; adult/student US$1.50/0.75; open 8am-6pm May-Sept). It displays period armour, maps, battle banners etc, and its cinema runs films about the battle. The ruin of the chapel erected by the Order a year after the battle in the place where the Grand Master is supposed to have died, is 500m from the museum.

Frequently visited by Poles, Grunwald is essentially a memorial to this glorious moment in Poland's history. Foreigners may find it less interesting. The shop by the entrance to the battlefield sells brochures in English and German, and the snack bar serves basic food.

There's a bus stop next to the snack bar, from which four or five buses go to Olsztynek daily (18km), Olsztyn (47km) and Ostróda (26km).

OSTRÓDA
☎ 89 • pop 35,000
Ostróda is the starting/finishing point for excursions through the Elbląg-Ostróda Canal, and if you take this trip you're likely to spend a night in town, either before or after the journey.

Places to Stay & Eat
Dom Wycieczkowy Drwęcki (☎/fax 646 30 35, ul Mickiewicza 7) Singles/doubles/triples/quads without bath US$12/16/22/26. Located 500m east of the bus and train stations, and just 100m from the boat landing site, Drwęcki is a popular, cheap place to stay, and has an unpretentious restaurant downstairs.

Kino Świt (☎ 646 27 03, ul Mickiewicza 34A) Beds in doubles or triples without bath US$7. The Świt cinema, 500m north of the Drwęcki, offers seven simple rooms, which gives you an alternative budget shelter.

Hotel Promenada (☎ 642 81 00, fax 642 81 01, ul Mickiewicza 3) Singles/doubles with bath & breakfast US$35/50. The reasonably new 50-bed Hotel Ostróda, next door to the Drwęcki, should appeal to those who need better facilities and comfort. It too has its own restaurant.

Getting There & Away
The train and bus stations are next to each other, 500m west of the wharf. Trains to Olsztyn (39km) and Iława (30km) run every couple of hours, and there are seven trains daily to Toruń (124km). There are no direct trains to Elbląg or Warsaw (239km), and only two to Gdańsk (150km). If you don't want to wait, go to Iława and change there as it's on the Warsaw-Gdańsk route and trains are frequent.

There's fairly regular bus transport to Olsztyn (42km), Olsztynek (29km), Grunwald (26km) and Elbląg (75km).

From 15 May to 15 September a boat to Elbląg leaves daily at 8am. See the following section for details.

ELBLĄG-OSTRÓDA CANAL
The 82km Elbląg-Ostróda canal is Poland's longest navigable canal still in use. It's also the most unusual: the canal deals with the 99.5m difference in water levels by means of a system of five slipways; boats are carried across dry land on rail-mounted trolleys.

The canal follows the course of a chain of six lakes. The largest is the considerably overgrown Lake Drużno near Elbląg, left behind by the Vistula Lagoon, which once extended as far as here.

The five slipways are on a 10km stretch of the northern part of the canal. Each slipway consists of two trolleys tied to a single looped rope, operating on the same principle as a funicular. They are powered by water.

There are also two conventional locks near the southern end of the canal, close to Ostróda, and a side canal leading west to Iława without either locks or slipways.

Boat Trips
From May to late September, pleasure boats sail the main part of the canal between

WARMIA & MASURIA

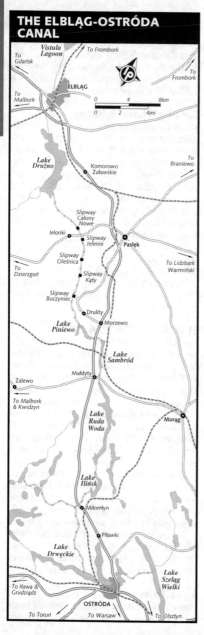

THE ELBLĄG-OSTRÓDA CANAL

Elbląg and Ostróda. They depart from both towns at 8am and arrive at the other end at about 7pm. The normal fare is US$20 or US$15 for people under 18 years. There are no ISIC student discounts. Bulky luggage (formally, anything larger than 20cm x 40cm x 60cm) costs US$4 extra, but it's US$6 for a bicycle.

Some boats from Elbląg go only as far as Buczyniec, covering the most interesting part of the canal, including all five slipways (US$15 or US$12 for under 18s, luggage/bicycle US$3/5). The trip takes five hours. The boat operator provides return bus transport from Buczyniec to Elbląg (US$3), returning by 2pm. This is a comfortable option for anyone not prepared for an 11-hour trip; indeed, the remaining seven-hour sail may be monotonous for some. This is also a good solution for motorists who have to leave their vehicles in Elbląg.

The boats, with a capacity of 65 passengers, only run when at least 20 passengers turn up for the trip. You can expect regular daily services in July and August but outside this period there may be some days off. You can ring the wharf a couple of days in advance to find out about the availability of tickets and the likelihood of the trip taking place (in Elbląg ☎ 55-232 43 07, in Ostróda ☎ 89-646 38 71). Boats have snack bars, which serve some basic snacks, tea, coffee, beer etc.

If you're not going to take the boat trip but have your own transport and want to see the slipways, it's best to go to Buczyniec between noon and 2pm, where boats pass on their way north and south. There's a small museum here and you can see the impressive machinery that powers the trolleys. There are two roads leading to Buczyniec, both branching off the Elbląg-Ostróda road: one near Pasłęk, the other one in Morzewo.

LIDZBARK WARMIŃSKI
☎ 89 • pop 18,000

Lidzbark Warmiński, 46km north of Olsztyn, is a peaceful if rather ordinary town. Its past is certainly more glorious than its present; it was the capital of the Warmian bishopric for over four centuries and was

The Elbląg-Ostróda Canal – a Wonder of 19th-Century Engineering

The rich forests of the Ostróda region have attracted merchants from Gdańsk and Elbląg since medieval times, yet the only way of getting timber down to the Baltic was a long water route along the Drwęca and Vistula Rivers via Toruń. Engineers considered building a canal as a short cut but the terrain was rugged and too steep for conventional locks.

In 1836, Prussian engineer Georg Jakob Steenke (1801–82) from Königsberg produced a sophisticated design for an Elbląg-Ostróda canal incorporating slipways, but Prussian authorities rejected the project as unrealistic and too costly. Steenke didn't give up, however, and eventually succeeded in getting an audience with the king of Prussia. Interestingly, the monarch was convinced not by the technical or economic aspects but by the fact that nobody had ever constructed such a system before.

The part of the canal between Elbląg and Miłomłyn, which included all the slipways, was built in 1848–60. The remaining leg to Ostróda was completed by 1872. The canal proved to be reliable and profitable, and cut the distance of the original route along the Drwęca and Vistula almost five-fold. Various extensions were subsequently planned, including one linking the canal with the Great Masurian Lakes 120km to the east, but none were ever built.

The canal was damaged during the 1945 Red Army offensive but was repaired soon after liberation and opened for timber transport in 1946. A year later, the first tourist boat sailed the route. It remains the only canal of its kind in Europe and continues to operate, though no longer for transporting merchandise; it's now a tourist attraction.

reputedly the richest and most cultured town of the region. Not much is left from that time, but the castle alone is enough to justify the trip – it's the best one surviving in Warmia and Masuria.

Lidzbark was a base for the Teutonic Knights' eastward expansion, but when the Warmian diocese was created in 1243, the settlement came under the administration of the bishops. Lidzbark received a municipal charter in 1308, and in 1350 the bishops chose it as their main residence and the seat of the whole bishopric. A castle and a church were built and the town swiftly became an important religious and cultural centre. Copernicus lived here in 1503–10, serving as a doctor and adviser to his uncle, Bishop Łukasz Watzenrode.

When the Reformation arrived in the 16th century Lidzbark, along with most of the province, became a citadel of Catholicism, and it remained so until the First Partition of 1773, when the Prussians took over the region. Deprived of his office, the last bishop, Ignacy Krasicki, turned to literature, to become Poland's most outstanding man of letters of the period, particularly noted for his sharp social satire.

Information

Bank Gdański, ul Świętochowskiego 14, opposite the train station, will exchange cash and travellers cheques and has an ATM. Cash can also be changed in a few kantors in the centre.

Castle

This mighty red-brick structure adorned with turrets on the corners is the most important sight in Lidzbark. The entrance to the castle is from the south through a palatial, horseshoe-shaped building, extensively rebuilt in the 18th century.

The castle was constructed in the second half of the 14th century on a square plan with a central courtyard, the whole surrounded by a moat and fortified walls. When the bishops' era ended with the Partitions, the castle fell into decline and served a variety of purposes, including barracks, storage, hospital and orphanage. Restoration was undertaken in the 1920s and within 10 years the building had been more or less returned to its original form. Miraculously, it came through the war unharmed, and today it is easily one of Poland's best preserved medieval castles.

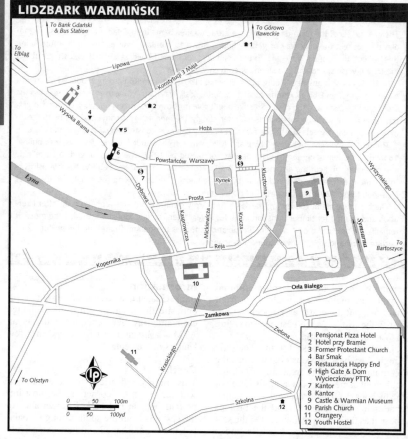

LIDZBARK WARMIŃSKI

To Bank Gdański & Bus Station
To Górowo Iławeckie
To Elbląg
Lipowa
Konstytucji 3 Maja
Wysoka Brama
Hoża
Powstańców Warszawy
Rynek
Prosta
Dębowa
Klasztorna
Wyszyńskiego
Łyna
Kasprowicza
Mickiewicza
Krucza
Symsarna
To Bartoszyce
Reja
Kopernika
Orła Białego
Zamkowa
Zielona
To Olsztyn
Krasickiego
Szkolna

0   50   100m
0   50   100yd

1 Pensjonat Pizza Hotel
2 Hotel przy Bramie
3 Former Protestant Church
4 Bar Smak
5 Restauracja Happy End
6 High Gate & Dom
   Wycieczkowy PTTK
7 Kantor
8 Kantor
9 Castle & Warmian Museum
10 Parish Church
11 Orangery
12 Youth Hostel

Most of the interior, from the cellars up to the 2nd floor, now houses the **Warmian Museum** *(Muzeum Warmińskie; ☎ 767 21 11, Plac Zamkowy 1; adult/student US$2/1; open 9am-5pm Tues-Sun June-Aug, 10am-4pm Tues-Sun Sept-May)*. The first thing you'll see is a beautiful courtyard with two-storey arcaded galleries all round it. It was constructed in the 1380s and has hardly changed since.

The 1st floor boasts the castle's main chambers, of which the vaulted Grand Refectory (Wielki Refektarz) is the most remarkable. The unusual chessboard-style wall paintings date from the end of the 14th century. The exhibition inside features works of medieval art collected from the region, including some charming smiling Madonnas. The adjoining chapel was redecorated in sumptuous rococo style in the mid-18th century.

The top floor contains several exhibitions, including 20th-century Polish painting and a collection of icons dating from the 17th century onward. The excellent two-storey vaulted cellars have some old cannons on display. These belonged to the bishops, who had their own small army.

Other Attractions

The 15th-century **High Gate** (Brama Wysoka) marks the entrance to what once was the Old Town and is now a nondescript postwar suburb. Destroyed in WWII, the historic quarter – regarded as one of the richest and most picturesque in the region – unfortunately hasn't been reconstructed.

Near the gate is the wooden **Protestant church** erected in the 1820s, believed to be based on a design by Karl Friedrich Schinkel. It's now used by the Orthodox community for infrequent Masses.

At the southern end of the Old Town looms the familiar brick **parish church**. Its structure retains much of the original Gothic shape, except for the top of the tower, which was struck by lightning in 1698 and rebuilt in baroque style. The interior is a mishmash of styles from different periods.

In the mid-17th century the bishops laid out the gardens to the south of the church, and built the **Orangery** (Oranżeria). Most of the gardens were turned into a cemetery at the beginning of the 20th century, but the Orangery stands to this day, though it's been altered and is now the local library.

Places to Stay

Dom Wycieczkowy PTTK (☎ 767 25 21, ul Wysoka Brama 2) Singles/doubles US$8/14, beds in triples, quads or larger dorms US$4. Enjoying an attractive location in the High Gate, the PTTK hostel is basic, but you won't find many 15th-century hotels for US$4 per head.

Youth hostel (☎ 767 24 44, ul Szkolna 3) Beds US$3-5. Open July & Aug. Based in the school building south of the Old Town, this is another basic, extra-budget place but only during the summer holiday period.

Pensjonat Pizza Hotel (☎ 767 52 59, ul Konstytucji 3 Maja 26) Doubles without/with bath US$24/31. Located in a stylish house with its own restaurant, the Pensjonat offers just three doubles sharing one bath and one double with its own bath.

Hotel Przy Bramie (☎/fax 767 20 99, ul Konstytucji 3 Maja 18) Doubles with bath & breakfast US$45. The best place to stay

in town, Przy Bramie offers just five comfortable rooms.

Places to Eat

Bar Smak (☎ 767 39 29, ul Wysoka Brama 4) Mains US$2-3. Bar Smak, close to the High Gate, has good food at very low prices.

Restauracja Happy End (☎ 767 58 21, ul Konstytucji 3 Maja 6) Mains US$4-6. Another good place in the same area, Happy End is more pleasant, and open longer, than Bar Smak.

Getting There & Away

The bus terminal is next to the defunct train station, about 500m north-west of the High Gate. Buses to Olsztyn (46km) depart every hour or so. There are two buses a day to Frombork (75km) and four to Gdańsk (157km). One bus runs eastwards to Kętrzyn (62km) passing Reszel and Święta Lipka on the way.

RESZEL

☎ 89 • pop 6000

Reszel ('Reh-shel') is a small market town, which came to life in the 13th century, as the easternmost outpost of the Warmian bishopric. A century later it evolved into a small fortified town, complete with a central square, castle and church. It didn't get much bigger, but was a prosperous craft centre before the wars of the 18th century brought about its decline. The town never really recovered, yet its minuscule centre still boasts the original street plan dotted with several historic buildings including the castle.

Things to See

Reszel's tiny Old Town, measuring no more than 250m x 250m, is centred around the Rynek with the town hall in its middle. One block east is the 14th-century brick **castle**, built at the same time as that in Lidzbark and likewise retaining much of its original form, except for the southern side, which was turned into a Protestant church in the 19th century, with a belfry and gable added on top. Today it's an **art gallery** (☎ 755 02 16, ul Podzamcze 3; adult/student US$1.50/0.75; open 10am-4pm Tues-Sun) featuring

WARMIA & MASURIA

modern art. Go to the top of the castle's massive cylindrical tower for a view over the red-tiled roofs of the Old Town.

The 14th-century **parish church** is a large Gothic brick construction with a tall square tower. It was refurnished and redecorated in the 1820s and has a harmonious though not outstanding interior.

North of the Rynek, on ul Spichrzowa, is a fine if derelict 18th-century half-timbered **granary**. A stone's throw east, at the entrance to the Old Town from Kętrzyn, is the unusually massive brick **Fishing Bridge** (Most Rybacki), built in the 14th century and recently so extensively restored that it looks like new.

Places to Stay & Eat

Hotel Zamek (☎ 755 01 09, fax 755 15 97, ul Podzamcze 3) Singles/doubles with bath US$30/40. Arranged in part of the castle, this is an attractive place to stay, and there's a charming vaulted cafe on the ground floor, with meals for guests.

Youth hostel (☎ 755 00 12, ul Krasickiego 7) Beds US$3-5. Not as atmospheric as the castle, but a bit cheaper, the hostel opens in July and August in the local school, 400m from the Rynek.

There are a few budget *snack bars* and *cafes* around the central streets.

Getting There & Away

Trains no longer call at Reszel, but bus transport is OK. The bus terminal is a five-minute walk north of the Old Town. There are plenty of buses east to Kętrzyn (19km) and all pass via Swięta Lipka (6km). A dozen buses go to Olsztyn daily (67km). Two buses run west to Lidzbark Warmiński (43km), and one of them continues to Gdańsk (200km).

ŚWIĘTA LIPKA
☎ 89

The tiny hamlet of Swięta Lipka (literally, the Holy Lime Tree; '**Shfyen**-tah **Leep**-kah') boasts arguably the most beautiful baroque church in northern Poland. It was built in 1687–93 and later surrounded by an ample rectangular cloister, with four identical towers housing chapels in the corners. The best artists from Warmia, Königsberg and Vilnius were commissioned for the furnishings and decoration, which were completed by around 1740. Since that time the church has hardly changed, either inside or outside, and is regarded as one of the purest examples of a late baroque church in the country.

The entrance to the complex is through an elaborate wrought-iron gateway. Just behind it, the two-towered cream facade holds in its central niche a stone sculpture of the holy lime tree with a statue of the Virgin Mary on top.

Once inside, the visitor is enveloped in colourful and florid but not overwhelming baroque. All the frescoes are the work of Maciej Mayer of Lidzbark, and display then fashionable trompe l'œil images.

Swięta Lipka Church – Product of a Miracle

The origins of Swięta Lipka church are linked to a miracle. The story goes that a prisoner in Kętrzyn castle had been sentenced to death. The night before the execution the Virgin Mary unexpectedly appeared and presented the prisoner with a tree trunk out of which to carve her effigy. The resulting figure was so beautiful that the judges took it to be a sign from Heaven and gave the condemned man his freedom. On his way home, he placed the statue on the first lime tree he encountered – as required by the Virgin – which happened to be in Swięta Lipka.

Miracles immediately began to occur, and even sheep knelt down while passing the shrine. Pilgrims arrived in increasing numbers; one of them was the last Grand Master of the Teutonic Order, Albrecht von Hohenzollern, who walked here barefoot, six years before deciding to convert to Lutheranism. A timber chapel was built to protect the miraculous figure, and was later replaced with a church, perhaps the most magnificent baroque church in northern Poland.

These are clearly visible both on the vault and the columns; the latter look as if they were carved. Mayer left behind his own image: you can see him in a blue waistcoat with brushes in his hand, in the corner of the vault-painting over the organ.

The three-storey, 19m high altar, covering the whole back of the chancel, is carved of walnut and painted to look like marble. Of the three paintings in the altar, the lowest one depicts the Virgin Mary of Święta Lipka with the Christ child.

The pulpit is ornamented with paintings and sculptures. Directly opposite, across the nave, is the **holy lime tree** topped with the figure of the Virgin Mary, supposed to have been placed on the site where the legendary tree once stood.

The pride of the church is its organ, a sumptuously decorated instrument of about 5000 pipes. The work of Johann Jozue Mosengel of Königsberg, it is equipped with a mechanism that puts in motion figures of saints and angels when the organ is played. Short demonstrations are held from May to September several times a day and irregularly the rest of the year. From June to August, organ recitals take place every Friday evening.

The cloister surrounding the church is ornamented with frescoes by Mayer. The artist painted the corner chapels and parts of the northern and western cloister, but died before the work was complete. It was continued by other artists but, as you can see, without the same success.

Święta Lipka is frequently visited by both tourists and pilgrims. The church is open for visitors 8am to 6pm except during Mass. The main religious celebrations fall on the last Sunday of May, and on 11, 14 and 15 August.

Places to Stay & Eat
Dom Pielgrzyma (☎ 755 14 81, fax 755 14 60) in the monastery complex next to the church provides 85 beds distributed in doubles, triples, quads and quins, for about US$5 per head, but it can often be full in July and August. Budget meals are available if requested in advance.

Some locals living near the church rent out rooms in their homes. A collection of food stands spring up in summer around the square in front of the church.

Getting There & Away
Buses to Kętrzyn (13km) and Reszel (6km) run every hour or so. There are several to Olsztyn (73km) and Mrągowo (19km), and a couple to Lidzbark Warmiński (49km).

The Great Masurian Lakes

The Great Masurian Lake District (Kraina Wielkich Jezior Mazurskich), east of Olsztyn, is a verdant land of rolling hills interspersed with countless lakes, healthy little farms, scattered tracts of forest and small towns. The district is centred around Lake Śniardwy (114 sq km), Poland's largest lake, and Lake Mamry and its adjacent waters (totalling an additional 104 sq km). Over 15% of the area is covered by water and another 30% by forest.

The lakes are well connected by rivers and canals, to form an extensive system of waterways. The whole area has become a prime destination for yachtspeople and canoeists, and is also popular among anglers, hikers, bikers and nature-lovers. Tourists arrive in great numbers in July and August, though after 15 August the crowds begin to thin out.

The main lakeside centres are Giżycko and Mikołajki, with two minor ones, Węgorzewo and Ruciane-Nida, at the northern and southern ends of the lakeland, respectively. They all rent out kayaks and sailing boats, though it may be difficult to get one in July and August.

Getting Around the Lakes
Yachtspeople can sail most of the larger lakes, all the way from Węgorzewo to Ruciane-Nida, which are interconnected and are the district's main waterway system. Kayakers will perhaps prefer more intimate surroundings alongside rivers and smaller lakes. The best established and most popular kayak

route in the area originates at Sorkwity and follows the Krutynia River and Lake Bełdany to Ruciane-Nida (see Kayaking Tours in the Olsztyn section). There's also a beautiful kayak route along the Czarna Hańcza River in the Augustów area farther east (see Augustów later in this chapter).

If you're not up to sailing or canoeing, you can enjoy the lakes in comfort from the deck of the pleasure boats operated by the Masurian Shipping Company. These large boats have an open deck above and a coffee shop below, and can carry backpacks and bicycles.

Theoretically, boats run between Giżycko, Mikołajki and Ruciane-Nida daily from May to September, and to Węgorzewo from June to August. In practice, the service is most reliable from late June to late August. In other times trips can be cancelled if too few passengers turn up. Examples of fares are US$9 from Węgorzewo to Giżycko, US$10 from Giżycko to Mikołajki, and US$9 from Mikołajki to Ruciane-Nida. There are no discounts for foreign students. Schedules are clearly posted at the lake ports.

The detailed Wielkie Jeziora Mazurskie map (scale 1:100,000) is a great help for anyone exploring the region by boat, kayak, bike, car or foot. It shows walking trails, canoeing routes, accommodation options, petrol stations and much more. It's normally available in the region but you're safer buying a copy in a city before you come.

KĘTRZYN
☎ 89 • pop 32,000

Kętrzyn ('**Kent**-shin') may be a stopover if you're wandering around the western fringes of the Great Masurian Lakes. The town hasn't major attractions but is a handy jumping-off point for two important sights nearby: the Wolf's Lair to the east and Święta Lipka to the west.

Kętrzyn was founded in the 14th century by the Teutonic Knights under the name of Rastenburg. Though partially colonised by Poles, it remained Prussian until WWII, after which it became Polish and got its present name. The name derives from Wojciech Kętrzyński (1838–1919), a historian,

scholar and patriot who documented the history of the Polish presence in the region.

Things to See
There are still some vestiges of the Teutonic legacy. The mid-14th century brick **castle** was damaged and rebuilt on various occasions; today it houses the **Regional Museum** (☎ 752 32 82, Plac Zamkowy 1; adult/student US$1/0.50; open 9am-4pm Tues-Fri, 9am-3pm Sat & Sun mid-Sept–mid-June; 10am-5pm daily mid-June–mid-Sept). It has a permanent display dedicated to the town's history, plus temporary exhibitions.

The Gothic **St George's Church** (Kościół Św Jerzego), a bit farther up the street, underwent fewer alterations to its structure, but the interior has furnishings and decoration dating from various periods. Note a fine pulpit and three tombstones in the wall near the entrance.

Places to Stay & Eat
All the hotels listed below are quite good and have their own restaurants.

Zajazd Pod Zamkiem (☎ 752 31 17, fax 752 20 41, ul Struga 3) Singles/doubles/triples/quads with bath US$22/32/38/50. Set in a stylish 19th-century mansion, next to the castle's entrance, the Zajazd has four rooms only, each furnished with four beds and a private bath.

Hotel Wanda (☎ 751 85 84, fax 751 00 88, ul Wojska Polskiego 27) Singles/doubles/triples with bath & breakfast US$26/ 34/42. This is another reasonable central choice.

Hotel Koch (☎ 752 20 58, fax 752 23 90, ul Traugutta 3) Singles/doubles with bath & breakfast US$35/50. The largest and the newest hotel in town, the Koch is also probably the best.

Getting There & Away
The train and bus stations are next to each other, a 10-minute walk from the town centre. The suburban bus No 1 to the Wolf's Lair in Gierłoż passes through here.

Train Two fast trains run to Gdańsk daily (269km) via Elbląg (189km). There are half

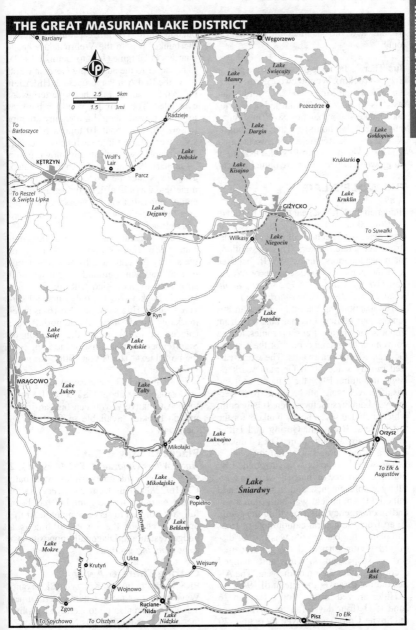

a dozen trains to Giżycko daily and Olsztyn, but check the bus timetable too on these routes.

Bus There's fairly regular bus transport to Giżycko (31km), Węgorzewo (38km), Olsztyn (83km) and Mrągowo (25km), plus one fast bus to Suwałki (122km). For Gierłoż (8km), take a suburban bus No 1 (in summer only, every 1½ hours) or the PKS bus to Węgorzewo via Radzieje. For Święta Lipka (13km), take any bus to Reszel, Olsztyn, or Mrągowo via Pilec – they are quite frequent.

THE WOLF'S LAIR
☎ 89

Hidden in thick forest near the tiny hamlet of Gierłoż, 8km east of Kętrzyn, there's an eerie place – 18 hectares of huge, partly destroyed concrete bunkers. This was Hitler's main headquarters during WWII, baptised with the name of Wolfsschanze or Wolf's Lair *(Wilczy Szaniec;* ☎ *752 44 29; adult/ student US$2/1; open 8am-dusk daily).*

The location was carefully chosen in this remote part of East Prussia, far away from important towns and transport routes, to be a convenient command centre for the planned German advance eastwards. The work, carried out by some 3000 German workers, began in autumn 1940; the cement, steel and basalt gravel were all brought from Germany. About 80 structures were finally built, which included seven heavy bunkers for the top leaders: Bormann, Göring and Hitler himself were among them. Their bunkers had walls and ceilings up to 8m thick.

The whole complex was surrounded by multiple barriers of barbed wire and artillery emplacements, and a sophisticated minefield. An airfield was built 5km away and an emergency airstrip within the camp. Apart from the natural camouflage of trees and plants, the bunker site was further disguised with artificial vegetation-like screens suspended on wires and changed according to the season of the year. The Allies did not discover the site until 1945.

Hitler arrived in the Wolf's Lair on 26 June 1941 (four days after the invasion of the Soviet Union) and stayed there until 20

November 1944, with only short trips to the outside world. His longest journey outside the bunker was to the Wehrmacht's headquarters in Ukraine (July to October 1942), to be closer to the advancing German front.

As the Red Army approached, Hitler left the Wolf's Lair and the headquarters were evacuated. The army prepared the bunkers to be destroyed, should the enemy attempt to seize them. About 10 tonnes of explosives were stuffed into each heavy bunker. The complex was eventually blown up on 24 January 1945 and the Germans retreated. Three days later the Soviets arrived, but the minefield was still efficiently defending the empty ruins. It took 10 years to clear the area of mines; about 55,000 were detected and defused.

Today, you can wander around the gruesome place. There's a board with a map of the site by the entrance, from which a red-marked trail winds around the bunkers. All structures are identified with numbers. Of Hitler's bunker (No 13) only one wall survived, but Göring's 'home' (No 16) is in remarkably good shape. A memorial plate (placed in 1992) marks the location of Stauffenberg's assassination attempt (see the boxed text 'The Hit on Hitler' for more information).

English- and German-speaking guides are available for about US$15 per 1½ hour tour. Alternatively, you can buy an information booklet (available in English and German).

Places to Stay & Eat
Hotel Wilcze Gniazdo (☎ *752 44 29,* ☎ *752 44 92)* Singles/doubles/triples with bath US$16/22/30. This former officers' hostel at the entrance to the complex has been fully refurbished to serve as a hotel. At the opposite end of the same building is a budget restaurant. Diagonally opposite is a basic *camping ground*.

Getting There & Away
PKS buses between Kętrzyn (8km) and Węgorzewo (30km) stop here several times a day. You can also go to Kętrzyn (in summer only) by suburban bus No 1.

The Hit on Hitler

Hitler used to say that the Wolf's Lair was one of the very few places in Europe where he felt safe. Ironically, it was here that an assassination attempt came closest to succeeding. It was organised by a group of pragmatic, high-ranking German officers who considered the continuation of the war to be suicidal, with no real chance of victory. They planned to negotiate peace with the Allies after eliminating Hitler.

The leader of the plot, Claus von Stauffenberg, arrived from Berlin on 20 July 1944 on the pretext of informing Hitler about the newly formed reserve army. A frequent guest at the Wolf's Lair, he enjoyed the confidence of the staff and had no problems entering the bunker complex with a bomb in his briefcase. He placed his briefcase beneath the table a few feet from Hitler and left the meeting to take a pre-arranged phone call from an aide. The explosion killed two members of Hitler's staff and wounded half a dozen others, but Hitler himself suffered only minor injuries and was even able to meet Mussolini, who arrived later the same day. Stauffenberg and some 5000 people involved directly or indirectly in the plot were executed.

Had the outcome of the plot been otherwise, it could have turned the whole course of WWII and the postwar period. A peace treaty between the Germans and the Allies might well have saved the lives of some five million people (including three million Jews) and the devastation of vast parts of Poland and Germany. One can also speculate that the former East Germany and perhaps a good chunk of Eastern Europe might have avoided half a century of Soviet communism.

WĘGORZEWO
☎ 87 • pop 12,500

At the northern end of the Great Masurian Lake District, Węgorzewo ('Ven-go-**zheh**-vo') is the northernmost lakeside centre for both excursion boats and individual sailors. Less overrun by tourists than its southern cousins, Giżycko and Mikołajki, Węgorzewo isn't quite on the lake shore but is linked to Lake Mamry by a 2km river canal.

You may end up at Węgorzewo while sailing or taking a pleasure boat cruise from Giżycko. If you turn up on the first weekend of August, you are here for a large craft fair, which has taken place for 25 years and attracted plenty of artisans from the region and beyond. From Węgorzewo you can continue by bus to Gierłoż and farther to the west (eg, Lidzbark Warmiński), or travel east along the northern, rarely used border route to the Suwałki region.

Information
The Biuro Informacji Turystycznej (☎ 427 50 80), ul Portowa 1, is open 8am to 6pm daily mid-June to mid-September. It has information about private rooms, yacht charter, kayak tours etc. Bank PKO BP, ul Chopina 7, has an ATM.

Places to Stay & Eat
Camping Nr 175 Rusałka (☎ 427 21 91) Triple cabins US$20-25, quad cabins US$25-40. Open May-Sept. With its pleasant wooded grounds, a restaurant, and boats and kayaks for hire, Rusałka is a good place and well run, though most cabins are pretty basic. The place is on Lake Święcajty, 3km from Węgorzewo along the Giżycko road plus 1km more to the lake. Infrequent PKS buses go there in season but if you don't want to wait, take any bus to Giżycko, get off at the turn-off to the camp site and walk the remaining distance.

Ośrodek Wypoczynkowy Wiking (☎/fax 427 21 82) Triples/quins in cabins US$50/70. Open year-round. Located on the Kal Peninsula, 2km south of the town centre, the Wiking is another camp site, better than Rusałka, but pricier.

Stanica Wodna PTTK (☎ 427 24 43, ul Wańkowicza 3) Beds in doubles or triples without bath US$7, singles/doubles/triples with bath US$18/24/34. Conveniently located in the town centre and facing the canal, Stanica offers cheap but basic rooms without bath in summer and the much better, but pricier, all-year rooms with bath.

Internat Garnizonowy (☎ 427 28 82, ul Bema 18) Singles/doubles/triples without bath US$10/15/18. This former army dorm,

1km from the centre on the Giżycko road, is an acceptable all-year budget option.

Pensjonat Pod Dębami (☎/fax 427 22 18, ul Łuczańska 33) Doubles/triples/quads with bath US$20/30/40. Pod Dębami is one of the cheapest pensions in town, and is one of the few that open year-round. It's 2km from the centre on the Giżycko road.

Pensjonat Nautic (☎/fax 427 20 80, ul Słowackiego 14) Singles/doubles US$25/40, suites US$50-150. Open year-round. Central and pleasant, Nautic is arguably the best place in town. All rooms have a private bath, satellite TV and include breakfast. The pensjonat has its own all-year restaurant, which is probably the best place to eat.

Getting There & Away

Trains no longer operate here but the bus terminal, 1km north-west of the centre, provides reasonable transport to Giżycko (26km) and Kętrzyn (38km); buses to Kętrzyn via Radzieje will drop you at the entrance to the Wolf's Lair bunkers. Several buses go to Gołdap (45km), from where you can continue to Stańczyki and Suwałki. Three fast morning buses run directly to Warsaw (278km); book in advance in high season.

From July to August, there's an excursion boat to Giżycko (US$9, 2½ hours).

GIŻYCKO

☎ 87 • pop 32,000

Positioned on the northern shore of Lake Niegocin, Giżycko ('Ghee-**zhits**-ko') is the largest lakeside centre in the Great Masurian Lake District. The town started life under the Teutonic Knights but was destroyed on numerous occasions by Lithuanians, Poles, Swedes, Tatars, Russians and Germans in turn.

Today, Giżycko is a rather ordinary place without much historical character. The town is essentially a transport hub and provision base for holiday homes and watersports centres that have grown up outside the town, and for hordes of holidaymakers who arrive en masse in the short summer season and take to the lakes. You'll find it's a useful springboard from where to take an excursion boat to Mikołajki or Węgorzewo, or rent a boat.

Information

The Centrum Informacji Turystycznej (☎ 428 52 65), ul Warszawska 7 (enter from ul Kętrzyńskiego), is open 7.30am to 3.30pm weekdays (8am to 6pm June to August and also 10am to 6pm Saturday).

Bank Pekao, ul Olsztyńska 17, exchanges travellers cheques and gives advances on Visa. There are several kantors in the centre including one in Orbis Travel, ul Dąbrowskiego 3.

Boyen Fortress

Named after the Prussian minister of war, General Hermann von Boyen, the Boyen Fortress (Twierdza Boyen) was built in 1844–55 to protect the border with Russia. Since the frontier ran north-south along the 90km string of lakes, the stronghold was strategically placed in the middle, on the isthmus near Giżycko.

The fortress, which consists of several bastions and defensive towers surrounded by a moat, was continually modified and strengthened, and successfully withstood Russian attacks during WWI. In WWII, it was a defensive outpost of the Wolf's Lair and was given up to the Red Army without a fight during the 1945 offensive. The fortifications survived in pretty good shape, though they're slowly being taken over by bushes. There's an amphitheatre and youth hostel here, while some of the old buildings are used as storage rooms. In the youth hostel building is a small museum (open in summer only) dedicated to the fortress.

Yacht Charter

Sailing boats are hired out by a number of local operators, including Almatur (☎ 428 33 88, ul Moniuszki 24); **Bełbot Yacht Charter** (☎ 428 71 35, ul Smętka 22A); **Osmolik** (☎ 428 86 86, ul Smętka 22); **PUH Żeglarz** (☎ 428 20 84, ul Kościuszki 1); **COS** (☎ 428 23 35, ul Moniuszki 22); **Polaris** (☎ 428 28 17, ul Nowogrodzka 21A); and **Grzymała** (☎ 428 62 76, ul Królowej Jadwigi 2).

The boat-charter market is volatile and operators often change. The tourist office is likely to have the current list of agents and can provide advice. It's also worth getting

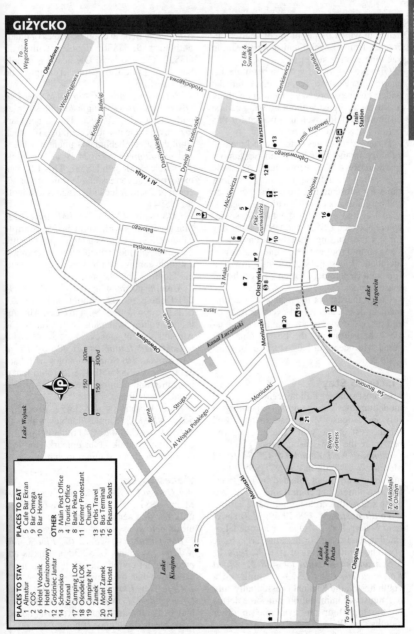

GIŻYCKO

PLACES TO STAY
1 Almatur
2 COS
6 Hotel Wodnik
7 Hotel Garnizonowy
12 Gościniec Jantar
14 Schronisko
  Krasnal
17 Camping LOK
18 Ośrodek LOK
19 Camping Nr 1
  Zamek
20 Motel Zamek
21 Youth Hostel

PLACES TO EAT
5 Cafe Bar Ekran
9 Bar Omega
10 Bar Hornet

OTHER
3 Main Post Office
4 Tourist Office
8 Bank Pekao
11 Former Protestant
  Church
13 Orbis Travel
15 Bus Terminal
16 Pleasure Boats

a copy of *Żagle*, the monthly yachting magazine, in which plenty of yacht-charter operators, from Giżycko and other Masurian yachting centres, advertise.

Giżycko has the largest number of yacht-charter agencies and, accordingly, offers the widest choice of boats, yet finding anything in July and August without booking can be difficult. Booking well in advance for this period is essential.

Boats are much easier to find in June (especially in the first half) and September (particularly in the second half). At these times, shop around, as prices and conditions can vary substantially from place to place and bargaining is possible with some agents.

In July and August, expect to pay somewhere between US$25 and US$100 per day for a cabin sailing boat large enough to sleep around four to five people, mattresses included. Prices are significantly lower in June and September – often half of the in-season prices.

Check the state of the boat and its equipment in detail, and report every deficiency and bit of damage in advance to avoid hassles when returning the boat. Come prepared with sleeping bag, sturdy rain gear, torch etc.

Places to Stay

Like most summer holiday centres, accommodation rates change notably, peaking in July and August. Many places stay closed for the rest of the year. The prices given below are the high-season rates.

Camping Nr 1 Zamek (☎ 428 34 10, ul Moniuszki 1) Beds in cabins US$5. Open mid-June–early Sept. Shaded by old trees, this is a simple but central and convenient camp site, with a collection of basic cabins.

Youth hostel (☎ 428 29 59, ul Turystyczna 1) Beds US$3-4. Open year-round. Located in the Boyen Fortress, the large, basic youth hostel has dorms of 10 to 12 beds.

Schronisko Krasnal (☎ 428 22 24, ul Kolejowa 10) Beds US$3-4. Similar to a youth hostel, the Krasnal is essentially July to August accommodation, but some dorms on the top floor are available in other months as well.

Ośrodek LOK (☎/fax 428 14 08, ul Św Brunona 4) Beds in doubles, triples or quads without bath US$6; doubles with bath US$20. The 150-bed LOK hostel is simple but cheap. LOK also operates a camp site on the waterfront.

Hotel Garnizonowy (☎/fax 428 14 14, ul Olsztyńska 10A) Singles/doubles/triples without bath US$13/18/26. The 35-bed Garnizonowy is clean and acceptable. It's back from the street, behind apartment blocks.

Motel Zamek (☎ 428 24 19, ul Moniuszki 1) Doubles with bath US$32. This 12-room motel provides a reasonable standard of accommodation. A locked garage is available for US$4.

COS (☎/fax 428 23 35, ul Moniuszki 22) Singles/doubles with bath US$25/35; triple cabins US$40. COS is a large sports centre on Lake Kisajno, which offers accommodation in cabins and hotel rooms. It has eating facilities and boat rental.

Almatur (☎/fax 428 59 71, ul Moniuszki 24) Double rooms without bath US$20; beds in cabins US$6. Next to COS, Almatur is another large waterside centre, run by the Almatur student agency.

Gościniec Jantar (☎/fax 428 54 15, ul Warszawska 10) Singles/doubles with bath & breakfast US$35/50. The 12-room Jantar is central and comfortable, and has a reasonable restaurant.

Hotel Wodnik (☎ 428 38 72, fax 28 39 58, ul 3 Maja 2) Singles/doubles with bath & breakfast US$40/60. Another central facility, the Wodnik is an upmarket option, complete with a restaurant to match.

Places to Eat

Bar Omega (☎ 428 37 63, ul Olsztyńska 4) Mains US$1-2.50. Omega is a modernised milk bar that serves some of the cheapest meals in town.

Bar Hornet (☎ 428 12 67, Plac Grunwaldzki 12) Mains US$2-3.50. This is another budget option, though it's a bit more expensive than the Omega.

Cafe Bar Ekran (☎ 428 21 09, Plac Grunwaldzki 1) Mains US$2-4. Another budget facility, the Ekran serves tasty homemade meals till 9pm or 10pm.

Should you need somewhere more up-market, the *Gościniec Jantar* and *Hotel Wodnik* have acceptable restaurants.

Getting There & Away

Train The train station is on the southern edge of town near the lake. Around eight trains run to Ełk daily (47km), Kętrzyn (30km) and Olsztyn (120km), and two fast trains to Gdańsk (299km) and Białystok (151km). Trains to Warsaw (353km) take a roundabout route – it's faster to go by bus.

Bus Next to the train station, the bus terminal offers a regular service to Węgorzewo (26km) and Mrągowo (41km). A dozen buses run to Mikołajki daily (31km), Kętrzyn (31km) and Olsztyn (104km), and five to Suwałki (91km). Two buses go to Lidzbark Warmiński (93km), and six fast buses to Warsaw (251km).

Boat Boats operate from May to September with extra ones in July and August. To the north, you can take a trip to Węgorzewo (US$9, 2½ hours). Southbound, you can either go to Mikołajki (US$10, three hours) or do a loop on Lake Niegocin (US$5, 1½ hours). The wharf is near the train station.

MIKOŁAJKI
☎ 87 • pop 4000

Mikołajki ('Mee-ko-**wahy**-kee') is far smaller than Giżycko but is also an important lakeside centre of the Great Masurian Lakes. It's more pleasant and has some style, which can be seen in its architecture and scenic location. Perched on picturesque narrows crossed by three bridges, the town has a collection of fine red-roofed houses and a lively waterfront packed with hundreds of yachts in summer. There's much development going on these days, with new pensions, eating places and other tourist facilities mushrooming.

The town is entirely geared to tourism and, like most other resorts of this kind, lives a high-speed life in July and August, takes it easy in June and September, and dies almost completely the rest of the year. As it lies on the main waterway linking

Giżycko with Ruciane-Nida, and is the gateway to the vast Lake Śniardwy 3km southeast of town, yacht traffic and pleasure-boat services are very busy here in summer.

Information

The tourist office (☎/fax 421 68 50) is at Plac Wolności 3, the town's central square. Several kantors in the centre change cash, and there's an ATM at Hotel Gołębiewski.

Yacht Charter

The Wioska Żeglarska (☎ 421 60 40), ul Kowalska 3, on the waterfront has sailing boats for hire or staff may know other companies that hire boats if they're booked out. Other places include Agencja Sagit (☎ 421 64 70) in Hotel Wałkuski, ul 3 Maja 13A; and Fun (☎ 421 62 77), ul Kajki 82. See Giżycko earlier in this chapter for more information about yacht charter.

Places to Stay & Eat

Plenty of small pensions have sprung up over recent years, and a number of 'zimmer frei' boards appear in summer, indicating rooms available. The language used is the result of the massive increase of German tourism in Mikołajki and throughout the region. On the whole, prices are flexible. Try not to arrive late in the day in midsummer as you could be forced to pay a lot for your room.

Camping Nr 2 Wagabunda (☎ 421 60 18, ul Leśna 2) Cabins US$15-25. Open May-Sept. The Wagabunda is the town's main camping ground. It's across the bridge from the centre and a 10-minute walk south-west. In addition to a camping area it has plenty of small bungalows that vary in standard and price.

Youth hostel (☎ 421 64 34, ul Łabędzia 1) Beds US$2-4. Open July-Aug. This youth hostel is in the large school next to the stadium, 500m from the main square on the Łuknajno road. It's perhaps the cheapest place to stay, but it only has large dormitories and facilities are poor.

There are several small pensions on ul Kajki, the main street that skirts Lake Mikołajskie, including *Pensjonat Mikołajki* (☎ 421 64 37) at No 18; *Pensjonat Na*

Skarpie (☎ 421 64 18) at No 96; and *Pensjonat Wodnik (☎ 421 61 41)* at No 130. They are all on the lake shore. Expect to pay US$20 to US$30 a double in any of these pensions.

There's another collection of pensions on the town's outskirts on the road to Ruciane-Nida. They include *Pensjonat Iwa (☎ 421 65 06)*, *Pensjonat Martyna (☎ 421 68 85)* and *Pensjonat Magda (☎ 421 68 86)*. You will find more pensions on the road to Ełk past the train station.

There are some all-year hotels in the town centre.

Hotel Król Sielaw (☎ 421 63 23, fax 421 68 75, ul Kajki 5) Doubles US$20-30. This 16-bed place is one of the cheapest of the central hotels.

Hotel Mazur (☎ 421 69 41, fax 421 69 43, Plac Wolności 6) Doubles with bath & breakfast US$50. Located in a stylish mansion on the main square, Mazur is a pleasant place with a lot of character.

Hotel Wałkuski (☎/fax 421 66 28, ul 3 Maja 13A) Doubles US$40-70. Another upmarket proposition, the Wałkuski provides decent facilities in the heart of town.

Hotel Gołębiewski (☎ 429 07 00, fax 429 07 44, ul Mrągowska 34) Doubles US$70-100. The largest and most expensive addition to the local lodging scene, this five-star 1200-bed hotel, across the bridge from the centre, has three restaurants, a nightclub, indoor swimming pool, sauna, tennis courts, marina and an elderly clientele bused in from Germany.

There are plenty of small eateries that operate in the town centre and along the waterfront during summer so it won't take long to find a pizza, some fried fish or a pork chop. These apart, all the hotels listed above have their own restaurants that vary accordingly in price.

Getting There & Away

Train The sleepy train station is 1km from the centre on the Giżycko road. It handles just a few trains a day to Ełk and Olsztyn.

Bus The bus terminal is in the centre, near the Protestant church. Buses to Mrągowo

(25km) run roughly every hour; change there for Olsztyn or Kętrzyn. Several buses go to Giżycko daily (31km), and there are two buses to Suwałki (122km). Two or three fast buses depart in summer to Warsaw (224km) and are much faster than the trains.

Boat From May to September, boats ply the main routes from Mikołajki to Giżycko (US$10, three hours) and Ruciane (US$9, two hours), the round trip to Lake Śniardwy (US$7, 1½ hours), and combination routes (eg, Mikołajki-Lake Śniardwy-Ruciane; US$10, 2½ hours).

ŁUKNAJNO RESERVE

The shallow 700-hectare Lake Łuknajno, 4km east of Mikołajki, shelters Europe's largest surviving community of wild swans *(Cygnus olor)* and is home to many other birds – 128 species have been recorded here. The 1200 to 2000 swans nest in April and May but stay at the lake all summer. A few observation towers beside the lake make viewing possible.

A rough road from Mikołajki goes to the lake but there's no public transport. Walk 3.5km until you get to a sign that reads '*do wieży widokowej*' ('to the viewing tower'), directing you to the left. Continue for 10 minutes along the path through a meadow (can be muddy in spring and after rain) to the tower on the lake shore. Depending on the wind, the swans may be close to the tower or far away on the opposite side of the lake.

RUCIANE-NIDA

☎ 87 • pop 6000

Ruciane-Nida ('Roo-**chah**-neh **Nee**-dah') is the southernmost base for the Great Masurian Lakes. Set on the banks of two lakes, Guzianka Wielka and Nidzkie, the town is surrounded by forest. As the name suggests, it consists of two parts: Ruciane, the holiday resort; and, 2km to the south-west, Nida, a collection of apartment blocks around the local paper mill. The two parts are linked by Al Wczasów, which runs through woods and is lined with holiday homes. About 1.5km north of Ruciane is the Śluza Guzianka, the only lock on the Great Masurian Lakes.

Ruciane-Nida is a handy point to stop on your trans-Masurian journey. From here, excursion boats go north to Mikołajki and south to the beautiful Lake Nidzkie. There are several marked trails originating from Ruciane. You can also use the town as a jumping-off point for exploring the Puszcza Piska (Pisz Forest), a vast area of thick woodland to the south-east. There are no marked trails there but many dirt tracks and paths crisscross the woods; most are OK for bikes.

Places to Stay

Dom Wycieczkowy PTTK (☎ 423 10 06, ul Mazurska 6) Beds in doubles, triples or quads US$7; beds in cabins US$5. Open year-round. The PTTK, a 10-minute walk north from the train station towards the Guzianka Lock, is the cheapest place around, but facilities are basic. Rooms are available year-round but cabins are only open in summer.

Farther down the same road are two small pensions, *Pensjonat Janus* (☎ 423 64 50, ul Guzianka 1) and *Pensjonat Bełdan* (☎ 423 10 94, ul Guzianka 5). Both have reasonable doubles/triples with bath for about US$25/30.

Dom Wypoczynkowy Perła Jezior (☎ 423 10 44, Al Wczasów 15) is a large holiday home that offers inexpensive rooms with shared facilities. The nearby *Ośrodek Turystyki Wodnej U Andrzeja* (☎ 423 10 12, Al Wczasów 17) has a camp site and cabins, and handles kayak and sailing-boat rental.

Places to Eat

There are several all-year restaurants on ul Dworcowa, including *Restauracja Kormoran* and *Restauracja Warmianka*. In summer, a number of places open between the train station and the wharf, and several more on the road to Nida.

Getting There & Away

Train Ruciane lies on the Olsztyn-Ełk railway line and trains to both these destinations go regularly throughout the day. There are also connections to Gdańsk and Warsaw (once a day), plus an additional train to Warsaw in summer.

Bus There are six buses to Mrągowo daily (37km) and three to Mikołajki (22km). One or two buses go as far east as Suwałki daily.

Boat Excursion boats operate from May to September with additional ones from June to August. Two boats go daily to Mikołajki (US$9, two hours). There's also one boat to Mikołajki which makes a detour to Lake Śniardwy (US$10, 2½ hours). A few boats a day depart for round trips south around Lake Nidzkie (US$4, one hour).

The Augustów-Suwałki Region

The far north-eastern corner of Poland, called Suwalszczyzna, is noted for its lakeland, but this one is quite different from the Great Masurian Lake District. Here the lakes (about 200 altogether) are smaller but deeper and even more crystal-clear than farther west. At 108.5m, Lake Hańcza is the deepest lake in the country, and perhaps in the whole Central European lowland. Forests cover only about 20% of the surface, but the terrain is rugged, with steep hills and deep valleys.

Suwalszczyzna is the coldest part of Poland; winter here is long and snow lies on the ground for 100 to 120 days a year. The average January temperature is -6°C, but during the occasional cold snap it may drop to -40°C. Summer is short, though the continental climate makes it pleasantly warm and even hot at times.

To the south, towards Augustów, the terrain becomes flatter and more forested. The area east of Augustów up to the national border is an uninterrupted stretch of woodland, the Augustów Forest (Puszcza Augustowska), cut in two by the Augustów Canal (Kanał Augustowski).

Despite its natural beauty, the region is far less visited than the Great Masurian Lakes. Yachting is restricted, as the lakes

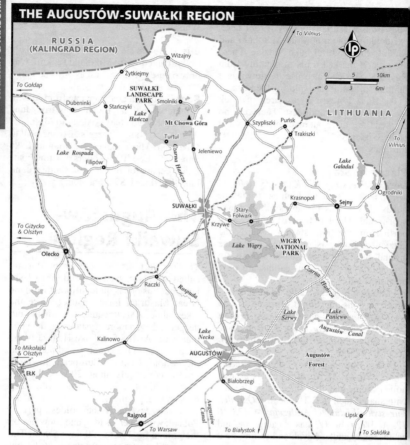

THE AUGUSTÓW-SUWAŁKI REGION

are smaller and not connected by channels, but canoeists will be in their element on the local rivers, which are among the best in the country. Walking and cycling are good too, and the last vestiges of a complex ethnic mix are an added attraction.

The first inhabitants of this land were Jatzvingians (Jaćwingowie). They belonged to the same ethnic and linguistic family as the Prussians, Latvians and Lithuanians, and lived off farming, fishing and breeding livestock. They were also warlike, and a bit of a headache for the Mazovian dukes, as they invaded and ravaged the northern outskirts

of the principality and not infrequently made their way farther south. On one occasion, in 1220, they got as far as Kraków. Their total population around that time is estimated to have been about 50,000.

In the second half of the 13th century, the Teutonic Knights expanded eastwards over the region, and by the 1280s they had wiped the tribe out completely, much as they had done earlier to the Prussians.

The region became a bone of contention between the Teutonic Order and Lithuania, and remained in dispute until the 16th century. At that time the territory formally became a Polish dominion but its colonisation was slow. Development was also hindered by the Swedish invasions of the 1650s and the catastrophic plague of 1710.

In the Third Partition of 1795, the region was swallowed by Prussia, and in 1815 it became a part of the Congress Kingdom of Poland, only to be grabbed by Russia after the failure of the November Insurrection of 1830. After WWI Poland took over the territory, not without resistance from Lithuania, but the region remained remote and economically unimportant, and in many ways still is.

Though today the population consists predominantly of Poles, it was for centuries an ethnic and religious mosaic comprising Poles, Lithuanians, Belarusians, Tatars, Germans, Jews and Russians. Traces of this complex cultural mix can still be found, at least in the local cemeteries.

There are only two important towns in the region, Augustów and Suwałki, which you may use as a base for further exploration. They are notably different from each other and provide access to different parts of the region.

AUGUSTÓW
☎ 87 • pop 30,000

Augustów ('Aw-**goos**-toof'), at the southern end of the region, is a small but sprawling town. It was founded in 1557 by King Zygmunt August and named after him. Located on the bank of the Netta River, the border between the Polish Crown and the Grand Duchy of Lithuania until they were united between 1569 and 1795, the town had trading potential but grew painfully slowly. Even 150 years after its foundation, it had no more than 500 inhabitants. Its development really began in the 19th century after the construction of the Augustów Canal, and was further boosted when the Warsaw-St Petersburg railway was completed in 1862.

The 1944 battle over the region lasted for a couple of months, during which time the town switched from German to Russian hands several times and 70% of it was destroyed. Predictably, there's not much to see of the prewar architecture, nor are there many sights.

What the town itself lacks in terms of special attractions, you'll find in its surroundings. The beautiful Augustów Forest begins just on the eastern outskirts of the town and boasts the spectacular Czarna Hańcza River and the unusual Augustów Canal (see Around Augustów later in this chapter). The town is a handy base for these places and has become the most popular waterside centre in this corner of Poland.

Information
Tourist Offices The Centrum Informacji Turystycznej (☎/fax 643 28 83), ul 3 Maja 31, is open 8am to 4pm weekdays (from June to August till 6pm and also Saturday 9am to 4pm).

Money Cash can be easily exchanged in any of several kantors, eg, Orbis Travel at the Rynek. Travellers cheques are cashed at Bank Pekao on ul Żabia, Powszechny Bank Kredytowy at ul 3 Maja and Bank Zachodni on ul Wojska Polskiego, and all have ATMs.

Email & Internet Access The most central is the Wypożyczalnia Grota (☎ 644 63 63), a video cassette rental outlet at Rynek Zygmunta Augusta 11. Alternatively, try Wypożyczalnia Videomaniak (☎ 643 53 39), ul 3 Maja 46.

Regional Museum
The most important sight in town, the Muzeum Ziemi Augustowskiej, is at two locations. The main section, featuring an ethnographic exhibition, is in the modern public library building (☎ 643 27 54, ul Hoża 7; admission US$0.50; open 9am-4pm Tues-Sun). There is also a section dedicated to the history of the Augustów Canal (☎ 643 23 60, ul 29 Listopada 5A; admission US$0.50; open 9am-4pm Tues-Sun 15 May-15 Sept).

Boat Excursions
From May to September, pleasure boats operated by Żegluga Augustowska (☎ 643 28 81) ply surrounding lakes and a part of the Augustów Canal to the east of town. All trips originate from the wharf at ul 29

WARMIA & MASURIA

AUGUSTÓW

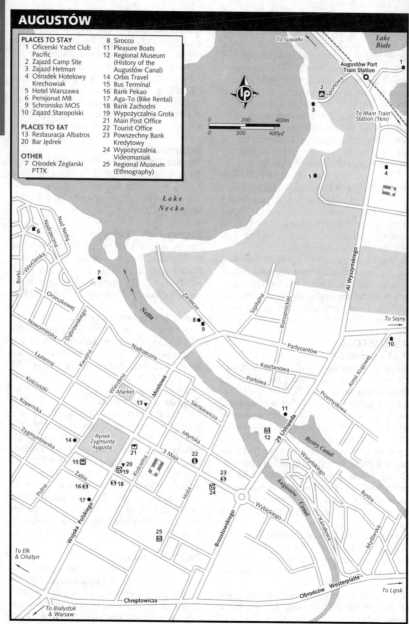

PLACES TO STAY
1 Oficerski Yacht Club Pacific
2 Zajazd Camp Site
3 Zajazd Hetman
4 Ośrodek Hotelowy Krechowiak
5 Hotel Warszawa
6 Pensjonat MB
9 Schronisko MOS
10 Zajazd Staropolski

PLACES TO EAT
13 Restauracja Albatros
20 Bar Jędrek

OTHER
7 Ośrodek Żeglarski PTTK
8 Sirocco
11 Pleasure Boats
12 Regional Museum (History of the Augustów Canal)
14 Orbis Travel
15 Bus Terminal
16 Bank Pekao
17 Aga-To (Bike Rental)
18 Bank Zachodni
19 Wypożyczalnia Grota
21 Main Post Office
22 Tourist Office
23 Powszechny Bank Kredytowy
24 Wypożyczalnia Videomaniak
25 Regional Museum (Ethnography)

0   200   400m
0   200   400yd

To Suwałki

Lake Białe

Augustów Port Train Station

To Main Train Station (1km)

To Sejny

Lake Necko

Netta

Nadrzeczna

Nad Netta

Borki

Wioślarska

Orzeszkowej

Nowomiejska

Dąbrowskiego

Łazienna

Kwiatna

Kościuszki

Kopernika

Zygmuntowska

Rynek Zygmunta Augusta

Market

Żabia

Polna

Wojska Polskiego

To Ełk & Olsztyn

To Białystok & Warsaw

Chreptowicza

Wierzbna

Mostowa

3 Maja

Kościelna

Hoża

Sienkiewicza

Młyńska

Brzostowskiego

Wybickiego

Obrońców Westerplatte

To Lipsk

Zarzecze

Szpitalna

Konopnickiej

Partyzantów

Kasztanowa

Portowa

29 Listopada

Al Wyszyńskiego

Armii Krajowej

Przemysłowa

Bystry Canal

Waryńskiego

Augustów Canal

Kanałowa

Bystra

Mydlińska

Listopada 7, and all are return journeys that deposit you back at the wharf.

The shortest trips (US$5, 1½ hours) will take you around the Necko and Rospuda lakes but don't go along the canal. More interesting are the cruises farther east along the canal system. The longest is the trip to Lake Gorczyckie (US$16, seven hours); the boat goes through two locks each way. It's scheduled on Wednesday in July and August only.

Kayaking

Kayaking tours are organised by several local operators, including **Szot** (*☎/fax 643 43 99, ul Konwaliowa 2*); **Sirocco** (*☎/fax 643 31 18, ul Zarzecze 5A*); **Necko** (*☎/fax 644 56 39, ul Chreptowicza 3/39*); and the **Ośrodek Żeglarski PTTK** (*☎/fax 643 38 50, ul Nadrzeczna 70A*). They all run various tours on different local rivers and can create a tour according to your requirements and time availability. Alternatively, kayaks can be rented (US$5 to US$6 per kayak per day), so you can go for your own tour.

The Czarna Hańcza River is the most popular kayaking destination in the region. The traditional route is designed as a loop, beginning in Augustów and leading along the Augustów Canal as far as Lake Serwy and up to the northern end of this lake. The kayaks are then transported overland to Lake Wigry or the village of Wysoki Most on the Czarna Hańcza, from where the canoeists follow the river downstream to the Augustów Canal and return by the canal to Augustów. The whole loop takes eight to 12 days and costs US$180 to US$220, all-inclusive (accommodation in tents on camp sites). Various shorter trips, being parts of the loop, are available with tour operators. For example, Shot organises one-day trips through arguably the most spectacular bit of the Czarna Hańcza, the 25km journey from Frącki to Mikaszówka (US$12 per person).

Other rivers used for kayaking trips by tour operators include the Rospuda (four to six days) and the Biebrza (seven to 10 days)

Places to Stay

There's a range of all-year hotels and hostels scattered throughout the town, which is

about 4km long from end to end. Also, plenty of holiday homes open in summer and accommodate individual tourists whenever they have vacancies. The prices listed are for the high season.

Schronisko MOS (*☎ 643 32 04, ul Zarzecze 1*) Beds in doubles, triples or quads US$5, in larger dorms US$4. Open July-Aug. MOS, a sort of a basic youth hostel, is one of the cheapest places in town, but it only opens in the summer season and it's often full with groups.

Zajazd Staropolski (*☎ 644 70 73, ul Armii Krajowej 28*) Beds in singles, doubles or triples US$7-10. The 20-bed Zajazd doesn't provide great luxury but it's pretty cheap. This is also a seasonal option that closes as soon as the tourist hordes thin out.

Oficerski Yacht Club Pacific (*☎/fax 643 34 96, Al Wyszyńskiego 1*) Beds in doubles or triples without bath US$8, doubles/triples with bath US$24/32. The Yacht Club, in a fine location on Lake Białe right behind the Augustów Port train station, has fairly good rooms with bath.

Zajazd Hetman (*☎/fax 644 53 45, ul Sportowa 1*) Doubles without bath US$18, doubles/triples with bath US$28/32. The Hetman, close to the Augustów Port train station, offers acceptable standard rooms with bath, but the rooms with shared facilities are nothing special. The building itself is a 1939-design by Polish architect Maciej Nowicki, later codesigner of the United Nations building in New York. The Zajazd runs a basic *camp site* opposite the entrance but it doesn't have cabins and the facilities are poor.

Pensjonat MB (*☎/fax 644 67 34, ul Spacerowa 4*) Doubles/suites US$24/32. MB is a small 18-bed guesthouse. All rooms have private facilities and provide a satisfactory accommodation standard.

Ośrodek Hotelowy Krechowiak (*☎ 643 20 33, fax 643 47 65, ul I Pułku Ułanów Krechowieckich 2*) Singles/doubles/triples with bath US$20/28/36. Extensively revamped over recent years, the Krechowiak now offers comfortable rooms with reasonable facilities.

Hotel Warszawa (*☎/fax 643 28 05, ul Zdrojowa 1*) Singles/doubles with bath &

breakfast US$40/60. Possibly the best place to stay in Augustów, the three-star Hotel Warszawa enjoys a fine lakeside location and provides good facilities.

Places to Eat

Bar Jędrek (☎ *644 64 01, Rynek Zygmunta Augusta 8)* Mains US$1-2. This basic milk bar servies up some of the cheapest meals in town.

Restauracja Albatros (☎ *643 21 23, ul Mostowa 3)* Mains US$4-8. Albatros has long been a popular local restaurant and it's not too expensive.

Hotel Warszawa runs possibly the best restaurant in town with mains costing around US$5-10.

Getting There & Away

Train Augustów has two train stations, but both are a long way from the town centre. The minor Augustów Port station is a more convenient place to get off, as it's closer to some of the hotels, but note that fast trains don't stop there. It doesn't even have a ticket office, so if you want to buy a ticket you need to go to the main Augustów station, 1km farther east.

There are three fast trains to Warsaw daily (282km). They all go via Sokółka and Białystok and cover the distance in about 4½ hours. Orbis Travel at the Rynek will book and sell tickets. There are also six trains a day to Suwałki.

Bus You can get around the region more easily by bus. The bus terminal is on the southern side of the Rynek and handles frequent services (every hour or so) to Białystok (91km) and Suwałki (31km). There are four buses directly to Warsaw (243km); all come through from Suwałki and can be full. Five buses a day run to Sejny (43km) and six to Grajewo (42km).

AROUND AUGUSTÓW
Augustów Forest

The Augustów Forest (Puszcza Augustowska) stretches east of Augustów as far as the Lithuanian-Belarussian border. At about 1100 sq km, it's Poland's largest continuous forest after the Bory Dolnośląskie in Lower Silesia. It's a remnant of the vast primeval forest that once covered much of this borderland of Poland and Lithuania.

The forest is made up mainly of pine and spruce, with colourful deciduous species such as birch, oak, elm, lime, maple and aspen. The wildlife is rich and diversified, and includes beaver, wild boar, wolves, deer and even some elk. Birds are also well represented and the lakes abound in fish. There are 55 lakes in the forest.

The forest was almost unexplored until the 17th century. Today there are paved roads, dirt tracks and paths crisscrossing the woodland, yet large stretches remain almost untouched.

You can explore part of the forest using private transport; roads will take you along the Augustów Canal almost to the border. Many of the rough tracks are perfectly OK for bikes, and on foot you can get almost everywhere except the swamps. Bikes can be rented out from several operators in Augustów, including Aga-To (☎ 644 54 72), ul Wojska Polskiego 14A. The Augustów tourist office can provide information, including brochures on bike routes in the forest. The detailed *Puszcza Augustowska* map (scale 1:70,000) shows all the roads, tracks and tourist trails.

Augustów Canal

Built in the 1820s, the Augustów Canal is a 102km-long waterway (80km within present-day Polish borders, 22km in Belarus), which connects the Biebrza and Niemen Rivers. Linking lakes and stretches of river with artificial channels, it's a picturesque route marked with old locks and floodgates. It's no longer used commercially; today it's a tourist attraction.

The canal begins at the confluence of the Netta and Biebrza Rivers and goes 33km north to Augustów through low and swampy meadows, partly using the bed of the Netta. It then continues eastwards through a chain of wooded lakes to the border. This part is the most spectacular.

The whole Polish stretch of the canal is navigable, but tourist boats from Augustów

180 Years of Augustów Canal

A remarkable achievement of 19th-century hydraulic engineering, the Augustów Canal (Kanał Augustowski) was built by the short-lived Congress Kingdom of Poland. It was intended to provide the country with an alternative outlet to the Baltic, since the lower Vistula was in the hands of the hostile Prussia, which imposed heavy customs barriers on river trade. The project aimed to connect the tributaries of the Vistula with the Niemen River and to reach the Baltic Sea at the port of Ventspils in Latvia. Despite the roundabout route, this seemed to be the most viable way of getting goods abroad.

The Polish part of the waterway, the Augustów Canal, linking the Biebrza and Niemen Rivers, was designed by an army engineer, General Ignacy Prądzyński, and built in just seven years (1824–30), though final works continued until 1839. About 7000 people worked daily on the site. It was the largest transport project realised by the Congress Kingdom, and it was a great engineering achievement. However, Poland was subjugated by Russia after the November Insurrection of 1830. The Russians were meant to build their part from the town of Kaunas via the Dubissa River up to Ventspils, but the work was never completed.

The Augustów Canal ended up as a regional waterway, and though it contributed to local development, it didn't become an import-export transport facility, as planned. Its route includes 28km of lakes, 34km of canalised rivers and 40km of canal proper. There are 18 locks along the way (14 in Poland) to bridge the 55m change in water level (15m upwards followed by 40m downwards).

The canal remains in its original form together with most of its archaic machinery, though not all locks are complete and in working order. Plans are to repair the inoperable locks and to open the canal as a tourist attraction. Meanwhile, applications have been submitted to include the canal on Unesco's World Heritage list.

---

only go as far east as Lake Gorczyckie. By kayak, you can continue to the border, but the locks beyond Lake Gorczyckie are closed. Contact tour companies (listed under Augustów earlier) for information, tour options and kayak-rental conditions.

SUWAŁKI
☎ 87 • pop 65,000

Suwałki ('Soo-**vahw**-kee') is the largest town in the region, and until 1998 was its provincial capital. In contrast to Augustów, Suwałki is not surrounded by lakes and forests, and is far less visited by tourists. There are no holiday homes here, nor much in the way of tourist facilities. It's a gateway to the surrounding countryside rather than a destination in itself.

Suwałki appeared on the map at the end of the 17th century as one of the villages established by the Camaldolese monks from Wigry. Isolated in this remote lakeland at the meeting point of different ethnic and religious groups, its small multinational community grew slowly; at different times it

included Jews, Lithuanians, Tatars, Russians and Germans, and there is still a tiny congregation of Old Believers, a peculiar religious group which split off the Russian Orthodox Church in the 17th century.

Information
Tourist Offices The Centrum Informacji Turystycznej (☎ 566 58 72, ☎ 566 54 94), ul Kościuszki 45, is open 8am to 4pm weekdays (till 6pm and also 9am to 2pm Saturday from June to August).

Money Bank Pekao has outlets at ul Noniewicza 95 and ul Kościuszki 72, and both have ATMs.

Email & Internet Access Internet facilities include S-Max (☎ 565 00 82), ul Noniewicza 35, and Grand (☎ 565 06 69), ul Korczaka 2A.

Things to See
The local **cemetery** gives a good picture of the town's ethnic and religious history. It

actually consists of several cemeteries where people of different creeds were buried.

There must have been a large Jewish community, judging by the size of its graveyard; in fact, at the beginning of the 20th century Jews made up half the town's population. Their cemetery was destroyed in WWII and only a memorial stands in the middle, assembled out of fragments of old grave slabs. The tiny Muslim graveyard is the last remnant of the Tatars, but the graves are now hardly recognisable.

At the back of the Orthodox Church cemetery is the Old Believers' graveyard.

A handful of followers still gather on Sunday at 6am in their church *(molenna)* at ul Sejneńska 37A, on the opposite side of town. The simple timber church dates from the beginning of the 20th century, but the icons inside are significantly older. Except during Mass, you have little chance of seeing them.

The main thoroughfare of the town, ul Kościuszki, retains some 19th-century neoclassical architecture. Here you'll also find the **Regional Museum** (*☎ 566 57 50, ul Kościuszki 81; adult/student US$1/0.50; open 8am-4pm Tues-Fri, 9am-5pm Sat &*

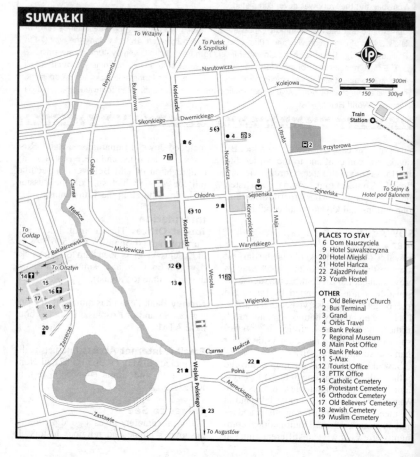

SUWAŁKI

To Wiżajny

To Puńsk & Szypliszki

Narutowicza

Kolejowa

Reymonta

Bulwarowa

Kościuszki

Dwernickiego

Sikorskiego

5 ●

● 4 ☐ 3

Noniewicza

Urata

☐ 2 Przytorowa

Train Station

0   150   300m
0   150   300yd

● 6

7 🏛

Gałaja

Czarna

Hańcza

8 ✉

Chłodna

Sejneńska

Konopnickiej

1 Maja

Sejneńska

To Sejny & Hotel pod Balonem

● 9

● 10

To Gołdap

Bakałarzewska

Mickiewicza

Kościuszki

Waryńskiego

To Olsztyn

14 🏛

15

16 🏛

17

18

19

12 ●

13 ●

Wesoła

11 ☐

Wigierska

Zarzecze

20 ●

Czarna   Hańcza

22 ●

21 ●

Polna

Mereckiego

Wojska Polskiego

● 23

Zastawie

To Augustów

PLACES TO STAY
6 Dom Nauczyciela
9 Hotel Suwalszczyzna
20 Hotel Miejski
21 Hotel Hańcza
22 ZajazdPrivate
23 Youth Hostel

OTHER
1 Old Believers' Church
2 Bus Terminal
3 Grand
4 Orbis Travel
5 Bank Pekao
7 Regional Museum
8 Main Post Office
10 Bank Pekao
11 S-Max
12 Tourist Office
13 PTTK Office
14 Catholic Cemetery
15 Protestant Cemetery
16 Orthodox Cemetery
17 Old Believers' Cemetery
18 Jewish Cemetery
19 Muslim Cemetery

Sun), which presents the little that is known of the Jatzvingian culture.

Organised Tours

The PTTK office (☎ 566 59 61, ☎/fax 566 79 47), ul Kościuszki 37, operates 12-day kayak trips down the Czarna Hańcza River. See Augustów earlier for details. The office also rents out kayaks (US$5 a day) and will provide information if you want to do the trip on your own.

Places to Stay & Eat

Youth hostel (☎ 566 58 78, ul Wojska Polskiego 9) Beds US$3-4. The small and basic youth hostel is open in July and August only.

Hotel Miejski (☎ 566 72 20, ul Zarzecze 26) Doubles/triples without bath US$14/16. Also known as the Hotel Wigry, this 42-bed sports facility next to the local stadium (close to the Jewish cemetery) is simple but acceptable.

Hotel Hańcza (☎/fax 566 66 33, ul Wojska Polskiego 2) Singles/doubles/triples with bath & breakfast US$24/34/40. The Hańcza has been refurbished and is perfectly OK and reasonably priced. It has a budget restaurant.

Zajazd Private (☎/fax 566 53 62, ul Polna 9) Doubles with bath US$30. The small Zajazd offers just six double rooms, all with bath and satellite TV.

Dom Nauczyciela (☎ 566 69 00, ☎/fax 566 62 70, ul Kościuszki 120) Doubles with bath & breakfast US$40-60. This former teachers' dorm has rooms of different size and standard, but the cheapest ones are nothing special. The hotel has a reasonable restaurant.

Hotel Suwalszczyzna (☎/fax 565 19 00, ul Noniewicza 71A) Singles/doubles/triples with bath & breakfast US$40/45/50. The central Suwalszczyzna is the most recent addition to the local accommodation scene, and arguably the best. It also has its own restaurant.

Getting There & Away

The train station is 1.5km north-east of the centre; the bus terminal is a little closer to the central area. Trains are useful mostly for longer journeys, with several departures a day to Białystok and Warsaw. Getting around the region is easier by bus. Buses also ply longer routes: to Gdańsk (one bus daily), Olsztyn (three buses, all via Giżycko) and Warsaw (four). There's one bus a week to Vilnius in Lithuania (US$5, 5½ hours).

AROUND SUWAŁKI
Wigry National Park
☎ 87

The Wigry National Park (Wigierski Park Narodowy) covers the whole of Lake Wigry and a wide, predominantly forested belt of land around it, sprinkled with about 50 small lakes. At 21 sq km, **Lake Wigry** is the largest lake in the region and one of the deepest, reaching 73m at its deepest point. It's also one of the most beautiful lakes. Its shoreline is richly indented, forming numerous bays and peninsulas, and there are 15 islands on the lake. The Czarna Hańcza River, a favourite among canoeists, flows through the park. The park's wildlife is diverse, with fish, birds and mammals, and the beaver is the park's emblem.

There is a **monastery** spectacularly located on a peninsula in Lake Wigry. It was built by Camaldolese monks (the monks of 'Memento Mori' – see the Las Wolski section in the Kraków chapter for more about them) soon after they were brought to Wigry by King Jan Kazimierz in 1667. The whole complex, complete with a church and 17 hermitages, was originally on an island, which was later connected to the shore. In 1795 the Prussians expelled the monks and confiscated the property, which by then covered 300 sq km and included over 30 villages. The monastery has been turned into a hotel, providing an atmospheric base for exploring the park.

There are marked trails throughout the park, which make it possible to visit some remote corners. You can walk all round Lake Wigry (49km by the green trail), provided you have three days. Lakeside camp sites along the trail are located within reasonable day-walking distances. If you are planning to walk in the park, the *Wigierski Park Narodowy* map shows the necessary detail.

The most popular access is from the Suwałki-Sejny road, which crosses the northern part of the park. The headquarters of the park (☎/fax 566 63 22) are on this road, in Krzywe, 5km from Suwałki.

Places to Stay & Eat There's quite a choice of accommodation inside and just outside the park's boundaries. The park's headquarters have a few simple rooms for visitors (about US$8 per person) and half a dozen hunting lodges scattered across the park (US$8 per person). There are also about 15 bivouac sites in the area. Another option is agrotourist farms open for visitors – Suwałki's tourist office will give you details. Other places include:

Dom Wycieczkowy PTTK (☎ 563 77 27) Beds in doubles, triples or quads US$5. The basic PTTK hostel, in the village of Stary Folwark, 9km outside Suwałki, offers beds in its derelict building, operates a *camp site* from June to August on the lake shore, and rents out kayaks.

Dom Pracy Twórczej (☎/fax 563 70 18) Doubles in main building US$40, doubles/triples in hermitages US$30/40. Open year-round. Attractively located on the lakeside in the former monastery building and the hermitages, the Dom offers quite good conditions in rooms with bath, and has a cafeteria that provides hot meals.

Getting There & Away The Suwałki-Sejny road is serviced by buses quite regularly. Buses between Suwałki and Stary Folwark run every hour or so. If you want to go directly to the monastery, take the bus from the main bus terminal to Wigry (four buses per day in summer).

Sejny
☎ 87 • pop 5000

Sejny, 30km east of Suwałki, is the last Polish town before the Ogrodniki border crossing to Lithuania, 12km beyond. The town grew around the Dominican monastery, which had been founded in 1602 by the monks from Vilnius. The order was expelled by the Prussian authorities in 1804 and never returned, however the two-towered silhouette of the **church** still proudly dominates the town from its northern end. It dates from the 1610s, but its facade was thoroughly remodelled 150 years later in the so-called Vilnius baroque style. Its pastel interior has harmonious rococo decoration.

At the opposite, southern end of the town is a large **synagogue**, built by the sizable local Jewish community in the 1880s. During the German occupation it served as a fire station and after the war as a storage room. Today it's an **art gallery** operated by the Borderland Foundation (Fundacja Pogranicze; ☎ 516 27 65) that focuses on the arts and culture of different ethnic and religious traditions from the region. The staff organise concerts and theatre performances, and they also sell various publications on ethnic issues.

Places to Stay & Eat *Dom Litewski (☎ 516 29 08, ul 22 Lipca 9)* Singles/doubles/triples without bath US$14/20/26, with bath US$18/26/32. This new Lithuanian House has a simple but neat and pleasant hotel and also has a cafe serving traditional Lithuanian dishes at low prices. It also shelters the Lithuanian consulate (☎ 516 22 73), your last chance to get a visa if you need one.

Hotel Skarpa (☎ 516 20 65, ul Piłsudskiego 13) Doubles/triples without bath US$14/18, doubles with bath US$18. Not as good as the Dom, but also budget and acceptable, with a restaurant.

Getting There & Away There is a regular bus service to Suwałki (30km). A few buses a day travel via a backwoods road to Augustów (42km).

Suwałki Landscape Park
☎ 87

Established in 1976, the 63-sq-km Suwałki Landscape Park (Suwalski Park Krajobrazowy) was the first nature reserve of that kind. It covers some of the most picturesque stretches of land in the region north of Suwałki, including 26 lakes (totalling 10% of the park's area) and patches of fine forest (another 24%).

A base for exploring the park can be the village of Smolniki, 20km north of Suwałki. There are several marked trails passing through the village. The *youth hostel* (open July and August) and several *ecotourist farms* will put you up for the night – inquire at the Suwałki tourist office for details.

The Smolniki neighbourhood is rugged, largely wooded, and dotted with a dozen small lakes, and there are three good viewpoints in the village, which allow you to enjoy some of this landscape. One of the numerous walking options is an hour's walk west to **Lake Hańcza**, the deepest lake in the country (108.5m). With its steep shores, stony bottom and amazing crystal-clear water, it's like a mountain lake.

Another handy base for hikes in the park can be the hamlet of Turtul, where the park's headquarters (☎ 569 18 01) is based. It has a few all-year budget dorms for visitors and rents out bicycles.

If you travel between Smolniki and Suwałki, it's worth stopping in Gulbieniszki at the foot of **Mt Cisowa Góra**. This 256m-high hill just off the road is cone-shaped like a volcano and provides a fine view over the surrounding lakes.

The *Suwalski Park Krajobrazowy i Okolice* map (scale 1:50,000) is good for exploring the area. It has all hiking trails marked on it and good sightseeing information in English on the reverse.

Stańczyki
☎ 87 • pop 200

Deep among forested hills close to the northern border, there's a pair of unusual

---

The Mysterious Bridges at Stańczyki

The two bridges at Stańczyki were built by the Germans, in what was then the territory of East Prussia, as part of the 31km Gołdap-Żytkiejmy railway track. The first bridge was constructed in 1912–14, just before WWI. About 12 years later the second identical bridge was built parallel to the first, just 15m to the south. The double line was used until late 1944 when the Red Army arrived, dismantled the tracks and took them to the Soviet Union, leaving the bridges inoperable, as they have been since.

There are some mysteries about the bridges. First of all, why was the railway line built in such a sparsely inhabited area with little economic importance? Was is to be a tourist line leading through a picturesque wooded land? Or maybe a facility for the transport of timber? Or perhaps some strategic military issues forced the Germans to build the line?

Another puzzle is, why were two bridges built, not just one? There were never many trains running through this route – the 1938 timetable reveals just three trains a day in each direction – so why such a monumental work with a separate bridge for each direction? Even if more traffic was expected, why not construct one bridge that was wide enough to accommodate two lines?

Next question: why were the bridges built at that precise point, in apparently the most rugged passage over the river? Just a few hundred metres to the south the terrain is much flatter, and the project wouldn't require constructions that were so high and expensive. It seems that the designers intentionally looked for difficulties to overcome them. Was it a challenge to demonstrate German technical advancement?

Another unanswered question concerns the bridges' concrete structure, which includes tree trunks sunk into it. It was initially thought that the trunks were used as the structural skeleton, partly replacing a heavy steel reinforcement, but engineering expertise has shown that the wooden structure wouldn't support the bridges' 30m-wide arches. Was it that the builders dropped the wooden pieces of scaffolding by accident and then filled over them with liquid concrete?

Whatever the answers are, though, the bridges are still there, looking like giant aqueducts brought from ancient Rome and dropped in this remote corner of Poland. And the mysteries perhaps just add to their attractiveness.

railway bridges that rise out of the woods. Linking the steep sides of the valley of the Błędzianka River, 36m above water level, these two identical 180m-long constructions were built next to each other. With their tall pillars supporting wide, elegant classical arches, they have the air of a Roman aqueduct. Now unused and without tracks, the bridges look like huge, surrealistic sculptures in the middle of nowhere.

You can walk on the top of both bridges and go down and look at them from below – it's really a weird sight. For a long time almost unknown and forgotten, they are now becoming a tourist attraction, and a car park with some basic facilities was built and is attended in summer.

Places to Stay & Eat *Pensjonat Biały Dwór (☎ 615 81 72)* Doubles without/with bath US$12/20, quads with bath US$35. Open May-Sept. This small guesthouse, near the bridges, offers simple but acceptable accommodation and has a restaurant that serves tasty budget meals.

Getting There & Away In July and August, there are two buses direct from Suwałki to Stańczyki daily. Alternatively, there's access from the Gołdap-Wiżajny road, serviced by about six buses in each direction daily. Get off at the turn-off to Stańczyki and walk 1.5km, and you'll see the bridges on your left. The Pensjonat is about 500m farther down the road.

Language

Polish is a western variety of the Slavonic languages found in central and eastern Europe, such as Czech, Russian, Serbian, Croatian, Slovak and Slovene.

Ideally, everyone who wants to travel in Poland should know some basic Polish – the more you know the easier your travel is likely to be and the more you'll get out of your time in the country. For a more comprehensive guide to the language, get a copy of Lonely Planet's *Polish phrasebook*.

The Polish Alphabet

Polish letters with diacritical marks are treated as separate letters, and the order of the Polish alphabet is as follows:

a ą b c ć d e ę f g h i j k l ł m n ń o ó p (q) r s ś t u (v) w (x) y z ź ż

The letters **q**, **v** and **x** appear only in words of foreign origin.

Pronunciation

Written Polish is phonetically consistent, which means that the pronunciation of letters or clusters of letters doesn't vary from word to word. The stress almost always goes on the second-last syllable.

Vowels Polish vowels are pure, consisting of one sound only, and are of roughly even length. Their approximate pronunciation is as follows:

a	as the 'u' in 'cut'
ą	a highly nasalised vowel; a cross between the 'awn' in 'lawn' and the 'ong' in 'long'
e	as in 'ten'
ę	also highly nasalised; like the 'eng' in 'engage' (where the 'ng' is one sound, not 'n' followed by 'g'); pronounced as **e** when word-final
i	similar to the 'ee' in 'feet' but shorter
o	as in 'not'

ó	the same as Polish **u**
u	as in 'put'
y	similar to the 'i' in 'bit'

Consonants Most Polish consonants are pronounced as in English. However, there are some very fine distinctions between certain consonants in Polish which English speakers may find difficult to produce. The following guide gives approximations only of the correct pronunciation – your best bet is to listen to and learn from native speakers:

c	as the 'ts' in 'its'
ch	similar to 'ch' in the Scottish *loch*
cz	as the 'ch' in 'church'
ć	similar to **c** but pronounced with the tongue a little further back on the roof of the mouth; pronounced as 'tsi' before vowels
dz	as the 'ds' in 'adds up'
dź	similar to **dz** but pronounced with the tongue a little further back on the roof of the mouth; pronounced as 'dzi' before vowels
dż	as the 'j' in 'jam'
g	as in 'get'
h	the same as **ch** (above)
j	as the 'y' in 'yet'
ł	as the 'w' in 'wine'
ń	as the 'ni' in 'onion'; written as 'ni' before vowels
r	always trilled
rz	as the 's' in 'pleasure'
s	as in 'set'
sz	as the 'sh' in 'show'
ś	similar to **s** but not as strident; written as 'si' before vowels
w	as the 'v' in 'van'
ź	similar to **z** but not as strident; written as 'zi' before vowels
ż	the same as **rz**
szcz	the most obtuse-looking cluster; pronounced as the 'shch' in 'fresh cheese'

The following consonants are unvoiced when they are word-final: **b** is pronounced as 'p', **d** as 't', **g** as 'k', **w** as 'f', **z** as 's' and **rz** as 'sz'.

Finally, here's the favourite Polish tongue-twister for you to test your pronunciation skills on: *Chrząszcz brzmi w trzcinie* (The cockchafer buzzes in the weeds).

Greetings & Civilities

Good morning.	*Dzień dobry.*
Good evening.	*Dobry wieczór.*
Hi/Bye.	*Cześć.* (informal)
Goodbye.	*Do widzenia.*
Good night.	*Dobranoc.*
Yes.	*Tak.*
No.	*Nie.*
Please.	*Proszę.*
Thank you (very much).	*Dziękuję (bardzo).*
You're welcome.	*Proszę.*
How are you?	*Jak się pan/pani miewa?* (m/f)
Very well, thank you.	*Dziękuję, bardzo dobrze.*
May I?	*Czy mogę?*
Excuse me/ I'm sorry.	*Przepraszam.*
OK.	*Dobrze.*
Mrs/Madam/Ms	*Pani*
Mr/Sir	*Pan*

Basics

I	*ja*
you	*ty*
he/she	*on/ona*
we	*my*
you	*wy*
they	*oni/one*
What?	*Co?*
Where?	*Gdzie?*
When?	*Kiedy?*
Who?	*Kto?*
Why?	*Dlaczego?*
How?	*Jak?*
and	*i*

Language Difficulties

Do you speak English?	*Czy Pan/Pani mówi po angielsku?* (m/f)
Does anyone here speak English?	*Czy ktoś tu mówi po angielsku?*
I don't speak Polish.	*Nie mówię po polsku.*
I (don't) understand.	*(Nie) rozumiem.*
Please speak more slowly.	*Proszę mówić wolniej.*
Could you repeat that, please?	*Proszę to powtórzyć.*
Please write that down.	*Proszę to napisać.*
What does it mean?	*Co to znaczy?*
How do you pronounce it?	*Jak się to wymawia?*

Getting Around

Where is (the) ...?	*Gdzie jest ...?*
airport	*lotnisko*
bus station	*dworzec autobusowy*
bus stop	*przystanek autobusowy*
petrol station	*stacja benzynowa*
train station	*stacja kolejowa*

What time does the ... leave/ arrive?	*O której godzinie odchodzi/ przychodzi ...?*
plane	*samolot*
boat	*statek*
bus	*autobus*
train	*pociąg*
tram	*tramwaj*

Two tickets to ... please.	*Poproszę dwa bilety do ...*

ticket	*bilet*
ticket office	*kasa biletowa*
timetable	*rozkład jazdy*
1st/2nd class	*pierwsza/druga klasa*
next	*następny*
first	*pierwszy*
last	*ostatni*
arrival	*przyjazd*
departure	*odjazd*
left-luggage room	*przechowalnia bagażu*

How do I get to ...?	*Jak się dostać do ...?*
How far is it?	*Jak to daleko stąd?*
Please show me on the map.	*Proszę pokazać mi to na mapie.*
Turn left.	*Proszę skręcić w lewo.*

Signs

Wejście	**Entrance**
Wyjście	**Exit**
Informacja	**Information**
Otwarte	**Open**
Zamknięte	**Closed**
Wzbroniony	**Prohibited**
Posterunek Policji	**Police Station**
Toalety	**Toilets**
Panowie	**Men**
Panie	**Women**

Turn right.	*Proszę skręcić w prawo.*
Go straight ahead.	*Proszę iść prosto.*

Where can I hire a ...?	*Gdzie mogę wypożyczyć ...?*
car	*samochód*
motorbike	*motocykl*
bicycle	*rower*

Around Town

town, city	*miasto*
village	*wieś*
road	*szosa, droga*
street	*ulica*
city centre	*centrum*
bank	*bank*
bridge	*most*
castle	*zamek*
cathedral	*katedra*
church	*kościół*
embassy	*ambasada*
monastery	*klasztor*
monument	*pomnik*
museum	*muzeum*
old town	*stare miasto*
old town square	*rynek*
open-air museum	*skansen*
palace	*pałac*
police station	*posterunek policji*
public toilet	*toaleta publiczna*
square	*plac*
synagogue	*synagoga*
town hall	*ratusz*
university	*uniwersytet*

money	*pieniądze*
cash	*gotówka*
travellers cheque	*czek podróżny*
commission	*prowizja*
credit card	*karta kredytowa*
ATM	*bankomat*

In the Country

beach	*plaża*
cave	*jaskinia*
coast	*wybrzeże*
forest	*las/puszcza*
island	*wyspa*
lake	*jezioro*
mountain	*góra*
river	*rzeka*
valley	*dolina*
waterfall	*wodospad*

Accommodation

hotel	*hotel*
youth hostel	*schronisko młodzieżowe*
room	*pokój*
dormitory	*sala zbiorowa*
Do you have any rooms available?	*Czy są wolne pokoje?*
May I see the room?	*Czy mogę zobaczyć pokój?*
How much is it?	*Ile kosztuje?*
Does it include breakfast?	*Czy śniadanie jest wliczone?*
bathroom	*łazienka*
bed	*łóżko*
key	*klucz*
sheets	*pościel*
shower	*prysznic/natrysk*
toilet	*toaleta*
cheap	*tani*
expensive	*drogi*
clean	*czysty*
dirty	*brudny*
good	*dobry*
poor, bad	*niedobry*
noisy	*głośny*
quiet	*cichy*
hot	*gorący*
cold	*zimny*

Post & Communications

post office	*poczta*
postcard	*pocztówka*
letter	*list*
parcel	*paczka*
stamp	*znaczek*
air mail	*poczta lotnicza*
registered letter	*list polecony*
letter box	*skrzynka pocztowa*
international call	*rozmowa międzynarodowa*
long distance call	*rozmowa międzymiastowa*
public telephone	*automat telefoniczny*
telephone card	*karta telefoniczna*
token	*żeton*

Shopping

Do you have ...?	*Czy są ...?*
How much is it?	*Ile to kosztuje?*
I (don't) like it.	*(Nie) podoba mi się.*
shop	*sklep*
shopping centre	*centrum handlowe*
market	*targ/bazar*
pharmacy	*apteka*
price	*cena*
cheap/expensive	*tani/drogi*
big/small	*duży/mały*
many/much	*dużo*
a few	*kilka*
a little	*trochę*
enough	*wystarczy*
more/less	*więcej/mniej*

Food

Only some basic words are given here. See the Food and Drinks sections in the Facts for the Visitor chapter for more terms.

I'm a vegetarian.	*Jestem jaroszem.*
the bill	*rachunek*
cup	*filiżanka*
dish	*danie*
fork	*widelec*
glass	*szklanka*
knife	*nóż*
menu	*jadłospis*

Emergencies

Please call a doctor/the police.
Proszę wezwać lekarza/policję.
Where is the nearest hospital?
Gdzie jest najbliższy szpital?
Could you help me, please?
Proszę mi pomóc.
I'm ill.
Źle się czuję.
I have a fever.
Mam gorączkę.
Could I use the telephone?
Czy mogę skorzystać z telefonu?
I want to contact my embassy.
Chcę się skontaktować z moją ambasadą.
Please leave me alone!
Proszę mnie zostawić!

accident	*wypadek*
ambulance	*karetka pogotowia*
dentist	*dentysta*
doctor	*lekarz*
hospital	*szpital*
medicine	*lek/lekarstwo*
police	*policja*

plate	*talerz*
spoon	*łyżka*
teaspoon	*łyżeczka*
bread	*chleb*
butter	*masło*
egg	*jajko*
fish	*ryba*
fruit	*owoce*
ham	*szynka*
meat	*mięso*
milk	*mleko*
pepper	*pieprz*
potatoes	*ziemniaki*
rice	*ryż*
salad	*sałatka, surówka*
salt	*sól*
sandwich	*kanapka*
sausage	*kiełbasa*
sugar	*cukier*
vegetables	*warzywa, jarzyny*
water	*woda*

Time & Dates

What is the time?	*Która godzina?*
time	*czas*

now	*teraz*	summer	*lato*
today	*dzisiaj, dziś*	autumn	*jesień*
tonight	*dziś wieczorem*	winter	*zima*
tomorrow	*jutro*	spring	*wiosna*
yesterday	*wczoraj*		
this week	*w tym tygodniu*		

Numbers

now	*teraz*
today	*dzisiaj, dziś*
tonight	*dziś wieczorem*
tomorrow	*jutro*
yesterday	*wczoraj*
this week	*w tym tygodniu*
next week	*w przyszłym tygodniu*
last week	*w zeszłym tygodniu*
morning	*rano*
afternoon	*popołudnie*
evening	*wieczór*
night	*noc*
midday	*południe*
midnight	*północ*
sunrise	*wschód*
sunset	*zachód*
minute	*minuta*
hour	*godzina*
day	*dzień*
week	*tydzień*
month	*miesiąc*
year	*rok*
Monday	*poniedziałek*
Tuesday	*wtorek*
Wednesday	*środa*
Thursday	*czwartek*
Friday	*piątek*
Saturday	*sobota*
Sunday	*niedziela*
January	*styczeń*
February	*luty*
March	*marzec*
April	*kwiecień*
May	*maj*
June	*czerwiec*
July	*lipiec*
August	*sierpień*
September	*wrzesień*
October	*październik*
November	*listopad*
December	*grudzień*

summer	*lato*
autumn	*jesień*
winter	*zima*
spring	*wiosna*

Numbers

1/4	*jedna czwarta*
1/2	*jedna druga*
0	*zero*
1	*jeden*
2	*dwa*
3	*trzy*
4	*cztery*
5	*pięć*
6	*sześć*
7	*siedem*
8	*osiem*
9	*dziewięć*
10	*dziesięć*
11	*jedenaście*
12	*dwanaście*
13	*trzynaście*
14	*czternaście*
15	*piętnaście*
16	*szesnaście*
17	*siedemnaście*
18	*osiemnaście*
19	*dziewiętnaście*
20	*dwadzieścia*
21	*dwadzieścia jeden*
22	*dwadzieścia dwa*
30	*trzydzieści*
100	*sto*
1000	*tysiąc*
100,000	*sto tysięcy*
one million	*milion*
1st	*pierwszy*
2nd	*drugi*
3rd	*trzeci*
percent	*procent*
once	*raz*
twice	*dwa razy*
three times	*trzy razy*

Glossary

You may encounter the following terms and abbreviations in your travels throughout Poland. For further Polish terms, see the previous Language chapter, the Food and Drink sections in Facts for the Visitor, and the Getting Around chapter.

Aleja or Aleje – avenue, main city street; abbreviated to Al in addresses and on maps
Almatur – the nationwide Student Travel & Tourist Bureau
apteka – pharmacy

bankomat – ATM
bar mleczny – milk bar; a sort of self-service basic soup kitchen which serves very cheap, mostly vegetarian dishes
barszcz – beetroot soup; one of Poland's national dishes
basen – swimming pool
bigos – sauerkraut and meat; another national dish
bilet – ticket
biuro turystyczne – travel agency
biuro zakwaterowania – office that arranges private accommodation

Cepelia – a network of shops that sell artefacts made by local artisans
cerkiew – (plural *cerkwie*); an Orthodox or Uniate church
cocktail bar – type of cafe that serves cakes, pastries, milk shakes, ice creams and other sweets
cukiernia – cake shop

Desa – chain of old art and antique sellers
dom kultury – cultural centre
dom wczasowy or dom wypoczynkowy – holiday home
dom wycieczkowy – term applied to PTTK-run hostels
domek campingowy – cabin, bungalow, chalet

grosz – unit of Polish currency; abbreviated to gr; see also *złoty*

jadłospis – menu

kantor – private currency-exchange office
kasa – ticket office
kawiarnia – cafe
kino – cinema
kiosk Ruch – newsagency
klezmer music – Jewish folk music
kolegiata – collegiate church
komórka – literally, 'cell'; commonly used for cellular (mobile) phone
kościół – church
kościół farny – parish church
księgarnia – bookshop
kwatery agroturystyczne – agrotourist accommodation; increasingly numerous and popular
kwatery prywatne – rooms in private houses rented out to tourists

LOT – Polish Airlines

miejscówka – reserved seat ticket
miód pitny – mead; a traditional Polish beverage obtained by fermentation of malt in honeyed water

na zdrowie! – cheers!; literally, to the health; what Poles say before drinking

odjazdy – departures (on transport schedules)
ogródek – literally, 'small garden', but also commonly used for any outdoor area of a cafe, restaurant or bar
Orbis – the largest travel/tourist company in Poland
otwarte – open

pensjonat – pension or private guesthouse, usually small
peron – railway platform
piekarnia – bakery
pierogi – dumplings made from noodle dough, stuffed and boiled
PKP (Polskie Koleje Państwowe) – Polish State Railways

PKS (Państwowa Komunikacja Samochodowa) – the state bus company
poczta – post office
Polonia – general term applied to the Polish community living outside Poland
powiat – sub-province; a unit of administrative division
pralnia – dry cleaner
prowizja – the commission banks charge on transactions
przechowalnia bagażu – left-luggage room
przychodnia – outpatient clinic
przyjazdy – arrivals (as seen on transport schedules)
PTSM – Polish Youth Hostel Association
PTTK – Polish Tourists Association
PZM or PZMot – Polski Związek Motorowy; Polish Motoring Association

rachunek – bill or check
rozkład jazdy – transport timetable
Rynek – Old Town Square

schronisko górskie – mountain hostel, providing basic accommodation and meals, usually run by PTTK
schronisko młodzieżowe – youth hostel
Sejm – lower house of Poland's parliament
skansen – open-air museum of traditional architecture
sklep – shop
smacznego – preprandial civility; *bon appetit*

specjalność zakładu – on a menu, speciality of the house
stanica wodna – waterside hostel, usually with boats, kayaks and other water-related facilities
stołówka – canteen; restaurant or cafeteria of a holiday home, hostel etc
szlachta – gentry or feudal nobility in 17th to 18th century Poland

Święty/a – Saint; abbreviated to Św (St)
Święty Mikołaj – Santa Claus

ulgowy (bilet) – reduced or discounted (ticket)
ulica – street; abbreviated to ul in addresses (and placed before the actual name); usually omitted on maps

wódka – vodka; the No 1 Polish brew
województwo – province; unit of administrative division (there are 16 in Poland), further divided into smaller territorial entities called *powiat*

zakaz wstępu – no entry
zamknięte – closed
zdrój – spa
złoty – the unit of Polish currency; abbreviated to zł; divided into 100 units called *grosz*
zniżka studencka – student discount

żubr – the European bison

Thanks

Many thanks to the travellers who used the last edition and wrote to us with helpful hints, useful advice and interesting anecdotes:

Ronald Aftanas, Beatrice Allen, Mark Allingham, Aaron Alton, Jorgen Alving, Nicholas Anchen, FR Antony, Gemma Arnold, Kerry Arthur, Peter Aspinall, Jorg Ausfelt, Michelle Austin, Artur Babecki, Stephen Barnard, Keith Baumwald, Dr J Belza, Jill Bennett, Henry Bercuk, Ben Bergonzi, Richard Beswick, David N Biacsi, Andrzej Bielecki, Jordan Blackman, Dennis Blazey, Esther Blodau-Konick, Cilla Bohlund, Lou Bolechala, Jerry Bollfrass, Jill Bowden, Graham Boyd, AJ Bradford, Alexander Brinkerink, Henry Briscoe, Janet & Christopher Brookes, Renay Buchanan, Hans J Buhrmester, Trevor Butcher, Steven Butler, Daniel S Byer, Flouis Bylsma, Cormac Byrne, Martin Cahn, Gill Callaghen, Joan Carles Gelabfroo, Annelise Carleton, Carlos Carneiro, Lachlan Carrick, Diane Caulkett, Jason Chapple, Bill Charette, Dave Chippendale, Marek Ciennik, Ray Coe, Tammy Colebrook, Lisa Collecott, Ian Collier, EJ Collins, Delta M Compo, Liam Connolly, Louise Cowcher, Phil Cubbin, Marek Czarnecki, Ake Dahllot, Paul Dalton, Alicia Darvall, Robert Davison, Anoek De Smet, Dave Depooter, Barbara Deskiewicz, K Deuss, Kristian Dillenburger, Nick Diouoyniotis, Julie & Jeff Dobslaw, Kelly Douglas, Gavin Doyle, Richard Draper, Paul Drooks, Marcel Droop, Kelly Duffy, Mavra Dundon, JR Dunn, Jon Durham, Michael Eckert, Honda Eiki, Jennifer Emmert, Fatima Entckhabi, Gert Eriksson, Nate Espino, Sheila Eustace, Ian Fair, Mario Falzon, M J Fey, B Filion, Ralph Fitchett, Hugh Ford, Tracey Ford, Vidar Frett, Marianne Fuchs, Brandon Furman, Daphne Gallagher, Alisoun Gardner-Medwin, Chad Garrett Randl, Halina & Ewa Gasinska, Sarit Gelbart, Lyall C Gibb, Tim Gilley, Bruce Gilsen, Leonard A Girard, Traci Gleason, Rynek Glowny, Felix Godwin, Owen Goldfarb, David & Lynne Golding, Stan Goodman, Kirsten & Arron Goodwin, Samantha Gordon, Ravi Gowda, Mark Grant, Chris Greenwood, Owen Groves, Gabriel Gruss, Genevieve Guay, Elio Gutierrez, Robert Gwalkoniak, Pat Hafeez, Michael Hall, Mikael Hanas, Louise Hannell, IW Harris, Sue Harrison, Shona Hawkes, Sarah Heckscher, Lorenz A Heinze, Jennifer Henderson, Miguel Herrera Martinez, Niall Hewitt, Elaine Hewson, Peter Hoogland, Jelka Hopster, Adam Howard, Bob Huber, Claudia Hueppmeier, Martin Hula, Judith Hunger, Marta Huscall, Colin Jacobson, Mary Jane Sheffet, Prashant Jayaprakash, Janaka Jayasingha, Tomasz Jelen, Oliver Johnston, Pamela Johson, Andrew Jones, Myrddin Jones, Stefanie & Jay Jordan, Nel & Martyn Kaal, Judith Kahan, Jennifer Kavanagh, Andrew Keeley, Alna & Ann Keenan, Mel Kempster, Gavan Kierans, John Killick, K Klidzia, Christian Knappe, Barbara Kocot, Fabiano Koich Miguel, Jeff Kolano, Stefan Korski, Andrei Koval, Roeland Krul, Hartmut Kuhne, Mike Kulowski, M Kulowski Sr., Margriet Lakeman, Diane & Ben Lapinski, Lyndal le Bas, Ronald Leganger, Bill Lehman, Manfred Lenzen, Adam Levy, MS Lewis, Susan & Vincent Lewonski, Jadwiga Lopata, Paul Andrew Lucrev, B Mackinnon-Little, Donald MacLeod, Maria Macur, J & M Malkiewicz, Charlotte Mariaggou, Charlotte Mariasson, Antoinette & Gerald Martin, Thomas Martin, Irving Massey, Phillip Matthews, Olivier Mauron, Eileen Mazur, K McDowell, David McGowan, Garry McKellar-James, Gregory McKenna, Christian McKenzie, Matiss Melecis, Warren Merel, John Michasiuk, Simon Miller, Elzbeta Mitura, Lee Gerard Molloy, Fiona Mooniariech, Una Morrison, Stacja Morska, Penny Moyes, Margot Munzer, Jameela Naseem, Chris Nelson, Pawel Neugebauer, Kate Nicholson, Batek Nitka, Sarah J Noceda, Dave Norris, Robin O'Donoghue, Katarina & Dick Oosthoek, Carlos Ortiz, Jacki Owen, RN Paech, Lee Palmer, Alec Parkin, Neil Parkinson, Jacinta Parsons, Donna Pasquale, Stephen Paton, Jan M Pennington, Mike Penrith, William Pentony, Dariusz Piotrowski, Leon PJ Drysdale, Robert Pluta, Adam Podgajny, Magdalena Polan, Miroslav Posta, Susan Prain, William D Preston, Anna Ptaszynska, Sophia Pugsley, Laura Pusey, Brandon Pustejovsky, Anin Rattan, Grant Reynolds, Jack Richards, Tony Richmond, Davina Rippon, Clifford Rogers, Piotr Romanowski, Kang Rong, Clare Rose, Cam Ross, Jarek Rudnik, Patrick Ryan, Magdalena Rybka, Piotr Rybka, Valerie Rzepka, Emily Sachs, Marcin Sadurski, Gladys Saenz, R Samuelson, Dorota Sarska, Nigel Saynor, Vicki Schwidden, Teresa Scollon, The Secher Family, Oliver Selwyn, Joe Sewell, Harvey Shaw, Christian Siggen, Ellen Skarsgard, PJM van der Sloot, Peter Sluijter, Captain RM Smyth, Carolyn Snell, George Soranidis, Vicky Southgate, Tina Souvlis, Juldborg Sovik, Phiana Stanley, George W Steed, Nicole Stewart, Patrick Stewart, Georgia Stone, Mildred Stone, Sarah Stratton, Bobbie Strich, Ken Swain, Prof. Nancy Swanson, Mike Sweeney, Chris Swiderski, Barbara Szczepanik, Henry Szot, Harry Taylor, Deborah Thatcher, Kate Thomas, Sinead Thornton, Brian Todd,

Janet Tomkins, Sylvia Tomlinson-Hoehndorf, James Travers-Murison, Arto Tuominen, Kevin van Damme, JWJ Van Dorp, Marek Verhoeven, Goran Verpoucke, Soren Vestergaard Hansen, Rudolf von Stein, Carl R Walkanshaw, Malcolm Wallace, Damian Wampler, Sally Watkins, Arnold Watson, Katherine Watson, Claire Weetman, Frederic Wehowski, Bill Wein, Jan Werbinski, Marek Wesolowski, Guy Westoby, Ian Wheeler, Ingrid White, Jarek Wieczorek, Maciej Wieczorek, Kate Wierciak, Di Wilson, Fiona Wilson, Eleanor Winters, Joseph and Elaine Wojtowicz, C Wolf, Nicholas Wood, Piers Wood, Philip G Woodward, Katherine Wrobel, Richard J Wyber, David Young, Harry Zapolski, Arek Zawada, Frans JL Zegers, Maike Ziesemer, Carolyn & Callon Zukowski

LONELY PLANET

ON THE ROAD

Travel Guides explore cities, regions and countries, and supply information on transport, restaurants and accommodation, covering all budgets. They come with reliable, easy-to-use maps, practical advice, cultural and historical facts and a rundown on attractions both on and off the beaten track. There are over 200 titles in this classic series, covering nearly every country in the world.

 Lonely Planet Upgrades extend the shelf life of existing travel guides by detailing any changes that may affect travel in a region since a book has been published. Upgrades can be downloaded for free from **www.lonelyplanet.com/upgrades**

For travellers with more time than money, **Shoestring** guides offer dependable, first-hand information with hundreds of detailed maps, plus insider tips for stretching money as far as possible. Covering entire continents in most cases, the six-volume shoestring guides are known around the world as 'backpackers bibles'.

For the discerning short-term visitor, **Condensed** guides highlight the best a destination has to offer in a full-colour, pocket-sized format designed for quick access. They include everything from top sights and walking tours to opinionated reviews of where to eat, stay, shop and have fun.

CitySync lets travellers use their Palm™ or Visor™ hand-held computers to guide them through a city with handy tips on transport, history, cultural life, major sights, and shopping and entertainment options. It can also quickly search and sort hundreds of reviews of hotels, restaurants and attractions, and pinpoint their location on scrollable street maps. CitySync can be downloaded from **www.citysync.com**

MAPS & ATLASES

Lonely Planet's **City Maps** feature downtown and metropolitan maps, as well as transit routes and walking tours. The maps come complete with an index of streets, a listing of sights and a plastic coat for extra durability.

Road Atlases are an essential navigation tool for serious travellers. Cross-referenced with the guidebooks, they also feature distance and climate charts and a complete site index.

ESSENTIALS

Read This First books help new travellers to hit the road with confidence. These invaluable predeparture guides give step-by-step advice on preparing for a trip, budgeting, arranging a visa, planning an itinerary and staying safe while still getting off the beaten track.

Healthy Travel pocket guides offer a regional rundown on disease hot spots and practical advice on predeparture health measures, staying well on the road and what to do in emergencies. The guides come with a user-friendly design and helpful diagrams and tables.

Lonely Planet's **Phrasebooks** cover the essential words and phrases travellers need when they're strangers in a strange land. They come in a pocket-sized format with colour tabs for quick reference, extensive vocabulary lists, easy-to-follow pronunciation keys and two-way dictionaries.

Miffed by blurry photos of the Taj Mahal? Tired of the classic 'top of the head cut off' shot? **Travel Photography: A Guide to Taking Better Pictures** will help you turn ordinary holiday snaps into striking images and give you the know-how to capture every scene, from frenetic festivals to peaceful beach sunrises.

Lonely Planet's **Travel Journal** is a lightweight but sturdy travel diary for jotting down all those on-the-road observations and significant travel moments. It comes with a handy time-zone wheel, a world map and useful travel information.

Lonely Planet's eKno is an all-in-one communication service developed especially for travellers. It offers low-cost international calls and free email and voicemail so that you can keep in touch while on the road. Check it out on **www.ekno.lonelyplanet.com**

FOOD & RESTAURANT GUIDES

Lonely Planet's **Out to Eat** guides recommend the brightest and best places to eat and drink in top international cities. These gourmet companions are arranged by neighbourhood, packed with dependable maps, garnished with scene-setting photos and served with quirky features.

For people who live to eat, drink and travel, **World Food** guides explore the culinary culture of each country. Entertaining and adventurous, each guide is packed with detail on staples and specialities, regional cuisine and local markets, as well as sumptuous recipes, comprehensive culinary dictionaries and lavish photos good enough to eat.

LONELY PLANET

OUTDOOR GUIDES

For those who believe the best way to see the world is on foot, Lonely Planet's **Walking Guides** detail everything from family strolls to difficult treks, with 'when to go and how to do it' advice supplemented by reliable maps and essential travel information.

Cycling Guides map a destination's best bike tours, long and short, in day-by-day detail. They contain all the information a cyclist needs, including advice on bike maintenance, places to eat and stay, innovative maps with detailed cues to the rides, and elevation charts.

The **Watching Wildlife** series is perfect for travellers who want authoritative information but don't want to tote a heavy field guide. Packed with advice on where, when and how to view a region's wildlife, each title features photos of over 300 species and contains engaging comments on the local flora and fauna.

With underwater colour photos throughout, **Pisces Books** explore the world's best diving and snorkelling areas. Each book contains listings of diving services and dive resorts, detailed information on depth, visibility and difficulty of dives, and a roundup of the marine life you're likely to see through your mask.

LONELY PLANET

OFF THE ROAD

Journeys, the travel literature series written by renowned travel authors, capture the spirit of a place or illuminate a culture with a journalist's attention to detail and a novelist's flair for words. These are tales to soak up while you're actually on the road or dip into as an at-home armchair indulgence.

The range of lavishly illustrated **Pictorial** books is just the ticket for both travellers and dreamers. Off-beat tales and vivid photographs bring the adventure of travel to your doorstep long before the journey begins and long after it is over.

Lonely Planet **Videos** encourage the same independent, tough-minded approach as the guidebooks. Currently airing throughout the world, this award-winning series features innovative footage and an original soundtrack.

Yes, we know, work is tough, so do a little bit of deskside dreaming with the spiral-bound Lonely Planet **Diary** or a Lonely Planet **Wall Calendar**, filled with great photos from around the world.

TRAVELLERS NETWORK

Lonely Planet Online. Lonely Planet's award-winning Web site has insider information on hundreds of destinations, from Amsterdam to Zimbabwe, complete with interactive maps and relevant links. The site also offers the latest travel news, recent reports from travellers on the road, guidebook upgrades, a travel links site, an online book-buying option and a lively travellers bulletin board. It can be viewed at **www.lonelyplanet.com** or AOL keyword: lp.

Planet Talk is a quarterly print newsletter, full of gossip, advice, anecdotes and author articles. It provides an antidote to the being-at-home blues and lets you plan and dream for the next trip. Contact the nearest Lonely Planet office for your free copy.

Comet, the free Lonely Planet newsletter, comes via email once a month. It's loaded with travel news, advice, dispatches from authors, travel competitions and letters from readers. To subscribe, click on the Comet subscription link on the front page of the Web site.

Lonely Planet Guides by Region

L onely Planet is known worldwide for publishing practical, reliable and no-nonsense travel information in our guides and on our Web site. The Lonely Planet list covers just about every accessible part of the world. Currently there are 16 series: Travel guides, Shoestring guides, Condensed guides, Phrasebooks, Read This First, Healthy Travel, Walking guides, Cycling guides, Watching Wildlife guides, Pisces Diving & Snorkeling guides, City Maps, Road Atlases, Out to Eat, World Food, Journeys travel literature and Pictorials.

AFRICA Africa on a shoestring • Botswana • Cairo • Cairo City Map • Cape Town • Cape Town City Map • East Africa • Egypt • Egyptian Arabic phrasebook • Ethiopia, Eritrea & Djibouti • Ethiopian Amharic phrasebook • The Gambia & Senegal • Healthy Travel Africa • Kenya • Malawi • Morocco • Moroccan Arabic phrasebook • Mozambique • Namibia • Read This First: Africa • South Africa, Lesotho & Swaziland • Southern Africa • Southern Africa Road Atlas • Swahili phrasebook • Tanzania, Zanzibar & Pemba • Trekking in East Africa • Tunisia • Watching Wildlife East Africa • Watching Wildlife Southern Africa • West Africa • World Food Morocco • Zambia • Zimbabwe, Botswana & Namibia
Travel Literature: Mali Blues: Traveling to an African Beat • The Rainbird: A Central African Journey • Songs to an African Sunset: A Zimbabwean Story

AUSTRALIA & THE PACIFIC Aboriginal Australia & the Torres Strait Islands •Auckland • Australia • Australian phrasebook • Australia Road Atlas • Cycling Australia • Cycling New Zealand • Fiji • Fijian phrasebook • Healthy Travel Australia, NZ & the Pacific • Islands of Australia's Great Barrier Reef • Melbourne • Melbourne City Map • Micronesia • New Caledonia • New South Wales • New Zealand • Northern Territory • Outback Australia • Out to Eat – Melbourne • Out to Eat – Sydney • Papua New Guinea • Pidgin phrasebook • Queensland • Rarotonga & the Cook Islands • Samoa • Solomon Islands • South Australia • South Pacific • South Pacific phrasebook • Sydney • Sydney City Map • Sydney Condensed • Tahiti & French Polynesia • Tasmania • Tonga • Tramping in New Zealand • Vanuatu • Victoria • Walking in Australia • Watching Wildlife Australia • Western Australia
Travel Literature: Islands in the Clouds: Travels in the Highlands of New Guinea • Kiwi Tracks: A New Zealand Journey • Sean & David's Long Drive

CENTRAL AMERICA & THE CARIBBEAN Bahamas, Turks & Caicos • Baja California • Belize, Guatemala & Yucatán • Bermuda • Central America on a shoestring • Costa Rica • Costa Rica Spanish phrasebook • Cuba • Cycling Cuba • Dominican Republic & Haiti • Eastern Caribbean • Guatemala • Havana • Healthy Travel Central & South America • Jamaica • Mexico • Mexico City • Panama • Puerto Rico • Read This First: Central & South America • Virgin Islands • World Food Caribbean • World Food Mexico • Yucatán
Travel Literature: Green Dreams: Travels in Central America

EUROPE Amsterdam • Amsterdam City Map • Amsterdam Condensed • Andalucía • Athens • Austria • Baltic States phrasebook • Barcelona • Barcelona City Map • Belgium & Luxembourg • Berlin • Berlin City Map • Britain • British phrasebook • Brussels, Bruges & Antwerp • Brussels City Map • Budapest • Budapest City Map • Canary Islands • Catalunya & the Costa Brava • Central Europe • Central Europe phrasebook • Copenhagen • Corfu & the Ionians • Corsica • Crete • Crete Condensed • Croatia • Cycling Britain • Cycling France • Cyprus • Czech & Slovak Republics • Czech phrasebook • Denmark • Dublin • Dublin City Map • Dublin Condensed • Eastern Europe • Eastern Europe phrasebook • Edinburgh • Edinburgh City Map • England • Estonia, Latvia & Lithuania • Europe on a shoestring • Europe phrasebook • Finland • Florence • Florence City Map • France • Frankfurt City Map • Frankfurt Condensed • French phrasebook • Georgia, Armenia & Azerbaijan • Germany • German phrasebook • Greece • Greek Islands • Greek phrasebook • Hungary • Iceland, Greenland & the Faroe Islands • Ireland • Italian phrasebook • Italy • Kraków • Lisbon • The Loire • London • London City Map • London Condensed • Madrid • Madrid City Map • Malta • Mediterranean Europe • Milan, Turin & Genoa • Moscow • Munich • Netherlands • Normandy • Norway • Out to Eat – London • Out to Eat – Paris • Paris • Paris City Map • Paris Condensed • Poland • Polish phrasebook • Portugal • Portuguese phrasebook • Prague • Prague City Map • Provence & the Côte d'Azur • Read This First: Europe • Rhodes & the Dodecanese • Romania & Moldova • Rome • Rome City Map • Rome Condensed • Russia, Ukraine & Belarus • Russian phrasebook • Scandinavian & Baltic Europe • Scandinavian phrasebook • Scotland • Sicily • Slovenia • South-West France • Spain • Spanish phrasebook • Stockholm • St Petersburg • St Petersburg City Map • Sweden • Switzerland • Tuscany • Ukrainian phrasebook • Venice • Vienna • Wales • Walking in Britain • Walking in France • Walking in Ireland • Walking in Italy • Walking in Scotland • Walking in Spain • Walking in Switzerland • Western Europe • World Food France • World Food Greece • World Food Ireland • World Food Italy • World Food Spain **Travel Literature:** After Yugoslavia • Love and War in the Apennines • The Olive Grove: Travels in Greece • On the Shores of the Mediterranean • Round Ireland in Low Gear • A Small Place in Italy

Lonely Planet Mail Order

Lonely Planet products are distributed worldwide. They are also available by mail order from Lonely Planet, so if you have difficulty finding a title please write to us. North and South American residents should write to 150 Linden St, Oakland, CA 94607, USA; European and African residents should write to 10a Spring Place, London NW5 3BH, UK; and residents of other countries to Locked Bag 1, Footscray, Victoria 3011, Australia.

INDIAN SUBCONTINENT & THE INDIAN OCEAN Bangladesh • Bengali phrasebook • Bhutan • Delhi • Goa • Healthy Travel Asia & India • Hindi & Urdu phrasebook • India • India & Bangladesh City Map • Indian Himalaya • Karakoram Highway • Kathmandu City Map • Kerala • Madagascar • Maldives • Mauritius, Réunion & Seychelles • Mumbai (Bombay) • Nepal • Nepali phrasebook • North India • Pakistan • Rajasthan • Read This First: Asia & India • South India • Sri Lanka • Sri Lanka phrasebook • Tibet • Tibetan phrasebook • Trekking in the Indian Himalaya • Trekking in the Karakoram & Hindukush • Trekking in the Nepal Himalaya • World Food India **Travel Literature:** The Age of Kali: Indian Travels and Encounters • Hello Goodnight: A Life of Goa • In Rajasthan • Maverick in Madagascar • A Season in Heaven: True Tales from the Road to Kathmandu • Shopping for Buddhas • A Short Walk in the Hindu Kush • Slowly Down the Ganges

MIDDLE EAST & CENTRAL ASIA Bahrain, Kuwait & Qatar • Central Asia • Central Asia phrasebook • Dubai • Farsi (Persian) phrasebook • Hebrew phrasebook • Iran • Israel & the Palestinian Territories • Istanbul • Istanbul City Map • Istanbul to Cairo • Istanbul to Kathmandu • Jerusalem • Jerusalem City Map • Jordan • Lebanon • Middle East • Oman & the United Arab Emirates • Syria • Turkey • Turkish phrasebook • World Food Turkey • Yemen **Travel Literature:** Black on Black: Iran Revisited • Breaking Ranks: Turbulent Travels in the Promised Land • The Gates of Damascus • Kingdom of the Film Stars: Journey into Jordan

NORTH AMERICA Alaska • Boston • Boston City Map • Boston Condensed • British Columbia • California & Nevada • California Condensed • Canada • Chicago • Chicago City Map • Chicago Condensed • Florida • Georgia & the Carolinas • Great Lakes • Hawaii • Hiking in Alaska • Hiking in the USA • Honolulu & Oahu City Map • Las Vegas • Los Angeles • Los Angeles City Map • Louisiana & the Deep South • Miami • Miami City Map • Montreal • New England • New Orleans • New Orleans City Map • New York City • New York City Map • New York City Condensed • New York, New Jersey & Pennsylvania • Oahu • Out to Eat – San Francisco • Pacific Northwest • Rocky Mountains • San Diego & Tijuana • San Francisco • San Francisco City Map • Seattle • Seattle City Map • Southwest • Texas • Toronto • USA • USA phrasebook • Vancouver • Vancouver City Map • Virginia & the Capital Region • Washington, DC • Washington, DC City Map • World Food New Orleans **Travel Literature:** Caught Inside: A Surfer's Year on the California Coast • Drive Thru America

NORTH-EAST ASIA Beijing • Beijing City Map • Cantonese phrasebook • China • Hiking in Japan • Hong Kong & Macau • Hong Kong City Map • Hong Kong Condensed • Japan • Japanese phrasebook • Korea • Korean phrasebook • Kyoto • Mandarin phrasebook • Mongolia • Mongolian phrasebook • Seoul • Shanghai • South-West China • Taiwan • Tokyo • Tokyo Condensed • World Food Hong Kong • World Food Japan **Travel Literature:** In Xanadu: A Quest • Lost Japan

SOUTH AMERICA Argentina, Uruguay & Paraguay • Bolivia • Brazil • Brazilian phrasebook • Buenos Aires • Buenos Aires City Map • Chile & Easter Island • Colombia • Ecuador & the Galapagos Islands • Healthy Travel Central & South America • Latin American Spanish phrasebook • Peru • Quechua phrasebook • Read This First: Central & South America • Rio de Janeiro • Rio de Janeiro City Map • Santiago de Chile • South America on a shoestring • Trekking in the Patagonian Andes • Venezuela **Travel Literature:** Full Circle: A South American Journey

SOUTH-EAST ASIA Bali & Lombok • Bangkok • Bangkok City Map • Burmese phrasebook • Cambodia • Cycling Vietnam, Laos & Cambodia • East Timor phrasebook • Hanoi • Healthy Travel Asia & India • Hill Tribes phrasebook • Ho Chi Minh City (Saigon) • Indonesia • Indonesian phrasebook • Indonesia's Eastern Islands • Java • Lao phrasebook • Laos • Malay phrasebook • Malaysia, Singapore & Brunei • Myanmar (Burma) • Philippines • Pilipino (Tagalog) phrasebook • Read This First: Asia & India • Singapore • Singapore City Map • South-East Asia on a shoestring • South-East Asia phrasebook • Thailand • Thailand's Islands & Beaches • Thailand, Vietnam, Laos & Cambodia Road Atlas • Thai phrasebook • Vietnam • Vietnamese phrasebook • World Food Indonesia • World Food Thailand • World Food Vietnam

ALSO AVAILABLE: Antarctica • The Arctic • The Blue Man: Tales of Travel, Love and Coffee • Brief Encounters: Stories of Love, Sex & Travel • Buddhist Stupas in Asia: The Shape of Perfection • Chasing Rickshaws • The Last Grain Race • Lonely Planet ... On the Edge: Adventurous Escapades from Around the World • Lonely Planet Unpacked • Lonely Planet Unpacked Again • Not the Only Planet: Science Fiction Travel Stories • Ports of Call: A Journey by Sea • Sacred India • Travel Photography: A Guide to Taking Better Pictures • Travel with Children • Tuvalu: Portrait of an Island Nation

Index

Text

Bold indicates maps.

Boxed Text

MAP LEGEND

CITY ROUTES

Freeway	Freeway
Highway	Primary Road
Road	Secondary Road
Street	Street
Lane	Lane
	On/Off Ramp

	Unsealed Road
	One Way Street
	Pedestrian Street
	Stepped Street
	Tunnel
	Footbridge

REGIONAL ROUTES

	Tollway, Freeway
	Primary Road
	Secondary Road
	Minor Road

BOUNDARIES

	International
	State
	Disputed
	Fortified Wall

HYDROGRAPHY

	River, Creek
	Canal
	Lake
	Dry Lake; Salt Lake
	Spring; Rapids
	Waterfalls

TRANSPORT ROUTES & STATIONS

	Train
	Underground Train
	Metro
	Tramway
	Cable Car, Chairlift

	Ferry
	Walking Trail
	Walking Tour
	Path
	Pier or Jetty

AREA FEATURES

	Building
	Park, Gardens
	Market
	Sports Ground
	Beach
	Cemetery
	Campus
	Plaza

POPULATION SYMBOLS

✪ CAPITAL	National Capital	● CITY	City	● Village	Village
◉ CAPITAL	State Capital	● Town	Town		Urban Area

MAP SYMBOLS

■	Place to Stay	
▼	Place to Eat	
●	Point of Interest	

✪	Border Crossing	⌂	Cave	🖥	Internet Cafe
☐	Bus Stop	☗	Chalet, Hut	☼	Lookout
☐	Bus Terminal	✚	Church, Monastery	⚲	Monument
☐	Cable Car, Funicular	☐	Cinema	🏛	Museum
⛺	Camping Area	☐	Embassy	✚	Police Station
☐	Castle	☔	Fountain	⚑	Ruins
☐	Cathedral	✚	Hospital	☒	Shopping Centre

🏛	Stately Home
🏊	Swimming Pool
✡	Synagogue
☐	Theatre
☐	Toilet
☐	Tomb
🐾	Zoo

Note: not all symbols displayed above appear in this book

LONELY PLANET OFFICES

Australia
Locked Bag 1, Footscray, Victoria 3011
☎ 03 8379 8000 fax 03 8379 8111
email: talk2us@lonelyplanet.com.au

USA
150 Linden St, Oakland, CA 94607
☎ 510 893 8555 TOLL FREE: 800 275 8555
fax 510 893 8572
email: info@lonelyplanet.com

UK
10a Spring Place, London NW5 3BH
☎ 020 7428 4800 fax 020 7428 4828
email: go@lonelyplanet.co.uk

France
1 rue du Dahomey, 75011 Paris
☎ 01 55 25 33 00 fax 01 55 25 33 01
email: bip@lonelyplanet.fr
www.lonelyplanet.fr

World Wide Web: www.lonelyplanet.com *or* AOL keyword: lp
Lonely Planet Images: lpi@lonelyplanet.com.au